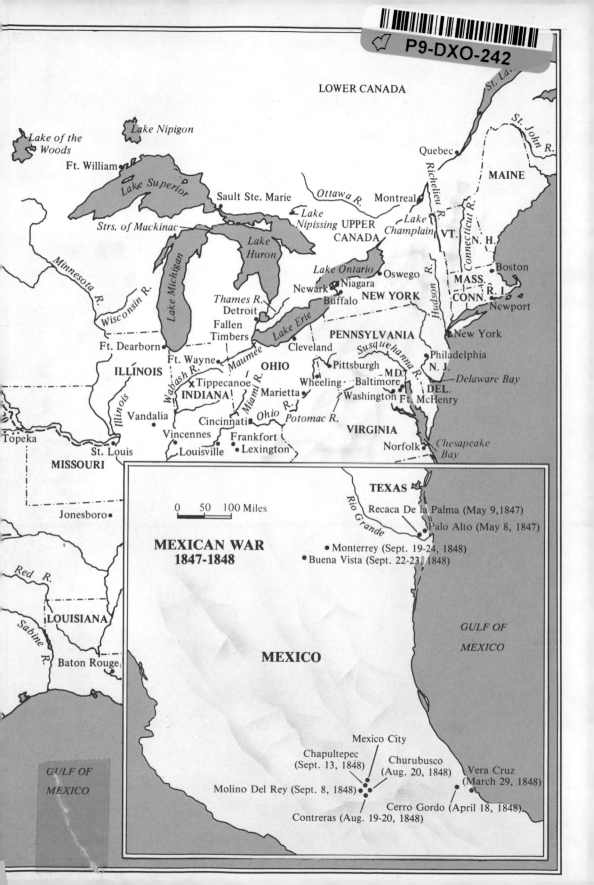

LOWER CANADA

Lake Nipigon

Lake of the Woods

Ft. William

Lake Superior

Sault Ste. Marie

Ottawa R.

Quebec

St. John R.

MAINE

Montreal

Richelieu R.

Lake Nipissing UPPER CANADA

Lake Champlain VT. N. H.

Connecticut R.

Strs. of Mackinac

Lake Huron

Minnesota R.

Wisconsin R.

Lake Michigan

Thames R.

Detroit

Newark Niagara

Lake Ontario Oswego

Buffalo

NEW YORK

Hudson R.

Boston

MASS.

R. I.

CONN.

Newport

Fallen Timbers

Lake Erie

Cleveland

PENNSYLVANIA

New York

Susquehanna R.

Philadelphia

N. J.

Ft. Dearborn

Ft. Wayne

Maumee

Wabash R.

×Tippecanoe

OHIO

INDIANA

Miami R.

Pittsburgh

Wheeling

MD.

Baltimore

DEL.

Delaware Bay

ILLINOIS

Illinois

Marietta

Ohio R.

Washington Ft. McHenry

Vandalia

Cincinnati

Ohio

Potomac R.

VIRGINIA

Topeka

Vincennes

Frankfort

St. Louis

Louisville

Lexington

Norfolk

Chesapeake Bay

MISSOURI

Jonesboro

TEXAS

Rio Grande

Recaca De la Palma (May 9,1847)

Palo Alto (May 8, 1847)

0 50 100 Miles

MEXICAN WAR 1847-1848

Monterrey (Sept. 19-24, 1848)

Buena Vista (Sept. 22-23, 1848)

Red R.

Sabine R.

LOUISIANA

GULF OF MEXICO

Baton Rouge

MEXICO

Mexico City

Chapultepec (Sept. 13, 1848)

Churubusco (Aug. 20, 1848)

Vera Cruz (March 29, 1848)

Molino Del Rey (Sept. 8, 1848)

Cerro Gordo (April 18, 1848)

Contreras (Aug. 19-20, 1848)

GULF OF MEXICO

THE
NATION
COMES OF
AGE

A
PEOPLE'S
HISTORY
OF THE
ANTE-BELLUM
YEARS

THE NATION COMES OF AGE

Page Smith

VOLUME FOUR

McGRAW-HILL BOOK COMPANY

New York / St. Louis / San Francisco

Hamburg / Mexico / Toronto

Library of Congress Cataloging in Publication Data

Smith, Page.
The nation comes of age.
Includes index.
1. United States—History—1815–1861. I. Title.
E338.S59   973   80–16889
ISBN 0–07–059018–4

For my brother, John Marshall Smith

ALSO BY PAGE SMITH:

James Wilson: Founding Father
John Adams (Two Volumes)
The Historian and History
As a City upon a Hill:
    The Town in American History
Daughters of the Promised Land:
    Women in American History
A New Age Now Begins:
    A People's History of the American
    Revolution (Two Volumes)
The Chicken Book
The Constitution: A Documentary
    and Narrative History
The Shaping of America: A People's History of
    the Young Republic

Contents

Introduction

The period covered by this volume—1826 to 1861—is the most remarkable era in American history, or even, it might be argued, in the history of the world. It extends from the deaths of Thomas Jefferson and John Adams on July 4, 1826, to the fall of Fort Sumter, a period of thirty-five years. The simple statistics are awesome. The population of the United States in 1826 is estimated to have been in the neighborhood of 11,000,000. On the eve of the Civil War it was nearly 33,000,000. The country had grown at the rate of more than 33 percent per decade and the population had tripled. Eight new states were added to the Union, carrying the stars and stripes to the Pacific Coast. The land area over which the federal government exercised control, including the territories of New Mexico, Utah, and Nebraska, almost doubled, from 1,749,000 square miles to 2,969,000.

There were no railroads in 1826; by the end of the era there were 31,000 miles of rails tying the country together. The value of farm produce increased from some four hundred million dollars at the beginning of the period to more than two billion at its end, a sixfold increase. Immigration, estimated to have been 13,908 in 1826, was 180,000 in 1861—a sharp decline from the peak year of 1851, when 474,398 immigrants entered American ports. Cumulative immigration for the period was in excess of 8,000,000.

But statistics only hint at a story of remarkable drama and complexity. In addition to the vast tide of immigration, there was the filling up of the Mississippi River Valley with settlers; the rise and decline of the fur trade, centering in the Yellowstone region; the annexation of California and Texas; the Mexican War and the Gold Rush—each episode following the other in such rapid succession that the implications of one had not been absorbed before it was eclipsed by the next. In all that wild ferment of chaotic growth and perpetual expansion an American consciousness was struggling to articulate itself. The Transcendentalists created a new kind of American religion, which apotheosized the individual. An American art and literature blossomed with an astonishing fecundity. In a single decade

Poe, Thoreau, Whitman, Hawthorne, and Melville wrote their most powerful and representative works, creating an American literature to which, one is tempted to say, subsequent literary efforts were hardly more than a footnote. In the preceding volume of this work I spoke of the American political and social system as releasing great new quantums of human energy. Those energies found their most remarkable expression in the era we now enter.

Two major themes dominate all lesser ones—slavery (and Abolition) and the extension of "democracy." A central theme continues to be the conflict in the American psyche between the yearning for the re-establishment of the true community and the attractions of competitive individualism with its promise of quick riches. The level of anxiety does not diminish; if anything, it is augmented. The upper classes in the various cities are dismayed by the "democratic" pressures from below, by the riotous urban mobs, the persistent violence and lawlessness, the corruption in politics and in business enterprise—often so closely allied. All classes suffer from perpetual anxiety about making or keeping money; about "going ahead" if they are behind, or staying ahead if they are in front, and doing so in the face of intermittent catastrophic panics or depressions. The Classical-Christian Consciousness is clearly everywhere on the decline, its last refuge the embattled elites of Boston, New York, and Philadelphia. The Secular-Democratic Consciousness is everywhere in the ascendant, raised to its epitome by the hero of democracy, Andrew Jackson. But the Protestant passion to redeem the United States from wickedness and error, from slavery, alcoholism, and a hundred other lesser but still troubling defects and deficiencies emerges in innumerable secular crusades as the most potent spirit of the age, moderating the unappeasable appetites of "the democracy," curtailing the most exploitative inclinations of "capital."

What is common to every caste and class is the conviction that, frequently as they may deviate from it, there is a moral order in the universe. That order is clearly ascertainable, verifiable, unimpeachable. It manifests itself in every area of human experience. All questions—social, political, literary, or artistic—may be referred to it in the confident expectation of an unequivocal answer.

Underneath that universal moral order particular creeds, religions, sects, and denominations may rise and fall, proclaim new truths or denounce new heresies, but the order stands solid and inviolable. Whether its adherents call themselves Calvinists, Baptists, Latter-Day

Saints, or Transcendentalists, they all acknowledge its ultimate authority. It is the only principle of coherence in a chaotic society. Republican
governments and democratic principles are perhaps its most striking
manifestations, the United States of America its appointed vessel. *His*
appointed vessel. The vessel of the Lord.

To the historian given to a simple division of history into the
exploiters and the exploited, the era might be read as "the rise of the
corporate state" or some such tag line anticipating the ascendancy of
modern capitalism. But a far more complex human drama was
unfolding. If the United States had taken on a tentative and imperfect
shape by 1826, in the decades that culminated in the Civil War we
achieved a hard-won measure of maturity. No longer an unruly child
in the family of nations, we approached the end of our first century as
a nation with far more confidence and brashness than our true
situation warranted. Teetering on the brink of ruin, we crowed over
past accomplishments and predicted brilliant new successes. If a nation
can have an "identity crisis" (and the United States seems especially
prone to them), ours was that of a country come of age, filled with
conflicts and confusions yet conscious of vast new powers it was
uncertain how to use.

In the period covered by this volume (and, indeed, considerably
beyond), we are fortunate in having five remarkable guides whose
perceptive observations on events and people will be quoted frequently and who are perhaps best introduced here. Four were lawyers,
members of the upper classes of their respective cities—Philadelphia,
New York, and Boston; one was a self-made businessman who became
mayor of New York and a power in Whig politics.

Sidney George Fisher was born in Philadelphia in 1808 and
graduated from the University of Pennsylvania. He began his diary in
the summer of 1834 when he was twenty-six years old. Philip Hone,
born in 1780 in New York, was the oldest of our five diarists. Of French
and German ancestry, he had started work in his brother's auction
business when he was sixteen. By the time he was forty he was, through
shrewd investments and hard work, one of the wealthiest men in New
York, a successful politician, a connoisseur of the arts, and a model of
fashion.

George Templeton Strong, another New Yorker, was born in
1820, the youngest of our five guides. He began his diary in the winter
of 1845 when he was twenty-five and continued it throughout a long
and active life. Richard Henry Dana, author of *Two Years Before the*

Mast, one of the great literary works of the nineteenth century, was born in 1815 and educated at Harvard. A lawyer and a founder of the Free Soil Party, Dana was frustrated in his political ambitions.

We are already acquainted with Charles Francis Adams, son of one president and grandson of another. He approached every issue, public or private, with the question How would an Adams behave under such circumstances? All five diarists viewed the United States from the perspective of the Eastern upper class, but taking that bias into account we will find them a remarkably astute and literate set of guides.

There is another level on which I am anxious that this history should function for the reader. I have, from time to time, complained that in modern times professional historians, writing primarily for each other, have ignored their traditional task—to mediate past generations to the present. We need history in order to breathe. To be without a history is to be without some essential element of one's own reality. We all exist (or should exist) in three dimensions of time: the past, the present (which we create anew every day), and the future. Missing any of these we are less than we might be, diminished, truncated. To attach us to our past is my ambition. Above all, I would make evident or (ideally) inescapable to the reader that, beyond praise or blame, our history has *been,* has actually happened.

I have insisted throughout this work that history is not a set of problems but a drama of extraordinary richness and power. The history of the past is made up of many lives fully lived (as well as those wasted or diminished by spiritual barrenness or desperate poverty). By entering sympathetically into past lives we enlarge our sense of our own potentialities. Perhaps more important, we discover what Alex Haley has properly referred to as our "roots," who we are as historic beings and where we belong in the strange movement of time that we call history.

The period we are dealing with in this volume is extraordinarily rich in the ennobling and enlivening lives of men and women we did not hesitate once to call heroes and heroines. To have lost the capacity to imagine heroes and heroines is to have lost something of ourselves, to have lost an awareness of the possibilities available to us. Every triumph over obtuse institutions, over life "as it is," over social inertia is an act of heroism—and one accessible to us all.

A modern humorist has written a characteristically American book entitled *If Life Is a Bowl of Cherries, What Am I Doing in the Pits?* We might rephrase the question somewhat as *If the United States Has*

Been Above Reproach Throughout Her History, What Are We Doing in the Pits? Life is clearly not a bowl of cherries, nor has the United States been immune to the complex trials, tribulations, and tragedies incident to the human condition. So, in a sense, this work contains a hidden theology, and since candor about our past (or at least a dogged attempt at it) has been a premise or promise of this work, I feel I owe it to the reader to be "up front." I am doing more than trying to tell the story of America; I am trying to enlarge the reader's (and my own) sense of the nature of history—which is the nature of man as it appears on a particular stage and in a particular time with all the "concrete fullness" written history invites us to try to achieve.

The late Eugen Rosenstock-Huessy wrote in his classic *Out of Revolution: The Autobiography of Western Man:* "Our passions give life to the world; our collective passions constitute the history of mankind." (An academic formulary, in contradistinction, might read "We understand history through logical analysis and aspire to control it through reason.") This work is, above all, a story of the passions, noble or ignoble, that shaped our nation. It is preeminently a story of men and women, some known and many, many more anonymous. With careful reservation for the Divine, I can discover no "forces," economic or astral, other than the individual and collective wills of human beings, that guide or direct human history. We hold to certain extremely fragile notions which we generally denominate "ideas," and we hold to these ideas passionately rather than rationally. How these ideas encounter the rough material stuff of the world, how they act *on* and react *to* the physical landscape seems to me the essence of history.

THE
NATION
COMES OF
AGE

1

The Election of 1828

At the conclusion of the preceding volume an unhappy and frustrated John Quincy Adams was the occupant of the White House. An intellectual's intellectual, rivaled in brilliance among all the presidents of the republic only by his grandfather, John Adams, and Thomas Jefferson, he had none of those small arts of accommodation so essential to the success of an American politician. In his inaugural address, Adams had proposed the vision of an enlightened and benign government establishing a national observatory, encouraging the arts and sciences, making the United States the rival of European powers in projects designed to enhance the cultural and intellectual life of its citizens. The address had been treated with contempt and derision by the great majority of the Congressmen; his national observatory was a special object of mirth to editorial writers.

Adams's presidency posed one of the classic problems of democracy. Were intelligence, vast experience, and personal rectitude to go unrewarded unless combined with the arts of ingratiation, with an affected affability and a willingness to pander to popular tastes and to flatter popular prejudices? Was hypocrisy the other face of democracy? It was a problem that was to trouble Adamses in every generation. There was another side of the question, of course. Didn't those "stiffened airs," that reserve, that aloofness, conceal a certain contempt for the common run of folks? Wasn't there some coldness of spirit, some lack of human warmth and generosity behind the glacial exterior, the "iron mask" that Adams's son Charles Francis so envied? That at least was what was said and would be said especially about New Englanders, despite their highmindedness and their tireless efforts to improve the world.

Ironically, the concurrent deaths of his father and Thomas Jefferson and the visit of Lafayette were the high points of Adams's administration. The most significant political event of his term of office might be said to have taken place far from the center stage of Washington. In Batavia, New York, a stonemason named William Morgan, an apostate Freemason, was preparing to publish a book exposing the secrets of the order. Masons in the area, hearing of the projected work, brought pressure on the printer to withhold publication. When this tactic failed, the printer's offices were set on fire and false charges were made against Morgan, resulting in his arrest and imprisonment for a debt of two dollars. During the night a man appeared, discharged the debt, and prevailed on the jailer to set Morgan free. He was immediately seized by a gang of men and carried off crying "Help" and "Murder." As far as it could be afterward ascertained, relays of carriages and horsemen bore Morgan off to an abandoned fort near Niagara where he simply disappeared. Morgan's partner in the enterprise, David Miller—the printer—was also abducted, but he managed to escape and published an account of Morgan's harassment and kidnapping along with his own sufferings at the hands of what were presumed to be outraged Masons. Before long the kidnapping of Morgan had become a cause célèbre, and the governor of the state was prevailed upon to offer a reward for information leading to the apprehension of his abductors and word as to his whereabouts. The result was a fierce wave of anti-Masonic sentiment. Excited meetings were held and proclamations were issued denouncing all secret societies and describing the Masons as murderers.

The episode was an odd one. Americans had already demonstrated a marked disposition to see conspiracies everywhere. The Reverend Jedediah Morse had warned years before of a conspiracy of the Illuminati, the freethinkers and revolutionaries of France, to use the Jeffersonian Republicans to rivet the chains of international atheism on the American people and subvert free institutions. The Republicans had replied that the real conspiracy was one of New England ministers against democracy and in favor of aristocracy and monarchy. That Freemasonry had about it a taint of the heretical was undeniable. On the other hand, so many active and ambitious Americans belonged to the order—including every president beginning with Washington —that it proved difficult to get a jury in Genesee County to indict or convict the individuals who confessed to playing prominent roles in the abduction of Morgan.

The enemies of the Masons charged that most local governments were in the hands of members of the order who gave political preferment to their fellows. One meeting declared "Freemasons unfit for any office of confidence." Three thousand angry citizens turned out for a meeting in Genesee and pledged to oppose a Mason's running for office. The rumor spread that Captain Brant, son of the famous Mohawk chief Joseph Brant, who like his father was a Mason, had been asked to dispose of Morgan. Brant denied any knowledge of Morgan or his whereabouts. The body of a drowned man was dug up on the shores of Lake Ontario and identified as Morgan; it was taken to Batavia and reburied with appropriate observances. The body was subsequently discovered to be that of a Canadian named Timothy Monro and was carried back to Canada, leaving the anti-Masons without a corpus delicti. But that did not modify their zeal. Armed with Morgan's book, *Illustrations of Masonry by One of the Fraternity Who Has Devoted Thirty Years to the Subject,* they carried their campaign to every corner of the state and substantially beyond. Soon they were a political force to be reckoned with.

Politically ambitious Masons began defecting by the hundreds. The incompatibility of Masonry with Christianity was stressed, and two alleged Masonic oaths were given wide publicity as demonstrating that a Mason was required to suspend or ignore common moral standards. Portions of the objectionable oaths read: "Furthermore do I promise and swear that I will aid and assist a companion royal arch Mason wherever I shall see him engaged in some difficulty, so far as to extricate him from the same, whether he be right or wrong" and "I swear to advance my brother's best interests by always supporting his military fame and political preferment in opposition to another." Thirty-two anti-Masonic newspapers blossomed in New York alone; soon Vermont and then the whole of New England were caught up in the exciting new political movement to purge the democracy of atheism and other alien doctrines.

That the popular reaction to the abduction and apparent murder of Morgan so far exceeded the provocation revealed more than anything else the uncertain temper of the American people, or at least those inhabiting New York and New England. If there is something in the American character especially susceptible to notions of conspiracy it may stem from an incapacity to deal with the unanticipated and coincidental quality of history itself. Americans have been generally inclined to think of themselves as being in control of their individual and collective destinies. Inexplicable or irrational events, hard times, or even natural disasters must, it was thought, be capable of explanation. Better a shaky conspiracy theory than no explanation at all. There was, moreover, the simple fact that the passionate attachment of many Americans to Freemasonry was an odd anomaly in an avowedly Christian country committed to open and democratic politics. Was Masonry to be best understood as one among many efforts at that "associational activity" which served to counteract, to a degree, the disintegrative effects of American life? In any case, the unfortunate Morgan was the posthumous founder of a political movement whose ripples were to be felt for years after his disappearance. Freemasonry would never again be quite the same.

The other major issue of Adams's administration (in which the President himself was very little involved) concerned a perpetually troubling problem: a schedule of tariffs on goods imported into the United States. The manufacturing interests, concentrated in the North and growing in power and confidence, insisted that high tariffs were necessary to protect and encourage American manufacturing, while the South viewed them as an unjust tax since the citizens of that region had to pay the higher prices of protected and—they argued—often inferior goods.

In 1824 New Hampshire had more than three hundred tanneries and six paper mills; Saco, Maine, was the site of the country's largest cotton mill. Manufacturing towns sprang up like mushrooms along New England's major rivers. There were 161 mills in Massachusetts, where Lowell was still the prototype. Providence, Rhode Island, employed more than thirty thousand people in 150 factories and considered itself the richest city of its size in the world. Philadelphia counted four thousand weavers, and in the nation as a whole two million men and women engaged in manufacturing, a tenfold increase in five years.

Since 1820 bills had been introduced at every session of Congress calling for higher tariffs but all had died, in most instances without debate. With the election of the Eighteenth Congress and the return of Henry Clay to the House, the forces for protection were substantially strengthened and a bill had been drafted that divided imported goods into two categories: items, mostly luxuries, that were not manufactured in the United States and on which a tariff for revenue was to be levied, and articles, most conspicuously items made of cotton, wool, iron, and glass, that were also manufactured domestically. The debate on the bill attracted petitions from the champions and enemies of protection. As in earlier agitations of the tariff question, agriculture and commerce were ranged against the manufacturers. At the heart of the controversy, of course, lay profound ideological differences.

Many Americans feared factories and manufacturing as tending to undermine morals and impoverish the workers. To them agriculture and democracy went hand in hand. Manufacturing was better suited to the reactionary regimes of Europe than to the republican spirit of the United States. To encourage manufacturing was to enter into a league with the Devil, the motive for which could be nothing more than desire for unholy profits. South Carolina argued, first, that the Constitution contained no provision for the encouragement of manufacturers and, secondly, that an increase in the tariff on imported cotton goods was nothing more than a tax on the cotton planters of Charleston. Another major Southern argument was that since two-thirds of its cotton was exported to Europe, any measure that, by constraining European trade, restricted the power of those nations to pay for Southern cotton with imported goods must work for the eventual impoverishment of the region.

Daniel Webster, closely allied with the commercial and maritime interests of New England, was initially an enemy of protection; Clay, as originator of the "American system," was its warmest and most skilled advocate. Speaking to the Congress, Clay invoked the "aid of the Most High" for a special dispensation of "power, moral and physical" to place the issue in its proper light. The Kentuckian began by depicting the economic situation of the country in the darkest possible colors— "successive crops of unthreshed grain . . . numerous bankruptcies . . . extending to all orders of society . . . a universal complaint of lack of employment . . . the reluctant resort to the perilous use of paper money. . . ." This distress "pervades every part of the union, every class of society. . . . What is the CAUSE of this wide-spreading distress, of this deep depression?" Clay asked, and answered that it was due to the fact that the American economy had been geared to the wars that had wracked Europe for a generation. Clay pointed up an interesting fact: the value of American exports in 1795 had been $40,764,097. Allowing for a growth in population of something more than 4 percent a year, or an increase in population between 1795 and 1825 of 120 percent, the value of American exports in the past year should have been $85,420,861; it had in fact been only $47,155,408.

The tariff bill, with Clay's astute management, passed the Senate by four votes and the House by five. The margin was a narrow one but the vote itself was one of those watersheds historians delight in identifying. It signaled the coming of age of American industry as a political power and, most important of all, provided a respectable rationale for its growth. The "American policy" or (as it came to be called) "the American system" had a reassuringly patriotic ring about it.

Less than two years after the passage of the bill from which so much had been expected, the manufacturers of woolen goods held an emergency meeting in Boston, petitioned Congress to impose a stiff duty on imported woolen material, and began a high-powered campaign to raise tariffs yet again.

While the South, led by South Carolina, showered Congress with angry petitions and warnings, the owners of failing mills and the growers of wool redoubled their efforts to get that body to pass legislation they believed would save them. The flood of petitions for and against increased tariffs seemed endless. They poured into the chambers of the Committee on Manufactures, dominated by Jacksonian antiprotection Congressmen, who held lengthy hearings and then—in a piece of misplaced strategy—proposed a bill with such sharp increases in the tariff schedule that the majority members of the committee assumed all moderate Congressmen would be frightened off and the bill must therefore fail of passage. By bringing in a bill that exceeded the hopes of the staunchest protectionists, the Jacksonians on the committee hoped to reconcile adherents of the American system in the Middle and Western states and ensure their support of Jackson in the coming election. The intention was, further, to put New England on the rack by increasing the duties on the raw wool its manufacturers imported to make cloth. Rates on imported items necessary to shipbuilding were also greatly increased with the expectation of driving off New England votes. The Jacksonians in Congress were determined to force a vote on the unamended bill, confident it would prove repugnant to a majority of the Representatives. The strategy failed. The House and Senate managed to amend out just a few of the bill's most obnoxious provisions. It passed and became promptly known as the Tariff of Abominations. As one senator put it, the tariff was "changed into a machine for manufacturing Presidents, instead of broadcloths and bed blankets."

News of the passage of the tariff bill brought renewed threats of secession from some regions of the South. Militant South Carolinians declared: "By all the great principles of liberty, by the glorious achievements of our fathers in defending them, by their noble blood poured forth like the waters in maintaining them, by their lives in suffering and their deaths in honor and glory, our countrymen, we must resist!" There were calls throughout the South for retaliation in the form of prohibition on the sale of Northern products. The students of South Carolina College pledged themselves not to "buy, consume, or wear any article of clothing manufactured north of the Potomac till the rights of our State shall be fully acknowledged." In Southern states the Fourth of July, 1828, was celebrated with such toasts as "Internal improvements and the tariff—the firebrands of discord. Let the South look to State rights and State sovereignty" and "Down with the tariff, the accursed upas [a mythical tree] beneath whose poisonous shade the prosperity, the life, perhaps, of this confederacy is destined to expire."

All over the South the issue of union versus disunion was hotly debated. The most fateful statement on the subject was a lengthy paper written by John Calhoun, the vice-president of the United States, developing in great detail the arguments against the constitutionality of the tariff act and in favor of the right of a state to nullify or ignore such acts. Circulated anonymously, it was adopted by the South Carolina legislature and came to be known as the South Carolina Exposition of 1828.

That resistance to the Tariff of Abominations did not pass beyond angry editorials and impassioned memorials was due in part to the fact that there was relatively little its Southern opponents could *do* but fulminate. The tariffs were collected by federal customs officials, primarily in Northern ports. Most important of all, the South anticipated the defeat in the coming election of John Quincy Adams by the hero of antiprotectionism, Andrew Jackson. With Jackson would come, presumably, a number of new Democratic Congressmen. There was thus every reason to assume the repeal of the obnoxious tariff.

The Tariff of Abominations did not bring prosperity to the North or ruin to the South. Its principal effect was to increase, if possible, the hostility and suspicion with which those two regions regarded each other and to initiate and define the basic opposing positions on the tariff question that would continue to trouble American politics for generations and that even today have not been successfully resolved.

John Quincy Adams's administration thus drew to a close much as it had begun, an "accidental" presidency, a vestige of "the old order" marked principally by an abortive piece of legislation, the Tariff of Abominations, that served to do little more than complete the demoralization of the National Republicans of whom Adams was hardly more than the nominal head. In a sense, therefore, this volume properly starts with the election of 1828 and the inauguration of what has been quite properly called the Age of Jackson.

The Jacksonians, who might be said to have begun the presidential campaign upon Adams's inauguration, found an invaluable ally in one of the "Old Republicans" of New York, Martin Van Buren, longtime foe of DeWitt Clinton and the Erie Canal. The completion of the canal was a serious setback to Van Buren's prospects in his home state, and he decided to re-establish the political bond between New York and Virginia that had brought Jefferson victory in 1800.

As an Old Republican and a supporter of William H. Crawford, committed to the Jeffersonian program of small government, free trade, and opposition to internal improvements, Van Buren was at odds with the National Republicans, whose leaders were Clay and Adams. But he was certainly an odd champion of Jacksonian Democracy. "He wore," an acquaintance wrote, "an elegant snuff-colored broadcloth coat with a velvet collar; his cravat was orange with modest lace tips; his vest of a pearl hue; his trousers were white duck, his shoes were morocco; his neat fitting gloves were yellow kid; his long-furred beaver with a broad brim was of a Quaker color." It was this sartorially resplendent figure whose remarkable political skills were now employed to advance the candidate of the people. In one of those familiar ironies of history, America's "coolest" politician joined forces with its "hottest." "If Gen Jackson & his friends will put his election on old party grounds," Van Buren wrote a friend, "preserve the old systems, avoid if not condemn the practices of the last campaign we can by adding his personal popularity to the yet remaining force of old party feeling, not only succeed in electing him but our success when achieved will be worth something." The "something" in this case was to be Van Buren's own eventual presidency.

Van Buren was the heir of Aaron Burr in his command of political tactics and organization. The "Little Magician" time and again had discomforted his popular rival, DeWitt Clinton, and had even succeeded for a time in halting the progress of the Erie Canal itself. Leaving the so-called Albany Regency behind to parcel out New York's patronage and run the political machine he had created, Van Buren established himself in Washington to take charge of the Jackson campaign. His principal coadjutors were the so-called Richmond Junto, led by the editor of the *Richmond Enquirer*, Thomas Richie; Duff Green of the *United States Telegraph*; Amos Kendall, editor of the *Argus of Western America*, a leading Jacksonian paper in Kentucky; and Vice-President Calhoun himself, who had moved into the Jackson camp soon after the election of 1824. Kendall, who had been a tutor to Henry Clay's numerous children, was the most intriguing figure of the Jackson brain trust.

The two issues to which Van Buren gave his closest attention were the development of local political organizations in all the states and the establishment of a nationwide chain of pro-Jackson newspapers. He advised Jackson to take as vague a stand as possible on the few issues of current public concern. Jackson thus described himself as a friend of the states but disavowed being an enemy "to domestic manufacture or internal works." He favored a "careful tariff" that followed a "middle and just course." He would, he assured his supporters, be ruthless in curbing the corruption and political favoritism rampant in Washington under the Adams administration. He vowed to "purify the Departments." All public officeholders "who are known to have interferred in the election as committeemen, electioneers or otherwise . . . would be unceremoniously removed," as would all who had been appointed "from political considerations or against the will of the people, and all who were incompetent." Adams, accused of installing political supporters in public office, had in fact been upbraided by members of his own faction for failing to do so and replied that he would not "dismiss or drop from Executive offices, able and faithful political opponents to provide for my own partisans."

Van Buren and his aides were notably successful at both organization and propaganda. Committees for Jackson were created on the community and county levels, with a state "central committee" to direct their activities and assist in raising money. Political events, the occasions for the "Hurra Boys" that had been so successful in creating sentiment for Jackson four years earlier, were revived—rallies, barbecues, and parades. In Baltimore, for example, Roger Taney, one of Jackson's more ardent supporters, arranged a "Grand Barbecue." Word was circulated that "three Bullocks are to be roasted, and each man is to wear a Hickory Leaf in his hat."

As the campaign ran its malodorous course, both sides engaged in relentless mudslinging. The Democrats attacked John Quincy, as they had four years earlier, for his father's supposed predilection for aristocracy and monarchy. He was, they charged, "trained up in anti-republican principles" by his father, who had been "poisoned with monarchy and aristocracy during his embassy in London."

Adams was accused of "royal extravagances" in the White House. "What sign was it," the editor of the Steubenville, Pennsylvania, *Ledger* asked, "that a *Billiard Table*—an instrument used by genteel and fashionable gamblers in high-life to play, and sport their money and time with an instrument seen at European courts and in the palaces of the 'nobility' . . . What sign was it, to see the *President of the United States* indulging either his taste for gentility, or for gambling, in expending the money, which is taken from the pockets of the people, in the purchase of *Tables and Balls, which Can be used for no purpose but for gambling*." In an effort to appeal to ethnic minorities, especially the Irish, Adams was accused of bigotry toward Catholics. Jackson, on the other hand, was declared "the son of honest Irish parents. . . . That natural interest which all true-hearted Irishmen feel in the fame of one who had so much genuine Irish blood in his veins, has drawn upon the head of that devoted people, the denunciation of the partisans of Messers. Adams & Clay."

Adams was also accused of "travelling through Rhode Island and Massachusetts on the Sabbath," a shocking impiety. In contrast, it was pointed out that Jackson attended a Presbyterian church (Adams was a Unitarian, which many orthodox Christians considered a heretical sect). "Does the old man [Jackson] have prayers in his own house?" Van Buren asked a visitor. "If so, mention it modestly."

Clay received almost as much attention in the Democratic press as Adams, since a main point of Democratic strategy was to depict Adams as the pliant tool of Clay. Duff Green in the *United States Telegraph* denounced him for using expensive writing paper made in England: "O fie, Mr. Clay—*English* paper, *English* wax, *English* pen-knives, is this your *American* System?" Democrats in Congress assisted by mailing out thousands of pieces of pro-Jackson campaign literature under their congressional franchises.

The National Republicans, friends of the administration, had neither the talents nor the taste for grass-roots organizing and the political hoopla that characterized the Jacksonian party. (It was really that—the personal party of Andrew Jackson, and serious political issues were hardly touched on.) Their principal tactic was to depict Jackson as a crude and uncultivated man, not fit for the high office of president. But they did not stop there. They went on to rake up the old scandal that centered on Jackson's marriage. His wife, Rachel, had been previously married to a Captain Lewis Robards. Jackson had lived in the same house, and Robards suspected him of having been too intimate with his wife. When Jackson (who had the reputation of being a ladies' man and who was certainly impulsive and capable of violence) heard that Robards had told a friend that he suspected Jackson of having an affair with Rachel, he confronted Robards and told him that if he ever again suggested such a liaison "he would cut his ears out of his head, and that he was tempted to do it anyhow." Aware of Jackson's reputation as a brawler and duelist, the alarmed Robards got a warrant for Jackson's arrest, but when he came to serve it, Jackson fingered a butcher knife while glancing at Robards with an implication that could not be missed. The irate husband took to his heels, and the judge dismissed the case in the absence of anyone to press charges. It was a typical "frontier" incident. Jackson thought it a great prank. It confirmed his contempt for Robards.

Jackson subsequently tried to persuade Robards that his friendship with Rachel was innocent but Robards flew into a rage and threatened to thrash Jackson; Jackson declined the challenge on the grounds that he did not have the "bodily strength" but offered to fight a duel.

Much obscurity and conflicting testimony surrounds the whole matter, although a few things seem clear. Lewis Robards was a notorious philanderer. Rachel was a high-spirited young woman, disposed to be flirtatious. Her husband was almost pathologically suspicious, bullied Rachel, and made unpleasant scenes. Jackson had from the first, as part of the Southern-chivalric-frontier code, a strong protective feeling for Rachel that doubtless soon developed into love. Soon afterward Robards left his wife and returned to his family's home in Kentucky. Later, according to Jackson, Rachel heard that Robards intended to return to Nashville to claim her, and she decided to flee to Natchez; Jackson accompanied her, ostensibly to guard against the Indians. Word reached Nashville in the spring of 1791 that Robards had obtained a divorce by an act of the Virginia legislature. Without investigating the report, Jackson hurried to Natchez and either simply began living with Rachel, as his enemies maintained, or married her (as both he and she claimed) in a service of which no record survives and which would, in any event, have been illegal because permission of the Spanish authorities of Natchez was not obtained. Thereafter the couple returned to Nashville, where they were accepted as husband and wife and entered into the social life of the city. Two years later it was discovered that Robards had not indeed obtained a divorce in 1791, but only authorization to sue for divorce. The divorce itself was not completed until 1793. So even assuming Jackson and Rachel had been married in Natchez, they had, in the eyes of the law and all pious and moral Christians, been living in sin for two years.

Jackson's friends urged him to marry Rachel at once, but he resisted for almost a year on the grounds that to marry would be to admit that they had been living in what the law termed adultery. On January 17, 1794, Rachel and Andrew Jackson were married by a justice of the peace in a simple civil ceremony.

These were the "facts," so far as could be ascertained, that had been first whispered about in the presidential campaign of 1824 and were now taken up with renewed enthusiasm by the newspapers and journals that supported the Adams administration. The *Cincinnati Gazette* was the first to play up the story, declaring Jackson a bigamist and an adulterer. "Ought a convicted adultress and her paramour husband to be placed in the highest offices of this free and christian land?" the editor asked. The story was quickly picked up by other papers.

Not satisfied with pillorying Jackson and his wife, one scurrilous paper charged: "General Jackson's mother was a COMMON PROSTITUTE brought to this country by British soldiers! She afterwards married a MULATTO MAN, with whom she had several children, of which GENERAL JACKSON IS ONE!!" If there was a factual basis for the charges of adultery, there was none for the attack on Jackson's mother. It was said that when Jackson read the sentences he broke down and wept, saying to Rachel: "Myself I can defend. You I can defend; but now they have assailed even the memory of my mother."

The election of 1828 was a landslide victory for Jackson. New Jersey went to Adams by a narrow margin and New England remained loyal. Delaware, where the electors were still appointed by the state legislature, remained in the Republican column. Maryland split its votes between the two candidates, as did New York. But everywhere else the Jacksonian tide proved irresistible. Jackson won by 56 percent of the popular vote (647,276 to 508,064), one of the largest margins in any nineteenth-century presidential election. The electoral vote was 178 to 83. Some additional statistics are revealing. The combined presidential vote in Massachusetts was 35,892 (29,876 for Adams, 6,016 for Jackson) out of a population of 610,000. The state had grown by less than 200,000 since the census of 1810. In Ohio, with a population of 938,000, the presidential vote totaled 130,995, divided almost equally between Adams and Jackson. Ohio had grown by some 700,000, almost a fourfold increase, in the same period. While the population of Ohio was approximately one-third greater than that of Massachusetts, the voter turnout was proportionally much higher. Similarly Kentucky, with 688,000 residents to Massachusetts's 610,000, turned out twice as many voters. Connecticut, with a population of 298,000, turned out only 18,500 voters, while in Illinois, with half that population, 14,000 voters went to the polls.

The figures suggest that the citizens of the Western states were far more eager to exercise their electoral franchise than their Eastern cousins. The disparity between the older states and the newer ones in popular vote also reflects the more liberal suffrage requirements of the newer states. But much credit must go to the new order of political managers, who left no stone unturned to get out the vote. "Considerable pains were taken to bring out the people," one party worker wrote; "flags were made and sent to different parts of the country [state], and the people came in companies of fifty or sixty with the flag flying at their head, and with the words 'Jackson and Reform' on it in large letters." Duff Green exhorted the voters in the *Telegraph:* "To the polls, To the polls! The faithful sentinel must not sleep—Let no one stay home—Let every man go to the Polls—Let not a vote be lost—Let every Freeman do his duty; and all will triumph in the success of Jackson, Calhoun and Liberty." All told, the popular vote was some 800,000 greater than four years earlier.

There was exultation in the Jackson camp and a conviction among his supporters that the country had once more been rescued from those aristocrats and monarchists who had threatened its freedoms ever since 1789. And, of course, there was consequent gloom among the supporters of the administration, one of whom wrote: "Well, a great revolution has taken place. . . . This is what I all along feared but to a much greater extent." To another Republican, "It was the howl of raving Democracy that tipped Pennsylvania & New York & Ohio—and this will be kept up here after to promote the ends of the Democratic party."

The presidential campaign of 1828 was one of the most disreputable in our history. No dishonorable tactic seems to have been overlooked. If the Democrats outdid the Republicans in scurrility they did so primarily through greater energy and better organization, not because the Republicans eschewed such tactics. It was all too painful for John Quincy Adams to record in his usually scrupulously kept diary: a gap in that remarkable record extends from August through the announcement of the popular vote.

The fact was that democratic politics were brutal and brutalizing. They encouraged, if they did not require, hypocrisy, double dealing, deceitfulness, lying, ruthlessness, the vilification of one's opponents, the exaggeration of one's own virtues, and the suppression of most decent feelings and sensibilities. They were an anomaly in a professedly Christian nation, and the verbal and sometimes physical violence that lay at their heart was one of the most conspicuous of the paradoxes in American society.

On December 3 Adams noted: "A continual stream of visitors. . . . Most of the Members of Congress who came were friends, and they had but one topic of conversation—the loss of this day's election. I have only to submit to it with resignation, and to ask that those who are dear to me may be sustained under it. The sun of my political life sets in the deepest gloom. But that of my country shines unclouded." His friends and supporters might despair of the republic, but he would hold to better hopes. He still had two months to serve before his successor would be inaugurated and he could retire like his father before him to Quincy. The prospect had a kind of horror for him. He had seen John Adams waiting for twenty-five interminable years to die—often cheerfully occupied, to be sure, but often sunk in gloom over the wreck of his political fortunes and the bland, unvarying pattern of his days. John Quincy was thus tempted when Ezra Bailey, a leader in Boston politics, asked him if he would accept an appointment as United States senator from Massachusetts were the Great and General Court to offer it. His rather ambiguous answer was that he was unwilling to displace an incumbent senator.

The general atmosphere in Washington, following announcement of Jackson's election, was depressing. The officers of the Adams administration prepared to depart with their families and many government workers feared for their dearly won jobs. The arrival of Jackson in the capital was shadowed by the death of his wife, a victim, Jackson was convinced, of the charges of adultery and immorality leveled at her by the Republican press. Henry Clay and his adherents were saddened by a tragedy in his family: his eldest son, a bright and promising young man, went insane and had to be committed to an asylum. Clay was so distraught that he could not sleep for weeks without potions, and Margaret Bayard Smith, wife of Sen. Smith of Maryland, noted in him a new "softness and tenderness with sadness." Yet in public he appeared as good-humored and ingratiating as ever, and Mrs. Smith heard him speak in small groups "of Genl. Jackson and the present state of affairs in a good humour'd and sprightly way." But to Adams Clay "spoke . . . with great concern of the prospects of the country—the threats of disunion from the South, and the grasping after all the public lands, which are disclosing themselves in the Western States"—an issue that had cost Adams precious votes in Illinois, Ohio, and Indiana. Adams's reply was that after March 3 he would consider his public life closed "and take from that time as little part in public concerns as possible. I shall have enough to do to defend and vindicate my own reputation from the double persecution under which I have fallen."

It seemed to John Quincy himself that he went into private life "with a combination of parties and of public men against my character and reputation such as I believe never before was exhibited against any man since the Union existed. Posterity will scarcely believe it, but so it is, that this combination against me has been formed, and is now exulting in triumph over me, for the devotion of my life and of all the faculties of my soul to the Union, and to the improvement, physical, moral, and intellectual, of my country. The North assails me for my fidelity to the Union; the South for my ardent aspirations of improvement. Yet 'bate I not a jot of heart and hope.' Passion, prejudice, envy, and jealousy will pass. The cause of Union and of improvement will remain, and I have duties to it and to my country yet to discharge."

The public calamity that turned John Quincy Adams out of office was followed by personal tragedies—chiefly the suicide of his favorite child, George Washington Adams—that greatly increased his depression and seemed for a time to threaten Louisa's sanity. Returning to Quincy and the old family manse, now badly run down, while building a new "stone house" nearby, the former president prepared to write a biography of his father, not a very cheerful undertaking in the gloomy old house so full of memories. Charles Francis busied himself with his father's business concerns, and father and son, so often at odds, established a new relationship, one of two adults rather than that of father and son, tied by bonds of mutual respect as well as familial affection. Charles Francis wrote in his diary: "It astonishes me more and more to perceive the extent and reach of the acquisitions of my father. There is no subject upon which he does not know a great deal and explain it with the greatest beauty of language. He has in the course of this day opened his information upon the subject of painting, of music and of historical characters—All of which have been handled with perfect ease and familiarity. He is a wonderful though a singular man, and now displays more of his real character than I have ever before seen."

So we leave John Quincy Adams in the old manse at Quincy, apparently prepared to spend the rest of his years vindicating the public careers of his father and himself.

2

President Andrew Jackson

One of the most surely fixed scenes in American history is the vast outpouring of democratic enthusiasm inspired by Jackson's inauguration. By some estimates more than 20,000 euphoric Democrats from every state in the Union poured into a Washington ill equipped to accommodate them. They were a different breed, in large part, from the political warhorses and insiders who had predominated at earlier inaugurations. To the Republicans who watched scornfully it seemed "like the inundation of the northern barbarians into Rome, save that the tumultuous tide came in from a different point of the compass." Daniel Webster, perhaps reflecting on his own presidential aspirations, noted: "I never saw such a crowd here before. Persons have come five hundred miles to see General Jackson, and *they really seem to think that the country is rescued from some dreadful danger.*"

At the inauguration ceremonies the crowd pressed forward so relentlessly to see the Hero of New Orleans that the official party was threatened. An observer wrote, "Never can I forget the spectacle which presented itself on every side, nor the electrifying moment when the eager, expectant eyes of that vast and motley multitude caught sight of the tall and imposing form of their adored leader, as he came forth between the columns of the portico." A vast, fierce cry of triumph rose from thousands of throats. "As if by magic . . . the color of the whole mass changed . . . all hats were off at once, and the dark tint which usually pervades a mixed map of men was turned . . . into the bright hue of ten thousand upturned and exultant human faces, radiant with sudden joy."

The oath of office was administered by Chief Justice John Marshall. Both men were relics of the Revolution. Marshall had been a young officer with Washington in the raid on Trenton; Jackson, scarcely more than a boy, had been wounded and captured by the British in the Carolina campaign. Marshall was a classic representative of the Old Order, a Virginia aristocrat, an intellectual, the indomitable defender of the Constitution. Jackson was the precursor of the New Order, rough, impatient, volatile, the prototype of the man of action. The two tall, thin old men standing side by side on the steps of the Capitol represented in their persons the polar extremes of American politics.

For Marshall it was the darkest moment in the history of the republic. He would as soon have sworn in the devil as president of the United States. He had survived the high tide of Jeffersonianism with its implacable hostility to the Court and to his own person. Now, in the last years of his life, when he would gladly have retired to the pleasures of his plantation and the reflections of old age, a new and even more formidable opponent had appeared with a popular mandate to make war on the Constitution as Marshall understood and interpreted it.

One of the spectators noted that the Chief Justice administered the oath of office "in a low and feeble voice, so that it could not be heard many feet beyond the steps of the eastern portico of the capitol." Jackson's brief inaugural address, "graceful and dignified," might have been taken to imply that he thought action more important than words. Margaret Bayard Smith, no partisan of Jackson, declared it "grand . . . sublime!" and noted that at its conclusion the new president then "bowed . . . to the people—Yes, to the people in all their majesty."

After the ceremony was over, the President made his way with difficulty through the masses gathered in front of the Capitol and mounted his horse to return to the White House, followed by "country men, farmers, gentlemen, mounted and mismounted, boys, women and children, black and white. Carriages, wagons and carts all pursuing him to the President's house." When Mrs. Smith finally found her way to the White House, the orderly procession of democrats had degenerated into a wild scene. She found "a rabble, a mob, of boys, negros, women, children, scrambling, fighting, romping. . . . No arrangements had been made no police officers placed on duty and the whole house had been inundated by the rabble mob. . . . The President after having been *literally* nearly pressed to death and almost suffocated and torn to pieces by the people in their eagerness to shake hands with Old Hickory, had retreated through the back way and had escaped to his lodgings at Gadsby's. Cut glass and china to the amount of several thousand dollars had been broken in the struggle to get the refreshments. . . . Ladies fainted, men were seen with bloody noses and such a scene of confusion took place as is impossible to describe—for those who got in could not get out by the door again but had to scramble out of windows." In Mrs. Smith's words, "Ladies and gentlemen only had been expected at this Levee, not the people en masse. But it was the People's day, and the People's President and the People would rule. . . . The noisy and disorderly rabble in the President's House brought to my mind the descriptions I had read, of the mobs in the Tuileries and at Versailles."

The scene at the White House, vividly described in newspapers everywhere, seemed to confirm the apprehensions of the National Republicans and of upper-class Americans generally. The lower orders of society, the "people," were on the march under the banner of Jackson and Democracy. Soon respectable persons, the well-to-do, the well-born, and the well-educated would not be safe in their beds. Margaret Smith was not alone in her reflections on the mobs of the French Revolution. Blown quite out of proportion, the White House "riot" became the symbol of a crude and "licentious" democracy.

The man who assumed office as the eighth president of the United States is certainly a compelling figure. He was that most intriguing of American types, the man of action. His whole career had been characterized by violent acts—against his enemies, against his friends, against Indians, against the British. He had fought his first duel as a young lawyer at twenty-one in Jonesborough, Tennessee. Believing that an older lawyer had spoken disparagingly of him in court, Jackson had demanded satisfaction. When the duel took place both men fired into the air and, honor satisfied, shook hands. His next duel came in 1805 as a consequence of a reported slur on Rachel by young Charles Dickinson. Believing that he could not equal Dickinson—reputed to be the best shot in Tennessee—in speed, Jackson determined to allow Dickinson to fire the first shot, to hold his own fire until he had recovered from the shock of the bullet's impact (assuming it did not kill him outright), and then coolly and deliberately to shoot his opponent. The duel went according to Jackson's plan. Dickinson fired quickly and hit Jackson in the chest. Jackson recoiled from the impact and with his teeth clenched against the pain placed his left arm across his chest. The dismayed Dickinson, expecting to see Jackson fall, thought for a moment he had missed him and stepped from his mark. Jackson's second aimed his own pistol at Dickinson and ordered him back. Jackson took his time aiming and firing at the defenseless Dickinson. His bullet hit below the ribs and tore a hole in the lower stomach. Dickinson fell forward and bled to death in a few moments.

Jackson, who later said "I should have hit him if he had shot me through the brain," walked some distance with his second and physician, neither of whom realized that Jackson had been seriously wounded. The first indication was that Jackson's shoe was full of blood. His coat and shirt were then cut off. Dickinson's bullet had smashed two ribs and lodged itself in Jackson's chest near his heart, where it remained to cause him constant pain for years to come. Dickinson was said to have bet three hundred dollars that he would kill Jackson; he had marked his outline on a tree and riddled it with bullets. Jackson had demonstrated his remarkable power of will and his remorseless temper. A few years later, his cordial reception of Aaron Burr after Burr's duel with Hamilton seemed to condone Burr's act, or—worse—celebrate it.

In 1813, after the Battle of New Orleans, Jackson took up the cause of a young officer in the Tennessee Volunteers, Captain William Carroll, who had gotten into a quarrel with one of the sons of the powerful Benton clan. Challenged to a duel, Carroll persuaded Jackson to serve as his second. Jackson instructed the two opponents in the etiquette of the duel—with which, needless to say, he was thoroughly familiar. The men must stand back to back, walk the prescribed distance (in this case five paces), wheel, and fire standing erect. Jesse Benton wheeled, crouched in the manner of a Western gunfighter, and fired, hitting Carroll in the thumb. Carroll's bullet plowed along Benton's buttocks. Benton had violated the dueler's code, but Jackson advised Carroll to ignore the matter since no fatal damage had been done.

When Thomas Hart Benton returned from Washington, where he had been doing his best to straighten out Jackson's accounts with the War Department, he was enraged to learn that Jackson had acted in behalf of Carroll against his brother. He angrily denounced Jackson. Troublemakers carried his words to the equally hot-headed general, who wrote to ask Benton if they were true: "Have you or have you not threatened to challenge me." Benton wrote a detailed reply, upbraiding Jackson for having allowed the duel to take place at all and accusing him of having conducted it "in a savage, unequal, unfair, and base manner." He had not threatened to challenge Jackson. "At the same time the terror of your pistols is not to seal my lips. What I believe to be true, I shall speak; and if for this I am called to account, it must be so."

Speak Benton did all over Tennessee, and Jackson, fiercely jealous of his public image, was infuriated by the stories that reached him. He announced he would horsewhip Benton the next time he encountered him. Forewarned, Thomas Benton rode into Nashville with his brother, took lodgings at a hotel near Jackson's, and prepared for the showdown. Jackson, ostentatiously carrying a whip, walked past the hotel where Thomas Benton stood in the doorway. Jackson went on to the post office, got his mail, and started back up the street. Now both Bentons were waiting with double-barreled pistols. When Jackson came abreast of his former friend and political ally he turned, waved his whip, and called out "Now, you damned rascal, I am going to punish you. Defend yourself." Benton reached as though for his gun but Jackson forced him to step back into the hotel. Jesse slipped through a door and along a porch where a window opened into the lobby. He fired and hit Jackson in the arm. As he fell, Jackson fired at Thomas Benton and missed. Benton in turn fired twice at the prostrate Jackson. Stockley Hays, a close friend of Jackson's, heard the shots, rushed into the hotel, and tried to stab Jesse with his sword cane. The slender sword broke on a button and Hays, a huge man, carried Jesse to the floor, where he stabbed him repeatedly with a dagger before he was dragged off by onlookers.

Jackson, badly injured, his arm and shoulder smashed, almost died from loss of blood before hastily summoned doctors could stem the flow. The consensus was that the arm should be amputated, but Jackson refused to allow the operation. The Indian remedy of slippery elm was used to treat the wounds and prevent infection, but it was three weeks before Jackson could leave his bed. When he did so it was with Jesse Benton's bullet in his shoulder.

Thomas Benton, after the affray, had marched around the town square denouncing Jackson as an assassin and crowing over his "defeat." But Benton soon experienced the pressure of Jackson's numerous friends. "I am in the middle of hell," he wrote a friend, "and see no alternative but to kill or be killed; for I will not crouch to Jackson; the fact that I and my brother defeated him and his tribe, and broke his small sword in the public square, will for ever rankle in his bosom and make him thirst for vengeance. My life is in danger . . . for it is a settled plan to turn out puppy after puppy to bully me, and when I have got into a scrape, to have me killed somehow in the scuffle." Benton moved to Missouri to become the political leader in that state and a United States senator. Ten years later, when Jackson was also a senator, the two men forgave each other and formed an important and enduring political alliance.

Considering the relationship of Jackson and Benton, one is moved to reflect that American men sometimes seem to have only two modes of relating, as we say today: social conviviality or shooting at each other. Often the modes were followed successively—intimate camaraderie, shooting to kill, and then camaraderie once more. Certainly that had been the course of the Jackson-Benton relationship. (Dueling was by no means an exclusively American social form, but in Europe it was confined to the upper classes and made far less lethal by the use, in most instances, of swords that left honorable scars but seldom resulted in death or disabling wounds.)

During the campaign against the Creek Jackson had ordered young John Wood court-martialed for mutiny. Largely at Jackson's behest the court-martial board had found Wood guilty and ordered him shot. Wood's "mutiny" consisted of abusing and threatening an officer who had peremptorily ordered him back to his post when he was eating breakfast. In the Florida campaign Jackson had strung up the two British traders Ambrister and Arbuthnut without ceremony and created a serious international crisis. Notorious for his terrible tempers, he had been insubordinate on more than one occasion. He was obstinate, vengeful, arrogant, volatile, something of a bully. He drank copiously if seldom to excess (in later years as an antidote to the constant pain of his wounds), loved horse racing and cockfighting and all the wild sports of the frontier. Small wonder many Americans, especially those north of Mason and Dixon's Line thought him little better than a savage.

On the other side of the ledger, he could be charming and courteous. He was often generous and invariably a man of his word. Certainly no one ever questioned his courage. If he had numerous vices, they were democratic ones and some were those much honored on the frontier—especially the Southern frontier. Above all, Jackson had remarkable qualities of leadership, qualities that we now call charisma, the power to draw and bind men and women to him. He was part genteel plantation owner, part frontier tough. Not intellectual in any sense, he was highly intelligent, with the shrewd practical intelligence so vital in democratic politics and so lacking in his rival, John Quincy Adams.

Beyond all these defects and positive attributes lay a quality much more important and profound. Unlike Jefferson in almost every other respect, Jackson was like him in his capacity to represent or epitomize a critically important set of ideals and aspirations held by ordinary men and women. Tall and thin, his presence recalled the power and dignity of a Washington. His long face with its strong features and his stiff white hair made him seem even taller than he was. Crippled as he was by his mostly ill-won wounds, his bearing was that of a soldier. In his suspicion of "Eastern" gentlemen, of intellectuals, Harvard professors, businessmen, and bankers he was typical of a very considerable number of his countrymen. His advocacy of the cause of "the people" was thus not a political gambit but the most central part of his consciousness. All his mature life he had resented the superior and patronizing ways of the Eastern elite and, most of all, their assumption that it was the wish of the Almighty that they should have in their hands the running of the country.

Like Washington and Jefferson, Andrew Jackson is one of those essential and inexhaustible heroes who, by embodying ideas important to the nation, have made possible crucial transitions in American society. Ideas in themselves are never enough to move history; they must be dramatized by charismatic leaders. Such individuals enter, as Jackson certainly did, into another realm or order of reality. The standards we apply to the common run of historical figures are inadequate to measure them.

Jackson's Cabinet appointments went to individuals whose principal qualifications were that they were his devoted followers. Van Buren was made secretary of state; S. D. Ingram of Pennsylvania was appointed secretary of the treasury; John Eaton of Kentucky, secretary of war; John Branch of North Carolina, secretary of the navy; John McLean of Ohio, postmaster; and John McPherson Berrien of Georgia, attorney general. Geography rather than talent was clearly the guiding principle. When Virginians complained that for the first time since the beginning of the republic there were no Virginians in the Cabinet, they were reminded that four years earlier Virginia had given her votes to Crawford and Adams in preference to Jackson.

The policy of firing the holders of public office under the preceding administration and replacing them with persons who had demonstrated their loyalty to Jackson was perhaps the most serious charge made against the new administration. Jackson was credited with having initiated the "spoils system" and William Marcy, a Jacksonian senator from New York, attached the phrase to the Democrats in a defiant speech in defense of Van Buren which he concluded with the observation that the Jacksonians "boldly *preach* what they *practice.* When they are contending for *victory,* they avow the intention of enjoying the fruits of it. . . . They see nothing wrong in the rule that to the VICTOR belongs the spoils of the ENEMY." Actually, in his first eighteen months in office Jackson replaced 919 officeholders out of 10,093, which is not exactly a clean sweep.

Much publicity was given in the Republican press to the hardships caused by the dismissals. A secretary in the Auditor's Office had committed suicide and a clerk in the State Department went mad. Amos Kendall, the editor of the *Argus* who had been rewarded for his support of Jackson by a job in the Treasury Department, wrote his wife: "I turned out six clerks on Saturday. Several of them have families and are poor. It was the most painful thing I ever did. . . . Among them is a poor old man, with a young wife and children. I shall raise a contribution to get him back to Ohio." More than three hundred postmasters were removed from office for having campaigned or simply voted for Adams.

To understand fully the effect of the remorseless weeding out of officeholders considered unfriendly to Jackson, the general economic insecurity that characterized American life must be kept in mind. There was a price for freedom, for mobility, even for "equality." The price was chronic insecurity and that insecurity was the greater the higher the status of the individual and the greater his ambition. As we have noted earlier, business and industry had not developed to the point where they provided any substantial number of jobs for middle-class youths. When one advanced from farming (which had its own multitudinous insecurities) to what we would call today white-collar employment, schoolteaching and the law—often engaged in successively—were the principal occupations. Schoolteaching was poorly paid and uncertain, and the law was so crowded with practition-ers that few could make a living at it. Besides law, public office was the principal hope of thousands of men with families to support whose nightmare was that they might sink down into the ranks of the laboring class from which some of them at least had only recently risen. If James Monroe, a former president of the United States and a member of the Virginian Establishment could fall in a few years into abject poverty, who was not threatened? Thus the competition for public office, the determination to achieve it or to hold onto it acquired, in early-nineteenth-century America, a quality of desperation that went far beyond the mere avidity for power so evident in all politics.

To John Quincy Adams, Jackson's appointments were "almost without exception . . . conferred upon the vilest purveyors of slander . . . and an excessive disproportion of places is given to editors of the foulest presses. . . . The custom-houses in Boston, New York, and Philadelphia have been swept clean, also Portsmouth, New Hampshire and New Orleans. The appointments are exclusively of violent partisans."

In addition to the large-scale removal of officeholders, the other issue that consumed much of the time of the new administration and held the fascinated attention of the country was that of Peggy O'Neale Eaton, the wife of the secretary of war. She had earlier been married to a purser in the navy named Timberlake; while he was at sea she had lived at a tavern owned by her father and there had met Jackson and Eaton, senators from Tennessee. Eaton had become enamored of the handsome Peggy, and after her husband died he had married her. There were rumors that they had been living together prior to her husband's demise and her reputation was not, in any event, "in good odor." In consequence, a number of the wives of Jackson's new Cabinet members refused to receive her at social functions or to attend those where it was known she would be. It was not clear whether their rejection of Peggy O'Neale was due to the fact that she was the daughter of a tavernkeeper or to the scandal that surrounded her marriage to Eaton. In Adams's words, "the Vice-President's wife, Mrs. Calhoun, being of the virtuous . . . remains in the untainted atmo-sphere of South Carolina." Jackson was furious and stood resolutely by his secretary of war, undoubtedly seeing in the opposition to Mrs. Eaton an analogy to the attacks on Rachel. As the controversy raged, Margaret Smith noted "Mrs. E. continues excluded from society, except the homes of some of the foreigners, the President's and Mr.

V.B.'s." At the Russian minister's Peggy Eaton was the first led to supper, which so enraged the wife of the Dutch ambassador that she and her husband refused to sit at the table.

Social life at the White House was characterized by an unprecedented degree of informality. "Persons of all ranks visit very socially," Margaret Smith wrote a friend, "and in return the family accept all invitations and visit the citizens in the most social manner, and live on more equal and familiar terms, than any other Presd. family ever has." But the matter of Peggy Eaton would not die. The female phalanx was solid and unrelenting. Even the President's great prestige and popularity was unavailing. And if Margaret Smith had originally been charmed by the President's courtesy and thoughtfulness, she was increasingly scandalized by his actions. She described him as "completely under the government of Mrs. Eaton, one of the most ambitious, violent, malignant, yet silly women you ever heard of. . . . The new Cabinet if they do not yield to the President's will on the point, will, it is supposed, soon be dismissed." Some took the cowards' way out by not bringing their wives to Washington and thus not being expected to entertain.

Every serious political issue remained in abeyance while the Eaton battle was fought to its conclusion. Word had it that John Branch, the secretary of the navy, whose wife had snubbed Peggy Eaton, was to be forced to resign, but two senators (Adams was told) had visited Jackson and warned him that if Branch were removed the senators from North Carolina "would join the opposition, and all the dubious nominations now before the Senate would be rejected. . . . Calhoun," Adams added, "heads the moral party, Van Buren that of the frail sisterhood; and he is notoriously engaged in canvassing for the Presidency by paying his court to Mrs. Eaton."

The "invisible" Amos Kendall was Jackson's alter ego, the classic self-effacing courtier. A native of Massachusetts and a graduate of Dartmouth College, Kendall had emigrated to Kentucky and been tutor to Clay's children and then a dedicated Jacksonian, helping to carry the state for the general in 1828. In his early forties, Kendall's hair was snow-white, his complexion sallow, evidence of bad health and overwork. He seldom appeared in public, but most of Jackson's important state papers were drafted by "this twilight personage," as Harriet Martineau called him—adding, "He is supposed to be the moving spring of the whole administration, the thinker, planner, and doer . . . work is done, of goblin extent and goblin speed, which makes men look about them with a superstitious wonder. . . . He unites with his 'great talent for silence' a splendid audacity." Martineau felt that Kendall imparted to Jackson's whole administration an air of mysterious potency "by the universal belief that there was a concealed eye and hand behind the machinery of government, by which everything could be foreseen, and the hardest deeds done."

On the rare occasions Kendall did appear in public he was the center of attention. The word would go around in a buzz: "Kendall is here"; "That is he." The Republican canard that Jackson was virtually illiterate gave Kendall an even greater importance in the public mind. Every paper that issued from the executive chambers was attributed to him. Although most presidents have had especially trusted advisers, the perfect harmony in which these two ailing men worked throughout the eight years of Jackson's administration has no parallel in our history.

When the new Twenty-first Congress assembled early in December, 1829, it was clearly in the hands of the Democrats. It was not long before a number of political brands were afire. Rumors circulated freely in Washington concerning Jackson's hostility toward the Bank of the United States. Jefferson and Adams, if they agreed on few other things, had agreed on the iniquity of banks. In their view banks made their profits on the manipulation of other people's money. They collected such funds, private or public, as they could get their hands on and then decided who should have the use of the money. Since they were invariably allied with the most conservative elements in their communities, their funds showed a disinclination to find their way into the accounts of Jeffersonian Republicans or Jacksonian Democrats. They lent money freely in good times and then, in bad times, when farmers and manufacturers desperately needed financial assistance, they foreclosed the mortgages and seized the security, usually land. Even their foreclosures favored the well-to-do. An abandoned factory was a liability for a bank. Idle machines rusted away. The bank had strong incentives to carry hard-pressed factories, but land was negotiable. In the depression of 1819, the Bank of the United States foreclosed more than fifty thousand acres of farmland in Ohio and Kentucky alone; the increase in value of those acres helped, a few years later, to save the Bank from collapse. The Jeffersonians had refused to recharter the Bank of the United States when its charter expired, but in the desperate need for money created by the War of 1812 the Bank had been rechartered after a bitter fight. The popular resentment against it had never waned and the events of 1819 had added fuel to the fire. If the "equality" celebrated in the Declaration of Independence meant, most essentially, equal opportunity to make money, equal access to money was the right of every American.

Nicholas Biddle, a member of the great Biddle family of Philadelphia, had been part of Joseph Dennie's Tuesday Club and a contributor to the *Portfolio,* a literary magazine that devoted considerable space to deploring the excesses of democracy. Essentially literary in his interests, Biddle had been gradually drawn into the affairs of the Bank of the United States, first as a member of the board of directors when the Bank was rechartered in 1814 and, nine years later, as its president. Not surprisingly, the Bank was a bastion of anti-Jacksonian sentiment. Year after year bills were introduced into Congress to clip the Bank's wings or suspend its charter. All were defeated, but with the election of Jackson the anti Bank forces took new heart. John McLean, the new postmaster general whose office was soon to be raised by the President to Cabinet level, wrote to Biddle urging that the officers of the branch of the Bank in Kentucky be drawn from both political parties. Biddle responded that to do so would "politicize" the Bank, which had remained scrupulously above politics.

The Democratic senator from New Hampshire was the next to take up the attack, charging that the president of the branch bank in Portsmouth, New Hampshire, was a "particular friend of Webster" and that, lacking in "conciliatory manners and intimate acquaintance with our business men," he had treated them with "partiality and harshness." J. D. Ingram, Jackson's secretary of the treasury, was soon involved in the correspondence with Biddle. Biddle was urged to appoint a new board of directors for the Portsmouth branch, consisting of six supporters of Adams's administration and four Jackson supporters. When Biddle resisted this proposal, Ingram warned that the government might remove United States deposits from the Bank and the President himself appoint five directors more amenable to his wishes. Biddle, seeing the handwriting on the wall, hastened to comply. He had an audience with Jackson and came away convinced that he had placated the President and reassured him about the nonpolitical role of the Bank.

In his first annual address to Congress, Jackson gave a résumé of the foreign relations of the United States with special attention to the unsettled state of affairs in South America, the dispute with England over the Maine-Canadian boundary, and the controversy with Mexico: slavery had been prohibited in Texas by the Mexican Congress, and the Mexican government refused to allow further settlement of Americans in the area in contravention of a treaty with the United States. Included in the address was a reference to the need for reform of the Tariff of 1828. Jackson also alarmed traditionalists by proposing an amendment to the Constitution to abolish the electoral college and provide for the direct election of the president and vice-president, who would be limited to one term of four or possibly six years. Jackson defended his "spoils system" by stating that in a democracy no person had any vested right in a public office. Such offices existed for the benefit of the people, not the officeholders. The President also reported that the national debt would soon be paid off through import duties and the sale of public lands and that the Treasury might, indeed, find itself with an embarrassment of riches, a large surplus which, Jackson suggested, should be distributed to the states on the basis of representation in Congress.

Like every president before him, Jackson had much to say on the subject of the Indians, toward whom he expressed the most benevolent intentions. He endorsed the notion of a vast Western preserve to be put aside for them, to which they should be encouraged to move voluntarily. If they preferred to remain within the boundaries of particular states, they must be subject to the laws of those states. Finally he raised the question of the Bank of the United States. It was, he insisted, of dubious constitutionality. Various criticisms had been leveled against it, many of them justified. Although its charter ran until 1836, it was not too early to begin to consider its replacement by an institution more compatible with the ideals of a democratic people.

Jackson's stricture on the Bank, included in his address against the advice of his closest advisers, had the effect of raising the issue to a level of symbolic significance early in his administration. It fixed him ever more firmly in the public eye as an opponent of the "interests."

The enemies of the administration found an abundance of grist for their mill in the President's message. Hardly an issue by Jackson failed to rouse anxiety or indignation in Republican bosoms. The proposal to remove the Indians proved one of the most inflammatory. Jackson had already alarmed the friends of the Indians by urging the Cherokee to remove beyond the Mississippi, telling them in effect that as long as they remained in Georgia they could expect no protection from the federal government. The Creek received a similar letter:

"Friends and brothers, listen. Where you now are, you and my white children are too near to each other to live in harmony and peace. Your game is gone, and many of your people will not work and till the earth. Beyond the great river Mississippi, where a part of your nation has gone, your father has provided a country large enough for all of you, and he advises you to remove to it. There your white brothers will not trouble you; they will have no claim to the land, and you can live upon it as long as the grass grows or the water runs, in peace and plenty. The land beyond the Mississippi belongs to the President and no one else, and he will give it to you forever."

The President's offhand dismissal of the Indians' claim that their treaties with the United States exempted them from the laws of the states in which their reservations were located aroused a furor in New England. Charles Francis Adams noted in January: "I went to a Meeting which was called in favour of the Cherokee and Creek Indians in the question with Georgia. It was very full. I never had seen a thing of the kind before. But it was not very famous for its soundness or its deliberation." One speaker "talked of sending a thousand regulars into Georgia with as much coolness as if he was going to take a breakfast" and received warm applause for his efforts. Resolutions denouncing treaty violations were adopted unanimously with the observation that such treatment of the Indians "would probably bring upon us the reproaches of mankind, and would certainly expose us to the judgments of Heaven." Charles Francis, who differed considerably from his father on the question of Indian policy, thought the speeches and resolutions "foolishly violent." In addition they gave him a headache. He wrote the elder Adams that he thought the matter should be decided on practical grounds "without reference to the abstract and impracticable views of the moralists." He was tempted to say so publicly. He received a sharp rebuke from his father, who urged him not "to make your first Essay at public speaking on the unpopular side of a great question of national policy," especially before he had gone thoroughly into the matter as a "question of justice—of Morals—of Politics—of Natural—Conventional—Constitutional, and federal Law—Of Natural History and of Political Economy. It is this and more."

In the Senate debate on the removal of the Cherokee, Henry Clay was at his most eloquent and impassioned. Word had spread in the House and throughout the city that Clay was to speak on behalf of the Cherokee, and the floor and the gallery of the Senate were crowded with foreign ambassadors, fashionable women of Washington who espoused his cause, and a solemn group of Cherokee chiefs. The audience was not disappointed. "His first sentences," Harriet Martineau wrote, "are homely, and given with a little hesitation and repetition, and with an agitation shown by frequent putting on and taking off of his spectacles, and a trembling of his hands among the documents on his desk." Then as Clay warmed to his subject, "the agitation changes its character. . . . His utterance is still deliberate, but his voice becomes deliciously winning . . . trembling with emotion, falling and swelling with the earnestness of the speaker . . . and his whole manner becomes irresistibly persuasive." Martineau saw "tears . . . falling on his papers as he vividly described the woes and injuries of the aborigines." Only Van Buren, who yawned ostentatiously, and the senators from Georgia seemed unmoved by Clay's speech.

The most outspoken opponents of the policy of Indian removal were the Christian missionaries among them. At a meeting at New Echota, North Carolina, in December, 1829, a group of missionaries resolved "That we view the Indian question, at present so much agitated in the United States, as being not merely of a political, but of a moral nature—inasmuch as it involves the maintenance or violation of the faith of our country—and as demanding, therefore, the most serious consideration of all American citizens, not only as patriots but as Christians."

3

The Webster-Hayne Debate

Early in 1830 the issue of Western lands had prompted a memorable
debate in the Senate over the nature of the federal Constitution. The
Mexican struggle for independence from Spain had drawn attention
to the relations between Mexico and the United States. In that struggle
the heart of the revolutionary cause had been the Order of Freemasons. Although certain priests had played a crucial role in the
revolution, the Church itself was disposed toward a monarchical rather
than a republican form of government. The Masons thus became the
intellectual rallying point for the champions of a Mexican republic.
Two political parties which took their names from Masonic chapters,
the Escoce and the Yorkino, soon became engaged in a bitter struggle
for control of the government. After months of uncertainty and days
of street fighting in Mexico City, the Yorkino triumphed and Vicente
Guerrero was elected president by Congress and Anastasio Bustamante vice-president.

The defeated Escoce sought help from the motherland, and four
thousand Spanish soldiers from Havana landed near Tampico. There,
without supplies or reinforcements, they were all captured a few weeks
later by Guerrero's army. Van Buren, as secretary of state, instructed
the American minister to Mexico, Joel Poinsett, to take advantage of

the upheavals in Mexico to try to buy Texas. (For all of the land east of the Rio Grande, Poinsett was authorized to offer five million dollars.) Matters were complicated by the fact that the Mexican government had induced a number of Shawnee, Kickapoo, and Cherokee to settle in Mexico to defend the Mexicans against raids by the Comanches.

Newspaper editors and democratic publicists in the Jackson network at once began cranking out a barrage of arguments in favor of the acquisition of Texas. Southerners were particularly attracted to the notion of acquiring Texas as an outlet for the surplus slave population of the South, a notion that of course horrified the North. One of Guerrero's first acts had been to issue a declaration freeing all slaves. Most whites in Texas owned slaves—and these to a man simply ignored Guerrero's proclamation, threatening to take up arms, if necessary, in defense of their property. At this point Guerrero, with enough other problems on his hands, exempted Texas from the edict. Guerrero believed that Poinsett, himself a Mason, had mixed indiscreetly in the internal affairs of Mexico and requested that he be recalled by Van Buren. Van Buren had no choice but to comply, but he took the opportunity to write a long letter recounting the friendship and sympathy of the United States for the Mexican revolution and charging Guerrero with ingratitude and bad faith. In the face of growing hostility between the two countries the notion of purchasing Texas became wholly impractical.

While the recall of Poinsett and the general deterioration of Mexican-American relations put the question of the acquisition of Texas to rest for the nonce, the issue had revived the anxiety of New Englanders about the disposition of Americans to move west, a movement perceived as disadvantageous to New England on two grounds. First there was the fact that the West for several decades had been bleeding New England of many of its most enterprising and energetic citizens; second, the influx of slaveowning Southerners into the lower reaches of the Louisiana Territory threatened to create so many new slave states that the North would be overbalanced politically and find itself powerless against the ambitions of the South. Because slaves were counted for purposes of representation in the House on the three-fifths basis, the South already had, in the opinion of the North, far more representatives in the House than it was entitled to. If more slave than free states were added to the Union, the North would lose the Senate. With these thoughts in mind, Senator Samuel Augustus Foot, a Connecticut Democrat, proposed that the Committee on Public Lands look into limiting the sale of public lands to those already in the market. Benton of Missouri, Jackson's old adversary and new ally, attacked Foot's resolution heatedly. It was evident that the New England senator wished to check or seriously inhibit the emigration westward. The selfish interests of Connecticut were evident, Benton argued. That state and her sisters wished to "force poor people in the East to work as journeymen in the factories, instead of letting them go to new countries, acquire land and become independent freeholders." It was part and parcel with the exorbitant tariffs, designed to ensure the profits of New England industrialists. Foot's resolution was intended "to inflict unmixed, unmitigated evil upon the new States and Territories. Such inquiries are not to be tolerated. Courts of law will not sustain actions which have immoral foundations. . . . The signs are portentous; the crisis is alarming; it is time for the new States to wake up to their danger, and to prepare for a struggle which carries ruin and disgrace to them. . . ." Benton took the occasion to review a long list of congressional actions inimical to the West.

At this point Robert Hayne of South Carolina saw Foot's resolution as a golden opportunity to separate the West from any lingering attachment it might have to the North and bind it tightly to a new alliance with the South. The original thirteen British colonies had secured their lands for little more than "a penny" or a "pepper corn." That policy was founded, Hayne said, "on the universal belief, that the conquest of a new country, the driving out 'the savage beasts and still more savage men,' cutting down and subduing the forest, and encountering all the hardships and privations necessarily incident to the conversion of the wilderness into cultivated fields, was worth the fee simple of the soil." Now the policy of the government seemed to be "not to settle the country, and facilitate the formation of new states, but to fill our coffers by coining our lands into gold."

Daniel Webster, alarmed at the sectional turn the debates were taking, proposed an indefinite postponement of the resolution but in doing so defended New England's role in the development of Western policy. Benton replied with an attack on the self-righteousness of New England in regard to slavery. "Slavery, in the abstract," he insisted, "has few advocates or defenders in the slave-holding States, and . . . slavery as it is . . . would have fewer advocates among us than it has, if those who have nothing to do with the subject would only let us alone." Benton then went on to argue that Jesus Christ himself had implicitly accepted slavery in the days of the Roman Empire. "Christ saw all this—the number of slaves—their hapless condition—and their white color, which was the same with his own; yet he said nothing against slavery; he preached no doctrines which led to insurrection and massacre. . . ."

Benton's arguments had already appeared a thousand times, and they would appear many thousand more. Do not criticize our peculiar institution, he told the North, or you will make us adhere to it more determinedly than ever. We acknowledge it to be wrong but we claim it is entirely consistent with the teachings of Jesus and the institutions of Christianity.

Webster, ignoring Benton, concentrated his fire on Hayne. When Hayne replied, the Senate gallery was packed and many members of the House deserted their chamber to listen to the South Carolinian. Hayne pushed the doctrine of nullification so dear to many South Carolinians, citing in support Jefferson's Virginia and Kentucky Resolutions. New England, he charged, had flirted with the doctrine of nullification on the eve of the War of 1812. Pressed by Webster, Hayne defended the principles that Calhoun had developed in the South Carolina Exposition and Protest.

The debate, which had started on January 20 with Webster's first speech on Foot's resolution, had now gone on almost a week, growing in the width and range of the issues discussed and accumulating public interest as it went. This was, after all, the age of oratory; what has come to be known as the Hayne-Webster debate was its most dramatic moment. When Webster replied to Hayne the Senate was again crowded. The New Englander disclaimed any "personal warfare" or party animus. He was motivated only by the dispassionate desire to search out the truth and illuminate the true nature of the Constitution. He began lightly enough by assuring his adversary that the oratorical arrows Hayne had discharged against him were "not to be found fixed and quivering in the object at which they had been aimed." Hayne had chided Webster for ignoring Benton's oration and concentrating on Hayne and implied that Webster felt himself "overmatched" against the Missourian. "Matches and overmatches!" Webster declared. "Those are terms more applicable elsewhere than here, and fitter for other assemblies than this. Sir, the gentleman seems to forget, where and what we are. This is a Senate, a Senate of equals, of men of individual honor and personal character, and of absolute independence. We know no masters, we acknowledge no dictators. This is a hall for mutual consultation and discussion; not an arena for the exhibition of champions. . . ." Webster's only concern, he insisted, was to discover the truth.

Having disclaimed taint of the merely personal or combative, Webster then went on to heap ridicule on his opponent's head—perfectly respectable debater's tactics. He clearly intended to obliterate the Carolinian, to weave about him such a dazzling net of rhetoric as would forever hold him prisoner. Webster assured the Southern members that he had no intention of tampering with slavery. The Constitution was plain enough on that point and Congress had affirmed that it had "no authority to interfere in the emancipation of slaves, or in the treatment of them in any of the States. . . ." For himself, "The domestic slavery of the Southern States I leave where I find it,—in the hands of their own government. It is their affair, not mine."

Hayne, in attacking the powers of the federal government and the whole American system, had asked what interest South Carolina had in a canal in Ohio, and Webster fastened on this spirit of parochialism: "Sir, we narrow-minded people of New England do not reason thus. Our *notion* of things is entirely different. We look upon the States, not as separated, but as united. We love to dwell on that union and on the mutual happiness which it has so much promoted, and the common renown which it has so greatly contributed to acquire. In our contemplation Carolina and Ohio are parts of the same country; States united under the same general government, having interests, common, associated, intermingled. In whatever is within the proper sphere of the constitutional power of this government, we look upon the States as one; we do not impose geographical limits to our patriotic feeling or regard. . . ." Webster and his constituents would gladly support a railroad that began and ended in South Carolina if it appeared to be "of national importance." "In war and peace we are one; in commerce one." There was a proposal before Congress to construct a road "in or through one of the new States." Certainly the government had the power and the constitutional right to "promote the common good" by assisting in the building of such a road.

"Mr. President," Webster declared, addressing Calhoun, "I shall enter on no encomium upon Massachusetts; she needs none. There she is. Behold her and judge for yourselves. There is her history; the world knows it by heart. The past, at least, is secure. There is Boston, and Concord, and Lexington, and Bunker Hill; and there they will remain forever."

This was all preliminary, the preface to the great volume of instruction on the nature of the Constitution. After a morning spent in what was, in view of Webster's grand design, almost frivolity, a brilliant curtain-raiser of corruscating oratorical gems, Webster was ready to proceed to "by far the most grave and important duty, which I feel is devolved on me by this occasion." That was the detailed explication of the Constitution. Webster had understood Hayne "to maintain, that the ultimate power of judging of the constitutional extent of its own authority is not lodged exclusively in the general government, or any branch of it; but that, on the contrary, the States may lawfully decide for themselves, whether, in a given case, the act of the general government transcends its power."

It was to this dangerous argument that Webster now turned his attention. He did not doubt that a majority of the citizens of South Carolina were opposed to the Tariff of 1828, "but that a majority holds to the right of direct State interference at State discretion, the right of nullifying acts of Congress by acts of State legislation, is more than I know, and what I shall be slow to believe."

Webster reserved his most eloquent words for his peroration. That was an impassioned exordium to the Union. "I profess, Sir, in my career hitherto, to have kept steadily in view the prosperity and honor of the whole country, and the preservation of our Federal Union. It is to that Union we owe our safety at home, and our consideration and dignity abroad. It is to that Union that we are chiefly indebted for whatever makes us most proud of our country. That Union we reached only by the discipline of our virtues in the severe school of adversity. . . . It has been to us the copious fountain of national, social, and personal happiness." He could not bring himself to look beyond it, "to hang over the precipice of disunion . . . while the Union lasts. We have high exciting, gratifying prospects spread out before us. God grant that, in my day, at least, that curtain may not rise." Not Liberty first and Union afterward, "But everywhere, spread over all in characters of living light, blazing on all its ample folds, as they float over the sea and over the land, and in every wind under the whole heavens, that other sentiment, dear to every true American heart,—Liberty and Union, now and for ever, one and inseparable!"

Webster's arguments will be familiar to those readers who have followed these volumes from the framing of the Constitution through the principal decisions of the Supreme Court in those cases affecting the relationships between the states and the federal government. They need not be repeated here. It is sufficient to say that they were marshaled with great skill and eloquence and substantial learning. We are not much of a mind today to attend to oratorical exercises as prolonged as Webster's great oration, but it can hardly be read even this far in time from the event without a profound sense of its potency.

The seeds of the Civil War lay as surely in Daniel Webster's reply to Hayne as they did in the devoted and as yet modest efforts of the Abolitionists. More than any other American the Massachusetts senator enhanced and dramatized the idea of the inviolability of the Union—that it was the keystone of national happiness and power, the mystic symbol of the present and future greatness of the American people. The notion of an indissoluble Union had often had hard going. First one section and then another had talked openly of secession. Ohio had been as contemptuous of federal authority as Georgia or South Carolina. Already some Abolitionists were saying that if the South would not rid itself of the curse of slavery the North must go its own way and thus be free of pollution. So it is evident that the *idea* of Union was nugatory. Webster made it predominant, at least in the North and West. The National Republicans were ecstatic over his speech. Although there was an inexplicable lapse of several weeks before the newspapers printed the text, it achieved instant fame, was reprinted everywhere, and passages were soon committed to memory by schoolchildren. Poets, inspired by Webster's words, wrote odes to the Union. In Washington alone forty thousand copies of the speech were sold and no less an authority on rhetoric than John Quincy Adams noted in his journal that "it is a remarkable instance of readiness in debate. . . . It demolishes the whole fabric of Hayne's speech, so that it leaves scarcely the wreck to be seen."

Webster's address was not, of course, the end of the debate but simply its climax. For five more weeks the senators harangued each other on all the issues that divided the country. The Senate chamber was filled with charges and countercharges, much heat and some light; but basically it was an airing of ancient animosities and irreconcilable differences.

During the debates, the President maintained his accustomed silence while orators on both sides of the nullification issue claimed his support. The South Carolinians and their adherents devised a plan to force the President's hand, confident that Jackson could be counted among the nullifiers. April 13 was Jefferson's birthday. A dinner would be held to honor his memory and revive his doctrines. The President, the members of his Cabinet, and noted political figures were invited, and to emphasize the political character of the event a list of proposed toasts was prepared, among them one to "The Virginia Resolutions, and Madison's Report of the Year '98—Text-Books in the Jeffersonian School. . . ." The Pennsylvania delegation to Congress thereupon refused to attend. Its absence was hardly noted in the endless Jeffersonian toasts, one for each state in the Union, now twenty-four. Hayne was the featured speaker, and the atmosphere was clearly one of challenging the authority of the federal government. Through it all Jackson remained inscrutable. Finally he was invited to propose a toast himself, and every eye turned to him. The expectation of the managers of the event was that the President would openly, or tacitly by his presence, identify himself with the good old Jeffersonian principle of nullification. But the President rose and proposed a toast that would have done Daniel Webster proud. Slowly, with strong and unmistakable emphasis: "Our *Federal* Union. It *must be preserved.*" The applause was restrained. Calhoun followed with "The Union; next to our liberties the most dear. May we all remember that it can only be preserved by respecting the rights of the States and distributing equally the benefits and burdens of the Union."

Van Buren was next: "Mutual forbearance and reciprocal concessions. Through their agency the Union was established. The patriotic spirit from which they emanated will forever sustain it." Those politicians who opposed the doctrine of nullification immediately claimed the President as their champion. To his name was soon added that of James Madison, the principal figure in the federal Convention, certainly the most notable member of that body still alive.

While the Webster-Hayne debate occupied the Senate, the House carried on its own extended debate revolving around the issue of internal improvements. One of the bones of contention was a proposed bill to use federal funds to build a highway from Buffalo through Washington to New Orleans. Its advocates argued that such an interstate highway would help to cement the Union, encourage trade in agricultural and industrial goods, and be an aid to national security by providing easier access between North and South in the event of war against some foreign power. Congressmen opposed to the bill denounced it as an attempt to increase the power of the federal government at the expense of the states. James Polk, a Congressman from Tennessee, charged that the proponents of the bill wished to find pretexts to keep taxes high; public works provided such a pretext. "The American System, as it is called, consists of three things," Polk declared; "it is a tripod that stands upon three legs. One is high prices for the public lands to prevent emigration to the West, that a population of paupers may be kept in the East and forced to work for low wages in the factories. Another is high duties, and high taxes to protect the manufacturer and produce a surplus revenue. The third is the system of internal improvements which is a sponge to suck up the excess revenue taken from the people." Since the War of 1812 there had been "a constant tendency to accumulate power in the Federal head and to encroach on the legitimate and reserved rights of the States. . . ."

A New York Democrat spoke heatedly of the bill's "cruelty . . . its injustice and its usurpation. . . ." In his view, it should be entitled "A bill to construct a road from the liberties of the country, by way of Washington, to despotism." After much acrimonious discussion, the bill was rejected, 78 to 111. A bill authorizing Congress to buy a portion of the stock of the Maysville and Lexington Turnpike in Kentucky passed, but Jackson vetoed it and took the occasion to spell out his views on internal improvements. In the President's opinion there were two points in question. The first involved the jurisdiction of the federal government over roads or canals built with federal funds. The second had to do with whether the federal government had, under the Constitution, the right to expend federal money for projects "undertaken by State authority." It seemed clear to Jackson that any such expenditure of federal funds within a particular state was an impairment of the sovereignty of the state and therefore unconstitutional. Further, such an expenditure was not among the enumerated powers of Congress and was therefore unconstitutional. Jackson expressed alarm that virtually every administration had "adopted a more enlarged construction of the power" of Congress to extend the enumerated powers by implication. The Maysville Road Bill appeared to Jackson as a project of a "purely local character" as opposed to a "national" one. He wished to make clear that he was not taking a position on the issue of internal improvements per se but only on the question of whether the Maysville Road could properly be included as a project warranting the use of federal funds. He then challenged the advocates of internal improvements to propose an amendment to the

Constitution clearly defining the nature of the internal improvements and the conditions under which public money might be expended on them.

There, for the time being, the matter rested, and Congress turned its attention to reforming the Tariff of 1828. Carolinians attempted to amend a bill to improve the collecting of duties by adding a provision repealing the Tariff of 1828. While there was a general disposition to modify that tariff, a substantial majority of the House was unwilling simply to repeal it. An acrimonious debate thus followed.

Once more, the exchanges were marked by bitter invective, most notably from the Southern members. George McDuffie of South Carolina declared, "No freak of tyranny ever committed by an absolute despot can exceed this outrage upon the principles of natural justice, which you are perpetuating under the perverted powers and prostrate forms of a free government." It was ironic that the principal charge of the Carolinians was that they were being "enslaved" by "Northern manufacturers." "If those who ought to cherish her as an old Revolutionary sister and confederate still persevere in ungenerous and unhallowed attempts to beggar and enslave her," McDuffie continued, "she will defy you, sir." Again there were the now familiar threats of secession.

Meanwhile the rift between Jackson and Calhoun, which had begun in the early days of the administration, came to a head. Calhoun had been indignant about the President's failure to choose a South Carolinian for his Cabinet. The rift deepened when Calhoun's wife, Floride, became a leader in the social resistance to Peggy Eaton. The final rupture was the revelation by William Crawford, whose physical health and political ambitions had revived, that Calhoun, as secretary of war during Jackson's foray into Florida, had urged President Monroe to disavow Jackson's actions and censure him or relieve him of his command. (Both Crawford and Calhoun had appealed to Adams, Monroe's secretary of state, whose vigorous defense of Jackson had brought Monroe to his view and undoubtedly saved the general's hide). Jackson at once confronted Calhoun, who replied with a fifty-two-page effort to exonerate himself, to which Jackson responded icily that "no further communication with you on the subject is necessary." When Calhoun tried to vindicate himself through the public press he only further compromised his cause with the President. Jackson was determined to rid himself of all of Calhoun's partisans in his administration, starting with the Cabinet. Van Buren, well aware of how the wind was blowing, offered to resign and thus provide an occasion for Jackson to bring pressure on the other members of the Cabinet to follow suit.

In the spring of 1831 Eaton resigned on the grounds that the uproar over his wife had made it impossible for the Cabinet to function effectively. Van Buren followed suit. For a time Jackson simply ignored the remaining members of his Cabinet, drawing advice from such trusted supporters as Van Buren, Amos Kendall, and Duff Green, who soon came to be known as his "kitchen cabinet."

Finally Jackson forced the resignation of Ingram, Branch, and Berrien. Edward Livingston of Louisiana was the new secretary of state; Lewis McLane of Delaware, secretary of the treasury; Lewis Cass of Ohio, secretary of war; Levy Woodbury, a New Hampsire Democrat, secretary of the navy; and Roger Taney of Maryland, whom we first encountered defending a runaway slave, was appointed attorney general. The second Cabinet go-round was much superior to the first. "Not a human being of any party regrets the loss of the services of any of the Secretaries," John Quincy Adams noted. Van Buren—in order, his enemies said, to preserve his neutrality in the contest between Jackson and Calhoun—prevailed on Jackson to nominate him ambassador to England.

When the nomination came before the Senate, Van Buren had already departed for Great Britain. The enemies of Jackson in the Senate, added to the enemies of Van Buren and augmented by the friends of Calhoun, could not resist the opportunity to make trouble. Van Buren was accused of having brought about the disruption of the original Jackson Cabinet and having "participated in . . . practices disreputable to the national character." After two days of acrimonious debate, the Senate divided evenly on approval of Van Buren, and Calhoun cast the deciding vote in the negative. The South Carolinian was reported to have turned to a colleague after the vote and said, "It will kill him, sir, kill him dead. He will never kick, sir, never kick." Jackson, furious, declared, "I have no hesitation in saying that Calhoun is one of the most base hypocritical and unprincipled villains in the United States. His course of secret session, and vote in the case of Mr. Van Buren has displayed a want of every sense of honor, justice, and magnanimity. His vote has dam'd him by all honest men in the Senate and when laid before the nation, and laid it will be, will not only dam him and his associates, but astonish the American people."

The President's second annual message to Congress was little more than a reiteration of the first. An amendment was again proposed to choose the President by direct election for one four- or six-year term. Reduction of the Tariff of 1828 was urged and the criticisms of the Bank of the United States reinforced. Rather surprisingly, all of Jackson's recommendations were ignored by Congress. A proposed amendment to the Constitution to limit the terms of the justices of the Supreme Court, a move prompted by the Court's action in calling the state of Georgia before it in the matter of the Indians, was likewise rejected. Evidently little was to be done by the expiring Congress. Its failure to take up the revision of the tariff was seen in the South as an especial affront to that section. The talk of nullification grew more intense. At a dinner in Columbia, South Carolina, Senator Hayne drank a toast to "The tariff; a thing too detestable to have been contrived except by Yankees; to be enforced except by Kentuckians; or to be endured except by 'the submission men' of the South." A month later George McDuffie, the South Carolina Congressman, gave a typical fire-eating speech calling the Union "a foul monster." On the Fourth of July the Unionists or "submission men" and the nullifiers held separate celebrations. The Unionists had invited Jackson, and although he could not come the President sent a letter that was read to the assembled crowd: "Every enlightened citizen must know that a separation, could it be effected, would begin with civil discord, and end in colonial dependence on a foreign power, and obliteration from the list of nations. But he should see also that high and sacred duties which must and will at all hazards be performed, present an unsuperable barrier to the success of any plan of disorganization, by whatever patriotic name it may be decorated, or whatever high feelings may be arrayed for its support."

Here was Jackson temper. An unequivocal challenge and warning. The Unionists spread it around the state and the nullifiers howled with rage. The state had been threatened and insulted. The Committee on Federal Relations of the state legislature could not find words to express its indignation. The United States was simply a confederacy of sovereign states any one of which could withdraw when it pleased without being intimidated by the President, who was "simply the agent of an agent."

While all of this was going on ex-President Adams, exiled in Quincy as his father before him, gave way to the gloomiest reflections. He read "the first Tusculan" upon "the contempt of death," noted in his diary: "Nature hath implanted in all animated beings a horror of death, and has made it doubly terrible by the agonies and convulsions which usually precede and attend it, as well as by that interest in the future which Cicero considers as an argument in favor of the immortality of the soul. . . . I have read this dissertation at the most favorable moment of my life for giving it all its weight, when I have no plausible motive for wishing to live, when everything that I foresee and believe of futurity makes death desirable, and when I have the clearest indications that it is near at hand." Yet, Adams added with that remorseless honesty that was so much a part of his character, "I should belie my conscience should I not acknowledge that the love of life and the horror of dissolution is as strong in me as it ever was at any period of my existence and that I deeply feel the hollowness of the whole argument of Cicero." In such a mood Adams was ready to listen receptively to a friend who came to urge him to be a candidate for Congress, arguing "that the service in the House of Representatives of an ex-President of the United States, instead of degrading the individual, would elevate the Representative character."

In that point, Adams replied, he had no hesitation. "No person could be degraded by serving the people as a Representative in Congress. . . ." On November 5, 1830, John Quincy Adams, formerly President of the United States, was elected Congressman for the District of Plymouth.

It was the proudest moment of a long and distinguished life, an instant of pure euphoria. Adams noted in a singular outburst in his diary: "My election as President of the United States was not half so gratifying to my inmost soul. No election or appointment conferred upon me ever gave me so much pleasure. I say this to record my sentiments; but no stranger intermeddleth with my joys, and the dearest of my friends have no sympathy with my sensations." Reading Adams's ecstatic words, one can hardly fail to recall his reaction at hearing that he had finally triumphed in the disputed presidential election of 1824: reportedly "he shook from head to foot and was so agitated that he could scarcely stand or speak." One witness remarked that from Adams's "hesitation, his manner and his words, he really thought he was going to decline."

Adams could not wait for the convening of the fall session of the Twenty-second Congress. He set out for Washington in December, stopping in New York on the way to visit James Monroe, who was in feeble health and to meet David Williams, the last survivor of the farmers who captured Major André during the Revolution and thus exposed Arnold's plot to betray West Point. Arriving in Washington in January, Adams entertained himself by reading Jefferson's memoirs. (Perhaps "irritated himself" would put it more accurately.) He was led to reflect on the character of his father's friend and rival. Jefferson's "loose morals" followed from his deistical thinking, Adams believed. His failure to believe in an afterlife had produced "insincerity and duplicity, which were his besetting sins. . . ." He had been a man characterized by "a rare mixture of infidel philosophy and epicurean morals, of burning ambition and of stoical self-control, of deep duplicity and of generous sensibility, between which two qualities, and a treacherous and, inventive memory, his conduct towards his rivals and opponents appears one tissue of inconsistency." Adams conceded that Jefferson's "love of liberty was sincere and ardent . . . not confined to himself, like that of most of his fellow slave-holders. He was above the execrable sophistry of the South Carolina nullifiers, which would make of slavery the corner-stone to the temple of liberty." He saw the gross inconsistency between the principles of the Declaration of Independence and the fact of Negro slavery and he could not, or would not, "prostitute the faculties of his mind to the vindication of that slavery which from his soul he abhorred." Yet, the Virginian's treatment of John Quincy's father had been "double-dealing, treacherous, and false beyond toleration." Adams was resolved to leave nothing undone to see that his father's reputation was restored. "I will vindicate the New England character," he wrote; "and I will expose some of the fraudulent pretences of the slave-holding democracy. I pray for temper, moderation, firmness and self-control; and, above all, for a pure and honest purpose. . . ."

The passage from Adams's diary is revealing. Jefferson, a Southerner and a slaveholder (albeit a reluctant one), had been "treacherous and false" to his father. John Quincy, in becoming the scourge of the South by exposing "the fraudulent pretences of the slave-holding democracy," might gain a measure of revenge for the way America had treated the Adams clan.

When the new Congress was organized, John Quincy Adams was a member. The occasion was a notable one. Margaret Smith wrote: "Mr. Adams received . . . marked and cordial attentions . . . every day, men of all parties, crowded round him to testify their respect and good will." For the first time in his life Adams felt like a genuine politician, the popular choice of the people's suffrages, his election untainted by deals and bargains. He wrote euphorically in his diary for February 20, 1831, "Being Monday, the States were successively called for presentation of petitions; a most tedious operation in the practice, though to a reflecting mind a very striking exemplification of the magnificent grandeur of this nation and of the sublime principles upon which our Government is founded. The forms and proceedings of the House, this calling over the States for petitions, the colossal emblem of the union over the Speaker's chair, the historic Muse at the clock, the echoing pillars of the hall, the tripping Mercuries [the pages] who bear the resolutions and amendments between the members and the chair, the calls of ayes and noes, with the different intonation of the answers from the different voices, the gobbling manner of the clerk in reading over the names, the tone of the Speaker in announcing the vote, the varied shades of pleasure and pain in the countenances of the members in hearing it, would form the subject for a descriptive poem." Adams was appointed chairman of the Committee on Manufactures. He presented fifteen petitions by "citizens of Pennsylvania, praying for the abolition of slavery and the slave-trade in the District of Columbia." The abolition of slave trade in the District he himself spoke in support of. The abolition of slavery elsewhere he felt would be too inflammatory an issue. He conferred with Clay and Webster on the matter of reducing the tariff and Webster declared he had no strong views on the subject. Clay, determined to protect his cherished "American system," was ready to drop all duties that were not protective of American industry. "The policy of our adversaries was obvious," Clay declared, "—to break down the American system by accumulation of revenue. Ours, therefore, should be specially adapted to counteract it, by reducing immediately the revenue to the amount of seven or eight millions this very coming year. He would hardly wait for the 1st of January to take off the duties; and he would adhere to the protective system, even to the extent of increasing the duties on some of the protected articles." Adams found Clay's manner "exceedingly peremptory and dogmatical." When Adams protested that such an unyielding stand would "be a defiance not only in the South . . . but defiance also of the President, and of the whole administration party" and probably could not pass, Clay responded that "he did not care who it defied. To preserve, maintain, and strengthen the American system he would defy the South, the President, and the devil." Clay and Adams clashed heatedly on the question of paying off the national debt. It was an obsession with Jackson, and Adams felt it both just and expedient to indulge him in it.

Indeed, Adams soon found himself the man in the middle on the tariff issue. He was convinced that substantial reductions were essential to placate the South and he had gone so far as to say as much to one of the South Carolina Congressmen. Clay, on the other hand, was ready to employ every expedient to force Adams and his committee to bend to his will.

Caught in the crossfire of the free-traders and protectionists, Adams fell prey to gloomy reflections. He noted in his diary that he had not long ago believed "this federative Union was to last for ages." Now, seeing all about him the rancor of sectional politics, he believed it could not last twenty—indeed, he doubted "its continuance for five. It is falling into the sere and yellow leaf." In March Adams asked the House to relieve him of his duties as chairman of the Committee on Manufactures. He had been appointed to a committee to examine the state of the Bank of the United States, a task more to his taste. The opponents of the tariff were at once alarmed and one after another exhorted Adams to reconsider. A New York Congressman declared that the fate of the Confederacy hung on the efforts of a few patriotic and disinterested men, and James Bates, a Maine Democrat, expressed as his opinion that Adams was the only man in the country who could draft and guide through Congress an equitable tariff measure. Adams relented and when Lewis McLane, the new secretary of the treasury, produced a bill to reduce the tariffs sharply it was referred to Adams's Committee on Manufactures. By its terms the tariffs would be limited to the amount of money needed to run the government, which McLane calculated to be $15,000,000 a year, of which $3,000,000 would be raised by the sale of Western lands. The duties designed to raise the necessary balance ($12,000,000) should be apportioned in such a manner as to protect "all the great national interests."

The Committee on Manufactures made modifications in the bill, which was then referred to the House and there denominated "the Adams Bill." Clay had channeled his bill through the Ways and Means Committee but the House preferred Adams's version, and although its members were flooded with protests from the advocates of high protective tariffs, the bill passed 132 to 65 and was signed into law by the President. The Adams Bill reduced many taxes while retaining the principle of protection. Duties on iron were reduced, those on woolens increased, and certain cheap raw wools of the type used to manufacture clothes for slaves were exempt. The new schedules were to take effect in March, 1833.

The Adams Bill satisfied no one, as it turned out. The adherents of the American system in the North took it to be a cowardly compromise with the free-traders. South Carolina once more took the lead in calling for open opposition to the federal government.

Meantime, the issue of the Bank of the United States, which had slumbered through the first three years of Jackson's administration, came to the fore. The House Ways and Means Committee, in response to Jackson's initial attack, had brought in a report strongly supportive of the Bank. Jackson had been furious and wrote to a political ally denouncing the Bank as a "hydra of corruption, so dangerous to our liberties by its corrupting influences everywhere, and not the least in the Congress of the Union."

As the Bank battle went on, Jackson developed a substantial degree of paranoia. When Van Buren returned from England and went to see the President, he found him looking pale and worn. Jackson took Van Buren's hand and said, "The bank, Mr. Van Buren, is trying to kill me, *but I will kill it.*" The words are almost too pat. Just as Jackson years ago had resolved to kill the insolent young Charles Dickinson in a duel, so he had resolved to "kill the bank."

Nicholas Biddle enlisted Albert Gallatin, himself now a banker, in defense of the Bank along with Madison and Monroe. Lewis McLane and Secretary of State, Edward Livingston, scion of the great New York family and one of the most prominent political figures in Louisiana, combined forces to prevail on Jackson to modify his opposition to the Bank and in his annual message to Congress in December, 1831, the President surprised his listeners by speaking of an accommodation with the Bank's supporters. The friends of the Bank, emboldened by Jackson's greater tractability, began to press for immediate rechartering, although the bargain with Jackson had rested on the assurance that the Bank would not apply for a new charter until after the presidential elections of 1832. The principal pressure came from Clay, who obviously hoped to benefit his own candidacy by appearing as a champion of the Bank.

4

Black Hawk's War

In the spring of 1832, fighting broke out between settlers and the Sac and Fox Indians in Illinois Territory. The Indians were led by Black Hawk, a Potawatomi whose father, a famous warrior, had become head chief of the Sauk (or Sac). Young Black Hawk had won glory in wars against the Osage and the Cherokee, and when his father was killed in a campaign against the Cherokee, he succeeded him. In 1830, the Sauk and Foxes had signed a treaty giving up all claim to their lands along the Mississippi, some seven hundred miles in extent.

A number of the Sauk and Foxes under the leadership of Black Hawk's rival, Keokuk, crossed the Mississippi to the area designated as their reservation. Black Hawk and a group of his followers refused to join them, but the land their villages were on was declared property of the United States by the territorial governor and sold by lot to white settlers. While Black Hawk and his band were on a hunting and raiding expedition the white claimants appeared, tore down the Indians' huts, and plowed up their fields.

Black Hawk returned to the villages in the spring and ordered the settlers off what he claimed were still Indian lands. While the frightened whites watched, his warriors destroyed fences, pulled down houses, and drove off or killed the cattle. When six companies of

49

United States troops, augmented by fifteen hundred volunteers and several bands of Oneida Indians, went in pursuit of Black Hawk, the Sacs withdrew across the Mississippi. Henry Dodge, colonel of Illinois volunteers, warned the Winnebago (who a few years earlier had been on the verge of rising against the whites) not to join with the Sac. But the next spring word reached the governor from friendly Indians that Black Hawk was back, determined to drive the whites from sites of the former Sac villages. A large motley force of Illinois militia volunteers was hastily assembled and started out in pursuit of Black Hawk.

The disorderly and undisciplined militia could not be controlled by their officers. There was no march discipline; making haphazard camps, they drank homemade whiskey and failed to observe the commonest precautions. When a party of Indians was sighted, the volunteers set out after them, shouting and hallooing. They were led into an ambush, and when the Indians charged they took to their heels—or rather their horses took to their hooves, their frightened riders clinging to their saddles. Eleven whites were killed in the rout and a number wounded. When word of the defeat spread through the frontier, the alarmed settlers began to build a series of small forts to protect their farms, most of them little more than houses reinforced by logs and palisades. The Indian tactics were to avoid direct engagements with the whites and direct their attention to any undefended farms or villages. Each day brought a fresh toll of murdered settlers.

Sioux and Menominie Indians, traditional enemies of the Sauk and Foxes, were recruited along with some Winnebago, often allies of the Sauk and Foxes; these Indian auxiliaries were especially useful in combating warfare such as Black Hawk was waging, with small bands attacking isolated farms. On one occasion, Colonel Henry Dodge, one of the original settlers engaged in lead mining and commander of militia by virtue of his prominence in the area, led a platoon of volunteers in pursuit of a party of Sauk who had killed four men working in a cornfield. The thirteen Indian raiders were overtaken at a riverbank and killed. Drawn by the sound of firing a band of Sioux arrived in time to take the Sauk's scalps and mutilate their bodies.

The fighting was mostly encounters between small parties of whites and Indians, often fiercely fought with mixed results. In a battle at the Rock River between a company of whites led by Major John Dement and some two hundred Indians led by Black Hawk, the Indians killed five white men and forty horses at a cost to themselves of "two young chiefs and seven warriors." Through May and June the

Indians, usually taking the initiative, killed some thirty whites, the majority of them caught outside their hasty fortifications. But the final outcome was foreordained. As larger companies of whites closed in on the area along the Rock River that served as Black Hawk's base of operations, the Indians were forced to drop back. When Black Hawk prepared to cross the Wisconsin River with his band of several hundred warriors, accompanied by a number of women and children, the pursuing whites led by twelve Winnebago scouts attacked. Vastly outnumbered, Black Hawk saw twenty or thirty of his braves fall while the American loss was one killed and eight wounded. Darkness saved the Indians, and under the cover of the night they made their way across the Wisconsin. Again the whites pressed their pursuit and finally overtook the Sauk, encumbered by their women and children, at the mouth of Bad Axe River, forty miles from the post at Prairie du Chien. A steamboat carrying a six-pound cannon blocked Black Hawk's flight across the Mississippi. Brought to bay at last, Black Hawk tried to surrender, but the Wisconsin and Illinois volunteers had come to kill Indians and were not to be deterred. The Indian leader insisted to his dying day that the whites had deliberately ignored his display of a white flag, and an American officer gave credence to the claim by writing later: "As we neared them they raised a white flag and endeavored to decoy us, but we were a little too old for them." The Indians were cut down mercilessly and the handful who escaped across the river, including women and children, were hunted down and killed by the Sioux. Black Hawk sought refuge with the Winnebago but two of their braves seized him, brought him to Prairie du Chien, and turned him over to Joseph Street, the Indian agent.

General Winfield Scott, who had been ordered to Rock River to join in the campaign against Black Hawk with nine companies of regular army artillery, arrived too late to share in the triumph. Cholera overtook his men on their way back to Chicago and more than four hundred died of the dread disease. The Americans lost some fifty volunteers in the scattered fighting of the "war," and half again as many settlers were killed in Indian raids. The Sauk and Foxes were estimated to have lost 230 in battle, with perhaps several hundred more dying of their wounds, disease, and starvation. If there was a hero on the American side it was Henry Dodge, who proved a determined and resourceful leader.

Black Hawk carried himself with a fierce pride and dignity that impressed his captors. Before he was carried off in chains he gave a defiant speech: "Black Hawk is an Indian. He has done nothing for which an Indian ought to be ashamed. He has fought for his countrymen, the squaws and papooses, against white men who came, year after year, to cheat them and take way their land. You know the cause of our making war. It is known to all white men. They ought to be ashamed of it. The white men despise the Indians and drive them from their homes. . . . An Indian who is as bad as a white man could not live in our nation; he would be put to death, and eat up by the wolves. The white men are bad schoolmasters; they carry false books and deal in false actions. . . . We were becoming like them, hypocrites and liars, adulterers, lazy drones, all talkers, no workers. We went to our great father [the President]. . . . His council gave us fair words and big promises, but we got no satisfaction. . . . There were no deer in the forest. The opossum and the beaver were fled. . . . The spirit of our fathers arose and spoke to us to avenge our wrongs or die. . . . The Heart of Black Hawk swelled high in his bosom when he led his warriors to battle. . . . He has done his duty. . . . Black Hawk is a true Indian, and disdains to cry like a woman. He feels for his wife, his children, and friends. . . . Farewell, my nation. . . . Black Hawk tried to save you, and avenge your wrongs. He drank the blood of some whites. He has been taken prisoner, and his plans are stopped. He can do no more. . . . His sun is setting. . . . Farewell to Black Hawk."

Black Hawk was sent as a prisoner under the charge of a young Southerner, Lieutenant Jefferson Davis, to the army prison at Jefferson Barracks. The "war" that bore his name was the first Indian War in almost a quarter of a century. As such it had been reported in extensive detail in the newspapers of the day, and Black Hawk and his warriors had many sympathizers—especially in Boston, with its tradition of championing the underdog. Numerous petitions were dispatched to Jackson protesting the continued confinement of Black Hawk and urging the President to pardon him. When Black Hawk reached Washington the President received him courteously, gave him a little lecture on the hopelessness of opposing the whites, and soon after pardoned him. Black Hawk was conveyed through a number of Eastern cities on a kind of triumphal tour. When he reached New York, the crowd gathered to see him was so immense that his party, made up of his wives and children, was unable to land. The farther white Americans were from the Indians, the more they romanticized them. To many of those who lined the street to watch Black Hawk pass, the fierce old warrior was a hero. Artists painted his picture, journalists interviewed him, politicians and socialites wished to meet him. Numerous individuals expressed their indignation at the treatment of his people and sought to dissociate themselves from the actions of their Western compatriots. Black Hawk dictated his autobiography, including his speech, and it became an immediate best-seller.

Keokuk, Black Hawk's rival for the leadership of the Sauk and Foxes, had kept that part of the combined tribes subject to his influence from going on the warpath. Now, to his indignation, he saw his defeated rival acclaimed and featured and, most annoying of all, loaded with presents. Keokuk was not slow to point out to the director of Indian affairs the lessons that other Indians might draw from this spectacle—the surest way to fame and honor with the whites was to kill a number of them, be finally defeated, make a moving and eloquent speech denouncing the white man, immediately become a celebrity, and go on a tour. Keokuk wanted a tour, too, and the government was eager to oblige. Having negotiated a treaty in Washington surrendering a million and a quarter acres of land, he set off with a retinue of squaws, papooses, and lesser braves "making a tour of the principal cities, receiving presents and being stared at for the benefit of theatre, fairs and lectures." Black Hawk joined the party, remaining sullen and aloof.

The Sioux, traditional enemies of the Sauk and Foxes, who had assisted in massacring the fleeing remnants of Black Hawk's people, had no intention of being left out. They were certainly as deserving of presents and attention as their enemies. So they made up another Indian road company and joined the tour, staying at different hotels in recognition of their ancient hostility. When Philip Hone went with thousands of other New Yorkers to see the Indians, they were seated on the ground distributing presents of colored cord which had been given to them. Hone was especially impressed with the son of Black Hawk, "a majestic man . . . one of the noblest figures I ever saw— perfect Ajax Telamon." The hands of the Indians were small and "femine," almost delicate, Hone noted, while their thighs and calves were heavily muscled. The pathos of absurdity hung over the whole scene, a perfect enactment of the ambivalent relationship of the two races.

Black Hawk returned to the reservation, where he lived four more years, enjoying his status as a celebrity. The white friends and admirers of the Indian who sought him out became as much a tribulation to the old man as the greedy settlers had been. Even after he was buried by the Mississippi River near present-day Des Moines, he had no peace. His bones were dug up some years later, it was said, and exhibited in the museum of the Historical Society at Burlington, Iowa.

5

Nullification

John Quincy Adams's ambitions were stimulated by his election to Congress. He entertained himself with the notion that the National Republicans, or what was left of them, might offer him the party's presidential nomination once again. If Clay got their support instead, there was this odd new party to which Adams had already given support and encouragement—the Anti-Masonic Party, which had its greatest strength in New York state and New England. It was undoubtedly the strangest political phenomenon of the era that a party whose only ostensible reason for existence was opposition to a secret society could, in the space of four years, become a political power to be reckoned with.

Getting a considerable jump on the two established parties, the Anti-Masons held a national convention in Baltimore in September, 1831, to choose a candidate for president of the United States. Perhaps the most revealing thing about the Anti-Masonic Convention was the caliber of individuals it attracted. John McLean, an associate justice of the Supreme Court, toyed with the idea of becoming the convention's nominee for president. Thurlow Weed, already a powerful political figure in New York, a supporter of DeWitt Clinton, and a newspaper publisher, was prominent at the convention along with William

Seward, just turned thirty—also a New Yorker, Clintonian, and warm supporter of Adams in 1824. Thaddeus Stevens was another leading figure at the convention. Born in Peacham, Vermont, of poor farm parents, he had graduated from Dartmouth College and studied and then practiced law in Pennsylvania. Stevens had taken a special interest in aiding in the escape and, when necessary, the legal defense of runaway slaves. Friendship for black people and hatred of slavery were to be the dominant principles of his career. Stevens was, if anything, more democratic than Jackson. But Jackson was a slaveowner and a Mason and an enemy of protective tariffs; he was thus an enemy of Stevens. Henry Dana Ward was the grandson of the Revolutionary general Artemas Ward. Born in Shrewsbury, Massachusetts, and a resident of Pennsylvania, Ward, at the time of the convention, was thirty-five, distinguished for his piety and millennial leanings.

John Spencer, at forty-four one of the older members of the convention, had been the prosecuting attorney in the investigation of William Morgan's death. This gave him a special weight and standing among the Anti-Masons. We have already encountered Samuel Foot, the Democratic senator from Connecticut whose resolution on restricting the sale of Western lands had triggered the Webster–Hayne debates. All of these delegates who played leading roles in the convention were under forty-five. All, with the exception of Henry Dana Ward, were to become prominent in national politics. The Anti-Masonic movement, otherwise such an odd political aberration, may thus best be understood as a protest movement of aggressive, politically engaged young men of strong democratic inclinations who could not stomach the Jacksonian Democrats because they considered the President and the Southern wing of his party hopelessly compromised by slavery, too tolerant of the extreme state's-righters and nullifiers in the South, and too draconian in policy toward the Southern Indians. The National Republicans appeared to them, on the other hand, a party of the past, dominated by an older generation of politicians whose ideas had been formed in an earlier era and were incapable of seriously challenging the Jacksonian Democrats.

The Anti-Masonic Party was thus a party of accident, a haphazard grouping of (for the most part) ambitious young politicians who had no other place to go. The new party was for them a kind of movement to affect the course of American politics. As much as anything else, it testified to the chaotic state of an America in transition, moving rapidly away from old political alliances that no longer corresponded to new realities. It was a catch-all for the discontented, of whom there proved to be—especially in Massachusetts, New York, and Philadelphia—a surprising number.

"The Address to the People" prepared by the delegates is also revealing. Its emphasis is almost exclusively moral. It began by listing the qualities of character necessary in a president—honesty, independence, prudence, wisdom, and patriotism. The principles that should guide an administration were equally vague and high-minded: equal justice, friendly commerce with all nations, states' rights, and "general suffrage." The enemy, "rich, disciplined, and wily," threatened these principles. Certainly the Anti-Masons represented, among other things, a strong distaste for politics as they existed, for the dubious tactics and desperate expedients all too evident in the maneuverings for the presidency. The intriguing question of course is how many of the intelligent and politically sophisticated men who gave their support to the Anti-Mason movement really thought that the country's greatest enemy was Freemasonry. Certainly their presidential candidates, William Wirt, a former Mason whose age and ill health made him a reluctant nominee, did not. He specifically disclaimed such notions to the convention itself, writing that he could regard Masonry "as nothing more than a social or charitable club, designed for the promotion of good feelings among its members, and for the pecuniary relief of their indigent brethren." One suspects that, interwoven with the dismay at the low state of political morality and growing frustration over the failure of the two major parties to deal with the current political issues, there was in the Anti-Masonic movement a substantial amount of class feeling. The dangerous Masons were those holding high Masonic office, high degrees, and these were in the main prominent and wealthy men, "the rich." Since America was ostensibly a classless society, Americans were constantly devising code words that stood for "upper class." We have seen many of them that were in fact quite explicit—aristocrats, the well-born, the nabobs, and so on. There were other names more subtle—Masons among them. Class animus could be understood to lie behind them. Like Thaddeus Stevens, most of the leaders of the Anti-Masonic Party were of modest origins, or at least outside the charmed circle of "first families."

There is another light in which the Anti-Masonic Party can be viewed. We have argued throughout this work that perhaps the most important clue to the nature of the American experience lies in the perpetual tension between the community and the individual. The disintegrative tendencies in America were so persistent and intolerable that Americans were constantly in danger of losing the sense of their own reality and thus were constantly coalescing into new combinations, new social groups, new parties, associations, lodges, communities, congregations and then flying apart again only to re-form. In the political realm the Masons gave rise to the Anti-Masons, the Irish Catholics to the Nativists, and on and on without end.

There was about the Anti-Mason meeting a disarming air of youthful energy and idealism that impressed even more cynical observers. Perhaps the sincerest compliment paid it was the organization of the Young Men's Republican Convention, also known as Clay's Infant School, which dutifully named Clay as its candidate, whereupon Clay arrived—the first time a nominee had appeared before a convention in person—and gave an eloquent address praising liberty and denouncing corruption.

In December the National Republicans held their convention to nominate a candidate for president. Only seventeen states were represented. The Deep South sent no delegates, nor did Missouri or Illinois. When the first vote was taken, 164 out of 165 delegates voted for Henry Clay. No platform was drawn up and the convention contented itself with attacking Jackson for instituting the infamous "spoils system"—he had, they charged, removed more officeholders in the first four months of his administration than all his predecessors in forty years; for appointing his supporters in Congress to federal offices; for vetoing internal improvement bills; for his betrayal of the Indians; and for his continuing assaults on the Bank of the United States.

In May, 1832, the Democratic delegates assembled in Baltimore for what may properly be regarded as the first national party convention. A rule was adopted that a two-thirds majority of the votes of the delegates would be required to secure the party's nomination and states were apportioned votes on the basis of their votes in the electoral college. Jackson was the unanimous choice of the delegates for president. The first ballot revealed 208 votes for Van Buren for vice-president to 49 for his nearest rival, Philip Barbour of Virginia.

As the presidential campaign of 1832 took shape, it became increasingly evident that the rechartering of the Bank would be the central issue; the tariff question was presumed to have been put to rest by the passage of Adams's bill. The Bank faction was anxious to press the issue, to secure the new charter on any terms acceptable to Jackson, and thus avoid having the Bank become a political football in the coming election. Trying to delay action by Congress, the opponents insisted on a thorough investigation of the Bank's affairs. Pushed by Biddle, a bill was introduced to extend life for the Bank for another fifteen years; it was passed after relatively little debate and sent to the President on July 3. Congress was scheduled to adjourn on the ninth, thus making it possible for Jackson to kill the bill with a pocket veto—simply not signing it into law. Clay, to force the President's hand, prevailed on Congress to delay adjournment until the sixteenth. Thus Jackson had to let the bill become law without his signature or veto it. Old Hickory was a dangerous man to back into a corner. He was profoundly suspicious of the Bank crowd—the more pressure they exerted the more they confirmed his feeling that they wielded too much power—and he may well have felt that Clay had hitched his wagon to a falling star on the Bank issue. In any event, he welcomed the opportunity to veto the bill and accompanied the veto with a severe indictment of the Bank that was as much a campaign document as a veto message.

The Bank enjoyed, Jackson declared, "a monopoly" of the government's support, and, as a necessary consequence, almost a monopoly of the foreign and domestic exchange. It was generally conceded that if the charter was renewed the value of the Bank's stock would increase greatly, thereby constituting a "gratuity of many millions to the stockholders." Since more than eight million dollars of the Bank's stock was held by foreign investors, they would be among the principal beneficiaries of the rechartering of the Bank. But more serious questions were at issue. "Every monopoly and all exclusive principles are granted at the expense of the public. . . . The many millions which this act proposes to bestow on the stockholders . . . must come directly or indirectly out of the earnings of the American people." The modifications in the existing charter were not, in Jackson's view, "such . . . as to make it consistent with the rights of the States or the liberties of the people." It had been argued that the constitutionality of the Bank had been settled by the Supreme Court, but Jackson rejected this argument. The fact was that "many of our rich men have not been content with equal protection and equal benefits, but have besought us to make them richer by act of Congress. . . . It is time to pause in our career to review our principles, and if possible revive that devoted patriotism and spirit of compromise which distinguished the sages of the Revolution and the fathers of our

Union." While resting his veto primarily on the ground of the unconstitutionality of the Bank, Jackson had much to say about the iniquities of the rich. "It is much regretted that the rich and powerful too often bend the acts of government to their selfish purposes" at the cost of "the humble members of society, the farmers, mechanics, and laborers, who have neither the time or the means of securing like favors to themselves. . . ."

Congress failed to override the veto and the Bank at once became a major issue in the upcoming presidential campaign. Jackson himself was pleased with the consequences of his veto. He wrote to Van Buren: "The veto works well, instead of crushing me as was expected and intended, it will crush the Bank." Van Buren concurred: "The Veto is popular beyond my most sanguine expectations. I will be greatly disappointed if its effect is not very considerable with the great body of people at the election."

To the businessmen and bankers Nicholas Biddle was a hero, their champion, the man on whom they depended to chasten the umbrageous President. Philip Hone, visiting Biddle in Philadelphia, looked fondly on the Bank of the United States and wrote in his diary, "The portico of this glorious edifice, the sight of which always repays me for coming to Philadelphia, appeared more beautiful to me this evening than usual, from the effect of the gas-light. Each of the fluted columns had a jet of light from the inner side so placed as not to be seen from the street, but casting a strong light upon the front of the building, the softness of which, with its flickering from the wind, produced an effect strikingly beautiful." Hone might have speculated on the symbolic significance of the fact that American banks commonly were built in the style of Greek and Roman temples, thus suggesting that for Americans the most sacred object was money.

The irony of the Bank battle was that Jackson's monetary views were, if anything, more conservative than those of the Bank's directors. He had been burned as a young man when he took bad promissory notes in payment of a debt. He disapproved of cheap money and easy credit. One of his objections to the Bank was that it issued paper money and that encouraged speculation and advanced credit. Jackson was a hard-money man. His economics were colored by moral fervor. He was a passionate agrarian in the mold of Jefferson and Adams, and he was forthright in telling a startled Nicholas Biddle, "I do not dislike your bank any more than all banks." What made Jackson's position the more ironic was that the vast majority of his supporters, especially those in the West, yearned for vast amounts of cheap paper money and unlimited credit so that they could indulge their insatiable appetites for speculation. But Jackson made the Bank issue appear essentially a class issue—and so it was for him. Even stronger than his suspicion of banks was his hostility to that class of men who controlled the Bank.

The re-election campaign for Jackson followed the by now well-marked paths: skillfully coordinated state and local organizations; rallies, parades, speeches, resolutions, bands, fireworks; pamphlets and newspaper editorials, most with a strong focus on the issue of the Bank. When news of Jackson's veto of the Bank bill reached one Western town, its citizens were soon "up and doing," as one of them wrote. "The roaring of cannon announced that some important occasion had called forth that token of national, patriotic feeling. . . . Immediately . . . a meeting of Democratic Republicans of this town . . . assembled at one of our public hotels, where the objections of the President on returning the bill were read and considered. Spirited resolutions, approving the course of the President were adopted. . . ." A typical resolution from such a gathering praised the President for preserving "the people from becoming enslaved by the corruptions of a moneyed aristocracy and desperate politicians."

The National Republicans did their best to depict themselves as the party of the people, and they copied the campaign tactics of the Democrats. In Philadelphia a large crowd turned out to hear orators denounce Jackson and his party. A Republican observer reported enthusiastically: "Thousands upon thousands were there and we consider this meeting as a death blow to the administration in this quarter. . . . It is evident that the mass of the people—the bone and sinew of the city and county—the patriotism and purity of the community, are opposed to the re-election of Andrew Jackson." The Irish had the delightful experience of finding themselves courted and flattered by both parties.

The principal Republican charge was that Jackson had seized the powers of a king or dictator. One newspaper headline proclaimed: THE KING UPON HIS THRONE: *The People in the Dust!!!* Jackson, the editor wrote, "has set at defiance the will of the people as strongly expressed by their Senators and Representatives . . . he has exercised a power that no Monarch in Europe dared . . . he has, by his frequent exercise of power which should never be ventured upon but in the most extreme cases, proved himself to be the most absolute despot now at the head of any representative government on earth." An Ohio newspaper declared that the coming election was perhaps the last opportunity "of strangling the monster of despotism before it shall have attained its full growth."

The Bank itself confirmed the Jacksonian charges against it by campaigning vigorously for Clay. Biddle so little sensed the temper of the country that he had thirty thousand copies of Jackson's veto message printed and distributed, convinced that it would cause a strong popular reaction in favor of the Bank. Estimates of the amount of money the Bank spent in its campaign to defeat Jackson have run as high as $100,000.

A French traveler, viewing a pro-Jackson parade "nearly a mile long," could compare it only to a religious procession he had witnessed in Mexico. "The American standardbearers were as grave as the Mexican Indians who bore the sacred tapers. The Democratic procession, like the Catholic procession, had its halting-places; it stopped before the homes of Jackson men to fill the air with cheers, and halted at the doors of the leaders of the Opposition, to give three, six or nine groans." The Frenchman's analogy to a religious procession is an arresting one. Americans were busy inventing political rituals that corresponded in many instances to the religious rituals of other peoples. They seemed determined to invest presidential campaigns with the rhetoric of apocalypse. The future of the country, perhaps of the world itself, rested, they seemed convinced, on the election of their candidate. To lose the election was to lose the hope of an earthly heaven and the promise of more than political salvation. If Andrew Jackson was the savior of his country in the eyes of the Democrats, Nicholas Biddle was "Old Nick," the devil himself, bent on destroying democratic government.

In popular votes Jackson received 688,242 to Clay's 473,462, while Wirt, who conducted virtually no campaign, received 101,051, the greater portion of them in New York and the New England states. The electoral vote was Jackson 219, Clay 49, and William Wirt 9. Clay took only six states—Massachusetts, Rhode Island, Connecticut, Delaware, Kentucky, and Maryland.

Historians have generally recognized that the election of 1832 cannot, like most elections, be understood in terms of the ostensible issues. The truth lies deeper, perhaps too much deeper to be entirely exhumed. The process of change in the United States had been, almost from the first instant, so rapid as to be virtually incomprehensible both at the point of change itself and, to a large degree, in retrospect. The country was not "saved" by the election of Andrew Jackson—at least not in the sense in which his supporters believed it to be—nor would it have been doomed by the election of Henry Clay. (It might be argued that the election of Clay would have resulted in the secession of South Carolina, but that is wholly conjecture.) The health of the nation's economy did not depend on the rechartering of the Bank or on its extirpation. Nor would higher tariffs have materially aided infant American industry, just as there is no evidence that the decline in the price of Southern cotton, which the South blamed on the tariff, would have been reversed had the tariffs been removed. As we have noted before, the American economy was unstable in the highest degree and would remain so for years to come regardless of what measures one administration or another might take to bolster it.

On November 24, in a convention held in Columbia, South Carolina declared the tariffs of 1828 and 1832 "null and void." Two weeks later, Jackson delivered his fourth annual message to Congress.

Notwithstanding the appearance of the dread disease of cholera in America, Jackson declared, "our country presents on every side marks of prosperity and happiness unequalled, perhaps, in any other portion of the world." Foreign affairs were marked by "amicable intercourse" and "friendly professions" by all nations. Business enjoyed a "state of prosperity and peace." There were a few troublesome incidents here and there—"a sanguinary struggle in Mexico," the unwillingness of Spain to live up to its financial commitments to the United States, reluctance on the part of Great Britain to reach an accord on the touchy subject of the northeastern boundary between Canada and the United States, "some agitations" with regard to Brazil and some difficulties with Peru and Bolivia.

The greatest cause for congratulation was the "extinction of the public debt," which meant that Western lands could be made available to settlers at a cost sufficient to cover merely the transactions. Furthermore, all tariffs could be abandoned and only such retained as were necessary to protect "those articles of domestic manufacture which are indispensable to our safety in time of war." High tariffs had produced "in the minds of a large portion of our countrymen a spirit of discontent and jealousy dangerous to the stability of the Union."

Jackson balanced his call for a further reduction in the tariff with a word of caution to the nullifiers. If they were disposed to resist the authority of the national government unlawfully, he was confident that "the laws themselves are fully adequate to suppression of such attempts." If necessary, however, he would immediately apply to Congress for the passage of such statutes as would give the President the requisite powers to force obedience to the laws.

For the Bank, whose charter ran until 1836, there was a warning that the government might withdraw its funds on the grounds that it was "no longer a safe depository of the money of the people."

A good deal of Jackson's message was devoted to the question of the public lands. "It cannot be doubted," he declared, "that the speedy settlement of these lands constitutes the true interest of the Republic. The wealth and strength of a country are its population, and the best part of that population are the cultivators of the soil. Independent farmers are everywhere the basis of society and true friends of liberty." The grim little Black Hawk War received passing mention: "The hostile incursions of the Sac and Fox Indians necessarily led to the interposition of the Government. . . . After a harassing warfare, prolonged by the nature of the country and the difficulty of procuring subsistence, the Indians were entirely defeated, and the disaffected band dispersed or destroyed."

As for the Creek and the Cherokee, Jackson was "happy to inform (Congress) that the wise and humane policy of transferring from the eastern to the western side of the Mississippi the remnants of our aboriginal tribes, with their own consent and upon just terms, has been steadily pursued, and is approaching, I trust, its consummation." With a few exceptions the Indians had accepted the fact that their removal "furnishes the only hope of their ultimate prosperity." The Cherokee alone continued to resist the "very liberal propositions" made to them. The government had offered "an ample indemnity . . . for their present possessions, a liberal provision for their future support and improvement and full security for their private and political rights."

Jackson ended with an admonition to his audience to keep always in mind that the framers of the Constitution had withheld from the "General Government the power to regulate the great mass of the business and concerns of the people," and that "the genius of all our institutions prescribes simplicity and economy. . . . Limited to a general superintending power to maintain peace at home and abroad and to prescribe laws on a few subjects of general interest not calculated to restrict human liberty, but to enforce human rights, the Government will find its strength and glory in the faithful discharge of these plain and simple duties."

It is ironic that the enunciator of these by-now standard pieties of American politics was a president who exercised the powers of the executive office more vigorously than any of his predecessors. From the time of Hamilton and Jefferson, almost half a century earlier, Americans had contended bitterly over the powers appropriate to the federal government and over the intentions of the framers of the Constitution. The Hamiltonians, who after all had been present at the creation, had all the best of the argument but generally the worst of the game.

The response to the President's annual message was more partisan than ever, if possible. John Quincy Adams wrote in his diary: "The message of the President gives great dissatisfaction to those with whom I converse. . . . He has cast away all the neutrality which he had heretofore maintained upon the conflicting interests and opinions of the different sections of the country, and surrenders the whole Union to the nullifiers of the South and the land-robbers of the West."

The degree of party rancor was dramatized by the brutal beating of Duff Green, the editor of the *Telegraph*, who had been originally set up in business to vilify President Adams. Green had later abandoned Jackson and thrown in with Calhoun and the nullifiers. As a Calhoun man, he excoriated the Unionists in South Carolina as "Tories"; one of them, General James Blair, a Congressman from South Carolina, a huge, powerful man, nearly killed him for it.

The South Carolina Proclamation of November 24, declaring the tariff acts of 1828 and 1832 null and void, had "further declared (it) to be unlawful for any of the constituted authorities of the State or of the United States to enforce payment of the duties." The proclamation also forbade the state courts to pass on the equity or constitutionality of the ordinance and directed that no appeal be allowed to the Supreme Court of the United States. In the event of any effort by the United States to enforce the collection of the tariffs in question, the people of South Carolina would "thenceforth hold themselves absolved from all further obligation to maintain or preserve their political connection with the people of the other States, and will forthwith proceed to organize a separate government. . . ."

To these bold statements Jackson replied as boldly. Three days after his annual message, Jackson issued a proclamation to the People of South Carolina. He had, under the Constitution, the authority necessary to force compliance with the laws, but the crisis was so grave that he thought it proper to state as fully and explicitly as possible the constitutional basis on which he was determined to act if the state persisted in its defiance. Nowhere could the champions of nullification find a word among the writings of the framers of the Constitution giving any color of legality to their argument. "The Constitution is still the object of our reverence, the bond of our Union, our defense in danger, the source of our prosperity in peace. It shall descend, as we have received it, uncorrupted by sophistical construction, to our posterity. . . . Fellow-citizens of my native State, let me not only admonish you, as the First Magistrate of our common country, not to incur the penalty of its laws, but use the influence that a father would over his children whom he saw rushing to certain ruin."

The President's manifest determination to enforce the laws was balanced by a promise to press for further reductions in the hated tariffs. Finally the people of South Carolina were warned that if they forced a showdown with the federal government the "primeval curse on man for the shedding of a brother's blood" must be borne by them.

Old Chief Justice John Marshall took new heart from the President's bold challenge. Associate Justice Joseph Story, who had been characterized by an angry Jackson as "the most dangerous man in America," was invited to the White House by the President. "But what is more remarkable," Story wrote to a friend, "since his last Proclamation and message, the chief justice and myself have become his warmest supporters. . . . Who would have dreamed of such an occurrence?"

Philip Hone took note of the nullification resolutions in his journal, calling them "rank treason" and adding "the leaders deserved to be hanged." He was surprised and delighted with Jackson's proclamation—which, he felt sure, "will take its place in the archives of our country, and will dwell in the memory of our citizens alongside the farewell address of the 'Father of his Country.' . . . I say, Hurrah for Jackson! . . ." The next day he added: "The effect of this noble paper has been astonishingly great in this city. The voices of all parties are raised in favor of the measure. . . . The doctrines are precisely those of the old Federalists, when Federalism and Patriotism were synonymous terms . . . in fact it is just such a paper as Alexander Hamilton would have written and Thomas Jefferson condemned."

Jackson's proclamation was a masterful document, making clear his determination to uphold the Constitution as he understood it but offering conciliation to the rebellious state. Its purpose was to prevent the state legislature from enacting the ordinances proposed by the convention, in itself a body of dubious legality. But Jackson's proclamation was defied. The South Carolina legislature met and passed, with only minor changes, the nullifying ordinance. The challenge of one duelist to the other had been offered and accepted (although Jackson, as we have seen, had done his best to offer the state a way out). It seemed to Old Hickory that his native state was, like the Bank, determined to kill him. But he would no more flinch than he had in his duel with Charles Dickinson many years before. On January 16 he sent a special message to Congress outlining the steps in South Carolina's resistance, including information that the state was preparing for a resort to arms. (Governor James Hamilton, Jr., had called for two thousand volunteers to take up arms at once and for another ten thousand to be organized into a State Guard.) In a long and able message the President asked Congress for the requisite powers to enforce the law as well as a bill further lowering the tariff.

John Quincy Adams, having just authored a bill to reduce the tariffs, believed that South Carolina should first be brought to heel before further reductions were made. Otherwise it might be assumed by many people that despite the President's rhetoric the state had, in the last analysis, gotten its way by threats and bullying. But Jackson was an enemy of the tariffs, as Adams was their friend, so he did his best to see that legislation giving him full power to force obedience to the laws was accompanied by bills to reduce the tariffs.

The most conspicuous of the new tariff bills was the so-called Verplanck Bill, and several weeks were spent debating its provisions. The familiar alignments were evident—the representatives of the manufacturing states of the North arrayed against the antiprotectionists of the South. As debate dragged on day after day, two improbable allies worked for a compromise. Calhoun, who apparently still cherished presidential ambitions, and his principal rival, Clay, put their heads together to produce a bill that pleased nobody but plainly proved better than nothing. By its terms tariffs were to be reduced a certain percentage each year until only a 20 percent *ad valorem* (percentage of the value of the imported goods) remained. The House, only a week away from adjournment, seemed deadlocked over the Verplanck Bill when one of Henry Clay's lieutenants rose to present a wholly new bill. Introduced late in the afternoon of February 25 as the members were preparing to leave the chamber, it came without warning, like a thunderclap, with all the weight that Clay and Calhoun could muster behind it. The New Englanders asked for a delay which was refused. It was this bill or nothing. John Davis of Massachusetts protested that the bill sacrificed the manufacturing interests of the North "as a burnt offering to appease the unnatural and unfounded discontent of the South." But pleas and protests were in vain. The Clay Tariff, as it was called, proposed (in Thomas Hart Benton's words) "when the members were gathering up their over-coats for a walk home to their dinners, was passed before those coats had got on the back; and the dinner which was waiting had but little time to cool before the astonished members, their work done, were at the table to eat it." It had passed by a vote of 119 to 85. A similar bill was rushed through the Senate, 29 to 16.

The preamble to Clay's bill was certainly the most ambitious ever appended to a tariff measure. It was designed "to prevent the destruction of the political system, and to arrest civil war and restore peace and tranquility to the nation." And, not entirely coincidentally, to advance Henry Clay's prospects for becoming president of the United States. Duties on imported goods were to be reduced gradually over a nine-year period, leaving a uniform 20 percent *ad valorem* tax on most imports.

Many members of Congress shared Benton's view of the compro-mise: "concocted out of doors, managed by politicians dominated by an outside interest—kept a secret— . . . it comprised every title necessary to stamp a vicious and reprehensible act—bad in the matter—foul in the manner—full of abuse—and carried through upon the terrors of some, and the interests of others . . . an outrage upon representative government."

When the members returned to the House, the bill requested by Jackson to enforce the collection of the revenue—the Revenue or Force Bill, as it came to be called—was immediately taken up. The debates grew, if anything, more rancorous and impassioned than before. In Benton's words, "The Bill was opposed with a vehemence rarely witnessed, and every effort made to render it odious to the people, and even to extend the odium to the President. . . ." In the Senate Webster carried the burden of debate for the advocates of the Revenue Bill and Calhoun was his principal adversary.

Calhoun developed what came to be called the theory of the "concurrent majority." His disquisition was the most ambitious effort to construct a rational argument, based on historical antecedents, for the doctrine of nullification and secession. Calhoun went back to the office of the Roman tribune, contending that the veto power of the tribunate was the highest degree of political wisdom. This had been designed to protect the people, the plebeians, from the exactions of the rich, the patricians. Thereafter "no measure of movement could be adopted without the concurring consent of both the patricians and the plebeians. . . . To obtain this concurrence, each was compelled to consult the good will of the other. . . . The result was that men possessing those qualities which would naturally command confidence, moderation, wisdom, justice, and patriotism, were elevated to office. . . ." The efficacy of this system "furnishes the real explanation of the power of the Roman state." In the United States, the principle embodied in the Roman tribunate must be translated into the right of "interposition" by a particular state—the right to interpose between an inequitable law passed by Congress and the citizens of the state. The real contest in the United States was between "power and liberty"— power represented by the larger numbers and greater wealth of the North and liberty by the South. Unless the South could establish a theoretical and practical basis on which to defend its own interests, its fate would be "more wretched than that of the aborigines whom they have expelled, or of their slaves."

Calhoun ended his remarks with an exhortation to his fellow Southerners. If they persevered in this noble fight for freedom "our section will become distinguished for its patriots and statesmen. But if . . . we prove unworthy of this high destiny, if we yield to the steady encroachment of power, the severest and most debasing calamity and corruption will overspread the land. Every Southern man, true to the interests of his section . . . will be forever excluded from the honors and emoluments of this government, which will be reserved for only those who have qualified themselves by political prostitution, for admission into the Magdalen Asylum [a notorious British institution for ill and aged prostitutes]."

If a nation, state, or region can suffer from collective paranoia, then surely the South had that affliction. The impassioned rhetoric of its politicians was full of violence, of rage, of fear and hostility. It does not take a heavy commitment to a psychological interpretation of history to be convinced that the perpetual and inescapable moral dilemma of slavery lay behind those dark torrents of oratory.

Calhoun's address had been delivered in a hoarse and often faint voice. When Webster began his reply, word spread through the city, and soon the galleries and the floor of the Senate itself were "crowded to suffocation." The House adjourned and members came to share seats with their colleagues in the Senate chamber. In an atmosphere of intense drama Webster spoke from five in the afternoon until eight in the evening to an audience that cheerfully suspended its dinner hour.

In his reply to Calhoun, Webster—the great defender, dramatizer, and explicator of the Union—extended the arguments he had employed against Hayne. The South Carolinian's doctrines, he declared, were revolutionary. They were directed not at the reform of government but at its destruction. "Sir, so soon as this ordinance (of nullification) shall be carried into effect, a revolution will have commenced. . . ." Nullification struck "a deadly blow at the vital principle of the whole Union." To believe that nullification must not lead inevitably to secession and to "the dismemberment of the Union and general revolution" was like believing that "if one were to take the plunge of Niagara, and cry out that he would stop halfway down. . . . Sir," Webster concluded, "the world will scarcely believe that this whole controversy" has "no other foundation than a difference of opinion, upon a provision of the constitution between a majority of the people of South Carolina, on the one side, and a vast majority of the whole people of the United States on the other." It must seem "incredible and inconceivable" that "a single state should rush into conflict with all the rest . . . and thus break up and destroy the world's last hope." When Webster finished he was rewarded by "a long, loud and general clapping of hands . . . from the floor and galleries."

A number of Calhoun's colleagues suggested that the real root of the controversy was Calhoun's thwarted ambition to be president. With the presidency within his grasp, Calhoun had committed a series of almost inexplicable political blunders, the last and most flagrant of which had been his patently malicious vote against Van Buren's confirmation as ambassador to Great Britain. It was now as though he had gone mad and with his coadjutors, Governor Hamilton and the inflammatory Congressman George McDuffie, was bent on pulling down the whole palladium of the Union in an apocalyptic disaster.

The vote on the Force Bill was 32 to 1, Calhoun and his supporters having left the chamber. Clay, determined not to alienate the South, avoided voting.

The Twenty-second Congress adjourned on March 3, 1833, at five in the morning. John Quincy Adams took Edward Everett home in his carriage and then walked on to his own lodgings, where he noted that the thermometer stood at six degrees above zero—the coldest night of the winter. As day dawned he went to bed, "exhausted and dejected but with blessings of gratitude to the Supreme Disposer of events for the merciful dispensation of His providence in bringing the affairs of the country to a condition more favorable to peace and union than it has been of late, and though still surrounded with dangers."

Two days later Andrew Jackson was sworn in for his second term. "The inaugural speech," Adams noted, "was brief, and full of smooth professions." The greater part of Jackson's second inaugural was concerned with the nature of the relationship between the states and the federal government. He was convinced that "the destruction of our State governments or the annihilation of their controls over the local concerns of the people would lead directly to revolution and anarchy, and finally to despotism and military domination. . . . Without Union our independence and liberty would never have been achieved; without Union they can never be maintained. . . . The loss of liberty, of good government, of peace, plenty, and happiness, must inevitably follow a dissolution of the Union." Jackson's role as president would be to foster "a spirit of liberal concession and compromise."

The day after Jackson signed the Force Bill and the Compromise Tariff into law the *United States Telegraph,* once a devoutly Jacksonian journal but later the voice of Calhoun and his adherents, appeared with a black border, announcing "here lies the remains of States rights. It is for this we mourn." The *New York Evening Post,* a Jacksonian paper, noted "A system founded on the most short-sighted selfishness has received its death blow. The experiment (protective tariffs) has been fully, almost fatally tried, and will be recorded in history only to be avoided."

South Carolina took the line that it had triumphed over the forces of evil. "This little state," one journal declared, "has defied the swaggering giant of the Union. Thirteen thousand Carolinians have not only awed the wild West into respect, compelled Pennsylvania stolidity into something like sense, New York corruption into something like decency, Yankee rapacity into a sort of image of honesty, but they have done all this loftily and steadily in the face of seventeen thousand betrayers of liberty (Unionists) of their own State."

It would be a serious mistake to assume that the nullifiers had anything like the unanimous support of the people of South Carolina. They were, by their own admission, a highly vocal minority and that fact, as much as the threat of federal power, caused second thoughts.

Even before Clay's Compromise Tariff Bill and the Force Bill had been passed by Congress, a number of the leading nullifiers had met at Charleston to reassert their principles but resolve it to be "the sense of this meeting that all occasion for collision between the Federal and State authorities should be sedulously avoided on both sides." Joel Poinsett, a South Carolina Unionist and supporter of Jackson, kept the President informed on an almost weekly basis of the state of affairs in South Carolina. The Virginia legislature went so far as to send a representative, Benjamin Leigh, to try to prevail on South Carolina to repeal its ordinance of nullification; his arrival in Charleston seems to have had a salutary effect on the nullifiers. In many towns and districts throughout the state, Unionists were forming into armed companies to oppose the nullifiers. Plans were made for a great rallying of pro-Union men as soon as the spring planting was over. (One Unionist described the nullifiers as "all the idlers, loafers, vagabonds and dandies who inhabit the cities and live by their wits.")

As each week passed it became clearer that persistence in the nullifying ordinance must result in severe internal conflict within the state as well as armed conflict with the federal government. When the nullifiers called for a convention to meet in Columbia on March 11 the Unionists responded by calling a convention of their own to convene a week later at Charleston. But the Nullification Convention, with a minimum of rhetoric, repealed the ordinance and the laws passed to support it and quietly faded away. The great secession crisis was over. The nullifiers, however, continued to proclaim their doctrine and insist that it was only the threat of secession that had brought a redress of their principal grievance.

Jackson himself was convinced that he had killed the serpent of secession in the egg. "I met nullification at its threshold," the old gunfighter wrote James Buchanan, then serving as ambassador to Russia. "My proclamation was well timed. It opened the eyes of the people to the wicked designs of the nullifiers sided by the union of Clay, Calhoun, the Bank, and the corrupt of all parties. Not a modification of the tariff, but a separation of the Union by the Potomac was sought. To-day advice informs us that South Carolina has repealed the ordinance of secession and all laws based upon it. Thus dies nullification and the doctrine of secession, never more to be heard of, only in holding up to scorn and indignation its projectors and abettors and handing their names to posterity as traitors to the best of governments." If Buchanan remembered Jackson's letter twenty-seven years later when, a lame-duck president soon to be superseded by the newly elected Lincoln, he watched seven Southern states secede from the Union, he must have reflected on the unpredictability of history.

Jackson had every reason for self-congratulation. He had steered a dangerous course through waters filled with shoals and rocks and had made a triumphant port. The historian can only reflect on the fortunate change of events that had placed him in the presidency at such a critical moment. Able and intelligent as John Quincy Adams was, it is impossible to believe that, given the political resources at his disposal, he could have prevented the secession of South Carolina. Jackson was, after all, the hero of the South and West. However much his actions might disappoint or enrage some of his partisans, he drew on an enormous balance of admiration and affection among the ordinary people of the South while Adams represented the quintessence of the New England enemy. With everything going for him, so to speak, it still took Jackson's remarkable political instincts and practical intelligence to weather the storm.

6

Jackson and the Bank

The President was not a man to rest on his laurels. The Bank had gone all out to defeat him and now it must pay the price. He was convinced that he had a mandate from the people supporting his political principles and policies. Clay declared himself "surprised and alarmed at the new source of executive power which is found as a result of a presidential election. I had supposed that the Constitution and the laws were the sole source of executive authority . . . that the issue of a presidential election was merely to place the Chief Magistrate in the post assigned to him. . . . But it seems that if, prior to an election, certain opinions, no matter how ambiguously put forth by a candidate, are known to the people, those loose opinions, in virtue of the election, incorporate themselves with the Constitution, and afterwards are to be regarded and expounded as parts of the instrument."

It is astonishing to think of the implacable old man in his sixty-seventh year, a semi-invalid, suffering so continually from the grievous physical wounds of his violent life that he had to take daily doses of pain-killing drugs, yet pressing on with his vendetta against Nicholas Biddle, "Old Nick," the Devil, and his instrument, the Bank of the United States. The charter of the Bank had only three years to run, and it was now clear to everyone that only a miracle could save it.

Jackson's closest advisers urged him to let well enough alone. But to him the issue was a moral, not a political one. It was simplicity itself: the Bank was evil; any compromise with evil was evidence of weakness or cowardice. The Bank had challenged him and tried to "kill" him. It was not enough that it must soon die of natural causes, he would kill it. The only question that remained was the particular weapon to choose. Secretary of the Treasury McLane, acting on Jackson's instructions, had informed Biddle that in July the government would withdraw six million dollars to pay off a 3-percent loan dating back to 1792. This required that the Bank in turn call in enough of its own loans to make up the necessary sum. Biddle pleaded for a delay. The financial condition of the country was highly unstable, he argued. The terrible cholera epidemic had put a damper on business activity everywhere. To call in large sums in loans would certainly aggravate the situation. When McLane consented to a four-month extension, Biddle entered into a secret agreement with the British banking house of Baring Brothers & Company, which held some three million dollars' worth of the paper of the Bank of the United States, to withhold those notes that were scheduled to come due for payment within the next year. When word of the agreement leaked out, Jackson was convinced that the Bank had been driven to such a measure by a shortage of funds. It thus followed that his obligation as President was to remove U.S. funds from the Bank. He requested Congress to look into the matter and recommend such action as seemed to it appropriate.

Young James Polk, the loyal Jacksonian Congressman from Tennessee, promptly brought in a bill to permit the sale of all Bank stock owned by the United States. When it was voted down, the House took up a majority and a minority report from the Committee of Ways and Means, the majority declaring the government deposits entirely safe in the Bank, the minority questioning its soundness. By a large majority the House then voted in support of the Bank. The vote confirmed Jackson in his conviction that the Bank bought and sold Congressmen and had more power than was good for it or the country. If the weapon was the removal of government moneys from the Bank, how was that weapon best employed? The always politically resourceful Amos Kendall proposed simply depositing future funds in certain state banks—banks favorable to the administration, so far as practical—and the gradual withdrawal of federal funds from the Bank of the United States to meet the operating expenses of the government.

When Jackson polled his Cabinet, several of them, including McLane, urged that the Bank's charter simply be allowed to expire. Postmaster General Barry supported the gradual removal of the deposits. Only Roger Taney, the attorney general, was emphatic in urging the prompt removal of the deposits. Word that Jackson was contemplating such action brought a flood of petitions from various state banks urging that they be made the depositories for funds withdrawn from the Bank of the United States. Among those whose advice Jackson solicited was Hugh White, senator from Jackson's home state. In his letter to White Jackson expressed his conviction that the Bank had become a tool of his enemies, Clay and Calhoun. White, like McLane, urged Jackson to take no immediate action but simply let the Bank's charter expire.

The resistance of McLane as secretary of the treasury was the first obstacle Jackson had to overcome. This was accomplished by transferring McLane to the office of secretary of state in place of Livingston, who was dispatched to France as ambassador. William Duane was then nominated and confirmed as McLane's successor, although Jackson had not taken the trouble to ascertain Duane's position on the matter of the removal of the deposits. About to depart on a presidential tour of the Northern states, Jackson summoned Duane and asked him to prepare an anti-Bank opinion to be ready when he returned to Washington.

When Jackson repeated Monroe's triumphal Northern tour in the summer of 1833, the Era of Good Feelings was a remote memory. The North was, in a real sense, enemy territory. But large and enthusiastic crowds turned out to greet the President. Jackson's visit to New York was the occasion for the greatest turnout in the city's history. "Broadway from the Battery to the Park," Philip Hone noted, "formed a solid mass of men, women, and children, who greeted their favorite with cheers, shouts, and waving of scarfs and handkerchiefs." The demonstration of popular affection for the Hero moved Hone to further thoughts. Jackson was even more popular, in his view, than Washington himself. Washington was "too dignified, too grave . . . and men could not approach him with familiarity." Jackson, on the other hand, "has a kind expression for each—the same to all, no doubt, but each thinks it intended for himself. . . . Talk of him as the second Washington! It won't do now; Washington was only the first Jackson."

Sidney George Fisher wrote bitterly on the occasion of Jackson's visit: "When we see a nation so infatuated, as in spite of all evidence and all reason, in spite of the grossest mismanagement, the vilest fraud & corruption, and actual & extensive suffering produced, to worship such a creature as Andrew Jackson, ignorant, passionate and imbecile . . . the tool of low adventurers & swindlers . . . it is enough to destroy all hope in the power of the people for self government, and dissipate forever the fanciful dreams of republicanism. . . . In every country there must be a mob, a canaille population, without property, without education, utterly degraded, & anxious to promote disturbance and revolution, because these cannot place them in a worse situation, & may place them in a better, and because scenes of violence afford opportunities for the gratification of their brutal passions." This class, still relatively small in the United States, would, in Fisher's opinion, increase until the "majority of the people, in whose hands is lodged the whole political power of the nation . . . unfit to possess that power . . . are . . . lead on to anarchy & revolution by designing and artful demogogues. . . ."

Bostonians heard with dismay that their city was on the President's itinerary. The Harvard Corporation concluded reluctantly that it had no choice but to invite Jackson to visit the college and receive the degree of Doctor of Law. Joseph Quincy, the great reformist mayor of Boston, now president of Harvard (which he had found, incidentally, more resistant to reform than Boston), visited John Quincy Adams, working in his garden at Quincy, to inform him of the proposed invitation and to ask Adams to attend. Adams replied that the President had treated him in such a fashion he "could hold no intercourse of a friendly character with him" and could not therefore accept the invitation. Then, in a flood of bitterness, Adams added that "as for myself an affectionate child of my Alma Mater, I would not be present to witness her disgrace by conferring her highest literary honors upon a barbarian who could not write a sentence of grammar and could hardly spell his own name."

The famous Dr. Benjamin Waterhouse, suspected of harboring Democratic sentiments, did attend and reported to Adams that he had been "much captivated by the ease and gracefulness" of the President's manner and by the cordial and complimentary words with which Jackson had greeted him. But to the doctor's experienced eye, the President looked so frail and ill that he doubted that he would survive the rigors of his tour. Adams was unrelenting. He suspected Jackson of being "one of our tribe of great men who turn disease to commodity, like John Randolph, who for forty years was always dying."

In fairness to Adams it must be said that to him and those of a like mind it seemed that the country was in the remorseless grip of a mad and vindictive old man. Certainly there was an element of extreme paranoia in Jackson. Harriet Martineau witnessed an attempt on Jackson's life in the Capitol following the funeral of a Congressman attended by all of official Washington. As Jackson was leaving the rotunda to join the procession to the grave, moving with difficulty and in obvious pain, a man named Robert Lawrence rushed forward and tried to shoot him. The pistol missed fire and the assailant was quickly overpowered and hurried away to prison. The effect on the President was startling. Convinced that he was the object of a plot by his political opponents, he flew into such a rage that those about him feared for his sanity. Harriet Martineau noted "it was found necessary to put him into his carriage and take him home," in "a tremendous passion." The President was convinced that the attempted assassination was instigated by George Poindexter, a senator from Mississippi and an inveterate enemy of Jackson's. Jackson had initiated the quarrel by criticizing Poindexter's private life and morals, whereupon the Senator had hinted at a duel. For the President of the United States to engage in a duel with a senator was too much even for Jackson to contemplate. It was agreed that the mutual satisfaction of honor must wait until the presidential term was over. Jackson was determined to charge the attempted assassination against Poindexter even though doctors certified Lawrence to be insane (he declared that Jackson had prevented him from becoming king of England). Jackson announced his views so publicly that Poindexter wrote to him expressing his incredulity and inviting the President to deny that he had made such an accusation. But Jackson would not let the matter rest and finally at Poindexter's insistence a Senate committee was appointed; it cleared him of any complicity in Lawrence's madness. Jackson's accusations against Poindexter, which Adams found "sickening . . . much as if we were running into the manners of the Italian republics," gave the emerging Whigs of Philadelphia an opportunity to make some political hay by giving "a magnificent banquet at the Arch Street Theatre" in honor of the Mississippi senator.

Denouncing Jackson had indeed become a favorite pastime of the upper classes. As Philip Hone put it, "Two or three of us were talking yesterday morning . . . and, as is the fashion nowadays, abusing Gen. Jackson and marveling at the undeserved popularity which he still enjoys in some parts of our country. . . ."

The state of Jackson's health did indeed force him to cut short his tour. When he returned to Washington in July, the President took up once more the question of the removal of the federal deposits from the Bank. In September he read the Cabinet a paper stating his intention of removing the deposits at once. When he had finished he handed the pages to Duane. "Is this a direction by you to me to remove the deposits?" Duane asked.

"It is a direction to you to remove the deposits," the President answered, "but on my responsibility. And if you will stand by me it will be the happiest day of my life."

Duane asked for a few hours to consider the matter. Jackson, not waiting for Duane's reply, announced through the *Washington Globe* that the deposits would be removed on October 1 and deposited in state banks in the principal cities. Duane at once sent Jackson a letter declaring that he was unwilling to remove the deposits and stating his reasons in detail. When Jackson returned the secretary's letter, Duane defiantly informed him that he would not participate in the removal and would not, moreover, resign the office to which he had so recently been appointed. Jackson thereupon dismissed him and made Roger Taney the secretary of the treasury.

The result of the President's action was a sharp curtailment of credit. As the Bank called in its loans, subsidiary banks experienced an acute shortage of cash. Interest rates and prices rose sharply. In many areas state bank notes circulated at a discount of from 8 to 12 percent. The sales of real estate dropped precipitously and the building trades languished. Two months later, in his fifth annual message to Congress, Jackson gave a lengthy defense of his motives in removing the Bank deposits maintaining that the Bank and its friends—not the removal —were responsible for the economic pinch.

Jackson devoted the major portion of his address to a lengthy review of foreign affairs, giving special attention to the failure of the French government to honor the terms of the Treaty of 1831 which settled spoliation claims against France dating back to Napoleon's Berlin and Milan decrees. To the subject of the constantly deteriorating relations with Mexico Jackson made only a passing reference. Interestingly enough for a president who believed in strict construction of the Constitution, Jackson called attention to the numerous fatal accidents caused by exploding boilers on steamboats and asked Congress to consider "precautionary and penal" legislation in cases where such accidents were due to "criminal negligence." And, finally, he repeated for the nth time his recommendation that the president and vice-president be directly elected by the people and their tenure limited to one term.

Jackson, complaining to a startled Harriet Martineau about the opponents of his policies in the Senate of the Twenty-third Congress, had assured her that the new Senate would be made up of a majority of solid administration men. That turned out not to be the case. The removal of the deposits proved too much for some Democratic senators to swallow. Those incongruous allies, Clay and Calhoun— united only by their hatred of Jackson—were determined to make as much trouble as they could. Clay opened the game by offering an insultingly worded resolution calling on the President to state whether his Cabinet paper on removing the deposits of the Bank, which had been widely published in the papers, was authentic and, if it was, to make it available to the Senate. With the tone somewhat moderated, the resolution passed and was sent to Jackson, who replied with a stinging lesson on the independence of the executive branch from the legislative: "I have yet to learn under what constitutional authority that branch of the legislature [the Senate] has a right to require of me an account of any communication, either verbally or in writing, made to the heads of the departments, acting as a cabinet council."

Clay had other arrows to his bow. A week or so later he offered a resolution to censure the President for exercising powers "not granted to him by the Constitution and laws, and dangerous to the liberties of the people" in dismissing two recalcitrant secretaries of the treasury and replacing them with an individual who could comply with his wishes. Another resolution, offered by Clay, declared that Taney's publicly stated reasons for removing the deposits were "unsatisfactory and insufficient." The debate that followed dragged on week after week, reflecting little credit on the Senate but giving a conspicuous demonstration of the general demoralization that existed in that body and of Clay's capacity to exploit it, as he apparently assumed, for his own political profit. Finally a vote of censure passed, to Jackson's fury.

Philip Hone noted that, as a result of the removal of the deposits from the Bank of the United States, "the times are bad, stocks are falling, and panic prevails which will result in bankruptcies and ruin in many quarters where a few short weeks since the sun of prosperity shone with unusual brightness. . . . We are smarting under the lash which the vindictive ruler of our destinies has inflicted upon us as a penalty for the sin which Nicholas Biddle committed in opposition to his election. My share of punishment amounts to $20,000, which I have lost by the fall of stocks in the last sixty days." But Hone had the honesty to add that "the gambling in stocks which has been carried on by the brokers to an extent disgraceful to the commercial character of the city" was a contributing factor.

Congress was flooded with memorials and petitions on the economic state of the country, the majority of which blamed the disordered state of financial affairs on the removal of the deposits. It is difficult to determine the degree to which protests were orchestrated by the Bank and its friends, but there was no doubt in Jackson's mind that he was the object of a carefully organized campaign to force him to reverse his policy in regard to the Bank. When delegations of apprehensive but determined citizens visited him to plead for some governmental action to relieve the shortage of currency and credit, Jackson received them with unfailing courtesy but then gave them angry lectures on the iniquities of banks and bankers, more especially the Bank of the United States. When the chairman of one such delegation from Baltimore asked the President to provide some relief from "the distressing situation of the currency of this country," Jackson broke in: "Relief, sir! Come not to me, sir! Go to the monster! . . . It is folly, sir, to talk to Andrew Jackson. The government will not bow to this monster."

"Sir," the unhappy chairman replied, "the currency . . . is in a dreadful situation. The State banks have not confidence in each other; they cannot give the trade facilities required."

"Sir, you keep one-sided company. Andrew Jackson . . . has more and better information than you, sir, or any of you. . . . The failures that are now taking place are among stock jobbers, brokers, and gamblers, and would to God they were swept from the land."

With more courage than wisdom, the chairman persisted—at least by his own account: "The people, sir, have not understood the character of a President, if he is unwilling to hear their calls and demands."

"The people! The people, sir, are with me. I have undergone much peril for the liberties of this people, and Andrew Jackson yet lives to put his foot upon the head of the monster, and crush him to the dust. . . . It is folly to talk to me thus, sir. I would rather undergo the tortures of ten Spanish Inquisitions than that the deposits should be restored, or the monster rechartered."

To another delegation Jackson used a biblical analogy. "I have read the Scriptures, gentlemen, and I find that when Moses ascended the Mount, the children of Israel rebelled and made a golden calf and worshipped it, and it brought a curse upon them. This Bank will be a greater curse." References to the golden calf and the Spanish Inquisition appeared in Jackson's replies to a number of his importuners. Finally, he refused to receive any more. He was Moses trying to lead his people into the Promised Land and he found that he must contend with the worshipers of the Golden Calf, Mammon, the Unrighteous, the Monster. But like a faithful Christian he would endure the fires of the Inquisition before he would betray his faith or his people.

7

The Indian Removal

Sandwiched between the clamor over the removal of the deposits from the Bank and the wrangling in the Senate over the authority of the President was the attempt to devise a final solution to the problem of the Indians. The Cherokee were so far from accepting Jackson's policy of removal that those Indians who tried to argue in its favor were frequently killed or banished. The complexities of the issue were suggested by a report submitted by Thomas McKenney, a longtime defender of Indian rights and head of the United States Bureau of Indian Affairs. McKenney had helped establish an ambitious program for "civilizing" the Indians that rested primarily on setting up numerous schools where the Indians were instructed in both practical and academic subjects. When McKenney visited the reservations in 1830 he was distressed at the conditions he found. There were a few Indians who had profited from the instruction, but "the rest was cheerless and hopeless enough. Before this personal observation," he wrote, "I was sanguine in the hope of seeing these people relieved, and saved, where they are. But the sight of their condition, and the prospect of the collisions which have since taken place, and which have grown out of the anomalous relations which they bear to the States, produced a sudden change in my opinion and my hopes."

The debate in Congress on the removal policy had ostensibly revolved around the question of what was best for the Indians. None of the speakers, however (either for or against), ever suggested that the Indians should be allowed to or encouraged to retain—or in most instances to re-establish—their own tribal life and customs. Such a course seemed manifestly impossible. Warfare, raids, and the hunting of wild animals were the essential elements around which tribal life was organized. Except for hunting, which was increasingly unproductive, these aspects of tribal life which gave form and order to aboriginal existence could not be tolerated within the boundaries of the states. To the degree that it might prove possible to sustain tribal life, the experiment could be tried only in the vast unsettled regions of the trans-Mississippi West. Even there it must be seriously inhibited by the promise of the government to protect all the tribes in their particularity and independence, a promise impossible to fulfill since many tribes bore for other tribes inveterate hatreds more deep-seated than their hostility to whites.

Lewis Cass, Jackson's secretary of war, exhausted all of his powers of persuasion trying to prevail on delegations of Cherokee chieftains to accept removal. They were adamant. "It was hoped," Cass wrote the new governor of Georgia, Wilson Lumpkin, "that the favorable terms offered by the Government would have been accepted. But some strange infatuation seems to prevail among these Indians. That they cannot remain where they are and prosper is attested as well by their actual condition as by the whole history of our aboriginal tribes." When they remained immovable, Jackson himself tried his hand, assuring them that "I am sincerely desirous to promote your welfare." They must join their "countrymen" who had already settled in the West: "And the sooner you do this the sooner will commence your career of improvement and prosperity."

The general issue of the Indians, with which John Quincy Adams had tried to deal, was complicated by the fact that Alabama and Mississippi followed Georgia's lead in passing laws placing the Indians under state jurisdiction. Requiring Indians to obey the laws of the states in which they resided seemed on the surface reasonable enough, but a Georgia law provided that "No Indian or descendant of any Indians, residing within the Creek or Cherokee Nation of Indians shall be deemed a competent witness in any court in the State to which a white person may be a party. . . ."

From all over New England memorials and petitions flooded

Congress protesting the administration's policy of, in effect, handing over the Indians to the hostile citizens of Georgia, Alabama, and Mississippi. One indignant Georgia representative charged that "these country fanatics [the New Englanders] have placed themselves behind the bulwark of religion and denounce the Georgians as atheists, deists, infidels and sabbath-breakers, laboring under the curse of slavery. . . . The Georgians arc described as the worst of savages; as men who can neither read nor write, and who never hear a sermon unless preached by a New England missionary."

The three Southern states made clear their intention simply to seize the Indian lands guaranteed to the tribes by treaty with the United States. The only question was how the President and Congress would respond. Jackson had made it clear that he had no intention of forcing the issue with the states. Indeed, he had taken the line that the best the federal government could do was to facilitate the removal of the Indians, although he had said specifically that such removal should be only with the consent of the Indians themselves. With this clue Congress, after warm debates, voted 103 to 77 to approve a bill providing land west of the Mississippi for the Indians and funds to assist them in moving. If there had been any doubt about the outcome, the discovery of gold in Georgia on land owned by the Cherokee settled the issue once and for all. By the summer of 1830 more than three thousand white men were frantically digging for the yellow metal. The Georgia legislature promptly passed laws forbidding the meeting of any Cherokee council or court under penalty of four years in prison. William Wirt, the famous constitutional lawyer, was now retained by the Cherokee to take their case to the Supreme Court. The Indian cause was given heightened drama by an incident in which an Indian named Corn Tassel, who had killed a fellow Indian, was sentenced by a state court to be hanged for murder. The verdict was appealed to the Supreme Court, which issued a writ directing the state of Georgia to show why Corn Tassel should not be released on the grounds that the state had no jurisdiction over him. On the urging of the governor of Georgia the writ was ignored and Corn Tassel was hanged.

The date set for the hearing of the Cherokee case before the full Court was in early March, 1831. Georgia refused even to appear on the grounds that the Court had no right to call a sovereign state before it. Wirt argued that the Cherokee nation had the same status as a foreign power. Marshall, for the Court, rejected Wirt's argument.

After reviewing the history of the relations between the federal government and the Indian tribes, Marshall concluded: "If it be true that the Cherokee nation have rights, this is not the tribunal in which those rights are to be asserted. If it be true, that wrongs have been inflicted, and that still greater are to be apprehended, this is not the tribunal which can redress the past or prevent the future." It is worth noting that two of the Northern justices on the Court, Joseph Story and Smith Thompson, dissented.

But that was not the end of the Supreme Court's involvement with the Indians. An act of the Georgia legislature directed that all whites in the Cherokee country must leave after March, 1831, or get a license from the state and swear an oath of allegiance to Georgia. Directed primarily against missionaries to the Indians, the penalty for failure to comply was four years' imprisonment at hard labor. Some stubborn spirits refused to leave and six were arrested. The case was tried before the superior court of Gwinnett County, with the defendants' lawyer taking the line that the Georgia law was unconstitutional on a number of grounds. It was ex post facto, after the fact, forbidden by the Constitution. It was in defiance of the guarantee that the citizens of each state are entitled to the privileges and immunities of the citizens of other states, and it called for unreasonable search and seizure. The court rejected all these arguments for the defense. Two of the prisoners were missionaries who were discharged on the odd grounds that they were authorized agents of the United States and thus exempt from the Georgia law.

The Jackson administration denied that the missionaries were agents of the United States and a few weeks later the Reverend Samuel A. Worcester and a colleague were ordered to depart in ten days. Worcester protested that his sick wife could not be moved, but he and ten other missionaries were arrested, "chained by the neck . . . to a wagon," and carried off to jail. All were sentenced by a Georgia jury to four years in the state penitentiary. The governor then offered to pardon the offenders if they would swear to comply with the law. Nine apparently did so and were released, but Worcester and Elizur Butler refused and were sent to jail. They appealed to the Supreme Court of the United States.

The Court thus once more took up the case of Georgia and the Indians. This time it accepted jurisdiction. Marshall reminded his audience: "From the commencement of our government Congress has passed acts to regulate trade and intercourse with the Indians; which treat them as nations, respect their rights, and manifest a firm purpose to afford that protection which treaties stipulate. All these acts, and especially that of 1802, which is still in force, manifestly consider the several Indian nations as distinct political communities, having territorial boundaries, and within which their authority is exclusive, and having a right to all the lands within those boundaries, which is not only acknowledged but guaranteed by the United States. . . . The act of the State of Georgia under which the plaintiff . . . was prosecuted is consequently void, and the judgment a nullity. . . . The Acts of Georgia are repugnant to the Constitution, laws, and treaties of the United States. . . ." The opinion this time was unanimous. Hearing of it, Jackson is reported to have said, "John Marshall has made his opinion, now let him enforce it." Georgia refused to release the two missionaries and denounced the verdict of the Court in unmeasured terms.

If Jackson had promptly dispatched a contingent of federal troops to Georgia to free the missionaries, the state would doubtless have submitted without armed resistance but it is unlikely that the situation of the Indians would have been materially improved. Alabama and Mississippi were, after all, as adamant as Georgia in their determination to claim the land of their unwelcome neighbors. Certainly such action on Jackson's part would have alarmed the Southern states and given added impetus to the talk of secession. It was not yet evident that Jackson was disposed to seek a second term, but the enforcement of the Supreme Court's decision in Georgia might well have alienated enough Southern votes to cost him re-election. The fact of the matter was that the case of *Worcester v. Georgia* was the wrong issue on which to assert the authority of the federal government, and Jackson was a shrewd enough politician to know it.

It did not appear in this light to the great majority of National Republicans or to the champions of the Indians' cause or indeed to those to whom the Supreme Court appeared as the only hope for the preservation of the Union. The Northern press was full of denunciations of Georgia. Faneuil Hall echoed with angry exhortations to Congress and the President to act in defense of the rights of the Cherokee and the Creek. Meetings were held in innumerable towns throughout New England and more petitions and memorials poured into Congress. In the face of manifest injustice, of open defiance of the Constitution and the government itself, nothing, it seemed, could or would be done. Marshall himself was so disheartened at the failure of

Jackson to support the Court's decision that he considered resigning. It seemed to him that the Court was in the twilight of its days. The words and actions of the President indicated that he was determined to reject the Court's authority over the executive and legislative branches of the government. Associate Justice Story took what comfort he could from his conviction that the Court had acted honorably. "Thanks be to God," he wrote a friend, "the Court can wash its hands of the iniquity of the Indians and disregarding their rights." But Marshall wrote his younger associate: "I yield slowly and reluctantly to the conviction that our Constitution cannot last. Our opinions are incompatible with a united government. . . . The Union has been prolonged thus far by miracles. I fear they cannot continue."

John Quincy Adams noted in his diary: "there is every prospect . . . the bullies of Georgia have succeeded in the project of extirpating the Indians, by the sacrifice of the public faith of the Union and of all our treaties with them." Yet Adams must have felt some relief that he had not had to make the decision as to whether or not to enforce, by the full weight of federal authority (whatever that might be), the decision of the Supreme Court. Indeed one can hardly escape the conjecture that had Adams been re-elected, his relentless sense of personal and public rectitude might well have precipitated the secession of the Southern states thirty years before that event finally took place and long before the rest of the country was morally or materially ready to contest the issue.

Samuel Worcester, it should be noted, was faithful to the end to his Indian friends. Pardoned by the governor of Georgia not long after the ignored decision of the Supreme Court, he accompanied the Cherokee when they finally embarked on their tragic journey west and he established the Cherokee Park Hill Mission and the first printing press in Indian territory.

While the Cherokee remained adamant, other Southern tribes yielded to pressure to remove. The Indian removal was not, of course, accomplished in a year or two. It was almost ten years between the time the most tractable Choctaw Indians began their long, arduous trek and the most obdurate Cherokee were pried out of their land by the bayonets of federal troops.

Much of the difficulty of removal lay in the extraordinarily varied nature of the Indians on the reserved lands. They were divided into two main categories—full-bloods and half-breeds. The full-bloods usually looked with contempt on the half-breeds, a feeling that was generally returned with interest. Many of the half-breeds dressed like whites and adopted white styles of living, sending their children to missionary-run schools, planting crops, owning slaves, and sometimes prospering notably. A substantial number, perhaps a majority, were Christian. The full-bloods were much more disposed to cling to their Indian dress and to their tribal life. They generally resisted the missionaries' evangelizing efforts and resented their influence over Christianized Indians.

A classic example of such a division was found among the Choctaw of Mississippi, the first tribe to sign a treaty—the Treaty of Dancing Bear Creek—under the terms of the federal legislation. The two most influential leaders of the Mississippi Choctaw were Greenwood Leflore, a half-breed, and the old chief, Mushulatubbe, who had fought with Jackson in the war against the Creek. Mushulatubbe had been deposed as head chief in 1826 by a half-breed named David Folsom on the grounds that he was too addicted to drink and too much under the influence of the whites to be trusted. Mushulatubbe, whose name meant Determined to Kill, was a powerful and imposing figure with a large head and strong features and was famous as an orator. He maintained two separate homes with a wife at each, owned eleven slaves, and cultivated thirty acres of land at the time of the Treaty of Dancing Bear Creek. We have an old daguerrotype of Greenwood Leflore in the formal dress of a white man, looking very much like a successful planter or frontier lawyer. (It is one of the ironies of the Indian situation that half-breeds often enjoyed more prestige in the tribes than full-blooded Indian chiefs. Certainly the quality of their intelligence, or consciousness, was conspicuously "whiter" than their full-blooded brothers'.) When Leflore undertook to manage the removal he soon found himself in conflict with Mushulatubbe and other chiefs, although the split was not simply along full-blood–half-breed lines. David Folsom, who had been educated by missionaries, had, after all, deposed Mushulatubbe.

Nonetheless, the first phase of the Choctaw removal began on an encouraging note. A group of Indian chiefs, accompanied by federal troops for protection against whites and hostile Indians, set off to look at the lands the Great White Father had reserved for them in Indian Territory. Each Indian was given a rifle, powder and ball, and winter clothing, and the party started out accompanied by George Gaines, an Indian trader liked and trusted by the Indians for his fair dealings and manifest sympathy for their cause. Every morning the hunters would spread out along the trail, Gaines wrote, "always bringing into camp in the evening plenty of game for the whole party, venison, turkeys, prairie hens and occasionally bear meat." The journey soon took on the air of an extended party: "an abundance of game, and fine weather to enjoy the chase, rendered each day and night joyous and happy." The lieutenant in command of the escort of soldiers and the surgeon sent along to care for the health of the soldiers and the Indians "were both jolly soldiers and good hunters and entered into our hunts in the day and feasts and jollification at night with great spirit and zest." Near the mouth of the Canadian River, Gaines and party were joined by a "Chickasaw delegation" on the same mission and they were invited by Gaines "to join us and travel with us to enjoy our sports; wild horses were now plentiful . . . large log fires at night . . . lengthened our social enjoyments. Our Choctaw hunting, war, love stories, and wit, were now seasoned by army stories and wit."

Reaching the designated lands, the Indians were "very much pleased" with the country, but there was an immediate awkwardness about which lands should be Choctaw and which Chickasaw, and threats of an attack by "Western" Indians forced the combined parties to prepare for hostilities. The younger braves looked forward to a fight with some anticipation so that they might judge the warlike qualities of their neighbors-to-be.

On the Red River they came upon an encampment of Shawnee who had been living there since the War of 1812. A half-breed woman, looking at Gaines, said, "You are a white man—I hoped never to see the face of another white man." Some of the land was already occupied with Choctaw and Chickasaw settlements, bands of Indians who had come west on their own. These Indians indicated that they would welcome Indian emigrants.

The happy expedition of Gaines and the Choctaw was one of the few bright spots in a story whose tragedies accumulated month by month. The demoralizing effects of intratribal struggles over removal that often resulted in murders and outbreaks of fighting among the Indians were accentuated by the uncertainties concerning the details of the government policy, the time when the actual removal would take place for those Indians who accepted it, and the flooding of white speculators and traders onto Indian lands before the removals had even begun, debauching the Indians with bad whiskey and cheating them on the sales of their homesteads. Some Indians expressed the wish to make the journey on their own—hoping, as it turned out, to feed themselves by hunting and to pocket the ten dollars allocated by the government for their food en route. When Gaines and his Choctaw returned from Indian Territory with glowing accounts of the country, seven or eight hundred of the Indians under Leflore's influence departed posthaste, hoping to get the first choice of the new lands. Most of these left "the aged and infirm behind," assuming that the government would bring them on later. The Reverend Alexander Talley went ahead with a small party to build a church at the site allotted to the tribe, but many of the Indians departed without adequate winter clothing, without sufficient food or supplies, and with no way to cross the Mississippi River. The winter was unseasonably cold and several Indians froze to death on the march.

Another Gaines, a United States Army Officer, wrote of the Mississippi Choctaw: "The feeling which many of them evince in separating, never to return again, from their own long cherished hills, poor as they are in this section of the country, is truly painful to witness; and would be more so to me, but for the conviction that the removal is absolutely necessary for their welfare."

Confronted by any unfamiliar problem, the Indians were quite helpless, waiting patiently for the whites who accompanied them to extricate them from the difficulty. When wagons carrying their meager goods got mired in the mud, the Indians stood about, reluctant to do anything that savored of physical labor. It was only by appealing to Christian congregations in the white towns they passed that Talley was able to keep his charges from starving. He had exhausted his own funds and his credit to buy supplies before venturing westward across the Mississippi River (when Talley appealed for reimbursement the secretary of war recommended against payment on the grounds that his disbursements had not been "previously authorized by the government").

It must be said that few emigrating Indians were allowed to proceed as improvidently as Leflore's Choctaw. In most instances there was at least a semblance of planning and organization. The real estate and the livestock and equipment that the Indians were unable to take with them were sold to whites at far less than their real worth. The aged and infirm were loaded into wagons and carts along with personal belongings, and hogs, cattle, ponies, and sheep were gathered up and driven along by the women and children. Sometimes pack horses, mules, and oxen were preferred to wagons. There was usually an escort of soldiers and a government agent responsible for disbursing funds and exercising general supervision. Where practical, the initial stage of the trip up the Mississippi to the Red River or the Arkansas was aboard steamboats on which the Indians were crowded with their livestock.

The first removals were, by and large, the most arduous. In many places roads and bridges had to be built. The military officers and civilian agents had to learn from scratch all the complex problems involved in moving large numbers of essentially passive and sometimes resistant people over long distances "through a country little settled and literally impassable to any thing but wild beasts." Viewed in one perspective, the purely technical one, the organization of the removal was a remarkable accomplishment. In addition to the building of roads and bridges, food and supplies for the emigrants had to be deposited at "stands" along the routes marked out for the journey. Cattle were driven along to provide a daily ration of meat.

That was the way it was *supposed* to work and occasionally did. More often all that could go wrong did. The most devastating of such disasters was cholera, a terrible epidemic of which coincided with the most active period of removal. One large party of Choctaw got lost in a swamp in the middle of winter; several hundred head of their horses and cattle died and the Indians themselves, who had been six days without food, were rescued only by the combined efforts of whites recruited by missionaries accompanying the Indians. From Lake Providence, some sixty miles from Vicksburg, an indignant white settler wrote the secretary of war describing a scene he had witnessed: a party of Indians had to cross a swollen river on rafts in a sleet storm "under the pressure of hunger, by *old* women and young children, without any covering for their feet, legs or body except a cotton underdress . . . before they reached the place of getting rations here, I gave a small party leave to enter a field in which pumpkins were. They would not enter without leave, though starving. These they ate *raw* with the greatest avidity."

By March, 1832, it was estimated that there were 4,500 Choctaw west of the Mississippi, but well over 8,000 remained in the state.

Ironically, the Indians on whom the removal policy might be said to have borne the hardest were those who had gone furthest in adapting to white ways. Such a one was the Choctaw chief Toblee Chubee, who—a convert to Christianity—had converted the members of his tribe and prevailed on them to live "sober, industrious lives, to abandon the habits of Indians and live like the better class of white people." In 1845, Toblee Chubee and his followers were finally persuaded to move; many suffered from disease and died in Indian Territory. Almost forty-five years later, when Indians remaining in Mississippi were invited to apply for lands in Indian Territory, more than 24,000, most of whom were predominantly white, did so. Of these 1,445 were accepted and added to the tribe.

The Creek in Alabama had a large list of grievances against the whites of that state, and in 1831 they sent two chiefs to Washington to appeal to the government for protection against the rapacity and exploitation of the whites. "Murders," they declared, "have taken place, both by reds and whites. We have caused the red men to be brought to justice, the whites go unpunished. We are weak and our words and oaths go for naught; justice we don't expect, nor can we get. We may expect murderers to be more frequent. . . . They bring spirits among us for the purpose of practicing frauds; they daily rob us of our property; they bring white officers among us, and take our property from us for debts that we never contracted. We are made subject to laws we have no means of comprehending; we never know when we are doing right."

They would not move west, they declared. "Our aged fathers and mothers beseech us to remain upon the land that gave us birth, where the bones of their kindred are buried, so that when they die they mingle their ashes together." One Chief, Eneah Micco, sent the United States Indian agent a list of whites living illegally on Indian lands. They numbered 1,500, among them many horse thieves and common criminals. Some were already marking the spots they intended to take over "by blazing and cutting initials of their names on the trees" around the homes of the Indians.

In Washington, the Creek chiefs met with the secretary of war and told him: "We have made many treaties with the United States at all times with the belief that the one making was to be the last . . . we have frequently given up large tracts of our country for a mere song; and now we are called on for the remnant of our land, and for us to remove beyond the Mississippi." There were then some twenty-five thousand Creek in Alabama, owning nine hundred slaves.

Colonel John Abert, directed by Cass to superintend the removal of the Alabama Creek, wrote a prophetic letter to the secretary of war in the summer of 1833. The Creek, he noted, "are incapable of such an effort and of the arrangements and foresight which it requires. Nor have they confidence in themselves to undertake it. They fear starvation on the route; and can it be otherwise, when many of them are nearly starving now. . . . A people who will sell their corn in the fall for twenty-five cents a bushel, and have to buy in the spring at a dollar or dig roots to sustain life; a people who appear never to think of tomorrow, are not a people capable of husbanding the means, and anticipating the wants of a journey, with women, and children, of eight hundred miles." Abert warned Cass that every area of good hunting, "every trivial accident, will occasion days of delay; and join with these their listless, idle, lounging habits, their love of drink . . . and what can be expected if the emigration is left to themselves? . . . You cannot have an adequate idea," he continued, "of the deterioration which these Indians have undergone during the last two or three years, from a state of comparative plenty to that of unqualified wretchedness and want." This was due primarily to the fact that the state, anticipating possession of the Indians' lands, had permitted whites to invade their nation, made "encroachments upon their lands, even upon their cultivated fields, abuses of their persons and property; hosts of traders, who, like locusts, have destroyed their substance and inundated their homes with whiskey, have destroyed what little disposition to cultivation the Indians may once have had. . . . Emigration is the only hope of self-preservation left to these people. They are brow beat, cowed, and imposed upon, and depressed with the feeling that they have no adequate protection in the United States. . . . They dare not enforce their own laws to preserve order, for fear of the laws of the whites." The heartbreaking consequence was that the more lawless Indians, freed from all constraints, murdered their fellows with impunity. In another report, Abert wrote of the Creek, "Their helpless ignorance, their generally good character, (for they are a well disposed people), instead of establishing claims upon good feelings, seem rather to expose them to injuries."

Cass, appalled by the stories that reached him, wrote to the governor of Alabama protesting the treatment of the defenseless

Creek. "Gross and wanton outrages have been committed" upon them. "The houses of the Indians have been forcibly taken possession of, and sometimes burnt, and the owners driven into the woods . . . their horses, cattle, hogs, and other property have been taken from them. . . . And, in addition to this, the deputy marshal reports that there are four hundred persons selling whiskey to the Indians on the ceded lands." When federal marshals and United States soldiers tried to arrest the most flagrant violators of Indian rights, they were arrested by state officials and tried in state courts.

In the summer of 1834, Jackson sent Francis Scott Key, the author of "The Star-Spangled Banner," to Alabama to report on conditions in the state. Key proved an able advocate of the Indian cause both before the legislature of the state and in Washington. He also reported that angry Alabamans were ready to lynch the soldiers and the officers charged with protecting the Indians. His estimate was that more than ten thousand whites were living on Creek lands; to evict them would require an army and result in widespread civil disorder.

The story that we are now familiar with from the experience of the Choctaw was repeated with the Creek, the principal differences being that the Creek were more resistant to moving and, if possible, less capable of coping with the problems involved. Despite an intense campaign of persuasion only 630 Indians enrolled for the trip under Captain John Page, a young regular army officer with strong compassion for his charges. "I have to stop the wagons to take the children out and warm them and put them back 6 or 7 times a day," he wrote. "I send ahead and have fires built for this purpose. I wrap them in anything I can get hold of to keep them from freezing. . . . Strict attention had to be paid to this or some must inevitably have perished. Five or six in each wagon constantly crying in consequence of suffering with the cold." When they reached the end of their three-month-long travail at the Creek agency at Fort Gibson, only 469 had survived the trip.

The great majority of the Creek refused to leave and every kind of pressure—including false reports that the Creek were on the warpath —was brought to bear on them until even the *Montgomery Advertiser* spoke out in protest: "The war with the Creeks is all a *humbug*. It is a base and diabolical scheme, devised by interested men, to keep an ignorant race of people from maintaining their just rights. . . . We do trust, for the credit of those concerned, that these blood suckers may be ferreted out, and their shameful misrepresentations exposed. . . .

The Red Man must soon leave. They have nothing left on which to subsist. Their property has been taken from them—their stock killed up, their farms pillaged—and by whom? By white men. . . . Such villains may go unpunished in this world, but the day of retribution will most certainly arrive." Georgia and Alabama citizens, alarmed at indications that the Creek, driven to desperation, were ready to turn on the nearest whites, sent an angry memorial to Congress asking that body to investigate "the most revolting facts known to the annals of history, disclosing scenes of turpitude and raping . . . clandestinely opening the flood-gates of savage assassination upon the defenseless women and children of this late prosperous country." The memorial was signed by seven hundred persons. The Alabama and Georgia Creek were now rounded up by federal troops, held in stockades, and then marched off, many in handcuffs, under heavy guards to the Indian Territory.

Behind the manacled braves came some two to three thousand women and children, "shedding tears and making the most bitter wailings." "It was a deplorable sight," an army officer noted, "but the wretchedness and destruction they have caused, and the diabolical cruelty which has characterized them during this warfare, demands the most ignominious punishment, and chains are worse to them than death." But the *Montgomery Advertiser* noted: "The spectacle exhibited by them was truly melancholy. To see the remnant of a once mighty people fettered and chained together forced to depart from the land of their fathers into a country unknown to them, is of itself sufficient to move the stoutest heart." All through the summer the doleful story continued. Now it was heat and dust that prostrated the Indians, and outbreaks of the dread cholera. By November eight thousand Creek had crossed the Mississippi at Memphis and another five thousand were camped waiting supplies and boats that would carry them across.

The Cherokee claimed 7,200,000 acres east of the Mississippi, the greater part of it in Georgia. The tribe was estimated to contain some 2,700 families (or 16,542 individuals), which worked out to roughly 2,666 acres of land per family. The kind of harassment they were subject to is indicated by the story of Joseph Vann, a Cherokee who had 800 acres in cultivation and a home of brick said to have cost ten thousand dollars. Charging him with having broken the law by employing a white overseer while he was absent, a state agent seized his property as forfeit. Two whites, claiming the house, fought for possession of it, finally setting it afire while Vann and his family fled across the Tennessee line.

The Cherokee removal began with deceptive smoothness. A first contingent of some two hundred reached Little Rock in January, 1830, where an observer noted that most of them were whites or half-breeds with Indian wives and mixed-blood children and slaves. A number of the "Indians" look more black than red, being the offspring, in many instances, of Indians and escaped or free blacks. But efforts to persuade full-bloods to emigrate met determined opposition. An Indian named Bushyhead returned from Indian Territory with dismaying tales of suffering and want. At this point word of the Supreme Court decision in the case of the Reverend Worcester caused widespread rejoicing among the Cherokee: "Councils were called in all the towns of the nation, rejoicings, night dances, etc, were had in all parts upon the occasion. . . ."

John Ross, one of the principal Cherokee chiefs (his Indian name was Coowees Coowe), led a delegation to Washington. He was a half-breed whose father had been a Scottish Loyalist married to a woman of one-fourth Cherokee blood. Ross had gone to a white school and served as an adjutant to the Cherokee Regiment that fought with Jackson at the Battle of the Horseshoe in the Creek War, and he had worked to develop schools and vocational training for Cherokee youth. On the return of the delegation from Washington with a treaty various factions of the nation became involved in bitter contentions over removal. Ross was opposed to leaving but Elias Boudinot—a graduate of the Indian School founded by the Pennsylvania philanthropist Elias Boudinot, whose name he had taken—supported the removal and was murdered as a result. Ross could not bring himself to believe that the federal government, or more specifically Jackson, would allow the dispossession of his people. Such an act was too opposed to every principle of American justice, to the Constitution of the United States, to the doctrines of the Christian religion which many Cherokee espoused.

John Howard Payne, a popular actor and playwright who was to be known to posterity as the author of "Home, Sweet Home," was present when the chieftains of the Cherokee met at Red Clay, Tennessee, to consider the treaty negotiated by their leaders with the secretary of war. He wrote a vivid account of the gathering: "Everything was noiseless. The party, entering, loosened the blankets which were loosely rolled and flung over their backs and hung them, with their tin cups and other paraphernalia attached, upon the fence. The chief approached them. They formed diagonally in two lines, and each in silence drew near to give his hand. Their dress was neat and picturesque; all wore turbans, except four or five with hats; many of them tunics, with sashes; many long robes, and nearly all some drapery; so that they had the oriental air of old scripture pictures of patriarchal processions."

The treaty was rejected and Ross instructed to return to Washington to continue the negotiations. To prevent him from leaving, twenty-five members of the Georgia guard arrested him and Payne on Tennessee soil and carried the two men to Georgia, where they were held twelve days. The *Cherokee Phoenix,* the Indian newspaper, was suppressed and the nation forbidden to hold councils at their capital, New Echota. When Payne was released his widely reprinted story of the persecution of the Cherokee roused a storm of criticism in the North and indeed brought protests from many Southerners as well.

What distinguished the Cherokee from the other Southern tribes was their determined resistance to removal. Among the Choctaw, Creek, and Chickasaw many had been prevailed upon to remove voluntarily, or at least had eventually yielded to white pressures; but with the Cherokee bribes, threats, confiscation of property, the cutting off of desperately needed supplies of food, and other harassments failed to budge the great majority. They preserved their solidarity and General Ellis Wool, given the thankless task of managing their removal, wrote to the War Department that "however poor or destitute," most of them would not receive "either rations or clothing from the United States lest they might compromise themselves in regard to the treaty. . . . Many have said they will die before they will leave the country."

Wool, whose sympathies were entirely with the Indians, found their plight "heartrending." He, like all other observers of the Indians' situation, favored removing them "beyond the reach of the white men, who, like vultures, are watching, ready to pounce upon their prey and strip them of everything. . . . Yes, sir, nineteen-twentieths, if not ninety-nine out of every hundred, will go penniless to the West." One Indian chief wrote to Jackson that the "lowest class of the white people are flogging Cherokees with cowhides, hickories, and clubs. We are not safe in our houses—our people are assailed day and night by the rabble. Even justices of the peace and constables are concerned in this business. This barbarous treatment is not confined to the men, but women are stripped also and whipped without law or mercy. . . . Send regular troops to protect us from these lawless assaults." The commanding officer of the Tennessee militia, called out to suppress a rumored uprising of the Cherokee, declared he would never dishonor Tennessee arms by assisting in enforcing a treaty so clearly opposed by a great majority of the Indians.

Finally, early in 1837, after almost eight years of resistance, some 466 Indians out of more than eighteen thousand, "the most wealthy and intelligent," those who had the most to lose to the depredations of the whites—were prevailed upon to start west. Half of the party were children. The hardships they suffered were not as severe as those of many other migrants, but there was an inevitable accompaniment of short rations, illness, disease and death in addition to the trauma of the move itself.

Other parties left for the West during 1837, but the mass of the Indians stood firm under the leadership of John Ross, suffering endless trials and humiliations in the process. In the spring of 1838 a petition signed by more than fifteen thousand Cherokee was presented to President Martin Van Buren asking that the charges of fraud and misrepresentation in regard to the treaty be investigated. When Van Buren tried to extend the time allowed to the Indians for their departure, the governor of Georgia threatened to take matters into his own hands. May, 1838, had been set as the final date for their removal and huge flatboats had been built to carry the emigrants down the Tennessee River. The boats were 130 feet long and two stories high. They carried stoves to keep the red-skinned passengers warm and hearths on the top deck for cooking. Some two thousand Indians had already made the trip west. Plans were now made to force the remainder to leave and the task was assigned to General Winfield Scott, who took command of a mixed force of militia, volunteers, and army regulars totaling some seven thousand men.

One of the most unnerving features of the removal was that wherever possible, crude churches and altars were erected and Cherokee preachers conducted services, often touching on the theme of the Children of Israel in Egyptian bondage. The ministers were tireless. "They never relaxed their evangelical labors," William Coodey, a Cherokee chieftain, wrote to Payne. "They held church meetings, received ten members . . . and went down to the river and baptized them. . . . Some whites present affirm it to have been the most solemn and impressive religious service they ever witnessed."

The line of March was led by "Going Snake, an aged and re-spected chief whose head eighty summers had whitened, mounted on his favorite pony. . . ." Coodey watched "my poor and unhappy countrymen, driven by brutal power from all they loved and cherished in the land of their fathers to gratify the cravings of avarice."

The nearly fifteen thousand Cherokee, concentrated in seven or eight camps guarded by soldiers, constituted by far the largest number of Indians ever moved west in a limited time. By steamboat, flatboard, train, wagons, on horseback and on foot they made their way along the "Trail of Tears," as the route came to be called in the Indian memory of their removal. Nine parties left in October, 1838, and four the next month. Again various illnesses struck down many Indians, bearing especially hard on young children. Skimpy rations, lack of proper sanitation, smuggled whiskey, bad water, the heat and dust and simple misery killed hundreds of Indians in each company of emigrants and thousands in the total. Those parties led by native Indian missionaries like Jesse Bushyhead and Evan Jones got permission not to travel on Sundays so that they could hold religious services. One company of more prosperous Indians included 645 wagons and some five thou-sand horses, besides many oxen. "It was like the march of an army," one observer wrote, "regiment after regiment, the wagons in the center, the officers along the line and the horsemen on the flanks and at the rear."

A Maine traveler, headed for Nashville, passed a unit of some two thousand Cherokee in western Kentucky and gave a detailed account of the procession: "The Indians carry a downcast dejected look bordering upon the appearance of despair; others a wild frantic appearance as if about to burst the chains of nature and pounce like a tiger upon their enemies. . . . One lady passed on her hack in company with her husband, apparently with as much refinement and equipage as any of the mothers of New England; and she was a mother of two and her youngest child about three years old was sick in her arms. . . ." When the last stragglers had passed, the anonymous Maine traveler "wept like childhood" at the thought that "my native country-men had thus expelled . . . those suffering exiles. . . . I wished the President could have been there that very day in Kentucky with myself . . . full well I know that many prayers have gone up to the King of Heaven from Maine in behalf of the poor Cherokees."

One of the parties that came through with the least loss of life was one whose Indian leader was the Reverend Stephen Foreman, a graduate of both Union and Princeton theological seminaries. Foreman's party began its journey with 983 men, women, and children, the great majority Christians. They lost 57 by death on the trip and had 19 births, thus numbering 921 on their arrival in their new home. The Christian Indians, having acquired with their faith that part of the white consciousness that was predominantly Christian, displayed the white's capacity for planning and organizing. Having in many instances prospered materially, they often started out with prudent provisions for the journey that helped to mitigate the inevitable suffering and hardship. Such individuals were Indians only in the most specific racial sense. Culturally they were white. They had no more in common with Comanche or Kiowa than did a pious New England farmer.

Over all the loss of life was enormous. Of the roughly fifteen thousand Cherokee removed, it is estimated that approximately four thousand died in the course of being captured, held in camps prior to their removal, or on the journey itself.

While in many ways the Cherokee removal was less terrible than that of the more southerly tribes, the fact that, under the leadership of John Ross, the great majority of the Nation resisted removal to the bitter end drew particular attention to their plight; that is why Indian removal has been associated in the popular mind with the Cherokee, though they were considerably outnumbered by the other tribes.

The soldiers "were sent to search out with rifle and bayonet every small cabin hidden away in the coves or by the sides of mountain streams. . . . Men were seized in their fields or going along the road, women were taken from their wheels and children from their play." A Georgia volunteer, who later served as a colonel in the Confederate army, wrote many years after the event: "I fought through the civil war and have seen men shot to pieces and slaughtered by the thousands, but the Cherokee removal was the cruelest work I ever knew."

One old Indian, his house surrounded by a squad of soldiers, called his family together and all knelt and prayed together while the discomforted soldiers looked on. William Coodey, the Cherokee chief, wrote to John Howard Payne, "Multitudes were allowed no time to take anything with them, except the clothes they had on. Well-furnished houses were left a prey to plunderers. . . . The property of many has been taken, and sold before their eyes for almost nothing—the sellers and buyers, in many cases having combined to cheat the poor Indians. . . . Many of the Cherokees, who, a few days ago, were in comfortable circumstances, are now victims of abject poverty . . . this is not a description of extreme cases. It is altogether a faint representation of the work which has been perpetuated on the unoffending, unarmed and unresisting Cherokees."

The most intractable Indian problem, so far as the "Eastern" and "Southern" Indians were concerned, was that of the Seminole of Florida—against whom Jackson had waged war almost twenty years earlier. Thoroughly at home in the labyrinthian recesses of the Florida swamps, they provided a hospitable refuge for runaway slaves. The Seminole, large, stout Indians, had a complex and sophisticated culture centering around sun worship. Like the other civilized tribes, they were excellent farmers, growing millet, sunflowers, pumpkins, melons, and tobacco. They made corn bread and hominy. From the whites they took over poultry and domestic animals as well as the cultivation of fruit trees.

When they found themselves included in the policy of removal, their leaders counseled them to accept the inevitable rather than engage in a futile war with the United States. A removal treaty had already been signed when the Seminole learned that no one of black blood would be allowed to accompany them. Such individuals would be sold into slavery. Since some Indian women were married to blacks, the edict meant tearing families apart and this the Seminole refused to do. In addition, some of the chiefs who had visited the lands reserved for their tribe reported that the neighboring Indians were "bad." A number of the Seminole yielded to the government's pressure, but a group led by a chief who, although he was the son of an English trader named William Powell, went by the Indian name of Osceola, refused to go. There were further negotiations. Jackson had, to be sure, declared on numerous occasions that no Indians would be removed against their will, but now he sent orders that they must go willingly or be transported in chains. An extension until the spring of 1836 was allowed, and Osceola and his fellow chiefs made good use of the time to prepare their resistance. The general in charge of the removal operation was startled to hear that five chiefs and five hundred Seminole who were willing to leave had had to flee for their lives to a federal fort on Tampa Bay.

Osceola's wife was the daughter of an escaped slave and an Indian.

As such she was, under Florida law, a black and a slave, and when she accompanied her husband to Fort King she was seized as a slave. When the furious Osceola challenged the commander of the fort, General Wiley Thompson, Thompson had him put in irons for insubordination. To secure his freedom Osceola pretended contrition, signed a document promising to remove, and once released began to raid plantations in the area.

When he received word that the main body of troops would be absent from Fort King, Osceola and some of his braves concealed themselves near the fort and when Thompson came out they riddled him with fourteen bullets. A sutler and his clerks were killed and scalped, the store robbed and set on fire. The Indians then ambushed a detachment of 110 soldiers in the Wahoo Swamp and killed and scalped the whole party with the exception of three who escaped. Two days later, with two hundred Seminole warriors and fugitive slaves, Osceola intercepted General Duncan Lamont Clinch at the head of six hundred soldiers moving from Fort Drane to the Withlacoochee River. Osceola was wounded in the engagement and the Seminole withdrew after several hours of bitter fighting.

Indians and blacks now roved the northeast region of Florida, adjacent to Georgia, killing whites and burning plantations and crops in the fields. Soon the whole region was depopulated as terrified whites fled to the larger towns and the government forts for protection. A thousand volunteers were raised from Georgia, South Carolina, and Alabama and placed under the command of General Winfield Scott. Ill-equipped and commanding untrained and undisciplined volunteers, Scott was no match for Osceola. Indeed, three generals—Gaines, Clinch, and Scott—were unable to bring the rebellious Indian to a decisive engagement. Scott was recalled and his command devolved on General Richard Call, an officer in the Florida militia. Osceola attacked American forces at Micanopy in June and, while he did not succeed in capturing the stockade there, he forced General Clinch out of Fort Drane. Scott's successor, General Thomas Jesup, was no more successful.

For more than a year Osceola baffled, harassed, and occasionally defeated the troops dispatched against him. Finally, in the spring of 1837, Jesup persuaded the Indians to meet in a peace conference at Fort Dade. A treaty which provided that the Seminole would "remove" and which guaranteed them "their negroes, their *bona fide* property," was signed and boats were assigned to carry them to New Orleans on the first leg of their journey to Indian Territory. Before the Indians could be loaded aboard, however, whites appeared to reclaim certain blacks as their former slaves. At this the blacks scattered, although Jesup was able to seize some ninety at Tampa Bay. The Indians, convinced that the terms of the treaty had been abrogated, took to the swamps and forests once again and the war resumed. In the fall Osceola and a band of his followers came to Jesup's command post to try to negotiate the release of two captured Indian chiefs. While talks were going on under a flag of truce, Jesup ordered the Indian camp surrounded and Osceola and other Indians seized. This act of bad faith raised a storm of protest in the North, but Jesup defended himself on the grounds that Osceola could not be relied on to observe the terms of any treaty. The Seminole chief was sent to Fort Moultrie off Charleston and died there a few months later.

There was widespread sympathy with Osceola and the stubborn Seminole. At the news of his death, Philip Hone, who had no toleration of the Irish of New York, the free blacks, or the tailors or carpenters, noted in his diary: "This noble Indian . . . had been brought a prisoner after being kidnapped by one of those breaches of good faith which we white civilized men do not hesitate to put in practice against unenlightened heathens, as we vaingloriously call them."

After Osceola's death Colonel Zachary Taylor (with a force of eleven hundred regulars, volunteers, and Indian auxiliaries) attacked a Seminole stronghold in the Okeechobee Swamp and after bitter fighting drove the Indians out. The American loss was twenty-six killed and over a hundred wounded, however, and Taylor was forced to withdraw. At last the federal troops abandoned the fray. Some Seminole were persuaded to emigrate, but most remained in their Everglade refuges, free from white harassment.

The policy of Indian removal was fashioned with a particular group of Indians in mind. These were the aborigines who had proved least assimilable, who doggedly maintained their tribal customs, whose young braves persisted in stealing ponies and cattle and periodically murdering stray whites, who were most readily debauched by unscrupulous white traders, and who often lived in conditions of desperate poverty and degradation, depending increasingly on government subventions for survival. These Indians were a particular offense to the whites who wished them out of the way. The fact that the policy included, willy-nilly, thousands of other Indians in various stages of assimilation was its harshest and most unjust feature. As President Jackson had said in his first annual message to Congress, the fifty-year-long policy of helping the Indians to accommodate themselves to white culture, to become "civilized," had plainly failed. But that was only part of the story. Much racial assimilation had certainly gone on. Many "Indians" were indistinguishable in their life-styles from whites—or, indeed, in their appearance. But for none of these variations in acculturation was there any provision in the policy of removal. Anyone living on Indian lands and having some degree of Indian blood must leave.

Even with the benefit of hindsight it is hard to understand what policy could have succeeded in making the life of the Southern Indians endurable. The state courts denied them justice; they were cruelly used and exploited by rapacious and unscrupulous whites. Even if the then current interpretations of the Constitution had allowed the federal government to intervene in behalf of the Indians, such intervention would undoubtedly have accelerated the talk of secession and would in any event have been impractical. Having said all that, the fact remains that the Indians were constantly cheated and exploited, robbed and sometimes killed by their white neighbors in those states in which they were found in substantial numbers. Part of the problem was that white men believed that they had as much right to cheat and swindle Indians as to cheat and swindle each other.

The whole issue of removal was complicated by the fact that the Five Civilized Nations of the South—the Choctaw, Chickasaw, Creek, Cherokee, and the Seminole—were in many ways more advanced than the Western tribes, being settled in villages and employing relatively sophisticated agricultural techniques. Tribes like the Kickapoo and Shawnee, more nomadic in character, had responded to white pressure or simply to the search for furs and game by moving westward of their own volition. To white Americans land was primarily real estate, something to be bought and sold, ideally for a profit. Such individuals simply could not conceive of the place-bound character of the Civilized Indians. The land had a particular power and significance for all Indians, settled and nomadic; it was filled with animated spirits and made sacred by the graves of ancestors. For the settled Indians it contained the essence of meaning of their existence. Whites gave their ultimate allegiances to abstractions—the Union, their states,

Georgia or Virginia, God or Progress. Such abstractions had no power for Indians. They worshiped the spirit in the concrete and particular, in trees and rivers, rocks and animals.

James Mooney, a pioneer ethnologist who was himself involved in the removal, wrote: "Cherokee removal of 1838 . . . may well exceed in weight of grief and pathos any other passage in American history." Certainly, if we take it with the removal of the other Southern tribes, it clearly constitutes the most tragic episode of our past, the Civil War excepted. The question is, Who was to blame? Clearly it was "the democracy," "the people" of Alabama, Mississippi, and Georgia. The people whose voice was said to be the voice of God. Or the Constitution, which allowed each state control over its own internal affairs and more particularly over police powers. What about the state officials? Certainly they were no help, rather the contrary; but they were, after all, only the servants of the people. Who were the people who robbed the Indians of their lands? They ranged from wealthy plantation owners and avaricious politicians to the most humble participants in the "free enterprise system." Americans have always shown a strong inclination toward criminality when the acquisition of wealth is involved. But there is still the feeling that even if the rights of the Indians had been scrupulously protected, their situation was an impossible one. It was, after all, the virtually unanimous judgment of those whites friendly to the Indians that removal was the only possible conclusion to "the Indian problem." The democracy was insatiable in its appetite for Indian lands and undoubtedly could not have been denied for long without tearing up the republic.

Americans are disposed to believe that all problems have solutions. If there is a higher order in the universe, if man is a rational animal, then there must be reasonable solutions to the most terrible dilemmas. But of course that is not necessarily so. There are "problems" that disintegrate into unmitigated tragedies. The entire Indian-white confrontation was a tragedy, but the Indian removal—perhaps because it was, on the part of the great majority of the people who fashioned it over almost a decade, well intentioned—was the most appalling chapter in a tragedy with so many acts.

Some modern historians have compared the removal to the Nazi Holocaust against the Jews, but the analogy is superficial and misleading. Official governmental policy was just the reverse of that of the Nazis toward the Jews. The purpose was not to exterminate the Indians but to *save them from extermination*. There is no doubt that many white Americans had an extermination mentality. John Holmes remembered that in the anti-slavery town of Masterville, Ohio, where copies of Garrison's *Liberator* were cherished mementos, the Literary and Debating Society discussed the question "Should the Uncivilized Indians be Exterminated?" If such a topic could be *debated* in liberal Masterville in the 1880s, it could certainly have been *done* in the Georgia of the 1830s and doubtless would have been done had the Indians not been removed by their guardian, the federal government.

On the credit side of the moral ledger must be placed the names of those individuals like the two Gaineses, John Page, William Armstrong, Alexander Talley, and many other named and unnamed soldiers, missionaries, and plain citizens who did their best to mitigate the sufferings of the Indians and some of whom devoted their lives to trying to improve the miserable conditions under which the great majority of the Indians lived.

Contemplating the horrors of the Indian removal, we can understand why D.H. Lawrence and others have seen America as a haunted land. The story of the whites and Indians is the story of the relationship of democracy to original sin. The Supreme Court's skirts were clean even if its injunctions were impotent. It had upheld the Constitution against popular clamor, against the democracy, the people of Georgia, Mississippi, and Alabama. When the Founding Fathers, in the name of equality, had invited the participation of *all* Americans (women and blacks and of course Indians excepted) in the political processes, subject to only those rather modest constraints made necessary by the effort to apply Divine law to human affairs, they had released hitherto inconceivable amounts of human energy and, inevitably, in the process a considerable amount of original sin. That was certainly unexceptional enough; no more than might have been expected, and the Founders themselves had been well aware of the risk. But since a primary article of the democratic faith, held by such exemplars of it as Jefferson and Jackson, was that "the people" were "good," we were forced into a kind of double-entry moral bookkeeping where the credit side of the ledger was constantly displayed and the debit side hidden. Moreover, God was commonly believed to be incapable of sin: thus if the United States was to take on itself the attributes of the Divine, it too must be without sin.

The Indian issue was the issue of the democracy. The reformers of New England and the aristocrats of New York were, for the most part, impeccable on the Indian issue. It was their anti-Bank opponents, the supporters of Andrew Jackson, the sturdy, honest, hard-working farmers who flunked. "The frontiers," wrote Gustaf Unonius, a Swedish immigrant, "are often settled by a peculiar kind of people who nourish inwardly a mortal hatred of the red man. They have been characterized, strikingly enough, by the statement that they have two kinds of conscience, one for whites, another for Indians. They are people whose behavior in their relations with their own race, whose kindliness—yes, whose often meticulous obedience to the commandments of religion—would entitle them to respect and esteem in any ordered community. For them, however, the red man's rights and privileges, his possessions, and his life weigh little on the scales, and they consider any injustice towards the Indians justifiable and permissible. Brave, seasoned, and enterprising, faithful, honest, benevolent, and hospitable toward a white stranger, they lack in their hearts all kindly feeling, all compassion for nature's wild children. . . ."

The obsession of Americans with the red man was subliminal, so to speak. Even when short-memoried newspapers carried no accounts of Indian wars or raids, of Indian cruelty or cruelty to the Indians, the Indian was there, in the novels of Cooper, in the paintings of Catlin or Bingham, in the poems of Whittier and Longfellow.

Philip Hone noted in his diary: "Indian stories are now all the rage in the United States and Canada. Col. McKenney's 'Indian Portraits' is a stupendous work, by which, I am told, the publishers will realize a profit of $100,000. . . . Washington Irving's 'Tour of the Prairies' and subsequently his 'Astoria' have aided in directing public attention to the annals of the red men. Latrobe also wrote an excellent book on the same subject, all of which are seen, heard, and read by learned men and fashionable ladies. . . ." McKenney had joined forces with James Hall, a capable artist, to publish the handsomely illustrated *History of the Indian Tribes of North America* which, as Hone indicated, became an immediate best-seller despite its very considerable cost.

Those Americans who sentimentalized or romanticized the Indians were usually deeply and desperately aware of the dehumanizing aspects of much of American life. They yearned for the noble and gracious and found it in the aborigine. The Indian recalled Plato's "the unreflective striving toward what is noble." In the white psyche reason/mind must dominate—the Nous—but in the savage, the center of life and vital energy was the thymos—the organ of courage and high spirit.

In perpetual contrast to the disintegrative effects of white society, there was the tribe. The Indian could not comprehend that strange, isolate being, "the individual," so prized by the whites. He only knew a Delaware, a Shawnee, a Caddo, or an Iowa. The almost chronic loneliness that many Americans experienced, even in the midst of crowded cities, was unknown to the Indian, who was secure in his tribe. He could not have understood the perpetually asked American question, "Who am I?" He was a Sioux, a Kiowa, an Arapaho, a Comanche. Against the incomprehensible velocity of change in white America, the Indian, with his fixed tribal culture, seemed as enduring as the earth.

In the troubled area of sexuality, the white man had again to confront the Indian way. Abstract sexuality, like abstract thought, was unknown to the Indian. He did not fantasize about sex, he simply engaged in it as naturally and spontaneously as an animal. He offered his wife to the white man as casually as he offered his hand—a gesture of friendship or a present which seemed to the white man depraved. Thousands of white men took Indian wives. Did they value the Indian women over their white sisters for their uninhibited sexuality?

The problem of the white American's relationship to the Indian was complicated by the fact that America was supposed to be the land of innocence. Europe represented old, worldly corrupt "artificial" civilization, America innocence and goodness, "natural man," close to nature, simple and democratic. But what was the Indian? Supernatural? Already there were numerous Americans comparing American "civilization" unfavorably with the "natural" spontaneous life of the American aborigine.

Although the removal of the Southern or civilized tribes was the most dramatic and tragic episode in the Indian–white relations because of the Indian resistance and because they had in so many instances accommodated themselves to white society, the same inexorable pressures drove the Indians out of the states of the Northwest. The last of the Sauk and Fox Indians had been driven from Illinois by the Black Hawk War and then forced to surrender in eastern Iowa. A series of Indian treaties was submitted to Congress in the waning months of Jackson's administration—treaties with the Caddo, who lived in the region of what was to become Nebraska and constituted a network of powerful tribes, the most prominent of which were the Pawnee; the Comanche, a warlike tribe that ranged across the Great Plains as far west as the Rockies and south to the Mexican border; the Ottawa and Chippewa, both related to the Algonquin and traditionally located in the Great Lakes region; the Wyandot, or Huron, who had been driven westward to present-day Wisconsin by the Iroquois generations earlier; the Potawatomi, allies of the Chippewa, also members of the Algonquin family, centered in that part of Indiana Territory that was to break off as Michigan. In every instance the effect of the treaties was to force the Indians off their hunting ranges.

8

Jackson at Bay

On July 6, 1835, John Marshall died. He had been troubled by stones in his bladder for years and was often in great pain. Old Philip Physick, the most famous surgeon of his day, had come out of retirement three years earlier at the age of sixty-five to perform an operation that had given the Chief Justice some relief. But the pain and infection had returned and Marshall had been brought to Philadelphia for a final and futile effort to save his life. Adams wrote a fitting if somewhat biased epitaph for him: "Marshall by the ascendancy of his genius, by the amenity of his deportment, and by the imperturbable command of his temper, has given a permanent and systematic character to the decisions of the Court, and settled many great constitutional questions favorably to the continuance of Union. Marshall has cemented the Union which the crafty and quixotic democracy of Jefferson had a perpetual tendency to dissolve."

The death of Marshall presented Jackson with the chief justiceship to fill. His choice was Roger Taney—who, as we have seen, shared his democratic aspirations and his sometimes misplaced faith in the goodness of the people. Marshall had been the stubborn defender of the Constitution interpreted in its broadest spirit, a spirit that seemed to the Jacksonians often to favor the well-to-do and powerful at the expense of the middle and lower orders of society. Now Jackson would place at the head of the Court a man known to be sympathetic to the rights of the states and suspicious of the "moneyed interests." At the height of the Bank controversy the Senate had refused to confirm Taney as secretary of state. Now fifteen die-hard senators voted against his appointment as chief justice of the United States, but he was confirmed by a comfortable margin—to the despair of all those who had come to look upon the Court during Marshall's tenure as the bulwark of the Constitution and the unwavering defender of property rights.

In the Senate, Clay and Calhoun continued to vie with each other to harass Old Hickory. The House, securely in the hands of the Jacksonians, ignored the excited clamors of the Senate and reaffirmed its support of the Indian removals. Thus House and Senate were pitted against each other. A resolution, again proposed by Clay and supported by Calhoun and passed by a vote of 28 to 18, declared that the President had "assumed an authority and power not conferred by the Constitution and laws. . . ." Back came another angry lecture from Jackson. The Senate refused to "receive" this paper, and Calhoun quoted Plutarch's account of Julius Caesar, "forcing himself, sword in hand, into the Treasury of the Roman commonwealth." Caesar at least was "intrepid and bold"; the present despoilers of the American Treasury were "artful, cunning and corrupt, politicians, not fearless warriors." Clay had spoken the truth when he declared that "we are in the midst of a revolution," but the true nature of the revolution went much beyond the issue of the Bank; it had to do with the usurpation by the general government of the rights of the states. The consequence was a "fearful crisis" with "alienation . . . hourly going on."

To all these effusions Martin Van Buren, as presiding officer of the Senate, had to listen. In accordance with the practices of that body, the senators ostensibly addressed their remarks to him. This was Clay's revenge. He charged Van Buren directly to convey to his master the indignation of the Senate at his despotic and unconstitutional rule. He must prevail on the President to abandon "his fatal experiment." "By your official and personal relations with the President," Clay declared, "you maintain with him an intercourse which I neither enjoy or covet. Go and tell him . . . the actual condition of this bleeding country. . . . Depict to him, if you can find the language to portray, the heart-rending wretchedness of thousands of the working-classes out of employment. Tell him of the tears of helpless widows . . . and of unclad and unfed orphans."

To this feverish oratory Van Buren responded with a gaze of bland innocence. When Clay had finished, the Vice-President left his presiding chair, went up to Clay, and asked him if he might borrow a pinch of "his fine maccoboy snuff"—received it, thanked him, and walked coolly off.

The episode, related by Benton with obvious relish, gives a revealing insight into the nature of political discourse in America. For Americans politics was, on a certain level, a game; a complex and often highly dangerous one, to be sure, but a game, nonetheless, or perhaps a play in which the politicians were actors who gave wild and impassioned speeches and then went off to dine together on oysters and good wine; who abused the President in the most intemperate fashion and then smiled and bowed agreeably as they arrived at the White House for a presidential fête. It was as though nothing was to be taken personally. It was all "part of the game," an act in the play. Players scored points or actors won applause by the skill with which they played their parts, the brilliance of their lines. In other political forums, a Van Buren might have approached Clay's counterpart with a sword or a knife in his hand. Van Buren's performance was pure bravura, of course, carried off with a style that even his enemies were compelled to envy. Envy, because it was the epitome of democratic (with a small d) politics. Only by understanding this crucial play element in political discourse can we understand how the country held together at all.

Somehow, the presidents all understood this, Washington first and most remarkably, for he had no precedent to go on and had to endure the calumny of all those who feared and distrusted the Constitution. Indeed, his greatest achievement as president may have been the establishment of a precious tradition of civility, a determination to preserve gentlemanly intercourse among the bitterly contending individuals and fractions who appeared so unnervingly in the first moments of the Republic. Dutifully he and his successors invited all the representatives and senators, generally in alphabetical order, to sit at table, to break bread, to talk of light social matters, and to affirm a kind of essential unity that seemed incredible or hypocritical to those observers who might have heard the diners, now chatting so amiably, only a few hours earlier breathing fire and destruction and predicting the immediate dissolution of the republic if the policies of the current administration were followed or not followed.

When Harriet Martineau visited the White House in such a company, Jackson offered her bonbons for the children of the friends with whom she was staying and talked of the children of his nephew and his adopted son, who had the run of the presidential mansion, all this "with a mildness and kindliness which contrasted well with his tone upon some public occasions." Jackson, Martineau wrote, "did the honours of his house with gentleness and politeness to myself, and as far as I saw, to every one else" whose name began with J, K, or L.

Perhaps subconsciously Congressmen and public officials sensed at some level both the terrible precariousness of the diverse nation—as little likely, on the surface of it, to mix as oil and water—and the profounder fact that strange and largely incomprehensible processes were going on that had little or nothing to do with the political deliberations and actions that so preoccupied them. The omnipotent eye of the Almighty floated above the pyramid on the reverse side of the Great Seal of the United States. Such an aerial perspective might see matters in their proper proportions—a small group of contentious men in a rough, unfinished town endlessly arguing and debating as though everything waited upon their actions, while out across the vast reaches of the country from Maine south to Florida, and then west to New Orleans and farther and farther west to the territories and beyond, people—always tending westward—were usually quite unaware of or unconcerned with the serious and self-important men in the Capitol. But they were all part of the game too. And for the most part they came forward quite faithfully at two-year intervals to play their parts, to echo the terrible prophecies of disaster if their candidates failed at the polls, to parade and caper and declaim, light bonfires and set off fireworks and then, the play over for the time being, to return to the deadly serious business of earning a living, to beat slaves, fight Indians, build ships, weave cloth, and, above all, to plow and sow and reap the fruits of the earth.

Life in Washington clearly had a debilitating effect on those who resided there even temporarily. The generally chaotic state of affairs —the bitter divisions in Congress, the mistreatment of the Indians, the fierce struggle over the rechartering of the Bank—all added to John Quincy Adams's growing pessimism. He, who had so resolutely affirmed his faith in the enduring nature of the Union on the heels of his own defeat in the presidential campaign of 1828, now wrote: "My hopes of the long continuance of this Union are extinct. The people must go the way of all the world, and split up into an uncertain number of rival communities, enemies in war, in peace friends." Like Jefferson and Madison before him, like his father (and indeed most of the Founding Fathers), Adams felt it a miracle that the country had held together as long as it had. To believe that it could survive much longer was to surrender reason to hope.

John Quincy Adams had a final cup of bitterness to drain. With George Washington Adams a suicide, his brother John had become a cross for his parents. He had made an unfortunate marriage, his business ventures proved uniformly unsuccessful, and his drinking and dissipation destroyed his health. He died in 1834 at the age of thirty-one after several years of "accellerating" decline, leaving debts of fifteen thousand dollars. The depth of the suffering and unhappiness John Adams caused his parents is perhaps best measured by the fact that all his letters were removed from the voluminous Adams papers.

Visiting John Quincy in Washington after his brother George's death, Charles Francis found his father's "nerves so shaken that he could not control his feelings at all. . . . It is very melancholy to an old man so bowed down, but *I* have contributed less to this than any member of the family. I have served him as well as I could although I had heretofore thought myself not cherished as I might have been." Charles Francis was moved to reflect that there was something "in the climate and habits" of Washington "very hostile to the happiness of the New Englanders. They are an active, enterprising race when at home, frugal in their habits and accurate in their plans. The relaxing climate, and indolent habits of the Washington Office holders rapidly take possession of these men and in a few years they cease to display any characteristics but mortification, disappointment and despair."

The exacerbation of political feelings was evident everywhere. When the Democrats won in the congressional elections of 1834, Philip Hone (who had campaigned actively for the Whigs) experienced popular hostility in the form of being kept awake much of the night "by the unmanly insults of the ruffian crew from Tammany Hall, who came over to my door every half hour and saluted me with groans and hisses . . . and what for? Because I have exercised the right of expressing my disapprobation of a course of measures which I conceive to be dangerous to the liberties of the people, and inimical to the free institutions of my native land." Hone then indulged in a little understandable self-pity. This was his reward for being "a member of all the public institutions, charitable, public-spirited, or patriotic, where time was to be lost, labor performed, and no pay to be had; my own affairs neglected, and my money frequently poured out like water; the friend and patron of the workingmen, without regard to party." Hone's last observation is an interesting one. He thought of himself as benevolent toward workingmen, but in his diary he never failed to denounce any workingmen who tried to strike for better wages or working conditions. Like many men of his class he gave generously to organizations founded to help the poor and needy, but he was indignant when the "lower orders" took common action to improve their situation. That was wholly unacceptable, an effort to whittle away the power of their "betters," the men who by their enterprise and initiative provided jobs. Workers should take with gratitude that which their employers gave them. Anyone who encouraged workingmen to fight for their rights was stirring up class feeling. More than once during the campaign for the state legislature, governorship, and mayoralty of New York in 1834, Hone had heard the Jacksonians declaring *Down with the aristocracy!* "They have succeeded in raising this dangerous spirit," he wrote, "and have gladly availed themselves of its support to accomplish a temporary object."

It was soon evident that the removal of the government's deposits from the Bank and their distribution among banks favorable to the administration's fiscal policies, institutions soon known as pet banks, had set in motion a chain of events quite unpredictable in their consequences. After the period of initial contraction of credit which brought the howls of protest that so offended Jackson, the state banks and pet banks began issuing notes at a rate sufficient to satisfy the greediest seeker of credit. It was soon apparent that the speculative fever was not confined to exploitative capitalists but was as common an American attribute as violence or the spirit of reform. No one was more startled or disillusioned by these developments than the President himself. He had been a wholehearted believer in the cardinal tenet of the Jeffersonian faith that "the people" were good, moral, and upright, and only "the interests" evil. Acting in accordance with that conviction, he had crushed the Mammon of Unrighteousness, placed his foot upon the head of the Beast so that the people would no longer be tempted to worship that Golden Calf. It turned out that the people would have their Golden Calf whatever the cost or in whatever form. Roger Taney wrote sadly to Jackson when the tide of democratic speculation was at its chaotic peak: "I remember your unshaken confidence in the virtue and intelligence of the people, and I trust they will yet, in due time, bring matters right. Nevertheless, I cannot conceal from myself that paper money and its necessary consequences —that is, speculation and the desire of growing rich suddenly and without labor—have made fearful inroads upon the patriotism and public spirit of what are called the higher classes. . . ." So it seemed Americans, high and low, aristocrats and democrats, were cut of one cloth. The Children of Israel had once again abandoned Moses in sight of the Promised Land.

With the Senate mired down in its rancorous exchanges with the President and the economic situation of the country increasingly chaotic, in large part because of the uncertainties created by the removal of the deposits, the second term of Jackson's administration drifted toward its conclusion. In the President's penultimate annual message to Congress, delivered in December, 1835, he extolled as usual "the unexampled growth and prosperity of our country. . . . Every branch of labor we see crowned with the most abundant rewards. In every element of national resources and wealth and of individual comfort we witness the most rapid and solid improvements." There were no domestic problems which "would not yield to the spirit of harmony and good will that so strikingly pervades the mass of the people in every quarter."

The report on the condition of the Indians was monotonously the same. The plan to remove "the aboriginal people . . . to the country west of the Mississippi . . . was adopted on the most mature considera- tion of the condition of the race, and ought to be persisted in till the object is accomplished . . . and as fast as their consent can be obtained. . . . A territory exceeding in extent that relinquished has been granted to each tribe." The Indians were being removed at the expense of the United States and supplied with food, clothing, arms, ammunition, and provisions of food for a year. Schools, churches, and council houses were to be constructed for the tribes with more settled habits, houses built for the chiefs, and "mills for common use." Funds had been established "for the poor . . . and blacksmiths, gunsmiths, wheelwrights, millwrights, etc., are supported among them. Steel and iron, and sometimes salt, are purchased for them, and plows and other farming utensils, domestic animals, looms and spinning wheels, cards, etc., are presented to them as well as an annuity of 430 dollars a year." Finally, preference was to be given in employing all persons on a reservation to the Indians themselves where they were qualified. Their land had been "forever 'secured and guaranteed to them.' . . . into which the white settlements are not to be pushed. . . . A barrier has thus been raised for their protection against the encroachment of our citizens and guarding the Indians as far as possible from those evils which have brought them to their present condition." We are aware by now of the vast gap between the professions of the President and the reality the Indians experienced.

The President had three other requests of Congress that, from constant reiteration, had virtually become entreaties: the drafting of a constitutional amendment to provide for the abolition of the electoral college and the direct election of a president limited to one term; the extension of the federal judiciary system to the Western states by establishment of additional justiceships; and the extension of every political right to the "citizens of the District of Columbia."

A few days after the delivery of his annual message, the President invited Congress to divide the Indiana Territory into two territorial governments, one that of Indiana and the other the Territory of Michigan. The inhabitants of the Territory of Arkansas had assembled at Little Rock, formed a constitution, and applied for admission to the Union as a state.

Despite all the ominous forecasts about the effect of the removal of the deposits, business revived notably in 1835 and Philip Hone noted: "All descriptions of property are higher than I have ever known them. Money is plentiful, business is brisk, the staple commodity of the country [cotton] has enriched all through whose hands it has passed, the merchant, mechanic, and proprietor of land all rejoice in the result of last year's operations." But the boom was to be short-lived.

John Quincy Adams noted in his diary in August, 1835: "There is a great fermentation upon this subject of slavery at this time in parts of the Union. The emancipation of the slaves in the British West India Colonies; the Colonization Society here; the current of public opinion running everywhere stronger and stronger into democracy and popular supremacy all contribute to shake off the fetters of servitude. . . ." In Adams's analysis, the democratic spirit had allied itself with "the precepts of Christian benevolence" and "the strength of organized association. It has linked itself with religious doctrines and religious fervor." The antislavery groups had raised large sums of money "to support and circulate inflammatory newspapers and pamphlets gratuitously, and they send multitudes of them into the Southern country, into the midst of the swarms of slaves." There were angry demands everywhere "to put down the Abolitionists." Their meetings were attacked and their buildings burned but they persevered. The activities of the Abolitionists increased with the paranoia of the South. At Charleston "mobs of slave-holding gentlemen intercept the mails and take out from them the inflammatory pamphlets circulated by the abolitionists, who, in their turn, are making every possible exertion to kindle the flames of insurrection among the slaves." Adams added: "We are in a state of profound peace and overpapered with prosperity; yet the elements of an exterminating war seem to be in vehement fermentation. . . ." The state legislature of Mississippi passed a law offering a reward of five thousand dollars for the arrest and conviction of any person "who shall utter, publish, or circulate within the limits of that State, *The Liberator,* or any other circular, pamphlet, letter, or address of a seditious character."

Philip Hone noted in August, 1835, that the rumor of a slave revolt in Vicksburg, Mississippi, had resulted in "murder and violence committed without the least color of the law upon the poor negroes and several whites who are accused of being their instigators." The slavery issue, he added, "has kindled a flame which may in time endanger the safety of our institutions throughout the Union. There is an awful tendency toward insubordination and contempt for law. . . . My poor country, what is to be the issue of the violence of the people and the disregard for law which prevails in all parts of it?" Hone took note of a wild riot in Baltimore directed against the Bank of Maryland, which had suspended payments a year earlier. The bank building and the house of the mayor were both destroyed. For three days the city was torn by violence. Troops were called out and fired on the mob, and word reached New York that twenty persons had been killed and almost a hundred wounded. At this point the troops withdrew, leaving the mob in control.

John Quincy Adams summarized the slavery question—"the most dangerous of all subjects for public contention. . . . In the South, it is a perpetual agony of conscious guilt and terror attempting to disguise itself under sophistical argumentation and braggart menaces. In the North, the people favor the white and fear the blacks of the South. The politicians court the South because they want their votes. The abolitionists are gathering themselves into societies, increasing their numbers, and in zeal they kindle the opposition against themselves into a flame; and the passions of the populace are all engaged against them."

The various denominations of antislaveryites, from the American Colonization Society to the out-and-out Abolitionists, solicited the support of Adams and he gradually became their spokesman in Congress. From simply being determined to assert their right to petition against the institution he went on more and more to involve himself in their cause. As he entered "upon the seventieth year of my pilgrimage" he spent several hours with Benjamin Lundy, editor of the *Genius of Universal Emancipation* and patron of William Lloyd Garrison, and then went with him to the home of James and Lucretia Mott, both leaders in the antislavery movement.

It was the custom of the House of Representatives when it convened after its summer recess to receive petitions from constituents on various public issues. On January 4, 1836, John Quincy Adams rose to present "the petition of Albert Pabodie and one hundred and fifty-three inhabitants of Millbury . . . praying for the abolition of slavery and the slave-trade in the District of Columbia." Adams then asked that the petition be received and "laid on the table." A delegate from Georgia protested. At once there was parliamentary wrangle over whether the petition had indeed been received and, if received, was subject to debate. A few days later Adams presented more abolition petitions, including one signed by 148 Massachusetts women. "For," as he noted in his diary, "I said I had not yet brought myself to doubt whether females were citizens." The petition of the women was especially offensive to the Southerners, most of whom felt that it was immoral for women to mix in political affairs. The moment was a significant one. From the beginning of the abolitionist movement women had played a prominent role. Lucretia Mott, whom Adams described as "sensible and lively, and an Abolitionist of the most intrepid school," was soon to be joined by hundreds and then thousands of equally intrepid ladies; the abolitionist movement became the political nursery school for women outraged by the institution of slavery, many of whom soon came to make analogies between the servitude of the Southern blacks and of American women under the legal and moral domination of their fathers and husbands.

The dilemma faced by the proslavery forces in the House was that even a debate on whether antislavery petitions should be received would provide a forum for antislavery Congressmen and give encouragement to the petitioners. The Southern strategy was therefore to prevent any discussion of their admissibility while rejecting them out of hand on the ground that Congress had no power to interfere with slavery in the states. But the District of Columbia was another matter. Here no one could dispute its jurisdiction. A New York Democrat, Gideon Lee, thus made a motion that the petitions be laid on the table—that is to say, made not a subject of debate. The parliamentary contest was resumed, and, proving heated but inconclusive, the whole subject was referred to a select committee headed by Henry Laurens Pinckney of South Carolina, the son of Charles Pinckney, a framer of the Constitution. In May the Pinckney Committee brought in a report which reaffirmed the contention that Congress had no right to interfere with slavery in the states. It was the opinion of the committee that since Congress "*ought not* to meddle with slavery in the District of Columbia" any discussion of that topic in the House could only be "disquieting." Therefore all petitions relating to slavery "shall, without being either printed or referred, be laid upon the table, and that no further action whatever shall be had thereon." The report, approved by a vote of 117 to 68, was soon known as the Gag Rule and became the subject of a long and dramatic struggle in the House over the First Amendment issue of free speech. Adams made the cause his own. Time after time he rose to present new petitions and protest the constitutionality of the Gag Rule. His demands to be heard invariably produced an uproar in the House, with shouts of anger and defiance from delegates and rulings from the Speaker declaring him out of order. But he persisted. Harriet Martineau, whose visit to Washington coincided with Adams's campaign against the Gag Rule, described him as "one of the most remarkable men in America . . . an embodiment of the pure, simple morals which are assumed to prevail in the thriving young republic." The Englishwoman was convinced that his notorious "eccentricity of thought and action . . . which renders him an impracticable member of a party" had its roots in honesty "mingled with a faulty taste and an imperfect temper. . . . Between one day and another, some new idea of justice or impartiality may strike his brain, and send him to the house warm with invective against his party and sympathy with his foes. He rises and speaks out his new mind, to the perplexity of the whole assembly, every man of whom bends to hear every syllable he says; perplexity which gives way to dismay on the one hand and triumph on the other." Beset by his colleagues and reduced to a minority of one, "he preserved a boldness and coolness as amusing as they were admirable." "He seems . . . reckless of opinion; and this is the point of his character which his countrymen seem, naturally, least to comprehend."

Adams had been told, he informed the members of the House, that "if a Northern abolitionist should go to North Carolina and utter a principle of the Declaration of Independence—" At once cries of "Order! Order!" were heard from Southern members; "the Speaker yelled among the loudest," Adams noted. Waiting until the clamor subsided, he added "—that if they could catch him they would hang him." More shouts of "Order!"

When the House prepared to vote on whether to receive antislavery petitions from William Calhoun, the Vermont Congressman, Adams rose and began to speak. Polk "roared out, 'The gentleman from Massachusetts must answer aye or no, and nothing else.' Order!" To which Adams replied, "I refuse to answer because I consider all the proceedings of the House as unconstitutional." More shouts and cries for order. They subsided and Adams said, in a firm and swelling voice: "A direct violation of the Constitution of the United States." Whereupon Polk, "with agonizing lungs, screamed, 'I call upon the House to support me in the execution of my duty!'" Adams coolly resumed his seat.

9

Jackson Vindicated

As the election of 1836 approached, Martin Van Buren was clearly in the ascendancy. Clay and Calhoun had blocked each other, as John Quincy Adams noted, and "are left upon the field for dead," while "men of straw" like William Henry Harrison and Daniel Webster were "thrust forward in their places."

The national convention of the Democrats met in Baltimore in May, 1836. Some six hundred delegates attended from every state except South Carolina, Alabama, Tennessee, and Illinois, and nominated Van Buren unanimously as the party's candidate for president. His running mate was Senator Richard Johnson of Kentucky, who was credited with killing Tecumseh at the Battle of the Thames during the War of 1812. (Indians certainly played a crucial role in advancing the political careers of anyone fortunate enough to have shot some of them.) Johnson had strong support from Westerners who loved Indian-killers but considerable opposition from Southerners because of his notorious relationship with a female slave, somewhat reminiscent of that of Jefferson with Sally Hemings.

The Whigs' "new" party depended on old-style legislative caucuses to come up with candidates, denouncing the Democratic convention as "degrading subserviency . . . at the shrine of mere party idolatry" and a "packed 'office-holders' convention." The result of the Whig approach was a profusion of candidates—Harrison, Webster, Senator Hugh White of Tennessee, and John McLean, postmaster general under Adams. To Adams all seemed third-rate. Particular states pushed favorite sons and rejected other candidates. Duff Green's *Telegraph,* having switched its allegiance from Jackson to Calhoun to Clay, now aligned itself with the Whigs but opposed Webster and wrote angrily: "Some of Mr. Webster's friends in Massachusetts are mad, mad with man worship; mad with a slavish devotion to the 'god-like man.'" An Ohioan noted that the Whigs of that state would find Harrison "a hard pill to swallow."

The election of 1836 marked several important developments in American politics. The Jacksonian "revolution," toppling old alliances and creating new ones, led to a redefinition of American politics and a basic realignment of parties that turned out to be of surprising durability. The anti-Jacksonians gradually coalesced into an odd assortment of National Republicans, Anti-Masons, and pro-Bank Democrats who denominated themselves Whigs—a name suggested by Philip Hone—reviving the name given to the friends of liberty on both sides of the Atlantic in the period of the American Revolution. Since the Jacksonians had preempted "Democrat," "Whig," with its echoes of Revolutionary struggle, seemed the next best bet. The Whigs were, in essence, the party of the outs, the antis, those to whom the policies and perhaps even more the style of the administration were objectionable. Although the Anti-Masonic Party made up only a modest portion of the new Whig coalition, its youthful spirit, its emphasis on morality in public life, and its vagueness on issues had foreshadowed the emergence of the Whigs. In place of principles and programs, the Whigs stressed party loyalty and party organization almost as though these were ends in themselves.

On the Democratic side, the suave Van Buren, "the reconciler of the estranged, the harmonizer of those who were at feud," as Horace Greeley described him, was a relief from the relentless partisanship of Jackson. For passion that often flirted with madness, Van Buren, "adroit and subtle" (Greeley again), substituted dispassion. It was he who, more than any other individual, had created the party apparatus the Whigs now emulated. The Whigs, conscious that if they intended to play down issues they must play up personalities, settled on William Henry Harrison, a general of very modest abilities who had managed to compensate for his poor performance in the War of 1812 by a narrow but important victory over the Indian forces gathered by Tecumseh and led by the Prophet at Tippecanoe, in present-day Indiana.

The Whig strategy was based on flexibility. In the South they emphasized their opposition to high tariffs; in the North they marched under the banner of Union; in the West they tried to outdemocrat the Democrats. The Illinois Whigs (of whom Abraham Lincoln was one) declared that they approved of "the democratic doctrines laid down by Jefferson in 1801, and by Jackson in 1829" and disapproved of the "convention system . . . forced upon the American people by the Van Buren party." The Virginia Whigs urged that "the Jackson dynasty . . . be exterminated root and branch." Much of the Whig fire was directed at the concentration of power in the hands of the President through the control of appointments to public offices, the excessive use of the veto, and the emphasis on party politics.

Richard Johnson, on the Democratic side, described the campaign as the "great and . . . final battle against thirty-five millions of money, against uncompromising nullification, against a scheme of protection and of its correlative, waste by internal improvement." The Whigs, he maintained, favored capitalists as opposed to ordinary people and temporized with the subversive doctrines of the nullifiers.

Under all the feverish political rhetoric lay the issue of slavery. "The geographic interests and impulses are coming to weigh down the scales of the election," wrote John Quincy Adams, who had perhaps done more than any other man to make this so by his determined campaign in behalf of the antislavery petitioners. "Vote for a Northern President from a free state and when the test comes, he will support the abolitionists," a Virginia newspaper editor warned. Another Whig paper, alluding to Johnson's mulatto mistress, declared, "It may be a matter of no importance to mere political automatons whether Richard M. Johnson is a *white* or a *black* man . . . or whether he is married to, or has been in connection with a jet-black thick lipped odiferous negro wench . . . but it should matter to all honest and self-respecting Americans." The reaction of the Whigs to Southern charges that they were soft on abolitionists was a flurry of resolutions disclaiming any shred of sympathy with the antislavery agitators and "fanaticks."

As Jackson's secretary of state, Van Buren had written several letters to the Vatican. These were exhumed and a Whig paper in Ohio trumpeted: "It is too palpable to be denied that Martin Van Buren has sought foreign aid to secure his election. His letter to the Pope of Rome is at once ridiculous and disgusting." Other papers took up the issue. Van Buren had "a strong Prejudice in favor of the Catholic religion," a typical editorial charged.

The Whigs meanwhile went so far as to make overtures to a group calling itself the Equal Rights Democrats, made up of followers of Robert Dale Owen and Fanny Wright, who had organized the now-defunct Workingman's Party and proclaimed their opposition to all banks and monopolies. The Equal Rights Democrats espoused every reform cause from public education to temperance. One of their slogans proclaimed the party's opposition to "Banks, banking, and paper money, labor-saving machines by which drones are enabled to grow rich without honest industry." The scheme of the Equal Rights Democrats to take over the regular party organization in New York City was narrowly averted. When they tried to pack a Tammany Hall meeting, a riotous scene followed. After a struggle between the regulars and insurgents to control the chair that degenerated into a fist-swinging brawl won by the Equal-Righters, the lights were extinguished and the hall plunged into darkness. At this point the reformers produced the new sulphur matches, locofocos, and "in a moment the platform was lined with fifty sperm lights. . . ." Henceforth to be known as Loco-Focos, the Equal-Righters immediately passed a set of resolutions calling for the direct election of the president, free public education, limited terms for all officeholders (rotation in office), and gold and silver currency in place of paper, and incorporated the Declaration of Independence into its statement. The Equal Rights Party with its hostility to banks, to business in general, to labor-saving machinery; with its affirmation that "every man is bound to contribute to the necessities of society," and its hostility toward the federal government and toward most state and national politicians, represented a profound disenchantment with the political scene and a passionate desire to return to an imagined better day when American society had been free of corruption, speculation, and exploitation.

Yet another splinter group appeared—the Native American Party. Its roots went back to the late twenties, when the seaport cities began to complain about the apparently endless flood of impoverished foreigners—many of whom, unable to find work, became public charges. It was said that in New York in 1830 out of 2,200 paupers housed and fed at municipal expense, 1,050 were recent immigrants. Similar figures were produced in Baltimore and other seaport cities.

The mayor of Baltimore had appealed to the state legislature for laws to check the invasion of "foreign beggars of both sexes and all ages who infest our streets." Throughout the 1820s hostility to immigrants, especially to the Irish and other immigrants from Catholic countries, grew stronger. Newspapers inveighed against foreigners, and "ethnic" riots grew frequent. Whites (most of them Irishmen) and free blacks, laying railroad tracks for the new Baltimore and Ohio Railroad, fought on two successive days. When the leaders of the Irish workers were arrested for disturbing the peace, four hundred of their countrymen appeared and demanded that they be set free. In city after city riots erupted over the most trivial issues.

The actual organization of the Native American Party—also called simply the American Party—was hidden by a cloak of obscurity quite intentionally thrown over its affairs. While its program called for the curtailment of the political rights of immigrants, the immediate objects of its concern were the Irish and, as a corollary, the Catholic Church. Its platform was simplicity itself: "Elevate no person of foreign birth to any office of honor, trust or profit in the United States."

One ugly evidence of anti-Catholic feeling was the burning of the Ursuline Convent in Charlestown, Massachusetts. The convent was a girls' boarding school with twelve nuns and some sixty pupils, most of them Protestants from upper-class Boston families. One of the girls "escaped" and spread stories of punishments and thrashing by the sisters; these stories were supplemented by lurid accounts of sexual misbehavior. When a dissident sister left the convent and sought asylum with friends, the officials inspected the premises and found nothing amiss, but before they could issue a report a mob attacked the convent, routed out the nuns, and set the building on fire. The next night the depredations were resumed, the garden and orchard of the convent demolished, and an attempt made to set a Catholic church on fire. The mayors of both Charlestown and Boston called public meetings where support was expressed for the Catholic citizens and the acts of the mob strongly condemned. Irish laborers from nearby towns were reported to be converging on Boston to protect their coreligionists, but the bishop of the diocese dispatched priests to stop them and assured the Catholics of the city that the civil authorities were competent and determined to protect their rights. Citizens formed a Vigilance Committee to patrol the streets and twelve men were eventually indicted, seven of whom were brought to trial in an atmosphere of considerable bitterness. The city was placarded by the anti-Irish with signs that read "Sons of Freedom! Can you live in a free country and bear the Yoke of Priesthood?" Anyone who testified against the rioters was threatened with assassination. For thirty-five years the burned-out convent stood in Charlestown as a reminder of the riot.

The confused state of political affairs can perhaps best be suggested by the fact that while the Virginia legislature had originally indicated support for Van Buren, it eventually endorsed White, while the Alabama legislature, having supported White, now shifted to Harrison.

The year 1836 witnessed another significant development in democratic politics. Heretofore the candidates for political office were men who had attained prominence in a nonpolitical realm—patriot leaders of the Revolutionary era, scions of prominent families, men who had held important appointive offices, protégés of powerful politicians—individuals like Madison, Monroe, John Quincy Adams. Now the assiduous party worker was to be preferred and advanced, along with the military hero. Van Buren's principal claim to the presidency lay not in his intellect, his oratorical skills, or his contributions to his nation's welfare as displayed in the outstanding discharge of important public duties, but in his skills as a political manager and in his loyalty to the leader of his party. Robert Johnson's selection as Van Buren's running mate was based not on his character [which was generally bad] or on his intellect [which was mediocre] but on his political activities as an enemy of the Adams administration. John Tyler, the Virginia Congressman who emerged as the vice-presidential candidate on the Whig ticket, was a cautious, undistinguished man whose principal asset was that he had offended no one. This lesson was not lost on ambitious politicians. Congressman James Polk of Tennessee was assiduous in his campaigning efforts for Van Buren and Johnson. To John Quincy Adams Polk appeared to have the talents of "an eminent County Court lawyer . . . no wit, no literature, no point of argument, no gracefulness of delivery, no elegance of language, no philosophy, no pathos, no felicitous impromptus; nothing that can constitute an orator, but confidence, fluency, and labor." Young Stephen Douglas of Illinois also drew favorable attention to himself by his efforts on behalf of the Democratic ticket.

Harrison proved a surprisingly strong candidate. Virginia-born, a member of the prominent and prosperous Harrison family, he affected a simple, democratic manner, trying as best he could to be all things to all men. His repeated failures in business after inconsequential terms in the House and Senate may have commended him to the voters as much as his chastisement of the Indians. The New York political leader, young Thurlow Weed, an organizer of the Anti-Masons and now a power in the Whig Party, was practical enough to see that Harrison had little chance in the coming election but he wrote to a friend that "General Harrison is capable of being made, under any other circumstances than the present, an invincible candidate."

The character of the presidential campaign only served to deepen John Quincy Adams's pessimism. The aim of his administration had been "to make the national domain the inexhaustible fund for progressive and unceasing internal improvements"—handsome public buildings, observatories, centers for scientific study and human learning, geological surveys and projects to raise the cultural and educational standards of the nation. But those splendid dreams had failed, "undisguisedly abandoned by H. Clay, ingloriously deserted by J. C. Calhoun, and silently given up by D. Webster." The democracy was interested in far more mundane matters, primarily money. "The prosperity of the country, independent of all agency of the Government," Adams wrote gloomily, "is so great that the people have nothing to disturb them but their own waywardness and corruption. They quarrel upon dissensions of a doit; and split up into gangs of partisans of A, B, C, and D, without knowing why they prefer one to another. Caucuses, County, State, and National Conventions, public dinners, and dinner-table speeches two or three hours long, constitute the active power of electioneering; and the parties are working-men, temperance reformers, Anti-Masons, Union and States-Rights men, Nullifiers, and, above all, Jackson men, Van Buren men, Clay men, Calhoun men, Webster men, and McLean men, Whigs and Tories, Republicans and Democrats, without one ounce of honest principle to choose between them."

As election day approached, the country was once again seized with its quadrennial political fever. The torchlit parades, the perfervid speeches, the rallies, barbecues, the whole wild hoopla were more extravagant than ever. It seemed almost as though the popular excitement varied inversely in relation to the stature of the candidates. "The remarkable character of this election," John Quincy Adams wrote, "is that all the candidates are at most third-rate men whose pretensions rest not on high attainments or upon eminent services, but upon intrigue and political speculation."

The vote itself showed a striking increase in the number of voters in most of the Southern states and a decline in others. Van Buren polled 50.9 percent of the popular vote—764,198 to the opposition's 736,147. Fifteen states with 170 electoral votes went for Van Buren and seven, with 73 votes, for Harrison. White got the votes of Tennessee and Georgia for a total of 26, while Webster got only the 14 votes of Massachusetts. Most encouraging to the Whigs was the fact that the Democrats lost strength in a number of states and the Whigs made conspicuous gains over the National Republicans' tallies four years earlier. In Illinois Abraham Lincoln, running as a Whig, was elected to the state legislature.

The lesson was clear to such party leaders as Thurlow Weed and William H. Seward. If the Whigs could hold their precarious coalition together until 1840 and settle on a single candidate, they should have reasonable expectations of success. The most striking aspect of the election was the apparent "nationalization" of the rival parties. Sectional differences had become blurred. The Whigs had shown surprising strength in the South, and the Democrats had made substantial gains in the North. As one historian has written, "For the first time in our history, a truly national two-party system was inaugurated."

But the results of the election of 1836 can be read another way. The real issue remained slavery. The country was not prepared to face that issue. A majority of Americans, North and South, preferred to hope that it would go away. In all the fatuous and inflated rhetoric of the campaign as little as possible was said about slavery and about Texas. The abolitionists became the universal whipping boys, with every candidate and every party within a party reiterating his or its abhorrence of their doctrines. Thus, in a curious way, the abolitionists served to neutralize the slavery question. Since both parties insisted that slavery was not an issue and did their best to wash their hands of it, the illusion was created and sustained for almost twenty-five years that the problem was not a problem, at least on the level of national presidential politics, that it would somehow go away or be resolved if sufficient time were allowed. What occurred was a classic case of suppression on a national scale and the result, as so often happens with suppression, was national schizophrenia. Denied a place in the most conspicuous forum of national politics, the quadrennial election of a president, the slavery issue continued to manifest itself in increasingly excruciating forms on every other private and public level of national life—in the courts, in Congress, in the churches, in private clubs and societies, in cities and towns and families. The consequence was that national presidential politics took on an air of unreality never equaled before or since in our history. For almost a quarter of a century the essential measure of presidential candidates was to be that they be absolutely indefinable on the most crucial issue facing the nation, that they be so "dough-faced" that they could be peddled in every region of the country as being without strong moral convictions on the issue of slavery.

Competing with the presidential election for public interest were the events in Texas. Americans had been infiltrating the vast, virtually unpopulated regions of Mexican Texas, sometimes encouraged by the Spanish and as often rebuffed and harassed. With the coming of the Mexican Revolution and the liberal constitution of 1824, modeled after the American Constitution, the American settlers in Texas had enjoyed a brief honeymoon, exchanging assurances of mutual respect and affection with successive governments. If Mexico was to be a federation of states on the American model, with each state having its own legislative body and a substantial degree of autonomy (much the same relationship as, say, Massachusetts or Georgia had to the federal government of the United States), Texans could be secure in the possession of their vast ranches and give allegiance as cheerfully to the government of Mexico as they had once given allegiance to the United States. But that dream was soon dissipated. The ups and downs of what passed for the Mexican government—or a dizzy succession of governments—were almost too fast for the eye to follow.

Anastasio Bustamante, who had won glory as a general by a conclusive victory over the Spanish at Juchi in 1822, took over the reins of the Mexican government in 1829 under the banner of liberal reform. Once in power, however, he displayed a thoroughly arbitrary disposition. Most infuriating to Texans was Bustamante's edict banishing slavery from all Mexican states. Soon the region swarmed with Mexican soldiers who were as high-handed as their president. The military commandant, General Teran, suspended civil government in the province and one of his lieutenants at Anahuac, on the Gulf of Mexico, arrested and placed in jail seven citizens without warrants or formal charges. John Austin immediately raised a band of armed men and besieged the town; the prisoners were freed and the commander forced to take to his heels. Meanwhile at Veracruz, Santa Anna had launched his own successful revolt against Bustamante's military regime. Austin assured Santa Anna that the American settlers in Texas did not wish to separate the region from Mexico. At San Felipe in 1833, a constitution was drafted for the state of Texas and a petition was prepared asking for the admission of Texas into the Mexican Union. Stephen Austin took the request to the new President, Santa Anna, and when Santa Anna made no response Austin incautiously wrote to some of his fellow Texans urging them to form a state regardless of the wishes or actions of Mexico. A copy of the letter reached Santa Anna, who had Austin arrested and thrown into jail—where he languished for eight months. Santa Anna, who had opposed Bustamante for his dictatorial behavior, now followed in his predecessor's path. He dismissed Congress and the Council of Government, set himself up as a virtual dictator, and peremptorily rejected the request of Texas to become a state.

The Texans reacted by creating revolutionary committees of safety and correspondence and by preparing to resist Santa Anna by force if necessary. To raise a war chest, the state legislature sold four hundred leagues of land to speculators. Santa Anna in turn dispatched an army to disband the legislature and arrest its members. Sporadic fighting followed and Stephen Austin, freed from his jail cell and back in Texas, helped to organize militia forces and make plans for attacks on posts held by Mexican troops. The town of Victoria was captured, Goliad seized, and Mission Concepcion captured by Colonel James Bowie [designer of the fearful knife that bore his name] and Colonel James Fannin. A large Mexican force at Bexar was besieged and captured and forced to cross the Rio Grande.

A convention of Texans that met in October, 1835, debated whether to declare Texas independent or to pledge loyalty to the liberal Mexican Constitution of 1824. Thirty-three delegates voted to adhere to the constitution and fifteen voted for independence. Texas would join forces with any other Mexican state that was determined to resist a dictatorial central government. A provisional government was formed with Samuel Houston chosen as major general of the military forces of the state, and generous allotments of land were promised to all lovers of freedom who would join Texans in their struggle for justice and republican government.

The response to this call for support was overwhelming. Men and money poured into Texas from every state in the Union, but predominantly from the Southern states bordering the Mississippi. Volunteers flocked to the Texas standard from Kentucky, Tennessee, Mississippi, Georgia, and—of course—Louisiana. Despite the rather half-hearted efforts of the federal government to halt the organization of expeditionary forces headed for Texas, Americans eager for action and land came from as far away as Philadelphia. Cincinnati, Nashville, and Louisville contributed substantial contingents—all this, it must be said, to the dismay of those Americans who deplored the whole movement westward and particularly the emigration of slaveholders into that part of Mexico known as Texas.

Meanwhile a General Congress dominated by Santa Anna met and established a new constitution in which the states were stripped of their legislatures and reduced to the status of provinces presided over by a military governor and a bishop.

The Texans reacted by calling a convention that met in March, 1836, and drafted a declaration of independence which listed the indignities they had suffered at the hands of the Mexican government, among them the fact that they had been denied freedom of worship, been ordered to surrender their arms, and had their soil invaded and their legislature disbanded. A constitution modeled on that of the United States was adopted and, pending elections, a president, vice-president, attorney general, and secretaries of state, war, and navy were chosen, along with three commissioners to represent the state in Washington. Even before the convention met, two volunteer armies had crossed the Rio Grande to engage Santa Anna on Mexican soil. Both Texas "armies"—each consisting of only a few hundred men— were wiped out by Santa Anna's troops who then entered Texas with three divisions under the command of generals Cos, Sesma, and Filisolar. Santa Anna's objective was the extinction of Texas. He captured the town of San Antonio, and its defenders, among them Colonel Bowie and Davy Crockett, the most famous frontiersman of the day, took refuge in the Mission of the Alamo nearby. There 188 Texans held off some 3,000 Mexican soldiers for almost two weeks. When the Mexicans finally stormed the improvised fortress, there were few Texans who had not been killed or wounded and these were cut down on the spot, leaving three women, two children, and a black boy as the only survivors. As a final indignity the bodies of the Texans were stripped and burned. The Mexican losses were 1,600 men killed or wounded. The Alamo at once became a code word for Mexican brutality and the heroism of the Texans. It was, indeed, an extraordinary episode and undoubtedly did more than any other event to create popular sympathy for Texas in the United States. "Remember the Alamo" became the battle cry of the Texans.

Colonel Fannin, who was in command of the Texas volunteers at Goliad, was ordered by Houston to abandon the town and withdraw to Victoria. A detachment of his small force, sent to the assistance of families at Mission Refugio, lost its way and was surrounded. After a brief fight against vastly superior odds, Fannin surrendered and his men were ordered shot as rebels by the Mexican general, Urrea. On Palm Sunday, 1836, 400 were executed.

Houston's force meanwhile retreated to the eastern border of Texas near the San Jacinto River, which flows into Galveston Bay. There Santa Anna came up with Houston, who commanded some eight hundred men near Buffalo Bayou. Up to this point the Texas "War for Independence" had been disastrous. Almost a thousand Texans and American volunteers fighting with the Texans had been captured and shot in addition to those who had been killed or wounded in battle. The greater part of the state had been swept clear of American settlers and a state of mind bordering on panic had resulted from the defeats, the massacres, and the month-long retreat of Houston's little army. But Houston was a remarkable leader of the Andrew Jackson–George Rogers Clark stripe. He kept the morale of his motley army high by his own example. Although Santa Anna commanded more than twice as many soldiers, the Texans were eager to attack and revenge the Alamo. A reluctant Houston, who realized that his army was all that prevented the complete subjugation of the state, finally gave the order to attack. The Texans, most of them mounted, formed a line some 200 yards from Santa Anna's army behind hastily constructed breastworks. Houston had ordered them to hold their fire until they were within 70 yards of the enemy. The Mexican artillery fired grape and canister at the advancing Americans, who came on despite their casualties, shouting and hallooing like Indians. When they fired at last the effects were devastating; they swept over the Mexican positions like a flood, killing 630 Mexican soldiers and wounding more than 200. Some 730 surrendered. Santa Anna fled but was captured the next day and taken to Velasco, where he signed two treaties agreeing to remove the Mexican armies from Texas, grant independence to the state, and accept the Rio Grande as the boundary between Mexico and Texas. The Mexican Congress, when news reached it of Santa Anna's capitulation and the signing of the treaties, declared that the government would not be bound by them. Imprisoned at Velasco, Santa Anna, at the insistence of his captors, wrote to Jackson urging him to recognize the independence of Texas and annex it to the United States.

The apparent success of the Texans in securing their independence and the agitation that was started at once for the annexation of the state to the Union aroused great anxieties among Northerners opposed to the extension of slavery. It was plain that Texas must come into the Union as a slave state. There was certainly strong support for annexation in parts of the Union—especially in the South, where the addition of another slave state had both practical and moral implications.

Congress was thus flooded with petitions protesting annexation. The fact that the opposition was strong enough to delay annexation was proof of the degree to which the issue of slavery had come to dominate every public question. Annexation had from the first a kind of inevitability about it. Texans who had emigrated from the various states of the Union far outnumbered native Mexicans. They looked to the United States as their parent; their heroic fight for independence against what had appeared for a time to be insurmountable odds recalled the struggle of the American colonies for independence from Great Britain. On every count—social, political, and economic—they belonged in the Union. Yet the antislavery men of the North were determined to exclude them.

When Jackson delivered his last annual message to Congress, on December 5, 1836, he had the satisfaction of appearing before that body, which included so many inveterate enemies, confident that his administration had been vindicated by the voters and his heir apparent installed in his place.

Much of Jackson's address was taken up with the problem of how to distribute a surplus of thirty million dollars in the federal Treasury and the dangers that must result in the future from the accumulation of such surpluses. They would be a constant incitement to corruption and contention and the government would be under pressure to use them to augment its powers unconstitutionally. Without such funds the government could not, for example, be accused of contributing to "that wild spirit of speculation which seeks to convert the [existing] surplus revenues into banking capital" in order to cure "the scenes of demoralization which are now so prevalent through the land." It was clearly Jackson's conviction that the country had brought its economic woes upon itself by sinful financial behavior and it must now learn its lesson through the inevitable suffering attendant upon sin.

The discussion of the surplus was followed by a stern lecture on the desirability of hard money and a defense of the removal of the deposits: "The lessons taught by the Bank of the United States," Jackson declared, "can not well be lost upon the American people. They will take care never again to place so tremendous a power in irresponsible hands."

The speech's most striking omission was any reference to the rising chorus of demands for the recognition of the independence of Texas. Two weeks later Jackson sent Congress a special message on the subject which surprised the advocates of recognition and nonrecognition alike. The gist was that "prudence seeks to dictate that we should still stand aloof and maintain our present attitude, if not until Mexico itself or one of the great foreign powers shall recognize the independence of the new Government, at least until the lapse of time or the course of events shall have proved beyond cavil or dispute the ability of the people of that country to maintain their separate sovereignty. . . ." On the last day of his administration the President complied with the request of the Senate that a "diplomatic agent" be sent to Texas by nominating Alcée La Branche to be chargé d'affaires to the new republic.

The following day, incident with the inauguration of Van Buren, Jackson issued his Farewell Address. In it he reminded his fellow Americans that "we have now lived almost fifty years under the Constitution framed by the sages and patriots of the Revolution. . . . Our Constitution is no longer a doubtful experiment, and at the end of nearly half a century we find that it has preserved unimpaired the liberties of the people, secured the rights of property, and that our country has improved and is flourishing beyond any former example in the history of nations."

The problem of the Indians had been solved: "The States which had so long been retarded in their improvement by the Indian tribes residing in the midst of them are at length relieved from this evil, and this unhappy race—the original dwellers in our land—are now placed in a situation where we may well hope that they will share in the blessings of civilization and be saved from the degradation and destruction to which they were rapidly hastening while they remained in the States. . . ."

The balance of Jackson's address was taken up with praise of the Union: "At every hazard and by every sacrifice this Union must be preserved." The preservation of the Union and the limitation of the government to the most narrow and essential functions, plus constant vigilance against the encroachments of the "moneyed power"—in such policies lay the hope for the future of the Republic. Foreign powers posed no threat, Jackson added. "It is from within, among yourselves —from cupidity, from corruption, from disappointed ambition and inordinate thirst for power—that factions will be formed and liberty endangered."

The most dramatic episode in the dying days of the Senate was Benton's campaign to expunge from the records the censure of the man who carried the wounds that Benton and his brother had inflicted on him. Eight of the senators who had originally voted to censure Jackson two years earlier had retired or been replaced and two senators had been seated from the new state of Arkansas. Benton was thus encouraged to make a motion calling for the vote of censure to be expunged. An injustice had been done, he argued, and it was time to redress it. The people had spoken through their state legislators; a number of senators and representatives had been elected to Congress "upon the express grounds of favoring this expurgation."

The Senate chamber, as always on such dramatic occasions, was jammed with enthralled auditors. Throughout the long afternoon and night few stirred. "No one went," Benton wrote, "no one could get in." The most formidable adversaries of expunging were Clay, Webster, and Calhoun, united on little else but their hatred of the President. Both they and Benton knew that a vote to expunge would also be a vote to measure the decline of their power in the Senate. There had been a day, not long ago, when their combined forces were irresistible, but that day was past. Benton and the expungers, aware that they had the votes necessary to carry the motion, were determined to keep the Senate in session until sheer weariness forced a vote. "Knowing the difficulty of keeping men steady to their work and in a good humor when tired and hungry," Benton had given orders "to have an ample supply of cold hams, turkeys, rounds of beef, pickles, wines and cups of hot coffee ready in a certain committee-room near the Senate-chamber." Thus fortified, the expungers sat back to indulge the three greatest orators of the day in their final excoriation of Andrew Jackson.

Calhoun declared himself unable "to argue against such contemptible sophistry. . . . You are going to violate the constitution and rid yourself of the infamy by a falsehood. . . . But why do I waste my breath? I know it is all utterly in vain. The day is gone; night approaches, and the night is suitable to the dark deed we meditate. There is a sort of destiny in this thing. The act must be performed; and it is an act which will tell on the political history of this country for ever. . . . This act originates in pure, unmixed, personal idolatry. It is the melancholy evidence of a broken spirit, ready to bow at the feet of power . . . an act like this could never have been consummated by a Roman Senate until the times of Caligula and Nero."

It was Clay's turn next and by general agreement it was one of the Kentuckian's greatest efforts, albeit [as was so often the case of late] in a lost cause. Even Benton, doubtless consoled by the thought of the waiting feast, was charmed by Clay's peroration. "It lacked nothing but verisimilitude," he wrote, "to have been grand and affecting." "The deed is to be done," Clay thundered, "that foul deed which, like the blood-stained hands of the guilty Macbeth, all ocean's waters will never wash out. Proceed then, with the noble work which lies before you, and, like other skillful executioners, do it quickly." Then the triumphant expungers could return to the people and tell them "that you have extinguished one of the brightest and purest lights that ever burnt at the altar of civil liberty. . . . Tell them, finally, that you restored the glorious doctrine of passive obedience and non-resistance. And, if the people do not pour out their indignation and imprecations, I have yet to learn the character of American freemen."

Webster spoke last, but not having the personal animus toward Jackson of his two colleagues, his heart was clearly not in the effort. He denounced the proceedings as "a ruthless violation of a sacred instrument" and "a contemptible farce." Even as he spoke two of the opponents of expunging approached Benton and said, "This question has degenerated into a trial of nerves and muscles. It has become a question of physical endurance." They were ready to capitulate to the foregone conclusion. When Webster finished speaking a hush of anticipation fell over the "dense masses." Then came the single word *question.* The large anti-Jackson crowd looked on so menacingly that some of the pro-Jackson senators sent out for firearms to defend themselves if attacked. The vote was 24 to expunge, 19 opposed, and as the ritual act of expunging the censure was performed on the records of the Senate, "a storm of hisses, groans, and vociferations arose. . . ." Van

Buren, as presiding officer, ordered the galleries cleared, but Benton protested. Only the Bank "ruffians" should be expelled. The innocent should be undisturbed.

And so the remarkable drama was concluded. Jackson's satisfaction was enormous. He gave a "grand dinner to the expungers." Too weak and ill to join them, he greeted them and withdrew, leaving Benton to take the seat of honor in his place. "That expurgation!" he told Benton, was the "crowning mercy" of his civil life, as New Orleans had been of his military.

The contrast between the subject that occupied the Senate in the final days before its adjournment and that which most concerned the House was instructive. While the Senate prepared to expunge the vote of censure against Jackson, the House writhed in anguish over the issue of slavery. The Senate event was pure politics, all wind and smoke. The House was pure terror, reality invading illusion.

Philip Hone noted on March 4: "This is the end of Gen. Jackson's administration—the most disastrous in the annals of the country, and one which will excite 'the special wonder' of posterity. That such a man should have governed this great country, with a rule more absolute than that of any hereditary monarch of Europe, and that the people should not only have submitted to it, but upheld and supported him in his encroachments upon their rights . . . will equally occasion the surprise and indignation of future generations." Of the new President, tainted as he was by Jacksonianism, Hone had better expectations. "As a man, a gentleman, and a friend," he wrote, "I have great respect for Mr. Van Buren."

On one point at least Hone was emphatically right. Jackson's administration has indeed excited "the special wonder of posterity." Historians have never ceased (and never will) to ruminate over its nature and its meaning. One of only two Presidents entitled to "an age" [as in "the Age of Jackson"], the Tennessean was a remarkable democratic catalyst and his eight-year reign was one of continual drama. Jackson might have made some Americans apoplectic and some ecstatic, but none was indifferent to him.

Dissimilar as they were in most respects, there was one striking similarity between Jackson and his principal rival, John Quincy Adams. They both had about them something of the angry, slightly mad Old Testament prophet Jeremiah, warning a wayward people of its sins, calling them to repentance. For Adams, those sins were slavery the Bank or the "moneyed interests." Jackson differed from Adams in his naïve faith in the natural goodness of the people and the natural badness of the "interests" [or the "Eastern Establishment," as we would call it today], but after the wild speculation let loose by the removal of the deposits from the Bank, a speculation that had no limitation to class or section, Jackson recanted. Though both men were exceedingly pious Christians they made the Union a second deity and called all Americans to worship at its shrine. Both men valued their own rectitude above all else and their self-righteousness often made them rigid and uncompromising. This spirit was in itself enough to put them out of step with their fellow politicians in an age when compromise with evil was revealed as the essence of democratic politics. Moreover, both men displayed marked evidences of paranoia—the belief that all men's hands were turned against them, seeking their destruction. They obviously derived considerable satisfaction from acting, as they believed, on the highest moral level, regardless of the consequences. Both were Puritan to the core. We do not know as much of Jackson's inner life as we do of Adams's. The General was not a subtle or a reflective man, and since he kept no diary we lack a daily record of his own feelings. We have, for instance, no clue to whether or not he experienced the dark periods of depression so common to Adams—to all the Adamses, it might be said—but we may doubt it. We do know of his fearful rages and his inveterate animosities. And his terrible wounds.

Adams epitomized the intelligent, dedicated public servant, placing his superior talents at the service of the republic, as his father and Washington had done, out of the promptings of civic virtue rather than out of ambition or the desire for power. Family, education, social position, some "independent" wealth, however modest, were the familiar elements in such a career. To Adams and those of his class, the mass of the people were perceived somewhat ambivalently as they had been by the Founders themselves. Rough, poorly educated, apt to be swept from their moorings by ambitious demagogues, they were—for better or worse—the essential material of a republic. They must thus be improved, educated as well as possible, instructed on the important issues of the day, and led by patriotic and highminded men.

Jackson, far more aristocratic in his bearing and mode of living than Adams, had ingrained in him the democratic sympathies that were a quality of his fellow Southerners. That ethos—the determination to meet all men on their own level—was deepened and strengthened by Jackson's frontier experience. Democracy was in his bones and ordinary men and women knew it to be there and loved him for it. While popular participation in the political processes had generally increased throughout the early decades of the century, it was still comparatively limited when Jackson came forward as candidate for the presidency. Things were then much as they had been in the earliest days of the republic. Democratic rhetoric filled the air but the running of affairs, North and South, was for the most part securely in the hands of representatives of the upper class. Jackson changed all that, in part by dramatic enactment. He combined the Old Testament's prophetic tone with a genuine affection for "the people" and, most important of all, a passionate attachment to the Union. Invoking all the old symbols of the Revolutionary era and drawing freely on the stern moral imperatives of Protestant Puritan Christianity, he carried America into a new age of vastly expanded popular participation in the political processes. There was, of course, a cost in such a dramatic broadening of the political base. It became harder to discuss real issues. Fireworks, parades, barbecues, and political hoopla replaced serious debate. Candidates were chosen for their popular appeal, their oratorical talents, their facades, and the number of Indians they had routed rather than for their intelligence and ability. Politics took on more and more the air of a perpetual circus; there was a conspicuous lowering of the level of political discourse and a denigration of certain humane values. Attitudes and attributes considered "upper class" were ridiculed and mocked; good manners, moderation, and civility were scorned. Reckless haranguing and extravagant promises were the common path to political preferment. If there was to be a "democracy," the cheapening of American political life seemed a necessary price to pay for it.

Quite aside from the critically important symbolic or psychosocial role Jackson played in extending and opening up heretofore undeveloped potentialities in American democracy, he must also be credited with certain practical political accomplishments, the most notable of which was his snuffing out of the dangerous fuse of nullification. Harriet Martineau had commented on Jackson's personal kindliness and tact, so different from his political style. But he could be astonishingly restrained and tactful in the political realm when he felt it expedient to be so, and the strategy by which he routed the South Carolina nullifiers was marked by great tact as well as by an iron will. Although Jackson had not, as he so ardently believed, buried the frightening specter of secession forever, he had laid it to rest for three crucial decades. It is doubtful if any other political figure of the day could have avoided a disastrous and perhaps fatal clash with the intransigent state of South Carolina, a clash that might well have led to an unraveling of the Union. So I would lay it to Jackson's account that he saved the Union, an accomplishment that alone merits "the gratitude of posterity."

The Bank issue is more obscure. Granting the by no means unreasonable proposition that the Bank was a dangerous or at least unhealthy concentration of power in the hands of an Eastern and Northern business elite and that Jackson was right in his instinct that it should be shorn of its power, the question of tactics remains. The Bank's charter was up for renewal in 1836, at which time Jackson might have delivered the coup de grâce with far less excitement and uproar than attended his removal of the deposits. Why did the man who had handled the nullification crisis with such skill and restraint turn on the Bank with impatient ferocity? Why was Jackson determined to "kill" the Bank? Obviously, on one level the answer has psychological roots. The Bank was the Eastern business establishment personified. Its directors were his enemies. The citizens of South Carolina, Jackson's birthplace, were simply misguided, but the Bank was EVIL and, as we have seen, there could be no compromise with evil. So Jackson expended untold amounts of energy and tens of thousands of words in his unrelenting attack on that institution. The removal of the deposits, a purely punitive act, caused a brief financial panic. The distribution of the funds to preferred state banks led to a greatly expanded currency and a period of wild speculation. Jackson's effort to arrest this widespread fiscal immorality by means of the Specie Circular resulted in an immediate contraction of the money supply and, in conjunction with the failure of several British banking houses, caused the Panic and Depression of 1837, which fell on the hapless head of Jackson's successor and was, not unnaturally, blamed on Jackson.

The most interesting aspect of Jackson's fiscal policies is, as mentioned earlier, their moral basis—paper money was evil, hard money was good—which, of course, was precisely the doctrine of those financial conservatives with whom Jackson was at war. He had forgotten or chose to ignore the lesson that he might have learned from the frantic period of wildcat banking activity that preceded the Depression of 1819. The lesson, quite simply, was that in a democracy the people were determined to have access to capital. Since soft money was invariably more abundant than hard money, they wished to have inexhaustible amounts of soft money even at the risk of devastating depressions. The hostility of many Americans toward the Bank of the United States was based not so much on the Bank's great reputed wealth and abuse of its powers as on the fact that it was perceived as an impediment to those outside of its charmed circle in making money. Deprived of access to capital, they were deprived of their right to make money. Deprived of the right to make money, they were deprived of the opportunity to become real Americans, deprived of the power of self-definition through money.

Democratic finances were of course not the only finances to be in a chaotic state during much of the nineteenth century. Monarchical finances suffered their own devastating fluctuations. Indeed, the two phenomena were closely related, since America was tied into European money markets, especially England's. If it seems reasonably clear that Jackson's fiscal policies helped to bring on the Panic of 1837, one of the most devastating in our history, there is no reason to believe that a depression of some degree of severity could have been avoided by any policy then available to Jackson. Chronic economic insecurity, like chronic personal insecurity (and of course very closely related to it), was part of the price Americans were forced to pay (and seemed, on the whole, willing to pay) for the opportunity to exploit the almost inconceivable riches of their vast continent. With this impulse morality, as it was increasingly clear, had very little to do.

Jackson was also implacable in his opposition to protective tariffs and internal improvement. Today these seem rather peripheral issues. The opinion of Jackson and those of similar views that American industry should concentrate on those articles in the manufacture of which, from the proximity of factories to natural resources or other geographical advantages, they enjoyed a competitive edge, was one to which we are, on the whole, sympathetic today. In the 1820s and 1830s manufactured items made up a very small part of what we call the gross national product. The fact that the manufacturing interests of the North and primarily New England were able to force the 1828 Tariff of Abominations through Congress was an indication of their disproportionate political influence. What the proponents of protective tariffs did not understand was that manufacturing, by its nature, was destined for continual obsolescence as new processes, new techniques, new products, and new markets developed. The manufacturer's equivalent of the farmer's uncertain weather was technological obsolescence and a public taste almost as unpredictable as the weather. The manufacturer yearned for an illusory security and was convinced that protective tariffs were the means thereto. Congress was prevailed upon to go along, primarily by Henry Clay's charm and by his genius in persuading his fellow legislators that high protective tariffs were the antidote to business recessions.

The fact is that many of the programs and policies adopted by successive administrations in the period prior to the Civil War were based on an unwillingness to accept the hard fact that perpetual prosperity was not the normal condition of America and Americans. They must be seen, therefore, in a sense as a persistent railing against an unkind fate.

Internal improvements were another matter. Although part of the same system—since it was the tariffs' revenues which, along with land sales, were to provide the funds for improvements—they had quite different implications. If John Quincy Adams's splendid vision of astronomical observatories, centers of scholarly research, and far-ranging geological expeditions left most of his countrymen cold, there was still the intensely practical issue of government assistance in building canals, highways, railroads, and dams. Here Jackson's dogged narrow-constructionism is more of a historical curiosity than anything else. The highways, canals, and railroads would, as he predicted, be built in any event by the limitless ingenuity and cupidity of private individuals.

Lastly, there is the matter of the Indian removal. In the light of revived interest in and sympathy for the American aborigines, Jackson has recently been severely criticized for supporting the removal policy. For Jackson, the most basic reason for endorsing Indian removal [which he, after all, had not invented] was constitutional. He was a devout believer in states' rights. To him the notion of stationing federal troops in the lands reserved to the Indians to protect them from the citizens of Georgia or Alabama and, if necessary, to fight the state governments to enforce the terms of the Indian treaties was inconceivable. Even if he had been a broad constructionist, entirely dedicated to what he conceived of as the best interests of the Indians (and we have no reason to doubt that he conceived himself to be the latter—that is to say, the friend of the Indians), it is hard to imagine that he could have undertaken to defy the states on the issue of removal. With Jackson it was first things first. The Southern states were already up in arms over the Tariff of Abominations and talking nullification and secession. His first task was to put a stop to such talk and, so far as possible, to isolate South Carolina—which had no Indian problem—from its neighbor states, especially volatile and irascible Georgia.

To run a final tally on Jackson's presidency is perhaps impossible. Certainly the good far outweighed the bad. And Jackson himself is such a compelling, totally American figure that we leave him reluctantly with a sense of areas still undefined. The President as gunfighter (he shared the common American enthusiasm for killing), as Jeremiah, as dignified and gracious plantation owner, as simple democrat, as stern but loving father of his people, as shrewd and skillful politician, even as a mad and vengeful old man, is caught in a hundred fascinating refractions of his character.

10

Tocqueville's America

The "Age of Jackson" was fortunate in having as a commentator upon it the most famous of all "visitor-writers," a young French count of liberal political sentiments, Alexis de Tocqueville. The spectacular efflorescence of Jacksonian "democracy" had focused attention on the nature and the future of political democracy in the United States and, prospectively, in the world. Another Frenchman, an immigrant, Hector St. John de Crevecoeur, had posed that perpetually fascinating question: "What is this new man, this American?" Tocqueville set out to answer it in the 1830s and did it so presciently, so sympathetically and wisely that we have ever since read his *Democracy in America* with astonishment that he could have struck off so brilliant a likeness.

Tocqueville, a philosopher and political theorist who had been trained as a lawyer, came to the United States in 1831, when he was twenty-six years old. His grandfather and an aunt had been guillotined at the time of the French Revolution and his parents imprisoned. The fall of the Bourbon dynasty in the July Revolution of 1830 was therefore a traumatic experience for him. It seemed to be yet another indication of the political instability of France. Soon afterward he and a young friend, Gustave de Beaumont, decided to come to America, ostensibly to survey American penal reform, actually to investigate American political and social institutions with an eye to their relevance for the young Frenchman's own country.

It seemed to Tocqueville that the march of history had been, for a thousand years or more, toward human equality, or what he called "a great democratic revolution." America had announced to the world that it had achieved the most advanced state of equality and its concomitant, democracy, in the world. The boast was true. In his stay in the United States, Tocqueville wrote, "nothing struck me more forcibly than the general equality of condition among the people. I readily discovered the prodigious influence that this primary fact exercises on the whole course of society; it gives a peculiar direction to public opinion and a peculiar tenor to the laws; it imparts new maxims to the governing authorities and peculiar habits to the governed. . . . The more I advanced in the study of American society, the more I perceived that this equality of condition is the fundamental fact from which all others seem to be derived and the central point at which all my observations constantly terminated."

In an age of advancing democracy "every addition to science, every fresh truth, and every new idea became a germ of power placed within reach of the people . . . throwing into bold relief the natural greatness of man"; knowledge became "an arsenal open to all, where the poor and the weak daily resorted for arms."

Tocqueville informed his French readers that his book had been "written under the influence of a kind of religious awe produced . . . by the view of that irresistible revolution which has advanced for centuries in spite of every obstacle and which is still advancing in the midst of the ruins it has caused." He wished to persuade his readers "that the gradual and progressive development of social equality is at once the past and the future of their history" with the "sacred character of a divine decree. To attempt to check democracy would be . . . to resist the will of God. . . .

"America, then, exhibits in her social state an extraordinary phenomenon. Men are there seen on a greater equality in point of fortune and intellect, or, in other words, more equal in their strength, than in any other country of the world, or in any age of which history has preserved the remembrance."

But American democracy—which, as Tocqueville had observed, was to be the world's fate—had certain obvious flaws and shortcomings. It was "wild," democracy undisciplined and unchecked. Democracy must be educated, its religious ideals reawakened, its morals purified. "A new science of politics is needed for a new world." The United States provided an observer with a field of observation and study where the strengths of democracy as well as its weakness might be closely observed. The government, by inheriting "all the privileges of which families, guilds, and individuals have been deprived," had replaced the oppressive power of the few with "the weakness of the whole community. . . . The poor man retains the prejudices of his forefathers without their faith, and their ignorance without their virtues; he has adopted the doctrine of self-interest as the rule of his actions without understanding the science that puts it to use; and his selfishness is no less blind than was formerly his devotion to others."

France had failed to moderate or channel its democratic passions into constructive political channels. But the United States was the "one country in the world where the great social revolution that I am speaking of seems to have nearly reached its natural limits. It has been effected with ease and simplicity; say rather that this country is reaping the fruits of the democratic revolution which we are undergoing, without having had the revolution itself." Tocqueville's wish has thus been "to find there instruction by which we may ourselves profit. Whoever should imagine that I have intended to write a panegyric would be strangely mistaken, and on reading this book he will perceive that such was not my design. . . . I confess that in America I saw more than America; I sought there the image of democracy itself, with its inclination, its character, its prejudices, and its passions, in order to learn what we have to fear or to hope from its progress."

Tocqueville, like a good political scientist, went back to the original establishment of the English colonies to trace the development of democratic institutions and attitudes, with particular emphasis on the New England town meeting. After discussing the framing of the federal Constitution, he plunged into the confusing maelstrom of American politics in the 1830s. The old Federalist party had disintegrated and the Jacksonian Democrats were in the ascendancy, but it was far from clear when Tocqueville wrote (and, indeed, for thirty years thereafter) whether two parties similar to the Federalists and Jeffersonian Republicans would emerge out of the political chaos. To the Frenchman it appeared that "at the present day the more affluent classes of society have no influence in political affairs; and wealth, far from conferring a right, is rather a cause of unpopularity than a means of attaining power. The rich . . . constitute a private society in the state which has its own tastes and pleasures. They submit to this state of things as an irremediable evil, but they are careful not to show that they are galled by its continuance. . . . Mark, for instance, that opulent citizen, who is as anxious as a Jew of the Middle Ages to conceal his wealth. His dress is plain, his demeanor unassuming; but the interior of his dwelling glitters with luxury, and none but a few chosen guests, whom he haughtily styles his equals, are allowed to penetrate into his sanctuary. No European noble is more exclusive in his pleasures or more jealous of the smallest advantages that a privileged station confers." Beneath an "artificial enthusiasm" for democratic institutions, Tocqueville wrote, "it is easy to perceive that the rich have a hearty dislike of the democratic institutions of their country. The people form a power which they at once fear and despise."

Another aspect of American political life which struck Tocqueville forcefully was that there was "so much distinguished talent among the citizens and so little among the heads of the government . . . the ablest men in the United States are rarely placed at the head of affairs. . . . The race of American statesmen has evidently dwindled most remarkably in the course of the last fifty years." This readily observable fact led Tocqueville to extensive reflections on its cause. It seemed to him that in a democracy popularity must necessarily rest on relatively superficial qualities that could be easily conveyed to the people at large—appearance, manner, oratorical skills. Moreover, there was an element of envy in popular government. "Democratic institutions," Tocqueville noted, "awaken and foster a passion for equality which they can never entirely satisfy. . . . The lower orders are agitated by the chance of success, they are irritated by its uncertainty; and they pass from the enthusiasm of pursuit to the exhaustion of ill success, and lastly to the acrimony of disappointment. Whatever transcends their own limitations appears to be an obstacle to their desires. . . ."

Tocqueville drew a sharp contrast between the type of politician elected to the House and that elected to the Senate. Of the House he wrote: "Often there is not a distinguished man in the whole number. Its members are almost all obscure individuals, whose names bring no associations to mind. They are mostly village lawyers, men in trade, or even persons belonging to the lower classes of society." Here Tocqueville's own biases showed. An assembly that contained at one time or another such men as John Quincy Adams and Abraham Lincoln was certainly not the collection of nonentities Tocqueville's remarks suggest.

The Senate, by contrast, contained "scarcely an individual . . .

who has not had an active and illustrious career . . . eloquent advocates, distinguished generals, wise magistrates, and statesmen of note, whose arguments would do honor to the most remarkable parliamentary debates of Europe." The reason Tocqueville gave such little credit to the House was due in large part to the fact that he personally favored the method of election of the Senate by the state legislatures over the direct popular election of the House. Only the "election by an elected body" could avoid the "risk of perishing miserably among the shoals of democracy."

Tocqueville noted that public officials in the United States wore no special costume to indicate their office. Such an official "is uniformly simple in his manners, accessible to all the world, attentive to all requests, and obliging in his replies." On the negative side, the United States was unable to develop broad administrative abilities in its public officials, agreeable as they might be, because of the instability of its political life. No adequate records were kept, "no methodical system . . . pursued, no archives . . . formed, and no documents . . . brought together when it would be easy to do so." The consequence was that "the only historical remains in the United States are newspapers. . . . " Thus everything had constantly to start from scratch, with no sense of a body of accumulated experience to draw upon. "In America," Tocqueville wrote, "society seems to live from hand to mouth, like an army in the field."

Of particular interest to the modern reader are Tocqueville's observations on the tendency of democracies to make large expenditures of public money. In a country that had universal suffrage, the poor—of necessity far more numerous than the rich—would always vote taxes that would fall on others but whose benefits would accrue to them. "In other words," Tocqueville wrote, "the government of the democracy is the only one under which the power that votes the taxes escapes the payment of them. . . . The thirst for improvement extends to a thousand different objects; it descends to the most trivial details, and especially those changes which are accomplished with considerable expense, since the object is to improve the condition of the poor who cannot pay for the improvement. Moreover, all democratic communities are agitated by an ill-defined excitement and a kind of feverish impatience that creates a multitude of innovations, almost all of which are expensive."

One of the most serious deficiencies of democracy in America, in Tocqueville's view, was that the future was sacrificed to the present. In his words: "The difficulty that a democracy finds in conquering the passions and subduing the desires of the moment with a view to the future is observable in the United States in the most trivial things." There were no laws against fraudulent bankruptcy because most Americans were more afraid of the consequences to themselves than anxious to chastise others. The relationship between crime and liquor was well established, but laws could seldom be enacted to remove liquor from the reach of those members of the lower class most prone to criminal activities just because of the class implications of such laws.

But it was perhaps in the conduct of foreign affairs that democracy seemed to Tocqueville most deficient. Democracy was "favorable to the increase of the internal resources of a state; it diffuses wealth and comfort, promotes public spirit, and fortifies the respect for law in all classes of society," but it could "only with great difficulty regulate the details of an important undertaking, persevere in a fixed design, and work out its execution in spite of serious obstacles. It cannot combine its measures with secrecy or await their consequences with patience." Interestingly enough, Tocqueville cited as an example of the volatility of foreign policy in a democracy the fact that Americans at the time of the French Revolution "declared themselves with so much violence in favor of France that nothing but the inflexible character of Washington . . . prevented the Americans from declaring war on England."

Tocqueville was impressed by the fact that in the American democracy the influence of the government was beneficial, "although the individuals who conduct it are frequently unskillful and sometimes contemptible." There seemed to be "a secret tendency in democratic institutions that makes the exertions of its citizens subservient to the prosperity of the community in spite of their vices and mistakes," while the reverse was true in aristocratic institutions.

American patriotism seemed to Tocqueville, as it did to so many others, something of a burden. "As the American participates in all that is done in his country, he thinks himself obligated to defend whatever may be censured in it; for it is not only his country that is then attacked, it is himself. . . . Nothing is more embarrassing in the ordinary intercourse of life than this irritable patriotism of Americans."

Perhaps most astonishing of all to Tocqueville was the political activity of Americans. Europeans in general were well aware of "the surprising liberty that the Americans enjoy; some idea may likewise be formed of their extreme equality; but the political activity that pervades the United States must be seen in order to be understood," Tocqueville wrote. "No sooner do you set foot upon American ground than you are stunned by a kind of tumult; a confused clamor is heard on every side, and a thousand simultaneous voices demand the satisfaction of their social wants. Everything is in motion around you; here the people of one quarter of a town are met to decide upon the building of a church; there the election of a representative is going on. . . . Meetings are called for the sole purpose of declaring their disapprobation of the conduct of the government; while in other assemblies citizens salute the authorities of the day as the fathers of their country." Every class and every portion of society seemed constantly engaged in politics. "It is impossible to spend more effort in the pursuit of happiness," Tocqueville added. "An American cannot converse, but he can discuss, and his talk falls into a dissertation. He speaks to you as if he was addressing a meeting; and if he should chance to become warm in the discussion, he will say 'Gentlemen' to the person with whom he is conversing."

In summing up the advantages of democracy, Tocqueville wrote: "Democracy does not give the people the most skillful government, but it produces what the ablest governments are frequently unable to create, namely, an all-pervading and restless activity, a superabundant force, and an energy which is inseparable from it and which may, however unfavorable circumstances may be, produce wonders."

On the negative side he placed the tyranny of the majority: "I know of no country in which there is so little independence of mind and real freedom of discussion as in America. . . . The majority raise formidable barriers around the liberty of opinion; within these barriers an author may write what he pleases, but woe to him if he goes beyond them. . . . The majority lives in the perpetual utterance of self-applause, and there are certain truths which the Americans can learn only from strangers or from experience."

To the Frenchman there seemed to be "an increasing despotism of the majority." It was as if "all the minds of Americans were formed upon one model, so accurately do they follow the same route." These tendencies were most apparent in the states where the opinion of the majority was most oppressive. "If ever the free institutions of America are destroyed," Tocqueville wrote, "that event may be attributed to the omnipotence of the majority, which may, at some future time, urge the minorities to a desperation and oblige them to have recourse to physical force." What is perhaps most notable in his discussion of the tyranny of the majority is that Tocqueville nowhere mentions the Supreme Court as an institution designed to protect the rights of dissenters and minorities. Perhaps the reason was, at least in part, that he was speaking of the states and the authority of the Court did not reach into the states.

Tocqueville's comments on the role of lawyers in American society are especially illuminating. He believed that the "government of a democracy is favorable to the political power of lawyers; for when the wealthy, the noble, and the prince are excluded from the government, the lawyers take possession of it, in their own right, as it were, since they are the only men of information and sagacity, beyond the sphere of the people, who can be the object of the popular choice. . . . Lawyers belong to the people by birth and interest, and to the aristocracy by habit and taste. . . . The English or American lawyer resembles the hierophants of Egypt, for like them he is the sole interpreter of an occult science. . . . In America . . . lawyers consequently form the highest political class and the most cultivated portion of society. They have nothing to gain by innovation, which adds a conservative interest to their natural taste for public order."

The evidence in support of Tocqueville's proposition is overwhelming. Virtually every prominent political figure in the first half of the nineteenth century was a lawyer.

Having described the positive and negative features of democracy, Tocqueville entered into speculations as to its future. "Americans have no neighbors," he wrote [ignoring the Mexicans and Canadians], "and consequently they have no great wars, or financial crises [Tocqueville wrote before the terrible depression of 1837] or inroads, or conquest, to dread; they require neither great taxes, nor large armies, nor great generals; and they have nothing to fear from a scourge which is more formidable to republics than all these evils combined; namely, military glory." The last was especially fortunate since Americans had already displayed a disconcerting devotion to a man whose only claim to their attention was his victory at the Battle of New Orleans. Moreover, the people thus carried away by the appeal of a military hero were "unquestionably the most cold and calculating, the most unmilitary, if I may so speak, and the most prosaic of all the nations of the earth."

Another factor contributing to political stability was the prosperity of the country. "The physical causes, independent of the laws, which promote general prosperity are more numerous in America than they have ever been in any other country in the world, at any other period of history. In the United States not only is legislation democratic, but Nature herself favors the cause of the people. . . . Everything is extraordinary in America, the social condition of the inhabitants as well as the laws; but the soil upon which these institutions are founded is more extraordinary than all the rest." Immigrants from Europe crowded into the seacoast cities along the Atlantic shore while the "Anglo-American" plunged "in his turn into the wilds of central America. This double migration is incessant. . . . No event can be compared with this continuous removal of the human race. . . . It would be difficult to describe the avidity with which the American rushes forward to secure this immense booty that fortune offers . . . for he is goaded onwards by a passion stronger than the love of life. . . . These men left their first country to improve their condition; they quit the second to ameliorate it still more; fortune awaits them everywhere, but not happiness. The desire of prosperity has become an ardent and restless passion in their minds, which grows by what it feeds on." But Tocqueville is careful to refute the argument used by many European critics of democracy, that the prosperity of the United States is due not to its form of government but to the apparently limitless riches its land offers. The vast, fertile land, the laws and the customs or "habits of mind" of the people were all crucial elements, he declared, pointing to the relative backwardness of South America and Canada as examples of the fact that the effect of ideas upon the landscape is decisive.

Tocqueville saw New England as the cradle of America's genius and described the process by which that section's ideals and values were diffused throughout the nation, reaching even to the distant frontier. On the frontier, in a crude log cabin, the traveler might encounter the pioneer; "everything about him is primitive and wild, but he is himself the result of the labor and experience of eighteen centuries. He wears the dress and speaks the language of cities; he is acquainted with the past, curious about the future, and ready for argument about the present; he is, in short, a highly civilized being, who consents for a time to inhabit the backwoods, and who penetrates into the wilds of the New World with the Bible, an axe, and some newspapers. It is difficult to imagine the incredible rapidity with which thought circulates in the midst of these deserts. I do not think that so much intellectual activity exists in the most enlightened and populous districts of France." Uninterested in theorizing, with "very few writers of distinction . . . no great historians, not a single eminent poet and woefully misinformed about the rest of the world," the American "learns to know the laws by participating in the act of legislation; and he takes a lesson in the forms of government by governing. The great work of society is ever going on before his eyes and, as it were, under his hands."

At the end of his discussion of the nature of American democracy, Tocqueville wrote, "The organization and the establishment of democracy in Christendom is the great political problem of our times. The Americans, unquestionably, have not resolved this problem, but they furnish useful data to those who undertake to resolve it."

The count concluded his first volume with a discussion of "The Present and Probable Future Condition of the Three Races That Inhabit the Territory of the United States." It seemed to him unlikely that the Union would disintegrate under the pressure of the slavery issue and other sectional differences (Jackson had just brought a chastened South Carolina into line); he felt that republican government was strong enough to survive any such cataclysm. The Union was only a confederation of states, but democracy was the irresistible will of the Almighty.

Predictably, Tocqueville's discussion of American blacks and aborigines is searching and perceptive. As for the Negro, "violence made him a slave, and the habit of servitude gives him the thoughts and desires of a slave; he admires his tyrants more than he hates them, and finds his joy and his pride in the servile imitation of those who oppress him. . . . Having been told from infancy that his race is naturally inferior to that of the whites, he assents to the proposition and is ashamed of his own nature. In each of his features he discovers a trace of slavery, and if it were in his power, he would willingly rid himself of everything that makes him what he is. The Negro, who earnestly desires to mingle his race with that of the European, cannot do so; while the Indian, who might succeed to a certain extent, distains to make the attempt. The servility of the one dooms him to slavery, the pride of the other to death." Even if slavery is abolished the Negro will have to contend with three prejudices, "the prejudice of the master, the prejudice of the race, and the prejudice of color." To induce the whites "to abandon the opinion they have conceived of the moral and intellectual inferiority of their former slaves, the Negroes must change; but as long as this opinion persists, they cannot change."

Prejudice against free blacks was greater in the North, Tocqueville declared, than in the South. In his words, "in those parts of the Union in which Negroes are no longer slaves they have in no wise drawn nearer to the whites. . . . Thus the Negro is free, but he can share neither the rights, nor the pleasures, nor the labor, nor the afflictions, nor the tomb of him whose equal he has been declared to be; and he cannot meet him upon fair terms in life or in death. . . . Among the Americans of the South, Nature sometimes reasserts her rights and restores a transient equality between the blacks and whites. . . . Thus it is in the United States that the prejudice which repels the Negroes seems to increase in proportion as they are emancipated, and inequality is sanctioned by the manners while it is effaced from the laws of the country." Which, of course, is what the white Southerner maintained.

Tocqueville had a final, somber word: "Slavery, now confined to a single tract of the civilized earth, attacked by Christianity as unjust and by political economy as prejudicial, and now contrasted with democratic liberty and the intelligence of our age, cannot survive. By the act of the master, or by the will of the slave, it will cease; and in either case great calamities may be expected to ensue."

The world of ideas inhabited by Americans was described by Tocqueville in these words: "They have a lively faith in the perfectibility of man, they judge that the diffusion of knowledge must necessarily be advantageous, and the consequence of ignorance fatal; they consider all society as a body in a state of improvement, humanity as a changing scene, in which nothing is, or ought to be, permanent; and they admit that what appears to them today to be good, may be superseded by something better tomorrow."

Tocqueville's study of democracy in America was written in the hope of providing a guide for the reform of the French political system, if indeed there was such a thing. He was far from believing, as he frequently insisted, that the United States was an infallible model. It revealed many weaknesses of a democracy that Tocqueville felt should be avoided. But it was the most vigorous example of a political democracy to be found in the world.

Democracy in America was a sensational success from the instant it came off the press. Within a year of publication it had gone through five editions in French, run through two British editions, had been translated into German and Spanish. Editions in Swedish, Hungarian, Russian, and Danish followed. Tocqueville, not surprisingly, decided to produce a sequel. In his first book he had concentrated primarily on the political aspects of democracy. Now he turned to its "social influence" in a volume that appeared in 1840. In the Preface he noted that democracy had created in the minds of Americans "many feelings and opinions which were unknown in the old aristocratic societies of Europe. It has destroyed or modified the old relations of men to one another and has established new ones. The aspect of civil society has been as much altered as the fact of the political world." It was thus to the effect of democracy on the family, on education, on the role of women, on speech, literature, and science, and on a dozen other areas that Tocqueville now turned his attention. Although Americans took little notice of philosophy in the traditional sense, they thought about the world in such a manner as to constitute what the Frenchman referred to as "the philosophical method of Americans." This "method" was distinguished by a disposition "to evade the bondage of system and habit, of family maxims, class opinions, and, in some degree, of national prejudices; to accept tradition only as a means of information, and existing facts only as a lesson to be used in doing otherwise and doing better; to seek the reason of things for oneself, and in oneself alone; to tend to results without being bound to means, and to strike through the form to substance. . . ."

By the same token Americans were convinced that "everything in the world may be explained, and that nothing in it transcends the limits of the understanding. . . . Everyone . . . attempts to be his own sufficient guide and makes it his boast to form his own opinion on all subjects. Men are no longer bound together by ideas, but by interests; and it would seem as if human opinions were reduced to a sort of intellectual dust, scattered on every side, unable to collect, unable to cohere." The result was a strange diffuseness in American life, the atomization of people and opinions.

This, in Tocqueville's view, contributed to the disturbing tyranny of the majority that he had discussed in his first book. For Americans "it may be foreseen that faith in public opinion will become for them a species of religion, and the majority its ministering prophet."

It had been truly said that America had no distinguished writers or poets or historians, but Tocqueville was confident that unhappy state of affairs would not last indefinitely. "As soon as the multitude begins to take an interest in the labors of the mind, it finds out that to excel in some of them is a powerful means of acquiring fame, power, or wealth. The restless ambition that equality begets instantly takes this direction, as it does all others. The number of those who cultivate science, letters, and the arts, becomes immense." In his discussion of the effect of democracy on the arts, Tocqueville is less convincing. The arts in a democracy, he believed, must be superficial imitations of those in aristocratic countries. The absence of great patrons, of schools for instruction, of time to develop and refine talent must all work to inhibit the creation of the highest quality work.

When an American literature was produced it would be character-ized, Tocqueville predicted, by a style that was "fantastic, incorrect, overburdened, and loose, almost always vehement and bold . . . there will be more wit than erudition, more imagination than profundity. . . . The object of the authors will be to astonish rather than to please, and to stir the passions more than to charm the taste." In these speculations he simply reflected the learned opinion of his time. American writers and artists would soon produce books and paintings fully worthy of comparison with their European counterparts. Indeed, James Fenimore Cooper and Washington Irving had already captivat-ed a large audience of European intellectuals.

But Tocqueville was disconcertingly correct when he predicted that democracy would produce mediocre writers by the thousands, men who would "at a cheap rate [achieve] a moderate reputation and a large fortune. . . . The ever increasing crowd of readers and their continual craving for something new," he wrote, "ensure the sale of books that nobody much esteems. . . . Democratic literature is always infested with a tribe of writers who look upon letters as a mere trade, and for some few great authors who adorn it, you may reckon thousands of idea-mongers."

In the realm of language, as in all others, a democratic people showed distinctive traits. Since they loved change for its own sake, change was as evident "in their language as their politics. Even when they have no need to change words, they sometimes have the desire. The genius of a democratic people is not only shown by the great number of words they bring into use, but also by the nature of the ideas these new words represent." Americans also had a taste for high-sounding but often empty abstractions, terms that were like boxes with false bottoms, into which you "may put . . . what ideas you please, and take them out again without being observed." Vague, windy terms, in other words, that did nicely as a substitute for thought.

Tocqueville also noted that "In democratic communities, each citizen is habitually engaged in the contemplation of a very puny object: namely, himself. . . . His ideas are all either extremely minute and clear or extremely general and vague; what lies between is a void."

Tocqueville believed democratic historians must "attribute hardly any influence to an individual over the destiny of the race, or to citizens over the fate of a people"; but rather "assign great general causes to all petty incidents," and "not only deny that the few have any power of acting upon the destiny of a people, but deprive the people themselves of the power of modifying their own condition, and they subject them to an inflexible Providence or to some blind necessity." Predicting the various deterministic schools of historiography that would arise in the Western world by the end of the century, Tocqueville was remarkably close to the mark. But a period would intervene during which democratic historians wrote history much as it had been written by aristocratic historians, as a drama in which individuals did indeed play a crucial role in shaping the course of history. What alarmed Tocqueville about the prospect of such a historiography was that it would instill in the citizens of a democracy the notion that they were powerless to effect the course of history and, by making them passive and skeptical, ensure the eventual demise of their nation.

Tocqueville is also illuminating on the tension between liberty and equality in a democratic society. In any contest between the two, he declares, equality must always win. While it was certainly true that "democratic communities have a natural taste for freedom . . . for equality their passion is ardent, insatiable, incessant, invincible; they call for equality in freedom; and if they cannot obtain that, they still call for equality in slavery."

One of the great deficiencies of democracy for Tocqueville was its encouragement of individualism, which "at first, only saps the virtues of public life; but in the long run . . . attacks and destroys all others and is at length absorbed in downright selfishness." Individuals felt "they owe nothing to any man, they expect nothing from any man; they acquire the habit of always considering themselves as standing alone, and they are apt to imagine that their whole destiny is in their own hands. Thus not only does democracy make every man forget his ancestors, but it hides his descendants and separates his contemporaries from him; it throws him back upon himself alone and threatens in the end to confine him entirely within the solitude of his own heart." But there were, fortunately, countervailing forces at work. The first of these was politics, which drew people together in common efforts to elect the candidates of their own choice. Benevolent associations worked to the same effect and a habit of mind attuned to helping others in need. "In democratic countries," Tocqueville concluded, "the science of association is the mother of science; the progress of all the rest depends upon the progress it has made. . . . The art of association then becomes . . . the mother of action, studied and applied by all."

Tocqueville's chapter on "Self-Interest Rightly Understood" is an extension of his comments on the American obsession with "well-being." Clearly self-interest was the motive power of American society, but inherent in it was the idea that self-interest also involves looking after the interests of others, since all are members of a larger community upon whose ultimate soundness the well-being of all depends. "The principle of self-interest rightly understood produces no great acts of self-sacrifice, but it suggests daily small acts of self-denial" and trains "a number of persons in habits of regularity, temperance, moderation, foresight, self-command. . . . Each American knows when to sacrifice some of his private interests to save the rest. . . . No power on earth can prevent the increasing equality of conditions from inclining the human mind to seek out what is useful or from leading every member of the community to be wrapped up in himself." Thus only an enlightened notion of self-interest, instilled primarily by moral training, by religion and education, can check the destructive tendencies of individualism, self-interest, and materialism.

"The passion for physical comforts is essentially a passion of the middle classes," Tocqueville wrote; "with those classes it grows and spreads, with them it is preponderant. From them it mounts to the higher orders of society and descends into the mass of the people." In America it appeared as "a tenacious, exclusive, universal passion." Americans desired "to be always making life more comfortable and convenient, to avoid trouble, and to satisfy the smallest wants without effort and almost without cost." The danger that lay in this preoccupation was that it tended to diminish the soul, "shut out the rest of the world and sometimes intervene between itself and heaven." It would "not corrupt, but enervate, the soul and noiselessly unbend its springs of action," until all that was grand, noble, and heroic dwindled to the merely comfortable.

In one of the most famous passages in his books, Tocqueville describes the restless American who "builds a house in which to spend his old age, and . . . sells it before the roof is on; he plants a garden and lets it just as the trees are coming into bearing; he brings a field into tillage and leaves other men to gather the crops; he embraces a profession and gives it up; he settles in a place, which he soon afterwards leaves to carry his changeable longings elsewhere. If his private affairs leave him any leisure, he instantly plunges into the vortex of politics; and if at the end of a year of unremitting labor he finds he has a few days' vacation, his eager curiosity whirls him over the vast extent of the United States, and he will travel fifteen hundred miles in a few days to shake off his happiness. Death at length overtakes him, but it is before he is weary of his bootless chase of that complete felicity which forever escapes him."

Looking ahead, Tocqueville was convinced that the chances of revolutionary upheaval in the United States were slight since not only did most Americans possess property or hope to, "but they live in the condition where men set the greatest store upon their property." The only revolution Tocqueville could imagine would be one brought about "by the presence of the black race on the soil of the United States." He returned repeatedly to the theme of the surprising changeability "of the greater part of human actions" in America "and the singular stability of certain principles. Men are in constant motion; the mind of man appears almost unmoved. . . . When ranks have been abolished and social conditions are almost equalized, all men are in ceaseless excitement, but each of them stands alone, independent and weak."

From having been convinced in his earlier volume that the states would gradually erode the powers of the federal government, Tocqueville argued in his second book that the tendency of the United States in the future would be toward more and more centralization of power: "It may be asserted that the older a democratic community is, the more centralized will its government become." Such a government willingly labors for the happiness of the people, "but it chooses to be the sole agent and the only arbiter of that happiness; it provides for their security, foresees and supplies their necessities, facilitates their pleasures, manages their principal concerns, directs their industry, regulates the descent of property, and subdivides their inheritances: what remains but to spare them all the care of thinking and all the trouble of living?" It seemed to Tocqueville that in the new democratic age: "Human existence becomes longer and property more secure; life is not adorned with brilliant trophies, but it is extremely easy and tranquil. Few pleasures are either very refined or very coarse. . . . Neither men of great learning nor extremely ignorant communities are met with; genius becomes more rare, information more diffuse.

. . . The ties of race, of rank, and of country are relaxed; the great bond of humanity is strengthened." All this was, in the main, salutary, yet, Tocqueville wrote, "when I survey this countless multitude of beings, shaped in each other's likeness . . . the sight of universal uniformity saddens and chills me and I am tempted to regret that state of society which has ceased to be."

Tocqueville clearly did not say the last word on the character and institutions of the United States, but he said one of the first words, and his analysis has retained its remarkable relevance for almost a century and a half. Certainly he posed questions to which we have yet to find answers and exposed blemishes that continue to plague us.

11

The Panic of 1837

The inauguration of President Martin Van Buren took on rather more the air of a going-away party for his predecessor. All eyes were fixed on Old Hickory. After the oath of office had been administered to Van Buren and Jackson descended the steps of the Capitol to enter his carriage, a vast shout rose from the crowd. "It was," Thomas Hart Benton wrote, "the affection, gratitude, and admiration of the living age, saluting for the last time a great man." Jackson took off his hat and bowed. The exultant roar swelled the louder and Benton, watching from a nearby window, was transported, seeing, he felt, a new kind of reality—"a real scene—a man and the people—he, laying down power and withdrawing through the portals of everlasting fame;—they, sounding in his ears the everlasting plaudits of unborn generations."

A cynic would have said that Jackson got out of town just in the nick of time. The storm clouds of what was to be the worst panic and subsequent depression yet to have engulfed the Union were already gathering on the horizon.

In his comparatively brief inaugural address, Van Buren reaffirmed the principles of the Jacksonian Democrats. Again there was the now familiar incantation, as inevitable as the appeals for Divine guidance: "Though not altogether exempt from embarrassments . . . yet in all the attributes of a great, happy, and flourishing people we stand without a parallel in the world." The new President was confident that "our great experiment" must succeed and that gloriously "new and inexhaustible sources of general prosperity have been opened; the effects of distance have been averted by the inventive genius of our people. . . . [a reference to the railroads]." As for slavery, the only possible element to disturb the domestic tranquillity of the country, Van Buren counseled against any agitation directed at that institution. He himself would "resist the slightest interference with it in the States where it exists." The President was confident that although there might be periods when such "dangerous agitation" was revived, it would, in each instance, grow weaker. For himself, he would take the Constitution "as a sacred instrument." He was the first president to make no reference to the Indians. That problem had presumably been solved by the removal of the Southern tribes and the defeat of Black Hawk.

In May, in the midst of a week of Whig festivities in New York during which Daniel Webster fulfilled everyone's highest expectations by speaking two and a half hours to a crowd of five thousand, the banking house of I. and L. Joseph, the facade of which had collapsed "with a crash like that of an earthquake" a week earlier, stopped payment, occasioning "great consternation in Wall Street." The cause of the bankruptcy was the news of the failure of the New Orleans house of Hermann & Company, who owed Joseph some two million dollars. Other banking concerns followed like a house of cards, "the forerunners of greater disaster." Accounts from England were equally alarming. "The panic," Hone noted, "prevails there as bad as here. Cotton has fallen. . . . The paper of southern and western merchants is coming back protested."

A few days later Wall Street insiders met and drafted a letter to Nicholas Biddle asking the Bank of the United States "to step forward in this most appalling crisis and save the commercial community of New York." Looking about him, Hone decided he had never "seen such an assemblage of woe-begone countenances. Despondency had taken the place of that indomitable spirit which usually characterizes the merchants of New York, and Nicholas Biddle, the insulted and proscribed of Andrew Jackson and his myrmidons, is the sun to which alone they can look to illumine the darkness. Did ever a man enjoy such a moral triumph?"

Sidney George Fisher was convinced that the country's troubles "are but the first fruits of that pernicious tree planted by Thos. Jefferson & nurtured & cherished by Genl Jackson, which has struck its roots broadly and deeply into our soil, & whose rank & spreading growth is now beginning to cast its poisonous and withering shade so widely over the land." To Fisher, Van Buren was "a sly, sneaking, adroit and practiced intriguer, and has risen from being the son of a grog-shop keeper at Kinderhook, and subsequently a pettifogging attorney . . . by management & trickery alone. . . ."

Bankruptcy sales were soon a familiar sight. Handsome furniture and fine paintings were sold for a fraction of their value, but the cost of food remained high and even shad, usually plentiful that time of year, were seventy-five cents apiece. Railroad and canal stocks fell to half their former value and city lots that had sold a few weeks earlier for $480 fell to $50. The same story was repeated in all the major cities from Boston to Savannah and westward to Cincinnati and St. Louis. "The immense fortunes which we heard so much about in the days of speculation," Hone wrote, "have melted away like the snows before an April sun. No man can calculate to escape ruin but he who owes no money. . . ." The three principal savings banks of New York—the Bowery, the Greenwich, and the Bank for Savings—were rumored to be on the verge of closing their doors. Savings banks had only made their appearance a decade or so earlier, hailed as a splendid incentive to those of modest means to put their money by for old age or a rainy day. Now "the poor and the laboring classes of the community," as Hone put it, "are withdrawing their funds in a most alarming manner." The state stocks of New York, Pennsylvania, and Ohio fell precipitately and buyers could hardly be found at any price.

Each day brought news of new failures. The mercantile house of Arthur Tappan, the antislavery leader who had helped get William Lloyd Garrison out of jail in Baltimore, failed in early May, 1837, with debts of $1,200,000. The Tappan failure was a special jolt to the abolitionist cause he had supported so generously. "It will produce a deeper sensation all over the country than would have remitted from the failure of any other mercantile house," a New York banker wrote. George Templeton Strong wrote unfeelingly: "Arthur Tappan has failed! Help him, ye niggers!" Strong heard talk of "political convulsion and revolution" and had to face the sobering fact that in the event of a complete financial collapse, and with it the loss of his family's fortune, he might "have to push my own way, entirely unsupported."

The coal mines of Pennsylvania closed down with the prospect of no fuel for the coming winter; thousands of miners were thrown out of work and faced starvation. It seemed as though there would be no end to the failures. "So they go—smash, crash. . . . Near two hundred and fifty failures thus far," Strong noted in his diary. The president of the Mechanics Bank was found dead in his bed; the rumor was suicide. The Bank for Savings, whose depositors, Hone wrote, were "generally of the poorest and most ignorant classes, weathered a run but the bank was jammed with depositors crying, 'Pay, pay,' women were nearly pressed to death, and the stoutest men could scarcely sustain themselves." There was a run on the Dry Dock Bank, headed by Strong's uncle, who was "almost dead with excitement and misery." The bank was forced to close its doors; when an angry mob gathered, it took all the persuasive powers of the mayor to prevail upon them to disperse without breaking in. In May the banks stopped payment in specie, and Strong wrote: "Glory to the Old General! Glory to little Matty, second fiddler to the great Magician!" Strong had not yet graduated from Columbia and, despite the financial crisis, the scholars played football on the college green. But the president of the college thought it no time for such an uncouth sport and knocked it up "tetotaciously" so that the students were "very savage" against "the old sap-head" and threatened rebellion. Strong, already a devoted bibliophile, took advantage of the panic to buy rare books at giveaway prices—Hobbes's *Leviathan* in "a very fine folio edition," Catullus, and an illuminated manuscript on vellum.

When the banks suspended specie payment, the city militia were called out as a precautionary measure; no riots occurred, although the streets were filled with restless crowds. "Posterity may get out of it," Hone wrote, "but the sun of the present generation will never again shine out . . . the glory has departed. Jackson, Van Buren and Benton were a triumvirate more fatal to the prosperity of America than Caesar, Pompey and Crassus were to the liberties of Rome."

As desperate as affairs seemed in the commercial centers and in the industrial cities and towns, among land speculators, merchants, and workers in the building trades, many farmers enjoyed considerable prosperity which, Philip Hone noted, "is perhaps unfortunate, as it prevents them from sympathizing with the merchants in their distress and uniting with them [in] a change of rulers." A truck farmer in Flatbush, Long Island, made $3,600 from his strawberry crop, which proved that some people still had money. To those disposed to see the hand of Providence in human affairs, it was of profound significance that at the same time that the Lord had chastened the proud and powerful by bringing their extravagant and immoral speculations to ruin, he had blessed the agriculturists of the land with the most abundant crops in memory. So he had brought down the mighty and exalted the lowly. The real suffering, of course, fell where it always fell in hard times: on the poor, on those least able to bear it; there it "touched life," in the vivid phrase of Daniel Raymond.

A party of New York merchants called on Van Buren and presented him with alarming figures. The real estate of the city had depreciated in value by some forty million dollars and twenty thousand workers had been turned out of their jobs in a few weeks. The petitioners wanted the Specie Circular rescinded and the Bank of the United States rechartered. Refusing those demands, Van Buren yielded to their plea for a special session of Congress.

Van Buren shared the belief of many Democrats that the panic was due to wild speculations and the heavy load of debt, especially to English merchants and banking houses. Philip Hone noted that a ship which sailed on August 1, 1837, "carried out a million and a half of gold and silver . . . this is as it should be. We must not buy any more goods . . . in Europe until we have paid all we owe there."

Van Buren's unwillingness to revoke the Specie Circular or recharter the Bank doubtless rested on a shrewd appraisal of his own class. They were certainly not above using the crisis to try to force his hand. As the months passed he suspected there was a good bit of crying wolf in the clamors of the bankers and merchants.

Addressing the special session of Congress, convened on September 6, the President warned against the tendency to blame the administration's policies for the "extensive embarrassment in the monetary affairs of the country" lest the issue become "connected with the passions and conflicts of party." Van Buren then proceeded to enrage his enemies by attributing the nation's financial difficulties to the Bank of the United States and "the rapid growth among all classes, and especially in our great commercial towns, of luxurious habits founded too often on merely fancied wealth, detrimental alike to the industry, the resources, and the morals of the people."

Van Buren's most effective point was that the same catastrophe had overtaken England for the same reasons—excessive speculation and the overextension of credit. The President confessed himself quite ready to acknowledge that the practice of placing government funds on deposit in state banks had had unfortunate consequences. Among other negative effects it had stimulated "a general rashness of enterprise." Van Buren's solution was the establishment "at a few important points of offices for the deposit and disbursement" of public funds, these offices to be under the direction of the secretary of the treasury. The scheme came to be known as the Sub-Treasury Plan. Van Buren also proposed uniform bankruptcy laws to apply to all banks, and a short-term issue of Treasury notes to help counteract the constriction of credit.

The Sub-Treasury Plan was the immediate object of violent attacks by the Whigs. It was not at all what the merchant-petitioners had had in mind. Philip Hone viewed it as a direct attack on the business community. Under its terms "government locusts" would "eat up the people's substance . . . but the merchants must be deprived of the use of any part of the money which their enterprise and intelligence have been the means of furnishing to the support of the government. . . . Was ever a commercial people cursed with such rulers?" he asked.

In the debate on the Sub-Treasury Bill, Calhoun, perpetually calculating his chances for the presidency and seeing no role for himself with the Whigs, put his weight behind the administration. He thus found himself arrayed once more against Webster and Clay. Calhoun gave a long speech in favor of the Sub-Treasury Plan, "studiously modeled upon Demosthenes on the Crown." And Webster, "the giant of Massachusetts, the defender of the Constitution," as Philip Hone wrote, replied with a speech of nine hours' duration, "said on all hands to have been the greatest speech he ever made, greater even than his reply to General Hayne. . . . " With Calhoun's support, the bill passed the Senate during the special session although its passage in the House was delayed until the beginning of the regular session in December.

While both houses wrangled over the bankruptcy bill, John Quincy Adams, in defiance of the President's admonitions not to agitate the slavery issue, took up once again the combined causes of antislavery and freedom of speech. Two weeks after the opening of the special session he presented "twelve petitions and remonstrances against the admission of Texas into the Union" and a week later "petitions for the abolition of slavery in the Territories; for refusing the admission of any slave-holding State into the Union; and for the prohibition of the inter-State slave-trade." The next day he presented

51 petitions against the Gag Law and then 150 others, saving as many again for the regular session in December.

Francis Pickens of South Carolina, an inveterate enemy of Adams and an ally of Calhoun, argued for the Sub-Treasury Bill in the House, aided by another South Carolinian, Hugh Legaré. Adams described Pickens as "pompous, flashy and shallow," Legaré as "much more polished, better educated, and better disciplined; a fine speaker, a brilliant scholar, but yet a shallow bottom." Pickens's speech was to Adams "a jumble of undigested political economy. . . . He said, if the abolitionists of the North would preach insurrection to the Southern slaves, he would retort upon them by preaching insurrection to the laborers against the capitalists of the North."

Legaré then delivered, in Adams's opinion, one of the most brilliant speeches yet given in the House, "dealing altogether in generalities; descanting upon the march of the intellect, the progressive improvement in the condition of mankind, the wonders effected by the modern system of credit, and the steam-engine."

The special session adjourned on October 14 without passing the Sub-Treasury Bill. Supporters of the administration were alarmed and Whigs exhilarated by news of Whig victories in elections in Maine and New York. Maine, Democratic in recent elections, had given the Whig candidate for governor a majority of ten thousand votes. The Whigs were confident that the rest of the nation would soon follow Maine's example.

The panic brought high prices with it. Again it fell hardest on the workingmen of the city, and a seething anger and discontent over the price of bread and flour finally revealed itself in posters nailed up around the city: "Bread, Meat, Rent, Fuel—Their Prices Must Come Down. The Voice of the People Shall be Heard, and Will Prevail. The People will meet in the Park, rain or shine, at four o'clock Monday afternoon to inquire into the cause of the present unexampled distress, and devise a suitable remedy. All friends of humanity, determined to resist Monopolists and Extortioners, are invited to attend."

The placards turned out thousands of aroused workers on a bitterly cold February day. Two prominent Loco-Foco politicians addressed the restless crowd, informing them that Eli Hart & Company had fifty thousand barrels of flour in their warehouse. This was enough to set the protesters off for the building on Washington Street, where they broke down the doors, scattered four or five hundred barrels of flour on the street, "and committed all the extravagant acts which usually flow from the unlicensed fury of a mob," Philip Hone noted. It took the efforts of the mayor, a solid Jackson man, reinforced by police officers and militia, to restore order after several days of violence directed against merchants selling flour.

The New York Whigs, convinced that the panic must help their cause, held a "Great Jubilee" in the city on November 22, 1837. Philip Hone, who had helped to arrange the affair, was ecstatic. "Such a day of continued excitement I have never experienced. . . . O, such a day, such a day of jubilee, sir!" he wrote in his diary. "So brilliant and exciting a scene was never witnessed . . . a member from each State addressed the meeting," Hone noted, adding, "It was perfectly astonishing that in this number of speakers, thus called together and most of them entirely unprepared, there were no failures; all spoke well—some of them with surprising eloquence." For five hours the flood of oratory poured over the enraptured crowd. The constantly reiterated message was that the rise of the Whigs meant that there was, after all, hope for the republic. The years of tyranny and misrule might be wiped from the slate, the nation might still be saved from anarchy and corruption. It was only necessary to elect enough Whigs. In the innocent exaltation of the moment—or, rather, of the hours—all things seemed possible. Then there was a splendid dinner at Niblo's and more speeches and innumerable toasts. "Never before," Hone wrote, "had there been such an assemblage of Whigs. A band of union and good-fellowship has been formed which will extend far and wide, and the delegates will go home . . . filled with confident hopes of a return of a national prosperity, and with a determination to restore the government of the Constitution and the laws." "Harry of the West," Henry Clay, was clearly the favorite of the delegates.

A week later there was a spectacular postlude to the Whig gathering. John Bell, a fellow Tennessean of Jackson's and a recent convert from the Democrats to the Whigs, arrived in New York City to try the political waters, and Hone arranged a splendid dinner at the Astor House to honor him as a repentant sinner. Some 220 guests sat down to eat at seven o'clock, and, reported Hone, "stayed all night." Speech after speech, interlarded with toasts, was given, and it was thus one in the morning before the featured speaker, Daniel Webster, rose. Due to the lateness of the hour, or earliness, he said, he would speak briefly. The hall was filled with cries of protest. He must go on; they must have their fill, so, "nothing loath," the famous and inexhaustible

Daniel spoke to his enthralled listeners "until *four o'clock.*" Hardly a soul had stirred. "What a wonderful gift is public speaking," Hone ruminated, "and what gourmands we Americans are when we get hold of a dish of popular oratory!"

If Philip Hone had no doubts about the exalted aims of the Whigs, his younger contemporary George Templeton Strong did. While Strong shared Hone's distaste for the "jacobinical spirit and the antipathy to law and order and the overthrow of everything worth preserving" which he believed to be the "unconscious principle" of the Democrats, he was almost equally contemptuous of the "commercial, speculating, bank-swindling, money-worshipping" motivations of the Whigs. "Certainly," he wrote, "since the downfall of Federalism there has been no conservative party in the country which has ventured to avow any higher aim than the cultivation of tariffs and credit systems, trade and manufactures."

As the depression continued its devastating course many Americans became profoundly pessimistic about the future of their country. "Never before," Sidney George Fisher wrote, "have ruin & embarrassment been so extensive & so deeply felt. The people are now feeling the effects, naturally produced, by placing power in the hands of ignorant & corrupt men." Yet Fisher went on a few sentences later to admit that the basic cause of the depression was the mania for speculation that affected all classes. There had been a time not long before when a man worth a hundred thousand dollars was considered wealthy; now no one was considered "well off" who did not have an estate of two or three hundred thousand dollars "and to be called wealthy a man must be worth half a million." Fisher, not notably sensitive to the needs of the lower classes, was concerned about the condition of the poor, although his concern was in large part based on fear that, persuaded by the radical press and by democratic politicians that "their distress is all produced by Banks, monopolies, aristocrats, capitalists, etc.," their passions would be so inflamed that they would wreak havoc on those they believed to be their oppressors.

When the Twenty-fifth Congress convened in December, 1837, Van Buren delivered his first annual message—which, in John Quincy Adams's words, was Jackson's message of 1832 "covered with a new coat of varnish." Van Buren declared the Panic of 1837 to be over—as well as the cholera, which had devastated sections of the country—"judicious legislation and the natural and boundless resources of this country have afforded wise and timely aid to private enterprise, and the activity always characteristic of our people has already in a great degree resumed its usual and profitable channels." Van Buren made another plug for the Sub-Treasury system and reported that more than seventy million acres of public lands had been sold in nine states containing three and a half million "souls" and sending one-third of the senators and one-sixth of the representatives to Congress. This vast movement westward had "formed a body of free and independent landholders with a rapidity unequaled in the history of mankind."

Perhaps the most serious problems were in the area of foreign affairs. The issue of the boundary between Maine and Canada had never been settled to the satisfaction of the residents of Massachusetts and Maine. The region had been constantly agitated by reports that Canadians were lumbering in the area and charges and countercharges were constantly exchanged about violations of what each party to the dispute considered the proper boundary. The question of where the line ran seemed impossibly complicated. The United States proposed a commission to decide the dispute, but Great Britain demurred and there the matter rested for two years, until Maine Congressmen began to agitate for federal action. The pressure for some kind of settlement mounted in 1837 as a result of two episodes that threatened to bring on general if undeclared fighting in the contested area, with the possibility of war between the United States and Great Britain. When a census taker, appointed by the state of Maine, tried to take the census of a town in "the highlands" over which Canada claimed jurisdiction, he was twice arrested by New Brunswick authorities and jailed. The American secretary of state, John Forsyth, called on the British to release the man immediately, but the British made no response. Meanwhile a revolt broke out in the predominantly French lower provinces of Canada against British rule, and the rebels called on Americans for aid. In border towns in New York, Massachusetts, and Maine meetings were held to collect money and provisions for the rebels and to organize a volunteer force to march to their assistance.

The leader of the insurgents, William Mackenzie, arrived in Buffalo to appeal for aid, and his tale of British brutality evoked so much sympathy that the flag of the rebels was raised over the Eagle Tavern and Mackenzie proceeded to establish a provisional government on an island in the middle of the Niagara River. From all over New England and from numerous towns in New York came offers of support. The uprising had uncovered a substantial residue of hostility toward the British dating back to the War of 1812. Cannon and shot were sent to the island and soon six hundred Americans and Canadians had collected for an invasion of New Brunswick. To the alarmed inquiries from the secretary of state word came back from every border state that plans to invade Canada were proceeding apace. The governor of Upper Canada took steps to forestall the threatened invasion by deploying troops at Chippewa across from the island chosen by Mackenzie as his staging area. A small steamer, the *Caroline*, had been hired by the insurgent "army" to carry men and munitions from Buffalo. The officer in command of the British force at Chippewa, Colonel McNab, organized a raiding party to seize and destroy the *Caroline* and dispatched it in seven rowboats carrying forty-two men. Under cover of darkness the Canadians boarded the *Caroline* and in the confused fighting that followed several people were killed and wounded. The rest were forced off the boat, which was then set afire, cut loose from its moorings, and allowed to float over the Niagara Falls. The next day, when news of the raid spread to the American shore, excitement ran high. Rumor had it that twelve men who had been on the steamer were missing and presumed lost in the destruction of the *Caroline*. American soil had been, in any event, invaded by hostile force, an act of war. When Forsyth demanded an explanation for the raid on American territory from the British minister, Henry Fox, the latter simply forwarded the report of the lieutenant governor of Upper Canada, who justified the destruction of the *Caroline* on the grounds that it was engaged in acts of piracy which the United States government seemed unable to prevent.

Mackenzie, meanwhile, had been arrested and released under heavy bail. Under pressure from the authorities, his little band dwindled away but the movement to "free Canada" had by this time spread to Michigan, where arms were seized from the state arsenal at Detroit and schemes hatched to launch an invasion from that state. Several hundred men were recruited and armed but thwarted by United States marshals. Before the winter was over two more abortive invasion attempts were mounted, primarily by Canadian refugees, and a Canadian steamboat plying the St. Lawrence, the *Sir Robert Peel*, was seized and burned in revenge for the *Caroline*. A number of the culprits were captured by New York militia, and it was determined that only a handful of Americans had been among the raiders. The most notable aspect of the whole affair was the enthusiasm with which the cause of the Canadian insurgents was taken up by Americans, so much so that state and federal authorities had their hands full trying to squelch warlike acts all along the northeast border. Lodges were formed of men pledged to assist the Canadians to obtain their freedom—the Canadian rebels called themselves Sons of Liberty, after the patriot leaders of the American Revolution. These so-called Hunters' Lodges were secret societies with an elaborate ritual of oaths and orders of rank, pledged to uphold republican institutions and root out all remnants of monarchy on the North American continent. The reports of government agents, sent to spy on their activities, suggested that thousands were involved.

The activities of the Hunters' Lodges pointed up the generally deteriorating state of British–U.S. relations. American bumptiousness and British arrogance provided a fertile soil for friction and misunderstanding. While the British and American upper classes maintained close ties and felt a strong mutual affinity, the British looked on the vast majority of Americans as crude and presumptuous lower-class types. While expressing great admiration for the federal Constitution, which they thought themselves in a substantial degree responsible for, they took an exceedingly dim view of American democracy and American Democrats. That Andrew Jackson, in British eyes little better than a barbarian, could ascend to the presidency of the United States appeared to them a confirmation of all their prejudices and undoubtedly affected the tone that Her Majesty's government was disposed to take in dealings with its transatlantic cousins.

Van Buren's administration had about it from the first something of the air of a lost cause. The accumulated grievances (the feeling that it was "time for a change"), the disaffections within the Democratic Party, and the increasing agitation of the slavery issue—to which the Democrats' only response seemed to be repression—all pointed to the likelihood of a one-term administration for Van Buren and an end to some twelve years of Democratic domination. Van Buren's optimistic predictions that the depression had run its course proved unfounded. The soup kitchens and bread lines, run primarily by volunteer women, which had done such noble service in the hard times of 1819, were revived in the major cities and contributions collected for the unemployed poor. Donations of free fuel were made and many cities and states allocated funds to assist the needy.

In the House of Representatives, John Quincy Adams renewed his fight on the matter of petitions. Starting with "all the petitions and memorials which I had presented at former sessions, and which had not been finally acted upon," he wrote, "[I] had them referred to the appropriate committees." He then presented the petitions calling for abolition of slavery and the slave trade in Washington; all were tabled. William Slade, a Vermont Democrat who had become a Whig, caught Polk, the new Speaker of the House, off guard and got the floor for a long antislavery address which, in Adams's words, "shook the hall into convulsions, Wise, Legaré, Rhett, Dawson, Robertson and the whole herd were in combustion. . . . The slavers were at their wits' end." Most of the South Carolina members left the chamber and when frantic efforts to adjourn finally succeeded, a call was made for all the slaveholding members to attend a special meeting in the chamber of the Committee on the District of Columbia. The following day a new Gag Law was introduced—"no petitions relating to slavery or the trade in slaves in any State, District or Territory of the United States shall be read, printed, committed, or in any manner acted upon by the House." When Adams's name was called for his vote, he rose and said, "I hold the resolution to be a violation of the Constitution, of the rights of petition of my constituents, and of the people of the United States, and of my right of freedom of speech as a member of this House." As he spoke there was "a perfect war-whoop of 'Order!'" When Adams asked to have his remarks recorded in the journal of the House, Polk ruled his motion out of order, at which Adams asked that his protest and the Speaker's ruling that it was out of order be entered in the journal. No answer from Polk.

The next day a Southern member named Boone told Adams that if the issue of slavery ever came to war, "the Southern people would march into New England and conquer it," to which Adams replied that he had "no doubt that they would if they could." Increasingly, Adams was preoccupied with little else than antislavery petitions. Other antislavery members were emboldened by his example to present petitions. On January 15 he brought in some fifty petitions and the next day received thirty-one more. The growing number of abolitionist newspapers and journals—most prominent among them the *Liberator,* the *Emancipator,* the *Philanthropist,* and the *Evangelist*—made him their hero and praised him so inordinately that he wrote, "I am in imminent danger of being led by them into presumption and puffed up with vanity." Fortunately for Adams's temptation to vanity, the praises were balanced by "treacherous, furious, filthy, and threatening letters" from the South.

Adams returned to the attack the following week, presenting a petition from a group of slaves asking for the abolition of slavery in the District and inquiring whether it might be debated. The House was immediately in an uproar again, with shouts and demands that Adams be censured for having insulted the dignity of the House by introducing a petition from slaves. By so doing he had, in effect, encouraged a black insurrection. To all of which Adams replied that he had not tried to present the petition but simply asserted that he held it in his hand—a brilliant ploy that served only to increase the rage of his opponents. They had been panicked by a symbolic piece of paper. In it slaves had somehow invaded the sacred precincts of the House. A series of resolutions of censure came tumbling forth charging Adams with "gross disrespect to his House" and with giving "color to the idea that slaves have the right of petition." The debate continued through the day, the fierce old man, former president of the United States, receiving the oratorical lances of his opponents with an unwavering resolution and an aloofness that still further enraged his adversaries. It was clearly the kind of combat he relished. One ancient warrior against a pack of wolves howling for his blood. A master of parliamentary tactics, Adams frequently tied his enemies in procedural knots that took considerable time and ingenuity to unravel. As the debate over censure dragged on day after day, tempers grew shorter, if possible. New motions were made, debated and voted down. A motion to drop the whole matter failed 21 to 137 and the debate continued until the House was distracted by more urgent business. But Adams, they would discover, was not done.

The Whigs won a notable victory in the New York municipal elections in the spring of 1838, and a month later there was news of a surprising Whig victory in a special election in Mississippi. One of the most significant developments in the congressional campaign that year was the circulation to the candidates of both parties of a questionnaire drawn up by the abolitionists "in rather a peremptory style . . . regarding slavery, and the political disqualifications of the free blacks." Philip Hone was indignant. "Such a course of inquisitorial scrutiny into men's consciences, if persevered in," he wrote, "will have the effect to destroy that lofty independence and integrity of mind which should characterize the representatives of the people."

In the spring of 1838 Congress repealed the requirement that all public lands be paid for in hard money. "This great event," Philip

Hone wrote, has "infused a joyful spirit of confidence amongst our New York folks. Verily Wall Street rejoiceth. Stocks have risen . . . and it would seem that the touch of Webster [who was credited with bringing it off] . . . has caused the corpse of public credit to rise to its feet and stand erect."

The general disorder in the political sphere was demonstrated in 1838 in Pennsylvania, where two rival parties, the Loco-Foco Democrats and the Whigs, both claimed victory and tried to take their seats in the state legislature. According to Philip Hone's hardly unbiased account: "Both parties elected their own Speaker and both proceeded to business in the same hall . . . brutal violence was resorted to and the hall was left in possession of the Loco-Focos, supported by a mob of ruffians in the galleries. The whole was a scene hitherto paralleled only by the . . . Jacobin Club of Paris in the horrid days of anarchy and bloodshed which ushered in the Revolution and led to the destruction of everything 'good and lovely and of good report' in that devoted country. God grant that the same causes here may not produce the same results!" The Whigs must get power through the electoral process and then subject "the rabble of Loco-Foco Jacobins to the power of the laws." (The strangeness of the political situation in Pennsylvania is perhaps best demonstrated by the fact that Thaddeus Stevens, an avowed friend of the slaves and recently a leader in the Anti-Masonic Party, now appeared as the Whig hero and was opposed by Charles Ingersoll, a moderate on the slavery issue, as the leading Democrat.) The governor of the state issued a proclamation stating that a "lawless, infuriated, armed mob" had seized the state capitol at Harrisburg and he alerted the militia. Further violence was averted and the Democrats took possession of the field.

The depression of 1837 brought with it, like the earlier depression of 1819, a revival of Puritanism. Evangelical ministers declared that the hard times were God's judgment on a froward and disobedient people. Much of their thunder was directed against the theater. "Shakespeare and Jim Crow come in equally for their share of condemnation," Philip Hone wrote, "and the stage is indiscriminately voted immoral, irreligious, and what is much worse, *unfashionable*." Lectures became "all the vogue." The Mercantile Library Association, the Mechanics Institute, the Lyceum, and the Historical Society all sponsored popular lecture series. For the Historical Society, the famous Harvard historian Jared Sparks, who had been busy publishing

bowdlerized editions of the papers of famous Revolutionary statesmen, was engaged to deliver eight lectures on "Events of the American
Revolution," which proved so popular that they had to be moved to the
Tabernacle, the "holdall of the city." "This is all right," Philip Hone
conceded; "it is more rational than the expensive parties for which
New York was formerly celebrated, where friendly intercourse was
stifled in a crowd of oyster-eating parasites, modest merit put to the
blush by reckless extravagance, and good fellowship voted vulgar by
parvenu pretension."

When Philip Hone returned from Saratoga Springs in the late
summer of 1839, he found that New York was still in the grips of
depression, with "Wall Street . . . in a state of consternation." Money
was "uncome-at-able. . . . A national bank is the only remedy. . . .
That, with a change of the Administration, are the only straws we have
to catch at." It would be interesting to be able to question Hone on
exactly how he thought a national bank and a new administration were
going to check the spirit of frantic speculation which, in his view,
lay—along with American dependence on British capital—at the
heart of the constant financial setbacks. Hone was so discouraged with
the state of affairs in New York that he fled back to Saratoga, which was
inundated by pleasure seekers, the dining room so full "that the brief
space of time allotted to the meal is a sort of running fight to secure
enough to eat: noise, confusion, elbowing, disputing for places." In
addition to the usual quota of summer visitors from New York, Philadelphia, and Boston, the town was filled with politicians, all preoccupied
with the coming presidential elections. Many members of Van Buren's
Cabinet turned up with a number of Congressmen and senators. The
arrival of Clay was the occasion for a great parade of "carriages, wagons,
horsemen and pedestrians . . . a mile and a half long," preceded by a
band of music. That night there was an elaborate dinner and an
elegant ball for eight hundred people, "comprising a greater number
of distinguished men and fine women than have probably ever been
collected in this country," Hone wrote. A few days later he noted:
"This is the meridian of the Saratoga season. All the world is here:
politicians and dandies; cabinet ministers and ministers of the gospel;
officeholders and office-seekers; humbugs and humbugged; fortune-
hunters and the hunters of woodcock; anxious mothers and lovely
daughters. . . ."

But gay though things might have been in Saratoga, New York
and the other "commercial cities" wallowed in the slough of financial

despond. The Democrats of Tennessee elected James Polk governor by a wide margin and Philip Hone noted: "The change has been dreadful in Indiana and our hopes in North Carolina are blasted. There seems to be a deadly warfare against the mercantile interests."

When Henry Clay arrived in New York at the end of August, he received a hero's welcome. He drove down Broadway in an open carriage accompanied, Hone noted, "by the greatest cavalcade I ever witnessed on such an occasion. All Broadway was filled with spectators; from the windows handkerchiefs were waved, and shouts ascended from the crowds collected at the corners." Hone could only compare it in popular enthusiasm with the reception accorded Lafayette fourteen years earlier.

A Loco-Foco candidate won the race for governor in Pennsylvania. Philip Hone wrote that "Ohio, which we thought our own, is, I fear, all wrong. But the strangest thing of all is our next-neighbor, New Jersey." It appeared to Hone that "The cause of the Constitution and the laws, the preservation of our precious institutions, are in the hands of the Whigs of New York." The auguries seemed favorable in Hone's home state and he was optimistic about the municipal elections in the spring of 1839, although he conceded that it would be "a hard battle," adding that "by the time the sun sets on Thursday, there will be lying, cheating, swearing and corruption enough to illustrate all the bright features of the universal suffrage system." The day after the election he wrote despairingly: "The Whigs are beaten. Violence, corruption, and immorality have prevailed." Isaac Varian, the Loco-Foco candidate for mayor of New York City, defeated only the year before, had won in a record turnout of voters, indicating that the working class of the city had gone to the polls in unprecedented numbers. "The whole affair is a farce," Hone added. "Cheating and false-swearing are the means by which our charter elections are carried . . . the republic cannot stand."

The fiftieth anniversary of Washington's inauguration was celebrated in 1839 and Hone was moved to some rueful reflections on the word *Federalism* "by which was designated in former times, the purest, wisest and most patriotic political party which ever existed" and was now "a term of reproach and the means of exciting bad feelings and prejudices of the people," used for "sinister purposes" by people "more ignorant of its meaning than they are of the Talmud." Hone and his fellows found it a bitter cup to drink that General Harrison "deems it necessary in order to gain the favor of the people to repudiate as the greatest calumny . . . the charge of having formerly been a *Federalist.* "

Clay was confident of winning the Whig nomination for the presidency in 1840. The popular enthusiasm generated by his political tour seemed to have made him the front-runner but Webster, who had been in England through much of the summer being lionized by the British, returned to the United States in time to use his vast influence to block Clay. Clay had also incurred the hostility of the declining Anti-Masonic Party, which had found an uneasy shelter under the Whig umbrella. In addition, a number of Whigs were opposed to slavery if unwilling to align themselves with the radical abolitionists, and these distrusted Clay as himself a slaveholder. So it was soon clear that stolid, innocuous old Harrison was the preferred candidate of the party faithful. The Whigs had invested too much in log cabins and Tippecanoe banners to turn readily to another candidate.

In December, 1839, a great Whig convention was held in Harrisburg, Pennsylvania, attended by some three thousand delegates. Harrison was promptly nominated and the meeting climaxed by "a grand procession, with banners, log-cabins, cider barrels, balls in motion, and every device which fancy could suggest." Hone acclaimed it "the most remarkable assemblage, in point of numbers, character, harmony, and zeal ever gathered together in these United States." Unfortunately, the procession was attacked, according to Hone, with stones and bricks by enraged Loco-Focos and two of the marchers were killed.

John Tyler was again the vice-presidential nominee, and while Hone would clearly have preferred Clay, he (like other loyal Whigs) was determined to support "the true, regular candidates of the United States." Hone was especially indignant that the slavery question had played an important part in sinking Clay. "The accursed question is destined to mix up with all national questions," he noted, "and in the end to alter the essential features of our government, if not to cause a separation of the States and a dissolution of the Union."

George Templeton Strong, attending a Whig rally in October, 1840, wrote: "There was an immense crowd and vast deal of fun—banners, bonfires, the old Hero staring grimly in plaster of paris, the 'Tippecanoe and Tyler too' in grand chorus, given with more effect than any effort of the Sacred Music Society." A week later he noted that "nobody can talk or think of anything else [but the election]. I suppose that enough money is staked on it to buy the consciences of nine-tenths of the politicians on both sides." There was another mass meeting with "a vast deal of fun and a little fighting. On the whole things looked well. . . . The only Loco procession I saw was the 'Albany Basin Rattlers'—a very rowdy gang of draggle-tailed black-guards." Another gathering of Loco-Focos was described by Strong as "a disgusting assemblage of the unwashed democracy, a . . . jailbird-resembling gang of truculent loafers. . . ."

Perhaps the most spectacular feature of the campaign was an enormous log cabin, fifty by one hundred feet, erected on Broadway near Prince Street and dedicated to Harrison and Reform. It held "an immense number of persons" and resounded constantly with the fervent speeches of Whig politicians.

Campaign songs and slogans had great currency: "Farewell, dear Van, you're not our man," "With Tip and Tyler / We'll burst Van's biler." Transparencies carried such messages as "Little Van's policy, fifty cents a day and French soup; Harrison's policy, two dollars a day and roast beef." The Whigs, signs proclaimed, would "teach the palace slave to respect the log cabin."

At Dayton, Ohio, it was said that one hundred thousand people, the largest throng in American political annals, had crowded onto a ten-acre field to sing, cheer, and chant for "Tippecanoe and Tyler, too." Daniel Webster, throwing his weight behind the party ticket, told an enthusiastic crowd in Boston that while he had not been born in a log cabin, his older brothers and sister had been. Perhaps the most effective slogan of the Whigs was that it was time for a change. Things were so bad they could only get better and a new administration was needed to put the country back on the right course. "Every breeze," a Whig slogan read, "says change! the cry, the universal cry is for a change." The highlight of the procession of Boston Whigs that wound onto the Common was "a whaleboat from New Bedford with all the apparatus for taking the whale and extracting the oil . . . manned by six old masters of whale ships," drawn by six gray horses. There was also a colossal shoe from Lynn, the shoemaking capital of the nation. Marblehead had a mammoth cod with the motto "A voice from the deep which seemed to say, 'For Benton a rod, And a bounty on cod.' "

The state of New York was Harrison's by a twelve-thousand-vote margin. Rhode Island and Ohio also fell into the Whig column. Day after day the word came in of other states added to the Whig tally until it was clear that they had swept the presidential elections and secured majorities in both houses of Congress as well as in numerous state legislatures. Before the electoral college met in December it was known that Harrison would get 234 votes to 60 for Van Buren. It was, Philip Hone noted, the end of the Jackson "dynasty." By his calculation the Democrats had reigned for forty years—which took in the Jeffersonian era—and now the country, having come to its senses, was in the hands of wise and conservative men who could be counted on to direct its affairs in the spirit of the Founders. "This is a beautiful illustration of the operation of a popular government," Hone noted. "There is not probably a country in the world where change of such prodigious magnitude could have been effected . . . in so orderly and decorous a manner."

Beneath the consoling figures was a reality somewhat different from what Philip Hone and his fellow Whigs perceived. While Harrison's electoral majority was great, his popular majority was small. Out of almost two and a half million votes cast, Harrison tallied only 135,000 more than Van Buren, while Van Buren received 350,000 more votes than he had four years earlier. The change was hardly of the "prodigious magnitude" Hone proclaimed it.

What is most striking about the campaign of 1840, besides the Whigs' enterprising use of political symbolism, was the extreme precariousness of the Whig alliance. Far from representing a profound shift in basic attitudes among the mass of Americans, the victory of Harrison was an odd amalgam of Eastern nostalgia for an old hero, Western assertiveness, a lack of enthusiasm for Van Buren as an arresting political figure, and the general disarray of Loco-Foco Democrats, disillusioned Anti-Masons, and antislavery people with no other place to go. Most striking of all was the fact that Americans, with the election of 1840, had clearly managed to do what no other people had perhaps done in history—turn politics into entertainment, into a national pastime, a game in which everyone could play; although one party was the loser, it could look forward in a relatively brief time to a new game which, as it was always ready to persuade itself, it had every expectation of winning. The bitterness of class and section that surfaced in virtually every election until the Civil War thus had an antidote in the sheer pleasure of this form of universal democratic entertainment. You could hardly sing and cheer, march and play, and then turn around and shoot your opponent (although, of course, a good many Americans did just that when "honor" was involved).

In addition to the play, there was clearly much rancor in political campaigns. Philip Hone wrote bitterly of the "scenes of violence, disorder, and riot" which "taught us in this city that universal suffrage will not do for large communities . . . in the heterogeneous mass of vile humanity in our population of 310,000 souls." The mobs of "political desperadoes" that Hone deplored were made up of those who felt themselves betrayed and exploited by the "aristocrats" who for the most part controlled the commercial and political life of New York and cities like it—the Irish, the Germans, immigrants generally, and "native" workingmen as well, all indeed who dared to protest against the existing state of things.

The scorn and hostility of people like Philip Hone toward "the masses" was returned with interest and expressed most potently by riots and disorders, by smashed windows and torn-up paving blocks, by bricks and stones flung by angry "ruffians" in the direction of indignant gentlemen, people of "quality" and "education." That such lower-class resentments, which obviously disturbed the dreams of the prosperous, did not in fact blaze up in sustained revolutionary activity (each riot, it might be said, was a revolutionary act of a kind) was perhaps due as much as anything else to the form that American politics took as popular entertainment. There are of course numerous other factors to be considered, prominent among them the fact that the discontented urban poor were confined to the large cities and constituted only a small fraction of the general population, most of whom, as we have had occasion constantly to be reminded, lived on farms or in rural towns.

Martin Van Buren was as cool and amiable in defeat as he had been in victory. When Philip Hone, a leader of the Whigs (and indeed the inventor, it was said, of their name), visited him in Washington after his defeat, Van Buren received him graciously and appeared "calm and unruffled as the bosom of a lake under the tranquil influence of a summer's sun."

It might be argued that the real victim of the election was poor old General Harrison—an agreeable and undistinguished man (certainly no great shakes as a general) and a political nonentity. He had simply been caught up on a kind of political tide which swept him into the highest office at the disposition of the people, his only clear recommendation being that he stood for little or nothing and therefore could not offend any of the remarkably mixed bag of voters who constituted the Whig "party." Harrison, sixty-eight at the beginning of his term of office, was clearly rather overwhelmed by what had befallen him. Hone was charmed to see the newly elected president, just a few days before his inauguration, mixing democratically with a crowd of Sunday churchgoers, "an elderly gentleman dressed in black . . . with a mild, benignant countenance, a military air, but stooping a little, bowing to one, shaking hands with another, and cracking a joke with a third—unattended and unconscious of the dignity of his position, *the man,* among men." To Hone it was "a sublime moral spectacle."

The Whigs, of course, descended on Washington for Harrison's inauguration in a tide. "Every hole and corner is filled," Hone noted, "and happy is the man who finds 'where to lay his head.' " A temporary building that seated four hundred people for meals and then was converted into "a vast camp-bed" was erected in the courtyard of Gadsby's hotel.

The inauguration itself was a splendid spectacle with gentlemen and ladies who on recent occasions had stayed away now present in great numbers. A vast procession made its way to the Capitol, made up of "several militia companies in uniform, Tippecanoe clubs, and citizens from different States" passing through the streets "amidst the shouts and hurrahs of fifty thousand men, and almost as many women waving handkerchiefs." The General's inaugural address was much too long and largely inaudible. The new President, feeling quite ill and faint, had then to repair to the White House to greet thousands of Whigs eager to shake the hand of their hero. In this at least they were disappointed; previous handshakers had left his hand so sore and swollen that his supporters had to be content with a smile and a nod. Indeed, the President confided to an aide that his duties had pressed so hard upon him that he had not had time to perform "the necessary functions of nature." That night at the inaugural ball, with (at least in Hone's opinion) "all the great men of the nation . . . there" and "an exceedingly brilliant collection of ladies," the President appeared at ten o'clock and passed around the room greeting friends. In a subterranean banqueting room reserved for the inner circle of Whigs, Hone found "Senators, Cabinet Ministers, military officers, and common men like myself, eating, drinking, laughing and joking, in a strain somewhat uproarious."

The new Cabinet promised well for the new administration. Webster was secretary of state, the able Kentuckian John Crittenden attorney general, John Bell of Tennessee secretary of war, and Francis Granger postmaster general.

A month to the day after his inauguration, the new President expired, exhausted by the enthusiasm of his admirers. Hone noted that he had expired with "a violent diarrehoea" related, in Hone's view at least, to the fact that his time was so much taken by supporters and petitioners (often one and the same) that he could not get to the bathroom regularly.

Philip Hone praised the "noble and virtuous old man" whose election had "lighted up the hopes of a dispirited people." The only sour note was sounded by William Cullen Bryant's *Evening Post*, which observed that it was unfortunate Harrison had not lived "long enough to prove his incapacity for the office of President."

The death of General Harrison provided the occasion for an extended period of mourning and a spectacular funeral. It was as though the Whigs, cheated of their stout old hero, were determined to make up for their loss by the extravagance of their grief. Businesses were closed, all public places, markets, hotels, and shops and many private homes were draped in black. The funeral procession included companies of militia, sixty clergymen, five companies of marines, Revolutionary veterans, a thousand firemen and their engines. "All was order and regularity in the tremendous mass of humanity," Philip Hone (one of twenty-six pallbearers) reported, "which formed the greatest civil and military procession ever witnessed in the city, for spectators occupied every window and housetop, or covered the entire streets. . . ."

The Whigs were determined to make the best of the new president, John Tyler. Philip Hone wrote in his diary: "Mr. Tyler is a fine, good-hearted gentleman, and I believe a disinterested patriot, but he has some Utopian notions of government which if he does not abandon, will leave him and his administration as they did poor John Quincy Adams, high and dry ashore. . . ." Chief among his "Utopian notions" was his refusal to turn out all the officeholders appointed by the Democrats.

12

Texas Becomes a Bone of Contention

John Tyler, the man on whose shoulders the mantle of office fell upon the death of poor old General Harrison, was the first vice-president to succeed to the presidency upon the death of the incumbent: the first "accidental president," as his enemies soon were calling him. An affable, ingratiating man with the charm for which Virginians were famous, Tyler, although a nominal Whig (he had resigned from the Senate rather than follow the instructions of the Virginia legislature to vote to expunge the Senate's censure of Jackson), was a low-tariff man and soon made it evident that he had little sympathy with the Whig businessmen who had intended to guide Harrison's footsteps.

Certainly Tyler's succession filled many Whigs with anxiety. "Never was there a time," Hone wrote, "when political measures were brought so closely home to men's bosoms, and men are compelled to be politicians in despite of their natural inclination. . . . All things are disjoined. Trade is at a stand; property diminished in value; confidence shaken to the center; and nothing thrives but party spirit and corporation taxes."

With Tyler as president, Clay took over the leadership of Congress and undertook to force through that divided and rather lethargic body a Whig program, the most prominent feature of which was the establishment of a new Bank of the United States.

Meanwhile the provisions of the Tariff of 1833 were about to expire and Congress rushed through a Little Tariff Bill to extend the existing tariff schedule for two months. The bill also contained a provision that suspended the distribution to the states of revenue from the sales of public lands. Tyler promply vetoed the bill, largely on technical grounds. Another tariff bill, Bill 472, which again provided for distribution to the states of the proceeds of land sales, was sent to the President a few weeks later. Tyler wrote another veto message, stating that the bill combined two matters "wholly incongruous in their character." More serious, it abandoned to the states the revenues from land sales needed by the federal government. The response of the Whigs in Congress was an open declaration of war on the President. Amid angry talk of impeachment, a proposal was made of an amendment to the Constitution requiring only a majority to override a presidential veto.

When the *New York Courier and Enquirer* under James Watson Webb attacked the President and his Cabinet for failing to pursue Whig policies, the fragile Whig coalition began to unravel. Webb's tirade was, in Philip Hone's words, "the signal for all the discordant elements of the Whig party to ferment and boil over. . . ." Finally the Bank Bill, known more generally as Mr. Clay's bill, was passed by the Senate and the House, in the latter by a strictly party vote of 128 to 97. Tyler vetoed it a week later with a message that Hone considered "one of the weakest and most puerile state papers we have ever had from the executive department," a "confused, egotistical, inconclusive argument" whose principal consequence, at least in New York, was to ally him with that "mammon of unrighteousness, Tammany Hall." The most interesting question was whether the Cabinet would now resign. All honest Whigs thought it must be done in good conscience. But that is not the way of officeholders generally. They stood fast and endured the obloquy of their party.

When Tyler intimated that he would sign a bank bill if it were redrafted to meet his most serious objections, the leaders of Congress tried again. But once more the tergiversating chief executive vetoed the bill, to the fury and despair of the Whigs; this time the Cabinet, with the exception of Webster, did resign. "Discouraging indeed is the prospect for future harmony in the Whig Party," Philip Hone wrote, "and the preservation of the union between the North and the South. . . ." Sidney George Fisher expressed a rather common view when he wrote that "Tyler is a poor, weak, vacillating fellow, heartily despised by everyone, and so completely a minority in Congress that he has no influence at all." George Templeton Strong called him "the old veto-grinder, Tyler the First." Again there was talk among the more adamant Whigs of impeaching Tyler.

Tyler had inherited the unsettled issue of the Maine–Canada border, the so-called Aroostook War. Moreover, the troubles along the New York–Canadian border flared up again. Tensions between the two countries were exacerbated by a revival of the *Caroline* affair. During the capture and burning of the *Caroline* an American named Amos Durfee had been shot. In the fall of 1840 an inebriated Canadian named Alexander McLeod boasted in a tavern on the American side of the border that he had killed Durfee. The burning of the *Caroline* was a bitter issue in the area; McLeod was slapped in prison and charged with murder and arson. The British demand for McLeod's immediate release on the grounds that the burning of the *Caroline* was an official act by a Canadian military force and that McLeod was, in any event, not a member of the raiding party was couched in such insolent language (referring to the *Caroline* as a "piratical steamboat") that American opinion was inflamed and the issue itself was blown up out of all proportion. The undiplomatic correspondence between the two countries escalated the quarrel and produced, as a byproduct, a report by congressional Democrats stating among other things that on no account should the United States submit to unjust demands "from any power on earth no matter what the consequences may be."

The problem was that the case was in the hands of a local upcountry court and an unfriendly jury. While the date for the trial was delayed, Britain made preparations for war. A change of venue from Niagara County to Oneida was secured and the United States District Attorney acted as counsel for the prisoner, who was tried in Utica, found not guilty, and discharged.

The most positive consequence of the McLeod affair was the Webster–Ashburton Treaty, ratified in 1842, which settled the troubled boundary question between Canada and Maine and in so doing marked a new era in the relations between Great Britain and the United States, disturbed only by the Oregon boundary question four years later.

On August 23 a revised tariff bill passed the House. The treaty and the passage of the tariff gave new heart to the Whigs and they held a great party rally, five or six thousand strong, in New York, addressed by Millard Fillmore, a native son who had guided the tariff bill through Congress as chairman of the Ways and Means Committee.

The slavery issue so penetrated every political question that Tyler's nomination of Edward Everett, former governor of Massachusetts and one of the great orators of the day, for an ambassadorial post was opposed in the Senate on the grounds that he was an enemy of slavery. "If the nomination is rejected," Philip Hone wrote indignantly, "it will be by the union of pseudo Whigs with exterminating Locofocos to punish a patriot and a statesman because he is in favor of the right to petition, which it would be treason in any public man to deny, and because he has refused to exclaim . . . that slavery is a positive blessing to the land."

Perhaps the oddest event of Tyler's administration was the so-called Dorr's Rebellion in Rhode Island. Once Rhode Island was the most radical colony in British America, governed by a charter procured in 1663 and notorious for its independent and contentious ways. But by the 1830s the state, still operating under a somewhat modernized version of its old charter, had the most limited voting franchise of any state in the Union. Voting was restricted to those who had freehold property to the value of $150. Agitation for universal manhood suffrage had been going on since the early 1820s. Finally a young Harvard graduate and Jacksonian Democrat named Thomas Dorr placed himself at the head of the forces of reform. He called on his fellow Islanders to appoint delegates to a convention to frame a new and liberalized constitution. The Rhode Island General Assembly met this tactic by calling a convention but then adjourning it indefinitely. Five years later, stimulated by the excitement of the presidential campaign of 1840, the reformers again called for a constitutional convention. Plainly the notion was to try to capture the state for the Democrats in the coming election. Once again the general assembly was unresponsive. This time three thousand placard-carrying men marched with such slogans as "Liberty shall be restored to the People; Peaceably if we Can, Forcibly if we Must." The reformers were summoned to a People's Convention which met in October and drafted a constitution featuring universal white suffrage. The constitution was submitted to the voters throughout the state. A total of 14,000 votes were tallied and the People's Convention announced that a new constitution existed. The assembly refused to accept the document or acknowledge its legitimacy. The so-called Freemen's Party, the creature of the assembly, called a rival convention and drew up a constitution clearly designed to limit the voting rights of newly arrived immigrants. Now there were two constitutions.

The assembly appealed to President Tyler to declare the Suffragists in a treasonable conspiracy against the state of Rhode Island and support the legitimate government with United States troops. George Templeton Strong wrote of the "Rebellion": "It's only a pity that things hadn't got a little hotter, that there hadn't been a little beheading and hanging there among the apostles of liberty . . . a pity because such a transaction . . . would add a little romantic interest to our history which yet it don't possess. . . . As to the rebels, not even an abstract democrat of the most mobcratic views can sympathize with them, for they're seeking not suffrage but plunder, they're literal anarchists, acknowledged banditti, gathered from the bullenders of this city of blackguards."

Philip Hone observed in *his* diary: "A terrible hubbub has been going on in the redoubtable little State of Rhode Island for some time past; a party of disorganizing, radical demagogues, unable to accomplish their object of changing the politics of this steady State and bringing themselves into office by fair means, have set about defeating the will of the people . . . and having made a Constitution of their own, have elected a governor (one Dorr) and State officers; while the sober part of the community, proceeding according to law and the Constitution, have reelected the present governor. . . . So the smallest State of the Union is the only one which can boast of *two* governors. . . ."

"Governor" Dorr carried "the case of the people" to Washington, where he conferred with President Tyler. On the way home he was received as a hero by the Loco-Foco Democrats of New York, among them William Cullen Bryant. Twelve thousand people showed up at a rally in support of the Dorr party and some went so far as to enlist in an expeditionary force to come to its assistance. Hone was indignant: "The Loco-focos in New York, high and low, leaders and led, seem determined to throw aside all regard for decency. They espouse openly the cause of the Rhode Island rebels, and respond to the call to send men and arms to support them in their opposition to the laws." Hone was prematurely elated at the news that the "supernumerary governor" of Rhode Island, Thomas Dorr, had "absquatulated, mizzled, made tracks." But a month later he was forced to take note of the fact that Dorr was "encamped at a place called Chessacket . . . with a force of about 800 ragamuffins, of whom a large proportion are volunteers, sympathizers from New York and Connecticut." The "constitutional" governor of Rhode Island had declared martial law, shut up the banks, and sent the students of Brown College home. No one could leave or enter Providence without a pass and three thousand troops had been assembled to suppress the rebels. "There was some little skirmishing," Hone wrote, "between a portion of the insurgents and the regular troops, in which one man was killed and two wounded; but the camp was taken quiet possession of, with the arms and ammunition, powder and pumpkins, guns and geese, pikes and potatoes, and by this time the good people of Providence have returned to their peaceful pursuits." Dorr was arrested, tried, and sentenced to prison for life. Meanwhile, a legislature favorable to reform was elected, the charter was replaced by a modern constitution with a liberal franchise, and after a year in jail Dorr was pardoned.

Outside Rhode Island, the Rebellion was important for the widespread sympathy it evoked among the Democrats and the fuel it provided them for their charges that a coterie of wealthy and selfish men was trying to run both the states and the country. To men like Fisher, Strong, and Hone the Dorr Rebellion was yet another indication of the radical sentiments circulating in the country, endangering good order and, indeed, the republic itself.

An indication of the volatile nature of public sentiment was to be found in the renewed activities of the Native American Party. In May, 1844, a group of Native Americans held a political rally in the Kensington district of Philadelphia, an Irish stronghold, where they were attacked by a party of paddies and "driven from the ground." Returning with augmented forces, they were fired upon, presumably by militant Irishmen. The next day there was a mass meeting of heavily armed natives who marched off to Kensington. There they were shot at from houses, so the story was, and in retaliation burned a number of them down. "Many," Sidney George Fisher wrote, "were killed & wounded & some, it is believed, were burnt in the houses"—all of this without any intervention on the part of the authorities of the city. A number of Irish barricaded themselves in St. Augustine's Church and from there held their enemies at bay. The mayor of Philadelphia at this point persuaded the defenders of the church to leave it under the protection of the city police, promising that he would protect it from the mob. With the church emptied, the mayor addressed the crowd, assuring them that he was determined to keep order, that the church had been abandoned and that they must disperse. At this word they rushed into the church and set it afire. In the following days two more Catholic churches and a total of forty houses were burned down. When Fisher arrived in the city it was like an armed camp. "Groups were at every corner, engaged in eager conversation, frightened . . . & distressed-looking women were standing at their doors or looking anxiously from the windows, bodies of troops were marching about, sentinels were seen stationed in all directions. . . ."

Martial law was proclaimed and the city divided into districts, citizens recruited to form volunteer companies under militia officers, marines brought from the Navy Yard and from the steam frigate *Princeton.* Governor David Porter came from the capital at Harrisburg with three regiments of volunteers from neighboring towns. Word was out that the mob was determined "that every Catholic church in the country shall be burnt & every Catholic expelled. . . ." Sidney George Fisher felt compelled to do his bit to restore order and joined a group of young lawyers defending a Catholic seminary at the corner of Fifth and Race streets. "There were about 40 of us," he wrote, "all very young men, perfectly undisciplined. . . . I mounted guard for two hours, & for the first time felt a musket on my shoulder. . . . I have no fancy for a soldier's life and consider that society is bound to protect me in person & property." But a few days later when he and his companions had discovered "some good wine in the cellar at our disposal & there was plenty of cold meat, bread & coffee & cigars," Fisher began "rather to like the excitement. It was an interruption to the usual dull monotony of life here, and produced emotions which varied the blank of Philadelphia existence. . . ." Little boys had been very prominent in the riots. "They were seen among the crowds shooting at people, several of whom were killed by little fellows scarce able to carry a musket. . . . Women, too, were busy, as in the French Revolution, cheering on the men & carrying weapons to them. These are strange things for Philadelphia," Fisher added. When it appeared that the trouble had passed, "a *volunteer* armed police of citizens" was formed "to hold themselves in readiness to assemble at a specified place whenever a riot occurs. . . ."

On the Fourth of July the Native American Party celebrated "by an immense procession with banners and all sorts of devices. . . . Everything was done to produce excitement. Those who were wounded in the May riot were paraded in a car," Fisher wrote. But the police were much in evidence and the day passed without trouble. The next day, however, word was spread about the city that guns and ammunition were being carried into the church of St. Philip de Neri in Queen Street. "This," Fisher wrote, "produced great excitement among the low population of the district, who gathered around it in considerable numbers." The sheriff arrived, searched the church, and took away the arms, but the crowd continued to grow. When General George Cadwalader appeared with several companies of volunteer citizens the crowd ignored his orders to disperse. The general then loaded an artillery piece and gave the word to fire, but before the gun could be discharged into the crowd a member of the sheriff's posse passed in front of it, thus screening the piece and preventing its discharge. The mob now dispersed but soon re-formed with two cannons of their own, which they aimed at the church. They then demanded that a militia company, the Hibernian Greens, leave the area with muskets reversed and firing pans open. As they filed away "they were attacked by the mob with stones & clubs, & after firing a few shots in defence, they broke & ran for their lives. Two were caught and most shockingly beaten."

Cadwalader, with 165 men, was then ordered to occupy and to defend the church. By now the crowd was "immense, of the very lowest class & greatly excited." The soldiers were loudly abused and some pelted with stones. Finally the captain of one of the volunteer companies had his sword wrested from his hand and was thrown to the ground, while others in the mob snatched at the muskets of the soldiers. At this the command was given by Cadwalader to fire and several people were killed or wounded by the volley. The crowd then dispersed but by dark many were back with firearms and a cannon. "The fight continued through the night," Fisher noted in his diary, "with constant firing on both sides, the mob shooting from the tops and windows of houses, & from alleys & street corners. . . . Among the military only two were killed & about 20 wounded. It is supposed that about 15 were killed among the mob and many more wounded."

The next day the city was once more in a turmoil. Certain companies of citizen volunteers refused to turn out since a number of Native Americans were included in them, and Fisher was dismayed to hear some individuals arguing that the troops ought not to have fired. "The mob," Fisher wrote, "were furious in their denunciations of Cadwalader, swore they would have his blood, that they would hang him, and we were in momentary expectation that his house would be attacked & that we should thus have war in the midst of us." Since the soldiers and Cadwalader were still besieged in the church a compromise was reached at last after daylong negotiations between the leaders of the mob and the city officials. Cadwalader and his men would leave the church and its defense would be taken over by the civil authorities. The night passed peacefully and the next day there was a meeting of "the better class of citizens . . . numerously attended by members of the bar, merchants, & men of education & property" to express the determination of those present to do their utmost to restore and maintain order. A fund of $10,000 was quickly raised for the relief of the wounded and slain among the soldiers and companies of volunteers poured into the city from nearby counties to help prevent any further outbreaks.

The simple facts of the riot reveal precious little about the state of mind that provoked them. One is reminded of the Lord George Gordon riots in London during the American Revolution, where what began as an anti-Catholic demonstration turned into a weeklong riot in which more than 300 people lost their lives and hundreds of buildings were pillaged or set afire. The Philadelphia riots were clearly aimed in two directions—at Irish Catholics and at what Fisher called "the better class of citizens," who rallied a bit belatedly to protect them. The degree of violence suggests a high level of class bitterness and resentment. One thinks of the Irish population of the city as constituting a substantial part of the "lower orders," but there was obviously a much larger depressed segment of the population who hated the Irish only somewhat more than they hated those Philadelphians at the top of the social order. Several points come to mind. The riots, along with similar but less serious disturbances in New York and Boston (George Templeton Strong referred to Philadelphia as "the most anarchial metropolis on this side of the Atlantic"), serve to remind us of the depth of class feeling in the larger cities, where the promise of equality contained in the Declaration of Independence was mocked by the dramatic contrast between the modes of life of the rich and the poor. The Irish hated the freed blacks in the Northern cities and seized any excuse to attack them. The "native Americans" of the working class in turn hated both the blacks and the Irish. These intramural hatreds prevented the lower classes—the three we have described—from making common cause against those who controlled the financial resources of the cities. The political leaders, for their part, played off one group against another (more particularly the nativists and the

Irish; the blacks were political ciphers), not as part of a deliberate strategy of "divide and conquer" but with the simple intention of retaining political power. Eager for the substantial blocs of voters represented by each faction, the "bosses" of the factions negotiated sufficient concessions with the middle- and upper-class managers of the two dominant parties to take the edge off the most serious social and economic grievances. Had it been otherwise the big Eastern cities would certainly have come close to social breakdown. We can hardly use the phrase "revolutionary activity" because the basis for a "revolution" clearly did not exist in the United States in the decades prior to the Civil War, outside of half a dozen of the larger cities. The Irishman's vote, which many more Americans than the activists who formed the Native American Party would like to have taken away from him, was—however badly he may at times have used it—his only protection against even more cruel exploitation.

We do not think of mid-nineteenth-century America as the scene of bitter class antagonisms if we think of it at all, but it is clear beyond question that they existed and that in a large degree they were mutual; the upper classes feared and hated the lower classes almost as enthusiastically as the lower hated the upper. Benevolent associations —Sunday schools and even temperance organizations—did something to ameliorate those antagonisms. The depressed and angry poor of the cities did not, with relatively few exceptions, go west for the reason that they were too sunk in poverty and degradation to make the psychological effort to go—or, more simply, were just too poor. The fact that there was no competing ideology was also of importance. It was not the American "system," not the Constitution or the political institutions per se that were resented by those at the bottom of the pile, but the fact that they did not *work* justly, that they had been appropriated by selfish and ruthless men to their own uses. Slavery played a role as well, if only because the party of the workingman in the North was also the party of the slaveholder in the South. The Democratic Party, by tying the greater mass of the Northern working poor to the slave system, rendered itself impotent as an agency of genuine social reform. By the same token, since the most aggressive and radical middle-class reformers, women like Lucretia Mott and men like Theodore Weld, were preoccupied with the cause of abolition which was an anathema to orthodox Democrats, the problems of the urban poor were little attended to by those people best suited to understand and to help remedy them.

One of the most sensational events of 1841 was the failure of the Bank of the United States. Nicholas Biddle had resigned as president almost two years earlier, but it was soon clear that his misuse of Bank funds was responsible for its failure. Sidney George Fisher noted: "Everyone is talking about the exposé . . . of the B.U.S. frauds. Astonishment & indignation are generally expressed. Indeed it is villainy on a most enormous scale. Yankees do nothing by halves, they always go the entire figure . . . I believe there has been more corruption & fraud in this country for the last five years than in all England for the last three hundred. . . . In the meantime the press is dumb. All bought, all indebted to the Banks, all bribed. A curious fact showing the power of these institutions. They have thus obtained control over the country by the mere power of money. They bribe legislators & the press, and by governing the interests, govern the opinions of an immense army of merchants, speculators, stockholders, lawyers, politicians, all in short who direct public sentiment. The 'monster' had verified the predictions of its enemies," Fisher wrote. "It had ended in bankruptcy & ruin, its corruptions & abuses were now exposed in open day. . . . The arch enemy of . . . 'the people' had met with a deserved fate. His true character was now brought to light with all his tricks and intrigues, together with the frauds, speculations, extravagance & luxury of the money mongers and gamblers, the mushroom 'aristocracy' with whom he was connected." In those private circles where "Mr. Biddle had been the delight & ornament . . . he was avoided . . . his name was mentioned with contempt & execration, many cut him & refused to speak to him in the street." As a final touch of drama, Biddle's criminal prosecution was conducted by St. George Campbell—whose mother, it was said, had been one of Biddle's mistresses.

When Biddle died early in 1844, Fisher—whose hostility to Jackson was so often recorded in his diary—devoted seven or eight pages of that journal to reflections upon Biddle's life and character. Through it all there runs the thread of a feeling that Biddle, by his lack of integrity, had done irreparable damage to his class and more widely to the financial and commercial interests of the country. The Protestant attitude toward money had been that its use was under God's judgment. Debtor laws were severe because Calvinist dogma had it that the payment of just debts was required by divine ordinance as well as by manmade laws, which reflected those of the Almighty. The fight between Jackson and the Bank, between Jackson and Biddle, was perceived by the forces on both sides as being above all a moral contest, a struggle between right and wrong. All the guardians of the flame of federalism, all the enemies of Jeffersonian democracy, of easy money and bad morals, all the conservative Christians, all the defenders of property cast their lot with the conceited little dandy, Nicholas Biddle, a gentleman, "one of us." And the gentleman let them all down. He turned out to be not a whit better or more moral than a blackleg, a Mississippi gambler, or a Kentucky freebooter. He was simply a pirate on a larger and more imaginative scale. He betrayed both his social class and the business and commercial interests of the country, categories which overlapped to a degree. He appeared to a vast number of Americans to have proved the truth of everything the Jacksonians had said about the ruthless power and corruption of the Bank and all that it represented. By his dereliction he had shattered once and for all the illusion—certainly already considerably battered —that the destinies of the country could be safely left in the hands of upper-class Christian gentlemen, men of unimpeachable integrity who could be trusted to manage its affairs in the best interests of all the citizens of the Union.

It is interesting to reflect on the possible consequences to the nation if Nicholas Biddle had possessed the relentless honesty of his adversary. Assuming that Jackson would, in any event, have destroyed the Bank, the failure of scandal to touch Biddle might, in the face of the economic collapse of 1837–1842, have greatly strengthened the position of the Bank's advocates. While it is impossible to predict the practical consequences of such a situation, it seems safe to assume that the "credibility," as we say today, of the Bank's supporters would have been greatly enhanced, and this credibility might well have translated itself into political power. No one could argue that radicals were in control of American politics from 1840 to the outbreak of the Civil War, but it was certainly the case that the conservative coalition represented by the Whigs and dominated by mercantile interests and business philosophy was, if not at once routed, thoroughly demoralized.

From the establishment of the Republic of Texas in 1835, the issue of the relationship of Texas to the United States had been a constant source of controversy. In 1842 the rumor that Mexico intended to invade and try to recapture Texas brought pledges of men and money from a number of Southern states. That rumor had hardly drifted away before word circulated that Great Britain was interested in developing a special relationship with Texas.

The abolitionists fanned the flames of Southern apprehension by appealing to the British government to assist in buying freedom for the slaves in Texas, for it was clearly the issue of slavery that aroused such passions on either side of the question. If Texas could be turned into a free state, Northerners reasoned, the issue of annexation could be defused. Indeed, the tables would be turned on the South, because a free Texas would prove a barrier to the establishment of slave states farther west. The Southern states were, conversely, equally determined to have Texas in the Union as a slave state.

Stephen Pearl Andrews, a lawyer, an abolitionist, a Texan whose eloquence had persuaded many of his neighbors to join the antislavery ranks without in some instances going so far as to free their slaves, traveled to England to enlist the enemies of slavery in Britain in his plan to buy the freedom of the slaves in Texas. The British Cabinet was favorably disposed to Andrews's proposal but it was soon clear that the reaction in the South was so extreme that Britain must run the risk of a war with the United States if Andrews persisted. Thwarted in his efforts and with his life in danger if he returned to Texas, Andrews sailed to Boston, where for the rest of his life he espoused radical causes and endeavored to found a new science of Universology. We shall meet him later.

Alarmed by word of Andrews's mission, Henry Wise, the Virginia hothead, declared "that unless by a treaty with Mexico the South can add more weight to her end of the lever of national power . . . the balance of interest is gone, and the safeguard of American property, of the American Constitution, of the American Union vanished into thin air." If Mexico reclaimed Texas "a horde of slaves and Indians and Mexicans" would "roll up to the boundary line of Arkansas and Louisiana. . . . And if England, standing by, should dare to intermeddle, and ask, Do you take part with Texas? the prompt answer should be, Yes, and against you."

John Quincy Adams replied by arguing that under the Constitution neither Congress nor the President could annex a foreign state to the United States.

Meanwhile, Mexico—alarmed by the growing talk of annexation —sent word to President Tyler that annexation would be "equivalent to a declaration of war against the Mexican Republic." Mexico still considered Texas a part of its territory and the government would declare war the instant the United States attempted to annex. Throughout the North a number of Whig conventions and certain state legislatures declared that the annexation of Texas must result in the destruction of the Union. Tyler, realizing that his only hope of re-election lay in securing the support of the Democrats—he had certainly been far more of a Democratic than a Whig president—saw the issue of annexation as his best hope of ingratiating himself with the Democrats. Texas was "the only matter," Tyler wrote Abel Upshur, Webster's successor as secretary of state, "that will take sufficient hold of the feelings of the South to rally it on a southern candidate and weaken Clay & Van Buren so much there as to bring the election into the House." Then, it was Tyler's hope, he would be put forward as a compromise choice. Upshur was meanwhile killed in the explosion of a gun on the warship *Princeton* and Calhoun appointed to succeed him. The South Carolinian proceeded to draft a treaty of annexation. The treaty stipulated that the United States would take over all unsold lands, forts, magazines, arms, and public buildings, along with the Texas navy and army. The citizens of Texas were to become citizens of the United States and the state's debts to the sum of ten million dollars were to be assumed by the United States.

The Northern view was well expressed by Philip Hone, who described the treaty as "a measure which many of our best and wisest citizens have looked at with most anxious apprehension. . . . The Executive incubus of the country, to gain Southern capital for his personal and political objects, has been for sometime past flirting with the Texan government." The rumor that annexation was imminent "and the dread that a majority of the Senate will ratify this alarming act of executive power, caused a panic in Wall Street. Stocks fell . . . men looked alarmed and shook their heads in fearful doubt. A war with Mexico would be the immediate consequence of this measure, and privateers would be fitted out in Mexican ports . . . to prey upon the immense commerce of the United States." Hone's anxiety proved well grounded.

A vote on the annexation of Texas was carried in the Senate at the end of February, 1844, by a vote of 27 to 25, and although the vote did not constitute a formal annexation, Hone wrote on hearing the news, "The Constitution is a dead letter, the ark of safety is wrecked, the wall of separation which has hitherto restrained the violence of popular rage is broken down, the Goths are in possession of the Capitol, and if the Union can survive the shock it will only be another evidence that

Divine Providence takes better care of us than we deserve." Charles Francis Adams wrote: "Thus is accomplished this enormous outrage upon the fundamental principles of our system of government . . . I see for the future nothing before me but grim darkness in political affairs."

Calhoun, encouraged by the virtually unanimous support for annexation among Southern Democrats and by the acclaim accorded him as the drafter of the treaty of annexation, dreamed once again of becoming president. Henry Clay had been touring the country to large and adoring crowds, building support for his own candidacy. The day Tyler signed the Treaty of Annexation, Clay wrote his so-called Raleigh letter (it was written in that city) and sent it to the *National Intelligencer*. In it he attacked the idea of annexation as "perfectly idle and ridiculous if not dishonorable," adding that "annexation and war with Mexico are identical. . . . I consider the annexation of Texas at the present time as a measure compromising the national character, involving us certainly in a war with Mexico, probably with other foreign powers, dangerous to the integrity of the Union, inexpedient in the present financial condition of the country, and not called for by any general expression of public opinion." This bold declaration solidified Clay's hold on the Whigs and assured him of that party's nomination, but it probably cost him the election.

Now attention switched to Van Buren. He was still the nominal leader of the Democrats, the heir of Jackson. While he had been defeated by Harrison, that defeat was considered something of a fluke. His supporters were determined to put him forward again. In the words of James Buchanan, "The old office holders who expect to be restored with Mr. Van Buren & the old editors who were liberally patronized by his Administration, are the regular troops in political warfare." They made a potent combination. Great pressure was now exerted on Van Buren to change his position on annexation, but the New Yorker, so often guided by practical political considerations, decided, perhaps at the insistence of Silas Wright, that the annexation of Texas, which he felt sure would bring about war with Mexico, "was a consideration which I was not at liberty to embrace. . . . We have a character among the nations of the earth to maintain," he wrote in explanation of his position, "and it has hitherto been our pride and our boast, that, while the lust of power, with fraud and violence in the train, has led other and differently constituted governments to aggression and conquest, our movements in these respects have always been regulated by reason and justice."

Van Buren left the door open a chink by stating that if Congress voted for annexation after the election, he would accept it. The chink, it turned out, was not wide enough. Things now turned about. One of Van Buren's staunchest supporters in Tennessee wrote him, "The Breeders of Mules and horses and hogs cry out 'let us have Texas right or wrong. . . .' If the British interfere we will give them New Orleans again. If those Mexicans come nigh we will eat them up."

Highminded as Van Buren's disavowal of annexation may have been, he was nonetheless surprised and embittered by the evident disposition of the South to abandon him on the issue. His supporters confessed to "smothered feelings that have no parallel in bitterness and indignation." It appeared that the United States was no less disposed to "aggression and conquest" than any other nation intoxicated by "the lust of power."

That left Calhoun the only clear annexation candidate; he and his supporters now concentrated their attention on trying to prevent a national nominating convention in favor of state conventions. Even in his own section Calhoun appealed primarily to those Southerners who, like William Gwin of Mississippi, wanted "a slave-holder for President . . . regardless of the man, believing as I solemnly do that in the next Presidential term the Abolitionists must be put down or blood will be spilt."

A recent student of the election of 1844 has written: "Outside the South, the Calhoun cause attracted a weird collection of the doctrinaire, the disaffected, the mercenary, and the opportunistic." By early 1844, the Calhoun campaign had collapsed. The Georgia Democratic Convention, which had earlier endorsed the South Carolinian, withdrew its endorsement, and conventions in a number of New England states declared for Van Buren. The disappointed Calhoun wrote to his son, "The whole affair is a gross fraud. . . . I am the last man that can be elected in the present condition of the country. . . . I am too honest and too patriotick to be the choice of anything like a majority." The tide now seemed to run irresistibly toward Van Buren. James Buchanan, who had tested the water, acknowledged that Van Buren "will obtain the nomination by an overwhelming majority. . . ." But those Democrats determined to have a proannexation candidate for president began a merciless campaign of bullying and arm twisting among the delegates to the coming nominating convention. Since it was clear that Van Buren would come to the convention with a majority of the delegates, it was essential to change the rule for nomination to a two-thirds majority of the delegates, thus enabling the proannexation minority to block the nomination of Van Buren or any other candidate opposed to annexation. To the New Hampshire delegates it was hinted that if the two-thirds rule were passed and Van Buren stopped, the nomination might well go to that state's favorite son, Levi Woodbury. The Michigan delegation was seduced by the notion that it might go to Lewis Cass and the Tennesseeans were shown, in the same way, that Polk would be nominated for president.

The Whigs met in Baltimore on May 1 in a great Clay extravaganza. The delegates from New York arrived in a large barge festooned with Clay banners and badges, flags, pennants, and streamers of every description proclaiming the hero of Kentucky. There were Clay hats everywhere and cages with live raccoons, the raccoon being a Clay symbol. Balconies displayed portraits of Clay and ladies wore sashes with the words "Clay Forever."

The Kentuckian was promptly nominated by acclamation and Theodore Frelinghuysen of New York was chosen as the vice-presidential candidate. Philip Hone, a delegate, was euphoric. Henry Clay, he wrote, was unanimously "recommended to the people of the United States . . . as President. . . ." "This," Hone added, "was certainly one of the most sublime moral spectacles ever exhibited: the twenty-six States of the American Union, by their representatives, consisting of the best talents, virtue, and patriotism of that portion of the several communities which constitute the great Whig party," had voted "without a doubt or shadow of dissent" for Henry Clay as the nominee of the party. "Thus in the most perfect harmony ended this sublime and exciting ceremony, the remembrance of which will never be effaced from my mind. I shall always rejoice that I was present," Hone concluded.

Following the nomination, ten thousand Whigs "came to Baltimore to ratify the choice"—in short, to have a parade. "This mass of noble, fine-looking fellows, from the granite hills of New Hampshire to the green prairies of the great West" formed in a procession "with flags and patriotic devices, badges and weapons of peace . . . cheered on by the bright eyes of the prettiest young women in the world. . . . The whole of Baltimore street, presented a pageant more bright and brilliant than any I ever beheld."

When the Democratic delegates convened three weeks later at the Odd Fellows' Egyptian Hall in Baltimore, Romulus Saunders of North Carolina called the meeting to order twenty minutes ahead of time, catching the Van Buren supporters by surprise, and jammed through the election of Hendrick Wright of Pennsylvania, an anti–Van Buren man, as president of the convention. A bitter struggle began at once over the adoption of the two-thirds rule. Replying to arguments in its favor, Benjamin Butler of the New York delegation "became white with excitement and actually . . . jumped up three or four times from the floor two or three feet high," a delegate noted. The two-thirds rule was nonetheless adopted and Van Buren's fate was sealed. On the first ballot Van Buren had the majority that would have given him the nomination, but under the new rule he was thirty-one votes shy of the necessary two-thirds and it was at once clear that he had no chance of getting them. For a time, as ballot after ballot was taken, Cass moved up until he had passed Van Buren. At this point the Van Buren men, aware that Van Buren could not be nominated, turned their efforts to stopping "the *damned rotten corrupt venal* Cass cliques." When the convention adjourned in the wake of "a *real western fight* —rough and tumble," with the Ohio delegates standing on chairs and shouting to be heard, George Bancroft devised a strategy to turn back Cass's bid. His solution was to put James Polk of Tennessee forward as a compromise candidate. Gideon Pillow, a leader of the Tennessee delegation, fell in with the strategy and Bancroft worked on the Ohio and New York delegations. Although Silas Wright was Van Buren's choice if he could not win the nomination himself, Wright had declined to have his name placed in contention. Nonetheless, Bancroft and Pillow joined forces with Benjamin Butler to fashion a Wright-Polk ticket or vice versa and tried to persuade Wright to change his mind. George Bancroft "went and saw the New York delegation, and they . . . perceived how the case lay. . . . Van Buren implacably detested the thought of Cass as a candidate." So it must be Polk.

Jefferson Davis meanwhile had asked James Polk what his position was on annexation. Polk replied in a letter, promptly printed in the *Washington Globe,* stating that he wholeheartedly supported annexation and believed in asserting the claim of the United States to the Oregon country.

The Tennessee delegation responded, not surprisingly, to Bancroft's proposal of Polk "joyfully, and distributed among themselves that part of the work which I thought they could best do," Bancroft wrote. "We went on in this manner. . . ." The result was that on the ninth ballot Polk was nominated, with Silas Wright as his running mate.

Polk had been the leader of the Jacksonian anti-Bank forces and a loyal supporter of Jackson's policies. He had served a term as governor of Tennessee and been defeated in two subsequent elections. Now, with Jackson's behind-the-scenes support, he had emerged as his party's nominee for president.

Philip Hone wrote in his diary: "Polk and Wright! . . . Alas for poor Van Buren! He is the best of the bunch by great odds, and to be so repudiated by his political friends who have so long been accustomed to swearing by him! . . . And then the idea of running Silas Wright subordinate to Gen. Jackson's chief cook and bottle washer, Col. Polk!" Wright declined the vice-presidential nomination and George Dallas of Pennsylvania was chosen in his place.

The most notable plank in the party's platform was the statement that "our title to the whole of the Territory of Oregon is clear and unquestionable . . . and that the reoccupation of Oregon and the reannexation of Texas, at the earliest practicable period, are great American measures. . . ." To Hone, Polk's nomination was "the beginning of the end. I have long thought," he added, "that the great question for the American people to settle would soon be whether the North or the South was to rule. . . . The abominable Texas question, the crowning enormity of Tyler's administration, will hasten the solution of these problems. Henry Clay's election may avert for a time the danger of a rupture, but come it must, and the present generation will see it."

There was an immediate outcry that Polk was a virtual unknown. The *Macon* (Georgia) *Messenger* asked: "Polk! Who is he? What has he done to give him prominence over Buchanan, Van Buren, Johnson, Cass, Calhoun?" A friend of Buchanan's wrote: "Polk! Great God, what a nomination! I do think the Democratic Convention ought to be d—d to all eternity for this villainous business." The battle cry of the Democrats came to be "Polk, Dallas, Texas and Democracy," but despite the outpouring of popular feeling for annexation, the Senate rejected the final Treaty of Annexation by a vote of 35 to 16.

The result was increased agitation in the South for separation from the Union. A gathering of citizens in Lawrence County, Alabama, resolved that "the possession of Texas is infinitely more important to us of this section of the Union than a longer connection and friendship with the Northern States, and if we have to yield either it cannot and shall not be Texas." The sentiments were repeated in meetings and in newspaper editorials all over the South.

A vivid illustration of party rancor was given in the House of Representatives, which Philip Hone called "the Five points of America," a reference to the slum section of New York City. A member, defending Henry Clay, was insulted by "a Mr. Rathbone," blows were exchanged, and a spectator from the gallery discharged a pistol, the bullet lodging in the thigh of one of the "House police."

The Whigs received a sharp setback to their hopes when the Liberty party, made up of antislavery men, nominated James G. Birney of Michigan as their presidential candidate. The principal effect of this development was that it drove an anxious Clay into trying to straddle both the annexation and the slavery issue. "I have . . . no hesitation in saying," he wrote to a Southern paper, "that, far from having any personal objection to the annexation of Texas, I should be glad to see it, without dishonor, without war, with the common consent of the Union, and upon just and fair terms." As for the problem of slavery in Texas, Clay felt that it would be unwise to refuse "a permanent acquisition" simply because of a "temporary institution," slavery, which must become extinct "at some distant day . . . by the operation of the inevitable laws of population."

Whatever those words meant to Clay, they aroused substantial anxieties among his Northern supporters. Seward was convinced that it would cost the Whigs New York. Meanwhile, a cousin of Clay's— Cassius Clay, the courageous Southern abolitionist—wrote a friend that he was convinced that his kinsman's "feelings are with the cause." A strong antislavery Congressman expressed his feelings of many antislavery Whigs when he wrote that Clay was "as rotten as a stagnant fish pond, on the subject of Slavery & always has been. Confound him and all his compromises from first to last. . . ."

Now the unhappy Clay began firing off letters and telegrams in all directions, one contradicting the other, leaving the image of a man without principles or convictions. A Missouri newspaper carried the widely copied verse:

> He wires in and he wires out,
> And leaves the people still in doubt,
> Whether the snake that made the track,
> Was going South, or coming back.

Meanwhile Polk had the sense to keep quiet and stay at home while Birney, like Clay, weakened his cause by writing letters denouncing banks and tariffs. To confuse matters further, the Native Americans showed signs of making a major comeback, electing two Congressmen and nine state legislators in Pennsylvania and making impressive showings elsewhere, although they had no presidential candidate in the running. It became increasingly clear that New York was the crucial state and both parties made extraordinary efforts to swing the balance in their favor there. Forged letters were circulated and rumors of bribery were everywhere.

The campaign itself was distinguished by what was, if not a new low in political invective (that would, to be sure, have been hard to imagine), at least one of the lower levels achieved in the history of presidential elections. Democrats attacked Clay "for his fiendish and vindictive spirit, for his disregard of the most important moral obligations, for his blasphemy, for his gambling propensities, for his frequent and blood-thirsty attempts upon the lives of his fellow-men." References were also made to his "debaucheries and midnight revels in Washington . . . too shocking, too disgusting to appear in public print."

Despite the efforts of the Northern Democrats to play down the annexation issue, it soon became the crux of the presidential campaign. Robert Barnwell Rhett of South Carolina called for a convention of slave states to demand a special session of Congress "when the final issue shall be made up, and the alternative distinctly presented to the free states, either to admit Texas into the Union, or to proceed peaceably and calmly to arrange the terms of a dissolution of the Union."

From the moment of his nomination Polk was under great pressure to reconcile his disappointed rivals for the nomination by promising not to run for a second term, thus keeping alive in their bosoms the hope of attaining that prize the next time around and encouraging, if not ensuring, their support for his campaign and, if elected, for his administration.

The outcome of the election was a terrible blow to the Whigs. The state of New York went for Polk by a margin of five or six thousand votes out of half a million, thereby swinging the election to the Democrats. This result, in Hone's view, had been "brought about by foreign votes made for the purpose. Mr. Clay is again defeated; the people have rejected their best friend, and repudiated the principles by which alone national prosperity and individual happiness might have been secured. . . . Mr. Clay's talents, public service, and sound principles are too much for this perverse leveling generation. The beauty of his character forms too strong a contrast to their deformity." The only ray of light was to be found in the fact that "Glorious old Massachusets, the cradle of American liberty, the last refuge of good principles, faithful among the faithless" had given Clay and Frelinghuysen a majority of 25,000.

In New York state the abolitionists had cast 14,000 votes for Birney. "If these mischievous men had gone with us," Hone wrote, "Mr. Clay would have been President."

Polk won in Pennsylvania by a bare 6,000 votes out of more than 328,000 cast. Ohio was lost by 6,000 and Birney polled over 8,000 there. The final tally showed 170 electoral votes for Polk to 105 for Clay, but the difference in popular votes was 1,337,243 for Polk; 1,299,062 for Clay, and 62,300 for Birney. Out of nearly 2,700,000 votes, Polk had a majority of 36,000 over Clay, less than 1 percent.

The election of Polk seemed to Sidney George Fisher to signal the triumph of "ultra democracy," which must continue to dominate American politics "until drunk with power it plunges into the anarchy which will destroy it. Everything here & in Europe," Fisher added, "indicates that the old order of things is to be destroyed, that the period of change has arrived. The masses are everywhere rising and claiming to govern society, to alter not only its political constitution but its organization, its relations, its life. What new forms will grow out of the chaos is a question which concerns a distant future. We, our generation & our time, have unhappily to suffer all the troubles & grief of the process of change, a fiery ordeal, of which the present foretaste is bitter enough."

To the casual observer it might have appeared that the closeness of the balloting indicated that the sentiment of the country was almost evenly balanced between the two major parties and that the country in consequence enjoyed a remarkable degree of political stability. But appearances were deceiving. The voters of both parties were heterogeneous in the extreme and their allegiance to one party or the other uncertain. The Democratic victory was determined by immigrant workers, the large Northern cities, and the almost solid slaveholding South. The Whigs had a core of high-tariff merchants and manufacturers to which were added such unstable elements as Native Americans, antislavery men alarmed by the radical aura of the Liberty Party, and opponents of the annexation of Texas. In such circumstances party affiliations meant little, especially in the case of the Whigs, whose various factions had little in common beyond a shared hostility to the Democrats.

Polk's election was taken to seal the annexation of Texas. "Here is the great question of severance between the North and the South," Philip Hone wrote, "which is one day to shake this overgrown republic to its center. The Southern States desire the annexation of Texas to the Union, to strengthen their position geographically and politically by the prospective addition of four or five slaveholding States. We of the North and East say we have already more territory than we know what to do with, and more slavery within our borders than we choose to be answerable for before God and man."

13

The Mexican War

James Polk had been born in North Carolina in 1795 and grown up in Tennessee on his father's farm. As a student at the University of North Carolina he had excelled in the classics and in mathematics and had given the Latin oration for his graduating class. He had attracted the attention of Andrew Jackson, become his protégé, mastered the art of oratory so thoroughly that he was known as the "Napoleon of the Stump," and been elected to Congress in 1825 at the age of thirty. From then on dutiful service to the Jacksonian Democrats had helped to advance his career. As chairman of the powerful Ways and Means Committee in the House of Representatives, he had supported the removal of the deposits from the Bank of the United States. He had been elected governor of Tennessee, but twice been defeated for re-election to that office. Now he was president of the United States.

Although Polk had won the presidency by the narrowest of margins he took his triumph as a mandate for the annexation of Texas, and it was certainly true that annexation had been the principal issue. Before Polk could even take office five bills and joint resolutions were introduced into the Senate, among them one by Benton, and several in the House, the principal one there being introduced by Stephen Douglas of Illinois. At the end of January the House produced a resolution calling for the annexation of Texas by a vote of 120 to 98. The Senate modified the resolution and for a time it shuttled back and forth between the two chambers. While the debate went on in Congress, it raged throughout the country. On March 1 Tyler signed the resolution passed by the House a month earlier, and when Polk was inaugurated three days later, in a pouring rain, papers were already on their way to Texas with the resolution.

In his inaugural address Polk, like his predecessors, protested his lack of qualifications for the office which had come to him "without solicitation . . . by the free and voluntary suffrages of my country-men." He invoked the aid of "the Almighty Ruler of the Universe," and pledged himself to uphold the Constitution and maintain "a plain and frugal government" characterized by "the strictest economy in the expenditure of public money. . . ." All sections and all classes would be treated fairly and equitably. As for Texas, it had once been part of our country, "unwisely ceded away to a foreign power." The "assent of this government has been given to a reunion," and it only remained for the two countries to come to terms on the conditions of such a reunion "to consummate an object so important to both."

The next serious issue that faced Polk was what Philip Hone called "the miserable Oregon question." We shall have more to say about Oregon subsequently. It is sufficient to note here that American claims to the region rested primarily on Gray's voyage up the Columbia River in 1792 and the visit of Lewis and Clark in the winter of 1805–1806. The British claim rested on the activities of the Hudson Bay Company in the region and their well-established trading post at Fort Vancouver.

Beginning in 1835 a vanguard of missionaries and settlers had begun filtering into the area of the Walla Walla River. Soon they were petitioning sympathetic members of Congress to have the United States exercise jurisdiction over the region. Blown on assiduously by politicians eager to find a popular cause, the Oregon spark soon blazed into a flame that manifested itself in an astonishing belligerence—"54° 40' or Fight," angry patriots declared. As a candidate for president, Polk had made statements on Oregon which caused anger in England and the deepest apprehension among the Whigs, especially those engaged in commerce with Great Britain. They were convinced that Polk's intransigent attitude would bring about war with England, war over a remote and rain-soaked piece of real estate that most Whigs would have gladly seen sunk in the Pacific before it should become a bone of contention between the United States and Great Britain.

Efforts at settling the issue dated from John Quincy Adams's tenure as secretary of state. Adams had accused the British of laying claim to everything in sight, including the moon. Polk had apparently determined on a deliberately inflammatory plan of attack. "This will do famously for the valley of the Mississippi, where they have all to gain by war and nothing to lose," Hone wrote. "But we on the seaboard must fight all, pay all, and suffer all. John Bull will roar furiously when he gets this gentle fillip. . . . We have but one chance. Congress may demur to these ultra measures. . . ." On the contrary, Congress seemed as disposed to belligerence as the President. Lewis Cass, the Democratic senator from Michigan (Philip Hone called him "the raw-head and bloody-bones of the West"), offered a resolution to prepare for war with England. Hone saw collusion between the South and West. "They have gotten Texas, through the instrumentality of their accidentally picked-up President; and now they must have Oregon—the whole, they won't abate a rod—and California too, and Cuba and Mexico; and finally the whole North American continent; and moreover they must have war with Great Britain, with or without a cause."

In June, on the eve of the war with Mexico, Andrew Jackson died at his plantation, the Hermitage, in Tennessee; he was seventy-eight. The country gave itself over to one of those national paroxysms of grief so congenial to the democratic spirit. Everywhere there were solemn services and observances. An unforgiving Philip Hone wrote, "This iron-willed old man has done more mischief than any man alive. Indomitable in action, he carried the fury of the warrior into the administration of civil affairs, referring all things to personal motives; his iron heel trampled upon the necks of all who stood opposed to his political measures, or dared gainsay his dogmatic opinions . . . he did more to break down the republican principles of government than all the rulers who went before him; and yet no man ever enjoyed so large a share of that pernicious popular homage called popularity."

When the resolution of Congress calling for the annexation of the Republic of Texas was delivered to Anson Jones, its president, he was uncertain whether to call a convention especially for the purpose of considering annexation or to submit the issue to the Texas Congress. News of the resolution caused joyful celebration. Militia paraded, cannons were fired, and bonfires ignited throughout Texas.

England had been active in encouraging President Jones to conclude a treaty with Mexico that would end the state of cold war between the two republics by assuring Mexico that Texas would never annex itself to any other country. Conversely, the word was that if Texas agreed to annexation to the United States, Mexico, which had seven thousand troops on the Rio Grande, would immediately invade Texas.

The Texas Congress met, accepted the terms of annexation, and rejected the treaty with Mexico the British chargé d'affaires to Texas had been attempting to negotiate. The constitutional convention met on July 4, drafted a state constitution much like the one Texas functioned under as a republic, and approved the terms of the treaty.

Polk was alarmed at the rumors of an imminent invasion of Texas by the Mexican army because he wished to buy California from Mexico and a war would put an end to that scheme. He therefore sent a secret emissary to President José Herrera with word that while the United States government was committed to the annexation of Texas, it wished to consider all other matters in an amicable spirit.

But the Mexicans were in an intractable mood. The ministers of the government felt that the country had endured sufficient humiliation at the hands of the Americans. There was, indeed, very little notion in Mexico of the military potential of the United States. North Americans were looked down on as a nation of farmers, little better than peasants, a people without a military tradition and without experienced military leaders. The well-trained and well-dressed Mexican army, made up of professional soldiers and led by generals in magnificent uniforms, would easily put the undisciplined and poorly attired Yankees to flight. Once this confidence had begun to spread among the officers and men of the army and among the public officials and citizens, a warlike spirit was soon generated that made the discussion of peaceful measures impossible.

American relations with Mexico were complicated by the so-called Mexican claims. These claims by American citizens for seizure of American property were extensive and, as submitted by Powhatan Ellis in 1837, included numerous incidents of arbitrary seizure of American vessels trading with Mexican ports, the abuse and, in some instances, the murder of American citizens; the detainment of Americans in Mexican prisons without formal charges being filed against them; illegal confiscation of American property by Mexican customs officials; and similar complaints. The claims, amounting to some millions of dollars, had been referred to the mediation of Prussia in 1838, but even after a decision favorable to the American claimants the Mexican government (or, more accurately, the bewildering succession of Mexican governments) made no payment. The government in fact had no money to pay and the renewed American demands touched sensitive Mexican pride. It thus became a tactic of Polk to insist on a final settlement of the claims, threatening war if Mexico did not comply. The constant state of revolutionary and counterrevolutionary ferment in Mexico further complicated the situation. President Herrera had indicated to Polk that he was willing to negotiate the differences between the two countries in hopes of avoiding war. Polk in effect offered Herrera a bribe. Knowing the desperate financial circumstances of the government, Polk instructed the American emissary to propose that the United States take over settlement of the claims as part of the price to be paid Mexico for the province of California. There would be an initial half million made available to Herrera, with the hope that he might thereby be able to stabilize his own precarious political situation.

Before Polk's special commissioner, John Slidell, could arrive in Mexico, Herrera had been deposed and a new government, headed by Mariano Paredes y Arrillaga, established. Paredes belonged to a faction eager for war with the United States. He therefore refused even to receive Slidell. Polk next turned to that battered but apparently indestructible political general Santa Anna, in exile in Cuba. Antonio Lopez de Santa Anna, a royalist general in the era of Spanish domination, had joined Iturbide in the war for independence, then led a revolution against Iturbide two years later. He had helped Anastasio Bustamante to power and then turned against him. Elected president for a term, he had established a right-wing dictatorship, been the villain of the Alamo in the Texas War of Independence, and been captured by Sam Houston's forces at San Jacinto in 1836. Losing a leg in the attempt to block the French landing at Veracruz had made him a hero again and won him another presidential term, which had been characterized by corruption and abuse of power. It was to this discredited but resilient politician-general, licking his wounds in Cuba and scheming to regain power, that Polk turned to promote his own plans for buying California. He dispatched Alexander Slidell Mackenzie, a naval officer, to negotiate with Santa Anna. It was ironic that the "Butcher of the Alamo" should now be appealed to to pull American chestnuts out of the fire. An agent of Santa Anna assured Polk that the general must soon return to Mexico to head a new government. He supported the Rio Grande as the Texas-Mexico border and a line from the Colorado River to the Bay of San Francisco as the northern boundary of Mexico. All the land beyond these boundaries could be purchased by the United States for thirty million dollars. Polk replied that Santa Anna must also promise to pay the American claims. Santa Anna's response was that no Mexican politician could make such a settlement and remain in office. He proposed to Polk that an American fleet sail into the harbor at Veracruz and demand payment under threat of war. Santa Anna would meantime return to Mexico, assume power, and—if provided with half a million dollars by the United States—would make a treaty that would include provisions for payment of the claims.

To cover his hand Polk sent word to Paredes that the United States would give his government financial assistance in return for a settlement of the boundary issue. When Paredes refused to consider such an arrangement, Polk asked his Cabinet for its support in sending a message to Congress recommending war. Only James Buchanan, his secretary of state, and Bancroft objected. In Polk's words, "Mr. Bancroft dissented but said if any act of hostility should be committed by the Mexican forces he was then in favor of immediate war." Buchanan was of somewhat the same mind. Such a message would undoubtedly have caused a storm of protest in many areas of the country, certainly in the North, but Polk was taken off the hook by word from Zachary Taylor that Texas had been "invaded" by a Mexican army which had attacked him and thereby created a de facto war.

When Texas voted to accept annexation, Polk had ordered Taylor, with fifteen hundred regulars, to cross the Nueces River and establish a base of operations near the Rio Grande with the ostensible mission of protecting Texas against the invasion that Mexico had warned would follow annexation. Since the area between the Nueces and the Rio Grande was in dispute, the gesture was plainly a provocative one, which gave force to the Whig charge that Polk intended to invite a war with Mexico as a pretense for seizing New Mexico and California. The Mexican government, in any event, seemed determined to play directly into Polk's hands. Taylor, reinforced by seven infantry companies and two companies of artillery, began to build Fort Texas across the Rio Grande from the Mexican town of Matamoros. A few weeks later the Mexican general Pedro de Ampudia, notorious for his cruelty, arrived in Matamoros with a large force and ordered Taylor to withdraw. When the American general refused, General Mariano Arista, one of Mexico's ablest officers, who had been sent to supersede Ampudia in command, crossed the river, engaged a party of sixty-three American dragoons, and killed or captured most of them. Word of this reached Polk early in May. With the aid of George Bancroft, Polk set about preparing his message to Congress stating the reasons for declaring that a state of war existed between the United States and Mexico. When Polk read a draft of his message to Senator Benton, the Missouri senator expressed his support for a proposal to appropriate ten million dollars and raise an army of 50,000 men, but he demurred at the idea of a war of aggression, which would be involved in any invasion of Mexican territory. Polk based his war message in part on "the long-continued and unredressed wrongs and injuries committed by the Mexican Government on citizens of the United States in their persons and property. . . ." Certainly much was ingenuous in the statement that the government had been guided by "the strong desire to establish peace with Mexico on liberal and honorable terms." Now, "after reiterated menaces, Mexico has passed the boundary of the United States, has invaded our territory and shed American blood upon the American soil. She has proclaimed that hostilities have commenced, and that the two nations are now at war."

Presenting his message to his Cabinet, Polk reiterated his goals of acquiring "California, New Mexico, and perhaps some others of the Northern Provinces of Mexico whenever peace was made. . . . In these views the Cabinet concurred," Polk noted.

Congress, with little debate, voted the President the funds he had requested and authority to raise an army of 50,000 men, but many citizens around the country questioned the necessity for the war, Polk's motives, and above all, his apparent intention of invading Mexican soil. Whigs and abolitionists were in general outraged, Democrats and proslavery forces exultant.

Sidney George Fisher shared the view of Philip Hone and George Templeton Strong that the Mexican War was "produced by an act of unjustifiable aggression on our part." The consequence was that "the sympathies, wishes and moral sense of the civilized world will be against us. . . . The cry will be raised by the demogogues for the *conquest* of Mexico."

Fate could hardly have found more oddly matched adversaries than Mexico and the United States. The United States was a self-proclaimed democracy that tolerated slavery and was based on conspicuous residues of Calvinistic Protestantism in which control, progress, individualism, science, and reason were dominant and often determining ideas. The Mexican Republic was, in contrast, almost unimaginably exotic. Republican ideals and principles of the European enlightenment were mixed with feudal Catholicism, much as Spanish blood was mixed with Indian. A rich, intricate life of ceremonial and festival offered distraction if not relief for peasant lives of grinding poverty. While generals and politicians fought for the control of power and usually used it to exploit the powerless, an enlightened portion of the beleaguered middle class struggled against corruption and the arbitrary rule of a succession of generals. Jacob Oswandel, a young Pennsylvania volunteer in the war, identified five different Mexican classes—"the real white foreigners, who are mostly very wealthy; second . . . a class of whites . . . the living descendants of the Spaniards . . . sometimes called Creoles; third . . . those who call themselves white and are partly mixed; fourth . . . the Indians and *leperos,* who sometimes live in huts, villages, and outskirts of all towns in Mexico; fifth . . . the *Mestizos,* or mixed Indian, who look like some of our mixed negroes in the South . . . but of all the classes of men . . . the *leperos* are the most miserable set of human beings you ever heard tell of." The *leperos* Oswandel believed to be the descendants of the Comanche Indians. Docile, lazy, and indifferent during the day, the *lepero* became a fearful raider at night. Darkness was his element, the silent assassination of unwary soldiers his special skill. Oswandel was an uneducated soldier and modern anthropologists may quarrel with his "class analysis," but he showed remarkably acute powers of observation and, however correctible in detail, his account suggests the heterogeneous character of the Mexican population. What we can say with some certainty is that its exotic mixture of feudal Catholicism, revolutionary principles, and native Indian subculture left it poorly prepared to enter a conflict with a people already far advanced into the new age.

Matters were further complicated on the Mexican side by the fact that the Republic was a republic in name only. Power was largely in the hands of a coterie of generals, usually at each other's throats. These were Spanish gentlemen, aristocrats, hidalgos who fought for the presidential chair as ferociously as medieval princes for a crown and had little sympathy with or concern for "democracy" or the depressed classes. Many of them were eager to have an opportunity to take on the cowardly Norteamericanos, farmers and shopkeepers, without a military tradition and with no professional army to speak of. The generals anticipated a string of brilliant victories through which they might consolidate their power, or reassert it if out of power, victories that would once and for' all put an end to the arrogant claims and expansionist tendencies of the United States.

Secretary of War William Marcy issued a call for 17,000 volunteers from states nearest the scene of the war and George Bancroft sent a message to the United States naval commander in Mexican waters to permit Santa Anna to enter Mexico in the hope that he would take power and negotiate a peaceful settlement. Santa Anna in turn sent a note urging that Taylor engage Paredes and defeat him in order to hasten his overthrow and pave the way for Santa Anna's return to power.

The two senior generals with whom Polk must wage his war were rather like Tweedledee and Tweedledum. It required considerable imagination to see in the large, stout, self-important, sixty-year-old Winfield Scott any trace of the handsome young officer who had led his troops so brilliantly in the battles of Chippewa and Lundy's Lane in the last months of the War of 1812. Zachary Taylor, two years older than Scott, had fought well in the defense of Fort Harrison and later against the Seminole in Florida and against Black Hawk. In addition to being similarly shaped, they had corresponding nicknames; Scott was known as Old Fuss and Feathers and Taylor as Old Rough and Ready.

Taylor, awaiting reinforcements, left his unfinished fort to block what he gathered was an attack by a Mexican army designed to cut him off from his base of supplies. In his absence General Arista crossed the Del Norte and surrounded the little fort, bombarding it for six days without inducing its commander, Major Harvey Brown, an artillery officer, to surrender. Taylor, having picked up recruits from New Orleans, made his way back and encountered Arista's army at Palo Alto. On May 8, Arista's cavalry, the pride of the army, attacked Taylor's right rear, while the infantry assaulted the left flank. Both attacks were repulsed by heavy artillery and musket fire. Arista withdrew his demoralized forces to Resaca de la Palma and the next day Taylor attacked him there, driving in his front lines and forcing him across the river. Taylor's forces numbered 2,288 to some 6,000 under Arista. The superiority of the badly outnumbered Americans at Palo Alto and Resaca de la Palma reflected, more than anything else, the excellent organization of the Americans, their ability to carry out orders with relative fidelity, and the capacity of the private soldiers to exercise a degree of initiative. Most important was the fact that the American artillery, commanded by West Point–trained officers, fired with deadly effect; their canister was devastating against the massed cavalry and infantry of the Mexican forces. Taylor's casualties at Resaca de la Palma were four killed and 34 wounded, while the Mexican casualties numbered some 800. The Mexican temperament, addicted to brilliant military displays, to gallant cavalry charges and daring acts of individual heroism, was ill-suited to a modern war of massed firepower and maneuver where organization and a degree of discipline rather than dashing feats of arms counted most.

Taylor, having returned to Fort Texas, renamed Fort Brown in honor of its commander, pushed over the Del Norte, occupied Matamoros, and awaited orders from Polk. When news arrived of Taylor's victories, Polk decided to try once more to negotiate a peace treaty with Paredes. Meanwhile the President was besieged with numerous requests for commissions. "The pressure for appointments in the new regiment of riflemen is beyond anything of the kind which I have witnessed since I have been President," Polk wrote. In addition Polk had to contend with a mutinous Winfield Scott, indignant because Polk had ordered him to take the field while he thought his duties as commander-in-chief required that he remain, at least for a time, in Washington to organize and equip the army. Polk was shown a letter from Scott to a friend which, in the President's view, "proved to me that General Scott was not only hostile but recklessly vindictive in his feelings towards my administration. . . . His bitter hostility towards the administration is such that I could not trust him. . . ." Scott had declared that "I do not desire to place myself in the most perilous of all positions—*a fire upon my rear from Washington, and the fire in front from the Mexicans.*"

Polk, well aware of the vogue for general-presidents started with Jackson and continued with Harrison, had naturally no interest in advancing Scott's presidential ambitions. When Scott, doubtless alarmed by the victories of his rival Taylor, expressed himself ready to proceed to Mexico to take command of the American forces, Polk ordered him to remain in Washington and announced the promotion of Taylor to major general by brevet "for his gallant victories over the Mexican forces on the Del Norte. . . ."

Before Polk's emissary could reach Paredes with new peace feelers, Paredes' government was overthrown and Santa Anna was made president for the duration of the war. Polk assumed that the new president would fulfill his pledge to bring the war to an end, but the war spirit was now so inflamed in Mexico that it is doubtful that Santa Anna could have undertaken peace negotiations even had he wished to; however he clearly had other fish to fry. Polk proceeded, innocently enough, to seek authorization from Congress for Santa Anna's agreed-upon stipend and such other money as might be thought of as a down payment on California and New Mexico. His supporters in Congress convinced him that he must make his intentions public, but as soon as a bill was introduced in Congress for the purpose of acquiring land from Mexico, David Wilmot, a Pennsylvania Democrat, introduced his famous proviso, which stated that slavery should be barred from any territory acquired from Mexico. The fat was immediately in the fire. Southerners were up in arms. Rather than attempt to deal with the issue, Congress abruptly adjourned and left the matter hanging.

This was the background against which Polk debated the proper strategy with the members of his Cabinet. Marcy sought Taylor's advice, noting: "A peace must be conquered in the shortest space of time practicable." Taylor, unresponsive at first, advised against a campaign against Mexico City from the Rio Grande region. Better to move from Veracruz or Tampico. Scott meanwhile had become an advocate himself of an attack on the port town of Veracruz followed by an investment of Mexico City. Supported primarily by Marcy, he prevailed on Polk to authorize the seizure of Veracruz.

While the debate over strategy was going on, Taylor added to his laurels by a successful attack on Monterrey, a well-fortified town protected by six strong redoubts; Ampudia had replaced Arista in command there. Taylor's strategy was to cut off the supply road from Saltillo while attacking the city from three directions. Although the American attack was poorly coordinated, the main force captured a redoubt—due primarily to the resourceful tactics of Jefferson Davis, who had fought so well under Taylor in the Black Hawk War. Davis, Taylor's son-in-law, was given the critical assignment of driving into the city, where every adobe house was a small fortress. His technique for city fighting, one later used by American troops fighting in Europe in World War II, was to break through the interior walls of the houses, driving the defenders back or forcing them to surrender. In this manner Davis's men fought their way to within a few blocks of the city plaza. Brigadier General William Worth had meantime pushed his way into the center of the town from the north. Elsewhere the Americans were repulsed with heavy losses, but Ampudia, unnerved by Worth's success, withdrew into a central citadel where he came under the massed fire of American artillery and after several days sued for peace.

Taylor, perhaps uneasy over his own lines of supply, accepted surrender terms that allowed the Mexicans to retain a portion of their arms and provided for an eight-week armistice. Taylor's excuse for such generous terms was that the enemy was still very well fortified while his own troops were poorly equipped, undisciplined, and weary from marching and fighting. Although he did not say so, he believed that a very bloody and difficult battle lay ahead of him, and he was surprised by and grateful for Ampudia's offer to surrender. Taylor's terms to Ampudia brought a stern rebuke from Polk, and the general was directed "to terminate the armistice . . . and to prosecute the war with energy and vigor." When he received these orders Taylor advanced down the Saltillo road to the town of that name; there dispatches overtook him, directing him to take up defensive positions at Monterrey and send the greater part of his more experienced troops to Veracruz to join an army, to be commanded by General Scott, for an advance on Mexico City. Taylor was furious at being stripped of fighting men (Polk insisted that he had left it to Taylor's discretion in the matter) and he joined Scott as a writer of insolent letters to his commander-in-chief, prompting Polk to write, "He [Taylor] is evidently a weak man and has been made giddy with the idea of the Presidency. He is most ungrateful, for I have promoted him, as I now think, beyond his deserts and without reference to his politics. I am now satisfied that he is a narrow-minded, bigoted partisan, without resources and wholly unqualified for the command he holds. . . . Taylor is no doubt brave and will fight, but he is not fit for a higher command than that of a regiment."

Polk meanwhile dispatched Stephen Kearny with the "army of the West," reinforced with a regiment of Mormons picked up west of Nauvoo, to California by way of Sante Fe, on the grounds that "it would . . . be very important that the United States should hold military possession of California at the time peace was made. . . ." The real question was what to do with Taylor's army at Matamoros. Polk felt considerable pressure of time. He had promised a quick and relatively inexpensive war (one of the conflicts between the President and his senior commander was that Scott felt obliged to plan for a protracted war). The longer the war dragged on, the more bitterly divided the country must become and the louder the agitation for peace. Taylor's victories had given an enormous boost to American pride and helped muffle the protests against the war, but a succession of relatively easy (though nonetheless glorious) victories was clearly needed to sustain public support for the war. At the same time an aggressive advance into the interior of Mexico would give fresh ammunition to those numerous enemies of the war who were already denouncing it as an unprincipled land grab and a ruthless attack upon a weak and innocent neighbor. With the introduction of the Wilmot Proviso, many Northerners who had feared the extension of slavery, and even more the augmented power of the slave states, seemed disposed to overcome their scruples about a war of aggression against a weak neighbor and discover reasons why the war was justified after all. But the South was beside itself at the prospect of being shut out of such a grand inheritance.

The President was on the horns of a classic dilemma. He disliked and distrusted Scott only slightly less than he disliked and distrusted Taylor. And yet they were his generals, the only instruments he had at hand to try to realize his extravagant vision of adding another quarter of the continent to the United States. He needed a quick victory over Mexico lest public opposition to the war mount to the point where the Democrats were replaced by the Whigs and the peace negotiated on terms far less favorable to the United States than those that Polk envisioned. But successful campaigns by Taylor and Scott must make them heroes and greatly augment their status as potential rivals for the presidency. Small wonder that Polk procrastinated, searching desperately for a way out. The solution he settled on did little credit to his good sense. He decided that he would try to wrest from Congress a new rank of lieutenant general and bestow it on the by-no-means-reluctant Thomas Benton, whose military experience did not extend far beyond brawling with Andrew Jackson, making him the supreme commander over Scott and Taylor. In this way he might divert attention from his contentious generals and push forward a proper Democratic general-hero-politician; hopefully, since Americans seemed so attracted to generals, Benton would be his successor as president. The Whigs seemed to have all the generals; the Democrats desperately needed one or two.

Democrats in Congress warned Polk that there was no chance that the body would approve Benton's receiving such a commission, but Polk persisted and Congress as firmly resisted the notion. The whole situation suggested the plot for a musical comedy rather more than a serious military venture by "a great and generous nation."

While Scott was completing the preparations for the attack on Veracruz, Santa Anna intercepted dispatches that revealed the American strategy—that Taylor had been required to detach a large part of his force for the support of Scott, that Scott was headed for Veracruz, and that Taylor's diminished army had been instructed simply to defend Monterrey. Santa Anna at once saw an opportunity to destroy Taylor's army. With a force of 20,000 men, he started up the San Luis Potosí road for Monterrey. Taylor, in defiance of his orders, left the town with its excellent system of defenses, and advanced to Saltillo with some 5,000 men and then down the San Luis Potosí road as far as Agua Nueva, where he encountered the advance elements of Santa Anna's army and withdrew to strong defensive positions in front of the hacienda Buena Vista. There, on the morning of Washington's birthday, 1847, Santa Anna confronted him and sent a message which read "You are surrounded by twenty thousand men, and cannot avoid being cut to pieces. I wish to save you this disaster, and summon you to surrender at discretion and give you an hour to make up your mind." Here was Polk's Mexican general, whom the President had assisted to return to power with assurances of his cooperation, about—it seemed —to annihilate the much smaller American force barring the way.

The outcome of the battle had probably been decided when Taylor laid out his positions. The terrain was all in favor of the defense. Deep arroyos, or gullies, ran from southeast to northwest diagonally across the battle front. High ground offered substantial protection for the American flanks. Artillery was placed to command the draws down which the Mexicans must advance.

The Mexican plan was to attack in three columns, a scheme that largely nullified their vastly superior numbers. The column under General Villamil was ordered to capture an artillery battery covering Taylor's right. A second column was to advance along a plateau toward the center of the American lines, and a resurrected Ampudia was to attack Taylor's rear. General Miñon was sent with several thousand men to cut off Taylor's line of retreat south of Saltillo. Santa Anna, it turned out, had divided his force into too many divisions for any firm control. Ampudia's attack was met with heavy enfilading shrapnel fire that drove his men back in disorder. The marching order of Villamil's column was broken up by the difficulties of the terrain over which they were forced to attack, and they came under heavy artillery fire from a battery at a strong point called La Angostura. The third column, under generals Lombardini and Pacheco, had better success. The Second Illinois Infantry assigned to protect Lieutenant O'Brien's battery broke and fled and one of O'Brien's guns was captured. The Second Indiana Infantry also decamped along with Arkansas and

Kentucky volunteers. Taylor's flank was about to be turned and the American positions overrun when Charles May's cavalry and Jefferson Davis's Mississippi Volunteers came down to restore the line. As a new attack formed the superior numbers of the Mexican army were felt acutely. Mexican soldiers were swarming everywhere. At this point the fire of the artillery batteries, most of them commanded by West Pointers, repulsed the Mexicans. At the end of the first day of fighting the outcome was still far from certain. In the words of Major William Wallace Smith Bliss, Taylor's chief of staff, the majority of the American force was "entirely *demoralised*. The commander of the Illinois volunteers had been killed, along with Henry Clay, the son of the Senator, and Colonel William McKee, commander of the Second Kentucky Volunteers, Archibald Yell, former governor of Tennessee, member of Congress and colonel of the First Arkansas Volunteer Cavalry. . . ." Jefferson Davis, "the best volunteer field officer in the army," according to Bliss, was wounded and delirious, "leaving the Mississippians helpless." At nightfall, with the battle halted, the Indiana regiment had fled. Taylor's officers urged him to go to the rear and attempt to rally the Americans who had fled. The general tried, with no success. The volunteers could not be persuaded to return to the battlefield. "The difficulty," as Bliss told it to Dana, "was want of discipline . . . circumstances had prevented them from being drilled much, & they had no confidence in each other, or in the *skill* of their Colonel. The same was the case with the Arkansas reg. They were good men but Yell had not only disparaged but ostentatiously neglected & derided discipline, & this caused his death & their disgrace."

When the fighting resumed the next day, the American cause seemed desperate. Bliss told Richard Henry Dana that it was only the resolution of Captain Braxton Bragg, in command of the artillery, in resisting the Mexican charge that saved the day. The supporting infantry regiments broke and fled, leaving his guns exposed, and when Bragg reported the fact to Taylor the latter declared, " 'Never mind, I'll take the responsibility. You must go into battery where you are.' Bragg went forward, came into battery, & the Mexicans came on in thousands. He had only three guns. . . . But he repulsed them with dreadful loss, & this saved the day." Equally important was the work of Captain John McCrae's Washington battery, which also played a crucial role in repulsing the Mexicans. Thomas West Sherman, West Point '36, Braxton Bragg, '37, George Henry Thomas, '40, all directed the fire of their guns with skill and crushing effect. The Mexicans, attacking with great courage and all the pageantry of traditional warfare, with bands, pennants, flags, and splendidly mounted cavalry armed with lances and swords, were cut down like grain. A final foray by a Mexican regiment against O'Brien's battery was repulsed, the Mexicans withdrew, and the Battle of Buena Vista was over.

A number of factors combined to make Buena Vista the most important single engagement of the war. First there were the purely military considerations—the great disparity in numbers, the heavy casualties on both sides (673 Americans were killed or wounded and more than twice that number of Mexicans), the closeness of the battle, the numerous individual acts of heroism, the crucial role of the artillery, and the brilliant performance of the West Point–trained officers. West Point had been under attack by the Democrats as a stronghold of Federalist and Whig policies, an elitist institution that catered to the sons of the upper class, an expensive luxury in a peace-loving society. The Mexican War—and, above all, the Battle of Buena Vista—was its vindication. No more talk was heard of abolishing it. The United States army was to have, for some years to come, a small but highly professional officers corps.

More important perhaps than the military aspects of the battle were the political. Taylor was known to be a "Whig general." He had been outspoken in his attacks on Polk's administration. It was the conviction of the Whigs that Polk, jealous of his earlier successes, had tried to clip Taylor's wings by detaching a major portion of his army to fight with Scott and assigning him an essentially passive role in an increasingly unimportant theater of operations—northern Mexico. Taylor had plainly outmaneuvered his commander-in-chief and won a splendid victory. The fact that he had done so in disobedience of orders, at great risk to his army, at high cost in American lives in a battle clearly not worth the consequences that must have ensued from an American defeat was lost sight of in national pride at the victory, a victory that (since it promised to provide the Whigs with a presidential candidate) was sweetest to those who were most strongly against the war.

Beyond all this, the dramatic effect of the battle was heightened by the fact that the initial reports were that Taylor had suffered a shattering defeat, that his army had been scattered and he himself wounded and captured. Close on the heels of this widely reported rumor came the true story and American enthusiasm knew no bounds. Despite Philip Hone's outrage at the war, he joined with his countrymen of whatever political coloring to celebrate the news of the American victory at Buena Vista. "The Americans, as usual," Hone wrote, "fought with the utmost bravery, and the contest was well-sustained by the enemy. The carnage was tremendous; four thousand Mexicans were killed and wounded by our accounts; but it is painful to relate that the blood of seven hundred to a thousand Americans was offered up to the Moloch of war and unjust aggressive hostility. . . ."

The consequence of Taylor's victory at Buena Vista was that the Whig press immediately began to puff him as their party's candidate for the presidency. Well before the war ended his name had come to be the most frequently mentioned as the Whig nominee. Despite all of Clay's years of service to the party, its managers were quite ready to toss him aside in favor of an untidy, wholly inexperienced old general, so keen was its appetite for victory.

Polk's reaction when he heard the news of Buena Vista was typical, it may be assumed, of most Democrats: pride and pleasure in the victory but indignation at Taylor's defiance of orders and at the long list of casualties, among them sons, brothers, and friends of many highly placed Americans. "Had General Taylor obeyed his orders, and occupied Monterrey and the passes beyond it," Polk wrote in his diary, "the severe loss of our army, including many valuable officers, would have been avoided. It was great rashness to take the position he did in advance of Saltillo. Having done so, he is indebted not to his own good generalship, but to the indomitable and intrepid bravery of the officers and men under his command for his success. General Taylor is a hard fighter but has none of the other qualities of a great general. From the beginning of the existing war with Mexico he has been constantly blundering into difficulties, but he has fought his way out of them but with very severe loss."

Polk's hopes of placing Benton in command of the Army of the South were ultimately frustrated by the refusal of Congress to create the rank of lieutenant general for him and Benton's angry rejection of a major generalcy. In spite of Taylor's victories—or in some instances because of them (the argument being that since Mexico had been sufficiently chastised and Texas protected against invasion, there remained no excuse for continuing the war)—criticism mounted. The Whig press was unsparing in its criticism of Polk's policies, and Whig politicians vied with each other in denouncing the war imposed on a peaceful country by slaveowning, imperialistic Democrats who, having squirmed into office by the most corrupt means and by the narrowest of margins, were bent on bankrupting the country by an expensive and unjust war, a war viewed with dismay by all lovers of peace and friends of humanity.

In Congress every argument was put forward a hundred times and a hundred times rebutted. Abraham Lincoln, Congressman from Illinois, subjected the government's case to a withering analysis. Lincoln challenged the President to prove that the blood of Americans had been shed, as Polk had claimed, on American soil—Polk's justification for declaring war on Mexico. "But if he *can* not, or *will* not do this," Lincoln continued, "—if on any pretence, or no pretence, he shall refuse or omit it then I shall be fully convinced, of what I more than suspect already, that he is deeply conscious of being in the wrong—that he feels the blood of this war, like the blood of Abel, is crying to Heaven against him. . . . As I have said before, he knows not where he is. He is a bewildered, confounded, and miserably perplexed man."

On Monday, February 21, in the midst of the debate on the war, John Quincy Adams attempted to rise to speak but fainted and fell back into the arms of Moses Grinnell, who heard him say "This is the last of earth; I am content." Adams died in his eightieth year without regaining consciousness. When Philip Hone heard, via the new Morse telegraph, of Adams's death, he wrote in his diary: "He died, as he must have wished to die breathing his last in the capitol . . . employed in the service of the people. . . ." Hone believed Adams to be "in many respects the most wonderful man of the age; certainly the greatest in the United States,—perfect in knowledge, but deficient in practical results. . . . He 'talked like a book' on all subjects. Equal to the highest, the planetary system was not above his grasp. Familiar with the lowest, he could explain the mysteries of a mousetrap. . . . I listened once, with Mr. Webster, at Mr. Adams' breakfast-table in Washington, to a disquisition on the subject of *dancing girls;* from those who danced before the ark and the daughter of Jairus . . . through the fascinating exhibition of the odalisques of the harem down to the present times of Fanny Ellssler and Taglioni." Hone's words constitute the most fitting eulogy to Adams of all the thousands of words pronounced on his demise. His body was brought from Philadelphia to New York on March 8 and there met by a military escort. "The streets on the line of march," Philip Hone wrote, "were filled to the edge of the sidewalks with the greatest body of men and women ever assembled in the city." From New York the coffin was carried on to Quincy, where Adams was buried in a simple ceremony by the side of his father and mother. Charles Francis Adams noted gloomily in his diary that his father's death left him completely alone in the world.

Polk acerbated the feelings of the critics of the Mexican War by charging them, in his second annual message to Congress, with giving "aid and comfort" to the enemy by their attacks, thereby prolonging the war and contributing to the loss of American lives. "The war," Polk declared, "has been represented as unjust and unnecessary, and as one of aggression on our part against a weak and injured enemy. . . . A more effectual means could not have been devised to encourage the enemy and protract the war than to advocate and adhere to their cause, and thus give aid and comfort."

Congress was thereupon given over largely to a debate on the morality of the war with charges and countercharges. At every point the issue of slavery obtruded itself. Joshua Giddings of Ohio, a warrior in every good cause, called for a clear statement of the purposes of the continuing conflict. News of the seizure of Santa Fe by Kearny and the announcement that it would henceforth be considered American territory was also denounced by the Whigs in Congress.

The most dramatic voice raised against the war was that of the old Jeffersonian democrat Albert Gallatin, now in his eighty-eighth year. He spoke with the authority of a founder, the friend and confidant of Jefferson and Madison. "Your mission," he told his countrymen, "was, to be a model for all governments and for all other less favored nations; to adhere to the most elevated principles of political morality; to apply all your faculties to the gradual improvement of your own institutions and social state; and by your example to exert a moral influence most beneficial to mankind at large. Instead of this, an appeal has been made to your worst passions; to cupidity, to the thirst for unjust aggrandisement by brutal force; to the love of military fame and false glory. . . . The attempt has been made to make you abandon the lofty position which your fathers occupied, to substitute for it the political morality and heathen patriotism of the heroes and statesmen of antiquity."

In all the clamor against the war the most notable single act was Henry David Thoreau's refusal to pay his taxes, his subsequent arrest and imprisonment, and his writing of "Civil Disobedience," the great tract on philosophical anarchy which went Tom Paine and Thomas Jefferson one better by stating "That government is best which governs not at all." The best-conceived governments were liable to abuse,

Thoreau argued. "Witness the present Mexican war, the work of comparatively few individuals using the government as their tool; for, at the outset, the people would not have consented to this measure." The role of the government, Thoreau argued, was to ensure justice and for the rest to get out of the way. "It does not keep the country free. *It* does not settle the West. *It* does not educate. The character inherent in the American people has done all that has been accomplished; and it would have done somewhat more, if the government had not sometimes got in the way. For government is an expedient by which men would fain succeed in letting one another alone. . . ."

Since Thoreau encountered the state only once a year in the person of the tax collector, it was to him that he must express his unwillingness to support an unjust government waging an unjust war. There was also the matter of the Fugitive Slave Law, which placed men who should be free in prison, both slaves and their abettors. "Under a government which imprisons unjustly," Thoreau wrote, "the true place for a just man is also in prison. . . . It is there that the fugitive slave, the Mexican prisoner on parole, and the Indian come to plead the wrongs of his race should find them."

Thoreau must respond to the promptings of his own conscience. It was a higher measure than the authority of the state or its system of coercive laws. "Is a democracy, such as we know it, the last improvement possible in government? Is it not possible to take a step further towards recognizing and organizing the rights of man? There will never be a free and enlightened State until the State comes to recognize the individual as a higher and independent power from which all its own property and authority are derived and treats him accordingly. . . . A State which bore this kind of fruit, and suffered it to drop off as fast as it ripened, would prepare the way for a still more perfect and glorious State, which also I have imagined but not yet anywhere seen."

Thoreau's famous essay did not shorten the Mexican War or mitigate its effects, but it did constitute the greatest modern statement of the supremacy of the conscience of the individual. It became the text for all who opposed the unjust exactions of any state: the United States in Mexico, in the Philippines, in Vietnam; the British in India, the Belgians in Africa. Its intellectual lineage ran from John Winthrop's *Model of Christian Charity,* written aboard the *Arabella* on the way to Massachusetts Bay in 1629. It was the perfect expression of the secularized Puritan conscience. There is a higher law, Thoreau said, and I have discerned it and placed myself in obedience to it. The state is powerless in the face of my intransigence. All it can do is place me in prison; it cannot coerce my conscience and thus it must give way at last to the power of the single conscience. We may call Thoreau's scandalous doctrine "romantic individualism" or "philosophical anarchism" or whatever other name pleases us, but it remains the rock on which the mightiest ships of state must break themselves if unjustly captained. Thoreau also revealed that persistent American millennial dream in his closing evocation of "a still more perfect and glorious State" that will be ushered in when democracy comes in time to regard the rights of each of its citizens as inviolable.

Like the other transcendentalists and reformers, Ralph Waldo Emerson hated the Mexican War and profoundly regretted the disposition of New England generally to accommodate itself to it and even to take pleasure in the victories of United States arms. "Mr. Webster told them how much the war cost," Emerson noted in his journal, "that was his protest, but voted the war, and sends his son to it. They calculated rightly on Mr. Webster. My friend Mr. Thoreau has gone to jail rather than pay his tax. On him they could not calculate. The Abolitionists denounce the war and give much time to it, but they pay the tax."

William Jay, son of John Jay, first chief justice of the United States and one of the authors of the *Federalist Papers,* spoke for the reformers and, more especially, the pacificists in his book *A Review of the Causes and Consequences of the Mexican War,* published at the war's end. In his introduction, Jay set the tone of his work: "The writer is a believer in the Divine authority of the Scriptures—he acknowledges no standard of right and wrong but the Will of God, and denies the expediency of any act which is forbidden by laws dictated by Infinite Wisdom and Goodness."

After a review of the events leading up to the war, characterized by a very evident hostility toward Texans—"booted loafers"—Jay went into the moral aspects of the war and the brutalizing effects of war in general. By carrying the war to the heart of the Republic of Mexico, the United States had "inflicted a cureless wound upon the self-respect of Mexico. . . . We have made an implacable enemy where we needed a friend. And so far as we have unjustly, by might and not by right, acquired . . . all of New Mexico and Upper California, we must sooner or later suffer the most condign punishment by the gigantic wrong. As surely as there is a God in heaven . . . the day cannot be far remote, when we shall be overtaken by the penalty of the law we have broken. Yes, our punishment has already begun. . . . Every interest of our beloved country, social, pecuniary, political, domestic, and moral has felt the shock of this war. . . . It is sufficiently evident to all, that this war has given our countrymen a taste for national aggrandizement, that will ask for more and more."

To Jay it seemed painfully evident that by the war America had turned away "from this sublime mission of realizing the kingdom of Christ on earth" and bowed down "to the base uses of Mammon and of Mars. . . . The tree of civilization withers and dies, when watered with human blood." Instead of sympathetic assistance to a neighbor struggling to build democratic institutions, we had taken cruel advantage of a weak and demoralized people.

Early in 1847 Scott set out with 13,000 men and a fleet of warships for Veracruz. Included in his invasion force was the better portion of Taylor's army. In fairness to the President and secretary of war, it must be said that it appeared to them that Taylor's operations in the north, successful as they had been, were doing little to shorten the war or bring Santa Anna to terms. It must also have been in Polk's mind that Taylor's reputation—and hence his political potential—had been greatly augmented by his victories. Polk had no disposition to allow him to continue accumulating fame in battles which had little discernible effect on the overall course of the war. Polk plainly wished to put Taylor on ice for a time. Moreover, he still hoped to supersede Scott with Benton and did his best to persuade Democratic Congressmen to back the move.

Scott landed with his army of regulars and volunteers on the island of Lobos, south of Tampico. From there the force sailed on transports to a point of debarkation three miles south of Veracruz. With typical thoroughness and attention to detail, Scott landed his troops and placed them on the hills overlooking Veracruz, a well-fortified city of some twelve thousand inhabitants. After almost a week of heavy bombardment the city surrendered and the way was open to Mexico City. Among the American soldiers who marched into Veracruz was Jacob Oswandel, a young bowman on a Pennsylvania canal boat who had responded a few months before to an appeal for volunteers to "support . . . our national honor and to sustain the flag of our beloved country which was then trailed and trampled in the dust on our frontier." Having "already started out into life for myself,"

Oswandel wrote, "being thus young and healthy, and naturally ambitious for new enterprises and excitement," he had enlisted with the Monroe Guard of Philadelphia and begun the long trip to Mexico with his newly enlisted companions-at-arms. Like many of his country-men he kept a meticulous journal of his experiences.

After the men had elected their officers, the regiment left Pittsburgh on a steamboat traveling down the Ohio to the Mississippi, thence to New Orleans for a brief period of training and then by boat to the island of Lobos, preparatory to capturing Veracruz by seige.

Oswandel estimated the number of prisoners taken in the capitulation of the city as some six thousand. "They were well uniformed and drilled," he wrote, "but they were nearly all what we called black men. Some were real negroes, while others were Mexican Indians, who are composed of all mixtures and all grades of color, which is naturally very dark and coarse. [The surrender] was one of the grandest spectacles that I have ever seen." The American losses were 17 killed and 28 wounded while the Mexican losses were over 1,100, "mostly all killed by the explosion of our shells and shots."

The largely ununiformed and often poorly armed Americans contrasted with the Mexican soldiers in their colorful costumes. Oswandel described his comrades, "some with straw hats, some with caps, and others with Mexican hats; some with one boot or shoe on, and others with no hats or boots or shoes; some had Mexican coats on, and some had hardly anything on except shirt and pants; in fact it looked more like a *fantastic parade* than a military one . . . " (another striking illustration of the law that the army with the worst uniforms invariably wins the wars).

D. E. Twiggs, brave, dependable, unimaginative, led the advance elements on the march inland, followed by Brigadier General Robert Patterson, who had served in the War of 1812, made a fortune as a commission merchant in Philadelphia, and fought well with Taylor at Palo Alto and Monterrey. Then came William Worth, an aide-de-camp to Scott at Lundy's Lane, where he had been decorated for bravery. It was to Worth that much of the credit must go for bringing Ampudia to terms at Monterrey.

At Plan del Rio, Twiggs found his way barred by an army of 13,000 under the command of Santa Anna. When all the divisions had come up and been deployed for an attack, Twiggs led off by driving the Mexican forces from the hill (El Telegrapho) where American guns were brought into battery to fire on Santa Anna's main positions on the knoll called Cerro Gordo. The next day a coordinated attack by the Americans swept up the knoll, through the Mexican breastworks to the top, capturing several generals and a number of their troops, while the defenders fled to Japala. Santa Anna's main force was still relatively intact when the general mounted a mule and headed for the rear, his men following. The booty from the battle amounted to three generals and 3,000 soldiers along with 5,000 stands of arms.

At the Battle of Cerro Gordo, Jacob Oswandel was among the soldiers who captured Santa Anna's field carriage after the general's flight. It contained "drawers under the seats, filled with papers, plans and maps and his field service, a splendid mounted saddle and several wooden or cork legs [the general had in reserve several artificial legs], and, best of all, over $60,000 in specie. . . ." The carriage was hitched to "three splendid black mules"; Santa Anna had fled on the fourth one.

Taylor's victory at Buena Vista had preceded by only a few weeks the triumph of Scott's army over Santa Anna at Cerro Gordo. In New York, a military review, a hundred-gun salvo, and "a general display of flags from all the vessels in the harbor, and from every public edifice in the city," celebrating Buena Vista had hardly ended before word arrived of the victory at Cerro Gordo. The fact that the Battle of Buena Vista took place on Washington's birthday made Philip Hone wonder what the great man would have thought of "the degradation of his countrymen in permitting a chief ruler, the accidental choice of a reckless faction, to exercise a power equally arbitrary and unconstitutional; and by usurping the people's rights . . . to involve the nation in an unjust and inglorious war of aggression upon a neighboring republic."

On the three-hundred-mile march from Veracruz to Mexico City, Scott's army was constantly harassed by Mexican guerrillas (Oswandel called them *lanza,* lancers) and rancheros. Stragglers or any soldiers who wandered beyond the periphery of the nightly camps were lassoed, most commonly around their neck "and dragged on the ground for some distance at full speed" after which, usually too weak and bruised to stand, they were stabbed to death with lances.

Day after day there was a growing roll of those killed or abducted as the poorly disciplined Americans disregarded orders to remain in camp. On several occasion parties of soldiers who pursued the guerrillas were cut off and killed. Oswandel calculated that more Americans were lost to the guerrillas than in the infrequent clashes between the opposing armies. The other persistent and, in the long run, most deadly killer of American soldiers was what Oswandel and his fellows called "diarrah blue." Every week saw more soldiers fall victim to the dreaded disease, wasting away in inadequate hospitals. Halfway to Mexico City the terms of enlistment of a number of volunteer companies expired and the men—resisting all appeals from their officers to re-enlist—decamped, declaring that "the United States Government had fooled and bamboozled them so often, that they have no faith in it; and seeing no re-enforcements arriving, they began to think that the Government is in no hurry to crush this war." "No ordinance, no ammunition, no stores, no wagons and teams, and worst of all, scarcely any soldiers fit to march further into the interior of Mexico," Oswandel added. The truth was that the vacillating Polk, launched on an unpopular war, kept delaying operations in the hope that Santa Anna or the Mexican government of the moment would capitulate. The fact of the matter was that the situation of Scott's army was dangerous if not desperate. Deep in Mexican territory, poorly supplied and constantly drained by guerrilla raids on the supply lines, the camps, the line of march along the National Road and by sickness, disease, and desertion, only the confusion and demoralization in the civil and military affairs of the Mexican Republic gave the Americans a reprieve.

When Jacob Oswandel and his unit were quartered in Perote on the road to Mexico City "there were at one time over five hundred men in this hospital with that disease called diarrhoea, which disease takes more to their graves than the enemy's bullet," he wrote in his journal. Desertion became such a serious problem that deserters when recaptured were summarily shot; on one occasion thirty men from a single company of Irish-Americans who had deserted en masse were executed.

"During the skirmish with the infernal guerrillas, we have suffered more frightfully than at the battle of Cerro Gordo with the regular Mexican army," Oswandel wrote. "In fact, we would sooner face ten of the regular Mexican army than one of these outlawed guerrillas." All of which suggests very strongly that if the Mexican government had put its major effort into organizing and equipping irregular forces for all-out guerrilla warfare, the American army in Mexico would have been in the greatest peril.

After the battle of Cerro Gordo Polk once more sent peace feelers to the Mexican foreign minister, who replied that no negotiations were possible while American soldiers were on Mexican soil. Still unconvinced that the Mexicans were determined to fight, Polk responded by sending a secret commissioner to join Scott with powers to negotiate a treaty. He chose a colorful and eccentric figure, Nicholas Trist, who had studied law with Jefferson and been private secretary to Jackson. Trist knew Spanish and was considered an authority on the Latin temperament. He was handsome and urbane but conceited and self-important. Trist was instructed to insist on a boundary line running along the thirty-second parallel to the Gulf of California and down the Gulf to the Pacific and to offer to pay as much as $30,000,000 for the lands so acquired. He soon let word of his mission leak out and found himself in an angry dispute with Scott over authority to conclude an armistice. Santa Anna sent word to Trist that if $10,000 were paid, followed by another million when peace was made, he would allow the army to penetrate close to Mexico City and then enter into negotiations for peace.

In August Scott's army pushed forward to Mexico City. The city was stoutly defended but Scott, having secured the approaches to it in fierce fighting, stopped to give Trist another chance for peace talks. Trist proved far more conciliatory than his principals, Polk and his Secretary of State, Buchanan. When word reached Polk that the Mexican government was resisting his terms, he recalled Trist and upped the ante. He wanted a larger chunk of Mexico. His annual message to Congress breathed fire. If the Mexican government did not capitulate promptly, Polk declared, "it may become proper for our commanding generals in the field to give encouragement and assurance of protection to the friends of peace in Mexico in the establishment and maintenance of a free republican government of their own choice. . . ." Thus would the war be converted into "an enduring blessing" to the Mexicans. "After finding her torn and distracted by factions, and ruled by military usurpers, we should then leave her with a republican government in the enjoyment of real independence and domestic peace and prosperity . . . in the great family of nations. . . ." If the United States were to withdraw before a treaty of peace had been concluded (as many Americans very evidently and vocally wished), Mexicans would be the sufferers, Polk solemnly declared. Mexico must be occupied until the American treaty terms were accepted. The more obdurate her wicked rulers were, the more they must be punished. The logic seemed badly flawed. On the one hand we were anxious to do everything we could for the well-being of the

Mexican people, but this apparently involved stripping them of an empire of almost unbelievable richness and forcing upon them a humiliating treaty that could only add to their impoverishment and demoralization.

The war must go on. The city itself must be invested by the United States forces. Then perhaps Mexico would capitulate. The key to the city, which was surrounded by lakes and marshes, was Chapultepec, a fortified hill. General John Anthony Quitman, a Mississippi lawyer and politician, led the main assault against it on September 13. Chapultepec taken, the city itself soon fell. Santa Anna resigned as president and placed himself at the head of a guerrilla army.

After the hasty departure of Santa Anna, Pena y Pen, president of the Supreme Court of Justice, headed an interim government. Although Trist had been ordered home by Polk, who had denounced him as "impudent, arrogant, very insulting, and personally offensive," he remained with Scott and pushed negotiations for peace, concluding the Treaty of Guadalupe Hidalgo on February 2, 1848, which established the boundary line between Mexico and the United States at the Rio Grande del Norte, then westward along the southern boundary of New Mexico to "the division line between Upper and Lower California, to the Pacific Ocean." Mexico thus abandoned its claims to Texas and ceded New Mexico and Upper California—a region vaster than the Louisiana Purchase, including almost all of the future states of California, Arizona, New Mexico, Nevada, Utah, and portions of Colorado and Wyoming. (Foreigners—Americans living in California— had already thrown off Mexican rule there and announced the birth of the Bear Republic.) For this vast empire, the United States agreed to pay Mexico fifteen million dollars and assume all the claims by United States citizens against the Republic of Mexico. The treaty further provided that all disagreements or differences that might arise in regard to the treaty or in the future relations of the country "should be settled by the arbitration of Commissioners, appointed on each side, or by that of a friendly nation."

When Polk received a copy of the treaty, he was at first disposed to reject it, but a majority of his Cabinet pressed him to send it to the Senate for ratification and it passed that body by a vote of 38 to 14.

Scott meanwhile involved himself in an unseemly wrangle with some of his senior officers. He brought charges of disobedience against Generals Gideon Pillow, James Duncan, and William Worth, three "political" generals with considerable influence in Congress, and placed them under formal arrest. When Polk heard of Scott's action he overruled the hero of Veracruz and Chapultepec, relieved Pillow and Duncan of arrest, advanced Worth in rank, and replaced Scott by General William Butler, a Democrat. The army was indignant. Jacob Oswandel wrote: "We . . . style it outrageous, unjust and infamous; a reproach to our civilization; a stigma of the deepest dye to our government forever." One of Scott's staff officers, Robert E. Lee, complained that Scott, having won the war for Polk, was now "turned out like an old horse to die." Scott wrote a long, rambling, self-congratulatory justification of his actions and on April 22, 1848, departed with the affectionate cheers of the army ringing in his ears.

One thing that could be said with confidence was that in this scandalous and unprovoked war only the soldiers and officers of the American army were worthy of praise. Many lost their lives in battle or by disease driving from Veracruz to Mexico City. Of course Scott and Taylor, Generals Tweedledum and Tweedledee, had their reputations greatly enhanced. Each in his own way was remarkably well suited for his particular task, Taylor for the rough and hasty campaigning in the north, Scott for the organization and management of the large-scale invasion force that fought its way into the heart of Mexico.

American casualties were 1,721 men and officers killed in battle or dead from wounds, 11,155 dead of disease. The cost of the war was estimated at more than $97,500,000.

"Scott's march to Mexico," Philip Hone wrote, "with his handful of men, through an unknown country filled with infuriated bands of armed guerrillas, and the occupation of the city by the American forces, is an event equal to the most brilliant recorded in history. But, alas! how dearly has this glory been purchased! . . . The best blood in the country has been shed." As we have noted, much of the spectacular success of American arms could be traced to the leadership of West Point graduates who made up a disproportionate number of the killed and wounded. Enumerating the West Point heroes, Philip Hone wrote, "Shame on the malignant demagogues who have labored to overthrow such an institution!" Schuyler Hamilton, grandson of General Schuyler of Revolutionary War fame and nephew of Alexander Hamilton, had been an aide to Scott. He had been badly wounded. Edward Webster, Daniel Webster's son, had died, as had young Henry Clay. Lieutenant Morris, another West Pointer, grandson of Robert Morris, the "financier of the American Revolution," had died of wounds.

"These are the trophies of West Point!" Hone added. "Shall it not be supported?"

The Mexican War was a kind of watershed in American history. Americans of conscience had agonized over the moral implications of slavery in a nation dedicated to freedom and democracy. They had deplored the treatment of the Indians and some had devoted their lives to trying with, on the whole, little success to mitigate the worst consequences of white contact with the American aborigines. But at least with respect to wars of conquest Americans had enjoyed a feeling of moral superiority. Other nations might bully, rob, or invade weaker neighbors, but the United States was too deeply committed to the ideal of national independence and too conspicuous in its sympathy for the underdog ever to engage in an act of aggression against another nation solely for its own aggrandizement. To such persons the war came as a further and more profound disillusionment. Northerners of liberal persuasion blamed the war on the South's insatiable appetite for Western lands and, above all, on the pernicious influence of slavery.

If we can overlook the farcical aspects of the war and assess it as a highly significant episode in our history (which it certainly was), we must face the issue of Polk's capacities as president. It has been the disposition of historians in recent years to give Polk high marks as a successful president based, in large part, on the "success" of his administration in annexing Texas (a process started before Polk took office) and his acquisition of the New Mexico Territory, California, and Oregon. Since those were such splendid acquisitions, it may seem ungenerous to fault him for the means he used to obtain them. Not only were the "means" entirely unscrupulous and corrupt—threats and bribery—they were also, as Benton, one of the President's closest confidants, subsequently wrote, "infinitely silly." Most important, they backfired badly. Santa Anna, restored to power with American connivance, made himself the backbone of Mexican resistance, and came within a hair of inflicting a crushing defeat on Taylor. His return to power cost "many thousands of Americans killed—many more dead of disease—many millions of money expended," in Benton's words. Indeed, as the Missouri senator pointed out, Santa Anna was as much a curse to Mexico as to the United States, "for, true to his old instincts, he became the tyrant of his country—ruled by fraud, force, and bribes, crushed the liberal party—exiled or shot liberal men . . . and put the nation to the horrors of another civil war to expel him again, and again; but not until he had got another milking from the best cow that ever was in his pen—more money from the United States." In Benton's words, the Santa Anna connection was "an intrigue laid for peace before the war was declared! and this intrigue was even part of the scheme for making the war. It is impossible to conceive of an administration less warlike or more intriguing, than that of Mr. Polk. They were men of peace, with objects to be accomplished by means of war; so that war was a necessity . . . to their purpose; but they wanted no more of it than would answer their purposes. . . . They wanted a small war, just large enough to require a treaty of peace, and not large enough to make military reputations, dangerous for the presidency."

Polk's estimate of a 90- to 120-day war, which he used to prevail on his Cabinet and on leading Democrats to suppress their misgivings about the invasion of Mexico, was a potentially serious delusion. His constant procrastinating and fiddling about to try to prevent the Whig generals, Scott and Taylor, from making political hay out of *his* war further demonstrated his disposition for intrigue and double dealing. Unfortunately for his reputation, Polk kept a diary which reveals him as a petty, conniving, irascible, small-spirited man whose able Cabinet served him much better than he deserved, a Cabinet that should, in the final analysis, probably be given credit for protecting him from his own destructive impulses. He was belligerent and tactless in his statements on the Oregon question, alienating the British ministry and inflaming public opinion at home and abroad. It must be said that no luckier man than Polk ever occupied the White House. Blundering and inept in his Byzantine plot to bribe Santa Anna, he was saved by the generals he distrusted and tried to supersede. The accidents of history gave him an army and a fate much better than he deserved.

There were other consequences of the Mexican War more difficult to assess. Even Philip Hone, shameless Anglophile, took pleasure in the changed tone of the British press with regard to the United States. He sounded positively chauvinistic when he wrote "They may occasionally abuse us as an arrogant people, grasping at extended territory, disregarding the rights of our neighbors, invading peaceful countries, fighting like lions, and negotiating like foxes. But the language of contempt is heard no more. . . . The Yankees may be ignorant of the most approved method of using the knife and fork; but it cannot be denied that they are competent to make a good use of the sword and musket; they use some queer expressions, but in defense of their rights are apt to talk much to the purpose."

Looking back on the main events of the war, we are reminded how precarious the American victory was. The United States narrowly escaped if not ultimate defeat at least devastating setbacks. Taylor's vastly outnumbered army was several times on the edge of defeat at Buena Vista, saved only by the extraordinary efforts of the artillery. Scott's army had dwindled away on the road from Veracruz to Mexico City, much more than decimated by guerrilla raids, disease, and desertion.

At the same time it must be said that Mexico was a mess. A succession of dictator-generals, most of them not much better than Santa Anna, interspersed with short-lived liberal regimes, had kept that country in a constant political and social turmoil and a state of financial insolvency. The principal sufferers were the Mexican people, primarily the peasants, who died in the interminable fighting or starved to death in periods of famine; who were murderously taxed and cruelly exploited by their rulers. Mexican notions of justice and due process were nugatory by American standards, and American emigrants and traders who came in contact with Mexican officials were often treated arbitrarily and sometimes brutally. In part for these reasons and in part because two more radically different character types than the Yankee-American and the Hispanic-Mexican could hardly have been imagined, there was a chasm of mutual hostility and, indeed, antipathy, between the two people which complicated all their relationships and would continue to do so down to the present day. That the Mexicans were as contemptuous of the Norteamericanos as the gringos were of the greasers is undeniable, as is the fact that the Mexican generals longed to teach their arrogant northern neighbors a lesson they would not soon forget about Latin courage and mastery of warfare.

But granted that the Mexican government (or series of governments) was almost impossible to do business with, that the rulers of Mexico were proud, fierce aristocrats without much sympathy for democratic principles, disposed to grind the faces of the poor, there were at the same time heroic spirits who took the cause of the peasants as their own and devoted their lives to fighting repressive military regimes. The wisest course, and the one most consistent with American principles, would have been to defend Texas (which had already shown a notable capacity to defend itself) against an invasion and beyond that, do whatever we could to strengthen the liberal and progressive elements in Mexico. There would certainly have been critics of such a course from both sides of the political spectrum—from those irrevocably opposed to the annexation of Texas and from those who wished to grab off as much of Mexico as we could get away with—but it would have been infinitely wiser and more humane than the policy followed by Polk.

The aftermath of the Mexican War was increased bitterness between the North and the South. Many Northerners, and certainly orthodox Whigs, considered the war a Southern war, carried on to extend slavery. They were determined to do all in their power to prevent the extension of slavery into the region of New Mexico. The fierceness of the struggle for control of Congress was indicated by the fact that, in a contest between Robert Winthrop of Massachusetts and Howell Cobb of Georgia for the speakership of the House, forty ballots failed to produce a victor. "Madness rules the hour," Philip Hone wrote, "faction, personal recrimination, and denunciation prevail, and men for the first time in our history do not hesitate openly to threaten a dissolution of the Union." Finally, when a Whig defection gave the office of speaker to Cobb, Hone wrote, "The new Speaker of the House of Representatives who was elected by a plurality of one vote, has evinced his determination to carry out the views of his party by rejecting all the leading Whigs from the important committees."

The antislavery Liberty Party chose as its candidate for the forthcoming presidential election the radical reformer Gerritt Smith, who was said to have told a friend that if he were president he would have brought the war to a halt, withdrawn all the troops, disbanded the army and navy, replaced the tariff by direct taxation, given the public lands to needy without charge, abolished all naturalization laws, and denied office to any man who supported the public sale of liquor or who owned slaves. A program, it turned out, far in advance of public sentiment.

A group that considered the Liberty Party beyond the pale but found itself increasingly unhappy in the Whig camp was led by Charles Sumner of Massachusetts and Salmon Chase of Ohio. Such men as Sumner, Seward, and Chase denounced the conservative Whigs for linking "the lords of the loom with those of the lash," as a historian has put it. With the formation of the Free Soil Party in 1848, Joshua Leavitt, one of its founders and a political abolitionist, declared, "The Liberty party is not dead but TRANSLATED." The motto of the new party was, after all, FREE SOIL, FREE SPEECH, FREE LABOR, AND FREE MEN. It was a slogan hard to argue with. Nothing was said about blacks or slavery. He who read as he ran might understand it to be no more than an affirmation of classic American principles.

The "pure" abolitionists, led by Samuel May and Garrison, who believed that the slavery issue should remain uncontaminated, by politics, were horrified at such a compromise. Garrison saw a ray of light in the fact that its formation must hasten the dissolution of the Union and May declared that the Liberty Party was "utterly annihilated . . . and their leaders . . . will soon fall to their true level of shame; the more they are known, the less will they be trusted." Frederick Douglass, committed to political action as he was, called it "folly and hypocrisy without advancing the cause of freedom at all."

14

Visitors

Foreign visitors had been coming to America in considerable numbers since the years immediately prior to the Revolution. The long, tedious, and often dangerous passage across the Atlantic and the expense of the journey restricted the trip for the most part to well-to-do members of the upper classes in the countries (England, Scotland, France, and the German principalities) from which most of the travelers came. They came, of course, with their own prejudices and perspectives, but by and large those who came were favorably disposed. They were to be counted among the more liberal or radical spirits in their homelands: those most interested in reform, in the lessons that might be learned in the new republic and carried back for application in the mother country.

As the nineteenth century wore on "freedom fighters" from various colonial possessions, especially the Spanish and Portuguese colonies of South America, fighting for *their* independence and then to establish republican governments with written constitutions, came to the United States to try to learn how it had been done and how it all worked, or failed to work.

The Germans were apt to be scientifically inclined aristocrats with a passion for sport shared by their English and Scottish counterparts.

They could hardly wait to rush to the frontier to shoot a buffalo or a grizzly bear. One of the German visitors, Moritz Busch, called the United States "this land of liberty and rudeness."

Englishmen tended to be rather patronizing and not infrequently outright contemptuous of many aspects of American life and manners. Usually, however amiably disposed they were, a strong class bias showed through. In 1839 Philip Hone wrote: "The present year has been prolific in that fashionable department of literature, the off-spring of the teeming portfolios of English travelers in the United States."

The French, on the other hand, having suffered the most extensive and violent revolution of modern times, a revolution followed by a temporary restoration of the Bourbon throne, came to the United States with a good deal more openness. Their revolution and ours had, after all, been conceived in somewhat the same spirit even if they had gone in strikingly different directions. The Democratic Party continued to identify itself with the French Revolution and with France despite the restoration of the Bourbons, while the Whigs aligned themselves with the British as the preservers of order and the exemplars of constitutional government.

While the preponderance of foreign visitors were from Northern Europe, the travelers came from virtually every country on the globe, from as far away as China and, after Perry's voyage, from Japan as well. It sometimes seems that most of them wrote books about the United States when they returned home. The books ranged from highly sophisticated analyses of American life and mores to practical guidebooks for the prospective immigrant. Some extolled our virtues; others dwelt on our numerous faults. All together they made up an extraordinary literature, a bibliography so vast as to be almost unencompassable, thousands and thousands of volumes, many of them not translated into English. What they demonstrate is the insatiable curiosity of the world about this strange new land and the peopling of it, an event that had plainly altered the course of human history and involved the rest of the species in the promise of its own future. The United States had become by some alchemical magic the future of the world. If one wished to know what the future looked and felt and smelled and tasted like, it was required that he or she go to America. What the traveler into the future found was often disconcerting.

This flow of visitors reached its high tide in the 1830s and early

1840s. Steamboats and canals and—soon—trains facilitated travel. Accommodations for travelers improved in a few decades from rough inns and taverns to elegant hotels that rivaled the best of Europe. Rapidly expanding trade established ties between commercial and banking houses in Europe and the United States, which also facilitated travel. Foreign investors came to inspect their holdings or in search of new fields for investment. The Wild West was an enormous attraction. Philadelphia or New York, interesting as they might be, were only lesser Londons or Parises. But the Wild West was the wonder of the world, full of Indians and frontiersmen, romantic and picturesque beyond the dreams of a romantic age obsessed by the picturesque, an age to which a log cabin in a wilderness clearing or a Sioux warrior mounted on his pony was as captivating as the legend of Troy or some tale of medieval knights.

Frances Trollope came to the United States to try to recoup her family's fortunes with the help of her friend Frances Wright, the famous woman reformer who had accompanied Lafayette on his triumphal American tour and had established the Utopian and short-lived interracial community in Nashoba, Tennessee. Mrs. Trollope brought with her her young son, Anthony, the novelist-to-be, and her two older daughters. A strong-willed and imaginative woman, Mrs. Trollope decided that her fortunes lay in the West and decided to open a bazaar in Cincinnati. By hook and crook she raised the money to build a kind of Byzantine shopping mall "which was to combine the specialties of an athenaeum, a lecture hall, and a bazaar." Designed by her, the building offended conventionally minded Cincinnatians by its miniature towers and minarets. She failed to attract sufficient business to make the extravagant venture profitable. Cincinnati society, such as it was, snubbed her and she returned home to take her revenge by writing an unfriendly book, *Domestic Manners of the Americans*, which was published in 1832. The book created an uproar in America. Another Englishman, traveling there the following year, wrote, "At every corner of the street, at the door of every petty retailer of information for the people, a large placard met the eye, with 'For sale here, with plates, Domestic Manners of the Americans, by Mrs. Trollope.' At every table d'hôte, on board every steam boat, and in all societies, the first question was, 'have you read Mrs. Trollope . . .' and the more it was abused, the more rapidly did the printers issue new editions."

Reading her work today, it is hard to realize what all the fuss was about. While she was hard on American manners in general, she spoke warmly of the "homely friendliness" of the people of Cincinnati and their "generous and abounding hospitality," which she found characteristic of the American people generally. But she was merciless with the social pretensions of middle-class Americans and the crudity and vulgarity of the common people.

Such passages as the following were particularly resented: "The total want of all the usual courtesies of the table, the voracious rapidity with which the viands were seized and devoured, the strange, uncouth phrases and pronunciation; the loathsome spitting, from the contamination of which it was absolutely impossible to protect our dresses; the frightful manner of feeding with their knives, till the whole blade seemed to enter the mouth; and the still more frightful manner of cleaning the teeth afterwards with a pocket knife, soon forced us to feel that we were not surrounded by the generals, colonels, and majors of the old world. . . ."

One Englishman "long resident in America" told Mrs. Trollope he had never "overheard Americans conversing without the word DOLLAR being pronounced between them. Such unity of purpose, such sympathy of feeling, can, I believe, be found nowhere else, except, perhaps, in an ants' nest. . . . This sordid object, for ever before their eyes, must inevitably produce a sordid tone of mind. . . ." Mrs. Trollope noted that while most Americans "in stature, and in physiognomy" were "strikingly handsome," she never "saw an American man walk or stand well . . . they are nearly all hollow chested and round shouldered." The Englishwoman was often offended by the deep-grained hostility she encountered toward England and all things English and amused by such comments as: "Well, I do begin to understand your broken English better than I did. . . ." Another woman conjectured whether Mrs. Trollope had left England "in order to get rid of the vermin with which the English of all classes were afflicted?"

At the same time she was startled by the "strong feeling against the Irish in every part of the Union, but they will do twice as much work as a negro, and therefore they are employed. . . . Details of their sufferings and unheeded death, too painful to dwell upon often reached us. . . ."

Frances Trollope's experiences "sojourning among an 'I'm-as-good-as-you-are' population" clearly left her in an unhappy frame of mind. "I suspect," she wrote at the end of her extensive work, "that

what I have written will make it evident that I do not like America."
Leaving aside "the small patrician band," situated primarily in the
large cities, she found "the population generally" distasteful. "I do not
like them, I do not like their principles, I do not like their manners, I
do not like their opinions." Nor did she like their government.

Perhaps all other criticisms might have been forgiven, all her
sometimes snide stories and sharp thrusts, but her subjects wished,
above all, to be *liked*. If she had ended her dissertation by saying
something like "Despite all their faults and shortcomings, I must say I
like the American people. They are a splendid breed," all might have
been forgiven.

A very different English lady followed Frances Trollope. Harriet
Martineau was one of the more remarkable representatives of that
remarkable tribe of women writers, reformers, and lecturers who
emerged on both sides of the Atlantic in the first half of the nineteenth
century. When she was in her early twenties, her father, a cloth
manufacturer, died—as did her fiancé and her elder brother. She was
thus left to make her own way in the world. Deafness precluded her
teaching, so she turned to work as a seamstress to make her living and
augmented her income by writing. Soon all she could turn out found
ready publishers. Interested in the economic conditions of her own
country, she decided to write a series of popular articles on economics.
They proved an enormous success and made her well known in
England and America. In 1834 she made her famous visit to the
United States, where she found more to admire than condemn.

Armed with her reputation, her ear trumpet, and innumerable
letters of introduction, she went everywhere and conversed with
literary figures, politicians, preachers, and ordinary folk. She heard
Henry Clay, "sitting upright on the sofa, with his snuffbox ever in his
hand," talking like a marvel "on any one of the great subjects of
American policy"; Webster, lounging, "telling stories, cracking jokes,
shaking the sofa with burst after burst of laughter"; Calhoun, "the
cast-iron man," whose remarkable forces seemed to Martineau "at best
but useless, and . . . but too likely to be very mischievous. . . . I know
of no man who lives in such utter intellectual solitude." Chief Justice
John Marshall won her sympathetic heart. She found in him "a
reverence for woman as rare in its kind as in its degree. . . . He was the
father and grandfather of women; and out of this experience he
brought, not only the love and pity which their offices and position
command . . . but a steady conviction of their intellectual equality with

men, and, with this, a deep sense of their social injuries." It always delighted Martineau to see Marshall "so dignified, so fresh, so present to the time, that no feeling of compassionate consideration for age dared mix with the contemplation of him."

In everything she wrote of, and particularly in her delineation of individual character, Harriet Martineau showed her innate good sense and humanity. She was surprisingly successful in overcoming the American suspicion of English lady writers but her outspoken opposition to slavery, an institution that horrified her, and her sympathy with the abhorred abolitionists soon made her unwelcome in many circles. She wrote of the common practice of white masters having sexual relations with the slave women of their plantations. "The personal oppression of negroes," she wrote, "is the grossest vice which strikes a stranger in the country." "It is well known," she added, "that the most savage violences that are now heard of in the world take place in the southern and western States of America."

In Cincinnati, Martineau noted, with some asperity, "Mrs. Trollope's bazaar . . . the great deformity of the city," with "Gothic windows, Grecian pillars, and a Turkish dome." She attended the city's first musical concert there, an evening of Mozart, marveling at the fact that what had lately been "a canebrake, echoing with the bellow and growl of wild beasts" now contained a salon where an admiring crowd listened to Mozart.

Harriet Martineau's own physical handicap made her especially interested in the institutes established for the education of the mute and blind. She was greatly impressed by the kindness and intelligence that had been devoted to attempting to draw them into the world and find useful work for them to do. "The generosity of American society," she wrote, "already so active and extensive, will continue to be exerted in behalf of sufferers from the privation of the senses, till all who need it will be comprehended in its care. No one doubts that the charity will be done."

Martineau was perhaps most taken with the large number of what she called "originals" in America. These were "the prophets and redeemers of their age and country." "The Americans appear to me," she wrote, "an eminently imaginative people. The unprejudiced traveller can hardly spend a week among them without being struck with this every day." There were, she noted, no traditional ways of doing things. The American imagination was not burdened with outmoded notions or frustrated by artificial constraints. The inevitable question was not "How has it been done?" but "How can it be done better?" It was the custom of visitors and of cultivated Americans themselves to deplore the lack of great American works of art and literature but Martineau was convinced that the same quality of imagination that had made "the organization of American commerce . . . the admiration of the world" would, in good time, reveal "a plenitude of power." Noah Webster, Emerson, and Father Edward Taylor (the famous untutored sailor-preacher who was to provide the model for Melville's Father Maple) were among Martineau's originals, as was William Lloyd Garrison. She had come to America to make friends, for friends were everywhere to be made where human spirits flowed through the superficial barriers of race and custom. And in her unfailingly cheerful spirit, she made friends everywhere and left in her *Retrospect of Western Travel* the kindly reflections of a friend on the oddly variegated inhabitants of the United States, a nation of "originals."

Another observant English lady traveler was Isabelle Lucy Bird, who, having conquered Canada and the United States, went on to write great tomes on Japan, Persia, Tibet, Korea, and China and to become the first woman member of the Royal Geographical Society. She ventured as far west as Illinois, where on a train delayed by a damaged engine she was charmed to encounter a party of "prairie men," "tall, handsome, broad-chested, and athletic, with acquiline noses, piercing grey eyes, and brown curling hair and beards. They wore leathern jackets, slashed and embroidered, leather smallclothes, large boots with embroidered tops, silver spurs, and caps of scarlet cloth, worked with somewhat tarnished gold thread. . . . Dulness fled from their presence; they could tell stories, whistle melodies, and sing comic songs without weariness or cessation: fortunate were those near enough to be enlivened by their drolleries. . . . Each of them wore a leathern belt—with two pistols stuck into it—gold earrings, and costly rings. Blithe, cheerful souls they were, telling racy stories of Western life, chivalrous in their manners, and free as the winds."

Her comments on American life and manners were invariably disarming and good-humored. What perhaps impressed her most strongly on her American visit was the "acts of hearty unostentatious good nature" that she experienced from ordinary Americans whenever she was in need of assistance.

A visitor with a very different outlook was Frederick Marryat, a former naval officer and British novelist who preferred the title of

Captain; a rather imperious gentleman, he viewed American democracy with the suspicion of an upper-class Englishman. His mother was a Boston Loyalist, his father a prosperous merchant and a member of Parliament. Marryat, already widely traveled, decided in 1837 to visit America to see "What were the effects of a democratic form of government and climate upon a people which, with all its foreign admixtures, may still be considered as English."

It was Marryat who took the most explicit notice of what many other visitors commented upon, the appearance of strain and anxiety, of "seriousness" on the faces of those one passed on the streets of the larger cities. He noted that when he walked down the streets of New York he had the odd impression that all the men he passed were in some strange way related. Finally he realized "that they were all intent and engrossed with the same object; all were, as they passed, calculating and reflecting; this produced a similar contraction of the brow, knitting of the eyebrows, and compression of the lips—a similarity of feeling had produced a similarity of expression. . . ."

Of all the visitors, Captain Marryat, with a novelist's ear for the nuances of speech, had most to say about the American language. He told of a New England girl who, asked if she had any suitors, replied, "well, now can't exactly say; I bees a sorter courted and a sorter not; reckon more a sorter yes than a sorter no." One man, telling Marryat of a speculation he had failed to make, declared that he would not only have doubled and trebled his money but would have "*fourbled* and *fivebled*" it, and when Marryat asked a lady why she drawled out her words, she replied, "I'd drawl all the way from Maine to Georgia rather than *clip* my words as you English people do."

The verb *admire* was often used in place of "like," as in "I would admire to go to Paris." A talkative woman would "talk to you like a book. . . . She'll talk you out of sight."

"I *suspicion* that's a fact."

"I *opinion* quite the contrary."

The word *considerable* was, Marryat found, in considerable demand in the United States: "My dear sister, I have taken up the pen early this morning, as I intend to write considerable." When Marryat asked a young lady if she was cold, she replied "some."

Inventiveness and exaggeration marked the American version of the English language. There was the ubiquitous "fix" for "mend"; "right away" for "immediately"; and "full blast" for "in the extreme" as "When she came to the meeting, with her yellow hat and feathers, wasn't she in *full blast?*" "I'm a *gone 'coon'* " meant "I am distressed or ruined or lost." Marryat heard a critic of the Shakespearean actor Edmund Forrest declare, "I do think *he piled the agony up a little too high in that last scene.*" Another man declared, "Well, I reckon that from his teeth to his toe-nail there's not a human of more conquering nature than General Jackson."

For Marryat the "one great luxury in America" was ice cream, "universal and very cheap." When he was having an ice "about a dozen black swarthy fellows, employed at the iron foundry close at hand, with their dirty shirt-sleeves tucked up, and without their coats and waistcoats, came in, and sitting down, called for ice-creams. . . . The working classes all over America can command not only all necessary comforts but many luxuries, for labor is dear and they are very well paid." (Skilled labor commanded a daily rate of $1.25.)

Marryat noted the American obsession for whittling. "A Yankee shown into a room to await the arrival of another," he wrote, "has been known to whittle away nearly the whole of the mantel piece. Lawyers in court whittle away at the table before them; and judges will cut through their own bench. In some courts they put down sticks before noted whittlers to save the furniture."

Marryat was severe in his strictures on majority rule. "Within the past ten years," he wrote, "the advance of the people has been like a torrent, sweeping and leveling all before it, and the will of the majority has become not only absolute with the government, but it defies the government itself. . . . The prudent, the enlightened, the wise, and the good have all retired into the shade, preferring to pass a life of quiet retirement, rather than submit to the insolence and dictation of a mob. . . ." Those who wished to gain and hold power must tell the people only what they wished to hear—how great, powerful, progressive, moral, and enlightened they were. "How can you expect a people to improve," Marryat burst out, "who *never hear the truth?*"

The Englishman defined the character of Americans as that of "a restless, uneasy people—they cannot sit still, they cannot listen attentively, unless the theme be politics or dollars, they must do something, and, like children, if they cannot do anything else, they will do mischief—their curiosity is unbounded, and they are very capricious. . . . They are good-tempered and possess great energy, ingenuity, bravery and presence of mind." These qualities "tempered by religious and moral feeling, would make them great and good, but without these adjuncts they can only become great and vicious."

At the time of the Declaration of Independence, Marryat believed, they were "perhaps the most moral people existing, and I now assert that they are the least so." The reason for the change was the decline of the native aristocracy which had "sunk the republic into a democracy. . . . The fact is that an aristocracy is absolutely necessary for America, both politically and morally, if the Americans wish their institutions to hold together, for if some stop is not put to the rapidly advancing power of the people, anarchy must be the result." The great achievements of the United States were due far less to the nature of the government, Marryat believed, than to the boundless resources of the country combined with "the credit and capital of England." The United States had indeed "proved to the world that, with every advantage on her side the attempt at a republic had been a miserable failure, and that the time is not yet come when mankind can govern themselves. Will it ever come? In my opinion, never!"

Marryat's book infuriated the normally urbane George Templeton Strong, who found the first part "sportively slanderous" but the balance "stupidly malignant . . . a farrago of lies." Philip Hone was equally indignant. Marryat's "manners were bad," Hone noted, "and he drinks grog with the vulgarity of a sailor." Since he was no gentleman he had had little contact with Americans of social standing and his observations were limited to "the vulgar and uneducated masses," who, Hone seemed to feel, were somehow not really Americans at all.

Another "captain" whose critical observations about Americans enraged us was Captain Basil Hall, a Scot, a British naval officer, diplomat, member of the Royal Society, and professional traveler. In 1827–1828 Hall toured through Canada and the United States and a year later published his *Travels in North America* in three volumes. A Tory and a firm supporter of the monarchy, he did not come to the United States in a frame of mind favorable to democracy and his book, a best-seller in Great Britain, clearly demonstrated that fact. His bias, however, did not prevent his making some shrewd assessments of American life and character and gave his more positive comments a special weight. One of his principal enthusiasms was American food, most particularly American breakfasts in the better hotels. He was in ecstasy over "great, steaming, juicy beefsteak," "mutton cutlets," and such native delicacies as shad, "almost worthy of a voyage across the Atlantic to make its acquaintance."

Hall was especially critical of Americans' treatment of the landscape and, like other European visitors, he was dismayed by the avidity with which Americans dropped trees. "Girdling" them was even more offensive. "An American settler can hardly conceive," he wrote, "the horror with which a foreigner beholds such numbers of magnificent trees, standing around with their throats cut, the very Banquos of a murdered forest!"

Hall had a revealing conversation with Noah Webster, "the famous lexicographer," about the differences between the English and the American language. Hall, not surprisingly, deplored the corruption of the mother tongue in the Western world and Webster defended it. To Hall's comment that "innovations" were to be "deprecated," Webster replied, "I don't know that. If a word becomes universally current in America, where English is spoken, why should it not take its place in the language?"

"Because," Hall replied, "there are words enough already; and it only confuses matters, and hurts the cause of letters to introduce such words."

Hall's strictures on American democracy caused bitter resentment in the United States and established a pattern to which many of his traveling compatriots adhered, which might be called something like "comic sketches of morals and manners in America, interspersed with observations of the decline of a people under the licentious system of popular government."

A British visitor who wrote sympathetically about the United States was George Combe, who traveled through the states lecturing and giving courses of instruction in phrenology. Phrenology was the psychology or perhaps the astrology of the nineteenth century. It attempted to analyze character from the shape of the head. The human personality was characterized as having various propensities: first, Feelings: "Amativeness—Produces sexual love, Philoprogentiveness . . . affection for young and tender things; Combativeness; Secretiveness; Acquisitiveness; Constructiveness, etc." Then Sentiments such as "Self-esteem" and "Benevolence." The proportion of these in each individual could be determined by examining the shape of the head. "Amativeness," for example, was situated at the base of the skull, "Combativeness" behind the ears. But phrenology did not stop there. Like all nineteenth-century reform movements it had a substantial ethical dimension. It was firmly rooted in Christianity. It was committed to self-improvement—certain "exercises" could improve the positive attributes and diminish the negative—and advocated a complete regimen which placed great emphasis on good ventilation and lots of exercise. Combe addressed substantial audiences wherever he went, met distinguished figures, and conferred with sympathetic "scientists."

Although Combe was far more liberal in his sentiments than Marryat and was generally sympathetic to the institutions of the United States, he, like virtually all other visitors, had reservations about democracy. "A democracy is a rough instrument of rule," he wrote, "in the present state of education and manners in the United States, and I have not yet met with a British radical who has had the benefit of five years experience of it, who has not renounced his creed and ceased to admire universal suffrage. But the coarseness of the machinery and its efficacy, are different questions. It is coarse, because the mass of the people, although intelligent, compared with the European masses, are still imperfectly instructed. . . . It is efficacious, however, because it is sound in its structure and its mainsprings are strong." When Americans were more refined and better educated the imperfections, he believed, would diminish. One of those imperfections was to be found in the fact that "the people worship themselves, as the fountains equally of wisdom and power. They bend all institutions in subserviency of their views and feelings. They are no longer led by, but they often dictate to, the wealthy and the highly educated."

Another of Combe's criticisms was directed at the wariness Americans displayed in their casual social contacts. As he traveled about New England he was struck by the taciturnity of his companions at public tables who turned to their eating with silent intensity. A friend explained that it was the consequence of the "fear of inferior people intruding themselves and fixing an acquaintance on persons of superior condition and attainments. All persons are pushing upwards in this country, and as there is no artificial rank, everyone guards his own station with extraordinary jealousy."

At the end of his sympathetic and open-minded survey of American life and politics, George Combe listed as "aberrations" of Americans: the cheating and "false swearing at your elections; the practice of betting on elections; your mobs, your Lynch laws, your wild speculations, your bank suspensions . . . ; your Negro slavery; your treatment of the Indians; the incessant abuse which one of your political parties heaps on the distinguished men of the other . . . ; the excessive number of bankruptcies; the very imperfect police for the prevention of crime which characterises some of your great cities, such as New York; the enormous and calamitous conflagrations which scourge your cities, the results either of recklessness or incendiarism; the great self-complacency of the mass of the people, who, although very imperfectly educated, are persuaded by political orators that they know every thing, and can decide wisely on every question; the general absence of reverence for authority or superior wisdom, displayed first in childhood and afterwards in the general progress of life. . . ." Admitting all these, "the irrefutable response," Combe declared, was that "you have proclaimed the supremacy of man's moral and intellectual nature over his animal feelings, and adopted this principle as the basis of your social order, and of your hopes." Providence had entrusted "the great cause of freedom" to Americans and they were thus bound "to exhibit *higher* intelligence, a *purer* morality, a *deeper* reverence for all that is great, good, and holy" than other nations of the world. And America might hope to do so if she responded to the imperatives of phrenology, which demonstrated that "to improve the human mind, we must begin by improving the condition of the brain; and that to attain success in this object, all moral, religious, and intellectual teaching must be conducted in harmony with the laws of physiology." Phrenology had, too, wide political implications. If the people of the United States learned its principles, they could, by choosing as their leaders only those persons with well developed bumps of Benevolence and Constructiveness and eschewing those whose craniums displayed Adhesiveness and Destructiveness, create a better and more humane social and political order.

In their desperate pursuit of self-improvement and the general advance of society at large, thousands of Americans listened sympathetically to the appealing doctrines of phrenology. When such men as George Combe proclaimed them, how could they fail to contain saving truths?

Of all the English visitors who came to the United States and went home (at least in American eyes), to defame her, none caused such pain and rage as Charles Dickens. Americans loved Dickens. All his writings were instantly pirated and eagerly read. The characters in his novels were as familiar to Americans as the names of their most eminent citizens. Wherever he went in the United States in 1842 thousands turned out to welcome and acclaim him. The "Boz Ball" in New York City was one of that metropolis's most spectacular events.

Politicians, socialites, literary lions all vied to do him honor. Only Lafayette had been so enthusiastically greeted.

The "Boz Ball" was, in Hone's phrase, "the greatest affair in modern times, the tallest compliment ever paid a little man, the fullest libation ever poured upon the altar of the muses." The hall was decorated with painted scenes from the Pickwick Papers and living tableaux were presented at intervals during the evening. More than two thousand guests attended—"everybody was there," Hone declared. As chairman of the ball, Hone made a gracious speech of welcome to the famous author and his wife. Dickens was "a small, bright-eyed, intelligent-looking young fellow . . . somewhat of a dandy in his dress, with 'rings and things and fine array,' brisk in his manner and of a lively conversation."

The arrival of Dickens in Boston was the occasion for another great public celebration. "The town is mad," Richard Henry Dana noted, adding revealingly: "I shan't go [to visit him] unless sent for. I can't submit to sink the equality of a gentleman by crowding after a man of note." Dickens did express an interest in meeting the famous author of *Two Years Before the Mast*. Dana was impressed by Dickens's manner—"perfectly natural & unpretending." "You admire him, & there is a fascination about him which keeps your eyes on him, yet you cannot get over the impression that he is a low bred man." In short, not a gentleman.

Despite such adulation, Dickens went home and wrote his *American Notes* and, later, the "American" novel *Martin Chuzzlewit*. The first copies of Dickens's *American Notes* reached the United States at six o'clock on a Sunday evening. Within nineteen hours the book had been reprinted to sell for twelve and a half cents a copy and within two days five thousand copies had been sold in New York City alone. In Philadelphia the three thousand copies that arrived there were all sold within thirty-five minutes. The question "Why?" rose like a great pained diapason from hundreds of thousands of victims of Dickens's merciless pen. The answer is perhaps suggested in his preface: "Prejudiced, I am not, and never have been, otherwise than in favour of the United States," he wrote. "I have many friends in America; I feel a grateful interest in the country; I hope and believe it will successfully work out a problem of the highest importance to the whole human race." Dickens came to the United States believing it to be the hope and promise of the world. What he found here deeply offended his very middle-class English sensibilities. The crudeness, the violence, the constant chewing and spitting of tobacco, the pretensions of the new rich, the universal preoccupation with money, and, above all, the horror of slavery, depressed and dismayed him. Great parts of his *Notes* are, to be sure, like those of other travelers, primarily descriptive and by no means hostile. He visited prisons and asylums, the Lowell factories, Laura Bridgman and Harvard University, attended lectures on transcendentalism and declared Emerson's essays to contain "much that is dreamy and fanciful," but "much more that is true and manly, honest and bold."

The man who wrote so powerfully of the seamy side of English life was tenacious in examining the underside of the American cities he visited, the low bars and dives, the "squalid" streets and "leprous houses" of Five Points, places where "dogs would howl to lie, women and men, and boys slink off to sleep, forcing the dislodged rats to move away in quest of better lodgings . . . hideous tenements which take their name from robbery and murder; all that is loathsome, dropping and decayed is here."

Dickens visited the holding cells at the Tombs and denounced them as places that "would bring disgrace upon the most despotic empire in the world!" He was horrified by the virulence of party spirit and the constant displacement of public officers by members of the party triumphant at the most recent elections. Every week he saw "some new most paltry exhibition of that narrow-minded and injurious Party Spirit . . . sickening and blighting everything of wholesome life within its reach." At the same time, he had much to praise and found the social life of the upper class more congenial than that of England. He "greatly liked" Philadelphia although he believed the new re-formed solitary confinement system of the Eastern Penitentiary "cruel and wrong." "I went from cell to cell that day," he wrote, "and every face I saw, or word I heard, or incident I noted, is present to my mind in all its painfulness." Indeed, it is in discussing conditions in prison that Dickens is most moving and most eloquent, and the reader is inevitably struck by his capacity to enter into the feelings of the desperate and despairing men and women with whom he talked.

In his travels Dickens encountered the apparently limitless tribe of peripatetic Americans and what he experienced displeased him exceedingly: their "coarse familiarity," "insolent conceit," and "the effrontery of their inquisitiveness" infuriated him.

As for the famous republican Congress, instead of heroes and champions of freedom Dickens saw "the wheels that move the meanest perversion of virtuous Political Machinery that the worst tools ever wrought. Despicable trickery at the elections; underhanded tamperings with public officers; cowardly attacks upon opponents . . . shameful truckling to mercenary knaves, whose claim to be considered, is, with every week, they sow new crops of ruin with their venal types . . . in a word, Dishonest Faction in its most depraved and most unblushing form, stared from every corner of the crowded hall."

Since Dickens could not write dully and since he had a marvelously keen eye for detail and the intonations of language, his *Notes* make continuously entertaining reading even when he is most splenetic. At the end of the *Notes* he conceded that Americans were "by nature, frank, brave, cordial, hospitable and affectionate," but he implied that these qualities were confined primarily to the upper class. The mass of people carried "jealousy and distrust into every transaction of public life," displaying an alarming fickleness and inconstancy. "Smart" dealing and unscrupulous business maneuvers were more often admired than censured, and everything revolved around trade. When thus charged Americans replied that they were forced by circumstances to be strictly utilitarian. "But," Dickens replied, "the foul growth of America has a more tangled root than this." And this root was to be found in its "licentious press." Indeed, it was for the press—"this monster of depravity"—that Dickens reserved his most sulphurous epithets. Its "ribald slander" blackened and defamed every aspect of American life and rendered all its potential virtues nugatory.

Finally, he wished for America greater "lightness of heart and gaiety, and a wider cultivation of what is beautiful, without being eminently and directly useful." Traveling about the country, he had been, like Captain Marryat, "oppressed by the prevailing seriousness and melancholy air of business; which was so general and unvarying, that at every new town I came to I seemed to meet the same people whom I had left behind me, at the last." Greater personal cleanliness, better eating habits (not "hastily swallowing large quantities of animal food, three times a-day, and rushing back to sedentary pursuits after each meal") must be developed to improve the general health; "the gentler sex must go more wisely clad, and take more healthful exercise," and "ventilation and drainage" must be improved.

It is interesting to speculate on the decline, at the book's end, from speculations upon the ethical principles of Americans to exercise and drainage, though it may well be argued that the latter are as important in the history of mankind as the former.

Some upper-class Americans read Dickens's *American Notes* with considerable sympathy. Washington Allston, the painter whom Richard Henry Dana so admired, read the *Notes* and told the younger man that he was "less of a Republican than ever, & . . . that if things go on as they promise now 'In 30 years there will not be a *gentleman* left in the country.' He says that the manners of gentility, its courtesies, deferences & graces are passing away from among us."

American readers had not yet recovered from the *Notes* when *Martin Chuzzlewit* appeared. In *Chuzzlewit* Dickens wrote of "That republic, but yesterday let loose upon her noble course, and but today so maimed and lame, so full of sores and ulcers, foul to the eye and almost hopeless to the sense, that her best friends turn from the loathsome scene with disgust." *Chuzzlewit* was published serially; the chapter on Chuzzlewit's arrival in New York gave special offense to New Yorkers and to none perhaps more than to the chairman of his reception committee, Philip Hone, who noted that he had often taken Dickens's part, thinking that he had been "ungenerously treated," "but he has now written an exceedingly foolish libel upon us, from which he will not obtain credit as an author, nor as a man of wit, any more than as a man of good taste, good nature, or good manners. . . . Shame, Mr. Dickens! Considering all that we did for you, if, as some folks say, I and others made fools of ourselves to make much of you, you should not afford them the triumph of saying, 'There! We told you so!'"

Dickens's dismay over much of American life and manners can best be accounted for on what might be called the "disappointed lover" theory. Appalled by the social conditions in England, he came to the United States like a lover to the arms of a mistress whose beauties existed primarily in his own fancy and whose very real blemishes thus acutely distressed him. Allowing for the justice of much of his criticism, it was delivered with a degree of asperity, one might say bitterness, which could only have come from exaggerated expectations. Indeed, Dickens came in time to confess as much, returning a penitent in later years.

Of all the Englishmen who visited and wrote about America, perhaps Alexander Mackay, an English lawyer and political radical, made the most thorough and sympathetic analysis of the country and the people. Mackay had lived in the United States for several years before he visited it in 1846–1847 as a reporter for the *London Morning Chronicle*. He had, moreover, the advantage of arriving in the United States at the end of the first wave of visitor-writers. Opinion about America had had more of a chance to take on a discernible form and the country itself an additional decade to mend some of its more egregious ways.

While Mackay was almost as offended by the constant chewing and spitting of tobacco as Dickens had been and took note of American boasting, he also took pains to analyze the reasons behind Americans' sensitivity to criticism of any kind. The American, he noted, had few of the local attachments so common to peoples of other countries. "His feelings are more centered upon his institutions than his mere country. He looks upon himself more in the light of a republican than in that of a native of a particular territory. His affections have more to do with the social and political system with which he is connected, than with the soil which he inhabits." This quality, which made an American think more of the institutions of his country than of its soil, was, Mackay argued, the reason for his abnormal sensitivity. "He is proud of it, not so much for itself as because it is the scene in which an experiment is being tried which engages the serious attention of the world. . . . He feels himself to be implicated, not only in the honour and independence of his country, but also in the success of democracy. He has asserted a great principle, and feels that, in attempting to prove it practicable, he has assumed an arduous responsibility." Mackay even viewed the preoccupation of Americans of all classes with "trade" sympathetically. Trade was, after all, "the rapid road to wealth; and wealth gives great, if not the greatest consideration in America. The learned professions are not regarded as one whit more honourable, whilst they are but slenderly remunerated. The youth who wants speedily to make a figure," Mackay wrote, "sees the shortest road to the attainment of his wishes through the avenues of business. It is thus that they flock in crowds from the rural districts to the towns, the farmer's sons preferring the yard stick, with its better prospects, to the plough."

The most serious rival to the successful businessman was "the busy, bustling politician, who plunges into the thick of the fight, and works his way to the influence which he covets, at the expense of his time, his convenience, and often his better feelings," cutting a path usually too arduous for his wealthy compatriots to follow.

Like Marryat, Mackay had a writer's ear for colorful speech. He reported that one of his fellow travelers on the way from New York to

Boston by train confessed himself "a spekelator . . . none of your dubitatious sort; I've lots for sale in Milwaukee, and Chicago. . . ." "Why, our people," he told Mackay, "can turn their hands to a'most anything, from whippin' the universe to stuffin' a mosquito."

At the end of his *Western World,* Mackay declared that the wealth of the United States was such that one must be led "however reluctantly, to the conclusion that the power of England must yet succumb to that of her offspring. There is however, this consolation left us," he wrote, "that the predominant influence in the world will still be in the hands of our own race. The powers which are destined to overshadow [Great Britain] are springing up elsewhere and are of her own planting. Of these the American Republic, or Republics, as the case may be, will both politically and commercially take the lead, when England, having fulfilled her glorious mission, shall have abdicated her supremacy, and the sceptre of empire shall have passed from her forever."

As the years passed the travelers came in ever increasing numbers. They wrote their books, proving, usually, what they had come to prove—that the experiment in republican government was a miserable failure or, conversely, that it was the hope of the world. They came, of course, not only from the British Isles but also from France, Germany, Italy, Switzerland, Sweden, Denmark, Norway, Moldavia. Tocqueville's friend Gustave de Beaumont wrote his own observations in the form of a novel. J. J. Ampère, professor of belles-lettres at the College de France and inventor in the electromagnetic field, published *Promenade en Amérique.* He noted that science in America was applied not only to industry but employed in the most common affairs as well. He was robbed of his purse at a presidential reception and commented on the "sadness of Sunday" in America. Godfrey de Vigney published his *Six Months in America* in both Paris and London.

Carl Postl, son of an Austrian vintner, who went by the name of Charles Sealsfield in America, wrote entertaining sketches of the "glorious and chaotic" America he both loved and deplored. "Democracy," he noted, "unites the population of the country into a homogeneous whole which day and night works for the public good and even ennobles their insatiable greed for money." The Americans "pay no attention to history and value only the present. They are no Hamlets but men of action, and with them world history rolls along ten times more rapidly than in Europe."

From Scandinavia came the novelist Frederika Bremer, who

found the way paved for Swedish females by her enormously popular compatriot Jenny Lind, the Swedish Nightingale. Bremer's *Homes of the New World,* written in the form of letters to her daughter, announced that she had come to the New World to allow "that great world's life to flow" into her own. Unabashedly romantic, she wished to penetrate its "living soul, a great character, an individual mind, with which I must become acquainted. . . . How I desire to see its characteristic features, to listen to its revelations, its unconsciously oracular words regarding its life and future!"

She was, predictably, charmed by Emerson, the only actual literary "Alp." Bronson Alcott, who had "lived for fifteen years on bread and fruit," had "suffered very much in acting up to his faith and love," and Thoreau had "built himself a hut and lived there—I know not on what." She met Bayard Taylor, just back from California with tales of gold, and she decided the Yankee, "the type of the 'go ahead American'—of Young America" was an individual "who makes his own way in the world in full reliance on his own power, stops at nothing, turns his back on nothing, finds nothing impossible, goes through every thing, and comes out of every thing—always the same. If he falls, he immediately gets up again and says, 'No matter!' and he begins again, or undertakes something else, and never stops till it succeeds . . . always working, building, beginning afresh, or beginning something new—always developing, extending himself or his country. . . ."

The Longfellows and the Howes were friendly to Miss Bremer. She visited all the expected places and spent months in the South, which she loved though she hated slavery. And when she left, she left sadly. She had come to observe "the commencement of the world's greatest governmental culture. That which I sought for was the new human being and his world; the new humanity and the sight of its future on the soil of the New World." The educational system and "aid of the unfortunate, schools and asylums" had impressed her most. She had hoped to find the vision of a redeemed humanity, "that kingdom of the Millennium where the lion shall lie down with the lamb; where every man shall sit in the shadow of his own vine and his fig-trees; where all people shall meet together in peace and heaven shall smile over a happy family of 275,000,000 of human beings . . .," but she had been forced to give up that "beautiful dream . . . I no longer have any faith in it. It is gone! The western land of the New World," she wrote, "will not produce any thing essentially different from the eastern. The New Paradise is nowhere to be met with on earth. . . . There will, however, be no deficiency of enlightenment among the people of North America," but in battle "between God and Mammon" she could only say of the outcome "*I did not know!*" America was clearly "not a Utopia, but—a judgment-day; that is to say, a more determined separation between the children of light and the children of darkness, between good and evil—a more rapid approach toward the last crisis." "The new man of the New World" had great opportunities and great advantages in that final combat. "And if I were to seek for one expression which would portray the peculiar character of the people of the New World, I could not find any other than that of *beautiful human beings.*"

One of the most perceptive and engaging of the travelers was Moritz Busch. Like his countryman and fellow revolutionary Carl Schurz, Busch came to the United States full of democratic idealism after the abortive German uprising of 1848. Without a wife, he ranged farther than Schurz and, without introductions to prominent persons, he fared less well and cared less for his new home—so little that he abandoned it after almost two years and took his chances in the land from which he had been forced to flee three years earlier. But Busch was nonetheless a keen observer, and if he found much to make fun of he also found much to admire.

He believed that the most conspicuous characteristic of Americans was the push toward democracy, "the government of all, by all, for all." This spirit was particularly manifest in New England, "and New England once was (and to a certain extent still is) the soil of America. . . . Wealth is . . . a secondary goal in the consciousness of the people. The passion for it has increased astoundingly since the beginning of the century, and the two roads leading to it—business and politics—are almost the only ones upon which the so-called better class is encountered." The *"idea of liberty"* appeared to Busch to stand out in the United States, "incontrovertibly as the character nucleus of the nation, and its unfolding to the earth-shading tree is the destiny of America in the organism of history."

But the "love for individual liberty" had certain negative side effects, the most conspicuous of which to Busch was "hostility toward all authority. Every single thing must state its reason and say why it exists and what justifies it to be so and not otherwise. . . . From this hatred of all authority . . . comes an aversion toward everything old. This is one of the explanations for the continual change in all affairs of the American. His house, his books, even his churches must always be new. . . . America is the land of heresies and sects, partly because it is hostile to any authority." Another American characteristic was "a questioning and searching after ultimate causes and general ideas. To be sure, one looks first for the facts, but then he looks immediately for the law of the fact and finally for the reason for the law." This trait helped to explain the American passion for lectures and the willingness of "shopkeepers and tailors" to "lend an attentive ear when Agassiz and Emerson, men who certainly do not speak in a very popular vein, announce a series of lectures." The American "intensity of living and striving" had its good side but it also had its bad. "It produces," Busch wrote, "haste, superficiality, and vanity. . . . One strives for the big, the many, and the spacious—not for strength and quality. . . . In education the goal is not to learn as much as possible but to snatch up rapidly as much as is absolutely necessary. . . . Everything is activity, running and rushing. One is so bent upon creating and working that one has no time for enjoying and hence enjoys very little of the poetry of life. . . . Everything is done 'in less than no time,' from the tanning of a cowhide to the training of a soul for the work and earning of life; and if flying is ever invented, it certainly will be done in the United States."

Americans, Busch wrote, seemed only able to measure worth in money. In Boston a man "believed he was praising a distinguished writer by remarking that his books had earned him more money than anyone else in the field." The desire to make money appeared (as it had earlier to Franklin and John Adams) to be an important incentive to progress. It was only "when money is sought as God and an excess of material goods as the final goal and not as a means" that the essential spirit of a people was threatened. "Never yet was a nation too rich," Busch added, "although many a nation has lost its soul in striving for material possessions." Such matters were secondary, Busch believed. "They do not belong to the basic idea of America and in their present form are even hostile to it." Once America had created its own abundance the nation would "proceed to the realization of its great national idea [the "idea of liberty"] and begin, first at home, and then over the entire earth (we hope), the sublime work that lies as a germ in the nucleus of its character. From new perceptions and previously unheard-of ideas new forms of social life will originate, compared to which the present day will appear like the barbarism of the Middle Ages. An American art will blossom—no tasteless imitation . . . but a fresh, independent weaving and working. An American literature will develop that satisfies the country and its character. . . . Finally, also, an

American church will be formed upon the ruins of present-day sectarianism—a marriage of the faith content with its present-day enemy, reason, and a recreation and renewal of aging Christianity by the spirit of liberty. . . . For this transformation of our race in and through the genius of the New World, this transfigured revival of the Old World in the New, *is* the Millennium!"

One of the most exotic visitors was Israel Joseph Benjamin, a Moldavian Jew, who reached the United States in 1858. Although Benjamin's interests were directed primarily at the status of Jews in the United States, he had many other comments, accurate and inaccurate, to make on life in America. He, like virtually all other travelers, was dismayed at the pursuit of wealth in the United States. "Almost every man is . . . driven to try to become a merchant, a banker, a speculator, a manufacturer, or tries to capture a position that will yield money," he wrote. "The child hears from its father, the pupil from his teacher, the student from his professor, that gold creates an almighty power in every circle of society. The greed for it is thus nourished with our life's blood at the expense of all nobler, better and higher feelings and at the sacrifice of our spiritual capacities and our happiness. Thousands sacrifice their health and their lives to the service of Mammon and as a result of this general and prevailing passion the human spirit is completely neglected. . . . This is the focal point of our corruption. . . . Herein . . . lies the root of the sickness and this is the dangerous cancer. The spirit of the American people is sick in a fashion that must arouse the greatest anxiety. . . ."

After a year spent in the East, "with its industrious and intelligent inhabitants, the West with its unpretentious prairies and woods, the sunny South and the stern North," Benjamin took passage to California, where we shall encounter him again.

In 1847 Domingo Faustino Sarmiento, an Argentine revolutionary, visited the United States to observe the functioning of the government and decide what in the American system might be applicable to his own new nation. He would return to help frame a new constitution, based in part upon that of the United States, and serve as president of the Republic from 1868 to 1874. "God," he wrote, "has ordained that in one nation only there should be joined together the following elements: the virgin soil that permits a society to expand ad infinitum without fear of poverty; iron that supplements human strength; coal that feeds the machine; forests that provide timber for naval construction; the public education that develops creative power in the people of a nation; religious liberty that attracts large masses to join the population; and the political liberty that looks with horror upon despotism and special privileges. In other words the Republic, strong, soaring heavenward like a young plant! All these factors are closely linked; liberty and the abundant earth, iron and the industrial genius' democracy and immense forests. . . ."

Sarmiento was especially impressed by the life and vitality of small towns. "The North American village," he wrote, "is a complete State, with its civilian government, press, schools, banks, municipality, census, its spirit and appearance." This was in sharp contrast to the villages in those countries which had been under Spanish colonial rule. There everything emanated from the capital. A swarm of petty officials carried out the orders of a centralized bureaucracy.

While Captain Marryat had predicted that the settlement of the West must bring about the dismemberment of the Union as the West asserted its own power in rivalry with the East, Sarmiento saw much more accurately that the westward movement produced a "constant reaffirmation of the national government," the principle of Union. Describing an overland journey of settlers to Oregon, he noted that once they had arrived, "the heads of families lay aside the axes with which they had been slowly clearing away the forests" and came together in a legislative assembly " 'with the object of establishing the principles of civil and religious liberty as the basis of all laws and constitutions that may be adopted in the future.' " The settlers thus carried with them, "organically, like a political conscience, certain constitutive principles of association." That seemed to Sarmiento the secret of the remarkable expansion and growth of the United States—the ability of ordinary citizens to do time after time as John Winthrop and the first Puritan settlers in New England had done more than two hundred years before—establish from scratch the classic institutions of a free people.

One especially observant traveler was a young Russian lawyer, Aleksandr Borisvich Lakier, who came to the United States a few years before the outbreak of the Civil War and recorded his observations about American customs and institutions. He had come, he assured a curious American questioner, not simply to "see how the Yankees live, how they use their freedom to shoot each other with revolvers, or how they get rich." He had a more serious purpose in mind. He wished to "answer for myself the question of how this youngest member of the family of mankind had managed to leave its older brothers so far behind in trade, shipping, and general productive activity. Why was it that the North American States were already serving as a model for Europe when from the first existence of America to the present day only a century and a half had elapsed? What promise did the future hold for this enterprising country? What could be derived for our own benefit and edification from the great experience represented by America? . . . Where was the core of that democratic equality which is quite incomprehensible to a European?" Peopled by a "race which had always stood in the vanguard of humanity's movement toward enlightenment, moral development, and material advancement," the United States had carried all these impulses much further than the lands from which it had drawn its heterogeneous population. Like Tocqueville, Lakier was constantly impressed by the absence of the "fossilized strata" that characterized European nations. "Each person is equal to every other in his right to discuss and interpret. There are no people inferior to others, there are only the rich and the poor."

The one issue on which Americans took irreconcilably different positions was on slavery and Lakier, on his passage across the Atlantic, was informed of all the arguments respecting that institution because among the passengers were two of Harriet Beecher Stowe's daughters. In his travels Lakier was delighted to find that "The American loves the Russian, for whom he predicts a great future and whom he wants to amaze with his own wealth, rapid growth, and present-day riches."

At the end of his visit Lakier left the United States with mixed feelings. He wondered why it was "that while much in individual Americans is not personally pleasing and offends our senses, yet from a distance one looks at these lively, clever, practical people and begins to have a reverential attitude for their boldness, their activity, and their realistic views of things? One may not love certain particulars in America, but one cannot help loving America as a whole or being amazed at what it has that Europe cannot measure up to—a people who know how to govern themselves and institutions that, unaided, give a person as much happiness and well-being as he can accommodate. . . ." Certainly there was much for a cultivated European to find fault with. But, Lakier concluded, "when your elbows no longer hurt from the blows of Americans on the run, and when you are no longer seated at the dinner table next to an American in a hurry, it is another matter. Then you love and marvel at him!"

We have discussed some of the more interesting commentators on the American scene to try to convey a sense of how large the United States loomed in the imaginations of the rest of the world and also because, in the words of one historian, they hold up a "mirror for Americans" in which we often see ourselves with startling if disconcerting clarity.

15

Hell in Harness

Tracks preceded trains. Enterprising entrepreneurs began laying crude tracks in the 1820s to carry horse-drawn carriages. The advantages were that a horse could pull a much heavier load faster and passengers much more comfortably on tracks than on the commonly rutted and unpaved roads of the time. Rails were usually made of wood with bands of iron on top. In Maryland experiments were conducted with stone "rails" covered with iron. The iron-covered wooden rails proved unsatisfactory as soon as the first steam engines were introduced; they had a tendency to tear loose and curl up, especially at the high rates of speed that the steam engines were soon capable of attaining—as much as fifteen miles an hour.

In England, steam engines at first seemed most promising in carrying passengers over ordinary roads and turnpikes. The Duke of Wellington's barouche was drawn by a steam engine and attained a speed of more than twenty-five miles an hour. English experiments in the use of rails were confined primarily to the hauling of heavy loads by horse or mule and, more and more frequently, by the use of some kind of steam engine.

In America, Peter Cooper, a successful businessman, saw the possibilities of combining rails and steam engines. While Cooper was neither an engineer nor an artisan, he did not hesitate to involve himself in the design of a locomotive, buying up unmounted gun barrels to use as tubes in the engine's boiler. When the locomotive failed to perform satisfactorily, Cooper turned the job of making a better one over to George Johnson, the owner of a machine shop and a skilled mechanic, who set to work with his young apprentice, James Milholland. While Johnson and Milholland were working on an improved version of Cooper's train, the *Stourbridge Lion,* imported from England, arrived in New York, followed by several other engines which were eagerly studied; the best features were quickly incorporated into the American machine.

Fourteen miles of railroad had meanwhile been laid between Baltimore and Ellicott's Mills, allowing horse-drawn carriages to make the trip in record time. The run to Ellicott's Mills was made by the horse carriage three times a day at a charge of twenty-five cents.

By May 30, 1830, Cooper's steam engine was ready to be tested. Cooper himself took the throttle of the *Tom Thumb,* with the president and the treasurer of the Baltimore & Ohio Company beside him. The *Tom Thumb* had a fourteen-inch piston stroke, weighed barely a ton, and developed slightly more than one horsepower, but it drew a weight of more than four tons at the rate of fifteen miles an hour. To draw attention to this new machine, Cooper advertised "a race between a Gray Horse and *Tom Thumb.*" The race took place on August 28, 1830, and a passenger on the coach drawn by the locomotive wrote: "The trip was most interesting. The curves were passed without difficulty, at a speed of fifteen miles an hour. . . . The day was fine, the company in the highest spirits, and some excited gentlemen of the party pulled out memorandum books, and when at the highest speed, which was eighteen miles an hour, wrote their names and some connected sentences, to prove that even at that great velocity it was possible to do so." It was on the way back to Baltimore that the famous race occurred. At first the horse, with quicker acceleration, raced out ahead but as the engine got up steam it overtook and passed the gray. Just at that moment the safety valve on the engine blew open and the train lost pressure and fell behind, despite Peter Cooper's frantic efforts to repair the damage.

George Stephenson, the great British engineer, had been working for almost a decade to perfect a practical engine. He had, in the process, built a dozen locomotives of various types in the well-equipped workshops of the Liverpool and Manchester Railroad and he had the stimulus of half a dozen active competitors. The United States had entered the field late and with far more modest resources, but within two years Cooper had produced the first practical passenger railroad locomotive. Engines designed by Stephenson soon outstripped the *Tom Thumb,* but American railroad building was on its way. When the Baltimore and Ohio offered a four-thousand-dollar reward for the most improved engine, Johnson and Milholland had one waiting. Its most serious rival was one designed and built by Phineas Davis, a watchmaker. Three other engines were also entered, each with important original features and all differing greatly in design. The *York,* built by Davis, won the first prize and Davis became an employee of the Baltimore and Ohio Railroad. It soon seemed as though every ambitious young engineer in the United States who could round up a few financial backers was making a locomotive. A year after the *Tom Thumb* made its historic run, the Mohawk and Hudson Railroad was completed and an engine named the *DeWitt Clinton* drew three cars at speeds that at times reached thirty miles an hour.

The Baltimore and Ohio Railroad Company had been formed on July 4, 1828, and the cornerstone laid by ninety-year-old Charles Carroll of Carrollton. But the course of the railroads, as they were soon called, proved far from smooth. They were opposed by the farmers, through whose lands their right-of-ways must run, in an alliance with the officers and stockholders of canal and highway companies (who rightly saw the railroads as dangerous competition), and by the teamsters (whose jobs were threatened). The engines themselves were so unpredictable that teams of horses had to be kept at way stations to pull broken-down trains to their destination.

Experiments in developing practical rails accompanied the constant experiments on improved engines. By 1832 the Baltimore and Ohio had carried 140,000 people between Baltimore and Washington over a wide variety of "rails"—iron on granite, wood and iron on stone blocks, wood and iron on wooden crossties on a bed of broken stones, and wrought iron.

By 1832—two years after *Tom Thumb*'s famous trip—Pennsylvania alone had sixty-seven railroad tracks from a few hundred yards to twenty-two miles in length, many of them constructed of wood. When the Baltimore and Ohio built a passenger carriage with seats on either side of a center aisle, there were strong objections that such an aisle would simply become an extended spittoon, but this seating arrangement soon became standard on most lines. (Davy Crockett was widely reported to have exclaimed at his first sight of a train: "Hell in harness, by the 'tarnal!")

Locomotives proved easier to build and to improve in efficiency than rails. Many rails were imported from England at an exorbitant cost. The six miles of railroad between Philadelphia and Germantown, for example, cost some thirty thousand dollars per mile and the rails, weighing thirty-nine pounds to the yard, were English-made.

On his way from Quincy to Washington in the fall of 1833 to take his seat in Congress, John Quincy Adams rode on the Amboy railroad from Amboy to Philadelphia. The train consisted of two locomotives, "each drawing an accommodation car, a sort of moving stage, in a square, with open railing, a platform and a row of benches holding forty or fifty persons; then four or five cars in the form of large stage coaches, each in three compartments, with doors of entrance on both sides." Each train ended with a high-piled baggage car, in which the passengers' luggage was covered with an oilcloth. The train sped along at almost thirty miles an hour, but after ten miles it had to stop to allow the wheels to be oiled. Despite this precaution, in another five miles a wheel on one of the cars caught fire and slipped off, killing one passenger and badly maiming another. Of the sixteen passengers in the coach only one escaped injury.

Boilers on the early trains were wood-fired and, like steamboats, trains had to stop frequently to take on fresh supplies of wood. The remarkable thing is that in spite of all these difficulties—the constraints imposed by state legislatures under the control of the canal and highway interests, the scarcity of money, the inadequacy of the rails themselves, the constant litigation, the restrictive municipal ordinances that for a time forbade the building of railroad stations in cities, the disastrous accidents that plagued every line, the barns and fields set afire by sparks that showered from primitive smokestacks— the building of engines and railway tracks went inexorably on.

Boston, which had seen the greater part of the vast commerce with the Mississippi Valley West go to New York with the construction of the Erie Canal, took the lead in developing railroad links with the West, thereby regaining much of its lost financial eminence. New York, anxious to protect the investment of the state and its citizens in the canal, did all it could to impede the development of competing railroads.

By 1850 there were some three thousand miles of track running from Boston to the principal cities of New England and westward to

Ohio, representing an investment of seventy million dollars. Of even greater significance was the fact that most of the lines made money.

The South was almost as well represented as the North in the initial stages of railroad development. South Carolina took the lead by ordering an engine from the West Point Foundry and building, by 1833, more than 137 miles of railroad, the longest line then in existence.

In Pennsylvania, when the Philadelphia–Columbia line was opened in 1834, an engine designed and built by Mathias Baldwin was placed in operation; it weighed almost twice as much as any earlier American locomotive and drew thirty cars, each carrying sixteen passengers. The cars resembled stagecoach carriages and were manufactured by carriagemakers.

The railroad mania exceeded, if possible, the earlier canal mania. Canals still continued to be built, of course, and fierce competition developed between canals and railroads, but an extraordinary amount of technical skill and ingenuity was channeled into the development of railroads and the locomotives and the cars that passed over them. Hardly a month passed without some important innovation which, as soon as it had proved itself (and often before), was adopted by other designers and builders. It was as though a particular quality in the American character, until now more or less dormant, had been activated. For forty years—from 1789 to 1830—the canal, the steamboat, and the bridge had been the primary fields of engineering development. Now, with the "discovery" of the railroad, the machine shop claimed equal importance with the farm or factory and Americans revealed more dramatically than ever before their astonishing facility for marshaling human energies and material resources to meet a particular challenge. Barns became foundries, warehouses were converted into machine shops. New tools were built and old tools improved. Moreover, the primary activity of building locomotives spawned a host of subsidiary and only indirectly related undertakings. Farmers with a bent for mechanics began working on an improved plow. Longer and stronger bridges had to be built to carry heavier and heavier trains, and there were tunnels to be built through mountains that blocked the way. It was clear that principles developed in making locomotives—such elements as pistons and valves—were adaptable to other processes. So there was a dizzying proliferation of inventions and improvements. Dedicated from the first moment to finding labor-saving methods and building labor-saving tools, thereby improving the ratio between work and its monetary return, a new breed of Americans—men like Peter Cooper and Mathias Baldwin and thousands of their less well-known compatriots—ushered in the "go-ahead age," the age of technology wherein any ambitious and dexterous farm boy might dream of becoming as rich as John Jacob Astor or Peter Cooper. A disposition to see the world in terms of practical problems to be solved was both the condition and the consequence of such a habit of mind, and it certainly contributed directly to the optimistic strain in American character. Wherever one looked he or she could see signs of "progress" and improvement in man's long war against nature. Everywhere "nature" was in retreat and civilization in advance. The Indian was nature, the natural man, and he was giving way to the determination of the American to cultivate the land and obey the biblical injunction to make it fruitful and to be fruitful himself, the determination to organize space and apply ideas to landscape with such single-minded zeal and unwearying industry that the landscape must succumb. Philip Hone noted proudly in his diary: "There was never a nation on the face of the earth which equalled this in rapid locomotion." A message had been carried from President Tyler in Washington to New York, a distance of some 225 miles, in twenty-four hours.

In the face of every obstacle the promoters of the railroads pushed ahead, raising their capital primarily by public subscription. A train of seventeen cars ran from Baltimore to Washington in 1835 in two hours and fifteen minutes, carrying relatives of Washington, Adams, Jefferson, and Madison. But antirailroad teamsters still waylaid trains and shot at crews from ambush, and two years later the Depression of 1837 brought railroad building to a virtual halt. It was eleven years before stockholders in the Baltimore and Ohio got any return on their investment and then it was a mere 2 percent. Construction had gone on during that period to connect Baltimore with the Ohio River commerce at the cost of $7,500,000, and only the intervention of the famous British banking house of Alexander Baring made it possible to avoid bankruptcy.

The biggest impediments to the railroads were laws designed to protect the investors in canals. The Chesapeake and Ohio canal, for example, cost $60,000 a mile to build and took twenty-two years to complete, by which time many of the original investors had died. The most notable feature of the canal was a tunnel 3,118 feet long which required the use of headlamps on barges passing through it, and despite the fact that the Baltimore and Ohio Railroad ran its tracks parallel to the river, the transportation of Cumberland coal down the canal brought in substantial revenues for years, although not enough to pay its enormous costs. Protracted and expensive as its construction was, the canal was by any standard one of the great engineering feats of the century, second only to the Erie Canal. Legislators were under enormous pressure to protect such a huge investment.

A number of states passed laws requiring the railroads, after they had recouped the cost of their construction, to pay all profits above 10 percent to rival canal companies. Other laws prohibited trains from entering into or passing through the incorporated areas of cities and towns. Some states included in railroad franchises the requirement that railroads sell their tracks and stock to the state after twenty years—at the state's evaluation. Other provisions limited the carrying of freight by train to those times of the year when the canals were frozen. Freight and passenger rates of trains were frequently tied to those of canal transportation to keep the trains from drawing off business. A more practical obstacle was the fact that virtually every railroad company, many of which ran no more than fifty to a hundred miles, had a different gauge, so that freight and passengers had to be unloaded and loaded again at the boundary of every company. Everything in America was bound to have a moral dimension; the railroads must be seen as not merely having a remarkable effect on commerce but as improving morals. In this spirit the Western Railroad Company of Massachusetts sent a circular to all the clergy of the state pointing out "the moral effects of rail-roads" and urging them "to take an early opportunity to deliver a discourse before your congregation, on the moral effect of rail-roads on our wide extended country"— thereby, presumably, encouraging investment.

Since nature and morality (and, indeed, religion) were intertwined, the railroad train must be somehow reconciled with nature. Emerson, who believed that everything worked for the best, had no trouble in effecting the reconciliation. He was entranced by the technological revolution ushered in by the train. In 1834 he wrote in his journal: "One has dim foresight of the hitherto uncomputed mechanical advantages who rides on the rail-road and moreover a practical confirmation of the ideal philosophy that Matter is phenomenal whilst men & trees & barns whiz by you as fast as the leaves of a dictionary. As our teakettle hissed along through a field of mayflowers, we could judge of the sensations of a swallow who skims by trees &

bushes with about the same speed. The very permanence of matter seems compromised & oaks, fields, hills, hitherto esteemed symbols of stability do absolutely dance by you." The railroads had introduced a "multitude of picturesque traits into our pastoral scenery," Emerson wrote, "the tunneling of the mountains, the bridging of streams . . . the encounter at short distances along the track of gangs of laborers . . . the character of the work itself which so violates and revolutionizes the primal and immemorial forms of nature; the villages of shanties at the edge of the beautiful lakes . . . the blowing of rocks, explosions all day, with the occasional alarm of a frightful accident." These all served to "keep the senses and the imagination active."

The train, Emerson believed, would complete the conquest of the continent, carrying Americans to every corner and making the United States "Nature's nation." The ambivalence of Emerson's own view of nature is suggested by his remark that "Nature is the noblest engineer, yet uses a grinding economy, working up all that is wasted to-day into to-morrow's creation. . . ." Thus nature was a good Puritan after all, a hard worker who wasted nothing.

In fairness to Emerson it must be said that, visiting the industrial midlands of England, he had second thoughts about the happy union of nature and technology. "A terrible machine has possessed itself of the ground, the air, the men and women, and hardly even thought is free," he wrote. Everything was centered in and conditioned by the omnipresent factory. In 1853, no longer rhapsodic about railroads, he wrote: "The Railroad has proved too strong for all our farmers & has corrupted them like a war, or the incursion of another race;—has made them all amateurs, given the young men an air their fathers never had; they look as if they might be railroad agents any day."

By the early 1840s the railroads had an irresistible momentum. Small lines constantly consolidated in an effort to increase their access to capital and improve their service. New lines were established and as soon as they proved themselves (or went bankrupt) they were taken up by larger lines and incorporated into a "system." This process of consolidation was noted by Sidney George Fisher in 1839. "The whole route from Washington to N. York," he wrote, "is now owned by gigantic corporations, who of course manage the lines solely with a view to profit, without reference to the convenience or accommodation of passengers. Heretofore the line on the Chesapeake has been unrivalled for speed, cleanliness, civility of officers & servants, and admirable accommodations of every kind. Secure now from any competition, & sure that all persons must travel by their conveyance, they charge what they please, and the fare & accommodations will I doubt not be as wretched as that of the line to N. York." British capital and the labor of Irish immigrants were two essential ingredients in the extraordinary expansion of the railroads in the decade of the 1840s. The prize was the produce of the Mississippi Valley, the great bulk of which had to be carried down the Mississippi and its tributaries to New Orleans. To carry it by rail to New York and the large East Coast cities and ports would generate enormous profits. The Pennsylvania Railroad took the lead in building a "through line" of uniform gauge (this meant a shift from primarily passenger service to freight and passenger) and in dressing its train "captain" or conductor in a uniform with blue coat and brass buttons. Coal was the principal freight on short hauls within states. Wheat and lumber were common loads on long hauls. Perhaps most important were the changes in the patterns of urban and rural life that the building of innumerable feeder lines brought about. Farmers within a radius of a hundred miles or more of a city could now ship fresh produce—milk, eggs, fruit and vegetables —to city markets. The farmer was thus disposed to specialize, to raise cash crops in sufficient quantity to make it practical to ship them to city markets. Dairy farms and one-crop farms thus began to replace general farming. As the farmer came to depend on distant city markets, he also became vulnerable to the operations of middlemen or wholesalers, who offered the lowest possible price for his produce, and from fluctuations in demand resulting from economic cycles. The farmer thus lost a measure of his cherished independence in return for more hard money. In turn the city, guaranteed a supply of essential foods, was able to grow at an unprecedented rate.

Much of the capital required to build railroads and develop coal mines as ancillary to them came from England. An English family named Morrison started the Hazelton Coal Company at Hazelton, Pennsylvania. Sidney George Fisher's brother Henry was the American representative for the coal company and for the Reading Railroad, which the Morrison family also owned. "The railroad," Sidney wrote, "is excellent, you roll along with great speed and great smoothness, and there is very little jar or noise, the cars are very comfortable, and there is but one source of annoyance, the cinders & smoke from the engine." The mining town of Tamaqua, not far from the Hazelton mine, was "a miserable village, wretched houses & population, produced by and dependent on the Little Schuylkill mines which are

all around the town & make the whole place black with coal dust."
Hazelton was a pleasant "new town" located in a pine forest under
which lay "immense and rich veins of coal." The ground was
undermined for miles around with diggings and the Morrisons, Fisher
reported, owned "1800 acres of the finest coal land in the state, the
buildings, mines, railroad & machinery."

In time the legal impediments to railroad building were struck
down by courts or repealed by state legislatures. The emphasis now
shifted to providing incentives for building railroads, especially in the
Mississippi Valley region, where vast expanses of lands were unsold
and unsettled because of their distance from markets. Most settlement
took place along rivers and waterways that provided access to markets.
Illinois set aside eleven million dollars in 1837, the year of the
depression, to build a railroad that would run through the center of
the state down to the Ohio River, but the state was in such desperate
financial circumstances that it was fourteen years before any substantial progress was made in building the Central Illinois Railroad to link
the Great Lakes with the Ohio and the Mississippi, making Chicago the
terminus for the proposed route. Irishmen again provided the
workers, and the death toll from disease was a heavy one. Cholera was
especially deadly in the crowded and unsanitary work camps. "Our
laborers," an engineer wrote, "numbered from 5,000 to 8,000 men. We
had to recruit in New York and New Orleans paying transportation to
Illinois . . . but the men would desert when the cholera epidemics
broke out and scatter like frightened sheep. Men at work one day, were
in their graves the next. In Peru, 130 died in two days. It was
dangerous during the summer months to eat beef, butter, or drink
milk. Our difficulties were increased by the groggeries and whisky that
got in our camps. Drunken frolics ended in riots, when a contractor
was murdered and state troops called out. One hundred and fifty
laborers left in a body after the riot."

Another account of the westward extension of the line reported:
"Two engines delayed 24 hours, while engineers and firemen went off
on a drunken spree. . . . North bound freight ran into a drove of
cattle, went down an embankment . . . nine cars with it. . . . Engine 72
went off trestle and sank in Lake, where it lies stranded with waves
breaking over it. . . . Work at standstill for 10 days, December, on
account of snow and ice. . . . Two of our Irish workmen shot by
groggery gang. . . . Cholera has broken out again."

The Central Illinois cost ten million dollars more to build than its projectors had estimated. The state gave the company 2,595,000 acres of land along its right-of-way. Abraham Lincoln was an attorney for the railroad; when he submitted a bill for $2,000 for his services and the railroad protested that that was more than Daniel Webster would have charged, Lincoln raised his fee to $5,000, took the railroad to court, and won his claim. Land through which the railroad passed rose in value from sixteen cents an acre to ten dollars an acre in a five-year period and a decade later to thirty dollars an acre.

The South now lagged behind the North and West in railroad building. All told, the feverish decade of building in the forties resulted in quadrupling the number of miles of railroad. This was all accomplished at enormous cost (the better part of it never recovered) and great loss of life (primarily Irish). When Alexander Mackay visited the United States in 1846 he found "an unbroken line of railway communication extending from Boston . . . to beyond Macon in Georgia, a distance of upwards of 1,200 miles." Lines reached out from Philadelphia to Pittsburgh, and the Baltimore and Ohio was pushing through the Cumberland Gap into the Mississippi Valley. Over 5,700 miles of railway had been completed, 2,000 of it within New England and New York state, and more than 4,000 miles of additional railway were under construction. In the 1850s the railroad mileage of the nation quadrupled once more.

Of all those who profited from the incredible expansion of the railroads none rose as dizzily as the city of Chicago. As Gustaf Unonius wrote in 1860, "The web of railroads which Chicago has spun around itself during the last ten years is the thing that more than anything else has contributed to its wealth and progress." The first locomotive reached the city in 1851. Seven years later it was the terminus of more than a dozen trunk lines. Three lines ran from Chicago to New York in less than thirty-six hours (it once had taken ten days to make the trip). Daily 120 trains, some of them hauling as many as forty freight cars, arrived and departed from the stations in various parts of the city. "It should be mentioned," Unonius wrote, "that all these railroads, altogether measuring five thousand miles in length, which radiate from Chicago as a central point in that immense iron web, the threads of which cross each other everywhere in the extensive Mississippi valley, are private undertakings." Private undertakings, as we have noted, with considerable public encouragement.

The passion to "go ahead," the endless emphasis on speed, exacted a heavy price in lives and serious injuries. In 1838 alone 496 persons died and many more were seriously injured in boiler explosions, not to mention those killed or injured in wrecks. Sidney George Fisher noted in his diary that there had been an accident on the North Pennsylvania Railroad in which thirty-nine persons had been killed and seventy-two wounded. One of the cars had caught fire and seventeen people had been burned to death. "These horrible scenes," he added, "are constantly recurring, and there seems no remedy." And Philip Hone wrote: "I never open a newspaper that does not contain some account of disasters and loss of life on railroads. They do a retail business in human slaughter, whilst the wholesale trade is carried on (especially on Western waters) by the steamboats. This world is going on too fast. Improvements, Politics, Reform, Religion—all fly. Railroads, steamers, packets, race against time and beat it hollow. Flying is dangerous. By and by we shall have balloons and pass over to Europe between sun and sun. Oh, for the good old days of heavy post-coaches and speed at the rate of six miles an hour!"

Captain Marryat ascribed such American "recklessness" to "the insatiate pursuit of gain among a people who consider that time is money, and who are blinded by their eagerness in the race for it. . . . At present, it certainly is more dangerous to travel one week in America than to cross the Atlantic a dozen times. The number of lives lost in one year by accidents in steamboats, railroads, and coaches was estimated . . . at *one thousand seven hundred and fifty*!" To Hone such disasters were "a stigma on our country; for these accidents (as they are called) seldom occur in Europe. . . . But we have become the most careless, reckless, headlong people on the face of the earth. 'Go ahead' is our maxim and password; and we do go ahead with a vengeance, regardless of the consequences and indifferent about the value of human life." His reflections were prompted by a report of the burning of the *Ben Sherrod*. The boat's crew, according to newspaper reports, was drunk and the wood took fire. "Out of 235 persons, 175 were drowned or burned to death." By the end of the year fifty-five steamboats had blown up, burned, or run aground and sunk on the Mississippi River alone; thirteen sunk on the Ohio and two on the Missouri.

When Marryat ventured by rail around the United States in the 1830s he wrote: "At every fifteen miles of the railroads there are refreshment rooms; the cars stop, all the doors are thrown open, and out rush the passengers, like boys out of school, and crowd around the tables to solace themselves with pies, patties, cakes, hard-boiled eggs, ham, custards, and a variety of railroad luxuries, too numerous to mention. The bell rings for departure, in they all hurry with their hands and mouths full, and off they go again, until the next stopping place induces them to relieve the monotony of the journey by masticating without being hungry." By the time Isabella Bird traveled west twenty years later there were numerous conveniences not available to Marryat. Bird reported that "water-carriers, book, bon-bon, and peach vendors" were "forever passing backwards and forewards." Baggage could be checked with metal checks, which was a novelty and a great convenience. Bird also discovered "through tickets," a single long ticket bought at the station of origin, for an entire trip of fifteen hundred miles on a dozen different lines.

Since Americans traveled so perpetually, travelers' accommodations were generally excellent, clean, and comfortable and virtually interchangeable. Marryat observed that "the wayside inns are remarkable for their uniformity; the furniture of the bar-room is invariably the same: a wooden clock, map of the United States, a map of the state, the Declaration of Independence, a looking-glass, with a hair-brush and comb hanging on it, *pro bono publico;* sometimes with the extra embellishment of one or two miserable pictures, such as General Jackson scrambling upon a horse, with fire and steam coming out of his nostrils, going to the battle of New Orleans, etc. etc."

The nature of travel in America was as different from travel in other countries as the American character was different. Since Americans of all classes traveled so constantly and, on the whole, relatively cheaply, they developed what we might call their own traveling style. Sidney George Fisher, snobbish as he was, preferred traveling by stagecoach to railroad or steamboat primarily because of the great opportunities for sociability. "There are more incidents," he wrote. "The change of passengers, of drivers & horses; the stoppings at the country inns, where you see new faces & groups & a thousand indications of the character of the people, all interest & occupy the mind. . . . The journey is enlivened by conversation, and your interest and attention are awakened by the collision of ideas, the varieties of manner & exhibitions of character. You also get information about the country thro which you are passing." Trains were far more socially constricting, if only because passengers sat in rows facing ahead. There were not on trains, moreover, the frequent stops and the opportunities for convivial drinks at taverns and inns along the way.

Traveling Americans were uninhibited and curious. Isabella Bird reported that on a train headed for Cincinnati a nasal "down-East" voice inquired, "Going west?"—"Yes." "Travelling alone?"—"No." "Was you raised east?"—"No, in the Old Country." "In the little old island? Well, you are kinder glad to leave it, I guess? Are you a widow?"—"No." "What business do you follow?"—"None." "Well, now, what are you travelling for?" And on and on.

Americans turned traveling into a form of popular entertainment; this was especially true on the innumerable steamboats plying the interminable rivers. Moreover, Americans in transit appeared at their best. They were almost invariably considerate of ladies, ready to help someone in trouble or excessively encumbered with luggage. Loving motion, they were usually cheerful in movement. Sidney George Fisher noted a great improvement in manners on a journey to western Pennsylvania in 1843 (a long jaunt for him). "Every one I met was civil, gracious and obliging without exception," he wrote; "whereas formerly surly tavern keepers, savage drivers, rude clowns were expected of course everywhere. We are certainly improving," he added. "It is evident in everything I saw, & the people say so themselves. Those with whom I conversed ascribe it to the diffusion of education by means of the public schools & to the reformation produced by the temperance movement."

The feverish railroad building of the 1840s and 1850s opened up a large part of the still undeveloped land of the Mississippi Valley and provided a tremendous stimulus to business activity, although it did not prevent the devastating Depression of 1857. Perhaps most important of all, it had tied the Old West or the Near West to the Northeast and thereby laid the foundation for preserving the Union.

One can only attempt to convey the nature of the railroad boom by such phrases as "reckless enthusiasm" and "extravagant passion." The American public, which had so recently fallen in love with canals, now made trains the objects of its collective affection. Canals suddenly seemed hopelessly pokey and out of date although they continued to be an important part of the transportation network. The loss of money and loss of life attendant upon the marvelous new invention seemed to most people an in-no-way unacceptable price to pay for the intoxicating sense of *speed*, of being drawn along as fast as the wind. So began a hundred-year-long love affair between Americans and railroads. If any one invention or device can be said to have had a determining effect on the history of a people, it was certainly the railroad train on the history of the people of the United States. In the beginning everything was aqueous. Water was the element on which Americans moved—lakes, rivers, and canals provided the initial circulatory system of American travel and American commerce. Now it was iron and soon it would be steel. The canal was an adaption of nature to human needs. The train, with its relentless disposition to go straight and level to its destination, was the subjugation of nature, man's greatest triumph over a world of curves and declivities.

16

The Near West

In the United States in the 1840s there were at least six "Wests," all quite definably different. There was, first of all, the "Old" West, or what we will call the "Near West," the upper Mississippi Valley which extended from the Great Lakes down to the Mississippi and its major tributaries to the Missouri. It included Ohio, Illinois, Michigan, Wisconsin, Indiana, Iowa, and later Minnesota and Nebraska Territory, the area covered roughly by the Northwest Ordinance. The "South" West ran from Missouri south to Louisiana and west through Texas to the Rio Grande. It also included western Kentucky, which retained its frontier character at least until the Civil War. The "Fur" West lay in the eastern foothills of the Rocky Mountains at the headwaters of the Missouri River and the region drained by the Yellowstone, containing the present-day states of Montana, Wyoming, and Colorado.

The fourth "West" was what came to be called the Great Basin region—the high plateau desert country between the Rockies and the Sierra Nevada range. This was the area of the future states of Utah, Idaho, and Nevada. Then there was the fifth "West"—the Pacific Coast West of California, the westernmost portion of the Far West. Finally, there was the "North" West of present-day Oregon and Washington.

When an Easterner or a European traveler spoke of "the West" it was often unclear which West or Wests he or she had reference to. The settlers in, or inhabitants of, all the Wests displayed certain common characteristics, and the original or Old West provided the great portion of the emigrants to the subsequent or new Wests. What distinguished these various Wests from each other was, then, less the character of their inhabitants than their astonishingly varied terrains. They thus provided a remarkable study of complex relationships of ideas to geography and the dominance of ideas over landscape. What is equally important to bear in mind is that American settlement leaped from the Old West—the Mississippi Valley West—over some two thousand miles of forbidding terrain to the Pacific Coast West, leaving the plains and Rocky Mountain–Great Basin West to fill up much later.

Tocqueville wrote of the vast tide of westward emigration: "This gradual and continuous progress of the European race towards the Rocky Mountains has the solemnity of a providential event; it is like a deluge of man rising unabatedly, and daily driven onwards by the hand of God. . . . No power on earth can shut out the immigrants from that fertile wilderness which offers resources to all industry and a refuge from all want. Future events, whatever they may be, will not deprive the Americans of their climate, or their inland seas, their great rivers or their exuberant soil. Nor will bad laws, revolutions, and anarchy be able to obliterate that love of prosperity and spirit of enterprise which seem to be the distinctive characteristics of their race. . . . The time will therefore come when one hundred and fifty million men will be living in North America, equal in condition, all belonging to one family . . . preserving the same civilization, the same language, the same religion, the same habits, the same manners, and imbued with the same opinions. . . . The rest is uncertain, but this is certain; and it is a fact new to the world, a fact that the imagination strives in vain to grasp."

The Old or Near West was distinguished geologically by the so-called Prairie Plains and the Lake Plains. The physical features of these contiguous areas were the product of enormous glaciers, sometimes a mile or more in height, that had over a million years or more moved from the north polar regions as far south as the Ohio River. In their slow grinding action they had converted the limestone mountains of the Great Lakes region into soil of remarkable richness. American land was like money. Marvelously fecund in many areas, it could often be bought for a few dollars an acre and almost immediately converted into cash. In many ways, its attraction was more akin to mining than to traditional farming. It yielded to the plow more readily than ore-bearing rock yielded to the miner's pick, and for the enterprising farmer was a much more reliable source of wealth. To sow such virgin land was often to recover much more than the original investment in the initial harvest. Not only had the glaciers produced a soil of great richness, they had most obligingly leveled the land rather in the form of a vast billiard table. The Indian practice of burning the prairies in hunting had left large regions free of trees and thus aided the pioneer farmer immeasurably.

Small prairies alternated with wooded areas. Tree-lined streams and rivers ran in a southerly direction and innumerable lakes dotted the region. The Grand Prairie began in northern Illinois. The Red River Valley of Iowa was predominantly mixed prairie, as was eastern Nebraska and Kansas. Native grass grew as high as a man's head in many areas and provided excellent grazing for cattle. The so-called oak openings, combinations of forest and prairie, were especially favored by pioneer settlers. Wood was available for building houses and barns and the terrible labor of clearing tree stumps was minimized. In the words of James Fenimore Cooper, between the oaks were "spaces . . . always irregular, and often of singular beauty [which] have obtained the name of 'openings'; the two terms combined giving their appellations to this particular species of native forest, under the name of 'Oak Openings.'" Northern Michigan, Wisconsin, and Minnesota had unsurpassed forests of white pine. It was the influx of settlers into the area of southwestern Wisconsin containing lead that had been the cause of the Black Hawk War.

The settlers in the southern portions of Illinois, Indiana, and Iowa were predominantly from North Carolina, Kentucky, and Tennessee. New Englanders, New Yorkers, and Pennsylvanians filled the northern portions of those states, thus ensuring a preponderance of free-state settlement and sentiment in the Near West. Tocqueville called the Mississippi Valley "on the whole, the most magnificent dwelling-place prepared by God for man's abode. . . ."

The Near West's most awesome feature was, of course, the Great Lakes. If the Mississippi River was its spinal column and nervous system, the Great Lakes were the lungs and the heart. Gustaf Unonius, the Swedish immigrant, wrote: "Of all the great bounties a good Providence has showered on the American continent there is perhaps none greater than this extensive navigable mass of water in the midst of the country, providing, as it does, even for the most remote regions, direct communication with the Atlantic Ocean. . . . In the innermost heart of the old country, where astounding new life streams are flowing forth, the real springs of the mercantile importance of the United States have their source."

The Lakes covered a surface of not less than 93,000 square miles and contained, it was estimated, five-sevenths of all the fresh water on the globe. Their waters held an apparently limitless supply of fish, their shores pine and fir trees beyond numbering as well as vast deposits of lead and coal. Over their surfaces passed every year more and more steamboats loaded with freight and passengers headed for the current frontier—Indiana, Iowa, Illinois, and Wisconsin.

In 1833 some 43,000 immigrants were taken by steamboat from Buffalo to various ports along the Lakes. Captain Marryat was told that over "one hundred thousand emigrants pass to the west every year by the route of the lakes," 30,000 of whom were from Europe. The rest of the world had little notion of "the vastness and extent of commerce carried on in these inland seas, whose coasts are now lined with flourishing towns and cities, and whose waters are ploughed by magnificent steamboats, and hundreds of vessels laden with merchandise. . . . In such places as Buffalo and Cleveland, everything is to be had that you can procure at New York or Boston. . . . It must be recollected that hundreds of new houses spring up every year in the towns, and that the surrounding country is populous and wealthy. In the farmhouses—mean looking and often built of logs—is to be found not only comfort, but very often luxury."

In the mining and lumber towns along the shores of the Great Lakes, Gustaf Unonius found frontier life at the rawest. Their isolation, the absence often of any women except prostitutes, the wide-open saloons "all give such communities," he wrote, "a spirit of brutality, savagery, and lawlessness." The lead mines of the state were soon producing over 15,000,000 pounds of lead a year.

The northern tier of states was strong on the leading reforms of the day, from abolition through women's rights, and Ohio was the center of such enlightened sentiments. The main line of the Underground Railroad ran through the region. Missouri was of course a slave state, as was Kentucky. South Illinois was predominantly Southern, while the northern half of the state was populated largely by Yankees. Frederika Bremer was so taken with the region that she declared if the millennium were ever to come, it would surely find its home in the area of the Mississippi Valley whose de facto capital was Cincinnati.

The Monticello Seminary for Young Ladies near Alton, Illinois, represented the progressive character of the region. Two graduates of Mt. Holyoke were among the staff of four "professors." "The mathematical course was as thorough as was to be found in any college," wrote Georgiana Bruce, who taught music there for a term. Latin, French, European history, moral and intellectual philosophy were also taught, as well as English composition "and a critical knowledge of the most noteworthy passing events." All the most advanced authors and liberal spirits of the day were read by the young ladies—Emerson, of course, and William Channing, Margaret Fuller, and Henry James, Senior, as well as the tracts and essays of Horace Greeley and Horace Mann. The Monticello Seminary was a church-supported school and the liberated young women were bored and annoyed by the reactionary, "tiresome, illiterate preaching" of hellfire and damnation that they were required to listen to twice each Sunday. When Georgiana Bruce asked the seminary's director why the staff did not resign rather than put up with such drivel, that good lady replied, "We are zealous and courageous in our labors; we know what are the best interests of those committed to our care. Would others as earnest and liberal take our places? The perfect situation occurs only in novels."

The center of this region of apparently inexhaustible natural riches was Cincinnati on the Ohio River. Its handsome buildings, clean streets, and enterprising citizens gave off an air of republican prosperity that was most attractive. There was no large population of depressed Irish laborers or indigent free blacks. And those that were to be found were usually the beneficiaries of some benevolent association organized to relieve their sufferings. Fifty-eight percent of the residents in Cincinnati were "native" Americans, 28 percent Germans, and 14 percent British or Irish. In contrast to the older Eastern cities, Cincinnati and her less notable sister cities exuded a "spirit of independence and good will," in the words of Georgiana Bruce. There was a feeling of well-being and abundance that was not observable elsewhere, "more food seemed thrown out of the back door than was taken in at the front door in New England." Bruce was most drawn to the "westernized Yankees, who had forgotten the cramped life of the East, but had not divested themselves of the neatness and good taste in which they had been trained, or the skill they had acquired in that excellent school." They subscribed to the *New York Tribune* or, if from New England, to the *Boston Evening Transcript;* and if they had strong antislavery feelings they subscribed to Garrison's *Liberator* as well.

Cincinnati was, in the words of Captain Marryat, "the pork-shop of the Union." (Moritz Busch, visiting there ten years later, called it "Porkopolis.") When Marryat arrived in 1838, he wrote that "the way they kill pigs here is, to use a Yankee phrase, *quite a caution.*" A hog was killed "upon the same principle as a pin is made—by division or, more properly speaking, by combination of labor." One man knocked it on the head as it was driven through a chute and then cut its throat, "two more pull away the carcass, when it is raised by two others, who tumble it in a tub of scalding water. His bristles are removed in about a minute and a half by another party, when the next duty is to fix a stretcher between his legs. It is then hoisted up by two other people, cut open, and disembowelled; and in three minutes and a half from the time the hog was grunting in his obesity, he has only to get cold before he is again packed up, and reunited in a barrel to travel all over the world."

It was estimated that some slaughterhouses killed and dressed more than 1,500 hogs a day by means of such techniques. From the slaughterhouse huge "rack-wagons" carrying 60 to 1,000 hogs at a time conveyed the carcasses to the packing houses. Moritz Busch recorded that 752 hogs were cut up and salted by six men in thirteen hours. By 1850, 500,000 hogs were being shipped from the city, along with 25,000,000 pounds of ham and 16,500,000 pounds of bacon, while thirty lard factories turned out some 1,500,000 pounds of lard. The largest "pork house" was that of Milward and Oldershaw, which covered two acres and held, on its roof, 4,000 animals. But pork was by no means the whole story.

Moritz Busch was taken through a bed factory that employed some 130 men. Five stories high, 70 feet deep, and 200 feet long, the factory used more than fifty steam-driven machines for sawing, planing, drilling, and turning and produced 130 bedsteads a day, ranging in price from $1.33 to $75. In the "gigantic" Johnston chair factory, 170 men turned out several hundred thousand chairs a year. Isabella Bird visited the factory and took note of the "baby-rocking cribs, in which the brains of the youth of America are early habituated to perpetual restlessness." Cincinnati also boasted "the greatest shoe factory in the world." "Two hundred male employees and no fewer women and children" worked in eight large halls turning 30,000 cowhides and 20,000 sheepskins into shoes every year. Ten other such shoe factories existed in Cincinnati along with forty-four iron foundries employing a total of 4,500 men; the largest foundry was owned by a German whose work force numbered over 350.

With all its bustling industry, the city maintained an intriguing frontier atmosphere. Isabella Bird saw men wearing "palmetto hats, light blouses, and white trousers . . . while Germans smoke chiboks and luxuriate in their shirt-sleeves—southerners, with the enervated look arising from residence in a hot climate, lounge about the streets—dark-browed Mexicans in *sombreros* and high slashed boots, dash about on small active horses with Mamelouk bits—rovers and adventurers from California and the Far West with massive rings in their ears, swagger about in a manner which shows their country and their calling, and females richly dressed are seen driving and walking about, from the fair-complexioned European to the negress or mulatto." In the stores, despite their gaudy window displays, Bird was surprised to find "the richest and most elegant manufactures of Paris and London."

Cincinnati was rich in benevolent institutions—the Deaf and Dumb Institute, with 130 pupils; the Asylum for the Blind, modeled after Samuel Gridley Howe's institute in Boston; and the Lunatic Asylum, with 400 separate rooms in which the "mentally ill are housed."

Moritz Busch noted that in the Mississippi Valley in 1852 Bunyan's *Pilgrim's Progress,* a life of the Indian chieftain Tecumseh, and Howe's *Historical Collection of Ohio* were the best-sellers, followed by "geographical and local historical collections" and novels about the West, usually sold in train stations and at steamboat landings. Macaulay's *History of England* had sold well, as had Rollin's *Ancient History.*

An increasingly serious rival to Cincinnati was the recently established town of Chicago. Its location at the southern end of Lake Michigan gave it access by water to Canadian ports and through Lake Erie and the St. Lawrence to the Atlantic. On a combined business (to inspect his Western real estate) and political (to help establish the Whig party in the West) trip, Philip Hone and his daughter made their way by steamboat up the Illinois River to Peru, beyond Peoria, and traveled by carriage the hundred miles or so to Chicago. That city was so crowded that father and daughter went from hotel to hotel searching in vain for accommodations. Acquired from the Winnebago Indians fifteen years earlier, "now it is a large town," Hone wrote, "beautifully situated at the head of Lake Michigan, a transcendentally beautiful

Mediterranean Sea . . . streets of stores and fleets of vessels, cottages for people of taste, brick houses for people of wealth, hotels for traveling people, and churches for good people." Ten thousand Whigs (of whom, Hone estimated, six thousand were delegates) thronged the city. No building was large enough to hold them all and they gathered under an enormous canopy on the courthouse grounds where they were addressed by Edward Bates, a Missouri Congressman, who gave a speech Hone described as "beautiful beyond description—brilliant and tasteful as Crittenden, seductive and captivating as Clay, powerful and convincing as Webster." Hone was not the only enthralled listener. The speech instantly made Bates a figure of national importance in the Whig Party.

Next to St. Louis, Isabella Bird found Chicago "more worth a visit than any other of the western cities." Even a day there was worth the voyage across three thousand miles of ocean. It seemed to her that the manner of its citizens proclaimed: "Stranger, I belong to the greatest, most enlightened, and most progressive nation on earth; I may be president or a *millionaire* next year; I don't care a straw for you or anyone else."

Fifteen years later, in 1855, when Gustaf Unonius visited the city, he was told that during the "navigation season" before the Lake froze, 6,610 ships had tied up at the city's piers, carrying a combined load of 1,608,845 tons of goods. It was already the greatest grain terminal in the world. In a single year one Chicago firm shipped 500,000 bushels of grain to Buffalo. Illinois alone produced, in 1855, 130,000,000 bushels of corn and 120,000,000 bushels of wheat. Between 1854 and 1856 the export of wheat increased two and a half times and that of corn nearly doubled. Along with oats, barley, and rye, Chicago saw more than 20,000,000 bushels pass through its warehouses and stations in the latter year.

Unonius, taken through a great grain elevator, found "something really sublime" in it, "a gigantic accomplishment in a city which in itself is one of the world's great wonders. . . ." The building was 203 feet long, 101 feet wide, and 117 feet high. Two railroad tracks ran along each wall, spurs from a main line. Six freight cars could be unloaded in six minutes in one of 148 bins, each 50 feet deep and holding 5,000 bushels of grain. A 500-bushel scoop lifted, weighed, and returned the grain to its bin. If a ship was to be loaded, it docked beside the elevator, the bottom of a bin was opened, and the grain ran through a spout into the hold of the vessel "with almost incredible speed." In less than an hour two ships, Unonius wrote, "are loaded with 12,000 bushels apiece." The elevator itself could hold 750,000 bushels. It employed no more than thirty men and most of its machinery was run by a 30-horsepower steam engine.

The only serious rival to grain was lumber. "Along the shores of the Chicago River," Unonius wrote, "there is nothing to be seen for a distance of six miles but lumberyard after lumberyard." In 1856, 457,711,267 cubic feet of boards and planks were imported into the city. "Great locomotive works, car shops, foundries, and all kinds of machine shops employing thousands of workmen" filled orders from all over the world. Prominent among them was Cyrus McCormick's factory for making several thousand harvesting machines a year. Twenty-five newspaper presses supplied the city's insatiable thirst for news and fifty churches cared for its soul. There were hotels "which in matter of elegance, comfort, equipment, and stock cannot only be compared with, but also surpass most establishments of that kind in the European capitals," Unonius noted.

The census of 1840 showed 212,000 people in Michigan and double that in 1850, with an impressive array of libraries, schools, and newspapers.

Iowa, originally part of the Missouri Territory, became part of Michigan and Wisconsin territories when Missouri achieved statehood in 1821. A district in 1832, Iowa was made a territory in 1838, two years later it had a population of 43,000.

By the end of the 1830s, Wisconsin Territory was all the rage. Milwaukee, advantageously located at the southern end of Lake Michigan, was a terminus for emigrants making their way into the interior. The number of steamships that arrived at Milwaukee in 1840 was 174, along with as many sailing vessels; the principal exports were wheat, furs, and pork as well as lead and copper. Ten years later the city had thirty churches—seven of them Lutheran—two musical societies, three orphanages, three Masonic lodges, five Odd Fellows lodges, several literary societies, and two temperance societies. Returning home by way of Milwaukee, Hone found it "another wonder of the Western world—an Aladdin's palace on a large scale—raised in a night . . . streets of business filled with wagons, some conveying merchandise of New York into the interior of the state, and others bringing in *new country* produce, and taking out *old country* immigrants; churches, printing-offices, markets and milliners—and all these in a place where 12 years ago there were just three log-shanties."

Among the early settlers in Wisconsin were the Christianized Stockbridge and Brothertown Indians, who had fought alongside the Americans during the Revolution. They came to Calumet County and by 1840 there were more than five hundred of them and only three whites—a missionary, a tavernkeeper, and a miller. They erected a grist and saw mill and for a time it was the only one in the region. Ten years later there were 1,746 whites in the county and, as one Stockbridge Indian put it, whites believing the Indians to be "poor degraded savages . . . scarcely dared to pass through our County, for fear of being scalped. But since they have learned that the Indians are an agricultural, mechanical, and manufacturing people, that they live, dress, and talk like other 'human critters,' that they have their own common schools . . . churches and preachers . . . they begin to entertain a little more respect for Calumet County and her population." The first steamboat on Lake Winnebago had been built by the Brothertown Indians, who had petitioned Congress for citizenship and received it, but the Stockbridge Indians turned out to be bitterly divided over the issue and the tribe split between those who wished citizenship and those who preferred to retain their special status as Indians and as wards of the government.

A very different settler, accompanied by his new bride, found his way to Wisconsin Territory in 1841, seven years before it was to become a state. Gustaf Unonius was a young Swede, educated at the University of Uppsala, whose opportunities were severely limited in his homeland. A clerk in a provincial accountant's office, he felt that his "hopes of a happy life, of freedom and independence" could best be fulfilled in the United States. "Its rich soil and industrial advancement right now offered a home, a means of livelihood, and an independent life to thousands of Europeans who in one way or another had found their hopes dashed in their own homelands," he wrote. "There every faithful worker had in his civic reputation his certificate of nobility. Conventional prejudices, class interests, petty public opinion, and the harlequin-wraiths of changing fashions did not cling to one's coat-tails or dog one's heels. American—what was there to prevent me . . . from going to that country, which like a new El Dorado appears before every venturesome youth? Her fabulous birth and history had excited our wonder from earliest school years; she realized . . . millions of hopes, had become a tomb for age-old prejudices, a cradle of true civil liberty, equality, and of such new social ideals as are destined to bring happiness to mankind."

At first Unonius's hope had been to find companions with whom to establish a Swedish colony in the American West. But this proved difficult and he finally decided to venture forth with his wife, her serving-girl, and a cousin. "I do not go to America," Unonius wrote, "to 'get rich quick.' Many labors, many difficulties, many privations await me. I shall have to do without the comforts to which I have been accustomed. In a literal sense I shall have to eat my bread in the sweat of my brow." Unonius also confessed that there was in him "a . . . radicalism that makes me see in the present institutions and social conditions of Sweden many things that are patched up, shrunken, and pitiful, and I have little inclination to become a cog in the worn-out machinery." He was convinced that he was only the vanguard of a vast tide of immigration who would soon seek to improve their lot in the United States where the simplicity of life and social policy and the rapid expansion of the nation's economy "make it possible for one and all . . . to forge their own future."

Unonius and his little party had first to be vigilant that they were not swindled by travel agents who swarmed around the newly arrived immigrants offering to sell them cut-rate tickets to the West, or, indeed, anything else they were disposed to buy, including the land itself. Once they were on a steamer, headed up the Hudson for the Erie Canal, a "strange fear" took possession of Unonius. The pushing, jostling crowd "awakened . . . scenes from stories I had sometimes read depicting the shadier side of American life. . . . Now we and our fellow travelers were alone in a strange land, among people that were total strangers, whose language we did not understand and to whom our own was still more strange; on our way to settle down in a far country about which we had only vague notions." On the Erie Canal, passing through its numerous locks, Unonius was deeply impressed by the engineering skill involved. "Everything," he wrote, "testifies to the wonderful power and immense resources possessed by a people whose energy when any great national undertaking is to be carried out, will allow nothing to bar its progress." Passing through the villages scattered along the canal, Unonius was struck by the "great number of churches and banks—evidence perhaps, in spite of the failures that occur in both these institutions, of the greater intensity of both spiritual and material activity here than in older communities . . . almost in every block [we came] across some temple erected for the worship of either God or Mammon."

Buffalo, at the western terminus of the canal, was a city that had literally sprung out of the wilderness. A scruffy village at the time of the War of 1812, it now boasted "comfortable five-story hotels, furnished with luxury and elegance . . . gas and water systems . . . fine buildings, private as well as public . . . numerous charitable institutions . . . literary organizations, printing offices, bookstores, and well-stocked public libraries. . . ."

The steamship *Illinois* was to carry them across the Great Lakes. The boat was filled with prospective settlers, "Yankees, English, Irish, Germans, etc.," whose heads were "full of plans for the future and how to establish themselves in a region of which they have only the slight knowledge to be derived from rather unreliable newspaper propaganda and guidebooks or the . . . highly colored descriptions given by fly-by-night land agents." The Yankee traveled light, "hardly more than the clothes he wears, a small trunk, a blanket, a few pieces of linen, an axe, a saw, and a few small tools. These will be the core of his personal effects in the log house soon to be erected, where his hardiness and inventiveness presently will supply him with everything he needs for his first home." The English invariably carried some prized piece of furniture "or some carefully cherished relics of an old china set," while the German immigrant bore along with him "plows, horseshoes, spades, harnesses, wooden tubs, chairs, old clocks, candlesticks, old engravings, and broken tobacco pipes. . . ."

From Detroit the steamer made its way up the Detroit River and into Lake Huron. Occasionally it stopped to take on wood and the passengers had a chance to stretch their legs. Mackinac had been the center of the northwest Indian trade and the town was full of Indians selling or trading furs, moccasins, baskets, and toy birch-bark canoes.

Unonius and his party had only the vaguest notion of their destination. Illinois was a name they had heard, so it was to Illinois they planned to go. A Swedish-speaking passenger informed them that the steamer stopped at Milwaukee, the largest town in the new Territory of Wisconsin. Unonius had never heard of the town or the territory before, but several of the passengers described it as one of the most attractive and fertile districts in the great West and, "after a family conference," Unonius decided "to look around in this region since everybody seemed to be going there." Milwaukee was an up-and-coming town. At their hotel Unonius found a piano in the parlor and on the center table the works of Byron, Longfellow, and other writers and poets as well as an English translation of *Don Quixote*.

They were told that Wisconsin Territory had grown in ten years from a population of scarcely 3,000 to 45,000. It appeared to be especially attractive to groups of settlers from Germany and the Scandinavian countries. "The natural resources of the country are being developed with astounding speed," Unonius wrote. "Here as elsewhere cities are springing up as by magic, agriculture, business, even manufacturing are beginning to flourish. . . . Before the streets have been leveled [in new towns] printing shops are established, and periodicals, religious, political, commercial, agricultural, and literary in content, are scattered in all directions throughout the new territory." Ten years earlier the first settlers had been fighting with the Indians. Now the stories of their hardships were legends "in the highest degree rich and exciting. One scarcely knows what to marvel at more," Unonius wrote, "the bravery and boldness of the hardy pioneers or the insatiable greed that always, at least to some extent, lay at the bottom of these perilous ventures."

Wisconsin, like the other territories of the West, was divided into square townships, six miles to the side, consisting of thirty-six sections, each one a mile square. A settler could register his land claim for so many parcels at $1.25 an acre but be excused from having to pay until the land was officially put up for sale. For the purpose of starting a university, Unonius noted, the government had given the state two townships for a total of 46,080 acres.

It was in an "opening" beside a small lake that the Unoniuses decided to make their new home. Once the site had been selected his wife, Lotten, and Christine, the maid, moved to a kind of cabin-hotel owned by an Englishman and his wife some fifteen miles away, while Gustaf and his cousin Carl built a crude lean-to made of small trees seven or eight feet long laid in a square on top of each other and covered it with some poles and a small supply of hay they had brought with them in a wagon. In this shelter they put a bed that Lotten had bought in Milwaukee. A few miles east were some other settlers, but to the north and west "was a vast expanse of forest in which no man had ever built his cabin. . . . We were still unacquainted with the wilderness, where our voice could not reach another abode." Winnebago Indians roamed through that region, hunting and fishing in the myriad lakes. "Taking all these things into consideration," Unonius wrote, "it was not strange that somber feelings should assail us when the darkness of night fell and we were to rest for the first time in our lonely, makeshift hut." The next day snow fell.

Gustaf and his cousin learned to use American axes through trial and error, cutting trees and hitching the oxen that had drawn their wagon to pull them to the building site. "Briskly and lustily we . . . kept swinging our American axes in the primeval forest," Unonius wrote, "and when the trees fell to the ground we cheered as lustily as the cry of 'Strike' on the bowling alley in Uppsala."

Almost before the cabin was finished, the location was known as New Uppsala; Unonius was often called Mr. Uppsala by neighbors who thought that was his name. While work proceeded on the cabin, Indians camped nearby. "I cannot say that this was a particularly pleasant surprise for one whose scant knowledge of North American Indians had been gathered from Cooper's novel," Unonius wrote. Yet he was soon on friendly terms with them, visited their camp, and noted all he could of their costumes and customs, awed by "their indomitable pride, their unfailing courage, their wild defiance. . . ."

When the logs had been cut for the walls of the cabin, Unonius and his cousin drove their wagon to a village—whose claim to even that modest status rested on a sawmill and a lumber mill—to get planks for the ceiling of their prospective cabin. The manager lived in a frame house built of boards, newly painted white, with glass windows and green shutters. Inside Unonius saw "carpeted floors, polished furniture, and an elegant bookcase."

Now it was time for the house raising and Unonius and Carl spread the word around the region. Most of the people to whom they spoke promised to come and also to notify others. "Far from showing any displeasure at such a call which involved walking, axe on shoulder, eight, ten, or even more miles from their homes and neglecting their own urgent affairs, the settlers appeared to take pleasure in coming to the aid of strangers." Handspikes were put in place and smooth trees for leaning against the walls as they mounted so that the next logs could be slid into place were prepared. By midmorning of the day set for cabin raising, there were twenty-three persons at work. The logs were quickly notched and lifted into place. By four o'clock in the afternoon, work had been completed. The house stood erect, 22 feet long, 18 feet wide, and 12 feet high. "The work," Unonius noted, "had proceeded cheerfully and heartily. . . . Many adventures were told from early pioneer days, jokes, witticisms, and laughter were the order of the day. A jug of whiskey had been placed by the side of a pail of fresh spring water. . . ." Unonius had brought with him a number of Swedish sheepskin coats and one of these was bartered for "two big, fat pigs" and ten bushels of corn. Then there were refreshments and

Unonius delivered a speech of thanks in broken English and Swedish. There was still much to be done: windows and, most important, a roof made of uncured oak planks covered with hay, which leaked copiously at the first rain. In the absence of stone, the chimney was built of clay packed between supported walls, the inside one of which was removed after the clay had hardened. Unonius and Carl then decided to splurge on an iron stove the next time they got to Milwaukee. Finally, the house was ready for Lotten and Christine, although the roof leaked and wind blew between the logs.

The cabin had no floor or even a door, "without chairs, table, or any other piece of furniture. . . . Still it was home . . . our home, built by our own hands, in a strange land. . . . To be sure it lacked every outward comfort, was wanting in every convenience that the most insignificant dwellings generally offered and yet it was home, and as we entered it, it seemed rich in all its poverty, rich in love, rich in friendship, rich in trust in God for His peace and blessing under that low roof."

After he had established himself with his wife and cousin on Pine Lake, Unonius discovered that only a mile away was the Bark River, which flowed into the Rock River, which in turn emptied into the Mississippi 165 miles south of the Wisconsin border. He thus could have traveled, had he wished, by canoe from Bark River, hardly more than a creek, to New Orleans.

The area around the Unonius farm soon filled up with settlers. Many were friends and relatives of Unonius or his wife from Sweden. Others were Norwegians, with whom the Swedes found surprisingly little in common, looking on them as a glum and joyless people. A school was built; on Sundays various religious denominations used it in turn, each succeeding the other "like regiments at the changing of the guard."

With the influx of Swedish immigrants, the Unonius house took on the character of a hotel, sometimes as many as eighteen people sleeping in the cabin. While Unonius always gave the newcomers a helping hand, he advised them to settle amid Americans rather than among other Swedes. In that way they would learn more quickly the American ways of doing things and better resist the temptation to cling to old customs. The Germans, he noted, were most inclined to cluster together, speaking their own language and observing their own feasts and festivals, in many instances not even attempting to learn English.

Among the new settlers was a Swede named Wester, who had been a rag collector in his motherland and now planned to set himself up as a Methodist preacher. Fleeced at a camp meeting by a fellow preacher, Wester declared, "Now I want no God but the dollar, and for him I will labor." He tried his luck as a barber and failed, tried religion again, moved to Illinois, and took up barbering once more. There he flourished at last, opened a general store and advertised his wares throughout the adjacent counties.

Unonius and his wife experienced all the hazards and setbacks that were part of pioneer life. Deer and rodents nibbled away at their small field of corn. Roving Indians stole a large stack of swamp grass Gustaf had cut for hay, and by spring they and their animals were near starvation. Their breakfasts were often burned-wheat coffee, potatoes, and an "ill-tasting brown sugar" called "nigger sweat." They took the straw from their mattresses to feed the ox and cow. Unonius prevailed on a prosperous farmer a few miles away to let him pick the furrows for half-frozen potatoes and turnips, and weak with hunger lurched home with a heavy sack. "My outward and my inward strength failed," he wrote, "and for the first time in my life I burst into tears with grief that for the moment seemed inconsolable."

At the first showing of spring buds, trees were chopped down and the tender shoots fed to the cattle. Soon there were grass and flowers, flocks of ducks on the lake and pigeons swarming in the trees. The cow gave milk and the chickens, guarded through the bitter cold of the winter, began to lay under bushes and in hollow stumps. Fifty Norwegian families arrived with money to buy what the Unoniuses could spare. Those immigrants who came with some substantial means soon found it eaten up in the cost of establishing themselves and were no better off than their poorer neighbors. The Norwegian immigrants were largely of the peasant class, "a vigorous, robust, and industrious people," Unonius noted, who generally fared better than the middle-class types who predominated among the Swedish settlers.

Unonius's life was further complicated by the fact that he decided to become an Episcopal minister and thus had to spend much time at the newly established seminary of that denomination at Nashotah. Ordained, he began to travel through the frontier settlements, performing services: marrying, baptizing, and evangelizing for his church.

Some Swedes made their way to the area of Pine Lake but many more pushed on to the plains of western Illinois, in Unonius's view the best destination for them. "The fertility of the soil," he wrote, "is surpassed by no other region on the American continent. . . . I hardly know of anything that can compare in freshness and invigoration with a clear summer morning on the wide prairie. . . . The cultivation of the prairie is as easy as its fertility is great. The farmer here is not compelled to waste his strength year after year hewing down giant trees of the primeval forest, and tearing out the stumps and roots to secure arable land. The plow can be put into the ground at once without any preliminary labor, and there are no rocks to impede its progress."

Unonius told of an Illinois farmer with a capital of $700, who, in 1847, purchased 20 acres of forest land and 160 acres of prairie. With a team of horses and a yoke of oxen he plowed and planted 55 acres of land his first year. The third year he plowed an additional 50 acres at the cost of $2 per acre. By the eighth year he sold his wheat for $2,000 and his capital had increased to $8,000 or $10,000. A laborer who spent five years splitting fence rails accumulated in that time $1,400. He lent $800 to a friend, bought a quarter section of land for $200, and spent $400 for cattle. In a few years he had acquired 7,000 acres of land with 2,700 under cultivation. In 1854 he sold hogs and cattle in Chicago for more than $44,000.

Another attraction of Illinois was the Illinois Central Railroad, which ran almost seven hundred miles from the southernmost point of the state to Chicago. The railroad owned hundreds of thousands of acres along its right of way, which it stood ready to sell at comparatively low prices and on easy terms to immigrants. Visiting the numerous Swedish settlements in the state, Gustaf Unonius was made homesick by a festival at Andover, Illinois, where the men and women displayed "the holiday garb of the Swedish country folk . . . the women checked-and-flowered kerchiefs on their heads, the psalm book and a posy wrapped in a white handkerchief in their hands; the men with their long, dangling watch chains dressed in their homemade frieze coats."

Unonius soon became Episcopal missionary to the Swedes of Wisconsin and Illinois, supported by home-missionary funds from Eastern congregations, but he found it difficult to make ends meet. Finally, through the interest of his countrywoman Jenny Lind and her financial contributions, he was able to collect a congregation and build a church in Chicago which included native Americans and Swedes in its membership. But as Lutheran ministers arrived in increasing numbers from Sweden, Unonius, rather than become involved in doctrinal quarrels or fights with rival ministers for church members, decided to answer a call to a congregation in Sweden, sold the land and little cabin, now deserted, in which he and his wife had begun life in the New World and where seven children had been born (four of whom had died), and returned to his homeland. Of all the narratives of immigrant life in America (not, indeed, that there are that many) few can equal the account of Gustaf Unonius, so wise, generous, and perceptive, a man whose story does credit to his native land as well as to his adopted one.

The upper Mississippi Valley was generally adjudged the most "American" section of the United States. Margaret Fuller, editor of the transcendentalist journal *The Dial,* had gone west "prepared for the distaste I must experience at its mushroom growth," but she discerned there "a new order, a new poetry . . . to be evoked from this chaos."

When the Swedish novelist Frederika Bremer visited the Mississippi Valley she believed she saw the prototype of the new man and woman. She predicted that "in consequence of the variety of nations by which it is populated, and from the variety in its scenery and climate," it "will at a future time produce a popular life of a totally new kind, with infinite varieties of life and temperament, a wholly new aspect of human society on earth." To accomplish this, "the inhabitants of the Mississippi Valley must become citizens of the world—the universal mankind, *par excellence.*"

Carl Schurz, after traveling about the East, decided to settle in the Mississippi Valley West, finding it "a new society almost entirely unhampered by any traditions of the past; a new people produced by the free intermingling of the vigorous elements of all nations . . . with almost limitless opportunities open to all, and with equal rights secured by free institutions of government" and "a warm, living interest in the progressive evolution, constantly and rapidly going on, the joy of growth."

Sidney George Fisher had very similar observations to make about a young Westerner he met from Chicago, George Smith. Fisher was "Much amused by his talk and manner. A thorough Western man, overflowing with animal spirits and very intelligent. He is a lawyer," Fisher added, "politician, stump orator, speculator—all combined, as is common enough in the West—married with three children & only 26. He talked eagerly, earnestly, and with all that exuberance of feeling & life which a young man in full activity with a wide field of enterprise before him in a new country would naturally exhibit. . . ." Fisher was plainly charmed by this ebullient Westerner and felt the attraction of the life he described as contrasted with his sense of the purposelessness and "unreality" of his own life. Sidney George Fisher could have no more escaped from the upper-class Philadelphia world which sustained him than he could have traveled to the moon. He might send some of his money west but he could never go. Nonetheless, he was fascinated by the effect that limitless landscape had on his fellow Americans. "There is something in the vast future, rapid growth, constant changes & large features of the West that has a great effect on character," he wrote. "Everything is in motion & constantly changing & people have to live fast to keep pace with the speed of all around them. Fortunes are so rapidly made, the conditions of men & things is so perpetually varying, and the resources of the country are in the course of such wonderful development, that, to use Mr. Smith's language, it keeps them in a constant state of excitement. . . . When we think of what it *must* be a century hence, the prospect is quite overwhelming."

George Smith's phrase "a constant state of excitement" is a telling one. There was a feverish quality to American life generally, a "go-ahead" velocity, but the go-ahead pace seemed to accelerate the farther west one traveled and it produced a kind of madness, a disposition to expend energy, money, and life itself with an astonishing prodigality. Perhaps the appropriate metaphor is that of discrete human particles ricocheting off the perimeters of the continent, hurtling from the Mississippi Valley to the Pacific Coast and back and, not infrequently, around the whole globe to Siam, to India, to China, to Lebanon, to Africa or the Sandwich Islands, so that all which was not old and rooted, like the Eastern urban upper class, was in perpetual restless motion and in "a constant state of excitement," further stimulated by liquor, tobacco, coffee, and an almost limitless capacity for fantasizing—the consequence, to a large degree, of the landscape itself. These particles of humanity, vibrating furiously in space, rushed together, coalesced briefly, and then flew apart again to form endless new combinations.

There were two not inconsiderable worms in the great succulent apple of the Mississippi Valley, two "fevers." One was the perpetual fever of speculation, which produced a financial instability hard to imagine. Like most Easterners, Sidney George Fisher was interested in investing in Western lands. A Philadelphia agent for Western real estate named Paul Engle spoke to Fisher "with great confidence of making very profitable investments for us in the West," Fisher noted in his diary: "Describes his life there as very unpleasant. The people are about half civilized, and savage in their manners. There are no distinctions of rank, he is obliged to eat with mechanics and people of the lowest order. Everyone goes armed. . . . Everyone is absorbed in the pursuit of money, not by steady industry but by speculation, which produces a gambling spirit, and is subversive of good morals."

The other fever was a physiological one, conveyed by the ubiquitous anopheles mosquito which lived in the ponds, lakes, and marshes with which the region abounded and brought its devastating chills and fevers into every frontier community.

The Southern "West" began in southern Illinois and reached its apogee in Missouri, the first "trans-Mississippi state" created by the Compromise of 1820—the Missouri Compromise. The state displayed a remarkable capacity for resisting civilizing influences. It remained for decades the model of a raw, crude frontier state. When the young Quaker Charles Pancoast traveled to Missouri in 1840 to make his fortune as a pharmacist, it was little different than it had been twenty years earlier.

St. Louis was the principal city in the state, "with whipping-posts, slave-pens, and auction blocks." Gangs of manacled slaves passed through, bound for the New Orleans market. Free blacks were charged six dollars a year simply to live there and many were despoiled of their property on the flimsiest of pretexts.

On his trip to Missouri to inspect his Western land holdings, Philip Hone stayed in St. Louis at the Planter's House, "one of those great hotels which astonish us in the great West." Hone's astonishment at the life and bustle of St. Louis was, in his words, "greater than I can describe." Fifty large steamboats were tied up at the docks taking on or discharging cargoes, "some constantly arriving from New Orleans and other ports on the Mississippi; Cincinnati, Louisville, etc., on the Ohio; from the great Missouri and its tributaries; the Illinois River . . . and the whole Western and Southern waters . . . whilst others are departing, full of passengers, and deeply laden with the multifarious products of this remarkable region. The whole of the levee is covered as far as the eye can see, with merchandise landed or to be shipped; thousands of barrels of flour and bags of corn, hogsheads of tobacco, and immense piles of lead. . . ."

Through the docks, Hone walked among "boatmen, draymen, and laborers, white and blacks; French, Irish, and German, drinking, singing, and lounging on benches." One of Hone's political bêtes noires, Thomas Hart Benton, the unbudgeable Democrat, called for Hone and his daughter in his carriage and took them on a tour of the city—the churches, the college, a convent, and the marketplaces.

St. Louis, like Cincinnati, had a large German population and was in its own way as cosmopolitan as New Orleans. Moritz Busch spoke of the wide variety of "languages and dialects" that could be heard in the streets—"the nasally lisping . . . New Englander, the rough-voiced trapper of the Rocky Mountains, the immigrant from 'Old Highland,' the Irish day laborer, the Spanish merchant from Santa Fe, the High German and the Low German, the Magyar, and the Frenchmen. . . ." Germans had come closer to attaining equality in St. Louis than in any Eastern city, where, Busch noted, they were "granted complete equality of rights only at election time." It was also true that the Catholics of St. Louis, like those of Cincinnati, were free of the harassments and prejudices endured by their coreligionists in such Eastern cities as New York and Philadelphia. Mormons were prominent in the city since it was a point of departure for the long trek to Salt Lake City and Moritz Busch, attending one of their services, noted the congregation was made up of "the prosperous middle class, judging by their appearance."

The traveler exploring the Southern West would turn down the Mississippi to its juncture with the Ohio at Cairo and cross to the east bank of the river. There the traveler could enter the western thumb of Kentucky. A state since 1792, Kentucky nonetheless retained much of the air of the frontier. "In this region," an acquaintance told Moritz Busch, "you'll still find real backwoodsmen in the sense in which the term is used in novels." Busch indeed soon made his way "past poor cabins surrounded by long cornfields and clearings, through brooks and marshes shaded by ancient, strangely outspread sycamores over whose white trunks, endless wild vines intwined, through beech and oak leaves piled a foot deep, across crude log bridges, through quiet valleys, through damp lowlands, the trees of which, gnarled and moss-covered, had worked their way out of the choking thickets and creeping vines, out from the shadows into the sunlight and back down again. . . ." Kentuckians were called Corncrackers, as Ohioans were Buckeyes, citizens of Illinois Suckers, and Missourians Pukers.

On the Kentucky frontier a typical salutation was "Chaw, stranger?," with which a malodorous plug of tobacco was extended, revealing the teethmarks of the latest chewer. Busch found in the frontier region a treasury of folktales of legendary heroes like Ludwig Wetzel, who killed and scalped one hundred Indians in the course of a long lifetime. The stories were told everywhere in almost the same words, "transmitted by oral tradition among the old settlers" in much the same way, Busch suspected, that the *Iliad* was passed down in ancient Greece.

Perhaps the most compelling sound on the frontier was the lonely tone of a farm woman summoning her husband and sons from the forest or from distant fields on a horn, sometimes six feet in length. Some women would play complete melodies on their crude instruments. "A person not accustomed to them is seized by a strangely solemn feeling," Busch wrote, "when, walking in the virgin forests of the West or sailing along its streams, he suddenly hears these sounds, evolving into a pious melody, resounding through the silent forests."

Roaming through Western Kentucky, Busch stopped at an inn where a young man, covered with mud and dust from having slept on the ground "under his nag," was "dancing to the growling of a jew's harp played with virtuosity by a redheaded, long-legged rascal sitting on the bar . . . a kind of roundabout or reel, similar in its position to the virtuous cancan of Parisian students," while others "with throats hoarse from yelling were practicing a new Negro song."

From Kentucky, the Southern West swung through Arkansas, which became a state in 1836, and then southwesterly to the Republic of Texas. Texas, again, was classic Southern frontier. To Philip Hone it was made up for the most part of "Americans of loose character, desperate fortunes, and disorganizing political principles. . . . Southern slave-holders and Western speculators. . . ." George Templeton Strong amused himself with a mock set of resolutions to set the terms on which Texas might be admitted to the Union. Number four read: "The Republic of Texas shall not be entitled to send any Representative to Congress who shall have become a citizen thereof after having been sentenced to be hanged in any state or territory of the Union."

We have often had occasion to note that the South virtually "invented" the West. From the time of George Rogers Clark's expeditions to Vincennes and Kaskaskia in the Revolution, sponsored by Virginia under the proddings of Jefferson, the South leaned determinedly westward. Yet out of that ceaseless ambition which in time claimed more than two-thirds of the continent for the Union, only four states—Louisiana, Arkansas, Missouri, and Texas—accrued to the South, while by the time of the Civil War eight "Northern" states had been carved out of that part of the West which lay north of the Missouri Compromise line. At the time of the Civil War those Western states provided the basis for the economic and military superiority of the North.

17

A Modest Competence

One of the most engaging and instructive nineteenth-century diarists was a young Hicksite Quaker named Charles Pancoast. In the introduction to the autobiography based on his journals and written in 1882, Pancoast noted that as a child he held strong religious convictions and "imagined myself to be more virtuous than the majority of Boys; and when I observe the common disrespect of Children as shown to their Parents, their presumptuous and aggressive manners, their thoughtless and rude treatment of unfortunate, aged, and decrepit People," he added, "I am assured that by reason of better feeling or better teaching I was morally superior to the average boy I meet at the present day."

Pancoast's father had sent all his sons to Philadelphia "when they arrived at a proper age to learn some Trade or Profession" except the two eldest, whom he had kept on the farm. But they too went to Philadelphia and entered into business for themselves when they were old enough. Through the efforts of an older brother, Samuel, Pancoast was apprenticed to a druggist in 1832 "to learn the Profession of an Apothecary." Charles, who was then sixteen, agreed to remain as an apprentice until he was twenty-one. His master, John Rowland, agreed, for his part, to furnish young Pancoast "with Board, Washing, and Clothing, and to send me for two terms to the College of Pharmacy at his expense." But Charles was to have no spending money, "for Father believed spending money to be the primary cause that led Boys into evil habits." Rowland nonetheless gave Charles a dollar a year—fifty cents at Christmas and fifty cents on the fourth of July. Pancoast's master had a patented "Tonic Mixture, a Remedy for the Chills and Fever" and entered into partnership with a young promoter to make his fortune, but the two men "pushed the Business too fast for the means of the Firm"; a year later they were bankrupt and Pancoast was out of a job.

Before Pancoast had much time to bemoan his bad fortune a doctor to whom he refers only as X hired him to assist his patent-medicine promotion. Now the young man quickly learned how to get ahead in the world of business. Doctor X was poor in worldly goods but rich in ingenuity. He bought a drugstore for $1,800, the greater part of which he borrowed from a relative. He had two specific remedies to market, "the Digestive Tonic" and his own "Cough Cure." To these he added "Professor Allibert's Hair Tonic, which had the effect of starting temporary Fuzz on the Bald Heads of many People." The hair tonic sold for a dollar a bottle and cost X some eight cents, including bottle and label.

The doctor gave Pancoast more and more responsibility, finally proposing that he go to St. Louis and open a drugstore there with X's nephew, "and take a general Agency for his Medicines in the States west of Ohio." Pancoast left Philadelphia for St. Louis in the spring of 1840, going first by train to Harrisburg and from there by canal boat up the Susquehanna to Pittsburgh. The canal trip was a lark for Charles. He and some of the younger blades entertained themselves by crying out "Bridge ahead! All Hands down!" and watching with glee as the passengers dropped hastily to the deck to avoid a nonexistent bridge. "Sometimes, at a Village," he wrote, "we would take on a gay Pick Nick Party, and we would then have Dances and Plays." After several days of such "Romantic and delightful Travel" Pancoast reached Pittsburgh. There he purchased glassware for the drugstore and took passage for Cincinnati on board the steamer *Boston*. Four days later he arrived in Cincinnati, "the most flourishing city west of Philadelphia and Baltimore." Then on to Louisville, Kentucky, and Paducah. The steamer landed its passengers at Paducah on a Sunday and there Pancoast was shocked to find "all the Stores, Taverns, and Gambling Houses open, and People . . . to be seen from the open

Street betting at the Gambling Tables. This," Pancoast added, "was my first introduction to this kind of Society, and I confess that although my own Religion was not very deep-seated, I was shocked at the spectacle."

As the steamer made its way down the Ohio, the passengers combated their boredom "by playing Poker and other Gambling Games from the time the Table was cleared in the morning until midnight, with much Merriment, and sometimes alarming Jarring; but to me," Pancoast added, "it all appeared like wicked folly, as I noted in the countenances of some of the Players a deep anxiety, and after the Play was over they manifested strong indications of sorrow and penitence."

St. Louis was a city of some 65,000. The southern part, called the Vide Poche, was the stronghold of the French-Canadian trappers and fur traders, "a miserable, ignorant and indolent People," Pancoast wrote, "who, when not employed by the Chouteaus' of St. Louis in the Fur Trade up the Yellowstone River and elsewhere" made their living cutting and selling wood in the city. St. Louis was, in Pancoast's phrase, a "transfer city." The mile-long docks on the river were lined with boats transferring freight from large Mississippi River steamers to the smaller steamboats that would carry loads up the Illinois and the tributaries of the upper Mississippi. This business made St. Louis "the most promising and progressive City in the United States" in Pancoast's opinion. But her days of commercial glory were to be short-lived. "The Rail Roads," Pancoast noted, "sneaked in at her back door and stealthily struck her at far-off Chicago. . . ."

Pancoast and his partner started their business with high hopes— "we were both young and looked mainly on the Rosy side of life. . . . Our Business opened in an encouraging manner. Many new Friends seemed to court our acquaintance; but we found afterwards to our sorrow that some of them were more interested in fleecing us than in our welfare."

St. Louis society was made up of old French families who had made their fortunes in the fur trade. In the back of Pancoast's store was a Chouteau warehouse where a hundred slaves "were constantly employed in receiving, preparing, drying, overhauling, and shipping Fur. . . ." Supplementing the French were slaveholders from the Southern states. This was Pancoast's first contact with slavery and he found it profoundly repugnant. "This new class of Settlers," he wrote, "were worshippers of the Institution of Slavery, with all its brutal tendencies, and the Spirit of 'Chivalry' prevalent in the Southern States; and although many Northern People were pouring into the City, when I arrived this Slave-holding class governed the City and dominated in all the Customs of Society. . . ." Duels were frequent; the week before Pancoast arrived a Colonel Biddle, cousin of Nicholas, had been killed in a duel on Bloody Island, the city's designated dueling ground. "So infectious was the Spirit of Chivalry," Pancoast wrote, "that a young Clerk who came to me from 'the Land of Steady Habits' . . . receiving what he conceived to be a mortal insult from a Drug Clerk in another Store . . . decided to appease his injured Honor by appealing to the Code. . . ." The seconds of the two clerks agreed to load their pistols secretly with pills and when the young duelists fired, no damage resulted except to their egos by the laughter of their friends.

Pancoast was shocked by the lynching of a slave. A constable had attempted to arrest the man for "some misdemeanor, the Negro resisted, and in the struggle killed the Constable with the blow of a Bludgeon." He was caught trying to flee and tied to a stake; wood was piled around him and set afire. Most horrifying to Pancoast was the fact that "during the burning a leading Citizen of St. Louis, a high professor of Religion and a Deacon in the Church . . . threw powdered Sulphir on the poor Slave while he was burning and appealing for mercy to his God and the brutal People that surrounded him."

When Charles Pancoast was taken sick in St. Louis, his doctor called in for consultation Dr. William McDowell. McDowell was the prototype of the ingenious, practical frontier doctor who performed more radical operations, following his own instincts and common sense, than his more learned and better-trained contemporaries in Philadelphia and New York. His famous uncle, Ephraim McDowell, had performed the first operation for the removal of ovarian tumors and had carried out twelve such operations with only a single death. He also did thirty-two successful operations for the removal of bladder stones as well as a number of radical operations for the reduction of hernias. His nephew, William, demonstrated the same experimental bent. He had performed a notable experiment on a French-Canadian trapper in St. Louis who had been shot through the stomach, leaving a wound that refused to heal properly. McDowell had inserted a tube in the opening, "through which," Pancoast wrote, "he inserted a tube whereby he could discharge the contents of his [the French-Canadian's] Stomach and thus test the digestive qualities of different kinds of food."

Illinois in that period was as crude and rough as any frontier. Pancoast, traveling with a Jewish friend, Elias Block, about the state to collect on bills owed to his store in St. Louis, encountered Abraham Lincoln at a hotel in Jacksonville. Charles and Elias had arrived almost frozen to death by a bitter prairie wind. When they were introduced to Lincoln by the proprietor of the hotel where they were staying, Lincoln "made only a few remarks, asked where I came from, spoke of our freezing Journey across the Prairie, and other commonplace remarks; and also remarked that he thought our Hebrew Companion was fortunate after all, for although his feet and ears were badly damaged he had saved his Stock in Trade." When Pancoast asked, "How was that?" Lincoln replied, "His Tongue was left intact."

Dining in a rude log cabin on the prairie on "Corn Donnick and Cracklings" Pancoast observed that his host and hostess were "a fair example of the rough, self-sacrificing, migrating People then to be found all over the State of Illinois. . . ." He was struck time and again by the dramatic difference between those towns settled by emigrants from New England and those settled by Southerners. Passing over into Indiana, he found Terre Haute "well laid out on elevated ground . . . and possessed of a number of delightful Dwellings with ornamented Grounds, large Stores, Churches, and Schools and two Hotels." The people of nearby Vincennes, by contrast, were "devoid of energy. . . . The town appeared to have been finished and deceased; the Houses were mostly old and dilapidated, without paint or ornament; and the People were ignorant and uncouth, without energy or care, resting quietly around the Stores and Hotels relying on Providence for support." Indianapolis Pancoast considered "the finest and most prosperous State Capital I had met with in the West." There he listened to a sermon by Lyman Beecher: "The Old Man was eloquent and very impressive, and said things so original they would adhere to you for a lifetime."

In Springfield, the capital of Illinois, a handsome new State House was under construction, "quite elaborate and well-planned and more substantial and imposing in appearance than Pennsylvania can boast of." The town itself was flourishing, with attractive houses and well-stocked stores. Pancoast went to the uncompleted State House to hear the legislature debate and was struck by their extreme youth.

"The Assembly appeared to be composed all of Young Men, some of them mere Boys; they forcibly reminded me of a Debating School of Boy Students. I was more amused than instructed. . . ."

At Keokuk, named for Black Hawk's rival, Charles Pancoast encountered the chief, Keokuk himself, "in full Indian dress, with a stuffed Rooster in his cap for an ornament."

Charles Pancoast's drugstore in St. Louis flourished in a modest degree, but the exactions of Doctor X, the extravagance of his nephew, and a $1,500 loan taken to help establish his partner's brother in business placed severe financial strains on the enterprise.

The heavy load of debt that Pancoast and his partner had incurred was made far more onerous by the chronically unstable state of the nation's economy. In 1842 banks all over the West suspended specie payments. The notes of the "suspended banks" were the only circulating medium. Banks refused to accept depreciated paper money in payment of debts and the only place the young partners could deposit their paper money was in a savings bank that "exploded," costing them a substantial part of their capital. "One Bank after another failed," Pancoast wrote, "causing us to lose more or less with each of them, until the failure of the Bank of Cairo, of whose notes we had about $1600," the greater part of their working capital. Pancoast, faced with the loss of his business, decided to travel to Kaskaskia, Illinois, where the Bank of Cairo was located, to try to retrieve something from that institution. On the way through woods infested with bears and wildcats, he thought ruefully that perhaps that was why such banks as the Bank of Cairo were called "wild cat" banks. In Kaskaskia the president of the bank gave Pancoast a revealing breakdown of the bank's assets, or lack thereof. It had $40,000 in coin, $30,000 in United States Bank notes, $15,000 "on broken Western Banks," $120,000 of "good Paper of responsible Persons . . . their issue of Bank notes was $150,000." The bank president flatly refused to pay Pancoast a nickel of his money. Pancoast then asked the proprietor of his hotel who in town owed the bank the largest sum of money. The proprietor suspected it was a local flour mill which was said to owe $10,000. Pancoast then went to the owner of the mill, who agreed to sell him 450 barrels of flour for shipping at $3.50 a barrel and take the Cairo bank notes in payment (which the Cairo bank would have to accept). Pancoast in turn shipped the flour to his largest creditor in New York, "who sold it at a trifling loss to us." The story is worth telling because it suggests the desperate expedients to which merchants had often to resort to find means of discharging debts or, conversely, of collecting them.

At this point, with most of the banks in the state defaulting and money impossible to obtain, our friend Doctor X appeared and demanded the money due on a note owed him by Pancoast (the doctor's nephew had departed months earlier), some $5,000. When Pancoast pointed out that they had outstanding claims worth $12,000 and asked for time to extricate themselves, the doctor refused. They must assign their reliable debts to him and the business besides ("including our bedroom furniture"), and he would undertake to pay off their other creditors, to whom they owed some $2,000. When Pancoast rebelled at such usurious terms, X threatened to have a sheriff's sale to collect his money. Pancoast gave in and Doctor X then offered to employ him at $75 a month to run the store until the stock was disposed of and the business terminated. Having taken advantage of his former apprentice's misfortune to deprive him of his business, the doctor departed, and Pancoast was left, as he put it, "alone and penniless to work out my future fortune alone. . . . My manhood and ambition had left me, and my pride was deeply wounded: the more so as I found many of my mushroom Friends that had theretofore courted my company now passed me by with an indifferent nod."

Pancoast set out by a Missouri River steamboat to try to find a town in which to practice his profession of pharmacy. At Lexington, Missouri, he found a drugstore run by a man who "appeared to understand his business, but was surly, unaccommodating and very unpopular. . . ." The people of the town encouraged Pancoast to set up his own store there. When Pancoast returned to St. Louis and tried to buy supplies to get his business started, the wholesale druggist to whom he applied refused credit and declared his plan impractical. But the indefatigable Pancoast found a partner in a young druggist who had just inherited a small fortune. With his backing, Pancoast was able to set himself up in Lexington, where he was soon "well patronized."

Pancoast found the people of Lexington "peculiar." "There were Merchants," he wrote, "generally prosperous, from all parts of the country; Mechanics and laborers, nearly all Virginians and Kentuckians; a few Gamblers and Slave Traders; and many others, apparently without business, were really Speculators in Farms, Stock, or Steam Boats." The farms around the town "all large and worked by Slaves, were chiefly devoted to raising Hemp, Tobacco, and Stock; very little grain was produced, and so little Garden, truck, Milk, and Butter (the

Farmers considering the raising of these products beneath their dignity) that the Merchants had to supply the People from St. Louis, 500 miles away by water."

In religion the residents were "Hard Shell Baptists, Campbellites, and Presbyterians (Blue Stockings)" leavened with a few Methodists. "All the Ministers (except perhaps the Methodists) boldly proclaimed that the Institution of Slavery was divine. . . ."

Increasingly Pancoast found himself in conflict with his partner in the Lexington pharmacy, which could supply only "one living." Finally, at the urging of a friend he had met on a steamboat trip, Pancoast decided to try his fortune in Warsaw, Missouri. The Osage River wound its way southwest from the Missouri and in the western quadrant of the state, not far from Indian Territory, was the town of Warsaw. Traveling westward from Lexington, Pancoast passed by large plantations worked by slaves. Beyond lay woodland with scattered clearings with log cabins and a few acres hewn out of the forest. In the "miserable Village" of Warrensburg he stayed at a "Log Hotel, where," he wrote, "I Procured a wretched Dinner served by a wild African Girl, six weeks in the country, who could not speak a word of any language but her own barbarous Jargon. She was tall, with a form symmetrical as any Woman I ever set my eyes on, but black as a Raven. She did not deem it necessary to wear Clothes above her waist, but was adorned with a red Tunic below, and wore brass Bridle Rings in her ears for ornaments."

At one farm, where he stopped to get supper, his hostess served him a half-cooked chicken without salt or seasoning. When she inquired where he came from and Pancoast replied that he had been born in New Jersey and brought up in Pennsylvania, she exclaimed, "La me . . . them are places we never heern on!" "This," Pancoast added, "was the kind of self-immolation to which these Pioneer Wives had to submit, and it not surprising that they were so grossly ignorant of the World; nor that the Children became as wild as the Negroes of the African Jungle. (I have frequently seen the latter run like Deer at the approach of a Stranger and hide in the Bushes or under the Buildings)."

But at another cabin, equally crude in appearance, Pancoast's host and hostess showed signs of "cultivated tastes." "The Man was a Virginian, and his Wife a down East Yankee. Both were devout Christians; the man asked a Blessing at Table, and made a Family Prayer before retiring."

On the road Pancoast fell in with the proprietor of "the best Hotel in Warsaw," who briefed him on the character of the town. His traveling companion told him that the man who had urged Pancoast to establish his drugstore there, a carpenter nicknamed "Black Jack Wilson," headed a "somewhat notorious" group called "the Warsaw 'Slickers' (Regulators)" who claimed to represent law and order in the county. The Slickers had been organized to rid the town of "a band of counterfeiters and other desperadoes known as the 'Bank of Niagara gang,' from the river of that name, where they made their headquarters." A feud had developed that took in several counties and resulted in considerable bloodshed.

When Pancoast arrived in Warsaw, the first and not particularly encouraging sight that greeted him was of "a man running out of a Groggery, pursued by another man shooting at him with a Pistol as he ran across lots." The next morning "Black Jack" Wilson introduced Pancoast to the "principal Citizens" and showed him around the town, which consisted of some 1,200 inhabitants with a court house (it was the county seat), "ten good Stores, and two Hotels." Pancoast rented a large store "with a handsome front and Show Window" from Colonel Dewett Ballou, "a good-natured, easy-going Gentlemen, a Lawyer, and a member of the Missouri Legislature," for $120 a year and headed back for St. Louis to collect his supplies.

Back in Warsaw Pancoast unpacked his goods and arranged them in his store, interrupted by a stream of curious visitors. One young man named Jim Piles asked Pancoast where he came from and when he answered, replied, "Why you are a Yankee!"

"We do not account ourselves Yankees," Pancoast replied. "We only recognize New England people by that name."

"Jerseymen are the damnest, meanest kind of Yankees," Piles replied. "There are too many damn Yankees here now, and we don't want any more of that breed."

Pancoast ordered his visitor out of his store on the threat of knocking his brains out with weights from a scales. Piles responded with "more impudence" and Pancoast pushed him out of his store and locked the door. "This Fellow," Pancoast added, "only came into the Store to try my grit and was always after that my firm Friend! but he and his Father were among the worst Desperadoes in Warsaw." The senior Piles was a blacksmith and one of the wealthiest men in town, and his son Jim was "the Town Dude, and lived on his Father's bounty, rarely working, as he had neither the Talent nor Education adapted for any business, even gambling." When Jim courted a respectable young lady in the town of Bolivar, one of the merchants of that town, knowing of the young man's bad reputation, informed the lady. "Upon this Merchant's next visit to Warsaw, while he was reading his Paper at the Hotel, Piles came in his rear and struck him over the head with a Chair; then drawing a Cow-hide while he lay helpless on the floor, whipped him until he was welted from head to foot, and had to be taken home in a Carriage accompanied by a Physician." "As in the case of other outrages committed in Warsaw," Pancoast added, "this man never received any redress through the Law."

At this point, Pancoast wrote, "I began to realize that I had cast my lot among People whose habits and education were inimical to all my preconceived ideas of what constituted a proper Social Community, endeavoring to conform to the Laws of God and Man." Pancoast was aware "that the Population that usually constitutes Society on the outskirts of Civilisation is made up of Adventurers: in Warsaw these were chiefly Nomads from the Southern States." For a time Pancoast was "lonely and heartsick," but he kept his spirits up with the hope "that I would yet find some congenial spirit under those rough exteriors." And indeed he soon found a young tailor, "intelligent and agreeable," who was elected to the state legislature, and a fellow Philadelphian, Zeb Bishop, who was clerk of the court and turned out to be a kindred spirit. "There were several other Young Men, of noble qualities but little cultivation . . . who proved to be true and devoted Friends." Without such allies, Pancoast wrote, "it would have been difficult to preserve my Life and Property among these desperate People." "Notwithstanding their rough characters," Pancoast found most of the people of the town "honest in their dealings. . . . They seldom resorted to duplicity or hypocrisy, in sharp contrast to more cultivated urbanites like Doctor X, but were outspoken and brave in all things, true Friends and dangerous Enemies." Most of them, even young boys, carried Bowie knives and did not hesitate to use them.

"The people of Warsaw," Pancoast noted, "were good-hearted and generous as a Class, full of life and jollity. They were fond of all kinds of Games, such as Cards, Ball, Quoits, Footraces and Horse-races; and while there were no Theatres, Circuses, or Shows of any kind, good Boating, Fishing, and Gunning were to be had all around the country. . . . They had not advanced far enough to have Pianos or Cabinet Organs, but as substitutes they had Mouth Organs, Jews' Harps, Banjos, Guitars, Accordions, Drums, Fifes, Flutes, the Violin and the Tambourine; and we had frequent Dancing-parties in the Dining Room of the Hotel."

The local humor was rough and sometimes lethal. Walking home one night, Pancoast heard a bullet whiz by his head. He drew his own pistol and started after a dim figure who turned out to be a local barkeeper known as Old Rascal, who, the story had it, had had to flee from Kentucky for chewing off a man's ear in a fight. He had fired at Pancoast to scare him, as a "joke," and was convulsed with laughter.

A few weeks after he had opened his store, Pancoast was startled to see people running in all directions with rifles in their hands. His friend Wilson appeared in a great state of excitement and called to Pancoast to get his gun and come to the Washington Hotel. At the hotel he was told to go to the second floor with his gun. There he found the leading men of the town "in earnest conversation. Pistols, Rifles, and Bowie Knives abounded everwhere." Dominating the room was a striking man almost seven feet tall with long dark hair hanging down the back of his hunting shirt. He wore "lye-colored Pants girded with a red Belt and silver Buckles, and high Boots," and was armed with a rifle, a pistol, and *two* Bowie knives. This was Tom Turk, chief of the Slickers of Benton County. He had arrived in town with word that three hundred "Horse-Thieves," as the Anti-Slickers were called, were on their way to town to seize him and the other leaders of the Slickers, intending to carry them off and murder them. Soon a party of mounted men appeared, led by "a notorious Bushwacker and Horse Thief named Ise Hobbs," and a corrupt Hickory County constable rumored to be in league with the Horse Thieves. The constable dismounted and approached the hotel, declaring he had a warrant for the arrest of Tom Turk. Turk consented to accept the warrant if he could have his hearing before the justice of the peace at Warsaw. This proposal was rejected. The defenders of the hotel had an old cannon which, at the command of Colonel Vaughn, head of the Benton County militia, was fired over the heads of the Horse Thieves, considerably discouraging them. They decided to accept Turk's proposition. He was arraigned and posted bail and the Anti-Slickers left town.

Having recounted the episode, Pancoast undertook to explain it. Wild as it must seem to someone from a more settled region, the episode had a more or less logical explanation. "These hardy, self-reliant People," Pancoast wrote, "had for generations dwelt on the outskirts of Civilization where the Executors of the Law were often impotent to enforce it against the outrageous Outlaws that infested Texas, Arkansas, and the southern part of Missouri, so that no honest Tiller of the Soil could peaceably enjoy the products of his labor or have security for his life." Thus, when justice became uncertain in the courts, "many honest People became enraged, and leagued together for the purpose of ridding the country of these pestiferous Fellows. . . ." Hence the Slickers or Regulators. In the comparatively brief time Pancoast lived in Warsaw, thirty murders were committed in Benton County and not one was punished by the law. There were political dimensions to the division between Slickers and Anti-Slickers as well. Slickers tended to be Whigs and Anti-Slickers Democrats. "Perhaps a majority of the leading men of Warsaw," Pancoast wrote, "were opposed to Slicker methods and desired the Laws to be enforced by the Courts."

The situation that Pancoast described is certainly a familiar one to any student of American history. The Reverend Charles Woodmason, an Anglican minister on the North Carolina frontier in the period prior to the American Revolution, gave an account of border towns in that region almost interchangeable with Pancoast's (the vigilante groups also called themselves Regulators) and many towns in the Far West used the same methods to deal with the same problems. All of which is to say that the American frontier, whether in western New York or western Pennsylvania or on the "old" Southern borderlands, displayed remarkably similar qualities in every era of our history. Vigilantes or Regulators were virtual institutions that made their way west.

With the warfare between Slickers and Horse Thieves much diminished, "a new enemy crept in" to complicate Pancoast's life. His Quaker education had given him a strong antipathy to slavery, but since Warsaw was a predominantly Southern town and filled with slaveowners and slaves, Pancoast kept a discreet silence on the subject. He was, however, much taken with a young Massachusetts schoolteacher, the daughter of a Methodist minister, who lived at his hotel. She "could not help expressing her sympathy with the poor slaves." One evening she showed Pancoast a note, written by his sponsor, Wilson, warning her to leave town within twenty days. When she asked Pancoast for his advice, he urged her to heed the warning. "She sobbed and shed many tears," especially for her abandoned pupils, Pancoast noted, but finally accepting the inevitable, she wrote her father, who lived in Illinois, asking him to come and get her. Her father arrived and put up at the hotel, but before he and his daughter could depart, a crowd of women gathered "with such horrid noisy Instruments," Pancoast wrote, "as I had listened to a few months before, when [a] Harlot was drummed out of Town. The difference was that this time the 'motley crowd' was headed by several of the leading White Women of the Town, who called themselves 'Ladies.' . . . The half-civilized Wenches and their Demon-Mistresses howled, clattered their noisy devices, and abused the Old Man and his Daughter with opprobrious and insulting epithets."

Then young Charles Pancoast added in a poignant footnote: "My heart goes out in profound sympathy to this noble, heroic Young Woman, who, enjoying a comfortable home and the society of worthy and loving Parents and appreciative Friends sacrificed all these to the noble aspiration of carrying the cultivation that God had blessed her with, to these Frontier Children who so much needed the light that she could impart; and I feel ashamed of my country (as well as of myself) that permitted the names of such heroic Women to die in obscurity, while the deeds of many a wily Statesman and destructive Warrior are emblazoned on the Nation's Roll of Honor."

The episode had an unpleasant aftermath for Pancoast. He had kept quiet because he was powerless and "knew that anything that I could do or say would only aggravate her troubles and bring certain destruction upon my own head." He did, however, mention to a friend that he thought the behavior of the leading ladies of the town deplorable and was sorry that they had not been cited for disturbing the peace. This word his friend promptly carried to the husband of one of the ladies, who appeared in Pancoast's store with the avowed purpose of caning him for insulting his wife. At this our young Quaker friend, in the best frontier style, drew his pistol and said calmly, "If you strike me, I will be compelled to shoot you."

Ultimately forced to leave Warsaw, Pancoast formed a partnership with his friend Abram Skinkle "to run a steamboat up the Osage in the spring when the river was high and thereafter on the Missouri. . . ." The two young men purchased an old boat, the *Otter*, carrying 350 tons of cargo and drawing eighteen inches of water. From St. Louis they headed up the Osage River with passengers and freight, making three trips during the season with a profit of about a thousand dollars on each trip. They were thus tempted to try another dash up the river, but this time the water was so low that they were hung up on numerous sandbars, had to wait for rain to raise the river, and lost over nine hundred dollars on the venture.

"The Drug business," Pancoast noted, "is slow and plodding and money can be made in it only by slow degrees. Steam Boating was the very opposite of this. Every trip was a venture; there was constant hurry and confusion and change of scenery, and constant anxiety about the success of your enterprise." One seemed always balanced between the possibilities of substantial profits and complete financial disaster, if, for instance, the boat should go aground, blow up, or be wrecked by a submerged tree trunk. "But the very adventurous nature of the business," Pancoast wrote, "seemed to have a charm for me, and I felt as if nothing could ever induce me to return to the dull confinement of a Drug Store again." Nonetheless the anxiety level often seemed to Pancoast disproportionately high. He and his partner had to depend "on the services of rough, insolent, and unreliable men . . . the wasteful Stewards; the dishonest Supply Men; the swindling Squatters who supplied us with Fuel along the River; the Engineers endlessly demanding money for repairs. . . . I soon found my natural Milk of Human Kindness eking out of me, and I was not half so good a fellow as I was before."

There were numerous unanticipated crises on every trip. Once Skinkle had to thrash an impudent and disobedient deckhand and knock down an "ugly-dispositioned Engineer." Shortly thereafter "a fire-eating New Orleans captain" tried to force his boat into a jam of craft tying up at a levee and when Skinkle cursed him and warned him off, the captain pulled out his pistol and fired at him.

One of the major hazards of the trips up the Missouri was the constant shifting of the river's main channel. The effort to discern the new channel was a nerve-wracking and unending one, and those river pilots who were especially skilled in reading the water and had the most recent knowledge of the river commanded large wages. Even with the best of pilots, few boats escaped going aground on sandbars and having to go through the exhausting process of "sparring"—a process in which long poles fixed to the boat's rails were used to pry it off the bar. Not infrequently a trip that in high, free water could be completed in three or four hours took as many days because of the difficulty of sparring off sandbars, all of which ate into the company's uncertain profits.

During the winter of 1847 Skinkle and Pancoast were caught in the river by an early freeze, but this time when the ice began to break up in March, a tide of water swept the boat onto a rock ledge on the riverbank. It took two weeks of hard work "with Spars, Tackle and Wedges" to get her afloat, but the *St. Louis Oak* was never the same again. She leaked and drew water despite the partners' best efforts. The *St. Louis Oak* began to lose money and the insurance company finally condemned her. A hundred miles from St. Louis, loaded with freight and passengers, the *Oak* "ran with great force on a Log Heap," staving in the hull. Uninsured, its cargo ruined, the boat was raised and repaired by a wrecker boat from St. Louis, but the partners had no recourse but to sell her at a large loss and settle up their debts, after which they found they had $150 to divide between them, the fruit of two years of hard labor. Pancoast was ready to confess himself whipped but Skinkle, "always full of energy and resource, was not willing to give up the River." He persuaded Pancoast to charter a steamer and two barges to bring railroad ties from the mouth of the Cumberland River to St. Louis. On the way back one of the barges ran onto a rock and it took two days to repair the damage. Now the partners, disenchanted with freight, decided to try taking passengers from Cincinnati to St. Louis, but here they found that they had to pay a drummer five dollars to get passengers aboard their boat—otherwise the drummer would spread word that the boat was old and dangerous and the crew inexperienced, thereby diverting prospective passengers to rival steamers. Skinkle at first refused to give in to the scam but Pancoast finally convinced him that "it would be much more to our interest to hire these Scoundrels than to pummel them." Pancoast immediately signed up the lot, some five, and "by evening we had two hundred and fifty Passengers."

The trip to St. Louis was "jolly," but when the partners had calculated their expense they found they were considerably out of pocket. At this point Pancoast decided to give up the steamboat business and parted company with the indefatigable Skinkle, who, he wrote, was "rash, but full of Spirit, Ambition, and Courage; persistent and energetic, honorable, loving, and compassionate; despising Meanness, Cowardice, and Duplicity; generous, merciful, and charitable . . .," in short, an unsung hero, the masculine counterpart to the "noble, heroic" young schoolteacher who had been driven out of Warsaw.

For almost ten years Charles Pancoast had struggled to establish himself in the world. Obviously well above average in intelligence, he had shown industry, initiative, and enterprise. He had not aspired to wealth but only to "a modest competence." "My ruling desire," he had written, "had always been to find a fixed location where I might spend a lifetime of rest." And yet he had failed in all his ventures.

Now, on the heels of the failure of the steamboat ventures, he found himself "afloat again in the cold World, without Friends to help me." He attributed his plight to a lack of that "financial Acumen that has contributed to the success of so many Young Men." Apparently it never occurred to him that the fault might not be his own. His failures, he conjectured, were due not so much to bad judgment as to the fact that he "lacked the willful determination to enforce my own conviction. . . ." Was he saying that he could not be as ruthless and conniving as his mentor, Doctor X? "I can now realise that Good Nature, in a business point of view, has been the bane of my life," he wrote in his old age. That is to say, thrift, hard work, a reasonable degree of piety, unusual intelligence, energy, and enterprise were clearly not enough. One had to give up "Good Nature" as well; be hard and calculating, "smart," forever on the lookout to take advantage of the occasion as well as of one's friends and associates.

Pancoast got a temporary job keeping a drugstore in St. Louis for a friend named Fisher, who declared that he was going on a vacation. The day after Fisher left the reason for his hasty departure became evident. A young woman appeared in the store inquiring after him, announcing herself as the departed Fisher's wife and demanding the day's receipts. A few weeks later the sheriff appeared with an order against Fisher for $800 and seized the store and its assets. Pancoast was once more unemployed. For weeks he searched unsuccessfully for a job. A friend who was watchman on a steamboat tied up for the winter let him live on board, and he spent most of the money he had left laying in a larder to carry him through the winter. Another friend offered to lease him the bar business in his boat but Pancoast declined a bit self-righteously, noting "I was in the very depths of poverty and on the verge of Starvation, but I was not yet poor enough to sell Intoxicating Liquors to my Fellow Mortals."

Finally, at the end of his rope, Pancoast offered himself as a pilot on the Osage River and was signed on at a hundred dollars for the trip by a captain with freight for Warsaw. Pancoast got the boat up and back safely and was on his way to a new career—riverboat pilot. It was something of a comedown from being an owner, but he was grateful for any kind of employment. Soon he had money in his pocket and found himself susceptible to another lure. Word had reached the East that gold had been discovered near Sutter's Fort in California. We shall encounter him again in the California goldfields.

The experiences of Charles Pancoast on the Mississippi Valley frontier—the Near West—do not, of course, comprehend the whole story of that remarkable and diverse region, but they serve to remind us that "the frontier" was as surely in Missouri in the 1840s as it had been in western Pennsylvania at the turn of the century and would be in Dodge City and Leadville a generation later.

18

The Fur West

After the Lewis and Clark Expedition, western exploration was put on the back burner, so to speak. The "Western issue," connected as it was with slavery, was an extremely delicate one, and without Jefferson's almost obsessive interest in the West governmental initiative waned. It was 1818 before President Monroe, doubtless prompted by Jefferson, took up the issue once more.

Stephen Harriman Long, a farmer's son, was born in Hopkinton, New Hampshire, in 1784. Bright and ambitious, he entered Dartmouth at twenty-one and graduated in 1809. Like most young men of similar background, he tried his hand at teaching for five years and then, bored with his young charges, enlisted in the United States army as a lieutenant in the Corps of Engineers. After two years of teaching mathematics at West Point he was transferred to the topographical engineers with the rank of major. His absorbing interest was in exploration and he prevailed on his superiors to appoint him to the command of what was originally conceived of as a military and exploring expedition to the Rocky Mountains. A thousand soldiers were to proceed up the Missouri to the Yellowstone and establish a fort there, the intention being to intimidate the Indians of the region and doubtless to lay a base for the extension of the fur trade into the region by American traders in rivalry with the Hudson's Bay Company. The ability of the British to attach the Indians to their cause had had serious consequences for the American frontier in the Revolution and in the War of 1812. Many tribes, besides being involved in the fur trade, primarily with Anglo-Canadian fur companies, came yearly to British posts in Canada to get gifts and supplies. The British were already well established at Fort Vancouver in one person of Dr. John McLoughlin, the formidable head of the Hudson's Bay Company post there, and they were expected to attempt to extend their influence eastward, through the French-Canadian trappers, to encompass the Oregon Territory as far as the Snake River and the headwaters of the Missouri. If American traders and trappers were to compete successfully with them, the Indians of the Great Plains and the Rocky Mountain region had to be placated or overawed. Although this motive was nowhere stated explicitly, it must have been in the minds of Monroe and his secretary of war, Calhoun, when they prevailed upon an inattentive Congress to authorize the expedition.

The military units of the Yellowstone Expedition were the first to depart. They were to be joined at Council Bluffs by the scientific detachment, led by Long and composed of a promising young ornothologist, Thomas Nuttall; Thomas Say, a young entomologist, conchologist, and zoologist who had already been on an important expedition to Georgia and Florida; and Titian Ramsay Peale, son of Charles Willson Peale and brother to Raphael and Rembrandt, as artist for the expedition. The combined party spent the winter at Council Bluffs, by which time Congress had had second thoughts about the enterprise. Dispatching such a large military force was bound to have both domestic and international repercussions. The Mexican Revolution was in its initial stages, introducing a further element of uncertainty into the Western picture. The military objectives were thus abandoned.

Long and the scientific detachment left Council Bluffs in the spring of 1820. In addition to Say, Nuttall, Peale, and Long, the dangerously small party consisted of Edwin James—"Botanist, Geologist, and Surgeon," as well as diarist—a lieutenant of artillery with the responsibility for keeping the official journal of the expedition, a French interpreter, a Spanish interpreter, two hunters and packers, a corporal, and six army privates. Edwin James made a detailed inventory of the trading goods desired by the Indian tribes— "strouding for breech clouts and petticoats, blankets, wampum, guns, powder and ball, kettles, vermillion, verdigris, mackasin awls, fire steels, looking glasses, knives, chief's coats, calico, ornamented brass finger rings, armbands of silver, wristbands of the same metal, ear-wheels, and bobs, small cylinders for the hair, breast broaches, and other silver ornaments for the head; black and blue handkerchiefs, buttons, tin cups, pan and dishes, scarlet cloth, etc."

Long's instructions directed him to "first explore the Missouri and its principal rivers, and then, in succession, Red River, Arkansas and Mississippi, above the mouth of the Missouri. The object of the Expedition, is to acquire as thorough and accurate knowledge as may be practicable, of a portion of our country, which is daily becoming more interesting, but which is as yet imperfectly known. With this view you will permit nothing worthy of notice to escape your attention. You will ascertain the latitude and longitude of remarkable points with all possible precision. You will, if practicable, ascertain some point in the 49th parallel of latitude, which separates our possessions from those of Great Britain. A knowledge of the extent of our limits will tend to prevent collision between our traders and theirs. . . . You will concili-ate the Indians by kindness and presents, and will ascertain, as far as practicable, the number and character of the various tribes with the extent of country claimed by each. . . . The Instructions of Mr. Jefferson to Capt. Lewis, which are printed in his travels, will afford you many valuable suggestions, of which as far as applicable, you will avail yourself."

The reference to the United States–Canada border and the respective trading spheres of those nations gives substantial support to the argument that the expedition was conceived of as a preliminary to the aggressive extension of the American fur trade into the Yellowstone region and perhaps beyond. The mention, at the end of the instruc-tions to Long, of Jefferson's instructions to Meriwether Lewis makes clear the line of descent from the Lewis and Clark Expedition to Long's and the direct or indirect influence of Jefferson in the plan for the expedition.

The winter months were utilized to visit Indian tribes in the vicinity of Council Bluffs and to make extensive observations on their cultures. The Kansa, who were close at hand, were already much corrupted by their contact with the whites and showed few traces of the "nobility" for which their most westerly cousins were noted. Charbon-neau, the husband of the famous Sacagawea, was of great assistance in smoothing the paths of the white explorers. The Oto, Missouri, Iowa, and Pawnee were likewise scrutinized. The party watched the Iowa do the "beggars' dance" for presents—tobacco or whiskey—a dance devised for whites. A chief rose to relate his martial exploits: "He had stolen horses seven or eight times from the Konzas; he had first struck the bodies of three of that nation slain in battle. He had stolen horses from the Ietan nation, and had struck the body of one Pawnee Loup. He had stolen horses several times from the Omahaws, and once from the Puncas. He had struck the body of two Sious." He was followed by Little Soldier, "a war-worn veteran," who "strained his voice to its utmost pitch whilst he portrayed some of the scenes of blood in which he had acted. He had struck dead bodies of all the red nations around, Osages, Konzas, Pawnee Loups, Republicans, Grand Pawnees, Puncas, Omahaws, and Sioux, Padoucas, La Plais or Bald Heads, Ietans, Sauks, Foxes and Ioways. . . ." Finally, he was interrupted by another warrior who placed his hand over his mouth and led him to his seat, an act of respect which signified that he had more exploits to his credit than the tribe had time to hear.

Among the Omaha, raids on other tribes were initiated by an individual warrior who first painted himself with white clay and then went through the village, calling out to other warriors to join him and enumerating the grievances against the tribe whose horses were to be the object of the raid. Then he gave a feast for all who were willing to accompany him and "made medicine," hanging out his medicine bag and haranguing his fellow warriors to seek fame and honor by warlike deeds. When such a party came within striking distance of the enemy, the warriors painted themselves and smoked tobacco from the medicine bag, which the leader suspended from his neck. Capturing a prisoner in such a raid was the supreme achievement. "Striking an enemy, whilst active," Edwin James reported, "appears to be the second in rank, of their great martial achievements. Striking his dead, or disabled body, confers the third honour. Capturing a horse may be regarded as the fourth; presenting a horse to any person, the fifth, and the shooting, or otherwise killing an enemy, by a missile, is the sixth in point of rank of military deeds. . . . The taking of a scalp is merely an evidence of what has been done, and, of itself, seems to confer no honour."

The wounded were killed and hacked to pieces by the victors. If squaws were present the bodies were turned over to them for dismemberment. "They sever the limbs from the bodies, and attaching them to strings, drag them about with vociferous exultation." The genitals were tied to the necks of the dogs and the dogs "driven before them, with much shouting, laughter, noise and obscene expressions."

Because of the great variety of languages among the tribes, the Indians had developed a universal sign language by means of which they could convey a substantial amount of information. The members of Stephen Long's expedition prepared a descriptive glossary of Indian sign language which ran to 104 remarkably expressive "signs" or gestures. Fear, for example, was suggested by "the two hands with the fingers turned inward opposite to the lower ribs, then brought upwards with a tremulous movement, as if to represent the common idea of the heart rising up to the throat. . . ."

James also commented on the strange optical illusions that appeared on the plains—mirages that looked like lakes or rivers and the distortion of forms by the light so that "an animal seen for the first time . . . usually appears much enlarged." What appeared to be a mastodon turned out to be an elk; an apparent bison, a hen turkey.

While they were visiting the Grand Pawnee, the scientists in Long's party tried to prevail upon their hosts to allow themselves to be inoculated against smallpox. Long himself offered his arm for a demonstration of the vaccination procedure but the Indians were unimpressed. The whites watched a game employing a hoop and pole, impressed by "that ease and celerity of motion in which the savages so far surpass their civilized neighbours . . . displaying a symmetry of proportion and beauty of form."

The "horse Indians" were as much the creatures of horses as their masters. Edwin James tells us that the Grand Pawnee, numbering not more than 1,500 warriors, had between six and eight thousand horses and the need to find fodder for them kept the Pawnee constantly on the move. Their agricultural efforts were especially hampered and James noted that at harvest time the Grand Pawnee burned their crops and moved on to new grazing ranges. In the winter they were restricted in their movements to creeks and rivers where cottonwood trees grew so that the ponies could eat the twigs and bark of the trees. If people or horses had to go hungry, it was better the people than the horses, although it was true that in extremity the poorer horses were often eaten.

The plains were covered with great herds of buffalo and James noted that they commonly mated beginning in late July and continuing until early September. The cows then separated from the bulls and calved in April; the calves stayed with their mothers for at least a year, sometimes as long as three. The cows were much prized over the bulls both for meat and for their hides, but the bulls were killed in large numbers—primarily for sport. As James wrote of the great animals, "In whatever direction they move, their parasites and dependents fail not to follow. Large herds are invariably attended by gangs of meagre, famine-pinched wolves, and flights of obscene and ravenous birds." Here James indulged himself in a reflection upon human odor. It was said that buffalo panicked at the scent of white men, and various theories had been advanced as to the reason. It seemed simple enough to James. Rather than the "frightful scent of the white man" it was more likely that it was "the impolitic, exterminating war, which he wages against all unsubdued animals within his reach." "It would be highly desirable," James added, "that some law for the preservation of game, might be extended to, and rigidly enforced in the country, where the bison is still met with: that the wanton destruction of these valuable animals, by the white hunters, might be checked or prevented. It is common for hunters to attack large herds of these animals, and having slaughtered as many as they are able, from mere wantonness and love of this barbarous sport, to leave the carcasses to be devoured by the wolves and birds of prey; thousands are slaughtered yearly, of which no part is saved except the tongues." The odor of the Indians, James added, "though very strong and peculiar, is by no means unpleasant . . . the Indians find the odour of a white man extremely offensive."

Long's party also passed large herds of wild horses "of various colours, and of all sizes. . . . Their playfulness seemed to be excited, rather than their fears, by òur appearance, and we often saw them, more than a mile distant, leaping and curvetting, involved by a cloud of dust, which they seemed to delight in raising."

From the headwaters of the Missouri, Long's party turned south in a great loop to the Platte, the Arkansas, and the Red, past the Comanche and Kiowa, Arapaho, Osage, Cheyenne, and the settlements of those Cherokee and Choctaw who had moved west. They found Fort Smith garrisoned by a company of riflemen "to prevent the encroachments of white settlers upon the lands still held by the Indians." Unauthorized white settlements had been made in the area of Skin Bayou and Six Bulls, but the officer in charge at Fort Smith had recently forced their abandonment. On their way down the Arkansas, the expedition came to Rocky Bayou, a Cherokee settlement, where they were received hospitably by the chief, Tom Graves. "His house," James noted, "as well as many we passed before we arrived at it, is constructed like those of the white settlers, and like them, surrounded with enclosed fields of corn, cotton, sweet potatoes, etc., with cribs, sheds, droves of swine, flocks of geese, and all the usual accompaniments of a prosperous settlement." Graves had named his son Andrew Jackson Graves and while he spoke no English, he offered the officers in the party an abundant meal served by two black slaves. There were other Cherokee settlements in the area, and the Cherokee were at war with the Osage over whose land they hunted. They had invaded Osage territory several years earlier, accompanied by a party of whites, and had burned a village and its crops and killed or taken captive between fifty and sixty old men, women, and children.

Perhaps most ironic of all, "the introduction of a considerable degree of civilization among the Cherokees," James wrote, "has been attended by the usual consequences of inequality in the distribution of property, and a large share of the evils resulting from that inequality." The poorer Cherokee, indignant at the notion of "exclusive possession"—private property—had made themselves free with the property of their more prosperous fellows; made themselves, in James's words, "troublesome neighbours—both to the wealthy of their own nation, and to those of the white settlers in their vicinity who have any thing to lose." The result was that the more prosperous Cherokee had formed a mounted troop of Regulators or vigilantes, "invested with almost unlimited authority," to catch and punish the thieves.

All through the region of the lower Arkansas, the Long party encountered single farms and settlements, some of them adjacent to Cherokee villages. Farther down river was a settlement of Delaware and Shawnee thoroughly intimidated by the more numerous whites. "It is painful to witness the degradation of a people once powerful and independent," James wrote, "still more so to see them submitting to the wanton and needless cruelties of their oppressors." This "miserable remnant" would soon, James suspected, be forced into the territory of the Cherokee and "their speedy and entire extinction . . . insured."

There was much truth in Stephen Long's statement that "the condition of the savages is a state of constant alarm and apprehension. Their security from their enemies, and their means of subsistence, are precarious and uncertain, the former requiring the utmost vigilance to prevent its infraction and the latter being attended with no regular supplies for the necessaries of life."

The consequences of Long's expedition have sometimes been described as "disappointing" by modern commentators, but its accomplishments were substantial. It greatly increased the general knowledge of the regions covered. The publication of a lively *Account of an Expedition from Pittsburgh to the Rocky Mountains,* compiled by Edwin James, gave widespread publicity to the expedition and the two volumes became the bible of subsequent geographers, geologists, and topographers. The *Account* contained a vast amount of interesting and generally accurate information, about the various tribes encountered on the way. The expedition's "collections," deposited in the Philadelphia Museum, comprised "sixty prepared skins of new or rare animals . . . several thousand insects, seven or eight hundred of which are probably new . . . between four and five hundred species of plants, new to the Flora of the United States, and many of them supposed to be undescribed." Peale's sketches amounted to 122, of which only 21 were finished, plus 150 landscape views by Peale's fellow artist, Samuel Seymour. Considering the physical difficulties under which the party labored, much credit is due Long and his companions. A vast miscellany, James's work remains well worth reading. Long was to go on to a distinguished career as an engineer and railroad builder. Say is honored as the father of American entomology.

The most disappointing aspect of the expedition, from the point of view of those among its sponsors who wished to promote Western settlement, was Long's opinion that the region was too barren and arid ever to support settlement by whites. Long's opinion was echoed ten years later by Josiah Gregg, the author of *Commerce of the Prairies,* who wrote that the Great Plains, from the Red River to the headwaters of the Missouri, were "uninhabitable—not so much for want of wood (though the plains are altogether naked), as of soil and of water; for though some of the plains appear of sufficiently fertile soil, they are mostly of a sterile character, and all too dry to be cultivated. These great steppes seem only fitted for the haunts of the mustang, the buffalo, the antelope, and their migratory lord, the prairie Indian."

Another kind of westward movement, to what might be called the Fur West, was also taking place in the same period. Stretching hundreds of miles west of the Mississippi Valley were the vast and uncharted regions of the Great Plains and, beyond them, the Great Basin area of the Rocky Mountains. Over this unsurveyed, unmapped, and largely unknown region a few fur traders of the Hudson's Bay

Company and John Jacob Astor's rival enterprise, the American Fur Company, made their way to trade for furs with the various tribes of Indians who controlled the fur trade. Since Lewis and Clark's expedition only a handful of Americans had penetrated the region, and none had traversed it to Oregon or California. John Colter, a member of the Lewis and Clark party, had been hired on the way home by two Illinois trappers, Joseph Dixon and Forest Hancock, to guide them for "sheers" (shares) of their fur profits. The three men went off to trap beaver in the Yellowstone Valley, the preserve of the Blackfoot and the Crow Indians, about as hazardous an undertaking as they could have embarked on. The Blackfeet were already involved in trade with the Hudson's Bay Company. The Indians did the trapping and carried the lustrous beaver pelts to rendezvous points, where they were collected by agents of the fur company, usually Frenchmen. Colter and his companions built a cabin and prepared to winter somewhere near the mouth of the Clark River but the restless Colter made a dugout canoe and headed down the Yellowstone, trapping as he went. Where the Platte flows into the Missouri, he encountered a party of keelboats that included three other veterans of the Lewis and Clark Expedition—George Drouillard, Peter Wiser, and John Potts. In the spring of 1807, under the leadership of Manuel Lisa, they were on their way to the Yellowstone to trade for furs. Lisa persuaded Colter to join the party. Among the other members of Lisa's group was a young Baltimore lawyer, Hugh Marie Brackenridge, the son of Hugh Henry Brackenridge, whose *Modern Chivalry*, one of the first novels of the new republic, had been a satire on the crudities of democracy. Brackenridge, who inherited his father's writing gift, described Lisa's keelboat in considerable detail.

It was "manned with twenty stout oars-men. . . . Our equipage is chiefly composed of young men, though several have already made a voyage to the upper Missouri, of which they are exceedingly proud [these were certainly the veterans of the Lewis and Clark Expedition]. . . . We are . . . completely prepared for defence. There is, besides, a swivel on the bow of the boat which, in case of attack, would make a formidable appearance. . . . These precautions are absolutely necessary from the hostility of the Sioux bands, who, of late had committed several murders and robberies on the whites, and manifested such a disposition that it was believed impossible for us to pass through their country. The greater part of the merchandise, which consists of strouding, blankets, lead, tobacco, knifes, guns, beads, etc., was concealed in a false cabin . . . in this way presenting as little as possible to tempt the savages." Despite the fact that the Sioux had waited on the river to prevent the passage of any trading boats, Lisa's party slipped by.

The principal tribes that inhabited the headwaters of the Missouri and the Yellowstone basin were the Blackfeet, the largest and most warlike tribe in the region; the Crow, reputed to be terrible in the attack but quickly discouraged if things did not go well; and the Shoshone or Snake Indians, who lived along that river and who had been so helpful to Lewis and Clark years earlier.

The Blackfoot Indians were remarkable in the fact that they were beset on all sides of their extensive range by tribes hostile to them and in many instances armed with the white man's musket. Thus pressed upon, they responded by developing the most efficient warmaking capacity of any of the Plains Indians with the possible exception of the Sioux. The Arikara harassed them from the north, the Cheyenne, Arapaho, and Comanche from the south. Discipline, cleanliness, good order, and unusual intelligence among their leaders characterized the Blackfeet when the first fur traders arrived in their domain. Initially in danger of being overwhelmed by the tribes adjacent to their vaguely defined "territory," which extended deep into Canada, the Blackfeet had encouraged the Hudson's Bay Company to set up trading posts within the area claimed by them to help thwart their enemies. Their real trouble began with the intrusion, after 1822, of Americans into the trade. Egged on by Canadian traders who wished to preserve their virtual monopoly, the Blackfeet continually attacked the American trappers, seizing their furs and selling them to Canadian traders. For a time this system seemed to the Blackfeet almost too good to be true. They were saved the very considerable labor of trapping the beaver themselves and had, in addition, the glory of killing white men and taking their scalps.

In a remarkable display of skill and determination, the Blackfeet, estimated between ten and eighteen thousand, held off the American trappers and fur traders or at least made them pay a very heavy price in lives and goods for their persistence in hunting the beaver. The downfall of the Blackfeet came with the terrible smallpox epidemic of 1836, which reduced some camps by two-thirds of their numbers and, overall, cost them more than half their population. The final blow was the penetration of the Blackfoot nation by "whiskey traders." These dealers in illicit merchandise found the Blackfeet, especially the younger braves, hopelessly vulnerable to the white man's liquor. A desperate struggle took place within the two various bands as the older chiefs, who foresaw the destruction of the tribe in the growing addiction of the younger warriors and braves to the deadly liquor, tried to prohibit its consumption.

The Snake Indians were large, noble-looking aborigines who were perpetually fighting for their lives against the more warlike Blackfeet and Sioux. At the time of the Lewis and Clark Expedition, they spent much of each year on the Pacific side of the Rockies to avoid the Sioux, coming onto the plains for hasty buffalo hunting forays and then slipping back over the mountains before the Sioux or Blackfeet could intercept them. They welcomed the coming of the white trappers as allies against their traditional enemies. Osbourne Russell, a young trapper, described them as "kind and hospitable to whites thankful for favors indignant at injuries and but little addicted to theft in their large villages. . . . I have found it to be a general feature of their character to divide the last morsel of food with the hungry stranger let their means be what it might for obtaining the next meal. . . ."

The Crow Indians roamed over a region that they had originally wrested from the Snake, bounded on the east and south by the Black Hills, on the west by the Wind River mountains, and on the north by the Yellowstone River. The smallpox, which virtually destroyed the Mandan, had reduced the Crow from some eight thousand to two thousand, of whom almost two-thirds were women. Russell described them as "proud treacherous thievish insolent and brave when they are possessed with a superior advantage but when placed in the opposite situation they are equally humble submissive and cowardly."

As with the Snake Indians, the chief was the one "who can innumerate the greatest number of valiant exploits . . . All the greatest warriors below him . . . are Councillors and take their seats in the council according to their respective rank." The Crow kept a "standing company of soldiers . . . for the purpose of maintaining order in the Village. The military leader, appointed by the Chief and the Counselors, had complete control over the internal police of the tribe subject only to the check of the body that appointed him." The Crow, "both male and female," Russell wrote, "are tall well proportioned handsomely featured with very light copper coloured skins." Sexual promiscuity was common among the Crow but intermarriage with other tribes was forbidden.

A stranger who stopped with the Crow, Russell reported, "can always be accommodated with a wife while he stops with the Village but cannot take her from it when he leaves." As with the Snake, children were cared for tenderly and it was "a high crime for a father or mother to inflict corporeal punishment on their male child." The Crow were notable for particular love of gaudy dress and display. A fur trader named Edward Denig described the tribe on the march: "When a camp is on the move in the summer, this tribe presents a gay and lively appearance, more so perhaps than any other. On these occasions both men and women dress in their best clothes. Their numerous horses are decked out with highly ornamented saddles and bridles of their own making, scarlet collars and housing with feathers on their horse's heads and tails. The warriors wear their richly garnished shirts, fringed with human hair and ermine, leggins of the same, and headdresses of various kinds, strange, gay and costly. Any and all kinds of bright colored blankets, loaded with beads worked curiously and elegantly across them, with scarlet leggins. . . . The bucks are fancifully painted on the face, their hair arranged . . . with heavy and costly appendages of shells, beads, and wampum, to the ears and around the neck. The women have scarlet or blue dresses, others white cotillions made of the dressed skins of the bighorn sheep . . . covered across the breast and back with rows of elk teeth and sea shells . . . the fringes . . . wrought with porcupine quills and feathers of many colors. . . . The young men take this occasion to show off their persons and horsemanship to the women. A good deal of courting is also done while traveling."

The Crow had a more varied cuisine than any of their neighboring tribes and paid greater attention to cleanliness. Among them the old retired warriors struck Russell as being remarkably healthy. They enjoyed great prestige and loved to sit smoking in a circle "conversing upon the good old times of their forefathers and condemning the fashions of the present age." One of the most notable things about the Crow was their determined resistance to whiskey. They called it "White man's fool water." If a Crow became drunk, he was considered not to be a Crow during the period of his inebriation.

The Crow had suffered much earlier in the century when one tribe was reduced from two thousand lodges to three hundred by smallpox. In 1832 another band contracted the terrible disease. In the words of the trader Larogue, "As soon as possible . . . the camp broke up into small bands each taking different directions. They scattered through the mountains in hope of running away from the pestilence.

All order was lost. No one pretended to lead or advise. The sick and dead alike were left for the wolves and each family tried to save itself. . . . More than a thousand fingers are said to have been cut off by the relatives of the dead [as a sign of mourning]. Out of 800 lodges counted the previous summer but 360 remained, even these but thinly peopled."

Smallpox, as we noted earlier, had virtually destroyed the once powerful and warlike Mandan. An epidemic in 1837 reduced one village from 1,600 to "13 young and 19 old men." One writer who observed the effects of a smallpox epidemic on the Arikara wrote, "Many . . . formerly handsome and stately in appearance, upon recovering their health committed suicide when they saw how they had been disfigured by the smallpox. Some of them leaped from high cliffs, others stabbed or shot themselves to death. The whole wide prairie has become an immense graveyard. . . . Women and children wander about in hordes, starving and moaning among the dead bodies."

Like many other tribes of "Rocky Mountain Indians" the Snake believed in "a Supreme Deity who resided in the Sun and in infernal Deities residing in the Moon and Stars but subject to the Supreme control of the one residing in the Sun. . . ." Snake warriors commonly had several wives with a system of divorce. Sexual promiscuity among the women was rare. They did all the labor of the tribe except caring for the horses and, in Osbourne Russell's words, were "cheerful and affectionate to their husbands and remarkably fond and careful of their children." Their government, according to Russell, was "a Democracy deeds of valor promotes the Chief to the highest points attainable from which he is at any time likely to fall for disdemeanor in office." Of a population of some six thousand, about half lived in villages and the rest in small detached bands of from two to ten families. These latter groups seem to have been composed of Indians who, in some degree, were failures in terms of the tribe's dominant values. They lacked skill in hunting or fighting and depended for their subsistence on gathering roots, seeds, and berries and catching fish. They had few horses—the Indian status symbol—and were more addicted to stealing and preying upon small parties of trappers. They were usually without muskets and depended on arrows pointed with quartz or obsidian which they dipped in poison from the fangs of rattlesnakes. The large villages of Snake seldom stayed more than a week or two in the same spot. In the period of the eight or nine years that Russell was in contact with the Snake, their principal chiefs died and the tribe began to break up into smaller bands "in consequence," Russell concluded, "of having no chief who could control and keep them together." "Their ancient warlike spirit seemed to be buried with their leaders and they are fast falling into degradation," he added.

Other tribes in the region were the Bonnack, the Piegan, the Blood Indians, the Flatheads, the Nez Percés, and the Gros Ventres, a dependency of the Blackfeet closely related to the Arapaho. In addition, a number of Eastern Indians, most prominently the Iroquois and Delaware, worked as individuals or in small groups for trading companies and these, of necessity, identified themselves with the whites.

It might be well at this point to say something about the fur-bearing mammal that was the object of so much avarice. Of all the animals on the American continent, the beaver was the creature whose fate was most intertwined with the American settlers. The buffalo had its relatively brief dominance in what we might call the era of the Great Plains, but the beaver was there at the beginning. When the first white settlers landed in New England they discovered the beaver and valued its pelt as an article of trade. The beaver pelt was the principal medium of exchange in all dealings with the aborigines. Many Indian tribes believed they were descended from an archetypal beaver and the beaver was thus sacred to them. The white man persuaded the Indian, in return for beads and cloth, dyes, knives, mirrors, and all the classic trading junk, to kill the sacred creature. A central issue in warfare among Indian tribes after the coming of the white man was which tribes were to control the lucrative trade in beaver skins. Many tribes moved from one watershed to another, exhausting the supply of beaver in a particular network of rivers and creeks and then pushing to another, often ousting a weaker tribe in the process.

The beaver itself was a marvelous creature, certainly worthy of the Indian's infatuation. It was a gifted engineer with an almost human facility for creating dams and houses. Beavers cut trees along the banks of streams and rivers and placed them in the water pointing diagonally upstream, interlacing the tree trunks with twigs and branches until a solid dam was created, forming a pond. Then on the dam, or sometimes along the shore when the water was too swift to dam, they built their houses, again brilliantly engineered structures approached through underwater tunnels. The inside of the house was lined with clean dry grasses and stocked in winter with a supply of green sticks and branches whose bark provided food for the often icebound beavers.

The female beaver produced each spring from two to six young, but she killed all except a single male and female in order to prevent overcrowding of the beaver range. The beavers' lodge was generally from four to seven feet in height, standing four to five feet above the water level.

The beavers' undoing was a potent yellow oil called castorum, a "gummy" yellow substance secreted in glands under their forearms. Whenever a beaver passed up or down a stream it took some mud or clay from the riverbottom in its paws, placed it on the riverbank, and supplemented it with castorum. In the words of a trapper, "should a hundred Beaver pass within the scent of the place they would each throw up mud covering the old castorum and emit new upon that castorum which they throw up." The Indians had learned to extract the castorum and carry it in a small vial or container. The Indian trapper would place some mud freshly mixed with castorum on the bank and anchor a trap below it, under the water, so that a beaver, coming up to add its castorum, would step on the trap and spring it. The trap itself, essentially the steel trap we are familiar with today, was the critical tool in the process. Attached to the trap was a dry piece of log some six feet long known as the float, designed to keep the beaver from sinking to the bottom of the river. The trap was set five or six inches below the surface of the water and staked down so that the beaver could not get to land, where he could gnaw a leg off and escape. Trapping beaver was arduous work. The traps themselves were heavy—a trapper would carry six or eight—and the trapper must immerse himself in the chilling waters of a creek or river to set his traps and enter the water again to clear and reset them. Rheumatism was, in consequence, one of the occupational diseases of trappers.

As white trappers gradually encroached on the preserve of the Indians by taking beaver themselves rather than simply trading with the Indians for the pelts, a bitter and remorseless struggle took place between them and the Indian tribes determined to preserve their monopoly of the trapping.

The standard equipment of a trapper consisted of a riding horse and pack horse. The riding horse carried an "eposhemore" (a square piece of buffalo robe much prized as a saddle blanket); a saddle and bridle; a gunnysack containing six beaver traps; a blanket; an extra pair of moccasins; powder horn and bullet pouch; and a belt holding a butcher knife and a small wooden box with castorum in it to bait the traps; a pipe and a sack of tobacco and implements for making a fire. The trapper's dress was a flannel or cotton shirt (both much preferred to buckskin shirts because they were far warmer and more comfortable and dried out more quickly); a pair of leather breeches and a blanket of buffalo skin; leggings; a coat made of a buffalo skin or a woolen blanket; and a hat or cap of wool or buffalo or otter skin. Besides the strictly utilitarian aspects of his costume, the white trapper was almost as colorful and bizarre in his dress as a Crow Indian. Indeed, it was often not easy to tell a white trapper from his Indian counterpart.

Emboldened by the success of his first venture, Manuel Lisa formed the Missouri Fur Company with Pierre and Auguste Chouteau and William Clark among his partners. Forty thousand dollars were raised and a party of 150 men set out in 1809, establishing trading stations among Arikara, Mandan, Minitari and Crow. Lisa defied the Blackfeet by building a substantial fort at Three Forks, the headwaters of the Missouri. But the Blackfeet were determined to protect their control of the fur trade and Andrew Henry, in command of the post, was driven back to the Snake River, where he and his men built a log fort and barely survived the winter. Thereafter the company pulled back to Council Bluffs below the Mandan villages there and established its main base of operations.

Lisa, the most enterprising and successful of the "first generation" of fur trappers and traders, was known as Uncle Manuel in St. Louis, where he brought his rich haul of furs every summer. He had married into the Omaha tribe and ascribed his success as a trader to the fact that "I put into my operations great activity; I go a great distance, while some are considering whether they will start today or tomorrow. I impose upon myself great privations; ten months in a year I am buried in the forest, at a great distance from my own house. I appear as the benefactor, and not as the pillager, of the Indians. I carried among them the seed of the large pompion, from which I have seen in their possession the fruit weighing one hundred and sixty pounds. Also the large bean, the potato, the turnip; and those vegetables now make a comfortable part of their subsistence, and this year I have promised to carry the plow. . . . I lend them my traps. . . . My establishments are the refuge of the weak and of the old men no longer able to follow their lodges. . . ."

The principal rival to the Missouri Fur Company was John Jacob Astor's American Fur Company. It was Astor's ambition to establish trading posts along the whole route of Lewis and Clark to the Pacific Ocean and Astoria. Astor's agent in this project was a young man named Wilson Price Hunt, who headed up the Missouri in 1811 with Lisa in hot pursuit. Rather than contest the region with Lisa, Hunt decided to take off on his own to try to find a passage to Astoria, almost fifteen hundred miles away. Lisa helped him buy horses from the Arikara Indians and Hunt set off with a party of sixty-four. The party arrived in Astoria after incredible hardships. Forced to abandon their trading supplies, they had been reduced to eating their moccasins. The expedition, desperate as its fortunes were, established the basis for Astor's challenge to the North West Company and the Hudson's Bay Company.

The Hudson's Bay Company, for its part, felt secure in its hold on the Columbia River basin. McLoughlin, the famous factor at Fort Vancouver, was reported to have said, "For all coming time we and our children will have uninterrupted possession of this country, as it can never be reached by families but by water around Cape Horn." The Yankees, he declared, "As well might . . . undertake to go to the moon."

At the mouth of the Big Horn, Lisa built a trading post, some halfway between the headwaters of the Yellowstone River and its confluence with the Missouri. This was the entrance to the beaver country. Lisa sent members of his party out to contact nearby Crow Indians, and Colter was given the assignment of bringing Indians to the post to trade. With this vague commission Colter set out on a journey of some five hundred miles to the Crow in the region of the headwaters of the Missouri. From Stinking Water River Colter turned south and east into what was later to be called Jackson Hole, rimmed by the Teton Range. From here he apparently found his way to Yellowstone Lake and from it followed an Indian trail along the river, doubling back to Stinking Water and then to Pryor's Creek and back to the Yellowstone and Lisa's camp. Colter's journey, which far exceeded his instructions, added substantially to the information that Lewis and Clark had gathered a few years earlier. Carefully recorded in the map that Clark kept at his headquarters in St. Louis, it encouraged other bold spirits to try to penetrate the beaver country of the Yellowstone Basin.

The next year when Colter set out to contact the Blackfeet and try to enlist them in Manuel Lisa's trading scheme, he fell in with a hunting party of Flatheads and Crow, both inveterate enemies of the

Blackfeet. By casually joining the party Colter made himself the enemy of the Blackfeet, who attacked the little band near the Gallatin River. Colter, badly wounded in the leg, managed to take refuge in a thicket and help fight off the Blackfeet. The next year trapping with a companion, John Potts, near the Jefferson, Colter and his friend were again ambushed by the Blackfeet. Potts, deciding that there was no hope of escape, fired his rifle and killed an Indian, whereupon he was filled with arrows. Colter surrendered, was disarmed and stripped of his clothes. The Indians chopped up Potts and threw pieces of his body in Colter's face. Colter was then turned loose, like a hare pursued by hounds. The Indian who could capture him first would get his scalp. Despite the fact that he had not fully recovered from the wounds of the previous year, Colter outdistanced all his pursuers except one. The brave tried to stab Colter with his spear. The white man evaded it and grasped the shaft, which broke, leaving the head of the spear in Colter's hand. He used it to dispatch the Blackfoot and then, with his enemies close behind him, headed for the Madison River, where he hid under a pile of driftwood until the Indians tired of searching for him. Then, clad only in a blanket he had taken from his pursuer, he made his way to Fort Lisa on the Yellowstone, a journey that took him nearly a week, "arriving there nearly exhausted by hunger, fatigue and excitement. . . . His beard was long, his face and whole body were thin and emaciated by hunger, and his limbs and feet swollen and sore. The company at the fort did not recognize him in this dismal plight," a friend wrote.

The War of 1812 led to the breakup of the Astoria enterprise since most of those involved were either Canadian or British and saw nothing to be gained in defending Astor's interests. The war also brought a virtual halt to the activities of the Missouri Fur Company. The loss of the foreign market for furs and the growing hostility of the Indians, egged on by agents of the British-Canadian fur companies, made trading unremunerative and exceedingly dangerous.

After the war, the United States government through the superintendent of Indian trade undertook to regulate and control the traffic in furs. Determined to open the fur trade to free enterprise, Thomas Hart Benton and John Jacob Astor formed an alliance to replace the government agents or factors by private entrepreneurs. Benton charged that the government factors were inefficient and corrupt, furnishing the Indians with inferior goods at inflated prices. Thomas McKinney, the able and enlightened superintendent of the Indian trade, argued that it was the private traders who debauched and exploited the Indians. Private enterprise won out. The government posts were abolished in 1822 and the trade thrown open to anyone energetic enough to seize it. The consequence was a decade or more of desperate competition, primarily between the Missouri Fur Company and Astor's reform American Fur Company.

Manuel Lisa had died in 1820. With the opening up of the fur trade William Ashley, lieutenant governor of Missouri, head of that state's militia and a leader in lead-mining ventures in Illinois territory, joined with Major Andrew Henry to revive the Missouri Fur Company. In March 1822, Henry ran an ad in the *Missouri Republican* which read: "TO ENTERPRISING YOUNG MEN the subscriber wishes to engage one hundred men to ascend the Missouri River to its source, there to be employed for one, two or three years. For particulars enquire of Major Andrew Henry, near the lead mines in the County of Washington. . . ." A few weeks later more than a hundred trappers and "campers," "many of whom," as a local paper noted, "had relinquished the most respectable employments and circles of society," reported to Henry.

Ashley also recruited a party (in the words of one member) from "the grog shops and other sinks of degredation," adding, "A description I cannot give but Falstafs Batallion was genteel in comparison." The truth about the types who signed on as trappers was certainly somewhere in between the description of Henry's men and those recruited by Ashley. What is most striking about the young men who became trappers besides their extraordinarily varied backgrounds— French, Spanish, Scottish, English, German, Southern, New England, half-breed Indian, a few black—was their relatively high degree of literacy and their lust for adventure. Though some doubtless hoped to make their fortunes, the great majority were drawn by the lure of the wild.

Andrew Henry's party suffered a severe setback a few hundred miles up the Missouri when one of the keelboats capsized and sank with $10,000 worth of trading goods. Above the Mandan villages a party of Assiniboin caught the trappers crossing the river and drove off fifty horses that had just been purchased from the Arikara. But Henry and his men pushed on and established a fort they named Fort Benton.

Two lieutenants of the Missouri Fur Company, Michael Immell and Robert Jones, headed up the Missouri in the spring of 1823 with

180 men, bound for Fort Benton. They trapped beaver in the area adjacent to the fort and then headed for the juncture of the Gallatin, Madison, and Jefferson—Three Forks—with twenty-seven men. After several weeks of trapping, they encountered a band of Blackfeet. The Indians made professions of friendship and received gifts from the trappers but twelve days later some four hundred Blackfeet ambushed the whites and killed Jones and Immell in the first onslaught. William Gorden, a clerk who had gone on ahead of the party, in his words, "escaped by a run of about seven miles across a plain, pursued only by footmen. . . ." Five other trappers were killed and four wounded. The remaining trappers held off the Indians long enough to improvise a raft and got off down the Yellowstone, abandoning all their furs, traps, horses, and equipment. The Blackfeet promptly sold the stolen furs to agents of the Hudson's Bay Company, who were well aware of their origin.

The agents of the American Fur Company and the Missouri Fur Company were ruthless in their fight for what was called "brown gold"—the prized beaver pelts. If the discovery of gold in California some twenty years later resulted in a Gold Rush, the abandonment by the government of the regulation of the Western fur trade resulted in a Beaver Rush. Many trappers and their auxiliaries—campkeepers, boatmen, and traders—lost their lives at the hands, primarily, of the warlike Blackfeet. A number died of disease, improperly treated wounds, of scurvy and camp fever.

Astor, in order to compete with the Missouri Fur Company, combined several of the old fur companies, among them that of the Chouteaus, originally partners of Lisa's, and Bernard Pratte and Company. In addition Astor signed on a number of former employees of the North West Fur Company, many of them Scotsmen with considerable experience in the trade and good relations with the Assiniboin and Blackfeet Indians. The company built a post named Fort Union at the mouth of the Yellowstone to carry on trade with the Assiniboin. The Missouri Fur Company established a post at Fort Piegan to control the Blackfoot territory, and Fort Cass, near Fort Benton, to serve as the center of trade with the Crow.

As more and more "forts" were established in connection with the beaver trade (they were, in fact, trading posts typically containing a few crude structures surrounded by palisades), they became a standard feature of the plains and Rocky Mountain area. Each collected its own characters and accumulated its own often brief but colorful history.

Edwin Denig, who had been in charge of Fort Union, wrote eloquently of the dangers at the posts and forts themselves (which appeared to the trappers as havens of refuge). Fort Union was under almost constant siege by the Blackfeet. When there were no Crow about to help defend the fort, "those who cut wood, guard horses, or go in quest of meat by hunting feel the murderous strokes of these ruthless warriors. Each and every year from 5 to 15 persons attached to the trading establishment have been killed since commerce has been carried on with the Crows in their own district. . . . Whoever went forth to procure wood or meat placed their lives in extreme jeopardy. Every hunter there has been killed, and the fort often reduced to a famished condition when buffalo were in great numbers within sight. The few horses kept for hunting were always stolen, and those who guarded them shot down. . . ."

Robert Meldrum, who had started out as trapper and lived for three years with the Crow Indians, was an intelligent and literate man. Promoted in Astor's American Fur Company to a position in charge of Fort Alexander near the mouth of the Rosebud River, he was later charged with building Fort Sarpy. Meldrum told of a typical incident —a Piegan squaw going to the river to get some water was surprised, killed, and scalped by a party of Blackfeet before anyone could come to her assistance. During a dance at Fort Sarpy some Blood Indians slipped into one of the houses where an old Assiniboin Indian was sleeping, "cut his throat then dragged him out about forty yards in front of the Bastion & commenced mutilating his body in a most horrible manner. . . ."

A clerk at Fort Sarpy charged that it had been turned into a "whore house," providing Indians and trappers alike with female companions. Squaws were often sold to trappers as "wives," but the price was usually high. The clerk at Fort Sarpy was offered "a dirty lousy slut" for "One horse one Gun one chief's coat one NW Blkt . . . two shirts one pr. leggins, six & half yards of Bed ticking one hundred loads ammunition twenty Bunches of Beads ten large Plugs Tobacco & some sugar Coffe Flour etc. . . ."

Archibald Palmer, the bookkeeper for a time at Fort Union under the Scotsman James McKenzie and married to the daughter of a Blood chief, was reputed to be an English nobleman who "always dressed in the latest London fashions" and took a bath every day. Attired in "ruffled shift fronts and . . . a great gold chain around his neck," he was "polished, scented, and oiled to the highest degree." McKenzie himself lived in considerable elegance with a well-stocked wine cellar. A visitor dining with him was astonished to see "a splendidly set table with a white tablecloth, and two waiters, one a negro. . . ." No one was allowed at table without a coat.

19

Jedediah Smith

In the spring of 1823, when General Ashley started up the river from St. Louis, young Jedediah Strong Smith was a member of the party. Smith's father was a native of New Hampshire who had emigrated to the New York frontier after the Revolution and then after the birth of the young Smith had moved, successively, to Erie, Pennsylvania, and then to Ashtabula, Ohio, producing a dozen children in the process. A doctor in Ashtabula had taken an interest in Jedediah and taught him the "rudiments of an English education and smattering of Latin." At the age of thirteen he got a job as a clerk on a Great Lakes freighter. In that rough and blasphemous world, Smith was distinguished for his industry, thrift, and, perhaps above all, his piety. At the age of twenty-three, with the poise and experience of a man many years older, he set out for St. Louis, not so much to make his fortune as to penetrate the heart of the continent. At St. Louis he signed on with Ashley for the Yellowstone expedition.

When Ashley and his men reached the Arikara villages which straddled the Missouri, they found the Arikara, or Rees, in a warlike mood, apparently intent on blocking the passage of the whites up the river. To add to Ashley's difficulties, the progress of the keelboats had become so slow as the river fell that the only practical way to continue the journey was by horseback. This meant buying horses from the hostile Rees. Word now reached Ashley from Fort Benton that Henry had been forced to abandon the Three Forks area and was in dire need of horses and further trading goods. The Ree towns contained 141 solid earth and log lodges, each of which held from five to ten Indians. The men on the keelboats could see that their appearance on the river had turned the villages into hives of activity. Ashley went ashore to parley with two Ree chieftains who were accompanied by a half-breed named Edward Rose, the son of a Scottish trader and a half-breed black woman. Rose, who had started life as a pirate in Louisiana, had lived with the Crows for years and was now a kind of subchief of the Rees.

A characteristically long and intricate exchange followed. Ashley had many men and guns; he also had many presents. He wished peace with the Rees and he wished to purchase horses from them to continue his trip. Everything seemed to go well. The horses were purchased, assembled along the riverbank, and hobbled preparatory to continuing the trip. That night there was a severe storm and, under the cover of it, the Rees launched an attack on Ashley's men, some of whom were guarding the horses on the shore with others asleep on the keelboats or along the shore. The Rees concentrated their fire on the horses, perhaps assuming that with the animals dead or scattered, the whites would be severely hampered in any attempt to escape. Jedediah Smith, one of the horse guards, tried to cut their hobbles and drive them into the river, but so many of the men on the riverbank were killed or wounded by the fire of the Indians that the effort failed. Thilless, a black man with bullet holes in both legs, loaded and fired from a sitting position, calling out in the dark, "They aint killed this niggah yet." The men on the keelboats, diminished as their numbers were, refused to go to the aid of their companions on the shore, some of whom wished to assault the Indian palisades. When Ashley sent skiffs ashore to pick up the wounded and the survivors, the men refused to enter the boats, declaring their determination to stay and fight it out; but when the keelboats began dropping down the river out of range, the men on shore swam after them and were taken aboard. Of the forty men in the party, eleven were either killed outright, drowned trying to regain the keelboats, or died of their wounds. The next day, when Ashley announced his determination to make another effort to pass the Ree towns, his men, to his "surprise and mortification," flatly refused. Ashley's next move was to try to contact Henry at Fort Benton more than two hundred miles away. He asked for volunteers to make the hazardous ride through Indian country to the mouth of the Yellowstone, but only Jedediah Smith came forward. A French-Canadian trapper named Baptiste was prevailed upon to accompany Smith. Two horses were captured and the men set off, traveling mostly at night and several times barely eluding capture by roving bands of Indians. Riding one night, their horses exhausted and pursuing Indians on their trail, they came on three Ree warriors asleep by a campfire with their horses tethered nearby. They killed the Indians while they slept and took their best horses; Smith was dismayed when Baptiste took their scalps as well. When Smith and his companion reached Henry, they brought him the unwelcome news that far from having horses and supplies for the men at the fort, Ashley himself was in dire straights.

Henry had no choice but to make out as best he could. He decided to spend the summer trapping. His party was augmented by a famous frontier character named Hugh Glass. A member of the party wrote, "Mr. Hugh Glass . . . could not be restrained and kept under Subordination he went off the line of march one afternoon and met with a large grissley Bear which he shot and wounded the bear as is usual attacted Glass he attempted to climb a tree but the bear caught him and hauled him to the ground tearing and lacerating his body in a fearful rate." Glass's companions killed the bear but Glass was so badly mauled that it seemed impossible that he could recover and Henry, anxious to not delay the party in Indian country, persuaded two of Glass's friends to stay with him until he died. A trapper named Fitzgerald and a young man named Jim Bridger remained behind to care for Glass. After five days, Glass, in a coma much of the time, still hung on, and his guardians, aware that the rest of the party was daily putting distance between them and anxious for their own safety, decided to leave the "old man" (Glass was in his forties) to his certain fate. They took his pack, rifle, and saddle and hurried after Henry. At the fort they reported that Glass had died. But Glass in fact was miraculously recovering. He got water from a nearby spring and found a few berries. For ten days he mended and then began to make his way to Fort Kiowa at the mouth of the White River nearly a hundred miles away. Much of the distance he crawled, too weak and severely wounded to walk. He reached Fort Kiowa, got food and essential supplies from the trader there, and then started for Fort Benton to settle his score with the men who had deserted him. He arrived at the fort on New Year's Eve when festivities were in full swing, looking very much like a ghost. Bridger he forgave because of his youth, and this was fortunate for western lore, because Bridger was to become more famous than Glass. Fitzgerald had wisely moved downriver, allegedly to Fort Atkinson near Council Bluffs. Glass and four companions set out after that unhappy man. They were waylaid by the Rees, who killed Glass's friends and stripped him of everything but "my knife and steel in my shot pouch." At Fort Atkinson, Glass found Fitzgerald, who had enlisted in the army. Fitzgerald was forced to return the rifle he had taken and Glass was prevailed upon to spare his life. Retrieving the gun was more important to Glass than killing Fitzgerald, for his gun was as legendary a weapon as ever existed in the West. It had been responsible for the deaths of countless savages and was as personal to Glass as a brother.

Glass had nine more exceedingly active years of life left to him. In the winter of 1833, he and two friends, Edward Rose, the ex-pirate, and a veteran trapper, Pierre Menard, were staying at Fort Cass in Crow country. Since the Crows were on peaceful terms with the trappers, Glass and his companions felt safe enough to venture down on the frozen Yellowstone to hunt beaver. There they were ambushed by a party of Arikara "who shot scalped and plundered" the three trappers. Glass's phenomenal luck had at last run out, but he was already a legend, one of a dozen or so "mountain men" whose names are forever intertwined with the Rocky Mountain fur trade. The apotheosis would begin at once as innumerable "western" writers and travelers repeated, often with embellishments, his heroic adventures. Soon it was said that Glass and his companions, surrounded by the Rees and despairing of their lives, had set fire to a powder keg and blown themselves to Kingdom Come though what they were doing hunting beaver with a powder keg was not explained.

The relationship between the trappers and Indians is suggested by a story told by Jim Beckwourth, a half-breed trapper. When General William Ashley and his party were on their way from the Green River, hundreds of Crow warriors came down on his camp like a whirlwind, brandishing their weapons and hallooing. Not knowing whether they were friendly Crows or hostile Blackfeet, the whites prepared to defend themselves, but the general ordered his men to hold their fire until he fired. As the Indians swept to within pistol shot of the camp, Ashley pulled the trigger of his rifle but the gun misfired and the Indians dashed into the camp. They were Crows. Jim Beckwourth, who told the story, was convinced that if Ashley's rifle had fired, followed by those of his men, killing and wounding some of the Indians, the trappers would all have been wiped out on the spot.

Recognizing some of his stolen horses among the Crow ponies, Ashley said to their chief, Sparrow-Hawk, "I believe I see some of my horses among yours."

"Yes. We stole them from you."

"What did you steal my horses for?"

"I was tired with walking. I had been to fight the Blackfeet, and, coming back, would have called at your camp. You would have given me tobacco but that would not carry me. When we stole them they were very poor. They are now fat. We have plenty of horses; you can take all that belong to you."

The winter and spring of 1824 saw a significant change in the procedures followed by Ashley and Henry. They decided to abandon the tortuous spring trip up the Missouri and depend, instead, on pack trains of mules and horses loaded with trading goods. The caravans would rendezvous at predetermined spots with the trappers who had been collecting beaver pelts. Pelts would be exchanged for goods needed by the trappers and further trade would be carried on with friendly Indian tribes. The cost and danger of trying to maintain trading posts in Indian country would thus be avoided, as would the risk and uncertainty of navigating the Missouri by keelboat. A further refinement was that of taking a substantial portion of the furs down the Yellowstone and the Missouri to St. Louis in bullboats. One consequence of the new procedure was that the trappers operated much more on their own. The risks were, if possible, even greater, since they now were more widely dispersed. A party of fifteen or twenty trappers would travel together to a major river basin—the Wind, the Green, or the Gallatin—and then split up into parties of two or three to work the creeks and tributaries. Thus isolated, they were in constant danger from hostile Indians, especially the Arikara, Blackfeet, and Pawnee. When the fall trapping season was terminated by the freezing of the creeks and rivers, the trappers would gather together, build a fortified camp, and hole up for the winter. The breaking up of the ice in the spring marked the beginning of a new trapping cycle in anticipation of the rendezvous. Another consequence of abandoning the dependence on "forts" was that the trappers ranged far more widely than before, opening up large new areas beyond the Yellowstone. In this development Jedediah Smith took the lead. From the time of the Arikara attack on Ashley's party, Smith displayed more and more conspicuously his qualities of leadership.

Trapping on the Big Horn in the winter of 1823, Smith, like Glass before him, was badly mauled by a grizzly. While he recovered, two of his trapping companions, who had been nursing him, were surprised and killed by a band of marauding Indians. Smith, hiding in the underbrush, barely escaped detection. The Indians made off with everything in sight—the horses, traps, saddles and blankets, and even the pans and kettles used for cooking. All that was left was Smith's rifle, knife, flint, and a Bible he always carried with him. He opened it and read: "He is chastened also with pain upon his bed, and the multitude of his bones with strong pain. . . . Yes, his soul draweth near to the grave, and his life to the destroyers. His flesh shall be fresher than a child's; he shall return to the days of his youth. He shall pray unto God and He will be favorable unto him. . . ." The next morning, Smith, unable to walk and in severe pain, dragged himself from one beaver trap to another until he found a beaver, laboriously retrieved it, made a small fire, and cooked the flesh. The next two days he went without food, finding consolation in his Bible. The third day Smith shot a fat buck that came to drink at the creek, and until the meat turned bad, he was well fed. Again he was without food and without dressing for his wounds. Again he read, "Yea, though I walk through the valley of the shadow of death, I will fear no evil; for Thou art with me." Three days later when Smith was nearly dead, a party of trappers, led by friends of Smith's who had gone for help after his encounter with the bear, arrived. A litter was improvised, Smith was fed and his wounds dressed, and the party headed down the Big Horn to the Yellowstone to join Henry's company. They were intercepted by Thomas Fitzpatrick, a partner of Henry's, who told Smith that a Crow Indian had given him directions to a trail along the Sweetwater River that would carry a traveler to a break in the Wind River Mountains, through which they could reach the Green. There, Fitzpatrick had been told, the land abounded with beaver.

At the mouth of the Big Horn, Henry's men had built winter quarters. The Crow Indians pitched their lodges nearby and the trappers settled in for a typical winter, trapping when the weather was warm and the ice had melted, finding other diversions when the creeks froze up. When the spring thaws came, Smith and Fitzpatrick got Henry's permission to work as "free trappers"—that is, to search for beaver on their own account, to be supplied by Henry and to pay him back with beaver pelts. Eighteen other trappers and camp keepers signed on with Smith and Fitzpatrick, and the party set out for the Wind River Valley. Some of the horses gave out on the difficult terrain leading from the Big Horn over "Bad Pass" into the Wind River area. It was thus decided that Smith would remain at the juncture of the Wind River and the Popo Agie, trapping in the region with a half-dozen men, while Fitzpatrick and the balance of the party pushed on to the pass that Fitzpatrick's Crow friend had told him led into the Green River Valley. After crossing through an arid region of red sandstone peaks and precipices, Fitzpatrick's men came to the Sweetwater, running along the base of the Wind River Mountains and then turning southwest. At first the going was deceptively easy. Then, as they advanced, the snow grew deeper and the weather sharp and cold. Finally the valley of the Sweetwater debouched on a high rolling plain. There the weather was warmer and the snow melting. They soon found themselves at what came to be called the Little Sandy, a river that flowed into the Colorado, which, in turn, ran to the Gulf of California. They had traversed the South Pass, probably the first white men through the pass that was to become the gateway to Oregon and California for hundreds of thousands of overland emigrants.

The valley of the Green River was all that the Crow chief had promised, and Fitzpatrick and his men took advantage of the virgin beaver streams and ponds to collect a rich bounty of furs; but before they could start back, a party of Snake Indians stole all their horses, some twenty in number, leaving them without the means to bring their packs of beaver skins back to the winter rendezvous. With the horses gone, the most prudent course would have been to cache the furs and return to the Popo Agie, where they could get horses from Jedediah Smith's party and return to retrieve the fruits of their summer's labors, but Fitzpatrick's men wanted the sport of following the Snake and recapturing their horses. They therefore cached their furs and set out in pursuit on foot—fourteen of them against many times that number of Snake. For eight days they followed the trail left by the band of horses, traveling the last part of their journey at night and lying concealed during the daytime, the scouts out a mile or more ahead. Finally they came on the Snake village of some twenty lodges. More than a hundred horses were loosely corralled nearby. The trappers' strategy was for each to seize a horse at a given signal, leap on its back, and drive the rest of the herd through the village and back down the trail in the direction of their own camp on the Big Sandy. Changing horses frequently and stopping only briefly to rest and eat, they got back to their cache in three days. For the twenty horses that had been stolen they now had forty, and what was as important, they had had a splendid adventure to yarn about in winter camp.

When Fitzpatrick and his men rejoined Jedediah Smith and his party at the Popo Agie and told them of the fabulous beaver trapping in the Siskadee country, Smith and William Sublette, another "captain" working as a free trapper under the general aegis of Ashley, decided to have a try themselves. While Fitzpatrick took their combined beaver packs in bullboats down the Sweetwater to the Platte and the spot designated for the fall rendezvous, Smith and Sublette went through the South Pass to try their luck on the tributaries of the Green.

Meanwhile, General Ashley had returned from St. Louis, determined to follow up Fitzpatrick's expedition through the South Pass. He recruited twenty-five men including Fitzpatrick himself, Jim Beckwourth, and Moses or "Black" Harris. Ashley made poor progress initially. It was bitterly cold and there was little grass to be found for his horses or game for his men. By the time they reached the village of the Loup Pawnee half their horses had died of starvation and exhaustion, and their thin, tough meat had been eaten by the party. The Pawnee sold them horses and a quantity of corn, dried meat, dried pumpkin, and beans. Leaving the Pawnee village, Ashley and his men encountered a terrible blizzard in which a number of their newly acquired horses died. For three weeks the party remained in camp on the South Platte while small detachments of trappers scouted for a passage through to the Green River Valley. At the end of February, Ashley and his men struck out through the snow and three days later penetrated the watershed of the North Platte. Now there was plenty of deer and buffalo and Ashley later wrote, "I was delighted with the variegated scenery presented by the valleys and mountains . . . and what added no small degree of interest to the whole scene were the many small streams issuing from the mountains, bordered by a thin growth of small willows and richly stocked with beaver." Trapping beaver as they went, Ashley and his men turned west from the river and crossed, on the twenty-sixth of March, the Continental Divide at a spot that was later named Bridger's Pass. The next night a band of Crow Indians stole seventeen of their horses and mules. Finally they reached the Big Sandy and started down the river, turning west for six days and coming at last to the Green after a journey of a hundred and sixty-six days in the dead of winter over country that no white men had traversed. It was one of the most remarkable journeys of that era of remarkable journeys, and it is worth remarking that while it could not have been accomplished without the assistance of the Pawnee, it was almost wrecked by the raid of the Crows. Ashley had covered a substantial part of present-day southern Wyoming on his peregrinations, penetrated into northern Colorado, and entered the Great Divide Basin. At the end of April he began a perilous journey down the Green in bullboats to a point some fifty miles south of its juncture with the Uinta.

Crossing the Unita Mountains, Ashley and his party reached what was later named the Weber River. Along its banks they encountered some of the trappers who had set out with Smith and Sublette the previous summer to retrace Fitzpatrick's course through the South Pass into the valley of the Green. With the Smith-Sublette party were twenty-nine deserters from the Hudson's Bay Company who had been persuaded by Smith to bring their furs to the Wind River rendezvous.

By the first of July, 1825, a hundred and twenty trappers had gathered at Henry's Fork on the Green. There they were joined by the train from St. Louis carrying its cargo of supplies—"flour, sugar, coffee, blankets, tobacco, whisky, and all other articles necessary for that region," as Jim Beckwourth put it. The free trappers constituted a kind of mountain aristocracy. As Joseph Meek, himself a free trapper, tells it, "They prided themselves on their hardihood and courage; even on their recklessness and profligacy. Each claimed to own the best horses; to have had the wildest adventures; to have killed the greatest numbers of bears and Indians; to be the favorite with the Indian belles, the greatest consumer of alcohol, and to have the most money to spend—that is, the largest credit on the books of the company. If his hearers did not believe him, he was ready to run a race with them, to beat them at 'cold sledge,' or to fight, if fighting were preferred —ready to prove what he affirmed in any way the company pleased."

It might be said parenthetically, that long after the heyday of the beaver trappers, enterprising journalists and ghostwriters wrote the "autobiographies" of many of the more famous mountain men, some of whom, like Beckwourth, were fond of drawing a long bow and became in fact professional storytellers. While there is no reason to doubt the practical details of daily life in their narratives, the rather formal and sometimes flowery language they are couched in is that of their amanuenses and not their own.

While Ashley and his men made their extraordinary circuit from Fort Atkinson to the Green River, Smith and Sublette had followed the Green to Horse Creek and from there to Hoback's River, which emptied into the Snake. Sublette made camp not far from the headwaters of the Yellowstone, while Smith went on some hundred miles down the Snake, trapping its tributaries. Thereafter he turned north with the hope of reaching Clark's Fork of the Columbia. He was now in the territory claimed by the Hudson's Bay Company and there he encountered a party of Iroquois who had been hired by the Hudson's Bay Company as trappers. They were starving and destitute and begged Smith to help them. They were operating out of Spokane House, a trading post on the river of that name, and they had a rich haul of furs from trapping in the Three Forks region at the headwaters of the Missouri and as far east as the Yellowstone. There the Snake Indians had made off with their guns, horses, and most of their furs. They still had nine hundred furs, worth some $5,000. Smith agreed to help them get back to their base of operations on condition that they would give him their remaining furs. Smith then took advantage of the opportunity to scout out the lay of the land in the Hudson's Bay Company's backyard.

Smith and his men were at the Flathead Trading House on the upper waters of Clark's Fork of the Columbia for almost a month before they started back with a party of Hudson's Bay trappers under the leadership of Alexander Ross. Separating from Ross near the Snake, Smith came upon the Great Salt Lake on his way to the Green. In Cache Valley on the Bear River, Smith was reunited with Sublette, who had made his winter camp there. During the winter, Jim Bridger had undertaken to follow the Bear River to its mouth. When *he* reached the Great Salt Lake, he was convinced that he had discovered an inlet of the Pacific.

At the 1825 rendezvous Ashley's trappers and the free trappers contracted to him brought in a hundred and thirty packs of beaver furs to the value of nearly $200,000—enough for Ashley to retire from the fur business. He took a dozen of his trappers down the Missouri with him to St. Louis for a farewell spree. When Ashley retired he sold his business to Smith and Sublette. They thereby advanced to the status called bourgeois by the French and "booshways" by the Americans.

It was soon clear that Jedediah Smith was less interested in collecting large sums of beaver skins than in exploring a passage through the Rockies to California. He thus set out in August, 1826, from the Great Salt Lake with eighteen men and fifty horses, leaving Sublette to carry on with trapping in the Green River Valley. The two parties were to meet at Bear Lake the next summer. Among those accompanying Smith was James Read, a hotheaded blacksmith; Harrison Rogers, a pious young man, much like Smith in temperament, who kept a careful journal of the party's progress; Peter Ranne, a free black; a half-breed, a Nipisang Indian, called, conveniently, Nipisang; Marion, an Umpquah Indian slave from the Pacific coast; Manuel, a "native Mexican"; two Kentuckians; two Scotchmen; John, a black slave; an Irishman; a German Jew named Emmanuel Lazarus; and three men from Indiana, Ohio, and New York, respectively.

As Smith wrote in the introduction to his journal, "In taking the charge of our western Expedition I followed the bent of my strong inclination to visit this unexplored country and unfold those hidden resources of wealth and bring to light those wonders which I readily imagined a country so extensive might contain. I must confess that I had at that time a full share of that ambition (and perhaps foolish ambition) which is common in a greater or less degree to all the active world. I wanted to be the first to view a country on which the eyes of a white man had never gazed and to follow the course of rivers that run through a new land."

Smith followed the Portneuf River from the southeastern end of the Great Salt Lake to Utah Lake, stopping to lay in a supply of dried buffalo meat. Near Utah Lake, Smith encountered the Ute Indians and negotiated a "treaty" with them "by which americans are allowed to hunt & trap in and pass through their country unmolested." Smith found the Ute "cleanly quiet and active." They were, in his view, "nearer . . . to civilized life than any Indians I have seen in the Interior." The Ute had captured two young Snake girls who, after having been forced to act as servants for Ute masters, were turned over to the women of the tribe to be tortured to death. Smith bought them from the Ute and they accompanied his party for a time, apparently as the companions of Manuel, the Mexican. When he deserted the expedition a week or so later, they went with him, as did the half-breed Nipisang.

Smith crossed over the Wasatch Range to the Price River, then turned west to the Sevier River (which he named the Ashley), following it south, crossing the Escalante desert, and picking up the Virgin River in what is now southwest Utah. Along the way he encountered the

Paiute, a degenerate branch of the northern Ute who lived primarily on roots and a kind of cake made out of grasshoppers and berries. The shy Paiute spread a warning of the white men's coming by setting small fires of grass and brush, so that Smith and his party got only occasional glimpses of them. They had no horses, were commonly naked, and were remarkably enduring and fleet of foot. Some days later, when the men had exhausted their supply of dried buffalo meat and found no game to appease their hunger, they met a tribe of Southern Paiute who traded with them for a very welcome supply of corn and pumpkins. Several times subsequently, when the party had run out of food, they encountered Indians (apparently Mohaves) who replenished their food supplies with squash and pumpkins. Here the Indians had horses and showed signs of a more advanced civilization. Smith's horses were now breaking down from the hard travel and poor grazing. For a time two Mohave Indians acted as guides, but they abandoned Smith and his men as they pushed down the Colorado.

The going was arduous in the extreme, the party often moving along narrow ledges far above the river where one misstep meant disaster. Finally Smith and his men came out in Cottonwood Valley, where there was grass for the horses. There Smith killed a mountain sheep. There also he encountered the first large settlements of Mohave Indians, who had obviously had contacts with the Spanish. The Indians greeted Smith hospitably. "Melons and roasted pumpkins," he wrote, "were presented in great abundance." The Mohaves were tall and well-built with light complexions. The men were commonly naked or wore a "Spanish blanket" thrown over their left shoulder. They wore "no head dress moccasins or leggings. The dress of the women," Smith noted, "is a petticoat made of material like flax. . . . The men appear to work as much in the fields as the women which is quite an unusual sight among the Indians." They collected locust pods and raised wheat, squash, corn, beans, and melons. The Mohaves told Smith that he was some ten days travel from the Spanish settlements in California. Smith, who had not informed his men that he had any intention of pushing on to California and later insisted to suspicious Spanish officials that such a notion had been far from his mind, now told his men they must go farther west on the not unreasonable grounds that the region that they had passed through was too barren to hazard a return trip.

After a day's travel without sighting water, Smith began to suspect that the Indians had deliberately given him instructions intended to draw him into a desert region where he and his men must perish from lack of food and water, the Indians thereby falling heir to all their belongings. His suspicion was strengthened when, retracing his steps, he found that Indians were following him. But peace was made and Smith prevailed on two Indians, who had escaped from the Mission at San Gabriel, to accompany him as guides across the Mohave Desert.

The passage across the desert was from one small brackish stream or spring to another until the party hit the mouth of the Mohave River a few miles beyond Soda Springs. The next day they encountered Vanyume Indians, poor cousins of the Serranos, who shared with the travelers small cakes of acorns and pine nuts and rabbits they caught in a long net. Two days later they saw signs of cattle and horses, which, Smith wrote, "awakened many emotions in my mind and some of them not the most pleasant . . . I was approaching a country inhabited by the Spaniards, a people of different religion from mine and possessing a full share of bigotry and disregard of the right of a Protestant that has at times stained the Catholic Religion. . . . They might perhaps consider me a spy imprison me persecute me for the sake of religion or detain me in prison to the ruin of my business."

Soon they were through the San Bernardino Mountains into the valley of the San Gabriel, dominated by the great mission there. The Indians working in the fields gazed at the strange, ragged band with astonishment. At a farm or hacienda, an elderly Indian greeted them in Spanish and asked the famished men if they would like to have a bullock killed. After a fine feast, Smith wrote a letter to the head of the Mission San Gabriel, Father Jose Bernardo Sanchez, a Franciscan, which was at once carried off to that dignitary, who replied in Latin. The father wished Smith to visit him and the trapper set off with his interpreter, arriving at "a Building of ancient and Castle-like appearance." "I was left quite embarrassed," Smith wrote, "hardly knowing how to introduce myself." The father took Smith by the hand and "quite familiarly asked me to walk in. . . . Soon bread and cheese were brought in and some rum. . . ." which the teetotaling Smith drank to be polite.

Their efforts to understand each other coming to naught, despite the interpreter, Father Sanchez sent for a young American, Joseph Chapman, who had been the first citizen of the United States to settle in Los Angeles. (He had been sent there as a prisoner after participating in a raid on Monterey.) Chapman was another "American original." He claimed to have been shanghaied in the Sandwich

Islands, or Hawaiian Islands as they were later called. He had made himself indispensable to the friars of the Mission of Los Angeles by his array of practical skills. He could construct a grist mill or a sailing ship, splint broken bones, pull teeth, fashion improved farm implements, and do a hundred other ingenious things.

While they waited for the arrival of Chapman, Smith was seated beside the father at dinner. "As soon as we were seated," Smith wrote, "the Father said Benediction and each one in the most hurried manner asked the blessing of heaven—and even while the last words were pronouncing the fathers were reaching for the different dishes." Smith described the meal in some detail, the good food, the wine and the cigars, adding, "I may be excused for being this particular in this table scene when it is recollected that it was a long time since I had had the pleasure of sitting at a table and never before in such company."

When Joseph Chapman finally appeared with a translator of his own, Smith learned that he and his men were, in effect, under detention until instructions were received from the governor of California at San Diego, which, it was predicted, might be a long time coming since that gentleman was notoriously indecisive.

While Smith waited for word from the governor, he and Harrison Rogers took note of mission life. The number of Indians attached to each mission varied from four hundred to two thousand and made up "with their dependencies" roughly three-fourths of the population of the province. The Mission San Gabriel, where Smith and his party landed, had some two thousand acres under cultivation in wheat, beans, peas, and corn, along with orchards of apples, peaches, pears, olives, "and a beautiful grove of 400 Orange trees." Within the walls of the mission compound, besides the quarters of the friars, there were apartments for visitors and a guard house for the soldiers who were assigned to protect the mission and keep order among the Indians. There were, in addition, store houses, a granary, a "soap factory," distillery, blacksmith, carpenters' and coopers' shops, and rooms given over to weavers. Rogers saw in a side room of the church "molten Images, they have our Saviour on the cross, his mother and Mary the Mother of James, and 4 of the apostles, all as large as life." He was presumably comforted to discover that the room was being used as a "sugar Factory."

For the friars meals were preceded by a glass of gin and some bread and cheese and Smith noted that "wine in abundance made our reverend fathers appear to me quite merry." Smith's two Indian guides were arrested and put in the mission's prison, to be punished as runaways, Smith noted regretfully, adding, "I thought them fine honest and well disposed boys."

The mission was a strange mixture of the authoritarian and benign. Most of the Indians had been forced to attach themselves to a mission and they were, for all practical purposes, confined to it and punished by flogging when they stole or fought or shirked their work or tried to run away. Rogers described the Indians as "compleat slaves in every sense of the word." He saw five "old men, say from fifty to sixty," whipped for not going to work when ordered, and a priest asked Jim Reed, the party's blacksmith, to "make a large trap for him to set in his orange garden to catch the Indians when they come up at night to rob his orchard." Rogers also noted that the soldiers at the mission "appear at times some what alarmed for fear the Inds—will rise and destroy the mission." Rogers also noted that while "friendship and peace prevail with us and the spanyards—our own men are continuous and quarrelsome amongst ourselves and have been since we started the Expedition." Rogers thought the Indian women "very unchaste." One came to his room, he wrote, "asked me to make her a Blanco Pickaninia, which being interpreted, is to get her a white child—and I must say for the first time I was ashamed, and did not gratify her."

It was certainly an exploitative system, yet its harshness was softened by the kindness of many of the friars and the paternalistic character of the relationship. Compared with black slavery in the American South, or with the treatment accorded the various Indian tribes by the enlightened and progressive government of the United States, the mission system doubtless had much to recommend it. After Mexican independence, the Indians had, of course, been formally emancipated but in most of the missions the fathers had used their authority and their powers of persuasion to prevail upon their charges to remain at their labors. Many of them had, indeed, no place to go to and faced starvation if they left the missions. Rogers noted that the mission "ships to Europe annually from 20 to 25 thousand dollars worth of skins and Tallow and about 20 thousand dollars worth of soap."

"The Missions," Jedediah Smith wrote, "setting aside their religious professions are in fact large farming and grazing establishments conducted at the will of the father who is in a certain degree responsible to the President of his order." The work required of the Indians did not appear to Smith "unreasonably hard."

Harrison Rogers, who had told Father Sanchez quite candidly that he was a Calvinist who "did not believe that it was in the power of man to forgive sins. God only had that power," had not suffered in the esteem of the urbane and tolerant padre. In January, 1827, in the absence of Jedediah Smith, who had gone to San Diego, Father Sanchez invited Rogers to deliver "a New Years Address" and Rogers cheerfully obliged, reviewing the life and teaching of Christ. "Reverend Father, remember," Rogers admonished him, "the whole world was missionary ground. Before the day of Christ Jesus our Saviour we never heard of missionaries to the Heathen," with the exception of Jonah. Paul aside, the missionaries of the early church, he reminded the father, "were not learned in the arts and sciences; were ignorant of books and of men: yet they went forth unsupported by human aid—friendless—opposed by prejudices, laws, learning, reasonings of Philosophy, passions and persecutions." "On the whole," he concluded, "we have no reason to doubt, on the Testimony, of history and tradition, that the last command of Christ was so obeyed, that in the Apostolic age, the Gospel was preached in every part of the Globe which was then known." How much of this remarkable discourse survived translation we cannot guess, but Father Sanchez, who had become much attached to this young American fur hunter, could hardly have failed to be astonished. Appearing with his companions out of the wilderness, looking as wild as an Indian, he seemed entirely at home in a thoroughly alien society and had delivered a sermon as learned and literate as any priest or preacher.

Early in December, Smith had been summoned to San Diego to be interrogated by Governor Echeandia. On the way to San Diego he was the guest of a large landowner, Don Yorba, who was described by another visitor a few years later as "a tall, lean personage, dressed in all the extravagance of his country's costume. . . . Upon his head he wore a black silk handkerchief, the four corners of which hung down his neck behind. An embroidered shirt, a cravat of white jaconet tastefully tied, a blue damask vest, short clothes of crimson velvet, a bright green cloth jacket with large silver buttons, and shoes of embroidered deerskin."

San Diego was a thoroughly unimpressive presidio, perhaps testifying to the qualities of the governor. Everything was rundown and in disrepair. For days the governor, obviously much embarrassed by his unwanted guest, vacillated. The governor must wait until he had received orders from Mexico; then Smith himself must go to the capital. Finally, after more than two weeks of waffling, Governor Echeandia at last proposed a solution. If the captains of the various American ships in the San Diego harbor would sign a paper saying they believed Smith's presence in California to be due to the circumstances he claimed he would be allowed to trade for necessary provisions and depart. But he must go the way he had come, a very severe constraint for Smith, who, the difficulties of the route aside, was determined to find a more convenient way back to the meeting with Sublette at Bear Lake.

Rogers parted from his friend Father Sanchez (he writes his name Sancus, Sannes, and Sanchius in his journal) most reluctantly. "Old Father Sanchius has been the greatest friend that I ever meet with, with all my Travels," he noted in his journal, "he is worthy of being called a christian as he possesses charity in the highest degree—and a friend to the poor and distressed, I shall ever hold him as a man of God . . . and may god prosper him and all such men. . . ."

The governor's requirement met, the party started back to Bear Lake. Two more men now deserted, although it was far from clear that the Mexican authorities would permit them to remain behind. Smith headed dutifully for the Mohave Desert as though to retrace his steps, but once out of the range of Mexican officialdom, he turned north along the Tehachapis to Kern Lake at the southern end of the present San Joaquin Valley. At Tulare Lake the party encountered a band of Yokut Indians who lived on an island in the lake and used rafts made of the tule that grew along the riverbanks bound together by grass thongs.

There Smith discharged one of his men, John Wilson, of "seditious disposition," and then continued his northward journey, passing a large Indian village of the Wukchmni Indians on Cottonwood Creek, and trapping for beaver as he went. The Wimilchi Indians were camped in a beautiful oak grove on the banks of the Peticutry, later the San Joaquin.

The San Joaquin River flowed up the valley that bears the same name and emptied into the San Francisco Bay; into it flowed the Merced, the Tuolumne, and the Stanislaus. Smith and his party made their way up the course of the San Joaquin, trapping beaver and shooting elk and antelope for food. Wild horses were everywhere in great abundance, as well as geese, brant, heron, cormorant, and many species of duck. Smith saw a California condor, one of the most majestic birds in the world. There were scattered bands of Indians —the remnants, Smith was told by an Indian guide, of those tribes that had been absorbed by the missions.

Smith was now in the region of the Penutian-speaking Indians of central California, estimated at some two to three hundred tribes or bands, whose main divisions were the Miwok, Costanoan, Yokuts, Maidu, and Wintun. Their food staple was the acorn from the great oaks that lined the foothills of the Sierras. The acorns were gathered and stored in bins until they dried, then they were pounded into a fine yellow meal which was placed in a sandy pit; water was poured over it to remove the poisonous tannic acid. When the meal was sufficiently leached out by this process, it was allowed to dry and bread was made from it. The Indians also hunted deer, rabbits, and squirrels and were provident in putting by food for the winter months. Their weapons were simple and since the weather was mild they seldom wore any kind of garment. They had developed their arts to a relatively modest extent, and, as contrasted with the dramatic and "noble" Indians of the eastern forests and Great Plains, they were mild and nonmilitant. Their culture had taken form around gathering rather than fighting. Thus they seem to present a classic example of Arnold Toynbee's concept of "challenge and response." In a salubrious climate, with a plentiful supply of food and protected by the Sierra Nevada from their more warlike eastern neighbors, they lived a happy existence, never really challenged to develop and extend their primitive cultures. They had, in consequence, been integrated into the missions with relative ease by threats and blandishments. Their experiences with the Spanish had made those who remained free of the missions understandably wary of white men, as Jedediah Smith's experiences were to prove, and increasingly militant, stealing horses and cattle from the missions and ranchos and killing stray whites when the opportunity presented itself.

Smith began to turn his thoughts toward the spring meeting with Sublette and Jackson near the Bear Lake. He had some two hundred beaver skins that he had collected on the way and his men were anxious to get back to what for them passed for home—Bear Lake and then Fort Atkinson for the fall rendezvous. The Sierra Nevada presented an apparently impassable barrier. Smith nevertheless turned eastward, searching for a pass. Following the foothills of the Sierra, he crossed the Mokelumne River and encountered an Indian village of several hundred mud lodges of the Mokelumne Indians, a branch of the Northern Miwok. There Smith found a Spanish-speaking Indian, a refugee from one of the missions. After a good deal of wandering about in the course of which his Indian guide absconded with two of his horses and he lost twelve traps in the Mokelumne, Smith found himself still stymied. Now the Indians were more numerous and bolder, and Smith and his men had several narrow escapes. On the American River, Smith pursued an Indian girl, intending to give her presents and through her to reassure the elusive Maidu Indians, but the girl died of fright and Indians soon pressed dangerously close on the party. Many of them had never seen whites nor heard a gun fired. Smith tried to convince them of his friendly disposition but to no effect. As the Indians continued to menace them, Smith ordered two of his best shots to fire at two of the most distant savages. At the report of the rifles the two Indians fell. "For a moment," Smith wrote, "the Indians stood still and silent as if a thunder bolt had fallen among them then a few words passed from party to party and in a moment they ran like Deer." The experiment was repeated once more and the Maidu thereafter kept their distance.

Going in advance of his men to try to discover some passage through the mountains, Smith was moved to reflect on the vanity of human pretensions. "I thought of home," he wrote, "and all its neglected enjoyments of the cheerful fireside of my father's house of the Plenteous harvest of my native land and . . . the green and wide spread Prairaes of joyous bustle and of busy life thronged in my mind to make me feel more strongly the utter desolateness of my situation. And it is possible thought I that we are creatures of choice and that we follow fortune through such paths as these. Home with contented industry could give us all that is attainable and fortune could do no more."

Blocked by the formidable range of snowcapped mountains before him, Smith decided to turn back and try the Stanislaus River once more. He planned to leave most of his men in a secure camp on the river and then try to find a way through the mountains with two of his hardiest and most reliable trappers. He would send back for the rest of the party once he had reached Bear Lake and made contact with his partners. Crossing the swift Cosumnes River, the horse carrying the party's ammunition was swept down the river. "This was a terrible blow," Smith wrote, "for if our ammunition was lost with it went our means of subsistence and we were at once deprived of what enabled us to travel among hostile bands feared and respected. But my thoughts I kept to myself knowing that a few words from me would discourage my men." The drowned horse and his load were fortunately recovered and the men continued to the Stanislaus. There friendly relations were established with a local village of Mokelumne Indians through the generous distribution of gifts to the old chief, Ti-me; meat was dried, horses shod, and grass collected for fodder. Harrison Rogers was left in charge of the camp on the Stanislaus. If he received no word from Smith by September 20, he was instructed to go to the Russian post on Bodega Bay, buy what supplies he needed, and try for Bear Lake himself. Alternately he and his companions might sign on for the Hawaiian Islands and then try to get a ship back to the United States from there.

On May 20, Smith, accompanied by Silas Gobel and Robert Evans, left behind a rather glum little party that hardly knew whether they were better off to stay or go, and headed up the river with six horses and two mules, sixty pounds of dried meat and a quantity of hay. For almost a hundred miles the three men made their way toward the summit of the Sierras before they were overtaken by a violent sleet storm that lasted two days and in the course of which they had to watch two of their horses and one mule freeze to death before their eyes. "It seemed," Smith wrote, "that we were marked out for destruction and that the sun of another day might never rise to us. But He that rules the Storms willed it otherwise. . . ."

The next day, the men passed through what came to be known as Ebbetts Pass and began the rapid descent of the east side of the Sierra Nevada. They had another nerve-wracking encounter with a party of Southern Paiute who surrounded their camp one evening with their bows and arrows in their hands and then carried on, in "loud and harsh" voices what was clearly a debate about whether to kill the white men. "After about two hours," Smith wrote, "they became peaceable and made a fire. I then offered them some tobacco they took it and smoked and remained all night. . . . I do not know how to account for the singular conduct of the indians. They did not appear unanimous for the massacre and perhaps saw our intention of making our scalps bear a good price."

The last leg of the journey to what Smith called the "Depo" was an endurance contest. Every few days another horse gave out and what little flesh was left on its bones was eaten by the travelers. Their progress was from creek to water hole in the burning sun across the present-day state of Nevada. Smith described the land as "extremely Barren" and a "desolate waste." The men were reduced to four ounces of dried meat a day. A rare rain gave them an opportunity to collect enough precious water to water the horses and fill their own canteens. Smith killed a hare and saw an antelope and a black-tailed deer, "solitary and wild as the wind."

Through the Grant Range and the Horse Range, through dry valleys and cruel mountains, finally to the tributaries of the White River they made their slow and painful way. For twelve days they were without fresh meat. On June 16 they ate their last portions of food. The hooves of the remaining horses were worn almost to the quick. They killed the most depleted horse and ate him, and the next day they covered thirty miles without water. The following day, when Evans had collapsed of thirst and been left behind, Smith and Gobel fell in with a party of fourteen Paiute. The Indians helped them find a small spring and bring water back to Evans, who revived enough to join his companions. The Paiute then gave the white men two small ground squirrels, which they eagerly consumed, and showed them a water plant that the Indians ate and which the famished white men "found . . . pleasant."

The next day some wild onions helped to make the remaining horse meat go down and again they met Indians who, once their fears had been assuaged, were endlessly curious. "All the indians I had seen since leaving the Lake [Bear Lake]," Smith wrote, "have been the same unintelligent kind of beings, nearly naked having at most a scanty robe formed from the skin of the hare peculiar to this plain which is cut into narrow strips and interwoven with a kind of twine. . . . They form a connecting link between the animal and intellectual creation and quite in keeping with the country in which they are located." If the California tribes could be taken to represent human beings insufficiently challenged to develop greater creative resources, the Indians of the desert country were clearly examples of human social groups living in an environment so demanding that the mere problem of existence allowed no margin for the development of higher culture.

At the Salt Marsh Lake near present Gandy, Utah, Smith and his companions encountered the Goshute Indians, perhaps the least prepossessing of all the tribes belonging to the general family of Shoshonian Indians since they inhabited a region most uncongenial to human life. As described by a later traveler, "They wear no clothing of any description—build no shelter. They eat roots, lizards and snails . . . and when the lizard and snail and wild roots are buried in the snows of winter, they . . . dig holes . . . and sleep and fast until the weather permits them to go abroad again for food. . . . These poor creatures are hunted in the spring of the year when weak and helpless . . . and when taken, are fattened, carried to Santa Fe and sold as slaves."

By June 24, Smith and his men were without food or water and their few remaining horses were so weak and lame that they could hardly walk. The men had to dismount and assist their exhausted animals. The soft sand underfoot made walking difficult in the extreme. "Worn down with fatigue and burning with thirst," they dug holes in the sand and "lay down in them for the purpose of cooling our heated bodies." Rising, they plodded on until ten o'clock at night hoping to find water, and then, lying down to sleep, dreamed "of things we had not and for want of which it then seemed . . . probable we might perish in the desert unheard of and unpitied. In such moments," Smith added, "how trifling were all those things that hold such a sway over the busy and prosperous world." After a few hours of fitful sleep the three men started on to take advantage of the cool of the night, conscious that they were very near the end of their resources and must soon die of thirst and exhaustion if they did not find water. By ten the next morning, Evans could go no farther. Smith and Gobel made him as comfortable as possible and hurried on to try to find water to save their companion's life. In three miles they came, to their "inexpressible joy," to a spring at the foot of the Little Granite Mountain. Gobel "plunged into it at once" and Smith poured it over his head and then drank it down in great gulps. Smith then took a small kettle of water and some meat and returned to the prostrate Evans, who was "indeed far gone being scarcely able to speak." When Smith had revived him Evans drank four quarts of water and asked for more. "I have at different times," Smith wrote, "suffered all the extremes of hunger and thirst. Hard as it is to bear for successive days the gnawings of hunger it is light in comparison to the agony of burning thirst. . . . Hunger can be endured almost twice as long as thirst."

For several days the men rested and tried to regain sufficient strength to continue. They were now near the Great Salt Lake and they reached a lone lodge of Goshute Indians who "cheerfully divided with us some antelope meat." For many years the Goshute told the story that the first white men they had ever seen were three tattered, starving men who appeared out of the Salt Desert.

On June 27, Smith, with his telescope, got the first glimpse of Salt

Lake. "Is it possible," he asked, "that we are so near the end of our troubles. For myself I hardly durst believe that it was really the Big Salt Lake that I saw." They were almost "home." The next night they ate the last of their horse meat. They now had a horse and a mule left, the mule carrying the pack of beaver skins and the horse the rest of the party's equipment. The three men "talked a little of the probability of our suffering being soon at an end. I say we talked a little," Smith wrote, "for men suffering from hunger never talk much but rather bear their sorrows in moody silence which is much preferable to fruitless complaint."

The next day Smith shot a fine buck and, he noted, "we . . . employed ourselves most pleasantly for about two hours and for the time being forgot that we were not the happiest people in the world. . . . So much do we make our estimation of happiness by a contrast with our situation that we were as much pleased and as well satisfied with our fat venison on the bank of the Salt Lake as we would have been in possession of all the Luxuries and enjoyments of civilized life in other circumstances."

From a village of friendly Snake Indians, Smith learned that his partners and their trappers were only some twenty-five miles away, and two days later Smith and his companions arrived at the rendezvous point where they had been given up for lost.

Smith's remarkable journey, arduous as it was, like the Lewis and Clark Expedition, could not have been carried through without the assistance of numerous tribes of Indians encountered along the way. It was thus, like so many other white ventures in the West—of the trappers, hunters, explorers, traders—a kind of cooperative venture, albeit unwittingly. Certainly, the lives of Smith and his companions were often in danger from hostile or suspicious Indians, but without the Indian guides, the food so often provided from the Indians' own meager supplies, and the information about the terrain, unreliable as it sometimes was, Smith and his men could never have reached California or, once there, gotten back to the "Depo" at Bear Lake.

Smith had little time to enjoy the pleasures of "home." Rogers and the men left on the Stanislaus were much on his mind. He was afraid they might try to follow in his footsteps and he knew they must perish in the attempt. Summer was getting on, and September 20 was the deadline he had given Rogers. He had only eight weeks to assemble a party and set out for California once more. Evans, understandably, had had enough, but Silas Gobel was ready to dare the now familiar hazards of the journey once more. Smith enlisted eighteen trappers, accompanied by two Indian women, and set out to retrace his steps down the Sevier to the Virgin River, thence to the Colorado and west across the Mohave Desert. With the experience gained in the first expedition, the party made good time and suffered relatively little hardship until they reached the Mohave Indians. Smith had spent fifteen days with them in amity on his original trip and he looked forward to replenishing his party's larder at the Mohave village. But in the intervening months Governor Echeandia had sent out orders to the free Indians to intercept any Americans who might pass through their territory. This time Smith traded with the Mohaves for three days in apparent friendliness and then, as he and his men were crossing the Colorado, the Indians surprised them and massacred the ten men of the party who had not crossed the river. Smith and the rest had to watch in horror as their companions, Silas Gobel among them, were killed and scalped. The eight survivors made a dash for the haven of the San Gabriel mission. This time Smith, knowing that any delay would make it impossible to catch Rogers' group on the Stanislaus, simply wrote a report to Governor Echeandia and started north up the San Joaquin Valley. He found the men he had left there hungry and demoralized. Competent as Rogers was, he was not a natural leader and the men had suffered in health and, more important, in morale. Smith's own party was little better off and he decided to appeal once more for help from a mission, this time the Mission of San Jose, a three-day journey. Governor Echeandia had by now established himself at Monterey, a far more congenial spot than San Diego. He must have thought he was having a recurring nightmare when the presumptuous American who had caused him so much vexation the year before made his unwelcome reappearance. It was now evident that Smith had failed to obey the governor's order to return the way he had come—back through the Mohave Desert—but had, instead, gone north, spreading, in the governor's view, trouble and unrest among the nonmission Indians. Once again Echeandia vacillated until four American ships captains whose vessels were tied up in the Monterey harbor came to his rescue, persuading the governor to accept a bond of $30,000 to guarantee that Smith and his men would leave California as soon as they were adequately supplied. The men in Smith's party had been sent to the village of San Francisco to await the outcome of their leader's negotiations with Echeandia. Smith, having posted his bond and bought horses, guns, and ammunition at Monterey, joined them there. From San Francisco, Smith and his men worked their way north along the Sacramento River, searching its tributaries for beaver. Smith also probed the lower reaches of the Sierras looking for a pass north of the one he had taken the previous winter. As the months passed, he decided to push north to the Columbia River and return to the region of the Green along the well-established route used each fall by the Hudson's Bay Company trappers. From the Sacramento to the coast proved an unexpectedly difficult and hazardous passage. One horse fell to its death and several others were injured. Harrison Rogers records the obstacles that the party had to surmount. Rogers and Thomas Virgin, who had recovered from serious wounds suffered in the Mohave attack months earlier, set out to reconnoiter a way to the ocean, but Indians ambushed them and shot a number of arrows at Virgin before he killed one and drove the rest off. Rogers, who had endured so much and been such a faithful scribe, felt his spirits sink under the conviction that Smith had led them into a hopeless impasse where they must fall victims to hostile Indians. "Oh, God, may it please Thee," he wrote in his journal, "in Thy divine providence to still guide and protect us through this wilderness of doubt and fear, as Thou hast done heretofore, and be with us in the hour of danger and difficulty. . . ." For two weeks the weary and demoralized men tried to find a trail to the ocean. Finally, defeated, they had to turn south "entirely out of provisions with the exception of a few pounds of flour and rice."

On June 8 they finally reached the mouth of the Klamath River and made their camp on the beach. From the river north they rode along the beaches, making rafts to cross the intersecting rivers. There were berries and clams and occasional fish bought from generally sullen and unfriendly Indians. Now they were in the region of the Klamath and Modoc tribes of lower Oregon. At the Umpqua River they encountered the Indians from which the river took its name.

The Umpqua were members of the great and extensive Athapas-can family whose tribes were to be found in western Canada, Alaska, and the Pacific Northwest. They belonged to the subfamily of Chastacosta and lived by fishing and gathering wild fruits and berries. More advanced in some ways than the California tribes, they were a far cry in their manner and appearance from the Crows, Sioux, Snake, and Blackfeet of the Great Plains and Great Basin regions. Perhaps their inferiority misled Smith in his dealings with them. Some of the Umpqua joined Smith's party to trade and one stole an ax. To force him to return it, Smith tied him up hand and foot, put a rope around his neck, and threatened to hang him. The other Indians watched the episode in silence. The ax was recovered and trading for otter and beaver skins resumed. Next day the Umpqua brought wild raspberries and blackberries and the trading resumed. The Indians gave the explorers the welcome information that the famous Multinomah (Willamette) River was not many miles distant.

Cheered by this word, Smith and another man pushed ahead of the rest of his party next morning, looking for the easiest passage north. Smith left orders that, despite the apparent friendliness of the Indians, none should be allowed in the camp during his absence. The orders were disregarded. The Indians crowded in and at a signal from their chief, who was the Indian that Smith had chastized for stealing the ax, they turned on the trappers and killed fifteen of them before they could reach their guns. Turner, the cook, seized a burning log from the fire, scattered his attackers, and ran in the direction that Smith had taken earlier. Another white man named Black, who had his gun in his hand, fired it at a group of Indians and then fled in the confusion that his shot created. Turner met Smith and his companion on his way back to camp and the three men set out to try to reach the Hudson's Bay Company post on the Willamette. While they struggled on to reach Fort Vancouver, Black followed the shoreline until he could go no further and then, "broken down by hunger and misery," threw himself on the mercy of the Killimour Indians, who "treated him with great humanity," and brought him to the fort at Vancouver. John McLoughlin, the factor at the fort, who had declared so confidently that there was as much chance of Americans reaching Oregon territory by a northwest route as there was of their going to the moon, was, in his own words, "One night in August, 1828 . . . surprised by the Indians making a great noise at the gate of the fort saying that they had brought an American. The gate was opened, the man [Black] came in, but was so affected he could not speak. After sitting down some minutes to recover himself, he told us he was the only survivor of eighteen men conducted by Jedediah Smith. All the rest, he thought, had been massacred."

McLoughlin, having heard from an Indian that other whites had escaped, immediately dispatched "Indian runners with tobacco to the Willamette chiefs to tell them to send their people in search of Smith and his two men, and, if they found them, to bring them to the fort and I would pay them, and telling them that if any Indians hurt these men we would punish them. . . ." Before a search party of forty men could depart, Smith and his two men reached the fort. McLoughlin then sent a party of men from the fort to try to recover all they could of Smith's property from the Umpqua. "The plan was," McLoughlin wrote, "that the officer [in charge of the party] was, as usual, to invite the Indians to bring their furs to trade, just as if nothing had happened. Count the furs, but as the American trappers mark all their skins, keep those all separate, give them to Mr. Smith and not pay the Indians for them, telling them that they belonged to him, that they got them by murdering Smith's people."

Everything went as planned. The furs were recovered, along with several of Smith's horses and some personal belongings, among them Harrison Roger's journal. McLoughlin paid Smith $20,000 for the furs in the form of a draft on a London bank and Smith procured horses, supplies, and ammunition from McLoughlin.

Since the fur company of Smith and Sublette was a serious rival of the Hudson's Bay Company and, indeed, had prevailed on a number of their trappers to desert to their company, McLoughlin's kindness is a great tribute to him. A friend described the Vancouver factor as "over six feet in height, powerfully made, with a grand head on massive shoulders and long snow-white locks covering them . . . a splendid figure of a man." The Indians of the region called him White Eagle and he exercised a remarkable influence over them. "He was a convert to Catholicism, and in no sense was he a bigot or lacking in Christian charity. . . . His policy to effect peace with the Indians was potent for good. . . . With his grand manner and majestic port, he was the embodiment of power and justice. . . . He was indeed, as he was styled, 'the Czar of the West.' His rule was imperial for a thousand miles, and his mere word was law." McLoughlin believed in living well in the wilderness. His house had something of the air of a Scottish castle with handsome paintings, a large library, fine wines, silver, and china, a band of bagpipers, and two Sandwich Islanders as servants. There was more than a little irony in the fact that devout Protestant Jedediah Smith's two principal benefactors at the southern and northern ends of the Pacific coast should have been Roman Catholics.

Smith and his three companions spent the winter at Fort Vancouver as guests of McLoughlin. In the spring the four men set out up the Columbia to the trading post on Clark's Fork and then south to the Snake. It was at Pierre's (later Jackson) Hole near the juncture of the Hoback and the Snake that a small party of Sublette's men found

Smith and his companions trapping in the streams of the valley. Joined by his partner, Smith and the trappers worked the area thoroughly and then spent the fall trapping in the country between the Missouri and the Yellowstone. The combined parties wintered on the Wind River while Sublette returned to St. Louis with the packs of beaver furs.

In the winter camp, Jedediah Smith wrote a revealing letter to his brother, Ralph. "It is that I may be able to help those who stand in need that I face every danger. It is for this that I pass over the sandy plains, in the heat of summer, thirsting for water where I may cool my overheated body. It is for this that I go for days without eating, and am pretty well satisfied if I can gather a few roots, a few snails, or better satisfied if we can afford ourselves a piece of horse-flesh, or a fine roasted dog; and most of all it is for this that I deprive myself of the privilege of society and the satisfaction of the converse of my friends!"

The letter he had written to his brother is one of the most remarkable and revealing of the considerable number of documents that survive from the era of the fur trade. It makes clear the manner in which the Protestant passion for personal rectitude invaded even such an improbable venture as the fur trade. It reminds us of Meriwether Lewis's on his thirtieth birthday, halfway across the continent of North America. Smith was thirty-one when he wrote his letter not far from where Lewis had written these words: "I reflected that I had as yet done but little, very little, indeed, to further the happiness of the human race or to advance the information of the suceeding generation. . . . I resolved . . . in the future to live for *mankind,* as I have heretofore lived *for myself.*"

Exactly how Jedediah Smith thought the sacrifices occasioned by his remarkable journeys were "to help those who stand in need of help" is far from clear. Was he amassing money from the fur trade to use in future philanthropic ventures? Surely the men and women who might follow the trails he had blazed to California were not the poor and the downtrodden, those "in need of help." Perhaps "thirst" was a clue. He had written eloquently of "thirst" in his journal. Thirst was far worse than hunger. If he had not consciously sought "thirst" on the Cimarron Desert, had he perhaps subconsciously invited it by not taking the precautions his experience told him he should take? To a devout Christian, "thirst" must be associated with Christ's death on the Cross and his most poignant human cry, "I thirst!" This may seem too bold a speculation by half, but it will serve its purpose if it does no more than remind us of the power of the idea of sacrifice for pious American Protestants in the nineteenth century. Whether Jedediah Smith associated his own terrible thirst, first on the Salt Desert and then on the Cimarron, with his Savior's thirst on the Cross we can never know, but we know beyond any doubt that he felt compelled to justify his restless passion for exploration and adventure, a passion that cost the lives of twenty-five of his fellows, by insisting that it was all done "to help those who stand in need."

The next summer saw the arrival of the first wagons to make their way up the increasingly well-marked trail from St. Louis to the headwaters of the Missouri. Smith and William Sublette were ready for new ventures. They had heard glowing reports of the trade between Independence and Santa Fe and they were determined to sample it. The fur trading firm of Smith and Sublette thus sold its assets to the Rocky Mountain Fur Company headed by Sublette's brother, Milton; Jedediah Smith's old friend, Thomas Fitzpatrick; Jean Baptiste Gervais; and Jim Bridger; and left to them the thankless job of battling John Jacob Astor for the control of the fur trade.

Smith and Sublette headed down the Missouri to St. Louis with a hundred and ninety packs of beaver to the value of some $80,000 and began to make plans to enter the Santa Fe trade. Smith's brothers, Peter and Austin, joined them, and on April 10, 1831, a party of eighty-five men with twenty-two heavily loaded wagons headed up the Missouri to Independence. There they turned southwest to the poorly defined trail that led to Santa Fe.

In three weeks the train reached the ford of the Arkansas, a distance of 392 miles from Independence. One man, who had wandered away from the train, had been captured and killed by the Pawnee, but the company was otherwise in good condition and spirits. Entering the Cimarron Desert, they neglected to lay in a sufficient supply of water. The summer was a dry one and the water holes they had counted on using had dried up. Some of the mules began to die of thirst and suddenly the train was faced with disaster. Josiah Gregg was told by a Mexican buffalo hunter what followed. Smith, desperate to find water, broke a cardinal rule of travel in Indian country and rode off alone to search for a creek or spring. After riding for some miles he finally sighted a stream that was, in fact, the Cimarron River. When he reached the riverbed he found that it was dry but, taking a stick, he dug down several feet and water slowly filled the hole. Intent only on quenching his thirst, he was unaware that a party of Comanche had come up behind him. His first intimation may have been when arrows struck him. According to the Comanche themselves, he killed two or three of their party before he died. Scalped and stripped, his body was never found and the details of his death were only subsequently pieced together by Gregg.

Was Jedediah Smith's recklessly invited death a propitiation for those deaths of which he had been the unwitting agent, by failures in the extraordinary leadership he normally exercised? On the surface his life seems the simple, unreflective existence of the classic man of action. But we know it to be otherwise. Jedediah Smith was an addict, an inebriate of the wild geography of western America. He prayed to God to sanctify his addiction so that, in the end, it might serve Him.

20

A Trapper's Life

Our best source for the life and feelings of a trapper is the account of Osburne Russell of the nine years between 1834 and 1843 that he spent trapping beaver in the Yellowstone basin area. By 1834 the fierce rivalry between the Missouri Fur Company and John Jacob Astor's American Fur Company—and later between the Rocky Mountain Fur Company and the Astor enterprise—was coming to a climax; shortly before the end of the era of the beaver hat, the struggle would end in the triumph of Astor's ruthless and irresistible endeavor. Russell, twenty years old at the beginning of his career as a trapper, had been born in Bowdoinham, Maine, one of nine children. He ran away to sea at the age of sixteen but soon tired of the disciplined life of a sailor and headed west. He spent three years in the region of Wisconsin and Minnesota, working for the Northwest Fur Trapping and Trading Company and then joined a party led by Nathaniel Wyeth, who was determined to take a group to the Oregon country under the banner of the Oregon Colonization Society.

The Oregon venture failed but Wyeth obtained a contract to deliver $3,000 worth of trading goods to Milton Sublette and Thomas Fitzpatrick, partners in the Rocky Mountain Fur Company, at the rendezvous of 1834. Russell signed on with Wyeth and his newly formed Columbia River Fishing and Trading Company for eighteen months at a wage of $250. When the Rocky Mountain Fur Company, pressed to the wall by the far better capitalized American Fur Company, defaulted on its contract to Wyeth, the latter decided to build a fort and establish his own fur trading operation. Fort Hall at the juncture of the Snake and the Blackfoot rivers was a stockade some eighty feet square built of cottonwood tree trunks sunk three feet in the ground and reaching a height of fifteen feet. Russell was left with nine other men to keep the fort while Wyeth pushed on for the Columbia.

Russell's first trapping expedition included ten trappers and seven camp keepers. They set out from Fort Hall on March 15 for the Bear River but the snow was so deep and the game so scarce that the party had to live for ten days on roots. A grizzly bear was shot and the camp keepers, who cooked the meals and guarded the camp while the trappers ventured off to set their traps, soon filled the kettles with delicious "fat bear meat cut in very small pieces."

In the "fall hunt," Russell was a member of a party of fourteen trappers and ten camp keepers dispatched in the direction of Yellowstone Lake. At the Salt River, the party, unable to ford the river, built a bullboat of buffalo hides to carry themselves and their equipment across, but young Abram Patterson, a Pennsylvanian, determined to try to swim his horse across, was swept away and drowned. Camped near Henry's Fork of the Snake, the party found itself surrounded by some sixty Blackfeet, a third of whom were mounted. There was a wild rush to round up the horses before the Indians drove them off but six escaped and were caught by the Blackfeet. Russell was then treated to a classic Indian deployment. While the unmounted Indians took refuge behind rocks and trees, their mounted companions rode back and forth just out of rifle range, shouting and hallooing, "brandishing their weapons and yelling at the top of their voices." It was like seeing a painting come to life. As Russell watched, enthralled, "the whistling of balls about my ears gave me to understand that these living Creatures were a little more dangerous than those I had been accustomed to see portrayed on canvass."

The experienced Indian fighters in the party directed some of the company to fire their rifles at the Indians scattered across the front of the camp while they slipped into the brush to attack the Blackfeet from the flank. Russell placed "a large German horse pistol" by his side as a precaution and then blazed away at the elusive foe. The Indians were armed with muskets, bows and arrows, spears and knives. None of these weapons was, of course, a match at long range for the rifles of the white men. The Indian strategy was to try to work their way within musket range, fire, and then try to close, shooting their arrows, five or six of which could be discharged while a rifleman was loading his piece. The arrows, though capable of being fired much more rapidly than the rifle bullets, were not nearly so lethal. A white trapper might and often did continue to fight with half a dozen arrows stuck in him unless they struck some especially vulnerable spot. Because the arrows might be poisoned, they had to be plucked out as soon as possible.

On this occasion, Russell, protected by a tree trunk, placed his hat on top of a nearby bush which he jostled from time to time with his foot, thereby drawing the fire of the Indians "and giving me a better shot at their heads." After two hours of such fighting, the Indians withdrew carrying their dead and wounded with them and setting up, typically, "a dismal lamentation."

One of the hunters had been wounded by musket balls in three places in his right leg and one in his left; another had received a superficial groin wound. Three horses had been killed and several more wounded. The next day the trappers found a spot where the Indians had stopped to bind up the wounds of their injured. They counted nine places where the crushed grass and bloodied soil indicated that bodies had been lying.

Cold, soaking rain fell for days, and while Russell's party was trying to cross the swollen Lewis River with a raft, all their equipment was swept away, including their rifles and ammunition. The next day, July 4, huddled at a sputtering fire in the drenching rain, Russell "thought of those who were perhaps at this moment Celebrating the anniversary of our Independence in my Native Land or seated around tables loaded with the richest dainties that a rich independent and enlightened country could afford or perhaps collected in the gay Saloon relating the heroic deeds of our ancestors or joining in the nimble dance forgetful of cares and toils whilst here . . . a group of human beings crouched round a fire which the rain was fast diminishing meditating on their deplorable condition not knowing at what moment we might be aroused by the shrill cry of the hostile savages with which the country was infested. . . ."

The next day, following the riverbank, they retrieved most of their goods and pressed on with the trapping. From a band of Snake they obtained "a large number of Elk Deer and Sheep skins . . . in return for awls axes kettles tobacco ammunition etc." With the improvement of the weather and the fortunes of the party camped in the beautiful Yellowstone Valley, Russell reflected, "I almost wished I could spend the remainder of my days in a place like this where happiness and contentment seemed to reign in wild romantic splendor surrounded by majestic battlements which seemed to support the heavens and shut out all hostile intruders."

Early in September Russell and his party encountered fourteen white trappers, members of a larger party of some sixty white men and twenty Flathead Indians under the leadership of Jim Bridger. It was a happy meeting, with the two parties staying up the better part of the night around a large camp fire exchanging mountain yarns and passing on "news from the States." Next morning a detachment of eight started off to set traps on the creeks leading into Henry's Fork. Soon they were back pursued by a large war party of Blackfeet. The Indians found places behind rocks on bluffs overlooking the camp and kept up a constant musket fire on the trappers below them. Unwilling to venture within range of the trappers' rifles, they did little damage except to the horses. Finally the Indians set fire to the dry grass to try to smoke the whites out. "This," Russell wrote, "was the most horrid position I was ever placed in death seemed almost inevitable . . . but all hands began immediately to remove the rubbish around the encampment and setting fire to it to act against the flames that were hovering over our heads." A change in the wind soon carried the fire toward the Indians, who were forced to beat a hasty retreat. Since Russell's small party had lost half its number through "the desertion of men and loss of animals," it joined forces with Bridger's band. Now hostile Indians lurked all about and the trappers had to be constantly vigilant. Leaving the forks of the Madison for a sweep through the network of rivers to the north, a Frenchman went out on his own to trap, despite warnings, and was promptly killed and scalped by a party of Blackfeet. Another smaller party was ambushed and narrowly escaped, finding refuge in a Flathead village of 180 lodges near the Beaverhead River. There Russell, grateful at having eluded the Blackfeet, noted, "The Flatheads are a brave friendly generous and hospitable tribe strictly honest with a mixture of pride that exalts them far above the rude appellation of Savages when contrasted with the tribes around them. They boast of never injuring the whites. . . . Larceny, fornication and adultery are severely punished."

Russell, restless with his fellow trappers, set out on his own, trapping along the Snake in a region that the Blackfeet avoided unless on a large-scale raid. Here he was comparatively safe. He now knew enough of the Snake language to carry on a conversation. At a Snake village of 332 lodges, he was welcomed warmly by the "Old Chief" and watched the slaughter of a thousand buffalo cows to provide food for the tribes. It was a brilliant display of Indian riding and hunting prowess. The Snake had recently been fishing for salmon at the headwaters of those rivers flowing to the Pacific, and were now following the cycle Lewis and Clark had observed, killing and drying buffalo and making pemmican to see them through the winter. Pemmican—dried buffalo meat, bone marrow, and berries mixed up together into a kind of cake—was the most nutritious and essential food of white and Indian alike in the Great Plains region.

It was Russell's first sight of an Indian buffalo hunt and he was an enthralled observer. A mounted brave rode toward the herd at an angle designed to bring him up to the running buffalo at the point where it was easiest for him to cut out a bull or cow and kill it. In Russell's words, "he gives his horse the rein and darts thro the band selects his victim reins his horse up along side and shoots and if he considers the wound mortal he pulls up the rein the horse knowing his business keeps along galloping with the band, until the rider has reloaded usually the hunter carried four or five cartridges in his mouth when he darts forward upon another Buffaloe. . . ." Cows were more desirable for their meat and there was an art to picking a cow or bull with the greatest amount of fat on it.

Buffalo were of course an essential source of food and hides of warmth and shelter for the Indian, the trapper, and plainsman. But the hunting of them was also the most exhilarating of sports for those who engaged in it. Russell wrote, "If Kings Princes Nobles and Gentlemen can derive so much sport and Pleasure as they boast of in chasing a fox or simple hare all day? which when they have caught is of little or no benefit to them what pleasure can the Rocky Mountain hunter be expected to derive in running with a well trained horse such a noble and stately animal as the Bison? which when killed is of some service to him." Certainly it was true that every foreign visitor with sporting instincts yearned to participate in a buffalo hunt and many of them did.

The old chief, Want a Sheep, put Russell up in his own lodge; told him in great detail of his life, his coups, his children and relations; and amused him "with traditionary tales mixed with the grossest superstition some of which were not unlike the manners of the Ancient Israelites." To which Russell added, "There seems to be a happiness in ignorance which knowledge and Science destroys here is a nation of people contented and happy they have horses and lodges and are very partial to the rifles of the white man. If a Eutaw has 8 or 10 good horses a rifle and ammunition he is contented if he fetches a deer at night from the hunt joy beams in the faces of his wife and children. . . ." Perhaps, in the last analysis, it was this sense on the part of the white man that the Indian was a "happy" being that was so compelling. Time and again we hear the same theme sounded—the happiness of a simple life with few wants and those easily satisfied, the absence of striving in the Indian's life, of competition and tension. A people dedicated to "the pursuit of happiness" but often finding little enough of it, saw it or, more properly, thought they saw it in the life of the aborigines—the carefree existence of the "noble" savage.

In many white reflections on savage life, the phrase "happy children of nature," or some variant of it, appears. What haunted Americans when they contemplated the Indians, what floated around in the buried depths of their consciousness, was the suspicion that with all their progressive, go-ahead civilization, they were missing out on happiness, that they were paying too heavy a psychic price for all these marvels. That was the question that the mere existence of the Indians perpetually posed and, it might be said, poses once again for a new generation of Americans, making a more self-conscious audit of the psychic costs of being an American.

Of course the notion that the Indian was a happy, carefree creature was only partly true. If one observed the life of an Indian village on "vacation" from warfare or hunting, with the games and play, the freedom and openness, the colorful pageantry, one might readily succumb to that charming illusion. But we have seen enough of various Indian tribes by now to know that they often suffered acutely from hunger when game was scarce, that the weaker tribes lived in terror of their more powerful enemies, that there were Indians who "failed" by the standards of their tribe just as there were whites who failed. What the white man saw that so intrigued him was that every Indian who preserved his tribal identity belonged to a close-knit group that supported him in every moment of his existence. With all the terrors of primitive tribal life there was one terror missing—the terror of being a discrete, single, atomized creature called "an individual," who was, in a particular excruciating sense, "on his own," at war with all other "individuals," an individual whose "tribe" was as vague and ill-defined as the state of Maine or Pennsylvania, or that most amorphous entity, the United States of America, and whose fate it was to be constantly searching for his "identity," having always to hold it precariously in his *mind* lest he forget who he was.

Russell soon rejoined a group of trappers under Jim Bridger's direction and began trapping on Blackfoot Creek. A few weeks later the party gathered with other bands of trappers and Snake, Bonnack, Nez Percé, and Flathead Indians for the yearly rendezvous near the Green. They made, in Russell's words, "a mixed multitude" that included "Americans and Canadian French with some Dutch, Scotch, Irish, English, halfbreed and full blood Indians of nearly every tribe in the Rocky Mountains." Not to mention some Iroquois, Delaware, Shawnee, and Mohawk. "Some were gambling at cards, some playing the Indian game of hand and others horse racing while here and there could be seen small groups collected under the shady trees relating the events of the past year all in good spirits and health for Sickness is a Stranger seldom met with in these regions." In this fashion the trappers passed the time until the "cavalcade" appeared. When it arrived early in July, led by Nathaniel Wyeth, it consisted of some forty men and twenty mule-drawn carts carrying supplies for the coming winter and headed, after the rendezvous, for Oregon. With Wyeth were Marcus Whitman and his beautiful wife, Narissa, as well as another couple on their way to establish a mission with the Cayuse Indians. The two women were the first white women most of the Indians had ever seen and they never tired of staring at them. One of the trappers shot a fat elk and juicy ribs and pieces of meat were soon suspended over a fire. After supper, "the jovial tale goes round the circle the peals of loud laughter break upon the stillness of the night. . . . Every tale puts an auditor in mind of something similar to it but under different circumstances which being told the 'laughing part' gives rise to increasing merriment and furnishes more subjects for good jokes and witty sayings such as Swift never dreamed of. Thus the evening passed with eating drinking and stories enlivened with witty humor until near Midnight all being wrapped in their blankets lying around the fire gradually falling to sleep one by one. . . ."

Such a life was, as Russell tells it, the archetypical camping trip, the ultimate male ritual of hardihood and companionship, hunting and playing—a life indeed very much like that of the Indians. It is easy to see why it cast such a spell on those young men of various nationalities who entered it. This was the magic relationship, "deeper than love," that D. H. Lawrence writes of in *Studies in Classic American Literature*. As old as Achilles and Patroclus, it reached to the profoundest levels of the masculine psyche and made all other modes of life seem bland and innocuous by comparison.

With the arrival of the cavalcade, "joy beamed in every countenance," Russell wrote. "Some received letters from friends and relations and Some received the public papers and the news of the day others consoled themselves with the idea of getting a blanket or a Cotton Shirt or a few pints of Coffee and sugar to sweeten it just by way of a treat gratis that is to say by paying 2,000 percent on the first cost." A pint of coffee thus cost $20 and tobacco $2 a pound. For several weeks after the cavalcade arrived the trappers reveled in their sense of well-being and camaraderie. They drank and ate excessively, enjoyed their new luxuries, disported themselves with Indian girls, played crude musical instruments, sang and danced together, and told their interminable mountain yarns, recounting in detail their skirmishes with the Blackfeet, their narrow escapes, or the death of a companion. Finally after several delightful weeks they divided into parties and turned back into the valleys and mountains where the beaver, in constantly diminishing numbers, awaited them.

Russell joined up with Bridger and a party of some sixty, mostly Americans. He found the group an especially congenial one. There were a number of New Englanders, including Elbridge Trask, a young New Hampshireman, who, like Russell, had started in as a camp keeper and who became Russell's closest friend. The party soon began breaking off into smaller and smaller groups and spreading out over as wide a range as possible. Russell and Trask, with five companions, found themselves working the waters in what is now Yellowstone Park; there they observed new wonders every day—geysers, blue pools of boiling water, a field covered "with a crust of Limestone of dazzling whiteness." At the forks of the Clark River Joe Meek, a famous trapper, and Dave Crow rode in and joined them. Blood was running down the neck of Meek's pony. The two men had been setting their traps on Prior's Fork, Meek told Russell and Trask, when they found "old Benj Johnson's boys [Meek's name for the Blackfeet] . . . just walking up and down them ar' streams with their hands on their hips gathering plums, they gave me a title and turned me a somerset or two shot my horse 'Too Shebit' in the neck and sent us head over heels in a pile together but we raised arunnin . . . and the savages jist squattin and grabbin at me but I raised a fog for about half a mile. . . ."

By the end of October the streams had begun to freeze over and Bridger established winter camp on the Yellowstone. This interlude was as highly ritualized as the rendezvous. From November through March, excepting those intervals when the weather was unseasonably warm, the trappers lived in their central camps, fifty or sixty to a camp, and entertained themselves by hunting (as Russell put it, "we had nothing to do but slay and eat") and in such other ways as their ingenuity might devise. The camp keepers' business in winter quarters was to guard the horses, cook, and keep fires. The trappers had "snug lodges made of dressed buffaloe skins in the center of which we built a fire and generally comprised about six men to lodge. The long winter evenings were passed away by collecting in some of the most spacious lodges and entering into debates arguments or spinning long yarns until midnight in perfect good humour," Russell wrote, adding, "I for one will cheerfully confess that I have derived no little benefit from the frequent arguments and debates held in what we termed The Rocky Mountain College and I doubt not but some of my comrades who considered themselves Classical Scholars have had some little added to their wisdom in these assemblies however rude they might appear."

One of the most fascinating aspects of the society of trappers, at least of the American trappers, was that far from coming from the lower classes, the urban or rural poor, they were, in the great majority, especially those from New England, the thoroughly literate sons of middle-class parents. Russell may indeed be taken as an excellent representative of the young men who made up the companies of trappers and hunters. Despite his practical disregard of commas and periods, he writes well and has obviously had a much better than average education.

Russell found the scenery a constant inducement to reflect upon the nature of the world and the proper ends of life. Looking at the incredible landscape, the flowers, "the scattered flocks of Sheep and Elk carelessly feeding or thoughtlessly reposing beneath the shade having Providence for their founder and preserver and Nature for Shepherd Gardner and Historian . . . wonder is put to the test. . . ." If many of the trappers were, like Russell, delighted to "argue and debate," others "never troubled themselves about vain and frivolous notions as they called them." The Scottish and English especially were prone to denigrate the American scenery and laud the castles and gardens of their native land. Russell recounted one conversation where an Irishman yearned to "fill my body wid good ould whisky 'yes' said the backwoods hunter on my left, as he cast away his bone and smoothed down his long auburn hair with his greasy hand, 'Yes you English and Irish are always talking about your fine countries but if they are so mighty fine' (said he with an oath) 'why do so many of you run off and leave them and come to America to get a living?' " which query ended the conversation.

Besides Osburne Russell with his knowledge of Shakespeare and the classics, there was the Virginian James Clyman, who wrote poetry and discussed sophisticated concepts of time and space. Edwin Denig, the son of a Pennsylvania physician, was an accurate observer of Indian life and customs. David Thompson, a Welshman, had gone to the Grey Coat School at Westminster, England. Jean Baptiste Trudeau had been a schoolteacher. These men were primarily traders, but the boundary line between traders and trappers was a very fine one.

In January, with the weather fine and warm, Russell and six other trappers decided to treat themselves to a buffalo hunt of some five or six days. Two days out of camp, "riding carelessly along with our rifles lying carelessly before us on our saddles . . . we came to a deep narrow gulch . . . when behold! the earth seemed teeming with naked savages A quick volley of fusees [muskets] a shower of balls and a cloud of smoke clearly bespoke their nation tribe manners and customs and mode of warfare: A ball broke the right arm of a man and he dropped his rifle which a savage immediately caught up and shot after us as we wheeled and scampered out of the reach of their guns. There was about 80 Indians who had secreted themselves until we rode within 15 feet of them They got a rifle clear gain and we had one man wounded . . . so they had so much the advantage and we were obliged to go to Camp and study out some plan to get even as by the last two or three skirmishes we had fell in this debt." The opportunity was presented several days later when some twenty Blackfeet were sighted. A party of trappers took after them at once and cornered them in an abandoned Indian fort. Four Indians were shot and killed by the trappers, their bodies pushed under the ice of a nearby stream by their fellows, and a half-dozen braves were wounded. The American casualties were one Delaware hit in the leg with a poisoned bullet and one trapper slightly wounded in the hip.

The next move was up to the Blackfeet. The score had now swung decisively in favor of Bridger's trappers and they might anticipate a raid in force by several hundred Blackfoot warriors. The next day Bridger, scouting with his brass telescope, saw the plains "alive with Indians." A palisade of cottonwood logs some six feet high and 250 feet square was quickly erected around the camp. The horses were brought inside and a double guard was mounted. That night there was a remarkable display of northern lights with a "deep blood red" spreading across the sky. The next morning a force that Russell estimated to number more than a thousand Blackfoot warriors drew up in a line facing the hastily improvised fort with the manifest intention, Russell wrote, "of rubbing us from the face of the earth." But apparently the sight of the rather formidable fortification coupled with the fiery display in the heavens of the night before, which the Indians took as an evil omen, deterred them and shortly they turned and rode off as swiftly as they had come, leaving Bridger and his men to amuse themselves "with playing ball, wrestling running foot races, etc."

By early April the trappers were out again setting their traps, their tracks dogged by parties of Blackfeet. Six men trapping on the Mussel Shell River had a trapper killed and lost all their horses and traps. Russell himself had a close call when he and two companions were ambushed by a war party and Russell's horse was shot from under him. He jumped up behind one of his comrades and they dashed off, shots whizzing past them.

The Blackfoot Indians were not the only hazard. The Crows, while enemies of the Blackfeet and ostensibly friends of the whites, could seldom be trusted. Russell, an Englishman named William Allen, the camp keeper, and two trappers named Greenberry and Conn were trapping on the Bighorn when they were joined by a party of Crows on the way, they said, to steal Blackfoot ponies. They pushed into the camp of the white trappers and grew, as Russell put it, "very insolent and saucy saying we had no right in their country and intimated they could take everything from us if they wished." The next morning they demanded that Russell and his companions divide their tobacco and ammunition with them and when they complied the Crows made as if to take it all. The trappers made clear they were determined to fight for their possessions and their lives whereupon the Crows put down their arms "and told us with an envious Savage laugh they were only joking. . . ." But the Indians followed them, stealing horses and traps until it became evident that they were bent on robbing and then killing them, whereupon Allen, who had lived two winters in a Crow village, made clear that the trappers were determined to be rid of their unwelcome companions. He knew their intentions. "If you follow or molest us we will besmear the ground with the blood and guts of Crow Indians and do not speak to me more for I despise the odious jargon of your Nation!" At that the trappers rode off, expecting a hail of arrows or musket balls in their back but they had gone little more than a mile or so before a chief caught up with them, approached them unarmed, and declared, "You are very foolish you do not know how bad my heart feels to think you have been robbed by men belonging to my village but they are not men they are Dogs who took your animals." If the trappers would return with him to the village he would see that they got their horses and belongings back. Otherwise he would have to bear the reproaches of "the Blanket Chief," Jim Bridger. The trappers, still suspecting treachery, refused and pressed on for the site of the winter camp. Stripped of much of their equipment and reduced at times to walking, the four made their way with great hardships and suffering to Fort William, where they replenished their supplies.

A few weeks later, Russell joined Bridger and a large party headed for the Madison. On their way, they came on a Blackfoot village ravaged by smallpox. The village was a large one and Bridger wished to detour to avoid a possible clash with Indians who might be healthy but his men protested, in Russell's words, "against trying to avoid a Village of Blackfeet which did not contain more than 3 times our numbers." They thus camped near the Indian village, prepared defensive works, and then set out in a party of twenty men to, in effect, challenge the Blackfeet to a battle. Approaching the unsuspecting Indians, the trappers fired three or four rounds apiece before the aroused warriors were ready to take the offensive. Then, pursued by the Blackfeet, they retreated to the camp. The Indians stationed themselves just beyond rifle range and kept up a musket fire for several hours, wounding a few horses. Finally a Blackfoot called out, saying the trappers were not men but women and should dress as such. They had challenged the Blackfeet to fight "and then crept into the rock like women." At this insult, an old Iroquois warrior who had lived long on the shores of Lake Superior, turned to the white trappers and said, "My friend you see dat Ingun talk? He not talk good he talk berry bad He say you me all same like squaw, dat no good, you go wid me I make him no more talk day way." With which the old warrior stripped off his clothes except for his powder horn and bullet pouch and began a war dance, uttering "the shrill wary cry of his Nation . . . which had been the death warrant of so many whites during the old French war," as Russell put it. Twenty whites rallied around the old man and followed him as he started up a long rocky slope of some three hundred yards to where the Blackfeet to the number of some hundred and fifty were stationed. In the face of heavy musket fire, the attackers reached the rocks without loss and without firing their rifles. Pausing to catch their breath, they jumped over the final barrier and, "muzzle to muzzle," drove the Indians ahead of them "like hunted rats among the ruins of an old building whilst we followed close at their heels loading and shooting until we drove them entirely into the plain where their horses were tied." Next morning the fighting was renewed, this time in the vicinity of the village, until the Indians were once again driven from the field.

It is clear from Russell's account of the battle that the fighting was, for the trappers, not much different from hunting buffalo: a more dangerous, but a far more exciting sport. One is inevitably reminded of the "fighting" games of children, shouting "pow-pow, you're dead"—the game of children here became the deadly game of grown men. Perhaps the most mysterious and fearsome line written by an American in the nineteenth century was the exclamation of the hero of Melville's novel *Pierre* as he kills his cousin, Glen, "Tis speechless sweet to murder thee!" The terrible secret that the trapper shared with the Indian was that it was "speechless sweet" to kill; that killing was an addiction, the most compelling game of all. Suffering from the constant raids and murders of the Indians in the California goldfields, Quaker Charles Pancoast found himself taking on his ruder companions' conviction that "the only good Indian was a dead Indian." One day, hunting, he came upon three Indians intent on skinning an animal and totally unaware of Pancoast's proximity. Pancoast raised his gun to shoot them when the thought came to him "that I should be taking the life of a Human Being without necessity or adding to my own security, and should perhaps regret the Murder." He was plainly startled at his almost instinctive impulse to kill the unoffending Indians and he subsequently "rejoiced that I did not pull the trigger of my rifle that day."

If we omit the first tentative ventures of Manuel Lisa and the Missouri Fur Company in the period prior to the War of 1812, the "beaver rush" had started with the expeditions of Ashley and Henry in the spring of 1822. Sixteen years later the era was over, a substantial period of time in terms of American capitalistic enterprise and one that left a residue of stories and legends, apparently inexhaustible in their retelling, one of the great romantic episodes in all history, a saga as compelling as the tales of Homer. The trappers, like Lewis and Clark, were men of the new consciousness. Their values, as the social psychologists put it, were "internalized"—that is to say, they were able to function as "individuals." Indeed they were the prototype of the "rugged individual," which is one reason that American captains of industry have been so obsessed with the "frontier ethic," the lonely individual making his way against all the terrors and hazards of the wilderness. John Jacob Astor, living in opulence in New York City, fancied himself a kindred spirit to Andrew Henry and William Ashley. Even Philip Hone, the ultimate urbanite, was charmed by stories of the West. He found Washington Irving's *Tour of the Prairies* "the very best kind of light reading. Killing buffaloes, hunting wild horses, sleeping every night on the ground for a whole month, and depending from day to day for the means of subsistence upon the deer, wild turkey, and bears which the rifles of their own party can alone procure, are events of ordinary interest to the settlers in the great west, but they are matters of thrilling interest to citizens who read them in their green slippers seated before a shining grate."

The Indians lived collectively, that is to say tribally, but they fought individually. The whites, on the contrary, lived individually but usually fought collectively—as an integrated unit with a preconceived strategy. Whites, experienced in fighting Indians, were thus always more than a match for considerably larger bands of Indians. It was not a matter of courage but of culture, specifically of organization. In order to organize people into new groups for various enterprises, from running a cotton mill or digging a canal to fighting the Indians, they had first to be broken down, so to speak, from the traditional corporate bodies to which they belonged, whether family, congregation, or community, into what we might liken to individual human molecules or atoms, and then reformed or reorganized into new corporate bodies. The disintegrative effects of American life accelerated that breaking-down process and meant that there were always innumerable free-floating "individuals," as we called them, available for every new venture. The fact that the breaking-down process was often an excruciating one for those individuals involved was the price that Americans paid for their capacity to form new human groups for new tasks with astonishing speed.

The Blackfeet were to have revenge, of a kind at least, on Russell. Trapping with three companions in the creeks that ran into Yellowstone Lake, Russell had set off with a trapper named White. Walking along a stream he glanced up to see the heads of Indians. His powder horn and bullet pouch, lying on the ground some distance away, were seized by an Indian before he could reach them. But cocking their rifles and aiming them at the nearest savages the two trappers made their way through a circle of warriors followed by a shower of arrows. White, struck in the hip, paused only long enough to pull out the arrow. Russell was also hit in the hip. Finally an arrow from the pursuing Blackfeet went through Russell's right leg above the knee. He fell across a log and the Indian who had shot him leaped forward with his tomahawk to administer the coup de grace. In Russell's words, "I made a leap and avoided the blow and kept hopping from log to log thro. a shower of arrows, which flew around us like hail, lodging in the pines and logs. After we had passed them about 10 paces wheeled about and took aim at them. They then began to dodge behind the trees and shoot their guns we then ran and hopped about 50 yards further in the logs and bushes and made a stand—I was very faint from the loss of blood and we set down among the logs determined to kill the two foremost when they came up and then die like men."

The Indians, searching through the down timber for their prey, twice passed within fifteen or twenty feet of the two men and then, more interested in dividing the spoils—the traps, horses, and equipment—they turned back, giving Russell and White a reprieve. The two wounded men then set off hobbling painfully toward the lake. Russell was so weak through loss of blood that he had to rest every few hundred yards. At the lake they patched their wounds as best they could and continued their tortuous progress along the shore. In the distance they could hear the shouting of the Indians over their booty. White, a Missourian, brought up, Russell wrote scornfully, as "the pet of the family" who "had never done or learned much of anything but horseracing and gambling," was convinced that he would die wretchedly in the wilderness far from his friends and doting parents. To such lamentations Russell replied, "If you persist in thinking so you will die but I can crawl from this place upon my hands and one knee and Kill 2 or 3 Elk and make a shelter of the skins dry the meat until we get able to travel." Russell's leg was so swollen that he could walk only with the aid of a crutch that White fashioned for him. The two men then took refuge in a grove of pines and had hardly done so when some sixty Indians appeared along the shore shooting at elk swimming in the lake. Returning to their original camp site, Russell and White found a French-Canadian trapper who had been one of their small party and a sack of salt overlooked by the Indians. Russell then bathed his wounds in warm salt water and made a salve of beaver's oil and castorum. The three men had not eaten since the Blackfoot attack. The Canadian shot several ducks and they had a meal of sorts. That night they camped at a hot springs where Russell was able to soak his swollen leg. Next day they shot a doe elk, cut the meat in thin slices, dried them over a fire to provide food for their journey back to the fort, and used the hide to make moccasins. By now Russell could limp along at a slow walk. The fall nights were growing increasingly cold and the three men, huddled around small fires and without blankets, could get little sleep. With infinite difficulty, they pressed on, sometimes going several days without food, to Fort Hall a hundred and thirty miles away, arriving there "naked hungry wounded sleepy and fatigued."

After ten days of rest and good food at the fort, Russell was out setting traps for beaver again, and by the end of October he had traveled to the region of the Jefferson River and back, finally making winter camp early in December with three companions, one from Missouri, one from Massachusetts, and one from Vermont. They felt themselves fortunate to find some books to read—Byron's works, Shakespeare, Sir Walter Scott, the Bible, and Clark's *Commentary,* as well as works on geology, chemistry, and philosophy. In May Russell was off trapping solo with "two horses six traps and some few books." After a summer and fall of trapping he joined a village of Snake Indians, and there a Frenchman with a Flathead wife invited Russell to pass the winter with him. The racial composition of the village provided an interesting insight into the process of amalgamation of various tribes with each other and with whites. In the lodge next to Russell's host was a half-breed Iowa with a Nez Percé wife and two children, his wife's brother, and another half-breed. The next lodge was that of a half-breed Ree, his Nez Percé wife, two children, and a Snake Indian. A third nearby lodge was occupied by a half-breed Snake and his Nez Percé wife and two children. The dwellers in the other fifteen lodges in the village were all Snake.

The Snake were far more casual about intermarriages than tribes like the Blackfeet and generally hospitable to Indians or whites who came to them in peace. Nez Percé women were particularly prized as wives by white men and half-breeds for their cleanliness and affection.

The whites and half-breeds living among the Snake felt a common bond at Christmas—"all who claimed kin to the white man (or to use their own expression, all that were gens d'esprit)." Russell was one of a party, only three of whom spoke English, that sat down to a Christmas feast of stewed elk meat, boiled deer meat, a boiled flour pudding prepared with dried fruit and four quarts of sauce made of the juice of sour berries and sugar, followed by cakes and six gallons of strong coffee. Large wood chips or pieces of bark served as plates and tin cups held the coffee. "The principal topic which was discussed," Russell wrote, "was the political affairs of the Rocky Mountains The state of governments among the different tribes, the personal characters of the most distinguished warriors Chiefs etc." It was the general opinion of the group that a certain Snake chief who was misusing his authority would soon be deposed and replaced by his brother. "In like manner were the characters of the principal Chiefs of the Bonnak Nez percey Flathead and Crow Nations and the policy of their respective govern-ment commented upon . . . with as much affected dignity as if they could read their own names when written or distinguish the letter B from a Bulls foot."

In the Yellowstone region Russell noted that "the trappers often remarked to each other as they rode over these lonely plains that it was time for the White man to leave the mountains as Beaver and game had nearly disappeared." After a futile hunt for mountain sheep, Russell himself decided to head for Oregon territory. He and Elbridge Trask "took an affectionate leave of each other," Trask to return to Vermont, Russell to push west. Russell prepared for his journey to the Willamette Valley by killing elk and drying the meat. Then climbing to a high peak in the Pont Neuf Range, he "sat down under a pine and took a last farewell view of a country over which I had travelled so often under such a variety of circumstances The recollections of the past connection with the scenery," he noted, "now spread out before me put me somewhat into a Poetical humour and for the first time I attempted to frame my thoughts into rhyme but if Poets will forgive me for this intrusion I shall be cautious about trespassing on their grounds in the future."

The impulse was more significant than the poem which was neither better nor worse than most of its genre, celebrating "the hoary icy mantled towers" and "crystal streamlets," the "smooth vale" where "skillful hands prepared a rich repast" and "hunters jokes and merry humor'd sport/Beguiled the time enlivened every face/The hours flew past and seemed like moments short/'Til twinkling planets told of nighttimes pace." But now "those scenes of cheerful mirth are done/The horned herds are dwindling very fast. . . ."

> Ye rugged mounts ye vales ye streams and trees
> To you a hunter bids his last farewell
> I'm bound for shores of distant western seas
> To view far famed Multnomahs fertile vale
> I'll leave these regions once famed hunting grounds
> Which I perhaps again shall see no more
> And follow down led by the setting sun
> Or distant sound of proud Columbia's roar

In the Willamette Valley Russell found some farmers and missionaries who had formed a company to erect a sawmill. He signed on as a worker and in a blasting accident lost the sight of his right eye. It seemed to him ironic that having survived every hazard of the wilderness, he should so soon become a casualty of civilization. Nonetheless he was soon a leader in the affairs of the valley, signing a petition to the "Legislative Committee of Oregon Territory," working to bring pressure on Congress to make good the claims of the United States to the region, and running for governor in 1845. He was elected to represent the recently formed Polk County in the Territorial Legislature in 1848 but when gold was discovered in California he, like many of his neighbors, headed for the goldfields. Although he was only thirty-five years old, the hardships he had endured in the Yellowstone country and the effects of the blast made it impossible for Russell to endure the rigors of mining, so he opened a store and boardinghouse near Gallowstown, now Placerville. He tried his hand at operating a trading ship between Sacramento and Portland and was swindled by his partner. He bought land for a farm but his title was challenged and he lost much of it. As the years passed he was increasingly troubled by nervousness, "bilious" attacks, and crippling rheumatism, until in his last years he was paralyzed below the waist. The persistent failure of his various business ventures was doubtless less indicative of flaws in Russell's character than of the terrible precariousness of all such ventures at the time. But he certainly must have looked back on his Yellowstone years as his own personal "golden age," full of danger and hardship but rich in romance and adventure and, above all, companionship: reading and "philosophizing" with friends in long winter camps, at the rendezvous, in the lodges of friendly Indian chiefs, on the hunt, with Elbridge Trask, and even in the exciting skirmishes with the ferocious Blackfoot Indians. For all its crudity and violence it was an Edenic world of savage innocence, endlessly compelling, the exhaustible material of myths and legends. Osburne Russell, we may hope, derived consolation in all his subsequent defeats and disappointments from the knowledge that he had not only been part of the legend, but, in recording it, had made it the more accessible to subsequent generations of his countrymen.

The rendezvous of 1838 brought word that the fur companies intended to discontinue all further operations. The American Fur Company had driven its less well capitalized rivals to the wall, but its victory, expensive in terms of men and money, was a hollow one. The halcyon days of the beaver trade were over. Fashion had created the insatiable appetite for beaver hats, and fashion ended it. Fashion now decreed that beaver hats must be replaced by silk, and beavers had a reprieve. The fur trading business would continue but in a much modified form. That branch of it based on the beaver had been a "brown gold rush," a boomtime business full of intrigue, unscrupulous maneuvers, desperate struggles for dominance among the competing fur companies, of dog-eat-dog competition and the ruthless despoiling of the Indians who were so often the eager instruments of their own undoing. It had been, in short, a classic capitalist undertaking, given a heightened color and intensity by the wildly romantic circumstances under which it took place. Individual trappers or small parties of trappers continued to carry on a greatly diminished trade. Many, like Osburne Russell, pushed on westward into Oregon territory to provide the nucleus of American settlements and strengthen American claims in that region. Most of those who were married to Indian squaws and had children by them remained in the region, living with friendly Indians and serving as army guides and scouts and, increasingly, as caravans of settlers began crossing the Great Plains for the Oregon country, as guides for emigrant trains.

The American frontier was the world's frontier, the most compelling and dramatic representation of the fact that the United States belonged to the world. The Fur West drew to it, irresistibly, representatives of a number of peoples or nations—French-Canadians, Spanish Americans, Iroquois, Shawnee and Delaware Indians, Scotsmen,

Irishmen, Germans, Dutchmen—and formed them into human groups, in this instance bands of trappers and traders, who, not even speaking the same language, ate, fought, played, and died or survived, welded together by the overwhelming power of the environment. The "language" of the frontier was a bizarre mixture of Indian signs and words, French words, Spanish words, English words, made-up words, a universal argot created out of the most practical necessities. We hear much today of the desirability for a *lingua franca,* a global language that all of the world's people might in time speak. But the experience of the American frontier reminds us that common tasks create their own forms of communication. The act gives rise to the word.

No account of the Trans-Mississippi West or indeed of the relations of white Americans to the Indians and trappers of the Old Northwest would be complete without mention of General William Clark. It was Clark's painful lot to watch from his strategically located post at St. Louis while the Indian nations were slowly destroyed by the westward migration his expedition had done so much to stimulate. While the Indians had been "strong and hostile" it had been the policy of the United States to weaken them. "Now that they are weak and harmless, and most of their lands fallen into our hands, justice and humanity require us to cherish and befriend them," Clark wrote. "To teach them to live in houses, to raise grain and stock, to plant orchards, to set up landmarks, to divide their possessions, to establish laws for their government, to get the rudiments of common learning, such as reading, writing and ciphering." These were the first steps to improving their condition. But before any of these steps could be taken, they must be removed from the corrupting presence of the whites to a land "where they could rest in peace, and enjoy in reality the perpetuity of the lands on which their buildings and improvements would be made."

The common practice of the United States government had been to "buy" Indian lands at treaty meetings where presents were given to those chiefs willing to enter into such negotiations and yearly "annuities" were promised to the tribes involved. Of the difficulties and complexities of such "purchases" we are well aware. Even where the Indian claims were extinguished with some shadow of fairness, the consequences of the "annuity" were demoralizing to the tribes. They came every year, warbonnets in hand, to receive their "annuity" in the form of supplies and baubles, ammunition and clothing. Or they awaited impatiently for it to arrive by steamboat up the Missouri or down the Mississippi. Clark was strongly opposed to the annuity policy. The value of the annuities was small enough but in the long run they made once-proud tribes mendicants, living from handout to handout.

Clark saw the basic problem with the Indians as one of poverty. It was a strange word to enter into the language of the Indian. He had always been "poor" in the sense that he lived very close to the margin of existence. However powerful a tribe he belonged to, a bad hunt, a hard winter, destructive storms might bring him to the point of starvation. But he had never considered himself poor. Now he saw the white as rich and himself, by comparison as poor. And soon his speech was sprinkled with that demeaning word: "The white man is rich. He has many horses and cattle. The Indian is poor. He begs his White Father to give him food and clothing. . . ."

Nothing of any enduring value could be done for the Indian until he was no longer poor, Clark argued. "It is vain to talk to people in this condition about learning and religion," he wrote. "They want a regular supply of food, and, until that is obtained, the operations of the mind must take the instinct of mere animals, and be confined to warding off hunger and cold."

Property had "raised the character of the southern tribes. Roads and travellers through their country, large annuities, and large sums for land from the United States, and large presents to chiefs," Clark wrote, "have enabled them to acquire slaves, cattle, hogs, and horses; and these have enabled them to live independently, and to cultivate their minds and keep up their pride. . . ." But all that they had accomplished was to count for little or nothing against the avarice of their white neighbors.

Clark, with Lewis Cass as an ally, made numerous suggestions to the federal government for laws "under which those scattered & miserable remnants of the people of America" might experience the "just & benevolent views of the government." In 1825, six months before Jefferson's death, Clark wrote his old commander-in-chief expressing his determination to continue his fight on behalf of "the people of America"—the Indians of the West. It would give him pleasure to find some way to improve "the conditions of these unfortunate people placed under my charge, knowing as I do their retchedness and their rapid decline It is to be lamented that the deplorable Situation of the Indians do not receive more of the human feelings of the nations."

When Clark died in 1838, the last year of the Yellowstone

rendezvous, things were no better for his Indian wards despite congressional legislation four years earlier that had followed his advice in part by strengthening the role of the military in protecting the Indians. His own life, much marred by personal tragedy and, in his last years, fear of financial insecurity (although he left an estate, largely in land, valued at $120,000), was a classic. One newspaper said of him truly, if a bit backhandedly, "he was more faultless, and more virtuous than almost any man who ever held so conspicuous a station for so long a time." That was so and much more. He had gone to the Pacific Ocean and back with his friend Meriwether Lewis.

21

The Southwest

In 1821, just before the beginning of the brown gold rush, traders' caravans, loaded with goods to trade in Santa Fe, started out from Fort Smith on the Arkansas River. Mexico had won its independence from Spain six months earlier and in the resultant euphoria trade with the United States was encouraged by the revolutionary Mexican government.

One of the first traders to take advantage of the new opportunity was Major Jacob Fowler who, with a party of twenty men, among them five Frenchmen and a black slave of Fowler's, departed for Santa Fe on September 6, 1821. The group, officially under the command of Colonal High Glenn, included "thirty Horses and mules Seventen of Which carried traps and goods for the Indean traid. . . ." They traveled along the Arkansas through the range of the Osage Indians, from whom, as Fowler, the recorder of the trip noted, they "got Some dryed meet Corn Beens and dryed Pumpkins. . . ." The next contact with the Osage was not encouraging, "These last Indeans," Fowler wrote, "appear more unfriendly and talk Sasy and bad to us but this is to be Exspected as the[y] . . . are Said to be a Collection of the Raskals from the other vileges."

Fowler's party followed the Arkansas to present-day Colorado but they found hard going. Buffalo were scarce and grass for the pack animals difficult to find. Soon they were in Pawnee country and they had to be ceaselessly vigilant lest their horses be stolen or their camps attacked. "We Have all Readey lost 13 Horses and two mules," Fowler noted on the sixth of November, "and the Remainder Hardly fitt for use"; "11 treaks of Indians Barfooded" were observed in the sand along the river. At the Purgatory River Lewis Dawson, who had left the party to pick grapes, was surprised by a "White Bare" or grizzly, which seized and shook him like a terrier with a rat. Fowler and the others were alerted by the "dredfull Screems" of the victim and the bear was finally driven off and killed. Dawson's head was terribly lacerated, but the wounds "Ware Sewed up as Well as Cold be don by men in our Situation Haveing no Surgen or Surgical Instruments. . . ." Dawson was conscious but convinced that his hours were numbered, declaring, "I am killed . . . I heard my skull break." Three days later he died.

Near the juncture of the North Platte and the Niobrara rivers Fowler's band encountered a party of Kiowa, allies of the Comanche, who "Came Rideing at full Speed With al their Weapons . . . in a florish as tho the Ware Chargeing uppon an Enemey but on their aproch the most frendly disposition appereed in all their actions as Well [as] gusters." It was a typically dramatic Indian encounter. As soon as the Kiowa discovered that the party was a trading expedition, they took it under their collective wing. They made it clear, through signs and gestures, that they would act as guardians and sponsors, expecting, of course, handsome presents in return for their services. The more enterprising tribes were always anxious to establish a close and profitable relationship with white traders. If that turned out to be impractical, their next intention was usually to steal what they could without excessive risk. As a last resort they robbed and killed the whites if the opportunity presented itself.

The Kiowa chief indicated that his tribe wished to trade. He prevailed on the uneasy traders to interrupt their journey. He then "took poesion and Charge of all our Horses," Fowler noted, while his band gathered and placed the trading goods in the chief's lodge for their "protection." Through the rest of the day Kiowa continued to arrive and set up their lodges so that by nightfall there was, in Fowler's words, "a large town Containing up Wards of two Hondrerd Houses Well filled with men Wemon and Children—With a great nombr of dogs and Horses So that the Hole Cuntry to a great distance Was Coverd. . . ."

On November 22 Fowler noted in his journal: "Remained in Camp al day Holding Counsels Eating and Smokeing and traiding a little with Indans . . . ." It snowed and turned bitterly cold and Fowler watched with astonishment several hundred naked Indian children "Running and playin on the Ice—Without the least appeerence of Suffering from the Cold."

As more and more Indians collected, including bands from several tribes friendly to the Kiowa, the traders grew understandably apprehensive. Next day came the shocker. A Comanche chief, who had recently arrived on the scene and assumed command, announced that the Indians were ready to receive the gifts in the traders' possession that "His father the President Had Sent them." Colonel Glenn replied that there were no such gifts. They were private traders on their way to Santa Fe. At this the chief flew in "a great Pashion" and told the colonel that he was a liar and thief and had stolen the goods from the President. He, the chief, would take charge of the goods and protect them and "He Wold kill the Conl and His men too upon Which the Conl and His Inturpreter With drew," leaving the Indians to confer about their fate. The issue boiled down to a conflict between the Kiowa and the Comanche, the Kiowa defending the traders, the Comanche denouncing them. So many Comanche had pitched their lodges along the river that they outnumbered the Kiowa. As Fowler put it with some understatement, "our Setuation Was not of the most plesent nature." At sundown a tall handsome Indian came running into the white camp, shaking hands all around and declaring, "Me Arapaho." The Arapaho, a third tribe included in the large Indian gathering, had declared for the traders. The Indian assured Colonel Glenn that the whites had nothing further to fear from the Comanche. Indeed, he was soon followed by the Comanche chief who had been so adamant about seizing the trading goods. Overborne by the other chiefs, he became all charm and compliance and "offered Conl glann and Mr Roy Each one of His Wifes—the greates token of friendship those Indeans Can offer."

Fowler estimated that there were from five to seven thousand Indians encamped on the plain stretching back from the river, among then Cheyenne, Paducah (a branch of the Comanche), and some Indians that Fowler called Snake but who could hardly have been members of the Shoshone tribe that most commonly bore that name. The white traders were, meanwhile, visited by "Spanish Indeans" from Taos in New Mexico and assured that they were on the right path and only six days easy travel from that Mexican post. Preparing to continue their journey, the white traders made camp a few miles down the river. There they learned from friendly Arapaho that the mercurial Comanche chief was preparing to attack them. As the traders erected hasty log palisades, a band of Arapaho set up camp around them, ostensibly for their protection against the Comanche. It soon appeared possible that the rumored Comanche attack was a ruse to give the Arapaho the opportunity to take charge of the expedition under the guise of defending it.

Amid indications that the gathering would soon disperse and the traders at last be free to proceed to Santa Fe, Fowler experienced a typical bit of Indian horseplay. He had lost one lens from his glasses and was startled when an Indian snatched the glasses from his head and ran off. "In a Short time," he wrote, "I heard great Shouting and laffing." The Indian who had absconded with the glasses was returning, leading another Indian wearing them. When he came up to Fowler, the latter saw that the Indian had only one eye—one eye, one eyepiece. The Indians were delighted with the joke. The glasses were returned and everyone was very merry. But before they could extricate themselves the traders needed to purchase some horses and, additionally, were confronted by another delicate bit of Indian diplomacy. Both the Arapaho and the Kiowa now claimed sponsorship of the traders. Both insisted that the whites must stay with them and for a time it looked as though the dispute might result in "a Ware With them and destruction to our Selves." The crisis was at least temporarily resolved by splitting the party into two groups, one for each tribe, but the Indians, anxious to delay their departure, refused to sell the needed horses. Finally enough horses were traded to allow the party to resume its journey, although both Kiowa and Arapaho showed every disposition to accompany them. When Colonel Glenn took leave of the Arapaho chief and presented him with some small presents that stoical warrior "threw himself on his bed in tears." And at the traders' camp that evening he appeared to spend one more night with his friend the white chief.

December 6, Fowler and his companions broke camp. The month that they had lived so precariously surrounded by the unpredictable aborigines had been instructive but nerve-racking, and they were glad to be on the move again. "It is but Justice," Fowler wrote, "to Say We find the Kiawa the best Indeans possessing more firmness and manly deportment than the arapoho and less arrogance and Hatey Pride than the Ietan [Comanche]. . . ." It should be noted that whites, almost invariably, found greater virtues in the tribes that were friendly to them than in those that were hostile.

A week later Fowler's group, still accompanied by some Arapaho warriors, encountered a party of Comancheros—Spaniards, or Mexicans, of mixed Spanish and Indian blood. When the two groups met there was a moment of uncertainty on the part of the Americans. For years the Spanish had been hostile and suspicious toward explorers and traders from the United States. Zebulon Pike had been arrested and held for several months when his expedition penetrated Spanish territory. But there had been a revolution. The Mexicans, like the Americans, had claimed their independence. Erstwhile enemies were now friends, both fighters in the cause of freedom. But had this new spirit of amity reached the frontier outposts of the newly proclaimed Republic of Mexico? It was soon evident that it had. The Comancheros, a miserable, ragged-looking lot, painted like Indians, "dismounted and embraced us with affection and friendship," Colonel Glenn noted, adding, "they are all creoles [mixed-bloods]. . . . The rather more literate seem well disposed—possess far less sence than the Indeans we are with, seem happy and possess a greater degree of Joy at seeing us then could be Immagined. . . ." Glenn was surprised to discover that the Arapaho treated the Mexicans "much as we command our negroes." One of the Arapaho ordered the Comancheros to kneel and pray "so that we may see their fashion which they readily agreed to and went through with the Catholic prayers, and afterwards prayed fervently for us. . . ."

Glenn went on with the Comancheros to Santa Fe, leaving "mager" Fowler in charge of the pack train, with instructions to make camp and keep a vigilant eye out for Indians. Fowler sent three of the party out to hunt for buffalo and they fell in with a war party of Crows, herding along some two hundred horses they had stolen from the Arapaho. The Crows took the hunters prisoner and relieved them of their ammunition and blankets, "giving them nine fine Horses in payment. . . ." While this negotiation was going on, the Crows were overtaken by a party of Arapaho seeking to recover their horses. In the fight that followed the hunters made their escape, leaving their horses, blankets, and ammunition behind.

The next day Fowler had to contend with "a mutney." When he ordered the hunters out of their beds to search for deer and buffalo, they refused to stir. Fowler's response was to yank the ringleader out of bed by his hair; the result was a "scoffel" in which Fowler triumphed. The men, it turned out, were convinced that Glenn would be arrested by the Mexican officials, in which case they were determined to divide up the trading goods among themselves as their pay for the expedition. Fowler told them that if they persisted in their plan he would send for the Arapaho chief, who would be glad to help him protect the goods. This threat brought capitulation. Peace was made and Fowler promised that if Glenn failed to return the hunters would be dealt with fairly.

Settling down to wait for word from the colonel, the party grew more restless and impatient with each passing day. Some thirty Crows, on their way to war with the Arapaho, moved in and "Recogniseing the three men the maid Prisnors . . . Exspressed much Joy to See them." After they had "don Eating Smokeing the Sung a long Song and all lay down and Slept tell morning." But before they departed, they stole everything they could carry. One Indian came into Fowler's tent "threw down His old Roab and took a new one." The bumptious savage then picked up Fowler's saddle bag as well. After a brief scuffle, Fowler retrieved his belongings and ejected the Indian from the tent. Similar scenes were being enacted in various parts of the camp. An appeal was made to the chief, who ordered the warriors to return whatever they had appropriated and "moved them all of[f] before Him," but when they had departed an inventory showed that the whites were missing a roll of brass wire, three blankets, five knives, and a smelting ladle. A few days later the Crows were back from their raid empty-handed. This time they tried to drive off the traders' horses and when they failed, they boldly "came to us as frends." Fowler gave them some tobacco and trinkets but he and his men remained on the alert. The chief professed to be hurt by the obvious wariness of the whites. He was their friend, he assured them. His only desire was to protect them from hostile Indians. While he orated "one of His Cheefs Stole a bridle and put it in His bosem." Fowler saw the theft and took back the bridle. There was another tense moment as the traders looked to the priming of their guns and the Crows drew off as though they were preparing to fight, but the moment passed and the head chief expressed his regrets at the actions of his warriors. The incident is a revealing one. The Indians generally had no notion of stealing as a crime. Members of a tribe were of course constrained from stealing from each other, although they sometimes did so—usually with fatal results for the thief. But other Indians, and especially whites, who always appeared to have such an abundance of things that they could well spare some, were fair game. Stealing horses was accounted part of a continuing game, demanding great stealth, skill, and daring. Stealing inanimate objects was not reprehensible, only less daring. What was, in effect, a cultural difference appeared to the white man simply another instance of Indian depravity and wickedness. In this instance it is easy to sympathize with the white man who heard the Indian profess devoted friendship while purloining his most essential possessions.

By the end of January word came from Colonel Glenn that the Mexican government was anxious to encourage trade with the United States and that he had secured permission to trap and trade "in the Spanish provences." Fowler and his men were at once on the move to join Glenn. The colonel met them near the village of San Cristobal and accompanied them to Taos, where they received a warm welcome and participated in a fandango, which the author Josiah Gregg later described as an assembly "where dancing and frolocking are carried on. . . . Nothing is more general, throughout the country, and with all classes then dancing. From the gravest priest to the buffoon—from the richest nabob to the beggar—from the governor to the ranchero —from the soberest matron to the flippant belle . . . all partake of this exhilerating amusement." The fiddle, the guitar, and the tombe or Indian drum were the standard musical instruments and they were so constantly played, fandango or no, "that," Gregg wrote, "one would suppose that a perpetual carnival prevailed everywhere."

At Taos, Paul, Fowler's black slave, enjoyed a great vogue. One of the older women of the town took a special fancy to him and "takeing Hold of Him and drawing Him to the beed Side Sot Him down with Hir arms Round His Sholders. and gave Him a Kis . . . Sliped Hir Hand down Into his Britches." "It Wold take a much abeler Hand than mine," Fowler added, "to discribe palls feelings at this time being naturly a little Relegous modest and Bashfull."

The trading goods were sold for hard Spanish dollars at Taos and Santa Fe, and for four months the party trapped beaver in the mountains and rivers of western Colorado and eastern New Mexico. They were constantly involved in close encounters with various Indian tribes, striving always to maintain a neutrality, often in as much danger from their Indian friends as their enemies. The Ute, whose range covered the Salt Lake and the Utah valleys as well as parts of present-day Colorado, and the Pawnee, roving over a region south and west of the Platte, were added to their inventory of tribes. By June they were on their way back to the Arkansas with a rich haul of beaver and specie. At Fort Osage on the Missouri, Colonel Glenn bought two canoes and the weary band floated down the river to St. Louis, spreading the word in the river settlements along the way that Mexico was independent and that trade had been opened with the United States.

Other expeditions were already on the way and soon the numbers increased dramatically. Although the risks and hardships were great there were high profits to be made. It was not unusual for an investment of $20,000 in trading goods to bring a return in the $200,000 range. For the next fifteen or sixteen years what Josiah Gregg called "the Commerce of the Prairies" flourished as an alternative to the rush for beaver in the Yellowstone. Gregg, who in 1831 took much the same route that Fowler had followed, wrote the classic account of the Santa Fe trade before the growing difficulties with Mexico led to its termination. Gregg was another American original, largely self-educated, who had tried schoolteaching, medicine, and law before becoming a trader on the Santa Fe route. He had been born in Tennessee, a farmer's son, but his father had moved, when he was three, to the St. Louis area. From there he moved soon again to Missouri Territory, settling near Cooper's Fort on the frontier and, finally, to Independence, the jumping-off point for everything and everybody going west. Gregg, an omnivorous reader, had taught himself French and Italian, learned to survey, and become a skillful cartographer. But it is also clear that he was highly eccentric and suffered a series of "identity crises" severe enough to leave him physically ill, or, in his words, "reduced and debilitated." His doctor, unable to find anything wrong with him, prescribed what was already a classic remedy—a trip west. So Gregg, more dead than alive, signed on as a kind of supercargo with a trading caravan headed for Santa Fe. Since Jacob Fowler's journey in 1821, wagons had largely replaced pack horses for the transporting of merchandise, and in the year of Gregg's departure 130 wagons carrying $250,000 in trading goods departed from Independence, Missouri, along a well-traveled wagon road.

At Independence, the leaders of the caravans recruited teamsters, hunters, trappers, cooks, and assorted hands. Wagons, generally made in Pittsburgh and floated down the Ohio, were purchased, as were mules to draw them. Cattle for butchering were part of most trains, as buffalo and deer became scarce along the much-traveled route, and horses for those who preferred not to walk or could afford to ride. The typical wagon carried some 5,000 pounds of merchandise and was pulled by ten or twelve mules. It was calculated that each man would consume during a six-week journey some fifty pounds of flour, a hundred pounds of bacon, "ten of coffee and twenty of sugar, and a little salt." Mules, once bought, had often to be trained to draw in tandem and respond to commands and to the teamster's whip. The wagons had to be expertly packed to avoid damage to goods on the long, jolting ride. The beginning of the trip, according to Gregg's account, was accompanied by a general mood of euphoria: "Harmony and good feeling prevail everywhere. The hilarious song, the *bon mot* and the witty repartee, go round in quick succession."

Gregg's caravan had hardly left Council Grove behind when his health revived astonishingly. His own reflections on the reasons for his remarkable recovery (it had been necessary to lift him onto his wagon a few days earlier) are worth noting: "The Prairies have," he wrote, "become very celebrated for their sanative effects. . . . Most chronic diseases, particularly liver complaints, dyspepsias, and similar afflictions, are often radically cured; owing, no doubt, to the peculiarities of diet, and the regular exercise incident to prairie life, as well as to the purity of the atmosphere of those elevated unembarrassed regions." Soon Gregg threw away the large supply of pills and medicines he had carried with him and dined voluptuously on buffalo meat.

Assuming Gregg's explanation of the curative consequences of prairie life to have some modest medical basis, one may be forgiven for doubting that a cure could be effected in *three days!* It seems far likelier that Gregg and the legion of valetudinarians who preceded and followed him found relief from the strains and stresses of American life, of what was rather loosely denominated "civilization," to be the greatest remedy for what ailed them—neurasthenia or bad nerves, typically manifested by a bad stomach or "dyspepsia," as it was commonly called.

At Council Grove, the various traders with their wagons or merchandise waited for a caravan to be formed. The purpose was to provide mutual protection against the Indians and to make formal arrangements for the organization of the train under the leadership of a captain, chosen democratically by a "grand council" of traders. "Even in our little community," Gregg wrote, "we had our 'office-seekers' and their 'political adherents,' as earnest and devoted as any of the modern school of politicians in the midst of civilization." The caravan was then divided into four divisions, each in the charge of a lieutenant. The lieutenants selected, or "formed," each day's encampment, assigned night watches, and distributed the major chores among the able-bodied members of the caravan. (Every caravan seems to have had its quota of invalids seeking to recapture their health who, along with the "tourists" and "genteel idlers," were exempt from the more arduous chores.) Gregg's caravan, when the roll was called, numbered some two hundred men. On May 27, 1831, the captain gave the cry "Catch up!" which was echoed through the camp and replied to by "All's set!" When the mules were harnessed and the wagons ready to move, "Stretch out," would be the captain's call, followed by the " 'heps!' of drivers—the cracking of whips—the trampling of feet—the occasional creaks of wheels—the rumbling of wagons. . . ."

The job of the captain was a thankless one. He had no real authority over his contentious and often quarrelsome charges. If an individual disobeyed him, he must bring the offender before a kind of informal court or council which, in turn, if it upheld the captain, could do little more than exercise moral suasion unless the offense was a heinous one such as stealing or murder; in such cases summary justice was commonly, though by no means invariably, inflicted. Captains and lieutenants who were too officious or demanding were often deposed. What was required in a captain, ideally, was considerable practical knowledge and experience, plus great tact and firmness in dealing with a polyglot and highly independent constituency.

Three elements governed all such caravans, whether traders in merchandise headed for Santa Fe, fur traders on the way to the Yellowstone, or emigrants headed for Oregon Territory: wood for the camp fires; water for cooking and for the stock—the mules, horses, and such cattle as accompanied the train; and grass as fodder for the animals. Without those three essentials no wagon train or caravan could go more than two or three days at the most and that at the cost of great hardship and suffering. This fact dictated the practical routes westward. They must all be along one of the great eastward-flowing rivers rising on the east side of the Rockies—the Continental Divide —and flowing to the Mississippi or the Missouri: the Missouri itself, the Arkansas, the Red, and the Platte. Where the route of the caravan departed from a major river system it must cover the ground in increments determined by smaller creeks, streams, or water holes.

The nature of the terrain and the winding course of the rivers necessitated frequent fordings and these were, generally speaking, the most hazardous obstacles of the journey. Major rivers, especially in times of high water, in early spring or after heavy rains, were deep and swift. They could in an instant sweep away horse, rider, wagon, and mules. So there was first a search up and down the river for a fording place where, hopefully, the wagons could be driven across. If no such spot could be found, the industry and ingenuity of the train was tested to the utmost. Sometimes crude rafts were built, the wagons loaded on them, and the rafts winched across by long ropes. This was a laborious and dangerous process. Ropes might break or the raft be overturned midstream and everything lost. The Platte and the Arkansas were broad and shallow and fordable at many places, but rivers like the Red, the Missouri, and the Yellowstone were formidable obstacles.

Traveling west from Independence, Gregg's train went along the Arkansas toward the Cimarron Desert, passing over the Great Plains, a grass-covered region often referred to as "the grand prairie ocean," flat as the proverbial pancake and seemingly limitless in its expanse. At the end of each day, when the lieutenants and their captain had formed an encampment, the wagons were drawn into a square or circle, famous from a thousand movie Westerns. When there was danger of imminent Indian attack, the mules, oxen, horses, and cattle were corralled in the center and the wagons attached to each other by heavy ropes or chains. This meant that grass had to be collected for the animals, which was an onerous chore for men already travel-weary and anxious to prepare their evening meal. The preference, of course, was to turn the animals loose to graze on the grass and brush that grew along the riverbed.

The attire of most members of the train was simple and utilitarian. In Gregg's words, most common was "the fustian frock of the city-bred merchant furnished with a multitude of pockets capable of accommodating a variety of 'extra tacking.' Then there is . . . the farmer with his blue jean coat, the wagoner with his flannel-sleeve vest," and of course the hunter with his hunting shirt and leather leggins. The hunter's indispensable arm was his rifle, but for other members of the party a shotgun or scatter gun was often preferred, a double-barreled fowling piece. By the time of Gregg's trip—1831—the repeating rifle had appeared and, as Gregg noted, "they are certainly very formidable weapons, particularly when used against an ignorant savage foe." In addition most travelers were "furnished . . . with a bountiful supply of pistols and knives of every description, so that [our] party made altogether a very brigand-like appearance."

The "kitchen and table ware" of a wagon consisted, typically, of a skillet, frying pan, sheet-iron camp kettle, a coffeepot, and, for each man, a tin cup and butcher's knife. Blankets of buffalo robes were spread beside the respective wagons on the outside of the perimeter. Tents were seldom used. If rain threatened, people slept under the wagons, or, space permitting, inside the canvas tops. Gregg judged the quantities of coffee drunk "incredible," adding, "It is an unfailing and apparently indispensable beverage, served at every meal—even under the boiling noon-day sun, the wagoner will rarely fail to replenish a second time, his huge tin cup."

The initial sighting of buffalo, especially for those who had never seen the famous animals, was always a sensation. In Gregg's description, "Every horseman was off in a scamper: and some of the wagoners, leaving their teams to take care of themselves, seized their guns and joined the race afoot. Here went one with his rifle or yager—there another with double-barrelled shot-gun—a third with holster-pistols—a Mexican perhaps with his lance—another with his bow and arrows—and numbers joined without any arms whatever, merely for 'the pleasures of the chase'—all helter-skelter—a regular John Gilpin race, truly 'neck or naught.' The fleetest of the pursuers were soon in the midst of the game which scattered in all directions, like a flock of birds upon the descent of a hawk." Gregg observed that the buffalo were fast diminishing through "the continual and wanton slaughter of them by travellers and hunters, and the still greater havoc made among them by the Indians, not only for the meat, but often for the skins and tongue alone (for which they find a ready market among the traders), are fast reducing their numbers, and must ultimately effect their total annihilation from the continent." Gregg added that the annual export of *"buffalo rugs"* (also called robes) from the prairies was a hundred thousand a year, and many more of the beasts were killed for meat.

Like the first sighting of buffalo, the initial encounter with Plains Indians was the occasion of great stir and excitement. To the Indians, the pack and wagon trains that made their way across the Great Plains to the Great Basin—whether they went southerly to Santa Fe and Taos or northerly to the Yellowstone and then north again to the Oregon country; whether they were fur traders, merchants, or, later, emigrants headed for the Pacific slopes—were, like the herds of buffalo, a form of game. They brought with them many attractive articles that the Indians coveted and, most important, food in the form of cattle and wealth in the form of horses and mules. The uniform intention of the various tribes was to acquire, at the least possible cost to themselves, as much of the white man's bounty as they could, including, ideally, his scalp. The strategy to accomplish this goal was, unless the tribe was notorious for its hostility to all whites, to approach the train with elaborate manifestations of peace and goodwill. This was generally done as Jacob Fowler described it in his earlier journey—attempting to achieve maximum dramatic effect by riding up to the train en route or, preferably, when making camp for the night, at full tilt in battle attire, bristling with arms and giving the impression of an all-out attack. As the alarm of "Indians!" was raised and whites dashed for their weapons and tried to round up their stock, the Indians would pull up at a safe distance and several of their chiefs come forward professing friendship and the desire to trade. The train captain and his lieutenants would confer with the Indian chiefs. A brief powwow might then follow, with the ritual smoking of the peace pipe. The chiefs not uncommonly spoke of the hardships of their tribe, the scarcity of game, their admiration for the white men, their need for tobacco and beads. The Sioux, especially since the days of Lewis and Clark, were shameless beggars. Behind the begging was always an unspoken threat. Part of the ritual was to give the chiefs presents, the best presents to the most important chiefs and so on down the line. Then the members of the train might barter with the warriors for Indian garments, bows and arrows, for pieces of finery, even scalps. The Indians would use every stratagem to insinuate themselves into the camp area and, as we have seen, while the trading was going on, help themselves to every object that was not nailed down or closely guarded by its owner.

Stealing horses and livestock from white trains was to the Indians an irresistible opportunity to minimize losses and maximize profits. It was far easier and less perilous to steal horses from white travelers than from other Indians. First off, the trains or caravans always contained a substantial portion of travelers inexperienced in the ways of the frontier, and this portion of course grew larger each year as more and more emigrants—as opposed to hunters and trappers —headed west. Most important, if fifty horses or mules were stolen out of a train's hastily erected and often inadequately guarded corral, the leaders of the train, while dispatching a party to try to overtake the Indians and recapture their animals, could not spend more than a few hours in the task. Above everything they had to push on, for time was their greatest enemy. If they dallied, winter might catch them on the trail. So the Indians were safe from protracted pursuit.

One variation of the stealing of horses and cattle came into play when the animals were too closely guarded to be gotten at, or when they were corralled inside the wagons. Then the Indians would often content themselves with shooting arrows at the dim forms in the hope of killing a few that, abandoned the next day by the train, would provide a hearty meal.

Every Indian tribe had its own range or territory along the main-traveled routes. A tribe usually confined its pillage of the wagon trains to its territory. Thus trains headed for the Yellowstone would pass successively through the territory of the Mandan, the Arikara, the Sioux, the Blackfeet, and the Crows as well as lesser and subsidiary tribes and each would take its proper turn. The all-out, large-scale attacks on trains so vividly depicted in many Western movies were relatively rare. For the most part these came only when a state of open war existed between a particular tribe and the whites—that is to say, when the Indians were on the "war path." What we might properly call the hunting of the white trains by the Indians, rather as they hunted the buffalo, was a peacetime activity. Relatively few travelers across Indian territory died in armed clashes. They were far more frequently killed when out hunting for meat for the train in small parties of two or three or when straying, for whatever reason, from the main body. Gregg did not think there had been more than a dozen deaths on the Santa Fe route from Indians and disease combined.

Often the chiefs of a tribe might genuinely deplore such isolated killings of whites—and even the raids themselves—and try to prevent them, but outside the immediate limits of the village their authority was often tenuous and even within the village it rested on moral force rather than legal sanction. Young braves anxious to qualify as warriors and warriors who coveted the rank of chief had constantly to find ways to prove themselves, to make "coup," to take the scalps by which an Indian's status was ultimately measured, to capture ponies, and to have dramatic stories to tell of their prowess. They were as swift and skillful as prestidigitators—their hands were often faster than the white man's eye.

When the gifts had been given and the possibilities of trade exhausted, the Indians would withdraw with additional assurances of friendship and ostensibly ride off to steal some horses from a rival tribe. Generally they shadowed the wagons or pack train for days, slipping in each night to try to drive off horses or mules or oxen. A tribe might double its collective wealth as measured in ponies by a single successful raid, or, conversely, be impoverished by a raid against it. Josiah Gregg tells of his caravan's suddenly being virtually swallowed up by several thousand Blackfeet and Gros Ventres who pitched a great tent city around the camp of the wagon train in the valley of the Cimarron River at the eastern edge of the desert; despite all efforts to keep them at arm's length, they swarmed through the camp. By nightfall, Gregg wrote, "we had perhaps a thousand of these pertinacious creatures, males and females, of all ages and descriptions, about us . . . every means, without resorting to absolute violence, was employed to drive them away, but without entire success." Soon it was discovered that they had made off with a "pig of lead" for bullets weighing almost a hundred pounds, as well as a number of smaller articles. Next day the Indians went their way only, it was learned later, to encounter the Sioux and lose almost half their company in a desperate battle.

One of the most picturesque figures of the Southwestern frontier was the Mexican Cioolero. Typically these buffalo hunters wore "leather trousers and jackets, and flat straw hats; while, swung upon the shoulder of each hangs his *carcage* or quiver of bows and arrows. The long handle of his lance being set in a case, and suspended by the side with a strap from the pommel of the saddle, leave[s] the point waving high over the head, with a tassel of gay parti-colored stuffs dangling at the tip of the scabbard." Even the hunter's musket had a "fantastically tasselled" stopper in its barrel.

A few days away from Santa Fe a party of customs officials met Gregg's caravan, ostensibly to escort them to Santa Fe. From a distance that town looked to Josiah Gregg like a cluster of brick kilns painted white. As he drew closer it was apparent that these were the adobe houses of the town and soon the travelers could hear the cries *"Los Americanos!"—"Los Carros!"—"La entrada de la caravana!"*

The cargoes of the wagons had to be deposited in the customs warehouses, inventoried, and duties paid (a process that involved a good deal of bribery); then they could be sold to Mexican factors and merchants. In some "ports" or places of entry into New Mexico, Gregg reported, the custom prevailed "of dividing legal duties into three equal parts: one for the officers—a second for the merchants—the other for the government."

In New Mexico the ranchos and haciendas had, of necessity,

grown into villages "for protection against the marauding savages of the surrounding wilderness," as Josiah Gregg put it. The land was mountainous, arid, and barren, with grass in the high hills that made excellent grazing for large herds of cattle. But it was the air and climate that most impressed such visitors as Gregg. He rhapsodized about it: "Nowhere—not even under the much boasted Sicilian skies—can a purer or more wholesome atmosphere be found." A strange enchantment hung over the land that makes up the southern end of the Great Basin, a unique geological region of the world, created only yesterday in terms of the earth's age by volcanic upheavals too immense to imagine. Rock and earth had been thrust up thousands of feet above sea level, tilted like a great plate; then the rivers had begun their carving and cutting of the land like fabulous masons, shaping battlements and towers, red and yellow and purple escarpments and minarets, plateaus as large as countries and chasms that seemed to have no bottom—a formidable and beautiful universe. The traveler, the hunter, the trader, could hardly escape the feeling that he had stumbled into a frozen panorama of the creation of the world. For the moment it existed primarily as a formidable barrier stretching across the land, dividing the golden shores of California and the rain forest of the Northwest from the rest of the continent. Nowhere could one find a better demonstration of the overwhelming power of geography—of landscape in ceaseless interplay with ideas.

There was in those who first saw this world a kind of astonished muteness in the face of such hitherto unimagined immensities. It was not evident whether it was beautiful or merely terrifying; it was all on a scale too vast to be comprehended under any existing aesthetic rubric. It seemed to call for an enlarged perception, a new way of looking at the world and at man himself, who appeared so dwarfed and impotent by comparison. So the first comers said little about the landscape as though they hardly knew quite what to say, conscious of the unbridgeable gap between what they saw and their power to render it in words. That muteness could not last, of course, and soon there were words enough, however inadequate, for Americans were loath to concede that there was any realm of human experience, any natural phenomenon, any artifact, however fantastical, that could not be summed up or summoned up or nailed down with words. To be sure, one needed new scales, new dimensions, new conceptions. The Indians, mysterious and protean and ultimately inexplicable, were hard enough to pin down, and now there was an additional and inescapable demonstration of the incomprehensible powers and forces of the natural world—the landscape and the Indians.

Everything was further complicated by the fact that in the "go-ahead age" human perspectives changed with bewildering speed. Experiences must be swallowed in great indigestible gulps. Perhaps that was what was wrong with the American stomach—perhaps gulping down too much undigested experience had given Americans a kind of collective stomachache. The fact that this fearful and awesome and—one could hardly call it beautiful; beautiful was for a very different scale—astonishing barrier *intervened* between the bustling East Coast and the benevolent waters of the Pacific was as profound a fact as any that entered into the composition of the American character, or psyche, or sense of the self in relation to the universe, or however we may put it when we try to say what America was and is.

The West entered the American consciousness in another way. The contours of the Great Basin made dramatically apparent what geologists had already been more than hinting at—that the earth was very much older than the Scriptures suggested. Hundreds of thousands of years had clearly been necessary for the Colorado River, for instance, to carve out the Grand Canyon and, indeed, for all the remarkable features of that terrain to be defined. For the orthodox, the findings of geology posed another problem for their faith. Even such a mild skeptic as Sidney George Fisher was troubled by the implications of "the truths revealed by geology. . . . The story of the creation taught in Genesis is much more ennobling to our race," he wrote. "It is a much more dignified idea that we were a special creation, made in God's own image, than that we are one link in a progressive series of development, from plants to worms, to fish, to birds, to beasts until finally a poet & a philosopher is produced of a species that began with a monkey, produced too by gradual changes of the earth's crust & temperature, by laws that are eternal & unvaried in their operation, chemical laws & laws of animal life." But while he mourned that passing of the wolf and buffalo Fisher derived comfort from the thought that higher forms of life were evolving. "The Indians . . . ere long will belong wholly to the past, as the aborigines of the West Indies do," he reflected. "Man destroys the animals, the strong races of man destroy the weak. This process is always going on and at the same time the superior races are advancing in knowledge & power." It seemed to Fisher that "in the vast spaces of time" climate and geography might well produce "changes as wonderful as those which geology teaches, and a million years hence, the ruling nations of the world may be as superior to those of today as these are to the Indians. The idea is vast and overpowering, whether we look to the past or to the future, but it is desolating to think that in this stream of humanity, our part is only the present moment, that the future is to us as the past and that we are mere bubbles upon a rushing current, coming whence we know not, going whither we know not, but not taking us with it. Nay, that man himself is to disappear like the mammoth and the buffalo and neither this earth nor any place to know him or have a habitation for him."

Josiah Gregg estimated in 1831 that no more than 70,000 "souls" inhabited the vast reaches of New Mexico and that of these only some thousand were what he called "white creoles," native-born Mexicans of pure Spanish descent. Mestizos, or "mixed creoles," he calculated to number some 59,000, while Indians of the pueblos he estimated at 10,000. Twenty United States citizens lived in the province and "not over double as many alien residents." "Agriculture," he wrote, "like almost everything else in New Mexico, is in a very primitive and unimproved state." Most peasant farmers used only a hoe, but Gregg took thoughtful note of a fact that would, in another day, determine the economy of the entire Great Basin. Since there was virtually no rainfall, all land planted in vegetables had to be artificially irrigated by water drawn from a stream or river by a system of crude canals and thus could grow much of the year without regard to rainfall. As Gregg put it, the Mexican farmer, primitive as his tools and practices, "is therefore more sure of his crop than if it were subject to the caprices of the weather in more favored agricultural regions."

The staple productions of the country were Indian corn and wheat. The corn was used principally to make tortillas, paper-thin cakes or crepes filled with meat or vegetables or cheese or simply with butter or salt. Indeed the ubiquitous tortilla, rolled up or dried, often served as both fork and spoon. The nut of the scrub pine, or piñon, was another prized delicacy. *El café de los Mexicanos* was a brew more potent than American coffee and more addictive among the "lower classes of Mexicans." With *frijoles* and *chile,* coffee or *atole* made up their principal fare. Red peppers entered into virtually every dish and every meal. Green peppers, *chile verde,* served both as a condiment and as a salad.

Goods were transported in New Mexico by mules, and Josiah Gregg was much impressed by the skill of the *arrieros,* or muleteers, in packing merchandise on the animals. In five minutes they could pack a mule so expertly that the load would hold tight over the roughest country. Like the *arrieros,* the *vaqueros* or cattle herders were excellent horsemen, usually mounted on handsome steeds, capable of performing "many surprising feats, which would grace an equestrian circus in any country, such, for instance, as picking up a dollar from the ground at every pass with the horse at full gallop." Even more impressive were the tricks they could perform with a *lazo* commonly made of horsehair or twisted sea grass "with a convenient noose at one end." As soon as the noose had been cast over the neck of a running horse, "the lazador fetches the end of his saddle, and by a quick manoeuvre the wildest horse is brought up to a stand." The same technique was employed with a runaway cow or ox, though a grown bull required the attentions of two *lazadors* to subdue it. While the *arrieros* and *vaqueros* were most skilled with the *lazo* all Mexicans were proficient in its use. As Gregg put it, "They acquire [the skill] from infancy; for it forms one of the principal rural sports of the children, who may daily be seen with their *lazitos,* noosing the dogs and chickens about the yards, in every direction." The *lazo* could also be used as a weapon and in skirmishes with the Indians a *vaquero* would often "throw this formidable object around the neck or body of the enemy," jerk him from his pony, and drag him along the ground until he was insensible or dead.

A Mexican marked his horse or mule "with a huge hieroglyphic brand," called his *fierro* or iron. When the animal was sold, it was marked with a *venta,* or sale brand, and Gregg noted that some frequently sold animals were covered with such a network of brands as to be undecipherable except by an expert.

The Mexican women especially caught the eye of American traders. Gregg described them as often possessing "striking traits of beauty" and "remarkable for small feet and handsome figures." They used a homemade suntan lotion to protect their complexions and gazed alluringly out from under large straw bonnets. The New Mexicans in general had, in Gregg's view, "inherited much of the cruelty and intolerance of their ancestors, and no small portion of their bigotry and fanaticism." They had "a highly imaginative temperament" (by no means a compliment) and "rather accommodating moral principles—cunning, loquacious, quick of perception and sycophantic. . . ." On the other hand Gregg found them remarkably generous to those in need and unfailingly courteous to visitors. "In their salutations," he added, "the ancient custom of close embrace, not only between individuals of the same sex, but between those of different sexes, is almost universal. It is quite a luxury to meet a pretty senorita after some absence."

The "marauding savages" were a very prominent part of the life of New Mexico. The Apache were famous for their horsemanship, for their daring raids and their cruelty. They had come to live, for the most part, on the cattle and sheep they stole from the ranchos and haciendas. Mules were reputed to be their favorite food and Gregg reported that the chiefs settled quarrels among warriors over possession of mules by killing all those in question. The Apache were the inveterate enemies, first of the Spanish, then, subsequently, of the Mexican government. In Gregg's words: "To such a pitch has the temerity of those savages reached, that small bands of three or four warriors have been known to make their appearance within a mile of the city of Chihuahua in open day, killing the laborers and driving off whole herds of mules and horses without the slightest opposition." By 1837 their raiding had become so daring and destructive that Mexican control over the entire province of New Mexico was threatened. The government reacted by putting a bounty on Apache scalps and dispatching government troops to try to exterminate the tribe. All such efforts merely made the Apache more vengeful and sanguinary, and it was not until after the Civil War, when the region was in American hands, that any serious check was put to their destructive raids. And that restraint was imposed only after a prolonged and bitter struggle.

The warlike Comanche augmented their ranks with young Mexicans captured in raids. "Strange as it may appear," Josiah Gregg wrote, "their captives frequently become attached to their masters and to the savage life, and with difficulty are induced to leave them after a few years' captivity. In fact these prisoners, it is said, in time often turn out to be the most formidable savages. Combining the subtlety of the Mexican with the barbarity of the Indian, they sometimes pilot into their native frontier and instigate horrid outrages." The Comanche, despite such periodic incursions, were on generally friendly terms with the New Mexicans. Famous horsemen in their own right, Josiah Gregg thought only the Mexican *vaqueros* and the Arabs could rival them. When they returned from a successful raid, the warriors and their chiefs would halt some distance from their village and send word ahead of their triumph. One of the "most respectable and aged matrons" of the tribe then came forward holding aloft a very long-handled lance to which the warriors fastened the scalps they had taken, "so arranged that each shall be conspicuous." The squaw then approached the wigwams "her scalp-garnish lance high in the air . . . chanting some favorite war-legend. She is soon joined by other squaws and Indian lasses, who dance around as the procession moves through the entire circuit of the village," to announce a celebration that might last for several days.

The Christianized Indians of New Mexico were known as Pueblos. Of the "wild tribes," the Navaho were the most numerous and the most "civilized." The Eutaws ranged as far north as the Yellowstone region. It was a Eutaw chief who had inspired Osburne Russell with such romantic reflections on Indian life.

Josiah Gregg estimated the number of Navaho in 1831 to be some 10,000. They were concentrated in the cordillera some hundred and fifty miles west of Santa Fe and they excelled in "original manufactures" in the making of silver jewelry and "a singular species of blanket, known as the *Sarape Navajo,* which is of so close and dense a texture that it will frequently hold water almost equal to gum-elastic cloth. It is therefore highly prized for protection against the rains." The Navaho cultivated all the grains and vegetables native to New Mexico and had large herds of sheep and goats to provide wool for their weaving; their horses and cattle were "celebrated as being much superior to those of the Mexicans; owing, no doubt to greater attention to the improvement of their stocks."

When Josiah Gregg left Santa Fe for Independence sixteen days later, his party consisted of twenty-three Americans and twelve Mexicans with seven wagons and two small fieldpieces. "The principal proprietors," Gregg wrote, "carried between them about $150,000 in specie and bullion, being for the most part the proceeds of the previous year's adventure."

Josiah Gregg took his last trading trip to Santa Fe in 1840. The next year he traded for mules in Texas and then traveled to Philadelphia to work on his book. There the ills and aches of civilization overtook him. He suffered severe headaches and lost his hair. A brief visit to New York increased his miseries and he was forced to take a "little jaunt" on the prairies to strengthen "the tone" of his stomach. At the University of Louisville he studied medicine and received an honorary degree.

At the end of *Commerce of the Prairies* Gregg had written a kind of epitaph for himself: "I have striven in vain to reconcile myself to the even tenor of civilized life in the United States; and have sought in its amusements and its society a substitute for those high excitements which have attached me so strongly to Prairie life." Yet not a day passed that he did not feel "a pang of regret that I am not now roving at large upon those western plains." As soon as New Mexico was in American hands, Gregg returned to his beloved Santa Fe. He spent much of his time botanizing, collecting more than seven hundred specimens of the Southwestern flora. Finally, attracted by news from the California goldfields, he headed for San Francisco. There, commissioned to search out a route between the Trinity River and San Francisco, the "old gentleman"—he was forty-three—fell from his horse and suffered a fatal injury.

22

John Charles Frémont

One of the indirect consequences of the Mexican War was the acquisition of California. We must therefore take account of an American adventurer whose name is indelibly associated with the establishment of the "Bear Republic." John Charles Frémont was the illegitimate son of Anne Beverely Whiting who, married to a man twice her age, ran off with a French painter of frescoes and portraits, Charles Fremon. John was born in Savannah, Georgia, in 1813. Five years later, Fremon died and Anne was left to provide as best she could for three small children. She settled in Charleston, South Carolina, where young John Frémont, as he preferred to spell his name, grew up. John was handsome, charming, bright, and ambitious. A patron paid for his education at a good preparatory school, where he distinguished himself by his academic brilliance and wild pranks. The principal of the school described him later, with the benefit of hindsight, as of "middle size, graceful in manners, rather slender, but well formed . . . of a keen, piercing eye and a noble forehead, seemingly the very seat of genius. . . . Whatsoever he read, he retained."

From school Frémont went on to Charleston College, where he distinguished himself similarly. Greek was one of his favorite studies and he immersed himself in Xenophon's *Anabasis,* a classic account of a military campaign against the Kurds. He also showed skill in mathematics and geometry. He was, however, rebellious and fickle in attendance, and the college dismissed him in his senior year for "habitual irregularity and incorrigible negligence." He later recalled that the two books which most influenced him were "a chronicle of men who had made themselves famous by brave and noble deeds" and a work on astronomy.

We would like to know more about Frémont's mother, Anne, who was to play, as did his wife Jessie, a central and continuing role in his life. It may have been through Anne that he acquired an important patron, Joel Poinsett, an ardent Democrat who had been appointed ambassador to Mexico by Jackson and went on to become Van Buren's secretary of war—and who, incidentally, gave his name to the flower.

Frémont's first important job was with the recently formed United States Topographical Corps as an assistant engineer, assigned to survey a projected railroad from Charleston to Cincinnati. He next served on a party that laid out the lands in Indian Territory for the Cherokee who were to be removed from South Carolina. But his real career began when he was appointed, apparently at Poinsett's behest, as an assistant to J. N. Nicollet to explore and map the area between the upper Mississippi and the Missouri. As secretary of war, Poinsett, who considered himself a disciple of Jefferson and Jackson in his preoccupation with the West, sponsored Nicollet's expedition. Nicollet was a French astronomer who had been trained at the Paris Observatory and immigrated to the United States in 1832. He was an experienced topographer and a pioneer in the use of the barometer to measure altitudes. Frémont learned a great deal from the Frenchman, who virtually adopted him. The Mississippi expedition was a success and Frémont subsequently assisted Nicollet in drafting his *Report Intended to Illustrate a Map of the Hydrographical Basin of the Upper Mississippi River,* which was published in 1843 and which has been called "one of the greatest contributions ever made to American geography."

The westward movement was a complex and many-faceted affair. On one level it took place as a kind of irresistible movement of people, of tough, independent individuals, of families, even of whole communities. On another level it took place in the minds of politicians, men like Thomas Hart Benton, John Floyd (the Democratic Congressman from Virginia and a relative of Mrs. Benton), Lewis Cass, all of whom, like Poinsett, considered themselves "disciples" of Jefferson. They were a closeknit group, tenacious and single-minded, and they drew support from individuals like John Jacob Astor, who had large investments in the fur trade. Frémont himself wrote of "Mr. Benton's unwearied interest in furthering knowledge of our Western possessions and bringing them into occupation." "The essential importance to the country of the great band of unoccupied territory which lay between the Mississippi and the Pacific coast," Frémont continued, "had been one of the chief subjects which Western members were endeavoring to force upon the early action of Congress. . . . Oregon was now coming to the forefront among political questions which were tending to embitter party politics."

The Long expedition to the Rockies in 1819–20 had been a keen disappointment from the political point of view because it reported very unfavorably on the prospects for the permanent settlement of the country that lay between the Missouri, the Arkansas, the Platte, and the Red rivers. Clearly it was important to have a more optimistic assessment of that vast region. A basic political rule is that if you want an optimistic report on some subject, you assign it to an optimist whose sentiments are known to be congenial to the positive side of the question. Poinsett was a loyal member of the Western lobby; indeed he shared its leadership with Benton. Through Poinsett, Benton came to know and like young Frémont. Poring over the Nicollet map, Benton realized the need for a similar work for the region to the south of the Missouri. He questioned Frémont about the requirements for such an expedition and Frémont wrote, "The interview left on me a profound impression and raised excited interest. . . . The thought of penetrating into the recesses of that wilderness region filled me with enthusiasm—I saw visions. . . . It would be travel over a part of the world which still remained the New—the opening up of unknown lands; the making unknown countries known; and study without books—the learning at first hand from Nature herself. . . ." Benton's house became the headquarters of the "Western members." Here they talked excitedly and extravagantly of their schemes, "and in this way measures were conceived and perfected which, by the strength behind them, carried their own fulfillment," Frémont wrote.

Two other developments were largely to determine the course of Frémont's career. His mentor, Nicollet, fell ill and clearly could not undertake such a demanding expedition. Among the hours spent in the Benton home discussing plans for the West, Frémont found some time to devote to Benton's second daughter, Jessie, "just in the bloom of her girlish beauty and perfect health." Soon he was infatuated with the pretty, animated young woman. Clearly she was no butterfly. As Fremont wrote of her years after, "she had inherited from her father his grasp of mind, comprehending with a tenacious memory; but with it a quickness of perception and instant realization of subjects and scenes in their complete extent which did not belong to his; and with these . . . tenderness and sensibility that made a feeling take the place of mind." She was only sixteen but she was as ambitious as her suitor and mature beyond her years. Mrs. Benton demurred and a year's "probation" was agreed upon but history hurried the young couple along. Benton was impatient for the topographical expedition to begin, but Nicollet was too ill to lead it. Frémont was the obvious replacement. His marriage to Jessie took place before he embarked in 1842. "This expedition," Frémont wrote, "was intended to be 'auxiliary and in aid to the emigration to the Lower Columbia'; it was to indicate and describe the line of travel, and the best positions for military posts; and to describe, and fix in position, the South Pass in the Rocky Mountains, at which this initial expedition was to terminate. At this time the South Pass, at the head of the Platte River, was the one most available for emigration, and already used. . . . The object of this expedition was not merely a survey; beyond that was its bearing on the holding of our territory on the Pacific; and the contingencies it involved were large."

Frémont set about gathering equipment for his expedition. He also designed and had built "an india-rubber boat with airtight compartments to be used in crossing or examining watercourses." His most valuable acquisition was a self-effacing German astronomer and topographer, Charles Preuss.

At St. Louis Frémont's way was paved by the aid of Benton's favorite niece. There, with the assistance of the ever helpful Chouteaus—Pierre and Auguste, grown rich in the fur trade —Frémont recruited twenty-one men, most of them Canadian fur trappers—L'Espérance, Lefevre, Gouin, Lajeunesse, Chardonnais, and Kit Carson. Carson and Preuss were to be involved with most of Frémont's adventures over the next decade. Also on the expedition were a great-nephew of Benton and Benton's twelve-year-old son, Randolph. The route that Frémont followed was by now a well-traveled one, but he and Preuss were assiduous in their observations and Frémont kept detailed notes from which he composed an attractive narrative of his expedition up the Platte to Fort Laramie and from there to the Wind River Mountains.

At Fort Laramie Frémont discovered that the Cheyenne and the Sioux were rebelling against the intrusion of white emigrants into their hunting range. They had recently attacked one party of emigrants, killed four whites, and driven off a number of horses and oxen and were now on the trail of a party guided by Thomas Fitzpatrick, Jedediah Smith's partner and the discoverer of the South Pass. Carson and Bridger both advised Frémont against pushing on, and word came from a council of Indians that Frémont and his party would be fired on. Frémont sought a parley. "We are soldiers of the great chief, your father," Frémont declared at the powwow. "He has told us to come here and see this country, and all the Indians, his children. . . . Before we came we heard that you had killed his people, and ceased to be his children; but we came among you peaceably, holding out our hands. Now we find that . . . you are no longer his friends and children. We have thrown away our bodies, and will not turn back. . . . We are few, and you are many, and may kill us all; but there will be much crying in your villages, for many of your young men will stay behind, and forget to return with your warriors from the mountains. Do you think that our great chief will let his soldiers die and forget to cover their graves? Before the snows melt again, his warriors will sweep away your villages as the fire does the prairie in the autumn." Not surprisingly the Indians were daunted by Frémont's assurance. They agreed to allow his party to pass.

At the South Pass Frémont and Preuss made detailed observations, carefully noting the altitude of various mountains, and producing the most accurate map of the region yet drafted. Back in St. Louis, where his bride awaited him, Frémont turned over his notes and journals to Jessie, who became his amanuensis, his editor, and perhaps even his "ghost," putting his manuscript into the form of a book. All the objects of his expedition had been accomplished, "in a way to be beneficial to science and instructive to the general reader as well as useful to the Government," Lewis Linn, Benton's fellow senator from Missouri, declared. Frémont's report, in the senator's view, "proves conclusively that the country for several hundred miles from the frontier of Missouri is exceedingly beautiful and fertile, alternate woodland and prairie, and certain portions well supplied with water. It also proves that the valley of the River Platte has a very rich soil, affording great facilities for emigrants to the west of the Rocky Mountains." To Linn and Benton it followed that settlement should be pushed aggressively.

Benton and the Western lobby used their considerable influence to arrange for a second Frémont expedition. The Oregon question was still up in the air, a dangerous bone of contention with Great Britain, and Frémont was hurried off in 1843 with instructions to go by way of the Arkansas, through South Pass, to Salt Lake and explore it and its environs.

Frémont took much the same party on his second expedition with the addition of Thomas Fitzpatrick as a guide, some ten additional trappers, two Delaware, and a howitzer to discourage the Indians. While Frémont was making his final preparations he received a message from Jessie urging him to depart as quickly as possible. Back in St. Louis at the end of his expedition he discovered why. Jessie had intercepted a letter from the head of the Corps of Engineers instructing Frémont to come to Washington to explain why he needed a howitzer to a make a topographical survey. If the motive of the Western lobby in dispatching him was primarily political, the effort to prevent him from undertaking the mission was undoubtedly also political. Instead of sending the letter on to her husband, Jessie, in a characteristic act, kept the order and replied that her husband was already beyond reach.

Reaching the Great Salt Lake, Frémont and his party passed up the Snake to the Columbia and along what was already being called the Oregon Trail to Vancouver and the post of the Hudson's Bay Company; there they were greeted cordially by Dr. McLoughlin, who had extended such generous hospitality to Jedediah Smith when he had arrived there fifteen years earlier, rather more dead than alive. Frémont found "many American emigrants at the fort; others had already crossed the river into their land of promise—the Willamette Valley."

Although McLoughlin warned Frémont of the hazards of attempting a return trip during the winter months, Frémont was determined to start back, turning south and searching for a pass through the Sierra Nevada. "This was our projected line of return," he wrote, "a great part of it absolutely new to geographical, botanical, and geological science—and the subject of reports in relation to lakes, rivers, deserts, and savages, hardly above the condition of mere wild animals, which inflamed [my] desire to know what this terra incognita really contained."

Frémont's winter trip was a dangerous, not to say reckless, venture. That he and his men survived was something of a miracle and striking testimony to his skill and enterprise as a leader. Beating their way through trackless forests, the members of the little band had to cope with subzero temperatures, lack of fodder for their mules and horses, snow drifts sometimes forty feet high, as well as hostile Indians. Working their way laboriously southward as far as the present-day Oregon-California border, they then turned back and found a passage through the upper end of the Sierras at Grant's Pass. They pushed on to the western edge of Nevada and again south once more, searching for a pass back across the Sierras into the Sacramento Valley. The way forward was often so difficult and dangerous that Frémont adopted the practice of not leaving one camp site until another suitable one had been found within a day's travel. In this way he inched along, constantly ranging ahead with Carson and another experienced mountain man, the French-Canadian trapper Alexis Godey. Frémont's most remarkable achievement was getting his party across a ten-thousand-foot-high pass over the Sierras to Sutter's Fort. Any faltering or bad decision would have meant disaster for the entire party. The presence of Carson and Fitzpatrick was doubtless an essential factor but it was, after all, Frémont who had recruited them and preserved their allegiance.

All this must be said because many of Frémont's subsequent actions were reckless and self-serving. He was, to a degree, a "political" explorer and it might be said that he who lives by politics shall die by them. When Frémont became a controversial political figure, his enemies undertook to discredit him. Not confining their attacks to those areas in which he was legitimately vulnerable, they attempted to strip him of credit for those achievements on which his fame and his political fortunes rested by saying that he explored no new territory and simply exploited the knowledge of the mountain men he recruited to accompany him. An unfairer charge could hardly have been made. Pompous, intensely ambitious, egotistical, and sometimes inclined to pull a long bow, Frémont was a conscientious and dedicated engineer and topographer, if not a brilliant one, and a courageous leader.

Having reached Sutter's Fort, Frémont turned south along the San Joaquin Valley. "Our cavalcade made a strange and grotesque appearance," Frémont wrote, "and it was impossible to avoid reflecting upon our position and composition in this remote solitude . . . still forced on south by a desert on one hand and a mountain range on the other; guided by a civilized Indian, attended by two wild ones from the sierra, a Chinook from the Columbia; and our own mixture of American, French, German—all armed; four of five languages heard at once; above a hundred horses and mules, half-wild; American, Spanish and Indians dresses and equipments intermingled—such was our composition."

Turning east by the so-called Spanish trail, a variation of the one by which Jedediah Smith had found his way into the San Bernardino Valley, Frémont and his men were constantly harassed by the Indians. Baptiste Tabeau, the French-Canadian half-breed who had been with Frémont on his first expedition, was ambushed and killed by Mohave Indians, a severe loss to the party.

At the oasis of Vegas de Santa Clara the party had a brief respite. Leaving there they encountered Joseph Walker, a frontier explorer and guide as famous as Fitzpatrick or Jedediah Smith. Walker had been the first man to cross the pass over the Sierras which bears his name and was perpetually hatching plans for extravagant and often illegal ventures. He belonged to that breed of frontiersmen who shot Indians on sight for the mere pleasure of exterminating them. It was said that he and a group of trappers under his leadership had shot and scalped twenty-one unaggressive Indians in a single episode. Walker gave Frémont valuable directions and some days later the party found themselves at Utah Lake. Frémont calculated that in eight months he and his men had made a circuit of 3,500 miles. Most important, Frémont had covered a substantial part of the Great Basin, given it its name, and described its physical character more completely than any predecessor. "The whole idea of such a desert," he wrote, "and such a people [the primitive "Digger" Indians of the region], is a novelty in our country, and excites Asiatic, not American, ideas. Interior basins, with their own systems of lakes and river, and often sterile, are common enough in Asia; people still in the elementary state of families, living in deserts, with no other occupation than the mere animal search for food, may still be seen in that ancient quarter of the globe; but in America such things are new and strange, unknown and unsuspected, and discredited when related."

As for the Northwest Coast, its value "commercially . . . must be great, washed as it is by the . . . Pacific Ocean; fronting Asia; producing many of the elements of commerce; mild and healthy in its climate; and becoming, as it naturally will, a thoroughfare for the East India and China trade." This was the kind of talk his father-in-law wished to hear.

Back in Washington in the fall of 1844, Frémont received an enthusiastic welcome from the Western lobby. Frémont took with him to Washington the Chinook Indian, who was called simply Chinook. There he had an audience with the new secretary of war, William Wilkins. The expansionist Polk would soon replace the cautious Tyler as president. There was abundant evidence that Texas would be annexed to the United States and a strong possibility that war with Mexico would result. In that case, California and New Mexico would be up for grabs and among the grabbers might be Great Britain, still clinging doggedly to her foothold in the Oregon country. Real or imaginary, this threat must be forestalled at all costs. The American "presence" in California must be discreetly augmented in any way possible. One obvious way was to dispatch eager young Frémont once more. Frémont had, indeed, become something of a public figure with his good looks, his flair for self-promotion, his influential sponsors. His lucid and interesting *Report* on his trip as Nicollet's assistant had been published and very favorably reviewed. General Scott promoted him to captain and praised him in a special order—"for gallant and highly meritorious services in two expeditions commanded by him."

When Polk was inaugurated, Frémont visited him with Benton. It was not an entirely successful meeting. Polk was disconcerted by Frémont's youth. Frémont spoke rhapsodically about California, "its delightful climate and uncommon beauty of surface . . . and its grand commercial position," and the President said something about the "impulsiveness of young men." Daniel Webster was much more openly skeptical. To him California was simply "a strip of sandy land along the Pacific Ocean with here and there an oasis of fertile soil; offering no inducements for us except the fine harbors indented upon its coast." That would be a New Englander's view of the matter—harbors and ports were all that mattered to them. Webster was convinced that England would never let California pass into American hands.

Frémont was well aware, of course, of the new President's ambitions. George Bancroft, secretary of the navy, the first three volumes of whose *History of the United States* had won enthusiastic acclaim, and James Buchanan, the secretary of state, were convinced that Mexico could not retain possession of California, which had already given indications of strong separatist tendencies. The only question was, Into whose lap would this particularly luscious plum drop? Frémont's future seemed assured. In his own words, "As chairman of the Committee on Military Affairs, [Senator Benton] was the center of information and conference."

Already a third expedition was being planned. "This was the situation," Benton wrote. "Texas was gone and California was breaking off by reason of distance; the now increasing American emigration was sure to seek its better climate. Oregon was still in dispute. . . ."

For the third expedition, as for the others, a varied crew was assembled that included twelve Delaware Indians; Edward Kern, a topographer and artist; and an assortment of Benton relatives. Frémont hired Fitzpatrick once more as a guide when he reached Bent's Fort on the Arkansas. Swinging by Kit Carson's spread on the Cimarron River, he found him "starting the congenial work of making up a stock ranch," but Carson cheerfully sold out, prevailed on his partner, Richard Owens, to accompany him, and signed on once more with Frémont. The party now consisted of sixty men, all experienced frontiersmen. They headed for the Oregon Trail, passed Fort Laramie, the South Pass, the Great Salt Lake, the Salt Desert, along the Humboldt to the Truckee and over the Sierras to Sutter's Fort in 1845. There Sutter told Frémont that the Mexican officials, having heard of his earlier expedition, had expressed a concern which Sutter tried to allay by assuring them that Frémont had been engaged in a geographical survey of the interior and had been forced to pass over into California in search of food. Frémont now began a leisurely journey back down the familiar San Joaquin Valley. His casual pace seemed to indicate that he was simply waiting for the next act in the California drama to begin. In the Santa Clara Valley he visited the ranch and hacienda of Don Antonio Sunol. From there he rode to Monterey and went directly to the merchant who acted as United States consul, Thomas Larkin. He asked Larkin to help him obtain the permission of Governor Pio Pico to equip and supply his men. The governor, it turned out, was in Los Angeles and Frémont applied to General José Castro for permission to refit his party, saying that he was a captain in the United States Army Corps of Engineers and engaged in surveying "the nearest route from the United States to the Pacific Ocean."

Instead of equipping his party and decamping, Frémont established a base at the William Fisher ranch, thirteen miles from San Jose. Here he held court, receiving Californians who visited his camp, engaging in horse races and shooting matches, and marveling at the vaqueros' horsemanship. He crossed the mountains from San Jose to the little mission town of Santa Cruz, where he saw the huge coastal redwood trees along the San Lorenzo River. He went through Gavilan Pass to the Hartnell Ranch and explored the Salinas Valley. There he was overtaken by a Mexican cavalry officer with a message from General Castro ordering him to leave California at once. Castro had undoubtedly heard that Frémont was making himself at home in a manner that was clearly unrelated to "finding the nearest route from the United States to the Pacific Ocean." Pico and Castro must have guessed that the uninvited guest was stalling for time. Frémont expressed "to the envoy my astonishment at General Castro's breach of good faith" and announced that he must refuse "compliance to an order insulting to my government and myself." He and his men then proceeded to build a small stockade near Gavilan Peak and raised over it the American flag. From their fortress they could see the Mission of San Juan, where Castro was gathering a force to attack them. After three days of defiance, Frémont packed up his camp and headed slowly north to the Shasta country, noting the wild life and vegetation of the Sacramento River Valley. It was in the vicinity of Mt. Shasta that a young naval officer named Gillespie overtook Frémont with important dispatches and an oral message. Nobody knows what message Gillespie had for Frémont. Gillespie died soon afterwards and Frémont was always coy. In his *Memoirs* he wrote, "The information received through Gillespie . . . absolved me from my duty as an explorer [which it must be said, parenthetically, he had given little attention to], and I was left to my duty as an officer of the American Army, with the further authoritative knowledge that the government intended to take California." Frémont's later summary of Gillespie's message was: "The time has come. England must not get a foothold. We must be first. Act discreetly, but positively . . . I saw the way opening clear before me. War with Mexico was inevitable; and a grand opportunity now presented itself to realize to their fullest extent the farsighted views of Senator Benton, and make the Pacific Ocean the western boundary of the United States."

Frémont's explorers had become soldiers. He headed for Sacramento to augment his small army with "foreigners," American emigrants who had settled in the area. There he began that period of his career which was to make him within a decade a candidate for president of the United States and cast a cloud over his ultimate reputation.

23

The Taking of California

Americans were an articulate people. Talking and writing came as naturally to them as breathing. It thus sometimes seems that every American who made his way across the endless reaches of the continent to the west coast wrote about his or her experiences. Certainly there was a vast tide of literature and an apparently endless supply of readers. Some of the works were simply forerunners of the ubiquitous how-to-do-it books that are the stock-in-trade of many publishers today. They were intended to inform migratory Americans of "how to" get from the Mississippi Valley to the mouth of the Columbia River. The advice they gave was often erroneous or misleading and always inadequate.

Edwin Bryant's *Journal of a Tour by the Emigrant Route and South Pass, Across the Continent of North America, the Great Desert Basin, and Through California* was a substantial cut above most such narratives, though it must be said that as a genre the genuine narratives (as distinguished from the quickie how-to's) made a body of fascinating, if often repetitive literature. Bryant, whose book had the catchy lead title *What I Saw in California*, quoted Dryden under his title: "All of which I saw, and part of which I was." Bryant and two traveling companions left Independence, Missouri, on the first day of May, 1846. Eighteen years had passed since Jedediah Smith and his party had returned from their fearful passage through the South Pass, down the Virgin and Colorado rivers, across the Mohave Desert to the Mission San Gabriel, but already thousands of Americans had passed through the South Pass, the great majority of them, to be sure, turning north along the Snake to Oregon Territory. We are already familiar with Independence as the supply and jumping-off point for the Yellowstone–Green River fur trade and the head of the Santa Fe trade. Now it was, increasingly, the staging area for settlers headed for the Pacific West. Its population numbered approximately one thousand men and women, largely occupied in supplying travelers, trappers, and traders. "Every man," Bryant noted, "seems to be actively and profitably employed." The transient population of the town was almost as large as the permanent residents and far more picturesque: New Mexicans in sombreros and serapes "on miserably poor mules or horses," half-breed Indians, and, hardly distinguishable from them, and indeed the same in many instances, trappers and hunters (the latter employed to hunt game for trains, or, as Josiah Gregg preferred to call them, caravans). Oxen had largely replaced mules in drawing wagons by 1846 and "huge tented-wagons" such as those used in the Santa Fe trade drawn by as many as ten or fifteen yoke of oxen were a common sight. With the appearance of wagons had come teamsters, tough, blasphemous men, who constantly cracked their long whips, the symbol of their trade, and shouted exhortations at their oxen or mules. Bryant and his friends bought three yoke of young oxen for $21.67 per yoke and a small wagon and hired a man "who had spent sometime in the Rocky Mountains as a servant of the trading and trapping companies, for our driver and cook."

Like travelers and traders headed for Santa Fe, the individuals and families setting out for California or Oregon must go in a train for protection from the Indians, so a party of sometimes as many as a hundred or more wagons must be assembled before any could depart. On the eve of the departure of the train to which Bryant and his friends had attached themselves, the Masonic Lodges of Independence celebrated the departure of those among the emigrants and traders who were Masons by "a public procession and an address, with other religious exercises." Bryant felt that the speakers were rather too ready to consign them all to desert graves. The ladies present wept, which was equally unnerving, and fearsome rumors spread through the town. Word was that five thousand Mormons, armed to the teeth and swearing hostility to all Gentiles, were on the trail ahead of them. Another was that five English agents had left Independence with the purpose of stirring up the Indian tribes along the way and thereby preventing the emigrants headed for Oregon (still claimed by the British) from arriving there.

Nonetheless the train started off and was soon overtaken by a violent rainstorm. The wagon of Bryant and his friends was filled with comforts and conveniences that the three travelers had been persuaded to buy, but everything had been indifferently packed and when they made their first camp they discovered that they had to move innumerable boxes and chests to reach their cooking and eating utensils and their food. In addition, "sundry pots, skillets and frying pans" which they had ordered and paid for were missing.

So day by day, the emigrant train shook down and learned by that exacting master, experience, how to survive on the trail. Bryant was enraptured by the country that stretched out before them to the horizon, an "illimitable succession of green undulations and flowery slopes . . . stretching away and away, until they fade from the sight . . . creating a wild and scarcely controllable ecstacy of admiration." Much of Bryant's journal was taken up with such effusions. "It would seem," he wrote typically on viewing some new prospect, "as if here the Almighty had erected a finished abode for his rational creatures and ornamented it with beauties of landscape and exuberance and variety of production far above our feeble conceptions or efforts at imitation." All along the way to Council Bluffs, where the train would be properly formed for its journey through Indian country, Bryant met entire families headed for California or Oregon. A Mr. West, seventy-five years of age, and his seventy-year-old wife were accompanying their daughter and her family to California in a party that included ten wagons. Emigrants from Missouri commonly stated that they were emigrating for reasons of health. During the summer and autumn they suffered from "ague and fever" (malaria) and in the winter pneumonia and flu. "They emigrated to the Pacific," Bryant noted, "in search of health, and if they can find this with a reasonable fertility of soil on their arrival, they will not only be satisfied but feel thankful to Providence for providing them such a retreat from the miseries they have endured."

Michigan, Virginia, and Kentucky were well represented among the emigrants. At Council Bluffs the process of electing a captain and lieutenants that Josiah Gregg has already described for us was carried out, and Bryant wrote of the "cheerful appearance" of the prairie "enlivened with groups of cattle numbering six or seven hundred, feeding upon the fresh green grass. The numerous white tents and wagon-covers before which the camp-fires are blazing . . . and men, women, and children . . . talking, playing, and singing around them with all the glee of light and careless hearts." Hymns and religious songs were special favorites with the emigrants, some of whom dwelt on the analogy between their journey and that of the Hebrews into the land of Canaan.

A Colonel Russell from Virginia was chosen captain of the train and former Governor Boggs of Missouri chairman of a committee to "draft rules or laws for the government of the party during their journey." Sixty-three wagons made up the train, 119 men and 59 women with 110 children and 58,000 pounds of flour, 38,000 of bacon, a thousand pounds of powder and 2,557 of lead, 700 head of cattle, and some 150 horses. To this point the trails taken by the Santa Fe traders and those of the emigrants to California and Oregon coincided, and a week or so out of Council Bluffs the emigrants passed a train for Santa Fe driving a thousand or so gaunt mules ahead of them. Bryant talked to one of the traders whom he found "intelligent, notwithstanding his soiled and ragged costume. . . ." His words were sobering. The journey to Santa Fe and Chihuahua was "one of great fatigue and hardship . . . but that the journey to California was infinitely more so; that our lives would be shortened ten years by the trip."

They soon encountered Indians in small parties, often a man and his wife. Two Sioux, dressed in white men's garb, rode into camp but were sullen and uncommunicative. A Potawatomi, wearing a calico shirt and buckskin trousers, appeared with moccasins to trade and several members of the same tribe rode up to try to trade for whiskey, the only white word they knew. They were a miserable, half-starved band who, in Bryant's words, "excited mingled emotions of loathing and commiseration." The next Indian visitor was chief of the Kansa tribe with two squaws and two warriors. The chief wore a medal around his neck on a buckskin string with the likeness of "Thomas Jefferson, President of the United States." "They came around us while eating supper, and begged something to eat, which we gave them. Their appearance was extremely wretched," Bryant noted.

As the train advanced, the hardships and stresses of the trip affected men's tempers and there were frequent instances of "petulance, incivility, and the want of a spirit of accommodation . . . wrangling and intrigue." Now many of the oxen began to falter. On one long day's travel without water, several collapsed, unable to proceed, and one died. When the train finally came to a stream a number of the beasts, "mad with thirst and heat," rushed into the river despite the efforts of their drivers to stop them. On the Kansas River they passed a Methodist mission, "an establishment for the education and christianization of the Indians, supported in part by the United States government." There was a blacksmith's shop at the mission and "an extensive farm under cultivation."

Seventeen wagons broke off from the train near the Kansas River to strike out on their own and a few days later nine wagons from Illinois joined forces with the Bryant contingent. The villages of the Kansa Indians that they passed varied widely in their character. One village contained fourteen lodges—which varied in their dimensions from twenty to thirty-six feet in length by fifteen feet wide—made of hickory saplings bent to form a roof eight or ten feet high interwoven with willow twigs and shingled with strips of linden bark about twelve inches wide and four or five feet long. "The bark-walls, on the outside were ornamented with numerous charcoal sketches, representing horses with men mounted upon them, and engaged in combat with bow and arrow. . . . There were various other figures of beast and reptiles . . . all done in a style so crude, as to show no great progress in the fine arts." Camping near a much larger village containing some hundred lodges, the travelers found themselves inundated by four or five hundred Indians. The hair of the braves was long and matted, the heads of the warriors were "shorn close to the skin, except a tuft extending from the forehead over the crown of the head down to the neck, resembling the comb of a cock," the scalp lock. "The faces of many," Bryant noted, "were rouged,—some in a fanciful manner, with vermillion. The eyelids and lips only, of several, were painted; the cheeks and ears of others, and the forehead and nose of others. There appeared to be a great variety of tastes and no prevailing fashion." Many of the men had holes in their ears "from which were suspended a variety of ornaments made of bone, tin, and brass. . . . Bread, meat, tobacco, and whiskey, they continually asked for. . . ." The Pawnee, Bryant learned, had recently raided the Kansa, killed a number of them, and burned a village.

Bryant's attitude toward the Indians that the train encountered was typical of the more enlightened of his fellow travelers. "This fair and extensive domain is peopled by a few wandering, half-naked, half-starved Indians," he wrote, "who have not the smallest appreciation of the great natural wealth of the country over which they roam in quest of such small game as now remains, to keep themselves from absolute famine. Having destroyed or driven further west all the vast herds of deer, elk and buffalo which once subsisted here upon the rank and nutritious vegetation, they are now starving and have turned pensioners upon the government of the United States, and beggars of the emigrants passing west, for clothing and food." Bryant then added a significant sentence: "Beautiful as the country is, the silence and desolation reigning over it excite irrepressible emotions of sadness and melancholy." Only a week or so earlier he had written of "an ecstacy of admiration" too powerful to express. Now he felt overcome by quite different emotions. Perhaps it was the growing distance from "civilization." Certainly there were unsettling developments in the train itself.

Many of the emigrants seemed disposed to dawdle along the way, slow to get going in the morning, anxious to make camp early in the afternoon as though they had no notion of the danger of being caught on the trail by the advent of winter snow and ice. They balked at the efforts of Colonel Russell to keep them moving, until he was ready to abandon his thankless job. Finally, he issued an edict. Either the laws and regulations adopted by the train must be faithfully and cheerfully observed or he would resign. "We are now a pure democracy," Bryant wrote. "All laws are proposed directly to the assembly, and are enacted or rejected by a majority. . . . These matters," he added, "I describe with some minuteness, because they illustrate emigrant life while on the road to the Pacific, where no law prevails except their will. So thoroughly, however, are our people imbued with conservative republican principles, and so accustomed are they to order and propriety of deportment, that with a fair understanding, a majority will always be found on the side of right, and opposed to disorganization. 'Our glorious constitution,' is their motto and their model, and they will sanction nothing in derogation of the principles of the American constitution and American justice." Nonetheless it was a slow and often laborious process. What was perhaps most remarkable about it was that, given the strains and stresses that the train was subject to, the process worked as well as it did. As Bryant put it, "the pugnacious and belligerent propensities of men display themselves on these prairie excursions for slight causes and provocations, the perpetual vexations and hardships are well calculated to keep the nerves in a state of great irritability."

That Bryant was much taken with the Great Plains is abundantly evident. The only drawback he could see was the lack of timber. "It possesses such natural wealth and beauties," he wrote, "that at some future day it will be the Eden of America. When that epoch arrives, he who is then so fortunate as to be a traveller along this route, may stand upon one of the high undulations, and take in at a single glance a hundred, perhaps a thousand villas and cottages, with their stately parks, blooming gardens and pleasure-grounds." But in this Eden, oxen dropped from hunger and exhaustion and two children died and were buried in lonely graves.

Two weeks out of Council Bluffs the train passed four trappers returning from the Rocky Mountains accompanied by a party of Delaware Indians. The trappers told the emigrants that there were large herds of buffalo ahead. "The costume of these men was *outré* surpassing description," Bryant noted.

Now they moved along the Platte River in the territory of the feared Pawnee who, like the Apache, lived by stealing horses and cattle from emigrants. On the banks of the Platte they met another party of trappers in bullboats, led by a man named Boudreaux from St. Charles, Missouri. "The whole party," Bryant wrote, "presented a half-civilized and half-savage appearance in their dress and manners. The Americans were all well formed, athletic, and hardy young men, with that daring, resolute, and intelligent expression of countenance which generally characterizes the trappers, hunters, and traders of the mountains."

At the South Fork of the Platte they encountered five men on their way from Oregon who informed them that they had counted a total of 470 wagons headed west, about half of them destined for Oregon, the rest for California. Now the emigrants were in buffalo country and they were able to supplement their corn bread and bacon with buffalo steaks secured by their hunters. By the end of June, the train was approaching the Wind River Mountains and Bryant wrote that the peaks and hills had the appearance "of the desolate and deserted ruins of vast cities, to which Nineveh, Thebes, and Babylon were pigmies in grandeur and magnificence."

Fort Laramie was surrounded by seven or eight lodges of the Sioux come to trade. The Sioux were in striking contrast to the unhappy Kansa. Bryant found the Sioux women "decidedly beautiful. . . . Their feet are small and exquisitely formed. . . . The men are powerfully made, and possess a masculine beauty which I have never seen excelled. Conscious of their superior strength . . . they are arrogant and exacting towards their more feeble neighbors; and have thus acquired a reputation for cruelty and duplicity."

Just before sunset the Indians and some of the hunters in the emigrant train had a shooting match "in which bow and arrow, rifle and pistol were introduced." The Colt revolving pistol, with which some of the travelers were armed, astonished and alarmed the Indians. Next morning the Sioux broke camp and set off while the enthralled emigrants watched. They appeared to Bryant to be divided into "numerous parties, at the head of each of which was a beautiful young female gorgeously decorated, mounted on a prancing fat Indian horse, and bearing in her hand a delicate staff or pole, about ten feet in length, from the point of which were suspended . . . brilliant feathers and natural flowers of various colors." The chiefs, in their finest regalia, followed and after them the women and children and pack animals with the warriors bringing up the rear. Thus splendidly caparisoned, they were off to raid the Snake and Crows. Two chiefs had recently returned from a foray against the Pawnee, bearing twenty-five scalps and a number of horses.

On the Fourth of July, the day was given over to celebration. The Declaration of Independence was read and "a collation was then served up by the ladies of the encampment, at the conclusion of which, toasts suitable to the patriotic occasion were given and drunk with much enthusiasm. . . ."

Four days later on the banks of the Sweetwater, approaching South Pass, the party saw Independence Rock, a hundred feet high and a mile or more in circumference, with several thousand names painted and carved on it by emigrants headed for Oregon. There were several deaths in the train during July and on the eleventh of the month Bryant noted that they had passed eight or ten dead oxen belonging to a party ahead of them on the trail. Near Fort Bridger —"two or three miserable log-cabins, rudely constructed"—Bryant met the famous Joseph Walker, the first man to cross the Sierras from the east. Walker was on his way back from California, where he had served as a guide to Frémont, and he and his men were herding five hundred horses which they intended to sell at St. Louis.

At Fort Bernard Bryant and his wagon mates took stock of their situation. The season for traveling was now more than half over and, judging from the slow progress of the train, it was evident to Bryant and his friends that their wagon had little or no chance of making it to California. They thus decided to trade it and those oxen who had not died on the trail for seven pack mules and saddles. Abandoning those items of their equipment that they could not sell, they packed the most essential articles on the mules, mounted themselves, and left the train to make its way as best it could.

From the Great Salt Lake, they turned northwest. Before them was an "appalling field of sullen and hoary desolation. It was a scene so entirely new to us, so frightfully forbidding and unearthly in its aspects, that all of us . . . felt a slight shudder of apprehension." Teased by mirages and other optical illusions, the little party traveled for seventeen hours and covered over seventy-five miles before they found a water hole. So it was, day after day, hurrying from one stream or spring to next, searching perpetually for some sign of a pass to the west through the mountains. When Bryant's party met a band of white men from Oregon who had been searching for a passage for emigrant trains headed for Oregon via Salt Lake, Bryant was moved to remark that while the federal government, anxious to establish its claim to the Oregon Territory, "had appropriated large sums of money" to try to discover a suitable route to the Northwest, all "of practical utility" had "resulted from the indomitable energy, that bold daring, and the unconquerable enterprise, in opposition to every discouragement, privation, and danger, of our hardy frontier men and pioneers, unaided directly or remotely by the patronage or even the approving smiles and commendations of the government."

By August 20 Bryant's little party reached the Truckee River on the eastern slope of the Sierras. Here they saw the welcome sight of "a line of willows, grass and other green herbage, and a number of *tall* trees," the first such sight in some five hundred miles. The hot and thirsty travelers rushed into the river to drink "copious draughts" of the clear water and cool themselves and their mules. As they made their way up the pass that Captain Walker and Frémont had traversed a few years earlier, Bryant was entranced with the scenery. He was convinced that even the Alps, "so celebrated in history," could not "present scenery more wild, more rugged, more grand, more romantic, and more enchantingly picturesque and beautiful. . . ."

A week later they were at the edge of the Sacramento Valley on Bear Creek. There they found the house of a Mr. Johnson, a simple adobe and log structure. The proprietor was away hunting and the party made camp nearby and prevailed upon an Indian boy to milk one of Johnson's cows and bring them a bucket of milk. When he returned, Johnson, "originally a New England sailor," told them that General Taylor had defeated the Mexicans in four bloody battles and that the whole of "Upper California" was in the hands of the Americans. From Johnson they received a copy of the first paper published in California—*The Californian*, printed and edited at Monterey. It was some two weeks old and the leading article called upon the people of California to form a territorial government, "with a view to immediate annexation to the United States." "This seemed and sounded odd," Bryant wrote. "We have been traveling in as straight a line as we could, crossing rivers, mountains, and deserts, nearly four months beyond the bounds of civilization . . . but here, on the remotest confines of the world as it were, where we expected to visit and explore a foreign country, we found ourselves under American authority, and about to be 'annexed' to the American Union. Events such as this are very remarkable, and are well calculated to excite the pride and vanity, if they do not always tally with the reason and judgment, of American citizens and republicans."

Now deer and antelope were abundant. The travelers saw huge herds of cattle and, as Jedediah Smith before them, large numbers of wild horses. Crossing the Rio de los Americanos, they arrived at Sutter's Fort. At the entrance to the fort were two Indian sentinels and sitting near them two Americans in buckskin trousers and blue sailors' shirts with white stars on the collars. Captain Sutter soon appeared and told Bryant that the fort had been taken over by a detachment of United States sailors and was thus no longer under his command, but he gave the party a generous quota of meat, salt, melons, onions, and tomatoes from his own garden. That evening Bryant reflected in his journal on the fact that the party, nine in all, had traveled from Fort Laramie to Sutter's Fort, a distance of almost 1,700 miles, "over trackless and barren deserts, almost impassable mountains, through tribes of savage Indians, encountering necessarily many difficulties and enduring great hardships and privations. . . ." Most important of all they had had no quarrels with the Indians. "We uniformly respected their feelings and their rights," Bryant wrote, "and they respected us."

One group of emigrants, made up of the Reed and Donner families, arriving late in the season at the foothills of the Sierras, had searched for several weeks for an alternate route to California. It was a delay that proved fatal in its consequences. When the party arrived at the entrance to Walker's Pass, they found that an early snow had made it impassable. They built crude cabins and one of the party set out to try to get help. When word of their plight reached San Francisco a public meeting was held and $1,500 raised to send a party to the relief of the emigrants. Sutter had already dispatched, at his own expense, a relief party loaded with provisions. On December 16 eight men and five women from the Donner party started out on snowshoes to try to find their way through the mountain with the aid of the two Indians from Sutter's Fort. The party, overtaken by a storm, made a crude shelter out of their blankets and thus kept themselves from freezing to death. But they had no food and one after another died, the survivors deciding to try to preserve their lives by eating portions of the dead. When the storm subsided, those who remained alive pushed on. Each day brought down one or two more of the survivors. Finally one man reached the settlement at Bear Creek. A rescue party was formed and six days later reached those who had remained behind in the cabins at Truckee Lake. Ten had died of starvation and those still alive had been eating bullock hides for four weeks. The rescuers decided to divide the food they had brought, and, leaving most of the men behind —twenty-nine in all—try to reach Bear Valley with the women and children and some of the older men. All were brought safely over the mountains and other relief parties set out for Truckee Lake to bring aid to those who had been left. Of the eighty-four members of two prosperous and extensive families and their friends who started out for California, forty died during the terrible winter months of 1846–47. Their deaths were accompanied by extraordinary tales of suffering and fortitude. The fact that almost half the members of the party were women and that the women endured the hardships as well as the men lent an additional interest. Most horrifying of all, of course, was the fact that several members of the party sustained themselves by eating portions of those who had died.

Bryant had known George Donner, Sr., "A respectable citizen of Illinois," well, and he received a gruesome account of the condition of the cabins when General Stephen Kearny reached them in the spring. Public horror at the Donner party disaster was increased by the most lurid and exaggerated stories that appeared initially in the *California Star* and were soon reprinted in other papers.

Bryant and his party remained for some days at Fort Sutter

finding Captain Sutter, a native of Switzerland and a former officer in the French army, a most congenial host. He was full of vivid and romantic tales of his experiences and, withal, a gentleman of the "old school . . . in manners, dress and deportment." He told Bryant that, besieged by Indians, he had lived for days on grass before he "succeeded by degrees in reducing the Indians to obedience, and by means of their labor erected the spacious fortification which now belongs to him." It was certainly a substantial adobe structure, some five hundred feet in length and one hundred and fifty in depth. Rows of shops, storerooms, and barracks lined the interior walls, and artillery pieces were mounted at embrasures at its corners. When Bryant reached the fort it was manned by some "fifty well-disciplined Indians and ten or twelve white men, all under the pay of the United States." It was doubtless at that moment the strongest "United States" post in Upper California. Sutter's principal crop was wheat, which he sent down the river to San Francisco in barges carrying some fifty tons.

Bryant was much impressed with the fertility of the soil and the remarkable resources of the region. "The day is not distant," he noted, "when American enterprise and American ingenuity will furnish those adjuncts of civilization of which California is now so destitute, and render a residence in this country one of the most luxurious upon the globe. . . . It is scarcely possible to imagine a more delightful temperature, or a climate which is more agreeable and uniform. The sky is cloudless. . . . At night, so pure the atmosphere, that the moon gives a light sufficiently powerful for the purposes of the reader or student who had good eyesight."

The missions that Jedediah Smith and Harrison Rogers had found so flourishing almost twenty years ago had degenerated strikingly, due, in large part, to the chaotic conditions in Mexico proper. There were still some twenty-seven missions and many Indians remained on them, their condition varying according to the competence and energy of the father in charge. Many of the Indians were crippled to one degree or another by venereal disease, and it was Bryant's observation that the rate of death far exceeded that of births.

With the secularization of the missions, most of the Indians had deserted and, like the Apache, took to horse stealing for their subsistence. The first famous horse thief was a neophyte of the Mission of Santa Clara, one named George, but he soon had hundreds of imitators. The best sources Edwin Bryant could find estimated that in the region between Monterey and San Francisco alone more than a hundred thousand horses had been stolen in the past twenty years, primarily for food. Settlers were constantly killed in the raids—twenty, to Bryant's personal knowledge.

In 1831, when the heyday of the missions was already over, the white population in California did not exceed 4,500, with 19,000 Indians on twenty-one missions. Eleven years later the white population had increased to some 7,000 and the number of mission Indians had dropped to no more than 5,000. The number of cattle, sheep, goats, and pigs had declined in proportion to the decline in the number of Indians, but five years later the quantity of livestock had increased so far as to exceed the numbers owned by the missions at their most prosperous.

The great majority of whites, called "people of reason" to distinguish them from Indians, lived in the principal towns. Most of them had come to California from Mexico proper as public officials in the service of the army or as settlers. Since a large part of California was claimed by the missions, the people of reason had difficulty obtaining titles to land. Bryant noted that those with government stipends were "entirely indolent, it being very rare for any individual to strive to augment his fortune." "Dancing, horse-riding and gambling, occupy all their time," Bryant added.

The population of the territory in the spring of 1846 was estimated at some 10,000 whites, of whom 2,000 were "foreigners" —that is to say, Americans. The Mexican officials had done their best since the first incursion by Jedediah Smith to prevent the settlement of Americans, most of whom had arrived by boat and at least initially justified their presence by being involved in trade which centered on hides. But the Americans could not be forestalled. They came in a constant trickle over the terrible mountains and deserts or in the eight-month-long journey around the horn of South America.

The year before, the foreigners had discovered an opportunity in a revolutionary movement headed by a group of Californians, among them Don José Castro and Pio Pico, to oust Alvarado, the governor of the territory. To this movement the Americans gave their enthusiastic support. The governor was deposed and Pio Pico assumed his office. General Castro took charge of the military. Once in power, the Mexican insurrectionists proceeded to treat the foreigners in a manner "highly offensive"—specifically, they ordered them to leave the country. An order by Castro to one of his lieutenants to bring some horses to his headquarters at Santa Clara was inflated into a rumor that several hundred soldiers were marching up the Sacramento Valley, intent on attacking the Americans in the vicinity of Fort Sutter.

At this point Edwin Bryant's fortunes became intertwined with those of John Frémont, who, when we took leave of him, had collected a band of "foreigners" in the Sacramento area and was preparing, in his words, to "make the Pacific Ocean the western boundary of the United States." Further rumors had it that Castro's next move would be to fortify all entry points to "prevent the ingress of the emigrants from the United States." The horses that were on their way to Castro were seized by Frémont's men, their herders stripped of their arms and set free, each with his own horse and the message to Castro that if he wished the horses "he must come and get them."

There was no turning back now. A party of American "revolutionaries," augmented to the number of thirty-seven, marched to Sonoma and took possession of the military post there, capturing General Guadaloupe, two Vallejos and Lieutenant Colonel Prudon. Frémont, having encouraged the foreigners to establish their own "Bear Republic," was appealed to by the Americans at Sonoma to take command. Recruiting more "soldiers" as he went, Frémont reached Sonoma in the middle of June and decided to move from there to the Santa Clara Valley to attack Castro.

Left behind in Sonoma was a garrison of some eighteen men under the command of William Ide, who, on June 18 raised the flag of the Bear Republic and issued a rather bold proclamation, considering the force under his command: "The Commander-in-chief of the troops assembled at the fortress of Sonoma, gives his inviolable pledge to all persons in California, not found under arms, that they shall not be disturbed in their persons, their property, or social relations, one with another, by men under his command." He and his fellows had been encouraged to come to California, the proclamation continued, by the promise of land and of "a Republican Government," but they had found instead a "military despotism" and had been threatened with extermination if they did not at once depart. It was the purpose of the foreigners "to overthrow a government which has seized upon the property of the missions for its individual aggrandisement; which has ruined and shamefully oppressed the laboring people of California. . . ."

"All peaceable and good citizens of California who are friendly to the maintenance of good order and equal rights" were invited to join the Americans "without delay, to assist us in establishing and perpetuating a Republican Government, which shall secure to all civil and religious liberty; which shall encourage virtue and literature; which shall leave unshackled by fetters, agriculture, commerce, and manufactures. . . . I furthermore declare, that I believe that a government to be prosperous and happy, must originate with the people who are friendly to its existence; that the citizens are its guardians, the officers its servants, its glory its reward." In its presumption and republican idealism William Ide's proclamation was a marvelously American document. Some forty men (his force had been swollen by new recruits) were claiming a region larger than most nations, encompassing millions upon millions of acres, and doing so in the name of popular government (although it was addressed to the residents of Sonoma, its implications embraced the entire territory). It boggles the mind to try to imagine what those Sonomans who could read English made of such an announcement.

At the time of the proclamation two young Americans set out of Bodega Bay. On the way they were captured by a party of Californians, which included a desperado known as Four-fingered Jack, tied to trees and stoned. One man had his jaw broken and a rope was then tied to the broken bone and the jaw dragged out. Pieces of the victims' bodies were than cut off and stuffed into their mouths and they were finally disemboweled. When news of the atrocity reached Sonoma, a party of eighteen Americans set out after the Californians who were said to number some eighty men, caught up with them near Santa Rosa, and attacked, killing eight of the enemy and wounding a number of others.

When word reached General Castro of the seizure of Sonoma, he replied with two proclamations of his own, one addressed to Californians and one to foreigners. Castro appealed to his fellow Californians to "rise 'en masse,'" against the "adventurers, who, regardless of the rights of men," had "daringly commenced an invasion." They must defend "our liberty the true religion . . . and our independence. . . ."

The proclamation to the foreigners denounced them for ingratitude, assured them of protection if they refrained from "revolutionary movements," and ended with a flourish: "I have nothing to fear—my duty leads me to death or victory. I am a Mexican soldier, and I will be free and independent, or I will gladly die for these inestimable blessings."

It was, in other words, "war by proclamation." The scene now shifted to the south. Frémont, having collected some hundred and seventy men, crossed the Rio de los Americanos to march on General

Castro at Santa Clara. Ten men were dispatched to capture San Francisco and word reached Frémont that Commodore John Drake Sloat of the United States navy, in command of the frigate *Savannah*, had arrived at Monterey. Sloat had heard of the first engagements between Taylor and Santa Anna on the Rio Grande, but he did not know that Congress had declared war on Mexico. Nevertheless he hoisted the United States flag over Monterey to the cheers of the foreigners there, fired a twenty-one-gun salute, and issued a proclamation of his own, this one with somewhat more authority behind it than Ide's. The central government of Mexico, it declared, had invaded the United States and thus brought about a state of war. Despite this fact Commodore Sloat did not come to the people of California an enemy but as " 'their best friend,' since henceforth it must be assumed [by whom?] that California will be a portion of the United States" and thereby "enjoy a permanent government, under which life, property, and the constitutional right and lawful security to worship the Creator in the way most congenial to each one's sense of duty, will be secured, which, unfortunately, the central government of Mexico cannot afford them, destroyed as her resources are by internal factions and corrupt officers, who create constant revolutions to promote their own interests and oppress the people." Under the United States, however, California "will rapidly advance and improve, both in agriculture and commerce." "A great increase in the value of real estate and the products of California" might also be anticipated.

Commodore Sloat ordered Commander John Montgomery, in command of a sloop-of-war in San Francisco Bay, to raise the American flag over that town and "a volunteer corps of American foreigners was immediately organized for the defense of the place." At Monterey another company of volunteers was organized, made up of sailors from merchant ships in the harbor and citizens of the town, and dispatched to the Mission of San Juan to raise the American flag there, but Frémont had arrived ahead of them and taken charge of the nine cannon and 60,000 kegs of cannon shot. Sloat thereupon sailed for the United States via the Isthmus of Panama to inform the government of his highly irregular actions and get instructions, leaving Commodore Robert Stockton in command. Stockton, who had served with distinction in the War of 1812 and later against the Algerian pirates, was one of the principal advocates of a steam-powered navy. In his new role he proved, if anything, more aggressive than his predecessor, sending Frémont with his party by boat to San Diego to seize that town and heading himself for San Pedro, the port of Los Angeles, at that point the capital of California.

In the meantime General Castro had joined forces with Governor Pico at Santa Barbara, creating thereby an "army" of some 600 men. This force marched to Los Angeles to defend the town. But when Stockton, with a battalion of sailors, marines, and foreigners, his cannon hauled by oxen, arrived in front of Los Angeles, Castro, apparently forgetting his pledge to die fighting, hastily retreated and Stockton marched into the City of the Angels without opposition. Several days later, Frémont, having captured San Diego and left a small garrison there, joined Stockton. It was Stockton's turn to issue a proclamation. "The flag of the United States is now flying from every commanding position in the territory," it announced, "and California is entirely free from Mexican dominion." The area would be governed by the laws of the United States. Meanwhile the people were "request-ed" to meet "in their several towns and departments . . . to elect civil officers." All those of whatever antecedents "who faithfully adhere to the new government" would enjoy its protection. Property would be secure and the freedom of all citizens to worship as they chose guaranteed.

Of all of these developments Bryant was a fascinated spectator and soon to be a participant. He found the Mission San Jose a scene of desolation. The buildings, "once inhabited by thousands of busy Indians, were now deserted, roofless, and crumbling into ruins. . . ." The abandoned mission structures covered fifty acres of ground. Bryant passed through "extensive warehouses and immense rooms, once occupied for the manufacture of woolen blankets and other articles. . . . Filth and desolation have taken the place of cleanliness and busy life." The calaboose, or jail for refractory Indians, was "a miserable dark room . . . without light or ventilation" and the stocks "and several other inventions for the punishment of offenders" still stood as a silent reminder of the basis of Indian "business." A few Indians still lingered about, engaged in farming or working as ranchers on a nearby ranch. On the way from the mission of San Jose to the pueblo, Bryant encountered a *carreta,* or California traveling cart, a large, awkward vehicle the wheels of which were cross-sections of a log. The wheels were coupled together by an axletree into which were inserted stakes some four feet in length, the whole covered with raw hides. Accompanying the *carreta* "freighted with women and children" were *excaballeros,* "riding fine spirited horses, with gaudy trappings. They were dressed in steeple-crowned, glazed *sombreros,* *serapes* of fiery colors, velvet . . . *clazoneros,* white cambric calzoncillos and shoes of undressed leather. Their spurs were of immense size."

At San Jose, Bryant met a Captain Fisher, a Massachusetts seaman who had married what Bryant called a "Hispano-American lady" of "fine manners and personal appearance," one of the commonest ways for a foreigner to obtain land. Bryant also met a Boston Dana running a flourishing ranch and married to another "Hispano-American lady," and in San Francisco he encountered one of the almost equally prominent du Ponts of Delaware, a family that had established its fortune making gunpowder in the War of 1812. Another foreigner named Livermore had followed such a bridal path and now owned a vast ranch and some 3,500 head of cattle as well as hundreds of sheep and innumerable horses. Señora Livermore was described by Bryant as having: "The dark lustrous eyes, the long black and glossy hair, the natural ease, grace, and vivacity of manners and conversation, characteristic of Spanish ladies." The children, "especially two or three *señoritas,* were very beautiful, and manifested a remarkable degree of sprightliness and intelligence," Bryant added.

The valley in which the pueblo and mission of San Jose were located appeared to Bryant one of the garden spots of the world. "For pastoral charms," he wrote, "fertility of soil, variety of productions, and delicious voluptuousness of climate and scenery, it cannot be surpassed. The valley, if properly cultivated, would alone produce breadstuffs enough to supply millions of population." The population was chiefly Californian. Their ranches were in the valley but their houses and gardens were in the town and Señor Sunol conducted Bryant and his friends through his orchard, where apples, pears, peaches, figs, oranges, and other fruits were growing in abundance and "grape-vines were bowed to the ground with the luxuriance and weight of the yield; and more delicious fruit I have never tasted."

To an austere Protestant eye, the California churches were monuments of ostentation and vulgar display. Bryant described the church at San Jose as "hung with coarse paintings and engravings of the saints, etc., etc. . . . the chancel . . . decorated with numerous images, and symbolic ornaments used by the priests in their worship. . . . gold-paper and tinsel, in barbaric taste are plastered without stint upon nearly every object that meets the eye, so that on festive occasions when the church is lighted, it must present a very glittering appearance."

"Gambling," Bryant noted, "is a universal vice in California. All classes and both sexes participate in its excitements to some extent." The games were conducted "with great propriety and decorum," Bryant noted. "The loud swearing and other turbulent demonstrations generally proceeded from the unsuccessful foreigners." Bryant was impressed by the differences between the native Californians and the foreigners in this respect. "One bore their losses with stoical composure and indifference; the other announced each unsuccessful bet with profane imprecations and maledictions." The reason for such different responses was, in Bryant's view, because the Californians played for sport and the foreigners for money.

Traveling down the San Joaquin Valley, Bryant and his party stopped at Mount Diablo at the ranch of Dr. Marsh, a New Englander and a graduate of Harvard who spoke Spanish fluently and was a storehouse of knowledge about Mexico and California. He owned some two thousand head of cattle, although he suffered constant depredations from the Indians and had started "an extensive vineyard" whose grapes exceeded in size and flavor any that Bryant had ever tasted.

What was perhaps most revealing about the courtesy and good spirit with which Bryant and his friends were received by Californians was the fact that this hospitality was extended in the face of the foreigners' takeover of the Californians' own territory. What it demonstrates most clearly is that far from being disposed to respond to General Castro's exhortation to die for the glory of Mexico, Californians were thoroughly disenchanted with the comings and goings of various claimants to the "presidency" of Mexico. As we have seen, daughters of the great ranch owners had, in many instances, intermarried with foreigners. They considered themselves Californians far more than Mexicans. To be a "state" in the Union of United States, with their property protected and their religious rights guaranteed, meant, for most Californians, the prospect of some order and stability in the affairs of government. Since native Californians outnumbered foreigners four or five to one, it was no accident that only a handful could be recruited by Pico and Castro who, after all, represented a "revolutionary" uprising against Mexican authority.

When Bryant reached San Francisco in the fall of 1846, it was a town of some two hundred persons, most of them foreigners. The transient population was perhaps three times as large and made up of the crews of merchant ships, whaling vessels, and sailors and marines from the sloop-of-war, the *Portsmouth*. The houses were modest frame and adobe structures, most of them without chimneys or fireplaces. He discovered that among the inhabitants it was "a settled opinion, that California [was] henceforth to compose a part of the United States, and every American who is now here consider himself as treading upon his own soil, as much as if he were in one of the old thirteen revolutionary states."

"The position of San Francisco for commerce," Bryant wrote, "is, without doubt, superior to any other port on the Pacific coast of North America. The country contiguous and tributary to it cannot be surpassed in fertility, healthfulness of climate, and beauty of scenery. . . . This place is, doubtless, destined to become one of the largest and most opulent commercial cities in the world, and under American auspices it will rise with astonishing rapidity." It was already transshipping flour, lumber, salmon, and cheese from Oregon and importing from the Hawaiian Islands sugar, coffee, and preserved fruits.

While Bryant was in San Francisco alarming news arrived from the southern part of the territory. The American garrison at Los Angeles had been besieged by a larger force of Californians, a relief party had been turned back, and the Americans had surrendered. Santa Barbara was likewise under attack. At this news Bryant and his friends undertook to raise a force of "emigrants and Indians" to go to the assistance of Frémont, who was determined to retake Los Angeles. Rounding up volunteers, including eighteen Walla-Walla Indians, Bryant and his party joined Frémont near the Mission San Juan Bautista. Including Indians and servants, Frémont now had 428 men under his command, many of whom had been only a few weeks in California. The force was organized into eight intermittently mounted companies of infantry and one of artillery constituting the "California Battalion." Through the early days of December, this motley group straggled south to recapture the capital, but before the California Battalion could reach Los Angeles, an American force under Stockton and Kearny landed at San Pedro and after two days of sharp fighting retook the town. Several days later Frémont and his men entered Los Angeles. "A more miserably clad, wretchedly provided, and unprepossessing military host, probably never entered a civilized city," Bryant wrote. "There were not many of us so fortunate as to have in our possession an entire outside garment; and several were without hats or shoes, or a complete covering to their bodies."

Kearny, acting on instructions from Secretary of State James Buchanan, had come up from Santa Fe with three hundred regulars of the 1st Dragoons. On the way he was disconcerted to be met by Kit Carson "with a party of sixteen men . . . with . . . an express from Commodore Stockton and Lieutenant-Col. Frémont," reporting that California was already "in possession of the Americans under their command; that the American flag was flying from every important position in the territory and that the country was forever free from Mexican control; the war ended, and peace and harmony established among the people."

Coming into California from the southwest by way of Caliente on the road to Sonora, Kearny found the situation rather different from the way in which Frémont had described it. On receiving Frémont's optimistic message, Kearny had left the greater part of his small force at Santa Fe. Now, entering California he found, instead of "peace and harmony," that he was outnumbered two to one by a force under the command of Andres Pico. The next morning his twelve mounted dragoons made a "furious charge" and, supported by fifty more mounted on weary mules, routed the Californians. Armed with carbines, lances, and swords, the Californians counterattacked and inflicted heavy casualties on the Americans. Three officers and fourteen enlisted men, including two sergeants and two corporals, were killed and Kearny himself wounded.

Stockton, who had retired from Los Angeles to San Diego, now joined Kearny with a party of sailors and marines, giving him a combined force of some five hundred men, including a battery of artillery. Thus reinforced, Kearny advanced on Los Angeles. At the San Gabriel River, he found his path blocked by some six hundred Californians and four pieces of artillery. The Americans again attacked and drove the Californians off. "The enemy," Kearny wrote, "mounted on fine horses, and being the best riders in the world, carried off their killed and wounded. . . ." The Americans lost one private killed and eleven wounded and two officers, one of them Captain Archibald Gillespie. The latter's death was a substantial loss to historians, for Gillespie was the bearer of Larkin's confidential message to Frémont, who had definitely jumped the gun with his unauthorized military activities at Sonoma. It had apparently been Buchanan's intention secretly to encourage the native Californians to rise against the government in Mexico City and then, having gained control of the territory, to apply to the United States for admission to the Union as a state. The first step of that process might have been the uprising against the legitimate governor of California by Castro and Pico. It was this scheme that Frémont's precipitous action negated. Historians have thus been disposed to charge Frémont with insubordination and bungling. But it must be remembered that Pico and Castro showed initially very little inclination to accommodate American foreigners, and there seems little reason to believe they would have fallen in with Buchanan's plans for a bloodless and "legitimate" annexation by the United States. The California leaders had several other alternatives. They may well have considered declaring California an independent nation, perhaps under the protection of Spain, which would doubtless have welcomed the opportunity. Certainly there was much pro-Spanish feeling in California, especially in what remained of the mission culture. It was equally the case that the "foreigners," i.e. the Americans, had no notion of accepting any status short of becoming a state in the Union. With or without Frémont, they would have resisted the government of Pico and Castro with its antiforeign bias. The most we can fairly charge Frémont with is the fact that while the actions of the foreigners were those of private citizens, he, as a commissioned officer in the United States army, acted without orders and without authority and that his rather pompous and flamboyant communiqué to Kearny clearly misrepresented the military situation and drew Kearny into an action that might well have been a disaster. Frémont, conscious of his support in high places, was often reckless and insubordinate. On the other hand, it can be argued that the proof is in the pudding. His energy and leadership undoubtedly helped to establish "foreign" control of California and advance the day of statehood. If Buchanan's plan had so far succeeded that the Californians established their independence from Mexico and then applied to be annexed as a state to the Union (a proposition in many respects dubious as we have noted), Polk might well have encountered determined opposition to annexation in Congress, where the northern members and the New Englanders in particular were already up in arms about the annexation of Texas and the Mexican War, which they believed to be the consequence of it. So Frémont, to the extent that he helped to force the issue, can be said to have contributed substantially to a resolution of the California question.

Frémont had gotten himself further in trouble by accepting the capitulation of Governor Flores, who had succeeded Pio Pico after his capture by the Americans. Stockton and Kearny had refused the terms proposed by Flores. The latter then sent emissaries to Frémont, still several days away from Los Angeles, and Frémont negotiated terms of capitulation. Again Frémont acted beyond his powers and enraged Kearny, already indignant over the misleading communiqué.

The peace and harmony that Frémont ascribed to the territory of California did not prevail in the little American army at Los Angeles. Kearny made his displeasure known to Frémont. There was a bitter quarrel between the two men, and Stockton became embroiled. Before the arrival of Kearny, Stockton had appointed Frémont governor of California. Frémont thus took the view that Kearny was subordinate to him. Stockton was disposed to take Frémont's side, and so the three remained at sixes and sevens until orders arrived assigning the command to Kearny.

After the recapture of Los Angeles, Edwin Bryant started for San Francisco. Everywhere he stopped, Californians expressed delight at the conclusion of the fighting. One man with whom Bryant stayed "stated that he and his family had refused to join in the late insurrection." Bryant assured them "that all was peaceful now; . . . that we were all Californians,—*hermanos, hermanas, amigos.* They expressed their delight at this information," Bryant noted, "by numerous exclamations."

When he reached San Francisco the rapid growth of the town —from two hundred residents to some fifteen hundred in eight months—moved Bryant to some reflections: "Wherever the Anglo-Saxon race plant themselves," he wrote, "progress is certain to be displayed in some form or other. Such is the 'go-ahead' energy, that things cannot stand still where they are. . . ." In San Francisco, "new houses had been established; hotels had been opened for the accommodation of the traveling and business public; and the publication of a newspaper had been commenced."

Bryant became a friend of General Kearny, who had not yet started for Washington. He described Kearny as "rising fifty years of age . . . about five feet ten or eleven inches . . . his features . . . regular, almost Grecian; his eye . . . blue" and having "an eagle-like expression, when excited by stern or angry emotion . . . unaffected, urbane, and conciliatory, without the slightest exhibition of vanity or egotism . . . the cool, brave and energetic soldier; the strict disciplinarian, without tyranny." The description is an interesting one in view of the fact that Bryant had served for several months under Frémont without ever making a personal reference to him in his journal. One feels that Bryant is, in practical fact, making an implicit contrast of Kearny with his rival. Kearny subsequently asked Bryant to be the alcalde or mayor of San Francisco, an office he held until Kearny started for the east with the intention of preferring charges of insubordination against Frémont. Before Kearny departed he added a final proclamation to the "war by proclamation," promising the people of the territory that the United States would provide "with the least possible delay, a free government, similar to those in her other territories" and once more promising protection of property. "California," the proclamation read, "has for many years suffered greatly from domestic troubles; civil wars have been the poisoned fountains which have sent forth trouble and pestilence over her beautiful land. Now . . . the star-spangled banner floats over California . . . and under it agriculture must improve and the arts and sciences flourish, as seed in a rich and fertile soil. The Americans and Californians are now but one people. . . . Let us, as a band of brothers, unite and emulate each other in our exertions to benefit and improve this our beautiful, and which must soon be our happy and prosperous home."

Kearny then set out for Washington with Frémont and at Fort Leavenworth filed charges against him for "mutiny," "disobedience of the lawful command of a superior officer," and "conduct to the prejudice of good order and military discipline." Frémont was placed under arrest, conducted to Washington and there, in a sensational court-martial that lasted three months, convicted as charged. (Bryant testified against him, incidentally.)

The principal result was to make Frémont a popular hero. His reports on his explorations—or perhaps more accurately expeditions, since his enemies claimed that he had discovered nothing new, but simply made well-publicized excursions over territory where others had preceded—had already made him something of a celebrity, and his eloquent accounts of the Oregon and California country had made him the idol of all those Americans with Western aspirations.

A majority of the court recommended clemency to Polk, who, needless to say, found himself under intense pressure to pardon Frémont. He confirmed the judgment of the court-martial with the exception of the charge of "mutiny" and suspended the penalty (the board had recommended Frémont's dismissal from the army). Frémont at once resigned his commission and set out on an expedition to find a passage to California by way of the Rio Grande.

24

The Gold Rush

Some eighteen months after William Ide raised the flag of the Bear Republic, James Marshall, a carpenter, was building a sawmill for Captain Sutter on the South Fork of the American River when he spotted in the millrace "something shining in the bottom of the ditch," as he recalled in his often told account of the historic moment. "I reached my hand down and picked it up; it made my heart thump, for I was certain it was gold. The piece was about half the size and shape of a pea. Then I saw another piece in the water. After taking it out I sat down and began to think right hard." Then he showed the nuggets to his fellow workmen. "Boys, I believe I have found a gold mine!" Marshall told his boss, Sutter, who although anxious to keep the matter a secret, could not refrain from mentioning it to his servants; from them the news got to the *California Star*, a modest sheet in San Francisco, which denounced the story as a "sham, as superb a takein as ever was got up to guzzle the gullible."

Sutter, Marshall, and the handful of men who knew of Marshall's find were happy enough, of course, to have it thought a "sham." They were busy prospecting. A rival storekeeper, Sam Brannan, was also in on the secret and busy on his own account, but he had a loose tongue, or so the story goes, and rode into San Francisco one day brandishing a bottle full of nuggets and calling out, "Gold! Gold on the American River!" The response was immediate and overwhelming. The alcalde at Monterey wrote that "the farmers have thrown aside their plows, the lawyers their briefs, the doctors their pills, the priests their prayer-books, and all are now digging gold." He might have added that the sailors had abandoned their ships in the harbor. Thus began the greatest movement of people—dislocation is perhaps an apter term —in modern history. The interim military governor of the territory of California, after a visit to one "mining" site, wrote to the secretary of war in Washington, D.C.: "The hill sides were thickly strewn with canvas tents and bush arbours; a store was erected, and several boarding shanties in operation. The day was intensely hot, yet about two hundred men were at work in the full glare of the sun, washing for gold." By the end of the year it was calculated that six million dollars' worth of gold had been washed out of the American River.

When Navy Lieutenant Edward Beale arrived in Washington in September, 1848 with 230 ounces of gold in a tea caddy, the rush was on. By the middle of December George Templeton Strong had written in his diary: "California gold fever raging furiously." Strong was concerned that the discovery of gold might depress the money markets, but soon a number of his friends were departing. "Bob Benson is going to California," he noted, "also Frank Winthrop; in short, there's no end to the emigration. I don't wish any harm to all these people, but it would give me considerable satisfaction if a sudden rise in the waters of the Pacific would overwhelm the gold region and the gold diggers, being provided with life preservers, could be floated off to the Sandwich Islands." The next day William Pennington headed west and Strong wrote, "It's a most weighty and momentous business, this California furor. Either it will be an era in the monetary concern of the world like the discovery of America, or posterity will have another chapter of delusion and mania and ruin and distress to wonder over. . . . The frenzy continues to increase every day. It seems as if the Atlantic Coast was to be depopulated, such swarms of people are leaving it for the new El Dorado. It is the most remarkable emigration on record in the history of man since the days of the Crusades; and as the country fills up with adventurers from every part of the world, and as they begin to crowd each other, some strange results will be seen. There is neither law nor social system there, scarcely a nucleus of civil order is yet visible at one or two points, the rest is mere chaos. Everyone is resolved to make a fortune and every one will soon begin to feel pressed for the necessaries of life and then crime and violence and disease and starvation will make a Pandemonium of the whole region." It was a startlingly accurate prediction.

One newspaper editor wrote: "The coming of the Messiah, or the dawn of the Millennium could not have excited anything like the interest." Between the middle of December and January 18 sixty-one ships with a total of three thousand passengers left Eastern seaports for San Francisco and all over the world steamers and sailing vessels canceled contracts to carry freight and passengers and headed for the United States to carry prospective miners to the goldfields. A month later sixty ships left New York and seventy sailed from Philadelphia. By the end of 1849 more than seven hundred ships had arrived in San Francisco, carrying some 45,000 passengers. Most of them lay at anchor or tied up to every foot of available wharf space while their officers and crews joined the passengers at Hangtown or Poker Flat or Rough and Ready.

In Philadelphia Sidney George Fisher noted in his diary, "The accounts of gold in California are marvelous in the extreme & at first were not believed, but subsequent information from many & respectable sources confirms them & the excitement produced is unparalleled. Many thousands have abandoned their pursuits & gone. . . . Thousands are going every day. . . . Not only here but in Europe the mania exists & increases."

The gold rush, Philip Hone wrote, encouraged talk of a "great national railroad across the Continent in a direct line from St. Louis to San Francisco. It is a great idea & would bring the commerce of Europe and the East across America. . . . Across the rails goods & passengers could be transported in a few days. Will it be done? Most probably, for if in the nature of things it *can* be done, the Yankees will do it."

Bayard Taylor, the New York literary critic who joined the rush, wrote that a party at Chagres on the east coast of Panama on their way to the mines encountered a returning Californian "with a box containing $22,000 in gold-dust, and a four-pound lump in one hand. The impatience and excitement of the passengers, already at a high pitch, was greatly increased by his appearance. Life and death were small matters compared with immediate departures from Chagres. Men ran up and down the beach, shouting, gesticulating and getting feverishly impatient at the deliberate habits of the natives, as if their arrival in California would thereby be at all hastened." Howard

Gardiner, who left New York City on March 15, 1849, with eight hundred other passengers and $475, was stuck for six weeks in Panama waiting for a ship to carry him and his fellow gold-seekers to San Francisco. The delay consumed the capital that he had counted on to get him started as a miner and he arrived in San Francisco with six dollars in his pocket.

The isthmus was a breeding ground for cholera and many emigrants died and were buried there. When Taylor reached Panama there were some seven hundred emigrants waiting for passage. "All the tickets the steamer could possibly receive had been issued," Taylor wrote. "And so great was the anxiety to get on, that double price, $600, was frequently paid for a ticket to San Francisco . . . I was well satisfied to leave Panama at that time; the cholera, which had already carried off one-fourth of the native population, was making havoc among the Americans, and several . . . lay at the point of death."

The passengers who attempted the 18,000-mile six-to-eight-month trip around the Horn were subject to almost as much hardship and suffering as those who went by land. Ships took on far more passengers than they were equipped for and their hastily recruited crews frequently had no other qualification than the desire to get to California. The vessels were often improperly rigged. Food, bad to begin with, got worse as the months passed. Water had to be rationed and scurvy and dysentery supplemented cholera in their assault on the passengers' internal organs. That any of them ever got to California was a wonder.

The principal overland routes were over the Santa Fe trail (the path Josiah Gregg had followed almost twenty-five years earlier) to the Gila River and down it to the Colorado (Jedediah Smith's route), or by way of the Platte to Fort Laramie and thence through the South Pass to the Humboldt River. Near the headwaters of the Humboldt, the emigrant either turned north to the Pitt River and then over the Sierra to the Sacramento or came by way of Truckee–Lake Tahoe into the southern end of the Sacramento Valley at New Helvetia or Sutter's Fort.

There were also a number of routes through Mexico. The so-called Texas Trail started at Galveston, crossed the Pecos, and ran along the Rio Grande to Tucson and the Gila River, then to Yuma and, finally, to San Diego; the Mexican Trail ran from Matamoros on the Gulf of Mexico to Mexican Monterrey and then turned north, running parallel to the Texas Trail as far as Tucson and beyond where it, too, connected with the Gila. Other Mexican routes ran across the peninsula to Acapulco, San Blas, and Mazatián.

When Mary Jane Megquier accompanied her physician husband to San Francisco in 1849, it was with the intention of making their fortune by starting a boardinghouse. They had the main beams for the structure precut and shipped around the Horn while they took the route across Panama and up the coast by steamship. From Panama Mrs. Megquier wrote her daughter that "in this miserable old town . . . 2,000 Americans" were waiting for coastal steamers to carry them to the regions of gold. "Womens help," she wrote, "is so very scarce that I am in hopes to get a chance by hook or crook to pay my way, but some women that have gone are coming home because they can get no servants to wait on them, but a woman that can work will make more money than a man. . . . They tell us . . . everybody is digging gold . . . in about one year you will see your mother come trudging home with an apron full, but without joking, gold is very plentiful and . . . we shall get it as fast as possible and start for home."

In San Francisco Mrs. Megquier had difficulty describing the scene to her daughter. "As for giving you a description of my situation and those around me," she wrote, "it is impossible, it is a complete farce, a change comes over one, that you can with difficulty recognize your intimate friends, the greatest dandies wear their beards long, their hair uncombed, a very dirty colored shirt, and coarse jacket, their skin brown from the sun and dust; some collecting dirty clothes for washing, others driving a mule and cart for which they get two ounces per day. Professor Shepard from one of the first institutions in the states is driving a cart from Sacramento city to the mines, from which he is coining a mint of money, every one must do something, it matters but very little what it is, if they stick to it they are bound to make money."

Mary Megquier calculated that if they could get their boarding-house up they could rent it for $30,000 a year. Renting a house at an exorbitant rate and taking in boarders, she had sometimes made $50 a day. They had been in San Francisco two months, she wrote, and had made more money than they could have made in two years at home. One of her boarders was a young Hungarian revolutionary who had taken an active part in the rebellion under the leadership of Kossuth and had been forced to flee for his life. A Dr. Robinson supplemented his income as a physician by composing and singing comic songs at a music hall in the city for $15 a night.

It was into this bizarre world that young Charles Pancoast decided to venture. "Here I was again about to plunge into a Sea of Troubles, with the distant hope that Fortune lay in the path before me. I could cheerfully bear Poverty and Hardship, but could not brook the idea of being a commonplace Young Man serving a Master who exacted of me routine service for a small remuneration. I had a kind of feeling always that when I had finished my Apprenticeship I should no longer serve any direct Master but my Lord; and I so courted this Freedom of thought and action that I preferred to endure any amount of hardship rather than to be under the command of anyone. This ambition led me to aspire to Wealth and honorable Position; but with my limited natural ability and still more limited Education, I was doomed always to encounter a continuous struggle."

So he joined the stream of fortune hunters making their way, in the face of almost inconceivable hardships and suffering, across the plains, deserts, and mountains to the land of gold. Those who went were, like Pancoast, predominantly young, middle-class males, though by no means exclusively so. All were prosperous enough or could borrow enough from complaisant friends and relatives to make the considerable outlay required to get them to California. This was, it might be guessed, no inconsiderable sum. It involved the supplies and equipment required for a three-or-four-month trip with little expectation of being able to replenish their supplies. A sturdy wagon of the Conestoga style was desirable if not essential, with from two to eight mules or oxen to draw it, along with a large supply of flour, bacon, and coffee. Fortunately by 1849 the gold rushers had available to them the cumulative experience of almost twenty years of overland travel, the greater part of it, of course, to Oregon. Unemployed or underemployed fur traders and trappers, men like Jim Beckwourth, Thomas Fitzpatrick, Jim Bridger, and Etienne Provost, were on hand at St. Louis and Independence to act as guides and as professional hunters.

Cholera, which had devastated the country for a decade or more, was abroad in the spring of 1849 when Charles Pancoast started the first leg of his "rush" to California. The steamer that left St. Louis for Fort Leavenworth was infected with it. Before the passengers were two days on the river seventeen were ill and nine dead. Pancoast, who knew the pilot, was allowed to stay in the pilot house and slept on deck. The next day twelve more died. They were buried "in the Wilderness in wooden boxes made by the Boat's carpenter."

At Jefferson City, where the steamer stopped to dispatch freight, the citizens of the town, having heard there was cholera on board, tried to prevent the boat from landing; a young passenger who went into the town to get a glass of brandy at a bar fell on his way back and died in the street of the disease. Pancoast wrote that "there was much in the circumstances to call out the nobler attributes of men, and much to bring out the innate meanness of brutalized Humanity." Passengers left the boat at every opportunity. Some passengers rifled the belongings of those who were ill. Others, Pancoast among them, tried to relieve the misery of those who had been stricken and were still alive. By the time the boat reached Westport (later Kansas City), sixty persons had died. There the cholera had been worse than anywhere along the river. Only one man and his wife remained in town, the rest having died or fled. Between Westport and Leavenworth five more passengers succumbed. Finally, the boat tied up at St. Joseph, its destination, and Pancoast began looking for a party headed west. Soon he found a pilot friend, Smith Philipps, who, with three companions, was about to start out. The other members of the party, in addition to Philipps, were his father, "an Old Soldier about fifty years of age . . . as tough as a pine knot," and Eugene and Myron Angel. Eugene was a lawyer from Peoria, Illinois. Myron was a West Pointer who had resigned from the Academy "to dig gold in California." Pancoast found that they had used up all their ready cash and he had to draw on his pilot's earnings to purchase four yoke of oxen, two riding ponies, and a good portion of the provisions for the trip.

The great gold rush migration was distinguished by the fact that, especially in the Mississippi West, parties were often made up of men from the same town. Thus the Philipps-Angel group were part of the Peoria Train consisting of some thirty-five men from that town. At Leavenworth, they found that the train had left without them and they decided that, rather than trying to hook onto a train from, say, Springfield, they would attempt to overtake the Peoria Train. The first day out they met a troop of United States cavalry whose captain warned them that they were in Indian territory and unless they could catch the Peoria Train within a few days they would all be slaughtered.

Outside of St. Joe, Pancoast and his friends passed through settlements of "half-civilized Wyandotte and Delaware Indians, who cultivated small Garden of Vegetables and possessed some miserable-looking Pigs and Ponies. The Indians," Pancoast added, "were generally squalid creatures, lamentably debauched and sunken in the scale of Humanity. . . ." This was plainly the result of their contact with the whites, and Pancoast noted that "such debauchery . . . was never found among the numerous tribes of Wild Indians with whom we afterwards came in contact. . . ."

A few days out from Leavenworth, Pancoast had the last of the sick headaches which had plagued him at biweekly intervals for years. Next day they had their first contact with "wild Indians": two Potawatomi who appeared silently beside the wagon before they were seen. "They were strikingly symmetrical in physique," Pancoast noted, "with marked but gentle dreamy countenances without paint, and were dressed rather tastily in brown cambric Tunics to their knees, bordered by a band of richly-colored Porcupine quills, sleeveless Jackets, and Belts decorated with quills of various colors."

So they passed through Kansas, encountering a few more Indians and an occasional train of rushers. Years later when he sat down to write his recollections, Pancoast observed, "When I look at the map of Kansas and see it thickly dotted with Towns where may be found magnificent Public Buildings and Dwellings with all the modern improvement and luxuries to be found in the great Cities of the East, and a Rail Road along this very Route that I have been describing, I am filled with Wonder and Amazement, and can hardly realize that all these things have come to pass in the space of half my lifetime. Surely no other Country on the face of the Earth has ever undergone such rapid changes as the great West of the United States."

The Angel-Philipps band caught up with the Peoria Train the fourth day out of Leavenworth. Pancoast was pleased to be able to report that the party had agreed not to travel on the Sabbath. That day was given over to singing religious songs and holding an informal church service during which they were addressed by a millenarian Millerite, a follower of William Miller who predicted that the world would end soon and all the faithful would ascend to Heaven. This made gold hunting seem foolish, Pancoast reflected, "if we are to ascend in so short a time."

The train of which the Peoria Train was a component was composed of forty-four wagons, seventeen of which were drawn by mules and the rest by oxen. It included two hundred men from different states and countries. "There were the ignorant and learned; generous and selfish; indolent and industrious; wild and erratic; and staid and sober Souls; jubilant and good Fellows, and crooked ill-natured Curmudgeons. There were Preachers, Doctors, Lawyers, Druggists, Pilots, Mechanics, Farmers, Laborers, Sailors, and representatives of many other occupations. . . . Some of the men were as old as sixty-five years; others were invalids when they started."

Jim Bridger of fur trapping days had been engaged as a guide, and it was rumored that he had killed friendly Indians to claim that bounty that the New Mexican government had offered for Indian scalps. The procedures followed on the march were those that we are already familiar with from earlier narratives. A captain and lieutenants had been elected by the members of the train at Fort Leavenworth and the train made camp each day by drawing the wagons in a circle. Pancoast described the excitement of the initial encounter with buffalo. Sixty men started out after the creatures and one man shot himself and another his horse while a third was thrown and never recovered his horse or his saddle.

And Indians. Near a Pawnee village they saw a row of poles with what appeared to be caps on them. When some of the men rode over to investigate they discovered that they were the scalps of Arapaho and Cheyenne Indians taken in a recent battle. A few days later they encountered some fifteen hundred Arapaho and Cheyenne, "each armed with Bow and Arrows, a ten-foot Spear, and a Shield of dried Buffalo hide, as hard as adamant, painted with many savage devices. Most of them were dressed in coats, moccasins, and leggings of Buckskin, ornamented with beads, Bear teeth, and colored Porcupine quills. . . . The Chiefs wore cloaks of Buffalo skins with the hair on, and to our excited eyes they appeared like giant Monsters." The men in the party looked to the priming of the rifles and prepared to fight for their lives but Bridger implored them to hold their fire, saying the Indians were displaying peace signals. In typical fashion they rode up to the train as though to attack it and then, at a command from the principal chief, dismounted from their horses and sat down, while the chiefs advanced to parley. The Indians were on the way to make a retaliatory raid on the Pawnee and they wished to trade for tobacco, whiskey, paints, and the like. Soon the squaws, children, and horses and cattle appeared in another division and the whites and Indians proceeded to trade "moccasins, Buckskin coats, and other Indian handiwork for trinkets, looking-glasses, Tobacco, Whiskey, and toy Paints, and offered to trade their Horses and Steers for Arms and ammunition, but these things we would not trade."

When the trading was over, the Indians challenged the whites to race horses with them, and then to foot race. A little bowlegged Illinois blacksmith offered to run against their fastest brave for five dollars. A splendid-looking brave came forth and the blacksmith easily beat him. Then the Cheyenne produced another lithe and muscular-looking savage and bet a buckskin coat against two of the blacksmith's shirts. Again the blacksmith won. Whereupon the Indians gathered around the winner and clapped him on the back, asking the captain of the wagon train if they could "have him."

"These Indians," Pancoast wrote, "both men and women, had the most beautiful forms and faces I have met with anywhere among the Indian Tribes. The men were all tall and straight, their forms perfect, and their countenances positive and fierce, yet extremely animated and expressive of intelligence and jollity. The Squaws were tastily, even beautifully, dressed, in Buckskin tunics to the knees, ornamented with beads, quills of various dyes, and other settings . . . They wore necklaces of showy beads, ear-rings, and armlets; some had gold bracelets on their ankles. They did not paint."

Charles Pancoast was a Quaker, an antislavery man, and uncommonly generous and humane in his relations with his fellows. His attitude toward the Indians may thus be taken with some confidence as representing, among those who had had a fair degree of firsthand contact with American aborigines, the more liberal end of the spectrum of white opinion about the Indians. "It is the belief of many good People," he wrote, "that the White Man is solely responsible for their decay and gradual extermination; but it appears to me that the White Man has been by no means the chief instrument in destroying these People. God has established universal Laws for the Government of all Mankind, making no exception in favor of Ignorance; and the Nation or Individual that violates His Laws shall surely die. God has given to these Indians the most beautiful portion of the Earth and all the necessary elements for its fructification, and commanded them as well as the rest of Mankind to earn their bread by the sweat of their brows, to increase and multiply, and to develop the elements of the Earth for their use and to the Glory of God. All of these Laws the American Indians have ignored. They do not appear to recognize any right of Man even to his own life, and entertain the idea that it is their right and duty to exterminate any other portion of God's Creation that claims to share His fruits with them; consequently they cultivated no Virtue except Heroism (and that of the most barbarous kind) which is to them the crown of all Virtues. This worship of Heroism inevitably leads to perpetual Warfare, which has been constantly taking place among the Tribes for hundreds of years. What with these incessant

Wars, the beastly treatment of their Women . . . the impure air of their Dwellings, severe exposure, and irregular and unwholesome food, is there any wonder that these People are being gradually extinguished? But the White Men cannot clear their skirts of furthering their destruction;—not so much by the Sword or Bullet (for where the White Man has destoyed one by these means the Indians themselves have destoyed a hundred), as by corrupting their Morals and furnishing them Whiskey, which has made of them a listless, shiftless, and debauched Race."

Here Pancoast displays the characteristic ambiguity of well-disposed whites toward the American aborigines. Although the modern reader might reject the main line of his analysis of the problem of the Indian, the fact remained that there seemed to be no way within the framework of either Enlightenment notions of man as a rational animal and progress as the goal of history or the traditional doctrines of orthodox Christianity to accommodate the savages of the American continent.

In a world that was rational, ordered, and progressive—a "go ahead" world—the Indian, mysterious and ultimately inexplicable, was a profoundly troubling anomaly. To put the matter as simply as possible, he was un-American. By his intractible "Indian-ness" he raised the most fundamental questions about the nature of man. If the Indian could not be "civilized" as Jefferson and all other partakers of the Secular-Democratic Consciousness were convinced that he could and must be—that his essential nature was, like all men's, rational —then the human psyche must be far more complex and impenetrable than the philosophers of the Enlightenment had imagined. On the other hand if it could be demonstrated that the Indians were the Lost Tribes of Israel they might at least be brought back into some comprehensible framework.

On the rushers went, day by laborious day, enduring all the dangers and hardships of the trail, losing mules from exhaustion and sometimes from the bites of rattlesnakes, going hungry when game was scarce, perpetually losing stock to Indian horse stealers, having the cattle stampeded by runaway buffalo, or, in one instance, by thunder and lightning, losing wagons in river crossings, and otherwise experiencing all the dangers and hardships of the trail.

On the Arkansas River the oxen took alarm one night, broke through the circle of wagons, and disappeared. Two days later most of them were found thirty miles away by Bridger. At Pueblo, on the Arkansas, a Delaware Indian appeared who promised to take the train to California by a shortcut for fifty dollars and a horse. Bridger advised against the venture but "these enthusiastic Gold Hunters had become monomaniacs on the subject," Pancoast wrote, "and their minds were so inflated with the idea of the great Fortune awaiting them in the California Mines if only they could get there before the thousands now on their way arrived, that they resolved then and there to start immediately with only this Indian for their Guide," even though they must abandon their wagons and all such goods as they could not get on the backs of their mules.

Pancoast later learned that the Indian guide had abandoned them in almost impassable terrain. At the Colorado River they had disputed the proper direction to go and split into two parties of some forty men each. One of these parties again divided and one group of some twenty, after living for ten days on acorns and small birds, reached the San Joaquin Valley in October tattered, barefoot, and emaciated. None of the rest—more than sixty men—were ever heard of again.

Near the Sangre de Cristo Pass in the Taos Mountains of New Mexico the train passed the ranch of Kit Carson. "Kit himself," Pancoast wrote, "was a superior representative of the genuine Rocky Mountain Hunter. His skin was dark and he wore his long black hair over his coat, giving him much the appearance of a Mexican. He dressed in first class Indian style in Buckskin coat and pants trimmed with leather dangles, and wore moccasins on his feet and a Mexican Sombrero on his head." Carson was full of stories of his adventures and of the raids of the Ute Indians against his horses and stock and showed the awed travelers "several Arrow and Bullet Wounds on his person that he had received in his encounters with the Indians, in which he gloried as much as could the most distinguished General."

Pancoast was most impressed by the Pima Indians of present-day Arizona. He considered them "the best type of Indian on the Continent." They lived in a large village on the Gila River and had dug a canal thirty miles long to irrigate a large plot of land. "The men did most of the labor," Pancoast noted, "and the Squaws bore an air of importance and independence not usually seen in other Tribes. . . . They had enclosures made so by planting Cactus so as to form a solid Hedge six feet through, so impenetrable that not even a Rabbit could get through it . . . They raised Horses, Burros, Cattle and Goats, Corn, Potatoes, Yams, Beans, Tomatoes, and other vegetables." Their chief was a splendid-looking man six feet four inches tall who exhibited "all the address and eloquence of a first-class cultivated Orator." The impression he made was augmented by the fact that he wore "a full Military Suit with the golden epaulettes of a U.S. General, and the regulation belt and sword." One of the Pima Indians had learned to speak some Spanish, which inclined him to put on great airs. He proudly presented Pancoast and his friends with what he called his "Letter of Recommendation," which read "This Fellow is a damned Rascal. Look out for him. Lt. Cook, U.S.A." "We all exclaimed, 'Mucho Bueno!'" Pancoast wrote, "and he smiled all over his face."

On the American desert a dispute arose about the best course to follow and a number of members of the train withdrew to hold a meeting. When others of the party, curious about the proceedings, tried to join the group, they were turned away with the statement that it was "a Masonic Meeting," and shortly after its termination what turned out to be the Masonic portion of the train, including twelve of the best-equipped wagons, started down the Gila River with no word of explanation to the rest of the train. Myron and Eugene Angel set out to follow, carrying their belongings on their backs in eighty-pound packs. The "Crippled Ducks," as Pancoast termed them, the rest of the train, followed the Gila River to Yuma, where it joined the Colorado, an arid expanse with little grass or water. Oxen fell of exhaustion and thirst and, as Pancoast put it, "our trials were incessant." On the other side of the Colorado, the famished animals were fattened up on mesquite beans and the train prepared for the final push to Los Angeles, loading their wagon with mesquite beans for the oxen before they left. A few miles out of Yuma they passed the bones of five yoke of oxen and the skeleton of a man.

Now the toll of dying oxen mounted. Pancoast's own team was reduced to two yoke, and twenty dropped in a single day. The last leg of their journey took the train through the Santa Anna Mountains and in the hundred miles from the mountains to Los Angeles they passed six or seven ranches, some of them ten miles square, where "thousands of cattle ranged over the Hills and Plains, as wild as Deer." Among the ranches was that of Isaac Williams, a former trader at Santa Fe, who now ran thirty thousand head of cattle and owned a hundred horses. "He had immense Drying-sheds partly full of hides, and five cemented Vaults about fifteen by forty feet in extent and ten in depth, all but one full of tallow. . . . He was loading a Vessel at San Pedro, and expected a ship from Liverpool in a few days. His bone pile was twenty feet high and covered near half an acre," Pancoast wrote. Pancoast and his party rested at Williams's ranch for several days and while they were there an emigrant train made up of men, women, and children from Iowa and Missouri passed by.

Charles Pancoast described the California landholding system as "the vicious policy" of "raising up a powerful aristocracy whose loyalty could be relied upon by the distribution of enormous land grants to a few individuals." Thus all lands in the San Jacinto and San Bernardino valleys had been granted to eight or nine proprietors and "all this vast extent of land maintained only by the families of these nabobs and about eight hundred miserable peons and half civilized Indians, low in intelligence and morality, and skilled only in equestrian Arts, but possessing a vast amount of dangerous untrained Heroism."

The "nabobs" owned most of the town of Los Angeles and there were in consequence no house lots for sale, only a few houses "Built to rent to poor People, Merchants, Doctors, etc. . . . The Lord," Pancoast noted, "did not intend that this vast range of land should remain always in the possession of a few Nabobs as a range for Wild Beasts alone."

Pancoast took note of the fact that there was an acute shortage of women in the region. One gold rusher in the Missouri Train had brought with him his wife and two daughters, one of whom was fifteen, the other seventeen. "The Father had not finished putting up his tent before several young Miners were hanging around the Girls and making love to them. Before they had been there three days a Young Fellow ran away with the youngest Daughter and married her and a few days later the other Daughter ran away with another Fellow. The Father, having poor luck at finding Gold in that locality, went off with a prospecting Party to a distant location, and when he came home found his Wife had also eloped with a gay Suitor."

From San Bernardino, Pancoast and what was left of the Peoria Train headed north to the Sacramento area and the "mines." On the way, some Mexicans joined the party, offering to direct them to the Mariposa. The next morning the mules and horses to the number of eleven were gone and the Mexicans with them, and a wagon had to be abandoned. Pancoast discovered later that their helpful friends had been a band of outlaws led by Joaquin Murieta and his lieutenant, Three-fingered Jack. Murieta was the most famous bandit of California; he made a business "of robbing and murdering Miners and

Chinamen." When the band was finally cornered and Murieta killed by soldiers who had suffered several defeats by the bandits, Murieta's head and the hand of Three-fingered Jack were cut off and taken to San Francisco, where Pancoast later saw them preserved in alcohol.

Finally, on February 15, 1850, in a snowstorm, Pancoast and his party, now shrunk to a handful, arrived at the Mariposa mines after a journey of nine months and seventeen days. Pancoast had fifty cents left, enough to buy a little tobacco. As he walked back to his tent with his purchase, he saw "the holes of the Miners full of water, rusty picks and shovels lying about in the Snow, nasty muddy clay everywhere and the whole aspect so repulsive and dismal that I returned to Camp sick at heart with the prospect of the new enterprise in which I was about to engage."

Pancoast and his friend Smith Philipps set out to scout the diggings along the Merced River. They had no idea how to go about panning or mining for gold and no one seemed willing to instruct them, so they learned by watching others hardly more experienced than themselves. Meanwhile, Philipps's father had sold the team of mules and the wagon that they had gotten to California with such labor for eight hundred dollars, of which they offered Pancoast one-third although he had "put in" over six hundred dollars at the beginning of the journey. The next day they built a rocker, made a cradle and a box for the hopper, and fashioned a sieve of sorts from a piece of perforated sheet iron. Under the hopper was a canvas apron "tacked loosely to a frame that sat on cleats attached to the rocker." "Being made of green wood," Pancoast wrote, "it was a heavy, clumsy affair, and we found it a man-killer to carry around the Mountain." For that was the procedure—to find a promising unoccupied spot on the river, not by any means easy to do, and lug the contraption to its banks, divert water from the river into the hopper, and shovel in gravel, allowing the flowing water to wash the flakes of gold into the sieve. The first day brought in less than five dollars in gold dust. The three men, Pancoast, Philipps, and his father, then worked a flat occupied by a number of miners and collected gold to the value of eight dollars. Hearing of a big strike made by a black man on Mariposa Flat, they moved in beside him. In two days they made forty dollars, while the black man made one hundred dollars. At that point a train of Pike County (Missouri) men arrived and proposed that everyone join in diverting the river to expose more gold-bearing gravel. When the black man and Pancoast and his friends joined in the scheme, the

Pike County intruders announced that they would all draw lots for the thirty-foot claims along the creek bed. Pancoast, the Philippses, and the black man, who had already staked their claims, refused, but they were "drawn out" of their claims and the next day they found them occupied by the Pike County crew. When the members of the group inquired from other miners about the means of redress, they were told that the miners had elected an "alcade" with jurisdiction over the whole creek and the power to adjudicate conflicting claims. He turned out to be an imposing Kentuckian. He went at once to the Missourians to tell them that they were violating the "rules" of the mines, to which they responded by asking "who the Hell he was." They had no more regard for his opinion than for "us or the Nigger." At which the "alcade" or mayor called his miners together "and they all eagerly agreed to go down and route out the Pike County men."

The next morning ninety armed miners appeared to expostulate with the intruders. "The Miners," Pancoast wrote, "did not wait for orders, but told us to put our tools back on our Claims, jumping into the Diggings themselves and throwing the tools of the Pike County men as far as they could. Not satisfied with this, they insisted that these Fellows should leave their Diggings, threatening otherwise to destroy their Goods and Teams. The Alcade tried to mollify them, but found his Volunteers hard to control."

In two weeks Pancoast and his friends washed out some five hundred dollars' worth of gold while their black neighbor took some three thousand dollars in the same period. "One evening," Pancoast wrote, "while we were working there came out to this Flat about fifty People, with Wagons, Pack Mules, and a Machine for crushing quartz. Among them were Store Keepers, Mechanics, Gamblers, Miners, a Restaurant Man and a Surveyor." This party immediately surveyed the flat and laid out a town right across a portion of the existing claims, ignoring the protests of Pancoast and the Philippses. This was the beginning of the town of Mariposa and since their holdings appeared mined out, Pancoast and his friends confessed themselves outnumbered and set out to search for new diggings near Yosemite Valley. They found a spot further up the Merced and hauled their crude rocker to the site where they were soon taking twelve to fifteen dollars a day in gold dust. In front of their tent was a small boulder that they used as a seat. One day a young miner inspected the rock and asked if he could have it as it seemed to contain some flecks of gold. Possessed of the stone, he sold it to the storekeeper from the new town of

Mariposa for two hundred dollars and the storekeeper in turn broke it up and extracted three thousand dollars' worth of gold.

At the mines a member of the Missouri Train named Roberts sold for sixteen dollars each a herd of sheep that he had bought for fifty cents apiece and brought with him on the cross-country trek; gave his slave, Green, his freedom, finding "he could no longer control [him] and that he was virtually free. . . ." And Green, in Pancoast's words, "like all Colored People at the Mines . . . had luck, and soon accumulated $1500." Roberts, seeing the money, told Green that he would have to buy his freedom for that sum, "and the thick-headed Fellow gave him the money, Roberts giving him a Paper he called an 'Emancipation Paper.'" Back in Missouri the paper was, of course, worthless and Pancoast heard later that Green was still a slave.

Mining was hard work and the profits split three ways were hardly sufficient to make Pancoast and his friends rich. They mined two diggings that were unproductive and then, reworking some abandoned claims with a friend named Elisha Douglas who had just joined them, found a solid gold nugget "about the size and shape of a Land Turtle," weighing over nine pounds. Before nightfall they had found another of three and a half pounds. After five days the gold ran out entirely and the party headed for the Stanislaus River where, they heard, a company had diverted the river and made a fortune. Adding several new recruits to their party, Pancoast and the Philippses decided to "turn the river" themselves. The plan was for a canal sixteen feet wide and four feet deep dug through a quarter of a mile of rocks and boulders to carry off the river. After two days of digging, the skeptical Pancoast calculated that it would take them two years to divert the river. Persuaded, the party turned to a less ambitious scheme of a dam and a much shorter canal. They worked on this project for four long, exhausting months before the river was finally turned. In the next two days, fifteen men working feverishly turned up sixteen dollars' worth of gold and several days later they abandoned the project, their months of back-breaking labor expended for nothing. The venture had cost each member of the party one thousand dollars. They now decided to disband and go their own ways searching for the elusive metal, but first they would spend their hard-earned sixteen dollars in a "jollification." A member was dispatched to the Mariposa store and returned with whiskey, lemons, sugar, and ginger cakes, all the sixteen dollars would buy.

"Jollification" was as much a part of the miner's life as digging.

Another young gold rusher named Amos Delano described the digging on the Feather River as including members of "almost every State in the Union, while France, England, Germany, and even Bohemia, had their delegates. As soon as breakfast was dispatched, all hands were engaged in digging and washing gold in the banks, or in the bed of the stream. When evening came, large fires were built, around which the miners congregated, some engrossed with thoughts of home and friends, some to talk of new discoveries, and richer diggings elsewhere; or, sometimes a subject or debate was started . . . I highly enjoyed . . . the wild life we were leading, for there were many accomplished and intelligent men; and a subject for amusement or debate was rarely wanting. As for ceremony or dress . . . we were all alike."

Life in the mining camps was reminiscent of life in the winter camps of the fur trappers. That is to say, there was a kind of ecstatic male comradery which encompassed all nationalities, classes, and races. French counts and German barons mixed with free blacks, half-breeds, and Indians as well as doctors, lawyers, ex-army officers, politicians, journalists, murderers, and common criminals. It was, again, this Whitmanesque "mystery of manly love," as D. H. Lawrence puts it, "the love of comrades" and of the "Open Road," the journeying. The miners established their own crude democracy, their ready-made justice. They worked and brawled and sang and danced together in their strange womanless world. Women were complication and "civilization," competition and anxiety. But life in the diggings was male life, life free of civilization, of women, of responsibilities, of politics. It was a world of back-breaking work and luck; a world where black men notoriously prospered over whites because they could work harder and had better luck. Civilization was minding one's manners, keeping clean, looking sharp, obeying the rules. Here the miners made their own rules, meted out their own often draconian but usually fair punishments, fleshed out their own fantasies.

The miners were, after all, not miners but all kinds and conditions masquerading as miners. The fantasy of buried treasure, the fantasy of picking up gold is as old as civilization, as old as precious stones and precious metals, and this is what this indescribably motley collection of individuals did; they picked up gold, washed it out of the creeks and riverbeds, knocked it out of the rocks. Very, very few of them made money, very few broke even, many of them lost everything but the shirts on their backs, a good many died miserable or violent deaths, a very few made fortunes and most of these gambled them away, squandered them on women and booze, or wildcat speculations. A few laid the foundations of great fortunes, but they were the cool, hard-eyed unscrupulous ones who turned all the bone-cracking work of others to their own accounts.

"California," Amos Delano wrote, "proved to be a leveler of pride, and everything like aristocracy of employment; indeed the tables seemed to be turned, for those who labored hard in a business that compared with digging wells and canals at home fared worse than the Irish laborer were those who made the most money in mining. It was a common thing to see a statesman, a lawyer, a physician, a merchant, or a clergyman, engaged in driving oxen and mules, cooking for his mess, at work for wages by the day, making hay, hauling wood, or filling menial offices." This was the democracy and equality that the Declaration of Independence had promised. The natural aristocracy of the placers was the aristocracy of muscle. "The consequence was," in Delano's words, "that starvation and misery stared them in the face, after all the trials they had encountered on the plains; for, notwithstanding public and private charity was extended for their relief to a great degree, their numbers were too great for all to be relieved, and many suffered and died for want of the care and proper nourishment which their way-worn and debilitated frames required. . . . It was found, too, that talent for business, literary and scientific acquirements, availed little or nothing in a country where strength of muscle was required to raise heavy rocks and dig deep pits. It was strength, absolute brute force, which was required to win the gold of the placers, and many a poor fellow, unable to endure the severe labors under a scorching sun, was finally compelled to give it up in despair."

Towns sprang up like mushrooms near the diggings. At a spot where Amos Delano forded the Yuba in September, 1849, there were only two crude adobe houses. When he returned a year later Yuba City consisted of a thousand inhabitants, "with a large number of hotels, stores, groceries, bakeries, and . . . gambling houses." "There seemed a speculative mania spreading over the land," Dalano wrote, "and scores of new towns were heard of which were never known, only through the puffs of newspapers. Not a single town was laid out on land where the title was indisputable; and as might be expected, litigations were frequent. Squatting followed, which resulted, in many cases, in riot and bloodshed." These instant towns had such names as Shinbone Peak, Murderer's Gulch, Delirium Tremens, Whiskey Diggings, You Bet. In Delano's words, "From one end of the valley of the Sacramento to the other innumerable towns were laid out, which would have required the concentration of the population of California to supply with inhabitants. . . ."

While some diggings were still productive word would come of a fabulous new strike and a new "rush" would be on. "Stores," Delano wrote, "were left to take care of themselves, business of all kinds was dropped, mules were suddenly bought up at exorbitant prices, and crowds started off to search for the golden lake. . . . The mountains swarmed with men, exhausted and worn out with toil and hunger; mules were starved, or killed by falling from precipices."

Out of all this extraordinary expenditure of energy, money, and even life, few benefited, although the total amount of gold scratched up more than doubled the world supply. But a subsidiary benefit was that "the country was more perfectly explored," roads were cut, trading posts established, and the remoter regions "opened up" to more orderly and permanent settlement; knowledge of California and its nonmetallic riches was widely disseminated and a new impetus given to its settlement as well as to that of the Oregon country, which was known to have its own gold rush or rushes.

Poking through an abandoned camp, Amos Delano came on a scarecrow in an old, torn shirt and ragged pantaloons. Pinned to the figure was a paper which read, "Californians—Oh, Californians, look at me! once fat and saucy as a privateersman, but now—look ye—a miserable skeleton. In a word, I am a used up man. Never mind, I can sing, notwithstanding,

> O California! this is the land for me;
> A pick and shovel, and lots of bones!
> Who would not come the sight to see,—
> The golden land of dross and stones.
> O Susannah, don't you cry for me,
> I'm living *dead,* in Californi-ee."

In September, 1850, word reached California that Congress had "grudgingly" accepted the territory "as a younger sister of the Union." The news set off an orgy of celebration "throughout the length and breadth of the land—for the people of California loved . . . the glorious Union of States which bound them in one common tie; and also ardently desired the 'star-spangled banner' should wave over her mountains and plains, a symbol that this too was 'the land of the free, the home of the brave,' " as Amos Delano put it. In San Francisco Bay hundreds of ships "were gaily decked with streamers." There were parades, orations, "odes and illuminations, the firing of cannon and general rejoicing."

The party that Pancoast attached himself to moved on to the Chinese Diggings, an area developed by Chinese immigrants, found them barren and headed for the Moccasin Creek Diggings. They remained there for a month, making eight to sixteen dollars a day—good wages but hardly the foundation of a fortune. The Moccasin mined out, they pushed on to the Tuolumne River. At Big Oak Flat they found an old Norwegian woman living in a hollow stump which she had converted into a boardinghouse and from which she dispensed a meal of pork and beans, dried apples and bread at a dollar a head—milk was a dollar a quart—and made much more money than most of the miners she served. At Big Oak Flat, Indians raided a miner's camp, stole a horse, and killed one miner and wounded another. The miners followed the Indians to their settlement some twenty-five miles away, and, with the braves absent, "killed Old Men, Squaws, and Children" to Pancoast's horror.

On the Tuolumne River the gold was so fine that it could not be caught with an ordinary rocker, so the party invested $250 in a "Quicksilver Machine." In this process quicksilver was put into "the sag of the apron" through which water washed. The quicksilver gathered the gold. At the end of the day it was placed in a buckskin bag and the water squeezed out, after which the gold and quicksilver were heated in an iron ladle causing the quicksilver to evaporate and leaving the gold. With this process they made about two hundred dollars a day for four weeks until winter overtook them, at which point they built a tidy log cabin and spent the time "throwing up dirt out of the Gulches," dirt which they would wash for gold in the spring and which they estimated would bring them each a thousand dollars or so. They also hunted deer and visited a nearby trading post and thus "spent the Winter merrily," as Pancoast wrote. But before he could harvest any of the fruits of his winter labor, Pancoast heard of rich gold strikes on the Trinity River hundreds of miles away, so he took leave of his companions and headed for San Francisco to find a coastal boat to carry him to the Trinity.

At San Francisco, the harbor was filled with the masts of sailing ships whose crews had deserted to go to the goldfields. There he was told that the nearest place on the coast to the new diggings was

Trinidad. From there to the mines was 150 miles, which must be covered by mule at a cost of two dollars a pound for transportation. Pancoast decided to buy his own mules, carry them by coastal schooner to Trinidad, and go into the packing business on the way to the mines. He thus bought six mules for $125 to $150 apiece and paid $30 apiece to have them transported. Leaving Golden Gate, the schooner sailed into a violent storm and the mules, tossed in the hold, were killed or so badly injured that they had all to be thrown overboard. For eight days the boat was buffeted, at the end of which time it was twenty miles south of San Francisco. When it put back to San Francisco for repairs, Pancoast took stock of his fortunes. He had lost some sixteen hundred dollars "in the turning of the Stanislaus," and lived for the winter months on the Merced River "without production." Now he had lost his mules and was down to his last ten dollars. "My continued Misfortunes and the prospect before me," he wrote, "were enough to crush the Spirits of almost any man; but Youth, Health, Spunk, Energy, and Perseverance" remained. He started once more for Trinity sans mules on an "old rattletrap Steamer" and once more was caught in a fearsome storm. The steamer nonetheless made its way to the mouth of Humboldt Bay, where it ran aground crossing the bar into the bay; Pancoast and the other passengers were carried by small boats to Eureka, while the steamer broke up rapidly under the pounding of the waves. At Eureka Pancoast, virtually penniless, got a job splitting cedar rails and palings to make fences, and a newfound friend from Belfast, Maine, lent him enough money to pay the proprietor of the pack train for carrying his equipment to the diggings. Five days of hard traveling over mountain trails brought Pancoast finally to the Trinity River. There he set to work once more to make his fortune, joining a party of four miners consisting of a sailor named Burr from New York, another sailor from Maine, a Scotsman, and an Irishman. The next day they were joined by seven Frenchmen. One of the Frenchmen, a hunchback named Dupont, persuaded Pancoast to go into partnership with him. For a time they mined twenty or thirty dollars of gold a day until a party appeared and located themselves on the claim of Pancoast and his partner. The Frenchman ran off and got his countrymen, who soon appeared "armed with Pistols, Blunderbusses and Picks," to drive off the intruders. The French party included a "Count," described by Pancoast as "a member of the Orleans Family, a profligate, good-hearted Fellow, and good company when sober."

The miners suffered constantly from the depredations of roving Indians, whose favorite trick was to kill and dismember a mule or horse so steathily that its owner never awoke. Pancoast lost a buffalo robe and all his blankets to a sick Indian he had befriended and the Count had his horse stolen while he slept although it was tethered to his wrist by a rope.

Pancoast found the constant physical exertion required of a miner increasingly onerous and finally decided to start a store to supply the miners, a less glamorous but more reliable way to make a living. Once again luck was against him. He had hardly opened his store with its modest but expensive stock of provisions when word came of a new strike on the Klamath River, sixty miles away, and his customers packed up and departed.

Disgusted with the life in the goldfields, which had turned out to be more arduous than that of a steamboat owner and as unremunerative as being a druggist or a door-to-door booksalesman, Pancoast set out for Weaverville and arrived there to find a crowd of miners with a "poor suppliant Fellow that they were hanging to the limb of a tree with a slip noose around his neck." He was suspected of having stolen several hundred dollars' worth of gold dust and his prosecutors were trying to extract from him its hiding place. He responded readily to save his neck but the gold could not be found and "believing him to be lying the miners hauled him up to the limb again and again until he was near dead. . . ." At that point the gold was found and the thief was let down from his limb; thereupon the miners formed a double line and forced the culprit to run the gauntlet to the accompaniment of kicks and blows. "This," Pancoast wrote, "was common Justice in California at that time."

At Weaverville that night Pancoast slept on the floor at a road house with some forty men and women. For three dollars the patrons got lodging, pork and beans, coffee without sugar or milk, and corn donnicks without butter. The next day Pancoast set off down the Shasta Valley past One Horse Town and Whiskeyville to Shasta City, which had a respectable hotel whose proprietor put Pancoast in a room with an ailing young man who died during the night of "Erysipelas of the head." Pancoast bought a mule, saddle, bridle, and "fittings" and set off down the Sacramento. "Here was I," he wrote, "who had not worn a coat or shaved for two years, assuming the Role of Traveling Gentleman." And so he went "putting up at Road Houses . . . with Omnibus Sleeping rooms and Pike County meals." Sitting beside the road, eating his breakfast and wondering what his next venture might be, Pancoast was delighted to see his old friend Myron Angel, with whom he had started out from Fort Leavenworth almost three years earlier and from whom he had parted company at the Gila River. Myron and his brother, Eugene, the erstwhile lawyer, had "squatted" on a land claim and were farming and raising cattle. Their adventures had been as colorful and strenuous as Pancoast's. They had arrived in San Diego, more dead than alive, "with swollen limbs, barefoot and ragged, out of money and Provisions." The American officer in charge of the United States interests in that town had helped them, along with a number of other emigrants in little better condition, to get to San Francisco by boat; there they had slept in the streets and worked with picks and shovels for three dollars a day. They had saved their money, bought a yawl, fitted it out with tools and provisions, and rowed it to Marysville where it was stolen. They had then signed on as packers for a mule train and thus gotten to the Yuba Mines, where like Pancoast they had carried on great labors with meager results.

The Angels easily persuaded Pancoast to join them on their ranch, a log cabin with a canvas roof, located at the juncture of a broad pond and a creek. Wild horses and antelope ranged the adjacent meadows and hillsides. Eugene had a plan to make their fortunes. From the famous filibuster General Walker, who lived near Marysville, the partners bought thirty-six hogs for fifteen hundred dollars, and from some Mexicans twenty-five chickens at sixteen dollars apiece and a dozen yoke of oxen, which exhausted their combined savings. All was industry and enterprise—a chicken house was built, a hog pen, a brush corral for the oxen, a little garden by the lake surrounded by paling to keep out the deer; six acres were sown in barley and one in potatoes. With sowing, reaping, building and repairing fences, and digging drainage ditches, Pancoast found himself doing more manual labor than he had done while mining. But the three young men had "good health" and good appetites and were surrounded "by Wild Animals, such as Elk, Antelope . . . California Lions, Coyotes, Rabbits, Squirrels . . . and sometimes Grizzly Bears and Wild Hogs . . . Otters . . . Geese, Ducks, Sandhill Cranes, Brant, Snipes, California Pigeons, Doves, and other Birds of value. We could go out at any time and shoot an Antelope, a Goose, or a Duck. . . ." Fish abounded in the river. But prairie wolves, hawks, raccoons, martens, and weasels inflicted a heavy toll on their sixteen-dollar chickens. Ground squirrels stole their sugar and flour and a grizzly bear carried off a hog. On one of his return visits they shot the bear, took off the choice pieces for themselves, and sold the balance in Marysville for forty dollars, suggesting the interesting calculation that a thousand-pound grizzly was not quite worth three chickens. The mountain lions also made themselves free with the partners' pigs and occasionally killed an old horse or mule. The most persistent menace was what Pancoast called the "mountain Indians," who made their homes in the mountains and carried off cattle or horses not carefully guarded. The "Valley Indians," who lived primarily on acorns and roots, were not a danger but they, from their proximity to whites, suffered terrible losses from disease, especially cholera, which ten years earlier had, it was estimated, killed half the Indians living in the Sacramento Valley. By Pancoast's time only one old chief was left of a tribe that had traditionally made its home in the area. He was employed as a butcher on a nearby ranch and lamented to Pancoast "the loss of his Tribe, and, appeared broken-hearted."

Idyllic as the life was, the ranch was slow to produce the fortune that Eugene Angel had predicted, and he was soon cooking up new ventures to augment the anticipated revenues from farming.

Another ambitious entrepreneur, "Mr. Munroe, the Prospector of Munroeville," was planning a stagecoach line to Marysville which would pass through the Angel-Pancoast ranch. If the partners would build a toll bridge across Butte Creek where it bisected their land he would pay them fifty dollars a year. If they would build a stable for the stage's horses he would add another twenty dollars a week. In addition they might wish to build a small hotel for the accommodation of travelers on the stage. "Eugene was not a man to linger," Pancoast noted, and soon the partners were hard at work building log cribs, cutting sleepers, and hewing main bearing timbers. In two weeks the work was done. Twelve cents for a "Foot Passenger, twenty-five for a Horseman, and fifty for a Team." One man could take the tolls and do haying in the fields nearby. The others winnowed the barley, dug a well, made fences, and lent a hand with the haying when they had nothing more pressing to do. Then one day a prairie fire swept down on the ranch and burned up the barley in the fields and the sacks of painstakingly winnowed grain piled beside the barn. Hastily set back-fires saved the bridge, the stable, and the hay.

Next came the hotel. It was to be an imposing structure thirty-six by forty feet, two stories high, with a stone foundation. While they labored to complete the hotel, their work slowed by lack of capital and the necessity to alternate as toll takers and farmers, a cattle drover named Thaddeus Pomroy appeared. Pomroy, a friend of Pancoast's from his druggist days in Lexington, Missouri, was looking for a pasture to fatten eight hundred scrawny cattle that he had driven across the plains and he offered the partners fifty cents per week per head to fatten his animals. Here was an undreamed of windfall, four hundred dollars a week.

One of the most striking aspects of the California gold rush was how often the rushers encountered friends or acquaintances from "back east." Charles Pancoast was typical in this respect. In the course of the somewhat more than three years that he was in California hardly a month passed that he did not meet, in some remote and unexpected spot, a friend whom he had known in one town or another. Such encounters serve to remind us of the perpetual mobility of many Americans. Eternally on the move over a relatively few well traveled trails and roads, they were constantly meeting and parting and meeting again. Taking a wagon load of barley to Colusa, Pancoast found a man named Majors who had bought out his drugstore in Warsaw running a raunchy hotel. Majors professed to be delighted to see him and put him in a flea-infested room for which he charged the outrageous price of four dollars for the night and a Pike County breakfast; when Pancoast went to pay him Majors weighed out his gold dust on a rigged scale and tried to take eight dollars' worth. So much for old times.

By December of 1852 Pancoast and his friends calculated that they had a property which, with improvements—houses, stables, fields, fences, wells, and stock—was worth at least seven thousand dollars. They had created it in a little more than a year out of an investment of less than a third of that sum and prodigious hard work. The hotel had been framed and an ice house built. Now the winter storms began. It rained almost constantly and the pond soon turned into a slough and the ranch was converted into "a great lake thirty miles in width." Each hour the water crept higher on the little rise that held the house and barn. Finally it was above the floor level and poured through the chinks between the logs until it was as high as the table top. There was nothing Pancoast and his friends could do but watch and pray. Finally the rains slackened and the waters began to recede, leaving more than fifty snakes in the house. It was a week before Pancoast and the Angels could leave the house and even then they were marooned without food. They ground up barley in a coffeemill and made coarse cakes and ate their sixteen-dollar chickens. As the water drained off and they had a chance to survey the damage it was apparent that they had been wiped out. The bridge, ice house, and half-finished hotel had all been washed away, the hogs drowned, the horses and cattle drowned or scattered. Worst of all, Pancoast was gripped by a relentless fever. As soon as he was able to walk he decided to head for Sacramento to try to find a doctor. So he took leave of the Angel brothers carrying a blanket and his last thirty dollars. The road to Colusa was strewn with evidences of the flood. The roadhouses had all suffered its consequences and at one where Pancoast stayed there was nothing to eat but biscuits made with mouldy black flour, poor bacon and weak coffee. From Colusa our friend made his way to Sacramento by steamboat and found the whole town of ten thousand people flooded and the "inhabitants sailing around the Town in Boats." Pancoast engaged one and was rowed to a hotel where he spent the night in "a third story Omnibus room" containing fifty other cots, most of them occupied. There his coughing so disturbed the other sleepers that the landlord next day requested him to find other lodgings.

Pancoast's situation was now desperate. He had what he called "pulmonary consumption," which frequently resulted in death. He was down to his last eight dollars and he had been unable to procure the services of a doctor. "There was no Alms House or Free Hospital in Sacramento," he wrote, "the able Poor could always get work, and the sick or disabled were expected to die." Through all his hardships, Pancoast had clung to some "rare and curious specimens of Gold Quartz." This he now sold to a "Jewish Broker" for sixty-five dollars, which enabled him to buy medicines to dose himself and pay for a hotel room. When he was able to get out of bed he went in search of a job as a druggist. He found a position with a South Carolina Jew named Dunbar and there he began to recoup his fortunes and his health. Word arrived from the Angels that they had rounded up some of the stock, the hogs and the horses, and proposed to hold a sale to dispose of what was left of their once flourishing venture. Pancoast decided to return to the ranch for the sale, settle up with the brothers, and shake the dust, gold and otherwise, of California from his shoes. After the sale, where the hogs went for fifty dollars apiece, they divided the modest proceeds, with Pancoast taking his third. Then they parted with tears and embraces. To Pancoast they were "two Noble Men, who approached as near to 'Angels' as Humans are capable of. Eugene was an educated Lawyer, but [the "but" is significant] very honorable in his business transactions. He was hopeful and visionary, and his conceptions were often far beyond his ability to execute; yet he had a vast amount of Industry, Energy, and Genius. Myron was still more cultivated than Eugene. He was a good Civil Engineer, and had a gentlemanly appearance and address, but was imperious and fiery in his Disposition. . . . They belonged to Professions not usually noted for their Integrity. . . . If any Reader of these remarks," Pancoast added, "should meet them, honour them, for an Honest man is the noblest work of God; and even if you meet their Children, honour them for their Fathers' sake."

Eugene was killed in an Indian massacre at Pyramid Lake, Nevada, in 1860. Myron became a successful journalist and died in San Luis Obispo half a century later.

The proceeds of the sale left Pancoast with five hundred dollars and he made his way back to Sacramento, where he took up his job with Dunbar for a time and then set out for San Francisco. Pancoast was less than impressed with the city: "the whole People seemed to be a set of Gamblers and Adventurers. They swarmed the Streets and Trade Marts, disdaining to keep to the sidewalks, and were constantly hustling each other, reminding me of Dante's Restless Spirits in his *Inferno*. There were neither Gas Lights nor Hydrant Water; we paid fifty cents per barrel for Spring Water, and Camphine furnished our lights. The Streets were in a wretched condition. Politics were corrupt; The City was controlled by Gamblers and their Friends, and the Courts were largely in the hands of the same power. Gambling Houses were to be found open to the Street, with attractive Bars, Lights, and bands of Musick; in some of them were perhaps fifty tables running day and night, Sundays not excepted. The use of deadly Weapons was an everyday affair. Villainous Women from China, Chile, Mexico, France, and New York, were imported by shiploads for Merchandise; all found Friends willing to pay their Captains their exorbitant charges, and many found faithful Husbands. Many other evils were rife which I will not attempt to unveil, and the Temptations to Youth were terrific," Pancoast concluded.

A Vigilance Committee was in the process of being formed to drive the thieves and gamblers out of the city. Pancoast encountered the gambler Burke who had accompanied the Peoria Train across the plains and who urged him to go partners in a plan to build a handsome hotel and gambling casino, the El Dorado Hotel. Pancoast resisted the "wild scheme"; Burke built his hotel by renting space in advance to gamblers, became a millionaire, lost his wealth in an "unfortunate

Speculation and went to destruction. So fast were Fortunes made and lost in San Francisco at that period," Pancoast noted.

"Robberies and murders were of daily occurrence," in Amos Delano's words. "Organized bands of thieves existed in the towns and in the mountains." There were no adequate prisons and such judges as there were were frequently corrupted by the criminals. A captain of police had three thousand dollars in gold stolen from him and some citizens were bold enough to wonder how he had accumulated such wealth. The flimsy buildings, some of them with canvas sides, were set afire to conceal a crime or distract attention while one was committed. "The whole length . . . of California," Delano wrote, "was now beset by unprincipled men who set law, order, and justice alike at defiance . . . so that for the peace of society, a general revolution became necessary." The "general revolution" was of course the taking of the law into the hands of outraged citizens. After a particularly lurid robbery and murder had gone unpunished, the newspaper the *Alta California* editorialized, "We do not wonder that the whole city is excited, that every honest man feels indignant against the vile miscreants who have fired our homes, robbed our citizens, and murdered them. This feeling is natural. And the present apparent and expressed determination to take the administration of the law into their own hands, is the inevitable result of a shameful laxity in the administration of our lower courts. To them alone, is chargeable the present state of public feelings." A month later the *Daily Courier* expressed similar sentiments: "It is clear to every man, that San Francisco is partially in the hands of criminals, and that crime has reached a crisis when life and property are in imminent danger. There is no alternative now left us, but to lay aside our business, and direct our whole energies, as a people, to seek out the abodes of these villains, and execute vengeance upon them."

On June 11, the *Courier* and *Alta California* carried notices proposing a meeting of all concerned citizens on the Plaza at three in the afternoon. The same morning a man was to be seen hanging from the porch of a house on Portsmouth Square. The Vigilance Committee was already at work. That night a man was in the act of robbing a safe. A "jury" was assembled on the spot, the culprit tried and hanged at once. "And this," Delano wrote, "was the commencement of the reign of justice in the criminal code of California."

The Plaza meeting brought out thousands of people who voted their approval of the existence and the actions of the Vigilance Committee and adjourned until the following day, when they met again to approve by acclamation a set of resolves which read in part, "we are constrained to believe that the crimes of grand larceny, burglary and arson, should be punished with death, disclaiming the right to inflict the penalty after a proper time has elapsed to obtain the voice of the people through the ballot box." The crowd then pledged "our lives, our fortunes, and our sacred honor, to protect and defend the people's court and officers, against any and all other jurisprudence." A person charged with a crime was promised "a fair and impartial trial by jury . . ." and the benefit of "any doubt."

According to Delano, the principal opposition came from lawyers who, in his skeptical view, "were losing a fruitful source of revenue in the defence of scoundrels." Again in Delano's opinion, the results were prompt and salutary: "An effective and active police was . . . formed, the rogues were either caught or banished, and the city soon relieved from the thralldom of their presence." Other towns and cities followed the example of San Francisco and formed Vigilance Committees to deal with the criminals and undesirables. Undoubtedly a good deal of injustice was done along with the much rough justice. The legislature responded by accepting as "capital" those crimes enumerated at citizen meetings, and the official organs of the law gradually reasserted their authority.

The population of California had risen from fifteen or twenty thousand in 1848 to 223,856 four years later. Even then tens of thousands had already returned home, disillusioned over the prospects of making a fortune digging for gold, many broken in health and fortune. In the same period $220,000,000 in gold had been mined and for the next fifty years, long after the gold rush was only a memory, the state continued to produce at least $10,000,000 in gold a year, much of it by large companies.

Even Amos Delano, who had himself succumbed to the lure of gold, was at a loss to understand the psychology that drew men in such numbers to the fields in the face of the multitude of letters and newspaper accounts which described very graphically "the difficulties and uncertainty of mining." "Gold," he wrote, "is not equally distributed in the earth, and the idea of picking up lumps in the mines, like gravel stones, is preposterous . . . and while now and then one miner may make a good strike, by far the greater number will make scarcely day-wages." In Delano's words, "An amount of treasure hitherto unparalleled in the annals of mankind has been taken out which threatens at no distant day to have an important bearing on the commercial and financial operations of the world." Its most important bearing, undoubtedly, was to ensure the acceptance of California as a state, a consequence that would have been by no means certain without the discovery of gold.

The gold rush was a prime example of what we might call "people's capitalism." Armadas of ships, vast caravans of wagons, tens of thousands of mules and horses and oxen had all to be assembled, virtually overnight. The most skilled military commissary with unlimited resources could not have organized such an immense army of citizen "soldiers" or gotten even a substantial portion of them to their destination. The force of American society might be centrifugal and disintegrative but those human particles whirling around in the great spaces of the continent could, if attracted by the magnet of money and adventure, coalesce in an instant. Thought of simply in terms of kilowatts of human energy expended, the gold rush becomes another major key to American history. All the human and material ingredients of the rush seemed to flow almost as though by magic to those centers from which the emigrants were to depart. Wherever there was a need, entrepreneurs appeared to meet it. Even such exotic items as rubber boats and air mattresses were produced in great quantities as though someone had waved a magic wand.

By concentrating on the gold and seeing the rush as a colorful aberration, we miss half the economic story. Gold aside, that awesome burst of energy involved in collecting it, that almost incomprehensible outpouring of largely misplaced activity, gave a tremendous stimulus to the entire national economy. It did, of course, more than that. Some American politicians had talked expansively about the "manifest destiny" of the United States to reach the Pacific. Many other Americans had expressed their abhorrence of the idea on constitutional, political, social, and moral grounds. For people like Philip Hone and George Strong, California was initially an irrelevance and then an embarrassment, important only so far as its largely unwelcome gold might affect the world's money supply and thereby their investments. But now several hundred thousand Americans had, at enormous cost, human and material, "manifested" that destiny in a fashion that could not be ignored, by going to the Oregon territory and by creating California.

More important than the gold, more important than the several hundred thousand Americans who made the desperately arduous journey to the goldfields, more important, even, than the emigrants who came by the tens of thousands each year following the rush to settle in the fertile valleys and coastal plains of California—more important than all these was the fact that the American imagination was "enlarged" by the rush to reach out to the shores of the Pacific and comprehend the continent. A stream of books—sketches, novels, reports, guides—as well as innumerable newspaper articles fleshed out and made vivid for stay-at-home Americans the practical, geographical reality of California, made them *conscious* of it in a new and compelling way. The tens of thousands of returnees also played a significant role. They might come back bitter and disillusioned and aged beyond their years, but they invariably came back with a repertoire of fascinating tales. Even those who died in California helped to make a connection between their native towns and the distant land. Correspondingly, the interminable space between—the Great Plains, the Great Basin, the Salt Desert, and the trackless Southwest—entered into the comprehension of Americans. Jefferson's westward-yearning imagination had become America's. What all this meant, in essence, was that the Union had grown stronger. Perhaps it could be said that the admission of California as a state consolidated the Union in the sense that it added an imponderable new element to the polarization of North and South, Free and Slave. The addition of California suggested a whole new set of possibilities. It helped to create a kind of interim, a political and social "space," wherein to reflect upon its meaning. It disturbed the delicate political equilibrium, but no one could at once be certain quite how or to what effect. The very substantial and growing sentiment in the North that the sectional divisions were irreconcilable and that the South must be allowed to depart from the Union in peace was checked. In such a division where would California and indeed the whole undeveloped trans-Mississippi West fit in? But more than such practical questions there was a sense that the Union was now too grand an edifice to be rudely dismantled. The gold rush, like so many events in our history, had dimensions and implications that it has, as yet, only partially disclosed and that, to a degree, we can only guess at. Among other notable things it provided a grand four-year distraction for the American people, which may have helped to draw their attention from that ultimate question slavery, and thereby postpone the day of reckoning.

In a sense, it also put the cap on the initial phase of the westward movement. From Stephen Long's expedition to the Rocky Mountains in 1820 through the "brown gold" or beaver fur rush of the 1820s and

30s, to the explorations of Jedediah Smith and the activities of the Santa Fe traders, to the beginnings of the emigration into Oregon Territory and on to the gold rush, there ran an unbroken thread of westward venturing in which the economic motive and a less-easily definable lust for adventure complimented each other to produce an era in our history of unrivaled, inexhaustible romance and drama. There were to be other "rushes," gold and silver, and other adventures in abundance in "settling the West," but nothing would quite equal the opening chapters, the stories of the "first-comers" to those fabulous lands.

In the spring of 1854 Pancoast took a boat for Philadelphia with the intention of going into the real estate business with his brother. Even on the steamer he encountered friends and acquaintances. Thaddeus Pomroy of Lexington, Missouri, whose cattle had been fattened at the Angel-Pancoast ranch, was a passenger. Pomroy had "galloping consumption" and was headed home to die. He had with him a metal-lined coffin filled with alcohol to preserve his body in case he failed to make it, and indeed he died the third day at sea, was sealed up in his coffin, and taken home for burial by the foreman of his ranch. Also aboard was the barkeeper of one of Pancoast's and Skinkle's Missouri steamboats. At San Juan del Sur, on the Nicaraguan coast, the passengers all debarked and took mules across the isthmus to Greytown; there they boarded another steamer for New York and thence went by train to Philadelphia, where Pancoast's friends found it difficult to recognize him after his "fourteen years of wandering."

We are singularly fortunate in having such an engaging guide to the Mississippi Valley frontier and to the gold rush itself. In his perceptiveness, good humor, and narrative flair, Pancoast calls to mind Joseph Plumb Martin, the "common soldier" of the Revolution. Even Pancoast's sufferings and hardships remind us of Martin's, and of the simple physical cost of creating America. In a sense the Revolutionary "war" continued for those Americans who ventured west. It was a war against nature, against a wild and intractable continent, against hunger and disease, against Indians, against a chaotic economy, and surely Charles Pancoast was a faithful soldier in that war. He is another American original and his autobiography abounds in revealing incidents, episodes, and observations, not the least of which are his reflections on what it took to get ahead in a "go-ahead" society. It is agreeable to report, in this regard, that Pancoast, who had covered so much real estate, prospered in the business of selling it, became a mainstay of the emerging Republican Party in Philadelphia, an alderman and a magistrate, married a handsome widow with two sons, and became a devoted husband and father.

He wrote his autobiography not, as he said with typical modesty, "with a view to Publication, but as a Memento" for friends and relatives and their descendants. His life had "not reached the full measure of my early Ambitions and expectations," but his disappointments had not been so great as "to interfere with my present Happiness. In the long and almost incessant struggles that I have encountered, [I only] regret that I have not done all the Good to my Fellow Creatures that I might have done, or obeyed the Laws and Commandments of my Maker as well as I should. . . ." To Pancoast it seemed that his life had been "somewhat void of Romance, and . . . Heroic Deeds and the accomplishment of extraordinary results. . . ." If the heroism of the commonplace is the only heroism available to most of humanity and, perhaps after all, the best part, Pancoast is certainly entitled to an honorable place alongside those anonymous heroes and heroines like the Massachusetts schoolteacher and the Angel brothers whom he celebrated in his autobiography. Romantic or not, it seemed to him that there were a few lessons to be learned from his own experiences, "the principal of which is that a Young Man with ordinary natural abilities, little Education, and small opportunities, meeting with repeated misfortunes and exposed to extraordinary Temptations and immoral Surroundings, may surely, by setting up to himself a high Moral Standard, together with Industry, Perseverance, and a stern determination to preserve his Honor and Integrity, acquire some Wealth, as well as the Respect of the Community in which he may dwell, and a peaceful and happy Old Age. And what more can a man covet, except the Eternal Blessing of our Lord." Charles Pancoast lived to his eighty-eighth year, to 1906, past the turn of the next century.

25

The Northwest

Until the establishment of the Bear Republic, California had been foreign territory that Americans entered, as we have seen, at considerable risk. The same could not be said of Oregon territory. The majority of Americans believed that it belonged by right to the United States and a number were determined to help substantiate that claim by going and settling there.

As early as 1829 the Oregon Colonization Society had been organized in Boston. Its purpose was to dispatch both missionaries to convert the Indians and settlers to strengthen the American claim to the region. Each prospective settler was required to give proof of good character and was promised a town lot of 500 square feet or 200 acres in the Multuomah Valley, but few people came forward and the project languished. By the mid-1830s the Yellowstone beaver rush and Jedediah Smith's explorations had revived interest in Oregon. In 1835 Marcus and Narcissa Whitman, with several other young missionary couples, stopped at the fur trapper's rendezvous at the New Fork River on their way to Oregon. The beautiful blond Narcissa charmed the trappers, and Whitman, a medical doctor as well as missionary, removed an old arrowhead from Jim Bridger's back. We have already taken note of the fact that the settlers who followed close on the heels of the missionaries besieged Congress with petitions to extend federal jurisdiction over the region. As president, Polk under the moderating influence of his Cabinet, pursued a more conciliatory course with Great Britain than that suggested by "54° 50' or Fight." Richard Pakenham, the British ambassador to the United States, was directed by Lord Aberdeen to propose the 49th parallel as the boundary between the United States and Canada, with Vancouver reserved to the British and free navigation of the Columbia River guaranteed to both powers. These terms were incorporated in a treaty that was confirmed by the Senate in July, 1846. The most important consequence of the treaty was a fresh influx of settlers to the Oregon territory. Among these was a young Virginian of New England antecedents named Samuel Hancock. Hancock set out, across the plains from Independence, Missouri, in a train of two hundred wagons, headed up the Platte to South Pass, and then on to Oregon territory, which, Hancock wrote, "seemed to our adventurous citizens, to possess the inducements necessary for them to go, and undertake the settlement, and there build up new homes, and if possible new everything. . . ." Hancock's party encountered all the classic hazards of the passage—rainstorms, floods, hostile Indians, cholera, hunger and thirst, exhausted stock, and internal dissension. At one point the presence of Indians caused first a mule and then the line of teams to stampede "and the whole train of forty wagons dashed across the plains, the drivers having no control over the frantic animals, and the women and children who were inmates of the wagons, screaming with all their voices . . . and it was some time before we could again exert any control over our teams and stop them; when we finally did it was ascertained that we had sustained considerable injury, some of our wagons lying on one side and teams detached from them in some instances, others with wheels broken, and the contents strewn promiscuously round, while some of our company were lying about with broken legs, and others seriously injured, the whole scene presenting a most disasterous appearance." The Crow warriors, the cause of the stampede, were interested observers.

Beyond Fort Laramie, Hancock observed Indians and half-breeds trapping crickets, filling baskets with them, drying them in a stone kiln, and then grinding them up in a kind of meal "which seemed to be regarded as a staple and delicate article of food among them, which they eat heartily and grow fat."

Dust was a terrible plague. Hancock found it "scarcely endurable."

It hung like a great choking cloud over the train, coating the faces and clothes of the emigrants and advertising the movements of the train for many miles. Everywhere they were accompanied by the Indians.

Crossing the Cascade Mountains, Hancock's party reached the Willamette Valley. "Each of us," he wrote, "felt that he had accomplished a great undertaking and been exceedingly fortunate in surviving all the perils and exposure to which we had been subjected on our long journey. . . . Everyone too seemed pleased with the country, presenting all the requisites of a rich and productive soil; money is rather scarce," Hancock added, "but with strong hands and stout hearts, what may we not accomplish." Meanwhile the emigrants were near to starvation and were forced to hire out to traders of the Hudson's Bay Company, splitting shingles for whatever wage they would pay. At Oregon City some settlers who had arrived the year before shared their wheat with the new arrivals so they managed to survive. For every family able to avail themselves of it the government of the territory offered a parcel of land a mile square in the two-hundred-mile-long valley which "being abundantly timbered and watered . . . all were soon comfortably settled, the land producing all necessary vegetables, while venison could be procured easily and in abundance, and those who had cattle were constantly increasing their stock."

But Hancock, without family responsibilities, was too restless to stay put long. He found an equally daring companion and they set out to explore the surrounding country, encountering Indians everywhere and moving as stealthily as the savages themselves. Here and there they found settlements of a few cabins, and at one a Methodist mission. All along there were beautiful clearings with deep rich soil and giant fir trees that took "two looks to enable one to see to the tops." At the Methodist mission they met the Reverend Mr. Campbell, "a very gentlemanly person, who had been at this place . . . for four years, preaching and doing all the good in his power to the benighted savages." They remained for a service, although to Hancock's eyes the congregation seemed "a rather hard set of Christians, coming to church without any very great regard to their appearance other than being painted in a way doubtless very satisfactory to themselves, but to us they looked perfectly hideous. Some of them were entirely without clothing . . . .What a contrast between the positions of this poor divine and the pampered ministers of the fashionable churches of our Atlantic cities." The minister gave a sermon in the tribe's native tongue. "When he commenced singing, he was joined by the entire assembly old and young, then they all kneeled and offered a prayer. . . . Indeed such was the devotion which prevailed that it imparted a solemnity to the occasion which quite astonished me besides hearing them sing familiarly the old Methodist hymns we used to hear at home."

Back in the Willamette Valley Hancock found the beginnings of a village started by "a Mr. Pettygrove," who had laid off part of his land at the confluence of the Willamette and the Columbia for a town to be named Portland. As Hancock noted, by 1847, "there were built at Portland, twelve or fifteen houses, mostly of logs, which were occupied by the people variously engaged in and about the town."

In the absence of money, settlers sold their produce to storekeepers in Oregon City and Portland for "orders payable in goods" and these circulated like currency. During the summer a trading ship arrived from the Sandwich Islands and one "from the Atlantic coast of our own country around Cape Horn, with an assorted cargo of merchandise. . . ."

The following year the settlers combined their efforts to build a sawmill on the Tum Water, a nearby stream, which provided them with lumber both for their own houses and for trading to the vessels which found their way each year in increasing numbers up the Columbia River. Into this classic scene of pioneer enterprise came the horrifying news of the massacre of Marcus and Narcissa Whitman by the Cayuse Indians. Fear of a general massacre swept through Portland and the adjacent settlements, and Hancock joined those men who volunteered to chastise the Cayuse. In Hancock's words, "they went forth to avenge the wrongs perpetuated by these Indians with all the cheerfulness of a people sanguine of best results from a full consciousness of doing right."

In the Portland region and as far away as Puget Sound to the north, new settlements flourished, interrupted only by news of the California gold rush, which drained off a substantial portion of the male population. Hancock himself headed for Sutter's Fort, part of a group of twenty-five men with as many wagons who left Oregon City "for the famous land of gold." Hunting for deer along the trail to the Sacramento Valley, Hancock saw an Indian in some bushes nearby who, he assumed, was stalking him. He fired at once, leaving the Indian "kicking on the ground . . . a fortunate thing for me, as he would have killed me, had I not been a little too fast for him. . . ."

Reaching the Feather River, Hancock and his party followed its waters to the Feather River mines. At the diggings, Hancock wrote, "we found every man hard at work washing the dirt with pans and rockers; they told us they were making from sixteen to thirty dollars each per day. . . ." (Substantially short of Hancock's "extravagant expectations".) They pushed on to the Yuba, "where there were reported very rich mines," but the miners there, it turned out, were doing no better than those on the Feather. Next try was the American River, where Hancock sold his wagon and oxen "to enable me to obtain provision enough to last me to the El Dorado of my expectations."

At the middle fork of the American River, Hancock met "four gentlemen" with whom he had crossed the plains three years earlier. They were making from thirty to two hundred dollars a day, they informed Hancock. Hancock's party set about diverting the river but after three days of prodigious labor a rain and flood washed away their efforts. This was enough for his companions, who departed. Hancock, panning in the bed of a diverted creek, took out $150 worth of gold the first day and $520 the second. Before he could pan any more, heavy rains came and once again altered the course of the stream, so Hancock made preparations for the winter, building a cabin and taking in six friends, "which we deemed sufficient to protect us against any incursions of robbers or murderers so numerous now in the mines." In the spring, Hancock and his friends resumed their mining activities and did "exceedingly well" for three months, then Hancock was taken ill and had to find lodging with an old friend from his emigrant days who kept a boardinghouse and grocery. He put Hancock up for eight dollars a day, and the doctor charged an ounce of gold per visit, or seventeen dollars. Hancock realized that he must objure his friend's hospitality while he still had some money left.

Traveling was extremely hazardous. Hancock armed himself with two Colt pistols and made his way, several times in danger from robbers, to the Leadsdolph ranch, where he bought a thousand dollars' worth of cattle, employing an Indian to help him herd them to Colma, near Sutter's Fort, to sell to the miners. The Indian soon abandoned him and joined five companions who kept up a rain of arrows until Hancock had killed two of them; whereupon the rest fled and Hancock, still weak from his illness, made his way to a roadhouse, where he recruited ten men to help him retrieve his cattle. At "Kelsey's dry diggings," occupied by a rough-looking group of "Spaniards and half-breed," Hancock sold his cattle at a handsome profit and went into the risky business of transporting merchandise by ox-drawn wagon from Sacramento to Colma, a distance of a hundred miles, for forty dollars per hundredweight. In a side trip to Mormon Island, another mining district, Hancock witnessed the hanging of a murderer and thief who, as the angry miners placed the rope around his neck, admitted that he had killed eight men. Another interested spectator was Charles Pancoast.

Hancock is an excellent example of those who came to the goldfields, had uneven luck mining, and then went into a variety of "business"—from transporting goods to running roadhouses and hotels and opening stores—and in doing so worked less hard and made more money than those who remained doggedly at work in the diggings.

While Hancock was making a living in the goldfields and even putting a little by, word reached him that the Oregon settlements were enjoying great prosperity because of the demand for lumber created by the gold rush in California. Hancock decided on Puget Sound as his headquarters, and the lumber business as his next venture. He sailed to San Francisco with a load of lumber, laid in a supply of merchandise, and returned to Puget Sound "with my goods, built a house and soon disposed of my supply." In San Francisco he had heard much talk of coal as the coming fuel, so he determined to go on an exploring expedition up the Columbia River looking for coal. He bought a canoe, hired seven Indians to paddle it, and started up the river. Everywhere he encountered curious and sometimes hostile Indians and had constantly to be on guard against surprise attacks. Hancock helped to negotiate a peace between the Snoqualmies and the Snohomishes, but found no coal.

Back in Puget Sound, Hancock decided to put all his remaining merchandise on board a ship bound for the Juan de Fuca Straits, running between Vancouver Island and Cape Flattery, and establish a trading post on the northwesternmost point of the Oregon Territory, Neah Bay. There Hancock and a friend built a house "that would answer for a trading establishment," and here he was soon visited by "large numbers of the most primitive looking creatures imaginable; some with furs covering parts of their bodies, others entirely without and some with blankets manufactured by themselves from the hair of dogs." These were members of a lesser Athapascan tribe, and Hancock's hopes of setting up as a prosperous trader were dashed when the Indians informed him that they wished him to leave at once.

When he demurred, saying, quite rightly, that he had no way to depart, he was visited by two hundred heavily armed warriors who ordered him to go. Hancock saved his hide by sitting before the chiefs and appearing to write a letter which, he informed them, would be sent to the Great Chief, the President of the United States, telling him of the treatment he had received at the hands of the Indians. This at once reduced the Indians to supplicants, pleading with him not to write the letter, offering him twenty baskets of potatoes, and promising not to molest him further. With this assurance, Hancock bought a canoe and enlisted three Macaw Indians to paddle him up the straits to Port Townsend. Once again he resumed his search for coal and found a "fine looking vein" up the Snohomish River, where he was befriended by the chief of the Snohomish tribe. Back at the site of a town to be called Olympia, he sold a half-interest in the mine and started back with his partner to explore the region more thoroughly and establish their claim. They passed Snoqualmie, Duamish, Puyallup, and Misqually villages. At Olympia, some weeks later, Hancock took passage on a ship bound for San Francisco, hoping to get back to his trading post at Neah. But the ship's captain was an inept navigator, so that when Hancock and several others of the ship's company pushed off in a long boat to try to find the entrance to Neah Bay they found themselves hopelessly lost and surrounded by curious Indians. For days they blundered about trying to catch sight of their ship or locate Neah Bay. Each day brought some potentially dangerous contact with one tribe of Indians or another and all Hancock's resourcefulness and, by this time, shrewd understanding of Indian psychology were required simply to preserve their lives. Again the situation was full of irony. On several occasions Indians saved them from starving and showed great kindness to the white man. In other situations the whites barely escaped being murdered. Finally they encountered a canoe manned by English-speaking Indians who told them they were only four days paddling away from Vancouver Island and the town of Victoria, where they met the ship and the captain who had abandoned them.

Convinced that he would have nothing but trouble with the Indians at Neah Bay, Hancock decided to relocate his trading post, with a sawmill added, at Clallam Bay, a hundred miles further up the Juan de Fuca Straits. But the carpenters and millwright struck for higher pay and Hancock, unwilling to meet their demands, refused to pay, and abandoned the project, turning his attention instead to the now flourishing settlement at Olympia. There he became a lumber contractor, buying lumber, shipping it to San Francisco, and bringing back merchandise needed in the town. It was a "lucrative occupation" but Hancock, always restless, was "determined to make another effort to locate at the lower end of the Sound." In the fall of 1852, he was back at Neah Bay with two men he had hired to build a house and trading post. This time the Indians appeared "greatly pleased" at the prospect of having a handy source of trading goods where they could bring their furs, oil, and salmon in exchange for cloth, beads, rings, ammunition, and a hundred other desirable items. "My coming," Hancock wrote, "seemed to have imparted new life to them; and stimulated them to habits of industry. . . ." They were skilled whalers and now, with an outlet for their whale oil, they repaired their canoes, sharpened their harpoons, and gave an attentive Hancock a striking demonstration of their prowess in whaling.

But the Indians resented the more and more frequent visits of trading vessels to the bay. Sailors going ashore sold whiskey to the Indians, cheated them, and debauched their women. Hancock became aware of a growing atmosphere of hostility toward him on the part of the natives. "On several occasions," Hancock noted, "nearly all the Indians . . . have been drunk fighting and brandishing their knives and threatening to kill me and my two men." Such demonstrations prompted Hancock to build a fort. A ship was anchored in the harbor and Hancock warned its captain that he should not permit Indians aboard his ship since they were in a warlike mood and might attempt to seize the vessel. Hancock then called a number of the most prominent Indians together and admonished them to conduct themselves in a manner more friendly to the whites, employing those classic elements of Indian diplomacy, threats and promises. Shortly afterwards, an old Indian chief told Hancock a story that helped to explain the attitude of the Indians in the area. Some years before, a ship had anchored in the bay to trade and after several weeks of amicable trading, natives had killed the captain and most of the crew and seized the ship, whereupon a wounded sailor had set the powder magazine afire and blown it up.

In the spring, Hancock happened to overhear two Indians, who had come in a party of forty canoes to trade, talking about plans to seize the fort and post, kill all the whites, and divide up their possessions. Once again Hancock made preparations to rebuff any attack and the Indians, seeing that their plans were discovered, paddled off. A few weeks later a ship from San Francisco put into the bay; aboard were two natives of the region who had the smallpox. The two went ashore and spread the disease, with disastrous consequences. "After resorting to every means in their power to arrest its progress and fatality in vain . . . those who had escaped became almost frantic with grief and fear, and conceived the idea of crossing the Strait and going to the Nitanat tribe living on Vancouver's Island. They of course carried the disease with them." "It was truly shocking," Hancock wrote, "to witness the ravages of this disease here at Neah Bay. The natives after a time became so much alarmed that when any of their friends were attacked, all of the other occupants who lived in the house would at once leave it and the sick person with a piece of dried salmon and some water . . . not intending to ever approach them again; sometimes the retreating ones would lie down anywhere on the beach till they died. I have, in walking along, encountered them lying in this situation where they would beg in the most supplicating manner for medicine or something to relieve them. . . . In a few weeks from the introduction of the disease, hundreds of the native became victims to it, the beach for the distance of eight miles was literally strewn with the dead bodies of these people, presenting a most disgusting spectacle." The Indians believed that Hancock could help them and many, as soon as they felt the onset of smallpox, came to his house and lay down in the yard. "They continued this until the dead were so numerous I could scarcely walk about around my house, and was obliged to have holes dug where I deposited fifteen or twenty bodies in each." Still they died. Some bodies were dragged to the beach to be carried away by the tide and the dogs "became fat on the bodies of their deceased masters."

The survivors blamed Hancock; when he managed to persuade them that he was innocent, they turned on one of the Indians from the schooner who had brought the disease ashore, placed him in a canoe, and set him adrift in the Straits without food or a paddle to die of hunger and exposure.

Soon afterwards, Hancock set out in the *Eagle* to trade with the Indians on Vancouver Island. The first were the Nitanats. After collecting their oil and salmon, the ship continued along the coast to the region of the Quachiniwhit tribe, north of Nootka Sound. These Indians, virtually naked otherwise, wore broad-brimmed waterproof hats of finely woven roots. While the trading was going on a storm came up and drove the *Eagle* on the rocks. The ship began to break up under the pounding of the waves, a sight that prompted the Indians, gathered to observe the scene, to "loud and wild" laughter. Hancock and the crew struggled to salvage some of the cargo, loading blankets into the ship's longboat and prevailing on the Indians to bring off some supplies in their canoes. As quickly as the Indians secured the blankets, they began tearing them into strips and distributing them around. Hancock stopped this sport by giving a number of blankets to the Indians to make "a favorable impression." As soon as the captain and the crew had abandoned the ship, it was surrounded by hundreds of Indians who swarmed over it stripping it of everything movable. There were now ten persons, eight whites and two Indians from Neah Bay, marooned among the Quachiniwhit Indians. The Quachiniwhits had no intention of letting them escape. Hancock distracted those who had been left to keep watch on them, while the looting of the ship went on, by scattering irresistible beads around in the underbrush. While their guards searched for the tiny glittering objects, the crew of the *Eagle* slipped away, four in a canoe and six in the longboat, paddling for their lives. Several days later, working their way down the coast toward the British post at Nootka Sound, the entire party was captured by another tribe of Indians who clearly planned to murder them. Hancock, noticing the large cedar boards that braced the chief's lodge, promised, if the chief would provide them with a canoe and some Indian paddlers, to come back with a ship full of trading goods in exchange for a number of such boards. The chief agreed but the men of the tribe refused to be party to the bargain. The chief therefore started out himself, the canoe paddled by his slaves, Indians of other tribes captured in war. But he, too, got cold feet and turned back.

In the midst of this dilemna, friendly Clyoquot Indians from the Nootka Bay region intervened to rescue the party. At Nootka Bay, Hancock found a ship headed for Olympia and took passage to get down to Neah Bay where he "found everything in good condition." The man he had left minding the store had been very successful in trading with the natives for oil, and Hancock's post was piled with barrels. But once more the Indians, still believing Hancock responsible for the terrible smallpox epidemic, became surly and threatening, insisting that he must leave the bay. So, trading for three large canoes, Hancock bound them together with cedar timbers, laid a platform across them on which he placed his supplies, and started for Whidby's Island, a hundred miles up the strait. By considerable effort and impressive seamanship, he reached his new haven, where, he wrote, "arriving in due time without any extraordinary adventures and completing them here in a short time with the *adventure of matrimony*, I then settled on a farm on this island, leading the quiet life of a farmer."

There are many notable aspects of Samuel Hancock's *Narrative*. Perhaps the most engaging is that quality which he shares with Charles Pancoast and a number of other similar narrators, of the simple, unadorned story, descriptions of hardships and terrors sufficient to make the reader's hair stand on end, rendered as casually as if he were describing the most commonplace events. Again Hancock displays in abundance that extraordinary *enterprise* with which we are by now familiar—time and time again defeated, time and again returning to the fray, turning his hand cheerfully to anything that offered to make an honest dollar; physical hardihood in the face of almost overwhelming obstacles, coolness in danger, wry humor, and a substantial degree of compassion for his fellows; above all, the stubborn unwillingness to accept any reverse as final; the infinite capacity for new beginnings.

26

Religion

Religion has to do with final and ultimate human concerns. It thus touches the profoundest levels of our experience as individuals and, collectively, as a people. America was most essentially shaped by the re-formed consciousness of Protestant Christianity, Calvinist division. American religious orientation had moved from the *community* of the faithful, where salvation was conceived of as primarily available through the community or congregation, to the notion of the salvation of the *individual* through piety, humility, sacrifice, and good works. The older faith was far more rigorous and was Old Testament–oriented. The later modifications of that faith were relaxed in various ways and New Testament–oriented. Christ the suffering servant was the model to be emulated. Calvinism had insisted (and Re-formed Christianity had taken it as its basic tenet) that man was by nature totally depraved (in the classic words of Jeremiah, "the heart of man is desperately wicked and deceitful above all things") and that men and women were "predestined" to salvation or damnation from the day of their birth and could do nothing, by piety or good works, to alter that condition. The first of those severe tenets to be abandoned, quietly and without fanfare for the most part, was predestination, which seemed to be in direct opposition to common sense and the notion of free will (although Jonathan Edwards had argued ingeniously that it was not). The second, around which a lengthy and bitter theological battle raged, was the total depravity doctrine. That also was argued against on the ground of free will. If men and women could earn salvation by living pious Christian lives, it seemed to follow that they could not be totally depraved; that even if they were "tainted" by original sin, they could do a good deal by the exercise of their free will, reinforced by Reason and Revelation, to remove that taint.

Congregationalism was the particular churchly or institutional form Calvinism took in the United States, with Presbyterianism as its first-cousin. Unitarianism began as what we might call a Congregational heresy, an infusion of rationalism into Calvinist orthodoxy. The Baptists and the Presbyterians were more successful in resisting the erosion of Calvinism, but they too "relaxed" the original dogmas. The movement from Trinitarianism to Unitarianism—from trinity to unity; from complexity to simplicity—traced very precisely a basic transformation in the American notion of ultimate reality. It was the theological correlative of the shift from the notion that the aim of life was to serve the Lord to the notion that it was to "pursue happiness"; from the belief that the real issue was the salvation of one's soul to the notion that it was the satisfaction of one's material needs, and finally, today, that it is the *expression* of that problematic entity "the self." New England became the capital of Unitarianism and thus, despite its marvelous intellectual flowering, its poets, preachers, philosophers, and novelists, could never come very convincingly to grips with the deeper and more troubling realities of American life.

Unitarianism's primary dogma was the rejection of the orthodox Christian notion of the Trinity. If history was in some fundamental and inescapable way a tragedy in which all human hopes and aspirations fell short of their aim, where the deaths of loved ones were only preludes to one's own deterioration and death, Christianity professed to have triumphed over that tragedy by the sacrifice of Christ on the Cross in an act by which he took on the sins of the whole world from the fall of Adam to the end of Time in order that all those who wished to might be redeemed into everlasting life. But the tension and tragedy must be borne by all who believed. The incomprehensible death of Christ on the Cross, the irrational death in which his human-ness was made inescapably explicit, as explicit as his Divinity, must be placed at the center of the Christian's consciousness. The doctrine of the Trinity—God in three persons, Father, Son and Holy

Spirit—was the conceptual framework, as we might say today, necessary to explain how it could be that God had, in the person of his Son, died on the Cross. The rational mind of the eighteenth century could not swallow the Christian paradox that Christ was both Man and God. It wished to avoid or suppress the paradoxical nature of the truth that Christianity endeavored to represent by defining it as superstition. Even the most dogged defenders of the doctrine of original sin, such exemplars of the Classical-Christian Consciousness as John Adams and James Madison, could not cope with those dimensions of human experience encompassed by the concept of Christ as the third-person-of-the-Trinity-resolver-of-the-tragic-nature-of-history-through-the-sacrifice-of-his-life. Adams wrote to Benjamin Rush, "The Christian religion, as I understand it, is the brightness of the glory and the express portrait of the eternal, self-existent, independent, benevolent, all-powerful and all-merciful Creator, Preserver and Father of the Universe. . . . It will last as long as the world. Neither savage nor civilized man without a revelation could ever have discovered or invented it." But he thought it intolerable to believe that the greatest power in the universe had been nailed by weak and sinful men to a cross. The Unitarian thus made Christianity a kind of modern Confucianism, the wise teachings of great men, timeless precepts for a useful and virtuous life to be rewarded by eternal life after death. The doctrine of the Trinity in its paradoxicality raised too many troubling questions for good republicans to deal with. Trinity must be reduced to Unity. Only in this way could the tragic character of human history, to which the doctrine had been a response, be obscured or glossed over.

In a certain sense all Americans became Unitarians—Presbyterians, Methodists, Episcopalians alike. That is to say, religion in America was increasingly disinclined to deal with the broader historical implications of Christ's death on the Cross and far more inclined to deal with moralism, with personal piety, and, especially on the frontier, with hell fire and damnation, with "spreading the gospel in foreign parts," and with the appropriate social behavior. It was increasingly disposed to perceive the United States not as being, like other nations, under God's judgment but as being His chosen vessel for the redemption of the world. So, finally, Unitarianism was a characteristic American form of evasion. It proved an ingenuous way of avoiding the issue; of being a church without doctrine, a church of the new religion of lectures and self-improvement.

In New York the Unitarian Church of the Messiah was, in Philip

Hone's words, "all the fashion." Crowds of ladies and gentlemen passed by Hone's house on Sunday morning on their way to the "handsome new church" to hear "doctrines somewhat out of the regular track of orthodoxy," presented by the famous apostle of Unitarianism Dr. William Ellery Channing. Unitarianism was in the air.

To George Templeton Strong, secure in his Anglicanism, Unitarianism might be "the fashionable and aristocratic faith" (in which case its most serious rival would be Episcopalianism) but it could never have a wide popular appeal. "Imposing no unpleasant restraints, requiring nothing but what decency requires . . . involving no points of belief above the reach of common sense, it will be very likely to become the favorite creed of those who want a religion at once convenient, compressible, and fashionable, for show—not use. But with the great mass of people, this cold-blooded system of combining the minimum of belief with the maximum of license will not *take*. It can never be a popular religion."

"Happiness as an end is unknown to Christianity," Strong added, "—its most deadly opponent is the desire of happiness for itself. To set self out of the question is its fundamental principle, and why doing good from the fear of future punishment is not identical with doing good for the sake of popular applause or through any other selfish motive, I'm really unable to see. . . ." Richard Henry Dana commented, "The Unitarian influence has been predominant at Cambridge for many years. This, though not so in its origin, has lapsed into Humanitarianism, a doubt of the divine authority of the Scriptures, a denial of the fallen nature & condemnation of man & of eternal punishment, & of the atonement of Christ. Unitarianism, especially with the young, was considered the only faith consistent with the advancement of man, freedom of thought & the dignity of our natures."

Dana noted that some wit had distinguished between the Unitarians and the Universalists by declaring that "the Universalists thought God was too good to damn them, & the Unitarians thought they were too good to be damned."

Thomas Hamilton, an acerbic and supercilious English visitor, declared that fully half the population of Boston, "and more than half of the wealth and intelligence . . . are Unitarians." "The New Englanders," he added, "are a cold, shrewd, calculating, and ingenious people, of phlegmatic temperament, and perhaps in their composition less of the stuff of which enthusiasts are made, than any other people in the world." Unitarianism thus seemed ideally suited to them. "An Unitarian will take nothing for granted but the absolute and plenary efficacy of his own reason in matters of religion. He is not a fanatic but a dogmatist."

The dogmatism was experienced by young Theodore Parker, whose Ordination Sermon, preached in Boston in 1841, was entitled "A Discourse on the Transient and Permanent in Christianity." According to Parker the heresies he espoused in it cost him his "reputation in the 'Christian Church'; even the Unitarian ministers, who are themselves reckoned but the tail of heresy," he wrote, "denounced me as 'no Christian,' and an 'Infidel.' They did what they could to effect my ruin—denied me all friendly intercourse, dropped me from committees of their liberal college, in public places refused my hand extended as before in friendly salutation; mocked at me in their solemn meeting . . . and in every journal, almost every pulpit, denounced the young man who thought the God who created earth and heaven had never spoken miraculously in Hebrew words bidding Abraham kill his only son and burn him for a sacrifice, and that Jesus of Nazareth was not a finality in the historical development of mankind. . . . Behold! said they, behold a minister thinking for himself afresh on religion! actually thinking! . . . He tells us God is not dead! that the Bible is not his last word; that he inspires men now as much as ever,—even more so." Some of Parker's critics went so far as to suggest he should be jailed for blasphemy.

The modern reader of Parker's sermon would be hard pressed to understand how his sermon could have aroused such bitter feeling. "There had never been an age," he declared, "when man did not crucify the Son of God afresh. But if error prevail for a time and grow old in the world, truth will triumph at the last, and then we shall see the Son of God as he is. Lifted up, he shall draw all nations unto him. Then will men understand the word of Jesus, which shall not pass away." But Parker went on to dispute the divinity of Christ, declaring that was a "heathen view" which robbed his life of much of its human significance.

The Episcopal Church, the American variation of the Church of England, or Anglican Church, was as fashionable as the Unitarian. The alliance between success and religion was consummated in the Episcopal Church, which discovered exactly the right balance between piety and worldliness that would appeal to the urban upper class and those aspiring to it. Even so conservative a character as George Templeton Strong was disturbed that "the church does nothing to relieve temporal sorrow and calamity; it only recommends individuals to do it when the opportunity comes their way. The church upholds the creeds and doctrines of the Catholic faith, but *as a church,* I see no works in its history since the sixteenth century." Strong's response was to take the lead in pressuring the Episcopal Diocese of New York to establish a hospital for the "sick poor." The hospital, called St. Luke's, was established and other denominations took similar steps to help alleviate suffering and hardship among the city's poor, most commonly through hospitals and orphanages.

When the national convention of the Episcopal Church met in New York City in 1847, Philip Hone wrote that he had no trouble identifying these "reverend visitors" who might be known "by their good-looking, complacent, self-satisfied countenances, well-brushed black coats and white neck-clothes, and gentlemanly, dignified deport-ment. Some of them may be seen with neat little wives, hanging on their arms, well dressed, each with a little satin bonnet, a little inclining to be gay. . . ."

At the consecration of the Trinity Chapel, his own church, Strong was caustic in his comments on the Episcopal clergy who assembled for the ceremony. He thought their faces "below the average trader, physician, attorney even in expression, moral and intellectual. There were sensual pig-faces, white vacant sheep-faces, silly green gosling-faces, solemn donkey-faces," but the prevailing type was that of the "commonplace fourth-rate snob, without any particular expression but mediocrity and grim professional Pharisaism. . . . Why does that profession attract so few men of mark, moral vigor, and commanding talent?" The answer had, undoubtedly, to do with the character of the church itself as a refuge for the respectable upper classes. Moreover, like all other major denominations, the Episcopal Church could not cope with the most critical moral issue of the day—slavery.

John Quincy Adams noted in his diary in the spring of 1838 that church attendance in the capital and elsewhere throughout the nation had fallen off noticeably in recent years. "There is in the clergy of all the Christian denominations," he noted, "a time-serving, cringing, subservient morality, as wide apart from the spirit of the Gospel as it is from the intrepid assertion and vindication of the truth. The counter-feit character of a very large portion of the Christian ministry of this country is disclosed in the dissension growing up in all the Protestant churches on the subject of slavery," Adams wrote. The abolitionists believed emphatically that it was a sin, and when they confronted the established churches with this proposition the churches waffled and procrastinated. Some went so far as to argue that "the Bible sanctions slavery; that Abraham, Isaac and Paul were slave-holders. . . . These preachers of the Gospel," Adams added bitterly, "might just as well call our extermination of the Indians an obedience to Divine commands because Jehovah commanded the children of Israel to exterminate the Canaanitish nations."

Slowly and inexorably, the last spark of publicly uttered antislavery sentiment was extinguished in the churches of the South. Undoubtedly it continued to burn in the hearts of many Southerners, but they came to be a beleaguered minority; they must remain silent or leave their homes. The conscientious objectors to the system were, indeed, never numerous. Antislavery sentiment was to be found primarily in the scattered Quaker communities of the South and in those border states with a strong tradition of religious dissent. In the suppression of antislavery arguments, the various Christian churches played a leading role. It was estimated that two-fifths of the Baptist clergymen of South Carolina owned slaves and two hundred traveling Methodist ministers held 1,600 slaves among them. Indeed, slaveholding by the clergy came to be a kind of test of a clergyman's loyalty to the slave system.

Thomas Roderick Dew, a political economist at the College of William and Mary in Virginia and a devout Christian, published in 1840 *An Essay on Slavery* which went further than earlier works in justifying slavery as a positive good. His insistence that slavery was divinely ordained became the text for innumerable sermons in Southern churches for the next twenty years. Calhoun read it and took it to heart. "Many in the South," he said, "once believed that [slavery] was a moral and political evil. That folly and delusion are gone. We see it now in its true light, and regard it as the most safe and stable basis for free institutions in the world." Robert Lewis Dabney described the strategy of the Southern clergy "to push the Bible argument continually, to drive Abolitionism to the wall, to compel them to assume an anti-Christian position." Until the publication of two books by George Fitzhugh—*Sociology for the South, or the Failure of a Free Society* which appeared in 1854, and *Cannibals All! or, Slaves Without Masters,* three years later—Dew's essay remained the basic proslavery text.

But if the issue of slavery was suppressed in the states south of the Mason-Dixon line, it continued to be the most bitterly divisive issue in the Northern churches, seriously compromising their effectiveness and dissipating their energies.

The tension between the churches and the opponents of slavery is suggested by the technique of the abolitionist Stephen Foster. Foster's method was to attend a church service and rise in the middle of it to denounce slavery and the Christian churches for acquiescing in it. Perhaps his principal contribution was a book entitled *The Brotherhood of Thieves, or a True Picture of the American Church and Clergy.* If it is a fair sample of the invective that he poured on the heads of startled church congregations, it is small wonder that he was frequently mobbed. He charged that "The American church and clergy, as a body, were thieves and adulterers, man-stealers, pirates, and murderers—that the Methodist Episcopal Church was more profligate than any house of ill fame in the city of New York—that the Southern ministers of that body were desirous of perpetuating Slavery for the purpose of supplying themselves with concubines from among its hapless victims—and that many of our clergy were guilty of enormities that would disgrace an Algerian pirate!! "

Perhaps, in the final analysis, the greatest contribution of institutional Christianity—the major Protestant denominations—was in the area of higher education. From the Tennant's Log College, an outgrowth of the Great Awakening of the 1740s, to Lane Seminary, Oberlin College, Antioch College, and a thousand other less well-known colleges and academies, the churches maintained their tradition of providing an educated clergy by establishing institutions to make a Christian "higher" education available to the children of the faithful. The first responsibility of such institutions was usually the production of missionaries, ministers, and teachers, and the education they provided was often modest in the extreme. But, taken together, they served the invaluable function of giving a leg up in the world to generations of young men and women who would otherwise have not had even the rudiments of higher education. In 1843 the Society for the Promotion of Collegiate and Theological Education at the West was organized in New York City to give support to Western Reserve, Illinois, Wabash, and Marietta colleges and the Lane Theological Seminary. "These colleges," the first report of the society read, "were all projected by religious men, most of whom were Home Missionaries

—they were established upon religious principles—have grown up under religious influence, and have all been repeatedly blessed with the converting influences of the Holy Spirit. In their infancy they were not only all approved and liberally aided by the Eastern churches—but the foundations of some of them were laid after very extensive consultation with leading benevolent minds in these churches."

It is ironic that one of the principal motivations in the establishment of Western colleges was the persistent fear of the growing power of the Catholic Church, with its attendant educational institutions— the parochial school and Catholic college. "The college," one pamphleteer wrote, "acts upon the public mind in a manner so peculiar, through such ages and classes, and through influences so various and subtle, so constant, noiseless and profound, that it can be successfully combated only by a similar institution. Place efficient Protestant colleges in the proximity of the Catholic, and the latter will wither. For all purposes of severe intellectual discipline of masculine reason, their education is soon found to be a sham. A spiritual despotism dare not, cannot, teach true history or a free and manly philosophy." Beyond that, the West was growing at such a pace that Christian colleges were desperately needed "to prevent the utter disorganization of society." On the one hand there was the "masked and political spiritual despotism" of the Catholic Church and on the other "a demagogic agitation, urged on too often by avarice, or ruffianism, or faction, or a sophistical but specious skepticism, or fanatical or superstitious or shallow religionism and socialism of every hue, against which orthodox Christianity was the only bulwark."

It is easy to be too severe with, or too patronizing toward, the established churches. It was they, after all, who supported the American missionary activity around the globe and underwrote hundreds of denominational colleges founded in every state in the Union. The mission field was for many young men and women of Christian convictions by far the most appealing way in which to bear witness to their faith. Missionary work almost invariably involved those much-to-be-desired elements of hardship, danger, and self-sacrifice that were the best way to serve Jesus Christ and the surest path to salvation. Those churches and congregations that could not cope with the slavery issue or the rights of women might salve their consciences by raising funds to convert the Indians of the East or West, the blacks in Africa, or the Muslims of the Middle East.

The slavery controversy split many congregations and eventually resulted in schisms between Northern and Southern wings of a number of Protestant churches. But quite beyond that, the fragmentation of established denominations continued at an accelerated rate. New varieties of Baptists and Methodists sprang up like mushrooms, especially in the rural and frontier areas of the country. The foot-washing Baptists split off from those to whom the practice was anathema. Then there were the Methodist Baptists and the Lutheran Methodists, the Unitarian Methodists and the United Brethren in Christ. There were the Bible Christians and the Jumpers, who leapt with ecstacy, and the African Methodists, "who accompany their services in the churches or in the field with horrible shrieks, bodily contortions . . . and convulsions . . ." and the Calvinistic Baptists, the Free Will Baptists, the Free Communion Baptists, the Baptists of the Ten Principles, the Fullerians, and the Universal Baptists. Among the German Baptists there were the Dunkers and the followers of Menno Simons, called Mennonites, and the Amish. The Universalists had gained many members, as had the Campbellites and the Swedenborgians.

"In America," Marryat wrote, "everyone worships the Deity after his own fashion; not only the mode of worship, but even the Deity itself, varies. Some worship God, some Mammon; some admit, some deny Christ; some deny both God and Christ; some are saved by living prophets only; some go to heaven by water, while some dance their way upwards. Numerous as are the sects, still are the sects much divided."

Marryat noticed the same phenomenon in families. He observed families "disperse as soon as they are out of the door—one daughter to a Unitarian chapel, another to a Baptist, the parents to the Episcopal, the sons anywhere or nowhere. . . . When anyone is allowed to have their own peculiar way of thinking," Marryat added, "his own peculiar creed, there is neither a watch nor a right to watch over each other; there is no mutual communication, no encouragement, no parental control; and the consequence is that by the majority, especially among the young, religion becomes wholly and utterly disregarded." At the same time it was evident to Marryat that in no other country was there "more zeal even to the sacrifice of life; no country sends out more zealous missionaries; . . . no country has more societies for the diffusion of the gospel; and . . . in no other country in the world are there larger sums subscribed for the furtherance of those praiseworthy objects as in the eastern states of America."

The "scandal" of American Protestantism—its ceaseless fragmentation—was also a strength. It meant that a new version of Christianity could be invented to meet the needs of every subdivision or faction in American society.

The most important manifestation of Christian zeal doubtless lay in the work of the Evangelicals. An Evangelical might be a Presbyterian, a Methodist, or even a Congregationalist. He was distinguished by a determination to make Christian morality a vital part of the everyday life of all Americans and in doing so to bring under judgment all the vices and injustices that disfigured the Republic. The center of the Evangelical movement, which had its roots in Jonathan Edwards's Great Awakening, was the experience of conversion, of being "born again" from infidelity or merely formal Christianity to an ecstatic devoutness in which one witnessed to the Lord, Jesus Christ, both by faith and by works.

Charles Grandison Finney was the virtual inventor of this form of active Christianity, which he adapted from the frontier revival, lessening the extreme emotionalism of that experience and adding generous amounts of "social conscience" to produce an amalgam suitable for more sophisticated urban audiences. He called his technique his "new measures." He advocated holding services at "unseasonable hours" and for greatly extended periods of time to shake people out of familiar patterns of worship. He employed emotional and exhortatory impromptu prayers and encouraged women to pray aloud. He used colloquial language and vivid and often frightening imagery, and made effective use of the "anxious bench," where those concerned for their salvation could sit under the gaze of the preacher. These techniques were so successful that the list of Finney's converts soon included prominent figures like Arthur and Lewis Tappan and Gerrit Smith. Hearing that he planned to hold revival meetings in Boston, Lyman Beecher, who considered that his own territory, told Finney, "I know your plan, and you know I do; you mean to come into Connecticut and carry a streak of fire to Boston. But if you attempt it, as the Lord liveth, I'll meet you at the state line, and call out all the artillery and fight every inch of the way to Boston, and then I'll fight you there." In 1832, Finney became pastor of the Free Presbyterian Church in New York and a few years later was installed as the enormously successful preacher of the Broadway Tabernacle.

It was ironic that Finney's most successful imitator was the son of his rival Lyman Beecher. From his pulpit in Indianapolis, Henry Ward

Beecher launched a vigorous attack on the disposition of organized religion in the United States to observe a division between the secular and sacred. This was of course the burden of the antislavery Christians, of whom Beecher counted himself one, but Beecher carried the doctrine a step further by inveighing from the pulpit against every moral evil in society. "How hateful is that religion," he declared, "which says, 'Business is business and politics is politics and religion is religion'; Religion is using everything for God; but many men dedicate business to the Devil and shove religion into the cracks and crevices of time and make it the hypocritical outdrawing of their leisure and their laziness." As John Burroughs, the friend and biographer of Whitman and a leading spirit in transcendentalism, wrote of Beecher, "His work was to secularize the pulpit, yea, to secularize religion itself, and make it as common and universal as the air we breathe."

David Macrae, a touring Scottish minister, wrote, "In America, Beecher is an independent power. Wherever he lectures or preaches people crowd to hear him; his sermons are printed in newspapers as far west as California; democrats abhor him; grog-sellers dread him; Princeton theologians shake their heads over his theology; but everywhere, liked or disliked, the name of Henry Ward Beecher is known, and his power recognized."

Macrae described him thus: "He stands erect with a brave look, one foot planted a pace forward. His white collar is turned over a black tie; his long hair . . . is brushed back behind his ears. His large, gray, light-floating eye is full of sunny light. . . . Altogether he has the look of a brave, strong man exulting in his strength."

Beecher was the special bain of the corrupt judges with which New York abounded. After one of his attacks the judges met to prepare a libel suit against Beecher. When Beecher heard of it he redoubled his attacks. "When a New York judge repents," he declared, "what a mighty change has to take place with him! . . . If such a man came to me and said, 'Sir, I have been the very chief of sinners,' and a thousand men should say 'Amen!' and he should say, 'I have corrupted the very fountain of justice—what must I do to be saved?' I should say, 'Quick! arise and confess those sins; and give back those bribes!' . . . If such men are ever to enter the kingdom of God, they must be born again; and when they are, there will be found scarce enough in them to make a fair-sized infant."

Beecher involved the Plymouth Church in the slavery issue in a most dramatic manner by producing one Sunday a beautiful mulatto slave girl. "This," he declared, "is a marketable commodity. Such as she are put into one balance and silver into the other. . . . What will you do now? May she read her liberty in your eyes? Shall she go out free?" The contribution plates were passed and the money raised to buy her freedom. On another occasion Beecher presented a nine-year-old black girl named Pinky—"too fair and beautiful for her own good"— and called on the congregation to buy her freedom. Rose Terry, a popular novelist, having no money, contributed her ring, which Beecher placed on the little girl's finger, saying, "Now remember that this is your freedom-ring." Such dramatic scenes infuriated the orthodox but enthralled the members of Beecher's congregation.

If nothing much could be done to curb the apparently insatiable appetite of American capitalism or to eradicate corruption in politics, there was at least some consolation in denouncing them. Stimulated by the exhortations of Finney and ministers of similar disposition, the revenues of the benevolent societies related to the churches grew to the vast sum of nine million dollars a year.

Beecher was not, he declared, interested in American power but in American compassion and justice. "I want influence for my country—not power. . . . I am not eager for her military superiority. . . . I am not eager for her commercial pre-eminence. . . . I am filled with a higher ambition. Let all arts and commerce thrive; let our influence extend and our example shine; but let it be as a *Christian* nation that we are known." He spoke enthusiastically of the "great evangelical assimilation which is forming the United States, a kind of supra-church binding the various denominations together in good works."

Isabella Bird, the English traveler, noted, "No class is left untouched by their benevolent efforts; wherever suffering and poverty are found, the hand of Christianity or philanthropy is stretched out to relieve them. The gulf which in most cities separates the rich from the poor has been to some extent lessened in New York; for numbers of ladies and gentlemen of education and affluence visit among the poor and vicious, seeking to raise them to a better position."

One major theological issue that emerged from the period of revivalism was what came to be called Perfectionism, the notion that "Christians could live perfect, wholly sanctified lives." Perfectionism had a long Christian tradition, reaching back at least to the days of the English Civil War and the Lollards and Levellers. But it was also clearly infused by Enlightenment ideas of human perfectability whose principal spokesman in America had been Thomas Jefferson. William Lloyd Garrison inclined increasingly to Perfectionism under the influence of its most impassioned champion, John Humphrey Noyes, who founded the Perfectionist Community at Oneida, New York.

If John Humphrey Noyes was the heretic of Perfectionism who carried the doctrine to an extreme from which the more orthodox drew back, Asa Mahan, the president of Oberlin, was the most effective expositor of the doctrine in a form acceptable to most Christians. Mahan emphasized that while no Christian could expect to achieve perfection, he or she might hope to grow "toward" it. Mahan based his argument on the verse from Matthew, "be ye therefore perfect, even as your Father in heaven is perfect." "In the Christian," Mahan declared, "perfection in holiness implies the consecration of his whole being in Christ." Perfectionism, on the other hand, was, in Mahan's view, worse than the worst form of infidelity. Perfectionism surrendered up the soul "to blind impulse, assuming, that every existing desire or impulse is caused by the direct agency of the Spirit, and therefore ought to be gratified."

It is not surprising that Finney's and Beecher's "great evangelical assimilation" brought a strong reaction from the threatened denominations that expressed itself in an increased emphasis on the peculiar doctrines of the various churches, on their historic origins, and on the sacramental character of Christian worship. The Mercersberg Movement, which began in the German Reformed Church, placed great emphasis on the "mystical presence" of Christ in the sacrament of communion. The "High Church" movement in the Episcopal Church went behind the Reformation to stress the "Catholic" character of the church, its "apostolic succession" (an unbroken line through the bishops of the church from St. Peter), and the centrality of the *Book of Common Prayer*, written in the reign of King John. A famous pamphlet by Charles Hodge, a Presbyterian clergyman, declared, "No such thing exists on the face of the earth as Christianity in the abstract. . . . Every man you see is either an Episcopalian or a Methodist, a Presbyterian or an Independence . . . no one is a Christian in the general." The nondenominational evangelist "stands therefore alone, in violent opposition to the whole Christian world."

Another phenomenon that we must take account of in the major Protestant denominations was what might be called "the feminization of the churches." While men remained firmly in charge of the business of the churches and women, with a few exceptions, were excluded from the pulpit and governing bodies of the various denominations, they came increasingly to dominate the work of the church, to be the most faithful attenders and to make up those legions who labored so indefatigably to do good for the needy. Their relationship with their pastors was often so intense as to take on the character of covert sexuality. Frances Trollope wrote that "the influence which the ministers of all the innumerable religious sects throughout America have on the females of their respective congregations" was in her view rivaled only by that of the priests in Catholic countries. "I think," she added shrewdly, "that it is from the clergy only that the women of America receive the sort of attention which is so dearly valued by every female heart throughout the world." In return for the minister's thoughtfulness and concern, American women "seem to give their hearts and souls into their keeping. I never saw, or read, of any country where religion had so strong a hold upon the women, or a slighter hold on the men."

Trollope might have added that the preacher's admiring ladies sometimes gave their bodies as well as their "hearts and souls" into the keeping of their pastors. Two Episcopal bishops, the Onderdunk brothers, bishops, respectively, of the dioceses of New York and Philadelphia, were both ousted from their episcopal sees on the grounds of improprieties with women in their congregations. Henry Ward Beecher was charged with having an adulterous relation with the young wife of his assistant and was tried in the most sensational trial of the nineteenth century. There were numerous other less spectacular scandals which, taken together, suggested that a strong undercurrent of not always suppressed sexuality characterized the relations between ministers and the feminine members of their flocks. It would, indeed, have been surprising if it had been otherwise. We have uncovered considerable evidence that the physical side of the relations between middle- and upper-class American husbands and wives was severely inhibited. In the constant and intimate contacts of a minister with his congregation, those of some force of character and personal charm must, almost inevitably, have come to be "loved" by their more susceptible charges, although seldom, of course, to the point of actual sexual liaisons. Nonetheless, the atmosphere in many urban churches must have hummed with a current of emotional intensity. One is tempted to the perhaps too easy conjecture that while the husband not uncommonly found an outlet for his own sexual drive in the arms of mistresses and prostitutes, the wife found in her church a less direct expression of similar but unacknowledged needs.

The most sensational religious movement of the era, aside from Mormonism, was the Adventist movement, based on the expectation of the imminent return of Christ to rule for a thousand years on earth before bearing off the redeemed to Heaven. The Adventist or millennial expectation had been a conspicuous element in Christian doctrine since the days of the primitive church. Some of the Founding Fathers of the Revolutionary period, including John Dickinson and John Jay, believed that the Revolution itself might turn out to be the beginning of the promised millennium. The millennial theme adorned revival sermons, as it had since the days of Jonathan Edwards. Since no man could tell when the hour of his own death might come, it behooved him to be in constant readiness so that he would not be taken with his unrepented sins upon him. In the same way, no one could foretell the hour of Christ's Second Coming and should, therefore, be always spiritually prepared for the advent, or coming. It was the inspiration of William Miller, a deist turned Baptist, to proclaim the day, which, it had often been thought (and by some Christians still is) was concealed in a scriptural riddle. Miller, studying the Bible, was convinced that he had found the key to unlock the riddle—Christ would return in the year 1843–44. Richard Henry Dana, with his consuming interest in Christian doctrine, attended a Millerite meeting. "Their preacher," he wrote, "had a map on wh. was represented the vision of Daniel, with all the beasts & figures, with their names & dates, all proving the end to be in 1843. He, too, had a full and attentive audience of respectable looking people, tho' the elements of fanaticism & at the same time of sincerity were . . . plainly visible in their faces. . . ." Miller demonstrated his proposition so persuasively that thousands were convinced. By the early 1840s Millerites were to be found in every part of the country. Excitement mounted as several dates set for the advent came and went. Finally, Miller, under great pressure from the faithful, declared October 22, 1844, the fearful and joyous day. When it, too, passed many Millerites fell away or returned to their own denominations. But many survived the trauma and formed new Adventist churches—the Seventh-day Adventists, the Advent Christian Church, the Church of God (Adventist), and the Life and Advent Union. These sects, not surprisingly, developed a pro-foundly other-worldly orientation. While they threw great energy into missionary activity, they eschewed social and political reform. The world seemed to them irredeemably fallen. The faithful Christian was concerned primarily with life hereafter, to which life on earth was merely a necessary prelude and preparation. Increasingly, and to an outside observer somewhat paradoxically, such churches tended to a brand of extreme nationalism in which the United States, with all its failings, was perceived as God's stronghold on earth with the rest of the world more or less under the dominion of Satan. It was as though in disappointment over the constantly postponed millennium the Adventists were determined to view the United States as at least a foreshadowing of the "Heaven-on-Earth" they so devoutly anticipated.

That was Moritz Busch's opinion. The millennial sects were, he thought, in large part the consequence of a "concealed but a hazy notion of the great future of the transatlantic world and of the transformation being readied there for a completely new era of history." Such a perspective was closely related to the so-called civil religion of the United States, the substitution of the United States—all-wise, just, omnipotent and eternal—for the Divinity.

It would certainly be wrong to suggest that Protestant Christianity had its way unchallenged in the first half of the nineteenth century. The Secular-Democratic Consciousness flourished, often, indeed, within the Protestant denominations, especially among the "democratic" sects and the rational denominations—the Congregationalists and the Unitarians. There was much anxious discussion in religious circles about the growing infidelity of America. One writer attributed it to "the disuse of the Bible as a classbook in our common schools; the importation of European infidelity and agrarianism by Owen, Fanny Wright, and others; the boastful and arrogant claims to reason, free inquiry, and independence of thought, so universally made by infidel writers and speakers, and so captivating to uninformed and uncultivated minds; and the natural preference of the human to error rather than truth. . . . No one can travel on our great highways, in steamboats, on canals, and railroads, and mingle with the moving masses he there finds, without being sensible of their dreadful effects."

On the Wisconsin frontier in the 1840s Gustaf Unonius, the Swedish immigrant who became a convert to the Episcopal Church, noted with dismay the decline in infant baptism. It "is crowded out," he wrote, "by the kind of liberalism which considers it wrong to influence the religious faith of the child, holding it should be let alone till its mind has been developed far enough to enable it to make its choice among the sects, or, in other words, between Paul and Confucius, Christ and Belial." It was in that same secular spirit that Sidney George Fisher, when he read the New Testament to his wife, Beth, in the evenings after tea, was careful to point out that it was done "not in any means as a religious exercise, but because it is a book exceedingly interesting in itself, full of fine thought, poetic imagery & noble sentiment, because it is the most dignified, affecting, impressive narrative that ever was written, & because from the vast influence it has had & has on the destinies of the world it deserves to be better known. As a source of pure morality, of profound wisdom, as a guide & teacher in the highest concerns of life, it cannot be too constantly or deeply studied."

Another challenge to Christian orthodoxy came from the fad for spiritualism introduced by the table-rapping Fox sisters of Rochester, New York. Judges, politicians, professors, and even young skeptics like George Templeton Strong were fascinated by the "Rochester knockings." "The production of the sounds is hard to explain," Strong wrote after attending one of the sessions, "and still stranger is the accuracy with which the ghosts guess of whom one is thinking—his age, his residence, vocation, and the like. They do this correctly nine times out of ten at least, where the inquirer is a stranger to the Exhibitors. . . ." Although Strong found the "demeanor" of the ghosts "trifling and undignified" he could not rule out the possibility on those grounds "for we know absolutely nothing of the laws of spiritual existence. . . ." It seemed to him "much more likely . . . that some obscure, occult, mysterious, but *natural* agency should be concerned, *if* anything but adroit humbug is concerned in the matter."

Richard Henry Dana's friend Thomas Appleton, "the prince of rattlers," was deeply into "Mesmerism and Spiritual Mediums." He told Dana "many stories of communications from the Spirit Land, and of table moving, music, etc. He says it confirms his belief in Christianity. . . ." So persuasive was the infatuation with spiritualism it was reported from Ohio that in 1850 there were forty people confined in the state insane asylum as a consequence.

James Russell Lowell said of a certain prominent Judge Wells, who was a practicing Spiritualist, he "is such a powerful medium that he has to drive back the furniture from following him when he goes out, as one might a pack of too affectionate dogs." Some of the mediums summoned up such figures as Benjamin Franklin, William Penn, and Sir Isaac Newton; Newton allegedly confessed that "he made a great mistake about the Law of Gravitation." "The development of this spiritual school has become very extraordinary and extensive," Strong noted. "Beside their quarterly periodical, they have one of two newspapers in this city, and I believe others published elsewhere." In addition a book had been brought out consisting of "communications" from George Washington, Andrew Jackson, Jefferson, and Margaret Fuller, "and a great many other people, all of them writing remarkably alike, and most of them using very questionable grammar. . . . Edgar A. Poe spells out bad imitations of the poetry he wrote while in the flesh. Tables loaded with heavy weights are made to dance vigorously. . . . It is a strange chapter in the history of human credulity at all events. . . . What would I have said six years ago to anyone who predicted that before the enlightened nineteenth century was ended hundreds of thousands of people in this country would believe themselves able to communicate daily with the ghosts of their grandfathers?—that ex-judges of the Supreme Court, senators, clergymen, professors of physical sciences, should be lecturing and writing books on the new treasures of all this, and that others among the steadiest and most conservative of my acquaintances should acknowledge that they look on the subject with distrust and dread, as a visible manifestation of diabolic agency. . . . Surely it is one of the most startling events that have occurred for centuries and one of the most significant. A new Revelation, hostile to that of the church and the Bible, finding acceptance in the authority of knocking ghosts and oscillating tables, is a momentous fact in history as throwing light on the intellectual calibre and moral tone of the age in which multitudes adopt it."

If Unitarianism was, in the minds of many Christians, a Congregational heresy, transcendentalism was Unitarian heresy, hard as that may be to imagine. Yet transcendentalism, difficult as it often was to describe or pin down, was undoubtedly the most vigorous and exciting intellectual and/or theological movement in the nineteenth century. The difficulty that it presents for the historian is that its cloudy theology hardly suggests the stimulus it provided for thousands of young men and women to whom it manifested itself as a modern revelation.

Before we discuss the rise of transcendentalism in the United States we must take at least brief notice of an eighteenth-century Swedish scientist-philosopher named Emanuel Swedenborg who, with a German, Immanuel Kant, had an extraordinary influence on

American philosophy and theology, more especially that of the transcendentalists. At the age of fifty-five, after a brilliant career as a scientist and inventor, Swedenborg had a revelation and began to talk with angels. Out of these conversations (and out of three classic Christian heresies—the Gnostic notion that everything is mind or spirit; the Manichean idea of the world as a perpetual battleground between God and the Devil; and the deistic concept of the single or unitary nature of the Divine) Swedenborg came perilously close to fashioning a new religion. What he did produce was a series of theological tomes that constituted a kind of grab bag of religious and philosophical ideas from which, for a hundred years following his death, European and American intellectuals and theologians drew forth whatever pleased their fancy. Rather than having the spirit world enter into the mundane world, Swedenborg entered into the spirit world as matter-of-factly as if he had gone down to the corner tobacconist.

Emerson considered Swedenborg one of his great "Representative Men," along with Plato, Napoleon, Shakespeare, and Goethe. Swedenborg did two things that made him irresistible to such men as Emerson: he detached the moral order of the universe from the context of traditional Christianity and he absorbed everything into "spirit." In his essay on Swedenborg Emerson states what perhaps is the most appropriate motto for us to nail above the portals of the nineteenth century: "The atmosphere of moral sentiment is a region of grandeur which reduces all material magnificence to toys, yet opens to every wretch that has reason, the doors of the universe."

Emerson writes of Swedenborg, in a marvelous sentence, "He is described when in London, a man of quiet clerical habit, not averse to tea and coffee, and kind to children." To Emerson, he was "one of the missourians and mastodons of literature not to be measured by whole colleges of ordinary scholars," for he had, in fact, discovered a new way of thinking and feeling about the world that shamed "our sterile and linear logic by its genial radiation. . . ." Man, Swedenborg argued, was free to know and respond to divine truth. With man's limitations, with his "fallen" nature, with the doctrine of original sin, Swedenborg had no truck. Creation had its origin in divine love and wisdom and since all things were created out of the divine love and wisdom they must "correspond" to ultimate spiritual realities. God was to be found everywhere, in nature and in the person, in the body specifically. Thus was traditional Christianity, with its basically tragic view of human history and its uneasiness about fleshly lusts and passions, turned on its head and made into the "religion of individualism," whereby, with the indwelling God, man is freed from earthly corruptions, from sin and mortality. "The thoughts in which he lived," Emerson wrote (and in which, it might be said, parenthetically, Emerson lived), "were,—the universality of each law in nature; the Platonic doctrine of the scale or degrees; the version or conversion of each into the other, and so the correspondence of all the parts; the fine secret that 'little explains large and large little,' the centrality of man in nature, and the connection that subsists throughout all things: he saw that the human body was strictly universal, or an instrument through which the soul feeds and is fed by the whole of matter." I am not sure that I understand all that, or that Emerson did, but what is clear is that Swedenborg spoke to certain deeply felt needs in the intellectual and religious life of the nineteenth century. Perhaps most basic was his insistence that God was imminent in man and nature and that the material was, in a sense, taken into the spiritual, that moral laws prevailed in the universe and that God existed. In a universe, the divine origins of which were increasingly being questioned by scientific skepticism, and which seemed indeed about to "fall apart," at least in the sense of the traditional assumptions about its origin and its destiny, Swedenborg, a scientist with impeccable credentials, sought, again in Emerson's words, "to put science and the soul long estranged from each other at one again."

Swedenborg's writings were sprinkled with such phrases as "Man is a kind of very minute heaven, corresponding to the world of spirits, and to heaven." The individual was a part of God. "God is the grand man," the sum of all men. To the Swedish theologian "the physical world was purely symbolic of the spiritual world." The notion of "correspondences" was especially appealing because it stated, in essence, that everything in the world is related to everything else. "To the withered traditional church, yielding dry catechisms," Emerson wrote, in an intensely self-revealing sentence, "he let in nature again, and the worshipper escaping from the vestry of verbs and texts is surprised to find himself a party to the whole of his religion."

In Emerson's obviously sympathetic paraphrase of Swedenborg: "All things in the universe arrange themselves to each person anew, according to his ruling love. Man is such as his affection and thought are. . . . We have come into a world which is a living poem. Everything is as I am. . . . Everyone makes his own house and state." For Emerson, Swedenborg's ultimate failure as a theologian was that he attached himself "to the Christian symbol, instead of to the moral sentiment, which carries unnumerable Christianities, humanities, divinities, in its bosom."

Oddly enough, Swedenborg's most famous follower, Emerson aside, was doubtless Jonathan Chapman, the legendary Johnny Apple-seed of the Mississippi Valley frontier. Distributing Swedenborgian tracts with his appleseeds, Johnny roamed the no-man's-land between the furthermost frontier settlements and the Indian territory clearing spots near the rivers and creeks to plant his seeds. A small, wiry, partially crippled man with "a long dark beard and black, sparkling eyes, quick and restless in speech and gesture," his clothing a coffee sack with holes for his head and arms, Johnny wore a cooking pot for a hat and also used it as a washbowl. Once, listening to a Methodist circuit rider exhorting a crowd with the question, "Where is the barefoot wandering Christian who is on his march to the kingdom of heaven?" Johnny, lifting his naked foot, called out, "Here, my man, here he is!" An American St. Francis, Johnny was opposed to killing any living creature and would endure clouds of mosquitoes rather than swat one. On one occasion, the story went, he was bitten by a rattlesnake. When a friend inquired what had happened to the snake, Johnny Appleseed replied, with tears in his eyes, "The poor thing! Hardly had it touched me than I, overcome by godless passion, cut off its head with my sickle. The poor, poor, innocent little animal!"

In 1823, after Emerson had graduated from Harvard and was headed for divinity school, he had written to a classmate, "When I have been to Cambridge and studied Divinity, I will tell you whether I can make out for myself any better system than Luther or Calvin, or the *liberal besoms* [innovators] of modern days. I have spoken thus because I am tired and disgusted with the preaching I have been accustomed to hear." Emerson had a number of coadjutors who, like himself, had graduated from Harvard College and attended the Divinity School. Neo-Platonic notions mixed with German idealism and conveyed to the American scene primarily through Thomas Carlyle and Samuel Coleridge drew on certain mystical elements from New England Congregationalism, from Puritanism, from the teachings of Jonathan Edwards, and as we have seen, from Swedenborg, to create a new amalgam which came to be called transcendentalism.

Emerson's famous sermon to the graduating class of the Harvard Divinity School in 1838, entitled "The American Scholar," is taken as the trumpet call of transcendentalism. "Truly speaking, it is no

instruction, but provocation, that I can receive from another soul,"
Emerson declared. "What he announces I must find true in me or
reject; and on his word, or as his second, be he who he may, I can
accept nothing. . . . As is the flood, so is the ebb. Let this faith depart,
and the very words it spake and the things it made become false and
hurtful. Then falls the church, the state, art, letters, life. . . . Once
man was all now he is an appendage, nuisance. . . . The doctrine or
inspiration is lost; the base doctrine of the majority of voices usurps the
place of the doctrine of the soul. Miracles, prophecy, poetry, the ideal
life, the holy life, exist as ancient history merely; they are not in the
belief, nor in the aspiration of society. . . . Life is comic or pitiful as
soon as the high ends of being fade out of sight, and man becomes
near-sighted, and can only attend to what addresses the issues. . . .
Jesus Christ belonged to the true race of prophets. He saw with open
eyes the mystery of the soul. Drawn by its severe harmony, ravished by
its beauty, he lived in it and had his being there. Alone in history he
estimated the greatness of man." The time had come for "new
revelations." Faith was almost dead and society with it. "The soul is not
preached. The church seems to totter to its fall, almost all life extinct."
The capacity for worship had diminished and when that happens in a
society, all things go to decay. "Genius leaves the temple to haunt the
senate or the market. Literature becomes frivolous. Science is cold.
The eye of youth is not lighted by the hope of other worlds, and age is
without honor. Society lives to trifles, and when men die we do not
mention them." He challenged the members of the graduating class to
"cast behind you all conformity, and acquaint men at first hand with
Deity. Look to it first and only, that fashion, custom, authority,
pleasure, and money, are nothing to you,—are not bandages over your
eyes, that you cannot see,—but live with the privilege of immeasurable
mind. . . . By trusting to your own heart, you shall gain more
confidence than other men. For all our penny-wisdom, for all our
soul-destroying slavery to habit, it is not to be doubted that all men
have sublime thoughts, that all men love the few real hours of life; they
love to be heard; they love to be caught up into the vision of
principles."

The religion that Emerson was propounding was, in its essence,
the religion of the "individual." The Protestant Reformation had
invented the individual, but he or she was an individual closely bound
up in a community of the faithful whose paramount desire was to serve
God. The new version of the individual of which Emerson became the

prophet was the free-floating, autonomous individual. And the exemplar of this individual was the poet and the orator. Emerson put this doctrine in a hundred seductive sentences: "Our private theatre is ourselves"; "Life consists of what a man is thinking of all day"; "The individual is the world"; "Nothing is sacred but the integrity of your own mind"; "The highest revelation is that God is in every man."

"Life is an ecstacy" was another Emerson aphorism. It was the free, uninhibited genius, the enraptured stargazer on the mountaintop who most plainly captured the meaning of life. Emerson seized on what was already so abundantly evident in American life—its atomized, disassociated, disintegrative character—and exalted it into the great central doctrine of his new religion. God in Man, God in Nature, Man in Nature, Man as God, Man as Poet, Poet as Articulator of the Mysteries, Poet as Priest of the Church of Transcendentalism. That was Emerson's genius—to take the negative aspects of the American experience and turn them into the positive. If Nature was often harsh and threatening, the poet-priest must make it benign. If American life was disintegrative, the poet-priest would turn those isolated individuals, whirling terrified, through space, into liberated spirits, filled with divine effluvia, consonant with Nature.

One of Emerson's most enthusiastic and successful disciples was Theodore Parker, whose ordination sermon had caused such a scandal. Parker was the grandson of Captain John Parker, who led the militiamen against the British regulars on the Lexington common on April 19, 1775. He graduated from Harvard Divinity School in 1836 and as pastor of a church in West Roxbury, Massachusetts, began preaching sermons so heretical that he was soon in hot water with his congregation. His friends banded together to help him organize a "new" Unitarian church where Parker preached the new religion of transcendentalism. "Christianity," he declared, "is a simple thing, very simple. It is absolute, pure morality; absolute, pure religion; the love of man; the love of God acting without let or hindrance. The only creed it lays down is the great Truth which springs up spontaneous in the holy heart—there is a God. Its watchword is: Be perfect as your Father in heaven. The only form it demands is divine life; doing the best thing in the best way, from the highest motives; perfect obedience to the great law of God. . . . The Christianity of sects, of the pulpit, or society, is ephemeral—a transitory fly. . . . It will pass off and be forgot. Some new form will take its place, suited to the aspect of the changing times." The Divine, whether Him or Her (Theodore Parker often spoke of

God as "Mother"), was single. God was "all-lovingness," a Being of "infinite perfection."

To Parker, transcendentalism was the doctrine that "man has faculties which transcend the senses; faculties which give him ideas and intuitions that transcend sensational experience." It included physics, politics, ethics, and religion. "It appeals to absolute justice, absolute right" whose source was in God. It was concerned with the "progressive" revelation of the truth through "harmonious development." Above all transcendentalism was grounded in "an immutable morality" and the individual was a "citizen of the universe" subject only to God. Transcendentalism thus "looks to a future, a future to be made; a church whose creed is truth, whose worship is love; a society full of industry and abundance, full of wisdom, virtue, and the poetry of life . . . a society without ignorance, want or crime, a state without oppression; best, a world with no war among nations to consume the work of their hands. . . . That is the human dream of the transcendental philosophy."

Americans, Parker insisted, "do not know how sick we are." "The Federal Government . . . just now is a vulture which eats the nations vitals out." Men dared not walk the streets of the capital city. "The Government is so busy filibustering against Cuba, Mexico, Central America, planting slavery in Kansas, that it cannot protect the lives of its own Congressmen in its own capital." And then there was slavery—"Every seventh man is property," and the "condition of women" who nowhere had her "natural right," who was imprisoned in loveless marriages "worse than celibacy." And, finally, drunkenness and crime. To Parker it was clear that there were two classes in America, "the victims of society, and the foes of society: the men that organize its sins, and then tell us nobody is to blame."

One of the distinguishing features of transcendentalism was its dogged optimism about the nature of man and the future of the species. In this it both reflected and enhanced that "democratic optimism" which was as such a prominent element in the American character. In the terms of our distinction between the Classical-Christian Consciousness and the Secular-Democratic Consciousness, we might say that with the appearance of transcendentalism Americans had finally invented a "religion" that was the perfect expression of the Secular-Democratic Consciousness. Understood in this light, transcendentalism had about it a kind of inevitability. To believe in predestination, original sin (or radical human depravity), *and* in the inevitable progress of the United States was to strain reason beyond reasonable limits. Since to believe *only* in the United States was insufficient for many people, especially in view of its prospective dissolution under the pressures of slavery, it remained to create a "religion" that allowed for faith in man's natural goodness, in progress, and in eventual "perfection." A clear line ran from Jefferson's religious speculations to Emerson and Parker and transcendentalism. Parker declared, "All the evil in the world is something incident to man's development, and no more permanent than the stumbling of a child who learns to walk. . . . It will be outgrown, and not a particle of it or its consequences shall cleave permanently to mankind. This is true of the individual wrongs which you and I commit; and likewise of such vast wickedness as war, political oppression, and the hypocrisy of priesthoods."

William Henry Channing was the nephew of William Ellery Channing, the high priest of Unitarianism. He, too, was a graduate of the Harvard Divinity School, class of 1832. He started a chapel for the poor in New York City, but the poor proved heedless and after a period of casting about he formed the Christian Union, committed to some form of Christian socialism. Four years later he took the lead in organizing the Religious Union of Associationists, a band of thirty-three, including George Ripley, who stated their faith in Universal Unity and the achievement of God's Kingdom on earth. In the first issue of a magazine called *The Present,* designed to spread the idea of Christian reform of the social and economic order, Channing declared that God, "through systems on systems, and worlds on worlds . . . crowns his creations by giving birth to hosts of spirits, destined originally, through revelations, forever brightening, to grow up in his likeness, and, by interchanges of good, to be united into families of immortal children, imaging in the heavens their holy father." If that proposition seemed impenetrable, Channing was clear enough in his denunciation of Americans as a people who had "allowed the excessive development of the animal passions, exaggerated the element of self; confused the judgments, weakened the power of the spiritual faculties; broken true society; in various degrees become incapable of receiving life from heaven; and so interrupted the divine order, and introduced depraved social tendencies, diseases, and natural confusions, which react to multiply evil." But all this would in time be dissipated by the goodness of the Eternal Father and it would become clear that "the worships and legislations, colonizations and empires of all ages, have been the steps to this progressive conquest of good over evil, by which mankind has been at once redeemed and educated. . . ." It was, in Channing's view, the destiny of the United States, "permitted to expand through an unobstructed, unexhausted, healthful, fertile, and most beautiful country—wondrously composed of representatives from every European state, who bring hither the varied experiences, convictions, manners, tastes, of the whole civilized world, to fuse and blend anew—this nation is manifestly summoned to prove the reality of human brotherhood, and of a worship of the heavenly Father. . . ." Certainly, Channing admitted, Americans "deserve the retributions, losses, disgraces, which our savage robberies of the Indians, our cruel and wanton oppressions of the Africans, our unjust habits of white serfdom, our grasping national ambition, our eagerness for wealth, our deceitful modes of external and internal trade, our jealous competitions between different professions and callings, our aping of aristocratic distinctions, our licentiousness and sensuality, our profligate expenditures, public and private, have brought and will continue to bring upon us." The day of the Lord would never come in all Christendom, "till, within our own borders, we secure for every individual man, woman, child, full culture, under healthy, pure, and holy influences; free exercise of their faculties, for the glory of God and the good of man."

Channing's essay abounds in the anguish and ambiguity that so many Americans who shared his perspective felt. God was good, God was just and loving, an active agent in the world. Yet the United States—his special vessel—was sunk in sin and depravity. So we have these inventories of evil and cries of hope.

Orestes Brownson was one of the most appealing figures in transcendentalism, perhaps because he came from the simplest antecedents, climbed from obscurity to fame, persistently championing the cause of the laborer and endlessly searching for his own religious "way," until, in abounding irony, he found himself in the Roman Catholic Church. Brownson, as a young man in his early twenties, had fallen under the spell of the Scottish reformer and "friend" of Lafayette, Frances Wright, and helped her to form the short-lived Working Men's Party in New York. The experience made him an enemy of capitalism. In 1836 he founded the Society for Christian Union and Progress and spelled out his views the same year in *New Views of Christianity, Society and the Church*. Two years later he published the first issue of the *Boston Quarterly Review*, perhaps the most radical Christian journal of the day. His essay on "The Laboring

Classes," which appeared in 1840, took the line that the condition of the Northern laborer was inferior in every respect but actual servitude to that of the Southern slave. "No one," he wrote, "can observe the signs of the times with much care, without perceiving that a crisis as to the relation of wealth and labor is approaching. It is useless to shut our eyes to the fact, and like the ostrich fancy ourselves secure because we have so concealed our heads that we see not the danger. We or our children will have to meet this crisis. The old war between the King and the Barons is well nigh ended, and so is that between the Barons and the Merchants and Manufacturers,—landed capital and commercial capital. The business man has become the peer of my Lord. And now commences the new struggle between the operative and his employers, between wealth and labor. . . . The laborer at wages has all the disadvantages of freedom and none of its blessings, while the slave, if denied blessings, is freed from the disadvantages. . . . We know no sadder sight on earth than one of our factory villages presents, when the bell at break of day, or at the hour of breakfast, or dinner, calls out its hundred or thousands of operatives. We stand and look at these hard working men and women hurrying in all directions, and ask ourselves, where go the proceeds of their labors? The man who employs them, and for whom they are toiling like so many slaves, is one of our city nabobs, revelling in luxury. . . . And this man too would fain pass for a Christian and a republican. He shouts for liberty, stickles for equality, and is horrified at a Southern planter who keeps slaves. . . . Wages is a cunning device of the devil, for the benefit of tender consciences, who would retain all the advantages of the slave system, without the expense, trouble, and odium of being slave-holders. . . . Our business is to emancipate the proletaries, as the past has emancipated the slaves. This is our work. There must be no class of our fellow men doomed to toil through life as mere workmen at wages."

The evil involved in the exploitation of labor for profit was "inherent in all our social arrangements," Brownson wrote, "and cannot be cured without a radical change of those arrangements." Brownson charged the evil of wage labor to religion and the clergy who had failed to speak out against so iniquitous a system. What was needed was, first of all, "legislation which shall free the government, whether State or Federal, from the control of the banks. The Banks represent the interest of the employer, and therefore of necessity interests adverse to those of the employed; that is, they represent the interests of the business community in opposition to the laboring classes, and may be made, nay, will be made, an instrument of depressing them yet lower. . . ."

Following the destruction of the banks "must come that of all monopolies, of all PRIVILEGE. . . . It will be seen at once that we allude to the hereditary descent of property, an anomaly in our American system, which must be removed, or the system itself will be destroyed. . . . A man shall have all he honestly acquired, so long as he himself belongs to the world in which he acquires it. But his power over his property must cease with his life, and his property must then become the property of the state, to be disposed of by some equitable law for the use of the generation which takes his place." Brownson had no illusion about the resistance of capitalists to such an equitable reordering of society. "It will come," he wrote, "if it ever come at all, only at the conclusion of war, the like of which the world has as yet never witnessed, and from which, however inevitable it may seem to the eye of philosophy, the heart of Humanity recoils with horror." The time had clearly not yet come for such radical measures, Brownson admitted, but the discussion of them and the preparation of the public mind for a radical reformation must begin.

"Democracy," Brownson declared, "is based on the fundamental truth that there is an element of the supernatural in every man placing him in relation with universal and absolute truth; that there is a true light which enlighteneth every man that cometh into the world; that a portion of the spirit of God is given to every man to profit withal. Democracy rests, therefore, on spiritualism, and is of necessity a believer in God and in Christ. Nothing but spiritualism has the requisite unity and universality to meet the wants of the masses." To Brownson it followed that the Democrats were the "Christian" party and the Whigs, because of their suspicion of democracy, were the party of "irreligion." It was talk like this that led George Templeton Strong to call Brownson an "infamous apostle of Jacobism" who "contents himself with talking suggestions about certain utterable blessings only to be enjoyed by the poor when wrested by a long and bloody struggle from the rich. . . ." Interestingly enough, a year later, when Brownson embraced the Catholic faith, Strong subscribed to his *Review* on the grounds that Brownson understood and was determined to expose the relationship between "Truth and Trade."

Brownson became increasingly conservative as he lost faith in the inherent goodness of "the people" and of the capacity of democracy to ensure justice for individuals. "We would think with the Radical," he wrote in 1840, "but often act with the conservative." The transcendental principles of his friends Theodore Parker and George Ripley with their rejection of all "authority" and of the institutional church, pushed him further toward a kind of Burkean fear of rapid change. He exalted the Old Americans, the Founding Fathers, with their profound respect for "order" and their emphasis on the necessary relationship between order and liberty, and denounced the Young Americans, misled by infidelity, selfishness, materialism, and the doctrines of Red Revolution.

From having held that it was "the mission of this country . . . to emancipate the proletary, to ennoble labor . . . and make every man free and independent," to do away with the division of society "into working men and idlers, employers and operatives," Brownson decided that America's true mission was "the sublime work of realizing the idea of a Christian society, and of setting the example of a truly great, noble, Catholic people. . . ." It was not that Brownson abandoned his concern for the poor and downtrodden, but rather that he became convinced that Protestant Christianity had gotten into bed with capitalism—"wealth is made a god, industry is a religion . . . poverty is a crime." Only a redeemed and purified Christianity could save the United States and indeed, Western Civilization. Where the destiny of the United States had been "progress" under God's providence, Brownson came to believe that "we must take our age as we find it, and accept it as far as we lawfully can, respect even its prejudices, where they are not sinful, in the hope of winning its regard for that higher progress proposed by the Church and possible only in her communion."

What is puzzling about the emergence of transcendentalism was that it attempted to reconcile elements of the American religious tradition, filtered through Unitarianism (which itself had been much influenced by the Enlightenment), with Enlightenment doctrines at the moment when those doctrines were most threatened by the persistence of reactionary politics and the imminence of large-scale tragedy in the conflict between the North and South. Jefferson, after all, wrote at that euphoric moment when it appeared that the revolutionary universalism of the American Revolution presaged the dawn of a new age and the beginning of a new human order. But fifty years or more of disaster had intervened between Jefferson and Emerson, quite enough tragedy to make the most sanguine spirit gloomy. Transcendentalism thus asserted its cheerful doctrines almost willfully, as it were, *against* the accumulated evidence. It was perhaps that which sometimes gave an air of desperation to the transcendentalists' pronouncements—or, at least, an air of unreality. It also underlay the involvement of the leading transcendentalists, most notably Bronson Alcott, Parker, and Ripley, in the reform movements of their time, and, even more, in a radical critique of American life and in the establishment of Utopian communities. If man was naturally good and good was progressive, and yet America seemed increasingly defaced by such social cancers as slavery, intemperance, prostitution, and the suppression of women, it followed that heroic efforts were required to bring about a general reformation and give effect to the promise of the New Age.

Seen in this light, transcendentalism accomplished three important tasks. It revived the optimistic faith of the Revolutionary Era, which, to be sure had never entirely died away, and gave it a mildly religious and theological setting. It ratified American "individualism" and cloaked it with positive connotations. Finally, one wing of it at least offered a radical critique of American "capitalism."

One of the most appealing aspects of transcendentalist thought was its openness to other "world religions," as we say today. The transcendentalists believed that God had revealed Himself in one fashion or another in all religious faiths and they were especially receptive to elements of Buddhism and Confucianism. Indeed it may be said that a sympathetic awareness of Oriental religions entered the United States through the agency of the transcendentalists.

The enemies of transcendentalism argued, with considerable force, that the movement seemed determined to worship man rather than God. Nathaniel Frothingham, minister of the First Unitarian Church in Boston, wrote in 1843, "The present era seems to be that of the apotheosis of human nature. Human nature is exalted above its own height. Man, who started into his first deviation from the truth by the worship of the surrounding universe, appears approaching, as his last delusion, to the worship of himself. Ah, poor worm!"

By the end of the decade of the 1850s Christianity was faced with its most serious challenge—Charles Darwin's *Origin of the Species,* published in the United States in 1859. The evolutionary explanation of the development of man from the higher apes was in direct contradiction to the Genesis account in the Old Testament and its publication stirred up a storm. The publishing house of D. Appleton and Company was charged with encouraging infidelity. George Templeton Strong, with his keen scientific interest and devout Episcopalianism, read the book with interest and wrote in his diary that he found it "a laborious, intelligent, and weighty book. The first obvious criticism on it seems this: that Darwin has got hold of *a* truth which he wants to make out to be *the* one generative law of organic life. Because he shows that the fauna and flora of a group of islands lying near a certain continent are so like those of that continent, though differing specifically therefrom, and so unlike those of regions more remote . . . he considers himself entitled to affirm that *all* beasts, birds, and creeping things, from mammal to medusa, are developments from one stock, and that man is the descendant of some ancestral archaic fish. . . . But I suspect that He who created and upholds this great marvelous system of various harmonious life is not obliged to conformity with any *one* Law of Creation and preservation that Darwin's or any other finite intellect can discover." Strong went on to point out that "man's experience for, we will say, only four thousand years furnishes no instance of the development of new functions or new organs by any animal or vegetable organism."

To Darwin, Strong wrote, "as to the physicists of the last one hundred years, the notion of a supernatural creative power is repugnant and offensive. He wants to account for the wonderful, magnificent harmonies and relations of the various species of life that exist on earth by reducing the original agency of supernatural power in their creation to a minimum." For Strong the distinction between the Christian view of creation and Darwin's came simply to this: "One is familiar to our senses, the other is proved by deduction. They are a priori equally credible, or incredible, whichever Mr. Darwin pleases. The inorganic world has its own internal harmonies and relations quite as distinct and unmistakeable as the organic. But no law of progressive development can be inferred from them."

Far more threatening to Protestant Christianity than slavery, schisms, spiritualism, transcendentalism, or Darwinism was its ancient enemy, the Mammon of unrighteousness, the Anti-Christ, the pope of Rome and his obedient minions. Protestant America feared and hated Catholic America. This hostility ran through all levels of American life. Missionaries like Marcus Whitman strove to save the Oregon country from Catholicism. Such liberal and enlightened spirits as Richard Henry Dana and Emerson himself had nothing good to say of the pope or his church. Reformers who fought for the abolition of slavery, the emancipation of women, and universal peace felt for Catholicism and those who practiced it only scorn. The common view was that it was an authoritarian religion, taking orders from Rome, entirely incompatible with American democracy. Only the Democratic Party took in its predominantly Irish and German practitioners. The greater part of the anxiety produced by Irish immigration centered on the fact that they were Catholics under the direct control of the pope.

The Church had flourished with the tide of immigration. By 1838, Captain Marryat estimated that there were more than "800,000 souls under the government of Rome, 12 Bishops, and 433 priests . . . colleges, 10; seminaries for young men, 9 . . . and seven Catholic newspapers." We are already familiar with the political and social manifestations of anti-Catholic sentiments in the form of consistent riots against Irish and German immigrants and the emergence of "native" political movements. While upper-class intellectuals like Strong and Fisher deplored the violence of "native" Americans, they spoke far more tolerantly of outbreaks against Catholic churches and convents than of attacks on banks. In the spring of 1842, George Templeton Strong noted "some hard fighting in the Bloody Sixth, and a grand no-popery riot last night, including a vigorous attack on the Roman Catholic Cathedral with brick bats and howls, and a hostile demonstration on Hughes episcopal palace, terminating in broken windows and damaged furniture." Sampling various church services, Strong found that of the Catholics "tolerable" but the sermon was "immensely absurd. . . . I never heard a comparable farrago of nonsense, false-hood, blunder, hibernicism, nonsense, fun, flummery, bad grammar, false logic and stuff."

The hostility toward Catholics astonished Harriet Martineau, who, noting the rapid spread of Catholicism in the Mississippi Valley, wrote that "its increase produces an almost insane dread among some Protestants." By the end of our period the number of Catholics had increased almost threefold with a corresponding increase in Protestant paranoia.

A typical example of anti-Catholic literature was a "portable" book entitled, *Foreign Conspiracy against the Liberties of the United States.* Published in 1835, it contained an endorsement by ministers representing the Episcopal, Presbyterian, Methodist, and Baptist churches which read, in part, "Learning that you are about to publish in a small volume, the articles . . . showing that a conspiracy is formed against the United States by the Papal powers of Europe, the undersigned . . .

have great pleasure expressing their approbation of your undertaking. . . . While we disapprove of harsh, denunciatory language towards Roman Catholics, their past history and the fact that they every where act together, as if guided by one mind, admonish us to be jealous of their influence, and to watch with unremitted care all their movements in relation to our free institutions.

"Americans! Friends of Liberty; Friends of order; examine this subject," the author exhorted, "and decide with your usual sagacity and discretion. You have a busy, a crafty, a powerful, a dangerous set of foreign leaders, controlling and commanding a foreign population, ignorant and infatuated, intermixed with your own population, and who at a single signal from the Pope or from Metternich, when the cause of despotism shall require, can spread disorder and riot through all your borders."

The Irish Catholics constituted a very particular kind of case. They were, in distinction to most immigrants, curiously unassimilable; you might say indigestible. They would not go down the great American gut and be turned into nourishment for the body politic. They lodged in the upper stomach under the standard of the Democratic Party and gave "native" Americans a vast collective bellyache. As their numbers grew, year by year, they came to constitute a kind of nation within a nation, stubbornly defiant of all the Protestant ethnics/ethics around them. Nothing tested the American system of constitutional government quite as severely as the immigrant Irish in the decades prior to the Civil War.

The middle- and upper-class character of American Protestantism was inescapable. For Moritz Busch, the German refugee from the Revolution of 1848, the alliance between Protestant Christianity and the business community was symbolized by the renting of pews in most churches. Christians of whatever denomination who paid their money for a particular space in a church to be built viewed their pews as their property. The pews were zealously guarded by formally attired ushers and woe to the working-class Christian who strayed into an Episcopal or Presbyterian church and tried to seat himself in the pew of a communicant. The consequences of this practice (which had been devised as a practical way to finance the building of churches) were commented on by Captain Marryat. "There is *no provision for the poor* in the American voluntary church system," he wrote. "Thus only those who are rich and able to afford religion can obtain it." The Catholic Church alone ministered to the religious needs of the working-class poor. If you were poor and not a Catholic in America, there was seldom a place to turn for the consolations of religion.

Jews made up a significant portion of the population in the major cities and, indeed, throughout the country as far west as the goldfields of California. George Templeton Strong noted their prominence in the cultural life of New York City. Attending a concert with a friend in the winter of 1845, he observed, "As usual, three-fourths of the assembly were children of Israel." If someone had risen in the hall, Strong wrote, and called out that the Farmer's Loan and Trust Company (a favorite bank for Jewish investors) had defaulted payment, "the announcement would have had an appalling effect on the hook-nosed and black-whiskered congregation. . . ."

Strong visited a Jewish synagogue and noted that the congregation all wore hats, "took a hearty and zealous part in the services and roared out their unintelligible responses with good will and strength of lungs. I like that," he added. "In our church it looks too much like going to heaven by proxy." Strong cited as evidence of a lack of prejudice against Jews the fact that Mordecai Manasseh Noah, former editor of the *New York Star,* former sheriff and surveyor of the port of New York—an office to which he had been appointed by Jackson—was named as associate justice of the New York City Court of Sessions. Similarly, George Combe could observe no hostility toward Jews in Philadelphia. "They are received in society according to their attainments and condition," he wrote. "Jewish physicians attended Christian patients, and *vice versa.* Jews fall in love with, and marry pretty Christian women, and within three generations the Jew is sunk and the family merges into the mass of the general population." There was a well-attended synagogue, but the "spirit of free discussion which has loosened the bonds of orthodoxy in other sects, has not been without some influence on the Jews. They use considerable freedoms with Moses and the prophets, preach and discuss general ethics and natural religion, and altogether wear the chains of Judaism so loosely, that probably their brethren in Europe would disown them."

Our best guide to the condition of Jews in the United States is Israel Joseph Benjamin, a Moldavian Jew who came to New York in 1858 with the intention of becoming an American citizen. He found in New York a flourishing but badly fragmented Jewish community consisting of twenty-three separate congregations, divided between German, Polish, English, French, Dutch, and Bohemian rituals, with German much predominating. The oldest and wealthiest was Shearith

Israel, made up of German and Portuguese or Sephardic Jews. B'nai Jeshurun, founded in 1825, followed the Polish ritual. Its rabbi, Dr. M. J. Raphall, had recently delivered the prayer at the opening of Congress.

"Lord, great and manifold have been Thy bounties to this highly favored land," Rabbi Raphall had declared. "Heartfelt and sincere are our thanks. While the vast despotisms of Asia are crumbling into dust, and the effete monarchies of the Old World can only sustain themselves by yielding to the pressure of the spirit of the age, it has been Thy gracious will that in this Western hemisphere there should be established a Commonwealth after the model of that which Thou, Thyself, didst bestow on the tribes of Israel, in their best and purest days." Raphall prayed that the Lord, "amidst the din of conflicting interests and opinions," would direct the legislators of the nation in "the way of moderation and equity; that they may speak and act and legislate for Thy glory and the happiness of our country . . . while the whole people of the land joyfully repeat the words of Thy Psalmist: 'How good and how pleasant it is when brethren dwell together in unity.'"

In addition to the synagogues, Benjamin enumerated forty-four "Jewish Charitable and Educational Societies" dedicated to a wide variety of benevolent activities, from visiting the sick and dying to caring for widows, supporting the poor, collecting funds for the poor in the Holy Land, running a hospital and orphanage, and promoting good literature. The Order of the B'nai B'rith (Sons of the Covenant) was a secret society "like the Freemasons, with passwords, signs, and the like . . . quite a new phenomenon" and, in Benjamin's view, "an unnecessary innovation."

Benjamin visited Philadelphia, Baltimore, Washington, Richmond, Cincinnati, Louisville, and New Orleans, everywhere with an attentive eye to the "various Jewish communities" and "the spirit of America." "If anyone has any doubts about the ever fresh and youthful strength of our religion that flourishes in all zones and regions of the earth," Benjamin wrote, "let him go to the United States and see what it has effected and produced there also." Benjamin listed the "rapid expansion" which Judaism had undergone, "the magnificent institutions that it has called into life, the great increase of congregations . . . the variety of religious viewpoints that are expressed with neighborly patience and without animosity and with the greatest of freedom."

The second Jewish emigration from Europe to the United States had begun in 1836 and increased yearly as persecutions in Germany and Poland had disposed Jews to look to "the modern Promised Land," the United States. The first Jewish immigrants had been "poor men looking to earn their bread by the sweat of their brow . . . without other means than the scanty possessions locked in their knapsacks or traveling-bags." Most of them followed the example of the Yankee peddlers. With their goods on their backs they set out to isolated towns and villages. Soon the shrewd and ambitious peddler prospered; he provided himself with a horse and wagon, "profits accumulated daily; and from his profits he sent, as a token of love and a sign of fortunate beginnings, sums to help his old and impoverished parents; other sums went along with these to pay for the passage of dear friends. The letters and the money so received were the missionary tracts of freedom, and immigration grew at an incredible rate." Soon many Jews were in business for themselves, thrifty and reliable, "with their own credit," so that "the name 'German Jew' soon fell pleasantly upon the ears of American importers, manufacturers and wholesalers; credit and profit increased rapidly, and in a few years the poor immigrant workingman was a respected and well-to-do merchant in his new fatherland . . . thousands of flourishing firms in . . . cities, towns and villages gave evidence of the prosperity that the Jews had gained in twenty-five years." Thrift, hard work, piety, and business astuteness were, after all, the qualities most admired by Americans, so much so that they were to be called "the Protestant ethic." They were, as it turned out, the Jewish ethic as well. "The political position of the Jews," Benjamin wrote, "kept pace with this rapid commercial development. Every office was open to all without distinction of religion or birth. As a result Israelites were represented, not only in all the states in the municipal and state offices, but they were also members of Congress, in the Senate as well as the House of Representatives." The Southern states outdid the North in their hospitality toward Jews: "The white inhabitants felt themselves united with, and closer to, other whites—as opposed to the Negroes. Since the Israelite there did not do the humbler kinds of work which the Negro did, he was quickly received among the upper classes and easily rose to high political rank." Louisiana and Florida both sent Jews to the Senate and in the former state the lieutenant governor was a Jew. Charleston, South Carolina, due in large part to the efforts of Charles Pinckney, had earlier wiped out all discrimination against Jews. It was also undoubtedly the case that the easygoing Southerners, often lacking in business acumen, welcomed the practical financial abilities of Jewish immigrants.

If Benjamin's account was, in some respects, overly optimistic, it was certainly true in the main. From the American Revolution to the latter part of the nineteenth century, the United States was, indeed, the promised land for the European Jews who found their way here. The relations between Jew and Gentile constituted a kind of golden age of interracial harmony and goodwill. Only the Catholics and the Irish felt the weight of religious and racial hostility.

Alexis de Tocqueville was especially interested in the state of religion in America because, like Orestes Brownson, he believed that Christianity was essential in a democracy. "The materialists are offensive to me in many respects," he wrote; "their doctrines I hold to be pernicious, and I am disgusted at their arrogance. . . . Materialism, among all nations, is a dangerous disease of the human mind; but it is more especially to be dreaded among a democratic people because it readily amalgamates with that vice which is most familiar to the heart under such circumstances. Democracy encouraged a taste for physical gratification; this taste, if it becomes excessive, soon disposes men to believe that all is matter only; and materialism, in turn, hurries them on with mad impatience to these same delights. . . ." It seemed to Tocqueville that there were many instances, the Puritans of colonial America among them, where religious peoples "while . . . they were thinking only of the other world . . . found out the great secret of success in this." Religion was directed at least in part toward the future, both toward the life hereafter and the well-being of subsequent generations on earth. It thus disposed men to resist "a thousand petty selfish passions of the hour" and it was only so that "the general and unquenchable passion for happiness can be satisfied." So governments must "apply themselves to restore to men that love of the future . . . and, without saying so, they must practically teach the community day by day that wealth, fame, and power are the rewards of labor, that great success stands at the utmost range of long desires, and that there is nothing lasting but what is obtained by toil."

The absence of common religious bonds tended to isolate men from each other, "to concentrate every man's attention upon himself" and lay "open the soul to an inordinate love of material gratification." For Tocqueville, following, doubtless unwittingly, in the footsteps of Benjamin Franklin and John Adams, well-being or what they called "luxury," was an essential engine in an egalitarian society. It was the impulse that energized people. The danger was that it would become the sole occasion of the society and thus destroy it. Only religion would be able "to purify, to regulate, and to restrain the excessive taste for well-being. . . ."

When all has been said, we may perhaps leave the last word on nineteenth-century American religion to another visitor, Moritz Busch. Busch wrote:

"Not since the fire of the Reformation was extinguished by dogmatism has the religious spirit expressed itself in any part of the Christian world as powerfully as among the people of the United States—and in no place so chaotically and strangely." Compared to Germany, "the life of the Christian Church in America seems almost like a remnant of the fantastically fluid primeval world alongside the solid regularity and rational dryness of present-day nature. Beneath the crust of a rigid and obstinate orthodoxy . . . has boiled since the arrival of the first Puritan ship on Plymouth's shores, and still boils and flows today, a volcanic wonder-fire. At times it runs through the land in the form of will-o'-the-wisps, so that rational people, confused, shake their heads about it; and at other times it flares up in intense revivals." Earlier principles of faith are overturned in desperate struggles. A new movement, "having ignited the minds of the masses with its fervor, . . deposits as slag the constitution of a new sect. The spirit which once descended upon the disciples in flaming tongues is still dispensed here in abundance, and every year thousands do not merely celebrate but actually experience a Pentecost."

27

Converting the Heathen

If many devout Americans in the middle decades of the nineteenth century were convinced that the United States could be redeemed by foreswearing liquor or giving women their rights or freeing the slaves, it is not surprising that large numbers were equally convinced that the path to salvation for the nation, and indeed the world, lay through the country of the heathen. Missions to the Indians went back, of course, to the days of John Eliot. There had never been a time, since the early days of the colonies, when there had not been missionaries laboring to convert the aborigines to the Christian faith. It could not have been otherwise. If the teachings of one branch or another of Christianity were the truth, it was the obligation of every Christian to spread the good news of salvation and eternal life. So God's work was carried on by his indefatigable servants generation after generation, in face of hardships sufficient to daunt the most saintly. To live among the aboriginal tribes was often dangerous in the extreme as the deaths of numerous missionaries at the hands of those they tried to convert proved. In addition to the unpredictability of their savage and often reluctant hosts, missionaries usually lived under conditions of extreme austerity, sustained by the uncertain largesse of the mission boards that dispatched them and by their own ingenuity and resourcefulness. If the tribes they lived among were subject to devastating white men's diseases, the missionaries were vulnerable to maladies that their charges were relatively immune to, such as rheumatism, pneumonia, consumption, and malaria.

At the sacrifice of all the comforts of civilization and often of their lives, thousands of men and women established missions with the great majority of Indian tribes, or, perhaps more accurately, with most of the tribes disposed to accept them. The greatest service the missionaries had to offer was the education of young aborigines, boys and girls alike, and it was here that they concentrated their efforts.

Captain Marryat, touring the Indian country, visited a missionary school for girls of the Dakota Sioux. There the children read and wrote English, French, and Sioux. "They are modest and well behaved, as the Indian women generally are. They had prayers every evening. . . . The warriors sat on the floor around the room; the missionary . . . his family in the center; and they all sang remarkably well. This system with these Indians is, in my opinion, very good," Marryat added.

In 1826 among fourteen eastern and southern tribes there were thirty-eight schools, maintained by the American Board of Foreign Missions, the Baptist General Convention, the United Foreign Mission Society, the Western Mission Society, the Methodist Episcopal Church, and the Protestant Episcopal Church. As with all benevolent enterprises carried on by Christians, there was a sharp division of opinion over whether each Protestant denomination should support its own missionary activity or whether all should contribute to a common missionary effort. For the year 1825, the various missionary agencies mentioned here contributed $176,700 out of a total expenditure of $202,070, the rest being contributed by the federal government, usually in compliance with some treaty agreement.

Year after year, labors of the faithful bore fruit, although usually in very modest quantities. The report for 1828 noted, "Among the Cherokee, Chickasaws, Choctaws . . . the preaching of the Gospel was attended with unusual success. At Brainerd, six natives were admitted to the church in May. In July, there were ten more who had hope of their own piety, most of whom appeared to be truly penitent. . . . On the 15TH of November, 29 Choctaws were admitted to the church. . . . It was supposed there were 3,000 anxious inquirers in the nation. More than 2,000 had begun to pray."

Missionary work among the Indians continued and indeed

increased with each decade. We have seen missionaries accompanying the Five Nations on the Indian Removal and settled with them in Oklahoma Territory. Marcus Whitman, who went to the Cayuse Indians as a medical missionary with his beautiful blond wife, Narcissa, turned his attention particularly to improving the health of the tribe and teaching its members improved agricultural techniques. The secretary of the American Board of Missions, which supported the Whitmans' work in Oregon Territory, wrote, "I fear from your account of what you have to do for the whites and the Indians, in respect to mills, fields and herds, that you will almost lose sight of the great spiritual object of your mission, and be too nearly satisfied with seeing the Indians advancing in industry, the arts of civilized life, and the means of comfortable living. Why should they not grow covetous and selfish, if their thoughts are mostly turned toward these things . . . ?"

The complaint was a common one from the spokesmen of the missionary boards that provided the money to sustain the work of the missions. They wanted results in the form of a harvest of Christian souls. The workers in "the field" were often far more conscious of what needed to be done to improve the physical condition of their charges before attention could be given to their souls. Whitman was, indeed, a remarkable figure. He was quite ready to admit that he was as much concerned with promoting emigration into the Oregon country as with converting the aborigines of the region. He took credit, in fact, for having directly assisted in the emigration of over a thousand settlers in the territory as well as having explored the most convenient overland route to the area. He excused himself for such worldly preoccupations by stating that without such efforts "Jesuit Papists" would have come to dominate the territory. To a friend who had been seduced by Millerism, Whitman wrote, "Come, then to Oregon, resume your former motto, which seemed to be onward and upward . . . in principle, action, duty and attainments, and in holiness . . . and then you will be cooperative and happy in Oregon. . . ." The country was a rich and fertile one. "Nor should men of piety and principle leave it all to be taken by worldlings and worldly men." If his brother-in-law came with a party of friends they could take up 640 acres of land "as a bounty," and "by mutual consent, set apart a portion for the maintenance of the gospel and for schools and learning. . . ."

The missionaries certainly did not solve the "Indian problem," which strictly speaking had no solution, but they did contribute far more than is generally realized to the amelioration of the condition of reservation Indians by establishing schools, missions, churches, and medical clinics. In the process they converted a number of Indians to Christianity, a substantial portion of whom passed over into the world of the white man. If this was not an ideal solution to those persons, Indian and white, who were anxious to preserve at least the major elements of tribal culture, it was often a form of worldly salvation for the converted and provided important links between the worlds of the white man and the Indian.

The missions to the aborigines, important as they were, were only part of the "home mission" effort. The rest was directed to establishing missions and missionaries on what was generally viewed in the East as "the Godless" frontier and at distributing religious tracts and, of course, Bibles throughout the length and breadth of the land.

The foreign missions extended around the globe. The first pioneers of what came to be in time a major missionary effort had arrived in India in 1813. The Sandwich Islands soon became a major missionary center. As early as 1801 a group of Congregational women in Boston started the Female Society for Propagating the Diffusion of Christian Knowledge, and a year later the first Female Cent Society was founded; its members contributed a cent a week to the work of missions. The Congregational Church had established the American Board of Commissioners for Foreign Missions, declaring, "The Eastern world . . . presents most extensive fields for missionary labors; fields which appear fast ripening for the harvest. All . . . are full of people sitting in darkness and in the region and shadow of death, and by experiments already made it has been abundantly evinced that it is by no means . . . vain . . . to attempt to spread the Gospel of salvation among them. . . ." In another statement the newly formed board announced, "Prophecy, history and present state of the world seem to unite in declaring that the great pillars of the papal and Mohammedan impostures are now tottering to their fall." The time was ripe for the conversion of a vast number of heathens. The board decided to direct its activities to four fields: "(1) peoples of Ancient civilizations (2) peoples of primitive cultures (3) peoples of ancient Christian churches (4) people of Islamic faith." It was under this general plan that a mission had been established in Bombay in 1813, in Ceylon in 1816, in the Sandwich Islands in 1820, on the Guinea Coast of Africa in 1833, Sumatra and Borneo a year later, among the Zulus in 1835, and then in Siam, Singapore, Madras, Amoy, Foochow and, in 1854, in Shanghai and Peking.

The Middle East soon became a major field of missionary activity. Missionaries came to the Armenians, Greeks, Bulgarians, and Syrians, to Turkey, to Arabia, and to Persia.

Loanza Gould Benton, who came to Syria with her husband in 1847, founded a girls' school in the remote mountains and raised two sons after her husband's death. A hundred years later, when one of her descendants visited the school at the end of World War II, the Syrian headmistress brought her charges out to greet the Americans and declared, "The memory of Madam Benton lingers in the hills of Lebanon like sweet perfume."

"Your views," the American Board instructed missionaries to the Sandwich Islands, "are not to be limited to a low or narrow scale; but you are to open your hearts wide, and set your mark high. You are to aim at nothing short of covering those islands with fruitful fields and pleasant dwellings and schools and churches; of raising a whole people to an elevated state of civilization." A historian of the board was not far off the mark when he wrote, "By and large it was discovered that friendliness expressed through loving concern for the poor and the sick, eagerness to learn and listen, patient endeavors to satisfy human curiosity, unwillingness to take offense, calmness under provocation and persecution and a disposition to be content with what seemed at first meager results—these characteristics of the missionary were in demand among Oriental peoples."

In all these efforts women played a central part, both as fund raisers to sustain missions and as the wives of missionaries who often established schools for native children and shared the tasks of their husbands. By 1838 there were 680 "ladies associations" with more than three thousand "local agents" collecting funds for the support of missionary activities. Judith Chace was appointed schoolmistress to the Cherokee in 1818 and in 1823 Betsy Stockton of Princeton, New Jersey, a black woman, was sent to the Sandwich Islands, the first unmarried woman sent overseas.

The great majority of the missionaries were graduates of such colleges as Williams, Amherst, Dartmouth, and Yale. Thirty percent died of disease or accident within the first ten years of their missions. Beyond that their efforts were beset by every kind of disappointment and frustration. In most places the harvest of souls was distressingly small, suggesting that the millennium must be long delayed. There were frictions between the missionaries in the field and the home boards and congregations which had dispatched them and which sustained them. In their dark, stiff clothes and their evangelical zeal, their fierce energy and relentless determination, they seemed to the people they had come to convert like creatures from another planet. In cultures that reckoned their history in centuries and, indeed, millennia, rather than decades, that were dominated by fatalism, by an ethic of simple survival, whose poorer classes lived among the accumulated refuse of ages, these odd individuals with their fetish about cleanliness, their teaching of a savior, and their promise of a better life, both here and now and in the hereafter, were listened to incredulously.

In their little mission churches they sang the hymns of Isaac Watts and in their schools they taught grammar, spelling, mathematics, and geography, all sprinkled with Christian piety and accompanied by ceaseless exhortations to be clean, the virtue next to godliness.

The greatest weapon in the evangelical armory was the printing press. Soon missionaries brought their own presses with them as the most essential piece of baggage. On them they turned out a vast tide of books of all kinds in native languages—dictionaries, histories, religious tracts and, by the end of the century, more than four million Bibles.

Persevering in the face of every discouragement, the missionary men and women came in ever increasing numbers with each passing decade, spreading out to every corner of the world that stood in need of God's word. Elias Riggs, a graduate of Amherst, went to Armenia in 1830 and remained there until his death, sixty-eight years later, producing, as did many of his fellow laborers in the mission field, a substantial progeny: three children, eleven grandchildren, and two great-grandchildren, all missionaries.

The missionaries from the United States joined missionaries from a number of European countries, most typically Germany and England, and formed, in time, a remarkable international Christian community whose members intermarried, often over the span of several generations. For missionaries to marry converted native women and for the daughters of missionaries to marry converted native men was also a familiar pattern.

Cyrus Hamlin started the Bebek Seminary in Constantinople in 1840 and organized "an industrial annex to teach the students to make shoes, clothes, and iron stoves." He started a bakery during the Crimea War and used the money he made selling bread to the soldiers, some $25,000, to erect thirteen churches. In 1863 Hamlin founded, at the Seminary, the first American institution of higher learning outside of the United States with five faculty members and four students. The "college" combined technical and classical training, and Hamlin sought faculty with "fervent symmetrical piety" as the college grew. Even here the Puritan covenant reasserted itself and a document survives in which two students, Pierre and Silvio, "two high contracting parties agree that in order to preserve peace . . . one shall not call the other a dog or a pig or a thief, robber, rowdy, pezevenk or other opprobrious epithet in Italian, French, Turkish, Greek, English, Bulgarian, Armenian or any other language spoken at the Tower at Babel or since that day. Silvio shall in no case strike Pierre or Pierre Silvio." Hamlin clearly had a sense of humor in addition to faith and erudition. When the American Board withdrew its formal support, Roberts College was kept going primarily through the beneficence of Christopher Roberts and several of his business friends, who contributed over $400,000 to the college.

Three years later the Syrian Protestant College opened in Beirut (later the American University) with sixteen students, using Arabic for instruction and boasting of a department of medicine and pharmacy. Daniel Bliss, its founder, at the cornerstone-laying ceremony for the college's first building, declared, "A white, black or yellow; Christian, Jew, Mohammedan or heathen, may enter and enjoy all the advantages of this institution . . . and go out believing in one God, in many Gods, or in no God. But it will be impossible for any one to continue with us long without knowing what we believe to be the truth and our reasons for the belief."

In 1840 the American Board of Commissioners for Foreign Missions, the Baptist General Convention, the missionary body of the Baptist Church, the Methodist Episcopal and the Episcopal Churches, the Freewill Baptist Foreign Mission Society and the Board of Missions of the Presbyterian Church cooperated in publishing a *History of American Missions to the Heathen from Their Commencement to the Present Time*. The chapter headings reveal the range of missionary activity. That of Chapter XII reads: "Death of Mr. Worcester. Deficiency of Funds—Bombay. . . . Death of Mr. Newell. Arrival of Mr. Garret.— Ceylon. Death of Mrs. Poor. Revival, Native Preachers licensed— Mission to Armenia suggested. Greek Revolution. Conversion among the Cherokees. . . . Conversions among the Choctaws. . . . Sandwich Islands. Opposition of foreign residents. First Chapel built."

A plan for a mission college in Ceylon stated as its objectives, "1. To impart a thorough knowledge of the English language, as the only way to unlock the treasures which that language contains. 2. The cultivation of Tamul literature; which is necessary in order to oppose idolatry most successfully, and in order to raise up a reading population. 3. The study of Sanscrit by a select few. . . . 4. To teach Hebrew, and in some cases Latin and Greek, to those native preachers who may be employed as translators of the Scriptures. 5. To teach, as far as the circumstances of the country require, the sciences usually studied in the colleges of Europe and America." Thirty-six pupils were enrolled, divided into three classes, and a school established for girls nearby. Two years later fifty missionary schools on Ceylon had enrolled more than 2,000 pupils, of whom 250 were girls.

The missionary work in the Sandwich Islands had, as one of its goals, the protection of the women of the islands from sexual exploitation by visiting whaling and trading vessels. There, as a missionary named Richards reported, when the islanders had passed a law "forbidding women to visit ships for immoral purposes," the captain of the British whaling ship visited the missionary and threatened to burn down his house and kill him unless he prevailed on the natives to revoke their new law. Richards and his ill wife refused to comply and natives defended their house against an attack by sailors, armed with knives and pistols, who announced that they would not return to their ships without women. The conversion of Kapiolani, a queen of one of the islands, did much to pave the way for other conversions. "Intemperance, and other gross vices disappeared, and numbers appeared truly pious." By 1830 forty schools were in operation on Hawaii alone and 600 pupils were graduated from the schools of Honolulu. But a year later the combined crews of several ships attacked the homes of chiefs on Honolulu, injured some of the natives, smashed the windows in the houses of the missionaries, and, under the leadership of a Lieutenant Percival, in command of the United States warship the *Dolphin*, finally succeeded in bringing women on board the ships, whereupon "a shout ran from one deck to another as if a glorious victory had been achieved." Despite such setbacks, it was estimated that by the end of 1826 more than 20,000 pupils were "under instruction" on all the islands and "2000 persons were known to be in the habit of family and secret prayers."

By 1840 missionary work was well established in the Chinese Treaty Port of Canton. A Christian hospital had cared for 6,540 patients and a campaign had been launched against the use of opium. A school with forty pupils and a printing press had been established in Singapore and 598,790 pages "all in the Chinese language" had been printed and disseminated. In Bombay the count was 25,826,000 pages with seventeen free schools and 822 pupils, a hundred of them girls; five boarding schools, three for boys and two for girls. The story was similar in Madras and Madura. In the latter Indian city there were eighty-two "native free schools" and 2,677 pupils, and in Ceylon 1,704 pupils were in free schools and the printing presses had turned out a total of 30,905,200 pages of reading matter in the native languages. And so it went in Turkey, Syria, Persia and Greece, South Africa, West Africa, and the perpetually fertile fields of the Sandwich Islands, which waxed even when other fields waned.

The cumulative statistics were impressive. Between 1826 and 1840 more than $20,000,000 had been collected by the American Board alone from 1,700 churches and 802 "monthly concerts" in 27 states and territories. Seventy-seven "stations were currently in operation, manned by 372 missionaries (694 had labored during the period of the board's existence). Native communicants were numbered at a comparatively modest 7,311 but the "number of children in common schools, more or less dependent on the missions of the Board for means of instruction" had been between 50,000 and 100,000 and an additional 20,000 had been yearly in schools maintained by the missions.

While the Baptist Convention offered no cumulative figures on schools and pages of religious tracts printed in native languages, their missions were as far-flung as those of the American Board, concentrating their efforts in Burma, with American Indian tribes, and in Southeast Asia, the general area of present-day Thailand, Cambodia and Vietnam. They were also in West Africa—Benin (formerly Dahomey)—and China, as well as France, Denmark, and Germany.

The Methodist Episcopalians, a relatively small denomination, confined their efforts primarily to American Indian tribes in the Oregon Territory and to the establishment of mission stations in South America and in Liberia in Africa. The African mission was a special challenge. The Reverend Melville Cox, a native of Maine, set out with several black aides but he died shortly after arriving in Liberia, and his last words were "Africa must be redeemed though thousands perish." Of three immediate successors, one died within months and another was so ill that he was forced to return to the United States, leaving an indefatigable lady, Miss Farrington, who remained to "offer her soul, upon the altar of God, for the salvation of Africa." She was soon joined by Francis Burns, "a colored local preacher, and Eunice Sharp, a pious female of color." From such a modest beginning the Africa venture grew in a few years to seventeen missionaries, ten teachers, the inevitable printer, and a physician, with 231 scholars and 300 pupils in the Sabbath schools. "Who can imagine," the historian of the mission wrote, "the gratitude to God that will swell the heart of the superintendent of that mission when he leads those new Christian Africans to the baptismal font . . . and thus ushers them into the enjoyment of Christ's Militant church . . . ?"

The missionaries came as heralds of the New Age to societies, to cultures, to tribes, to peoples locked into traditional consciousnesses characterized by stolid acceptance of rigid, virtually impenetrable class barriers, perpetual poverty, and, with few exceptions, the entire subordination of women. They came full of subversive notions of the preciousness and the equality of all souls in the eyes of God, Christ's preference for the poor over the rich, the promise of everlasting life in the hereafter and of vastly improved life on earth, of new dignity and status for women, and, finally, of the unity of all peoples in Christ— the brotherhood of man, and, equally important, the sisterhood of woman; and they came armed with the principal instruments of redemption—schools and printing presses. No stranger confrontations have ever taken place. The fellahin of Islamic lands and the untouchables of India were told that Christ cared as much for them as for the proudest Amir or Brahman.

In India wife killing was a common practice. Indians who would not kill a cat or a dog or a sacred cow did not hesitate "on the slightest quarrel" to hack their wives to death. The Englishman Sir Charles Napier described an incident where a seventeen-year-old girl, who was suspected of being unfaithful to her thirteen-year-old husband, was led to the front of the house by her father who "twisted her long hair in his hands, and held her on tiptoe while her brother hacks off her head." Unwanted daughters in many Eastern societies were simply killed. The Amirs of India gave their mistresses potions to cause miscarriages, and if that failed, Napier wrote, "they chop up the child with a sword. . . . In Cluthc they kill daughters who do not marry quickly." In Todas, near Goa, "infant daughters are drowned in milk or trampled to death by water buffaloes and among the Belochis the girls are killed with opium." One missionary woman wrote that in her view the greatest single argument in favor of Christianity was its attitude "toward women and children as over against the attitude of every other religion of the world toward women and little children."

Every missionary was a dramatic embodiment of the "life-style" of the United States. Clothes, expressions, gestures, stance, and intonation taught as much as the spoken, and, increasingly, printed word.

If their initial efforts to convert native peoples met with varying degrees of success, the record was less ambiguous in terms of the creation of an educated middle class (which in most tribal societies promptly became the upper class) but which was characterized by "Western" democratic political and social ideals instilled in them by their missionary teachers. It is impossible to overestimate the role that missionary-educated native men and women played in the transformations of their own countries. While the missionaries, export agents of the Protestant Passion, conveyed in a thousand direct and indirect ways an awareness of the outlines of the New Age to native peoples, they were also re-transmitters of the exotic cultures to which they came. They became the scholars, the translators, the anthropologists, and the interpreters of non-Western cultures. In order to ensure a flow of funds from home to sustain their activities, they had to involve the "home folks" in the remarkable pageant of these alien cultures. So they went back periodically to fire the imaginations of their supporters with vivid and touching stories of "their people." They brought costumes and artifacts and, soon, daguerreotypes and magic lanterns with stereopticon cards. Loanza Benton brought her children with her from Syria and, attired in native costumes, they played Syrian instruments and sang Syrian songs. It is safe to say therefore that the members of the First Congregational Church of Pittsfield, Massachusetts, or the Free Will Baptists of Sidon, Ohio, had a much more intimate knowledge and feeling for exotic cultures than many of their college-trained descendants do today. Not only did the missionaries convey to those at home some sense of the astonishing variations of the human species, they and their offspring took the lead in founding departments of Oriental languages in many of the major universities and in inserting historical and, later, anthropological studies of non-Western peoples into the curriculums of colleges and universities. As we might be disposed to put it today, they were involved not only in converting heathens into Christians, in which they were relatively unsuccessful, but in raising the consciousness of the West in regard to the East, and vice versa, and thus ensuring that the twain should, eventually, meet.

Undoubtedly there was a substantial amount of racial arrogance and ethnocentricity among the missionaries of all Western nations in their contact with native peoples. They were, after all, human, and it would have been surprising if it had not been so. The missionaries came because they thought the culture of Western Christendom superior to that of "the East." And what they saw, by and large, confirmed their convictions, especially in the degraded state of the lower classes and of women.

An indirect consequence of the work of the missionaries was an increasing number of immigrants to the United States from non-Western nations, especially those of the Middle and Far East. Although only two or three out of ten of those who immigrated were Christians (most natives converted to Christianity remained to work as missionaries with their own people), their awareness of the United States and their faith in its "promise" was largely the result of missionary activity. The heroes and heroines of the missionary church knit the world together.

The Greek Slave. Sculpture by Hiram Powers.
(The Newark Museum Collection)

Kindred Spirits. Painting by Asher B. Durand.
(The New York Public Library)

The Titan's Goblet. Painting by Thomas Cole. *(The Metropolitan Museum of Art. Gift of Samuel Avery, Jr., 1904)*

Study for Belshazzar's Feast. Painting by Washington Allston. (*Courtesy of Museum of Fine Arts, Boston. Bequest of Ruth Charlotte Dana*)

Eel Spearing at Setauket. Painting by William Sidney Mount.
(New York State Historical Association, Cooperstown)

Fur Traders Descending the Missouri. Painting by George Caleb Bingham.
(The Metropolitan Museum of Art, Morris K. Jesup Fund, 1933)

Strutting Pigeon. Painting by George Catlin.
(National Collection of Fine Arts, Smithsonian Institution)

The Jolly Flatboatmen in Port. Painting by George Caleb Bingham.
(The St. Louis Art Museum Purchase)

Waiting for the Stage. Painting by Richard Caton Woodville.
(In the collection of the Corcoran Gallery of Art, Museum Purchase, Gallery
Fund, William A. Clark Fund, and through the gifts of Mr. and Mrs. Lansdell
K. Christie and Orme Wilson)

Great Blue Heron. Painting by John James Audubon.
(Courtesy of The New-York Historical Society, New York City)

28

The Mormons

Joseph Smith grew up near Palmyra, New York, a rather feckless youth, given to tall tales and digging for buried treasure. In his own words "as is common with most or all youths, I fell into many vices and follies," but none, he insisted, had resulted in "wronging or injuring any man or society of men." In whatever adventure he was involved, he was clearly the leader, a youth with a powerful physique, prominent, commanding eyes that gleamed with a luminous zeal, and large features. Joseph Smith's father was a dreamer and a visionary, as were his grandfathers. His mother was a woman of great independence and force of character.

Palmyra, the center of Smith's activities, was in the heart of the so-called burnt-over district of western New York state, where repeated revivals kept the population of the area in a constant state of enthusiasm. Lucius Fenn, of Covert, New York, wrote to his friend Birdseye Bronson in Connecticut telling of the fever of religion in the region. "As it respects religion," he noted, "there has been considerable of an attention paid to it this winter . . . and there has been considerable many as we humbly hope have been renewed by the grace of God." Martin Harris, who was one of the first converts to Joseph Smith's teachings and had mortgaged his farm for $3,000 to pay for the first printing of five thousand copies of *The Book of Mormon,* had been subject to frequent visions, heard voices, and been tormented over the state of his soul. But if the burnt-over district was notorious for its susceptibility to new and bizarre religious movements as well as plain, old-fashioned revivals, it was in that respect no different from most of rural America. Reading the diaries and letters of the period, especially those of individuals whose struggle to remain solvent was constant and often distressingly arduous, the anxiety over the state of their souls is abundantly evident as well as their susceptibility to "visions." A religious ferment of dreams and "fearful omens" worked like yeast in the psyches of many practical farmers and small-town businessmen.

In 1826 Smith was brought to court on the charge of being "a disorderly person and an imposter." He confessed to indulging in "magic arts" and digging for gold. In this latter obsession he was not alone. The editor of a Vermont newspaper wrote in 1825, "We could name, if we pleased, at least five hundred respectable men who do in the simplicity and sincerity of their hearts believe that immense treasures lie concealed upon our Green Mountains, many of whom have been for a number of years industriously and perseveringly engaged in digging it up." The item is a fascinating one that evokes a strange picture of the fantasy life of sober New England farmers. The dream of riches, that if the meager crops in flinty soil would not make their harvest rich there must be treasure buried beneath it, was persistent and deep-seated. The Indians had buried it, perhaps centuries before, or so the faithful were determined to believe, and the discovery of an occasional artifact lent credence to the notion. A "professional" treasure hunter named Walters stirred up the town of Palmyra with promises to locate Indian treasure with his system of divination. He read to those who fell under his sway in an unfamiliar language which he claimed to be an ancient Indian manuscript but which the editor of the *Palmyra Herald* declared was actually Cicero's *Orations.*

Digging a well for a neighbor, Joseph Smith discovered an odd stone, "not exactly black but rather dark in color," as Smith's wife later described it, and one of his friends declared that Joseph could see in it "ghosts, infernal spirits, mountains of gold and silver." One of Joseph Smith's principal backers in his treasure-hunting days was the prosperous and eminently respectable Josiah Stoal, the leading citizen of Harmony, Pennsylvania, who swore in court that Joseph Smith with his "seek stone" "could see things fifty feet below the surface of the earth."

In later years Smith described a conversion experience which had taken place, he said, when he was fourteen years old. "I saw a pillar of light," he wrote, "exactly above my head, above the brightness of the sun, which descended gradually until it fell upon me. . . . When the light rested upon me, I saw two personages, whose brightness and glory defy all description, standing above me in the air. One of them spake unto me, calling me by name, and saying . . . 'THIS MY BELOVED SON, HEAR HIM.'" Smith, who had been unable to decide which of the numerous Protestant denominations was the true instrument of the Lord, boldly asked one of the figures, "which of all sects was right (for at this time it had never entered into my heart that all were wrong) . . ." What Smith said the figure replied was "that all their creeds were an abomination in his sight; that those professors were all corrupt . . . they teach for doctrine the commandments of men, having a form of godliness, but they deny the power thereof."

Years later another "personage" appeared to Smith, "exceedingly white and brilliant," who introduced himself as a messenger of the Lord, Nephi (later changed to Moroni), and told him "that God had work for me to do, and that my name should be had for good and evil among all nations, kindreds, and tongues. He said there was a book deposited, written upon gold plates, giving an account of the former inhabitants of this continent, and the source from whence they sprang. He also said that, the fullness of the everlasting Gospel was contained in it. . . . Also that there were two stones in silver bows (and these stones fastened to a breastplate, constituted what is called Urim and Thummin) deposited with the plates and the possession and use of these stones was what constituted seers in ancient or former times, and that God had prepared them for the purpose of translating the book. . . ."

Smith went to the place indicated by the angel and found there in a "stone box" the plates and the translation stones. But the messenger told Smith that the time had not yet arrived to remove the stones and translate them. Not until 1827 was Smith told to transcribe the stones, after which the angelic messenger took them away.

The translation took place, according to one account, in a tent divided by a partition; Smith sat on one side with his seer stones, translating the golden plates and dictating them to a friend on the other side who transcribed them. The result was *The Book of Mormon*, a most remarkable work. It is divided into a series of "Books" of prophets, most of them unknown to the Bible. Nephi, Joseph Smith's messenger, is the principal prophet and leader of the tribe of Nephites. Mormon and his son, Moroni, are among the other prophets who include Jacob and Enos, as well as Omni, Mosiah, Zeniff, Alma, and Ether. The language is biblical as in Chapter 20, Verse 17, Nephi I: "And thus saith the Lord, thy Redeemer, the Holy One of Israel; I have sent him, the Lord thy God who teacheth thee to profit, who leadeth thee by the way thou shouldst go. . . . O that thou hadst harkened to my commandment! then had thy peace been as a river and thy righteousness as the waves of the sea. . . ."

Much is said of the iniquity of the rich and the proud. The day will come when the Lord will "burn them up . . . for they shall be as stubble. And they that kill the prophets and the saints, the depths of the earth shall cover them and the whirlwinds shall carry them away. . . ." But the chosen ones shall be carried into a New Jerusalem, a new Zion, "the land of promise, which was choice above all other lands, which the Lord hath preserved for a righteous people." Much of *The Book of Mormon* has to do with the preparation and preservation of the tablets and the stones to which Joseph Smith was directed and much with wars between the Nephites and the Lamanites. In the Book of Ether it is foretold that certain of the tribes of Israel shall inherit this choice land. These are the Indians and Joseph Smith adds a note, "The Lord brought them upon the western coast of North America."

Not all of Joseph Smith's neighbors were attracted to his novel doctrines. Martin Harris reported one skeptic who declared, "Damn him! Angels appear to men in this enlightened age! Damn him, he ought to be tarred and feathered for telling such a damn lie!" To which Harris quoted "Old Tom Jefferson," who declared that it did not matter to him whether a man believed in one god or twenty. It did not rob his pocket or break his shins. "If you should tar and feather all the liars, you would soon be out of funds to purchase the material."

Even before he had completed the book, Smith had to flee with his plates concealed in a flour barrel to avoid harassment by indignant neighbors. When the printing of the book began, unknown persons broke into the shop and destroyed a portion of the manuscript. After that episode, Smith, or one of his close supporters, was always present to protect the precious pages, and the finished sheets were carried home each night.

When *The Book of Mormon* was finally finished (the future United States governor of Utah, Stephen Harding, was present by coincidence when the title page was struck), Smith gathered a little company of friends and relatives, including a number of his eight siblings, into a congregation of the Church of Jesus Christ of the Latter-Day Saints. These thirty were, to Smith, the vanguard of a great Christian empire to be established in the West as a prelude to the millennium. One of his original followers, Oliver Cowdrey, joined with Martin Harris, Smith's brother Samuel, and Smith himself, to sell the "Gold Bible" as *The Book of Mormon* was commonly called. The story of the origin of the Gold Bible had generally preceded them and missionaries of the new faith were often turned rudely or violently away. But here and there they found a convert or two, the most important being the Young brothers, Brigham and Joseph.

Another convert who was to play a crucial role in the early history of the "kingdom" was Parley Parker Pratt, who had lost his farm when he could find no buyer for a bumper crop. "I had met," he wrote, "with little else but disappointment, sorrow and unrewarded toil. . . ." He thus determined to go west. "There, at least, thought I, there will be no buying and selling of lands—no law to sweep all the hard earnings of years to pay a small debt—no wrangling about sects, and creeds, and doctrines. I will win the confidence of the red man; I will learn his language; I will tell him of Jesus; I will read to him the Scriptures; I will teach him the arts of peace; to hate war, to love his neighbor, to fear and love God, and to cultivate the earth." On the frontier, living alone in a cabin in the woods, Pratt began "to understand the things which were coming on the earth—the restoration of Israel, the coming of the Messiah, and the glory that should follow." Clearly Pratt was ripe for conversion to Joseph Smith's new church. And thousands like him who believed that *"darkness covers the earth, and gross darkness the people."* When Pratt came upon *The Book of Mormon* he knew his prayers had been answered. "I esteemed the Book . . . more than all the riches of the world," he wrote. "Yes, I verily believe that I would not at that time have exchanged the knowledge I then possessed, for a legal title to all the beautiful farms, houses, villages, and property which passed in review before me."

As the number of converts mounted unto the hundreds and then thousands, the crucial question came to be, Where were the faithful to be "gathered"? Where was the kingdom to be? For Mormonism was not to be, like other denominations, a congeries of congregations. It was to be the great Christian empire. "The poor," Joseph Smith said, would have "a land of promise, and a land flowing with milk and honey." The meek would inherit the earth. Kirtland, Ohio, was their first home. Several hundred of the faithful sold what they had, moved to Kirtland, and turned over their money to the common treasury. But Kirtland was, in Joseph Smith's vision, simply a way station. The original Garden of Eden had been, according to his calculations, in Missouri, and Smith and his elders were soon looking for a site for the New Jerusalem in the western part of that state. Meanwhile whole congregations of Campbellites and Universalists converted en masse to Mormonism, joined by numerous Methodists, Baptists, and even Presbyterians. Established in Independence, Missouri, then a small, raw, frontier town, the jumping-off point for the Yellowstone fur trappers and traders and the Santa Fe trading caravans, the Mormons were soon embroiled with the "old settlers," men and women who had reached Missouri a decade or so ahead of the Mormons and bitterly resented the newcomers' announced intention of making the state into headquarters of the new Zion.

The first Mormon Sunday service was indeed enough to alarm the citizens of the town. In the words of a modern historian, "It was a motley gathering of settlers, vagabond Indians, renegades, traders, and Negro slaves." Smith himself reflected upon the magnitude of the task ahead and, "looking into the vast wilderness of those that sat in darkness," thought "how natural it was to observe the degradation, leanness of intellect, ferocity, and jealousy of a people that were nearly a century behind times, and to feel for those who roamed about without the benefit of civilization, refinement, or religion; yea, and exclaim in the language of the Prophets, 'When will the wilderness blossom as the rose? When will Zion be built up in her glory, and where will Thy temple stand, unto which all nations shall come in the last days?' "

Soon the suspicion and hostility of the old settlers was felt in numerous tangible ways. Shots were fired at houses occupied by Mormons and stones thrown through windows; haystacks were burned and individual Mormons abused and cursed. On the Fourth of July, 1833, the enemies of the Mormons drew up a "Secret Constitution" listing their charges against the Saints. The next move was to order the Mormons to depart and, when they refused, to destroy their print shop and then to tar and feather one of the elders. The church was demolished.

Much of the hostility toward the Saints seems to have stemmed from their acceptance of free blacks as members. A newspaper account of a meeting of the old settlers is revealing. The gathering, we are told, was made up of "gentlemen from every part of the country, there being present between four and five hundred persons. . . ." The Mormon band was made up, it was charged, of the "very dregs" of other communities, "elevated . . . but little above the condition of our blacks, whether in regard to property or education" and had already exerted "their corrupting influence on our slaves." More alarming was the report that the Mormons expected to acquire the lands of the Gentiles by the work of a "destroying angel, the judgement of God, or the arm of power." Mormon missionaries were busy in every state and since the converted were required, "as soon as convenient, to come to Zion, the name they have thought proper to confer on our little village," it was clear that the Gentiles would soon be inundated. Word was that the Mormons had invited "the free brethren of color in Illinois to come up like the rest to the land of Zion. . . . With the corrupting influence of these on our slaves and the stench both physical and moral, that their introduction would set off in our social atmosphere . . . our situation here" would soon be "unsupportable."

The Saints found no recourse in the courts, which were in the hands of the Gentiles, and after several armed clashes in which three or four people were killed, the Mormons began to leave Jackson County and establish themselves in the more sparsely settled Clay County to the west. Two hundred empty Mormon houses were burned by the Gentiles in the spring.

Joseph Smith's response was to organize a small Mormon army, which he called "Zion's Camp," well armed and accompanied by twenty supply wagons. With it Smith set out to reclaim Zion. Included in the force was Brigham Young, already a trusted lieutenant of the Prophet. The Mormon "War" fizzled out, however, and the displaced followers settled in Clay County. Smith, meanwhile, returned to Kirtland, where many Mormons still resided, and the town now became the church's headquarters; a handsome stone temple was erected there, built in conformity with a design revealed to Smith by the Lord. At Kirtland the emphasis was on study and seventy men were enrolled in a Hebrew class taught by a rabbi named Joshua Seixas. A visitor found the Saints "by no means, as a class, men of weak minds," adding, "perhaps most fanatics and visionaries have intellects peculiarly though perversely active. . . ."

The depression of 1837 left the Kirtland Mormons bankrupt and heavily in debt. There were charges of mismanagement, self-seeking, abuse of power, of lying and counterfeiting money. In the aftermath of bitter divisions, many members scattered, and Smith himself took refuge in Far West, Missouri, a Mormon town. Once again, as Mormons began to pour into Clay County, the Gentiles grew uneasy. After two years, Smith and the leaders agreed to move on. This time violence was avoided. Indeed, the citizens of the county subscribed money to facilitate the Mormon move to Shoal Creek in the northwest corner of the state. Here they requested their own county, to be called Caldwell, bought 250,000 acres from the government, laid out two thousand farms, built 150 houses, four stores, six blacksmith's shops, and two hotels. Soon Far West, the county seat, was "a thriving town of some three thousand inhabitants." But once again the now familiar drama was enacted. As more Mormons came and spilled over into adjacent counties, the Gentiles became prey to the same anxieties that the Mormons had aroused in Independence. Moreover, there was constant dissension within the church. Extremists gained control and two of the original Saints were read out of the faith. The militants rallied around Sidney Rigdon, who declared in a widely reprinted sermon given on the Fourth of July, 1838, "we warn all men in the name of Jesus Christ, to come on us no more forever; for from this hour, we will bear it no more. . . . And that mob that comes on us to disturb us, it shall be between them and us a war of extermination. . . ."

Rigdon's "ultimatum" served only to inflame feelings among the Gentiles and a state election aroused the old fears of a Mormon takeover. The old settlers stated publicly their determination that "Mormonism, emancipation and abolitionism must be driven from our State," and the Mormons prepared to fight for their rights. The smaller Mormon towns were attacked, houses burned, and cattle killed. Mormons were robbed and beaten by roving gangs and struck back in raids and pillagings of their own. The response of Governor Boggs was to declare, "The Mormons must . . . be exterminated, or driven from the state if necessary for the public peace." At Haun's Mill nineteen Mormon men and boys were murdered. Brigham Young's brother, Joseph, barely escaped with his life. An old man, a veteran of the Revolution, was killed with his own gun, and a nine-year-old boy was shot in cold blood with the comment, "Nits will make lice, and if he had lived he would have become a Mormon."

Badly outnumbered, the Mormons surrendered. Joseph Smith, his brother Hyrum, and five other leaders were sentenced by summary court-martial to be shot at a public execution in the town square "as an example." Cooler heads prevailed and the prisoners were taken in chains to Independence and there charged, along with forty-nine other Mormons, with "treason, murder, arson, larceny, theft and stealing." Five were indicted for treason and five for murder, but there was considerable public support for the Mormons in other states, and after six months, the state authorities arranged for the prisoners to escape.

The next seat of empire was in Illinois. Brigham Young displayed striking qualities of leadership in conducting the retreat northward to a site on the Illinois River which was called Nauvoo, the Hebrew name for beautiful. The legislators of Illinois, Abraham Lincoln among them, anxious to attract settlers, assigned a county to the refugees with a municipal charter that gave the Mormons virtual autonomy, and when Joseph Smith joined the colony he was given a state commission as head of his Mormon legion.

At Nauvoo a large number of English men and women who had been converted by Mormon missionaries in Great Britain arrived to join in the work of establishing the new kingdom. For a time it seemed that the church had at last found its capital, a center from which its power would radiate out over the nation and the world, gathering in new Saints and preparing for the millennium. Charles Francis Adams and his friend Josiah Quincy paid the Prophet a visit at Nauvoo, obviously attracted by this reanimated Puritan Commonwealth on the frontier. Quincy described the Prophet, now thirty-nine years old, as a "hearty, athletic fellow, with blue eyes standing prominently out upon his light complexion, a long nose and a retreating forehead," wearing "striped pantaloons, a linen jacket which had not lately seen the wash-tub, and beard of some three days' growth." He seemed to Quincy "endowed with that kingly faculty which directs, as by intrinsic right, the feeble or confused souls who are looking for guidance. . . . He had little enough of that unmixed spiritual power which flashed out from the spare, neurasthenic body of Andrew Jackson. The prophet's hold upon you seemed to come from the balance and harmony of temperament which reposes upon a large physical basis."

The two Bostonians were plainly fascinated with the general, as Smith was commonly called, and his followers. Smith displayed a keen grasp of practical politics and "mingled Utopian fallacies with his shrewd suggestions," Quincy wrote. "He talked from a strong mind utterly unenlightened by the teachings of history," and hinted to his visitors that he might one day be president of the United States. Quincy marveled that, born in poverty "and with the homeliest of all human names . . . he had made himself a power upon the earth. Of all the multitudinous family of Smith, from Adam down (Adam of the 'Wealth of Nations,' I mean), none had so won human hearts and shaped human lives as this Joseph. His influence," Quincy added, "whether for good or evil, is potent today, and the end is not yet."

A friend of Sidney George Fisher's who visited Nauvoo about the same time reported that the Mormons were "a depraved & ferocious band of gloomy fanatics, sunk in ignorance & every species of vice, but formidable from numbers, discipline, hardihood & skill with the rifle."

Our observant friend Charles Pancoast visited Nauvoo and described it as centered around "a broad street that led up to a large circular Plaza, ornamented with grass Plots and Flowers. Around this Plaza were located the Temple, Hotels, and Business Places." The town was laid out in perfect squares and each was allowed a view of part of the inner temple "all frame and very capacious. . . . The Baptismal Pool stood on the backs of twelve Oxen carved of wood and was a Wonder in Art." When Pancoast and his fellow travelers from Missouri attended a camp meeting, Joseph Smith denounced all Missourians for their intolerance and persecution of the Mormons and when they left for their steamer, Pancoast wrote, "a crowd of miserable-looking Mormons began to hoot and abuse us. Our officers and elders appealed to us to pay no attention to them; but when they commenced to throw Stones at us our Men became infuriated and chased them away." The sightseers were hurried on board their steamer but the Mormons had recruited more men "and showered us with Stones. Pistols were fired on both sides; many of us were hurt by Stones, and one or two by Bullets, but no one was dangerously wounded."

Richard Henry Dana went to a Mormon meeting in Boston to "hear from their own mouths what doctrines or shows they were able to make" that enticed so many followers. At the Boylston Hall, "a noisy, vulgar, ranting, screaming fellow, ignorant & with a beastly expression of countenance, was holding forth to 5 or 600 persons, of both sexes & all ages, most of whom had respectable appearance, though some of the elements of fanaticism were plainly exhibited in their countenances." After the sermon, "a mere disjointed series of screamings & whisperings upon matters sacred and scriptural, five converts were received into the faith." To Dana "it was a shocking scene, I had no question of it being blasphemous & immoral. The priest, I was persuaded, was a thorough villain, & the converts were some deluded & some as bad as their teachers. Of the converts, one was a demure looking old man, one of the ugliest old women I ever saw, & two others were dressy & suspicious looking young women." But John Greenleaf Whittier attending a Mormon service in Lowell, Massachusetts, was impressed in spite of himself. "In listening to these modern prophets," he wrote, "I discovered, as I think, the great secret of their success in making converts. They speak to a common feeling; they minister to a universal want. They contrast strongly the miraculous power of the gospel in the apostolic times with the present state of our nominal Christianity. They ask for the signs of divine power; the faith, overcoming all things, which opened the prison doors of the apostles. . . . They speak a language of hope and promise to weak, weary hearts, tossed and troubled, who have wandered from sect to sect, seeking in vain for the primal manifestations of divine power. . . ."

There was already serious trouble among the Saints when Adams and Quincy visited Nauvoo. Smith had come, increasingly, to rule as an iron-handed dictator. He had taken the position that no Illinois law could apply in Nauvoo until he had approved it. Anyone criticizing the church was subject to punishment. He maneuvered to have Nauvoo declared federal territory, free of state control, and, finally, he practiced and sanctioned for a few of his inner circle "plural marriage" or polygamy. A dissenting party in the church issued the *Expositor,* a newspaper critical of Smith's rule and calling for reform. As mayor, Smith prevailed on the city council to order the press destroyed. If its owners protested, Smith was said to have declared, they should be ripped "from the guts to the gizzard." Setting up headquarters in Carthage, the dissident editors secured a warrant for Smith's arrest. At the center of the uprising was the scandal of "a plurality of *living* wives," as one indignant Mormon wife wrote. The Prophet had had a revelation that the Saints could have as many as "ten living wives at one time. I mean certain conspicuous characters among them. They do not content themselves with young women, but have seduced married women. . . . Those who cannot swallow these things and came out and opposed the doctrine publicly have been cut off from the Church without any lawful process whatever. . . . Any one needs a throat like an open sepulchre to *swallow down* all that is taught here."

In reply to the warrant for his arrest Joseph Smith and his brother, Hyrum, went to Carthage where they lodged in jail for their own protection. The militia, which had been called out by the governor to preserve order, turned out to be bitterly anti-Mormon. Its members stormed the jail and killed Smith and his brother.

John Greenleaf Whittier, hearing of Joseph Smith's murder, wrote, "Once in the world's history we were to have a Yankee prophet, and we have had him in Joe Smith. For good or evil, he has left his track in the great pathway of life; or, to use the words of Horne, 'knocked out for himself a window in the wall of the nineteenth century,' whence his rude, bold, good-humored face will peer out upon the generations to come," leaving behind him "a temple unique and wonderful as the faith of its builder, embodying in its singular and mysterious architecture, the Titan ideas of the Pyramids. . . ." But the temple, unfinished at the time of Joseph Smith's death, was to remain unfinished. Nauvoo was soon to be abandoned by the Mormon remnant under pressure of the Gentiles and the half-finished temple destroyed.

The death of the Prophet accelerated the fragmentation of the faithful. Some followed Sidney Rigdon, others gave their allegiance to Brigham Young and "the Twelve," while James Strang, a prominent elder, headed another faction. All were under severe pressure to depart from Nauvoo—from the Gentiles of the state, from Governor Ford, who was anxious to be rid of his troublesome guests, and from men like Stephen Douglas, who was anxious to see the Rocky Mountain West and California occupied by American citizens of whatever religious persuasion. In the dead of winter, 1846, those who remained at Nauvoo began their exodus. The plan was for a "pioneer corps," the "Camp of Israel" as it was called, to go five hundred miles west, "build a village, and put in a spring crop." Those who followed after would then have food and shelter when they arrived at the way station. The process would be repeated until the various echelons arrived at their destination.

Now began the classic hegira of the Mormon battalions, one of the great movements of people in history, thousands of men, women, and children making their way under the leadership of Brigham Young across the Great Plains and the arid regions of the Far West to the valley of the Great Salt Lake.

A reporter who visited Nauvoo wrote that despite the desperateness of their situation, and their "inability to procure the necessary equipments and provisions—with an indefinite journey before them, a journey of months, probably years through plains and over mountains . . . destitute of the assistance which might be expected of a civilized country," the faithful displayed a "lightness of heart, apparently cheerfulness, and sanguine hopes," convinced of "the rewards which they were to receive in heaven for their present sacrifices. . . . Their enthusiasm, or fanaticism, is stimulated by songs and hymns, in which their men, women and children join, and contained allusions to their persecutions; and the names of Oregon and California, and the hopes that await them. . . ."

It was estimated by observers of the exodus that some three thousand wagons with perhaps ten thousand persons made up its various trains. Its greatest pride was its splendid band, recruited in England, in a body, it was said. "Their office now was to guide the monster choruses and Sunday hymns and like the trumpets of silver . . . to knoll the people into church. . . . It had the strangest effect in the world, to listen to their sweet music winding over the uninhabited country."

Although there was talk of California, Brigham Young set his course for the valley of the Great Salt Lake and one of his lieutenants, William Clayton, an Englishman, looking over the mountains leading into the valley saw the lake, "its dark blue shade resembling the calm sea" and "the intervening valley . . . well supplied with streams, creeks and lakes. There is but little timber in sight anywhere, and that is mostly on the banks of creeks and streams of water which is about the only objection which could be raised in my estimation to this being one of the most beautiful valleys and pleasant places for a home for the Saints which could be found. . . . When I commune with own heart and ask myself whether I would choose to dwell here in this wild looking country amongst the Saints surrounded by friends, though poor, enjoying the privileges and blessings of the everlasting priesthood, with God for our King and Father; or dwell amongst the gentiles with all their wealth and good things of the earth, to be eternally mobbed, harassed, hunted, our best men murdered and every good man's life continually in danger, the soft whisper echoes loud and reverberates back in tones of stern determination; give me the quiet wilderness and my family to associate with, surrounded by the Saints and adieu to the gentile world until God says return and avenge you of your enemies."

With the Saints gathered in the Kingdom of Deseret and converts making their way in increasing numbers along the Mormon Trail, it seemed that the Empire had at last been established. The government was theocratic, with Brigham Young as its head. Richard Burton, the explorer, visiting Salt Lake City, described Joseph Smith's successor in these words: "Altogether the Prophet's appearance was that of a gentleman farmer in New England—in fact, such as he is; his father was an agriculturist and revolutionary soldier. . . . He is a well-preserved man. . . . His manner is at once affable and impressive, simple and courteous; his want of pretension contrasts favorably with certain pseudo-prophets that I have seen. . . . He shows no sign of dogmatism, bigotry, or fanaticism. . . . He impresses a stranger with a certain sense of power; his followers are, of course, wholly fascinated by his superior strength of brain."

Under Young's direction, the Church flourished and two years after the first parties found their way to the valley, the Elders issued a report which, after enumerating the accomplishments of the Saints, declared: "While kingdoms, governments, and thrones, are falling and rising; revolutions succeeding revolutions; and the nations of the earth are overturning; while plague, pestilence and famine, are walking abroad; and whirlwind, fire, and earthquake, proclaim the truth of prophecy, let the Saints be faithful and diligent in every duty, and especially in striving to stand in chosen places, that they may watch the coming of the Holy One of Israel."

But fate pursued them still. The gold rush of 1849 brought streams of emigrants headed for California through the Kingdom of Deseret. While the passersby were, with one terrible exception—the Mountain Meadows Massacre—treated with circumspection by the Saints, the migration served to draw the attention of the United States government to the Great Basin region. Government officials, territorial judges, and a governor were given a hard time by the understandably paranoid Mormons and withdrew with stories of persecution and harassment. By 1857 relations had grown so strained that President Buchanan, who could decide little else, dispatched 2,500 federal troops from Fort Leavenworth under the command of Colonel Albert Sidney Johnston to bring the Deseret Kingdom under the authority of the United States flag. The reaction of the Saints to the news that United States soldiers were on their way was one of fury. Brigham Young promised to destroy Salt Lake City before he would allow it to be occupied by the Johnston expeditionary force. "Before I will suffer what I have in times gone by, there shall not be one building, nor one foot of lumber, nor a stick, nor a tree, nor a particle of grass and hay that will burn, left in reach of our enemies. I am sworn . . . to utterly lay waste this land. . . ." Johnston sent one of his staff officers ahead to open negotiations with Brigham Young but the officer found Young adamant. No United States soldiers would be allowed to enter Salt Lake Valley. Young then announced that Salt Lake City and the adjacent Mormon settlements would be abandoned at the approach of the troops, the population settled in the hills, and the city set afire. Young declared martial law and ordered units of his legion to harass the federal troops in every way possible and intercept and destroy supply trains and emigrant wagons. The party of United States officials and soldiers spent the winter in an improvised camp near Fort Bridger. The interval allowed time for Young and the Mormon leaders to consider the long-range consequences of their intransigence. By spring Young, hearing that troops were being recruited in the Mississippi Valley states for a large-scale invasion of Deseret, displayed a more conciliatory mood. Colonel Thomas Kane, a friend and defender of the Mormons, had been recruited by Buchanan to carry on further negotiations with Young. Kane conferred with Young and then with the new governor, Alfred Cummings, who went to Salt Lake City where he told the Mormons that it was his responsibility to establish the authority of the federal government in the territory and that he would not use force unless Deseret refused to recognize him as governor of Utah. Brigham Young, while continuing to carry on talks with Cummings, sent orders to the Saints to abandon their settlements and take refuge in the hills to the south.

In a proclamation issued in April of 1858, Buchanan declared: "Fellow-citizens of Utah, this is rebellion against the Government to which you owe allegiance; it is levying war against the United States, and involves you in the guilt of treason. Persistence in it will bring you to condign punishment, to ruin, and to shame. . . ." The President went on to offer "a free and full pardon to all who will submit themselves to the just authority of the Federal Government." Informed by peace commissioners of the President's proclamation, Young accepted the inevitable. The federal troops were to march through the deserted city and make their camp some distance away. The Mormons now began returning to their communities and the "Mormon War" was thus peaceably concluded due, in large part, to a rare exercise of statesmanship on Buchanan's part or to his disposition to procrastinate. Since he could claim few enough laurels it would be ungenerous to deny them to him in the matter of handling of this dangerous confrontation of 1857–58.

It was especially fortunate that forebearance was shown because a force of Mormons and Indians had provided an occasion for severe action against Deseret by attacking an emigrant train of some 140 men, women, and children at Mountain Meadows on September 7, 1857. After a three-day siege, the Mormon commander, John Lee, had persuaded the men of the train to surrender their arms on the assurance that they would be conducted to the Mormon settlement at Cedar City. When they complied, they were all murdered, except seventeen children under seven years of age. The emigrants' possessions were then divided among the Indians and the Mormon guerrillas and everyone pledged to secrecy. Word of the massacre nonetheless leaked out. By some accounts it had been the work of Indians in retaliation for whites' having poisoned their wells. All that can be said in exculpation of the Mormons was that they had been harassed, persecuted, and killed for years until they felt the hand of every man against them. Now word had come that federal troops were on the way to drive them from the final refuge in the desolate mountains of the Great Basin. Paranoia infected them all and expressed itself in this single murderous act which, for almost a century, was to be used by the enemies and critics of the Saints as conclusive evidence of their wickedness.

The growing crisis over the slavery issue and then the onset of the Civil War itself would give the Saints another seven or eight years to build up Zion. Mormon missionaries by the hundreds brought in converts by the thousands, principally from the British Isles and the Scandinavian countries. A perpetual Emigrating Fund, established to help converts make their way across the Great Plains to the Great Basin, provided for those too poor to pay for their own travel, and hundreds came pushing handcarts containing their belongings over the by now well-worn trail.

Brigham Young had declared, "We cannot talk about spiritual things without connecting them with temporal things. . . . We, as Latter-Day Saints, really expect, look for, and we will not be satisfied with anything short of being governed and controlled by the word of the Lord in all our acts, both spiritual and temporal. If we do not live for this, we do not live to be one with Christ." Perhaps it was this, above all, this melding of the spiritual and temporal, or material, that exerted such a powerful attraction to men and women who were trying to live by a set of Christian precepts which they saw violated all around them and which they themselves felt called on to violate if they were to "make their way in the world." By establishing Christian dominion over every aspect of life, and perhaps, most particularly over the economic sphere, the church of the Saints healed that basic schizophrenia, to which we have often referred, that tormented so many pious Americans. The belief in the golden tablets was a small price for converts to pay for the healing of the wounds inflicted by a competitive, individualistic society. It is not surprising that a system which offered "absolute integration" to a generation tormented by disintegration attracted believers by the tens of thousands from all corners of the "modern" world.

Where Americans suffered from an excess of freedom, from the generally chaotic character of American life, the church of the Saints offered a reassuring sense of order, a voice that spoke authoritatively on every issue from appropriate dress to proper food and drink. (Smoking and drinking were both forbidden.) And what of the terrible feeling of rootlessness, the lack of continuity, or the breaks in the links between generations that characterized America? Well, this too, it seemed, could be repaired. The long-dead ancestors could be retroactively baptized and brought within the circle of the Saints. For the defeated, the embittered, the lonely women and marginal men, the "failures," those whom life had dealt a bad hand, the Church of the Latter-Day Saints offered fresh hope. So whatever one thinks of its bizarre origins and eccentric creeds it must be acknowledged that from a purely sociological point of view it was a brilliant solution to many of the most destructive aspects of our society. It has thus to be read as a kind of social litmus paper, a psychological profile, a seer's "print" or tracing of the American soul. It rose up boldly in seeming defiance of all the dominant values in American life—individualism, strict monogamy, reason, the lessons of history, the revealed truths of Christianity, competition, capitalism, free enterprise, success, the sanctity of private property. Indeed there was hardly an accepted "value" left unchallenged. That was, of course, what alarmed and, eventually, enraged a vast number of Americans. The quite literally sensational success of the Mormons demonstrated that all was not as it appeared to be in the United States. Otherwise how to account for these defections? That the Mormons should be persecuted, should be hunted from pillar to post, was, however regrettable, inevitable. They were bold in proclaiming their doctrine, arrogant in denouncing the Gentiles as an abomination in the eyes of the Lord, fearsome in their manifest intention of turning the United States into a theocratic empire. They were militant, not humble. They carried guns and made it clear that they intended to defend themselves against the heretics and blasphemers who lived in adjacent towns.

In their determination to convert the world the Mormons substituted religious intolerance for racial intolerance, for they desired to gather in the nations of the earth. They laid hold of the passage from Daniel, the touchstone of all Christian utopian expectation: "And in the days of these kings shall the God of heaven set up a kingdom, which shall never be destroyed; and the kingdom shall not be left to other people, but it shall stand forever." In 1844, Joseph Smith wrote, "I calculate to be one of the instruments of setting up the kingdom of Daniel by the word of the Lord, and I intend to lay a foundation that will revolutionize the whole world."

So there it was. The United States should be "a gathering of nations." It was, through the guidance of Smith, to "revolutionize the whole world." John Winthrop's expectation of redeeming the world had manifest itself at the time of the American Revolution as the desire to spread the benefits of America's secular political revolution over the globe, to "emancipate a world," as the Reverend Samuel Thacher put it in his Fourth of July sermon in Concord in 1794. It had been Joseph Smith's intention to accomplish that goal through the worldwide theocratic government of the Church of the Latter-Day Saints.

Reading *The Book of Mormon* (certainly a strange exercise for a nonbeliever), one is struck with Smith's genius, for it seems clear that many Americans wished, in the depths of their hearts, to believe in a new, purified order of humanity in the United States. They wished to be free of the burden of history, full as it was of tragic ambiguity. They wished to claim the land, in good conscience, if possible, but, good or bad, to claim it and possess it. They wished to reestablish the true community of the fathers and to sanctify the process of material acquisition. They wished to solve the dilemma of sexuality and to preserve the family inviolate against the disintegrative forces of the insatiable land. For all these often desperate needs Joseph Smith was the master therapist. The structure of American society seemed to present its members with this tormenting choice. Hold to the old values, labor and pray and preserve the faithful community, but pay the price in meagerness of life, in chronic insecurity, in a corrosive sense of personal failure. Or, adopt the cunning of the jungle and fight your *individual* way to wealth and esteem, to success. The choice is yours. It must only be said you can't have it both ways. And, of course, even if you pursued wealth and success with feverish and unscrupulous determination, there was no guarantee it would, in the end, be yours. But Joseph Smith proclaimed a startlingly different doctrine. If you followed him and the Angel Moroni you could, indeed, have it both ways. You could prosper in the world and prosper in the sight of God and in the hope of salvation. Smith was not the promoter of a new denomination, a new sect with a new interpretation of Scripture; he was the recipient of a new revelation accompanied by a new testament that superseded all older revelations and all subsequent interpretations of them. For this "the Book" was essential. That Joseph Smith should have perceived this and performed the enormous task of creating (or transcribing) it was the most essential mark of his genius. Against the disintegrative forces of American life, he created a counterforce, not simply another choice but the radical reordering of all history. There was, and remains, such an air of breathtaking daring about it that it is hardly to be wondered that hundreds of thousands of people were in time persuaded of its authenticity. It seemed as though for every psychic need and every anxiety-producing paradox, Joseph Smith had a solution.

Were the Indians an uncomfortable riddle? Many Americans had believed, from the first moment of colonization, that the aborigines were the Lost Tribes of Israel. Smith placed them solidly within his whole scheme of redemption. Now whites and Indians might share the land and the Indians be gathered up, with a place of special dignity and honor, in the company of the Saints.

The position of the black man was another quandary for many Christian Americans. It turned out, according to Smith, that as the accursed descendants of Ham they were irredeemably inferior. Therefore while they, like the Indians, had a place, it was a subordinate one to the white man. Did money rest under God's judgment? Well, yes, but the material inhered in the spiritual. The spiritual was also the material. Money could be readily sanctified by subordinating its acquisition to the common good of the community, of all the Saints. Were many Americans tormented by financial insecurity, by fear of losing their jobs or their money? Joseph Smith and his Latter-Day Saints would provide for the needy out of the common stores.

Smith could even accommodate the widespread yearning for the millennium. Although he was vague about when it would come—one revelation suggested in forty years—he was convinced of its relative imminence. We will encounter the Mormons again in the course of this history. It is perhaps sufficient to say here that in their turbulent history we find one of the essential keys to the psyche of nineteenth-century America.

29

"This Huge Misery": Slave Life in the South

Undoubtedly the most dreadful aspect of slavery was the buying and selling of slaves. Virginia alone exported almost nine thousand slaves a year to the deep South and the *Natchez Courier* stated that during 1836 Alabama, Mississippi, and Arkansas imported two hundred and fifty thousand slaves from the slave states of the upper South.

A former slave named Robinson, who had been the overseer of a Washington slave pen, told Richard Henry Dana something of its operation. When prospective purchasers came, "the boys had their faces washed & greased to make them shine. 'Many a time have I greased the faces of the boys & girls where they were tallowy complexioned, to make them look glossy.' The purchasers go around, make the slaves open their mouths, that they may look in, as they would a horse, feel of their limbs, strip them, & make them run, jump & try all their physical powers. In the cases of the girls, they often lift up their clothes & feel of their legs, feel their bosoms, & try all their feminine points. . . ."

A slave "coffle" was usually made up of forty to fifty slaves, accompanied by a light wagon to carry "the camp equipment, provisions & clothes." They were expected to walk some twenty-five miles a day, guarded often by no more than two men with dogs and the greater number unchained.

Testimony on the life of the slaves is surprisingly voluminous, considering that few slaves were literate and fewer still wrote accounts of their experience as slaves. Yet no segment of any society in history was as carefully observed and as fully described. In addition to the numerous travelers through the South—the most famous of these being a young American landscape architect, the designer of Central Park, Frederick Law Olmstead, who wrote two substantial volumes, *Travels Through the Seaboard Slave States* and *The Cotton Kingdom*—a number of escaped slaves dictated accounts of their lives to Northern journalists. Since we are primarily concerned here with penetrating to the inner life of the slave, we have chosen two guides of totally different backgrounds. Frederick Douglass was a fugitive slave who became the most famous of all the black abolitionists. Fanny Kemble was one of the most beautiful and gifted women of the age, a brilliant actress and interpreter of Shakespeare.

When Kemble first appeared in New York at the Park Theatre, Philip Hone noted that she had chosen a part "well calculated for a display of the strongest passions of the female heart—love, hate, and jealousy." Hone had never witnessed "an audience so moved, astonished and delighted . . . the expression of her wonderful face would have been a rich treat if her tongue had uttered no sound . . . and the curtain fell amid the deafening shouts and plaudits of an astonished audience." Attending another of her readings, he reported that "delicate women, grave gentlemen, belles, beaux, and critics, flock to the doors of entrance, and rush into such places as they can find, two or three hours before the lady's appearance. They are compensated for this tedious sitting on hard seats, squeezed by the crowd, by an hour's reading—very fine, certainly, for Fanny Kemble knows how to do it—the favorite plays of the immortal bard. She makes $2,000 or $3,000 a week. . . ."

In 1834 Fanny Kemble married Pierce Butler, the grandson of the Pierce Butler who participated in the Convention that framed the Constitution. Butler was rich and handsome, and he owned a large plantation in Georgia, the income from which enabled him to live in grand style in Philadelphia, where Fanny was a great adornment to the social life of the city. Sidney George Fisher, who came to know her well during her years in Philadelphia, described her at a Philadelphia ball as "superb in a gold turban and dress of maroon velvet. Such a costume well suits her magnificent style of beauty. She is certainly the most beautiful woman here, tho a little faded. Her manner is very gracious, and perfectly simple & unaffected."

Several years after her marriage to Butler, Fanny set off with her husband and two small children for a visit to the plantation that provided their livelihood. It was a painful experience for a woman who hated slavery. She kept a journal which was later published under the title *Journal of a Residence on a Georgia Plantation,* one of the most penetrating and compassionate accounts that survive of plantation life in the deep South. Her book is especially important for what it tells us of the lives of slave women.

Fanny Kemble was torn between her sympathy for the degraded condition of the slaves and irritation over their shiftless ways. "Their laziness, their filthiness, their inconceivable stupidity, and unconquerable good humor," she wrote, "are enough to drive one stark-staring mad." When she and her husband arrived at the plantation they were greeted by "Negroes, jumping, dancing, shouting, laughing, and clapping their hands (a usual expression of delight with savages and children), and using the most extravagant and ludicrous gesticulations to express their ecstasy at our arrival."

White mistresses who deplored the objectionable odor of blacks did not hesitate to have their infants suckled by black mammies, "nor almost every planter's wife and daughter from having one or more little pet black sleeping like puppy dogs in their very bedchamber, nor almost every planter from admitting one or several of his female slaves to the still closer intimacy of his bed. . . . The stench in an Irish, Scotch, Italian, or French hovel is quite as intolerable as any I have ever found in our Negro houses," Fanny Kemble wrote.

The strange capacity for extravagant joy that dwelt in the slaves despite their degradation fascinated Fanny. She had seen Jim Crow performances in the North which professed to represent the black, but "all the contortions, and springs, and flings, and kicks, and capers you have been beguiled into accepting as indicative of him are spurious, faint, feeble, unimportant—in a word, pale Northern reproductions of that ineffable black conception," she wrote. "It is impossible for words to describe the things these people did with their bodies, and, above all, with their faces, the whites of their eyes, and the whites of their teeth, and certain outlines which either naturally and by the grace of heaven, or by the practice of some peculiar artistic dexterity, they bring into prominent and most ludicrous display."

Overwhelmed by the filth and disorder in which most of the slave families lived, Fanny Kemble struggled to introduce the most elementary principles of cleanliness and sanitation, but the fact that the women were "condemned to field labor" and had no time to give to the rearing of their children defeated all her efforts. Women who had had from five to ten children were expected to keep up with young female workers "in the prime of their strength," a practice that seemed to her "cruel carelessness." When women were flogged for trifling offenses, Mrs. Butler was especially angered and disturbed. "I had a long and painful conversation with Mr. [Butler]," she wrote, "upon the subject of the flogging which had been inflicted on the wretched Teresa. These discussions are terrible: they throw me into perfect agonies of distress for the slaves, whose position is utterly hopeless; for myself, whose intervention on their behalf sometimes seemed to me worse than useless; for Mr. [Butler], whose share in this horrible system fills me by turn with indignation and pity." She was moved to wish "that the river and the sea that bounded the plantation" would "swallow up and melt in their salt waves the whole of this accursed property of ours." Her horror of slavery in general had narrowed down "to this most painful desire that I and mine were freed from the responsibility of our share in this huge misery. . . ."

The sight of pregnant women laboring in the fields along with the men made Fanny miserable. When a group of them gathered to plead with Butler for some alleviation of their work load, his wife wrote, "I did not stay to listen to the details of their petition, for I am unable to command myself on such occasions, and Mr. [Butler] seemed positively degraded in my eyes as he stood enforcing upon these women the necessity of fulfilling their appointed tasks. . . . I turned away in bitter disgust. I hope this sojourn among Mr. [Butler's] slaves will not lessen my respect for him, but I fear it; for the details of slaveholding are so unmanly, letting alone every other consideration, that I know not how anyone with the spirit of a man can condescend to them."

And so it was, each day bringing some fresh revelation of this apparently unfathomable horror of slavery. One day it was the pregnant women forced to labor in the fields under the imminent threat of the lash. Another it was mothers and children ill and untended in the "infirmary," and yet another an old slave dying, "panting out the last breath of his wretched existence like some forsaken, overworked, wearied-out beast of burden, rotting where it fell! I bent over the poor awful human creature," Mrs. Butler wrote, "in the supreme hour of his mortality; and while my eyes, blinded with tears of unavailing pity and horror, were fixed upon him, there was a sudden quivering of the eyelids and falling of the lower jaw—and he was free."

What was most distressing to Fanny Butler was the acceptance by the slaves themselves of the notion that they were irredeemably inferior to whites. Whenever a slave woman spoke in a demeaning way of herself or her race, Fanny Butler expostulated with her. She tried to explain "that the question is one of moral and mental culture—not color of an integument—and assure them, much to my own comfort . . . that white people are as dirty and dishonest as colored folks when they have suffered the same lack of decent training. If I could but find one of these women," she wrote, "on whose mind the idea had dawned that she was neither more or less than my equal, I think I should embrace her in an ecstasy of hopefulness."

Fanny Kemble noted that where slaves were given responsibilities they underwent striking changes in manner and even appearance. A slave assistant to the plantation's overseer was "clear-headed, well judging, active, intelligent, extremely well mannered . . . always clean and tidy in his person," and exhibiting "a strong instance of the intolerable and wicked injustice of the system under which he lives."

A Southern friend told Fanny Kemble that teaching slaves to read "impairs their value as slaves, for it instantly destroys their contentedness, and, since you do not contemplate changing their condition, it is surely doing them an ill service to destroy their acquiescence in it." To which Fanny Kemble added her own reflections. "A slave ignorant; he eats, drinks, sleeps, labors, and is happy. He learns to read; he feels, thinks, reflects, and becomes miserable. He discovers himself to be one of a debased and degraded race, deprived of the elementary rights which God has granted to all men alike. . . ."

It seemed to Fanny Butler that the women had the hardest lot of all. The very young male slaves were idle and "the very, very old, idle and neglected too"; the middle-aged men did not appear overworked. It was on the women that the greatest burdens fell, especially those who were pregnant, as many of the women were a good part of their childbearing years.

One of the most poignant aspects of the situation of slave women was their resourcefulness in discovering means of preventing conception or aborting fetuses that were the result of sexual unions forced upon them against their will, either with a black or white overseer, with the master, or as the consequence of a "marriage" with a male slave they did not like. After the Civil War a former slave named Rose Williams told how her master had forced her to accept a slave named Rufus as her husband when she was only sixteen years old, with the expectation that she would produce children by him. "Dere am one thing [my master] does to me what I can't shunt from my mind," she declared. "What he done am force me to live with dat nigger, Rufus, 'gainst my wants." Rose Williams didn't like Rufus because he was "a bully." Initially, she didn't realize that she was supposed to do more than cook and "look after" Rufus, but the first night she spent in a cabin with him she was rudely disabused. When she had gotten in bed, "dat nigger come and crawl in the bunk with me 'fore I knows it. I says, 'What you mean, you fool nigger?' He says for me to hush de mouth. 'Dis my bunk, too,' he say. 'You's teched in the head. Git out,' I's told him, and I put de feet 'gainst him and give him a shove and out he go on de floor 'fore he knew what I's doin. Dat nigger jump up and he mad. He look like a wild bear. He starts for de bunk and I jumps quick for de poker." Thus armed Rose hit her importunate suitor over the head and rebuffed him, but when she appealed to her master he declared he would have her whipped until she consented to accept Rufus as her mate.

A Georgia physician wrote that "the planters believe, the blacks are possessed of a secret by which they destroy the fetus at an early stage of gestation. . . . All country practitioners are aware of the frequent complaints of planters" concerning the "unnatural tendency in the African female to destroy her offspring." A Tennessee doctor reported that slave women tried to produce a miscarriage by medicine, violent exercise, and "external and internal manipulation." The roots of the cotton plant and cotton seed were both, ironically, used as abortives, along with Indian herbs. It was said that one master had six slave women he bought as breeders, but that in a period of twenty-five years they produced only two children among them.

One Southern historian has blamed the sexual indulgence of white masters on slave women. "The heaviest part of the white racial burden," he wrote, "was the African woman, of strong sex instincts and devoid of a sexual conscience at the white man's door, in the white man's dwelling." And another historian wrote, "Under the institution of slavery, the attack against the integrity of white civilization was made by the insidious influence of the lascivious hybrid woman at the point of weakest resistance. In the uncompromising opposition of the white mother and wife of the upper classes, lay the one assurance of the future purity of the race." The latter passage is a particularly revealing one. It was doubtless true that young slave women did, on many occasions, seduce their masters for the preferred status that usually accompanied the fathering of the master's child.

Although it was relatively rare, there were cases where male slaves seduced, or were seduced by, their mistresses or a daughter on the plantation. Peter Neilson, a traveler in the South, mentions an instance "wherein a white woman was captivated by a Negro . . . a planter's daughter having fallen in love with one of her father's slaves, had actually seduced him; the result . . . was the sudden mysterious disappearance of the young lady." The story was told in North Carolina of a white woman who drank some of her black lover's blood in order to be able to swear that she had black blood and thus be legally permitted to marry him. John Rankin reported "several instances of slaves actually seducing the daughters of their masters! Such seductions sometimes happen even in the most respectable slave-holding families."

Fanny Butler was increasingly conscious of the fear that hung over plantations. "Truly," she wrote, "slavery begets slavery, and the perpetual state of suspicion and apprehension of the slaveholders is a handsome offset, to say the least of it, against the fetters and lash of the slaves. Poor people, one and all, but especially poor oppressors of the oppressed! The attitude of these men is really pitiable; they profess . . . to consult the best interests of their slaves, and yet shrink back terrified from the approach of the slightest intellectual or moral improvement which might modify their degraded and miserable existence. I do pity these deplorable servants of two masters more than any human beings I have ever seen—more than their own slaves a thousand times. . . . I know that the Southern men are apt to deny the fact that they do live under a habitual sense of danger; but a slave population, coerced into obedience, though unarmed and half-fed *is* a threatening source of constant insecurity, and every Southern *woman* to whom I have spoken on the subject has admitted to me they live in terror of their slaves." Yet Fanny Butler praised the manners and "breeding" of Southerners; she maintained that "the shop is not their element; and the eager spirit of speculation and the sordid spirit of gain do not infect their whole existence, even to their very demeanor and appearance, as they too manifestly do those of a large proportion of the inhabitants of the Northern states."

She found a good measure of hypocrisy in the North on the issue of slavery. "The North," she wrote, "with the exception of an inconsiderable minority of its inhabitants, has never been at all desirous of the emancipation of the slaves. The Democratic party, which has ruled the United States for many years past, has always been friendly to the slaveholders, who have, with few exceptions, all been members of it (for, by a strange perversion both of words and ideas, some of the most democratic states in the Union are Southern slave states . . .). The condition of the free blacks in the Northern states has of course been affected most unfavorably by the slavery of their race throughout the other half of the Union." Mrs. Butler was convinced that it had been the "deliberate policy" of the North to degrade free blacks by keeping them in a menial and dependent status, thereby not challenging the South's image of the incompetence of the black. "Northern politicians," she wrote, "struck hands with the Southern slaveholders, and the great majority of the most enlightened citizens of the Northern states, absorbed in the pursuit of wealth and the extension and consolidation of their admirable and wonderful national prosperity, abandoned the government of their noble country and the preservation of its nobler institutions to the slaveholding aristocracy of the South."

Oversimplified as Fanny Kemble's analysis may be, there is substantial truth in it. The Democratic Party held power by accommodating the Southern slaveholders and the Irish and German immigrants. It was a strange alliance whose effect was to mitigate the hardships and sufferings of the immigrants by extending political power to them, while giving tacit approval to the system of slavery and the degradation of free blacks in the North.

It is not surprising that Fanny Kemble Butler and her husband soon came to the parting of the ways. He sued for divorce on the grounds of infidelity (a charge that was ironic since his affairs were notorious) and requested custody of the children. Fanny wrote from England in 1843, "For God's sake and for your children's sake, Pierce, my husband, oh still my most tenderly beloved, let us be wise before it is too late. . . .I implore you by that love which you once had for me, by that unalterable love which I still bear you, forgive me, forgive me. . . ."

Of the numerous ex-slaves who made effective public speakers, Frederick Douglass emerged as by far the most powerful and eloquent.

Elizabeth Cady Stanton, that indefatigable champion of the rights of women, who began her public career as an abolitionist speaker and often shared a platform with him, wrote of one such occasion, "He stood there like an African prince, conscious of his dignity and power, grand in his proportions, majestic in his wrath, as with wit, satire, and indignation he portrayed the bitterness of slavery."

Undoubtedly Douglass was the most dramatic personal embodiment of the ex-slave. In his classic autobiography, he told of his childhood and youth as a slave who, as his master's son, enjoyed special privileges. With twenty or thirty other black children, Fred, as he was called, went to learn the Lord's Prayer from an old black preacher, Uncle Isaac Copper, who switched his charges when they were dilatory. "Everybody in the South," Douglass wrote, "seemed to want the privilege of whipping somebody else. Uncle Isaac, though a good old man, shared the common passion of his time and country.

"A man's character always takes its hue, more or less," Douglass wrote, reflecting upon the effects of slavery on Southern whites, "from the form and color of things about him. The slaveholder as well as the slave was the victim of the slave system. Under the whole heavens there could be no relation more unfavorable to the development of honorable character than that sustained by the slaveholder to the slave. Reason is imprisoned here, and passions run wild."

It was so with Douglass's master. "Even to my child's eye he wore a troubled and at times a haggard aspect. . . . He seldom walked alone without muttering to himself, and he occasionally stormed about as if defying an army of invisible foes. . . . He was evidently a wretched man at war with his own soul and all the world around him. I have seen my old master when in a tempest of wrath, and full of pride, hatred, jealousy and revenge, he seemed a very fiend."

The slaves on Frederick Douglass's plantation received "as their monthly allowance of food, eight pounds of pickled pork, or its equivalent in fish. The pork was often tainted and the fish were of the poorest quality." With this they got a bushel of unbolted Indian meal and a pint of salt; "this was the entire monthly allowance of a full-grown slave, working constantly in the open field from morning till night every day in the month except Sunday." The yearly allowance of clothing was equally meager—two tow-linen shirts, one pair of linen trousers for summer and woolen trousers and a woolen jacket for winter, a pair of yarn stockings, and "a pair of shoes of the coarsest description." Children under ten had two shirts per year, no trousers, no shoes—and when the shirts wore out they went naked.

The fare in the Great House was, by comparison, lavish beyond description. Beef, veal, mutton, venison, "chickens of all breeds, ducks of all kinds, wild and tame . . . guinea fowls, turkeys, geese, and peafowls . . . partridges, quails, pheasants, pigeons . . . rock perch, drums, crocus, trout, oysters, crabs and terrapin with every kind of vegetable and fruit—figs, raisins, almonds, grapes from Spain, wine and brandies from France, teas of various flavors from China, and rich, aromatic coffee from Java, all conspiring to swell the tide of high life, where pride and indolence lounged in magnificence and satiety."

As a child Douglass had a protectress in the daughter of his first master, Miss Lucretia Anthony, who gave him bread for singing and "sympathy when I was abused by the termagant in the kitchen," a black woman. The half-naked slave children were like a pack of animals. Their food was cornmeal mush, which was placed in a large tray on the kitchen floor, "or out of doors on the ground, and the children were called like so many pigs, and like so many pigs would come, some with oyster shells, some with pieces of shingles, but none with spoons, and literally devour the mush. He who could eat fastest got the most."

The days between Christmas and New Year's were the slaves' holiday. Frederick Douglass described how the time was spent on his plantation. "The sober, thinking industrious [slaves] would employ themselves in manufacturing corn-brooms, mats, horse-collars, and baskets, and some of these were very well made." They might be used or sold to provide a few dollars income. "Another class spent their time in hunting opossums, coons, rabbits, and other game. But the majority spent the holidays in sports, ball-playing, wrestling, boxing, running, footraces, dancing, and drinking whisky, and this latter mode was generally most agreeable to their masters. . . . Not to be drunk during the holidays was disgraceful. The fiddling, dancing, and 'jubilee beating' was carried on in all directions. . . . Once in a while among a mass of nonsense and wild frolic, a sharp hit was given to the meanness of slaveholders:

> We raise the wheat,
> Dey gib us corn;
> We bake de bread,
> Dey give us de crust;
> We sift the meal,
> Dey gib us de huss;
> We peel de meat,

Dey gib us de skin;
And dat's de way
Dey takes us in;
We skim de pot,
Dey gib us de liquor,
And say dat's good enough for nigger."

"These holidays," Douglass added, "were . . . used as safety-valves
to carry off the explosive elements inseparable from the human mind
when reduced to the condition of slavery. But for these the rigors of
bondage would have become too severe for endurance, and the slave
would have been forced into a dangerous desperation."

Frederick Douglass tells us that to sing as he or she worked was
virtually required of slaves: "A silent slave was not liked, either by
masters or overseers. 'Make a noise there! Make a noise there!' . . .
were words usually addressed to slaves when they were silent. This and
the natural disposition of the Negro to make a noise in the world, may
account for the almost constant singing among them when at their
work." But on "allowance days," days without work when the slaves
collected their allowances of food and clothes, "they would make the
grand old woods for miles around reverberate with their wild and
plaintive notes," Douglass wrote. "They were indeed both merry and
sad. Child as I was those wild songs greatly depressed my spirits. . . . I
did not," he added, "when a slave, fully understand the deep meaning
of those rude and apparently incoherent songs. . . . They breathed the
prayer and complaint of souls overflowing with the bitterest sadness."

Miss Lucretia married Thomas Auld, and young Fred was sent to
Baltimore to be a servant in the house of Thomas's brother Hugh,
where he found another amiable mistress in "Miss Sophia—kind,
gentle and cheerful"—the wife of his new master. Sophia had never
owned a slave and took an immediate liking to the bright, handsome
young black boy. Deeply devout, Miss Sophia was "much given to
reading the Bible and to chanting hymns of praise when alone."
Hearing her read the Bible aloud awakened Fred's curiosity "in respect
to this mystery of reading, and aroused in me a desire to learn."
Douglass asked his mistress to teach him and she, in all innocence,
undertook to do so. Soon he had mastered the alphabet and learned to
read a few words and Sophia Auld, delighted at his quickness, boasted
of him to her husband. "Master Hugh was astounded beyond measure
and, probably for the first time, proceeded to unfold to his wife the
true philosophy of the slave system. . . ." She was forbidden to give

Douglass any further instruction. In the first place it was against the law. Beyond that it was "unsafe"; " 'if you give an nigger an inch he will take an ell. Learning will spoil the best nigger in the world. If he learns to read the Bible it will forever unfit him to be a slave. He should know nothing but the will of his master. . . . If you teach him how to read, he'll want to know how to write, and this accomplished, he'll be running away with himself.' "

Years later Douglass made a remarkable analysis of the subtle but profound change produced in the Auld household by Hugh Auld's edict. Her husband had, in effect, ordered her to treat the young black slave, for whom she had obviously come to feel an affection akin to that she felt for her son, as less than human—as, in Douglass's words, "a chattel," a piece of property—but "she felt me to be more than that. I could talk and sing; I could laugh and weep; I could reason and remember; I could love and hate. I was human, and she, dear lady, knew and felt me to be so."

In the struggle between her conscience and her duties as a wife, Mrs. Auld changed from a happy, loving mother to her own son and guide and protector of her black charge, to a repressed and sometimes cruel mistress. "Conscience cannot stand such violence," Douglass wrote. "If it be broken toward the slave on Sunday, it will be toward the master on Monday. It cannot long endure such shocks. It must stand unharmed, or it does not stand at all. As my condition in the family waxed bad, that of the family waxed no better." Mrs. Auld "finally became even more violent in her opposition to my learning to read than was Mr. Auld himself. Nothing now appeared to make her more angry than seeing me, seated in some nook or corner, quietly reading a book or newspaper. She would rush at me with the utmost fury, and snatch the book or paper from my hand."

But Douglass was not to be denied access to the alluring world that he had glimpsed in his initial efforts to read. He enlisted his young white playmates. He carried with him a copy of *Webster's Spelling Book*, "and when sent on errands, or when my playtime was allowed me, I would step aside with my young friends and take a lesson in spelling." With the money he made blacking boots, Douglass bought, for fifty cents, *The Columbian Orator*. In it was the story of a young slave who engages in a dialogue with his master on the evils of slavery and persuades him to set him free. It also contained "Sheridan's mighty speeches on the subject of Catholic Emancipation, Lord Chatham's speech on the American War, and speeches by the great William Pitt and by Fox. . . . I had now penetrated to the secret of slavery . . . and had ascertained their true foundation to be the pride, the power, and the avarice of man." And knowing, he became stubbornly resolved to be free whatever the cost. Mrs. Auld, of course, could not know his thoughts; she could only perceive that they grew daily further apart, and thus she grew harsher and more unhappy and blamed the young slave for her unhappiness and the changed nature of the life of the household, now tense and strained where it had been happy and open. In Douglass's words, "Poor lady . . . she aimed to keep me ignorant and I resolved to *know*, although knowledge only increased my misery. . . . It was *slavery*, not its mere *incidents* that I hated. . . . She had changed, and the reader will see that I, too, had changed. We were both victims to the same overshadowing evil, she as mistress, I as slave. I will not censure her harshly." The whole literature of slavery has not a wiser nor more penetrating analysis of the psychological effects of slavery on slaveholders themselves.

More and more Douglass heard the word "abolitionist" used with anger, always in connection with slavery. "This made the term a very interesting one to me. If a slave had made good his escape, it was generally alleged that he had been persuaded and assisted to do so by the abolitionist. If a slave killed his master, or struck down his overseer, or set fire to his master's dwelling, or committed any violence or crime out of the common way, it was certain to be said that such a crime was the legitimate fruit of the abolition movement." Finally, in the *Baltimore American* Douglass found the key to the riddle. The *American* reprinted some of the petitions that John Quincy Adams had tried to submit to Congress and the young slave discovered that "I was not alone in abhorring the cruelty and brutality of slavery. . . . I saw that there was fear as well as rage in the manner of speaking of abolitionists, and from this I inferred that they must have some power in the country. . . . Thus the light of this grand movement broke upon my mind by degrees, and I must say that ignorant as I was of the philosophy of the movement, I believed in it from the first, and I believed in it, partly, because I saw that it alarmed the consciences of the slaveholders."

As early as his thirteenth year, Douglass recalled, he felt in his "loneliness and destitution" the longing for some one to whom I could go as father and protector. Hearing a white Methodist minister named Hanson preach "was the means," he wrote, "of causing me to feel that in God I had such a friend. He thought that all men, great and small, bond and free, were sinners in the sight of God; that they were by nature rebels against his government; and that they must repent of their sins, and be reconciled to God through Christ."

Heretofore, as represented by the slaveholders, God had appeared to Douglass to confirm the slave system; now he had another vision of God's mercy and justice and underwent the classic experience of conversion. "I loved all mankind, slaveholders not excepted, though I abhorred slavery more than ever. I saw the world in a new light. . . . I gathered scattered pages of the Bible from filthy street-gutters, and washed and dried them, that in moments of leisure I might get a word or two of wisdom from them." A pious old black man named Uncle Lawson became Douglass's "spiritual father." The old man told the young one "that the Lord had great work for me to do, and I must prepare to do it; that he had been shown that I must preach the gospel. . . . He fanned my already intense love of knowledge into a flame by assuring me that I was to be a useful man in the world. When I would say to him, 'How can these things be? and what can I do?' his simple reply was, 'Trust in the Lord!' When I told him, 'I am a slave, and a slave for life, how can I do anything?' he would quietly answer, 'The Lord can make you free, my dear; all things are possible with Him; only have *faith* in God. "Ask, and it shall be given you." If you want liberty, ask the Lord for it in faith, and He will give it to you.'"

In 1833, Thomas Auld, who had inherited Douglass from Lucretia at her death, ordered him back from Baltimore and brought him to the home of his second wife, Rowena Hamilton, at St. Michaels on the Eastern Shore of Maryland—"an unsaintly, as well as unsightly place," in Douglass's view. The Hamilton plantation was an abode of desolation where the most barbarous cruelties were inflicted for the slightest offenses. There, the proud and rebellious young Fred, who now had escape constantly on his mind, was in constant conflict with his master. Finally, he was farmed out to a man named Edward Covey, "who enjoyed the reputation of being a first-rate hand at breaking young Negroes." A steady supply of slaves was sent to him by their masters to be made tractable. "Cold, distant, morose, with a face wearing all the marks of captious pride and malicious sternness . . . with a pair of smallish, greenish-gray eyes, set well back . . . the creature presented an appearance altogether ferocious and sinister. . . ." Here Douglass, experiencing every day the most degrading punishments and hostility, came to despair of ever gaining his freedom. When he was too ill to stand and complained of a terrible headache, Covey, declaring, "If you have got the headache, I'll cure you," took a hickory slab and struck him so hard on the head blood flowed down Douglass's face.

When he had recovered his health, Douglass vowed to himself that, come what may, he would never again allow Covey to beat him. The next time the slave breaker came after him to administer a whipping, Douglass grappled with him. "The fighting madness had come upon me," he wrote, "and I found my strong fingers firmly attached to the throat of the tyrant, as heedless of consequences at the moment, as if we stood as equals before the law. The very color of the man was forgotten. I felt supple as a cat, and was ready for him at every turn. Every blow was parried, though I dealt no blows in return. I was strictly on the defensive, preventing him from injuring me, rather than trying to injure him. I flung him on the ground several times when he meant to have hurled me there. . . . He held me, and I held him. . . . My resistance was entirely unexpected and Covey was taken all aback by it. He trembled in every limb. 'Are you going to resist, you scoundrel?' said he. To which I returned a polite 'Yes, sir.' " The enraged Covey called to his cousin, Hughes, for help and when he tried to come to his assistance, Douglass kicked Hughes in the stomach and "sent him staggering away in pain." Now Covey was clearly frightened "and stood puffing and blowing, seemingly unable to command words or blows." So they struggled on, neither man willing to yield in a terrible contest of muscles and will. The minutes stretched into two hours and finally Covey loosened his grip on Douglass and said, "Now, you scoundrel, go to your work. . . ."

For the remaining months that Douglass was hired out to Covey, the white man never touched him again. "This battle with Mr. Covey," Douglass wrote, "undignified as it was . . . was the turning-point in my 'life as a slave.' It rekindled in my breast smoldering embers of liberty. I was nothing before—I was a man now. It recalled to life my crushed self-respect, and my self-confidence, and inspired me with a new determination to be a free man. A man without force is without the essential dignity of humanity. Human nature is so constituted, that it cannot honor a helpless man, though it can pity him, and even this it cannot do long if signs of power do not arise. . . . I had reached the point at which I was *not afraid to die*. This spirit made me a freeman in *fact*, though I still remained a slave in *form*. When a slave cannot be flogged, he is more than half free. He has a domain as broad as his own manly heart to defend, and he is really 'a power on earth.' "

Slowly, under almost inconceivable disadvantages, Douglass's plans for escape took shape. He had now to be doubly on guard, for masters developed a kind of sixth sense for a potential runaway. Many of them had "learned to read, with great accuracy, the state of mind and heart of the slave. . . . Unusual sobriety, apparent abstraction, sullenness, and indifference—indeed any mood out of the common way—afforded grounds for suspicion and inquiry." Douglass recruited five other slaves, all older than himself, though vigorous young men. Every Sunday night they met to consider the means of escape. As the leader, Douglass carried a heavy burden of responsibility. Maps were almost impossible to come by. "I knew something of theology," Douglass wrote, "but nothing of geography. I really did not know that there was a State of New York, or a State of Massachusetts. I had heard of Pennsylvania, Delaware, and New Jersey, and all the southern states, but was utterly ignorant of the free states."

The scheme determined on at last was simple enough. The six men on the Saturday night before the Easter holidays were to steal one of the canoes, "launch out into the Chesapeake Bay and paddle with all our might for its head, a distance of seventy miles." Then they would be beyond Baltimore and they would travel north at night following the North Star. Douglass wrote each of them a pass and signed his master's name. But before they could leave, someone betrayed them, and their master, accompanied by constables, came down on them as they were working in the fields a few days before the day of flight. One of the slaves, ordered to cross his hands to be tied so that he might be conducted to jail, refused, and in the fierce struggle that followed to subdue him, Douglass and the others were able to destroy the passes which would have incriminated them. After jailing them for a week, their masters, unable to persuade any of them to confess, and lacking sufficient evidence, brought them back to St. Michaels. Douglass was separated from his friends and for a time feared he was to be "sold south"—to Georgia or Alabama—the fate most dreaded by slaves in the upper South. But Thomas Auld decided to send him back to his brother Hugh's in Baltimore, to be apprenticed as a carpenter in the Baltimore shipyards.

Working in a Baltimore shipyard, "at the call of about seventy-five men," Douglass discovered a new dimension of American society—the prejudice of white working men toward black men, slave or free. "Hullo, nigger! come turn this grindstone," . . . "I say, darkey, blast your eyes! why don't you heat up some pitch?" Douglass learned the hard way "the conflict of slavery with the interests of white mechanics and laborers. . . . The slaveholders," he wrote, "with a craftiness peculiar to themselves, by encouraging the enmity of the poor laboring white against the blacks, succeeded in making the said white man almost as much a slave as the black man himself. The difference between the white slave and the black slave was this: the latter belonged to one slaveholder, while the former belonged to the slaveholders collectively. . . . Both were plundered, and by the same plunderers. The slave was robbed by his master of all his earnings, above what was required for his bare physical necessities, and the white laboring man was robbed by the slave system of the just results of his labor, because he was flung into competition with a class of laborers who worked without wages. The slaveholders blinded them to this competition by keeping alive their prejudices against the slaves as *men*—not against them as *slaves*." The slaveholders conveyed the impression "that slavery was the only power that could prevent the laboring white man from falling to the level of the slave's poverty and degradation. . . . The feeling was, about this time, very bitter toward all colored people in Baltimore, and they—free and slave—suffered all manner of insult and wrong."

It was this spirit that made Douglass's work a grievous burden to him. His fellow apprentices "began . . . to talk contemptuously and maliciously of 'the niggers,' saying that they would take the 'country,' and that they 'ought to be killed.'" When they struck him, Douglass, physically a match for any of them, struck back. Finally four of them set on him with bricks and staves and almost killed him. Fifty white workers witnessed the assault on Douglass and "no one said, 'That is enough,' but some cried out, 'Kill him! kill him! kill the damned nigger! knock his brains out! he struck a white person.'"

Douglass's master, more angry at the damage to his property than at his slave's wounds and bruises, tried to have charges brought against the apprentices, but the constable told him that no white men would testify to the assault and that Douglass's own testimony was inadmissible since he was a slave.

Hereafter Douglass, having mastered the elements of caulking a ship's planks, worked more and more as an independent contractor, finding his own jobs and paying his wages to Hugh Auld. There were other young slaves and some free blacks working in the shipyards and throughout the city on the same basis, and a group of them formed the East Baltimore Mental Improvement Society to read and discuss books and to debate issues of the day. Although his situation in Baltimore was far better than it had been on the Hamilton plantation, the fact that Douglass found his own jobs and was paid for his skilled labor only increased his determination to be free. His escape was a comparatively simple matter. Every free slave in Baltimore was required to carry identification papers which had a description of the individual and which had to be renewed periodically. It was a common practice for slaves to borrow the papers of a free black whom they resembled, use the papers to make their way to freedom, and then mail them back to their owner. It was a great risk for a free black to lend his papers for such a purpose since the punishment was severe if the subterfuge was discovered, but many gladly took the chance.

Douglass borrowed the papers of a free black sailor whom he resembled only slightly and dressed himself in a sailor's costume. Thus attired, he waited until the train to Philadelphia was already pulling out of the station and then jumped aboard, trusting that the conductor would only give a cursory glance at his papers. On the train and on the ferry crossing the Susquehanna, Douglass saw three or four men he knew but they either failed to see him or simply kept their peace. Twenty-four hours later he was in New York, a free man.

What we call today the consciousness of the slave has been endlessly explored and speculated on by historians. The *life* of the slave, his or her daily activities, the character of plantation life in the various sections of the South, the habits and outlook of white Southerners are all "documented," as historians like to say, in almost overwhelming detail. Frederick Douglass's autobiography alone is a document of incomparable richness in what it tells us of the thoughts and emotions of a black man, who, if he was typical of his fellow slaves in certain essential matters, was clearly unusual if not unique in others.

What did the slave *think?* we ask repeatedly. How did he or she *feel* about being a slave, about his or her relationship to her master or mistress? Many Southerners came to feel (it was clear that few did earlier) that the slaves were happier in their enslaved condition than when they were free in the North or the South. They pointed constantly to the singing, dancing, hand-clapping happy black man as proof of their contention. And certainly, as we have seen, there were innumerable accounts that did describe slaves as happy, carefree, childlike, and so on. The enemies of slavery, oddly enough (or perhaps understandably), felt obliged to try to rebut every such claim, not realizing that it was beside the point. The point was simple enough. It was that slavery was a moral horror and an unendurable stain on the good name of the United States, that it was brutalizing and inhuman, that it degraded master and slave alike. Jefferson and George Mason and many other Southerners had understood that very well. That slaves were sometimes happy; that they had a curious and enviable capacity for expressions of spontaneous and exuberant delight; that they professed to "love" their masters and mistresses and indulged in the most extravagant expressions of joy when they returned to the plantation from a trip, or of sorrow when they departed—all of these were undeniable but entirely irrelevant to the question of whether slavery was a better material condition for black people to be in than freedom, or of whether the great majority of slaves were happy and content with their condition. The evidence to the contrary is mountainous. We have, hopefully, encountered a representative sampling of it in the course of this chapter. But historians, and especially white historians, have commonly been uneasy, especially in recent years, in dealing with the question of black consciousness. It has been, in fact, black historians who have been most inclined to recognize the existence of a "slave mentality" or consciousness among perhaps the great majority of slaves. The reasons for this uneasiness are clear enough. Historians have feared that their acceptance of the notion of a slave mentality or consciousness would seem "racist"—that is to say, to imply that blacks had some racial inferiority. It is an understandable reaction to the theories of white supremacy that have been so evident throughout our history. But it is, of course, quite a different question. The tragic fact is that one of the by-products of slavery was the instilling in the minds, first of slaves and then, as a kind of inevitable consequence, in the minds of the vast majority of black Americans, of the notion that they were inferior simply by virtue of being black. Dominant groups or classes always do this to those they dominate. Men have done it for centuries to women. Conquerors have invariably done it to the conquered. Powerlessness destroys the faith of the powerless in their own capacity to exercise even a modest degree of power, but, fortunately for the history of the human race, it does not do this *ad infinitum*.

What distressed Fanny Kemble most was the disposition of the slaves on her husband's plantation to, as we say today, put themselves down, to speak of themselves as hopelessly inferior to white people. That was the slave mentality in its essence: fatalistic acceptance that, come what may, God or Providence had ordained that black should be ineradicably and perpetually inferior to white. That was, of course, what, in the last analysis, prevented mass slave revolts in the South. More important, it continued to cast its shadow over the lives of black people when slavery was only a dim memory. It was slavery's most terrible legacy. We know, by the record of what they endured, of the dreams of freedom they clung to, of the risks they ran to achieve it, that there were many heroic men and women among the slaves of the South, men and women of much more than ordinary courage, intelligence, and resourcefulness, of compassion and humanity, for the most part nameless heroes and heroines. But very few, even of these, can be assumed to have escaped the dark cloud of unknowing, of accepted inferiority.

To say that slaves had, to a remarkable degree, the capacity for joy is not to say that they were happy in slavery; nor to say that they had, in the mass, a slave mentality. It is not to make a judgment about them, as human beings, but a judgment on the system that degraded them and consciously and systematically sought to deny them the experiences that would have made the claim of inferiority far more difficult to support. And then, finally, there was, of course, the fact that in all questions of inferiority or superiority, the white man was the measure and the master. He could change the rules of the game as he wished, raise the ante at will, define the terms on which the question was to be answered. If, for instance, he conceded that the black man had "a better sense of rhythm" than the white, it was, on the one hand because he was convinced that "technology" was as superior to "rhythm" as work was to music, and, on the other, that he could point to that "rhythm" as proof that the black was more primitive, i.e., was, not long ago, beating drums in the jungle.

What was most remarkable about the slaves, as we have had occasion to note before, was how they preserved their humanity in the face of brutalizing conditions. Black families, for example, showed remarkable stability and coherence over generations, if they were not torn apart. There is something of mystery about how they *created* their consciousness. One school of historians has been disposed to argue that blacks were simply what whites made them. Another school has insisted upon the importance of their increasingly dimly remembered tribal antecedents, their Africanness. Both notions have a substantial degree of truth about them. But they both scant the fact that the great majority of slaves were profoundly religious, most typically in some form of Protestant Christianity, and while it is true that their religion came to them as the "white man's religion," it is also most abundantly true that they made it profoundly and uniquely their own. The white master tried to persuade his slaves that the Bible justified and legitimated slavery, but the great majority of slaves read it differently and, regardless of what they were told, or how they read it, they experienced the redemptive power of the Christian faith as perhaps only the most desperately deprived can experience it—*in a way totally different from that of their masters and mistresses.* Christianity had, after all, begun its life as the religion of the rejected, the despised, the outcast, the meek, the humble, the oppressed. Christ had been whipped and crucified. And it was this strain in Christianity that impelled the abolitionists to "identify" with the enslaved black. Christianity is not the religion of the rich and successful, however much Americans may have tried to make it so. The slaves of the South took Christianity and preserved it in their slave cabins and around their midnight fires.

30

The Church of Abolition

W e have taken note, in the previous volume of this work, of the origins of abolitionism in Benjamin Lundy's *Genius of Universal Emancipation* and of the early efforts of the so-called Underground Railroad. Abolitionism was destined to become the most powerful and compelling movement for reform in the era preceding the Civil War.

The summer of 1831 witnessed an event that greatly increased the paranoia of the South. In 1800 Gabriel Prosser had organized a formidable uprising against the whites in Virginia; the plans for the uprising had been betrayed and a number of those accused of being involved had been hanged or deported. Twenty-two years later, Denmark Vesey's conspiracy had likewise been betrayed. Vesey had purchased his freedom with a winning lottery ticket in 1800 and had prospered as a carpenter and businessman. In recruiting followers, he had placed his primary emphasis on the Bible and on the challenge: "You are in God's eyes equal to your masters; will you fight for that principle?" In 1822 Vesey and a number of his followers had been executed.

Now another conspirator appeared, perhaps the most compelling figure of all, a Virginia slave named Nat Turner. Turner was a field hand, as distinguished from his more sophisticated predecessors,

Prosser and Vesey. Turner was also a religious visionary. He prayed and fasted, looking for a sign that would confirm his role as leader of a black rebellion. His visions, his impassioned rhetoric, and his supreme confidence in his own powers made him a natural leader among the slaves. Aware of the danger of enlisting large numbers of slaves, he initially recruited only six trusted friends. In a few weeks the number had grown to some sixty men who could obtain horses and who were supplied by Turner with arms of various kinds. On August 22, 1831, the band began a reign of terror, killing sixty-one white men, women, and children, most of them owners of small farms and a few slaves, whose treatment of blacks was more enlightened than that of many large plantation owners.

At Levi Waller's his wife and ten children were butchered. At the Vaughan farm old Mrs. Vaughan, her daughter-in-law, and her fifteen-year-old son were shot amid bitter curses and abuse. When word of the murders spread, the whole state was swept by fear and panic. Rumor said that more than a thousand armed blacks were on a rampage of killing and looting. Three or four hundred women and children crowded into the village of Jerusalem in Southampton County, protected by a contingent of some 250 federal troops sent from Richmond and hundreds of heavily armed whites. In retaliation blacks with no connection to the conspiracy were killed in cold blood "without trial and under circumstance of great barbarity," some by "decapitation." One white man claimed to have killed between ten and fifteen blacks himself. For two months Turner evaded capture and then, betrayed by two black women, he was captured and put in jail to await trial. While in jail he dictated to his lawyer his famous "Confession."

At the age of three, Turner told his scribe, he had discovered the gift of prophecy and on May 12, 1828, "I heard a loud noise in the heavens, and the Spirit instantly appeared to me and said the Serpent was loosened, and Christ had laid down the yoke he had borne for the sins of men, and that I should take it on and fight against the Serpent." Turner then went on to relate, most matter-of-factly, the bloody details of the murders. What was most unsettling to those who read his Confession was the ecstatic religious tone that permeated it and the promise in his vision that "the time was fast approaching when the first should be last and the last should be first." That hinted at a general slave uprising throughout the South and rumors of such an uprising circulated for months after the trial and execution of Turner. The fortitude and resignation with which Turner faced his death also made a strong impression, especially in the North.

William Lloyd Garrison, son of a drunken sea captain who had abandoned his family when Garrison was still an infant, had been apprenticed by his mother successively as a shoemaker and a cabinet-maker. In each instance he ran away. Finally apprenticed at the age of twelve to a printer, he became an expert compositor and journeyman printer. From there it was only a step to writing pieces himself, and at the age of twenty-two he became editor of the *National Philanthropist,* the first newspaper in the country devoted to prohibition. His next enthusiasm was the antislavery cause. He read Benjamin Lundy's *Genius of Universal Emancipation* and became a subscriber and a disciple of Lundy. Impressed by Garrison's passionate feelings on the issue of slavery, Lundy engaged him as editor of his paper but Garrison's style was too bold and inflammatory for the Quaker Lundy. In one issue Garrison described the owner of a slave vessel as a "highway robber and murderer." He was prosecuted for libel, convicted, and ordered to pay a fine of $450. When he refused he was put in jail and there he stayed for some weeks until one of the famous antislavery Tappan brothers sent a check to Lundy with a note declaring, "I have read the sketch of the trial of Mr. Garrison with that deep feeling of abhorrence of slavery and its abettors which everyone must feel who is capable of appreciating the blessings of liberty." Unnerved by Garrison's militancy, Lundy, who was a gradualist on the matter of slavery, parted company with him, and the younger man decided to establish his own antislavery journal. He visited his benefactor, Arthur Tappan, his face shining, as Tappan later recalled, with "conscious rectitude" and asked for a contribution to help him get started. Tappan gave the rather dandified young man a hundred dollars. Other prominent New England reformers, Lyman Beecher and William Ellery Channing, recoiled from the solicitations of this pushy young abolitionist whose radical notions alarmed them. Undaunted, Garrison found a partner, Isaac Knapp, and on January 1, 1831, the two young men published the initial issue of the *Liberator.* In its first year, the four-page weekly had six subscribers; the next year, fifty-three. "I *will* be harsh as truth," Garrison warned his readers, "and as uncompromising as justice. On this subject, I do not wish to think, or speak, or write, with moderation. No! No! Tell a man whose house is on fire, to give a moderate alarm; tell him to moderately rescue his wife from the hands of the ravisher; tell the mother to gradually extricate her babe from the fire into which it has fallen O but urge me not to use moderation in a cause like the present. I am in earnest—I will not equivocate—I will not excuse—I will not retreat a single inch—AND I WILL BE HEARD."

Powerful, and to many sincere opponents of slavery, distasteful words, but certainly among the most famous uttered in the nineteenth century. The South, pathologically sensitive on the slavery issue, reacted at once to the *Liberator*. Indeed it might not be amiss to say that its influence, in its early years, was far greater in the South than in the North. Southerners seized on it as an example of the fanaticism of the antislavery faction in New England. The fact was that Northern antislavery men and, to a lesser extent, women were almost as embarrassed by Garrison's journal as the South was enraged by it.

Garrison viewed Turner's uprising as the fulfillment of "What we have long predicted. . . . The first step of the earthquake, which is ultimately to shake down the fabric of oppression, leaving not one stone upon the other. . . . The first drops of blood, which are but a prelude to a deluge from the gathering clouds, have fallen. . . . The first wailings of a bereavement, which is to clothe the earth in sackcloth, have broken upon our ears. . . . What was poetry— imagination—in January, is now bloody reality." It was not just the hands of the South which were stained with blood, blood was on the hands "of the people of New-England and of all the free states. The crime of oppression is national. The south is only the agent in this guilty traffic." A "war of extermination" had begun in "a nation of oppressors." But for the South there were especially fierce words: "Ye patriotic hypocrites! ye panegyrists of Frenchmen, Greeks and Poles!! ye haters of aristocracy! ye assailants of monarchists! ye republican nullifiers! ye treasonable disunionists! be dumb! . . . Ye accuse the pacific friends of emancipation of instigating the slaves to revolt. Take back the charge as a foul slander. The slaves need no incentive at our hands."

Denying that the abolitionists had ever tried to justify "the excesses of the slaves," Garrison nonetheless compared the rebellious blacks to the Greeks who killed Turks in their fight for freedom, "or our fathers in slaughtering the British." Garrison professed to be "horror-struck at the late tidings." He had exerted his "utmost efforts to avert the calamity . . . preached to the slave the pacific precepts of Jesus Christ . . . appealed to Christians, philanthropists and patriots to accomplish the great work of national redemption through the agency of moral power—of public opinion—of individual duty."

And at the end: "Woe to this guilty land . . . ! IMMEDIATE EMANCIPATION can alone save her from the vengeance of Heaven, and cancel the debt of ages!"

There was more than a little plain madness in Garrison's response to Nat Turner's revolt, just as there was madness in the revolt itself. So, one might say, the madness of slavery produced the madness of abolition. The notion that the solution to slavery was to free the slaves immediately was of course wildly impractical. The result, as every Southerner knew, must be instant chaos: the complete impoverishment of the South, where slaves represented the principal capital of the region—a sum almost beyond calculating and far beyond the capacity of the federal government to compensate slave owners; and acute suffering for the slaves themselves, quite unable to provide for themselves or make their way in the white world. And such a dark prognosis was to ignore the most terrible possibility of all, one that haunted the dreams of all Southerners and which Garrison and other abolitionists did their best to cultivate—that the freed slaves would turn against their former masters and mistresses and murder them by the tens of thousands. The doctrine of the abolitionists thus seemed to Southerners the most dangerous kind of insanity aimed at robbing and murdering them. Northerners of general antislavery sentiments comforted themselves, as Daniel Webster did, with the thought that slavery was a Southern problem which the South must work out in its own way. There were of course a substantial number of Northerners who had no moral objections to slavery at all and deplored any agitation of the question; who hated black people and believed they should all be enslaved or at best shipped back to where they came from. The true story of the four decades preceding the outbreak of the Civil War revolved around the process by which a substantial number of Northerners—probably never a majority but enough—came, under the relentless proddings of the abolitionists and the ferocious response of the South, to think the unthinkable—that the slaves must somehow be freed.

Critics of Garrison, North and South, did not hesitate to recommend that he be put in jail or in an asylum. Indeed it became one of the principal grievances of the South that Northern authorities appeared unable or unwilling to muzzle its most relentless detractor. William Lloyd Garrison was a presumptuous representative of the lower class, a humorless fanatic, a working man without proper connections or education, a marked deviation from the high-minded,

Harvard- or Yale-educated men who just were beginning to speak their minds rather more openly on the dangerous and complex issue of slavery. He rushed matters along in his impetuous, hasty way. He was unpardonably crude and violent in his language, unreliable in his financial dealings, pretentious in his manners; no one could mistake him for a gentleman. But heard he was, forcing his rough way into the quiet studies of Unitarian ministers, pacific Quakers, liberal lawyers, and antislavery politicians. Deplore him as they might, they could not ignore him. He would let no uneasy conscience rest. Slowly at first and then more rapidly, he began to change the rules of the game. He would be the Tom Paine of the abolition of slavery, expressing thoughts that no one else dared to express in language almost as violent as an angry blow, a knife thrust, or the impact of a bullet. Very few dared to defend him but they read him and he was satisfied with that.

The roots of the abolitionist movement lay in the growing power of evangelical Christianity, which was appalled at the wickedness and injustice evident in so many areas of American life. Businesses were rapacious and dishonest, banks misused their customers' money, cities were sinks of iniquity and licentiousness; many Americans drank to excess, denied the rights of women and free blacks, abused the Indians, threatened the Mexicans, talked recklessly of war with Great Britain for a remote portion of territory in the Pacific Northwest. Above all, above everything else, "the land of the free" denied freedom to millions of human beings whose only crime was the color of their skin. Evangelical Christianity had about it, certainly, a touch of hysteria, and a degree of fanaticism, the hysteria that was so evident in camp meetings and revivals, the fanaticism that refused to be quiet about the terrible sin of slavery in the face of constant admonitions from the respectable and violence from the "lower orders." Blacks were the modern prototypes of the "suffering servant." Their suffering and servitude brought to the orthodox Christian mind the servitude of the Jews in Egypt, the suffering of Christ on the Cross. By sharing, through physical and material sacrifice, the sufferings of the black man and woman, the white Christian might identify himself or herself with the Savior. One thing was clear enough: America stood in desperate need of redemption.

American reformers worked in virtually every area, but it was as abolitionists that the champions of Christian redemption made their greatest impact. William Jay, the son of John Jay, wrote, "I do not depend on anyone as an abolitionist who does not act from a sense of religious obligation." That was the key.

Abolitionism was, to be sure, merely a branch of a larger antislavery movement. Anyone who disliked slavery and was willing to say so was eligible to join one of the numerous antislavery societies that sprang up in such profusion during the late 1820s and the 1830s. The antislavery movement was, moreover, international, or at least Anglo-American. British middle-class Protestant reformers had been tireless in their efforts to have slavery abolished from the British West Indies, and they made common cause with their American cousins. What became, increasingly, the dividing line in the antislavery movement was "immediatism" versus "gradualism." The immediatists declared that no compromise could be made with the institution of slavery. Slavery must be abolished "immediately," or, at the very least, its abolition should *begin* immediately. It was not enough to declare that slavery must *eventually* be abolished; "eventually" sounded more and more like "never." But "immediately" posed serious problems for the abolitionists, as those espousing that doctrine came to be called. Obviously they were unable to effect anything immediately; or perhaps anything at all. Year after year, they appeared to be doing virtually nothing to hasten the day of emancipation. Speeches, however eloquent or numerous, could not free the slave. Or could they? In retrospect one is much less sure. Because proponents of slavery, or friends of the Union (the Northern enemies of the abolitionists claimed, in most instances, to be opposed to slavery but to be equally opposed to opposition to it since such opposition must eventually bring about the dissolution of the Union), tried their best to suppress all discussion of the issue, the question of slavery became attached to the issue of free speech, which proved more potent, in the long run, than the slavery issue. Even abolitionists argued about whether the federal Constitution supported, or condoned, or militated against slavery, but no one could deny the fact that it protected free speech.

That was the ground on which John Quincy Adams stood to goad Congress relentlessly, like the abolitionists themselves. The members of that body might have their own views about the constitutionality of slavery, but freedom of speech and its corollary, freedom of petition, were irrefutably granted in the First Amendment to the Constitution, the first article of the Bill of Rights. So speech, it turned out, was the crucial element. The first thing that had to be done about slavery, however remote and impractical it might seem, was *to talk about it!*

And that was quite rightly perceived by the friends of slavery, or by those who had no strong feelings on the subject one way or another and simply wished to avoid rocking the ship Union, as being more dangerous than artillery broadsides or bombs. The more desperately the sensible, moderate men (and the angry, rancorous ones) struggled to prevent its being talked about, the more bitterly they denounced or threatened the speakers, tarred and feathered them, burned their halls, beat and on occasion murdered them, the more clearly the issue of freed slaves appeared to be linked to the issue of free speech and the more deeply the two sank into the consciousness and disturbed the consciences of ordinary folk who loved the Union and cared little for blacks, slave or free.

In Boston, the home territory of abolitionism, the venerable Harrison Gray Otis of Hartford Convention fame presided over a meeting of some 1,500 citizens who expressed "their disapprobation of the proceedings of the fanatics who are seeking to sow the seeds of discord among our fellow citizens of the South, and to excite the slaves to revolt against their masters." A similar meeting was held in New York at Central Park.

Important as speech was, it was not, it appeared to many of the enemies of slavery, enough. Help must be given to those slaves who wished to be free to escape from bondage and, once free, they must be helped to find havens in the free states of the North and Northwest. In addition, the legal and political disadvantages that free blacks suffered in those states must be removed, and free blacks, as well as freed slaves, must be assisted by training and education to take their places as the equals of whites. The Underground Railroad was the practical arm of the abolitionist movement. It was a daily, dramatic manifestation of the determination of slaves to be free, free in the face of every hazard, and of the determination of thousands of whites to aid and abet them. The Underground Railroad was the more remarkable in that it ran directly in the face of the American respect for property. Every slave helped to escape by a white man or woman appeared to Southerners, and to many Northerners as well, to be stolen property, and those who aided them no better than bank robbers or burglars. Each theft encouraged among other slaves the hope of being "stolen," so that the analogy must encompass the notion of an epidemic as well as a theft, a cancerous disease as well as an assault on property. *Every single escaped slave made the system tremble.* The monetary loss, while it came in time, as the number of runaways mounted, to a considerable sum, was far less important than the psychological effect on the owners of slaves and, in the North, on the general public who, the abolitionists made sure, were informed of every detail of every dramatic escape. Between thirty and forty newspapers and journals carried the antislavery message. The most prominent, next to the *Liberator,* were the *National Anti-Slavery Standard,* the *Philanthropist,* the *Anti-Slavery Bugle,* the *Herald of Freedom,* the *Emancipator,* and the *National Era. The Slaves' Friend* was directed at children and the *Liberty Bell* was an annual compendium of poems, essays, and thrilling accounts of slave escapes. These went, to be sure, primarily to the converted, but many newspapers had an antislavery bent and, more important, news was news. Besides what appeared in the papers, many communities experienced at first hand the drama of a fugitive slave pursued by slave catchers or, later, by a United States marshal. No newspaper account, however vivid, could equal the impact of seeing a black man or woman who had escaped slavery being captured and returned to servitude. It made the theoretical and abstract excruciatingly actual.

So the task was repentance and redemption for a nation mired in sin, and abolitionism (as seen in this perspective) was an offshoot of the movement to convert the United States to Christianity starting, logically, with the most heinous sin. In the words of Amos Phelps, a Boston clergyman, "The doctrine of immediate emancipation is nothing more or less than that of immediate repentance, applied to this particular sin." The idea of gradual emancipation "throws the charge of guilt back on the past or on the future, and brings in a plea of innocence for the present." It was thus powerless to "awaken conviction of guilt—the indispensable prerequisite to all genuine repentance. . . . Slavery, in its true and real character in the sight of God, is a moral evil—a sin—a crime, and not a mere undefined evil, or calamity, or misfortune. And every man who is in any way implicated in the matter is implicated in sin, and not merely in a misfortune or calamity." Americans could talk until doomsday of slavery as a "great evil," but as long as it was spoken of simply in this way it was an impediment to emancipation because it absolved the speaker of the necessity of *doing* anything to remedy it. The solution of the "immediatists" was for the slaveholder at once to "cease to hold or employ human beings as property." Slaves should be freed and employed "as free hired laborers" with a choice as to whether to remain in the employ of their former masters. Thereafter the master "should at once *begin* to make amends for the past, by entering heartily on the work of qualifying them for, and elevating them to all the privileges of freedom and religion;—thus doing what he can to emancipate them . . . from the *consequences* of slavery, as well as from the thing itself."

All this was to be achieved, most abolitionists believed, by conversion rather than by force. The abolitionists, at least initially, disclaimed "all physical force, and all unconstitutional legal interposition." If the hearts of slaveholders and their proslavery adherents in the North were to be changed they must be changed by "light and love" on this subject, as well as on others. Through the "pulpit and the press" the country must be aroused to understand that emancipation was "the plan of Jesus Christ . . . on which he has been acting, and is now acting, in conjunction with his people, for the conversion of the world. It is simply the application of his plan for the abolition of every sin to the abolition of a particular one."

The moral reformation of America was to take place through means of a national society "whose business it shall be to superintend this great movement, to collect facts, print tracts and send them abroad upon the winds, to enlist the press and the pulpit, to employ agents . . . address popular assemblies . . . form auxiliaries, etc., etc. . . . ; until every section of the land shall be pervaded with it, and the *people* with one consent shall rise and say to the oppressed, 'Go free.' "

First the North must be converted and then the work could begin in the South, initially among the clergy and "among others of those broken-hearted mothers and deserted wives, who are doomed to weep night and day over sons and husbands that have fallen victim to the shameless licentiousness, which slavery everywhere begets. . . . The thing proposed, then, can be done. To say that it cannot is to deny the efficacy of the gospel."

In the third annual report of the New England Anti-Slavery Society the delegates defined what they meant by immediate abolition. "It means, in the first place," the report read, "that all title of property in the slaves shall instantly cease, because their Creator has never relinquished his claim of ownership, and because none have a right to sell their own bodies or buy those of their own species as cattle." Beyond that every husband should have his own wife and all parents should have control over their own children. All the laws should be extended to protect the rights of blacks as well as whites.

The freeing of the slaves would result in great benefits to every segment of society, annihilating "a system of licentiousness, incest, blood and cruelty," and opening up "an immense market to our mechanics and manufacturers; for these two millions of free persons will need, and will make every exertion to obtain, hats, bonnets, shoes, clothes, houses, lands, etc., etc." Every former slave should be educated in "morals, science and literature" and supplied with a Bible. The children could be placed "in infant schools," and transferred into primary and secondary schools and Bible classes, and "by the assistance of the Holy Spirit, from Bible classes into the christian church. Thus they will become ornaments to society—capable men, good citizens, devoted christians—instead of mere animals." The South, in turn, would "exhibit the flush of returning health, and feel a stronger pulse, and draw a freer breath. . . .

"Abolish slavery, and the gospel will have free course, run, and be glorified; salvation will flow in a current broad and deep. . . . In fine, immediate abolition would save the lives of the planters, enhance the value of their lands, promote their temporal and eternal interests and secure for them the benignant smiles of heaven."

When an antislavery convention was held in Boston, Richard Henry Dana attended and was very unfavorably impressed. "Nothing," he wrote in his diary, "can exceed the wildness & fanaticism of that collection of people. . . . Two conceited, shallow-pated negro youths named Remond & Douglass were among the chief speakers. They seemed to have been entirely spoiled by the notice taken of them & evidently had but little strength of mind by nature. The expression of conceit was so evident upon their countenances as to be perfectly laughable. . . . Two or three women also spoke, but their speeches were painful from the sense they gave one of incoherency & excitement amounting almost to insanity." Wendell Phillips was a more difficult case for Dana since he was "a gentleman & scholar & speaks as such. . . . Garrison has logic & force, but is a fanatic by constitution, & a hater of everything established & traditional, & an infidel & socialist. Phillips, however, advocates exciting the blacks to insurrection & war. . . . The elements of which this convention was composed are dreadful. Heated, narrow minded, self willed, excited, un-christian, radical energies set to work upon a cause which is good, if rightly managed, but which they have made a hot bed for forcing into growth the most dangerous doctrines to both church & state. They are nearly all at the extreme of radicalism, socialism & infidelity."

The same year, the antislavery groups of Boston and New York joined forces to found the American Anti-Slavery Society. John Greenleaf Whittier, the poet, was prominent in the New York branch of the movement and helped to draft a Declaration of Sentiments in the spirit of the New England Report, which pledged the association to a policy of moral suasion—"the destruction of error by the potency of truth—the overthrow of prejudice by the power of love—and the abolition of slavery by the spirit of repentance." While the New England Society had pledged obedience to the law, the Declaration of Sentiments stated that "all those laws which are now in force, admitting the right of slavery, are . . . before God utterly null and void; being audacious usurpation of the Divine prerogative, a daring infringement of the law of nature, a base overthrow of the very foundations of the social compact. . . ."

At the same time, the Declaration, in an apparent contradiction, recognized "the sovereignty of each state, to legislate exclusively on the subject of the slavery which is tolerated within its limits. We concede," the document continued, "that Congress, *under the present national compact,* has no right to interfere with any of the slave states. . . ." But the federal government had not been content to stop there. It was the active aider and abettor of slavery by virtue of recognizing slaves as property under the Constitution, i.e., the provision counting the slave population as three-fifths of the white population for purposes of representation. This relationship between the federal government and the slave state was "criminal and full of danger," and "MUST BE BROKEN UP." The trust of the abolitionists was "solely in GOD. *We* may be personally defeated, but our principles never, TRUTH, JUSTICE, REASON, HUMANITY, must and will gloriously triumph . . . whether we live to witness the triumph . . . or perish untimely as martyrs in this great, benevolent and holy cause." The delegates then resolved that "With entire confidence in the overruling justice of God, we plant ourselves upon the Declaration of Independence and the truths of divine revelation. . . . We shall organize anti-slavery societies, if possible, in every city, town and village in the land. We shall send forth agents to lift up the voice of remonstrance, of warning, of entreaty and rebuke. We shall circulate unsparingly and extensively anti-slavery tracts and periodicals."

At the heart of the abolitionist policy then lay an assumption and a strategy. The assumption was that hearts could be changed and Americans converted to abolitionism-Christianity. The strategy was to try, by such a change, to induce the federal government to stop the illegal slave trade, to halt the interstate traffic in slaves, to prevent the extension of slavery to the territories and to new states, to change the basis of representation and, on every level, to withhold support for the slave system, thus adding political pressure to moral pressure. As the limitations of moral suasion became apparent, and the Constitution was repeatedly invoked by the defenders of slavery (or the opponents of abolition), the Garrison wing of the movement became increasingly hostile toward that document and disposed to sever the irredeemably sinful portion of the body politic—the South—from the Union. This was certainly moral rectitude with a vengeance. The slave would thus be left to languish in perpetual servitude in order to free the consciences of Northerners from the guilt of slavery. For many abolitionists such a resolution of the issue was completely unacceptable, and within a period of ten years the movement was seriously split.

The major effect of the abolitionists was to enhance enormously the paranoia of the South and thereby drive Southerners into positions and acts that seemed indefensible to many Americans. As long as one could be "against" slavery without feeling the necessity to do anything about it, Northerners and Southerners could unite or concur in an agreeable unanimity. Slavery was an evil that *in time must be done away with.* But if slaveholding or any association with slavery was a personal sin that placed one's soul in danger of eternal damnation—well, that was obviously a different matter. Now the South began to defend slavery, in a certain sense, to save its soul. And every step in that direction deepened the awareness of non-Southerners and Southerners of conscience that slavery was a wound that time could not be trusted to heal.

The devotion of the Tappans to the cause of abolition was especially offensive to the South. They were rich and successful men, members of the inner circle of merchants and bankers who controlled the financial life of the nation's most flourishing city. A delegation of Arthur Tappan's fellow merchants had exhorted him to abandon such a disreputable cause but Tappan had declared, "I will be hanged first." But even his enemies were appalled to learn that Georgians had offered a $12,000 reward to anyone enterprising enough to kidnap Tappan. New Orleans raised the pot to $20,000. The severed ear of a slave was sent to him. Bankers refused to lend him money and insurance companies refused to insure his business on the grounds that it was in perpetual danger of being put to the torch by antiabolition mobs. Rumors circulated through the city that hired kidnappers or assassins were lurking about to seize or murder the Tappans. Lydia Maria Child wrote, " 'Tis like the times of the French Revolution, when no man dare trust his neighbor."

The year 1835 saw the high tide of violence and harassment directed against the abolitionists. In Canaan, New Hampshire, the citizens hitched up a hundred yoke of oxen and dragged the main building of the Noyes Academy into a nearby swamp, all because the school had admitted two young black students. In Boston, more than a thousand of that city's most respectable citizens met in Faneuil Hall, "the cradle of liberty," to denounce the abolitionists. The cry was everywhere much the same. Agitation of the slavery question must cease. It endangered the Union and was apt to have serious economic consequences.

In Canterbury, Connecticut, a young woman named Prudence Crandall kept a school for girls. When a black farmer asked her to accept his daughter as a student, she readily complied, raising in the town a furor which was considerably increased when she advertised in the *Liberator* that she was prepared to teach "colored little misses." When she resisted public pressure to refuse admission to black girls, the Connecticut legislature hastily passed a law forbidding the establishment of schools for nonresident blacks, and legal proceedings against her were started at once. One of the few people to rally to her cause was a Unitarian minister from a nearby town, the Reverend Samuel May. May was one of the champions of universal reform, extending from temperance and women's rights through abolition to international peace. He undertook to find lawyers to defend her and prevailed on Arthur Tappan to open his apparently bottomless purse to pay her legal fees. Prudence Crandall, convicted in the local court, won on appeal to the state supreme court, but the residents of Canterbury forced her to close the school. Her brother, Dr. Reuben Crandall, was meanwhile thrown into jail in the District of Columbia for distributing abolitionist literature. May himself became one of the warhorses of the abolitionists. He aided runaway slaves on the Underground Railroad and constantly risked life and limb by preaching his unpopular doctrines wherever he could find an audience. He calculated that in Vermont alone he had been harassed by mobs five times in the month of October, 1835.

The arrival in the United States of George Thompson, the famous British abolitionist, added fuel to the already bitter feelings against the abolitionists. In Boston the Female Antislavery Society had invited Thompson to lecture to them and the call went out through the city to tar and feather the British intruder. The abolitionist women, one handbill declared, must be shown that their proper role was "attending to domestic concerns instead of sowing the seeds of discord in the antislavery rooms."

Thirty women, among them several blacks, gathered on October 21 for the meeting, which was also attended by Garrison. Outside the hall several thousand furious males jeered and chanted. The mayor arrived and implored the militant women to adjourn: "Ladies if you do not wish to see a scene of bloodshed and confusion, go home!" Beautiful young Maria Weston Chapman, the president of the society, whose social connections were impeccable, answered defiantly, "If this is the last bulwark of freedom, we may as well die here as anywhere."

Garrison felt that he was the principal object of the mob's wrath; if he left, the women would be safe. But before he could escape from the building, the mob broke down the door and stormed up the stairs. The mayor helped Garrison escape through a second-floor window and the women, blacks and whites, in pairs, walked out of the building and through the abusive crowd that cursed and taunted them. Garrison meanwhile was discovered hiding in a nearby carpenter's shop. A rope was tied around him and he was dragged into the street; evidently the mob was under the impression that he was George Thompson. Someone, recognizing him, called out, "Don't hurt him—he is an American." He was led through the throng of people in the streets, his arms bound and, some observers noted, a slight smile on his lips. As the crowd passed State Street with its victim, the mayor and a group of constables sallied out and rescued him, hurrying him into City Hall where he remained until nightfall. Under the cover of darkness the mayor tried to get him to the Leverett Street jail but the mob, still milling around the hall and calling for Garrison's blood, intercepted the carriage and tried to break off its doors and unhitch the horses. Constables drove them off with staves and whips, and Garrison and his guards reached the jail, where he was booked for disturbing the peace and placed in a cell for his protection. John Greenleaf Whittier, who had already written a poem hailing Garrison as the hero of the age, came to visit him with Alcott and other friends and supporters, and the next day the charges against him were dismissed. He had written on the wall of his cell, "William Lloyd Garrison was put into this cell on Monday afternoon, October 31, 1835, to save him from the violence of a respectable and influential mob, who sought to destroy him for preaching the abominable and dangerous doctrine that all men are created equal, and that all oppression is odious in the sight of God."

The scandal was that the leaders of the mob included some of Boston's "better sort," who had encouraged the riot "to assure our brethren of the South that we cherish rational and correct notions on the subject of slavery."

In Reading, Connecticut, a normally peaceful little town, the Baptist church was blown up because the church had been used for abolition meetings. In Troy, New York, a city official was one of the leaders of a riot against Theodore Weld. "Twice a rush was made up the aisles to drag me from the pulpit," Weld wrote. "Stones, pieces of bricks, eggs . . . were thrown at me while speaking." John Rankin estimated that he had been mobbed more than a hundred times, while Henry Stanton, Elizabeth Cady's husband, tallied a hundred and fifty attacks on him.

In Utica, the same day that the Boston Female Antislavery Society was being driven from its meeting hall, six hundred antislavery delegates to the New York State Anti-Slavery Convention were beset by a similar mob and forced to abandon a Presbyterian church where they had been meeting. Gerrit Smith, the grandson of James Livingston and one of the richest men in the state, had gone to the convention as an observer. He was so incensed by the actions of the mob that he threw his considerable energies and large fortune into the abolitionist cause without abandoning his activities in behalf of temperance and vegetarianism.

The name carried on copies of the *Liberator* as the publisher of the paper was that of R. G. Williams, a New Yorker. The governor of Alabama called on the governor of New York to extradite Williams to Alabama to face charges of stirring up slave revolt. Although Williams had never even visited Alabama, the extradition was urged on the grounds that he had been there "in spirit" through the pages of the *Liberator*. That such tactics could only backfire was understood very well by the abolitionists and even by the more moderate Southerners. Williams himself wrote, "Our opposers took the wrong course to accomplish their purpose. Instead of putting us down they put us and our principles up before the world—just where we wanted to be."

Even the governor of Alabama declared, "Arthur Tappan and the infuriate demoniacs have never acquired any considerable notoriety until this opposition [in the South] commenced." A Virginian wrote in a letter that found its way into the *Emancipator,* "When I think of the myriads of . . . papers . . . from the prolific press in New York . . . diffusing at once delusion and bitterness through the North, and exasperation through the South; of our own imprudences in offering rewards for Tappan . . . of our lynchings and excessive irritability throughout this whole season of agitation, how is it possible to avoid fearing the worst?" Henry Foote, a brilliant young Mississippi lawyer, wrote, "Never was there an instance of more extraordinary or even maddening excitement amid a refined, intelligent and virtue-loving people than that which I had the pain to witness in the counties of central Mississippi. . . ."

The events of 1835 hastened the schism between the evangelical Christians who constituted the shock troops of abolition and the established churches. The Congregationalists in 1836 rejected all advocates of immediatism and the Methodists followed suit, abjuring "any right, wish, or intention to interfere with the civil and political relation between master and slave." The Presbyterians took the position that slavery was a political not a moral issue, and when a substantial number of Northerners refused to accept that dictum, the church split into Northern and Southern branches. To the abolitionists, the action of the clergy was proof of their charge that churches and their ministers cared more for protecting property than saving souls or doing justly. Christianity was the handmaiden of capitalism. Garrison attacked the churches with bitter invective and the churches replied in kind.

David Nelson was a Presbyterian clergyman and president of Marion College, Missouri, an institution founded by the church. When Nelson, at a meeting of the Missouri synod, read a paper urging that slaves in Missouri be freed and their owners compensated by the state, a melee followed in which a man was badly wounded and Nelson was forced to flee for his life to Illinois. There he founded his own college and assigned students to assist in the escape of runaway slaves, sending them out to patrol the Missouri side of the river and help fugitives to get across to safety. Finally the institute was set on fire and Nelson barely escaped the flames.

James Birney, the reformed Southerner who had been converted to the cause by Theodore Weld and driven out of Kentucky, had established himself and the *Philanthropist* in Cincinnati. There, in the summer of 1836, a mob sanctioned by some of the leading businessmen, clergy, and lawyers of the city broke into his printing office, destroyed the presses, and scattered the type. Next day Birney repaired his press and printed a new edition of the *Philanthropist*. Indignant public meetings were held and a handbill distributed which read "Abolitionists BEWARE. The citizens of Cincinnati, embracing every class, interested in the prosperity of the city, satisfied that the business of the place is receiving a vital stab from the wicked and misguided operations of the abolitionists, are resolved to arrest their course." Once again the office was broken into, and this time the press was thrown into the river. Salmon P. Chase, a graduate of Dartmouth College and a rising young lawyer, went to Birney's aid, placing himself in the doorway of his house and defying a mob, which turned its attention to the black section of the city. There it was met by gunfire from embattled blacks. For three days the city was on edge, with groups of armed whites roving the streets. Finally order was restored and the publication of the *Philanthropist* resumed, with Chase its most conspicuous contributor.

The aftermath of the mobbings and lynchings was a spectacular growth in the number of antislavery societies from some two hundred in May of 1835 to 527 a year later. Fifteen thousand new subscribers had been added to the readers of abolition literature. Well might Garrison write triumphantly: "What have I done? In seizing the 'trump of God' I had intended indeed to blow a jarring blast—but it was necessary to wake up a nation slumbering in the lap of moral death. . . . Within four years I have seen my principles embraced by thousands of the best men in the nation. I have seen prejudices which were deemed incurable utterly eradicated from the breasts of a great multitude. I have seen the press teeming with books, pamphlets, tracts, and periodicals, all in favor of the bondman and against his oppressors. I have seen crowds rushing to hear the tale of woe and blood. I have seen discussions of slavery going on in public and in private, among all classes and in all parts of the land; and more spoken, and written and printed and circulated in one month than there formerly was in many years."

One of the most notable recruits to the abolitionist cause was William Ellery Channing, the Unitarian minister who shared with Lyman Beecher the reputation of being the foremost preacher of the day. Channing's book *Slavery*, while a temperate tract, declared black servitude to be inconsistent with the principles of Christianity.

Soon there was hardly an important literary figure, intellectual, or popular minister in New England who was not in the antislavery camp.

An important convert was Richard Henry Dana, who had been so contemptuous of the abolitionist "fanatics" a few years earlier. Dana contributed his services as a lawyer to runaway slaves. The bitterness aroused by his defection was so great that lifelong friends ceased to speak to him. Dana's close friend George Hilliard said to him "he hoped there would be no interruption of social relations." "In tenderness of pity & I hope of magnanimity too, I said no, certainly not . . ." Dana wrote. But Hilliard then went so far as to say that if someone "lives in Boston & feels about her position & action as you do . . . he ought to either keep silent or leave the city. . . . I told him that the principle would do in a Club or Society, but not in a community of equal rights. I told him that the sentiment came from persons who thought Boston was a club—their club, said I, 'this must be fought out here & now.'"

One of the most spectacular converts, brought into the fold by Weld himself, was the Kentucky planter and slave owner Cassius Clay, who freed his slaves and took up the abolitionist cause. Dana dined with Clay at John Palfrey's in the company of Charles Francis Adams and was impressed by his "noble eye, soft as a woman's, with a watchfulness & resolution lying in wait at the bottom of it which bespeaks him full of courage & conduct." One of Clay's political enemies had told Palfrey that Clay "had more moral & physical courage than any man he ever met. . . . Once when addressing an assembly he was set upon by three men, brothers, [whose] object was to kill him. He defended himself gallantly with his bowie knife, but wounded before & behind, he was sinking under the cowardly assault, when his boy, only 12 years old, ran into the midst of the combat & handed his father a pistol. Mr. Clay raised it & shot dead the leader of the assailants. This saved his life, although he was taken up for dead."

In November, 1837, friends of the antislavery cause and freedom of speech were outraged by the murder of Elijah Lovejoy, a dedicated abolitionist, in Alton, Illinois. Lovejoy had grown up in Maine, graduated from Waterville College, and gone to St. Louis to establish a school. There he underwent a religious conversion and decided to become a Presbyterian minister as his father had been. After graduating from the Princeton Theological Seminary Lovejoy returned to St. Louis and began to publish a church paper called the *Observer,* in which he inveighed against slavery. A public meeting was called to protest the *Observer*'s editorials. The meeting passed resolutions affirming that the Bible sanctioned slavery and that the abolitionists were bent on destroying the Union. The rights guaranteed to Americans under the First Amendment must not be interpreted to permit abolitionists "to freely discuss the question of slavery, either orally or through the medium of the press." Lovejoy, at this point, decided to move to Alton, Illinois, further up the river. He shipped off his press but before he left town a black man stabbed and killed an officer who was arresting him. A mob of angry whites carried him from the jail, hanged him from a tree, and burned him alive. When an effort was made to bring the leaders to justice, the judge enunciated the doctrine that acts that would be criminal when performed by an individual or two or three persons, were when committed by a mob "beyond the reach of the law." This legal approval of mob violence was denounced by Lovejoy, in reply to which the mob tore down his office.

Meanwhile his press arrived in Alton where his notoriety preceded him. A mob discovered the press, smashed it, and threw the pieces in the river. A meeting of the more responsible citizens of the town abjured any sympathy with abolitionism but deplored the actions of the mob in the destruction of private property and took up a collection to replace it. Lovejoy, back in business, wrote mostly of religious matters but in the issue of July 4, 1837, he advocated forming a state antislavery society. He was told that the citizens of Alton did not wish him to mention the subject of slavery any further, and when he refused to accept that edict, his press was destroyed and the office housing it demolished. Lovejoy now issued a general appeal to all persons who supported the principle of a free press. With the aid of abolitionists around the country, he procured a new press but before it could be set up a dozen masked men broke into the warehouse where it was stored, carried it off, and smashed it. Lovejoy now made plans to produce a fourth press, this time contributed by the Ohio Anti-Slavery Society. He and his coadjutors, including his younger brother Owen, who had joined him in Alton, were determined to protect this press by arms if necessary. When it arrived it was stored in a warehouse and a guard placed over it. Several days later a mob collected and demanded that Lovejoy surrender the press. When he refused, stones and bricks were thrown through the windows. Someone fired a shot. More shots rang out and one of the crowd, a man named Bishop, was shot and killed. Chastened, the mob withdrew but when Lovejoy opened the warehouse, five shots struck him.

The incident aroused a storm all over the country. In the South, and among those in other sections friendly to slavery or determined to suppress it as a public issue, it was said that Lovejoy had gotten no more than he deserved. Elsewhere there was great indignation. Meetings and memorial services were held to express the sense of outrage, and Lovejoy's name was thereafter constantly evoked by the abolitionists and an increasing company of "fellow travelers," individuals sympathetic in one degree or another to the fight against slavery, but unwilling to take a public stand on the issue. Lovejoy had written to John Quincy Adams months before, praising his efforts in behalf of the antislavery cause and soliciting his assistance in publishing his paper. "He was a man of strong religious, conscientious feeling," Adams wrote, "deeply indignant at what he deemed the vices and crimes of the age. Such men are often fated to be martyrs; and he has fallen a martyr to the cause of human freedom." His murder seemed to Adams "the most atrocious case of rioting which has ever disgraced this country. . . ."

In Boston, the stronghold of abolition sentiment, a meeting was held at Faneuil Hall to denounce Lovejoy's murderers. In Philadelphia at the new Hall for Free Discussion, Theodore Weld spoke bitterly of American hypocrisy: "The empty *name* [of freedom] is everywhere,— *free* government, *free* men, *free* speech, *free* people, *free* schools, and *free* churches. Hollow counterfeits, all! FREE! It is the climax of irony, and its million echoes are hisses and jeers, even from the earth's ends. FREE. *Blot it out.* Words are the signs of *things.* The substance has gone! Let fools and madmen clutch at shadows. . . . Rome's loudest shout for liberty was when she murdered it. . . . The words and sound are omnipresent masks, and mockers! An impious lie! unless they stand for free *Lynch Law,* and free *murder;* for they *are* free."

In May, 1838, the Pennsylvania Hall for Free Discussion, just recently completed, was burned down by an angry mob. "The mob," Philip Hone noted, "still further instigated . . . by the wanton outrage of public opinion in the exhibition in the public streets of white men and women walking arm in arm with blacks, . . . broke into the hall, destroyed everything they could find, and set fire to the building, which was entirely destroyed. . . . A large proportion of the Abolitionists assembled in the hall were females, of whom several harangued the meeting, and were foremost in braving the excited populace. This dreadful subject gains importance every day," Hone added, "and reflecting men see in it the seeds of the destruction of our institutions." The rioting continued for several days. Having destroyed Pennsylvania Hall, the rioters were reported to have their sights set on Temperance

Hall, where the abolitionists had continued their meetings. Sidney George Fisher wrote in a similar vein of the destruction of the hall "by a mob of well-dressed persons, the police scarcely interfering & the firemen not being allowed to play on the fire. So much for the supremacy of the laws, which cannot be executed in opposition to popular feeling. To be sure, there was great provocation. The cause is unpopular & justly so, and the fanatic orators openly recommended dissolution of the Union, abused Washington etc. Black & white men & women sat promiscuously together, & walked about arm in arm. Such are the excesses of enthusiasm. . . . Such is the hatred of abolition here, that many respectable persons, tho they do not defend these outrages, blame them faintly & excuse them."

One of the fundamental issues which split the abolitionists was the degree to which the movement should involve itself in party politics. At the annual meeting of the American Anti-Slavery Society in 1839 in New York City, this division became dramatically apparent. Lewis Tappan opened the session brandishing slave whips in one hand and in the other a bowie knife with "Death to Abolitionists" carved on the handle. The particular objects of his scorn were the New York merchants and manufacturers who connived at the slave system by buying and selling slave-produced cotton. Next under attack were those clergy who kept silent on the issue.

After Tappan's speech, the delegates considered the question of the right of women attending the convention to vote and approved their enfranchisement over the protests of Tappan and the more conservative delegates. The next issue was James Birney's motion to reject Garrison's doctrine of "no politics" and nonresistance. Birney had a special status among the abolitionists. With his upper-class origins and Princeton education, he was wary of Garrison's impetuousness and infatuation with moral purity. Far more pragmatic than the Bostonian, Birney was determined to politicize the movement and saw the formation of an antislavery party as the best hope for furthering the cause. In 1839, he and Gerrit Smith made an effort to wrest control of the American Anti-Slavery Society from Garrison on the grounds that he and the Bostonians were too narrow and dogmatic in their approach.

Defeated at the convention of 1839, the more moderate New York faction formed the American and Foreign Anti-Slavery Society and set about, with the help of such veterans of lost causes as Myron Holley and Alvan Stewart, who had helped to organize the Anti-Masonic

Party, to form a political party committed to the principle of abolition. The result was the hastily organized Liberty Party, which nominated Birney for president in the election of 1840. The fact that Birney got only 7,000 votes failed to discourage those abolitionists who advocated political action. William Seward increasingly distressed his friend Philip Hone by markedly gravitating in the direction of abolition, and Salmon Chase, the shrewd Ohio politician who counted himself in the antislavery ranks, declared, "we think it better to limit our *political action* by the *political power*, explicitly and avowedly, rather than run the risk of misconstruction by saying that we aim at *immediate and universal emancipation by political action.*"

Four years later, Birney ran again, aided by more seasoned politicians and a widespread campaign led by the New York faction of the movement; he polled 62,000 votes, too few to indicate that a single-issue antislavery party could ever take charge of the government. Lewis Tappan himself admitted "that the Liberty party, in order to accomplish much, must be a *reform* party" and "include other subjects of reformation. . . ."

Anxious to find figures with a broad popular appeal, the political abolitionists tried to prevail upon Seward, who had expressed strong antislavery sentiments as governor of New York, to run under their standard, but Seward, though sympathetic to the cause, was too shrewd a politician to accept.

George Templeton Strong was distressed, with Dana, Fisher, and Hone, to see abolition introduced into politics. It might, he thought, "play the devil with our institutions and . . . is at any rate a new force brought into the system, with an influence now almost inappreciable, but which may grow greater and greater till it brings the whole system into a state of discord and dissension, from which heaven preserve it!"

Meanwhile the champions of moral suasion, vindicated—at least in their own minds—by the general disarray of the cause in the political realm, carried on their indefatigable campaign, lecturing, writing, working for the betterment of free blacks, assisting slaves to escape, and, above all, praying. Two of the most notable recruits to the abolitionist cause were the Grimké sisters of South Carolina, Sarah and Angelina. They and their brother, Thomas Smith Grimké, all shared a moral rectitude and spirit of reform which they had absorbed from their stern father, a judge and a strong Unionist. While Thomas, a graduate of Yale, devoted himself primarily to educational reform, Angelina and Sarah moved to Philadelphia, joined the Society of

Friends and the ranks of abolitionist lecturers and writers. Sarah, born in 1792 and thirteen years older than Angelina, had been encouraged by her father to study mathematics, geography, world history, Greek, and natural science. One of her most vivid childhood recollections was of seeing a slave whipped. She had run sobbing from her house. "Slavery was a millstone about my neck," she later wrote, "and marred my comfort from the time I can remember myself." Every Sunday afternoon she taught Bible classes to the slave children and although there was a large fine for anyone "who shall teach any slave to write," Sarah taught her own slave girl to read and write. "The light was put out, the keyhole screened, and flat on our stomachs, before the fire, with the spelling book under our eyes, we defied the laws of South Carolina."

Sarah Grimké recalled that as a teenage girl she visited a neighbor known as a devout churchgoer and saw at her plantation a runaway mulatto woman who had been brutally whipped; she was wearing a heavy iron collar with three long prongs attached to it and one of her front teeth had been extracted as punishment. The slave "could lie in no position but on her back which was sore from scourging. . . . This slave, who was the seamstress of the family, was continually in her mistress' presence, sitting in her chamber to sew, or, engaged in other household work, with her lacerated and bleeding back, her mutilated mouth, and heavy iron collar, without, so far as appeared, exciting any feelings of compassion."

Some years later, returning to Charleston from a visit to Pennsylvania where she had met Lucretia Mott, the Quaker abolitionist, Sarah Grimké wrote, "it seemed as if the sight of their condition [the slaves] was unsupportable, it burst on my mind with renewed horror . . . deprived of the ability to modify their situation, I was as one in bonds looking at their sufferings I could not soothe or lessen. . . . Events had made the world look like a wilderness. I saw nothing in it but desolation and suffering. . . . I was tempted to commit some great crime, thinking I could repent and thus restore my lost sensibility."

Sarah, without a mother, raised Angelina in a spirit as bold and compassionate as her own. The younger sister had to go frequently to a workhouse in Charleston where slaves were sent to be punished by masters too squeamish to inflict punishment themselves. There slave women as well as men were whipped for a price. The worst torment was the treadmill, with broad steps which revolved rapidly. The slave's arms were secured to a beam above it. When a slave could no longer keep up with the revolving steps, he hung from his arms while the steps struck his back and legs and a "driver" lashed him with a heavy whip. "No one," Angelina wrote, "can imagine my feelings walking down that street. It seemed as though I was walking on the very confines of hell. This winter being obliged to pass by it to pay a visit to a friend, I suffered so much that I could not get over it for days and wondered how any real Christian could live near such a place."

In Philadelphia, the sisters were often subject to public ridicule for their uncompromising attitude about the mixture of the races. It was "the duty of abolitionists," Sarah wrote, "to identify themselves with these oppressed Americans by sitting with them in places of worship, by appearing with them in our streets, by giving them our countenance in steamboats and stages, by visiting them at their homes and encouraging them to visit us, receiving them as we do our white fellow citizens." Angelina was more militant than her sister. She joined the Philadelphia Female Anti-Slavery Society and in 1836 published her *Appeal to the Christian Women of the South,* which infuriated Southerners because it came from a *Southern* woman, a traitor to the cause.

Much of Grimké's essay was devoted to a detailed refutation of the argument that the Bible sanctioned slavery. After reviewing the history of human servitude, Angelina Grimké exhorted her Southern sisters: "Read . . . on the subject of slavery. Search the Scriptures daily, whether the things I have told you are true. . . . Pray over this subject. When you have entered into your closets, and shut the doors, then pray to your father, who seeth in secret, that he may open your eyes whether slavery is *sinful.* . . . Pray also for all your brethren and sisters who are laboring in this righteous cause of Emancipation in the Northern States, England and the world. . . . Speak on the subject. . . . Speak then to your relatives, your friends, your acquaintances on the subject of slavery. . . . Act on the subject. Some of you *own* slaves yourselves. If you believe slavery is *sinful,* set them at liberty."

Angelina Grimké was described by Wendell Phillips as possessing an "eloquence such as never then had been heard from a woman. Her own hard experience, the long, lonely, intellectual and moral struggle from which she came out to conquer, had ripened her power and her wondrous faculty for laying bare her own heart to reach the heart of others. . . ."

Our history surely offers us no more complex irony than that of the Grimké family. Among the brothers and sisters of Sarah and Angelina Grimké were Thomas, Frederick, and Henry. Thomas

Grimké, who graduated from Yale in 1807, opposed the position of his home state in the nullification controversy of 1832 and worked for peace, for educational reform, and for the temperance cause. Frederick, who also graduated from Yale, where he was Phi Beta Kappa and senior orator, moved from South Carolina to Ohio after the death of his father and there served on the supreme court of the state, resigning in 1842 to write his great treatise on the American political system entitled *The Nature and Tendency of Free Institutions*. A perceptive and scholarly book that can still be read with profit, it is little known, perhaps in part because in it Frederick Grimké supported the institution of slavery to which his sisters were so strongly opposed. Henry, a younger brother, was restless and unhappy, obsessed with suicide, with, in his brother's words, "a distaste and a disgust for life." After his early death, it was discovered that in addition to a white wife and children he had fathered three children by a family slave. In his will he left instructions that his "black" sons should be freed, but his son Montague, his executor, refused to do so on the grounds that they were part of a heavily encumbered estate. When Montague Grimké tried to sell his half-brother, Francis, the latter escaped and became the orderly of a Confederate officer. After the war Francis Grimké and his brother Archibald went to Lincoln University in Pennsylvania. When the Grimké sisters heard for the first time that they had black nephews, they visited the two young men, claimed them as their nephews, and helped with their education. Francis went on to Princeton Theological Seminary and became a minister in a black church in Washington, D.C. and a trustee of Howard University. Archibald Henry Grimké graduated from Harvard Law School, lived and practiced law in Boston, wrote biographies of William Lloyd Garrison and Charles Sumner, and was appointed consul to Santo Domingo by Grover Cleveland. The two brothers became allies of W. E. B. Du Bois and leaders in the fight for the rights of black people.

In 1837–38 Angelina and Sarah Grimké went on a nine-month speaking tour, during which they spoke at eighty meetings in sixty-seven towns and cities to an estimated forty thousand people. As the climax of the tour Angelina appeared before the Massachusetts State Legislature to speak in behalf of abolition, armed with the signatures of twenty thousand Massachusetts women protesting slavery. She appeared, she said, on their behalf, and to those who declared that social and political questions lay outside the sphere of women, she replied, "Are we aliens, because we are women? Are we bereft of citizenship because we are mothers, wives and daughters of a mighty people? Have women *no* country—*no* interests staked in public weal—no liabilities in common peril—no partnership in a nation's guilt and shame? . . . I hold, Mr. Chairman, that American women have to do with this subject, not only because it is moral and religious but because it is *political*, inasmuch as we are citizens of this republic and as such our honor, happiness and well-being are bound up in its politics, government and laws."

But it was slow work for women, winning the right to speak. When Abby Kelley was granted permission to speak at a meeting of the Connecticut Anti-Slavery Society in 1840, the chairman of the meeting resigned his post, declaring, "I will not sit in a chair where women bear rule. I vacate this chair. No woman shall speak or vote where I am moderator. I will not countenance such an outrage on decency. I will not consent to have women lord it over men in public assemblies. It is enough for women to rule at home. It is woman's business to take care of children in the nursery. She has no business to come into this meeting, and by speaking and voting lord it over men. Where women's enticing eloquence is heard men are incapable of right and efficient action. She beguiles and blinds men by her smiles and her bland and winning voice. . . . *I have had enough of women's control in the nursery. Now I am a man, I will not submit to it.*" There is, to be sure, a kind of poignance in the poor chairman's reactionary outburst. It must be said to his credit that his fear of feminine power was clear and unequivocal.

If New England and New York together constituted one axis of the antislavery movement (however much at times they were at swords' points with each other), the other axis was the state of Ohio. While it was certainly true that there was much antiabolitionist sentiment in the Mississippi Valley states, it was equally true that the abolitionist movement was deeply rooted there. It was almost as though, in their migration from New England and New York, the settlers of the Ohio country had been strengthened in their devotion to the principles of freedom.

Charles Grandison Finney had joined with the Tappans and a handful of Ohio philanthropists to establish the Lane Theological Seminary in Cincinnati as a stronghold of evangelical Christianity. Lyman Beecher, described as "the most prominent, popular and powerful preacher in our nation," was hired as president of the new institution. Theodore Weld, who had been a convert of Finney's, was the leader of the student body and president of his class. Shortly after

Beecher's arrival, Weld organized a series of debates on the slavery issue—what would be called today teach-ins. The debates lasted for nine consecutive nights and resulted in the conversion of most of the students and some of the faculty to immediate abolition. The students voted unanimously to seek to improve the black population of the city through "social intercourse according to character irrespective of color." Lyman Beecher was alarmed that the students would stir up "the slumbering demon of pro-slavery fanaticism. . . . You are taking just the course to defeat your own object and prevent yourself from doing good," he wrote Weld. "If you want to teach colored schools I can fill your pockets with money, but if you will visit in colored families and walk with them in the streets you will be overwhelmed." So spoke the voice of orthodox antislavery sentiment in Cincinnati. Beecher's apprehension was understandable. He himself was under heavy fire from the Ohio presbytery, who considered him a heretic in doctrinal matters. While Beecher, Professor Calvin Stowe, and other faculty members were in the East during a school recess on a money-raising expedition, the trustees of Lane, under considerable public pressure, announced the discontinuation of the student abolition society and prohibited further discussion by the students on slavery issues. The entire senior class of forty students thereupon withdrew from the seminary. Asa Mahan, a Southerner and a faculty member, also withdrew with the students. They were kept alive by Arthur Tappan, who contributed a thousand dollars to sustain the group in a boardinghouse on the outskirts of Cincinnati, which the community referred to as "the Anti-Slavery Patmos." The Reverend John Shipherd, a Congregational minister who had already established a religious community of New Englanders at Oberlin along the shores of Lake Erie and was busy trying to gain support for a college in the wilderness dedicated to the ideals of Christian austerity, came to Arthur Tappan in New York to solicit his support and prevailed on him to settle his Lane rebels at Oberlin. Tappan had relatives who held property in Ravenna, Ohio, only a few miles from Oberlin, and he was receptive to Shipherd's proposal. He and his brother stipulated that to the "life of simplicity," "special devotion to church and School, and . . . earnest labor in the missionary cause," already stated as the goals of the college, be added the clause "the broad ground of moral reform, in all its departments, should characterize the instruction in Oberlin."

The settlers at Oberlin balked at rumors that the college would have a strong abolitionist bent and Shipherd, to reassure them, wrote "to all the beloved in Jesus Christ. . . . I did not desire you to hang out an abolition flag or fill up with filthy stupid Negroes; but I did desire that you should say you would not reject promising youth who desired to prepare for usefulness. . . ." Opposition crumpled and the faculty and students soon put in an appearance. Arthur and Lewis Tappan, apparently not too favorably impressed by poor Shipherd, stipulated that Asa Mahan be president, and Charles Grandison Finney headed the department of theology. Black students were admitted from the first and, with continued and generous contributions from Arthur Tappan, the Oberlin Institute soon became a mecca for radical Christians from every state in the Union.

Of the young men who migrated to Oberlin, Theodore Weld was the most outstanding. He was thirty years old and had already converted the Tappans and a number of prominent figures in the abolition movement to the cause when he assisted in establishing Lane Seminary and enrolled in it as a student. After graduating from Oberlin, Weld traveled throughout the West, New England, and the Middle Atlantic states recruiting and organizing abolitionist chapters and holding training sessions. Handsome and eloquent, he had a quality that drew people to him irresistibly. Yet he was always modest and self-effacing, embarrassed by the adulation he inspired. In Philadelphia he held a training session attended by Angelina Grimké. There they met—the hero and the heroine of the abolitionist movement and, of course, fell in love.

The sisters had recently thrown themselves into the nascent women's rights movement with characteristic zeal, and Angelina was distressed when Weld tried to dissuade her from continuing to support the movement. In reply he assured the sisters that he was of one mind with them on the subject. "In a debating society when a boy, I took the ground that *sex* neither *qualified* nor *disqualified* for the discharge of any functions mental, moral, or spiritual"; he wrote "that there is no reason why *woman* should not make laws, administer justice, sit in the chair of state, plead at the bar or in the pulpit, if she had the qualifications. . . ." But to him the Grimkés were unique resources for the abolitionist movement. "Now *you two* are the ONLY FEMALES in the free states to combine all these facilities for antislavery effort: 1. Are southerners. 2. Have been slaveholders. 3. For a long time most widely known by the eminence of friends. 4. Speaking and writing power and practice. 5. Ultra Abolitionists. 6. Acquaintance with the whole subject, argumentative, historical, legal and biblical. Now what unspeakable responsibilities rest on *you*—on YOU! Oh my soul! that you but *felt* them as they are." They must leave the "lesser work" to others. "Let us all *first* wake up the nation to lift millions of slaves of both sexes from the dust, and turn them into MEN and then when we all have our hand in, it will be an easy matter to take millions of females from their knees and set them on their feet, or in other words transform them from *babies* into *women*."

John Greenleaf Whittier had written in a similar vein, and the sisters replied very firmly to their "Brethren beloved in the Lord." What was at issue in their view was their "right" to labor in the cause and that right rested on their common humanity with men. It did not rest on Quakerism, "but on the only firm basis of human rights, the Bible. . . . Antislavery men are trying hard to separate what God hath joined together. I fairly believe," Angelina Grimké wrote, "that so far from keeping moral reformations entirely distinct that no such attempt can ever be successful. They are bound together in a circle like the sciences; they blend with each other like the colors of the rainbow; they are parts only of our glorious whole and that whole is Christianity, pure *practical* Christianity." Lay Christians, men and women alike, must go out and "declare the *whole* counsel of God to the people. The whole Church Government must come down, the clergy stand in the way of reform, and I do not know but what this stumbling block too must be removed *before* slavery can be abolished, for the system is supported by *them*." It is hardly surprising that Theodore Weld's reply was somewhat defensive and cautionary.

As the date set for her wedding to Weld approached, Angelina was beset by anxiety over whether she was guilty of placing her own personal happiness ahead of the "cause." In a touching exchange of letters, she expressed her doubts to her fiancé, who replied: "We marry, Angelina, not *merely* nor *mainly* nor *at all comparatively* TO ENJOY, but together to do and dare, together to toil and testify and suffer . . . to keep ourselves and each other unspotted from the world, to live a life of faith . . . rejoicing always to bear one another's burden. . . ."

They were married soon after Angelina's triumphant appearance before the Massachusetts legislature to plead the cause of abolition. A black baker made the wedding cake, using only "free sugar." There was no formal exchange of vows but "only such words as the Lord gave them at the moment." A black minister prayed and then a white minister. Two days later Angelina gave her last public speech on the subject of abolition at the antislavery convention in Philadelphia. Outside the hall an angry mob tried to howl her down. "Men, brethren and fathers—mothers, daughters and sisters, what came ye out for to see? A reed shaken in the wind? Is it curiosity merely or a deep sympathy with the perishing slave, that has brought this large audience together?"

With constant reference to the raging mob who interrupted her speech by throwing rocks through the windows of the building, she persevered. "As a Southerner I feel that it is my duty to stand up here tonight and bear testimony against slavery. I have seen it—I have seen it. I know its horrors that can never be described. I was brought up under its wing: I witnessed for many years its demoralizing influences, and its destructiveness to human happiness." When she could no longer "endure to hear the wailing of the slave" she had fled to the land of Penn. Here "the people were kind and hospitable, but the slave had no place in their thoughts." She was determined to "lift up my voice like a trumpet, and show this people their transgression, their sin of omission towards the slave, and what they can do towards affecting Southern mind, and overthrowing Southern opposition. . . . There is nothing to be feared from those who would stop our mouths but they themselves fear and tremble. . . . A few years ago, and the South felt secure, and with a contemptuous sneer asked, 'Who are the abolitionists? The abolitionists are nothing. . . .' (Mob again disturbed the meeting.) We often hear the question asked, 'What shall we do?' Here is an opportunity for doing something now. Every man and every woman present may do something by showing that we fear not a mob, and in the midst of its threatening and revilings, by opening our mouths for the dumb and pleading the cause of those who are ready to perish."

The realm of the antislavery petition was the special realm of women abolitionists. As Sarah Lewis, president of the Women's Anti-Slavery Society, put it, "It is our only means of direct political action. It is not our right to fill the offices of government, or to assist in the election of those who shall fill them. We do not enact or enforce the laws of the land. The only direct influence we can exert upon our Legislatures, is by protest and petitions. Shall we not then be greatly delinquent if we neglect these? . . . Slavery is annually increasing the number of its wretched victims. . . . Ought not the number of our petitions, this year, testify that we remember this mournful fact? Our beloved country is annually increasing her guilt and danger. . . . We know, dear sisters, that this is weary work. . . . We know how painful it is to endure the scornful gaze, or rude repulses of strangers, as journeying from house to house to solicit their sympathy for the crushed and broken-hearted slave, we see them turn away in hot displeasure or cold indifference." The petitioners should be supported in such moments by the knowledge that the principal hope of the slave for freedom lay in the knowledge that he had "friends in the far North, who are striving to rescue him. . . ."

So the petitions rolled in, filled chests and, finally, rooms, were presented and rebuffed, and with each rebuff some small increment of antislavery sentiment was added to the growing realization that slavery was, above all, a moral affliction, a national "sin."

Poets and newspaper editors aided the cause. John Greenleaf Whittier was coadjutor of Weld and Garrison. Under the title *Poems Written During the Progress of the Abolition Question in the United States Between the Years 1830 and 1838*, Whittier published his antislavery poems, the most famous of which was "The Hunters of Men":

> Oh! goodly and grand is our hunting to see,
> In this "land of the brave and this home of the free."
> Priest, warrior, and statesman, from Georgia to Maine,
> All mounting the saddle—all grasping the rein—
> Right merrily hunting the black man, whose sin
> Is the curl of his hair and the hue of his skin!

In addition to his poems, many of which were published in the *Liberator* and other antislavery journals, Whittier was himself the editor of a succession of journals and newspapers all of which had a strong antislavery bias.

William Cullen Bryant, the editor of a Jacksonian paper, the *New York Evening Post*, and the dean of American poets of nature, was another champion of the antislavery cause. Increasingly, his considerable editorial influence was felt on the side of the abolitionists.

Though Emerson came to be a strong supporter of the cause of antislavery, he did not lend it his poetic talents. Garrison's fierce partisanship put off the spokesman of transcendentalism. But Henry Wadsworth Longfellow, who would share with Whittier and Bryant the poetic laurels of the century, was a loyal abolitionist. "The Slave's Dream" was a romantic evocation of the themes of death and slavery, and in "The Warning," Longfellow wrote of slavery as a modern Samson:

> The poor blind slave, the scoff and jest of all,
> Expired, and thousands perished in the fall!
> There is a poor, blind Samson in this land,
> Shorn of his strength and bound in bonds of steel,
> Who may, in some grim revel, raise his hand,
> And shake the vast pillars of this Commonweal,
> Till the vast Temple of our liberties
> A shapeless mass of wreck and rubbish lies.

James Russell Lowell had graduated from Harvard in the class of 1838 and from Harvard Law School two years later. He belonged to that fortunate class of "independent" gentlemen who, like Sidney George Fisher and George Templeton Strong, had sufficient income from family investments to indulge in the literary life. Even before his marriage to an ardent abolitionist, he had written "Stanzas on Freedom," proclaiming:

> Men! whose boast it is that ye
> Come of fathers brave and free,
> If there breathe on earth a slave,
> Are ye truly free and brave?
> If ye do not feel the chain,
> When it works a brother's pain,
> Are ye not base slaves indeed,
> Slaves unworthy to be freed?
> . . . .
> They are slaves who fear to speak
> For the fallen and the weak;
> They are slaves who will not choose
> Hatred, scoffing and abuse,
> Rather than in silence shrink
> From the truth they needs must think;
> They are slaves who dare not be
> In the right with two or three.

Two years later, Lowell wrote "The Present Crisis," a bold call to his countrymen to rally to the cause of freedom:

For mankind are one in spirit, and an instinct bears along,
Round the earth's electric circle, the swift flash of right or wrong;
Whether conscious or unconscious, yet Humanity's vast frame
Through its ocean-sundered fibres feels the gush of joy or shame;—
In the gain or loss of one race all the rest have equal claim.
. . . .
New occasions teach new duties; Time makes ancient good uncouth;
They must upward still, and onward, who would keep abreast of Truth;

Lo, before us gleam her camp-fires; we ourselves must Pilgrims be,
Launch our Mayflower, and steer boldly through the desperate winter
sea. . . .

Lectures, poems, articles, and essays in the cause of abolition,
important as they were, would have weighed little without the
endlessly recurring drama of escaped slaves. The Southerner's perpetually reiterated defense of slavery was that the slaves themselves
accepted their status and were, in the main, carefree, happy creatures,
devoted to their kindly masters and mistresses. Every black man or
woman who escaped gave the lie to the story of the contented slave,
and gave it in a peculiarly striking fashion by enduring great hardship
and danger, including cruel punishment and even mutilation if caught
and returned to his/her master. The so-called Underground Railroad,
one of the most remarkable clandestine operations in all history, grew
up gradually to assist fugitive slaves to reach freedom. Each year, as
the moral outrage over slavery grew in the North, new recruits were
added until the Railroad had thousands of conductors and hundreds
of escape routes that reached from the Pennsylvania and the Ohio
borders to Canada.

Certain names emerged from that valiant band to become symbols
of the enterprise. Levi Coffin was a North Carolina Quaker who moved
to Newport, Indiana, where he became a prosperous businessman,
president of the town bank, and one of the most active conductors on
the road—so much so, indeed, that he became known as "the President
of the Underground Railroad." He turned his business talents to
improving the organization of the escape routes. His home in Newport
became a kind of switching yard for refugees coming up from the
South as well as those moving east and west seeking refuge in New
York state or Canada. One night seventeen runaway slaves were
brought to his home in two wagonloads by agents. They had hardly
been fed and sent on their way before word reached Coffin that fifteen
Kentucky slave hunters were on their track. Coffin arranged for the
fugitives to be scattered across a number of tracks and the slave
hunters, after three or four fruitless days, gave up and recrossed the
Ohio.

Thomas Garrett was another almost legendary hero of the Underground Railroad. Garrett, a Pennsylvania Quaker, established himself
as a shoe merchant in Wilmington, Delaware, a crucial spot on the
route north for slaves escaping from Virginia and Maryland. When he

was only twenty-four, he pursued men who had kidnapped a black servant of his mother and rescued her. It seemed to him that the Lord spoke to him, in the midst of his pursuit, telling him that his lifelong calling was to work to free the slaves. Although Delaware was a slave state, for more than twenty years Garrett passed slaves along the Railroad. Under constant surveillance, he managed, nonetheless, to assist in the escape of almost three thousand slaves. Maryland slaveholders offered a reward of $10,000 for him, dead or alive, and there were so many threats against his life that free blacks often maintained a night guard around his house. Like all good conductors, Garrett was an excellent actor. On several occasions, he dressed female fugitives in his wife's clothes and bonnets and drove them past slave hunters and their agents.

To avoid the danger of blacks being employed as spies, each fugitive slave had to deliver a note from the conductor at the previous station to the conductor of the next. Needless to say, the "trains" on the Underground Railroad ran irregularly. A light tap on a door or window any hour of the night or early morning might announce the arrival of a new "shipment of black wool."

Finally, in 1848, Garrett was arrested and brought to trial in Newcastle, Delaware, along with John Hunn, for aiding in the escape of two slave children. The verdict of guilty was accompanied by a judgment that forced Garrett to sell his home and business. He was a tall, dignified man with white hair, then sixty years old, and when the sentence was pronounced he rose and said, "Judge, now that thou hast relieved me of what little I possessed, I will go home and put another story on my house. I want room to accommodate more of God's poor." Garrett then turned and gave an hour-long oration to the courtroom on the sin of slavery. When he had finished a juror came up to him, took his hand, and asked, "Give me your forgiveness, and let me be your friend." "Freely given," Garrett said, "if thee ceases to be an advocate of the iniquitous system of slavery."

Garrett's friends bought his property at auction and returned it to him. He was given a bank loan and built the extra story on his house. The story of his trial was printed in every abolitionist paper and money was sent from as far away as England to help him to carry on his work. Until the end of the Civil War, Thomas Garrett continued to give shelter to fugitive slaves and extended his philanthropic activities to include the cause of women's rights and of white working men and women.

Daniel Drayton was a sea captain who had sailed in ships carrying slaves from Africa. One night when his boat was tied up to a Washington wharf a black man came aboard and began to query him on his views about slavery. Finally, the black man came to the point. A slave woman and her five children were trying to escape to join her husband, a free black. The black man asked Drayton to help them escape. Drayton, who had never considered himself an abolitionist or anything more than mildly antislavery in his feelings, agreed. The woman and her husband were reunited in Philadelphia and soon Drayton got a message asking him to help two more families. Drayton thus found himself drawn into the business of helping blacks to escape. His waterborne branch of the Underground Railroad ran down the Chesapeake, around Cape Charles, and up the Delaware to Philadelphia. On his second trip he carried seventy-eight slaves from Washington. But a hack driver had betrayed the ship and it was overtaken, captured, and brought back to Washington. There the city was in a turmoil, and a mob attacked and ransacked the office of the *National Era,* an antislavery paper.

Bail for Drayton, for the owner of the ship, and the mate, was set at $228,000. Horace Mann, William Seward, and Salmon Chase defended the three men, but Drayton was convicted and was fined $10,000.

In 1837 Calvin Fairbank, a graduate of Oberlin and an ordained Presbyterian minister, who had come under the influence of Theodore Weld, started down the Ohio River in charge of a raft of lumber. At Wheeling, Virginia, he had the intoxicating experience of helping a slave escape across the river. When he reached Kentucky a slave woman enlisted his help in the escape of her seven children whom he ferried across the river. Most railroad "conductors" assisted slaves to escape by maintaining "stations," i.e., their homes and barns along well-established escape routes, but Fairbank and a few daring whites ventured into Southern territory to encourage slaves to flee their masters and to act as guides to get them to free territory. Fairbank became famous for his mastery of disguises for both himself and his runaways. He often dressed men in women's clothing and vice versa to throw off pursuers.

A slave named Lewis Hayden, who appealed to Fairbank, was owned by one master while his wife and child belonged to another. Fairbank rented a carriage and recruited a Miss Webster to ride with him while they picked up Hayden, his wife and child and drove away with them as though they were a white slaveholding couple out for a casual ride with their slaves. They crossed the Ohio River on a ferry and drove to the nearest station of the Underground in Hopkins, Ohio, and started their charges north. When they returned to Lexington they were arrested and charged with slave stealing, and Fairbank was sentenced to five years in the state prison.

A Washington newspaper in 1839 carried an angry editorial on the Underground Railroad. "The abolition incendiaries are undermining, not only our domestic institutions, but the very foundations of our capital. Our citizens will recollect that the boy, Jim, who was arrested while lurking about the Capitol in August, would disclose nothing until he was subject to torture by screwing his fingers in a blacksmith's vise, when he acknowleged that he was to have been sent North by railroads; was to have started from near the place where he stood when discovered by the patrol. He refused to tell who was to aid him—said he did not know—and most likely he did not know. Nothing more could be got from him until they gave the screw another turn, when he said, '*the railroad went underground all the way to Boston.*'"

A tobacco planter named Colonel Hardy in the District of Columbia had lost five slaves, the paper reported, and although "they were pursued by an excellent slave catcher," they disappeared. The first word of their whereabouts was a letter in an abolitionist paper, marked and sent to the slaves' owners: "Arrived this morning by our fast line three men and two women. They were claimed as slaves by Colonel Hardy . . . but became dissatisfied with the Colonel's ways and left the old fellow's premises last Sunday evening, arriving at our station by the quickest passage on record."

The experience of Colonel Hardy's slaves was a kind of textbook study of the way the Underground Railroad functioned. Jo Norton, one of the fugitives, told the story of the escape to a reporter for an abolitionist journal. Norton had been determined for some time to try to escape north with his wife and child. One night Norton met on a dark road a man whom he identified by his voice as a Northerner. Several weeks later he met the man again and told him of his desire to escape and was informed of the facilities of the Underground Railroad. He was told to return in three weeks to a certain spot late at night. At the rendezvous he met his "conductor" and four other slaves—two men and two women—of Colonel Hardy's, all terrified at the prospect of going under the ground. They were to follow the road some thirty miles in the direction of the north star until it came to a railroad and walk along the tracks until they encountered a man. If he said "Ben," they were to accompany him. They found Ben just as dawn was breaking, and he hid them in bundles of cornstalks. That night someone appeared and led the two women to a road where a carriage waited to take them to Baltimore, where they were hidden. The men were fed by Ben, a free black, and remained concealed in his corncrib. Meanwhile the item in the abolitionist journal describing their arrival in Albany was printed and sent to Colonel Hardy, who called off his slave hunters on the assumption that their quarry was out of reach. Only then did the flight continue. In Baltimore the fugitives were supplied with pocket money and told to behave naturally, mingling with the crowds and keeping track of a thirteen-year-old black boy who was to act as their guide. The boy led them to the edge of the city just at nightfall and from there they traveled by night, staying during the daytime at the homes of Quakers along the route. From Philadelphia they went by fishing boat to Bordentown, New Jersey, and from there on a train to New York, the women dressed in handsome clothes with veils to conceal their faces and riding first class, the men hidden in the baggage car. Jo Norton returned later to lead his wife and child to freedom.

When the abolition movement fell on hard times in the 1840s, with money difficult to come by and memberships in the antislavery societies declining, the stories of slave escapes, published and widely read, helped to keep the issue alive. It was in these years that what was undoubtedly the most famous escape of all took place. A Kentucky slave named Eliza, hearing that her master planned to sell her, took her youngest child and headed for the Ohio in the middle of winter. When at dawn she reached the river, which at that time of year was often frozen over, she found that it was filled with ice floes. She stayed with a white couple in their nearby house during the day hoping that the river might freeze over during the day. At night when she returned to try to cross, she saw that the floes were still loose. As she was about to return to the house she saw slave hunters ride into town. She decided to risk the river and, wrapping her baby in a shawl, she began to leap from one ice floe to the next. In this way, drenched and half-frozen, she made her way across the river and was guided to the house of the Rankins. From there she was passed along the Underground Railroad to Levi Coffin's and he gave her the name of Harris. At Sandusky she cut her hair and attired herself in man's clothes. Once in Canada, Eliza Harris decided to go back for her other five children. She came back on a Sunday in June, gathered up her brood, and with two hundred pounds of household goods distributed between them, she headed back for the river where John Rankin and his sons were waiting with a boat on the other side. Close on the heels of Eliza and her children came the slave hunters and their hounds. Eliza and the children hid in the reeds by the riverbank where the bloodhounds could not pick up their scent. One of the Rankin sons, dressed as a woman, crossed the river in a rowboat and decoyed the hunters away while another, under the cover of darkness, rowed over and picked up the runaways. For two weeks Eliza and her children stayed with the Rankins, and then they were hidden in a wagon, covered with sacks of flour, and taken on to the next station, and so, by stages, to Canada. Of Eliza, John Rankin said, "She was a heroic woman, if ever one lived." She was immortalized by Harriet Beecher Stowe, in whose *Uncle Tom's Cabin* she is forever fleeing across the broken ice.

One of the most famous escapes was that of William and Ellen Crafts, who fled from Georgia in 1848. Light-skinned Ellen Crafts posed as a silent young white male slave owner, while her dark-skinned husband acted the part of his slave. The story of their journey north was widely recounted in newspapers and antislavery journals.

The Southerners meanwhile complained of losing hundreds of thousands of dollars' worth of their property every year. A Congressman from Maryland, which through its proximity to free states was especially vulnerable, stated that the loss amounted to $80,000 a year, which might be calculated to represent eighty to a hundred slaves. The estimate was that Virginia had losses "too heavy to be endured . . . increasing year by year" and already in excess of $100,000. South Carolina claimed to lose $200,000 a year from runaways and it was said that in the District of Columbia the number of slaves had declined in ten years from 4,694 to 650 due to the Underground Railroad and felonious abductions. Southerners estimated that by 1850 thirty thousand escaped slaves with a value of $15,000,000 were living in the North.

Levi Coffin mounted a campaign to boycott cotton grown on slave plantations. To this end he took numerous trips through the South, searching out small farmers—many of them Quakers—who raised cotton but owned no slaves, and contracting with them to buy their cotton for sale in the North as "free cotton." All such moves fanned the paranoia of the South. Even slaves who had escaped and been recaptured were considered a menace. The South Carolina legislature passed a law forbidding slaves who had been north of the Potomac River, to the West Indies, or to Mexico from being brought into the state. They were presumed to be tainted by aspirations of freedom. The governor of North Carolina declared that the workers of a country, whether "*bleached or unbleached*," were a threat to all legitimate authority and predicted that the free workers of the North would have to be enslaved in order to prevent them from overturning the republic. Six Southern states passed resolutions calling on their sister states in the North to pass legislation outlawing the abolitionists. When Amos Dresser, a Southerner and one of the Lane seminarians who had finished up his education at Oberlin, went to Tennessee to sell Bibles and do some covert recruiting to the abolitionist cause, he was seized, and when no law could be found under which to prosecute him, the local Vigilance Committee condemned him to be given twenty lashes at midnight in the public square before several thousand attentive watchers, including a number of slaves. Aaron Kitchell, a Northern schoolteacher in Georgia, was tarred and feathered and ridden out of town on a rail. Mobs killed three white men in South Carolina and three in Georgia for "association with Negroes." In Charleston, a mob that included a number of the most prominent citizens of the town and a sprinkling of clergy broke into the post office and seized and burned antislavery literature. The clergy emphasized their sympathy with the forces of disorder by closing the Sunday schools attended by free blacks.

In the so-called Prigg case of 1842, a slave hunter, Edward Prigg, captured a runaway named Margaret Morgan in Pennsylvania without obtaining a warrant. He was arrested, charged with kidnapping, and convicted. When he appealed to the Supreme Court that body ruled that while state laws could not prevent a master from recapturing an escaped slave, state authorities were not required to assist in such captures. The result was a rash of what were called "personal liberty laws" passed by various states, prohibiting such assistance by state authorities and thereby vastly complicating the slave hunter's task.

Cases that made a particular impact on public opinion were those in which a fugitive slave had lived for years in the North and established himself or herself as an honest and reliable citizen. Such a case was that of George Latimer, a resident of Boston, who was captured by a slave hunter. When a lawyer, acting for Latimer, tried to secure his freedom on a writ of *habeas corpus* to the Massachusetts

Supreme Court, it was refused. A protest meeting was called in Faneuil Hall and four thousand people crowded into its historic chambers. Charles Lenox Remond, a free black, who was one of the most popular abolition orators, and Frederick Douglass were shouted down by the throng that turned out to contain a pro-slavery majority, but Wendell Phillips managed to gain their attention long enough to declare: "We presume that the Bible outweighs the statute books. When I look upon these crowded thousands and see them trample on their consciences and the rights of their fellow men at the bidding of a piece of parchment, I say, my curse be on the Constitution of the United States." That was highly subversive doctrine to many who heard Phillips's words, but others were inspired to raise the money to buy Latimer's freedom.

In Ohio, a farmer named John Van Zandt, although defended by Salmon Chase, was convicted of giving a ride in his wagon to nine blacks. He was fined $1,200, which in effect bankrupted him but provided a new hero for the abolitionist cause. Another was Jonathan Walker, who had gone to Florida to help to build a railroad. When the railroad was completed, Walker tried to help seven slaves to escape to the Bahamas in a small boat. They were intercepted and brought back to Pensacola. Walker was chained in prison for fifteen days, placed in a pillory and pelted with eggs, and then, by order of the court, had the letters SS, for "slave stealer," branded on his hand. Freed through money raised by Northern abolitionists, Walker was soon featured at antislavery meetings.

Another technique developed by the abolitionists was that of flooding the country with antislavery pamphlets. Tens of thousands were printed on abolitionist presses and sent through the mails to Congressmen and state legislators, to ministers with requests to distribute them to the members of their congregations, to schools, to editors and lawyers. They were left on steamboats and railroad cars and in hotels and saloons. Millions were smuggled into the South, although in several states it was a capital offense to own or be apprehended reading an abolitionist document.

The abolitionists suffered a setback when Amos Kendall, the postmaster general, authorized postal officers to remove abolitionist literature from the mails in the slaveholding states, on the grounds that "we owe an obligation to the laws, but a higher one to the community in which we live, and if the former be perverted to destroy the latter, it is patriotism to disregard them." This seemed to Philip Hone to be little better than open defiance of the law by one of the highest government officials. It was, he wrote, Lynch Law or "Jackson's Law." In Maryland the penalty for circulating such literature was ten to twenty years in jail.

Among the flood of antislavery books and pamphlets that poured from the presses three deserve special mention. Theodore Weld's *American Slavery as It Is*, published in 1839, was one of the inspirations for *Uncle Tom's Cabin*. Weld's book contained both a plan for action against slavery and a compendium of horror stories, most of them culled from Southern newspapers. He called on all those who viewed slavery as a crime to sacrifice "our persons, our interests," and "our reputations" if necessary to bring about "the triumph of justice, liberty, and humanity, or perish untimely as martyrs in this great, benevolent, and holy cause."

The work of Richard Hildreth had a particular weight because, next to George Bancroft, Hildreth was the nation's most respected writer of American history. His book, published fifteen years after Weld's, was entitled *Despotism in America, an Inquiry into the Nature, Results and Legal Basis of the Slave-Holding System*. Hildreth's approach was both historical and sociological. He described the origins of the slave system and its social and economic consequences. He gave an especially perceptive picture of the "small planter, who can neither read or write" but has managed to purchase a few slaves. He was often "the most mild and indulgent master," who "works with his slaves in the field . . . converses with them and consults them." If any of his slaves "exhibits any peculiar shrewdness or good judgment, the master perceives it, and avails himself of it; and such a slave often becomes his owner's chief confidant and adviser."

Hildreth was most effective in describing the psychological effects of slavery upon the masters and mistresses and the constant fear of slave insurrections which was such a conspicuous fact of Southern life. "That terror," he wrote, "levels all distinction between slaves and freemen, and so long as it lasts, no man's person is secure." The great plantation owner's anxiety about a slave uprising had its counterpart in the anxiety of the small slave owner with only two or three slaves that a substantial part of his property might run away. Finally, Hildreth described at length the economic inferiority to which the South was condemned by the institution of slavery. The picture that emerged from Hildreth's work was one which we have emphasized in this work before—the perpetual and corrosive sense of anxiety and insecurity, mounting at times to outright terror, that was the inevitable by-product of the system and which, in time, drove the South into a kind of collective insanity.

The most sensational assault on the slave system was undoubtedly that of a North Carolinian, Hinton Helper, who as an up-country farmer of modest means, deplored the economic consequences of slavery in a book entitled *The Impending Crisis*. Hinton's unpardonable crime was that he as a Southerner attacked the system of slavery. Southerners had long ago dismissed the moral arguments against slavery but Helper's economic statistics were peculiarly disconcerting to defenders of the system, and his rhetoric was designed to rally the poor whites and nonslaveholders of the South against the slaveholders, a tactic of whose dangers the owners of slaves were only too well aware. "Now, chevaliers of the lash, and worshippers of slavery," Helper wrote, "considering how your villainous institution has retarded the development of our commercial and manufacturing interests, how it has stifled the aspirations of inventive genius; and above all, how it has barred from us the heaven-born sweets of literature and religion," should not the nonslaveholders demand compensation? By his calculation, the sum due the nonslaveholders, as the principal victims of the system, was roughly six billion dollars. "Do you," he asked the slaveholders, "aspire to become the victims of white non slave-holders' vengeance by day, and of barbarous massacre by the negroes at night? Would you be instrumental in bringing upon yourselves, your wives, and our children, a fate too horrible to contemplate. . . . Sirs, you must emancipate them—speedily emancipate them, or we will emancipate them for you. . . . Slavery has polluted and impoverished our lands; freedom will restore them to their virgin purity." Helper then went on to demonstrate that the South would actually profit economically from emancipation and at the end he proposed an eleven-point program to bring about abolition including (point 5) "No Recognition of Pro-Slavery Men, except as Ruffians, Outlaws, and Criminals."

Under the circumstances it is perhaps not surprising that the report that Thaddeus Stevens, the principal candidate for speaker of the House, had read and endorsed Helper's *The Impending Crisis* created one in the chambers of Congress. A Missouri member introduced a resolution declaring that no one who approved of Helper's book was fit to be speaker, and in the feverish debate that followed Stevens was physically threatened by a group of Southern representatives who crowded around him on the floor of the House.

Helper's book is a fascinating document. The combination of bitter accusation and statistical analysis is startling, as is the author's insistence that he spoke for the nonslaveholders of the South. Actually the book, by tracing such a dramatic disparity of interest between the two classes, serves to raise, in a most insistent form, the question of why the nonslaveholders of the South identified themselves, for the most part, with the slaveholders and why the movement that Helper called for failed to materialize.

The most famous proslavery book was undoubtedly George Fitzhugh's *Cannibals All!* "We are all, North and South, engaged in the White Slave Trade," Fitzhugh wrote, "and he who succeeds best, is esteemed most respectable. It is far more cruel than the Black Slave Trade, because it exacts more of its slaves, and neither protects or governs them. We boast, that it exacts more, when we say, 'that the *profits* made from employing free labor are greater than those from slave labor.'" The capitalist thus deprives the free laborer of a substantial part of the fruits of his skill. The slave owner, on the other hand, "allows the slave to retain a larger share of the results of his own labor, than do the employers of free labor." The free laborer was left to take care of himself and his family "out of the pittance which . . . capital have allowed him to retain. When the day's labor is ended, he is free, but is overburdened with the cares of family and household which makes his freedom an empty and delusive mockery." The labor practices of the North were, Fitzhugh charged, "moral Cannibalism," the greedy devouring the "free" laborer's substance. Indeed, "all good and respectable people are 'Cannibals all,' who do not labor, or who are successfully trying to live without labor, on the unrequited labor of other people." Society was thus divided into four classes: "The rich, or independent respectable people, who live well and labor not at all; the professional and skillful respectable people who do a little light work, for enormous wages; the poor hard-working people, who support everybody, and starve themselves; and the poor thieves, swindlers sturdy beggars, who live like gentlemen, without labor, on the labor of other people." To Fitzhugh all those who lived on their "capital," the income from the money they had earned rather than on the money itself, were cannibals, whether the labor was white or black. The respectable way of living in the United States was "to make other people work for you, and to pay them nothing for doing so—and to have no concern about them after their work is done. . . . You, my virtuous, respectable reader, exact three thousand dollars per annum from white labor (for your income is the product of white labor) and make not one cent of return in any form. You retain your capital, and never labor, yet live in luxury on the labor of others!"

Such arguments had about them the sting of truth, but Fitzhugh was not content to rest there; he felt obliged to declare that "The negro slaves of the South are the happiest, and, in some sense, the freest people in the world. . . . Free laborers have not a thousandth part of the rights and liberties of negro slaves." Fitzhugh, like Orestes Brownson before him, had surely placed his finger on a terrible flaw in the system of industrial capitalism—its exploitation of labor and its indifference to the laborer's fate—but he vastly diminished the trenchancy of his argument by employing it for the defense of the slave system. In doing so Fitzhugh demonstrated what was perhaps the major reason that the Northern spokesmen for the working man never succeeded in developing an adequate theoretical rationale for a full-fledged labor "movement." To all attacks on the exploitation of the free laborer, the apologists for Northern industrialism replied by contrasting free labor with slave labor. Burdened by the defense of slavery, Fitzhugh's argument fell to the ground, far short of its legitimate target.

In the 1840s, with the decision of the more conservative abolitionists like the Tappans and James Birney to venture into politics, the emphasis shifted from the moral exhortation of the 1830s to political engagement. Garrison was too fervent and mercurial to maintain the leadership of the movement which he, more than any other man, had started. By eschewing politics he ensured his own decline. Unrealistic and uncompromising, viewing politics as the devil's work, denouncing the churches and flaying the Constitution as "a covenant with death and an agreement with Hell," he nonetheless continued to exercise a remarkable influence within the abolition movement. Perhaps the greatest flaw in his thinking was his willingness to cut the North free of the South. The Union that Webster spoke for meant little to Garrison as long as it included slaves. But if the Union were to be dissolved and the South turned out or allowed to go in peace, who would free the slaves? Garrison, elevating his own rectitude into a false God, seemed willing to abandon the slave to his master rather than be contaminated by the system he abhorred.

When Garrison came to an antislavery convention in New York, James Gordon Bennett, editor of the *New York Herald*, called on "the merchants, men of business, and men of property to frown down on the meetings of these mad people, if they would save themselves." "Look at the blacks and white brethren and sisters, fraternizing, slobbering over each other, singing, praying, blaspheming and cursing the Constitution of our glorious Union," he wrote. The final breech between Garrison and those abolitionists who were committed to preserving the Union came in 1855 when Garrison, speaking in New York, declared: "The issue is this: God Almighty has made it impossible from the beginning, for liberty and slavery to mingle together, or a union to be founded between abolitionists and slaveholders—between those who oppress and those who are oppressed. *This Union is a lie; the American Union is a sham, an imposture, a covenant with death, an agreement with hell, and it is our business to call for a dissolution. . . . I say, let us cease striking hands with thieves and adulterers,* and give up to the winds the rallying cry, 'No union with slaveholders, socially or religiously, and up with the flag of Disunion.'"

Garrison had accomplishments of crucial importance to his credit. He had led the fight to make slavery a moral rather than a political issue; to plant and nourish the seed of the idea that it was the blackest kind of sin to hold another human being in perpetual bondage—and that every American, whether a slaveholder or not, shared in that sin. That was the Gordian knot. In order that the slave might ever be free that knot must be cut. All the immediatists who had fallen under his spell had preached that doctrine. The issue of slavery could no longer be postponed or dismissed as a Southern problem. Historians who have been disposed to be critical of Garrison for his fanaticism and rigidity have missed the point. The first voice to speak out in unmistakable accents against a social injustice that the rest of society has come to take largely for granted *must* speak violently and intemperately. He has to shatter carefully constructed defenses, penetrate ears tuned out to his message. Shock and trauma are his necessary and inevitable weapons. In the minds of most Americans, slavery had become, by the 1820s, primarily a political problem to be "solved" or at least contained by such measures as the Compromise of 1820, which so horrified Jefferson. Garrison made it transcendently a moral issue for what proved to be a sufficient number of Americans. It was perhaps inevitable that it should remain exclusively a moral issue for him; that he remained, like some unconquerable landmark, to hold to the moral pole while the issue was repoliticized, but this time bearing the ineradicable stamp of its ultimately moral character. What

Garrison and his coadjutors had accomplished was to prevent the issue of slavery from ever becoming *simply* a political issue. Most of those who parted from him on doctrinal or strategic ground continued to love him for his irrepressible hopefulness and his simple trust in the final triumph of God's justice.

An ally of Garrison's and a frequent critic, Lydia Maria Child, made one of the best evaluations of the abolitionist leader when she called him "a disinterested, intelligent, and remarkably pure-minded man, whose only fault is that he cannot be moderate on a subject which it is exceedingly difficult for an honest mind to examine with calmness. Many who highly respect his character and motives, regret his tendency to use wholesale and unqualified expressions; but it is something to have the truth told, even if it be not in the mildest way. Where an evil is powerfully supported by the self-interest and prejudice of the community, none but an ardent individual will venture to meddle with it."

Garrison himself seemed never to feel discouragement. He wrote to a friend at the nadir of the movement, "Apparently the slaveholding power has never been so strong—has never held such complete mastery over the whole country—as at the present time; and yet never has it in reality been so weak, never has it had so many uncompromising assailants, never has it been so filled with doubt and consternation, never has it been so near the downfall as at this moment."

Edmund Quincy, Harvard graduate, son of Josiah, the great reform mayor of Boston, and pioneer in the antislavery ranks, wrote a friend, "Garrison is in good spirits as he always is, and as we all have a trick of being." Elizabeth Cabot Follen, whose German husband, Charles, had been fired from Harvard for his proabolition sentiments, told Quincy that "when she wants to be put in spirits, she goes among the abolitionists, and there she is sure to find cheerfulness, wit, humor and fun. And who should be cheerful and merry in this country but the abolitionists?" Quincy added.

They made up a strange company, these unflinching servants of the Lord, from Boston aristocrats like Wendell Phillips and Richard Henry Dana to ex-slaves like Douglass and ex-slaveholders like Birney and Cassius Clay, to businessmen like the Tappans and Gerrit Smith, Quakers like the Motts, preachers and lawyers and men and women of the simplest backgrounds like Garrison himself. They formed a society within the larger society. They met in their constant conventions and corresponded when they were not meeting. They married each other and their children intermarried. With all their factions and divisions they constituted a faith. Within the churches they constituted a church, the Church of Abolition, the most powerful congregation in the country.

31

Free Blacks

Free blacks in the North and the South lived in a kind of social and political limbo, discriminated against in both sections of the country. Each passing decade saw new legislation designed to restrict further the few rights enjoyed by "free" blacks, who were more free in name than in fact.

In the words of Fanny Kemble, Northern blacks while "not slaves indeed . . . are pariahs; debarred from all fellowships save with their own despised race—scorned by the lowest white ruffian in your streets, not tolerated as companions even by the foreign menials in your kitchen. They are certainly free but they are also degraded, rejected, the offscum and offscourings of the very dregs of your society; they are free from the chain, the whip, the enforced task and unpaid toil of slavery; but they are not less under a ban." Southerners and Northerners alike had pointed to the condition of free blacks as an argument for slavery and for the racial inferiority of the black, but Kemble burst out impatiently, "How, in the name of all that is natural, probable, possible, should the spirit and energy of any human creature support itself under such an accumulation of injustice and obloquy? Where shall any mass of men be found with power of character and mind sufficient to bear up against such a weight of prejudice."

Captain Marryat wrote: "Singular is the degree of contempt and dislike in which free blacks are held in all the free states of America. ... In fact, in the United States, a Negro, from his colour, and I believe his colour alone, is a degraded being. Is not this extraordinary, in a land which professes universal liberty, equality, and the rights of man?" Blacks continued to be confined to the most menial tasks. Richard Henry Dana, visiting Philadelphia, noted that "nearly all the porters & hackmen were blacks, & an ill dressed, uncouth-looking set they were, very civil, touching their hat to every man they asked to take a cab, talking all the time, good natured, free & easy. Some of them were giants in stature, & wore long drab coats wh. made them appear yet taller."

If upper-class whites patronized free blacks and confined them to such jobs as waiters and porters, lower-class whites hated and abused them. In the late summer of 1842 a mob of Irishmen in Philadelphia attacked a Negro temperance procession. "This," Sidney George Fisher wrote, "produced a fight and great excitement. For three days, the Negroes were beaten, the houses torn to pieces, and two of their churches were burnt down in spite of the police, and when all was over & the rascals had done all they wished, the troops were called around." Most unjust of all, in Fisher's view, was that the city commissioners tore down a small temperance hall built by blacks "on the ground that it *produced excitement.*"

In many Northern states free blacks were denied the franchise. In the South a web of restrictive laws controlled every aspect of their lives and, by the 1850s, a number of Southern states had passed legislation that forced free blacks to leave the respective states under the penalty of being reenslaved.

Discrimination in the North was constant and galling, especially for those blacks of superior education and intelligence who found all doors closed to them. Ira Aldridge, the son of a free black and an actor of great power and promise, had to go to England to find roles. There he was praised for his performance as Othello and toured Europe playing with Edward Kean. As we have noted, the Noyes Academy in Massachusetts had been towed to the swamp because it admitted two black students. One of the students, Alexander Crummell, went to Cambridge, England, to study the classics and theology. Henry Highland Garnet, the grandson of an African chief, was the other Noyes student: he went on to study with Beriah Green at the Oneida

Institute and soon was one of the most popular and most radical of all the abolitionist orators, rivaled only by Frederick Douglass.

Garnet's cousin, James W. C. Pennington, was a young black Presbyterian minister who had escaped from slavery and joined Garnet, Brown, Douglass, and others on the lecture circuit. Heidelberg gave him an honorary degree, but in the United States he was not allowed to speak at Yale College.

Of the blacks who played leading roles in the abolitionist movement, the best known was Frederick Douglass, whom we left in New York, having just made his escape from slavery. New York was filled with slave hunters, and some free blacks were willing to betray runaways for a portion of the reward. An escaped slave named Jake warned Douglass not to go to the wharves or to any colored boardinghouse, for such places were closely watched by the hunters. So Douglass found himself in a strange city "without home, without acquaintances, without money, without credit, without work, and without any definite knowledge as to what course to take or where to look for succor." Any man, black or white, to whom he spoke might betray him. Standing on the sidewalk in the Tombs, completely at loose ends, Douglass saw a sailor looking at him in a friendly manner. The man approached him and Douglass asked him for help. The sailor took the young runaway slave home with him for the night and the next morning delivered him into the hands of members of the New York Anti-Slavery Society. Its secretary was a free black named David Ruggles.

Ruggles hid Douglass in his home for several days. Now Douglass was a passenger in the famous Underground Railroad. There he was joined by a free black woman from Baltimore and they were married by a Presbyterian minister. Ruggles decided that since Douglass was trained as a ship's calker the best place for him to go was New Bedford, Massachusetts. With his new wife, Douglass set out for the seaport town. There free blacks, the Nathan Johnsons, took the young couple in and guided them through the difficult steps of getting adjusted to their new home and new life. The first thing to be done was to find a name for Frederick. Slaves commonly had no last names, but Frederick's mother had "named" him Frederick Augustus Washington Bailey, which he had shortened to Frederick Bailey in Baltimore. In his escape he had called himself Johnson, but New Bedford was full of Johnsons so Frederick left it to his host to choose a name; since his wife had just finished reading the romantic poem *The Lady of the Lake,* whose hero was a member of the Douglass clan, Nathan Johnson chose the name of Douglass.

The North was a continual revelation to Douglass. There he found "even the laboring classes lived in better houses, that their houses were more elegantly furnished and were more abundantly supplied with conveniences and comforts, than the houses of many who owned slaves on the Eastern Shore of Maryland." The same could be said of free blacks. Johnson "lived in a nicer house, dined at a more ample board, was the owner of more books, the reader of more newspapers, was more conversant with the moral, social, and political conditions of the country, than nine-tenths of the slaveholders of all Talbot County."

Douglass was also struck by how much more efficient and productive labor was in the North and the constant recourse there to labor-saving devices. "With a capital of about sixty dollars in the shape of a good-natured old ox attached to the end of a stout rope, a New Bedford man did the work of ten or twelve thousand dollars, represented in the bones and muscles of slaves, and did it far better. . . . Here were sinks, drains, self-shutting gates, pounding-barrels, washing-machines, wringing machines and a hundred other contrivances for saving time and money." Soon Douglass was experiencing the unfamiliar delights of free enterprise. On his way down Union Street to look for work, he passed the home of the Reverend Ephraim Peabody and, seeing a large pile of coal in front of the house, went to the kitchen door and "asked for the privilege of bringing in and putting away this coal. 'What will you charge?' said the lady. 'I will leave that to you, madam.' 'You may put it away,' she said." The pay was the princely sum of "*two silver half dollars*," Douglass's first wages as a free man, and it struck him with the force of revelation "*that it was mine—that my hands* were my own."

But New Bedford, idyllic as it seemed, was not without its racial prejudices as Douglass soon found out. When he applied for work in the shipyard as a calker, the owner of the yard, an antislavery man, was glad to take him on; but the other workers informed him "that every white man would leave the ship in her unfinished condition if I struck a blow at my trade upon her. . . . The consciousness that I was free—no longer a slave—kept me cheerful under this and many similar proscriptions which I was destined to meet in New Bedford and elsewhere on the free soil of Massachusetts." The New Bedford Lyceum refused to allow blacks to attend their lectures, a rule that was not relaxed "until such men as Hon. Charles Sumner, Theodore Parker, Ralph W. Emerson and Horace Mann refused to lecture in their course while there was such a restriction."

Denied the opportunity to practice his trade, Douglass "sawed wood, shoveled coal, dug cellars, moved rubbish from back-yards, worked on the wharves, loaded and unloaded vessels, and scoured their cabins"—all unskilled work for which he received substantially less money than he would have made as a calker.

Some five or six months after he arrived in New Bedford, a young man came to Douglass's door to sell him a subscription to the *Liberator*. When Douglass said he was too poor to pay for a subscription, the young man added his name to the list without a charge, and "from this time," Douglass wrote, "I was brought into contact with the mind of Mr. Garrison, and his paper took a place in my heart second only to the Bible. . . . I loved this paper and its editor. . . . His words were full of holy fire, and straight to the point." Not long after Douglass began receiving the *Liberator,* Garrison himself appeared in New Bedford to lecture at Liberty Hall. "On this occasion he announced nearly all his heresies. His Bible was his textbook—held sacred as the very word of the Eternal Father. He believed in sinless perfection, complete submission to insults and injuries, and literal obedience to the injunction if smitten 'on one cheek to turn the other also.' . . . All sectarianism was false and mischievous—the regenerated throughout the world being members of one body, and the head Jesus Christ. *Prejudice against color was rebellion against God.* Of all men beneath the sky, the slaves, because the most neglected and despised, were nearest and dearest to His great heart . . . those churches which fellowshipped slaveholders as Christians, were synagogues of Satan, and our nation was a nation of liars. He was never loud and noisy, but calm and serene as a summer sky, and as pure. 'You are the man—the Moses raised up by God, to deliver His modern Israel from bondage,' was the spontaneous feeling of my heart, as I sat away back in the hall and listened to his mighty words, mighty in truth, mighty in their simple earnestness."

For three years Douglass worked at whatever jobs he could find, read omnivorously and faithfully attended every antislavery lecture in the city. In 1841 "a grand antislavery convention" was held in nearby Nantucket. Douglass went, and there a New Bedford abolitionist who had heard Douglass "speaking to my colored friends in the little schoolhouse on Second Street . . . sought me out in the crowd and invited me to say a few words to the convention." Overcome with anxiety, Douglass stammered out a few sentences about his experiences as a slave. Garrison followed, and taking Douglass's remarks as his text, spoke with unusual power and eloquence, displaying the "fabulous inspiration" that so often marked his speeches. Afterwards Douglass was asked by John Collins, general agent of the Massachusetts Anti-Slavery Society, to become a worker for the cause "and publicly advocate its principles." With many misgivings, Douglass consented to a three-month trial period. "Young, ardent, and hopeful," Douglass wrote, "I entered upon this new life in the full gush of unsuspecting enthusiasm. . . . My whole heart went with the holy cause."

But Douglass found that like other escaped slaves on the abolitionist lecture tour, his white friends had a definite and limited role for him to play. He was the "thing," the "piece of property," the "it" that could speak like a man, a living demonstration of the horror of slavery; his "act" was to recount certain of his grimmest experiences. It was left to the white orators to develop the larger theological, social, and political implications of slavery. "Fugitive slaves were rare then, and as a fugitive slave lecturer, I had the advantage of being a 'brand new fact'—the first one out." "Give us the facts," a white friend said, "we will take care of the philosophy." Even Garrison pressed that part upon him. "Tell your story, Frederick," he would whisper to him on the platform when Douglass showed a disposition to philosophize.

But Douglass refused to be denied. He began to give free rein to his own remarkable powers as an orator, with the result that he was soon being denounced as an impostor. No ex-slave could think with such clarity or speak so fluently and literately. "People said I did not talk like a slave, look like a slave, or act like a slave, and . . . they believed I had never been south of Mason and Dixon's line." Douglass's position was further complicated by the fact that he could not tell his real name or his master's or give any of the details that would have verified his stories because he was still legally a slave and might be recovered by his master if his whereabouts became known. But Douglass finally established his credentials as a genuine ex-slave and was soon one of the most successful orators on the abolitionist circuit. His allies were such white men as Stephen Foster; Wendell Phillips, a graduate of Harvard, class of 1831, who had first gained fame for his remarkable speech at a meeting called at Faneuil Hall in 1837 to protest the murder of Elijah Lovejoy; and, of course, Garrison himself. "They received me as a man and a brother," Douglass wrote. When steamboats, railroad cars, and hotels refused to admit Douglass, his white companions insisted on sharing his lot, whether it was the Jim Crow car of a train or the forward deck of a steamer. "True men they were, who would accept welcome at no man's table where I was refused." When Douglass found towns that would not allow him to use a public hall, he held his meetings in the open. At Hartford, Connecticut, he, Foster, Garrison, and the beautiful and eloquent Abigail Kelley, a young Quakeress, held a well-attended outdoor meeting, and at Grafton, Massachusetts, when Douglass was denied a hall, he borrowed a dinner bell and passed through the streets of the town ringing it and calling out, "Notice! Frederick Douglass, recently a slave, will lecture on American Slavery, this evening at seven o'clock. Those who would like to hear of the workings of slavery by one of the slaves are respectfully invited to attend." The common was crowded and thereafter "the largest church in town was open to me," Douglass wrote.

Once Douglass, traveling alone on the Boston-Portland line, refused to sit in the Jim Crow car, which led to a physical contest with the conductor and brakeman. Since Douglass was a large, powerful man, it took six trainmen to eject him and the head of the railroad thereafter decreed that the train would not stop in Lynn where Douglass lived. When Lynn abolitionists protested, the head of the line replied that a railroad was neither a "religious or a reformatory body, that the road was run for the accommodation of the public, and that it required the exclusion of colored people." When the Christian churches no longer barred colored persons from their pews the railway company would follow suit.

The black abolitionists were untroubled by the moral suasion versus political action question except as it divided and demoralized their white colleagues. The political arena was largely closed to them. They worked to organize societies of "colored citizens" to work both for the advancement of the free black and for the end of slavery. Prominent among the black abolitionists was William Wells Brown, who had been hired out by his master to Elijah Lovejoy, who had taught him to read and write. He had subsequently been a coachman, a sailor, and a printer. He ran away from his master, signed on a Great Lakes vessel, and was soon involved in helping fugitive slaves to get from Cleveland to Canada. In a period of nine months during 1842 he helped sixty-nine slaves to escape. The next year he came across a copy of the *Liberator* and fell under Garrison's spell. Brown was a strikingly handsome man and soon became a well-known abolitionist orator.

In 1843, a Convention of Colored Citizens was held in Buffalo and Henry Highland Garnet declared, "Brethren, arise, arise! Strike for your lives and liberties. Now is the day and the hour. Let every slave throughout the land do this and the days of slavery are numbered. Rather die freemen than live slaves! In the name of God we ask, are you men? Where is the blood of your fathers? Awake, awake, millions of voices are calling you! Let your motto be resistance; no oppressed people have secured their liberty without resistance. Remember you are four million!" Garnet's militant stand was disclaimed by the delegates but by the margin of only one vote.

William Nell, a free black and a Bostonian, devoted much of his life to desegregating Boston's schools. Nell recalled that when Harrison Gray Otis, then mayor of Boston, had visited his "colored school," where Nell had won one of the highest awards of merit, the boy had been given a book on the life of Franklin rather than a Franklin Medal, awarded to white students who excelled in the public schools, and had been denied the right to be present at the award ceremony in Faneuil Hall. Nell prevailed on some of the black waiters at the party to smuggle him in in the guise of a waiter. This experience made Nell determined to devote his best efforts to "hasten the day when the color of the skin would be no barrier to equal school rights." In this battle "it was the *mothers*," he wrote, who carried on most courageously the "attack upon the fortress of Colorphobia."

Nell did not stop with school desegregation. An ally of Garrison's, he was a renowned orator and a historian, writing a book on *Services of Colored Americans in the Wars of 1776 and 1812,* and another entitled *Colored Patriots of the American Revolution.* When the Boston schools were desegregated in 1855, Nell was the featured speaker. "To the colored boys and girls of Boston," he declared, "it may now in truth be said, 'The lines have fallen to you in pleasant places.' Behold you have a goodly heritage. . . . Do not waste your spring of youth in idle dalliance, but plant rich seeds to blossom in your manhood and bear fruit when you are old. The public schools of Boston are the gateways to the pursuits of honor and usefulness, and if rightly improved by you, the imagination almost wearies as future prospects dawn upon its vision. . . ."

Another prominent black orator was James Holly, who became a champion of the black republic of Haiti and cited it as proof that black people could govern themselves. One of the first public advocates of "racial separation," Holly viewed the indifference of slaves to the issue of American independence in 1776 as evidence of the slave's sense of where his own interests lay. The slave "remained heedless of the effervescence of liberty that bubbled over in the bosom of the white man, and continued at his sullen labors, biding his time for deliverance." His "cool self-possession" was "a miracle." Holly's message was that all free blacks should migrate to Haiti, the native land of the black hero Toussaint, "the unswerving friend and servant of God and humanity." Holly's mission was "to establish, before the world, the Negro's equality with the white man in carrying forward the great principles of self-government and civilized progress." He was determined to arouse "the minds of my race . . . to a full consciousness of their own inherent dignity . . . thereby increasing among them that self-respect which shall urge them on to the performance of those great deeds which our age and the race now demand at their hands." The success of black Haiti, in the light of Christianity and civilization, would redound to the ultimate benefit of the African homeland by providing enlightened black leadership for the Dark Continent. Holly took his own advice and moved to Haiti.

Charles Langston, an Ohio black, waged war on the Fugitive Slave Law. When he assisted in the escape of a fugitive slave named John Price at Wellington, Ohio, and was arrested and tried under the provisions of the Fugitive Slave Law, he made one of the most moving speeches by a black man in the ante-bellum era, pointing out that his father had served in the Revolution under Lafayette, and yet, Langston said, quoting Taney's words in the Dred Scott Case, "the colored men have no rights in the United States which white men are bound to respect." "The law under which I am arraigned," he declared, "is an unjust one, one made to crush the colored man, and one which outrages every feeling of humanity, as well as every rule of right." Langston's most effective point was that he had not been tried by a jury of his peers since the white jury shared the "universal and deeply fixed *prejudices* against black people. . . . I was tried by a jury who were prejudiced, before a court that was prejudiced, prosecuted by an officer who was prejudiced, and defended, though ably, by counsel that was prejudiced. And, therefore, it is, your Honor, that I urge by all that is good and great in mankind that I should not be subjected to the pains and penalties of this oppressive law, when I have not been tried, either by a jury of my peers or a jury that were impartial." The judge, obviously moved by Langston's speech to the court, gave him a far lighter sentence than his white codefendants but Langston had, nevertheless, to pay a fine of one hundred dollars and spend twenty days in jail.

An important black leader was James McCune Smith, the son of a slave, who was educated in the African Free School in New York City and received his B.A. and his medical degree at the University of Edinburgh in 1837. After working in clinics in France, Smith returned to New York and an outstanding career as an abolitionist leader, a physician, and a writer. Smith concentrated his fire on the argument that blacks were inherently inferior to whites, taking Jefferson's statement to that effect in *Notes on Virginia* as his special target. Smith was well aware that the abolition of slavery was only part of the problem of the black person in the United States. The other was a reluctance among *all* whites to accept black men and women as their equals. Smith tackled the issue directly. "Can they be elevated to the same rank with the white citizens of this great Republic?" he asked. "Is the standard occupied by whites really elevated above that occupied by the black population? What is the standard of mind—of excellence? Is it ingenuity in constructing machinery? Is it in morals? Is it in physical courage? Or is it to be measured by the tone of a 'shopkeeping gentility'?" It was a question not easily answered and, in Smith's opinion, it obscured a far more important one: "Can the black and white live together in harmony under American institutions, each contributing to the peace and prosperity of the country, and to the development of the problem of self-government in American institutions?" Smith quoted from the Song of Solomon, "I am black but comely," adding from Ephesians, "For we are all His workmanship." "Such testimony," he wrote, "is enough to show that there is nothing essentially hideous or distinctly deformed in a black complexion."

Men like Nell, Holly, and Smith, not to mention Frederick Douglass, were, of course, in themselves the best argument against the theory that blacks were inherently inferior to whites. Highly intelligent men and eloquent orators on behalf of the rights of blacks, they had made their way in the white world against massive prejudice.

One of the most notable of the black abolitionists was Robert Purvis, a black man only by the broadest extension of that word. He had been born in Charleston, South Carolina, the son of a wealthy English merchant and a half-Jewish, half-Moorish mother. Purvis's father, knowing his sons would encounter strong prejudices in the

South, sent Purvis and his brothers to Philadelphia to be educated in private schools; he died when Purvis was fifteen years old, leaving an inheritance of over $125,000. Purvis graduated from Amherst, lived in a handsome house in Philadelphia and devoted his life to the antislavery cause, contributing money to the *Liberator,* helping to found the Pennsylvania Anti-Slavery Society, and organizing the Philadelphia branch of the Underground Railroad.

As opposed to most of the underground stations or networks, Purvis and the Philadelphia committee kept careful records from the time it began its operations in 1831 until it terminated its activities thirty years later. In that period nine thousand runaways received assistance from Purvis and his associates. "The funds for carrying on this enterprise were raised from our antislavery friends, as the cases came up and their needs demanded it," he wrote. "Many of the fugitives required no other help than advice and directions how to proceed. The most efficient helpers or agents we had were two market women who lived in Baltimore, one of whom was white, the other colored. By some means they obtained a number of genuine certificates of freedom which they gave to slaves who wished to escape. They were afterwards returned to them and used again by other fugitives." One of Purvis's most efficient agents was the son of a New Bern, North Carolina, slaveholder who smuggled slaves aboard coastal lumber ships headed for Philadelphia.

Initially black abolitionists had their own societies and their own newspapers but gradually they were drawn into white abolitionism, although, as we have seen, the main-line abolitionists often stopped short of personal contacts with free blacks. In addition the ranks of the abolitionists were increasingly augmented by runaway slaves. At first the escaped slaves were presented as little more than props for white antislavery speakers. Their role, like that of Frederick Douglass, was limited to telling stories illustrating the inhumanity of slavery and lending a note of the practical and immediate to what was otherwise often abstract. In the words of John Collins, an agent of the American Anti-Slavery Society, "the public have itching ears to hear a colored man speak, particularly a *slave.*" The black orators were eager to oblige. Illiterate, their tradition was an oral one, their consciousness was oral. They spoke in singing cadences with all the expressiveness of the black tongue. The Southern black had a quality that even the most eloquent white speaker lacked—an ability to speak immediately, poignantly, without any sense of an intervening, censoring self-consciousness. So he—or she, because two of the greatest black ex-slave orators were women: Sojourner Truth and, later, Harriet Tubman—led their entranced listeners into the strange, hidden world of the slave with unbounded pathos and often hilarious humor, imitating a Southern master or mistress, recreating a dialogue, their richly musical accents rising and falling for dramatic emphasis. Sometimes they sang black spirituals of faith and freedom, of the yearning to "Lay My Burden Down." A typical audience "cheered, clapped, stamped, laughed and wept, by turns."

At the fifth annual meeting of the Massachusetts Anti-Slavery Society in Boston in 1837, "Mr. Johnson, a colored man, was introduced, who said he could tell something about slavery. He *knew* what it was;—I was born in Africa, several hundred miles up the Gambia River. Fine country dat; but we are called heathen in dis Christian—no, I don't know what to call it—in dis *enlightened heathen country* (Laughter). But the villagers in that country are very kind. When you go into house, the first question is, have you had any thing to eat? Bring water, you wash, and den eat much you want; and all you do is tank them for it—not one fip you pay. If you are sick, nurse you, and make you well—not one fip you pay . . . (Applause). When I was nine years old, I was out with my aunt to get figs. . . . I had to crawl amongst de bushes; when all at once I feel something pull my leg. I look around and could see no aunt, nothing but man of my own color; and I never seed my aunt since. . . . First white man I ever see was Capt. Boss, of Newport, R.I., and I tot he was de devil (Laughter). My own color told me he was a man, but I could not believe it." "Mr. Johnson" completed his simple story with an account of being auctioned off in Savannah, Georgia, to a master. "One day my master was dining with a gentleman who had a wife as black as dat hat. A young colored woman, as likely *for her color* as any lady in dis assembly (a laugh), waited on table. She happened to spill a little gravy on the gown of her mistress. The gentleman took his carving knife, dragged her out to the wood pile and cut her head off; den wash his hands, come in and finish his dinner like nothing had happened! Do you call dat a Christian country? I never saw the like in Africa. My master dropped his knife and fork, and eat no more . . . I have seen a Christian professor, after the communion, have four slaves tied together, and whipped raw, and then washed with beef brine." He had seen mothers hoeing in the fields who had stopped to nurse crying babies, whipped for falling behind in their quota of work. " '*Slavery is the most cruel ting in de world.*' Mr. J here expatiated very sensibly upon the peculiar evils of slavery in this country, and very suddenly pointed to Mr. Garrison, and said, 'Dat man is de Moses raised up for our deliverance' (tremendous applause)."

The account of Johnson's speech ends with these words: "The story became still more interesting and amusing, so that the reporters dropped their pens, and enjoyed the sallies of his wit with the audience." Reading the account of Johnson's speech it is easy to see why ex-slave speakers were so much in demand at antislavery gatherings.

Another popular black lecturer was Lunsford Lane, whose story received wide publicity in the North. Lane had been a slave in Raleigh, North Carolina, and had bought his freedom for a thousand dollars, money that he had earned as a carpenter. He had then negotiated with the owner of his wife and children to buy them for twenty-five hundred dollars. After Lane had raised and paid six hundred and twenty dollars to the owner of his family, the North Carolina legislature passed a law forbidding free blacks to remain in the state. Lane found a white lawyer who helped him draft a petition to the state assembly asking for an exemption so that he could remain and continue to work to buy his family's freedom. The petition, signed by some of the leading men of the city, was summarily rejected by the assembly when it convened. Lane was then taken to court to determine if he should not be enslaved for remaining in North Carolina in defiance of the law. Before the case could come to trial, Lane was advised by his white lawyer to flee north. He did so, taking one child with him. In Boston he secured the help of the abolitionists and went from door to door soliciting money to complete the purchase of his family. Having raised fifteen hundred dollars, Lane wrote to the governor of North Carolina asking for permission to return and buy his family. The governor could give no official permission, Lane was told, but he was assured he could come into the state for twenty days "with perfect safety." He had hardly arrived in Raleigh before he was arrested for giving antislavery lectures in Boston. So charged by the judge, Lane reviewed his efforts to buy his family's freedom. He had simply told the story "from house to house, and from store to store, and from church to church. . . ." Could this be called antislavery lectures? Supported by many of the largest slaveholders in the city, Lane was freed and had his hands shaken by the governor but he had hardly been released before he was seized by a mob of angry whites who ransacked his luggage and then carried him off to a gallows with threats to hang him. Instead they stripped him and tarred and feathered him. And then, in the most revealing moment in the entire episode, his tormentors turned him loose, saying, "You may do what business you please and you shall not be hurt. We merely wished to let the aristocracy know that they should not have their own way."

The next day a crowd larger than "when Lafayette went through Raleigh," gathered around Lane and his wife and children and his mother, who had been given her freedom by her owner. The mood of the gathering was uncertain. Some who espoused Lane's cause were afraid the crowd might try to prevent him from boarding the train for the North, so he was smuggled to a point on the railroad tracks outside of town and arrangements were made for the conductor to stop the train to pick him up there.

After Lane told his story, his wife and children were introduced to the audience. The children "rose or were raised before the meeting, exhibiting the bright countenances of young immortals," the reporter for the *Anti-Slavery Reporter* noted, "such as the people of this nation buy and sell as they do swine. Now, said [Lane], as he concluded his story, I have not a dollar in my pocket; yet I think there is not one here who feels richer or happier than I." Lane's story was told in an autobiography, which enjoyed substantial sales, and in a number of subsequent platform appearances.

Lydia Maria Child gave an account of another such meeting addressed by a former slave. She had, she wrote, "seldom been more entertained by any speaker. His obvious want of education was one guaranty of the truth of his story; and the uncouth awkwardness of his language had a sort of charm, like the circuitous expression, and stammering utterance of a foreign tongue. . . . His mind was evidently full of ideas, which he was eager to express; but the medium was wanting, 'I've got it in *here*,' he said, laying his hand on his heart; 'but I don't know how to get it out.' However, in his imperfect way, I believe he conveyed much information to many minds; and few that knew him went away without being impressed by the conviction that he was sincerely truthful. . . ." His name was Lewis Clarke. He had been a slave in Kentucky and his father had fought in the American Revolution. His grandmother had been her master's daughter and his mother *her* master's daughter and he had been his master's son, "so you see, I han't got but one-eighth of the blood." He did not wish to dwell upon the whippings a slave was subjected to, "though I'm the boy that's got 'em, times a plenty. . . . But what I want to make you understand is, that A SLAVE CAN'T BE A MAN!"

Two things are evident in reading such literature. One is simply the terror of slavery, its day-to-day brutality, which could never be balanced by the greatest kindness and benignity on the part of indulgent masters. This horror sank into the souls of the auditors and with it a vast amount of homely detail about the daily lives of slaves. The crowning irony was that it was, for the most part, only the ex-slave who had such a voice. The tens of thousands of free blacks in the North were speechless. No rapt audiences gathered to hear them tell of the restraints and prejudices they encountered at every turn from their white neighbors.

In addition to those escaped slaves who went on the abolitionist lecture circuit, dozens of others told their stories to eager white scribes who wrote them down and published them in one or another of the numerous abolitionist journals. Indeed, it is not too much to say that for a good many Americans through the middle decades of the century their most absorbing reading matter was the moving and dramatic tales of escaped slaves.

The white men and women who listened to black orators—the prim Quakers, the Calvinistic Presbyterians, the rational Unitarians, the teetotaling Methodists—got tantalizing glimpses into the slave world, where the spontaneous and expressive life of black people was in sharp contrast to white anxieties and repressions. It was as though blacks had access to some secret source of vitality and humor. Perhaps that was what impressed their audiences more than anything else— that black speakers could turn their manifold sufferings into humor and thereby both increase their poignance and give testimony to the indestructability of their own spirits. What the white listeners got, in essence, was a larger sense of human possibilities. It was evident that in many instances the brutal and dehumanizing circumstances in which the ex-slaves had existed had increased rather than diminished their humanity. They seemed to adumbrate new human possibilities, perhaps a new human type, a type in whom *joy* might make *happiness* seem a counterfeit coin, in whom ecstacy might assuage anxiety and despair.

If others sensed that, Harriet Beecher Stowe articulated it. "If ever Africa shall show an elevated and cultivated race," she wrote, "—and come it must, some time, her turn to figure in the great drama of human improvement,—life will awake there with a gorgeousness and splendor of which our cold western tribes faintly have conceived. In that far-off mystic land of gold, and gems, and spices, and waving palms, and wondrous flowers, and miraculous fertility, will awake new forms of art, new styles of splendor; and the negro race, no longer despised and trodden down, will, perhaps, show forth some of the latest and most magnificent revelations of human life. Certainly they will, in their gentleness, their lowly docility of heart, their aptitude to repose on a superior mind and rest on a higher power, their child-like simplicity of affection, and facility of forgiveness. In all these they will exhibit the highest form of the peculiarly *Christian life,* and, perhaps, as God chasteneth whom he loveth, he hath chosen poor Africa in the furnace of affliction, to make her the highest and noblest in that kingdom which he will set up, when every other kingdom has been tried, and failed; for the first shall be last, and the last first."

"Gentleness," "lowly docility," "child-like simplicity of affection" may seem negative stereotypes to present-day blacks, but clearly they were the noblest Christian virtues Harriet Beecher Stowe could conceive of and it is equally certain that her vision was formed from her associations with black Americans.

Lydia Maria Child, whose book *An Appeal in Favor of Americans Called Africans* was one of the basic tracts of the abolitionists, had early addressed herself to what many of the women abolitionists felt was the most crucial issue of all—racial hostility toward the blacks in the North. While those we might call the "radical" abolitionists split on such issues as gradual emancipation and even more on nonresistance and the eschewing of politics, they were of one mind on the issue of Northern racism. They were appalled by the professed enemies of slavery who wished to have nothing to do with free blacks in the North. Child addressed herself particularly to this question in an essay, written in 1833, entitled "Prejudices Against People of Color, and Our Duties in Relation to the Subject." It was true, she told her readers, that the form of slavery did not exist among them, "but the very *spirit* of the hateful and mischievous thing is here in all its strength. . . . Our prejudice against colored people is even more inveterate than in the South. The planter is often attached to his negroes, and lavishes caresses and kind words upon them, as he would a favorite hound; but our cold-hearted ignoble prejudice admits of no exception—no intermission." Southerners had offered in rebuttal the argument that "Northern ships and Northern capital have been engaged in this wicked business; and the reproach is true. . . . Those who are kind and liberal on all other subjects, unite with the selfish and proud in their unrelenting efforts to keep the colored population in the lowest state of degradation. . . ." Segregated schools and colleges were the special objects of Child's scorn. Wesleyan had refused a well-qualified young black who sought admission. A Boston school had turned away a black boy until his mother threatened legal action. A black man had been refused a pew in a Philadelphia church. The list was a long and damning one.

Sarah Lewis, like Lydia Maria Child and the Grimké sisters, called for an end to such racial attitudes at the Anti-Slavery Convention of American Women in Philadelphia in 1839. "The opposition we have to encounter as a convention of American Women,—the scorn which we excite in some, and the unaffected concern which we awaken in others," she declared, "render it incumbent upon us to address you upon that subject which, above all others, has drawn upon us odium and reproach—the admission of our colored sisters to intercourse with us, which their moral worth demands."

Many of her listeners encouraged black efforts at self-improvement and general advancement "in all those branches of education necessary to the mechanic or tradesman," but if a black person went so far as to try to mix with whites, "you frown him back with scorn and contempt. . . . Would it be believed that our museums, our literary and scientific lectures, our public exhibitions, which contribute so much to the intelligence of a people, are generally closed against this portion of our population. . . . Women of America! we entreat you to ponder these things in your hearts; to consider how far you are 'guilty concerning your brother.' It is in your power, to roll back this tide of cruel prejudice, which overwhelms thousands of our fellow creatures, equally gifted with ourselves by our common Father, though ruthlessly robbed of their heritage."

Two black women achieved fame second only to Douglass as abolitionists. One was Harriet Tubman, a Christian mystic, whose exploits in conducting slaves to freedom were the most remarkable in the annals of the Underground Railroad. As a thirteen-year-old child, Harriet Tubman had been accidently struck in the head by a heavy iron bar when she tried to intercede to prevent a slave from being whipped. Thereafter she suffered from fainting, or "sleeping," spells, when she would be unconscious for minutes at a time. During a prolonged illness she prayed constantly to God to convert her master, but after his death she heard that she and her brothers were to be sold south to settle the estate. "Pears like, I prayed all de time," she told her biographer, "about my work, eberywhere; I was always talking to de Lord. When I went to the horse-trough to wash my face, and took up de water in my hands, I said, 'Oh, Lord, wash me, make me clean.' . . . When I took up de broom and began to sweep, I groaned, 'Oh, Lord, whatsoeber sin dere be in my heart, sweep it out, Lord, clar and clean.'" Much given to visions and trusting to her intuitions, Harriet Tubman felt the Lord had directed her, "Arise, flee for your life." She saw beckoning hands of "lovely white ladies" summoning her and saw herself flying through the air, looking down on the land beneath her. The slaves were the Israelites. The South was Egypt; the North the land of Canaan. She was to be the Moses of her people. She would start with her own brothers. She passed among the slave cabins singing a familiar spiritual:

> When dat ar ole chariot comes,
> I'm gwine to lebe you,
> I'm bound for the promised land,
> Frien's, I'm gwine to lebe you.

They were only a few miles from the plantation when the courage of the brothers deserted them and they turned back. Harriet went on, following the north star, "For," she said, "I had reasoned dis out in my mind; there was one of two things I had a *right* to, liberty or death; if I could not have the one, I would have de oder; for no man would take me alive; I should fit for liberty as long as my strength lasted, and when de time came for me to go, de Lord would let dem take me."

Tubman traveled only at night, hiding during the day and instinctively managing to search out the persons who would help her rather than turn her over to the authorities. Finally, she discovered she had passed the magic boundary, the Mason-Dixon line. "I looked at my hands," she said, "to see if I was de same person now I was free. Dere was such a glory ober eberything, de sun came like gold trou de trees, and ober de fields, and I felt like I was in heaven." She determined to return and free her friends and relatives. She had found white men and women along the way who were already conductors on the Underground Railway, the most notable being Thomas Garrett, the Quaker businessman and manufacturer of shoes who gave every runaway who came to his door food, money, and often railroad tickets and a new pair of shoes. Befriended by abolitionists, she saved her wages, begged money, and returned time and again to bring out, first her brothers and cousins, then her mother and father, and finally any slaves courageous enough to risk the long, hazardous, and exhausting trip to the North. She often carried a rifle and invariably a pistol. When one of her black charges grew fainthearted and threatened to betray the others by panicking, she would place her pistol at his head and declare, "Dead niggers tell no tales; you go on or die."

In time the escapes she engineered became legendary and perhaps fabulous. It was said that she went back nineteen times into Maryland and Virginia and, in the course of some fifteen years, brought more than three hundred slaves with her out of bondage. So she did become the Moses of her people. A reward of forty thousand dollars was placed on her head dead or alive by furious slaveholders whose property she had stolen or who lived in fear that she would carry off their slaves. The most experienced and ruthless slave hunters dogged her trail time and again and she and her charges had hairbreadth escapes. Always she trusted her instincts. She seemed to sense when slave hunters were nearby and took alternative routes. On one occasion, riding north on a train, she realized that a handbill offering a reward for her capture was posted almost over her head. She decided that the best way to disarm suspicion was to transfer to a train headed south. She returned to her own plantation disguised as an old woman and hid out there until the hue and cry had died down. When infants were brought out with their parents, Tubman had their mothers administer paregoric to keep them asleep so that their crying would not alert pursuers. And when they were safe, Tubman and her charges would sing the spiritual forbidden in the South:

> Oh go down, Moses,
> Way down into Egypt's land,
> Tell old Pharaoh,
> Let my people go.

When the Fugitive Slave Law was passed in 1850, Harriet Tubman's escaped blacks were no longer safe in New York. Now she conducted them to Canada. Although she was too much engaged in her activities on the Underground Railroad to become a regular on the abolitionist lecture circuit, when she did speak she transfixed her audiences with her wit and eloquence. "I always tole God," she declared, "I'm gwine to hole stiddy on to you, and you got to see me trou." When people expressed astonishment at her indomitable courage and remarkable fortune, she replied, "Jes so long as He wants to use me, He'll take ker of me, and when He don't want me any longer, I'm ready to go."

William Seward assisted her, and wrote, "a nobler, higher spirit, or truer, seldom dwells in human form." She was a friend of Emerson, the Alcotts, and Horace Mann. She became the friend, supporter, and fellow conspirator of John Brown, whom she declared she had first encountered in a dream before she had met or heard of him. Frederick Douglass wrote to her that her "labors and devotion" to the cause of the enslaved were much superior to his own. "Most that I have done or suffered . . . has been in public, and I have received much encouragement every step of the way. You, on the other hand, have labored in a private way. I have wrought in the day—you in the night. I have had the applause of the crowd and the satisfaction that comes of being approved by the multitude. . . . The midnight sky and the silent stars have been the witnesses of your devotion to freedom and of your heroism." Only John Brown had endured more "perils and hardships to serve our enslaved people."

The other black woman who became a central figure in the abolitionist movement was one who called herself Sojourner Truth. Given the name Isabella Baumfree by her owner, she had been born in slavery a few years before the turn of the century to a Dutch master in Ulster County, New York. Her brothers and sisters were sold and she was sold twice, the second time to a farmer, John Dumont, who raped her and then married her to another slave by whom she had five children. Her five-year-old son was sold as a slave. When slaves were manumitted by law in New York, she was freed and sued to recover her son, Peter. She worked as a servant in a New York household and joined a religious community where she, like Harriet Tubman, talked with God and was told to become an evangelist against slavery. She thereupon abandoned her friends and possessions and started out on foot as an itinerant preacher, changing her name to Sojourner Truth. The Lord had told her that she was to be a sojourner—a wanderer on earth—and to carry His truth to all who would listen, hence Sojourner Truth. "When I left the house of bondage," she later declared, "I left everything behind. I wa'n't to keep nothin' of Egypt on me, an' so I went to the Lord and asked him to give me a new name."

With her new name, Sojourner became a compelling orator, preaching where she could find a hall or an audience. Camp meetings were favorite spots. She carried in her ample pockets white silk banners with texts such as "Proclaim liberty throughout the land unto all the inhabitants thereof." "I sets up my banner, an' then I sings, an' then folks always comes up round me, an' then I preaches to 'em. I tells them about Jesus, an' I tells them about the sins of his people. A great many always comes to hear me; an' they're right good to me, too, an' say they want to hear me agin."

Harriet Beecher Stowe tells of meeting Sojourner Truth, "a tall, spare form of great dignity." "I do not recall ever to have been conversant," Stowe wrote, "with any one who had more of that silent and subtle power which we call personal presence than this woman. In the modern spiritualistic phraseology, she would be described as having a strong sphere. . . . She was dressed in some stout, grayish stuff, neat and clean, though dusty from travel. On her head she wore a bright Madras handkerchief, arranged as a turban, after the manner of her race. She seemed perfectly self-possessed and at her ease,—in fact, there was almost an unconscious superiority, not unmixed with a solemn twinkle of humor, in the odd composed manner in which she looked down on me.

" 'So this is you!' she said.

" 'Yes,' I answered.

" 'Well, honey, de Lord bless ye! I jes' thought I'd like to come an' have a look at ye. You's heerd o' me, I reckon?' she added.

" 'Yes, I think I have. You go about lecturing, do you not?'

" 'Yes, honey, that's what I do. The Lord has made me a sign unto this nation, an' I go around a-testifying, an' showin' on 'em their sins agin my people.'

"So saying, she took a seat, and, stooping over and crossing her arms on her knees, she looked down on the floor, and appeared to fall into a sort of reverie. Her great gloomy eyes and her dark face seemed to work with some undercurrent of feeling; she sighed deeply, and occasionally broke out,—

" 'O Lord! O Lord! O the tears, an' the groans, an' the moans! O Lord!' "

Harriet Beecher Stowe, who had been entertaining a group of distinguished clergymen and academics, including her brother, Henry Ward Beecher, when she had been called downstairs to meet Sojourner Truth, now asked them to join her and meet the Libyan Sybil, as the black abolitionist was often called. "No princess," Mrs. Stowe wrote, "could have received a drawing-room with more dignity than Sojourner her audience. She stood among them, calm and erect as one of her own native palm-trees waving alone in the desert."

When Harriet introduced her pompous and famous brother to Sojourner as "a very celebrated preacher," she replied, looking down on him, "Ye dear lamb, I'm glad to see ye! De Lord bless ye! I loves preachers. I'm a kind o' preacher myself."

When Beecher asked if she preached from the Bible, Sojourner Truth replied that she couldn't read a letter. She had just one text, "When I found Jesus." And then she proceeded to preach to the company of preachers, telling of her conversion and ending by singing "in a strange, cracked voice," a hymn of salvation. "She sang it with the strong barbaric accent of the native African, and with those indescribable upward turns and those deep gutturals which give such a wild, peculiar power to the negro singing,—but, above all, with such an overwhelming energy of personal appropriation that the hymn seemed to be fused in the furnace of her feelings and come out recrystallized as a production of her own. . . . Sojourner, singing this hymn, seemed to impersonate the fervor of Ethiopia, savage, hunted of all nations, but burning after God in her tropic heart, and stretching her scarred hands towards the glory to be revealed."

It was certainly an odd encounter. The small, blond Harriet and the tall, gaunt Sojourner. Two of the most remarkable women of the age, they shared a common devotion to their Lord and to the cause of abolition. Sojourner stayed several days at the Beecher house, helping to care for a member of the family who was ill. "One felt," Harriet wrote of her, "as if the dark, strange woman were quite able to take up the invalid in her bosom and bear her as a lamb, both physically and spiritually. There was both power and profound sweetness in that great warm soul and that vigorous frame."

On the occasion of an abolition meeting at Faneuil Hall in Boston, Sojourner Truth shared the platform with Frederick Douglass and Wendell Phillips. Douglass, carried away by his recital of the wrongs done to the slaves, ended "by saying that they had no hope of justice from the whites, no possible hope except in their own right arms. It must come to blood; they must fight for themselves, and redeem themselves, or it would never be done." When Douglass finished a hush fell over the house and Sojourner's voice sounded out, "Frederick, *is God dead?*"

"The effect," according to Wendell Phillips, "was perfectly electrical, and thrilled through the whole house, changing as by a flash the whole feeling of the audience."

Harriet Tubman and Sojourner Truth lived and spoke in the tradition of Christian mystics. To audiences receptive to the language of sin and redemption their words and actions had a unique power. America was sunk in depravity. Slavery, the ultimate sin, was only the sign and symbol of the others.

Other free blacks besides the remarkable Harriet Tubman were prominent in the Underground Railroad. John Mason, who had escaped to Canada, returned to Kentucky to help others to freedom. In a period of less than two years he assisted 265 slaves to escape. Finally, pursued by bloodhounds, he and a party of slaves were overtaken and captured. Mason had both arms broken and his flesh torn by the teeth of the hounds. He was at once sold south but escaped again and a year and a half later was back in Canada. Over a thousand more slaves reached freedom primarily through his efforts.

Josiah Henson fled with his wife and child, making his way through Indiana and Ohio, aided by the Underground Railroad and, finally, by a tribe of Indians who helped him cross the Canadian border. In Canada, Henson organized committees to help ex-slaves who, with few skills, had great difficulty finding employment. Unaccustomed to such a harsh climate, they suffered excessively from the cold and from pneumonia and respiratory diseases. Henson realized that freedom from slavery was only the first step in enabling the fugitives to function in white society. He instructed them in agricultural techniques and in such simple matters as the management of the small sums of money they made.

Henson too went back to the South a number of times to lead parties of slaves to freedom, two hundred in all by 1840. That year he traveled to England with abolitionist friends and there met Queen Victoria. More important, he met Harriet Beecher Stowe and became her model for Uncle Tom.

Grim as were the stories of fugitive slaves recaptured in their flight, along with heart-rending accounts of escaped slaves who had established themselves as free men and women only to be snatched back into slavery, there were even more horrifying reports of free blacks who were simply kidnapped by slave hunters and sold into slavery. Such was the case of Solomon Northrup, a thirty-two-year-old free black man who lived with his wife and children at Glens Falls, New York. His mother and father had been slaves of a family named Northrup and had been given their freedom at their owner's death. Solomon Northrup, literate and intelligent, was a skillful performer on the fiddle. His story was a classic, if modest, American success story. He worked as a laborer on the Champlain Canal, saved his money, bought two horses and became a rafter, hauling timber rafts from Lake Champlain to Troy, New York. When the canal closed down he worked as a lumber contractor and finally was able to buy the farm his father had worked on as a hired man. With a cow, a pig, and "a yoke of fine oxen," Northrup raised corn and barley and played his fiddle at local dances. His wife worked as a cook at a local coffee house and they led "a happy and prosperous life." After a stint of farming, the Northrups moved to Saratoga Springs, where Solomon Northrup hoped to improve his fortunes as a businessman and musician. There he met two flashily dressed young white men who represented themselves as agents of a circus. If he would go with them to New York City, they promised him three dollars a performance and a dollar a day for expenses in addition to the cost of his ticket from Saratoga to New York and back. The two men were classic mountebanks whose "circus" consisted of juggling, "dancing on the rope, frying pancakes in a hat, causing invisible pigs to squeal and other like feats of ventriloquism and legerdemain."

At New York, the men persuaded Northrup to continue on to Washington, promising him higher wages. In Washington, he was drugged and sold as a slave, apparently for the sum of $650, to a dealer named James Burch. When the effects of the drug wore off Northrup found himself in William's Slave Pen. He insisted that he was a free man and could not be sold; whereupon Burch had him whipped and beaten until he was silent and then told him that if he ever again claimed to be a free man he would kill him. From Washington Northrup was sent by ship to the New Orleans' slave market with a half-dozen other slaves. Among them was a man named Robert, who, like Northrup, had been born free and had a wife and two children in Cincinnati. He had been hired by two white men to help them move merchandise to Washington and there had suffered the same fate as Northrup. The boat carrying Northrup and the others put in at Norfolk, where several other blacks were brought aboard, among them a man named Arthur who told Northrup that he was a free black who had worked for years as a mason in Norfolk and had been kidnapped by a gang, beaten insensible, and sold in that condition to a dealer who had him brought on board the boat.

When the vessel reached New Orleans, white friends of Arthur were there to meet it. His kidnappers had been identified and jailed, and his friends had come to rescue him and take him back to his family.

Northrup, on the other hand, after being kept for several weeks in the New Orleans slave pen, was sold to a planter named William Ford, a Baptist preacher who owned a lumber mill on the Red River near the Texas border. There Ford proved a kind master, but Northrup's troubles began when Ford fell on hard times and had to sell seventeen slaves, Northrup among them, to a man who was a notorious slave driver. From this point on his treatment grew harsher and more brutal and his life more degraded. Finally, after twelve years, Northrup managed to get a letter out to the white family that had owned his parents informing them of his whereabouts and pleading with them to help him regain his freedom. Evidence proving that Solomon was a free man was produced and a court order freed Solomon.

Back in Glens Falls, Northrup, with the assistance of a local newspaperman, gave a remarkably detailed and accurate picture of slave life in the deep South that under the title *Twelve Years a Slave* became a best-seller.

Northrup's book appeared two years after *Uncle Tom's Cabin,* and thus cannot be said to have had a major effect on public opinion, but it did serve as a reminder of one of the grimmest abuses produced by the slave system. Southerners protested that such cases were rare and that, when discovered, justice was done. But the fact remains that while in a slave population of over four million the number of free blacks kidnapped and sold into slavery may not have numbered more than a few thousand, each instance was a bitter personal tragedy.

Some free blacks formed colonies or settlements on the Western frontier or in Canada, but these had an uncertain fate. Moritz Busch, the German refugee from the upheavals of 1848, came on such a town in Mercer County, Indiana. It had been established by a white philanthropist, a Mr. Wattles of Connecticut, who had recruited the community from the depressed black population of Cincinnati. Wattles purchased the land and moved onto it with some two hundred blacks. Five years later the colony numbered over four hundred and eventually it evolved into the Emlen Institute for the education and training of black youths but, as the country around it filled up, the colony was subjected to "all sorts of torment and mistreatment," Busch wrote, so that many of the blacks abandoned their farms and returned to Cincinnati, where at least there was strength in numbers.

In Shelby County, Ohio, another colony of some three hundred fifty blacks, many of them the former slaves of John Randolph of Roanoke, lived a marginal rural existence. Near Georgetown, in the same state, the freed slaves of Samuel Gist, who originally emigrated from Virginia in 1818, survived. Such ventures were usually unsuccessful since blacks had neither the skills nor the motivation to compete with their aggressive white neighbors. The victims of both prejudice and ignorance, they were easy marks for unscrupulous whites. Deprived, in most instances, of the basic rights of citizenship, they lacked self-esteem and the protection of the law.

Free blacks in the South were, of necessity, in constant contact with whites, and these relationships were complex and infinitely subtle. They varied from the associations of upper-class free blacks and mulattoes in New Orleans with their white counterparts (to whom, it might be said, many were related), to the alliances between white criminals and those free blacks who lived, in large part, by petty theft. Some free blacks were engaged in business with white "fronts" or partners. This was especially true in saloons, hotels, and brothels. A gambling den in Baltimore in 1854 was run by three whites and a free black. In Nashville, Tennessee, a free black was the owner of "a contraband business in wet groceries, in the management of which Mrs. Nancy Walker, a white woman, is the ostensible representative."

White thieves often set up "night cribs" where blacks could bring stolen goods to be fenced. A few whites went so far as to conceal blacks for whom the police were looking or write passes for them to help them escape to other areas. Some fugitive blacks paid white men or women to pretend to be their masters. A Richmond paper reported in 1860 that "not only free Negroes but low white people can be found, who will secrete a slave from his master in order to get his services. . . ."

In Charleston, South Carolina, blacks with the names of prominent white families—the Hugers, Legarés and Poinsetts—were leaders in free black society and mingled, in special circumstances, with their white namesakes. Adam Bingaman, a wealthy Mississippi politician with a black mistress, was on familiar social terms with William Johnson, a black barber and "banker," and his wife. Southern towns and cities, moreover, had no black ghettos such as those that disfigured Northern cities. Black and white, rich and poor lived jumbled together. As the historian Ira Berlin puts it, "At times the indiscriminate distribution of free Negro and white residences threw the two castes together in striking combinations; wealthy whites and impoverished freemen, elite free Negroes and poor whites. . . ."

Much the same was true in the countryside where, at the lower economic levels, blacks and whites mixed far more freely than in the North. A patrol in South Carolina, attracted by the sound of revelry, came on "a collection of free blacks, slaves and some white folk, fiddling and frolicking generally." In Florida a census taker noted that the majority of free blacks were "mixed blood almost white and have intermarried with a low class of whites—have no trade, occupation or profession. They live in a Settlement or Town of their own, their personal property consists of cattle and hogs. They make no produce except Corn Peas and Potatoes and very little of that. They are a lazy, indolent smooth assed race."

A Richmond, Virginia, newspaper account of a raid on a gambling house described "a very interesting kettle of fish, at a negro den . . . where white, yellow and black congregate to eat, drink and be merry." In a "den of male and female reprobates" in Petersburg, Virginia, the night watch discovered "George Addington and Susan Evans, white; and George Bartley, Susan Smith and Sarah Smith, mulattoes; all of whom were found lying together promiscuously, upon a bunk redolent with the fumes of whiskey." Again in Richmond police found "two youthful white girls, not of uncomely figures or shape . . . pandering for lucre's sake to the passions of negroes."

Against all such lower-class "mixing" upper-class white leaders exerted constant social and legal pressure. While relatively few plantation owners forebore to have sexual relations with the slave women on their plantations and many members of the white aristocracy in such cities as Charleston and New Orleans had black or mulatto mistresses, they plainly felt threatened by any evidence of genuine equality in the relations between the sexes.

Another aspect of race relations in the South was the resistance of slaves to contact with the more prosperous free blacks, some of whom themselves owned slaves. Free blacks who had prospered materially in the white world were often more puritanical and morally strict than whites, looking down on lower-class free blacks for their laziness and promiscuity. William Johnson, the black barber and real estate dealer of Charleston, was indignant when he caught several of his slaves sparking a black girl. "Oh what Puppys," he wrote, "Fondling— beneath a Levell. Low minded Creatures. I look upon them as Soft." Johnson gave his daughters music lessons, bought large numbers of books, and bred racehorses.

Andrew Durnford was a free black who owned a plantation in Louisiana worked by seventy-five slaves. But Durnford showed no more inclination to criticize the system than any white slaveholder. Like them he complained frequently of the laziness of his "rascally negroes" and bought and sold them without compunction. Yet no black man, however well-to-do and however assiduous in imitating white ways, was ever accepted as an equal in white Southern society. Disliked by the poor men and women who made up the vast majority of the free blacks for their pretensions and mocked by the slaves, they lived in their own limbo.

The situation of the free black in the North was hardly better than that of his Southern counterpart. Confined to noisome and unhealthy ghettos and constantly embroiled in bitter conflicts with white working-men and Irish immigrants, the Northern black carried heavy burdens. There was much in George Fitzhugh's charge that the South at least afforded security to its old workers by providing for them in their declining years while the North turned them out of their jobs and left them to make out as best they could.

Sidney George Fisher worried about the fate of an old black hand at his Mt. Harmon farm in Maryland. "He is free," he wrote, "and an old, broken-down Negro in a slave state is an unfortunate being. Indeed, so is an old laborer in any state. This is a problem yet to be solved by society, how to combine liberty with subordination & to afford protection & support when needed & deserved without destroying self-reliance and self-respect."

North and South, Americans who were "black" in the slightest identifiable degree suffered humiliating and dehumanizing con-straints. When the American Anti-Slavery Society met in New York City in May, 1860, Robert Purvis, the featured speaker for the occasion, had been for thirty years a leader in the abolitionist movement. For the government that "declares one part of its people— and that for no crime or pretext of a crime—disenfranchised and outlawed," he could, he declared, have "no feeling but of *contempt, loathing* and *unutterable abhorrence!*"

The code of Draco, Purvis declared, was mild compared with "the hellish laws and precedents that disgrace the statute books of this modern democratic, Christian Republic!" Liberal whites professed to deplore the racial attitudes of "native Americanism," but what was "tenfold more base and contemptible" was "your piebald and rotten democracy—that talks loudly about equal rights and at the same time tramples one sixth of the population of the country in the dust." The free blacks of Pennsylvania had been disenfranchised by the state legislature in 1832, in large part because of the political pressure generated by Pierce Butler, grandson of one of the framers of the Constitution, and his allies in the assembly, the same Pierce Butler who had married Fanny Kemble. What Purvis would not let his predominantly white audience forget was that the status of free blacks in the North had declined markedly in the progressive, go-ahead age since the drafting of the Constitution.

32

Utopian Communities

We have already encountered in an earlier volume of this work two classic types of utopian communities: the Rappites, German pietists who wished to establish their own form of Christian communism in the New World, and Robert Owen's intensely secular but highly moralistic New Harmony, planted on soil first cultivated by the followers of George Rapp.

The Shakers, followers of Mother Anne (Christ returned in the person of a woman), were one of the scenes that most foreign visitors wished to view. With their highly organized and strikingly successful communal life, they ranked with Niagara Falls and American women as objects of interest to European travelers. In a century obsessed with the issue of community, the quiet, peaceful life of the Shakers—their material well-being, their charming music, even their celibacy—had enormous appeal to men and women trying to cope with the "real" world. The interest was not limited to foreign visitors. John Humphrey Noyes, the founder of the Oneida Community, spent seven months observing and analyzing what made the Shakers "work" when so many other, more sophisticated efforts failed.

Moritz Busch was charmed to hear the Shakers of Watervliet, New York, sing:

> O heavenly love surges, precious love flowers!
> Hallelujah! La la la!
> Up! Let us bend and let us bow,
> Interweave into a dance now . . .
> And let's drink happily as we sing
> Of the mildly flowing love
> That comes to us from above,
> From the Mother's inexhaustible spring.

The Rappites, though more exotic than the Shakers, were also the subject of much interested study. A Hungarian traveler named Sándor Farkas de Bölön, accompanied by the wealthy Transylvanian, Count Francis Béldi, visited the Rappite colony of Economy, Pennsylvania, in 1831. Farkas noted that the accounts of the Rappites that circulated in Europe were contradictory. "One depicts Rapp's Society as a society of united industry, of perfect equality, and dedicated to the purest moralities. Others depict it as a society of simple Germans, blinded by Rapp's foolish lures, of people who are selfishly and intellectually exploited by Rapp, and who will have to dissolve upon Rapp's eventual death. . . . The main principles of the Rappists, or Harmonists, are: perfect equality, common property of all earnings—no one has private wealth, all belongs to the community. Everyone has equal rights to the otherwise indivisible common wealth—that may be used by anyone— but everyone has to work in some way and to add to this common property. Idle members have no place in the Society; everyone has to take up some endeavor according to his strength and intellectual capacity."

Economy was flourishing. The count and his young traveling companion saw "in the tremendous fields—50–60 ploughshares; in the fenced pastures we saw especially beautiful herds; elsewhere very attractive Merino sheep; again colts, cows . . . and in such large herds as we are accustomed to see on the great Hungarian estates. On the road we met many groups of laborers, in Rhenish and Swabian dress. Haystacks, wheat crosses, brick ovens, and other farm sheds stood around. Had we not known where we were, we might have thought that we were entering the estate of a wealthy aristocrat." The village itself had "beautiful, wide streets . . . with a double row of trees." Every house had its own garden plot and there was a "luxurious inn" and a simple church in the center of town.

The elder Rapp had brought twelve hundred immigrants from Wurttemburg and "kept them together," Farkas noted, "with his intellectual leadership," raising them from "their erstwhile poverty" to prosperity. Rapp, who was then about seventy, appeared in "a long, old-fashioned, large buttoned coat, with a big, knobby cane; his steps were lively, his blue eyes shone vividly from under his bushy eyebrows, he had an extraordinary face, smiling cheeks, and simple gestures." George Rapp told his visitors that since his childhood he had read the Scriptures and early felt that Christianity had parted "from its original moral simplicity." He found that many of his neighbors, farmers and peasants, shared his convictions and they had finally decided to emigrate to the United States. Economy contained, in addition to its fertile fields, a woolen mill, a flax breaker, a brewery, a distillery, and large flour mills, all driven by steam.

The Hungarians found Economy "a great school of practical philosophy and of practical life! What is done here, is clear: these simple morals, this placid domesticity, this disregard of worldly glitter which nevertheless brings a plentitude of wealth—all of this would seem a pious dream, had we not seen it and been convinced of its true existence. Does not this Society," Farkas wrote, "hamper the higher strivings of the intellect? Or curb the proud self-consciousness of man's will to be superior? Or do these simple patriarchial pleasures, this secure wealth, and this spurning of worldly vanities satisfy the soul amid all this constant work? Of all this different minds will possibly decide differently. I left this place with admiration, richer with the discovery of a new philosophy."

The Rappites did not marry, yet the community was full of the children of members who had joined the community as families. They were also millenarians, who believed in the imminent second coming of Christ.

Interesting as the Shakers and the Rappites were, theirs were modest ventures with limited appeal. Above all, they were retreats. They had no ambition to reorganize or redeem a fallen world. They simply sought refuge for the faithful. The 1830s and '40s witnessed quite a new phenomenon, one akin to Robert Owen's New Harmony —social experiments whose avowed purpose was to create a model for the more humane reorganization of society. They were all, in one degree or another, socialistic or communistic and they were clearly protests against the cruelly exploitative aspects of a burgeoning industrial capitalism.

The most widespread of these ventures were the Fourier "pha-lanxes." Charles (François Marie) Fourier was a French reformer who envisioned a world made up of cooperative units of production organized in what he called phalanxes or common buildings. Intensive agriculture was to be the basis of the economic life of the phalanxes. The common earnings were to be divided between labor, capital, and talent, with the largest portion going to labor. The members were to own shares in the phalanx, which in turn was to provide such common amenities as a community center, school, library, health clinic, bank and "shoppers' mall."

Work assignments were to be rotated regularly, so that no member would be stuck with menial or unrewarding tasks. Members were organized for their work in "series" and "groups." There was the Farming Series, the Domestic Series, and various other Series. These were in turn divided into the Cattle Group, the Milking Group, the Plowing Group, the Nursery, and the Culinary Groups. It was all marvelously French and quite unworkable. The phalanx itself was conceived of as a unit of some six thousand acres, the core of which was the phalanxtery, a double row of buildings seven hundred yards long, one of which contained dining rooms, kitchens, apartments, and workshops; the other storage chambers, stables, and granaries. Needless to say, no phalanxteries were ever built, but thousands of individuals collected at prospective phalanxes.

Fourier, who apparently had little practical interest in establishing phalanxes (for fear, possibly, that they would be badly managed and thus discredit his ideas), found an enthusiastic advocate in Arthur Brisbane, an American journalist who wrote a Fourier-influenced book called *The Social Destiny of Man* and then, with a column in Horace Greeley's *New York Tribune,* promoted the cause of Utopian socialism. It was Brisbane who was primarily responsible for the vast number of phalanxes that sprang up in the early 1840s.

In his *History of American Socialisms,* Noyes counted some eighty utopian or socialist experiments, many of them in one degree or another religious in inspiration. Thirty-four were Fourier phalanxes. The others ranged from Jemima Wilkinson, "the Universal Friend," and her community, established in 1780, through Frances Wright's Nashoba community, to the Association of All Classes of All Nations, the Brotherhood of the Union, and the Communial Working Men's League. Fifty-seven were established in the decades of the forties and fifties, thirty-nine in the five-year period between 1840 and 1845.

Few lasted as long as a year. The North American Phalanx in New Jersey survived for twelve; Hopedale, in Massachusetts, for seventeen.

Noyes paid particular attention to Hopedale. It was, he wrote, "intensely religious in its ideal. As Brook Farm was the blossom of Unitarianism, so Hopedale was the blossom of Universalism." Under Aldin Ballou, "it came nearest to being a religious community—it commenced earlier, lasted longer, and was really more scientific and sensible than any other experiments of the Fourier epoch." Ballou wrote of it, "it insists on supreme love to God and man. . . . It enjoins total abstinence from all God-condemning words and deeds; all unchastity; all intoxicating beverages; all oath-taking; all slave-holding and pro-slavery compromises; all war and preparation for war; all capital and other vindictive punishments; all insurrectionary, seditious, mobocratic and personal violence against any government, society, family or individual; all voluntary participation in any anti-Christian Government . . . all resistance of evil with evil; in fine, from all things known to be sinful against God or human nature. . . . It is a Civil State, a miniature Christian Republic . . . it is the seedling of the true Democratic and Social Republic, wherein neither caste, color, sex nor age stands proscribed. . . . It is a universal religious, moral, philanthropic, and social reform Association. It is a Missionary Society for the promulgation of New Testament Christianity, the reformation of the nominal church, and the conversion of the world. . . . It solves the problem which has so long puzzled Socialists, the harmonization of just individual freedom with social cooperation." Ballou believed that all man's wants, rights, and duties could be comprehended in seven spheres, reaching from individuality to universality. These could be comprehended in four distinct kinds of communities which, in turn, would be built into larger social units up to a "grand Fraternity of Nations, represented by Senators in the Supreme Unitary Council." After some seventeen years of precarious existence, Hopedale foundered on the rocks of insolvency in 1858.

Brisbane comforted himself after the collapse of most of the phalanxes with the thought that "if Fourier has failed, if he has not discovered the laws of natural organization, or has not deduced rightly from them, he has opened the way and pointed out the true path. . . . He has shown how the human mind is to create a Social Science, and effect the Social Reconstruction to which this science is to lead. . . . Fourier is the Kepler of new science. . . . Other great minds will be required to complete the science. It will have its Galileo, its Newton, its Laplace . . . it is the crowning intellectual evolution, which human genius is to effect in its scientific career."

To Noyes the weakness of Fourierism was that it was not founded, like Oneida and Hopedale, on a devout and pervasive Christianity. In his *History of American Socialisms,* Noyes was careful to distinguish between what he called "revivalism" and "socialism." Socialism, without a strong religious dimension, must fail because only religion could tame the baser instincts of the human heart. Revivalism without "social science" or scientific socialism must prove equally impotent because the enthusiasm created by the revival experience must soon be dissipated if it was not given a formal social and economic structure.

Noyes charged Brisbane with damaging the cause of socialism in the United States by "spending all his energy drumming and recruiting," encouraging the establishment of dozens of hastily conceived and inadequately planned phalanxes. Not only had socialism been given a bad name, social science—"which is really the science of righteousness"—had suffered a setback by being divorced from Christian morality. Thus the "Shakers and Rappites, whom Mr. Brisbane does not condescend to mention, are really the pioneers of modern Socialism," Noyes wrote, "whose experiments deserve a great deal more study than all the speculations of the French schools. . . . Thus it is no more than bare justice to say that we are indebted to the Shakers more than to any or all other social architects of modern times."

Arthur Brisbane and John Humphrey Noyes make an instructive contrast. Brisbane was a spokesman for the new "objective" science. He was impatient with the Shakers and Rappites who so intrigued Noyes. Religion was irrelevant in an increasingly secular society. *Science was the religion.* Noyes, on the other hand, spoke for the older tradition, rooted in the Puritan vision of a redeemed Christian commonwealth. Moral issues lay at the heart of his social science, pragmatic experimentation was essential, deductive reasoning was the enemy. Christian faith was the *given;* understanding its social and economic implications and translating those into human groups in a pragmatic spirit was the task of the new social science.

Of this extraordinary efflorescence of socialist experiments on the Fourier model several things may be said. Part was simply fad, of course, the readiness of Americans to chase after any new nostrum or panacea. Part was the never entirely buried vision of the true commonwealth. Part was a profound disillusionment with the direction in which American history seemed to be moving with increasing velocity. And closely related was a deep feeling of alienation and despair on the part of ordinary Americans, who felt the stress and pressure of American life too heavy a load to bear.

Another French political theorist and socialist, Etienne Cabêt, advocated complete equality between men and women, the suppression of self-interest, and freedom of religion; he was reputed to have enlisted hundreds of thousands of French, Germans, Swiss, and Italians in his cause and he brought 480 of his followers (called Icarians) first to Texas, and then, that effort having failed, to the town of Nauvoo in Illinois, recently abandoned by the Mormons. Like so many other similar ventures, the colony proved long on ideals and short in practicality.

Undoubtedly the most famous of the utopian communities, in large part because of the famous literary figures attracted to it, was George Ripley's transcendentalist colony at Brook Farm, Massachusetts—the Institute of Agriculture and Education, to give it its proper name, established in 1841. A refuge for Emerson, Hawthorne briefly (Thoreau avoided it), and a dozen other lights of the transcendental movement, it sought, like most of the other communities, to create a noncompetitive, harmonious "space" where physical labor and high thinking would compliment each other. As Ripley put it, he and his fellows "wished to prepare a society of liberal, intelligent and cultivated persons, whose relations with each other would permit a more wholesome and simple life than can be led amidst the pressure of our competitive institutions."

William Ellery Channing, the famous Unitarian minister, was one of Brook Farm's spiritual godfathers. Its principal appeal was to the young men and women of Boston with liberal inclinations who shrank from the gross materialism of American life. Emerson's great declaration in his Phi Beta Kappa address on "The American Scholar" was a creed for the young idealists of Brook Farm. Emerson had announced: "We will walk on our own feet; we will work with our own hands; we will speak our own minds. The study of letters shall no longer be a name for pity, for doubt, and for sensual indulgence."

George William Curtis, the editor-to-be of *Harper's Weekly*, recalled his own youthful enthusiasm and desire to express "boundless protest against the friction and apparent unreason of the existing order." The young transcendentalists outraged their elders as much by their dress as by their ideas. They appeared in public "with hair parted in the middle and falling upon their shoulders, and clad in garments such as no known human being ever wore before—garments which seemed to be a compromise between the blouse of the Paris workman and the *peignoir* of a possible sister."

While the leaders of the community were drawn from Harvard classrooms and Unitarian pulpits, the residents of the Institute were a heterogeneous lot, "young farmers, seamstresses, mechanics . . . the industrious, the lazy, the conceited, and sentimental. . . ." If there was a notable lack of practicality about the venture, there was an amplitude of brilliant conversation and good spirits. In Curtis's words, "there were never such witty potato patches and such sparkling cornfields before or since. The weeds were scratched out of the ground to the music of Tennyson or Browning, and the nooning was an hour as gay and bright as any brilliant midnight at Ambrose's."

Virtually everyone who visited Brook Farm and most of its members wrote about it. One of the most engaging accounts is that of Georgiana Bruce, a young Englishwoman who joined Brook Farm soon after it started. She found it a stimulating refuge from the practical world. Work and study were interspersed with delightful conversations, sometimes with Orestes Brownson, "the unpolished, vehement, and positive man," as Georgiana Bruce put it, "who had been foremost in his assaults on our vicious social system [and] had now dropped his sledge-hammer and other modern tools, and walked backwards into the Catholic Church." When Brownson appeared there were heated debates. It was clear that he got on mild-mannered George Ripley's nerves. One night Ripley "dreamed that he had become a Catholic, and that Brownson had been appointed his confessor." After he had confessed his sins, Brownson said to him: 'Kneel, my son, and for penance repeat after me the 58th psalm in the Vulgate.' Upon which the dreamer in mortal agony cried out: 'O Lord, my punishment is greater than I am able to bear!' and woke up trembling from head to foot."

As the fame of Brook Farm spread, letters poured in asking for admission "from German political refugees whose possessions consisted of radical ideas and the classic tongues; from small traders who were being cut out by large capitalists; from widows with helpless children, whose only property was a few hundred dollars."

Much attention was devoted to education. In conventional education "we stuff our children with dry facts, overloading their memory, while leaving the higher faculties dormant," Georgiana Bruce wrote. If at Brook Farm a freer, more inspiring system of education could be developed that would expand the imagination and enhance the reasoning and intuitive faculties "then we should have a right to anticipate great and original qualities in the coming generation" and the nation "might have its 'rise and progress' without any 'decline.'"

The school was perhaps Brook Farm's most successful institution. In addition to the regular curriculum, work on the farm was mixed with study and much emphasis was placed on music, dancing, and drawing. The works of Beethoven, Mozart, and Haydn were part of the curriculum. There were plays, concerts, poetry and dramatic readings. "Brook Farm," Georgiana wrote, "was a grand place for children, and I am sure they had never before been so happy. They were given the right sort of care, and left the right kind of freedom." George Ripley's wife, Sophia, "read aloud the best books within their comprehension." They learned to dance and feasted on fruit and gingerbread. "Farmers', artists', sea captains', and cooks' children found themselves on the same plane of opportunities."

George Ripley told those who accused Brook Farm of being a nest of infidels who never went to church that the church had done its best to destroy Christianity. "Jesus," he declared, "instead of a friend, is held over us as a rigid taskmaster. We live in formality and dead forms, and the end and aim of our services is not freedom, growth, fraternal love, but a stolid safety from all these." The members of the Brook Farm community were "emancipated from all the churches, and worship more generally in the discharge of their duty and in the admiration of God's universe, than in any house. . . . One hour's talk with a true and loving spirit is of more worth to me than the litanies of a cathedral, or the eloquence of an archangel."

Like many others, Georgiana Bruce left Brook Farm after a residence of a little more than a year, but she was convinced that the experience had changed her life in important ways. The reformers and intellectuals she had met there "inspired the young with a passion for study, and the middle-aged with deference and admiration, while we all breathed the intellectual grace that pervaded the atmosphere. All the newest and most beautiful thoughts of the time seemed to find us out, and thus we were kept *en rapport* with the noblest of all lands, and quite secure from any petty feelings. . . . We . . . hopefully await-ed the time when intelligent capitalists and skilled artisans converted to the cooperative ideas, should, by the establishment of factories, place our enterprise out of the reach of any possible danger. . . . We believed . . . that the times were ripe for the abandonment of the miseries and falsehoods of the social order termed 'civilization.'"

The desire to serve and care for each other produced the "griddle-cake crisis." "Those eating their breakfasts declared that they could not enjoy the hot cakes while oppressed by the thought of two or three friends leaning over the stove cooking them." A meeting settled the question by having the eaters then turn about and serve the cooks.

After a time it was evident that Brook Farm needed "skilled mechanics in place of transcendental enthusiasts." The members decided to convert Brook Farm into a Fourier phalanx. But somehow, for all Brook Farm's high-minded democratic principles, the new "Fourieristic" mix did not work. "The charm was swiftly dispelled," Georgiana Bruce wrote. Fourierism "frightened away the idealists whose presence had given the spot its chief attraction and injured the pastoral bloom which beautified it. The reputation of Brook Farm for brilliancy, wit, and harmless eccentricity was seriously compromised. The joyous spirit of youth was sobered. The outside community henceforth regarded the enterprise as a mechanical attempt to reform society, rather than a poetic attempt to regenerate it."

In 1847, after a disastrous fire, Brook Farm closed its doors. Despite its short life, it was a kind of enchanted moment in our history. While many critics denounced it as socialistic and un-American and others poked fun at it, none of those who came in close contact with it could ever quite shake off its spell. Emerson wrote that its founders "Should have this praise, that they made what all people try to make, an agreeable place to live in. All comers . . . found it the pleasantest of residences. . . . There is agreement that it was to most of the associates, education; to many the most important period of their life, the birth of valued friendships, their first acquaintance with riches of conversation. . . . It was a perpetual picnic, a French Revolution in small, an Age of Reason in a patty-pan," and he wrote of his own involvement, "I wished to be convinced, to be thawed, to be made nobly mad by the kindlings before my eye of a new dawn of human piety. But this scheme was arithmetic and comfort . . . a rage in our poverty and politics to live rich and gentlemanlike, an anchor to the leeward against a change of weather; a prudent forecast on the probable issue of the great questions of Pauperism and Poverty."

Georgiana Bruce wrote: "What a royal time we had. The days were full of affection and sunshine. . . . The very air seemed to hold more exhilarating qualities than any I had breathed before." Hawthorne, who was often a skeptic and whose *Blithedale Romance* satirized Brook Farm, wrote in the final chapter, "Often in these years that are darkening around me, I remember our beautiful scheme of a noble and unselfish life, and how fair in that first summer appeared the prospect that it might endure for generations, and be perfected as the ages rolled by, into a system of a people and a world. . . . More and more I feel we struck upon what ought be a truth. Posterity may dig it up and profit by it."

Perhaps the oddest phenomenon of the latter days of Brook Farm was the conversion of a number of its members to Catholicism, among them, Richard Henry Dana's sister, the brother of Charles Sumner, and, most startling of all, Sophia Ripley. "How *could* they take such a step?" Georgiana Bruce asked herself. "What induced them to do it? . . . Perhaps it was the disappointment of the breaking up of our hopes. Perhaps the speculative intellect needed rest. . . ." Perhaps it was the compelling character of Brownson himself and a feeling that all the marvelous talk had come to nothing.

Georgiana Bruce refused to believe "that there was no result from the too early attempt to reorganize society. Every loving word and deed produces results according to its kind," she wrote, "and an incalculable impetus to rational and generous thought was afforded by the apparent failures."

Bronson Alcott, thinking Brook Farm too worldly a venture, was determined to found his own Utopia. "Our freer, but yet far from freed, land," he wrote, "is the asylum, if asylum there be, for the hope of man; and, there, if anywhere, is the second Eden to be planted in which the divine seed is to bruise the head of Evil and restore Man to his rightful communion with God in the Paradise of Good."

Alcott found a partner in a half-crazy English visionary named Charles Lane, whose money enabled the vegetarian reformer to start his Fruitlands on ninety acres of land some fifty miles from Concord. He collected an oddly variegated lot—Isaac Hecker, a radical labor leader from New York who was to become a Catholic priest; Lane, who advocated the overthrow of the United States government; several local farmers; and Alcott's wife and four young daughters. If fun and high spirits characterized life at Brook Farm, Fruitlands was all austerity. Its diet was primarily apples, potatoes, and whole wheat bread. Since cotton was produced by slaves and wool stolen from sheep, the colonists were forced to wear linen garments. The crops were neglected in favor of writing tracts and giving lectures about the advantages of the community.

Georgiana Bruce reported that at Fruitlands, "One old man kept a cow on an adjoining farm and drank all the milk himself. The children's governess had cheese in her trunk, and another unregenerate son of Adam had salt fish hidden on the premises." When one farmer asked his neighbor who did all the work at Fruitlands, the latter replied, "Mrs. Alcott and the girls."

After a few months Lane took his son and his money to a nearby Shaker settlement, Alcott fell ill, and his poor wife grew infinitely weary of the whole experiment. It lasted barely six months and Louisa May, in a story written years later called "Transcendental Wild Oats," has the character that is obviously her father exclaim: " 'Ah, me! my happy dream. How much I leave behind that never can be mine again. . . . Poor Fruitlands! The name was as great a failure as the rest,' continued Abel, with a sigh, as a frost-bitten apple fell from a leafless bough at his feet."

If the Fourier phalanxes were the most numerous of the mid-nineteenth-century utopian communities and Brook Farm the most famous, Noyes's Oneida Community was the most interesting. John Humphrey Noyes was one of those Americans described by Harriet Martineau as "originals," types unique to the soil of the New World. He was a Vermont boy who had attended Dartmouth College and studied law and theology at Yale. Somewhere along the line he began to develop his own unique combination of Christian socialism. A later-day socialist, George Bernard Shaw, described him as "one of those chance attempts at the Superman which occur from time to time in spite of the interference of Man's blundering institutions." Noyes decided that the Second Coming of Christ had already taken place. The Kingdom of Heaven was already on earth. From this conviction a number of consequences followed. For those who believed they were "perfected," the government of Christ was superior to any mundane institutions. Since there was, according to the Scriptures, no marrying and giving in marriage in heaven, all the faithful or perfected were married to each other, in what Noyes called "complex marriage." Sexual relations were "amative" as a particularly intimate expression of love—or "propagative," for the propagating of children. Children were the common responsibility of the community, therefore no one in the community should have propagative relations without the agreement of the community. Indeed even amative intercourse was controlled by the older women in the community. A rather taxing form of birth control was required—*coitus reservatus,* whereby the male stopped short of emission. Before young men could have sexual relations with women their own age, they had to have such relations with older women who had gone through menopause. With them they perfected the practice of "male continence." "Every woman was free to refuse any, or every, man's attention." Noyes defended the constant attacks by outsiders on the "free love" practices of the community by pointing out the superiority of complex marriage over conventional marriages. "It is the theory of the equal rights of women and men," he wrote, "and the freedom of both from habitual and legal obligations. . . . It is the theory that love *after* marriage and always and forever, should be what it is *before* marriage—a glowing attraction on both sides, and not the odious obligation of one party and the sensual recklessness of the other."

After some preliminary effort of Noyes and his followers to live and practice their beliefs in existing communities, to the great scandal of the other residents, Noyes drew his flock into a community at Oneida in New York state in 1847, the year that Brook Farm went out of existence. Some 250 persons made up the core of the community of Perfectionists, as they were called. The aim was that everyone "should be surrounded with circumstances favoring the best development of heart, mind and body."

Noyes regarded the Oneida Community as a continuation of Brook Farm, which he knew by firsthand observation. Like the Brook Farmers, the Perfectionists had their own school, run on advanced principles, which emphasized plays, games, concerts, picnics, and dances. "We insist," Noyes wrote, "that God's appointed way for man to seek the truth in all departments, and above all in Social Science, which is really the science of righteousness, is to combine and alternate thinking with experience and practice, and constantly submit all theories, whether obtained by scientific investigation or by intuition and inspiration, to the consuming ordeal of practical verification."

From the first the community had a press which poured out a stream of material, most of it written by Noyes. The soul, in Noyes's view, was the indestructible, guiding element in the human body. The world was the scene of a constant battle between God and Satan, God creating an internal pressure that counteracted the external pressure created by the Devil. The Perfected man or woman was guided and controlled by the spirit of the Almighty. The reborn person would have a clear and rational mind and a loving heart in which all selfishness was extinguished. Above all he or she would seek spiritual improvement.

The daily life of the Perfectionists revolved around their work. No laborious and menial work was directly assigned, but when such work needed to be done "Bees" were organized in which a number of persons pitched in voluntarily. As one member of the community wrote, "Anyone who has the responsibility of a job or has a special interest in having it done, mentions it in the evening before with an invitation to a general Bee, and the red rising sun of the next morning greets us in the field. One morning it is the kitchen group which invites to a Bee in the meadows for gathering cowslips for dinner. This system is particularly useful applied to those monotonous kinds of work which in detail would tire out one or two workers; done by storm by a large company, there is, as the phrase is, 'nothing but fun.' "

There were no distinctions of sex in the kind of work done. The Perfectionists favored "*the mingling of the sexes in labor. . . .* We believe," a member wrote, "that the great secret in securing enthusiasm in labor and producing a free, healthy, social equilibrium, is contained in the proposition, 'loving companionship, and labor,' and especially the mingling of the sexes, makes labor attractive."

Despite such doctrines, the Perfectionists had great difficulty making financial ends meet and it was not until a recruit appeared with an improved steel trap of his own invention that the community was established on sound financial ground. Sewell Newhouse turned his trap over to the community and helped develop methods of mass production that enabled the group to turn out a large number of traps at a low price. Soon they were hiring outside labor and branching out into spoon and bag factories. The members themselves never received wages for their work; all money went into a common fund to provide for the common needs. Those too old to work were provided for, as were the ill and the children of the community. Constance Noyes described a typical work scene at Oneida. "Our great omnibus, which holds fifteen or sixteen persons on a squeeze, starts from the house at six and a half o'clock in the evening, and we get fairly at work a little before seven. Sometimes we put together links to be 'fitted,' then again some of us rivet jaws, try swivels, and arrange the chains for testing. The noise of the machinery, the flickering of dozens of little kerosene lights, the talking, laughing, and occasional singing of the people make a lively attractive scene. We women and girls like the work very much. . . ."

Speaking of the general atmosphere of the community, Noyes

wrote, "Certainly we could not wish for better surroundings for a child to make him—not indeed a distorted professional, or a hard-faced speculator—but to make him a gentle, thoughtful man of use and improvement. I hope he will be ever kept from the mercenary idea of doing things for pay, or making riches for himself. . . . Let him [also] remain free from the absurd notion that one kind of employment is more honorable than another, which causes so much mischief in the world. He will be taught in the Community that it is not the kind of work that dignifies a man, but that by good spirit and good manners the man dignifies *every kind* of work; and that he is the truest gentleman who is capable of doing the most useful things."

Dress reform and the equal education of women were other principles of Noyes and the Perfectionists. The women cut their long hair short, wore comfortable, practical pantaloons, and learned to play ball with the men. Noyes wrote of their role in the community, "I can truly say that I am proud of our women, young and old. I see that in will and principle, and to a good extent in practice and feeling, they have conquered the fashions of the world in themselves, and are substantially free from bondage to the spirit of dress and ornament. . . . They have, in many respects, had to bear the brunt of the battle for Communism. . . . They have proved themselves good soldiers; and they will have their reward."

For more than thirty years the faithful company of the Perfected scandalized their fellow Americans and proved the viability of Noyes's ideas.

The reader must keep in mind that we have been talking here primarily about utopian socialistic or communistic communities, characterized by a determination to work cooperatively and to share the fruits of the common labor. For every such heavily ideological enterprise, there were literally hundreds of more modest utopias. I have classified American communities into two types, the cumulative and the covenanted or colonized. The cumulative community was (and is) a community started in response to some economic opportunity—a mine, a river junction, a natural power source. Cumulative towns have been collections of heterogeneous individuals whose motivations have been essentially material. The colonized towns were made up of friends and relatives sharing the same vision. Their establishment was often preceded by a covenant or agreement that was a direct descendant of the Mayflower Compact, by means of which the founders of the community pledged themselves to a common goal. When a group seeking a purified community emigrated from Granville, Massachusetts, to Granville, Ohio, they drew up a covenant and a constitution and transplanted pastor, deacons, and church members to their new home. Their first act on reaching the settlement was to hold a service of worship in the forest. One of the band later wrote that "they wept when they remembered Zion."

Oberlin, in Lorain County, Ohio, was another transplanted New England community. The colonists pledged themselves to "a life of simplicity, to special devotion to church and school, and to earnest labor in the missionary cause."

By 1840 Illinois could count at least twenty-two colonies of transplanted New Englanders or New Yorkers in the northern or central regions of the state. The so-called Union Colony, which established itself in Vermontville, Michigan, originated in Putney, Vermont. Its members agreed, "As we must necessarily endure many of those trials and privations which are incident to a settlement in a new country, we agree we will do all in our power to befriend each other; we will esteem it not only a duty but a privilege to sympathize with each other under all our trials, to do good and lend, hoping for nothing again, and to assist each other on all necessary occasions."

Some such communities were, as the decades passed, temperance communities, hoping for redemption through total abstinence; others sought salvation through vegetarianism or hydropathy. The utopian socialist communities, secular or Christian, shared with the covenanted colonized communities the impulse to counteract the disintegrative effects of American life. They were, at the same time, a kind of index to the severity of the disintegrative forces constantly at work and there is thus, about them, a special poignance. Idealistic and impractical— visionary—as they seemed to the great majority of Americans, they kept circulating through the larger and generally indifferent society ideas of social change and reform, many of which are reclaiming our attention today; ideas that, impractical as they may seem, we dare not ignore since they contain much of what is best and most aspiring in our culture. "Dreamers of the American Dream," one historian has called these utopians.

The ubiquitousness of the success ethic in the United States has often inclined us to ignore or patronize the ventures that fail, but the true heroes and heroines of our society have been those men and women who endured (or invited) ridicule and obloquy on behalf of people and causes that had no other champions. By being too soon, they enabled us eventually to be "on time." They were the salt that gave savor to the vast, indigestible lump that was the United States. So we are drawn back again and again to them and their sometimes loony but noble dreams of a more just and humane social and economic order.

33

Reform

The Protestant passion for reform was insatiable. It reached into every nook and cranny of American life. It searched out every public vice, every secret blemish. It was not "reform" as we think it today—a strenuously secular, liberal spirit of social improvement. It was rather full of redemptive ardor. Its referent was the Protestant Reformation directed at the reformation of Christendom and then, of course, of the world. The Friends of Universal Reform wished, as the word "Universal" suggested, to reform everybody and everything.

When the Friends met in Boston in 1840, Emerson, who attended some of their meetings, described them as "Madmen, mad-women, men with beards, Dunkers, Muggletonians, Groaners, Agrarians, Seventh-Day Baptists, Quakers, Abolitionists, Calvinists, Unitarians, and Philosophers—all came successively to the top, and seized their moment, if not their hour, wherein to chide, or pray, or protest." He was struck, nonetheless, by the "prophetic dignity" of the speakers.

Prominent among the reformers were the reformers of the American diet, vegetarians primarily, whose most notable leader was charming, gentle, visionary Bronson Alcott, father of a brilliant daughter, Louisa May. When George Templeton Strong met Bronson Alcott, he noted in his diary, "The great Alcott is a vegetarian, and I think attributes most of the sin and evil in the world to our carnivorous habits. 'We are what we eat.' 'We make our flesh out of the substance of sheep and pigs, therefore, we make ourselves like sheep and pigs,' was the substance of his argument on that head."

The principal theoretician of the vegetarian forces was Sylvester Graham, who preached that meat eaters could not enter heaven. Not only was the killing of animals a sin (Alcott would not wear any article of clothing made of leather, including shoes), eating meat accentuated the animal appetites of man, most especially the sexual. Vegetables and grains moderated those lusts. To help redeem society Graham invented a whole-grain cracker which came to bear his name.

Abolition of slavery aside, the most persistent reform effort was temperance reform. It enlisted more Americans, expended more energy, survived longer (and one is tempted to say accomplished less) than any other reform movement in our history.

Spirituous liquors have occupied a central place in our history from the instant the first Puritans set foot on "the rock" (if, of course, they stepped on it at all). Getting stoned, fizzled, sloshed, or just plain blind drunk has been Americans' favorite indoor sport for considerably more than three hundred years. From which I think we must conclude that there has always been something in the nature of American life that has impelled us to the use of stimulants and narcotics in excessive amounts.

To live by the "will," the naked assertion of self, is, itself, a great strain on the nervous system. To compete, to be always on the competitive edge of life is another strain. The landscape with all its untamed terrors and awesome grandeur was another source of anxiety. In the go-ahead age the collective American nervous system was as strung-out as the electro-magnetic telegraph lines.

Sidney George Fisher (and many others) spoke of the "excitement" of life in the Mississippi Valley West. "Excitement" is a key word. Excitement worked on the nerves and the nerves cried out for sedation. Liquor was the primary and essential, though by no means exclusive, sedative.

In 1843 George Templeton Strong noted in his diary that "opium chewing prevails here extensively." Strong blamed it on the temperance movement, adding, "Nothing more natural—a 'movement' of that sort never moved away the *principle* of any vice, though it may drive this or that development of it into the background for a while."

Americans were always in motion—a perpetually restless people

—whittling, chewing and spitting, smoking and, above all, drinking. We know drunkenness to be a "social disease." That is to say, the incidence of alcoholism in a society is at least roughly equivalent to the inability of its members to cope with the burden of daily life which the society places on them.

In addition drinking was, on a simpler level, a way, as we say today, of "relating," of establishing contact, "breaking the ice." Captain Marryat declared: "Americans can fix nothing without a drink. If you meet, you drink; if you part, you drink; if you make acquaintance, you drink; if you close a bargain, you drink; they quarrel in their drink, and they make it up with a drink. They drink because it is hot; they drink because it is cold. If successful in elections, they drink and rejoice; if not, they drink and swear; they begin to drink early in the morning, they leave off late at night; they commence it early in life, and they continue it, until they soon drop into the grave. To use their expression, the way they drink is 'quite a caution.' As for water, what the man said, when asked to belong to the Temperance Society, appears to be the general opinion: 'It's very good for navigation.'"

Temperance, while it had some obvious overlap with the woman's rights movement in the sense that it carried a load of latent hostility toward men as well as a measure of sexual anxiety, was far more amorphous. Was it directed toward getting every individual American to sign "the pledge," to swear off alcohol in any form? Or was it directed to prohibitory laws which would forbid the manufacture and sale of spirituous liquors from wine and beer up (although there were divisions on that question as well)? The trouble with the individual redemption approach was that it was wildly utopian to believe that enough Americans could ever be persuaded to abandon the bottle or even be "temperate" in their use of such beverages. The prohibitory approach, of which more and more was heard as it became apparent that the moral redemption approach was unsuccessful, ran in the face of cherished American ideals of individual freedom. Who were the "prohibitionists" to tell their neighbors that they could not enjoy a social glass of beer or wine, or of rye or bourbon for that matter, simply because some benighted individuals imbibed excessively? The fact was that drunkenness was one of those problems, not uncommon in our history, for which there was no satisfactory solution. Which did not, of course, keep innumerable Americans from trying to devise one. Drunkenness was clearly part of the price Americans had to pay for the disintegrative effects of American life—the high level of anxiety in all social classes and the often desperately harsh conditions and profound sense of loneliness and alienation so often associated with life in big cities and on the frontier. Yet there were as many chronic drunkards in the classic agricultural villages of New England as there were on the Wisconsin or Missouri frontier, perhaps more. In the recollection of William Goodell, who grew up in a small Massachusetts town: "In those days everybody drank, old and young, rich and poor, male and female; and our whole country seemed rapidly descending on the steep and slippery side of the hill towards ruin. But New England at length arose in the greatness of her strength, and, in the firmness of her principles, signed the temperance pledge; 'and the land had rest for forty years.'"

So the appalling extent of drunkenness in America, which was apparent from the time the first English settlers landed in the New World, must be seen as symptomatic of the terrible strains and stresses in American life (as well perhaps as an indication of the absence of folk ceremonies and festivities in which drinking was "socialized" and contained within what, in other cultures, was often a religious context and thereby robbed of its most demoralizing consequences).

The intimate connection between Protestant Christianity and the temperance movement is indicated by an address delivered by the Right Reverend Charles McIlvaine, an Episcopal bishop, on the occasion of the founding of the New York Young Men's Temperance Society in 1833. The bishop assured his audience that "great strides have already been accomplished; that much greater are near at hand; and that the whole victory will be eventually won if the temperance portion of society are not wanting in their solemn duty. . . ." The civilized world had expressed horror at the loss of life in a single battle of the Napoleonic Wars but far more Americans lost their lives every year to the evil of drunkenness. "Enough is known of the intemperance of this country," the bishop declared, "to render it undeniable by the most ignorant inhabitant, that a horrible scourge is indeed upon us. . . . *The time has come when a great effort must be made to exterminate this unequalled destroyer.* . . . In order to exert ourselves with the best effect . . . let us associate ourselves into *Temperance Societies.* We know the importance of associated exertions. . . . The whole progress of the temperance reformation, thus far, is owing to the influence of *societies;* to the coming together of the temperate, and the union of their resolutions, examples and exertions, under the articles of temperance societies."

When Amelia Bloomer, Susan B. Anthony, and Nette Brown gave three public temperance lectures in New York in 1853 in conjunction with the yearly convention of the Temperance Society, they addressed audiences estimated at between three thousand and five thousand persons. George Templeton Strong's response was less than enthusiastic: "Great shindy between Bloomers and anti-Bloomers, at the Temperance Convention in session here." He noted in his diary, "As for the 'Rev.' Antoinette Brown & Co., I should be glad to see them respectfully jumped upon by a crowd of self-appointed conservators of manners and morals, though perhaps they have womanhood enough left in spite of themselves to be worthy of better usage. The strumpets of Leonard and Church streets are not *much* further below the ideal of womanhood than these loathsome dealers in clack, who seek to change women into garrulous men without virility. I'm glad I'm too stolid tonight for full realization of their folly. It would surely lead to a sick headache tomorrow. Womanhood is still reverenced in this irreverent age and country, as every omnibus and railroad car can testify. Destroy its claim to concession and protection and courtesy by putting it on an equality in everything but physical strength with manhood and manhood is gone, too."

Philip Hone took note of a great temperance meeting at the Tabernacle to honor the Washington Temperance Guards. A succession of orators "and the voices of a hundred male and female vocalists" praised "Washington and water, the triumphs of temperance and the prowess of patriotism. The total abstinence men, among whom is the learned and eloquent Chancellor Frelinghuysen of the New York University . . . would fain claim the *pater patriae* as a cold water man." Frelinghuysen, a Princeton graduate, former attorney general of New Jersey and a Whig senator from that state, had been one of the leading opponents of Indian Removal.

Reading of the extraordinary popularity of temperance lectures, one is disposed to feel that the American propensity to turn everything into entertainment played a substantial role in the large turnout of audiences. The temperance lecture evoked something of the spirit of the camp meeting revival. It was marked by an unabashedly religious fervor and it dealt with those perpetually interesting questions of sin and redemption, in the tangible and simplified form of drinking (sin) and stopping drinking (redemption).

A popular temperance lecturer was Thomas Marshall, a former Kentucky Congressman—a "fierce, impassioned declaimer," Philip

Hone called him. In New York he "went from place to place, to tabernacles, churches and fire engine houses, all of which overflow when it is announced that he is to speak, inveighing against the use of all liquors from wine down to whiskey, and extolling water as the only panacea for soul and body."

As with virtually all other reformers, the temperance reformers declared that universal temperance would redeem the United States from the sin and folly in which it was sunk. The Fourth of July, 1841, was the sixty-fifth anniversary of American independence. Firecrackers, blank gun charges from "the juvenile lazzaroni of the city, to the bitter annoyance of all persons of quiet habits and sensitive nerves," in Philip Hone's words, characterized the day. No one apparently thought it odd or ironic that "added to all these, and the divers amusements at theatres, gardens, and other public places, there was a great procession of temperance societies, with banners, water-carts, and other diluting emblems and devices. . . ." Sixty-five years after the Declaration of Independence, the speakers of the day, among them Benjamin Butler, the prominent Democratic politician of whom Hone wrote that he doubtless adhered to temperance "in all things but politics and honesty," suggested that the promise of the early days of the republic might be fulfilled if Americans could only be persuaded to stop drinking to excess.

Maine had the distinction, under the leadership of Neal Dow, of pointing the way to reform by its "prohibitory" law. In 1830 thirteen distilleries in the state had turned out one million gallons of rum, much of it dispensed through five hundred taverns. With a population of four hundred fifty thousand, Maine had two thousand places where intoxicating liquors were sold and the sales amounted to twenty dollars a year for each resident of the state. In 1846 Maine "gravely and solemnly" enacted a law prohibiting the manufacturing and sale of liquor and five years later the legislature passed a much stiffer law, which came to be known as the Maine Law.

Vermont followed Maine's example, and in 1855 New Hampshire fell in line. Massachusetts was "wonderfully roused on the subject of Prohibition" and passed a law in 1855 that "grappled with the monster traffic in the great rum citadel, the City of Boston."

Rhode Island passed a law in 1852 "for the suppression of drinking-houses and tippling shops," and the "Maine Law" was introduced in the New York legislature in 1855. "It won't pass," George Templeton Strong predicted, "though the demented fanatics who back it all spare no effort. If it should pass, and were enforced in this city (which it never could be), I'm not sure but that its effect would be wholesome." It passed, despite strong opposition from the Democrats, but Governor Seymour vetoed it and Strong approved. It seemed to him a high-handed and arbitrary law, impossible to enforce. "The democratic despotism of a majority is a formidable element of injustice and oppression, but it is the power to which we are subject and which will determine the question," he wrote.

Michigan passed a prohibitory law in 1853, repealed it a year later, and then tried again in 1855. Delaware was also a backslider, taking the pledge in 1847 in a law which was declared unconstitutional, trying again in 1855, and then giving up the struggle. The Whigs of Iowa got through a law in the peak temperance year of 1855 which forbade "the manufacture and sale of intoxicating liquors, except for medicinal, medical, culinary, or sacramental purposes," which, it turned out, constituted a generous set of loopholes. Pennsylvania prohibited liquor in 1855 and repealed the law the following year. The Whigs of Illinois did likewise.

The solid South, in contrast, remained total abstainers from prohibitory legislations. There the mint julep held undisputed sway.

Two points might be made here. Prohibition (as distinguished from temperance) was, like so many other things, a political issue. The Whigs and the Free Soilers (later the Republicans) included in their ranks many ardent prohibitionists, in return for whose political support they committed themselves to prohibitory legislation. The Democrats, by and large, were opposed, seeing the prohibitory legislation as being directed primarily against the workingman.

The notion of prohibition also served to dramatize the issue of individual redemption versus the coercive powers of the state (or states). Many sincere temperance advocates were repelled by the idea of police powers being invoked to control the behavior of individuals. To do so threatened to undermine character and replace redemption by legislation. Considering the weight of tradition and even of constitutional theory opposed to such legislation, it is astonishing that it enjoyed such a vogue.

Although the temperance movement clearly had a symbolic dimension to it (it seemed to offer an opportunity *to do something* about a serious blemish on the body politic), it would, I think, be a mistake to underestimate the seriousness of the problem it addressed itself to.

The extent of the temperance movement is difficult to comprehend today. At the Centennial Temperance Conference held in Philadelphia in 1885, twenty-eight church temperance groups were represented and twelve independent temperance organizations, from the Congressional Temperance Society (excessive drinking by Congressmen had become a national scandal) to the Cadets of Temperance (for young men) and the Citizens' Law and Order League, and these did not by any means exhaust the list of societies and associations dedicated to temperance. Governors, bishops, senators, the greatest preachers of the day—men like Charles Grandison Finney, Lyman Beecher and his son, Henry Ward, and William Lloyd Garrison—were all conspicuous in temperance reform along with virtually all the women prominent in the woman's rights movement. By 1860 the temperance movement was, like its sister, the woman's rights movement, just at the threshold of its greatest days, growing in strength and in confidence that it was doing the Lord's work.

Benjamin Rush, who was the father of the temperance movement, also fathered another long-lived offspring—the anti-capital punishment movement. Unlike prohibition, the fight against capital punishment reached its apogee in the 1830s, when it became a nationwide crusade. In New York the American Society for the Collection and Diffusion of Information on Punishment by Death was founded, with William Cullen Bryant as its president, and in almost every Northern state opponents of capital punishment pressed their legislatures to outlaw the death penalty primarily on the grounds that it was un-Christian to take a life. It was pointed out that the poor—especially the Irish and free blacks—were the principal victims. Well-to-do criminals were seldom executed. The advocates of capital punishment did not say so, but with many of them prejudices against the Irish and the free blacks made them strong supporters of that draconian measure. Significantly, it was Maine, with few immigrants or free blacks, that first abolished capital punishment in 1837. Rhode Island and Michigan followed in Maine's footsteps, but in a few years a reaction set in. By 1852 petitions were being passed about in Rhode Island urging the restoration of the death penalty for murder and similar steps were taken in Michigan, where crime had increased since the abolition of the death penalty.

In Massachusetts six crimes—robbery, burglary, rape, arson, treason, and murder—were punishable by death, although such punishments were rarely invoked for robbery and burglary. The result of the agitation against capital punishment in that state was to narrow the range of crimes for which the offender might be hung to rape, treason, and murder. It is perhaps worth noting that there was often considerable support for the abolition of the death penalty among politicians and legislators, but whenever the issue was submitted to popular vote it was roundly defeated.

Closely related, of course, to the issue of capital punishment was the whole question of prison reform. The Auburn, New York, system was one of cell blocks with common dining quarters and work areas. The rule of silence was maintained. Prisoners were marched to and from work and severely whipped for disobedience to the prison rules. The principal effort at rehabilitation was by means of sermons, exhortations, and Christian tracts.

Auburn was supplemented by an improved plan at Sing Sing on the Hudson. Tocqueville and Beaumont spent more than a week there, and both men were impressed by the cleanliness and good order of the convicts. Tocqueville wrote: "One cannot see the prison of Sing Sing and the system of labor which is there established without being struck by astonishment and fear. Although the discipline is perfect, one feels it rests on a fragile foundation; it is due to a *tour de force* which is reborn unceasingly and which has to be reproduced each day, under penalty of compromising the whole system of discipline—it seems to us impossible not to fear some sort of catastrophe in the future."

One feels that the Auburn and Sing Sing systems contain some critical clue to the American psyche or consciousness. A constantly renewed effort of the will, manifest in this case, by the enlightened and reformed prison system ultimately creates in prisoners and custodians alike an unbearable tension which *must* explode. Is there a metaphor here for American life, one wonders? Criminals are individuals unable or unwilling to observe society's social constraints or "norms." They are individuals, above all, with inadequate or perverse "wills." The task of the "correctional" system is to *break* the perverse wills and reinforce the weak ones. Silence, order, and exhortation were the means chosen in the spirit of reform (rather than simply punishment). Punishment for wickedness had been the traditional "Christian" method of dealing with "sinners," i.e. those whose sins were a threat to society. The directors of the Massachusetts state prison at Charlestown had declared in 1815 that the discipline should be as severe as the law of humanity will by any means tolerate. The inmates should be "reduced to a state of humiliation." Prisoners had the words Massachusetts State Prison tattooed on their arms.

The emphasis on punishment was gradually replaced, in part, by reform or "correction." The job of the prison was no longer to punish the evildoer but to alter character and condition the will. A vast change in attitude toward the nature of the person and his or her relation to society was, of course, contained in this new rational, humane system and it is noteworthy that two of the most sensitive and perceptive critics of American life, Tocqueville and, after him, Charles Dickens, were horrified at the human consequences of American prison reform.

Tocqueville and Beaumont were much impressed by the fact that nearly a third of the inmates were involved in making things used in the prison's own economy, which brings us to the issue of prison "work." It was certainly not coincidental that work by convicts was a major element in the new ethic of prison as an agent of reform. Work was perceived, increasingly, as a channel of salvation. The way to rehabilitate criminals was, therefore, to require them to work. They would thus presumably have both a practical skill and a disciplined will.

The most serious rival to the Auburn system was that of the Eastern Penitentiary northwest of Philadelphia. In contrast to Auburn, it was based on "separate and solitary confinement at labor" (at Auburn the inmates worked in common work areas), and was designed "for proving the efficacy of solitude on the morals of these unhappy objects." The cell blocks radiated out from a central guard tower. When a prisoner arrived he was examined by the warden, given a prison uniform (which was considered an important innovation), blindfolded, taken to his cell, and there interrogated as to his "former life." Locked up with a Bible and religious tracts, he was left for some days to meditate in silence and isolation upon his evil ways. In every cell there was a water pipe and "a kind of water-closet, a bed, a chair, and the implements of the convict's labor. . . . The men receive a towel, a razor, and shaving apparatus. . . . The punishments inflicted for breach of discipline are deprivation of exercise, diminution in the quantity of food, and confinement in a dark cell. No flogging is allowed, and very little punishment of any kind is required." Most conspicuously lacking, in the view of the English phrenologist, George Combe, were teachers and instructors, individuals who would inculcate "day by day the principles of temperance and religion." The inmates' bodies were reasonably well cared for, Combe observed, and they were trained in a trade, but their intellectual and moral selves were largely untouched. Reformers were loud and persistent in their criticisms, but the state legislature paid little attention.

In their report for 1838 the inspectors of the Pennsylvania prison, citizens appointed by the state legislature, laid heavy emphasis on the "necessity of an asylum for discharged convicts intermediate between the prison and common society. The situation and the sufferings of discharged convicts," the report noted, "have excited our attention and sympathy. . . . This class of men, as well as a large portion of the laboring poor, need advice and assistance to help them along the rugged pathway of life."

It was Tocqueville's conclusion, after studying the Auburn and Pennsylvania systems, "that the penitentiary system in America is severe. Whilst society in the United States gives an example of the most extended liberty, the prisons of the same country offer the spectacle of the most complete despotism."

So here again was one of those tormenting ambiguities. Setting out to extend to the most marginal members of society the fruits of enlightened policy, American reformers succeeded only in demonstrating the split between the impulse to punish and the desire to rehabilitate, ending up with a system or systems in some respects more dehumanizing than the admittedly scandalous situation they replaced.

We get an illuminating perspective on efforts at prison reform from Georgiana Bruce, who, fresh from her term at Brook Farm, got a job as a matron at the women's prison at Sing Sing under Eliza Farnham, one of the great company of reforming women. Mrs. Farnham, who, at twenty-eight, was only a few years older than her matrons, undertook to introduce reform into the prison. Mrs. Farnham was, Bruce wrote, "so evidently fearless, and at the same time so gentle in manner and speech, so regardful of their welfare, that [the inmates] learned to reverence and bless her. . . . Interesting, thoughtful books were read to them," and the prison library was expanded from the religious tracts which had made up its entire inventory to the novels of Dickens, the tales of Mrs. Sedgewick, and other more challenging works. Classes were instituted to teach the women inmates, many of whom were black, to read and write. Georgiana Bruce was moved to reflect on the fact that she had allied herself "to the civilization we condemned." "Locking the base products of false conditions into narrow cells was an unworthy occupation," she reflected. Eliza Farnham shared with Charles Dickens the conviction that the "attempt to enforce continuous silence between human beings in close proximity to each other was worse than useless." There was another aspect of the prison that troubled Georgiana. "Colored people," she wrote, "were at that time convicted and given long terms on the flimsiest testimony." The same was true for the Irish.

One of the most serious problems was that of the transition to society of the released convict who had served his or her term. Turned out without money or guidance, most were forced to take up their old habits simply to exist, "starve or steal" as one inmate put it to Georgiana Bruce. To meet this problem a Prisoner's Aid Society had been started by the venerable old Quaker reformer Isaac Hopper, whose life had been spent "assisting the prisoner, the slave, and the outcast." Hopper undertook to find employers who would give jobs to released criminals and raised money to help them make the transition from prison to the world outside. "I trust this admirable society still exists," Bruce wrote years later, "for, if we insist on continuing the social conditions which *create* the criminal, the least we can do is to give him a chance to live decently after his incarceration for a crime. This, besides, is the cheaper and safer method of procedure."

Having been a member of the Brook Farm community and a coadjutor of Eliza Farnham in that indefatigable lady's efforts to improve the condition of female prisoners at Sing Sing, Georgiana Bruce decided that her mission in life was to teach young blacks. In her words, "The pitiless hatred of a colored skin, manifested by white Americans, was incomprehensible to me, and struck me as a form of insanity, a sort of monomania, which I could only partly account for on the principle that we dislike, and often calumniate, those we have wronged. Education, good looks, business capacity, in persons of mixed blood, evidently increased the virulence of the prejudice." Frustrated time and again in her efforts to establish a school for blacks, Georgiana finally took a position as a governess for the five children of Robert Purvis, the well-known black abolitionist. She described him as "elegant and distinguished in appearance, gracious and charming in his manners. . . . There was in him a rare combination of tenderness, magnanimity, and refinement. . . ." For eighteen months Georgiana was tutor and governess for Purvis's children and in that period observed numerous instances when Purvis, rich, cultivated, and light enough in complexion to pass for white, was insulted as a "nigger."

Much less ambiguous than prison reform was the question of the treatment of the insane. This became the particular province of Dorothea Lynde Dix.

Insanity was especially common in the rural towns of New England. In New Hampshire, George Combe calculated that the rate of insanity was in the neighborhood of two per thousand. In 141 towns there were 312 insane persons. Combe noted that while the private benevolent agencies were numerous and often well financed, the public agencies, the "Civic Pauper Lunatic and Prison Establishments," were often poorly supported and badly run. The reason, he believed, was the candidates for public office vied for favor by promising economies. Such improvements as a vast public water system like the Croton Reservoir had many enthusiastic advocates, but there were comparatively few to speak for the poor, the criminal, and the insane. Moreover, Combe wrote, "it is an *unpopular duty* to expose the imperfections of any American institutions, and hence the actual conditions of some of these establishments is really unknown to the great body of upper classes of the city, who would otherwise be well disposed toward their improvement."

As a child, Dorothea Dix had lived in a desperately unhappy home from which she fled to live with her grandmother in Boston. Her grandmother was a severe and undemonstrative woman who helped to instill in Dorothea the desire to serve the Lord by doing good. She was a remarkably precocious child who was teaching school at the age of fourteen and a few years later started her own school for girls. William Ellery Channing, who was so ardent an advocate of Christian reform, was the principal influence on her. He sent his daughters to her school and encouraged her bold experiments in education. At the age of thirty-three, after almost twenty years of keeping school, Dorothea Dix fell victim to one of those strange, undefinable maladies that so often affected middle-class American women in the nineteenth century. She left the school and traveled to England, but when she returned to the United States several years later she was still a virtual invalid.

Encouraged by Samuel Gridley Howe and young Charles Sumner, she began visiting the jails and poorhouses in Massachusetts, taking careful notes of everything she saw. After two years she was ready to make known the results of her "investigations." "I shall be obliged to speak with great plainness," she wrote, "and to reveal many things revolting to the taste and from which woman's nature shrinks with peculiar sensitiveness. . . . I proceed, gentlemen, briefly to call your

attention to the present state of insane persons within this Commonwealth, in cages, closets, stalls, pens—chained naked. Beaten with rods.
Lashed into obedience." At Danvers she had seen a young woman,
"clinging to or beating the bars of her caged apartment, the contracted
size of which afforded only space for increasing accumulation of
filth—a foul spectacle, gentlemen—and there she stood with naked
arms, disheveled hair, the unwashed frame invested with fragments of
unclean garments, the air so offensive that it was not possible to remain
beyond a few minutes. . . ."

Declaring that the "sight of Babylon in ruins was not so melancholy a spectacle as madness," Dix began the most remarkable
personal crusade of the nineteenth century. With a cause to command
her remarkable energies and intelligence, her health improved
strikingly. She had great political acumen, taking her revelations to
influential and public-spirited men who became advocates of her cause
with politicians and legislatures.

The best hope of reform, Dorothea Dix realized, was to enlist
intelligent young men and women, with a high sense of moral
obligation, as directors of such institutions. Having brought about
important reforms in Massachusetts, Dix moved on to New York,
Rhode Island, New Jersey, and Pennsylvania. Everywhere her technique was much the same—careful investigation, a detailed report of
horrors, the enlisting of influential men and women, and the recruit-
ment of idealistic young people to staff the institutions. In eight years
she traveled over ten thousand miles, covering every state in the Union
except Texas, North Carolina, and Florida.

In Michigan, when the stage on which she was riding was held up,
she upbraided the bandits. One of them looked at her and exclaimed,
"My God, I know that voice." He had heard her speak on prison
reform in the Walnut Street jail in Philadelphia. The passengers'
belongings were promptly returned to them.

Dix estimated that she saw in the course of her travels over nine
thousand insane men and women as well as epileptics. One wonders
how she endured such scenes. By 1852 eleven states had built hospitals
for the insane directly as a result of Dorothea Dix's crusade. Not
satisfied, she left for a tour of England and the Continent with a view
to achieving similar reforms there.

Philadelphia was far in advance of other states in its treatment of
the insane. When Sidney George Fisher visited the Pennsylvania
Hospital for the Insane in 1841, he found "a noble institution, 40 acres

of undulating and wooded ground are enclosed by a stone wall. This space is planted and to be kept in nice order for the exercise and recreation of the insane. The house is very large, in good taste, admirably contrived, handsomely furnished and replete with every convenience for the purposes intended. The unfortunate inmates have every possible comfort and attendance and are made as happy as their situation permits. They are treated with the greatest kindness and every amusement they can enjoy is afforded them. Within the enclosure are a large and excellent house for the resident physician, stables, farmhouse, gardens, etc. . . . ."

The Alms-House in Philadelphia, built at the cost of over a million dollars, was so handsome that it was called "the Pauper Palace." "Its fame stands so high," George Combe noted, "and has extended so widely, as affording comfortable quarters for the destitute, that some of them have been known to walk two hundred and fifty miles to reach it." There were some eighteen hundred inmates, which seemed to Combe a large number for a city of two hundred thousand "situated in a young fertile and prosperous country where labor is greatly in demand." Most of them were immigrants whom we would categorize today as unemployable because of physical or psychological handicaps, the most common in the latter category being simply the inability to function in so unfamiliar an environment.

In South Boston a House of Refuge for Juvenile Offenders was maintained for "employment and reformation [of] all children who live an idle and dissolute life, whose parents are dead, or, if living, from drunkenness or other vices, neglect to provide any suitable employment, or exercise any salutary control over said children." George Combe noted that "they are taught a trade, and receive instruction in the common branches of learning, and in morals and religion."

The Pennsylvania Institute for the Blind was another exemplary enterprise. Sidney George Fisher visited it with a cousin who served as its corresponding secretary. He noted that the pupils were "taught music by ear, and attain great proficiency. It is one of their principal exercises, and must be a great solace and source of enjoyment to them. Reading they learn by means of raised letters, to which they apply their hands and acquire astonishing facility. It was a melancholy sight," he added, "altho delightful to see the defects of nature so far remedied, and light, knowledge and enjoyment afforded to minds which would else be so dark, inert and miserable."

In New York, Silas Jones, who had "a large head . . . large Benevolence, and Love of Approbation" and was "the very picture of joyousness and health," according to George Combe, ran the Asylum for the Blind. It was a spacious, well-ventilated structure and Combe noted that the residents were "good musicians, and take great pleasure in playing in concert. They weave rugs and mats, and make baskets and other articles of simple construction."

Samuel Ward Howe, the beau ideal of reformers who had fought for Greek independence from the Turks and married the brilliant Julia Ward, ran the Boston Institute for the Blind and had made it the most enlightened such institution in the country. Not only did Howe develop the use of braille or raised letters for reading, he encouraged his charges to undertake a "variety of exercises . . . by climbing up poles, jumping over beams, and performing other athletic feats." Laura Bridgman was Samuel Howe's most famous pupil. She had been born deaf, dumb, and blind and Howe and the other teachers at the Boston Institute had taught her "the finger-alphabet" and even how to write. When George Combe visited her she wrote, laboriously, "Laura glad see Combe." She could count, add and subtract, and was usually "gay and frolicsome."

The intense concern with teaching the handicapped—especially the blind and deaf—to be self-reliant and independent was a very important aspect of the reform spirit of the age, for it reached to the center of the question of the nature of man and his perfectability, or, at the very least, his capacity for moral and spiritual improvement. Those children who were deaf from infancy and more especially those blind at birth had been considered as little better than perpetual invalids, charges on their families or, if indigent, on society. Their status was further clouded by the feeling that their disabilities were in some way a divine judgment, although it was never quite clear on *whom*.

So to penetrate into that world of silence and sightlessness was as remarkable and exciting a venture as to uncover the secrets of electromagnetism; to do so was to prove in a particularly definitive and dramatic fashion what Julia Ward Howe called the "dignity and ability of human nature." Laura Bridgman thus became, in a certain sense, another triumph of or for transcendentalism. Horace Mann, the great educational reformer, a transcendentalist fellow traveler, wrote to Howe, "I should rather have built up the Blind Asylum than to have written Hamlet, and when human vitality gets up into the coronal region every body will think so." Both Howe and Mann were apostles of phrenology, the science of the cranium, with its very sensible emphasis on exercise and proper ventilation.

Since Americans wished so passionately to improve the universe, it was not surprising that from the time of the American Revolution onward, there were a substantial number who wished to do away with war.

The roots of the peace movement went back at least to David Low Dodge's essay "War Inconsistent with the Religion of Jesus Christ," published in 1811. Several years later New York and Massachusetts peace societies were formed, the latter under the leadership of William Ellery Channing, but it was not until 1828, at the beginning of the era of "benevolence," that the American Peace Society was formed. It was dogged from its beginning by a division between the all-out pacificists and those persons who were willing to fight in defense of the country in the event of an invasion. The "total" pacificists, led by William Lloyd Garrison, soon went their own way, leaving the American Peace Society to occupy a more moderate position. George Beckwith, a Congregational minister and a leader of the society, published what he called *The Peace Manual* in 1847. In addition to giving an array of arguments against war, the pamphlet reveals the roots of a number of the dominant anxieties of American Protestants. "Would you fain convert our seamen to God?" Beckwith asked. "Alas! war would soon carry them beyond your reach. . . . Would you check the tide of impurity? War would multiply its reeking Sodoms all over the land. Would you follow hard upon the farthest wave of Western population, or tread the dark alleys and lanes of our cities, to gather the young into Sabbath schools . . . ? War would thwart you at every step. . . . Would you plant in the very confines of the wilderness, churches that shall one day make the moral desert there bud and blossom like the rose . . . ? War would drive your home missionaries from their field, or well-nigh neutralize their power."

The moving spirit in the peace movement became William Ladd, born in New Hampshire, educated at Harvard, who had made a fortune as a cotton merchant in Georgia and as a planter in Florida. In 1812, at the age of thirty-four, Ladd "retired" to the life of a gentleman farmer in Maine. Meeting Dodge, Ladd was inspired to take up the cause of peace. The principal plank in Ladd's platform was the notion of "submitting national differences to amicable discussion and arbitration; and finally, of settling all national controversies by an appeal to reason, as becomes rational creatures and not by physical force as is worthy only of brute beasts; and that this shall be done by a congress of Christian nations whose decrees shall be enforced by public opinion that rules the world."

Ladd joined forces with George Beckwith in publishing the journal the *American Advocate of Peace*. A prize was offered for the best essay on "A Congress of Nations for the Prevention of War" and the best papers were printed in a single volume in 1841.

The most valuable recruit to the cause was Emerson, who in a public lecture termed war "epidemic insanity." Peace could be best achieved "by private opinion, by private conviction, by private, dear and earnest love." William Jay, the "universal" friend of reform, was another active worker in the cause; we have already encountered his volume on the wickedness of the Mexican War.

While the reformers, for the most part, wished to redeem the world by changing drunkards into sober citizens or slaves into free men, the philanthropists and that vast company of Americans who organized and ran the innumerable benevolent associations had more modest goals. They wished primarily to relieve want and suffering in the working class and among the indigent. They took their inspiration in large part from such interdenominational Evangelical preachers as the Beechers. In New York Christians with missionary impulses were quick to point out that while there were sixteen churches in the upper- and middle-class area in lower Manhattan there was only one in the seventh ward, which had twice as many residents. The fact that two thousand prostitutes plied their trade there was viewed as by no means coincidental. The Female Missionary Society for the Poor of the City of New York had been established in 1816, followed not long afterward by the New York Evangelical Missionary Society of Young Men, which recruited four hundred part-time missionaries to work both in western Pennsylvania and western New York as well as in the Five Points section of the city. The fact was that it was both safer and more productive to work in the areas of rural poor than to try to penetrate the dock areas and slums of the city itself. Boston, inspired apparently by New York's efforts, gave birth to the Boston Society for the Moral and Religious Instruction of the Poor. Its aims were to establish Sunday schools for the children of poor parents, to suppress vice, distribute Bibles, and preach the gospel with the hope of conversion. The New York Sunday

School Union Society, which had started in 1816, was especially successful. In a year it recruited 50 superintendents and 170 teachers with 2,000 boys and adults, while girls were served by twenty-one schools with 250 teachers and 3,163 pupils.

Thirteen years later New York City had five thousand more children enrolled in Sunday schools than in public schools. Those children who completed the five-year course of instruction would, it was estimated, have read 167 improving books, whose benefits "in most cases, will last throughout eternity." Interestingly enough, the effort to provide special instruction and special facilities for the children of the poor on the British model, was resisted, moving Dr. Stephen Tyng, a leader in the missionary Sunday school movement to write, "the characteristic of American poverty, is everywhere discontented poverty, aspiring poverty and must be dealt with as such."

Since cleanliness was, in the spirit of Benjamin Franklin, next to godliness, Sunday pupils of whatever class were expected to be clean and those whose parents were too poor to dress them properly had clothes provided for them. Undoubtedly, one of the most important duties of the teachers was visiting the homes of their pupils. Middle- and upper-class young men and women thereby acted as social as well as religious evangelizers, urging middle-class styles of life and middle-class social values on the parents of their students. The auxiliary of the Sunday school was the religious tract. In 1829 the New York City Tract Society embarked on the ambitious program of distributing one tract a month throughout the entire city. The wards of the city were divided into districts of some sixty families. Arthur Tappan, the bankroller of the abolition movement, was in charge of Ward Five and his brother, Lewis, presided over Ward One. The Tappans and their lieutenants applied the same practical techniques to religious evangelism that had made them highly successful businessmen. *The Institution and Observance of the Sabbath* was one of the first tracts and it was distributed to 28,383 families in March of 1829, followed by *Address on Intemperance* in April, and a pamphlet with the titillating title of *The Dairyman's Daughter* the following month.

In Boston a team of a hundred and fifty voluntary distributors passed out tracts to 7,500 families. Cincinnati, Pittsburgh, St. Louis, and Charleston all followed suit. In those cities markets received 146,500 pages of tracts to be distributed free to customers, and steamboats 79,000. Hospitals, almshouses, and prisons were also attended to. It seemed that the benevolent societies which we have already encountered in considerable numbers were destined to increase beyond enumerating. The Society for the Encouragement of Faithful Domestic Servants, a rather self-seeking organization, it seems safe to assume, hailed the time as "the age of benevolence." "Scarcely a new want discovered, or a new field presented in the moral waste of the world," the author of its yearly report wrote in 1827, "where the benevolent may labour with a prospect for doing good, but numbers may be found ready to gird themselves for the duty, however humble or self-denying may be their office."

In New York the Association for the Relief of Respectable, Aged, Indigent Females applied to the city for funds to assist their clients, while the Magdalen Society attempted to reform some of the city's estimated twenty thousand prostitutes.

George Templeton Strong, already a convert to benevolence, was pleased to find in the basement of Calvary Church a "crowd of little Irish and German emigrant children who had been picked up . . . from utter poverty and deprivation and reclaimed and humanized by the Industrial School" connected with the parish. "They were feasting on turkey and roast beef, a dinner provided for them by a few of the congregation, and looked clean, well cared for, and most happy. . . . And among them, active, busy, sympathizing, and accustomed to such society, were a score of the young ladies of Calvary Church, in their costly furs and silks and wonderful little bonnets, ministering to the hungry crowd. Thank God for the impulse He has given to the wealthier classes to seek out and aid the poor," Strong wrote. "It is a symptom of great good to be set off against manifold signs of social degeneracy and disease. Personal intercourse and contact and individual effort to benefit individuals is better than very many dollars subscribed to any charitable mechanism or organization. . . ."

Strong had considerable reservations, however, about the growing disposition of wealthy New Yorkers to put on "charity balls" for worthy causes which, in his opinion, simply enabled the rich to pursue their expensive pleasures without guilty feelings about the sufferings of the poor. "To a poverty-stricken demagogue, the plan of feasting the aristocracy on boned turkey, and *pâté de foie gras* that the democracy may be supplied with pork and beans, and assembling the Upper Ten in brocade and valenciennes that the lower thousand may be helped to flannel and cotton shirting would furnish a theme most facile and fertile." Such doubts did not deter him from helping to plan a money-raising ball for St. Luke's hospital featuring "the St. Vitus dance, the tetanus polka, and appropriate waltzes."

The efforts to provide religious and moral instruction for the poor, outside of the system of organized Sunday schools, seemed destined to failure and prompted an increasingly bitter debate in philanthropic circles. The question was one of "character" and "dependency." The officers of the Boston Society for the Moral and Religious Instruction of the Poor, when that organization went out of business in 1834, argued at some length that both private and public charity were demoralizing and encouraged the poor to live off handouts. The more charity available through "the pure and generous" instincts of the benevolent, the more "poor" appeared to claim it, thus developing a "paralyzing dependence on legal charity." All public provisions for the poor should thus cease, they maintained. There was one important exception. Those families of respectable workingmen whose breadwinners suffered from general financial crises should be engaged in a system of public construction or public works at somewhat below standard wages.

Reform and benevolence went hand in hand in the sense that both were directed at removing or ameliorating the harshest aspects of American life. Benevolence was largely the preserve of the established churches. Reform was, in a sense, its own church. It dealt with larger, more dramatic issues and it viewed benevolence as timid and compromising, dedicated to dealing with the consequences of social injustice rather than with the causes. Benevolence was burdened with upper-class respectability; reform was radical and thoroughly middle class.

34

The Women

The most notable by-product of the abolition movement was the woman's rights movement. Things had not been going well for American women for a generation or more. The status that they had enjoyed in colonial times, especially in Puritan New England, had declined sharply. The shift from an overwhelmingly agricultural society to one in which urban life and urban values came to be of increasing importance worked to the disadvantage of women. In the rural community the woman's role in the economy of the farm was self-evident. In the city the woman's sphere was largely circumscribed by household duties. And in upper middle class families these duties were increasingly performed by servants. So in practical terms the wife's role was reduced to the supervision of servants.

Rather than being a producer of income with her contributions to the economic life of the farm, the wife was now exclusively a consumer of the income her husband earned; by her style of living, the clothes she wore, and the furnishings and decorations of her house, she was expected to advertise her husband's ascent of the ladder of success. She paid and received calls, attended balls and parties, and acquired a few appropriately feminine accomplishments like playing the piano and singing. Her successful husband became more demanding, more harried, less a "partner" and more a proprietor. He expected his wife to maintain an establishment whose basic if not almost exclusive function was his own comfort and convenience. She herself was increasingly confined—the things she could do, the opinions she could express, the friends whose company she could enjoy were largely subservient to her husband's career and a steadily narrowing range of appropriate behavior. Those women who were too outspoken, too independent, too aggressive in espousing "causes" suffered from the disapproval of their more conventional sisters and, what was more restricting, their husbands suffered as well. It was clear that an ambitious husband needed a compliant wife.

Occasionally a wife, rich and secure far beyond her sisters, might defy such social pressures, especially if her money was her own. Mrs. James Rush, the daughter-in-law of Dr. Benjamin Rush, had an inherited fortune of several million dollars, and Sidney George Fisher thought her "a person of remarkable qualities, with virtues and defects, strongly marked, much intellect, cultivated by books, society and traveling . . . excitable passions, and sentiments altogether elevat-ed and free from anything petty or mean. On the other hand," he continued, "her mind was ill-regulated, without high culture, and led her to opinions and conduct at times so extravagant that she seemed partially insane." One of her eccentricities was to declare "that she found agreeable people in every circle and therefore visited all and invited all to her house. Her parties, therefore, were very mixed and those were brought together at them who would not and could not mingle."

Fanny Kemble Butler, the beautiful and talented wife of Pierce Butler, experienced the same kinds of constraints. As the wife of a man who had inherited a fortune of seven hundred thousand dollars she was treated badly by Butler, who expected complete submission on her part. Sidney George Fisher wrote of her: "she is a woman of genius of noble impulses and kind feelings. Too much will and vitality and force of character, however, to be very happy in domestic life. . . ."

George Templeton Strong echoed his Philadelphia counterpart when he wrote, "Special force of character and intellect are dangerous things in a woman; unless combined with high religious principle, I believe they're apt to make her unhappy, and to be as scourges and scorpions unto that forlorn and woeful caitiff, her husband."

At the same time there was virtually complete agreement by foreign visitors that American women enjoyed unique privileges and

universal deference and were, for whatever reason, superior representatives of their sex. While it was true that they received universal
admiration and the most flattering attentions, these served to limit
their powers. "When men *respect* women," Marryat wrote, "they do not
attempt to make fools of them, but treat them as rational and immortal
beings, and this general adulation is cheating them with the shadow,
while they withhold from them the substance."

Yet these exemplary creatures had, for the most part, to get along
with a minimum of attention from the opposite sex. Mrs. Trollope
noted that "in America, with the exception of dancing which is almost
wholly confined to the unmarried of both sexes, all the enjoyments of
the men are found in the absence of the women. They dine, they play
cards, they have musical meetings, they have suppers, all in large
parties, but all without women." The women, Mrs. Trollope wrote,
were confined to "the sordid offices of household drudgery. . . . They
are tender and attentive in the nursery," she added, "bustling and busy
in the kitchen, unwearying at the needle, and beautiful in the
ballroom; but in the drawing room—they are naught." Featured,
flattered, and applauded as girls, as married women they quickly
receded into the background. "It is in vain," Frances Trollope wrote,
"that 'collegiate institutes' are formed for young ladies, or that
'academic degrees' are conferred upon them. It is after marriage, and
when these young attempts upon all the sciences are forgotten, that
the lamentable insignificance of the American woman appears. . . ."

In a society that valued "morality" above all other virtues or
attributes, women were assigned the guardianship of those precious
morals. Thus at the "semi-centennial" of Washington's inauguration,
held in New York City in the spring of 1839, a splendid dinner was laid
on by the Historical Society at which the thirteen toasts began with
"George Washington; his example was perfect," and ended with
"Women; the best teachers and guardians of sound principles."

To Captain Marryat it was clear that "the women are more moral,
more educated, and more refined than the men. . . . If the American
women had their due influence, it would be fortunate; they might save
their country by checking the tide of vice and immorality, and raising
the men to their own standard."

Some of the sharper feminine observers of the American scene
(and a few of the men, Captain Marryat among them) noted that the
"worship" of women as purer, more refined, more spiritual, and more
exalted than men, had the subsidiary effect of curtailing their range of

activity and creating a stereotypical female who was too delicate for any physical effort beyond a languid game of croquet; too refined to discuss, let alone engage in, politics; and too pure to do more than tolerate sexual relations. We have already given some attention to the practical effects of the astonishing prudery of middle- and upper-class urban women. The situation vis-à-vis sex only got worse. Women encased themselves, with an unconscious symbolism, in layers of impenetrable garments. An ardent and reckless male, if he once unsheathed such a lady, came at last to whalebone or metal "stays," designed to constrict her internal organs in conformity with the ideal of a slender waist. Tiny hands and feet, indeed any physical attribute or article of clothing that suggested weakness and "delicacy," were highly prized. What the relation of this cult of female purity was to the general crudity, violence, and disorder of American life we should perhaps leave to the consideration of the psychologist. Clearly it suggested what psychologists like to call overcompensation. It was as though women's assignment was to represent those aspects of life most conspicuously missing in the merciless give and take of the working, speculating, practical world.

There were clearly advantages as well as drawbacks for American women in being so excessively venerated by men. The American woman, Aleksandr Lakier noted, "enters life boldly, moves through it alone if fate does not send her a husband, works as much as possible, and writes and teaches. . . . And it must be admitted," he added, "that American women, feeling that men have placed a halo over them, take full advantage of their position."

Israel Joseph Benjamin was one of the few travelers who viewed American women unfavorably. Although he conceded that they had "dignity and refined features, are very delicate in physique and, above all are those who of all women in the world know best how to dress," were very "cheerful" in conversation, "always lively and . . . passionately fond of music, singing and dancing," he felt they made indifferent mothers, had an "inherited and ineradicable aversion to any work and household management and delight in sweets and tid-bits." The result was that their teeth decayed early and the United States was full of dentists—"nowhere in the world are there so many dentists as in America, and yet they are all doing well." Some women, Benjamin observed, "have rows of their teeth pulled, as I myself witnessed, to obtain more beautiful ones. . . ."

Visitors commented on the fact that many American families lived in hotels rather than in private homes, in large part, it appeared, because their wives did not wish the trouble of housekeeping, and enjoyed the lively social life of such institutions. Harriet Beecher Stowe and her sister, Catharine, who presumably had more firsthand experience, considered the American wife a disaster as a home keeper and invented the "science" of domestic economy to teach her to do better.

Fanny Kemble's remarks about American women in the travel book she wrote before she settled in the United States were much resented. "The women here, like those of most warm climates," Kemble had written, "ripen early and decay proportionately soon. They are, generally speaking pretty, with good complexions and an air of freshness and brilliancy, but this, I am told, is very evanescent and whereas in England a woman is in the bloom of health and beauty from twenty-five to thirty, here they scarcely reach the first period without being faded and looking old." According to Fanny Kemble, "The reasons for such 'early fading'" were that American girls were "brought up effeminately . . . take . . . little exercise, live in rooms like ovens, and marry . . . early."

The Reverend David Macrae found American women "paler and more ethereal" than English women. "Pale features of exquisite symmetry, a delicately pure complexion, eyes radiant with intelligence, a light, graceful, often fragile form—this is the vision of loveliness that meets the eye in almost every American drawing-room." But closer observation convinced Macrae that American women were "*too* pale and thin," nervous and dyspeptic. They worried about being too thin and were "constantly having themselves weighed . . . every ounce of increase is hailed with delight, and talked about with the most dreadful plainness of speech. . . . Every girl knows her own weight to within an ounce or two, and is ready to mention it at a moment's notice. It seems to be an object of universal interest." Even babies were weighed at the instant of birth—their weight was faithfully recorded—and then weighed subsequently at regular intervals. The paleness and nervousness of American women, Macrae decided, was due to "too much metaphysics, hot bread and pie. . . . Pie," he added, "seems indispensable. Take everything away, but leave pie. Americans can stand the prohibition of intoxicating drinks; but I believe the prohibition of pie would precipitate a revolution."

James Silk Buckingham, an English visitor, a social reformer and former member of Parliament, was much impressed by the "general good sense, amiability, intelligence, and benevolence" which marked the conversation of American women. He found them "always equal to the men, and often superior to them, in the extent of their reading and the shrewdness of their observations. . . . There are perhaps ten times the number of women in good society in New York, who interest themselves in the support and direction of moral objects and benevolent institutions, that could be found in any city of the same population in Europe." Much of the money acquired by their busy husbands was "directed by the benevolent influence of their wives into useful and charitable channels." At fashionable parties the gentlemen "appeared far less handsome in person and less polished in manners than the ladies; and many whom we saw were evidently very ill at ease, and had their thoughts occupied by other subjects. . . ." It seemed to Tocqueville that "the singular prosperity and growing strength" of the American people "ought mainly to be attributed . . . to the superiority of their women."

Unmarried American girls were allowed a remarkable degree of freedom. "Long before an American girl arrives at marriageable age," Tocqueville wrote, "her emancipation from maternal control begins; she has scarcely ceased to be a child when she already thinks for herself, speaks with freedom, and acts on her own impulse. The great scene of the world is constantly opening to her view." What struck Tocqueville most forcibly was the contrast between the free state of the unmarried woman and the confined state of the married. The girl who had found "her father's house an abode of freedom and pleasure . . . comes to live in her husband's as if it were a cloister." The reason for such a constrained life for the wife, in Tocqueville's view, was that the Americans were "at the same time a puritanical and a commercial nation; their religious opinions as well as their trading habits consequently require much abnegation on the part of woman. . . ."

Another essential element in the rising dissatisfaction of women was the fact that many of them were the daughters of fathers who took their education and their "humanity" with the utmost seriousness and encouraged them to develop their minds and talents. Indeed there is some evidence that a good many fathers who, quite illogically, expected their wives to play dependent and submissive roles, encouraged their daughters to develop a sense of themselves and their capacities quite incompatible with the role of a submissive wife. Many women who as daughters had been stimulated and challenged by their fathers faced the prospect of marrying men who were thoroughly unsympathetic with their aspirations. To use a modern phrase, such women were in a double bind. To form an enduring tie with one man—a husband—they had to reject another—the father. Such putting off of the father tie for that of the husband is inherent in all marriages or mature female-male relationships, but for many nineteenth-century women that transition was greatly complicated by what we might call conflicting role definitions. As we shall see, some strong-minded women solved this dilemma by not marrying at all. Others solved it by marrying weak and compliant men. A few, like Angelina Grimké, were fortunate enough to be able to find men like Theodore Weld who were sympathetic and supportive of their aspirations. Some married rather conventionally minded men and simply went their own different ways, leaving their husbands to make the best of it.

Contributing to the unhappiness of upper-class urban wives was the polarization of sexuality that we have spoken of in an earlier volume of this work. Uninhibited female sexuality had come increasingly to be associated with lower-class women and with a lack of self-control and self-restraint. Mixed in was the notion, increasingly promulgated by the churches, that sexual intercourse, even between married couples, was tainted with sin. The sin of Adam was increasingly depicted not as disobedience to the Lord but as the act of intercourse with Eve. Some such ideas had been inherent in Puritanism from the early years in America, but they had been modified by rural practicality and the "forgiving spirit" of the community. Now they asserted themselves with a disconcerting fierceness. One result was the growing disposition of upper-class males to seek sexual pleasures with lower-class women, prostitutes, and mistresses. Sidney George Fisher, commenting on General Thomas Cadwalader's magnificent establishment, added, "He is a fine animal, with great energy and practical ability which have made him successful in all his pursuits of sportsman, man of pleasure, soldier and man of business. He is immensely rich. He is also coarse, ignorant and profligate, keeping a mistress now openly at his place in Maryland." At the general's funeral his mistress was conspicuously present.

Even in the utopian socialist communities, only the Shakers, the Rappites, and the Perfectionists tackled the sexual issue head on. Noyes was most critical of Fourier for saying nothing about the "Woman Question." "In fact," Noyes wrote, "women are rarely mentioned [by Fourier] and the terrible passions connected with distinction of sex, which . . . the religious communities have had so much trouble with, and have taken so much pains to provide for or against, are absolutely left out of sight."

Those "terrible passions" clung to the nineteenth-century psyche like an incubus. There seemed no way to control or exorcise them. Slowly they crept into the rhetoric of the woman's rights movement— thinly veiled allusions to man's unappeasable sexual appetites, so often sated on defenseless wives, or, more terrifyingly, on diseased women of the streets who infected their casual partners who, in turn, came home to infect their innocent wives and unborn children. Stories of such dreadful occurrences circulated among women and increased their loathing of sex as something vile and unclean.

Sexual anxieties took an interesting literary form in popular novels most of which were written by women for other women. Blond or fair women were almost invariably the heroines, dark women the villainesses, the seducers, the destroyers of homes and families, creatures of fatal sexual attraction. One can only wonder what frame of mind this produced in the predominantly brunette female population of the United States. Such novels, wildly overdrawn and insipidly romantic as they were, throbbed with a strange, covert sexuality. One heroine exclaims that women "are secondary objects of creation . . . nor have we any right to require of superior men an example of the virtue in which he would train us. . . . Our state of society is a dependent one, and it is ours to be good and amiable, whatever may be the conduct of the men to whom we are subjected." Dr. Gregory, in a popular manual for young ladies, wrote, "the possession of even an average share of vitality and animal spirits [is] something less than fashionable and more than feminine."

The consequences of the relentless suppression of "animal spirits," the enforced inactivity, the impossible clothes, and the hopeless sexual muddle was to make the average middle- and upper-class American woman a physical and psychological wreck. Deploring the notorious ill health of American women, George Combe noted that "they rarely take systematic and daily exercise abroad, which ought to be inculcated on them as a moral duty, as on its regular performance will greatly depend the easy and successful discharge of their other duties, both moral and religious."

Catharine Beecher devoted more and more of her time to the subject of women's health. She took informal polls on her tours around the country and reported eight women of ten "ailing" or "in poor health" in this city, seven out of ten in that. Women fainted at the drop of a scented handkerchief, had the "vapors," and took endless cures for disturbed nerves. They suffered unidentifiable aches in unmentionable portions of the body, bore innumerable children, and died at a comparatively early age. It was not uncommon for a husband to outlive several wives and sire a dozen children.

What all of this added up to was that by the middle decades of the nineteenth century, for a variety of reasons, women had lost ground in the sense of having the opportunity to live useful and fulfilling lives. Some, but by no means all, of these disabilities can perhaps be ascribed to the development of what we must call, I suppose, for want of a better word, capitalism—that is to say, the intense preoccupation of most upper- and middle-class males with making money. This impression is strengthened by the fact that leaders of the woman's rights movement soon came to be the most outspoken critics of a competitive system based on making money by fair means or foul. One consequence of the rather unfocused feeling of upper-class women that "something was wrong" was their heavy involvement in those reforms that became so prominent in the 1830s and '40s. We have mentioned abolition. Temperance was a serious rival, and the activities of temperance women clearly contained a substantial measure of hostility toward males. It was, after all, men who made up by far the greater part of the ranks of drunkards. It was drinking men who squandered their money on liquor and abused their wives and children.

As in so many other matters of "liberation," the Quakers, as a sect, led the way in the emancipation of women from their diminished and dependent role. The essential character of the Quaker meeting, with its manifest equality and its emphasis on inner light and religious spontaneity, worked very clearly in that direction and it was thus no accident that a Quaker women, Lucretia Mott, was one of the first women to protest, from within the antislavery movement, the discrimination against women. Despite the critically important part women had played in the antislavery movement from the first, they had been segregated in female societies and denied full participation on an equal basis with their male counterparts.

Lucretia Mott was the daughter of a sea captain who, as she put it, "had a desire to make his daughters useful." He had taken pains with their education and instilled in Lucretia his own determination to improve the world. A Quaker "preacher," married to a man who, like herself was actively engaged in reform, Lucretia Mott was also the mother of six children. She was the guide and sponsor of the Grimké sisters, encouraging their own inclinations to champion the cause of women's rights. "My sympathy," she wrote, "was early enlisted for the poor slave, by the class-books read in our schools, and pictures of the slaveship. . . . The unequal condition of women in society also early . . . impressed my mind . . . I early resolved to claim for my sex all that an impartial Creator had bestowed." She was also deeply concerned with the oppression of the working class by capitalists, the low wages and the inequities of a society in which, it seemed clear to her, the rich were growing richer and the poor poorer.

Besides being the friend and counselor of the Grimké sisters, she was a kind of godmother to young Elizabeth Cady Stanton. The daughter of Judge Daniel Cady and a cousin of Gerrit Smith, Mrs. Stanton told in her memoirs how her father had encouraged her to pursue inclinations (such as breaking and training horses and studying law) that were commonly thought to belong exclusively to the masculine sphere. To his "sober, taciturn, and majestic bearing," was added "the tenderness, purity, and refinement of a true woman," Elizabeth Cady Stanton wrote.

When her adored older brother died and Elizabeth, still a child, crawled into her father's lap to comfort him, he patted her distractedly on the head and said, "O, my daughter, I wish you were a boy!" To this the ten-year-old Elizabeth had replied, "Then I will be a boy . . . and I will do all that my brother did."

If Elizabeth Cady needed an incentive to become a leading advocate of wider rights and opportunities for women, the judge's words provided it. When she married Henry Stanton, a lawyer, a liberal journalist, and agent on the Underground Railroad, they agreed that the word "obey" should be omitted from the marriage ceremony. After their marriage Elizabeth and her husband sailed for London to attend the World Anti-Slavery Convention. In England Elizabeth met many members of that remarkable company of middle-class evangelical reformers whose greatest triumph had been the abolition of slavery in the British possessions, most particularly the West Indies—the Barrets, the Sturgeses, the Reverend John Scobie, George Thompson (whose visit to America had roused such a storm), the Braithwaites, and Mary Rawson, who, when she offered William Lloyd Garrison a glass of sherry, was instantly converted by him to teetotalism. The American contingent included William Ellery Channing, the famous preacher whose *Essay on Slavery*, published five years earlier, had established his credentials as a strong antislavery man disposed to waffle on immediatism. The black abolitionist Charles Lenox Remond was a member of the large American delegation, as were Wendell Phillips and the Motts.

The convention was less notable for what it accomplished—like many such gatherings it revealed a hundred shades of opinion about the character of slavery and the tactics appropriate for suppressing it—than for the fact that its managers refused to allow women to sit on the floor of the convention hall with the male delegates. They were banished to a draped gallery where, presumably, they could not inflame the less noble passions of the male delegates. Garrison and Remond, refusing to accept the decision of the chair, joined the ladies "upstairs."

One of the main hopes of the Americans—that their British cousins might be persuaded to lead a movement to boycott all cotton or sugar produced by slaves—was disappointed. The British speakers proved fertile in antiboycott arguments, and antiwomen ones as well in Lucretia Mott's view. Charles Stuart, a retired British army officer, seemed "swallowed up in the littleness of putting down women" and the newly formed Free Produce Society. One of the most significant entries in Lucretia Mott's notes on the convention reads "H. B. Stanton not so strong in confidence in moral power as desirable . . . Elizabeth Stanton gaining daily in our affections—hope she may be a blessing to her H.B.S." Elizabeth soon proved a much more powerful figure than her well-intentioned but rather ineffectual husband. What was most important was that under the influence of Lucretia Mott, and angered by the discrimination against the women delegates, Elizabeth Cady Stanton was soon a leader in the incipient movement to advance the rights of women.

The last day of the convention was a tense one as the Americans were determined to present a resolution protesting the exclusion of women. Abby Kimber, an American delegate, wrote a note of protest to the managers of the convention: "Since we left America, the *man* question has, it seems, split the National Anti-Slavery Society, therefore it [the resolution] has a tremendous significancy in our country. . . ." The American Anti-Slavery Society, meeting in New York, and in the absence of many of the abolitionists most sympathetic to the full participation of women, had split on the subject and the seceders, led by the Tappans, had formed the American and Foreign Anti-Slavery Society. If the convention intended to side with the New York seceders, it should have the courage to say so publicly.

While Elizabeth Stanton's impressions of the convention differed in some minor points from Lucretia Mott's notes, Mrs. Stanton wrote enthusiastically of "the lovely Quakeress . . . the first liberal-minded woman I had ever met," and added, "nothing in all Europe interested me as she did." Elizabeth Cady had read the standard works on the role of women. "But," she recalled, "I had never heard a woman talk of things, that, as a Scotch Presbyterian, I had hardly dared to think." And when she heard Mrs. Mott preach in a Unitarian church, it seemed to her "like the realization of an oft-repeated happy dream."

In the words of Elizabeth Cady Stanton, "While walking the streets of London, Mrs. Mott and I resolved on a Woman's Convention, as soon as we returned to America." But it was eight years before the two friends found an opportunity to call a "convention." As we have noted in the correspondence between Theodore Weld and Angelina Grimké, the issue of women's rights constantly threatened to divert women abolitionists, usually to the dismay of their male colleagues who, even though they might, like Weld, be thoroughly sympathetic to their aims, deplored any activity that tended to drain energy from the primary cause. Not only was the issue of the rights of women a divisive one within the antislavery movement—serious enough, as we have noted, to lead to a dangerous schism—but it contributed substantially to the general public image of the antislavery movement as a collection of nuts and fanatics. The male abolitionists thus found it difficult to refrain from hinting that the growing preoccupation of abolitionist women with the issue of women's rights was perilously close to selfishness. It was perhaps such considerations as these that accounted for the hiatus between the resolve of Elizabeth Cady Stanton and Lucretia Mott at the World Anti-Slavery Convention and the actual calling of the first convention on women's rights at Seneca Falls, New York, in 1848. Seneca Falls was, not coincidentally, Elizabeth Cady Stanton's home town. The prestige of her father, the judge, and the remoteness of the town from city mobs enabled her to undertake such an alarmingly radical action with some confidence. Lucretia Mott, the "Benjamin Franklin of the woman's rights movement," as Elizabeth Cady Stanton called her, was "the ruling spirit," and the small group of delegates who assembled were, for the most part, friends of Lucretia

Mott's and, to a lesser degree, Elizabeth Stanton's, recruited from the antislavery movement.

James Mott presided—Elizabeth and Lucretia thought it improper to have a woman "call a promiscuous assembly to order"—and among those leading discussion sessions were Frederick Douglass and Lucretia Mott's sister, Martha Wright, who soon displayed considerable gifts as a presiding officer at woman's rights meetings.

Elizabeth Cady Stanton drew up a "Declaration of Sentiments," patently modeled on the Declaration of Independence. Over the objections of Lucretia Mott, she included a plea for woman's suffrage —for the right of women to vote in local, state, and national elections.

"When, in the course of human events," the Declaration began, "it becomes necessary for one portion of the family of man to assume among the peoples of the earth a position different from that which they have hitherto occupied, but one to which the laws of nature and nature's God entitle them, a decent respect to the opinions of mankind requires that they should declare the causes that impel them to such a course.

"We hold these truths to be self-evident: that all men and women are created equal. . . ." And so it continued in the words of the Declaration of Independence, modified to cover the cause of women's freedom. "The history of mankind," Stanton wrote, "is a history of repeated injuries and usurpations on the part of man toward woman, having in direct object the establishment of an absolute tyranny over her. To prove this, let facts be submitted to a candid world."

Then followed an impressive list of male "tyrannies"—the lack of the franchise, the necessity to obey laws "in the formation of which she has no voice"; the oath of obedience in the marriage vows; the unfairness of the divorce laws; the exclusion of women from many jobs and professions ("as a teacher of theology, medicine, or law, she is not known"); and the creation of "a different code of morals for men and women, by which moral delinquencies which exclude women from society, are not only tolerated, but deemed of little account in men."

In effect, man "has endeavored, in every way he could, to destroy [woman's] confidence in her own powers, to lessen her self-respect, and to make her willing to lead a dependent and abject life." The delegates, therefore, insisted "that they have immediate admission to all the rights and privileges which belong to them as citizens of the United States" while at the same time anticipating "no small amount of misconception, misrepresentation, and ridicule. . . . We hope this Convention will be followed by a series of Conventions embracing every part of the country."

It was a remarkably comprehensive document and it was, of course, an inspiration to cast it in the general terms of America's most sacred document. Although it demanded "immediate admission" to all the rights of white male citizens, it established in fact a women's rights agenda for at least the next hundred and fifty years. It was a manifesto so bold, so daring and radical that a horrified Judge Cady was heard to express regret that he had lived to see a daughter of his express such heresies.

Little public attention was paid to the handful of plainly "unbalanced" women who gathered at Seneca Falls. The reformist editor of the *New York Tribune,* Horace Greeley, was one of the few who deigned to notice it. But there was already in existence a network of women's antislavery, temperance, peace (or nonresistance) societies and indeed a dozen more such reformist organizations, and the Declaration of Sentiments that issued from Seneca Falls passed quickly and readily through that network—read by many, to be sure, with disapproval, but firing the imaginations of many others, particularly those of the rising generation, the younger women.

Prominent among the newcomers to the antislavery movement were two young graduates of Oberlin College. Having admitted blacks from its inception, Oberlin soon opened its doors to women. Lucy Stone had been born in West Brookfield, Massachusetts, in 1818, of fundamentalist Presbyterian parents. She did not see the justice of her brother's being sent to college, "while she and her sister remained at home to work on the farm." After considerable discussion the parents were converted to her view. She borrowed money for the train fare and the tuition and headed for Oberlin, "where, with great economy, management, self-denial, and untiring application to her studies, she graduated with high honors," as the author of a biographical sketch wrote.

At Oberlin her dearest friend was Antoinette Brown. Antoinette had been born in Henrietta, New York, in 1825. At the age of nine she had joined the Congregational church and sometimes "spoke and prayed in the meetings," displaying a precocious gift for religious expression. Her ambition was to become a preacher, and by the age of sixteen she was teaching school during the summer and attending

Henrietta Academy during the winter. Graduating from the academy, she was admitted to Oberlin in 1844 and soon she and Lucy Stone had joined forces to fight the discrimination practiced against them by men even in the most radical institution of higher learning in the country. After several years of teaching, Antoinette returned to Oberlin to get her degree in theology. Although she completed her work with high grades, the college refused to give her a license to preach because she was a woman. Interestingly enough, Nette, as she was called, found numerous opportunities to preach in Ohio towns around and about Oberlin, indicating the liberal sentiments of communities in that region. Lucy Stone and Nette Brown were two members of the younger generation of Christian reformers who were drawn to the woman's cause by the Declaration of Sentiments.

The Seneca Falls Convention was followed by one held at Rochester a few weeks later. There, despite Lucretia and Elizabeth's misgivings, Abigail Bush, wife of a Columbia professor, presided, "and did us all great credit." The editor of the *Albany Register,* writing about the Rochester Convention, declared: "People are beginning to inquire how far public sentiment should sanction or tolerate these unsexed women, who make a scoff of religion, who repudiate the Bible and blaspheme God; who would step out from the true sphere of the mother, the wife, and the daughter, and taking upon themselves the duties and business of men, stalk into the public gaze, and by engaging in the politics, the rough controversies, and the trafficking of the world, upheave existing institutions and over-turn all the social relations of life."

State conventions were held a year or so later in Indiana and Ohio and at each successive convention women spoke and acted with greater assurance and self-confidence. Lucy Stone soon emerged as the most arresting public speaker on the subject of woman's rights. She had discovered at Oberlin that she could hold her own with any of the male students in debate. In Elizabeth Cady Stanton's words: "Young, magnetic, eloquent, her soul filled with the new idea, she drew immense audiences, and was eulogized everywhere by the press. . . . Her style of speaking was earnest, fluent, impassioned appeal rather than argument." She excelled in telling touching incidents and amusing anecdotes. Although she was a paid agent of the American Anti-Slavery Society, she spoke as often for the cause of women's rights, traveling from one large town or city to another with her alarming new gospel. Small, almost diminutive, with dark brown hair, gray eyes, rosy cheeks, "fine teeth . . . and . . . a sparkling, intellectual face," she had a voice that was "soft, clear, and musical. . . ."

Nette Brown was also an effective speaker but her initial concern was with finding a congregation that would accept her as an ordained pastor. Finally, after three or four years as a kind of itinerant preacher, she was called to a church in South Butler, New York, in 1853. There, with Gerrit Smith and Samuel May in attendance, she was ordained a Congregational minister.

An important aspect of the woman's rights movement centered on the issue of dress. Amelia Bloomer was already a popular lecturer on temperance when she decided to wear a pantaloonlike garment fastened at the ankles that gave her more freedom of movement and was far more comfortable than the cumbersome skirts and petticoats then in style. She had not invented the costume that was to bear her name, but it proved singularly upsetting to males generally; and since such woman's rights champions as Lucy Stone and Nette Brown promptly adopted "bloomers" as a kind of uniform, they became the object of innumerable vulgar satires and heated newspaper editorials. When Nette Brown invited Lucy Stone to visit her in South Butler where she was minister, Lucy wrote back protesting that Nette must have enough problems without complicating her life by having so controversial a visitor. Nette reassured her friend, "You are the biggest little goose and granny fuss that I ever did see." The congregation knew Lucy wore bloomers and was an "infidel" but they were still prepared to welcome her. Two of the girls in the congregation wore bloomers and all believed in free speech.

Unhappily Nette Brown achieved her ambition to be a minister at the very time when she had begun to have grave doubts about the doctrines of the church, and after less than a year she resigned and turned her energies to abolition, temperance, and, increasingly, to the woman's rights movement.

Perhaps the most important recruit to the women's cause was a tall, thin, classic spinster schoolteacher, Susan B. Anthony. Anthony, born in 1820 in Adams, Massachusetts, was the daughter of a Quaker cotton manufacturer who took a strong interest in her education, encouraged her to work in his factory, and even organized a school in his own home which she attended until she was seventeen. Susan felt that a slight cast in one eye so marred her appearance that she had no hope of marriage, and while she was teaching school she found herself drawn into the temperance movement as a lecturer. It was at a temperance convention, called by Susan Anthony in Albany, New York, that she and Elizabeth Cady Stanton first met. They discovered an immediate affinity. Susan Anthony felt a strong sense of indignation that she was paid only eight dollars a month as a teacher while her male counterparts received three or four times as much. When she was denied a seat at the Men's State Temperance Convention at Syracuse, she was ready to become a full-time champion of the cause of women. Again in Elizabeth Cady Stanton's words, "At this time Miss Anthony's life and mine became nearly one. . . . Wherever we saw a work to be done, we would together forge our thunderbolts, in the form of resolutions, petitions, appeals, and speeches, on every subject— temperance, anti-slavery, woman's rights, agriculture, education, and religion—uniformly accepting every invitation to go everywhere, and do everything." Susan B. was "the reform scout, who went to see what was going on in the enemy's camp, and returning with maps and observations to plan the mode of attack. Wherever we saw an annual convention of men . . . filled with *brotherly* love, we bethought ourselves how we could throw a bombshell into their midst, in the form of a resolution, to open the door to the sisters outside, who had an equal interest with themselves in the subjects under consideration. In this way, we assailed, in turn, the temperance, educational, and church conventions, agricultural fairs, and halls of legislation." The men attending the yearly educational convention besieged for ten years, grew apprehensive "the moment Miss Anthony, with her staid Quaker face and firm step, walked up the aisle. . . ." Finally, they gave way and "women were permitted to speak and vote in the conventions, appointed on committees, and to make reports on various subjects." The brilliance of the tactics was that the women, under the tutelage of Stanton and Anthony, concentrated their attacks on just those areas of masculine concern—the great reform projects of the age—where men were most vulnerable to the appeal to morality, to equality and justice.

Susan B.'s style of speaking was "rapid, vehement, concise, and in her best moods she is sometimes eloquent," her coadjutor, Stanton, wrote. Most important of all, Susan B. Anthony had organizational abilities sorely needed in the emerging woman's rights movement. As a single woman, unencumbered by husband or family, she occupied the command post and provided "the connecting link" between those workers in the cause who were, to a degree, tied to their homes and families, and "the outer world." From 1852 through most of the two succeeding decades she was the "acting secretary and general agent" of the often amorphous movement. In the winter of 1854–55 alone she presided over fifty-four conventions in the various counties of New York state "with two petitions in hand,—one demanding equal property rights, and the other the ballot,—and rolled up ten thousand names."

We have already mentioned that Sojourner Truth was as eloquent on the rights of women as on the subject of slavery. Frances Gage tells a revealing story of a woman's rights convention where Sojourner Truth suddenly appeared, uninvited, to the dismay of many of the delegates. There were immediate murmurs and complaints, cries of "An abolition affair!" "Woman's rights and niggers!" "I told you so!" "Go it, darkey."

The convention was liberally sprinkled with men, many of whom came to hiss and hoot at the gathering of "strong-minded" and presumptuous women. Just when the tide seemed to be running against the women, Sojourner Truth slowly rose from her seat. Several women whispered to Frances Gage not to give her the platform but Sojourner Truth "moved slowly and solemnly to the front, and," in Gage's words, "turned her great speaking eyes on me. There was a hissing sound of disapprobation . . . I rose and announced 'Sojourner Truth,' and begged the audience to keep silence for a few minutes.

"The tumult subsided at once, and every eye was fixed on this almost amazon form, which stood nearly six feet high, head erect, and eyes piercing the upper air like one in a dream. . . . She spoke in deep tones, which, though not loud, reached every ear in the house, and away through the throng at the doors and windows.

" 'Wall, chilern, whar dar is so much racket dar must be somethin' out o' kilter. I think dat 'twixt de niggers of the Souf and de womin at de Norf, all talkin' 'bout rights, de white men will be in a fix pretty soon. But what's all dis here talking 'bout?

" 'Dat man ober dar say dat womin needs to be helped into carriages, and lifted ober ditches, and to have the best place every-whar. Nobody eber helps me into carriages, or ober mud-puddles, or gibs me any best place!' And raising herself to her full height, and her voice to a pitch like rolling thunder, she asked, 'And a'n't I a woman? Look at me! Look at my arm!' (and she bared her right arm to the shoulder, showing her tremendous muscular power), 'I have ploughed and planted, and gathered into barns, and no man could head me! And a'n't I a woman? I could work as much and eat as much as a man—when I could get it—and bear the lash as well! And a'n't I a woman? I have borne thirteen chilern, and seen 'em mos' all sold off to slavery, and when I cried out with my mother's grief, none but Jesus heard me. And a'n't I a woman?' "

Then there was the matter of Eve: " 'If the fust woman God ever made was strong enough to turn de world upside down all alone, dese women together . . . ought to be able to turn it back, and get it right side up again! And now dey is asking to do it, de men better let 'em.' Long continued cheering greeted this . . . Amid roars of applause, she returned to her corner, leaving more than one of us with streaming eyes, and hearts beating with gratitude. She had taken us up in her strong arms and carried us safely over the slough of difficulty turning the whole tide in our favor. I have never in my life," Frances Gage added, "seen anything like the magical influence that subdued the mobbish spirit of the day, and turned the sneers and jeers of an excited crowd into notes of respect and admiration."

I have argued elsewhere that in the simple act of speaking in public women changed the male image of them as dependent and inferior beings, or as sweet and gentle creatures too refined for the rough male world. Since they spoke, on the whole, more powerfully and passionately than men, it was a doubly daunting phenomenon to those hostile but fascinated males who turned out in increasingly large numbers to hear them. The psychological effect on the women in their audiences was different but equally powerful. They saw at once new capacities and possibilities in themselves; they felt a thrill of pride at the courage and eloquence of their sisters. If in addition to speaking of "essential things," the speakers were young and pretty, the effect was of course much heightened. So, in a sense, it did not matter so much whether women talked about abolition, temperance or the rights of women; the important thing was that they talked! That changed the perception of them almost as much as what they said.

The path of reform was not always smooth nor the reformers always harmonious. Nette Brown, having attended the Woman's Convention in Rochester in 1852, wrote to Lucy Stone: "Some things were good and glorious but they quarreled a good deal of course. Douglass and Remond grew painfully personal. . . ." Even Lucy and Nette fell out briefly because Nette wore artificial flowers in her hat and Lucy, thinking them a sign of vanity and frivolity, burst into tears.

Lucy was also alarmed by indications that there might soon be a number of woman's rights groups with differing programs and aims.

The movement must be organized upon "true grounds," not a "narrow minded partial affair of some stamp that will shame the cause and retard its progress. . . . We may have a dozen ephemeral woman's rights organizations like successive crops of mushrooms springing up and dying one after another as the temperance parties have done," she wrote Nette.

The antislavery movement was the means of entry into American political life of a vast number of women who organized, chaired meetings, prepared agenda, made motions, debated issues, circulated petitions, and did all of this in the face of passive and often active resistance from most men, from virtually all the "media," and from the great majority of their sisters. The woman's rights movement, to which we have been here introduced, was the most significant outgrowth of the abolition movement, but its heyday was reserved for the post Civil War era when, with the issue of slavery settled, the "woman question" might be addressed more wholeheartedly.

It would be the height of presumption to try to summarize the thoughts and feelings of American women in the decades covered by this volume. It was doubtless true that the great majority of them were entirely preoccupied with those domestic duties that most men insisted were their proper and indeed exclusive sphere. But a new spirit was certainly stirring and it is difficult to overstate its importance or the debt it owed to first dozens and then hundreds and finally thousands and tens of thousands of remarkably able and intelligent women who felt that, however much politicians and publicists might trumpet the power and the glory of the United States, there were many things seriously amiss in the republic.

One of the most famous women of the nineteenth century was Margaret Fuller, editor of the transcendentalist *Dial.* In her book *Woman in the Nineteenth Century,* the boldest and, in a real sense, the first statement of American feminism (if we take feminism, as distinguished from the woman's rights movement, to be concerned with the subtler questions of the male and female psyche), Margaret Fuller ranged over the whole history of the female sex from antiquity to her own day. If she emphasized the mysterious inner life of the sexes, she boldly stated her social and political premises: "We would have every arbitrary barrier thrown down. We would have every path laid open to Woman as freely as to Man. Were this done and a slight temporary fermentation allowed to subside, we should see crystallizations more pure and of more various beauty. We believe the divine energy would pervade nature to a degree unknown in the history of former ages, and that no discordant collision but a ravishing harmony of the spheres would ensue." The romantic effusion established a tone that would come to characterize much feminist writing. It was not simply that women had been denied their "rights"; a new and more wholesome relationship between men and women would bring with it some "ravishing harmony."

How was this to be achieved? In a thinly disguised autobiographical interlude, Fuller wrote of a girl named Miranda whose father "cherished no sentimental reverence for Woman, but a firm belief in the equality of the sexes . . . he addressed her not as a plaything but as a living mind. . . . A dignified sense of self-dependence was given as all her portion, and she found it a sure anchor. Herself securely anchored, her relations with others were established with equal security." The sentences concealed as much as they revealed. Margaret Fuller paid a high price for her father's encouragement and in a painful sense of her own difference that bordered on the neurotic. But the important thing was that she triumphed over her youthful traumas and in her brief lifetime achieved a substantial measure of the fame she wished for so ardently.

"Male and female," she wrote in one of her most compelling (and to male readers infuriating) insights, "represent the two sides of the great radical dualism. But in fact they are perpetually passing into one another. Fluid hardens to solid, solid rushes to fluid. There is no wholly masculine man, no purely feminine woman . . . now the time has come where a clearer vision and better action are possible—when Man and Woman may regard one another as brother and sister, the pillars of one porch, the priests of one worship. . . . I wish Woman to live first for *God*'s sake. Then she will not make an imperfect man her god, and thus sink to idolatry. Then she will not take what is not fit for her from a sense of weakness and poverty. Then if she finds what she needs in Man embodied, she will know how to love and be worthy of being loved."

In her *Summer on the Lakes,* Margaret Fuller, like a good transcendentalist, reveled in the scenery of the Great Lakes region and scattered through her accounts of nature Emersonian reflections on life. "Only the dreamer shall understand realities," she wrote, "though in truth his dreaming must not be out of proportion to his waking!" In an imaginary dialogue between Free Hope and Good Sense, she wrote, "Subject to the sudden revelations, the breaks in habitual existence, caused by the aspect of death, the touch of love, the flood of music, I never lived that I remember what you call a common natural day. All my days are touched by the supernatural, for I feel the pressure of hidden causes and the presence, sometimes the communion, of unseen powers."

Having conquered the American literary scene and established herself as both a champion of the cause of women and one of the foremost literary critics of her day, Margaret Fuller set out to conquer the world. She visited Carlyle with a letter of introduction from Emerson, who called her "this wise, sincere, accomplished, and most entertaining of women. . . . She is full of nobleness, and with the generosity native to her mind and character appears to me an exotic in New England, a foreigner from some more sultry and expansive climate. . . . In short, she is our citizen of the world by quite special diploma." Carlyle found her "a high-soaring, clear, enthusiast soul; in whose speech there is much of all one wants to find in speech. A sharp, subtle intellect too; and less of that shoreless Asiatic dreaminess than I have sometimes met with in her writings. We liked one another very well, I think. . . ."

Margaret was on her way to live a dream of romance, to fall passionately in love with, marry, and have a child by an Italian nobleman, the Marchese Giovanni Angelo Ossoli, a revolutionary follower of Mazzini and champion of a new and united Italy. So Margaret Fuller of Boston became Marchesa Ossoli to the astonishment of her Boston friends, who had, in the main, a rather low opinion of Italians. Mazzini's revolution was, for the time, defeated, and the Ossolis, with their infant daughter, Angelina, died in the wreck of their ship off Long Island on their way back to the United States.

Her friend William Channing penned a fitting epitaph for her. Speaking of the tragedy of her unrealized promise as a writer and thinker, he wrote, "But the tragedy of Margaret's history was deeper yet. Beyond the poet was a woman—the fond and relying, the heroic and disinterested woman. The very glow of her poetic enthusiasm was but the flush of trustful affection; the very restlessness of her intellect was the confession that her heart had found no home."

At one of Margaret Fuller's famous "conversations" held at Elizabeth Peabody's West Street Bookshop in Boston, a young visitor from New York was an enthralled listener. Julia Ward was the carefully raised daughter of a prominent New York banker with reform interests, Samuel Ward, who had recently died. Julia Ward showed

Margaret Fuller some of her poems and the older woman was struck by their promise. "I saw," Margaret Fuller wrote later, "in her taste the capacity for genius, and the utmost delicacy of passionate feeling." In the summer of 1841 Julia Ward met a man twenty years her senior, the beau ideal of the romantic reformer, Samuel Gridley Howe. Byron was Howe's hero, and Howe had achieved a measure of world fame by fighting in the Greek war for independence. Julia had read his *History of the Greek Revolution* in her father's library.

Returned to a hero's welcome, Howe had been offered the post as director of the Perkins Institute for the Blind and had won fresh fame in his new career. "Deep in his heart," Julia Ward wrote, "lay a sense of the dignity and ability of human nature. . . . The blind must not only be fed and housed and cared for; they must learn to make their lives useful to the community; they must be taught and trained to earn their own support."

A year later Howe became her suitor and a New Yorker reported in his diary that he had seen the pretty "blue stocking," Miss Julia Ward, walking down Broadway with Dr. Howe. "They say she dreams in Italian," he wrote, "and quotes French verses. She sang very prettily at a party last evening, and accompanied herself on the piano. I noticed how white her hands were." Julia Ward and Samuel Gridley Howe were married in 1843 and Julia, to indicate her own independence, called herself Julia Ward Howe and not Mrs. Samuel Gridley Howe.

The married relationship of Julia Ward Howe and her husband is an instructive one. Both were "emancipated," both interested in all the leading reforms of the day. Both believed in the "rights" of women, but it was increasingly clear to Julia that they defined them quite differently. She found Howe a rigid and demanding husband and she wrote her sister from their extended honeymoon in Rome, "We are fulfilling the destiny of women, we are learning to live for others more than for ourselves, and in following thus the guiding of Providence, we have acted more wisely than we would have done in marking out an eccentric course of our own and adhering to it." But it was clear that this expression of pious resignation did not solve the problem. Julia wrote poetry that was published in various journals and was invited to read her works in public, but Howe was stubbornly resistant. Such a display, he insisted, would be unsuitable. With all his reform activities, he had little time for his wife and, soon, children. "My husband has scarcely half an hour in twenty-four to give me," she wrote. "So, as I think much in my way, and nobody takes the least interest in what I think, I am forced to make myself an imaginary public. . . . While I am employed in fictions my husband is dealing with facts. . . ."

By the early 1850s Julia had found a spiritual father in Theodore Parker, who encouraged her aspirations to write and teach and helped her endure what she called "the frozen ocean of Boston Life." Her closest friend was young Horace Binney Wallace, to whom she wrote, "I miss you so much, and life is so short, and friendship so precious, ah me!" She told him she had been reading Comte and Dante and completed "two long headache-compelling poems." She published a book of poems, which one reviewer called "impassioned wails of suffering," with thinly veiled references to the unhappiness of her marriage. Howe was deeply wounded by the poems and Julia wrote her sister that he "has been in a very dangerous state, I think, very near insanity. . . . We have had the devil's own time of it. . . ."

The Kansas-Nebraska Act and the rush to settle Kansas by both pro- and antislavery forces involved both the Howes. Samuel Howe addressed a mass meeting in Faneuil Hall, raised ten thousand dollars to aid in emigration to that state, and then set off for Kansas himself. Julia, in his absence, wrote a play called *The World's Own*, which scandalized her friends by its theme of illicit love. When the *Atlantic Monthly* appeared under the editorship of James Russell Lowell, in 1857, she flooded him with her poems, and when he refused to publish them she excoriated him for his lack of critical acumen. Now she threw herself wholeheartedly into the abolition cause, accompanying her husband on his next trip to Kansas. Back in Boston she met John Brown, "a middle-aged, middle-sized man, with hair and beard of amber color, streaked with gray. He looked a Puritan of the Puritans, forceful, concentrated, and self-contained." Two years later she wrote "The Battle Hymn of the Republic," the most popular song of the Civil War.

Women on the frontier presented a special case. It was Margaret Fuller, on her Western tour, who made the most accurate analysis of the situation of many women settlers on the frontier. In her view they were ill suited for the rigors of the wilderness. Their presence there was, almost invariably, the choice of the men, "and the women follow as women will, doing their best for affection's sake but too often in heart-sickness and weariness. Besides, it frequently not being their choice or conviction of their own minds that it is best to be there, their part is the hardest and they are least fitted for it. The men can find assistance in field labor, and recreation with the gun and fishing-rod. Their bodily strength is greater, and enables them to bear and enjoy both these forms of life." Women could seldom find anyone to help them in their taxing domestic duties: "All its various and careful tasks must be performed, sick or well, by the mother and daughters to whom a city education has imparted neither the strength nor skill now demanded." The wives of the poorer settlers thus often became "slatterns," unkempt and old before their time. The determinedly middle-class women struggled desperately "under every disadvantage to keep up the necessary routine of small arrangements."

The other side of the coin was that frontier women preserved and indeed extended the status that they had enjoyed in colonial New England. In a purely economic sense, the urban male did not need a wife—a serving woman could keep his house and cook his meals, a mistress satisfy his sexual needs. But in Wisconsin or Indiana or Missouri or Oregon a wife was almost indispensable and she was usually correspondingly valued. Tocqueville noted that most of the settlers on the frontier "who rush so boldly onwards in pursuit of wealth" took "their wives along with them and make them share the countless perils and privations that always attend the commencement of the expeditions." He had often met on the "verge of the wilderness" young women who had been gently reared "amid all the comforts of the large towns of New England," and who had passed from a prosperous parental home "to a comfortless hovel in a forest." But "fever, solitude, and a tedious life had not broken the springs of their courage. Their features were impaired and faded, but their looks were firm, they appeared to be at once sad and resolute."

Three years after the passage of the Kansas-Nebraska Act, William Dorsey moved his wife and eight children from Indianapolis to Nebraska, drawn by the opportunity to buy a hundred and sixty acres of land at $1.25 an acre. Among William Dorsey's eight children was an eighteen-year-old girl named Mollie, who decided to "commence a diary, or daily Journal, to note passing events, to have as a confidante or bosom friend, now that I am to leave so many near and dear. I go among strangers, into a strange land, and it may be a long time before I find one to whom I can confide my joys and sorrows. I have thought for years that I would keep a Journal," Mollie wrote, "I know it is a source of improvement and pleasure, and have only postponed it, because I have thought my life too monotonous to prove interesting." Now, on the eve of a great adventure, she took up her pen. "Indianapolis," she wrote, "has been my home for years. Here I have had the benefits of schools, churches, and the best of society. I go to a wild unsettled country, where I shall be deprived of all of these; but I go with my dear parents, to share their burdens and their lot whatsoe'er it be."

The family traveled from Indianapolis by train to the Mississippi River and across it on a steam ferry to St. Louis, where they bought supplies for their push west. "Going to New Brasker?" people asked. "Nothing to eat there." From St. Louis they headed up the Missouri on the handsome steamboat *Silver Heels,* with a "motley crew, persons of every form, size, and color. Fussy old ladies with their poodle dogs. Anxious mammas in moral terror lest their youngsters should fall overboard; giddy girls, frolicksome children, fascinating young gents, and plenty of bachelors."

Nebraska City was the immediate goal of the Dorseys. They found temporary quarters there and the father searched out a land claim in the country that stretched westward. The best accommodations they could find were "a small dilapidated log house with one small room and a three-cornered kitchen." It was a dismal beginning. "Father tried to look cheerful," Mollie wrote, "but I could see the tears in Mother's eyes, and *I,* well *I* have started out to be a heroine, a *brave, brave* girl, and I said, 'it would be jolly.' (I did not *think* so)." In a place where women were scarce, Mollie and her older sisters drew men like flowers draw bees. "Mr. Andrew Jackson Cook came to pay his distresses to me the other day," she wrote in her diary. "He said he was on the hunt for a wife, and hearing there was a 'hull lot of girls' here, he thought he would 'come around.' I tried to freeze him but I don't think I did. . . . Mr. Alexander Mapes, came through going to Neb[raska] City. He was sick all day here. I dosed him on pepper tea and toned him up with a good supper, which placed him under such great obligations that he asked me to deal out his rations thro life." Mr. Cook proved a persistent suitor. He wrote a letter proposing matrimony and a few weeks later he was back, "looking too innocent for anything," to press his cause, upon which Mollie told him, "You are a goose, Mr. Cook, to want a young girl like me. You are old enough to be my father. *Yes,* my grandfather."

The Dorsey claim was near Nebraska City, a few dozen rickety houses. "Here," Mollie wrote, "there are nothing but rude cabins and board shanties not even plastered. I see such lots of men, but very few ladies and children. I heard one fellow shout, 'Hurrah for the girls' as father marched his brood into the hotel parlor, and Mrs. Allen, our landlady, said, 'I'm glad to see the girls.' . . . She says the place is full of gamblers, topers, and roughs of every description. . . ."

Mollie was incurably romantic. When the family finally reached their homestead on the Little Nemaha River, she wrote, "I never felt more relieved and thankful now that we had come through safely and were coming to a home of our own once more. The sunrise was glorious! the trees full of singing birds, ringing out a welcome. Soft zephyrs floated o'er us, bright flowers gave out their perfume, and all nature was glad. Father had named the place 'Hazel Dell,' and we christened it by singing that sweet song. And such a chorus as went up from those lumbering wagons! Birds stopped their carols to listen, and festive chipmunks flew from their hiding places bewildered with the noise. . . . Mother hardly enters into extacies [sic]. She no doubt realizes what it is to bring a young rising family away from the advantages of the world. To *me*, it seems a glorious holiday, a freedom from restraint, and I believe it will be a blessing to we girls. We were getting too fond of style, too unhappy not to have the necessary things to carry it out."

Mollie went on a three-day rampage, "exploring the woods, catching fish, and helping in the garden, for altho late, Mother says, we must have some vegetables. We *all* seem content. Even *Mother* has caught the inspiration and lost her care-worn look and, Mother, dear, we will try and make you happy yet."

Soon, however, Mollie was writing poignantly, "If the country would only fill up, if there were only schools or churches, or even some society. We do not see a woman at all. All men, single, or bachelors, and one gets tired of them."

She helped her father put a new roof on the house and noted, with obvious satisfaction, "it seems I can put my hand to almost anything." She fretted about the state of her soul and her neglect of her prayers and about her future. "Will I be a happy beloved wife, with good husband, happy home, and small family, or an abused, deserted one with 8 or 9 small children crying for their daily bread? Or won't I marry at all? If I live to be an *old maid*, I will be one of the good kind that is a friend to everybody and that everyone loves. If I *do* ever marry it will be someone I *love very, very, very* much, better than anyone yet, except—except." The "except" was Byron Sanford, the "yallar mule driver" who found his way to the Dorsey cabin more and more regularly; soon Mollie was calling him "my" Mr. Sanford.

William Dorsey's brother arrived with plans to lay out a town site nearby. The girls put up berries and currants and wild apples, milked the cow and made cheese. The "town" was named Helena and a store and a post office were built. Two young men were hired to run it and boarded with the already crowded Dorseys. Word came from Grandfather Dorsey that he was planning to emigrate himself. Soon the Dorsey house, with a shed attached, was serving as modest hotel for travelers on their way from Nebraska City to another new town, Beatrice, twenty miles down the line. The burden of the additional cooking fell on Mollie. She also had charge of the skittish cow and often had to hunt through the woods for her. Her brother, Sam, was bitten by a rattlesnake and frantically doctored with home remedies. Mollie's high spirits constantly broke out in pranks and practical jokes until her mother feared "I am losing all the dignity I ever possessed." While the two storekeepers of the town of Helena were "having a good time," doubtlessly drinking, "some marauding Indians . . . walked off with most of their supplies," thereby putting an end to Helena. But the Dorsey grandparents arrived with a cousin, driven out by Byron Sanford and his mules, and gradually the land in the vicinity was taken up, some by friends and relatives from Indianapolis, some by strangers. One holiday twenty-two members of the Dorsey family sat down at table.

William Dorsey was often away, working as a carpenter in and about Nebraska City. Mollie's feelings for "By" Sanford had ripened into love. It was understood that they were to be married, but meanwhile Mollie must go to Nebraska City and find a job as a teacher or seamstress to help make ends meet in the economy of the family. She left "Hazel Dell" a little sadly. It had become to her "the sweetest spot on earth," but she reminded herself: "I must expect to suffer with the world. I know the path is not strewn with roses to one that has to make her own way, but I have a strong, brave heart, and a faith that teaches me that the Lord will help those who help themselves."

In Nebraska City Mollie worked as a seamstress for a Mrs. Burnham whose "morose and tyrannical" husband was away in the East on business. Mrs. Burnham's apartment was in a building on the main street and she and Mollie could sit at the front window and watch the "ox teams loading up to start on a trip to Utah. All is commotion,"

Mollie wrote, "the hallowing of the drivers, the clanking of chains and wagon-masters giving orders." Mollie joined the church choir, made new friends, and spent much time with By. It was now agreed that they would be married when she was twenty-one and he had saved enough money to build a house.

By fall Mollie was back at Hazel Dell. The abandoned Helena general store had found use as a church. Mollie noted in her journal, "People are settling all around us, and Sundays there is quite a congregation at the 'church,'" where a Methodist circuit-riding minister preached periodically. Mollie had chills and fever and, exempt from household duties, spent much time with her "precious Grandma," and with her journal, writing sentimental poetry—"A Dying Girl's Dream" and having "many seasons of sublime and poetic thoughts" which often carried her soaring "above the cares of life into a world of my own. . . . It is well perhaps," she added, "that I have to battle with stern realities. I might become an idle dreamer, for I have not talent enough to make much of myself. I used to dream of being an author, of climbing the steps of fame, but *Fate* has led me from the realms of Poesy and Thought into a sea of perplexities and cares." She found comfort in the thought of By's "thoroughly matter-of-fact and practical" temperament that "will help equalize my romance and sentiment. He often brings me from my airy flights. He is good and sensible and, bless his heart, *I live in him*. . . . Our associations here are not congenial, the people rough and ignorant. I suppose I ought to go to work and do something to help and elevate them. But where shall I begin?"

In February, Byron Sanford and Mollie Dorsey were married. Mollie had baked the wedding cake while Byron rode to Tecumseh, the county seat, to get the license. The event was given a heightened drama by the fact that Byron, unable to track down the justice of the peace, arrived for the ceremony five hours after the guests had assembled. "We were married in the kitchen!" Mollie wrote. "Start not! ye fairy brides. Beneath your veils and orange blossoms, in some home where wealth and fashion congregate, *your* vows are no truer, your heart no happier, than was this maiden's, in the kitchen of a log cabin, in the wilderness of Nebraska. Time may change, and I may have more attractive surroundings, and I may smile at this primitive wedding, I only trust my heart may ever be as brave and true as then and as happy as now."

Byron and Mollie made their way across the plains to Denver, drawn by the Colorado gold rush, and we will encounter them again; but in her journal Mollie Dorsey Sanford gives a classic picture of a young woman meeting, with an indomitable spirit, the rigors of life on the Nebraska frontier.

Western women—women of the Mississippi Valley frontier—were quite different from Eastern women, just as city women differed in their manner of living and their expectations from rural and small-town women. What can be said, I think, with some certainty, was that the American woman, generally speaking, *was* a new breed. Despite all the efforts, most of them emanating from the circles of higher fashion, to limit and confine American women (and it is not clear that these efforts were by any means entirely chargeable to men; women often seemed eager accomplices), they broke by far the greater part of those barriers that confined them. We have seen them active in all the reform movements and, increasingly, in a movement for their own "reform" or, as we say today, liberation. Indeed, if we except the antislavery movement, the century-long struggle of American women for their rights is the most dramatic and important social development of that age, rivaled only perhaps by the technological revolution.

35

Immigration

Immigration in its simplest form is statistics. At the beginning of our period—the year 1826—the number of immigrants entering the United States totaled 10,837, of whom 9,751 were of European origins. Approximately 2,300 were from England, 5,408 from Ireland, and only 511 from Germany. Over five thousand listed "no occupation"; 190 listed "professional," 1,943 "commercial," 2,129 "skilled," 1,382 "farmer." Immigration thereafter rose and fell increasing almost eight times to 79,340 in 1837, of whom 12,218 were from Great Britain, 28,508 from Ireland, and 23,740 from Germany. The depression years from 1837 to the early 1840s saw a general decline in immigration due primarily to the hard times, but in 1842 the Irish potato famine sent more than 50,000 Irish to the United States.

The boom period of almost eight years, 1846 to 1854, saw a dramatic increase in immigration, rising to 427,833 in the latter year, of whom 101,606 were Irish (a sharp decline from the peak year of Irish immigration of 221,253 four years earlier) and 215,009 were German (a number exceeded only once—in 1882—in our entire history). For the remainder of the decade of the fifties the number of immigrants each year ran between 121,000 and 251,000.

The decade of the fifties saw more than three million immigrants enter the country, the majority of whom listed "no occupation." The number described as servants rose sharply, as did the category of laborers, which increased from 716 in 1826 to 31,268 in 1860. Farmers and the skilled came in roughly equivalent numbers except in the peak years of German immigration, when farmers far outnumbered any other category. Indeed one wonders that there were any farmers left in Germany, since some 360,000 came to America in that decade, out of a total German immigration of well over a million.

But immigration is also people and we are already familiar with some, at least, of the story of what happened to immigrants who arrived in the United States in this era. Isabella Bird went to view a group of some seven hundred English immigrants who had arrived in New York. "They looked tearful, pallid, dirty and squalid. . . . Many were deplorably emaciated, others looked vacant and stupefied. Some were ill, and some were penniless; but poverty and sickness are among the best recommendations which an emigrant can bring with him, for they place him under the immediate notice of those estimable and overworked men, the Emigration Commissioners, whose humanity is above all praise." The stolid Germans seemed to have been most successful in surviving the ardors of the voyage while "the goods and chattels of the Irish appeared to consist principally of numerous red-headed, unruly children and ragged-looking bundles tied round with rope. . . . Here [the immigrants] found themselves in the chaotic confusion of this million-peopled city, not knowing where to betake themselves and bewildered by cries of 'Cheap hacks.'"

The Germans and Irish were treated, for the most part, as badly as possible, considering the limits set by the laws and the fact that they constituted an essential labor supply. They were cheated and swindled when they arrived in the United States (often, to be sure, by their own countrymen). They were looked down on and discriminated against by earlier immigrants, so-called native Americans, and frequently attacked and beaten or killed. They lived in filthy ghettos, as they came later to be called, and, in appalling numbers, died of disease, excessive amounts of bad booze, and killing labor. They had neither the glamour of the Indians or the dramatic appeal of the black slaves of the South.

Fanny Kemble was one of the relatively few reform-minded persons whose feeling for the misery of the slave's plight extended to the Irish poor. They were, in her view, "not only quarrelers, and rioters, and fighters, and drinkers, and despisers of niggers—they are a passionate, impulsive, warmhearted, generous people, much given to powerful indignation, which breaks out suddenly when not compelled to smolder sullenly. . . ." She dared to hope they might overcome their repugnance to blacks, "and then" she wrote, "I leave you to judge of the possible consequences." It was true that "in Ireland nothing can be more savage, brutish, filthy, idle and incorrigibly and hopelessly helpless and incapable than the Irish appear; and yet, transplanted to your Northern states, freed from the evil influences which surround them at home, they and their children become industrious, thrifty, willing to learn, able to improve, and forming, in the course of two generations, a most valuable accession to the laboring population."

They were perceived by "native" Americans as the source of all urban problems—disease, crime, crowded living conditions, alcoholism, and prostitution. "This state of things," Philip Hone wrote, describing the breakdown of law and order in New York City, "has been hastened in our case by the constant stream of European paupers arriving upon the shores of this land of promise. Alas! how often does it prove to the deluded emigrant a land of broken promise and blasted hope!"

If America had only her own poor to provide for, she could get along tolerably well. Public and private charity, Hone wrote, "might save us from the sights of woe with which we are assailed in the streets." A constant stream of petitioners made their way from house to house seeking food or a few pennies. "Nineteen out of twenty of the mendicants" were, in Hone's opinion, "foreigners cast upon our shores, indigent and helpless . . . deceived by the misrepresentations of unscrupulous agents, and left to starve among strangers. . . ." The cost of a bottle of wine at the lavish dinner he had recently left would "alleviate the distress of those miserable objects who stretch out attenuated arms of wasted poverty, or display the haggard countenance of infantile deprivation." Many of the rich were "liberal and charitable," but the contrast between their "lavish expenditure" and the "absolute destitution" of the city's poor dismayed him, though he seems to have had no notion what might be done to remedy such ills. Ironically, New Yorkers seemed readier to raise money for "the suffering people of Ireland," than for the Irish poor of their own city. Nine thousand dollars was collected in a few days among the city's merchants to send a shipload of wheat and other foods to Cork, and collections were taken up in a number of churches. Immense shipments of flour and corn were dispatched from every port on the east coast to Ireland, as were, oddly enough, forty-two boxes of clocks. The Relief Committee in New York alone raised over fifty thousand dollars. A priest declared that four thousand persons, many of them children, had died of starvation and disease in the county of Cork. Through disease, starvation, and emigration the population of Ireland declined by two million—one-third—in the period of a few years.

The news from abroad was of economic upheaval and desperate hardship. "Ireland is no longer the exclusive abode of suffering humanity," Hone wrote. "Every part of Europe is uttering the appalling cry of bread! bread! and (strange and wonderful state of things) the New World supplies the wants of the Old, the mother derives nourishment from the child. . . . All Europe is coming across the ocean; all that part at least who cannot make a living at home; and what shall we do with them? They increase our taxes, eat our bread, and encumber our streets, and not one in twenty is competent to keep himself."

Hone's worries about the flood of Irish immigration were typical. They had, he wrote, "brought the cholera this year and they will always bring wretchedness and want. The boast that our country is an asylum for the oppressed in other parts of the world is very philanthropic and sentimental, but I fear that we shall before long derive little comfort from being made an almshouse and place of refuge for the poor of other countries."

George Templeton Strong also deplored the flood of immigrants and the "increasing tendency of the Whig party to absorb all the wealth and respectability, and of the Democratic (so called) to take in all the loaferism of the nation, a tendency which may bring us finally to be divided into two great factions, the rich and the poor; and then for another French Revolution. . . ." Strong went to the hall where immigrants were seeking naturalization and wrote that it was "enough to turn a man's stomach. . . . Wretched, filthy, bestial-looking Italians and Irish, and creations that looked as if they had risen from the lazarettos of Naples for this special object; in short, the very scum and dregs of human nature filled the clerk of C[ommon] P[leas] office so completely that I was almost afraid of being poisoned by going in. A dirty Irishman is bad enough, but he's nothing comparable to a nasty French or Italian loafer."

Prejudice against immigrants had a long and, indeed, respectable history in the United States. It was none other than Jefferson, the patron saint of democracy, who had expressed a classic apprehension about "the unbounded licentiousness" of immigrants. He did not believe American democracy, rare and exotic plant that it was, could survive an influx of foreigners with different ideals and traditions. They would, he predicted, "infuse into [the United States] their spirit, warp and bias its direction, and render it a heterogeneous, incoherent, distracted mass." That, in fact, was what the United States appeared to many Americans, especially those who called themselves Whigs, to have become by the 1840s—"a heterogeneous, incoherent, distracted mass"—and that, certainly, was the way in which most visitors described it.

If the Irish were disposed to congregate in the Eastern seaport cities of Boston, New York, Philadelphia, and Baltimore (more and more made their way west to work on the railroads), the Germans and Norwegians headed for the "Near West," the Mississippi Valley region, what we call today the Midwest. Chicago became the terminus for many. Often Swedish and Norwegian immigrants arrived there packed into freight cars like cattle. On one occasion when the freight car doors were opened four dead bodies were found. On the outskirts of Chicago, the "Garden City" as it was called, Irish and Swedish immigrants had put up improvised shacks. "The materials for the warrens, by courtesy called houses," Unonius wrote, "consisted mainly of slabs and pieces of boards begged from the lumberyards."

The mortality rate was often shocking. Unonius reported that in 1849 during the cholera epidemic half of the poor Swedish immigrants who made their way to Chicago died—"entire families died within the space of a few weeks." Many children were orphaned and Unonius helped to find foster parents for them. In the summer of 1855 so many Swedish immigrants died that Unonius found himself with "more than twenty fatherless and motherless children in the house." His appeal for help was met immediately by the members of his congregation. He received "beds and bedding for them to sleep in, money to buy the food for them, suitable food and drink prepared for their immediate needs, medical aid for the sick, and fine, noble people to watch at their bedsides. . . . Where else but in America," Unonius wrote, "could a thing like that have been done? I dare not say nowhere, but I doubt that in any other country the aid would have come so speedily, so willingly, and been so freely given as on that occasion. . . . In spite of their faults—and what people, what individual is without faults?— [Americans] have proved that their hearts possess as great treasure as the ground on which they tread." In the month of October alone fifty-five Swedes who had died in private homes were buried at public expense.

So far as they could, immigrants formed their own communities. The Germans, Swedes, and Norwegians, with language barriers, were especially disposed to do so. Of the Germans, Gustaf Unonius wrote, "They have their own schools and their own justices of peace and other municipal officers. Supplied with newspapers in their own language, of which there are published in America almost as many as in all of Germany, and associating mainly with each other . . . many do not even trouble to learn the language or teach it to their children."

By and large the Germans fared much better than the Irish, but Moritz Busch, the German refugee, was saddened by "the contempt" in which his countrymen were held "by the great mass of Anglo-Americans." He blamed that contempt in part on the Germans' own exclusiveness, their "thickheaded peasant's conceit," and their "factionalism," with "hundreds and hundreds of little groups persecuting, goading, and stigmatizing each other, and then, above all, in the great cleft between the old immigrants or the 'Grays,' and the newcomers, or the 'Greens.'" The Grays had come in an early period of migration to improve their material situation; the Greens were refugees from the revolutionary upheavals, intellectuals, reformers, and radicals. The typical Green was "a bearer of new ideas, and an admonisher of the vices and ugliness that have developed in the New World along with much excellence." The Gray, "caring only for 'the almighty dollar,' patronises or fleeces his newly arrived compatriot. Money counts in America and the newcomers have no money, therefore no status in the older German community." This, at least, was how things struck Busch, himself a potential Green. "America," he wrote, "is the land of extremes and contrasts, and upon this many a fool turns his somersaults—none, however, is a more woeful figure than the German who in this way is ashamed of his mother."

Busch reserved some of his most scornful comments for the radical newspapers of "Red Socialism" published by the refugees of 1848. One of these, the *Schnellpost,* he described as "sensually lewd, blasphemous, and coarse in opinion and language. It reprints the dirtiest slop of irreligion, holds the satisfaction of sensual desire to be the highest goal, and carries communism so far as to calculate the amount that every individual in our cities would receive through a division of all property. . . ."

The most gifted of the German revolutionaries—the Greens—

was a young man named Carl Schurz. Like Kossuth and Mazzini, Schurz had been forced to flee when a reactionary government snuffed out the revolution. After lingering for several years in England with Kossuth, Mazzini, and a host of other radical exiles, Schurz and his new bride came to the United States, arriving in New York in the fall of 1852, where, "with the buoyant hopefulness of young hearts, we saluted the new world," as Schurz wrote.

Handsome and gifted, an ardent idealist and visionary, Schurz was only twenty-three years old when he arrived in America. At their first meal in the New World at a hotel called the Morton House, the Schurzes were astonished to see a corps of black waiters who served their meal in a bizarre ballet of uniform movements commanded by "a portly colored head-waiter in a dress coat and white necktie, whose manners were strikingly grand and patronizing." Mrs. Schurz fell ill almost at once, perhaps as much from the strangeness of her surroundings as from a specific malady, and young Schurz, surrounded by men and women whose language he could hardly speak, experienced "the most melancholy hours of my life . . . in the great Republic, the idol of my dreams, feeling myself utterly lonesome and forlorn." But in Philadelphia the Schurzes found both hospitable countrymen and helpful Americans and set out to learn English and adjust to the strange ways of their new home. Schurz was introduced to Lucretia Mott. "I thought her," he wrote, "the most beautiful old lady I had ever seen. Her features were of exquisite fineness. . . . Her dark eyes beamed with intelligence and benignity. . . . She expressed the hope that, as a citizen, I would never be indifferent to the slavery question. . . ."

Needless to say, America was not the country the young idealist had imagined. "The newly arrived European democrat," he wrote, "having lived in a world of theories and imaginings without having had any practical experience of a democracy at work, beholding it for the first time, ask[s] himself: 'Is this really a people living in freedom? Is this the realization of my ideal?'" Soon he comes to realize that the real world is made up of imperfect people. In a free society man thus "manifests himself, not as he ought to be, but as he is, with all his good qualities, instincts, and impulses: with all his attributes of strength as well as all his weaknesses; that this, therefore, is not an ideal state, but simply a state in which the forces of good have a free field as against the forces of evil. . . ." "Here in America," he wrote a German friend, "what there is . . . of great institutions of learning, of churches, of great commercial institutions, lines of communication, etc. . . . almost always owes its existence, not to official authority, but to the spontaneous co-operation of private citizens. Here you witness the productiveness of freedom."

The volume of immigration is almost as hard to comprehend as is the suffering of those who immigrated. The causes of immigration were, of course, various, but they can perhaps be grouped into three or four general headings. There were those, who, like the Irish preeminently, were driven by the most desperate need, by the literal threat of starvation. Even these needed somehow to find passage money. It might be lent by relatives (or sent by those already in the United States), given by those in charge of the poor in a parish, or by some benefactor, or, on occasion, the government itself. Except in times of desperate famine, the poorest people could not come because they could not raise even the modest sum required to pay their passage.

A substantial degree above the impoverished Irish were marginal farmers or peasants whose worldly goods, painstakingly acquired, could be disposed of in order to provide them with their fare on a crowded and often pestilential sailing ship. Then there were mechanics and artisans, those with a skill or trade, tin- or iron-smiths, or cabinetmakers. When bad times pinched them severely, they could again, in many instances, liquidate their main possessions or borrow money to cross the ocean.

There were those members of the middle class like Gustaf Unonius who felt themselves hemmed in by a future as a petty provincial functionary, or who saw military commissions and professional offices monopolized by the aristocracy.

There were also the younger sons of the lesser nobility whose futures were cramped or uncertain and there were those who were well-to-do but hoped to do very much better. Many young men came to escape the draft in one European country or another. Married couples, like Gustaf and Lotta Unonius or Johannes and Anna Schweizer came. Extended families came with uncles and cousins; more rarely, whole communities, or substantial portions of them, came.

It should be noted that the more who came from a particular village, or province, or country, the easier it was for their successors to find help and succor in a strange land. The nationals of every country constituted in the United States unofficial (and sometimes official) immigrant aid societies where compatriots, friends, and relatives who spoke the same language, ate the same food, and observed the same customs stood ready to lend a helping hand.

What cannot, perhaps, be sufficiently emphasized is that conditions of the poor in many European countries were so desperate that any hazards seemed worth facing in the hope of something better. It must also be said that reports from those who had made the journey almost invariably understated the arduousness of the undertaking and overstated their own "success" in their new environment. In addition land agents roamed through Europe with glittering promises of fortunes to be made in America. Where a few precious acres of carefully tended land constituted a modest fortune, the vision of millions of acres of virgin soil awaiting the bite of the plow was enormously alluring.

The vast majority of immigrants underwent the misery that Isabella Bird observed and Gustaf Unonius (and many others) described. The psychological consequences of such a massive trauma are, of course, difficult to assess, but they were assuredly vast, reaching the profoundest levels of human experience, and including alienation from the Motherland (or Fatherland), disease, homelessness, and simple terror. The grandmother of Max Ways, the former editor of *Fortune* magazine, was a child of seven when her parents died in an Irish famine. A tag was placed on her, addressed to relatives in America, and she was sent on board a ship across the ocean like a package. To her dying day, she could never speak of the voyage without weeping. We know that the collective residual memory of such experiences must be one of the most important elements in the American consciousness.

36

Urban Life

The large Eastern cities grew, during the period we are presently considering, from what today would be considered hardly more than small towns to great metropolises numbering hundreds of thousands of people. In the process they acquired the character and the problems of the modern city. All of them had large populations of depressed poor as well as substantial middle classes and small but powerful upper classes. What is hard to comprehend today is the constant ferment of social unrest and bitterness that manifested itself almost monthly in violent riots and civic disorders. In New York or Philadelphia the most trivial incident might trigger a riot that would last for days. In New York City, in the fall of 1831, when an English actor named Anderson who had been reported to have spoken critically of America appeared in a Sir Walter Scott play, *Rob Roy,* he was hissed and his voice drowned out by shouts of "Off! Off! Go back to England! Tell them the Yankees sent you back!" The next night "apples, eggs and other missiles were showered upon the stage," Philip Hone reported. The following night there was more rioting. The theater was attacked, the windows smashed, and the doors battered down. The next day a large crowd again collected in front of the theater, but the city watch and the mayor succeeded in persuading them to disperse.

At the municipal elections in New York in April, 1834, there were "dreadful riots between the Irish and the Americans," Philip Hone noted. "A band of Irishmen of the lowest class came out of Duane Street . . . There was much severe fighting and many persons were wounded and knocked down. . . . The mayor arrived with a strong body of watchmen but they were attacked and overcome, and many of the watchmen severely wounded." According to Hone the police, more commonly called watchmen, did little to quell disorder since they had been appointed "as a reward for party services performed at the polls, not to quell riots created by the very fellows who assisted to place" them in office.

The year 1834 was remembered as the "riot year" in New York. One of the most violent was the "stonecutters' riot," brought about by the city's decision to use convicts to cut the marble for a building of the recently established New York University on Washington Square. In July a mob attacked the Bowery Theatre on the rumor that an English actor playing there had, like Anderson, disparaged America. When Edwin Forrest managed to quiet the crowd, many in it turned their attention to a meeting of abolitionists. What particularly offended the mob was the fact that blacks and whites had appeared on the same platform. Collecting at the handsome Rose Street house of Lewis Tappan, a leader of the abolitionists, the mob broke into it, "destroyed the windows and made a bonfire of the furniture on the street." For three days the riots continued. The home of the Reverend Samuel Cox, a Presbyterian minister, one of the founders of New York University and a director of the Union Theological Seminary, was nearly demolished. The African Episcopal Church was destroyed "and many of the houses of black people, particularly in Leonard Street and at the Five Points," were torn down or badly damaged. It took three thousand militia "with a strong body of citizens organized as special constables" to bring some semblance of order to the city.

The citizens of the larger cities were alarmed at the breakdown in law and order. Many people felt it was unsafe to go out on the streets after dark. Juries became notorious for freeing culprits and judges for imposing light sentences. Philip Hone wrote that "a man must have great luck to get himself hanged in this country," adding, "It is certainly a melancholy proof of the depravity of our morals that the most flagrant offenses against the laws, and the most atrocious violations of the peace and good order of society, go daily 'unwhipped of justice' by the misjudging leniency, if not the base corruption, of men elected to preserve as jurors the purity of our legal institutions."

New York City, like Philadelphia and Baltimore (Boston being something of an exception), was plagued by gangs of toughs and bullies. Philip Hone complained to his diary of the "degeneracy of our morals and the inefficiency of our police." There had been a number of ugly robberies and stabbings. Gangs of young men "generally . . . between the ages of twelve and twenty-four" patrolled the streets "making night hideous and insulting all who are not strong enough to defend themselves." They frequented low bars in the Bowery and along Canal Street "and some even in Broadway, where drunken frolics are succeeded by brawls, and on the slightest provocation knives are brought out, dreadful wounds inflicted, and sometimes horrid murder committed."

Such gangs ran their districts virtually unchallenged by the officials of the city. In Philadelphia it was the Moyamensing section where "various organized gangs of ruffians" were "suffered to do as they please without interference," in Sidney George Fisher's words. One especially serious outbreak was put down by employing gangs from a rival district deputized as police. "There could hardly be a worse policy," Fisher added.

When times were bad, robberies, thefts, and holdups increased alarmingly. In the Philadelphia suburbs there was an outbreak of burglaries and holdups following the Panic of 1837. Sidney George Fisher was awakened one night by the sound of someone in his house. He intercepted robbers who fled. "Many country houses in the neighborhood have been robbed during the winter," he noted; five on his road and six on Chestnut Hill within a few weeks. Incendiarism was also rife. Barns had been "burnt in all directions, some of them very valuable, and a week scarcely passes that one or two are not destroyed. These things have produced such a sense of insecurity," he added, "that no one feels safe or likes to leave home, and probably there is scarcely a house within ten miles of the city where firearms are not kept loaded for defense, a thing unheard of a few years ago."

In New York George Templeton Strong reflected in his diary that the time had perhaps come to form a vigilance committee of citizens to supplement the inadequate police force and suppress "rowdyism." The high crime rate moved Strong to reflect: "Cities are bad enough at the best, but a rich commercial city (like this) I regard as a *hell*—a sink of vice and corruption and misery—lightened on the surface by the false glare of unhealthy exhalations. . . ."

James Silk Buckingham, the visiting Englishmen, noted that notwithstanding the "number and efficiency of the benevolent institutions of New York, there is still a large amount of misery and crime, of destitution in its most abject state, and of intemperance in its most fearful forms. . . . A very painful part of this picture," he added, "is the indifference, and even levity, with which the subject is treated in the public papers. . . ." Buckingham was dismayed at the numbers of deaths "from destitution and want . . . in a country . . . where food of every kind is abundant and cheap, and where labour of every description is largely remunerated."

"In New York," the Reverend David Macrae wrote, "all that is best and all that is worst in America is represented. Fling together Tyre and Sidon, the New Jerusalem, Sodom and Gomorrah, a little of heaven, and more of hell, and you have a faint picture of this mighty Babylon of the New World. City of colossal wealth and haggard poverty; city of virtue, with an abortionist occupying the most palatial residence in Fifth Avenue; city of churches and Bible houses, where one of the foremost citizens is a man who keeps his wife on one side of the street, and his mistress on the other."

If Americans generally were pleasure loving, active, restless, and competitive, New York epitomized all these traits. When Charles Francis Adams visited the city he was highly critical of its atmosphere of mad hurry and bustle. "The activity of competition glares in every street," he noted. "Here is a livery stable built of half burnt bricks and clay mortar painted to imitate a Roman temple. . . . A man advertises his blacking in large chalk letters upon the wooden fences of every vacant lot and another man builds a house to the clouds that *his* painted letters may be seen for half a mile glaring over the intervening houses. Then there is such an intermixture of fashion and poverty." Adams found that many of the prominent old families were yielding to newcomers. "The new ones are coming forward on the strength of wealth suddenly acquired and which in all probability will be as suddenly lost."

The most shocking event of the summer of 1849 was the cholera epidemic that swept New York City. It had started, Philip Hone noted, "in Orange Street, in the abodes of filth, destitution, and intemperance, in houses where water was never used internally or externally, and the pigs were contaminated by the contact of the children." St.

Louis and Cincinnati were also hard hit. The disease was most severe in the poorer sections of cities, but no class or area was spared. "Poor New York has become a charnel house," Philip Hone wrote at the end of August; "people die daily of cholera to the number of two or three hundred. . . . But this mortality is principally among the emigrants in the eastern and western extremities of the city, where hundreds are crowded into a few wretched hovels, amidst filth and bad air, suffering from personal neglect and poisoned by eating garbage which a well-bred hog on a Western farm would turn up his snout at." Two weeks later, Hone reported that the cholera continued in New York and elsewhere, noting, "There have been many cases of whole families dying." The death toll in New York alone was set at five thousand, and many schools were turned into makeshift hospitals. Finally Hone himself was stricken but survived.

The gangs of toughs, the restless unemployed, and the prevalence of disease were all less of a threat than fire, and this in spite of the teams of volunteer fire fighters in all the major cities. George Combe, who witnessed the celebration in Philadelphia of the hundredth anniversary of that city's fire companies, was impressed to see in their "grand jubilee" "a train of engines fully a mile in length, with all their apparatus necessary for extinguishing fires, maintained in the highest order, by unpaid citizens." Twenty to a hundred men made up a team. As soon as the alarm sounded a wild race began between the various companies to get to the scene of the fire first. The first team there was in command and the others must obey. "When two engines arrive . . . at the same time," Combe noted, "the companies occasionally fight for the first place, and then a desperate and bloody battle will rage for a considerable time while the flames are making an unchecked progress." From having considered the volunteer fire companies as unparalleled examples of civic zeal, Combe came to view them as "a convenient apology for excitable young men indulging in irregular habits, which, if not clothed with an official and popular character, would expose them to censure by a strictly moral community."

In New York hardly a week passed without a dangerous conflagration. The most serious took place on December, 17, 1835. Philip Hone described it as "the most awful calamity which has ever visited these United States . . . nearly one half of the first ward is in ashes; 500 to 700 stores, which with their contents are valued at $20,000,000 to $40,000,000, are now lying in an indistinguishable mass of ruins." The fire had started at nine o'clock at night and the efforts to check it had been thwarted by the fact that most of the fire hydrants were frozen. The Merchants' Exchange, "one of the ornaments of the city," had been burned down. Hone's son and son-in-law and nephew all had lost their businesses and the fire-insurance companies were bankrupted. Looters were soon prowling in the ruins and Hone heard such remarks from working-class types as "Ah! They'll make no more five percent dividends," and "This will make the aristocracy haul in their horns." "Poor deluded wretches," Hone added, "little do they know that their own horns 'live and move and have their being' in those very horns of the aristocracy, as their instigators teach them to call it. This cant . . . forms part of the warfare of the poor against the rich . . . the politicians of Tammany Hall . . . find now that the dogs they have taught to bark will bite them as soon as their political opponents."

Hone was proud of the spirit with which the merchants of the city responded to the crisis: "There is no despondency; every man is determined to go to work to redeem his loss, and all are ready to assist their more unfortunate neighbors." The federal government was called on to appropriate twelve million dollars for disaster relief. Hone wrote that "goods and property of every description" were to be "found under the rubbish in enormous quantities, but generally so much damaged as to be hardly worth saving. Cloths, silks, laces, prints of the most valuable kind, are dug out partly burned, and nearly all ruined. A mountain of coffee lies at the corner of Old Slip and South Street."

A new city literally rose from the ashes. Burned-out lots sold for more than they were worth before the fire with buildings on them. A fever of speculation took hold of normally sensible citizens. Everyone with a dollar to spare got into the game. One result was a precipitous rise in prices. It was estimated that living costs of the average workingman had risen 66 percent in little more than a year. Workmen made their displeasure known by a series of strikes. Philip Hone noted that "the stevedores and other laborers employed along-shore made a demand for an increase of wages. . . ." The employers yielded, "but this concession," Hone wrote, "encouraged further demands . . . an immense body of malcontents paraded the wharves all yesterday and attacked the men who refused to join them. . . . While this disgraceful scene was acting out on the wharves, a large body of laborers assailed the men who were at work removing the rubbish from the ruins of the fire, with clubs and brickbats."

Not ten years later another devastating fire swept New York City.

This time the losses were estimated in the neighborhood of five million dollars. Philip Hone had just started an insurance company a few years earlier, and the company had claims against it of more than three hundred fifty thousand dollars which he could not pay. "The stores in Broad Street," Hone wrote, "some of the finest in the city, on one of the broadest streets, were instantly overthrown. . . . Like the fire of 1835, the progress of the flames was so rapid, and its approach so unexpected, that scarcely anything was saved." Some three hundred buildings were burned to the ground. "My prospects," Hone added, "are all blasted in the destruction of this company. . . ." Three weeks later he wrote, "the masses of ruins are smoking yet in many places . . . and in the heart of this region of desolation fine stores are being built."

The most problematical aspect of the large cities was that most troubling of all American ambiguities—sex. Prostitutes roamed the streets. Luxurious brothels catered to the well-to-do, while sleazy taverns and rooming houses served the poor. Richard Henry Dana "cruised" the tenderloin districts of the cities he visited in disguise, "determined to see the whole of this new chapter in the book of life." In New York he cruised the extensive red-light district. As he put it, "I had a sudden desire to see that sink of iniquity & filth, the 'Five Points.'" There the streets were peopled with drunken men and women, prostitutes, sailors and laborers, sounds of music and laughter punctuated by shouts and imprecations drifting from darkened houses. "Men & women were passing on each side of the street, sometimes in numbers together, & once or twice a company of half a dozen mere girls, ran rapidly, laughing & talking loud, from one house to another. These I found gradually were dancing houses." Dana was frequently accosted by women walking the street, sitting in doorways, or simply standing on the sidewalks. At one house, where a madam and her girl were standing together, Dana accepted their invitation to step in. The living room had a bar and a few pieces of furniture. The girl then asked Dana to come to her bedroom. He did so and asked how much she charged for her favors. Half a dollar. "I was astonished at the mere pittance for which she would sell her wretched, worn out, prostituted body," he wrote.

Dana, of course, ran a considerable risk in his strange cruises and, not surprisingly, he worried about the consequences "if a row should take place in the neighborhood, a descent made by the police & I taken up among others, or I should meet injury or an accident which should render me helpless. . . ." In such circumstances he could "ill account" for being found in the red-light district of the city. Yet the fact that he was willing to take such chances is an indication of the strength of his obsession and illustrates, almost too neatly, the nature of that sexual schizophrenia which characterized his time and his class. "I felt," he wrote in his diary, "as though I was wandering in a dream made up of strange extremes & unnatural contrasts. How wonderful, wonderful, fearful, fearful are the relations of man with man, & man with God! 'Who can understand his errors? Cleanse thou me from secret faults.' Am I any better in the sight of an *all*-seeing God than these filthy wretches? I have done things worse *in me,* than brought some of them to that condition; & their subsequent course has been a matter of necessity, inevitable."

George Templeton Strong, who clearly feared the lustful temptations of the city, wrote in his diary in the winter of 1853 that among the young men of the city there had never been "so much gross dissipation redeemed by so little culture and so little manliness and audacity of the watchman-fighting sort. It has grown to be very bad, the tones of morals and manners has, even among the better class of young men about town." One of Strong's young cousins had involved himself notoriously in "drunkenness, whoremongering, insubordination and total worthlessness." Strong did some cruising of his own (although he did not call it that). When he ventured down to Eighth Street he found that "whores and blackguards make up about two-thirds of the throng . . . one cannot walk the length of Broadway without meeting some hideous troop of ragged girls, from twelve years old down," he wrote, "brutalized already almost beyond redemption by premature vice, clad in the filthy refuse of the rag-picker's collections, obscene of speech, the stamp of childhood gone from their faces, hurrying along with harsh laughter and foulness on their lips. . . . And such a group I think the most revolting object that the social diseases of a great city can produce. . . . Meanwhile, philanthropists are scolding about the fugitive slave law, or shedding tears over the wretched niggers of the Carolinas who have to work and to eat their victuals on principles inconsistent with the rights of man, or agitating because the unhanged scoundrels in the City Prison occupy cells imperfectly ventilated. . . . And what am I doing, I wonder? I'm neither scholar nor philanthropist nor clergyman, nor in any capacity a guide or ruler of the people, to be sure—there is that shadow of an apology for my sitting still. But if Heaven will permit and enable me, I'll do something in the matter before I die—to have helped one vagabond child out of such a pestilential sink would be a thing one would not regret when one came to march out of this world—and if one looks at FACTS, would be rather more of an achievement than the writing of another *Iliad*."

Strong took note that some of the prostitutes who strolled the streets in the better sections of the city were attractive women. "Now and then as one walks Broadway at night," he wrote, "the gaslight shines on faces so pretty, innocent, and suggestive of everything antipodal to profligacy and impurity that one is shocked at our indifference and inertness in regard to this calamity and scourge and feels as if the whole city should go into mourning over it, were there but one woman so fallen."

All this took place, as we have had occasion to note before, against a background of extraordinary prudishness and repression, that extended from the drawing rooms of New York's elite to the Nebraska frontier. When George William Curtis's book of travels in Egypt came out, its cautious references to exotic sexual practices in the mysterious Near East caused general shock and dismay, and Eleanor Strong, the wife of George Strong's cousin Charles, having a chapter read aloud to her, was thrown "into a state of indignant excitement which might have injured her in her present delicate condition [she was pregnant]." Mollie Dorsey, on the Nebraska frontier, told of a suitor who could not bring himself to tell her where the rattlesnake's rattles were because he would have to use the word "tail." Finally Mollie helped him: " 'On the end of its tail, Mr. Mann,' 'Yes! Yes!' he gasped, 'on the end of its t-a-i-l.' "

The reform mayor of New York, Fernando Wood, directed a campaign against what Strong called "the noctivastrumpetocracy," the prostitutes who swarmed the streets and solicited honest (and dishonest) burghers. The mayor's measures were designed not to close down the houses of pleasure but simply to suppress "the scandal and offence of the peripatetic whorearchy . . . for its conspicuousness and publicity are disgraceful and mischievous and inexpressibly bad," Strong wrote. But there was a question of whether his "*means*" were "legal and right, or lawless and wrong." Strong thought the policy "dangerous and bad. It enables any scoundrel of a policeman to lay hands on any woman whom he finds unattended on the streets after dark . . . and to consign her for a night to a station house." Illicit relations were not confined to prostitutes. Any slightly "lower class" woman was eligible, although maids were preferred.

In Boston, the descendants of John Hancock were notorious for lechery and incontinence. Richard Henry Dana had a client named Elisa Butler, a "poor, pretty & simple girl" who had been persuaded to live in the Hancock family. "The whole house," she told Dana, "was a den of iniquity. The old man and his sons equally bad, rich & licentious." For four months she had held out and then left "to save herself from crime." Whereupon the younger son, who had always treated her better than the others, came to visit her, took her for a ride in his carriage, coerced her into intercourse, and got her pregnant. Dana brought suit against the young Hancock, and he settled out of court for three hundred dollars, which seems to have been the going price for seduction of a serving girl resulting in pregnancy.

When Samuel Gridley Howe died, his beautiful and talented wife, Julia Ward, discovered that he had had a mistress and numerous assignations in his office at the Perkins Institute for the Blind.

Deferred marriages were believed, probably correctly, to encourage "licentiousness," that is, the frequenting of houses of prostitution or keeping a mistress. In addition, the emphasis on fashion and the inclination of many young women to live idle lives led, apparently, to an alarming rise in the rate of abortions and the use of various methods of birth control. A preacher named Philo Tower wrote of the New Orleans upper class, "No young man ordinarily dare think of marriage until he has made a fortune to support the extravagant style of housekeeping, and gratify the expensive tastes of young women, as fashion is now educating them; many are obliged to make up their minds never to marry." There was substantial evidence that hundreds of "couples" lived together as man and wife without marrying. It was also common for Northern men, whose business took them regularly to New Orleans, to have a second family there, typically a mulatto mistress and sometimes children by her. "The extent of licentiousness and prostitution here," Tower wrote, "is truly appalling, and doubtless without a parallel, and probably double that of any other place in the civilized world." Tower estimated that in one section of the city "three-fifths at least of the dwellings and rooms . . . are occupied by prostitutes or by one or the other class of kept mistresses."

Edward Mansfield, writing in 1845 on the legal rights of women, was dismayed at the spread of abortions. "In the larger cities it is, we fear, practised frequently. . . . Indeed public advertisements, shameless as they are, have been published in the newspapers, directing the child of fashion or of vice, where she might find a woman to perform that service," and a professor of medicine, writing ten years later, deplored "the evil effects [on] educated, refined, and fashionable women; yea in many instances women whose moral character is in other respects without reproach. The contagion has reached mothers who are devoted with an ardent and self-denying affection to the children who already constitute their family." By the same token a variety of birth-control methods were practiced with usually indifferent results, the most successful, of course, being the sick headache or "the vapors" as they were commonly called. Bad health, real or feigned, was the only infallible control.

So it might be said with some confidence the cities throbbed with sexuality and violence, with their constant traffic in the unmentionable sin.

But that of course was by no means the whole story. The cities were vibrant with life and, above all, with economic activity. They grew in size and wealth with every decade and again New York was the prototype. It led the way in population growth, in civic inprovements, in entertainment, and, above all, in wealth. In May, 1831, Hone noted in his journal, "The city is now undergoing its usual annual metamorphosis; many stores and houses are being pulled down and others, altered, to make every inch of ground productive to its utmost extent." A few years later he wrote, "The spirit of pulling down and building up is abroad. The whole of New York is rebuilt about once in ten years."

Hone also took note more than once in his diary of the speculation so evident everywhere: "The rage for speculating in lands on Long Island," he wrote, "is one of the bubbles of the day. Men in moderate circumstances have become immensely rich merely by the good fortune of owning farms of a few acres of this chosen land." Abraham Schermerhorn, the father-in-law of Hone's daughter, Mary, had sold land that four years earlier he had offered for twenty thousand dollars with no takers, for one hundred two thousand dollars, "and regrets that he sold it so cheap."

The new Merchants' Exchange on Wall Street, a "superb edifice" designed to advertise the power and importance of the business men of the city, was completed and dedicated to money. The ground on which "this costly temple of mercantile pride" stood had cost $750,000 and the building itself well over a million dollars—all this in the midst of a severe depression in which businesses and banks continued to fail and states to repudiate their debts. The stock of the Bank of the United

States had, by the fall of 1841, fallen from 122 to 4; that of the Farmer's Trust from 113 to 30; the Harlem Railroad from 74 to 18; and the American Trust Company from 120 to zero. But property values went up and up. When Henry Brevoort, one of the leading citizens of New York, died in 1841, at the age of ninety-four, his farm—located on Broadway—which had cost him a few hundred dollars, was worth half a million dollars to his heirs.

Hone was enthusiastic over the continued growth of the city, especially the spread of stores along Broadway. But the fact that they were often hastily and improperly constructed was emphasized by the fact that two buildings in the process of construction collapsed "with loss of life, and dreadful mutilations of the workmen," Hone wrote in his diary. "Laws should be passed, and inspectors of buildings appointed with arbitrary power, to prevent the erection of these man-traps." By 1844 the population of New York City was in excess of three hundred fifty thousand, of whom fifty-four thousand were voters. Some of its land was now worth a million dollars an acre, Philip Hone estimated.

As the entertainment capital of the United States, New York had five theaters, the most famous being Niblo's, as well as innumerable lecture halls. In 1844 Castle Garden was converted into an open-air summer theater capable of seating eight thousand people. "The pit or area of the pavilion," Philip Hone wrote, "is provided with some hundred small white tables and movable chairs, by which people are enabled to congregate into little squads, and take their ices between the acts."

The city was a mecca for tourists and conventioneers. Philip Hone noted that the theaters were sustained, to a substantial degree, by visitors to the city. The annual meetings of "all the great national societies for religious and benevolent objects" were held there—the Bible Society for distributing Bibles among the poor and in the Western regions of the country, the Africa Colonization Society, the Sunday School Union, a number of missionary societies. They had, Philip Hone noted in the spring of 1835, "poured upon us a host of respectable, good-looking, well-dressed men, clergy and laymen, some of them in black clothes and shoes. . . ."

The stores of Broadway glittered with expensive merchandise. Isabella Bird saw a diamond bracelet priced at twenty-five thousand dollars. The greatest retail merchant of the city was A. T. Stewart, whose emporium Bird described as "spacious and magnificent beyond anything of the kind in the New World, or the Old either. . . ." The most spectacular feature of Stewart's was the windows, nearly level with the street, formed of plate glass six feet by eleven to display the store's goods to passersby. Philip Hone's first thought was that they would soon be smashed by someone filled with "jealousy, malice, or other instigation of the devil. . . ." In 1854 Stewart's was housed in an immense building of white marble, three hundred feet long and six stories high. Four hundred clerks were employed and in the material department silk was for sale at as much as twenty-five dollars a yard.

Isabella Bird rhapsodized over "stores of the magnitude of bazaars, 'daguerrean galleries' by the hundreds, crowded groggeries and subterranean oyster-saloons, huge hotels, coffeehouses, and places of amusement . . . the pavements present men of every land and colour, red, black, yellow, and white, in every variety of costume and beard, and ladies, beautiful and ugly richly dressed . . . groups of emigrants bewildered and amazed, emaciated with dysentery and sea-sickness, looking at the shop windows; representatives of every nation under heaven, speaking in all earth's Babel languages; and as if to render this ceaseless pageant of business, gaiety and change, as far removed from monotony as possible, the quick toll of the fire alarm-bells may be daily heard." Private homes were impressive brick and brownstone buildings, with large plate-glass windows. But the city was indescribably dirty and jammed with traffic. In Bird's words: "Scarlet and yellow omnibuses racing in the more open streets . . . carts and wagons laden with merchandise—and 'Young Americans' driving fast-trotting horses, edging in and out among the crowd. Often wheels were locked and horses fell, throwing their passengers into the street and occasionally, the whole traffic of the street comes to a dead-lock, in consequence of some obstruction or crowd." The New York cab drivers were "licensed plunderers, against whose extortions there is neither remedy or appeal."

In the midst of all this opulence, pigs still rooted in the streets and when it rained Broadway became, in Strong's words, "a long canal of mud syrup, all the sidewalks greasy with abominable compound like melted black butter," so that citizens inhaled "at every breath . . . vaporized decomposing gutter mud and rottenness."

The frequent outbreaks of cholera gave greater impetus to leaving the city for the summer. Strong noted that more and more of the common crowd were seeking summer refuge in the suburbs around

New York City, most conspicuously on weekends. For a radius of thirty miles about the city "the civic scum ebbs and flows on Sundays and holidays," he wrote, "gent, snob, blackleg, fast-man, whore, and Bowery gal, some or all of them radiate from New York in every direction to infest Long Island and Richmond County; and all conveniently accessible hotels and boardinghouses are overrun by the vermin that hot weather roasts out of its homes in town. Coney Island, for instance, seems to be nothing more than Church Street transported bodily a few miles out of town."

Finding some suitable material to pave the much-traveled streets of the city proved exceedingly difficult. The streets were thus often in a sorry state and constantly being pulled up and repaved with some improved material. In 1835 Broadway was dug up to a depth of two feet, covered with a layer of broken stone, then a layer of round stones, and the whole covered by "a compact course of wooden blocks . . . one foot in length and placed vertically," the interstices filled with liquid tar. It proved little better than earlier compositions.

Horse-drawn omnibuses carried New Yorkers around the rapidly growing city. Philip Hone noted that if he did not wish to walk from his home to the Wall Street area, "I can always get an omnibus in a minute or two by going out of the door and holding up my finger." Strong described a ride uptown on a "choky, hot railroad car . . . drawing stale, sickly odors from sweaty Irishmen in their shirt sleeves; German Jew shop-boys in white coats, pink faces, and waistcoats that looked like virulent prickly heat; fat old women, with dirty-nosed babies; one sporting man with black whiskers, miraculously crisp and curly, and shirt collar insultingly stiff, who contributed a reminiscence of tobacco smoke—the spiritual body of ten thousand bad cigars." The streets were puddles of "festering filth" and Center Street a "reeking, fermenting, putrefying, pestilential gutter." In winter, when the snow was heavy, the tramways were unable to run and sleds replaced them. "These insane vehicles," Strong wrote, "carry each its hundred sufferers, of whom about half have to stand in the wet straw with their feet freezing and occasionally stamped on by their fellow travelers, their ears and noses tingling in the bitter wind, their hats always on the point of being blown off. When the chariot stops, they tumble forward, and when it starts again, they tumble backwards, and when they arrive at the end of their ride, they commonly land up to their knees in a snowdrift."

The municipal authorities were notoriously corrupt. The members of the city's governing body, the Common Council, were known, unflatteringly, as the "Forty Thieves" for their disposition to sell valuable city franchises for ferries, docks, and transportation for substantial bribes. Three aldermen were indicted in 1854 for gross corruption in connection with the sale of franchises but a majority of the judges in the Court of Sessions were aldermen, so that the prospects for successful prosecution of the culprits were poor.

Yet in the fall of 1850 George Templeton Strong would write in his diary, "How this city marches northward! The progress of 1835 and 1836 was nothing to the luxuriant, rank growth of this year. Streets are springing up, whole strata of limestone have transferred themselves from their ancient resting-places to look down on bustling thoroughfares for long years to come. Wealth is rushing in upon us like a freshet."

Strong and Hone were especially proud of two great achievements of the city. First there was the construction of the Croton Reservoir to supply the city with an almost unlimited flow of potable water. The reservoir was divided into "two equal compartments which together will contain nineteen million gallons," Hone wrote. "The walls are granite of prodigious thickness, finely wrought on the exterior . . . I doubt whether there is a similar work in Europe of equal extent and magnificence with the Croton Aqueduct, its dams, bridges, tunnels, and reservoirs. . . . The Philadelphians crack about their Fairmont Water Works," Hone added, but the New York system was vastly superior.

When water finally flowed through its huge pipes to the city in abundant quantities, the citizens of Gotham became intoxicated with the limpid stream. "Nothing is talked of or thought of," Philip Hone wrote, "but Croton water; fountains, aqueducts, hydrants, and hose attract our attention and impede our progress through the streets." The dedication of the reservoir was the occasion for a great parade, five miles long, with companies of soldiers and fifty-two companies of firemen, including several from as far away as Philadelphia. "A day for New York to be proud of," Hone concluded. For many of the older spectators it brought back memories of the opening of the Erie Canal.

The year 1853 saw the erection of the Crystal Palace at a cost of $750,000 in Reservoir Square, in imitation of the London original, and more important, the beginning of Central Park, the architect of which was George Templeton Strong's friend, Frederick Law Olmstead.

Central Park slowly took shape under Olmstead's direction, and

Strong visited it from time to time to observe the progress. He was confident that it would be "a feature of the city within five years and a lovely place in A.D. 1900, when its trees have acquired dignity. . . . Perhaps," he added, "the city itself will perish before then, by growing too big to live under faulty institutions corruptly administered. . . . Many beautiful oases of path and garden culture have sprung up, with neat paths, fine greensward, and hopeful young trees. The system and order and energy of the work are very creditable, considering especially the scale on which it's conducted. Some three thousand men are employed and there are no idlers."

Central Park seemed to George Templeton Strong to represent all that was most promising in the age, most opposed to the chaos and anarchy that he saw around him. "Central Park and Astor Library and a developed Columbia University," he wrote, "promise to make the city twenty years hence a real center of culture and civilization, furnishing privileges to youth far beyond what it gave to me in my boyhood."

New York was the center of the publishing business. Two or three thousand persons were "daily employed in the various departments of bookmaking, binding, publishing, etc."

In many ways, 1853 was "the last good year" prior to the cataclysm. Eighteen hundred and fifty-four was the fateful year of the Kansas-Nebraska Bill. Fernando Wood, who, to men like Hone and Strong, was the epitome of corrupt machine politics, was elected mayor of New York in the mid-term Whig debacle of 1854. Wood surprised his numerous detractors by launching a whirlwind cleanup campaign to introduce a modicum of honesty and efficiency into the administration of the city's business.

Wood's attack on the "whorearchy" mentioned earlier proved to be largely window dressing instead of a prelude to genuine reform. Gangs of thieves and robbers, thought to be acting with the connivance of public officials, created a reign of terror in the city. Strong noted that street crime had reached epidemic proportions: " 'Garotting' and highway robbery" occurred on frequented streets in the early evening. "Most of my friends," he wrote, "are investing in revolvers and carry them about at night . . . though it's a very bad practice carrying concealed weapons."

Armed robbery, often accompanied by savage beatings and stabbings, became so serious an issue that the state legislature undertook to erode Fernando Wood's powers by a series of bills designed to create a metropolitan police force with jurisdiction over

New York, Kings, Westchester, and Richmond counties. The police were to operate under a board of five commissioners, but as soon as they attempted to exercise their authority they were blocked by Mayor Wood, backed by the old police force, reinforced by "a miscellaneous assortment of suckers, soap-locks, Irishmen, and plug-uglies," in Strong's words.

For a time it looked as though open warfare would ensue but the National Guard's Seventh Regiment helped to preserve order for a time and the courts ruled against the man Strong called "the King of Scoundrels . . . the arch-knave of our civic structure." But two weeks later a riot broke out in the notorious Sixth Ward. Downtown streets were made impassable by barricades. There was open fighting at Five Points with numerous casualties. Rioters established themselves on rooftops and fired on the police and on members of rival gangs. Finally suppressed by the police, the fighting broke out again the next day between the Dead Rabbits and the Bowery Boys. In New York on a visit, Richard Henry Dana witnessed the fight between the rival gangs. It went on all day during the Fourth of July with the popping of gunfire, which Dana at first thought was firecrackers. Armed with clubs, bricks, rocks, and guns, the gangs left a trail of blood and of dead and wounded. When Dana asked why the police made no effort to stop the fray, a bystander told him "that the men of the Sixth Ward had vowed to kill them all, if they came there." When Dana protested that the police were backed by the force of the whole state, his informant replied, " 'The Sixth Ward, Sir, is the strongest power on earth.' He repeated this, & fully believed it," Dana noted, adding, "Nor is it strange he should. It has given the great Democratic Majority every year, & is the only hope the Demo. Party has of carrying the State, & [its inhabitants] have enjoyed almost an impunity in their violences & wickednesses." Walking through the section, Dana was deeply depressed by the "brutalized" look of the men and women alike.

After a week of uneasy truce, a mob of over five hundred Irishmen, among whom were a number of Wood's discharged police, attacked the new police force, bringing them under heavy fire at a police station and wounding several before they were driven off by the "new" police. Finally some semblance of order was restored in the Sixth Ward, but for the rest of the summer the city lived in the shadow of an uncertain truce.

Another cholera epidemic threatened during the summer's heat and, to cap it all, by the middle of September there were indications of a financial panic on Wall Street that recalled the dark days of 1837. "Prophets of evil," George Templeton Strong wrote, "say that if it lasts a week longer everything must go down in wreck, that this is the beginning of trouble, and that a general smash is certainly close at hand." The prediction was an accurate one. Every week brought a new tally of commercial failures. The Reading Railroad, the Erie, the Delaware, Lackawanna & Western, the Illinois Central, and the Michigan Central all had failed by the end of October. Baltimore and Philadelphia banks suspended specie payment and runs began on the New York banks, the kingpins in the nation's financial structure. "All confidence in the solvency of our merchants is lost, for the present," Strong wrote, "—and with good reason. It is probable that every one of them has been operating and gambling in stocks and railroad bonds. . . . Panic is very dreadful in Wall Street. . . . Depression and depletion are going on without sign of any limit and promise to continue till we reach the zero point or universal suspension. This attack is far more sudden, acute, and prostrating than that of 1837."

The depressed economic situation helped to trigger the religious revival of 1857, which began with noon prayer meetings in New York City and soon grew into great mass gatherings and prayer meetings that spread to other cities.

One of the most bizarre events of the 1850s was the attack on the Quarantine Station on Staten Island by angry mobs. Since the yellow fever epidemics of 1856, the Staten Islanders had been demanding that the hospital be closed on the grounds that it was a health hazard. Complaints were also made that it provided poor service and was operated at excessive cost to the taxpayers. When yellow fever broke out again in the summer of 1858, a gang of what Strong called "screeching blackguards" carried most of the patients out of the hospital and set fire to it. A dozen buildings were burned, including some containing patients with smallpox who were saved from being burned to ashes by the nurses. Since a few of the buildings survived, the assault was renewed the next night, led by the captain of the Staten Island fire police and the police justice. The large central hospital, one of the most up-to-date in the country, was burned to the ground, the patients left scattered around the grounds. It was ironic that the attack was made in the midst of the celebration over the completion of the Atlantic cable.

Strong noted, "We are a very sick people just now. The outward and visible signs of disease . . . are many. Walking down Broadway you pass $200,000 buildings begun last spring or summer that have gone up two stories, and stopped, and may stand unfinished and desolate for years. . . . Almost every shop has its placards (*written*, not *printed*) announcing a great sacrifice, vast reduction of prices, sales at less than cost. In Wall Street every man carries Pressure, Anxiety, Loss, written on his forehead. This is far the worst period of public calamity and distress I've ever seen. . . ."

As usual the greatest burdens fell on the poor. It was estimated that between thirty and forty thousand were out of work in New York City, and other major cities suffered proportionately. The high rate of unemployment made it "a difficult matter to maintain peace and order in the city through the winter," in George Templeton Strong's words. Isabella Bird reported that fifty-nine thousand paupers in New York received public relief and of these 75 percent were Irish.

Fernando Wood recommended to the city council that it spend "a few hundred thousand dollars in buying provisions for the poor and inviting attention to the difference between 'the rich who produce nothing and have everything and the poor who produce everything and have nothing.'" Strong and others suspected him of "subterranean operations to get up some movement among the 'dangerous classes.'" And whether in response to Wood or their own hungry stomachs, workingmen had been "marching in procession—holding meetings in Wall Street—listening to seditious speeches—passing resolutions that they were entitled to work and the wages of work, and that if they were not provided with work they would take the means of subsistence *vix et armis*."

City Hall was in a state of virtual siege, "all its front portico and a large space in the park occupied by a mob," Strong reported, while several hundred policemen watched and as many soldiers and marines were posted in the Custom House to be ready to respond to any call. Listening to the orators who addressed the crowd, Strong was impressed, in spite of himself, by their "ease and . . . command of forcible and accurate language, and . . . great intensity of feeling. . . ." Martial law was declared and groups of citizens were organized into quasi-military units to help keep order. "People are fast coming to the conclusion that democracy and universal suffrage will not work in crowded cities," Strong wrote.

We have taken New York as the representative city as earlier we took Philadelphia, but every city had its own character. Boston, for instance, was admired by upper-class intellectuals like Strong. He found it far superior to New York, writing, "Boston is an exceedingly glorious place. I wish my lot had been cast there instead of in this pestilential hogsty, New York. . . . The whole city's one huge pigstye, only it would have to be cleaned before a prudent farmer would let his pigs into it for fear of their catching the plague." To Isabella Bird Boston was "stately, substantial and handsome" with "an air of repose" about it. Its crooked streets were crammed with people and vehicles, but it was "very clean and orderly, and smoking is not permitted in the streets," she noted, adding, "There is a highly aristocratic air about it. . . ."

At the American House in Boston, Bird observed "an enormous lobby, a lofty and very spacious hall, with a chequered floor of black and white marble," and "lounges against the wall, covered over with buffalo-skin; and except at meal-times, this capacious apartment is the scene of endless busy life, from two to three hundred gentlemen constantly thronging it, smoking at the door, lounging on the settees, reading the newspapers, standing in animated groups discussing commercial matters, arriving, or departing." Piles of luggage stood about all this to the accompaniment of "the incessant sound of bells and gongs, the rolling of hacks to and from the door. . . . The trampling of innumerable feet, the flirting and talking in every corridor" made the hotel seem to Bird "more like a human beehive than anything else."

Most striking of all, a guest could get his laundry done in a single day in a "churn-like machine moved by steam, and wrung by a novel application of the principle of centrifugal force; after which the articles are dried by means of being passed through currents of hot air, so that they are washed and ironed in the space of a few minutes." There were also barbershops and hot and cold baths.

Philadelphia, in the words of Charles Francis Adams, had "something solid and comfortable about it, something which shows *permanency*. Everything looks neat, the steps are white, the entries clean, the carriages nice, the houses bright. . . . New York is all display, Baltimore is upstart, Washington is fashion and politics. Boston is unbending rigidity." If Philadelphia had a fault it was "tameness." But Boston was clearly the superior of its sister cities in its patronage of the arts. "Indeed," Adams noted, "for public spirit Boston is incomparably beyond all the Cities."

Captain Marryat considered "the public institutions, such as libraries, museums, and the private cabinets of Philadelphia . . . very superior to those of any other city or town in America. . . ." And in no city was "there so much fuss made about lineage and descent; in no city are there so many cliques and sets in society, who keep apart from each other." To George Templeton Strong, Philadelphia was "the most anarchical metropolis on this side of the Atlantic. . . . I would not live in such a hornets' nest as the City of Brotherly Love appears to be," he wrote in the aftermath of the protracted nativist riots in 1844. "One can't look out of his window without the risk of being knocked down by some stray bullet or other that was intended for somebody else entirely, or fired on speculation, without meaning anything against anybody in particular. . . . Such a pitiable scene of feebleness, irresolution, and old grannyism in general as the civic potentates of that place have enacted for the amusement of posterity isn't to be found anywhere. . . . It's some consolation that Philadelphia is worse governed than we are." Allowing for some degree of civic rivalry, there was much truth in Strong's comments. Philadelphia, constantly plagued by riots between "natives," Irish, and free blacks frequently seemed to be verging on anarchy.

If New York, Boston, and Philadelphia shared a number of qualities, Washington was a different matter entirely. It was emphatically a Southern town (one even hesitated to call it a city), with the relaxed and slightly disheveled atmosphere common to Southern communities, plus the odd air of impermanence and unreality characteristic of municipalities whose only reason for existence is political. Foreign visitors enjoyed it because they could observe, undistracted by the usual diversions of a real city, what they imagined to be the workings of the government of the United States, featuring the famous debates in the Senate and the House, and including conversations with compliant politicians. Harriet Martineau found it the most American of cities and reveled in its diversity. It was, in her view, a "society, singularly compounded from the largest variety of elements: foreign ambassadors, the American government, members of Congress, from Clay and Webster down to Davy Crockett, Benton from Missouri . . . flippant young belles, 'pious wives' dutifully attending their husbands, and groaning over the frivolities of the place; grave judges, saucy travellers, pert newspaper reporters, melancholy Indian chiefs, and timid New-England ladies, trembling on the verge of the vortex; all this was wholly unlike anything that is to be seen in any city in the world, for all are mixed up together in daily intercourse, like the higher circles of a little village, and there is nothing else. You have this or nothing; you pass your days among the people, or you spend them alone."

We have already discussed Cincinnati, the "Queen of the West," and Chicago, the railroad hub. New economic opportunities produced new cities which started as "cumulative communities" and grew, sometimes in a few years, to metropolises. Pittsburgh—the "Birmingham of America"—was such a flourishing city. It was at its most spectacular at night with "bright flames issuing from foundries, glass and gas works, and rolling mills, steam-engines puffing like broken-winded horses, and heavy clouds of smoke making the night's darkness darker." Philip Hone, visiting the city in 1847 on his way to Wisconsin to inspect his investments in land, was much impressed. "This is one of the most active, business-like places I have ever seen," he wrote, "with every appearance of present prosperity and future greatness; manu-factures of iron, glass, and machinery are carried on extensively, and under great advantages; iron abounds in every valley, and bituminous coal of the best quality comes cantering down from the surrounding mountains. . . . A place so situated must rise to greatness. I have seen nothing like it in Pennsylvania."

When Charles Sealsfield, an Austrian journalist, wrote of "glori-ous and chaotic" America, he obviously had much more in mind than its great Eastern cities, but chaotic they certainly were—filled with class and racial hatreds, violence, disease, sex, and corruption. At the same time they were centers of energy, vectors of change and growth without parallel in human history. Through them flowed the enliven-ing (and, many felt, corrupting) influences of "civilization," of culture, art, literature, learning, science and technology. Through them flowed also goods and people and, above all, money; the money that fed the insatiable needs of the endless continent. No wonder that it seemed at times to George Templeton Strong and others as well to be "Hell." But if New York was Hell, Heaven was nowhere in sight, and if it had been I suspect Strong would have declined to move. And so it was, in their respective ways, with Dana in Boston and Fisher in Philadelphia (though it must be said that the Fishers moved to Bryn Mawr where they could enjoy the pleasure of Philadelphia without its disadvantages).

Technically "urban" covered towns as opposed to rural areas, including the innumerable small towns of the Near West. Gustaf

Unonius gave a classic description of such a community. The weary traveler might inquire of a passerby, "How far to X-town?" Why this is X-town, he would be told. "You look around," Unonius wrote, "and finally behind a clump of trees you discover a house which you learn later is the courthouse, since the place may be the county seat. . . . A little further away you notice another building, which proves to be the schoolhouse, and after you have traveled a little further still, you glimpse among excavations in a sandy hillside three or four houses which seem to have been erected not with a view to permanence, but rather for temporary use—holes to crawl into. One of these houses is naturally a hotel; another may contain only two rooms, one of which is occupied in common by a lawyer and a druggist who is also a physician. While the attorney is attending to his legal matters, his roommate is standing behind the counter, dispensing medicines, sometimes selling tobacco and snuff, cigars, pocketknives, dyestuffs, beverages, coffee, sugar and a variety of other groceries, all of which in a pioneer community belong to a well-stocked drugstore, which at the same time is also a depot for Bibles, hymnbooks, and cheap reprints of the novels of Bulwer, Dickens, Eugene Sue, and others. The other room, temporarily the bedchamber of the two busy young gentlemen, is also utilized as a carpenter shop. . . ."

Unonius's frontier town was a far cry from New York or Boston, but no one was insensible to the fact that Cincinnati and Chicago had equally humble origins. Just as it was said that any American boy, however humble his origins, might become president, any hastily constructed collection of shacks might aspire to become another New York City, a Memphis, or an Athens.

37

Entertainment

Americans were mad for entertainment. They could never get enough of it. It was, it turned out, an essential element of democracy. Most Americans had so filled up their lives with work that they had little capacity for coping with "non-work" or with "play." Instead of "play" they sought entertainment or diversion. Moreover, the absence of traditional cultural forms imposed an extra burden on the American psyche, as we have seen in numerous other areas. Most historic peoples had been (and many still are) sustained in their daily lives by a web of associations, ritual activities, and cultural forms which filled up their lives. Lacking these, Americans were acutely conscious of the empty spaces in their lives that threatened them with that most corrosive disability, boredom. From the beginning of the republic Americans fled boredom as they fled the Devil and showed characteristic ingenuity in devising means for keeping it at bay. Yet fond as Americans were of entertainment, Frances Trollope found them singularly lacking in the capacity for real enjoyment of the casual pleasures of life.

Charles Dickens had similar observations. He was struck by the absence in American cities of the festive air that characterized the streets of his native London. "How quiet the streets are," he wrote.

"Are there no itinerant bands, no wind or stringed instruments? No, not one. By day there are no Punches, Fantoccini, dancing dogs, jugglers, conjurers, orchestrinas, or even barrel-organs? No, not one. Yes, I remember one. One barrel-organ and a dancing monkey. Beyond that nothing lively, no, not so much as a white mouse in a twirling cage. Are there no amusements? Yes, there is the lecture room and evening service for the ladies thrice a week, and for the young men the counting-house, the store, the barroom and the fifty newspapers the urchins are bawling down the street. These are the amusements of the Americans."

What struck many foreign visitors about Americans was that with all their infatuation with entertainment, they engaged in no active physical sports with the exception, on the frontier and in rural areas, of hunting.

Reflecting on the poverty of American celebrations, the absence of folk festivals and "bacchanalian routes," it is notable that New Orleans and St. Louis with their strong French traditions were the only American cities that had official festivals—the Mardi Gras or "Fat Tuesday," the beginning of Lent in New Orleans and in St. Louis.

Americans would go to see *anything*: Italian opera, a beached whale, freaks of nature, Shakespeare's plays, poor old Black Hawk (indeed, any Indian), Louis Kossuth, a mangy buffalo, tumblers, boxers, acrobats, high-wire artists, horse races, and cockfights. They loved noise—fireworks, bands, politicians speaking. Not satisfied with those things defined more or less formally as entertainment, they did their best to turn *everything* into entertainment, even such incongruous matters as politics and medicine.

We have already had numerous occasions to take note of the "play element" in American politics. The differences between the respective parties seemed superficial to foreign visitors. The Englishman Thomas Hamilton was surprised "at the harmony in regard to the great principles of government" contrasted with "the clamor and confusion" that characterized party politics. Members of one party praised themselves and abused the other party unsparingly, but to Hamilton "the praise and the abuse seemed to rest on a foundation too narrow to afford support to such disproportionate superstructures. Parties there evidently were, but it was not easy to become master of the distinctions on which they rested." The puzzled visitor "looks for the broad distinction of political principle, and he finds men fighting about

Masonry, or other matters which have no apparent bearing on the great doctrines of government."

Edwin Forrest was the outstanding Shakespearean actor in America. After a successful tour in England, he returned to America, where Philip Hone saw him in *Othello* and noted that he was "much improved; his acting . . . more quiet . . . in person, deportment, and voice, the Senate in its most palmy state never had so magnificent a commander, black or white,—nor ever Desdemona so good an excuse for her misplaced affection."

It is significant that Forrest's principal devotees were to be found among the "lower orders." The actor's anti-British sentiments were exactly suited to his fans; and his extravagant style, which so offended theatergoers like Strong and Dana, delighted "the multitude." Sidney George Fisher noted: "I do not like him, he is too violent, rants and distorts his features too much & sadly over-steps the modesty of nature." The Philadelphia theater itself had, in Fisher's view, become a gathering place for the unwashed. "The crowd of horrid, vulgar people disgusts me," he wrote, "and the wretched performance of most of the actors except the 'star' of the evening destroys the pleasure one would otherwise feel in seeing a good character well played." The fact was that Americans were especially addicted to the "star" system. Rather than a skillful and well-balanced troupe, they wished to see a spectacular star such as a Forrest or William Macready.

When Macready appeared in *Macbeth* at the Astor Place opera house in New York, his rival, Forrest, played the same part at the Broadway Theatre. The supporters of Forrest, whom Hone characterized as "vulgar, arrogant loafers," raised a riot at Macready's appearance. He was showered with rotten eggs, hooted and jeered at until the play was stopped, "and the vile band of Forresters left in possession of the house." For two days mobs raged through the city. When the "friends of good order" invited Macready to continue his performances and assured him of their support, the announcement, in Hone's words, "served as a firebrand in the mass of combustibles left smoldering from the riot. . . . Inflammatory notices were posted in the upper ward, meetings were regularly organized, and bands of ruffians, gratuitously supplied with tickets by richer rascals, were sent to take possession of the theatre."

This time the police were on hand in substantial numbers, the troublemakers were expelled and some arrested, but "the war raged with frightful violence in the adjacent streets. The mob—a dreadful one in numbers and ferocity—assailed the extension of the building, broke in the windows, and demolished some of the doors." Sixty cavalry and three hundred infantry were dispatched to disperse the rioters, but when the militia appeared at Lafayette Place "they were assailed by the mob, pelted with stones and brickbats, and several were carried off severely wounded." At this orders were given to fire. Twenty people were killed and a large number wounded, and when Philip Hone ventured out the next day to the scene of the battle where a number of buildings were marked with bullet holes, he found groups of people standing around discussing the affair, a "large proportion" of whom "were savage as tigers with the smell of blood." That night troops remained under arms near the theater and a thousand special deputies patrolled the streets.

Several things might be said about the riots. The laboring and lower middle classes of the large Eastern cities were as anti-British as their "betters" were Anglophile. Such feelings were exacerbated by the traditional hatred of the Irish, who made up a substantial portion of New York's lower class, for the British. There is ample evidence that the hostility to Macready contained a considerable element of animus toward the upper class who applauded Macready and treated Forrest with contempt. Political differences also contributed to the intensity of feeling. Loco-Focos rallied to Forrest and Whigs to Macready. What the riots do demonstrate, in conjunction with other riots over matters almost as inconsequential, was the depth of class feeling in the major cities, especially in New York, Philadelphia, and Baltimore.

The larger cities enjoyed a constant fare of excellent music— Beethoven, Mozart's *Don Giovanni*, and Donizetti's *Favorita* were being performed in New York during the summer of 1851—and George Templeton Strong and his wife, Ellen, were frequent attenders. When the opera *Somnambula* played at Castle Garden it drew an "immense crowd." "Everybody goes," George Templeton Strong wrote, "nob and snob, Fifth Avenue and Chatham Street, side by side fraternally on the hard benches. Perhaps there is hardly so attractive a summer theatre in the world as Castle Garden."

The child singer Adelina Patti made her first appearance in America in the fall of 1851 and was almost as much of a sensation as Jenny Lind. And Patti was followed by the sensuous and exotic dancer Lola Montez.

The black was already being parodied by observant whites who mimicked the songs and dances of slaves. So the minstrel show was born. Its greatest practitioner was Thomas Dartmouth Rice, who, in blackface, introduced the "Jim Crow" song and dance at the Southern Theatre in Louisville, Kentucky, in 1828. Soon he was touring the country to large, ecstatic crowds with his "Ethiopian Operas." He went on a triumphal tour of England where, Philip Hone noted, "He entertains the nobility at their parties; the ladies pronounce his black face the 'fairest of the fair' and his bowed legs and crooked shins the perfect 'line of beauty.' " The Crow Club was established in London in his honor. In New York the Italian opera had to give way to minstrel shows. Philip Hone went to see the " 'Ethopian Serenaders' who sing and play on banjo, accordian, and bone castanets. Negro songs, glees, and other refinements of the same kind," he wrote scornfully, "helped along by wornout conundrums, form this refined amusement, which is very popular and fills the theatre, in which so lately the scientific strains of Italian music floated over empty benches."

One of the great sensations of the year 1842 was the match race between Fashion, a mare owned by a Mr. Gibbons of New Jersey, and Boston, belonging to a Colonel Johnson. It was like the famous race a decade earlier between the horses Henry and Eclipse. The race was held at the Union Race Track on Long Island. As Philip Hone wrote, "the tens of thousands of the sovereign people who wished to see this race made their arrangements to go by railroad from the South Ferry, but the numbers were so great that the locomotives refused to draw. . . . The mob who had provided themselves with tickets, finding it 'no go,' became riotous, upset the cars, placed obstructions on the rails, and indulged in all sorts of violence, in which some persons were hurt."

Swiss bell ringers, "seven robustious fellows," toured the major cities in 1844 and played to full houses. A few years later Ole Bull, the Norwegian fiddler, arrived in the United States. Even so fastidious a critic as Sidney George Fisher was charmed and astonished at the virtuosity of Ole Bull. "Never heard such tones from a violin," he wrote. "They . . . resemble the clear whistle of birds, the wailing of winds, the rustling of leaves and the human voice. His execution fills you with amazement. The notes stream as if spontaneously from the instrument in a liquid flow of melody or seem to fly like sparks of fire from the strings."

There were museums everywhere that ranged from the rusty artifacts of early settlers in small town museums to the Philadelphia

Museum, where George Combe saw "every kind of object and article illustrative of the Chinese life . . . arranged, labelled, and beautifully displayed": a Chinese silk store, its shelves filled with bolts of silk and "the shop-keeper, as large as life . . . showing a piece of black silk . . . to a customer also in full dress" along with "mandarins of various grades . . . with their secretaries behind them; ladies of rank in full dress; every variety of china, earthen-ware, a japanned utensil used in ordinary life, including a beautiful and elegant collection of lamps. . . ." In the first week it was opened eight thousand people visited the exhibition.

Captain Marryat found most American museums a strange jumble—fossil mammoth bones beside "the greatest puerilities and absurdities in the world—such as a cherrystone formed into a basket." Wax figures of prominent murderesses were mixed in with replicas of famous persons, the most popular being General Jackson at the Battle of New Orleans. "The present collections in the museums," Marryat wrote, "reminds you of American society—a chaotic mass, in which you occasionally meet what is valuable and interesting, but of which the larger portion is pretence."

The premier American entertainment was, of course, the Fourth of July. Americans gave themselves over to the celebration of that day with an exuberance that astonished Marryat, who wrote, "the little boys and the big boys have all got their supplies of rockets, which they fire off in the street. . . . What sea-serpents, giant rockets scaling heaven, Bengal lights, Chinese fire, Italian suns, fairy bowers, crowns of Jupiter . . . Tartar temples, Vesta's diadems, magic circles, morning glories, stars of Columbia, and temples of liberty, all America was in a blaze; and, in addition to this mode of manifesting its joy, all America was tipsy." George Templeton Strong described a similar Fourth in his diary: "It's a beautiful sight the city presents. In every direction one incessant sparkle of fire balls, rockets, roman candles, and stars of all colors shooting thick into the air and disappearing for miles around. . . . A foreigner would put it in his book of travels as one of the marvels of New York, and compare it to a swarm of tropical fireflies gleaming in and out through a Brazilian forest."

But even the Fourth of July was not immune to the ubiquitous reformer. Uncle Ellis, Richard Henry Dana's Maine guide, lamented the disappearance of the old muster days "& the old style of celebrating public days, when they had dancing in the tents & all kinds of fun going on. 'Yes,' says the old man, 'Yes! Faith! Now . . . you can't have any Independus as you used to but there must be a d——d Sunday School or Bible Class! If you inquire for some place where [they're] going to celebrate, they say, 'Oh, yes, there's going to be one down to such a place.' 'Well, what is it going to be? What's the bill?' 'And it turns out to be some d——d child's play of Sunday School!' "

Most of the larger cities had "citizens' balls" to raise money for charitable purposes. In Philadelphia such a ball was held yearly to raise money for "the Firemen's fund," and Sidney George Fisher so forgot his snobberies to attend. He confessed himself "much pleased with the respectable appearance, & proper quiet behavior of the multitude. There were certainly many ridiculous & awkward figures, but I question very much whether any other country could show from the same classes of society so many well dressed, & well behaved people. . . . These public balls have a good effect," he added, "in bringing the different classes together occasionally, & tend to produce more kindly feeling on both sides. The higher order are impressed with respect by witnessing the multitudes of decent, good-looking people, among those they are apt to regard with contempt, & the lower are gratified by being in the same room with persons whom they consider above them, by having an opportunity of seeing and observing their appearance and manner, & by feeling, that they do not disdain to mingle with them and partake of the same amusements with themselves."

There was a "buffalo hunt" in Hoboken, New Jersey, which attracted thirty thousand "men, women and children . . . but the buffaloes became the hunters instead of the hunted. One of the herd being caught by the lasso broke through the enclosure, and followed by the rest dashed into the crowd, overturning everything in their way and occasioning such screaming and scampering among their persecutors as was never heard of in the peaceful precincts of the Elysian fields. One man was killed by falling from a tree to which he had fled for refuge," Philip Hone reported.

In Philadelphia a Frenchman named Goddard ran a chartered balloon service. A party of six landed on the lawn of Henry Fisher's country estate. "They were invited in & entertained liberally," Sidney Fisher noted, "& being but common fellows some of them got tipsy."

An increasingly popular form of entertainment was the county fair, usually sponsored by the local agricultural society. Sidney George Fisher and a number of gentlemen farmers were members of such a society, the New Castle County Agricultural Society. When Fisher arrived at the society's "exhibition" he was disconcerted to find that there was a "large multitude assembled" and that "the great majority were evidently an inferior class, attracted not by objects interesting to a farmer, but by the race track, an attraction which has recently been introduced on these occasions for the express and avowed purpose of making money and which will destroy agricultural societies if persisted in." Gambling and "other meretricious attractions" had been permitted and "there were several tents where humbugs & catchpennies, dwarfs, deformed women, etc. were. Two or three vendors of quack medicine were haranguing gaping crowds about the grounds. . . ."

One of the most popular new sports was boxing, imported from England. Hone described it "as one of the fashionable abominations of our loafer-ridden city. . . . The parties, their backers, betters, and abettors, with thousands and tens of thousands of degraded amateurs of this noble science, have been following the champions . . . out of the jurisdiction . . . of the authorities of New York; and the horrid details, with all their disgusting technicalities and vulgar slang, have been regularly presented in the *New York Herald* to gratify the vitiated palates of its readers, whilst the orderly citizens have wept for the shame which they could not prevent. . . . Two men, named Lily and McCoy, thumped and battered each other for the gratification of a brutal gang of spectators, until the latter after 119 rounds fell dead in the ring, and the other ruffian was smuggled away and made his escape from the hands of insulted justice. . . . The fight lasted two hours and forty-three minutes. McCoy received a hundred square blows and was knocked down eighty-one times."

City and country, East and West, Americans loved to dance. It was a national addiction. A "German wanderer beyond the Mississippi" attended a frontier dance where, when the fiddler passed out from excessive draughts of whiskey, "a tall lad placed himself in front of the chimney, turned up his sleeves with the utmost gravity, bent his knees a little, and began slapping them in time with the palms of his hands; in two minutes all was going on with as much spirit as before." Old Uncle Ellis told Dana "that dancing was the greatest enjoyment of his life, & that a violin set him crazy. 'The other day I was driving into Monson in a wagon with Joe Anstiss, & I heard a fiddle playing a dancing tune & the room a-shaking with the folks dancing,—I threw the reins to Joe & says I, "Here, take the reins, let the horses go to h-ll," I'm in there, & I jumped 15 feet, & was in the middle of 'em before they knew the door was open.'"

America's obsession with entertainment made Phineas Taylor Barnum one of the most famous men of the century. A poor boy born in Bethel, Connecticut, in 1810, son of an innkeeper who died when Barnum was fifteen, he worked as a clerk in various stores, opened an unsuccessful store in his hometown, and ran a lottery. He started a newspaper, the *Herald of Freedom,* was convicted of libel, and sent to jail for two months. In 1834, at the age of twenty-four, he was already twice a failure, encumbered with debts and uncertain of his future. On a trip to Philadelphia he saw "on exhibition" an ancient colored woman, Joyce Heth, advertised as the nurse of George Washington. Her owner claimed she was 145 years old and displayed an ancient bill of sale dated 1727. Barnum borrowed a thousand dollars and bought Joyce Heth. She unobligingly died less than a year later, a risk obviously inherent in the transaction, but by that time Barnum, through extravagant promotion of the old woman, had made tens of thousands of dollars.

An autopsy performed on Joyce Heth indicated that her real age was nearer 70 than 145. This finding encouraged Barnum. It showed him how easy it was to make money in the United States by humbug. But there were still obstacles to be overcome. A traveling show through the South went bust and Barnum returned to New York, borrowed a substantial sum of money, and bought Scudder's American Museum across the street from Philip Hone's house. He renamed it Barnum's Museum, dusted off the medley of odd objects, and added substantially to them. Promotion was the key to his success, and from the first the enterprise flourished. Isabella Bird described Barnum's Museum, rather caustically, as "a gaudy building, denoted by huge paintings, multitudes of flags, and a very noisy band. The museum," she added, "contains many objects of real interest, particularly to the naturalist and geologist, intermingled with a great deal that is spurious and contemptible." Among other features were a dog with two legs and a calf with six, "disgusting specimens of deformity," in Isabella Bird's opinion, "which ought to have been destroyed, rather than preserved to gratify a morbid taste for the horrible and erratic in nature."

A year after his museum opened Barnum discovered the young man who was to make his fame and fortune. Charles Stratton of Bridgeport, Connecticut, was in every way quite an ordinary young man except that he was only two feet tall and weighed less than twenty pounds. Barnum immediately signed him to an exclusive contract, renamed him Tom Thumb and promoted him to general. General Tom Thumb soon became one of the authentic wonders of the world. After a trip to Europe, where he was said to have earned something in excess of three hundred thousand dollars, Tom and P. T. returned to New York, where the General made a thousand dollars a day by "performing four or five times . . . to a thousand or twelve hundred persons; dances, sings, appears in a variety of characters with appropriate costumes, is cheerful, gay, and lively . . . kisses the good-looking women . . . and in one way and another sends his audience away well satisfied with their outlay of a quarter of a dollar each," a visitor reported. Philip Hone took his daughter Margaret to see Tom Thumb, "the greatest *little* mortal who has ever been exhibited; a handsome well-formed boy, who is twenty-five inches in height and weighs fifteen pounds . . . lively, agreeable, sprightly, talkative, with no deficiency of intellect. . . . When I entered the room he came up to me, offered his hand, and said 'Howd'ye do, Mr. Hone?'—his keeper having apprised him who I was."

Along with General Tom Thumb, Barnum's most famous promotion was the great singer Jenny Lind, the Swedish nightingale. When Jenny arrived at New York she was met at the wharf by "thousands of silly bird-fanciers," in Philip Hone's words. Barnum had offered a prize of two hundred dollars for the best song written for her to sing in the United States. There were seven hundred entries and the prize was won by Bayard Taylor for a piece called "Welcome to America." Already adored, Jenny Lind added to her popularity by contributing half of her salary to the charitable and benevolent institutions of the city, headed by the fire department, to which she gave three thousand dollars. George Templeton Strong wrote, "Miss Jenny is a young lady of very great musical taste, possessed of a larynx so delicately organized that she can go up to A *in alto* with brilliancy and precision and sing with more effect than any other living performer." No sooner had she been established at Irving House than twenty thousand persons crowded the streets outside, and at midnight she was serenaded by the New York Musical Fund Society. Strong's diary is sprinkled with entries on Jenny Lind's visit: "Jenny Lind mania continues violent and uncontrolled. Auction of seats for her first concert Saturday; Genin the hatter took seat No. 1 at $225. . . . Lindomania unabated . . . it's a prevalent morbid passion for assuming the form of an ass and paying six dollars and so on for the privilege of drinking in her most sweet voice through the preternaturally prolonged ears of the deluded victims of this terrible new disorder."

When Strong finally went himself to hear the marvelous Jenny he was disappointed to find that she "runs too much on music written for the altitudes"—that is to say, she sang inferior songs to display the remarkable range of her voice. "I always find that sort of thing a bore," Strong wrote, with the self-conscious sniff of a musical connoisseur.

In 1855 Barnum retired to his oriental villa at Bridgeport, Connecticut. He played the role of a philanthropist with as much zeal as he entertained and hoodwinked his countrymen, planting trees along the streets of the town, building a natural history museum for Tufts College in Massachusetts, lecturing on temperance and on getting ahead. He served in the Connecticut legislature for four terms and once as mayor of Bridgeport. It must also be reported that some fast talkers inveigled him into signing one million dollars worth of bad notes. His own fortune was virtually wiped out in consequence, and he and the General had to hit the road again to recoup.

When Charles Darwin's *Origins of the Species* appeared in 1858 with an attendant public furor, the incorrigible Barnum immediately introduced into his museum the "What-is-it?" which he suggested was the "missing link" between apes and man. George Templeton Strong went with thousands of other New Yorkers to view the What-is-it? and decided it was "clearly an idiotic negro dwarf," adding, "his anatomical details are fearfully simian, and he's a great fact for Darwin." Strong found other creatures in Barnum's establishment such as a "grand grizzly bear from California, a big sea lion," and "a pair of sociable kangaroo" much more interesting.

The career of Barnum reminds us that a conspicuous element in the American psyche was the pleasure that citizens of the republic seemed to take in being "fooled." Any number of travelers noted that a highly admired American type was the "smart" man, the hustling, unscrupulous dealer who sold wooden nutmegs to unsuspecting farm wives, paste jewelry for real, brass watches for gold, swamp land for fertile pasture, and so on. Isabella Bird was startled by how often stories told to appreciative audiences involved tricking or swindling someone. "Fully half the stories told," she wrote, "began with, 'There was a cute 'coon down east,' and the burden of nearly all was some clever act of cheating, 'sucking a greenhorn,' as the phrase is. There were occasional anecdotes of 'bustings-up' on the southern rivers, 'making tracks' from importunate creditors, of practical jokes and glaring impositions.'"

We find a characteristic ambiguity on the subject even in so moral a young man as Charles Pancoast, who, while he could not bring himself to emulate his unscrupulous employer's methods for making a fortune, could not entirely suppress a grudging admiration for the man's ingenuity. They were everywhere, confidence men of every stripe and degree, from Cornelius Vanderbilt and John Jacob Astor with their ruthless manipulations, to the comparatively harmless "snake oil" salesmen with their patented medicines. The big business men rigged stocks and cornered commodity markets. The small ones sold mythical gold mines and large chunks of imaginary real estate or preyed on poor immigrants, selling them worthless or overpriced tickets to Wisconsin or Illinois. Indeed, it sometimes seemed as though the United States were one vast, ceaseless hustle, everyone a greedy entrepreneur with the soul of a riverboat gambler, each one "smarter" than the next, trading a horse or a steamboat or a hotel, or dispatching settlers to an imaginary "city" on the bare plains of Nebraska.

Moritz Busch, generally a friendly critic of America, expressed this feeling when he wrote: "Brass is their [Americans] stock in trade." He felt disposed to shout: "Brass, humbug—all America is a single enormous Mock Auction!"

There was, then, clearly something in the American psyche that responded to the "con," the swindle, the financial sleight-of-hand. Sidney George Fisher deplored the manner in which the promoters of the Reading Railroad and similar ventures bought and sold legislators and was ashamed of the modest amount of law work he felt forced to perform for the company. Yet he enjoyed the fringe benefits from the fortune amassed by his ambitious and successful brother. Richard Henry Dana and George Templeton Strong had similar qualms, but a vast number of Americans admired the "smart" men and longed to be "smart" themselves.

P. T. Barnum was the symbol of the confidence-man-as-millionaire. He catered most successfully to the insatiable American appetite for the novel, the grotesque, the spectacular. Out of his capacious bag of tricks he pulled innumerable rabbits, mixing the genuine with the phony, offering the public Jenny Lind and "the wild man from Borneo," a deformed black man from Paterson, New Jersey. The exit to his museum was marked "Egress" and visitors, charged a nickel to see the Egress, were delighted at the trick and reminded their friends to be sure to see the Egress.

There was a kind of hecticness, an urgency in most American entertainment, as though time were being stolen from more serious and pressing concerns; there was little joy in it and it was that absence of joyousness and genuine "play" that so distressed Dickens, who perceived in the poorest London Cockney a quizzical pleasure in life and the capacity to celebrate it that seemed to be missing in the rush and press of the go-ahead age, whose most characteristic ceremony was the ubiquitous lecture.

Americans were, as we have said, great starers, like curious children, always looking. Foreigners found that perpetual staring disconcertingly rude; to the Indians it was an insult answerable by death to stare a man in the face. But the relentless democratic eye was ready to "stare down" every other eye. That Faustian element, what Oswald Spengler called the "pure lordship of the eye," reigned supreme in America and made P. T. Barnum one of the great men of the age because he knew how to gratify the insatiable eye by an array of endless things to be stared at. Thus did the democratic spirit assert itself over the world, animate and inanimate. If the inquisitive passenger on a steamer or lounger in a saloon could *catch your eye,* he had caught you and considered himself entitled to lay claim to your time and attention. This obsession with looking made Americans ideal spectators. They would go as far to look at some grotesquerie of nature as they would to hear a renowned stump speaker.

It is rather a puzzle why Americans were so attracted to humbug, to extravagance that ran on into trickery. It had, doubtless, to do with the notion of *living by one's wits.* Somehow the world lay there waiting to be mastered, overpowered or, best of all, *out-witted,* conned, deceived. All people knew, for example, in at least one part of their consciousness, that American politics was a vast, immeasurable humbug, a swindle on a gigantic scale. And yet, seen in another perspective, it was the means of survival, the only hope of the republic, the shield against an always threatening chaos, the only game in town. Perhaps humbug was an antidote to tragedy. Moreover, humbuggery had in it a measure of self-mockery, while it commonly was free of any corrosive sense of shame. Many other societies, especially those of the East, revolved around the notion of maintaining "face," of avoiding any experience that would imperil one's standing in the opinion of others. In America the laugh might be on you but it was a reassuringly good-natured laugh without malice that cheerfully included you in the limitless ranks of the gullible. We are all fooled by life, it said, the rich and poor alike. Only the foolishly pompous, the "stuck-up" and self-important, are unwilling to immerse themselves in the great sea of democratic humbug. So it was a kind of test. If you could risk appearing ridiculous, if you could laugh at yourself, you were a good American, someone who considered himself no better than others, a good fellow, a "good hoss."

Thus American affection for humbug was double-edged (like so much else in life). It comprehended the sometimes grudging admiration for those who lived by their wits—Slick and Smart, Incorporated —but it went further and took in one of the most essential aspects of the democratic spirit. Wary, cautious, closed in so many other ways, the American democrat was disarmingly open in this. The humbug, the joke, the *practical* joke—that is to say, the joke enacted, the joke made flesh—was essential to the American psyche. The joke transcended all classes, all races, all divisions; if Americans, scattered in their endlessly fragmented sects, could not worship together they could at least laugh together. So the joke was like a prayer or the pledge of allegiance, a ritual prelude to any proper political speech, and laughter was a sacrament. It said "we are together here in this space; we are brothers and sisters because we have laughed together." Then the speech could start.

38

High Society

In the large Eastern cities upper-class Americans like our five diarists created a closed world of "society" with rules as strict as any Brahmin. In fact, the upper class of Bostonians were called, appropriately, "Boston Brahmins." While the rules varied from city to city, with some more exclusive than others (New York the least, Philadelphia the most), access to the higher circles was carefully guarded against intrusions from those below. Money in sufficient quantities usually was an entrée but it needed aging and sometimes it took at least a generation of philanthropic activities to entitle new money to a place among the elect.

We have already noted the anxieties of Dana, Strong, and Fisher at being exposed to contact with individuals who were not ladies and gentlemen. The ideal of a Christian gentleman, to which Dana subscribed so fervently, was not simply a matter of birth, though birth was essential. We have the description of the type in Richard Henry Dana's enumeration of the virtues of his friend Robert Wheaton, who died in his thirties: "he was," Dana wrote, "pure-minded, elevated, intellectual, religious, literary, accomplished in manners, arts & letters, fond of high topics & great questions, just, humane, kind, polite, with a high degree of pride & reserve, yet truly modest." Dana knew and liked William Cullen Bryant; he had "good feelings, good principles & a beautiful mind but I was never in company with him, & especially when he was the entertainer, that I have not been made to feel unpleasantly & to wish he had been taught the artificial, the insincere, if you choose, habits of a gentleman." There were well-born persons who were "no gentlemen" by Dana's standards, but voice, manner, dress, a kind of reserve, a certain style were virtually prerequisites. The matter was different in England, Dana gathered. In Canada when he met the Young brothers, British officials who held important public posts, he found them "so ordinary in their appearance & manners, & in fact . . . so *under-bred*" as to be hardly worthy of notice. Yet in conversation they were "well informed in all parts of literary knowledge. I am told," Dana added, "that this inferiority of caste is noticeable as soon as you get out of the aristocracy & upper gentry with hereditary estates & old names, among men whose education & professions would entitle them to the first rank in America, & who educated to that among us, would probably have had the manner which marks high breeding."

If some intelligent, handsome, prosperous middle-class men like Bryant might be admitted on a kind of provisional basis to the casual company of upper-class males, the case was more difficult with women. When Sidney George Fisher, who enjoyed the company of young Peter Engel (who acted for him as an investment agent for Western lands), met Engel's new wife, he wrote in his diary, "His marriage and associations, which are in a sphere entirely different from mine, will necessarily put an end to our intimacy. He is a very good fellow, but his opinions in politics, and his manners are not to my taste." Richard Henry Dana had used almost the same words in talking of his friendship with William Cullen Bryant.

The upper class was enthusiastically pro-British. In 1850 Dana encountered Ralph Waldo Emerson on the train from Boston to Concord. Emerson invited his former pupil to come home with him after a political rally and stay the night. "We sat up until nearly midnight," Dana wrote in his diary, "talking, mainly about England. How much he likes England & Englishmen! Their masculine, manly appearance & manners, their intonations, their culture, their personal independence!" It was clear that Dana shared his host's feelings.

In his devotion to the British, Fisher rivaled Dana. He was quite ready to condone the "contempt in their manner towards foreigners

. . . since in everything they see, the immeasurable superiority of their native land must be suggested to their minds." Americans on the other hand could have "no strong national feelings. We have no past, with its thousand recollections, associations and monuments. We have no distinct national character, but our population is almost as varied in its traits as the inhabitants of the different nations of Europe. And then our territory is so vast, and the interests of its parts so distinct and often so conflicting; and we are poor, and coarse and unrefined, and what with slavery, southernism and Yankeeism, and Western barbarism, and Lynch law, and mob law and democracy, there are so many things to disgust & feel ashamed of, that I really think the true way is to insist on our claim of relationship to England & feel proud of her glory and greatness, and keep up our complacency, in that way for the next hundred years, when if there is no civil war, or servile war, or agrarian war, & if the Railroads and steam engines go on increasing, we may have something to brag of ourselves."

In another diary entry, Fisher wrote: "An Englishman feels that he belongs to the greatest nation that ever existed upon the globe. Who can blame him or dispute him. It is a nation to be proud of. She has been the salt of the earth & the Israel of the Christian faith for the last four centuries." To George Templeton Strong, Britain was simply "the greatest empire the world has ever seen." Those Americans who, like Fisher, Dana, Strong, and their friends, were fervent Anglophiles winced at reports that the British felt "only hatred and contempt for our bullying, coarse & unjust conduct . . . and for the frauds in business & banking which have produced severe distresses among the numerous English families who have invested their fortunes in our stocks." Equally embarrassing were tales of American nouveaux riches who, visiting England, behaved in gauche ways. The wife of the American ambassador to England entertained a party of Philadelphians with "anecdotes . . . of the awkward behaviour and mortifying exhibitions of some Americans being presented at Court. . . ."

Dana, sailing to Halifax for a vacation, found himself hard pressed to defend his country against the criticisms of some English passengers. "The African slave trade, our own slavery, *repudiation*, loco-focoism, the Rhode Island rebellion . . . the rule of faction, removals from office for party purposes" left Dana with "nothing to say." When "a New York radical" defended removal from office of members of a defeated party and Dana protested, "the radical replied that I was in favor of aristocracy & conservatism, & the reason was because I belonged to an old family, known in the history of the country, & wished to see family privileges preserved."

Like Dana, Fisher was highly critical of the United States and when he was taken to task by his friends for denouncing his country in the presence of the British consul in Philadelphia, he replied with asperity "that a large portion of the educated men in the country were opposed to democracy & its influences, considered that all the evil we suffered & none of the good we enjoy were ascribable to it, and that the experiment in self-government had already failed in producing any of the higher and more desirable results of civilization."

Fisher fretted over the decline in the quality of Philadelphia social life. "The good, respectable, old-family society for which Philadelphia was once so celebrated is fast disappearing, & persons of low origins & vulgar habits, manners & feelings are introduced, because they are rich, who a few years ago were never heard of. If they are agreeable, cultivated, intelligent or beautiful there would be some compensation for their innovation, but they are all commonplace & uninteresting, many of them vulgar, stupid and ugly." If Sidney George Fisher was contemptuous of the parvenues who tried to push their way into Philadelphia society, it must be said he was equally caustic about the so-called "men of *pleasure*," the city's sports, who could "think & talk of nothing but play, bets, horses, dogs & women."

The upper class continued to maintain its dominance by controlling the marriages of its sons and daughters. There were strong social pressures, as we have noted earlier, on men to defer marriage until they were able to provide "properly" for a wife. Such pressure moved George Templeton Strong to write: "If it be true that two young people who like each other can't marry on $5,000 a year, then has snobbishness made greater strides towards universal empire in New York than I had deemed possible. . . . Better that a sans-culotte mob should invade the Fifth Avenue, better that Wm. B. Astor's estate be subjected to a 'benevolence' for fifty per cent, better that vested rights and the sanctity of property be all trodden down into the mire of democracy and Fourierism, than that we should all become snobs together. . . ."

Sidney George Fisher was distressed when his brother, Henry, married at the premature age of twenty-four. "He has assumed care & responsibility too soon," he wrote in his diary. Although his wife was an heiress, "he must . . . live plainly & economically." As for Fisher himself, he felt he could not marry until he had an income of at least four thousand dollars a year (perhaps the equivalent of twenty-five thousand dollars today). It was important to marry a woman of one's own class, as well as one, preferably, who had money although, to be sure, the two usually went together.

Lavish parties and handsome balls provided much of the social life of the cities. New York and Philadelphia were notorious for extravagant entertainments. In the former city the high point of the summer social season in the spring of 1838 was the appearance in the United States of the nineteen-year-old Prince de Joinville, son of the French monarch, Louis Philippe. French naval vessels anchored at Newport gave a lavish party for the young prince, and the steamboat *Cleopatra* was chartered to take the elite of New York to Newport. Delmonico's, the famous New York restaurant, catered the affair, and the wine alone for six hundred and fifty guests was said to have cost more than three thousand dollars.

New Yorkers, with their expensive parties even in the midst of hardship and depression, were indignant at the determination of James Gordon Bennett and his *New York Herald* to give firsthand accounts of the festivities. One such affair was a fancy dress ball given in February, 1840, the very month when Hone had lamented the demoralized state of the city's finances. Given by the wealthy Brevoorts, the "splendid pageant" drew the aristocracy of the city. Hone went as Cardinal Woolsey, "in a grand robe of new scarlet merino," and his daughter went as Day and Night. Many of the costumes were "superbly ornamented by gold, silver and jewelry. . . . " The whole scene "dazzled the eyes and bewildered the imagination." But there was one of Bennett's reporters, attempting, by giving a detailed account of the whole affair, "to sow the seeds of discontentment in an unruly population. . . . This kind of surveillance is getting to be intolerable," Hone noted, "and nothing but the force of public opinion will correct the insolence."

Bennett, having given a straightforward account of the costume ball, enraged Hone, and presumably most of the other guests, by adding, "This is one of the most remarkable, curious, droll, incomprehensible cities, the capital of one of the greatest countries, that God ever tried to save from damnation, or the devil ever worked like a horse to get down below." It was clear to the most casual reader that Bennett numbered among the cohorts of the devil the upper-class revelers at the ball. Hone recorded in his diary his indignation that "this filthy sheet" should have a wider circulation than any other paper in the city. When Bennett showed "his ugly face in Wall Street" he felt the weight of the business community's displeasure.

Fisher contrasted New York and Philadelphia society very much to the disadvantage of the former. Philadelphia was "unpretending, elegant, cordial & friendly containing many persons not rich, but few whose families have not held the same station for several generations, which circumstance has produced an air of refinement, dignity & simplicity of manner, wanting in N. York and also a great degree of intimacy among the different families who compose our society, as their fathers & grandfathers knew each other & associated together in former years. . . . In N. York, there is all the vulgarity, meanness, ostentatious parade of parvenuism. Wealth is the only thing which admits, & it will admit a shoe-black, poverty the only thing which excludes & it would exclude grace, wit & worth with the blood of the Howards. In this country & age of speculation & enterprise, large fortunes are frequently made in a very short time, & this has been & is particularly the case in N. York, and as money is the only test, the society is composed of people from every rank in life, even the lowest. . . . The love of money there is the absorbing passion; every other feeling is made to yield to it; the immense fortunes made in the West by speculation have produced a wild gambling spirit, which has seized upon the whole population & amounts to monomania." Yet even in Philadelphia the rich "parvenues" could not entirely be excluded.

In the spring of 1839, Fisher noted in his diary that he had attended "a small, but very beautiful recherché party at Mrs. Geo. Cadwalader's. . . . Walls & ceilings painted in fresco by Monachesi, curtains, chairs, divans, ottomans of the richest white damask satin *embroidered*, vases, candelabra, chandeliers, enormous mirrors in great profusion, chairs, white & gold, beautiful carpets, etc. etc." The elegant rooms were filled with "about 50 well-dressed and well-bred men & women, sitting in quiet talk. . . . Very different from the gaudy show, crowded glitter and loaded tables of certain vulgar people here, who by mere force of money have got into a society to which they are not entitled by birth, education or manners." A few months later he went to a fancy dress ball in Philadelphia where there were "a great many shepherdesses, peasants & old-fashioned court dresses." Edward Biddle was in the court dress of a Spanish grandee and Pierce Butler wore "a very rich velvet dress of an English nobleman for a former century, covered with lace & embroidery." Fisher himself wore the costume of an Austrian peasant.

Masculine clubs were the inner sanctums of the urban elite. Hone joined with some Brinkerhoffs, Coldens, Renwicks, Stuyvesants, Fishes, and Irvings to form a Knickerbocker Society "as a sort of an off-set against St. Patrick's, Saint George's, and more particularly, the New England." Not by any means satisfied with that, he helped to form the Union Club, limited to four hundred members, and the Hone Club, limited to twelve. In addition he belonged to the Book Club, which had little to do with books and concerned itself primarily with gourmet meals and good fellowship. "They sup, drink champagne and whiskey punch, talk as well as they know how, and run each other good-humoredly"—that is to say, "ragged" or teased each other.

Visiting and leaving "cards" was a ritual social exercise most heavily indulged in on New Year's Day. Philip Hone noted in his diary that at the turn of the New Year of 1843 he made forty-odd visits. "The ladies smiled and looked beautiful," he wrote, "the fires sparkled and looked warm, the furniture shone and looked comfortable, the whiskey-toddy smoked and looked strong, and everything was gay as it used to be in good times." For the day people forgot that the old year had been "marked by public calamity and individual misfortune" with "business unprofitable, confidence impaired, stocks and other personal property of little value, taxes nearly doubled, rents reduced, tenants running away, debts wiped out . . . and Loco-focoism triumphant."

Social life grew more hectic with each passing year, New York of course far surpassing its rival cities. George Templeton Strong was moved to complain in his diary. "How many hours," he wondered, after an evening at such a function, "could a man survive under this terrible combination of nervous irritants and stimulants, the crash of brassy music, glare of gas, and a shifting, fluctuating, high-colored crowd? Not many," he answered, "even without the terrible drain on the vital forces produced by the constant, agonized, fruitless effort to evolve commonplaces and secrete small-talk. . . ."

One of the diversions of the young social crowd in New York in the winter of 1848 was sniffing chloroform. "It seemed an innocent kind of amusement not followed by any reaction or other unpleasant symptoms" George Templeton Strong wrote. "I think it altogether probable that its use may be instrumental in bringing to light important truths in the science of 'psychology,' or rather in that department of physiology which relates to the connexion between mind and matters, the functions of the nervous system and so forth . . . I think I'll write 'confessions of a chloroform-smeller' some of these days after the manner of the English Opium Eater, though I've as yet but little to confess. It's curious stuff, is chloroform—and very curious indeed are its temporary effects on one's system. The dreams are so strange it fills one's mind with, the apparent duration of its effects so much longer than one's watch indicates. The sensations of a week are crowded into two minutes. The last time I dosed myself I heard most distinctly the performance of a part of Mozart's *Requiem*. . . ."

Strong also wrote at considerable length of his "silly experiments with Hashish, or rather with the official extract of *Cannabis Indica*." "The prominent feature of my mental condition," he wrote, "was that I was distinctly in a dual state. I was two gentlemen in one night shirt." Strong "No. 1 was in an agreeable, mild delirium, unable to control and hardly able to follow the swift current of incoherent images that were passing through his head." Strong No. 2 was the detached observer. The "flow of images was wonderful and unprecedented, each distinct and keen. . . . When I closed my eyes, a phantasmagoria of living and moving forms kept pace with this current of delirious thoughts."

Since everything in American life must finally yield to organization, the leaders of New York society decided to set up a committee, of which, incidentally, George Templeton Strong was a charter member, "to take charge of polite society, regulate its interests, keep it pure, and decide who shall be admitted hereafter to 'Bachelors' Balls' and other annual entertainments. The committee is perpetual and fills its own vacancies. It is to pass on the social grade of everybody, by ballot—one blackball excluding."

Boston's upper class had a markedly more literary and intellectual bent. It went in for "evenings" of cultivated talk and general sociability and deplored New York's extravagance. On June 19, 1851, Richard Henry Dana noted in his diary, "A beautiful little re-union at Longfellow's to take leave of Mr. & Mrs. James R. Lowell, about going to Europe for a few years. We had Longfellow & wife, Lowell & wife, Wm. Story & wife, Ames & wife, Sarah & myself. . . . We sat around a beautiful circular table, covered with flowers, & furnished with fruits, ices & wines, from 10 o'clock until 1, midnight having passed without our knowledge. I never saw so many beautiful married ladies together before, in a group. Mrs. Longfellow, so queen-like, Mrs. Ames so Italianly beautiful, Mrs. Story so lovely & gentle, & Mrs. Dana so graceful & airy, & Mrs. Lowell in wretched health, but with the remains of beauty, young enough to be revived, if health will permit. The men, too, were agreeable, clever & accomplished. It was a golden evening."

Despite the lively social and cultural life of the cities, their upper-class residents found them dirty, noisome, and dangerous and got away from them whenever they could. Although Philip Hone had suffered severe financial reverses in the Panic of 1837, he went off every summer with his family to Saratoga where, typically, he had a suite of two parlors and four bedrooms, "in the delightful South wing." Governor Seward was there and in the summer of 1839, Henry Clay and Webster were among the distinguished guests. Hops were in great vogue, featuring besides endless dancing, "champagne, and ice-cream, and blanc-mange."

By the 1840s the move from city to country houses had begun. These were as vast and elaborate as the wealth of their builders permitted—often more so—and were situated within commuting distance of their owners' city offices, banks, or mercantile businesses. More remote were the older summer places where prosperous upper-class families went for the summer months. For Philadelphia it was Schooley's Mountain, near Morristown, New Jersey, although New York families like the Roosevelts also spent the summers there along with the Dickinsons and Cadwaladers. Sidney George Fisher noted in his diary in the fall of 1847, "The taste for country life is increasing here very rapidly. New & tasteful houses are built every year." Henry Fisher followed suit with a magnificent estate in Germantown that his brother estimated cost over a hundred thousand dollars to build and half as much more to furnish.

Philip Hone visited the still unfinished mansion of William Paulding in Tarrytown, "an immense edifice of white or gray marble resembling a baronial castle, or rather a Gothic monastery, with towers, turrets, and trellises; minarets, mosaics, and mouse-holes; archways, armories, and air-holes; peaked windows and pinnacled roofs in it; great cost and little comfort. . . ."

Even the provincial cities shared in the growing display of wealth and luxury. When Sidney George Fisher visited Albany in 1847 he was much impressed with the "many handsome residences, glittering shops, fine hotels, all imitations of the 'Broadway Style.'" Both the buildings and the legislators were handsome and respectable in appearance. "Yet," he added, "we know that this legislature is the seat of the grossest corruption & that in it radicalism and demagogues

reign triumphant. There anti-rentism finds support and encouragement, partisan passions rule & riot and every species of political
dishonesty & vice has its familiar dwelling."

Driving outside the city in a rented carriage, Henry and he passed
the handsome country seats of the wealthy. "Nothing," Fisher wrote,
"can show more forcibly the superiority of New York to any other state
in wealth & civilization. The Van Rensselaer brothers' mansions facing
each other across the Hudson were especially splendid, William's
running for more than six miles back from the river."

While Saratoga remained a favorite resort for New Yorkers, by
1827 the isolated island of Nahant had become the summer "watering
place" of proper Bostonians. The rooms of the Nahant Hotel were
described by a summer visitor as "gaily decked and lighted; violins,
tambourines, and drums echoed through them, and the ladies dressed
in full ball costume, were dancing lightly and merrily. . . . Flowers,
manufactured by Nicollati, and perfumed by Richardson, lent their
artificial brilliance to the loveliest of Nature's works; feathers, laces and
gauzes. . . . Matrons, in gay attire, not weary of a winter's campaign of
light amusement, were there . . . the very paraphernalia of a Beacon
Street drawing room." The Lawrences, Amos and Abbott, the greatest
textile manufacturers in America, took up summer residence followed
by the Lowells, Appletons, and Brookes (Charles Francis Adams's
father-in-law), the Searses and Motleys and Prescotts—William Hickling Prescott, already with a worldwide reputation for his great history
of the *Conquest of Mexico*. Colonel Thomas Handasyd Perkins, who had
built the Nahant Hotel, had interests in a woolen factory, land
speculations in Michigan, and opium in China. The British consul,
Thomas Grattan, derided Perkins's "pretensions to 'aristocracy'"
while "descending to very low methods of money-making."

Newport, Rhode Island, far outshone Nahant with its ineffable
New England frugality and moral superiority. Social life in Newport
centered on the Ocean House, described by George William Curtis as a
"huge, yellow pagoda factory." "Nahant," Curtis wrote, "would not
satisfy the New Yorker, nor, indeed, a Bostonian, whose dreams of
sea-side summering are based on Newport life. The two places are
entirely different. It is not quite true that Newport has all of Nahant
and something more. For the repose, the freedom from the fury of
fashion, is precisely what endears Nahant to its lovers, and the very
opposite is characteristic of Newport."

A Harvard professor was more explicit: "Hither [to Newport]

comes the youthful dandy, with the suspicion of a mustache on his lip, and a cigar in his mouth. Middle aged men and old men, fat men and lean men, stout ladies and slender ladies, disport themselves on the rocks, and repair the waste of exercise by the daily chowder, prefixed to the far fetched luxuries of a city dinner. . . . The morning concerts and evening dances at the hotel fill up the time and employ the heels and voices of the performers, as well as the ears and eyes of the spectators in a most agreeable manner."

Fanny Kemble came to Nahant in the summer of 1858 and wrote to her daughter, "How you would open your eyes and stop your ears if you were here! The enormous house is filled with American women, one prettier than the other, who look like fairies, dress like duchesses or *femmes entretenues*, behave like housemaids and scream like peacocks."

To the dismay of the proper Bostonians, eccentric Frederick Tudor, the Ice King, opened an amusement park on Nahant that featured a dance hall, an ice-cream parlor, a croquet field, a shooting gallery, two tame bears (Ben Butler and Jeff Davis), Indians weaving baskets, a bowling alley, giant swings and seesaws, a photographer, and a seller of balloons.

The literary elite joined the financial elite on Nahant. Henry Wadsworth Longfellow had a cottage there. Horatio Greenough, the sculptor who had spent eight years on his famous statue of Washington, died there at the age of forty-seven as he was building his own house. Wendell Phillips spent many summers there and Louis Agassiz, the great Harvard zoologist, built himself a kind of mini-laboratory to study the ocean creatures that abounded in the island's rocky coves.

Class lines were not of course confined to the larger cities of the East. Cincinnati, St. Louis, and even brand new Chicago had their own elites who sedulously imitated the older cities. Even on the frontier class lines, although blurred, were visible. Gustaf Unonius compared two families he encountered on the Wisconsin frontier, both of whom lived in the same kind of modest cabins. In one case the husband was an uncultured and uneducated backwoodsman, strong, hardened and experienced in all the difficulties and circumstances of frontier life and "not lacking in a certain social ease, and considering his place in society, had a kind of breeding generally characterizing even the laboring classes in America. . . . The wife, probably even more ignorant and uncultured than her husband . . . smoked her clay pipe, loaded with strong virginia. . . . Her patched calico dress was the only sign of femininity about her. . . ." In the other cabin the husband was "a complete gentleman" and his wife obviously a lady. There were books in view and some sheets of music. The wife conversed knowledgeably with Unonius about Linnaeus and Berzelius, a famous Swedish chemist. The husband had been a well-known and successful businessman who had been ruined in the depression of 1837. "Wealth," Unonius added, "is the only mark of rank, the only thing that in itself serves to erect a wall . . . between the lower and the so-called better classes, for even education and culture, if not accompanied by riches, must . . . carry the stamp of a standard of living better than the average if they are not to be put on the same level."

Disinterested observers differed on the degree of political power exercised by the upper class in the three cities on which we have concentrated our attention. It seems clear that in Boston and, indeed, to a large extent in Massachusetts, upper-class domination was generally accepted. In New York it was strongly and often successfully contested by the Loco-Foco wing of the Democratic Party. In all three cities the upper class gave ample evidence of its hostility toward the lower classes and its determination to exclude the middle class from its own charmed circle.

39

"The Devil Is in the People"

T he evidence of deep-seated class antagonism in nineteenth- century America is massive and irrefutable. The working class (or we should say classes since "native" workingmen, Irish, and free blacks all constituted distinctive "classes") suffered most acutely from the succession of financial crises. Their efforts at improving their condition were denounced as intimations of "red revolution."

We need, I think, to distinguish between two types of working-class protest. The most common was expressed in the numerous riots that were endemic in the larger Eastern cities. Such episodes as the Forrest-Macready riot and the nativist "war" in Philadelphia in 1844 were random lashings out, devoid of ideological content, which revealed depths of rage against a cruelly inequitable system. The other form of social action centered on demands for the redress of specific grievances. While this latter "action" was usually characterized by acquiescence in the political principles of the republic, it gave, on occasion, clear evidence of a radical "socialist" or "communist" critique of American capitalism and called on occasion for other social and economic systems.

In the early 1830s workingmen's parties revived. The ten-hour day and free public education were the most prominent planks in their platform. Now, under the influence in New York City of Robert Owen, the English reformer, and Fanny Wright, the young Scotswoman who had accompanied Lafayette on his American journey, the Working-men's Party broadened its political range to take in such issues as the reform of debtors' laws (which in most states still permitted imprisonment for debts as low as five dollars), temperance, and the abolition of business monopolies. Owen and Wright edited a radical magazine called the *Free Inquirer,* which advocated free love, liberalized divorce, equality for women and free blacks, and abolition of slavery. That was a diet much too strong for most American stomachs. Philip Hone heard Fanny Wright lecture and wrote scornfully of her as a "female Tom Paine. . . . Her doctrines are similar to those of Paine, Godwin, and other modern philosophers who would unsettle the foundations of civil society, and subvert our fundamental principles of morality if people were fools enough to believe them." There was, in addition, considerable talk of "agrarian laws"—laws that took property from the rich and distributed it among the poor. George Templeton Strong wrote in his diary that "theorists begin to dream of Agrarian Laws and Locofocos to talk of 'the rich against the poor.' " Richard Henry Dana, equally alarmed, noted that antislavery meetings were used (or abused) to raise the most unsettling social issues. He wrote that at the adjournment of a Boston antislavery convention a meeting was announced for that evening "to discuss the subjects of the right of man to hold property, & the re-organization of society,—'very simple subjects,' " the speaker added. When Dana attended the discussion he discovered "a new exhibition of radicalism. The speakers took the ground that no man had a right to any private property, not even the products of his own industry. They were answered by a man named Ballou [Alden] who wound them up completely, by putting questions to them wh. they had to answer *ex tempore.* In this way he made them take the ground that an idle man, or a robber, who could work & would not, had the same right to my crop which I had planted & cut, as I had myself. This upset them with the audience, & raised a shout of applause for Mr. Ballou."

Thomas Hamilton, the Scottish aristocrat who was so disposed to patronize the United States, was struck by the separation of classes. "That proportion of the population whom the necessity of manual labor cuts off from the opportunity of enlarged acquirement," he wrote, "is in fact excluded from all the valuable offices of the state. As matters are now ordered in the United States, these are distributed exclusively among one small class of the community, while those who constitute the real strength of the country, have barely a voice in the distribution of those loaves and fishes, which they are not permitted to enjoy. There does exist then—they argue—an aristocracy of the most odious kind,—an aristocracy of knowledge, education, and refinement, which is inconsistent with the true democratic principle of absolute equality." Some went so far as to "boldly advocate the introduction of an AGRARIAN LAW, and a periodical division of property." In Philadelphia, Albany, Troy, Buffalo, and Dorchester, Massachusetts, chapters of the Workingmen's Party were established, largely through the influence of Frances Wright, and candidates nominated for municipal and state offices. A dozen labor papers were started, most of them short-lived, with names like the *Democratic Mechanic's Free Press* in Philadelphia, the *Workingmen's Bulletin* (Buffalo), *The Farmers', Mechanics' and Workingmen's Champion* (Albany).

A convention of workingmen from all parts of New England met in Boston in 1833 and drew up resolutions opposing child labor in factories and imprisonment for debt and supporting lien laws for laborers (by means of which they could recover their wages on projects that went bankrupt) and equal taxation of all property on the grounds that the wealthy householder was more lightly taxed than the poor. It also issued a call for workingmen in the Middle States to hold a similar convention and proposed a national convention the following year.

When the Journeymen Tailors of New York went on strike for higher pay, Philip Hone wrote, "a set of vile foreigners (principally English) who, unable to endure the restraint of wholesome laws, well administered in their own country, take refuge here, establish trade unions, and vilify Yankee judges and juries." Twenty of the tailors were convicted of a conspiracy to raise their wages. The conviction caused an immediate uproar in the working-class areas of the city and a handbill was circulated which read:

"The *Rich* Against the *Poor*! Judge Edwards, the tool of aristocracy, against the people! Mechanics and Workingmen! A deadly blow has been struck at your *Liberty*! The prize for which your fathers fought has been robbed from you! The freemen of the North are now on a level with the slaves of the South! With no other privilege than laboring, that drones may fatten on your life-blood." The judge and jury had "established the precedent that workingmen have no right to regulate the price of labor, or, in other words, the rich are the only judge of the wants of the poor man." The workers of the city were called on to assemble to protest "the hellish appetites of the aristocra-cy."

Judge Edwards imposed heavy fines on the striking tailors and a mass meeting held in City Hall Park on June 13, 1836, drew what was estimated by some to be the largest public gathering in the city's history. While the Whig leaders and newspapers applauded Edwards's sentence, the *Evening Post* spoke for the Loco-Focos and the Demo-crats, declaring, "If this is not slavery, we have forgotten its definition. Strike the right of associating for the sale of labor from the privileges of a freeman, and you may as well bind him to a master, or ascribe him to the soil." Some advocated direct and violent action, but more moderate counsels prevailed. What was clear from the meeting was that a substantial number of the workingmen of the city perceived their interests to be directly opposed to those of the mercantile community.

"Real estate is high beyond all the calculation of the most sanguine speculators," Hone wrote in 1836. "Immense fortunes have been made . . . within the last few months, and everything is dear but money." Under such circumstances, with prices highly inflated and wages low, the condition of the workingmen about whom Hone professed to be solicitous became acute. There was widespread resentment and hostility toward the speculators and profiteers which expressed itself, to a degree, in frequent riots, the result of anger and frustration, and in acts of vandalism. The carpenters and cabinetma-kers of the city were indignant at the fad for expensive imported furniture, which they felt was taking money out of their pockets. At a sale of French furniture at the City Hotel, cabinetmakers "went to the place where the furniture was exhibited, and cut and scratched it in such a diabolical manner that the injury exceeds a thousand dollars." "The devil is in the people," Hone wrote.

In Boston the shipwrights and caulkers agitated for a ten-hour day and, when the shipyard owners refused, went on strike. The owners took the high moral ground that wages and hours should be regulated by the open market. Unions were conspiracies to control the "natural" fluctuations of prices and wages and as such un-American and unconstitutional, immoral and un-Christian. But the efforts to union-ize went on. In New York carpenters struck for a wage of a dollar and a half a day. In Connecticut carpet weavers struck for higher pay and were convicted of conspiracy by the courts.

In January, 1839, the workingmen of Philadelphia issued a report on the condition of workers in the state. The committee which prepared the report "cheerfully" assented "that the interests of the whole people are identical under our republican form of institutions; but," the report went on, "this equality or reciprocity of rights is no longer regarded—the great principles which aroused the energies of freemen . . . are now lost in corporate interest which controls nearly all the avenues to wealth, absorbs the whole attention of the legislature, while it leaves you, who are the majority, in a state of abject servitude. . . . We also admit, that no system can be introduced which will free, perhaps, a majority of the people from manual labor; but we do insist that a better system than the present, which inflicts upon them perpetual toil and eternal poverty, can be devised. What argument can be adduced why a *more equal distribution of wealth should not be made?*" The workingmen of the city had been accused of "wishing to level down society and appropriate to yourselves the proceeds of others' industry." They should throw the charge back, for the workingmen knew "that the mass are levelled almost below the common feelings of humanity, and your toil appropriated to fill others' coffers." The workingmen were for a system which "will level up instead of down." They did not wish "the hackneyed system of education" which was the order of the day and which served little purpose but to perpetuate "the same prejudices." The workingmen called for "a democratic republican education which regards all the children as equals, and provides food and clothing during the period they are receiving their education to fit them as members of society and component parts of a free government; so . . . they may start equal in the accumulation of wealth, or in the pursuit of the honors of the government. This is the levelling system we desire . . . an equal and perfect system of education." The report ended by recommending the formation of "trade societies and associations and a literary and scientific institute."

A number of things might be said about the joint report of the workingmen's societies. It manifested a strong spirit of resentment toward the increasing tendency of wealth to accumulate in the hands of the few. But it saw the solution to this problem in the greater accessibility of educational opportunities to the sons and daughters of workingmen. This was curious in itself. It was as though workingmen themselves forfeited any hope of materially improving their own circumstances and placed all their hopes in greater opportunities for their sons. In this the document was touchingly and typically American. The economic system was exploitative and unjust; the remedy was education. Indeed, there were those prepared to offer it as the universal panacea. To slavery, intemperance, injustice of every kind, education was presented as the cure. Historians have speculated almost endlessly over the reasons for the absence of a radical labor movement in the United States committed to changing "the system." The Philadelphia workingmen's report calls for "levelling up" through "a democratic republican education." It looks to the achievement of that "levelling up" not in the present but in the next generation. In that sense it is also entirely compatible with the inclination of Americans to wish, above all, for the upward mobility of their children.

There were, of course, other factors at work in the period before the Civil War to blunt the very widespread hostility aroused in the working classes by the striking disparities between the well-to-do and the poor. One was racial. The native workingmen viewed the most depressed and exploited class, the Irish immigrants, with unconcealed contempt and hostility. Without some degree of sympathy and cooperation between the two groups, no unified labor movement was possible. For the Irish, on one hand, the Catholic Church was their union. It did not work to improve the wages or conditions of the workers, but it did provide an essential center, a social, political, and religious rallying point. It was the Irish workingman's social club and welfare system all in one. Beyond that the "native" workingmen were tied to the reactionary politics of the South through the Democratic Party. Their very genuine radicalism consisted of a persistent evocation of the ideal of "equality" and they were ready to follow wherever that ideal might carry them, but they had no inclination to make common cause with those major segments of the depressed classes, the Irish and the free blacks. All these workingmen—native, Irish, and black—expressed their mutual hatred by dangerous riots directed, for the most part, not against the "exploiters" but against each other.

In addition to the severe economic hardships inflicted upon the poor and working classes of the larger mercantile cities by the prolonged depression that followed the Panic of 1837, the union movement was nipped in the bud. When thousands were jobless and businesses failing daily, there could be no talk of common action to raise wages. Not only did prices rise steadily, wages dropped and the plight of the workingmen became desperate.

The feelings of ordinary people might be judged by the attacks on banks. "Every day," Sidney George Fisher wrote in Philadelphia, "some outrage is committed by the populace, & life and property rendered insecure. . . . A wild, radical, agrarian spirit is abroad, which is constantly fired by incendiary presses, & designing demagogues for their own purposes."

When Frances Wright, her money and energy expended, departed for England in the summer of 1839, conservative Americans heaved an almost audible sigh of relief and Philip Hone wrote in his diary of Wright as "the quondam friend of Lafayette, who was thought to make desperate love to him, the apostle of infidelity, the idol of the Loco-Focos, and the oracle of the sub-treasury politicians," adding, "Let her go home or to the Devil, so that she never visits us again."

Philip Hone, always ready to see an incipient French Revolution in a demand for higher wages or a riot over the cost of flour, was horrified at a revolt of the tenants of the great Van Rensselaer estate in the region of Albany. It was General Van Rensselaer who, acting, his detractors said, on the orders of his wife, had voted for John Quincy Adams in the House and thus given the crucial vote of New York State and the presidency to John Quincy Adams in the disputed election of 1824. On his death in 1839, it was discovered that the general had provided that the back rents on his lands should be used to pay off his debts. Although the rents were nominal, they had, in many instances, gone unpaid for years and now amounted to some four hundred thousand dollars. With the country in the depths of a depression, many tenants could not raise money to pay their arrears. The general's heir, Stephen Van Rensselaer, proceeded to secure writs of ejectment to oust the defaulting tenants. This move was met by armed resistance on the part of the tenants. A sheriff, with seventy hastily deputized followers, set out to execute the orders of the courts but he found himself confronted by several thousand armed and mounted men who swore "by Dunder and Plitzen that they would pay no more, nor surrender their farms to the rightful owner." Hone clearly felt no sympathy for the embattled farmers. What was at issue was an attack on private property, "nothing more than a carrying out of the Loco-Foco principles of the people of the State. . . ." The conservative Whig press was filled with denunciations of the recalcitrant farmers, while Democratic journals espoused their cause and denounced the remnant of feudalism that had kept them in tenancy.

William Seward, governor of New York, called out the militia to restore order. "All the mighty Men of War of the city of Gotham—all our little great men—are in a state of turmoil, bustle, excitement, fuss, and fury unparalleled," George Templeton Strong wrote; they were impatient to "be at" the refractory tenants and teach them a lesson about the sanctity of private property. Yet when Strong heard that the Democrats were planning to hold a sympathy rally for the beleaguered tenants, he wrote in his diary, "This is the worst thing I've heard of The Democracy yet, and if it be an act of the party, it fully justifies all that has been said of their agrarian, disorganizing, law-defying character."

For almost seven years the "war" dragged on through the courts and in the state legislature, with periodic outbursts of violence. In August, 1845, three hundred renters, disguised as Indians, stopped the sheriff and his deputies from selling the property of tenants who refused to pay their rent. A deputy sheriff was killed in the fray and the Democratic governor, Silas Wright, declared the "disaffected counties in a state of insurrection," accompanying the proclamation, however, with conciliatory phrases. Wright then guided legislation through Albany liberalizing the state's essentially feudal laws on tenancy and the war was finally over.

The ferment of social protest and radical turmoil that culminated in Europe in the year of revolutionary upheaval—1848—helped to generate a more militant spirit in American workingmen in the industrial cities of the North. Their principal demands were for the enactment by state legislatures of laws limiting the workday to ten hours and forbidding the employment in factories of children. Hard times had undermined the bargaining power of workers in all trades, but a revival of the economy in the late forties and early fifties stimulated renewed efforts by workingmen to improve their salaries and sometimes their working conditions. The workday was commonly from sunup to sundown. Boston bakers declared that they worked eighteen hours or more, and a committee of the state legislature appointed to examine the subject reported that the average workday in most trades and industries was in excess of twelve hours. Faced with the obduracy of employers, many workers went out on strike. In the cotton mill town of Chicopee, Massachusetts, women operatives went out on strike and were dismissed. The Female Industry Association was formed in New York by women who were employed in various small-scale industries. The president, who was a seamstress, said that her wages were only eighteen cents a day.

A convention of workingmen was called in New England, and the New England Workingmen's Association was formed to encourage the formation of unions, support workingmen in strikes for better pay and working conditions, and work through political channels for legislation to protect workingmen. The mill hands of Fall River, Lowell, and Andover presented petitions to the Massachusetts legislature signed by 2,139 workers describing the conditions under which they did their jobs. They were required to be at work by five o'clock in the morning and worked until seven in the evening, with half an hour for breakfast and three-quarters of an hour for supper. Salaries ranged from seven or eight to twenty-three dollars a month.

An industrial congress held in New York called for limitations on the amount of land any one person could own, a ten-hour day, and free homesteads for settlers on government lands. Legislatures in several states responded by setting a limit of ten hours in certain industries and stipulating that no boy or girl under fifteen could work more than ten hours without the written consent of a parent. The failure of many of the strikes led to talk of workers' cooperatives and to a sympathetic hearing for the theories of Fourier and Saint-Simon. The workingmen of Boston sent fraternal greetings to the working-men of France, called for the end of slavery for both white laborers and black slaves, and proposed that a labor department be established by the government to look after the rights of workingmen.

Cooperative workshops were actually opened by Boston tailors after a futile fourteen-week strike, and to Philadelphia "tailoresses," Arthur Brisbane, champion of Fourier's phalanxes, declared, "We must do away with servitude to capital. Capital locked up by selfishness is the infernal tyrant of to-day, and what we want to know is how to change, peacefully, the system of to-day. The first great principle is combination. You are slaves because of no concert of action. You produce the wealth of the world, and you have not got it, because you allow a certain class of men to be your merchants, bankers, employers."

A German immigrant tailor spoke in even more forceful terms, asking, "We came here because we were oppressed, and what have we gained? Nothing but misery, hunger, oppression, and treading down. But we are in a free country, and it is our fault if we do not get our rights. Yes, stand out for them in fire and water rather than submit to the tyranny of the capitalists, the aristocrats, the oppressive employers. Let those who strike eat; the rest starve. . . . We must have a revolution. We cannot submit any longer."

The question of free land for settlers soon became a national issue. Andrew Johnson, Congressman from Tennessee, took the matter up in the House and proposed a homestead bill to give land to poor settlers on the condition of their occupying it and farming it for a specified period of time. Opponents of the bill declared that it was un-American and socialistic; that it would undermine the initiative of those who received land free and encourage the passage of agrarian laws.

That the grievances of workingmen were of substance cannot be doubted. If the United States was measured against its original professions rather than against the oppressive monarchial governments of Europe with their depressed and exploited masses, the gross inequities in American society were all too apparent. The abundant wealth of the United States, the wonder of the world, was clearly going, in excessive amounts, into the pockets of its most ruthlessly competitive citizens. It was small wonder that workmen went on strike and there was talk of socialism in the air. Nor was the discontent confined to the working class. The transcendentalists in general and the reformers specifically expressed their profound disillusionment with an economic system that seemed to put a premium on chicanery, that exploited white labor while pointing a finger of scorn at the slavery in the South.

In the United States in 1855 the depression continued, bearing heavily on the urban poor. Strong noted that "unemployed workmen, chiefly German, are assembling daily in the Park and listening to inflammatory speeches by demagogues who should be 'clapt up' for preaching sedition. . . . Large majority of the distressed multitude," he added, "is decently clad and looks well fed and comfortable. People anticipate riot and disturbance . . . Friday night it was rumored that a Socialist mob was sacking the Schiff mansion in the Fifth Avenue. . . . Certainly the destitute are a thankless set and deserve little sympathy in their complaints. The efforts to provide employment and relief, the activity of individuals and of benevolent organizations, the readiness with which money is contributed does credit to the city. More could and ought to be done, of course, but what is done is beyond precedent here, and more than our 'unemployed' friends had a right to count on." The passage, like so many others in Strong's diary, displays a profound ambivalence. The unemployed are sympathized with in one sentence and excoriated in the next. It is clear enough that the urban upper classes were torn between their benevolent instincts and their uneasiness at any manifestation on the part of laborers, employed or unemployed, of an intention to improve their own condition. Such agitations all smacked of "socialism" and attacks on "property," that most sacred of sacreds. Strong comforted himself with the thought that "there has been a vast improvement during the last three or four years in the dealings of our 'upper class' with the poor; not merely in the comparative abundance of their bounty, but in the fact that it has become fashionable and creditable and not unusual for people to busy themselves in personal labors for the very poor and in personal intercourse with them. . . . Perhaps it may be a short-lived fashion, but it is an indication most encouraging of progress toward social health. . . ."

Transient as it proved to be, the workingmen's party movement, if it can be called that, was of considerable significance. Confined almost exclusively to the industrial cities of the North and centered in New York state and Massachusetts, it demonstrated enough enterprise and organization to elect a number of candidates in local elections, made its endorsements of candidates in the established parties sought after, drew attention to labor's social concerns, and contributed very substantially to such causes as reform of the laws involving debtors and creditors. Perhaps its most important practical by-product was the increasing disposition of laborers to form trade unions and strike for better working conditions, most specifically the ten-hour day. The movement was also characterized, as the participation of Owen and Wright indicated, by an alliance of workingmen with middle-class reformers and radicals. It was, to be sure, an uneasy alliance for the most part. White workingmen harbored strong prejudices against free blacks whom they feared as cheap competition and toward whom they felt, in most instances, strong racial antagonism. Similarly, those who were "native Americans" were apt to be found in the ranks of the anti-Irish mobbers and solidly arrayed on the side of high protective tariffs and restrictive immigration policies. Favorably disposed to temperance reform, they were only slightly less hostile toward the abolitionists than were Southern slaveholders.

Along with the crippling ethnic splits, there were numerous other factors at work to prevent the development of a full-fledged labor movement, or an even more radical or revolutionary movement of workingmen. The notion of moral uplift had its place in the working-class consciousness as well as in that of the middle and upper classes. It followed that some of the ablest potential working-class leaders were drawn into such moral uplift enterprises as the temperance movement or the drive to improve and extend free public education. The fact that American workingmen, as opposed to most of their European counterparts, were, for the most part, unimpeded in their efforts to form unions and "protective associations" encouraged the feeling that they could achieve their aims within the system, as we say today. The excitement generated by Fourierism and the establishment of numerous phalanxes also turned the attention of workingmen and their champions to utopian schemes and away from the practical problems of labor organization.

The constant fluctuations of the economy—the cycle of boom and bust—were a further inhibiting factor. When masses of men were out of work, their attention turned away from union organization and strikes to agitation for public works and relief for them and their families. In boom periods, labor activity invariably accelerated and there were frequent strikes for higher wages and better working conditions. The subsequent and inevitable bust set all such activities back. In addition, there was the perpetual dream of escaping from the mill or factory to the West, starting a farm and thereby becoming an independent entrepreneur. The frequency with which workingmen's resolutions and petitions included the demand for free homesteads and even, in some instances, substantial government subsidies to help prospective farmers get started, shows that the dream was a persistent one. The great historian of the West, Frederick Jackson Turner, speculated that the region served as a "safety-valve" for labor unrest, for workingmen angry at their exploitation by greedy "capitalists." It seems clear that relatively few workingmen, and they only the worst paid and most unskilled, thought of themselves as permanent members of a "working class."

There was also, as a powerful neutralizing force against labor organization, the American self-help philosophy and a dogged individualism that was related to the philosophical anarchism that had been a continuing American tradition since Roger Williams and Tom Paine, and was currently expressed in the writings of Thoreau and, to a degree, of Emerson himself.

As we have noted, workingmen had a strong if sometimes reluctant ally in the Democratic Party, whose strength in the North was based on the vote of Irish and German immigrants; and when the Democratic regulars faltered in their support of the cause of immigrant laborers, the Loco-Foco wing of the party took it up. Add persistent nativism, which undermined all efforts at working-class solidarity, and, finally, the endless influx of new immigrants desperately seeking any job that would put bread in their mouths and the wonder is that there was any workingmen's movement at all. That there was one and that it spoke out repeatedly in loud and angry accents is an indication that workingmen shared a very deep sense of social and economic injustice and that, while those injustices on the whole got worse instead of better, the various factors that we have described continued to blunt or deflect all major efforts to improve the condition of workingmen.

Many middle-class reformers identified themselves with the cause of the workingmen, used the same rhetoric in attacking the banks, the factory owners, the railroad tycoons, the land speculators, and the moneyed interests in general, and insisted that the "system" must be made more equitable. There was, thus, a vital link preserved between the working class and the liberal middle class, the latter more radical in its sentiments. Moreover there was a constant dispersion of energy caused by the continuing debate about whether the whole system was corrupt beyond reform or whether the problem was simply that of creating greater opportunities for everyone to become a capitalist in one degree or another. That issue, of course, was never to be entirely resolved, although the great weight of opinion always favored trying to make it work better.

Finally (there seems to be an endless list of "finalies"), there was the issue of slavery, which activated the workingman's schizophrenia. All could perhaps agree that labor was demeaned when confined to slaves. It therefore made sense for free white workingmen to be opposed to the institution of slavery, but this, as we have seen, did not mean any interest in or sympathy with blacks, slave or free; quite the contrary. And since in the North the only channel of political expression open to the workingman was in the Democratic Party, the party whose political power, in the final analysis, rested on its alliance with the slaveholding South, the Northern workingman was caught in a classic political double bind. The implications of this paradox, as we have noted before, extended, of course, far beyond the mill "operative" or bricklayer. All American society was involved in this political and moral conundrum. If the "ideological" Northern Democrats, following the simplest demands of logic, had severed their connections with the Southern Democrats and formed a party that genuinely represented their political and social philosophy, they would have condemned themselves to complete political impotence and turned over the country to the moneyed interests to do with as they wished. Moreover had the Democratic Party split along sectional lines, the South, condemned to permanent political inferiority, would undoubtedly have seceded and done so at a time when it would have been far more difficult to bring Northern sentiment to the point of seeking to prevent secession by force of arms. So it may be said, with some assurance, that the incongruous alliance of Northern workingmen and Southern slaveholders (the constituencies were, of course, far broader than that) saved the country for a number of decades from political chaos, from secession, and perhaps from revolutionary upheaval.

Another factor that must be mentioned was the work of the innumerable benevolent associations which served, in their very considerable aggregate, to ameliorate some of the harshest aspects of the lives of the urban poor and, in times of depression, of the jobless. As important as the material assistance afforded by these groups, with their insistent Christian message, was the connective tissue that they formed between the prosperous, Christian, reform-minded middle class and those at the lower levels of society.

Nor should we neglect the response of particular state legislators. Numerous legislatures passed laws limiting work hours and restricting child labor. The hopes engendered by the movement to establish workers' cooperatives such as that started by the tailors of Boston and the tailoresses of Philadelphia also served to draw attention away from more radical solutions.

40

Technology

American technology centered on saving time and human energy by making work simpler and easier and traversing space more rapidly. While canals reduced the arduousness and the cost of the transportation of freight over long distances, they were too slow for a go-ahead people and they were soon challenged by steam engines on tracks—by trains. The other major area of technological innovation was agricultural tools, most notably plows.

The years between 1826 and 1860 not only witnessed a development in the use of steam to power boats and then trains, but witnessed the birth of the "machine age" as a prelude to the post–Civil War era of large-scale industrialism. Americans had already modified and perfected numerous tools to make everyday tasks and crafts quicker and easier. The machines were a natural outgrowth of the tools and in the first moment of their fabrication they were as splendid as any work of art. Modern critics have accustomed us to the notion of the "beauty of machinery," focusing on their austere functionalism and gleaming surfaces. But the first makers of tools considered themselves artisans with an emphasis on the *art*. The pistons, cylinders, cast-iron casings and supports, the tempered metal surfaces, the brass castings were all objects of great aesthetic potency both for those who made them and for those who saw them. Since iron would rust, it must be painted, often in several colors—white and red, green with gold letters with eagles, flags, and other emblems in brilliant tones. Each machine was, in its gleaming perfection and all that it suggested of the skill and ingenuity of its designer and of its maker, a work of art as compelling in its own way as a DaVinci or a Rembrandt.

The steamboat was, of course, the archetype of this wedding of art and technology. Traveling from New York to Newport, Rhode Island, on the *Bay State,* Sidney George Fisher called it "another wonder of modern art. . . . The machinery is bright as silver & exhibited thro large panes of plate glass set in gilded frames. The saloons, cabins & staterooms are all painted & gilded in the most splendid style & sumptuously furnished. Brilliant Saxony carpets, chandeliers, marble tables, sofas, ottomans, armchairs of every pattern, well-cushioned & covered with the richest stuffs, silk curtains, French china, cut glass, mirrors. . . . The servants are well dressed & well drilled & order, cleanliness & comfort reign throughout." While it seemed to Fisher that nothing could exceed it in elegance, he had no doubt another year would see a yet more splendid vessel. "The vast multitudes, increasing every year, who throng the great routes of travel," he wrote, "sustain & justify this lavish expenditure whilst competition produces all this comfort & lowers the price." The fare to Newport was a dollar without a stateroom and three dollars with one.

Returning to New York from Albany on the *Hendrick Hudson,* Fisher wrote: "Thro the enchanted scene the magnificent steamer swiftly glided like a thing of life, her speed, her size, her power, her splendor and the associations of the wonderful art by which she was produced & impelled according well with the majestic scenery of the mighty & bountiful river." He tried to imagine the future when the river would carry "the trade of mighty nations & be thronged with millions yet unborn. All this," he added, "exists in the future as certainly as N. York & Albany, the *Hendrick Hudson* & my humble self existed in the future when the Indian built his wigwam where the Albany demagogues now rave & plot, ignorant of the rapacious & conquering white man who has driven him from his home, & of the wonderful civilization which has usurped his dominion, & of which he can neither comprehend the acts nor partake the benefits." Fisher was in good literary company. After visiting a ferryboat engine room Walt Whitman wrote, "It is an almost sublime sight that one beholds there;

for indeed there are few more magnificent pieces of handwork than a powerful steam-engine swiftly at work!"

All this elegance and speed had a price in human lives, which were expended with a prodigality hard to comprehend today. In a period of two months in 1841, eight steamers sank between St. Louis and the mouth of the Ohio and in four years 138 sank in the Mississippi at a loss estimated in excess of three million dollars. On July 28, 1855, the steamboat *Henry Clay,* on a run between Albany and New York City, began to race a rival, the *Armenia.* The *Henry Clay* caught fire and ninety passengers were drowned or burned to death. Among the victims was the famous landscape architect Andrew Jackson Downing. A few weeks later the boiler of the steamboat *Reindeer* exploded on the same run and thirty-three passengers in the dining salon were scalded to death. George Templeton Strong expressed a general outrage when he wrote in his diary, "It is time that this drowning and burning to death of babies and young girls and old men to gratify the vanity of steamboat captains were stopped. I would thank God for the privilege of pulling the cap over the eyes of the captain and owners of this boat the *Henry Clay,* and I feel as I completed my hangman's office that I had not lived utterly in vain. . . . What a sagacious people we are with our 'reverence for human life' and our increasing scruples about the lawfulness of capital punishment!"

Each month seemed to bring some important technological innovation. One of the most significant was the development of the oceangoing steamship. This was possible, in large part, through the use of anthracite coal. In the summer of 1826, the first voyage of a steamboat propelled by anthracite coal was made from New York to Albany. The cost of fuel for the trip up the Hudson was one hundred dollars. Wood, the then standard fuel, would have cost almost two and a half times as much. Coal, in consequence, became an increasingly important product. In 1820 the whole amount "sent to market" in Pennsylvania was only 365 tons from the town of Lehigh. Twenty years later the same town shipped out a million tons of anthracite.

The new technology charmed Ralph Waldo Emerson. By means of "the useful arts" man need no longer wait "for favoring gales, but by means of steam, he realizes the fable of Aeolus's bag, which carries the two and thirty winds in the boiler of his boat. To diminish friction, he paves the road with iron bars, and, mounting a coach with a shipload of men, animals, and merchandise behind him, he darts through the country, from town to town like an eagle or a swallow through the air. . . . Machinery & Transcendentalism agree well. State Coach & Rail Road are bursting the old legislation like green withes." Poets and inventors were blood brothers. "Readers of poetry," he wrote in his essay "The Poet," "see the factory-village and the railway, and fancy that the poetry of the landscape is broken up by these . . . but the poet sees them fall within the great Order not less than the beehive or the spider's geometrical web. Nature adopts them very fast into her vital circles, and the gliding train of cars she loves like her own." Lyman Beecher wanted Christian morality to control the use of the new technology. Emerson trusted the mission to the poet. Melville, reading Emerson's effusion, wrote dryly in the margin, "So it would seem. In this sense Mr. E. is a great poet."

The British ship *Great Western,* the largest steam-driven vessel yet built, caused a sensation when she arrived in New York in 1838. She was 234 feet in length, weighed over sixteen hundred tons, and was driven by engines developing 450 horsepower. Against strong head winds she had made the passage from Bristol in fifteen days. "Our countrymen," Philip Hone prophesied, " 'students of change and pleased with novelty,' will rush forward to visit the shores of Europe instead of resorting to Virginia or Saratoga Springs; and steamers will continue to be the fashion until some more dashing adventurer of the go-ahead tribe shall demonstrate the practicability of balloon naviga- tion, and gratify their impatience on a voyage *over* and not *upon,* the blue waters in two days instead of as many weeks. . . . Then they may soar above the dangers of icebergs. . . ." Although such a project was already being advocated, Hone remained "still skeptical on the subject."

When the *Great Western* sailed in May, "All the city went to behold the sight. The Battery was a mass of living witnesses to this event," Hone wrote, ". . . and all the adjacent wharves and houses were thronged with spectators"; she was accompanied by hundreds of smaller craft with many steam vessels among them.

A few months later the citizens of New York were enlightened by "the wonderful process lately discovered in France by M. Daguerre," as Philip Hone noted. "The pictures he has are extremely beautiful. They consist of views of Paris and exquisite collections of the objects of still life. The manner of producing them constitutes one of the wonders of modern times, and like other miracles, one may almost be excused for disbelieving it without seeing the very process by which it is created. . . . Every object, however minute, is a perfect transcription of the thing itself; the hair of the human head, the gravel of the roadside, the texture of a silk curtain, or the shadow of the smaller leaf reflected upon the wall, are all imprinted as carefully as nature or art has created them. . . . How greatly ashamed of their ignorance the by-gone generations of mankind ought to be." No invention seemed more "American" or was more readily adopted than the camera. Within a few years Americans were photographing everything in sight. The camera comported perfectly with the American penchant for staring.

But the most astonishing and miraculous invention of all was just around the corner. Samuel Finley Breese Morse was the son of that fierce old Calvinist, Jedediah Morse, the enemy of the "Illuminati." Samuel F. B., as he was generally called, had graduated from Yale in 1810, studied painting with Benjamin West and Washington Allston, and been admitted to the Royal Academy. Back in the United States, he found that he must paint portraits to support himself. Naturally gregarious and anxious to raise the standard of American painting, Morse formed an association of artists who met to sketch and socialize, feasting on "milk and honey, raisins, apples and crackers." The group evolved into the National Academy of the Arts of Design of which Morse was the first president. Deeply interested in science, Morse also attended the lectures of Professor James Dana on electromagnetism and electricity. Back in Paris to continue his studies in painting, Morse confided to James Fenimore Cooper "his ideas on the subject of using the electric spark by way of a telegraph." Morse was encouraged by the experiments of the French physicist Ampère. The critical question was, Would the velocity of the electricity be impeded by the length of the wire over which it was transmitted? Benjamin Franklin had already conducted experiments that indicated "electricity passes instantaneously over any known length of wire." "I see no reason why intelligence may not be transmitted instantaneously by electricity. . . . If it will go ten miles without stopping, I can make it go around the globe," Morse is reported to have said. On his way back to the United States, he devised a system of signals, a code. Appointed professor of the literature of the arts of design at New York University, Morse spent the next five years designing and testing a transmitter and receiver for his electrical signal.

In the meantime he was forced to surrender his professorship and was often "without a farthing in my pocket, and have to borrow even for my meals. . . ." Reduced to penury, Morse laid siege to Congress to try to persuade that body to appropriate thirty thousand dollars to build a telegraph line between Baltimore and Washington. At last, in February, 1842, by a vote of 90 to 82, in the waning hours of the congressional session, sixty thousand dollars was appropriated, with half to be used for experiments in animal magnetism, or mesmerism, one of the great fads of the day. It is ironic that without the alliance between the advocates of animal magnetism and electromagnetism, Morse would never have gotten his money. Now the line was quickly erected. On May 11, 1844, Morse sent the important if uninspiring message to his assistant, "Everything worked well."

The first important message transmitted from Baltimore to Washington was of the nomination of Henry Clay by the Whigs for the presidential election of that year.

Morse was now ready for a public demonstration, which took place in the chambers of the Supreme Court. Annie Ellsworth, the daughter of the Commissioner of Patents, was given the honor of making the first "official" transmission and she chose the words, "What hath God wrought!" What indeed! The country and the world were struck with awe and astonishment. Messages sent instantly over hundreds and perhaps thousands of miles! It was as dramatic and symbolic a moment as the century afforded.

Richard Henry Dana wrote: "How incredible are the powers of the magnetic telegraph! . . . This is incredible. My faith is staggered. I see that the result is produced, but I have no faith of the understanding of it." Philip Hone, equally impressed, noted: "Strange and wonderful discovery, which has made the 'swift-winged lightning' man's messenger, annihilated all space, and tied the two ends of a continent in a knot." Alexander Mackay, the Scottish visitor, spoke for millions of others when he wrote: "The effect which this invention, as thus developed, has produced, and that which it is still likely to produce on many of the operations of society are almost beyond comprehension."

The *Ladies' Repository*, a Methodist journal for women, hailed the telegraph as a "noble invention" intended to be the "means of extending civilization, republicanism, and Christianity over the earth. It must and will be extended to nations half-civilized, and thence to those now savage and barbarous. Our government will be the grand center of this mighty influence. . . . The beneficial and harmonious operation of our institutions will be seen, and similar ones adopted. Christianity must speedily follow them; and we shall behold the grand spectacle of a whole world civilized, republican, and Christian. Then will wrong and injustice be forever banished. Every yoke will be broken, and the oppressed go free. Wars will cease from the earth . . . for each man shall feel that every other man is his neighbor—his brother. Then shall come to pass the millennium. . . ."

The telegraph spawned an immediate progeny of stories and jokes. Dana told of one "Western man" who although in a state of "half incredulous extacy" was determined to be blasé about the wonderful new magnetic telegraph. He walked up to a man making transmissions and said, "Can you send me a message to Baltimore?" "Yes, sir." "How long will it take?" "Five minutes," said the clerk, expecting the man to register astonishment. "Can't wait," said he, walking off.

Almost as remarkable as its invention was the rapid extension of the telegraph. Four years after Morse had prevailed on Congress to try the experiment of establishing a telegraph line between Washington and Baltimore, more than five thousand miles of telegraph wire had been stretched around the country and three thousand more were under construction. "Every year, almost now," Philip Hone wrote, "brings with it some new victory of man over nature, of mind over matter, changing the course of civilization and increasing the accommodations of life."

One immediate consequence of the development of the telegraph was the increased importance of the press. News stories were soon being reported "instantly" from all corners of the country to newspaper offices. On a visit to New York, Richard Henry Dana visited Horace Greeley's *Tribune,* where he met his star editors and reporters, among them two relatives, Charles Dana and George Ripley, "all at work at their separate tables." What impressed Dana most was the newspaper's technology, "the great enginery of the 19th century, steam engines in every part of the huge building, four editors at humble tables, with pen & scissors in hand, preparing for 100,000 readers & more, with telegraphic despatches every hour, from all parts of the Union." (Horace Greeley, the great reform editor of the day, impressed Dana as "coarse & cunning.")

Philip Hone wrote in the same spirit: "We live now on steamers, and newspapers have become the most agreeable of all reading, so exciting & wonderful are the movements and events of the age. By the magic aid of steam & Morse's telegraph, the nations think simultaneously, opinion forms itself with unequalled rapidity, and everything that occurs of the slightest public importance is almost instantly known throughout the civilized world. We have every morning news from all parts of the Union up to the previous evening and every week a steamer comes to astonish us with the wonderful things that are happening every day in Europe. Each arrival is like the rising of the curtain at a theatre for a new act in some interesting drama, and the picture thus daily presented to our view of the exciting present and the vast working of society is so interesting and so instructive that even the eloquent pages which describe the past are forsaken for the London *Times* and the *New York Herald*."

In January, 1850, three steam vessels, built at an aggregate cost of more than one million dollars, were launched: the *New World*, 216 feet long and 27 feet in the beam, intended for the rivers of California; the *Boston*, designed to run between Boston and Bangor, Maine; and the *Atlantic*, for ocean commerce. The *Atlantic* was the most impressive vessel of all. She was the largest ship ever built in the United States, a "great specimen of American enterprise and skill in naval architecture and mechanical science . . ." Philip Hone wrote. Only a yard short of a hundred yards in length, with a width of beam of forty-six feet and a burthen of 3500 tons, she boasted "cabins decorated with all the splendor and extravagance for which our Yankee marine palaces are famous the world over."

There were, of course, setbacks. Robert Stockton, a captain in the United States navy, was a pioneer advocate of the screw propeller–driven man-of-war made of steel with an armanent of heavy guns. The *Princeton* was the fruit of his efforts and he received permission from the secretary of the navy to sail his improved warship, with its battery of heavy guns, to Washington to give a demonstration of its speed and firepower for the members of Congress. President Tyler, his Cabinet, and a number of senators and representatives with their wives and friends were on board the ship on March 2, 1844, to witness the firing of its larger guns, one of which, designed by Stockton and called the Peacemaker, was capable of throwing a 250-pound shell some three or four miles with amazing accuracy. The gun exploded in firing, killing Abel Upshur, secretary of state; Thomas Gilmer, secretary of the navy; several other naval officers and spectators; and severely wounding ten sailors. Fortunately, the President and most of the ladies aboard were in the dining room enjoying champagne, oysters, and chicken salad at the time of the accident. Stockton himself was knocked down by the discharge and the papers announced that the blast had burnt his hair off, but it turned out it was only his wig that had suffered.

Samuel F. B. Morse had also conducted experiments in the process of Daguerre, whom he had met in Paris, and with Professor John Draper, Morse made the first photographs of a living person, a moment almost as significant as the first pulse of electricity over his wire.

Even before Congress appropriated money for the Baltimore-Washington line, Morse had conducted experiments on transmitting messages under water. Now the daring idea of laying a transatlantic telegraph cable along the ocean's bottom was taken up by a remarkable duo: Cyrus Field and Peter Cooper. Cooper was another American original, a classic self-made man. The son of a hatter, some of his earliest recollections were of plucking fur from rabbit skins to make felt. With no more than a few months of schooling, young Cooper showed an innate inventiveness and ingenuity. Apprenticed to a carriage maker, he promptly designed a machine to mortise the hubs of carriages, but he refused his master's offer to set him up in business on shares and opened his own machine shop to manufacture machines for shearing cloth. When the demand for his machines declined, Cooper turned to making cabinetware. He added a grocery store and then a glue factory. All his ventures flourished, and in 1828 he bought three thousand acres of land in Baltimore and erected the Canton Iron Works. Here, as we have noted earlier, he built *Tom Thumb*. Selling his Baltimore properties at a large profit, Cooper shifted his operations back to New York; building an iron foundry, he used, for the first time in the United States, anthracite coal for puddling iron. Next, three blast furnaces were built near the anthracite coalfields at Easton, Pennsylvania, and there Cooper manufactured the first wrought-iron beams for use in multistoried buildings.

In addition to his triumphs as an inventor-capitalist, Cooper was indefatigable in pursuing good works; his favorite cause was the education of workingmen, to which end he established the Cooper Union, which George Templeton Strong considered such a visionary enterprise.

Cyrus Field, one of three very able brothers, was the son of David Dudley Field and Submit Dickinson. The elder Field was a Congregational minister and amateur historian and scholar. Cyrus began his career at the age of fifteen as a clerk in Alexander Stewart's department store in New York City. Before he was twenty-one he had established a flourishing paper factory and in 1853, at the age of thirty-four, he "retired" and began looking for a new field to conquer.

The idea of a transatlantic cable seemed to him a project worthy of his attention. He enlisted Cooper's enthusiastic support and for the next thirteen years the two men worked to bind Europe and the United States by a wire. Not even Peter Cooper's fortune was sufficient to meet the enormous costs involved, and Field made over a dozen trips to Europe seeking financial backing. The actual laying of the cable was a formidable task. The enormous weight of the heavily insulated cable caused it to break time and again, and it often seemed that the obstacles were too great to be surmounted. But Field refused to be discouraged, and in 1858 the first message was conveyed across the Atlantic.

The news that the Atlantic cable had been completed caused a sensation. "Everybody all agog about the Atlantic Cable," George Templeton Strong wrote. "Telegraph offices in Wall Street decorated with flags of all nations and sundry fancy pennons beside, suspended across the streets." In towns all over the country celebrations were held to mark the most sensational accomplishment of the go-ahead age. The *Herald* declared the cable to be the modern manifestation of the Angel in the Book of Revelations "with one foot on the land, proclaiming that Time shall be no longer." "Moderate people," Strong wrote, "merely say it is the greatest human achievement in history. . . . If your great revolutions or cataclysms don't throw mankind off the track they've been traveling for the last half-century, if the earth doesn't blow up or get foul of a comet and not be rebarbarized by Brigham Young or Red Republicanism, it will be a strange place in 1958, most unlike what it is now. The diverse races of men certainly seem tending toward development into a living organic system, telephone wires for nerves, and the London *Times* and New York *Herald* for a brain." A week later Queen Victoria and President Buchanan exchanged messages. In Great Barrington, Massachusetts, where the Strongs were taking hydrotherapy treatments, the citizens of the town turned out with a fife and drum and torches, parading up and down the main street. In New York, Strong noted, "the triumphant pyrotechnics by which our city fathers celebrated this final and complete subjugation by man of all the powers of nature—space and time included—set the City Hall on fire, burned up the cupola and half its roof. . . ."

The celebration over the completion of the Atlantic cable was marred in New York by the raids on the Staten Island Quarantine Station, and Strong wrote in his diary, "I fear that this millenium over which we have been braying is made of gutta-percha and copper wire and is not the real thing after all." The final blow was that after three or four days of transmission, the cable ceased to operate. The celebrations, it appeared, had been premature. It would be years before sufficient capital was accumulated to put the cable back in service again.

The steam engine, the railroad locomotive, the transatlantic steamship, the telegraph, and the camera together virtually completed the conquest of nature by the go-ahead age. What followed were, in effect, refinements. The telephone and the wireless radio were already anticipated in the electromagnetic telegraph. The camera, as it turned out, could also be hitched to electromagnetic devices to project pictures as well as signals and words. Even the increasingly anticipated conquest of the air would, in essence, be no more than an added convenience. Its effect was simply to turn days into hours. It was the shortening of months into days by the railroads that was the basic revolution in transportation. The technological innovations that we today take so much for granted appeared to our ancestors astonishing beyond belief; they were understood to presage the transformation of the world.

Farming technology, centering on the plow and on the mechanical reaper, was the other branch of technology in which Americans were to excel. There had been little improvement in plows since man first began to cultivate the soil. The inadequacies of the instrument were felt most keenly in the United States, where virgin soil had constantly to be put under the plow, a process as hard on the plow as on the plowman. If there were rocks and boulders in the flinty soil of New England to break wooden plows, the problem was as acute in the prairie regions of the Old Northwest, where the matted roots of grass several feet deep impeded the progress of the most advanced plowshare. Thomas Jefferson had been one of the first Americans to make a scientific study of the moldboard in order to delineate the most efficient shape, but Jefferson did nothing to publicize his experiments, and it was left to Jethro Wood, a New York Quaker, to make the first notable innovations in that ancient instrument. In 1819, drawing on Jefferson's calculations, Wood designed an iron plow with replaceable parts. Resisted initially as a crackpot invention, the plow soon demonstrated its superiority and was immediately copied and Wood's patent stolen, so that he was forced to spend the last years of his relatively short life fighting infringements. Effective in ordinary soil and soon widely used, the face of Wood's plow would not "scour" or throw the soil from its face easily. John Lane, a Chicago blacksmith, improved on Wood's plow by making a wood plow and share, to the face of which he screwed saw steel. The result was a vastly improved plow. In Grand Detour, Illinois, a powerful young blacksmith named John Deere, much of whose work consisted of repairing plows, began experimenting with a plow similar to Lane's with a tempered steel face, thicker and curved much in the manner suggested by Jefferson's drawing forty years earlier. The result was a strong plow so light that Deere could carry it on his shoulder. Deere converted his shop into a small-scale factory, imported his steel from Germany, and soon had more orders than he could fill. Gustaf Unonius, the Swedish immigrant to Wisconsin, noted that "like all other tools and equipment in use here, plows are constructed with a view to making physical labor easier. The plowman walks very erect, and if the plow is properly adjusted . . . he does not have to use much physical strength to press and keep the plow in the ground. . . . On a prairie a man with four horses can plow about two acres a day." James Fenimore Cooper wrote, "Though there is scarce such a thing as a capital picture in this country, I have seen more beautiful, graceful, and convenient ploughs in positive use here, than are probably to be found in the whole of Europe united. In this single fact may be traced the history of the character of the people, and the germ of their future greatness."

Close behind the plow came a mechanical planter built by a Michigan farmer. In it the amount of seed dropped in a furrow was geared to the distance traveled by the machine. The drills were stopped or started by the motion of the seeder. It was not until after the Civil War that grain drills were widely used. Meanwhile a practical corn planter had been built in 1839 by a man named D. S. Rochwell, but it failed to be generally adopted.

Next to plowing, reaping—done by hand—was the farmer's most arduous task. A number of farmers had devised horse-drawn reapers in the early years of the century, but they failed to perform up to their designers' expectations and it was not until a Massachusetts sailor, Obed Hussey, and a Virginia farmer, Robert McCormick, went to work independently on the problem that a practical mechanical reaper was devised. Hussey's contribution was a cutting blade in which the teeth moved from side to side, cutting the grain. After seven years, when the dominance of his machine was threatened by one designed by McCormick's son, Cyrus, Hussey sold out his interests and turned his attention to trying to build a steam-driven plow. Young Cyrus McCormick, in the first test of his machine, reaped six acres of grain in a day. A man with a scythe was expected to reap an acre in the same time. McCormick had many problems to solve before his reaper could be produced on a mass scale, however. His father gave him financial backing but the depression of 1837 wiped out both father and son. Cyrus enlisted his three brothers and three sisters to help him build reapers, and by 1844 he had sold ninety for approximately $150 a piece. Encouraged, he opened a factory in Chicago, and by 1857 he had sold over twenty-three thousand reapers and was a millionaire.

If the railroad locomotive was the most spectacular achievement of American engineering skill and the improvements in agricultural technology the most characteristically American inventions, they were supplemented by a remarkable range of inventions designed to make work easier and living more comfortable. It sometimes seemed as though every American who found himself saddled with some tiring and monotonous job had to set out to find a machine to do it for him and, in the process, to make his fortune. Moreover, since help was expensive and disposed to head for the California or Colorado goldfields without a moment's notice, proprietors, who in many instances had begun their careers as inventors, were under continuous pressure to devise new labor-saving machines to increase their output and their income while, at the same time, reducing the number of skilled employees they must train and retain.

Since Americans had a unique addiction to the printed word, improvements in printing presses were at a premium and hundreds of patents were taken out each year for improved presses and faster methods of setting type. Eli Whitney had helped to give practical effect to Americans' constitutional right to bear arms by developing the assembly-line and interchangeable-parts technique of manufacturing guns, thereby making them so cheap that any bloodthirsty American could afford them.

While Americans were to have a long and ardent love affair with guns, they were almost equally distinguished by an anxiety about the passage of time. It was therefore appropriate that America should lead the rest of the world in the manufacture of inexpensive time-pieces. A Connecticut Yankee named Chauncey Jerome adapted Whitney's techniques to the making of wall clocks and turned out clocks that cost little more than a substantial meal at a classy hotel.

Having saturated the American market, Jerome decided to export his clocks to England. The British customs officials could not believe the prices on Jerome's invoices so they invoked their right to buy up at invoice price all goods they thought had been undervalued to evade tariff duties. Jerome was delighted and sent another large shipment. When these were claimed in the same manner, Jerome sent over a shipload and the customs officials capitulated.

There were a thousand other commonplace articles invented, from cooking utensils to everyday farm implements, butter churners, improved stoves, better pots and pans, cheaper screws and nails, more efficient pumps. Rubber was vulcanized in 1839 and soon there was an abundance of rubber shoes, raincoats, hats, rubber gloves, pails and drinking cups, tents, water beds, life preservers, inflatable rubber rafts, hot-water bottles, teething rings, "cushions of every description," nipples for babies' bottles, elastic bands and "erasive rubber," syringes, and washers. Sidney George Fisher wrote that his wife, Bet, "has a sewing machine which is a great pleasure to her now that she is able to work it with skill. How these inventions come, one after another, to facilitate labor & multiply & cheapen the comforts & accommodations of life! This ingenious little machine performs in an hour as much work as could be done with a needle in a day, and it is a very pleasant employment to use it—many ladies become very fond of the occupation and prefer it to a piano." Walt Whitman saluted a new gas-fired hot-water heater with as much enthusiasm as a blade of grass:

> By thud of machinery and shrill steam-whistle undismay'd,
> Bluff'd not a bit by drain-pipe, gasometers, artificial
>   fertilizers,
> Smiling and pleas'd with palpable intent to stay,
> She's here, installed amid the kitchenware.

Bet Fisher's sewing machine was an example of the vital connection between invention and promotion. Elias Howe was a Massachusetts farm boy who worked in a Lowell cotton factory from the time he was sixteen until the Panic of 1837 cost him his job. Working for a Boston machinist, young Howe hit on the idea of a machine to sew cloth. For five years he worked on it in his spare time and finally patented his machine in 1846, when he was twenty-seven. The artisans of Boston who made their living sewing were so strongly opposed to the new machine, which they were convinced would put them out of work, that they refused to use it. Howe was forced to take a job as a railroad engineer and soon afterwards had a nervous breakdown. He tried to peddle his invention to England but after two frustrating years he worked his way back to the United States as a common sailor, arriving penniless to find there had been numerous infringements of his patent during his absence. One of those was Isaac Singer, a machinist and inventor who, with the backing of a wealthy lawyer, had started his own factory for the manufacture of the new machine. Howe won the rights to royalties on all the machines produced by Singer, whose genius lay in what we would call today marketing and promotion. Both men were classic eccentrics. At the outbreak of the Civil War Howe, by then a rich man, entered the Union army as a private. Singer, vastly richer, toured the world, finally settling in England in a bizarre mansion that he built. Howe's genius as an inventor and Singer's genius in developing a market for the new machine, more captivating than a piano, made the new instrument the first mass produced "home appliance," the perfect artifact of the go-ahead age. Time payments enabled even families in modest circumstances to own one of the marvelous new devices.

When the Crystal Palace opened in New York in 1853 it featured American accomplishments in the arts and sciences. The ambitious Exhibition of the Industry of All-Nations was a kind of migratory world's fair.

The cotton gin was on display, along with Colt's famous repeating revolvers and Morse's telegraph. A typewriter and an electric motor were exhibited as well as many large, steam-driven power tools, lathes and drills, gear-cutting machines, and, most striking of all, George Corliss's sixty-horsepower reciprocating steam engine. Corliss, born in New York state in 1817, was one of the authentic geniuses of the age. Son of a doctor, he tried storekeeping but soon began experimenting with devices to improve the efficiency and safety of steam engines. He sold his machines to skeptical manufacturers by guaranteeing savings in fuel that would soon repay the cost of his engines.

The Exhibition of Industry in 1853 was the first major expression of American leadership in the field of industrial technology. Many of the machines displayed were highly satisfying aesthetic objects as well as precursors of the age of industry. The *New York Illustrated News* wrote: "Science and art are in an amicable wrestle for the smile of beauty; the loom and anvil laughing out the jocund sound of profitable labor; the steam-engine snorting out its song of speed; the telegraph flashing its words of living flame; the subdued ocean bridged with golden boats. . . . The Crystal Palace may be termed the Iliad of the Nineteenth Century, and its Homer was the American people."

An invention that beguiled the dreams of innumerable would-be inventors was a "perpetual motion machine," a device calculated to run forever on its own energy. Some visitors noted that the American need only discover himself—in perpetual motion, his jaws constantly chewing tobacco, his mouth expectorating streams of juice, his hands whittling, his rocking chair rocking.

Alonzo Potter, later to be the Episcopal bishop of Pennsylvania, saw technology as God-given. Man, in a state of nature, was "one of the most defenseless and wretched" of creatures. Now, with technology, "Not only animals, with their fleetness and strength, but even winds, and waves, and heat, and gravity, have been trained to obey him; and, operating by means of machinery, they now fabricate for him, almost without intervention on his part, the choicest food and raiment; transport him, with the celerity of the deer or antelope, from place to place; and surround him with all the comforts and conveniences of life." Lyman Beecher insisted that technology placed a new burden on Christianity. Great as its blessings might be, it could become an instrument of destruction if it was not rigorously subordinated to Christian morality.

The great majority of the inventors were what we call, rather loosely, Yankees, of whom Eli Whitney was the prototype. That is to say, they were individuals who were, on the one hand, used to using their hands, and, on the other, anxious to save themselves labor wherever they could. It was not that such Americans *disliked* work. It was rather that they wished to minimize it; to make it as unlaborious as possible. Work was the curse that God had placed on the descendants of Adam for his disobedience. It was, to be sure, necessary to do it well and do it as a form of praise of God, but it was also perfectly appropriate to attempt in every reasonable and rational way to lessen the "curse" of work and increase the productivity or "fruitfulness" of the worker. Emerson described his countrymen as "an ardent race . . . as fully possessed with that hatred of labor, which is the principle of progress in the human race, as any other people. They must & will have the enjoyment without the sweat. So they buy slaves where the women will permit it; where they will not, they make the wind, the tide, the waterfall, the steam, the cloud, the lightning, do the work, by every art and device their cunningest brain can achieve."

Traditional societies used traditional tools. The tool took on a kind of sacred or talismanic character. It was revered and passed on from father to son. To change it was unimaginable, an assault on the established order. Yankees freed tools from the quasi-religious character that had inhered in them. The same spirit that created new theologies in such profusion created new tools with equal facility. Yankees were notoriously ingenious, constantly devising things, using their eternally restless hands to fabricate, to shape, if only to whittle a piece of wood or make a child's toy. But it was at this crucial juncture, beginning in the 1820s, that the transition took place from the tool to the machine. It was a change in degree that quickly became a change in kind. The machine was more than simply a larger, more intricate tool. It opened up a new vision of life. It went far beyond mere convenience or ingenuity to suggest new dimensions of human nature. *It was a new way of thinking, a new way of experiencing the world.* It was contagious. Those who caught the disease of invention sacrificed everything to it. They became obsessive. Every story of an important invention was the same: tireless, unremitting labor and experiment, frustration, disappointment, apparent defeat, and then triumph. The problem finally solved. Of course, at any one time there were hundreds and possibly thousands of anonymous "inventors" working at the solution of the same problem. How, for example, to build a machine that would tie up the bundles of wheat that had to be tied laboriously by hand? How to improve the ratio of fuel to power in a steam engine? And so on. Only a relatively few survived in this fierce and largely unrecorded struggle. Even those who succeeded, after years of devoted application, in making the first or most practical machine for performing a particular function, discovered that someone else was right on their heels or, more commonly, did not scruple to infringe or challenge their patent. Indeed a whole legal industry arose to challenge or defend patents. Fortunes were lost in endless litigation that often dragged on for decades, sometimes with millions of dollars at stake. The "inventor," who was soon metamorphosed into the "engineer," joined the minister and the lawyer and the missionary as a classic American type. Indeed it was he who became most clearly identified with the notion of progress because it was he who most clearly demonstrated its marvelous, endless "improvement." The intellectual and practical antecedents of "the inventor" in the first instance derived from the Protestant Reformation in the formation of a character-type who believed himself autonomous, capable of functioning outside traditional contexts. For him the world became malleable, plastic. He asserted himself against nature;

even, if need be, against his own nature, or at least against his lower, more animal instincts. He believed that the order of the universe could be discerned by reason and by revelation. Just as there were laws governing human affairs which the framers of the national government had attempted to discover and incorporate in a particular document called a constitution, there were clearly laws governing the natural world which might also be discovered by reason, by a process, essentially logical, of trial and error, of, in short, experimentation.

Edward Everett, one of the apostles of technology, declared, "There is an untold, probably an unimagined, amount of human talent, of high mental power, locked up among the wheels and springs of the machinist; a force of intellect of the loftiest character." Everett praised, "This stunning din, the monotonous rattle, this tremendous power, and the quiet, steady force of these humble, useful, familiar arts [which] resulted from efforts of mind kindred with those which have charmed or instructed the world with the richest strains of poetry, eloquence, and philosophy." The inventor "kindles the fires of his steam engine, and the rivers, the lakes, the ocean, are covered with flying vessels. . . . He stamps his foot, and a hundred thousand men start into being; not, like those which sprang from the fabled dragon's teeth, armed with the weapons of destruction, but furnished with every implement for the service and comfort of man."

Thomas Ewbank, the United States commissioner of patents from 1849 to 1852, was not content that science and invention should have parity with the arts; he plugged for supremacy. He believed that God had made "the world a giant workship" and it was thus man's Christian duty to labor in it. Machines were "poems carved out of wood and forged out of metals. . . . A steamer is a mightier epic than the Iliad, . . . and Whitney, Jacquard, and Blanchard, might laugh even Virgil, and Milton, and Tasso, to scorn." Such fine phrases flowed through Ewbank's reports of his department, prompting Henry Foote, the Mississippi senator, to call them "more poetically grand, more brilliant, more fanciful, more Byronic than any of the most fanciful poems that Lord Byron ever produced."

Christianity was enlisted in the apotheosis of the engineer and inventor. John Kimball wrote in the *Christian Examiner:* "It is notorious that nearly all poets and philosophers, nearly all theologians, too, have something mean and little about them, all inventors something heroic and grand." In the final sanctification of machinery, Kimball depicted Christ as the chief engineer, the supreme inventor: "The great driving wheel of all earthly machinery is far up in the heavens, has its force and direction supplied immediately from Omnipotence."

The hand was essential, too—the hand as fabricator, as tool user. American hands were thus large, long-fingered, powerful in grasping and holding, as American feet were large and broad for perpetual walking, or for following a plow. Undoubtedly, the fever of invention was stimulated in certain fields by the fortunes that were to be made through the creation of some much-needed machine. Prior to the 1830s the great majority of American fortunes had been made in oceangoing commerce (as in New England most particularly), in the mercantile trade (New York and Philadelphia), or in the large-scale production of cash crops (cotton in the South, wheat and corn in the West, or lumber anywhere), and, finally, real estate. These ventures required the command or accumulation of large amounts of capital. Access to them by ordinary men without advantages of birth and education were, if not blocked, certainly much impeded. In the North they remained largely in the hands of urban elites, in the South of the landed aristocracy. But any enterprising poor boy, fired by a dream of self-improvement and handy with tools, could dream of becoming rich by virtue of a brilliant invention. The readiest ladders for upwardly mobile young men, the most obvious paths to riches on the one hand, or fame on the other, were to be an inventor or a politician. The accumulation and manipulation of capital—symbolized by the banks —would remain the commonest ground for wealth in the United States, but the new partner in the development of American capitalism—the inventor/engineer—would become the central figure in the flowering of American industrial technology. It would, of course, be wrong to suggest that invention was an exclusively American phenomenon; England had preceded the United States by decades and Germany followed, but neither country rivaled the extraordinary effusion of inventions that marked America's entry into the age of technology. And in no other Western nation did invention become a quality of character in the way that it did in the United States.

In all the confusion and disorder of American life, the crudity and violence, the disappointed dreams, the noisome cities and the lonely farms, the bitter cycles of boom and bust, joblessness, anxiety, defeated ambitions, the horror of slavery, the evil of intemperance, only the physical world seemed manageable. Its conquest became a metaphor. More and more engineers and inventors came to rival or surpass ministers and lawyers as culture-heroes. Only they seemed to be able to produce, year after year, new miracles of progress, perpetually renewed promises of prosperity, convenience, comfort, speed, power. And, more than any man-made object or artifact, the steam locomotive, metamorphosing with bewildering speed through dozens of tentative forms toward an archetypal image, was the perfect symbol of power transmuted into movement, the ultimate American creation. The locomotive, on its endlessly converging rails, was the perfect instrument for subduing a continent that not long before had seemed so vast and intractable as to be perhaps forever unconquerable.

If Emerson was, at least initially, quite untroubled by any notion of a conflict between technology and nature, Nathaniel Hawthorne wrote a sharp satire on those Americans who put their faith in trains and steam engines. His "Celestial Railroad" retold the story of *Pilgrim's Progress*. Instead of accompanying Christian on his laborious journey, Hawthorne's characters took the train from the City of Destruction to the Celestial City. The conductor, Mr. Smooth-it-away, assured them they would get to the Celestial City much faster and more safely without any toil or inconvenience. Instead of having to climb the Hill of Difficulty, they would whiz through it in a tunnel. The Valley of the Shadow of Death was gay with gas lamps. The travelers enjoyed a stay in the City of Vanity Fair, which was given over to liberal religion that promised everything good without stint. But as the train approached the Celestial City, the passengers were seized by a terrible anxiety, and when they transferred to a steamboat for the last leg of their journey they discovered that their conductor, Mr. Smooth-it-away, was the Prince of Darkness and their destination was Hell.

In much the same spirit Oliver Wendell Holmes, noting the American passion for turning everything into money, wrote, "The mountains and cataracts, which were to have made poets and painters, have been mined for anthracite and dammed for water powers."

41

The Economy

A nation's "economy" is how its inhabitants earn and use their money. In considering the American economy it is necessary to keep in mind that it was, in a basic sense, "out of control."

In order for the landscape of ideas to impinge on the physical landscape, imagination, greed, and enormous amounts of what was called, in its various forms, "money" were essential. This so-called money came in a wide (and wild) variety of forms, from slips of paper printed up by individual storekeepers, which promised to pay the bearer as little as five cents, to Spanish pieces-of-eight and English silver shillings. Commercial paper, bank certificates, I.O.U.'s all circulated as "money." Credit was freely extended and as quickly withdrawn. In such a system or nonsystem, fraud and sharp dealing were endemic.

Credit was what lubricated the wheels of American business enterprise. "The advancement of America," Captain Marryat wrote, "depends wholly upon it. It is by credit alone that she has made such rapid strides, and it is by credit alone that she can continue to flourish. . . ." Even so, there was not nearly enough money or credit to be had in the United States to finance all the extravagant enterprises that the American imagination was capable of conceiving. From the early years of the republic English capital was actively sought to finance American ventures and, as the century wore on, that trend became more and more evident. The hard times of 1837 were caused in large part by the contraction of British credit due to a sharp recession in England. Philip Hone was moved to somber reflections on an economy tied so directly to events three thousand miles away. "The United States of America, by the grace of God free and independent as they style themselves, have, by a course of extravagant speculations, aided by bad management of the government, and the indulgence of personal spite of 'the Greatest and Best' [an apparent reference to Van Buren and his Cabinet], brought themselves into a state of thraldom to their old masters nearly as great as that which existed previous to the Declaration of Independence. All we undertake to do is predicated on the chance of borrowing money from John Bull. . . . Cotton, the only thing we have to pay with, is placed at the mercy of our creditors, and the Bank of England becomes the arbiter of the fate of the American merchant." By 1840 British bondholders had invested between a hundred and ten and a hundred and sixty-five million dollars in American state and territorial bonds alone.

One of the conspicuous features of the economy was the rapid growth in large fortunes and ostentatious styles of living. When John Jacob Astor died at the age of eighty-five, Philip Hone wrote in his diary that his wealth was estimated at between twenty and thirty millions, "and this immense, gigantic fortune was the fruit of his own labor, unerring sagacity, and far-seeing penetration. He came to this country at twenty years of age; penniless, friendless, without inheritance, without education, and having no example before him of the art of money-making, but with a determination to be rich. . . . All he touched turned to gold. . . ."

Stephen Whitney, a cousin of Eli, was a large-scale cotton speculator and real estate manipulator who left some fifteen million dollars when he died. He had amassed his huge fortune—second only, it was said, to that of John Jacob Astor—"without doing the least good to himself or anyone else," George Templeton Strong noted, adding, "His last act was characteristic and fitting. He locked up his checkbook and died."

The sixth national census, taken in 1840, showed roughly ten million people living along the Atlantic coast from Maine to Florida and inland to the Appalachians, and more than six million in the

Mississippi Valley and along the Gulf of Mexico. The free states contained 9,561,176 whites and 1,134 slaves. In the South were 4,634,519 whites, 2,486,321 slaves, and 215,569 free blacks. In the entire North and West, there were fewer than 200,000 free blacks.

The proportion of the population engaged in farming had declined from almost 90 percent in 1783 to slightly less than three-fourths. Eight hundred thousand were employed in "trade and manufactures." Almost ninety thousand made their living as sailors on oceangoing vessels or as boatmen on canal barges and steamboats. Lawyers and doctors accounted for approximately sixty-five thousand. Eight and a half percent of the population lived in "cities" of over eight thousand inhabitants.

In an economic sense there were two Americas that predominated. The first was the business and commercial world, the world of "merchants" and the captains of a small but growing world of industrial enterprise. They were concentrated in the large Eastern cities where they held the levers of economic power (which Jackson had been so determined to wrest from them) and, sporadically, political power, when they could persuade a large enough portion of the electorate that they represented more than simply their own interests, or, conversely, that their own interests were synonymous with those of the "people at large."

It was estimated that the total capital invested in manufacturing enterprises in the United States in 1840 was close to $268,000,000. Of this New York state accounted for some $55,000,000, Massachusetts $42,000,000, Pennsylvania $32,000,000, and Ohio next with an estimated $16,000,000. Eight years later the capital invested in manufacturing had risen to an estimated $350,000,000, an increase of 30 percent in eight years. The capital invested in cotton manufacturing had increased to $64,000,000, a gain of about 25 percent. The value of cotton goods was roughly $58,000,000. The manufactures of the states were calculated at the value of $340,000,000, while the worth of agricultural products was above $560,000,000.

As for the growth of industry, it, like so many other "progressive" developments, exacted a heavy human toll. Reports began to circulate that all was not well in those manufacturing havens of Lowell and Lawrence. There were rumors that long hours, increased work loads, and unhealthy working conditions were producing illness and disease rather than culture and high thinking among the "operatives." As the work became more arduous, the young ladies who had charmed the world with their nimble fingers and literary accomplishments were gradually replaced by Irish laborers. It was said, more commonly every day, that the "lords of the loom" were as harsh and tyrannical as the "lords of the lash," and that they were fit companions for each other. Amos Lawrence encouraged a Unitarian minister to write a gushy work praising the whole operation and commending "the moral machinery" of the factories (which now employed over twenty thousand men and women) as well as the physical, indeed implying that they were hardly to be distinguished in their beneficent effects.

But George Templeton Strong saw things in quite a different light. When the Pemberton mill in Lawrence collapsed, killing or maiming several hundred young women workers, Strong wrote in his diary, "News today of a fearful tragedy at Lawrence, Massachusetts, one of the wholesale murders commonly known in newspaper literature as accident or catastrophe. A huge factory, long notoriously insecure and ill-built, requiring to be patched and bandaged up with iron plates and braces to stand the introduction of its machinery collapsed into a heap of ruins yesterday. . . . Of course, nobody will be hanged. Somebody has murdered about two hundred people, many of them with hideous torture, in order to save money, but society has no avenging gibbet for the respectable millionaire homicide. Of course not. He did not want or mean to do this massacre; on the whole, he would have preferred to let these people live. His intent was not homicidal. He merely thought a great deal about making a large profit and very little about the security of human life. . . . It becomes us to prate about the horrors of slavery! What Southern capitalist trifles with the lives of his operatives as do our philanthropes of the North?"

A month or so later several tenements burned down in New York with heavy loss of life and two factories in Brooklyn blew up, killing a number of workers. Again Strong noted, "We are still a semi-barbarous race. . . . If a few owners or builders of factories and tenement houses would be hanged tomorrow, life would become less insecure."

The cotton-growing South and the mercantile and industrial North were completely interdependent. If boll weevils chomped excessively on the cotton bolls in Southern fields the effects were soon felt on Wall Street, on the Boston exchanges, and in the homes of mill hands in Pawtucket and Lowell. It was because of this economic dependence of the North upon the South that the activities of the abolitionists made many Northerners so frantic. It was evident that the abolitionists posed far greater dangers to the economy of the North than all the boll weevils in the South.

We are sometimes disposed to think of the great period of expansion in the production of cotton as following almost immediately upon the development of the cotton gin, but in the years between 1830 and the Civil War, the production of cotton rose from 731,452 bales to 4,541,285 annually, a sixfold increase. Unquestionably Southerners were right when they declared that much of the prosperity of the United States rested on the enormous output of slave labor. Moreover, such statistics strengthened Southerners in the conviction that the North simply could not afford to go to war to prevent the secession of the Southern states. Simple self-interest would force the North to enter into negotiations with the South to ensure a continuing supply of cotton for Northern mills. Without Southern cotton Northern industry must wither, banks must fail, and financial ruin must prevail.

Foreign trade was the merchant's lifeblood. A summary of American exports in 1838 listed trade with more than sixty countries and regions ranging from Russia and Prussia through the West Indies to Manila, China, "Asia generally," and the South Seas, and Chile and Peru. England and her possessions received by far the larger portion. Spain and her West Indian islands, the most important of which was Cuba, were next, followed by France and then Brazil and Chile. Holland was an important customer, as were the Dutch East and West Indies. Much American shipping was engaged in the "carrying trade." Almost 70,000 pounds of tea, for example, were transported from China to England that year and another 230,282 pounds to Brazil. More than a million pounds of coffee were carried to the French Mediterranean ports and a half million pounds to Belgium. Sugar was another article carried from the West Indian islands to numerous European and Mediterranean ports. Of articles processed or manufactured in the United States, dried fish went to the Caribbean islands, whale oil to Holland and the towns of the Hanseatic League. More than eight million pounds of pork products—ham, bacon, and lard, primarily—were exported, the greater part to Cuba. Flour in large quantities went to Brazil and Cuba, as well as many other South American countries. Rice was another major export commodity and, again, the greater part went to Cuba. Tobacco to the value of more than seven million dollars was shipped to the Hanse towns, England, and France. Soap, nails, refined sugar, gunpowder, and cotton cloth, the latter valued at $3,250,130, were sent primarily to Brazil, Mexico, Chile, and China. American exports came to a total of $96,033,821, with Great Britain and her possessions counting for $56,493,217 of that total. Of the American exports, cotton was valued at $61,556,811 and tobacco at $7,392,094. All other agricultural products came to only $9,105,514, while the total of manufactured goods was a comparatively modest $8,483,321. More than six thousand American vessels with a total tonnage of 1,302,974 tons were engaged in foreign trade; 65,000 men and boys manned them, or an average of slightly more than ten sailors to a ship.

Goods valued at $113,717,404 were imported into the United States during the same year (1838), much the greater part in American ships. Included were eighty-two million pounds of coffee and fourteen million pounds of tea. Raisins were another major item of import, as were silks, gold bullion, spices, wool, pottery, wines, molasses, sugar, and bar iron.

The cotton, tobacco, and rice of the South constituted almost two-thirds of the total exports of the United States. At the end of our period—1860—the dollar value of imports and exports had increased more than threefold—exports to the value of roughly $316,000,000, imports to $354,000,000.

Joel Barlow in his epic poem *The Vision of Columbus* had predicted the day when commerce would unite the world in one common human family governed by a "general council" of the "fathers of all empires." Each "remotest realm by friendship join'd,/Links in the chain that binds all human kind,/The union'd banners rise at last unfurl'd/And wave triumphant round the accordant world." If any Americans recalled that turgid work, it must have seemed to them that things were proceeding on schedule. American commerce was busy forging the "links" that Barlow had foreseen.

It appeared to Tocqueville that the principal appeal of commerce was that it appeared to most Americans the quickest road to fortune. "In democracies there is nothing greater or more brilliant than commerce; it attracts the attention of the public and fills the imagination of the multitude; all energetic passions are directed towards it." Moreover, since all Americans were engaged "in productive industry," they were able to combine their efforts to achieve some practical goal with remarkable speed and efficiency. The most striking examples were "the immense public works." On the other hand it was apparent to Tocqueville that as industry flourished an increasing division of labor resulted, with the consequence that "the workman becomes more weak, more narrow-minded, and more dependent. The art advances, the artisan recedes."

Industry was quick to take advantage of this development by exploiting labor, offering minimum wages, and calling on the courts to block efforts at labor organization on the grounds that it constituted conspiracy against the employers. "I am of the opinion," Tocqueville wrote, ". . . that the manufacturing aristocracy which is growing up under our eyes is one of the harshest that ever existed in the world; but at the same time it is one of the most confined and least dangerous." Tocqueville believed that "if ever a permanent inequality of conditions . . . again penetrates into the world . . . this is the gate by which it will enter."

The closest reading of the business mind was perhaps to be found in Freeman Hunt's *Merchants' Magazine and Commercial Review*. Hunt was a New York journalist who had served his apprenticeship with Sarah Hale on the enormously successful *Ladies Magazine*. In 1839 he published the first issue of *The Merchants' Magazine*. Thirty-eight volumes followed, until his death in 1858. With Hunt's magazine the apotheosis of the businessman began. The monthly journal contained a vast amount of useful information on such matters as prices, foreign and domestic, for various commodities; the state of the money market; abstracts of government reports on foreign trade; the price of gold; information on government bond issues; and many matters of interest to the business community.

In addition Hunt included death notices of prominent merchants and biographical sketches. In these, cumulatively, a new American type was defined—the pious, hardworking, moral, upright, philanthropic businessman of whom Alexander Henry was an exemplar. Scotch-Irish, born of prosperous and "respectable" parents, Henry came to the United States in his eighteenth year and got a job as a clerk in a Philadelphia dry goods store. So great was his "diligence, tact, and energetic zeal" that within two months he was made "superintendent of a branch of the house." Soon he went into business for himself, and, abundantly endowed with "that noble integrity which scorns concealment and abhors deceit; that liberality which relieves distress, and by its golden alchemy transmutes despair into hope," plus a dutiful submission to "the all-seeing Eye," he promptly acquired a fortune. No person was ever turned away by this merchant prince. "Many a half-ruined tradesman, many a broken-hearted woman . . . the widow and the orphan . . . went forth from the presence of Alexander Henry with glad tidings of relief. . . ." A pillar of the Presbyterian Church, he was also a founder of the American Sunday-school Union and a faithful distributor of Christian tracts.

In addition to his biographies, all of which had a numbing sameness about them, Hunt published essays on such subjects as "The True Mercantile Character"—excellent, needless to say. "Without unduly magnifying the calling of merchants," one such article began, "it must be conceded that they do now exert, and will continue to exert, a greater amount of influence for good or evil than any other class. All history attests to the truth of this maxim."

Hunt decided, in 1854, to collect and augment the biographical sketches and publish them in a book entitled *Lives of American Merchants*. "We have lives of the Poets and the Painters; lives of Heroes, Philosophers and Statesmen; lives of the Chief Justices and Chancellors," he wrote. But there was "a class of men whose patronage of art has been princely in its munificence, as their wealth has equalled that of princes, whose interests have become a chief concern of statesmen, and have involved the issues of peace and war; whose affairs afford a leading subject of the legislation of States . . . who can boast the magnificence of the Medici, and the philanthropy of Gresham and of Amos Lawrence; and whose zeal for science and zeal for philanthropy have penetrated to the highest latitude of the Arctic seas. . . ." These splendid, princely figures are, of course, the merchants. Hunt has thus embarked on the " 'Plutarch's Lives' of trade." The merchants were clearly not satisfied with simply being rich. They wished, like all Americans, to be morally justified and this the accommodating Hunt set out to make them.

The second economic world was that defined by agricultural production. Its agents were the millions of farmers scattered over the whole twenty-six states. They were relatively immune to the wild fluctuations of the world money markets, although any prolonged depression hurt them and was especially damaging to the rural towns on which they depended for goods and services and to their source of money, the banks, which usually failed at the mildest economic shock.

Corn and wheat were the staples of the Northern farmer. In 1850, 592,071,104 bushels of corn were produced in the United States. Pumpkins were commonly planted between the rows and the corn husking was one of the few interludes of play and hilarity that a farmer's life afforded. "Corn," Gustaf Unonius wrote, "plays such an important role in the life of the new settlers that one can hardly form a conception of pioneer life in America without visualizing a corn patch, a hoe, a corn crib . . . and inside the house ears hanging on the walls to dry, ears in the kettle, ears on the table." Nine-tenths of the hay and potatoes and two-thirds of the wheat of the country were grown in the North. The value of Northern wheat alone was twice that of all the major crops of the South with the exception of cotton.

If commerce and manufacturing on the one hand and agriculture on the other constituted the basis of the country's economy, they were both subject to severe financial shocks and dislocations. The Panic of 1837 was, in reality, the beginning of a depression or of a series of financial crises that lasted more than six years. By summer 1839 the financial news was gloomy in the extreme. Hone noted that "Wall Street looks blue. . . . Stocks have fallen, confidence is shaken; and money not to be bought." The mood of the business community was as "disastrous and gloomy almost as that of the great crisis three years ago. . . . Many of the millers and cotton-planters are ruined. . . . The natural consequence of all this is a recurrence of dreadfully hard times. The jobber cannot collect his debts or sell his goods; the capitalist grips his money with the hand of death." In Hone's opinion the new crisis was the result of "the bank difficulties in the Southern and Western States, occasioned by a premature resumption of specie payments. . . . Stocks have fallen suddenly; trade is at a standstill. New York cannot collect her debts and the banks are looking to their own safety." In the meantime prices rose so that, in Philip Hone's words, "how the poor man manages to get a dinner for his family passes my comprehension." In the midst of these new troubles he had the heretical thought that even "turning out Van Buren and his scurvy pack" would do little to improve things. In every state there was heated debate about the repudiation of the state's debts. The Democrats, by and large, supported repudiation on the grounds put forth by the *Democratic Expounder* in Detroit: "Undoubtedly the plighted faith of the State should be kept; but if it cannot be kept she must do the best she can consistently with her first duty—the public weal. All morality does not consist in keeping faith in dollars and cents." Michigan repudiated her state debt. Florida followed suit. Many states passed stay and exemption laws, the former preventing the seizure of a debtor's property to satisfy claims against him, the latter exempting a portion of the debtor's property from sale; in Georgia, for instance, twenty acres of land, and five more for each child under fifteen, a horse or mule, ten hogs, thirty dollars' worth of provisions, and dwellings and improvements to a value of not more than two hundred dollars were exempt. Kentucky excluded a saddle, bridle, six chairs, a bedstead, all chickens, turkeys, geese and ducks, one cow, five sheep, and six months' supply of fuel. In state after state laws providing for imprisonment for debt were repealed. One Southerner described Mississippi in 1840 as ruined. "Her rich men are poor and her poor are beggars. . . . The people are running their Negroes to Texas and Alabama and leaving their real estate and perishable property to be sold. So great is the panic and so dreadful the distress that there are a great many farms prepared to receive crops and some of them actually planted, and yet deserted, not a human being to be found upon them."

In Hone's view, "All this comes from the rage for speculation here, the desire to grow rich in a short time." The grower or commodity trader thus hoarded crops, waiting for the best price, and then, when the market collapsed, went down with it. What is worth noting about the passage is the relatively small role in the process that Hone, so hostile to the Democratic administration, assigns to the "bad management of the government." His condemnation of those who wish to "grow rich in a short time" comes somewhat ironically from a man who made a large fortune before he was forty. Hone was now relatively "old money," and he could indulge himself in criticism of those scrambling to achieve the financial eminence on which he rested.

The issue of indebtedness to British investors was an especially touchy subject in the business community, which was horrified by the disposition of state governments to repudiate their debts. "The English papers," Philip Hone wrote, "do abuse us shamefully for swindling, repudiation, cheating, and other trifling departures from rectitude," which was all the harder to bear, Hone felt, because it was, in large part, true. New York state, which had remained solvent, had to suffer for "the rascality of our brethern [in] Pennsylvania, Mississippi, Ohio, Indiana, and Illinois," all states that had repudiated their debts.

A different point of view was expressed to Richard Henry Dana by "the *Honorable* Thomas Laighton," formerly governor and now senator from New Hampshire, a radical Loco-Foco, whom Dana met on a trip to that state. He encountered Laighton "seated on the pier, dressed in the roughest manner, with a coarse dirty handkerchief about his neck, with an unwashed & uncombed appearance, a bloated vulgar face, chewing tobacco & whittling a stick with a jackknife. . . . I thought he

was the rankest specimen of a vulgar demagogue I had ever seen."
When Dana was introduced, the senator "kept his seat, & kept
whittling & chewing as before. . . ." Dana tested him with a question
about why so many Americans seemed "hardly to be trusted to manage
money matters?" Laighton's answer was that "foreign luxuries &
foreign notions . . . had corrupted our republican simplicity." But why
was it then that the old corrupt countries seemed to have higher
standards of fiscal responsibility? Dana asked. Laighton's reply was
that "money was everything here, & all could make it & he who could
make the most was at the head of society; while in England this was
qualified by hereditary rank & blood, wh. no money can buy. The
competition & the temptation was less universal & overpowering."

Early in 1842, after a brief economic revival, "the inflated banking
system with all its enormities" came crashing down. In Philadelphia the
Girard Bank, thought to be the soundest in the city, closed its doors
and, Sidney George Fisher noted, "fears were entertained that the
Girard Bk. would be attacked by the mob. If the other Banks go in the
same manner, with a large circulation of small notes in the hands of
the lower classes, a serious riot may be the result, and how far tumult &
bloodshed once commenced may extend it is not easy to predict."
Several days later Fisher expressed the opinion in his diary that only
heavy rains had prevented a serious riot.

A month later the pot was still boiling. Fisher wrote that "mobs
have assembled nightly in immense numbers opposite the Banks &
brokers' offices threatening violence. A deputation of 1000 men was
sent to Annapolis to *petition* the legislature, and marched in a body to
the hall. Volunteer companies are under arms every night, and a row is
constantly expected. So we go. In every part of the country confusion,
alarm, distress, violence and fraud. The people discontented and
turbulent, & property insecure, the government corrupt, imbecile,
impotent, debt, taxation, infamy; these are the results of our blessed
institutions. . . . Nothing but a village in the West can be more stupid,
triste, and village-like than Phila now. No society, no life or movement,
no topics or interest of any kind. Everybody has become poor & the
calamities of the times have not only broken up the gay establishments
& put an end to social intercourse, but seem to have covered the place
with a settled gloom. The streets seem deserted, the largest houses are
shut up and to rent, there is no business, no money, no confidence &
little hope, property is sold every day by the sheriff at a 4th of the

estimated value of a few years ago, nobody can pay debts, the miseries of poverty are felt by rich & poor, every one you see looks careworn & haggard. . . ."

The winter of '43–'44 saw an upturn in business, but by summer there was what Hone called "one of those astounding Wall Street revolutions gotten up by gamblers, and by which the turn of a day makes nabobs and beggars, and unsettles the minds of men who watch the brokers' books with anxiety equal to that which of old attended the development of the sibylline leaves." Stock prices had been inflated "by the process of bubble-blowing" to prices double and quadruple those of a week or so earlier. "Many who had 'sold ahead,' as it is called in Wall Street, were ruined by the change, and fortunes were made by men who had not sense or judgment to make a living at an honest calling." The inflated prices lasted some three days and then the manipulators of the market sold, stocks fell, and they "pocketed their gains, and laughed at their dupes."

The perpetual building of new railroad lines, new inventions, and advances in technology (the most spectacular of course being Samuel F. B. Morse's telegraph) all helped to fuel a new boom by 1845. Mining had assumed great importance with the growing demand for iron and coal. In Illinois the lead mines appeared to be virtually inexhaustible, while a vast coalfield was discovered stretching from southern New York to Alabama, estimated to be twelve times the extent of all the coalfields of Europe. As New England was the center of manufacturing, Pennsylvania was the seat of coal and iron. Alexander Mackay reported that the state had ten thousand square miles of coalfields, of both bituminous and anthracite coal, the latter employed especially in smelting, forging, and casting. Starting with an output of three hundred sixty-five tons of coal in 1820, the state's output had increased to almost a million and a half tons by 1848. The capital expenditures for canals and railroads in the Lehigh Valley alone amounted to over seven million dollars, while those in the Schuylkill region were calculated at over nineteen million.

Added to these stimuli were the Mexican War and, finally, at the end of the decade, the discovery of gold in California. Euphoria followed. "Individual prosperity has increased in this part of the Union," Philip Hone wrote; "men have grown rich in supplying the wants of the starving population of Ireland, palaces have been erected out of the freights of nine shillings sterling for flour; and the extravagance and love of show to which people are prone have had ample scope in the successful mercantile operations of the year." Sidney George Fisher's relative Henry Gilpin, a lawyer, had gotten a fee of sixty thousand dollars for helping to settle claims growing out of the Mexican War. This he had invested "in lots in some of the growing towns of the West—Milwaukee, Chicago, etc.—and they increased so rapidly & greatly in value that his fortune is now estimated at half a million," Fisher wrote.

Once again there were wild speculations, fortunes made and spent overnight, and an alarming rise in prices, but the cycle of boom and bust was disconcertingly rapid. A panic in 1854 was followed by a boom and then another, more devastating panic in 1857. A three-year cycle hardly allowed investors, speculators, and ordinary businessmen time to catch their breath.

Under the heading of September 20, 1857, Sidney George Fisher wrote: "There is now a panic & pressure in business similar to the disastrous year of 1837. Several of the oldest & strongest houses have failed and more trouble is anticipated." There was a run on the City Bank and the Bank of Commerce and "many families, lately rich, are plunged into actual poverty. Nearly all the factories have stopped work and thousands of the poor are thus thrown out of employment, now, at the approach of winter. Severe and extensive suffering will be the consequence, and very probably riots & popular tumult." Before six months were out, Fisher speculated, New York and Philadelphia would be "under the rule of vigilance committees or martial law. . . ." The cataclysm that most closely affected Fisher was the collapse of the Reading Railroad. "This vast corporation," he wrote, "with a capital of over 20 millions, employing thousands of laborers, and owned all over the country as an investment, stopped today."

As the depression deepened, Fisher noted, "The distress among the poor is becoming painfully evident already. Two men came here today for food. They said they could get no work & looked very wretched. One came to Henry's while we were there. The factories and workshops have all stopped and thousands are without employment. . . . It is feared that the roads, that our houses will not be safe."

Economic instability was the price that Americans seemed willing to pay for access to money or credit in whatever form and whatever the consequences. As one American explained the matter to George Combe, "this is a new country, and we must encourage enterprise; although we have many speculators and numerous bankruptcies, yet these are always helping forward the general advance of the country;

the individuals may fall, but the results of their speculations remain and add to the general wealth."

We have stressed throughout this work the theme that being an American has always been a "high anxiety" state. Nowhere is this more evident than in the economic sphere. Economic anxieties supplemented sexual anxieties. Clearly Americans must go ahead at all costs. Dubious credit went with dubious practices. Extravagant expectations collapsed into despair. Sidney George Fisher's diary carried a constant note of anxiety about the economic conditions of the country. In a typical entry he wrote, "everything looks so gloomy & uncertain, the business of the country, thro fraud & mismanagement is in so deplorable a condition, and the politics of the country so debased and ignorant, that there is no security for anything."

The most persistent anxiety—"a fifty-pound weight of foreboding" that George Templeton Strong felt—related to financial insecurity. Although he was often oppressed by fears of "all sorts of nameless calamities . . . first and worst is that standing bane of man's existence on earth—the fear of want of money—tenfold worse than the reality, bad as that would be. . . . It's a periodical disease with me, a causeless attack of insane, gnawing, corroding, burning, suffocating anxiety and despair about my own resources and prospects, my ability to fight my way through the world and carry my little wife through it in comfort and honor. When the disease is upon me I'm a pitiable case, sick at heart, disgusted with myself, and able to exist only by working hard and drinking coffee."

The point to be stressed is that year in and year out, whatever might happen in the stock markets, however many banks might fail or merchants be forced to close their doors, American farmers planted and reaped vastly larger crops and, allowing for the inevitable natural disasters of drought and flood, developed cheaper and more expeditious methods to get them to markets, domestic and foreign. In that endless and largely uninterrupted growing, the nation's economy also grew, so to speak, in spite of itself—by the labors of millions of farmers moving relentlessly westward and putting each year millions of new acres under their insatiable plows, turning up dollars as they plowed up the virgin earth. In the face of that elemental fact the chaotic state of the economy assumed a relative unimportance. Every financial disaster would, in time, be retrieved. The vast continent existed to be turned, if possible, into money—the land, the animals on it, the forests, even the mountains laced with valuable ores. Philip Hone was ecstatic at the news that a party of hunters had arrived in St. Louis in the summer of 1839 with twenty-four thousand buffalo robes and "a quantity of beaver, worth altogether $100,000." "Twenty-four thousand buffaloes," he rhapsodized, "what a sublime idea for any man who has ever seen a buffalo or a drawing of one or heard him described . . . the imagination cannot keep pace with the magnificent scale on which the works of nature are represented in the regions of the great West."

Most of the "professional" discussions about the American economy started with the Scriptures. Henry Vethake was professor of mathematics at the College of New Jersey but he taught and wrote extensively on economics. He was concerned over the fact that the theories of economists "have been sometimes suspected as leading to conclusions inconsistent with the precepts of revealed religion." In "An Essay on the Moral Relations of Political Economy" Vethake urged that the unemployed poor be provided with work at public expense but at a rate lower than that of "the independent labourer," so that they would have an incentive to seek work in what we call today the private sector. Otherwise their moral fiber would deteriorate. Vethake was insistent that capital formation was the essence of a progressive economy, that savings were of primary importance but, since spending was essential to stimulate the economy, saving should be balanced by spending. This not particularly illuminating reflection was characteristic of much economic theorizing.

Vethake was a devoted advocate of property rights, which he identified with the most basic moral principles. Trade unions were, on the other hand, a terrible bane to a society since they interfered with free competition and used coercion to increase the wages of their members at the cost of the employer. Equally reprehensible were laws reducing working hours, since their effect was to raise wages. Moreover, it might be anticipated that hours so gained would be spent in dissipation. It followed that shorter hours would be unhealthy for the workingman. To Vethake, economics was a reenforcement to Christianity, since by providing the theoretical basis for the protection of property it ensured orderly progress and demonstrated "unequivocally that the physical condition . . . of mankind, or . . . the command which each individual of a community, on the average, enjoys over the necessities and luxuries of life, depends . . . on moral causes."

The economists of the period, so far as they deserved the name, split on the issue of free trade versus protection (or the American

System) depending, in part, on their sectional origin, but they preserved a solid front on the sanctity of property and in their view of the workingman and his wages. The poor should receive the minimum assistance to prevent actual starvation because, as a popular economics text put it, "Where poor rates are the highest, the poor will be found the most discontent and lawless and the most inveterate against the rich." The accumulation of wealth was, like everything else in the universe, subject to divine laws. "Everyone, for instance, knows that no man can grow rich without industry and frugality," the Reverend Francis Wayland declared in his *The Elements of Political Economy*.

These pious observations hardly take account of Smart and Slick, Incorporated, and suggest how far Wayland and his colleagues were from engaging the real economic issues of American life. Sidney George Fisher was a much sounder economist when he wrote: "In making money the great thing is to get a start & the command of capital. With this & judgment to use it, such is the rapid increase in the value of property in our growing cities, it is easy enough to get rich." This was the source of most of his brother Henry's wealth. "He buys a lot for 40 or $50,000, cuts it up, lets it on ground rent sometimes at a profit of 2 or 300 per ct., &, as soon as the lots are improved, sells the grd. rents. He now has 150 houses building on various lots."

What the German sociologist Max Weber called the Protestant Ethic—thrift, piety, and hard work (along with "early to bed and early to rise")—was supposed to make a man "healthy, wealthy and wise," though of course it did none of these things, and the way to wealth was clearly through the shrewd and often unscrupulous manipulation of money and power.

By 1850 the working population of the United States had grown to 7,700,000, of whom 4,900,000 or roughly 65 percent were farmers. Twenty-five thousand were listed as involved in lumbering or fisheries and 90,000 in mining. Manufacturing and skilled crafts, such as shoemaking and building, accounted together for 1,260,000 and "trade"—stores and shops—for 420,000.

Ten years later, in 1860, with a total population of 31,443,321, there was a white working population of 10,530,000, an increase of almost three millions; the number of farmers had increased by something over a million while miners had almost doubled and the category of manufacturing and construction had grown by half a million, a much larger proportional increase.

Wages remained remarkably stable over the entire period, approximately seventy-five cents a day for common labor—rising in 1839 to a dollar and then declining to seventy-five cents again—a dollar twenty-five for carpenters, and a dollar fifty to a dollar seventy-five for masons. Farm workers were paid approximately forty cents a day for casual labor and eight to ten dollars a month as regular hired hands.

What these figures reveal is a steady and, indeed, accelerating shift from an economy based almost exclusively on agriculture to an increasingly "mixed" economy in which manufacturing, building, handicrafts, mining, "trade," and common labor played an important role. Jefferson would have been dismayed at such a development, Hamilton, presumably, delighted. Jefferson would doubtless have derived some comfort from the growth of "democracy" although mid-nineteen-century American democracy was a far cry from the independent yeoman-farmer democracy that he had celebrated. And Hamilton, if he would have applauded the growth of business and industry, would certainly have been more convinced than ever of the "bestiality" of the people and their indifference to the principles of sound government.

42

Education

Whatever else might divide them, on one point most Americans seemed in accord—education was a highly desirable, indeed almost sacred, thing and the United States could hardly get enough of it. One of the important reforms of the age had to do with making elementary and secondary education available to more pupils. Workingmen's associations, rejecting the pauper schools established by benevolent societies because of the stigma of poverty associated with them, had agitated more actively for free public schools than for any other beneficial legislation.

In Massachusetts, Horace Mann, secretary of the newly established state Board of Education, a reformer, a Unitarian transcendentalist, and a practical politician, founded a state teaching or "normal" school to develop standards and teach teachers.

Teaching had, to this point, been largely an amateur operation. Typically it was done by young women waiting to be married or by young men studying law or looking about for a profession. Mann professionalized teaching, working tirelessly to improve the conditions under which teachers taught, to raise their salaries to the point where able young men and women were attracted to teaching, and to give them professional training. School terms were extended, the curricu-

lum expanded, and specialized subject matter introduced. Elected to
Congress in 1848, Mann worked there to promote the principle of at
least a free elementary school education for every child in the country.
A man of great personal charm, Mann recruited a company of
idealistic young men and women to disseminate his ideas.

After Mann's death in 1859, his friend Theodore Parker wrote, "I
think there is but one man in America who has done the nation such
great service—that is Garrison; the two were much alike in their
philanthropy and hatred of all oppression, in their asceticism and
puritanic austerity, in their cleanness of life and readiness to sacrifice
their own interests for a general good. . . . Mann had benevolence in
the heroic degree. I have known none who more deeply and heartily
wished for the welfare of mankind. . . . He took up the common
schools of Massachusetts in his arms and blessed them. Here was the
great work of his life. . . . How he did work! How he did fight! how he
licked the schoolmasters! . . . His good work here will live; one
hundred years hence three generations will have tested its blessed
influence, the last and deepest of all."

In 1835 there were only seven hundred sixty-two public schools in
operation in New York. Four years later there were five thousand
"common schools, thirty-eight academies, and seven female seminaries," in addition to a number of private schools. All were locally
supported, with additional appropriations from the state. By 1846
there were more than ten thousand school districts and the amount of
money expended for education by the state was $456,970. Alexander
Mackay, the English visitor, calculated that if England spent money for
elementary education at a comparable rate, it would spend ten times as
much as it had spent in the same year. In addition there were more
than six hundred private academies and grammar schools, as well as
Columbia College, New York University, and Union College in
Schenectady. There were in the same year (1846) one hundred nine
colleges scattered about the states, the vast majority of them
denominational or "sectarian" institutions.

A divisive issue among New York Whigs was the question of the
use of public money for the establishment of schools for the children
of foreigners to be taught in their own language and by teachers of
their own faith. The most inflammatory aspect of the proposal was, of
course, public support for Catholic parochial schools. William Seward,
the liberal governor of the state, made the grave political mistake of
supporting the legislation. The party was at once seriously split.

In the common schools of Boston, the master had to be able to teach "orthography, reading, grammar, geography, history, writing, arithmetic, and book-keeping" and where a majority of the "parents of the children require it, he must also teach German," George Combe noted. Combe was critical of the conditions in the public schools. The pupils were often crowded in poorly lit and poorly ventilated rooms. They were not taught "the laws of health, the laws by which the production and distribution of wealth are regulated, or the laws which determine the progress of society." The student thus comes forth "a free-born, self-willed, sanguine, confident citizen, of what he considers to be the greatest, the best, the wisest nation on earth, and he commences his career in life guided chiefly by the inspirations of his own good pleasure."

Combe had another interesting observation. He noted that parents put great pressure on teachers in the public elementary or "common schools" simply to teach their children to read without particular attention to the meaning of what they were reading. A teacher told Combe that the parents "complained . . . of time spent in explaining words and teaching objects as being 'lost' "; and the school boards, "to satisfy them, desired her to make them 'read,' and not to waste time in giving explanations. She obeyed, and certainly the children read with great fluency; but the meaning of the words is to a great extent unknown to them."

By 1850 there were in the country 80,985 public schools with 91,966 teachers, indicating that a large number were one-room, one-teacher schoolhouses. There were 119 colleges and 44 schools of theology.

By the time Isabella Bird arrived in the United States in 1854, schools in the larger cities were commonly housed in "extremely handsome" buildings "and are fitted up at great expense, with every modern improvement in heating and ventilation," she wrote. "Children of every class residing within the limits of the city, are admissible without payment." Several of the schools that Bird visited in New York City had more than two thousand pupils. "It is not uncommon," she noted, "to see the children of wealthy storekeepers side by side with those of working mechanics." Each school had a large assembly hall and spacious classrooms with "substantial mahogany desks only holding two. . . . The common school is one of the glories of America, and every citizen may be justly proud of it. It brings together while in a pliant condition the children of people of different origins; and besides diffusing knowledge among them, it softens the prejudices of race and party, and carries on a continual process of assimilation." Isabella Bird also noted that "to encourage those habits of order and self-reliance to which so much weight is attached in the States each pupil is made responsible for the preservation and security of her books and all implements of education."

The New York City Board of Education had established a Normal School on the model of those started in Massachusetts by Horace Mann. Most of its students were "assistant-teachers in the common schools and attended the normal schools on Saturdays, to enable themselves to obtain further attainments, and higher qualifications for their profession."

If Horace Mann was the brilliant organizer and reformer of primary and secondary education, his coadjutor, William Holmes McGuffey, provided the essence of the curriculum in his famous *Eclectic Readers*. President of Cincinnati College at the age of thirty-six and then of Ohio University from 1839 to 1843, McGuffey accepted the chair of moral philosophy at the University of Virginia and sat in it for almost thirty years.

McGuffey *Readers* were a remarkable amalgam of pious essays and literary pieces by well-known authors, heavily interspersed with scriptural texts. The intention of Christian nurture was plainly stated. One typical selection read, "God has given you minds which are capable of indefinite improvement; he has placed you in circumstances peculiarly favorable for making such improvements; and to inspire you with diligence in mounting up the shining course before you, he points you to the prospect of an endless existence beyond the grave."

Another passage pointed out the wickedness of an excessive love of money: "Of all God made upright and in their nostrils breathed a living soul, most fallen, most prone, most earthy, most debased is the miser who lives for money. He is also the greatest fool for those in material abundance often die of utter spiritual want." Pupils were promised, "You will see the throne of God. . . . You will see God, the Savior, seated on that majestic throne, and Angels in numbers more than can be counted, will fill the universe with their glittering wings and their rapturous songs."

McGuffey believed that the universe was a wondrously interwoven manifestation of God's wisdom and benignity, and he desired his *Readers* to convey that message. "From its stupendous magnitude," he wrote, "its irresistible energies, and its unequivocal evidences of design, we ascribe to its cause the attribute of infinite power controlled and directed by infinite wisdom. This would seem to be the lowest character of the Creator deductible from his works, even in ruins."

The famous *Fourth Reader* contained fifty-one poems and seventy-nine prose selections, including Shakespeare, Milton, Bacon, Byron, Washington Irving, and Harriet and Henry Ward Beecher, in addition, of course, to copious extracts from the Bible. As important as the material included was McGuffey's emphasis on "grading"—that is to say, selecting readings that would be suitable to the age of the reader and would advance with his or her developing comprehension. It was said that McGuffey tried out his selections on children of different ages before including them in his readers. Each selection was followed by a series of questions, designed to assure understanding of its meaning. The selections were meant to be read aloud with special attention to pronunciation and the quality of expressiveness.

In the words of one reviewer, "The books are such as to impart clear and well defined ideas to the minds of the pupils. The proper gradation is observed in the selection and arrangement of lessons, keeping pace with the increasing ability on the part of the reader to overcome new difficulties. . . . A fine moral effort is made in these lessons which should be ranked among the prominent merits of these books."

Taken together, the *Readers* contained a complete "system" of the universe and moral precepts covering every aspect of personal behavior. It was a remarkably coherent and ordered world that emerged from them. Good is rewarded; evil is punished. The child is loved by God and his or her immortal soul is in God's keeping. In addition, Americans are clearly God's chosen people, the special recipients of his grace.

It is important to note that as the century wore on and subsequent editions appeared, some long after McGuffey's death, the emphasis on the *Readers* shifted markedly from "piety" to "moralism." That is to say, where the early *Readers* contained an explicit theology covering life on earth and in the hereafter, the later editions stressed moral behavior, industry, temperance, honesty, kindness, perseverance in the face of adversity.

The first McGuffey *Reader* was published in 1836 and by 1850 over nine million had been sold. By 1920 over one hundred twenty million had passed through the hands of small readers. Thus it does not seem farfetched to assume that McGuffey may well have had more influence on the shaping of American values and American minds in the last two-thirds of the nineteenth century than any other individual or event of that era.

Given the American preoccupation with the word, it is not surprising that the elementary and high schools emphasized rhetoric and elocution. One such text instructed the pupil to master:

"A well-defined Principle associated with each Emotion . . . Articulation . . . Inflection, Stress, Emphasis, Pause, Tremor, Circumflex . . . Spirited Declamation. Gay, Brisk, and Humorous Description . . . Dignified Sentiments; Solemn and Impressive Thoughts; Deep Solemnity, Awe, Consternation."

In a section on "Rate or Movement of the Voice" the novice speakers were exhorted to use "Slow Movement" to suggest "Melancholy, Grandeur, Vastness," and "Lively Movement" to suggest gaiety and lightheartedness. The main body of the book was taken up with selections from a wide variety of writers—from Shakespeare to Washington Irving—meant to give proper range to all the elocutionary nuances and all themselves making an improving or uplifting moral. Class recitations were constant and students were required to memorize poetry by the yard. Mixed in were lavish portions of the patriotism that we have noted before—the United States as all-powerful, just, virtuous, and immortal.

Gradually the curriculum expanded and became more demanding. In Boston in 1858, Aleksandr Lakier, the young Russian tourist, noted that at the boys' high school, and at the girls' high school as well, in a three-year course the "young people . . . are taught ancient geography, general history, algebra, geometry, trigonometry as applied to measurement, surveying navigation, astronomy, more on the United States Constitution, bookkeeping, drawing, French and Spanish." Those who wished to stay an extra year and pursue their studies further could take philosophy, logic, mechanics, "the engineering arts and higher mathematics."

By 1858 attendance at primary school was compulsory for every child residing in the city. Lakier was fascinated to discover that an official called a "truant officer" tracked down children who did not attend school and made "the parents or relatives send the children to the nearest school . . ." where each teacher was responsible for some fifty children. Lakier was "amazed at the speed with which the children answered questions that were quite complicated for their age, and solved arithmetic problems."

There is substantial evidence that at least in the private boys' schools attended by the sons of the Eastern upper class the experiences of the pupils were anything but enlivening. Richard Henry Dana's school life was dismal. In addition to frequent beatings he recalled that one master "had a mode of punishment rather peculiar to himself; that of pulling the ears of boys, & dragging them about by their ears. He sometimes dragged boys a good part of the way across the school room, & over the benches in this manner."

George Templeton Strong remembered with repugnance his days at the Grammar School of Columbia College and "the foul, ill-ventilated den in which I was bullied, insulted, and tormented from October 1832 to October 1834. . . ." Years later, as a trustee of Columbia, Strong signed the report recommending the abolition of the school "with a thrill of keen satisfaction" and "a feeling that long-cherished views of vengeance were fulfilled at last. In no decade of my life since 1834 has there been one hundredth part the sense of misery (oppression, terrorism, subjugation, tyranny) that I was wilting under every day of those dark years of suffering at the Grammar School." Strong had been "an ambitious and interested" student "far beyond the average schoolboy standard," but he had received little help or encouragement from his masters, conventional "gentlemen" who performed their pedagogical tasks in a thoroughly uninspired manner.

Charles Francis Adams, Jr., looking back on his own education at what was reputed to be the best boys' school in the country, Boston Latin, felt it had been a disaster. "The school building," he recalled, "was a cold, dreary, granite edifice, of the stonemason style of architecture in vogue about 1840." Like George Templeton Strong, Adams was delighted when it was torn down: "I rejoiced to see it go! It effaced to a degree a hateful memory," he wrote. He had spent three years at the Latin School and "loathed it." "Not one single cheerful or satisfactory memory is with me associated therewith. Its methods were bad, its standards low, its rooms unspeakably gloomy. It was a dull, traditional lifeless day-academy, in which a conventional, common-place, platoon-front, educational drill was carried on. I absolutely languished there. . . ." Years later Adams asked a classmate who had been an outstanding scholar if he had sent his children to Boston Latin. The classmate turned on Adams "and vindictively snapped out, 'Latin School, I wouldn't send a dog to the Latin School!'" "I think of the period I spent there still as the dreariest, the most depressing and the most thoroughly worse and profitless of my life," Adams wrote in his autobiography.

The testimony of Dana, Strong, and Adams is supported by others of their social class. It seems reasonably clear, especially when we compare the traditional private-school education that upper-class Americans were subjected to with the far freer and more imaginative courses of instruction that prevailed at Brook Farm and Oneida, that private secondary education in the period we are concerned with in this volume was an educational wasteland, far less concerned with education in any real sense than with imposing on its victims a rigid and repressive pattern of thought and behavior. "A perfect system of education, if it could be devised," Adams wrote, "would be one which, while developing to the fullest extent all the faculties, would allow free play to the special aptitude. But this," he added, "is just what our American school system fails to do, and does not aim at. In that a child is—a child! and all children are cast in the same matrix."

Moritz Busch was impressed by the widespread network of American educational institutions, especially in New England and the Mississippi Valley West. But he described it as a "training system for moneymaking." On the other hand, he praised the elementary schools, "in regard to both the instructional method and the selection of the subjects of instruction"—reading, writing, arithmetic, geography, and English grammar. In Cincinnati the city schools, supported by state school funds and local tax monies, were supplemented by parochial and private schools. After elementary school many young men and women went on to academies or "high schools," where mathematics and world history were taught in addition to American history, natural science, the state and federal constitutions, geometry and surveying. Colleges commonly offered what was called, rather vaguely, "a thorough classical education" along with professional training in law, medicine, or theology. If all three were offered the college claimed to be a "university." For those students who had not the time or money to attend college, a "central high school" had been established in Cincinnati with a modified college curriculum; "in this way," Busch wrote, "the children of the poor have a sort of 'free university' in which the talented and ambitious among them have tuition-free access to the higher studies, such as the ancient languages, astronomy, chemistry and political science."

Like most larger cities Cincinnati offered "additional means of instruction in the lyceums, where traveling scholars give lectures; in scientific societies, such as the local *Mechanics Institute*; and in the libraries, among which the *Mercantile* Libraries occupy a most respected position."

There was also a college in Cincinnati which specialized "in the training of dentists—the number of which, by the way, is extraordinarily large in all American cities," Moritz Busch wrote. In addition, Cincinnati had four business schools and five colleges of theology run by various denominations.

If denominational rivalries led to the founding of innumerable colleges in virtually every state in the Union (Ohio led by a substantial margin), the pressure to perpetuate them induced trustees and faculty in time to deemphasize the denominational character of the institutions in order to appeal to more prospective students. At the same time the denominational colleges looked on themselves as bulwarks against infidelity and political and social radicalism. Certainly there was much truth in Francis Wayland's statement that "the legislatures of this country have never done for even professional education one tithe of what has been done by the various denominations of Christians among us. In many cases the state has done nothing; at best it has generally done but little. . . ." Philip Lindsley, trained at Princeton and president of the University of Nashville, deplored "abolitionism, and radicalism, and agrarianism, and ultraism, and amalgamationism, and Loco-Focoism, and Lynchism, and Fanny-Wrightism" which were "all the rage."

In the older and more prestigious institutions of the East such as Harvard, Yale, and Princeton, a sharp struggle took place over the nature of higher education and, more specifically, the question of "classical education" with a heavy emphasis on Greek and Latin, versus a more practical and professionally oriented education. It was, in effect, the old debate that John Adams and Benjamin Rush had carried on almost a generation earlier, Adams favoring the classical, Rush the practical. This debate was gradually overshadowed by another one which hinged on the nature of scholarship itself, on rigorous academic training as opposed to an emphasis on character, on moral training and deportment, on the development of certain upper-class manners and attitudes that constituted what a few bolder spirits still dared to call "a gentleman."

The famous Yale Report of 1828 declared that Yale's purpose was not to teach that which is peculiar to any one of the professions; but to "lay the foundation which is common to them all." "Classical discipline" formed "the best preparation for professions of divinity and law. . . ." In the words of one of its advocates, a classical education was "especially adopted to form the taste, and to discipline the mind, both in thought and diction, to the relish of what is elevated, chaste, and simple."

When young American scholars began to travel to the new seats of learning at Göttingen and Heidelberg another element entered the equation. To the argument as to whether higher education should be "practical" or "classical" was added the question of whether it should not, above all, be "scholarly." George Tichnor and George Bancroft had gone to Göttingen and there been intoxicated by the serious and searching character of German scholarship, which in its rigor and thoroughness made American and English colleges look like finishing schools for the sons of the well-to-do. Tichnor had written enthusiastically to Jefferson as early as 1815 that the new scholarship had brought the German universities "forward in forty years as far as other nations have been three centuries in advancing & which will yet carry them much further." Tichnor was impressed by the "unwearied & universal diligence among their scholars—a *general* habit of laboring from fourteen to sixteen hours a day—which will finally give their country an extent and amount of learning of which the world before has had no example." The German university, for better or worse, made modern Germany. They did this, as Tichnor perceived, by working professors as hard as day laborers and inducing them to compete more fiercely than Mississippi River steamboat captains or American business tycoons. To the young men who made their way to the great German universities it was a revelation. American colleges were mere nurseries. Only in Germany could one get a glimmering of the power and excitement of intellectual things.

Francis Lieber, a student of Barthold Niebuhr, the great German historian, a political refugee from Germany in 1827 and the "father" of American political science, attributed the remarkable achievements of German scholarship to the fact that "the German's life is entirely within him." Barred from political activity, he must perforce turn his energy and his intelligence into the "private" realm of scholarship, "because almost the only field of ambition of a German, I mean that ambition which looks beyond the life of the individual and seeks for another distinction than that of wealth and titles, is science. . . ."

After wandering about the Continent and lingering for a time in Spain Tichnor returned home to take a chair in Spanish literature at

Harvard and write his great work on that subject, but he was determined to reform Harvard along the lines of the German university. Tutors must be replaced by lecturers or at least made subordinate to the lecturers. The lecturers should be the most outstanding scholars in their field. The old system had revolved around a text and a classroom recitation, presided over too often by a drowsy tutor. Such was mere rote learning, conducted at the droning pace to inattentive youths. Tichnor was convinced that only by creating specialized departments of study could genuine intellectual rigor be achieved. George Bancroft, echoing Tichnor's enthusiasm, added a characteristic American caveat. He wished to transplant German historical scholarship, which had made the "the darkest portions of history become almost transparent," to America "if we could engraft it on a healthy tree, if we could unite it with a high moral feeling, if learning could only go to school with religion." It was wonderful to see what "German perseverance" could do when united with "reason and acuteness . . . every author is read, every manuscript is collected, every work perused, which can be useful, be it dull or interesting, the work of genius or stupidity . . . the most trifling coins and medals, the ruins of art. . . ."

Tichnor's efforts at reform were rebuffed by the Harvard faculty, who reaffirmed their faith in the classical curriculum, but Tichnor was able to organize a department of literature within the college and within that students could "elect" to take courses of special interest to them rather than following a rigidly prescribed curriculum. The seed was planted. By 1842, Francis Wayland, the president of Brown University, was able to say, "the lecture room has become a center of universal attraction."

As a young intellectual interested in many of the issues addressed by George Tichnor at Harvard, George Templeton Strong was deeply concerned by the fact that many of the older Columbia professors had settled into their chairs and abandoned any pretense of keeping up with the advances in their fields. This was especially serious in the fields of engineering and in the sciences. One of the liberal Columbia trustees argued that "professors may be prevented from degenerating into drones . . . by requiring of them to accomplish something every year or every six months, making it a condition of holding office that at certain periods they produce some essay, memoir, or investigation in their respective departments. . . ." It was a notion Strong sympathized with. His efforts to have a first-rate chemist chosen by the trustees to fill a vacant chair in the science faculty having failed because the candidate was a Unitarian and the Board of Trustees was dominated by Episcopal "fogeys," George Templeton Strong reflected ruefully that his college was probably destined to be "a sleepy, third-rate high school for one or two generations more." Although Strong was anxious to reform his alma mater, his notions of educational change fell far short of Peter Cooper's plans for an institute that would stress practical and aesthetic studies for the workingman. "Cooper," Strong wrote, "is very well meaning but very silly for a self-made millionaire. All his conceptions of his future university . . . are amorphous, preposterous, and impractical."

Fraternities were established at Columbia as early as 1836. Twenty years later George Templeton Strong noted with sharp disapproval the hold they had on students; a friend of his removed his son from the college because "the youth belonged to some mystic association designated by two Greek letters which maintained a sort of club room over a Broadway grocery store, with billiard tables and a bar."

An area of growing tension lay in the conflict between autocratic boards of trustees and faculty members increasingly concerned with improving the standards and the standing of their profession, and convinced that they were better judges of most academic matters than the trustees who were commonly successful businessmen. Francis Wayland was anxious to expand the Brown curriculum to make it more useful to "merchants, farmers and manufacturers." He wished to see undergraduate students learn "a *smaller* number of things *well*. By learning one science well, we learn *how to study*, and how to master a subject. Having made this attainment in one study, we readily apply it to all others."

Since only a relatively few Americans attended colleges or universities, these institutions came under frequent attack as undemocratic, attacks similar in spirit to that of William Manning, the Billerica farmer who had complained in 1792 of people who were "always crying up the advantages of costly collages, national acadimyes & grammer schooles, in ordir to make places for men to live without work." Annoyed by such criticisms, Philip Lindsley expressed his willingness to call them anything the people wished—lyceums or "popular intellectual workshops," if that sounded more democratic. He was quite ready to accept the principle that if "liberal" education was an aid to happiness, everyone should have access to it. He looked forward thus to the day "when it will not be deemed anti-republican for the labourer to be intellectual and to comprehend the Constitution." This clearly put Lindsley in William Manning's camp but in opposition to the great majority of his colleagues, who continued to think of colleges either as training schools for ministers and missionaries, and, less often, for lawyers and doctors, or as institutions where those whose parents could afford the tuition learned the manners and assembled the rather lightweight intellectual baggage needed to maintain their upper-class or upper-middle-class social position or, in many instances, to ascend to it.

One of the most serious problems faced by all colleges was the failure of students to complete the work required for their degrees. At Iowa State University in the 1860s only fifteen students graduated out of six hundred who entered. At Harvard the percentage of graduating students was much higher—20 percent it was said. Things were not so different in Great Britain, where, David Macrae reported, only 39 students out of 661 at Aberdeen received their M.A. degrees; at Edinburgh it was 53 out of 661.

Iowa, like Oberlin, admitted women without discrimination. Like many others, the Reverend David Macrae, who visited both institutions, expressed doubts about the effects of coeducation. Women, he was convinced, gained intellectually, "and in some respects morally." But he felt that such education might impair "the delicate modesty and refinement" which constituted their principal charm. When he quizzed a young male Oberlin graduate, he confessed that "the idea of kissing a girl who had studied anatomy, and knew quadratic equations, alarmed me at first, but after making the experiment, I found the kiss the sweetest I had ever got in my life."

When we speak or think of private American colleges and universities in the middle decades of the nineteenth century, we are apt to have in mind such venerable places as Harvard, Brown, and Amherst, but there were also hundreds of others, most of them almost as ephemeral as the fruit fly. They ranged from high-minded and underfunded ventures directed at the reform of existing educational practices to fly-by-night diploma mills where rather than acquiring a legitimate and negotiable sheepskin the pupil got fleeced instead. There were, for example, in the state of Tennessee alone in 1848, twenty-five "colleges" and "universities" with the authority to award degrees, institutions which were "bought and sold on the open market." A decade later only six were still in business. Nonetheless, in the aggregate this class of academic ephemera managed to give a leg or legs up to tens of thousands of ambitious youths in modest circumstances. So far as I know no one has ever bothered to compile an inventory of them all but I am confident they would number in the thousands and their students in the hundreds of thousands.

It is easy enough to determine the curriculum of one college or another. It is much more difficult to discover how it affected the students who were subjected to it. Again we have the testimony of Charles Francis Adams, Jr., as to the Harvard Class of '56 of which he was a resigned member. "In one word," he wrote: "the educational trouble with Harvard in my time was the total absence of touch and direct personal influence as between student and instructor. . . . It was not good form—it was contrary to usage—for the instructors and instructed to hold personal relations. Our professors in the Harvard of the 'fifties' were a set of rather eminent scholars and highly respectable men. They attended to their duties with commendable assiduity, and drudged along in a dreary humdrum sort of way in a stereotyped method of classroom instruction. But as for giving direction to, in the sense of shaping, the individual minds of young men in their most plastic stage, so far as I know nothing of the kind was even dreamed of; it never entered into the professorial mind. This was what I needed, and all I needed—an intelligent, inspiring direction; and I never got it, nor a suggestion of it. . . . No instructor produced, or endeavored to produce, the slightest impression on me; no spark of enthusiasm was sought to be infused into me." It would be a mistake to extrapolate from Charles Francis Adams, Jr., to all Harvard undergraduates in the period 1826–1860, or from Harvard to the wide variety of institutions of so-called higher education in the United States. There is no question that in many of them, and perhaps for some fortunate individuals even at Harvard, students found inspiring teachers and enjoyed that close personal contact that Adams so yearned for and without which, one is tempted to say, no genuine education can take place. What is undoubtedly true is that Harvard, increasingly, became a model for other institutions to strive to emulate and one of the consequences of that effort at emulation was an increasing formal and distant relation between teacher and student. If that was the way Harvard did it, many ambitious tank-town colleges concluded, that must be the right way.

What we can say, I think with some confidence, is that, with a few exceptions, the colleges and universities that existed in the first half of the nineteenth century played a very modest role in the intellectual life of the nation. Their curricula were both undemanding and rigid; the performance of academic tasks by pupils and their masters was little more than perfunctory; their social bias was strongly Federalist-Whig-conservative—institutions like Lane Seminary and Oberlin College, with strong radical Christian leanings, being notable exceptions. Certainly whatever there was of radical social criticism was lodged in such institutions. Yale and Harvard were already inclining toward the Germanic ideal of scholarship, which saw the professor as a figure above the battle, someone who viewed the world, so far as possible, with a degree of distance or objectivity. A distinction was beginning to be made between "practical" or "applied" studies and "pure" research which had no immediate practical end in view but was concerned with the more general task of what came to be called, in a disarmingly American phrase, "advancing the frontiers of knowledge."

43

The Kindly Killers

American medicine has always ranked somewhere between technology and entertainment. In the first half of the nineteenth century, medicine advanced little from the era of Benjamin Rush. What improvements were made were on the side of medical "technology."

The reader will recall that when Samuel F. B. Morse finally prevailed on Congress to appropriate money to erect his Baltimore-to-Washington telegraph line, that body included an equal sum for the study of mesmerism. A by-product of the mesmerism fad was the appearance of "painless" dentists, who claimed to be able to mesmerize their patients and extract teeth painlessly. One dentist, Horace Wells, watching a demonstration of nitrous oxide, or laughing gas, decided that it could be used to deaden pain during extractions, and offered himself as a subject. The experiment was successful and American dentistry scored another first, although Wells himself abandoned the method. His successor was William Morton, a Boston dentist who knocked himself out for eight minutes with sulphuric ether. The ether was next tried on a patient and a tooth was removed without pain. Then, in October, 1846, Morton administered ether to a patient of Dr. John Collins (nephew of Dr. Joseph Warren, the hero of Bunker Hill) at the Massachusetts General Hospital before an operation, and with the successful use of that anaesthetic a new era in surgery was opened. It was probably not entirely fortuitous that Americans pioneered new ways of preventing pain. The discovery of anaesthesia was, of course, of enormous importance. Since whatever improvements had been achieved were largely in the field of surgery, anaesthesia provided an additional impetus by making operations easier on both surgeons and patients.

It is interesting to note that Sidney George Fisher, so contemptuous of the law, had little more regard for medicine as a profession. He spoke of a wealthy Philadelphia surgeon, John Rhea Barton, as "a vulgar man, with talents, but a commonplace limited mind & no culture either as a gentleman or a scholar" whose life had been devoted "to a mere mechanical pursuit like surgery, in which dexterity of manipulation is the chief merit & object. . . ." A person in such a profession was "not likely to possess superior tastes & enlargement of mind." Medicine alone seemed more or less immune to the progressive developments in science. The College of Physicians and Surgeons in New York was referred to quite accurately by George Templeton Strong as "the old fossil Medical College" with a staff of "Heroic Phlebotomizers, the extreme right conservative orthodoxy."

But hospitals were marvels of efficiency. While Isabella Bird was visiting the New York Hospital on Broadway, half a dozen serious accident cases were trundled in, wounds sewn up, and broken limbs set. She was especially impressed by the female ward in which fourteen broken legs were being treated, the legs having been set and supported by "two long straps of plaister . . . glued from the knee to the ankle, and . . . fixed to a wooden bar, with a screw and handle, so that the tension could be regulated at pleasure."

The two major divisions of what we might call "popular" or "democratic" medicine had to do with home remedies, often traditional herbs and so-called patent medicines. It was on the patent medicine side that "medicine" was often indistinguishable from entertainment or, more accurately, humbug and swindle. Americans loved medicine, snake oil, Indian remedies, cough syrups, elixirs, tonics, whatever was guaranteed to make them feel better. The quantity of such concoctions consumed by the citizens of the republic in the last century would doubtless have filled a good-sized lake. The great inside joke was that the tonics taken in vast quantities by teetotaling old ladies had such a high alcohol content that the dosees were generally in a mild state of inebriation.

There was a consuming interest in Indian remedies, which were reputed to be especially efficacious (and often were). Thus many sellers of patent medicines advertised their stock as "Indian" and displayed a wood replica of an Indian or, not infrequently, a bona fide Indian or a white man disguised as an Indian, who was prepared to descant on how his "tribe" had preserved the health of its members for hundreds of years with the potion contained in this particular bottle. The fact that patent medicines were so ubiquitous suggests that a lot of Americans felt bad much of the time.

Most visitors remarked on the American disposition to diseases of the nerves. "The general nature of the American diseases are neuralgic, or those which affect the nerves," Marryat wrote. "Eye infection and inflammation was common and the *tic douloureux,* a neuralgic spasm of the face," was very common, according to Marryat, especially among women. "Nerves" and "excitement" come to be mentioned more and more frequently by visitors as the century wears on. Some, like Captain Marryat, ascribe them to the climate, others to the hectic and competitive character of American life.

This was certainly the case with most of those who submitted to the various "cures" that were so popular. These were touted for those suffering from "nerves," or "nervous debility," or any of a wide range of ailments whose vagueness suggested psychosomatic origins.

That doctors were aware of the psychosomatic character of many American illnesses was indicated by their frequent prescriptions of placebos, inert pills that had no medicinal properties but which, represented to the patient as remedies, made him or her feel better. The rise of placebos was also a consequence of the shift from a belief in the efficacy of "heroic" or massive doses of drugs to a growing conviction among the younger generation of doctors, influenced by the cult of Nature, that the body should, wherever possible, be given the opportunity to assert its own curative powers. The "heroic" treatment of bloodletting and purges which still, to be sure, survived, belonged to an age when Nature, i.e. the body, was perceived of primarily as something to be subdued or overcome. If Nature was benign, then the less the doctors intervened the better. One critic of "heroic" therapy was Dr. Marion Sims, a famous surgeon. When he was a young doctor in South Carolina, Sims went with an older physician to attend a young woman dying of consumption. The older man insisted on bleeding her. "Now she will be better," he said. But she died promptly and Sims wrote: "The practice was heroic; it was murderous. I knew nothing about medicine, but I had sense enough to see that doctors were killing their patients; that medicine was not an exact science; that it was wholly empirical, and that it would be better to trust entirely to Nature than to the hazardous skill of the doctor." Calomel (mercurous chloride), a severe purgative, remained the physician's stock-in-trade. It was supplemented, by many physicians of the older school, with "copious doses of opium." In the words of a prominent Massachusetts doctor: "The lancet, the leech, the cupping glass, the Spanish fly, croton oil, tartarized antimony, 'pecaouanha and mercury,' are instruments of power and of great utility when skillfully used."

The new treatment abandoned bleeding. Quinine, so effective in the treatment of malaria, replaced the much more "heroic" calomel in the doctor's medicine chest. Water and brandy were substituted for more radical measures and "the general tendency of therapeutics," a doctor wrote in 1860, "is, to use a favorite and expressive clinical phrase, 'building up,' sustaining and stimulating."

The asthenic notion was based on part on the theory that industrial and urban life had produced a marked decline in the vitality and basic health of individuals subject to such conditions and no persons in such weakened condition could withstand "heroic" measures. They could best be treated by rest and nourishing food supplemented by brandy or whiskey.

Homeopathy was the "scientific" doctrine that the proper treatment of a disease consisted of dosing the patient with a medicine that, if given to a person in good health, would produce the same symptoms as those observed in the ill. Thus if a patient had a severe headache the "remedy" might be to give him or her a medication designed to give a headache to a person without one. The dangerous inanity of this notion was somewhat mitigated by the doctrine that "medicines are more efficacious the smaller the dose."

Allopathy, on the other hand, tried to cure the patient by administering a dose that would produce a *different* symptom in a healthy person. Hence if you had a severe headache the remedy might be to induce "a vomit."

Thomsonism, which had a great vogue in the 1830s and '40s, was an extension, one might say, of Benjamin Rush's republican medicine, where individuals took a democratic interest in their own health and became in effect their own doctors. Samuel Thomson was a New Hampshire farmer who acquired an extensive knowledge of botanic medicine from a local woman who was an herbalist. Thomson believed illness was related to cold and he therefore heated his patients and used an Indian emetic called lobelia. Thomson developed his system at some length, enrolled people in the Friendly Botanic Society for twenty dollars, and sent them a booklet entitled *Family Botanic Medicine*.

Daniel Drake, a frontier doctor and president of the Ohio Medical College, wrote that Thomsonism was practiced by "Respectable and intelligent mechaniks, legislative and judicial officers, both state and federal barristers, ladies, ministers of the gospel, and even some of the medical professors 'who hold the eel of science by the tail' have become its advocates and puffers." Thomson sold over one hundred thousand copies of his booklet, which, in effect, told the purchasers how to make their own medicine with herbs and he estimated that three million people used his "system." He had numerous imitators who put out such works as the *Medical Pocket-Book*, the *Guide to Health, Domestic Medicine*, and for vegetarians, *The American Vegetable Practice*.

One of the principal advantages of Thomsonism was that women avoided "the necessity of consulting the other sex with all its attendant indecency and mortification." The Thomsonian physician "instead of dealing out poison would deal out advice to his fellow men to live according to the dictates of nature."

One of the most popular cures was hydropathy, invented by a Silesian peasant named Vincent Priessnitz. Catharine Beecher, Harriet's sister, took it religiously, and Harriet herself spent more than six months taking a water and "walking" cure. Hydropathy called for the patient to give up all liquor and rich foods, to take regular exercise in the open air, drink large quantities of water, and bathe regularly. The Brattleboro Water Cure House was one of the best known of the American spas. George Templeton Strong, who tried it with his family, described it as "plunge bath, sitz bath, half bath, wave bath, douches of every grade of intensity, and lastly 'packing,' not a pleasant way of spending an hour. The packed patient . . . looks like the pictures of the gravid female white ant."

Horatio Greenough, the American sculptor who was living in Florence, took his ailing wife to the source—Priessnitz's sanatorium at Gräfenberg—and wrote to Hiram Powers describing the curative effects of the daily cold baths. To another friend he wrote: "I have seen upwards of a thousand patients treated for very complicated and severe maladies with water. From . . . leprosy to croup and common colds. . . . The whole syphilitic family—small pox of the worst and most virulent character included." And of this great company of ailing only four had died. "I conceive this system great and valuable as it is to the sick and suffering to be still more important to the sound and healthy—a system which enjoins labour—which makes it clear that idleness is decay and excess and vice suicide must have important moral results—perhaps the day will come when cleanliness will be preached when decency will consist of showing a wholesome clean and well developed body instead of hiding a dirty one."

Among hydropathy's principal American practitioners was Mrs. Mary Grove Nichols, a staunch advocate of women's rights, who wrote that in the water cure, "Mothers learn to not only cure the disease of their families but, what is more important, to keep them in health." The women practitioners of hydropathy placed strong emphasis on women taking proper care of their bodies.

An important convert to hydropathy was Ellen White, a prophetess in the Seventh-Day Adventist Church who published a journal entitled *The Health Reformer* and, most important, enlisted John Harvey Kellogg, who became the editor of her magazine and later a famous food reformer who established his headquarters at Battle Creek, Michigan.

One of the most ingenious cures of the day was that devised by a Scottish doctor named Mitchell who decided that the cool dry air of the Mammoth Caves of Kentucky would make an ideal sanatorium for persons suffering from tuberculosis. He built cottages, shops, and tea houses in the caves. There were "strolls to distant parts of the cave," a contemporary visitor noted, "and music, dances, and songs filled those mournful, quiet places where bats cluster." The experiment proved short-lived. The smoke from constantly burning lamps and a feeling of depression from being kept underground accelerated rather than cured their illness. According to Aleksandr Lakier, the patients died off, one by one, and the doctor with them.

Considering patent medicines along with the innumerable "cures" (the patent medicines were middle and lower class; the cures middle and upper class), it seems evident that American health, especially in the larger cities, was deplorable. Most ironic of all was the fact that the best medical care was available to slaves. Since their owners had a vested interest in keeping them healthy, no expense was spared in doctoring them when they were ill or injured.

On the frontier, doctoring was, in large part, a woman's work. In addition to her multitudinous duties as a wife and mother, the rural and frontier woman acted as doctor for a host of maladies. Some were diseases such as cholera, smallpox, diphtheria, and ague (malaria), which were common to the frontier. Others, like scarlet fever and measles, were typical childhood diseases. In still another category were broken bones, bruises, and cuts. Harriet Conner Brown, who settled in Amesville, Iowa, where her husband ran a store, was constantly "doctoring." Even when doctors were to be found, their notions of treatment were often so primitive that women like Harriet Brown steered clear of them, convinced that they could do better with their own home remedies and herbs grown in their gardens or picked in the woods. Her second child, Charlie, was born during a temperance rally while a band in a fine red wagon played at the picnic ground. So Charlie, perforce, became a prohibitionist and was "wonderful fond of music ever since." When three of her children came down with scarlet fever, Harriet Brown took care of them herself. She gave them no medicine and no food except the juice of grapes and canned peaches. Slippery-elm water was a common housewife's remedy and many supplemented family medical lore with Dr. Gunn's *The House Physician,* "which told how to take care of the sick and make them remedies from the herbs that grew all around us. Whatever the ailment," Grandma Brown recalled, "from hiccups to tapeworms, I consulted Dr. Gunn. . . . Whenever one of my children was ailing, the first thing I tried to do was to clean him thoroughly, inside and out, to open skin and bowels, and then put him to bed. The warm bath would bring out any latent trouble. . . . One time I came to Eben Foster's house when he was very sick with bloody flux—very low indeed. I went to the drug store and bought some slippery elm and laudanum, grated the slippery elm and beat it to a fine cream, added some fifteen drops of laudanum, got my brother to give his son an injection with a baby syringe, put a hot plate on his abdomen. He rested all night. 'Good morning, doctor!' he called to me when daylight came."

When her son Herbert cut off three of his fingers cutting sheaf oats for his pony, his mother "washed them, fitted them together carefully, and bound them up so that they grew into perfectly good fingers again."

Gustaf Unonius, the Swedish immigrant to Wisconsin, was impressed by the competence of American doctors who, on the frontiers, he believed, compared favorably with their professional brethren in Europe. It was difficult to be certain, however, who had genuine credentials and who had simply declared himself to be a physician. "A person I had seen going about working as a mason served for a couple of months as an assistant in a drugstore in Milwaukee," Unonius wrote, "whereupon he laid aside the trowel, got himself some medical books, and assumed the title of doctor." Such unlimited freedom, if it had given the "opportunity for many humbugs to flourish," Unonius reflected, had, at the same time, "called forth many able men and . . . spurred them on to greater efforts."

What was most extraordinary about the "kindly killers" was that the profession of medicine grew in numbers and maintained the respectability that it had established at the time of the Revolution. Outside the field of surgery, it was the political, social and, in a real sense, psychological, rather than the medical, role of the doctors that was important. They were comforters and consolers of the ailing and even though their attentions were frequently lethal, they themselves were appreciated and admired by the general run of the citizenry. What was most important was that they made great sacrifices. They came miles—in wintertime in drafty buggies or on horseback, in the dead of night, in the midst of storms—to manifest a human concern for a human need. If they were, on the whole, no better than witch doctors with their eccentric notions of disease, they at least gave the illusion that something was being done and that undoubtedly made the patient and his/her family feel better. They were performers of rituals rather than healers. What they knew was less important than what they professed. Thus, they bore witness to the growing power of professionalism in American society.

It was clearly on the practical side that American doctors excelled. Ephraim McDowell, who practiced in Danville, Kentucky, pioneered in abdominal surgery, performing what was probably the first ovariotomy. By 1829 he had carried out twelve such operations with only one death, as well as a number of operations for direct hernias and thirty-two on gall bladders. McDowell had no formal medical training but he displayed the same qualities of enterprise and inventiveness so evident in men like Elias Howe and George Corliss.

In Marion Sims's engaging autobiography, he tells of numerous "cases" in which, knowing his own limitations, he had the good sense to do nothing except offer his patients whatever reassurance he could give. Sims himself suffered from a terrible attack of malaria and ill as he was, learned much from observation and experience—especially how often mortality followed the practice of doctors. "I became exceedingly conservative; I never bled and gave as little medicine as possible."

When Sims moved to Montgomery, Alabama, his first patients were "free niggers." If he was cautious in his medical treatment, he was remarkably bold in surgery. He operated successfully on a clubfoot and for strabismus or cross-eye, and, in his words, "performed all sorts of beautiful and brilliant operations." When a young woman came to him with a harelip, no teeth, and a seriously disfigured face, he did a series of operations in what we would call today "plastic surgery" and reconstructed "a very presentable mouth" while a dentist made her a set of teeth. In Sims's words, "Her life . . . was enlivened and revolutionized."

Sims had never treated "any of the diseases of women" until he was summoned to help a slave woman who had been in labor for three days. Sims found that the child's head was "impacted in the pelvis." He made a forceps delivery but a few days later he discovered that the mother was suffering from a vesico-vaginal fistula, a tear in the bladder that created a channel into the vagina and made it impossible for her to retain urine. Soon other cases came to Sims's attention, all among young slave women who had recently given birth. Sims had "a little hospital of eight beds, built in the corner of my yard, for taking care of my negro patients." Using a bent spoon, he "saw everything, as no man had ever seen before. The fistula . . . as plain as the nose on a man's face." It came to him with the force of revelation that he could "repair the torn bladder and effect a cure—I felt sure I was on the eve of one of the great discoveries of the day."

Sims went to work to devise instruments that would enable him to carry out the operation. He added a floor to his hospital, scoured the plantations round about, and collected seven cases of "incurable" vesico-vaginal fistula. Without anaesthesia and with a dozen fellow physicians watching, Sims began his first operation. The fistula was closed and a catheter placed in the bladder to allow the urine to drain. Other operations followed but in every instance infection developed, usually from the suturing material. For almost three years, Sims worked with his black patients to solve the problem of infection, keeping them in his little hospital at his own expense. He trained them to assist him in his operations and told those friends who tried to prevail on him to admit defeat that he was determined to persevere "if it costs me my life." Finally he hit on the notion of silver sutures. He chose a slave girl named Anarcha for the experiment. It was the thirtieth operation performed on her and it was at last successful. There was no infection, no cystitis.

Two things might be said about Sims's achievement: There was genius in his original concept of repairing the torn fistula and astonishing tenacity and technical skill in pursuing the experiments through a hundred failures to his final success. But most astonishing of all was the cheerful persistence of his patients who endured the operations without anaesthesia and assisted Sims in performing them. Lucy, Betsey, Anarcha, and their unnamed sisters were heroines in their own right.

44

Home Life

The American child was pampered, featured, indulged, and beaten as perhaps no other child in the world. Captain Marryat believed the permissiveness was the consequence of discipline being left in the hands of the mother. He told of a child three years old whose mother summoned him:

"'Johnny, my dear, come home.'

"'I won't,' cries Johnny.

"'You must, my love, you are all wet, and you'll catch cold.'

"'I won't,' replied Johnny.

"'Oh! Mr. ————, do, pray make Johnny come in.'

"'Come in, Johnny,' says the father.

"'I won't.'

"'I tell you, come in directly, sir—do you hear?'

"'I won't,' replies the urchin taking to his heels.

"'A sturdy republican, sir,' says his father to me, smiling at the boy's resolute disobedience."

George Combe, the visiting phrenologist, made the same observations. "Many American children appear to be indulged in their appetites and desires, and to be too little restrained in the manifestation of their propensities. Egotism, or the idea that the world is made for them, and other persons must stand aside to allow them scope, is a feature not infrequently recognized." At the same time the male child was constantly beaten. This odd combination of "soft" psychology and "hard" discipline may be assumed to have affected the child's psyche in particular ways.

The precociousness of American children, David Macrae, the touring Scottish divine, attributed to their being brought to the table with adults at an early age, where they began to acquire "an interest in general affairs, and to acquire the ideas and language of grown people." "A small boy of eight," Macrae wrote, "will stand up to you and say, 'What do you think, sir, of the present state of the country?'" Children did not hesitate to admonish their parents. When a friend of Macrae's tried to describe "how some comical Frenchman had spoken at a public meeting," his young daughter said, "Papa, don't be foolish."

He heard another infant, when his mother told him to wipe his mouth, respond, "Say *please.*" "Well, darling, *please.*" "Precocity wiped his lips solemnly, as if an important moral lesson had been given, and requested to be lifted down from his chair." To control an American child, Macrae observed, "you must appeal to [its] reason and good sense—not merely to your own authority.

" 'Remember who you are talking to, sir!' said an indignant parent to a fractious boy: 'I am your father, sir.'

" 'Who's to blame for that? . . . It ain't me!' "

After a series of such experiences, Macrae felt that he understood better what a young New England mother had meant when she said, "I am learning to be a *docile* parent!" " 'Parents obey your children in all things' is the new commandment," Macrae added.

Certainly childhood was grossly sentimentalized. The traditional Christian notion that the child was born in a state of "original sin" and had to be carefully and lovingly trained up to a state of grace was gradually replaced by the notion that the child was "naturally good," in a state of happy innocence uncorrupted by the world. The Enlightenment, the reader will recall, postulated a good (and reasonable) nature corrupted by prejudice and superstition. If Man in the form of the child was "naturally" good, it was necessary only to protect that built-in goodness and allow it to grow in its own way and own time. It may have been the penetration of this Enlightenment notion of man-child, reinforced by a rising tide of romanticism, that explained parental permissiveness. And it may have been the residual Christian notion of original sin that explained the ubiquitous "rod." In any event, it was an inherently schizophrenic situation that the American child faced. Moreover, a world was described for him/her that was clearly and sharply defined. It was painted in vividly contrasting colors of good and evil, right and wrong. To every problem there was a clear-cut solution, and the answer was usually to be found in the Holy Scriptures or the nearest minister's gloss on them. All ambiguity was banished; paradox was obscured. Life thus appeared deceptively simple. The child, however, received conflicting signals. He was told that his duty to his Maker required him to be honest, generous, kindly, and self-sacrificing, but the other message that his society conveyed was that he must be "smart and slick" to get ahead in the world. He (and, to a lesser extent, she) was given great freedom, but it was continually impressed on him that self-discipline and above all "control" were essential to worldly success (and not to succeed was to run the risk of not "being"; not quite, in a sense, to exist). Americans were thus expected to serve *both* God and Mammon and they were constantly torn by those conflicting imperatives. Charles Pancoast was shrewd enough to perceive that if you had wealthy friends and a Harvard or Princeton education you had a far better opportunity to resolve the paradox, to make a "competence," to live comfortably or even luxuriously on "moral" money rather than grubbing for "immoral" money. That was perhaps the greatest luxury that American life could afford, not to have to grub for immoral money and thus to enjoy the moral superiority of looking down on those who did. If you did not have wealthy friends, family, education then you had to experience daily the tension between God and Mammon.

What this meant in many cases was an abbreviated or truncated childhood. Captain Marryat wrote: "At fifteen or sixteen, if not at college, the boy assumes the man; he enters into business, as a clerk to some merchant or in some store. . . . He frequents the bar, calls for gin cocktails, chews tobacco and talks politics. . . . Boys are working like men for years before they would be in England; time is money, and they assist to bring in the harvest." All of which, Marryat noted, contributed to the great American obsession with "going ahead." What seemed more remarkable to Marryat was the fact that "society has been usurped by the young people, and the married and old people have been, to a degree, excluded from it."

There were many others who shared Marryat's view of growing up in America. Thomas Colley Grattan, an Irishman who acted as British consul in Boston in the years from 1839 to 1846, condemned the "hard precocity" of American youth. The fact was they had no youth. "It might almost be said," he wrote, "that every man is born middle-aged in that [Boston] and every other great city of the Union. The principal business of life seems to be to grow old as fast as possible. The boy, the youth, the young man are only anxious to hurry on the gravity and care of 'the vale of tears.' . . . The toils of life—the destiny of the poorer classes in Europe form the free choice of the rich man of America, always excepting the indolent Southern planters." There were no athletic games to give "gracefulness or strength to body or mind, all that is left is chewing, smoking, drinking, driving hired horses in wretched gigs with a cruel velocity. . . . Young men made up of such materials as I describe are not young men at all. . . . They follow business like drudges and politics with a fierce ardour. They marry. They renounce party-going. They give up all pretensions in dress. . . . They assume and soon acquire a pursed-up, keen, and haggard look. Their air, their manners, and conversation are all alike contracted. They have no breadth, either of shoulders, information, or ambition. . . . The money-making faculty is alone cultivated. They are incapable of acquiring general knowledge on a broad or liberal scale. All is confined to trade, finance, law, and small, local, provincial information."

We have taken note in an earlier volume of this work of the enormous importance of the family in American history. Families provided the training, the social cohesiveness, the sense of purpose and direction, the dominant values for the individual. Thus we must pay particular attention to the process of transmission by which values were sustained, modified, and passed on from parents to children. The family felt particular pressures in this respect because in mobile, constantly moving American families, grandparents and older relatives were seldom available to assist in such transmissions. Even communities were usually in a state of flux, of change and transition, of extraordinary and delirious growth or worrisome decline. All of which meant that the family, and essentially the mother and father, had to bear a very heavy burden. They had, in many instances, the denominational churches to help them, but even the churches were often in a state of confusion as to what constituted orthodoxy. The consequence was that there were temperance families, missionary families, abolitionist families, women's rights families, families that for generations produced, let us say, Presbyterian ministers, or lawyers, or doctors, and that particularly in the families of reform, intermarried generation after generation, sustaining an original commitment to a cause, or, more typically, congeries of causes.

There was another aspect of the American family that we should take note of—American sons (and sometimes the daughters) left home typically at the age of fifteen or sixteen to make their way in the world and assume the responsibilities of an adult. Thus the period of parental supervision and nurture was considerably shorter than that in traditional societies, where a child might spend much of his or her life under the dominance or influence of parents. In the looser, more permissive atmosphere of the American mobile home, values were transmitted with a particular urgency just because of the sense of transience. In a world in constant motion moral values alone seemed stable, ideas dominated feelings—or such, at least, was the intention. Indeed one has the impression that only this precarious process of "family transmission" held the United States together, kept it from one moment to the next from simply flying apart, as it so often appeared ready to do.

In traditional (or non-American) societies class was the determining factor. The aristocracy was defined *as a class*. The identification of a person born within that class was with the class and its values. The individual was defined *by his class*. It stipulated what he should wear, how he should conduct himself, whom he should marry, and what callings he might appropriately pursue or how he should spend his leisure hours if he pursued no career. The careers were, generally speaking, the church, the military, the court, or politics, to which was added in time foreign service. In the United States, on the other hand, there were no such ready-made definitions. There were, of course, classes, but as we have argued before, individuals maintained themselves in those classes (limited, in large part, to major Eastern cities) only by making money, and they were always in danger of falling out of their class in stormy economic seas. But it was not just the upper class that had a problem of identification; so did all those "below," those struggling to mount higher or those merely trying desperately to maintain themselves on the particular rung on which they found themselves deposited by birth or fortune.

The consequence was that a host of particular socializing functions devolved on the family. The family was a school of moral and social values and the primary "shaping" institution of the larger society. Families made up of powerful and self-confident individuals exerted remarkable influences on their children. It was by no means simply a matter of money—the Beechers, for example, were always comparatively poor, and the Alcotts were really poor—or social position, although those helped. It was far more a matter of "character" and training.

Such families varied greatly in the nature of their emotional life. The middle-class reform-minded families like the Beechers and Alcotts were often full of fun and exuberance, games and play, dramatics, the reading aloud of the classics, singing and the playing of musical instruments. Others were more than anything else systems of discipline, hard schools of morality and "duty." Charles Francis Adams felt his family was his cross. "When I recur to the question of family," he wrote in his diary, "a creeping dread comes over me and I see distinctly as I think, that the world has lost its force to me already in this life. I feel that I am an insulated being. . . ." Similar themes appear in the diaries of Fisher, Strong, and Dana, a persistent worry that the protecting character of their family life had denied them an important range of human experience. However intense the spirit of family might be, the vast majority of Americans were far more apt to conform to Grattan's description of "growing up in America" than the self-contained, protective situation of our diarists.

Families lived, for the most part, in houses—much larger and more spacious houses than those in which the vast majority of peoples of other cultures lived. They were also distinguished by the fact that they could be built relatively inexpensively (commonly out of wood, less frequently out of local stone) and very quickly by a simple framework of two-by-four studdings and light cross ties. In many societies even the homes of peasants might take years of arduous and intermittent labor to build (and of course be owned by someone else). In the United States the so-called balloon-frame house not only could be built quickly by a carpenter of limited skill, it could be moved from place to place. When the site of a dwelling became too valuable for its comparatively modest purpose, it was simply trundled off to a new location, usually during the night, and a store or bank hastily and often badly erected in its place. In Cincinnati, Gustaf Unonius wrote, "even three-story buildings travel down the street, pulled by a horse-powered capstan over planks and rollers. . . . I have seen houses on the move," he wrote, "while the families living in them continued with their daily tasks, keeping a fire in the stove, eating their meals as usual, and at night quietly going to bed to wake up the next morning on some other street."

The most influential architect-builder and landscape architect was Andrew Jackson Downing, who when he died in the aforementioned steamship explosion at the age of thirty-six, had already left his mark on innumerable homes and public buildings. Downing was born in Newburgh, New York, to a nurseryman who died when Downing was still a child. When he left school at the age of sixteen he joined his brother in the nursery business, married a great-niece of John Quincy Adams's, and soon became a much-sought-after architect and, more important, an architectural theorist. He wrote the first important American work on landscape gardening, *A Treatise on the Theory and Practice of Landscape Gardening, Adapted to North America in 1841*, when he was twenty-six, which went through numerous editions, and his *Cottage Residences* a year later. *The Architecture of Country Houses*, his most famous work, went through nine printings. Downing was true to his own modest origins and to the moral precepts of his age in warning against the building of "great houses." "We see signs showing themselves," he wrote, "with the growing wealth of the country, of expenditure in domestic architecture quite unmeaning and unwise in a republic. Fortunes are rapidly accumulated in the United States and the indulgence of one's taste and pride in the erection of a country seat of great size and cost, is becoming a favorite mode of expending wealth. And yet these attempts at great establishments are always and inevitably, failures in America. And why? Plainly because they are contrary to the spirit of republican institutions; because the feelings upon which they are based can never take root, excepting in a government of hereditary right; because they are wholly in contradiction to the spirit of our time and people."

Downing began his *The Architecture of Country Houses* by stating the reasons "why my countrymen should have good houses. The first is, because a good house (and by this I mean a fitting, tasteful and significant dwelling) is a powerful means of civilization. . . . With the perception of proportion, symmetry, order, and beauty, awakens the desire for possession, and with them comes that refinement of manners which distinguishes a civilized from a coarse and brutal people. . . . The second reason, is because the *individual* home has great social value for a people . . . in America, not only is the distinct family the best social form, but those elementary forces which give rise to the highest gains and the finest character may, for the most part, be traced back to the farm house and the rural cottage. . . . The third reason is, because there is a moral influence in a country home. . . .

Much of that feverish unrest and want of balance between desire and the fulfillment of life, is calmed and adjusted by the pursuit of tastes which result in making a little world of the family home, where truthfulness, beauty, and order have the largest dominion."

Andrew Jackson Downing represented the spirit of Jacksonian democracy applied to architecture. His apotheosis of the "single-family dwelling" is our most eloquent evocation of that central American institution, the nuclear family.

The reforming spirit thus spread to the actual physical arrangements of American homes. Harriet Beecher Stowe and her sister Catharine combined their formidable common talents to write the pioneering books on "Christian" *Domestic Economy.* In their view most American homes were barren wastelands and until they became humane and gracious abodes of light and air and love and democratic happiness, centers of the moral life, all other reforms were exercises in futility.

Within houses there were interesting shifts in the allocation of space for private and social functions. The private parts of upper- and middle-class American homes grew larger and more comfortable, and the "social areas" diminished, perhaps reflecting the more intimate nature of American marriages. Isabella Bird noted that American bedrooms were, typically, "large, lofty, and airy; and . . . furnished with all the appurtenances which modern luxury has been able to devise. . . . There are bath-rooms generally on three floors, and hot and cold water are laid on in every story."

Dining rooms were small by English standards, but the wealthy often had large ballrooms in their houses, testimony to the American infatuation with dancing, common to every class of citizens.

Most foreign visitors agreed with Thomas Colley Grattan on the horrors of overheating. "Casual visitors," he wrote, "are nearly suffocated, and constant occupiers killed. An enormous furnace in the cellar sends up, day and night, streams of hot air, through apertures and pipes, to every room in the house. No spot is free from it, from the dining-parlour to the dressing-closet. It meets you the moment the street-door is opened to let you in, rushes after you when you emerge again, half-stewed and parboiled, into the wholesome air." The epitaph of most Americans should read, in Grattan's view, "died of a furnace."

The lavish houses of the rich in the cities were usually austere on the outside to avoid arousing the envy of the poor or the attention of thieves. More and more the wealthy were disposed to live in comparatively modest urban houses and build splendid mansions in the countryside well beyond the city limits. Such structures tended increasingly, like William Paulding's mansion on the Hudson, to resemble miniature Gothic castles. The directness and simplicity of the Federal architecture or the Classical Revival gave way to crenellated turrets and architectural oddments such as towers and dormers.

Every home that could afford it was full of "conveniences"; American ingenuity and inventiveness was evident there as elsewhere. Gustaf Unonius was impressed, when he landed in New York, with the conveniences in American kitchens. In houses with furnaces it was possible to have hot water day or night. "In another corner of the room," he wrote, "was another piece of furniture, in appearance a small cabinet, but in reality an icebox, or refrigerator, in which a supply of ice for the day was kept. Every morning at sunrise the wagons of the ice company would make their rounds and deliver ice at the gate." His wife was charmed by the simplicity and convenience of these arrangements. Even the laundry was done more quickly and easily than in Sweden by means of "a small washboard . . . made either out of wood or zinc, with horizontal grooves or corrugations against which the clothes are rubbed."

With the constant influx of Irish and German immigrants and the growing prosperity of the middle class, more and more families had more and more servants. A cook was supplemented by a maid or a butler and a coachman or valet or combination of both. Throughout our period more and more immigrants listed their occupation as "servant," and the invasion of the home by a vast body of servants— that "silent, observing army" as Charlotte Perkins Gilman called them—was certainly one of the crucial domestic transformations in the nineteenth century (it reached its apogee after the Civil War).

The greatest difficulty that the Reverend David Macrae encountered in his travels in the United States was getting his boots polished. The specific problem was ancillary to the general problem of servants, or, as most of them insisted on being called, the help. American servants were more often defined, it appeared, by what they wouldn't do rather than what they would—wouldn't brush boots, wouldn't open the door, etc. "It is," Macrae wrote, in despair over his muddy boots, "one of the great miseries of life in America." It was the principal reason, in Macrae's view, that many American families lived in hotels. "I did have a home of my own," one such hotel dweller told Macrae,

". . . but I was driven here for want of proper service. Why, sir, I had to get up and kindle the fires in the morning; I had to brush my own boots; I had to do fifty things of that sort that servants should have done."

The difficulty of training and keeping servants disposed Americans to "socials," to evenings of entertainment rather than formal dinner parties. At such gatherings, David Macrae noted, there were "charades, readings, talk, songs, music, just as the spirit moves; though most of the time is generally spent in conversation, in which Americans greatly excel. At some of these 'socials' you will find men of all classes—senators, merchants, lawyers, shopkeepers, army or navy officers, professional and business men of all kinds, with their wives—meeting and enjoying themselves together on terms of perfect equality." Such was the case at least in all but the highest social circles.

In most households the relation between the mistress and her servants was one of what Macrae called "armed neutrality." He concluded this obviously painful subject by noting "America might almost be defined as a land of glorious liberty, qualified by the necessity of brushing your own boots."

The presence of servants affected the psychological atmosphere of the home in a variety of ways. The wife-mother (nurses for the children would soon make their appearance, modeled after the English nanny) was freed for social or philanthropic activities or simply to read novels and eat bonbons. Instead of being perceived as the essential provider of food and nurture, she exercised largely managerial functions. Even her increasingly restricted clothing suggested dramatically her reduced utility and freedom of movement. Her garments grew so elaborate and constricting that she needed a maid to help her struggle into them.

Fanny Kemble was among a number of sensible women who protested "the various abuses of our constitutions, and infractions of God's natural laws. The mere items of tight stays, tight garters, tight shoes, tight waistbands, tight arm-holes and tight bodices . . . must have a tendency," she wrote a friend, "to injure irreparably the compressed parts, to impede circulation and respiration, and in many ways which we are not aware of . . . destroy the health of the system, affect disastrously all its functions, and must aggravate the pains and perils of childbearing. . . . Pitiable women!" Fanny Kemble was quite ready to admit that there were doubtless additional causes for the bad health and agitated nerves of middle-class women, but she was convinced "tight-lacing, want of exercise, and a perpetual inhaling of over-heated atmosphere" were the principal culprits.

The destructive consequences of such regimens were not, of course, confined to women. "Americans generally," Kemble noted, "have little or no regard for the laws of health." Middle-class American men were notorious for bad nerves and poor physiques; that was doubtless why so many of them thrived in the face of the physical ardors of westward migration. The American male on the frontier was the picture of masculine vigor and good health. The American male in New York City was usually the reverse. Like George Templeton Strong, he lived on coffee and sleeping potions. While the dress of women grew more and more elaborate, expensive, and constricting, men's clothes became increasingly utilitarian, somber, and "democratic." Trousers had long since replaced knee breeches, wigs had disappeared, and hair was worn shorter. Philip Hone spelled out the attitude of his class toward masculine dress. "Great men, statesmen, divines, eminent lawyers, physicians, and magistrates should dress well. It gives them consideration and raises their several professions in the eyes of their fellow men; black is safest—it is peculiarly the garb of a gentleman, and never goes out of style." As much as he admired Webster, Hone could not reconcile himself to his flashy manner of dressing. He met the great orator in Wall Street, "at high noon, in a bright blue satin vest, sprigged with gold flowers, a costume," he added, "as incongruous for Daniel Webster as ostrich feathers for a sister of charity."

Of course the modest and comfortable female costume of ankle-length trousers or slacks *plus* a short shirt worn by the Bloomerite reformers filled the orthodox with horror and rage and was denounced as lewd, lascivious, and a denial of feminity, which seems somewhat paradoxical. Dr. Mary Walker, a leader of the Practical Dress Reformers, dedicated her attack on conventional female dress in a book entitled *Hit*, to the dress reformers, "the truest friends of humanity, who have done more for the universal elevation of woman . . . than all others combined. You, who have *lived* the precepts and principles that others have only *talked*—who have been so consistent in your ideas of the equality of the sexes, by dressing in a manner to fit you for the duties of a noble and useful life." Such ladies were "living martyrs . . . the greatest philanthropists of the age. . . ."

On the frontier and in rural communities men and women wore simple, practical clothes, although the Sunday-go-to-meeting costume was as austere as the businessman's black frock coat. The frontier trapper, trader, or mountain man dressed in his own colorful quasi-Indian attire, definitely outré, and in the South, Southern gentlemen affected a much richer and more colorful attire than their drab Northern cousins. Southern and Western costumes were as "loose" as Eastern clothes were "tight."

Finally there was the strange potency of hair. We went from wigs, which really are a very odd notion—to wear hair not your own if you have perfectly good hair—to the "wind-blown" style popularized by the French Revolution and then to hair up above the ears (sideburns allowed). But in all that time not a hair was allowed on the chin or lip. For two hundred years Americans had been totally beardless. When a radical innovator in Framingham, Massachusetts, undertook to grow a beard in 1840, his furious neighbors attacked him and when he defended himself, he was thrown in jail. But in that remarkable decade the 1850s, when so much else of an extraordinary nature transpired, hair crept onto male chins and lips. Beginning modestly enough as "imperials," goatees, and mustaches, there was soon a wild efflorescence of hair, an enormous collective whiskery thicket that covered the country. The significance of that dramatic change was certainly profound if obscure.

Americans ate, by the standards of other peoples, enormous quantities of food, especially meat, pork, and beef—in part, one suspects, because meat was, in the countries from which many Americans came, one of the marks of affluence. The prodigious consumption of meat was denounced by vegetarian reformers like Bronson Alcott on the grounds of both physical and psychic health. Meat made its eaters coarse, sensual, aggressive, and animallike, with aggravated lusts. It was, in short, brutalizing. It also made them prone to numerous ailments and diseases.

But what perhaps most distinguished Americans' attitudes toward food was the speed with which they consumed it. In other societies eating was a ritualized, quasi-religious act. In the United States it seemed often more akin to the hasty feeding of a human perpetual-motion machine. Captain Basil Hall was disconcerted by "the imperturbable silence and gravity" of Americans engaged in the serious and hasty business of eating. He was taken to a "fast-food" emporium where the diners sat in booths and were attended by "urchins, imps and gnomes" who took their orders and bawled them out to an invisible cook. "It was still more marvelous," Hall wrote, "that within a few seconds after our wishes had been communicated . . . the things we asked for were placed piping hot before us. It was quite an Arabian Nights' Entertainment, not a sober dinner at a chop-house."

Aleksandr Lakier noted that "someone has compared Americans at the dinner table to sharks. The comparison," he added, "is rather good, and the reason for the haste is the same: the desire to get down to business and not waste time."

David Macrae made the same observation. At the Opera Restaurant in Chicago he timed "five or six gentlemen at their dinners," he wrote, "and found the average time taken by each to be three and three-quarters minutes. All of them had two courses; one of them had three. There were no seats; the customers swarmed in front of a long metal counter like a public house bar. A man would come in, walk briskly to the counter, order brown soup, shoot it down, order chicken and ham, give it the run of his teeth as it flew in bits into his mouth, would snap up a blackberry tart, pay his money, and be off. This was dinner."

George Combe also noted that Americans wolfed down their food, which was hardly conducive to dinner table conversation. At one hotel table, he calculated that a hundred and fifty people were fed in fifteen minutes. "You Europeans," one diner remarked, "eat as if you actually enjoyed your food!" To which Combe's reply was, "Assuredly we do—and you Americans will never escape from dyspepsia and headaches until you learn to enjoy your meals."

In *The American Democrat*, James Fenimore Cooper joined in the indictment of American eating habits. "The art of eating and drinking," he wrote, "is one of those on which more depends, perhaps, than on any other [branch of civilization] since health, activity of mind, constitutional enjoyments, even learning, refinement, and, to a certain degree, morals, are all, more or less, connected with our diet. The Americans are the grossest feeders of any civilized nation known. As a nation their food is heavy, coarse, ill prepared and indigestible. . . . The predominance of grease in the American kitchen, coupled with the habits of hasty eating and of constant expectoration, are causes of the diseases of the stomach so common in America."

There was general agreement among visitors and upper-class Americans alike that the mass of the people had execrable manners. The spitting that so annoyed Dickens also repelled Sidney George

Fisher, who, visiting a small town in western Pennsylvania, went to the Court of Common Pleas and found it held in "a miserable room, the furniture of the commonest kind, the crowd coarse & dirty looking, the lawyers vulgar and shabby, the Judge, respectable in his appearance & a fine head & face, but sitting with his feet cocked up à l'Américain over the bar, and almost every individual in the room chewing tobacco. Such an incessant spitting I never heard. It was positively nauseating. . . ." Gustaf Unonius pointed out that foreign visitors "sometimes forget that this class in Americans should be compared with the lower classes in Europe rather than with the upper, or, as they sometimes are, even with the highest classes at home. . . . Those whom we in Europe should account the lower, uneducated class are often here the half-educated, and instead of doing them justice because of the higher plane they have attained to, we are inclined to speak of their rudeness and offensive manners as if they were representative of the higher or educated classes, which is entirely erroneous."

Americans, like other humans, were born, grew up in families, ventured into the world, succeeded or failed (and often did both successively throughout their lives), grew old and died—by disease, gunshot wounds, steam boiler explosions, and drowning. In their reckless disregard for life and limb, many Americans did not survive to old age. Infant and child mortality was distressingly high. It was not uncommon for only half the children in a family to reach maturity. So death was all about, an ever present reality that might bring one down without warning or carry away a loved one long before his appointed hour. It was perhaps this omnipresence of death that accounted for Americans' preoccupation with that final event in life's drama. People observed the death of loved ones with the closest attention—John Trumbull painted his wife dying—gave way to paroxysms of grief, and kept prolonged periods of mourning. Richard Henry Dana's mother died when he was six but he never forgot his father's grief "which no description we have read of agony short of madness has equalled," Dana wrote. Dana himself "connected her constantly with some notion of rising from the dead, the resurrection of our Saviour, the raising of Lazarus, & other instances of miraculous restorations of life haunted my imagination, & I spent hours in picturing to myself her coming to life, & went into the minutest details of the manner (always supernatural & by divine interposition) in wh. it would be done. . . . My thoughts were only of coming to life & breaking away from [the] power of the grave, the church-yard, the tomb, the coffin & the grave-clothes, & coming among us pure, holy & giving life & spreading joy."

When Dana's seven-year-old cousin, Frank Dana, died, the child's aunt and uncle, Sophia and George Ripley, the leaders at Brook Farm, were devastated, their grief "incontrollable & uncontrolled. Mr. Ripley wrings his hands & cries out like a child. He is almost insane. Cousin Sophia seems overpowered & helpless & hopeless." The child was buried in Cambridge "in the company of the dead of his own flesh & blood of five generations. . . . There was something interesting & consoling in seeing the remains of all one family preserved together in care & kept in this communion. . . . All the family went down into the tomb, & the chief mourners say they were glad they went. It made them feel more definitely about the body & took off some of the terror & strangeness of the tomb."

Sidney George Fisher's niece, Henry's "darling little Emily, my brilliant & beautiful pet and companion," was seized by what Fisher called "the bilious cholic" and died after an illness of only a few days. Fisher, who with his brother sat through her last hours, gave a detailed account of her death throes. "She was in fact dying," he wrote. "She had a succession of spasms each of which looked like death & were thought by all of us to be death as they occurred. . . . There she lay, panting, talking incoherently & wildly with a face of startling strength & sweetness, her beautiful face rapidly changing its expression, assuming from time to time as the struggles proceeded, strange, unnatural, ghastly & elfish looks which made us shudder. . . . This lasted for three hours, and each minute seemed to have a different character & feeling as her countenance altered & life ebbed." Five pages of Fisher's diary are given over to the graphic account of the last hours of Emily's life.

The fact that death was so much a part of life—that life was so "cheap"—would, one would think, have inured people to death. That they so often gave way to what appears to us excessive and often immobilizing grief is a fact of profound psychological implications. The intense concentration on the *instant of death* was undoubtedly in large part the consequence of a keen interest in "psychology," the relation of what George Templeton Strong referred to as the "ego" or soul to the body, of the "animal" to the spiritual. When a person died, the "soul"—destined, most Americans believed, for eternal life—left the body. That instant was the strangest and most mystifying event in all of life—its conclusion. Could the soul be seen to fly out of the windows of the eyes? What clue lay there for the living? It was obviously more complicated than that. Was it that science and reason, questioning the Christocentric notion of the world, at least by implication, and with it the idea of life hereafter for which this world was merely a preparation, had encouraged this fascinated, obsessive attention to death? The final irony was what happened after death— the elaborate funeral arrangements, the extended period of mourning, the handsome and expensive headstone or crypt or mausoleum. American cemeteries, like Niagara Falls and American women, were an object of great curiosity to most visitors. It seemed as though whatever equality existed in life was to be at once overthrown in death. In the cemetery conspicuous display ruled.

Isabella Bird visited the Greenwood Cemetery in Brooklyn, to which, she wrote, "most of the dead of New York are carried. . . . There are family mausoleums, gloomy and sepulchral looking, in the Grecian style; family burying grounds neatly enclosed by iron or bronze railings. . . . There are tombs with epitaphs, and tombs with statues . . . and nameless graves marked by numbers only." The numerous graves of children had "toys in glass cases placed upon them . . . wooly dogs, and lambs, and little wooden houses. . . ." There was a statue in memory of a sea captain's wife with the captain himself in marble "taking an observation, on the top." Whenever he returned from a voyage, Bird was told, "he spends one whole day in the tomb, lamenting his bereavement." The tomb of a fireman who died rescuing a child bore a statue of the hero "with an infant in his arms, and the implements of his profession . . . below." But the most spectacular of all was the tomb of a young woman killed in a runaway carriage accident. She stood "under a marble canopy supported by angels . . . in her ball-dress." The cost was said to have been in excess of fifteen thousand dollars in a day when a professor's salary was fifteen hundred to two thousand dollars a year.

45

Work and Nature

Work lay at the heart of American life and the attitude of Americans toward it was characteristically ambivalent. As we have had occasion to note from time to time, work was, in the view of people like William Manning, physical labor. But it soon came to be anything people did to make money. For Americans it was a way of serving and praising the Lord, of authenticating the self and of earning a living. At the same time the Scriptures stated quite plainly that work was the primal curse, God's punishment of man for his disobedience.

Americans, however much they may have been divided in their inner beings about the nature of work, developed a new relationship to it. An essential part of that relationship was to make work as close to play as possible, as "light" as possible, to mitigate the curse. Americans loved, above all, to dance; they thus brought into physical labor something of the dance. Observers as different as Richard Henry Dana and Gustaf Unonius noticed the same quality of lightness and gracefulness. "In the matter of work I must note in passing," Unonius wrote, "how native Americans differ from most European immigrants. I have often had occasion to see the former at work with, for example, Swedes and Norwegians. It is hard to tell when an American is really working. He appears to be merely playing with the implements. If anyone by chance passes by, he may spend a long while in conversation with him. Communal affairs and questions of the day are discussed with a vigor that might lead one to imagine this was his real work, and that axe, scythe, plow, or the very busy knife was something held just to keep the hands occupied. The immigrant workman, on the other hand, keeps everlastingly at it, works almost without cessation, silent and sober, seldom rests, undoubtedly uses more muscular power, and yet in the end accomplishes far less."

Unonius quoted a traveler who had written: "Put a Yankee with a horse and an axe on a country road, and he will go into the woods and make a sled of his own invention. Put him in the wilderness," Unonius added, "and he will build a house, in which every small detail is the work of his own hands. In a masterly way he can with his own hands and such materials as he happens to have available make all sorts of things that are generally bought in stores but which he lacks money or the opportunity to buy, or both. So wood is made to do in place of iron, old barrels serve as chimneys, wood stumps as easy chairs, and so forth. American energy is manifested in these comparatively trivial matters as well as in more important inventions. There is nothing a genuine American believes he cannot accomplish, even if he has had no previous experience in it, if necessity or his own advantage urges him to the undertaking."

Sailing to Halifax, Dana and a friend watched the sailors, a mixed crew of Englishmen and Americans, "working & handling . . . the sails. . . . The national characteristics were obvious . . . —the English slow, heavy, old fashioned, strong & sure, the American light, active, quick, ingenious & inventive."

Coupled with the desire to lighten work not merely by the most economical (and thus usually the most graceful) use of the body was, as we noted in the chapter on technology, the disposition to lighten it with the use of tools and of methods, "by analysing the job and devising the easiest way to do it." This constant application of grace and ingenuity to manual labor was, of course, the consequence of the fact that self-employed entrepreneurs did a great part of the gross physical labor required to run the economy, so they had a vested interest in doing it easily and quickly, thus turning labor into money.

But the proposition seems to break down when we turn to those tasks that did not require actual physical labor, tasks that Manning would have refused to call work. These, to be sure, were often done with an equivalent degree of mental skill and ingenuity, but those who did them suffered a depressing attrition of their affective life.

Most visitors remarked on the pale, anxious expressions and nervous debility of American males involved in business or the professions. (Aleksandr Lakier wrote, "The black faces of Africa were far brighter than the pensive somber faces of their masters.") Of our five diarists four—Fisher, Strong, Dana, and Adams—suffered excessively from headaches, stomach disorders, sleeplessness, and periodic depression.

Speaking of the law for which he had been trained, Fisher wrote, "I dislike the profession, & everything connected with it. . . . Most deeply do I thank my stars, which made [me] independent, 'tho not rich. I know of nothing more narrowing to the mind, more debasing to the soul than this same struggle for business at the bar to which so many of our young men are obliged to devote themselves; and nothing has ever disgusted me so much with human nature as to witness the moral qualities which it produces or develops and cherishes."

When a contraction of his income as the result of the prolonged depression that began in 1837 caused Sidney George Fisher to consider seriously pursuing his law practice, he was sunk in gloom. "The idea of being obliged to work is horrible," he wrote in his diary. "It is to me a change of all the habits & feelings of my mind & life & involves an abandonment of my cherished tastes & the bias of my mind . . . I detest business in all its forms, and am unfit to mix in the stir & struggles of the world. Entire freedom & independence are essential to my happiness. . . ."

George Templeton Strong was given to long spells of melancholia, triggered by his "abominable headaches." In addition to homeopathy, Strong tried shower baths and exercise. In October of 1847, Strong wrote in his diary that he had been dosing himself with every drug he could procure to try to relieve "this blighting, paralyzing, disgraceful, hideous, unspeakable disease of nervous dejection and instability that has been down on me like ten thousand tons of granite for the last two years."

Richard Henry Dana, struggling to make a living as a lawyer in Boston and to fight off spells of incapacitating depression, wrote, "God grant that the care of this life may not destroy me. I feel that if I were independent of my profession, & my wife were spared to me, & we could together give ourselves to contemplation, to religious exercise, to nature, to art, to the best of reading & study, spending more of our time at the dear dear shore, we should be more elevated, more tender, more fit for a spiritual world. My only stay at such times, is the thought that God assigns us our duties. My duty is clear. I must support my family, & earn a competency for them, by my profession. This requires indefatigable labor. All I can do is to aim at a life of rectitude & integrity. . . ."

Even Philip Hone hinted at severe emotional difficulties when he noted that he had been reading Lockhart's *Life of Sir Walter Scott,* a book which gave, Hone wrote, "a sort of wild, disjointed history of his mental struggles, disordered feelings, and philosophical reflections." "I have been intensely but painfully interested in all this," Hone wrote. "Perhaps it is that I find a resemblance in his case to my own."

Samuel Gridley Howe, on the other hand, seemed to speak in a much more characteristically American view when he wrote to Charles Sumner: "Life without labor is nothing, nothing, not even love can load the wings of time with those delightful recollections which come from a consciousness of usefulness in its widest sense." But Howe, after all, had the intoxicating experience of breaking through Laura Bridgman's silent world, "work" more exciting than discovering the North Pole.

"Work," unfortunately, was related to "success," and there the real trouble began. Of all our diarists, Sidney George Fisher was the one most frequently moved to reflect upon the cost of success, for the obvious reason that his brilliantly successful brother was there to remind him. Henry presented him, within his own family, with the dilemma of work/wealth. Henry had become rich at an early age not through luck but as "the legitimate consequence of industry, talent, honorable conduct & knowledge of business and of men. . . . I never saw a more happy family," Fisher added, "or one by whom happiness & prosperity was more fully deserved." Yet his large-scale and ambitious business concerns, constantly threatened by the general economic instability of the country, were a constant worry and concern to Henry Fisher. His brother noted in the fall of 1845 that Henry was "well nigh used up by fatigue, anxiety & excitement." He had made thirty-five thousand dollars in the past year and lived in lavish style, but it was clear that he paid an increasingly heavy price in strain and worry. With the severe depression of 1857, Henry found himself dangerously overextended and the diarist was worried about him. "The labor & excitement of carrying his immense business thro these difficult times are wearing him out," Fisher wrote. "He says he has no enjoyment in life and does not sleep at night. What good does all his money produce? Toil, anxiety, no time for thought or mental improvement, and the sword of Damocles hanging over his head. . . . As business is conducted in this country, it is so nearly allied to gambling that any one who has a competence is very foolish not to be satisfied. But the excitement of a career, love of action, of influence, pride of display and want of mental resources lead most men from one enterprise to another, until to stop is difficult, even if they desire it, and the temptation to make still more too great to be resisted and so life passes & is gone, without real enjoyment or worthy purpose accomplished." Fisher continued to be, through his brother, dependent to a degree on the Reading Railroad and to resent that dependence bitterly, indirect though it was. "My connection with this company," he wrote five years later, "and all that it revealed to me have completed & confirmed my aversion and disgust at all business and businessmen. They live in a very base and inferior world, and I would prefer a thousand times poverty and obscurity to any degree of fortune or influence that can be obtained only by a sacrifice of all that is best and worthiest in life. The only way to have property is to inherit it, and the universal feeling of the world that makes this the basis of the position of a gentleman is founded in truth and nature." For Fisher to have had to work at a mundane job "would have been intellectual suicide, the abandonment of knowledge, truth, beauty, thought, independence, leisure, of everything that I was accustomed to enjoy & for which I wished to live."

The key word here was "independence." The problem with "work" for members of the upper class was that it meant "dependence" and usually the sacrifice of one's standards of right and wrong, a loss of precious integrity.

Besides his successful brother, Fisher was clearly fascinated, if repelled, by the classic American high achiever. George Cadwalader, scion of one of the great families of the city, had been involved in the bloody native American riots several years earlier as commander of the city forces and then gone off to win laurels for himself in the Mexican War. He told Fisher that "campaigning is a delightful life. . . . Among other things, he said that when cannon shot struck a company of men, you can distinctly hear the blow & the bones crack. . . . Cadwalader is a remarkable person," Fisher noted. "He has a fine physique, great strength & activity, a handsome manly figure & face, an appearance of exuberant vitality & power, energy, boldness, decision of character. . . . Hence his remarkable success in all he undertakes. He has made a large fortune & lives in more luxury & style than any man in town. . . . Withal he is a gentleman in his manners as he is in birth and breeding. On the other hand, he is uncultivated, unintelligent, selfish & heartless, addicted wholly to money-making & sensual enjoyments." The type was not, of course, confined to Philadelphia. As a trustee of Columbia, George Templeton Strong sat on a board made up, in large part, of "rich merchants, illiterate and purse-proud." What, he asked, could be expected "from such a lot of men but vulgar pride in power and abuse of authority and absolute ignorance of courtesy as well as scholarship?"

His father-in-law's wildly fluctuating fortunes led Strong to reflections on the American struggle for success strikingly similar to those of Fisher's. Samuel Bayard Ruggles was heavily involved in coal mines and in the Erie Railroad. In addition he undertook to build the Atlantic Docks. Overextended, some of his loans were called and at once his financial empire came crashing down, plunging the whole family into the deepest gloom and involving a number of Ruggles's friends and associates. "What a lesson this miserable business is against speculation!" Strong wrote in his diary. "Talents, genius, that could have gained a fortune in ten years' steady legitimate labor, bearing no fruit but insolvency, bitter self-reproach, and the memory of a life's unavailing struggle, of a long series of harrowing cares and sickening uncertainty—and ruin at last." Although to his son-in-law, just turned thirty, the senior Ruggles doubtless seemed ancient, he was still a comparatively young man in his late forties and having survived the debacle of the Atlantic Dock venture, he was soon rebuilding his fortune by only slightly less perilous financial ventures. Strong deplored "the system that makes the utmost fruit of steady industry vulgar and cheap when compared with the glittering results" of speculation which, although the exception, "occur often enough to lure the multitude and make us a nation of gamblers, easily classified as a minority of millionaires sprinkled through a majority of beggars. . . . That is the worst of our wretched 'financial' system. It degrades, debases, demoralizes its victims. They look men in the face whom they have ruined by breaking their promises, and have nothing to say but that it was a 'business transaction.' It dissolves out all the sterling integrity there may be in the great mass of people, and leaves the dross and dirt behind. The practical question for the merchant and the

financier becomes, 'For how much is my credit good in Wall Street?'—
not, 'Shall I be able to keep my promise and pay this debt I'm
contracting?' . . . Mr. Ruggles suffers from the system into which
brilliant and sanguine men, possessed of energy, fertility, and ambition, must inevitably be led in this age and country."

"Is it the doom of all men in this nineteenth century," Strong
asked himself, "to be weighed down with the incumbrance of a desire
to make money and save money, all their days? I suppose if my career
is prosperous, it will be spent in the thoughtful, diligent accumulation
of dollars, till I suddenly wake up to the sense that the career is ended
and the dollars dross. So we are gradually carried into the social
currents that belong to our time, whether it be the tenth century, or
this cold-blooded, interest-calculating age of our own. . . ."

The passage is one of the most poignant and revealing in all of
Strong's journals. No one, he had come to feel, could entirely escape
"the social currents of" his time.

Money, as we have argued before, is the essential ordering
element in American life. Most posttribal societies have had elaborate
systems of "ordering." In France and England there were three
traditional "estates," or orders—the nobility, the clergy, and the
commons—recognized in the political and legal arrangements of those
nations. The commons represented the middle class, the substantial
property holders, and the lower classes were virtually unrepresented,
subsumed under burghs or populated places owned often by a
member of the nobility. Or they belonged to guilds of craftsmen. In
the United States nobody "belonged" anywhere. Money was the only
principle of order, the only thing that defined the individual and
placed him in some recognizable social context. Thus money occupied
a place in American society that it did in no other modern or ancient
society. It was not just a medium of exchange, it was a badge of
identification, it was class, guild, corporation rolled into one. In class
societies access to money was controlled by those who held power and
access was denied to the powerless. Americans knew instinctively that
"equality" and "democracy" were empty words if they were not
accompanied by general access to money. Money was, therefore, the
essence of politics, and nothing aroused the emotions of Americans as
much as the issue of its availability. As we have seen, they would
willingly, if not gladly, endure the most chaotic economic conditions if
that was the price that had to be paid for their access to money. It was

futile and beside the point for foreign visitors (and many native Americans) to bemoan American greed and materialism, to deplore the fact that most Americans talked excessively of money. It was well and good for an English gentleman, living on the rents from tenants or dividends from industrial stocks, to talk condescendingly about the obsession of Americans with money; money was all the great majority of Americans had to *define* them, to identify them to their fellow citizens. It was not by chance that Americans so commonly asked what a man was "worth," as though he were a prize steer or a winning racehorse. Was he worth two hundred thousand dollars? Five hundred thousand dollars? If the notion that men were born equal was not a lie or a fraud, it could only mean that every American had, at least theoretically, an equal opportunity to define himself by making money. Increasingly there came to be other ways of self-definition, most typically professional careers, college education, inherited money and social standing, a historic name, outstanding skill or talent in a particular line, active work in "reform," often in trying to combat the evil effects of money. But money preceded and underlay them all. It is not too much to say that the most critical question every young American male had to work out in the period of his initial "identity crisis" was what his relation was going to be to money. Would he devote his life single-mindedly to the acquisition of it? Or would he limit himself to enough to live comfortably and do "good works"? Or would he, with God's help, leave it to take care of itself and devote his life to a "calling," a vocation, like the ministry or abolitionism or temperance, or perhaps even politics.

The most instructive nineteenth-century dialogue on the question of money versus "service" may be the exchange of letters between John Quincy Adams and his prickly, hypersensitive son, Charles Francis. The son was clearly irritated with the father for not coming back to Quincy after he was defeated by Jackson, taking care of his business interests and settling placidly into old age. Instead the old man insisted on making a national spectacle of himself by his eccentric refusal to respect party lines and his determination to subject every issue to the measure of his conscience. The irritation was plainly mixed with pride but the former emotion came out clearly in the letters Charles Francis wrote chiding his father for being so indifferent to his worldly interests which were, of course, Charles Francis's interests too, since he was the only surviving son. When Charles Francis complained to his mother about his father's tactlessness, his mother urged him to be patient and restrained—"do not be hurt at any expression, for his mind is too much engrossed by self to remember or enter into the feelings of others."

Charles Francis's immediate annoyance stemmed from his father's admonition, "you like others must be the maker of your own fortunes, and if you are frightened or disheartened by the turbulence, and dangers and disasters of all political adventure, learn to number your days so as to apply your heart unto wisdom. Turn your attention to making money. Get rich, apply all the faculties that God has given you to hoarding up treasures, and see if *that* will secure to you a happier state of existence than that which has been the lot of your father and grandfather." It was a cruel and wounding letter and it is not surprising that Charles Francis replied to it with some asperity. "The only basis of public conduct which I can find in any direction," he wrote, "is private interest, the desire of personal aggrandisement. This desire, according to your own showing leads every man entirely to overlook or disregard the rights of others, it produces a perpetual exacerbation of feeling against some person or other who may momentarily be an obstacle. . . ." By which Charles Francis appeared to be saying that what we would call today ego satisfaction was "the only basis of public conduct." Some people derived their satisfaction from making money, others from exercising political power. His father "pled for higher motives and feelings than you give credit for to any body else." The son could not go so far as to gainsay him; he left that to his own conscience and sense of rectitude. "I am unable to contest the goodness of your reasons for remaining in public life," he added. Such a career was not to his liking and if it had not been for the obligation placed on him by being an Adams, Charles Francis would gladly have stayed out of politics entirely. "Of the acquisition of Wealth as an *end* of life, I trust I understand pretty accurately the value. Of its possession as a *means* of independent action in all its relations. . . . I do not believe that I can think too highly. To be a slave to a game of chance would be as bad as to be a slave to the game of reputation [is he charging his father with the latter crime?]. They are both and equally contrary to the injunctions of the gospel and the doctrines of all enlightened philosophy." The son was convinced that the only hope for peace of mind came "from the power of rigid self-regulation—a power which is never acquired as your own letters bear witness in the storms of political faction, nor in the fluctuations of the Exchange." Did his father truly derive his "winter's satisfaction" from such ephemeral events as the applause of his colleagues in the House when his resolution on the conflict with France passed, or "the little breeze of popular favor" that followed his eulogy of Lafayette? There was bitterness behind the candor and the dialogue was inconclusive. Charles Francis seemed to say that an iron will and relentless self-control behind an imperturbable mask was the path if not to happiness at least to some measure of equanimity in the face of the tragedies and disappointments of life. All the rest—political fame or material wealth—was an illusion.

Gustaf Unonius had some shrewd comments to make on American materialism. "We are living in an industrial age," he wrote, "and Americans . . . want to make money; but so do the Swedes and Europeans in general. The only difference is that Americans seem to know better how to do it. . . . The American is a speculator rather than a servant of Mammon in the real sense of the word. . . . With his wealth he often supports liberally undertakings for the welfare of his country. As he plans his own future, he often has in mind also the advancement and improvement of his community. He does not hover greedily over the gold he has accumulated; he does not keep his wealth in idleness. . . . He is avid for money, but he is not mean and avaricious." He generously supported universities and "hundreds of other institutions established and maintained for the good of society. . . ."

The American was a generalist, a jack-of-all-trades. In the words of Philip Hone "there is a striking difference between the people of Europe and those of our own country, which arises perhaps from the nature of our political institutions and the newness of everything around us, which affords greater freedom of action and a larger scope of imagination." The difference "consists in the larger proportion of men in the old countries who know each of them some one thing better than any one else, in science, mechanics, or philosophy, whilst they are comparatively ignorant of everything else; persons who make one study, one pursuit, one occupation the business of life to the exclusion of every other, and become in time, on that point, the oracles and instructors of their fellow men. . . . We, on the contrary, know a little of everything and nothing to perfection. Everybody here of a decent education writes tolerably well, speaks with fluency, has a calculating head and skillful hands; but his knowledge from being more diversified is more superficial. . . . An American blacksmith would think meanly of himself if he could not argue a point of law with the village lawyer."

Moritz Busch met a German immigrant who had been a tailor's apprentice in the motherland. "Here he had become a farmhand, had changed himself into a pedlar, and had crept out of this chrysalis to become a trapper. Then, through a goodly number of metamorphoses—during which he taught the mysteries of the ABC in Missouri, was a steamboat fireman in Illinois, worked as a commercial clerk in Kentucky, as a sexton in Indiana, and as a preacher in Virginia, depicted heaven and hell to visitors at camp meetings—he had become one of the most esteemed lawyers in Ohio."

In addition to the constant "metamorphoses" in American life, things were seldom what they appeared to be, which was particularly unsettling for visitors. The man that Moritz Busch saw sweeping out a bank in an Ohio town turned out to be not the janitor but the president. The young dandy was not a touring aristocrat but a clerk; the fashionably dressed young lady was actually a young lady's maid. The building that looked like a temple was a bank and the structure that rather resembled a bank turned out to be a church. The man dressed like a preacher was a riverboat gambler; the man dressed like a riverboat gambler might well be the apostle of a new and flourishing religious sect. What looked like a carnival was a political meeting or a religious revival.

Since Americans were not fixed to a class or a social role, they had every inducement to play any number of "parts." All America seemed at times to be engaged in a vast stage play. The "play element" which was so conspicuous a part of American life began with the individual player.

"Nature" like "duty" or "progress" was one of the key words in the American lexicon. The infatuation with nature was, to a discernible degree, an upper-middle-class antidote to the increasing intractability of the human world. Many sensitive souls turned from contemplation of man in America, a scene of almost indescribable chaos and disorder, to Nature, which ambivalent as she might be, gave hints of some design. Richard Henry Dana sought constantly in nature relief from the corrosive anxieties and periods of despondency that beset him. Vacationing in New Hampshire, he walked the craggy shores and found, among the rocks, "the most delicate, tender, little flower in nature. . . . I took it up, & for the first time in my life made the flower completely a person. The impersonation was so entire that I unconsciously talked to it as to a hearing & feeling thing. How perfect, I felt, is the system of the universe. . . . I could not forbear kissing the delicate little thing with a feeling of gratitude, pity & protecting care. What a world is this! What beasts, what sinners, what insensible creatures fill this earth! What is to be the end, the explanation of this mystery? May my heart be kept open to all that is simple & pure in nature! I need such helps, or my state will be fearfully hard & cold."

"Man," Dana wrote in another passage, "has dominion over the birds of the air, the beasts of the field, & the fish of the sea. In its extent, this dominion is unlimited except by the laws of humanity. There must be no cruelty, no needless suffering inflicted, & no more taking of life than the wants of man, in the way of food, clothing, labor, or science or art, perhaps also exercise & recreation justly warrant. Whatever we may say or feel about the taking of life, is not this the truth? Is it not the truth of Scripture & of reason?"

Crawford's Notch, the Indian Pass of the Adirondack, and Mt. Washington were all mountains that Dana climbed and about whose scenic wonders he wrote ecstatically in his diary: "The view from the Grand Stairs [at Mt. Washington] is one [of] the most beautiful & grand I ever saw. . . . Eye hath not seen nor ear heard nor hath it entered into the heart of man to conceive, anything more gorgeous, more magnificent . . . I . . . wandered about the rocks, alone, gazing at them, lost in wonder, & able only to call out—'Great God—Great God!!' I was overpowered with the scene, as if I had been taken up upon an exceeding high mountain apart & admitted to a slight revelation of the beauties & grandeur of 'the world that is to come.' " The air was like a tonic—"I stood & sucked it in, inhaled it with all the force of my organs, feeling that every breath was of the essence of life. The thought came across me,—could I only be able to make this very wind, in its exact present state, to blow for eight & forty hours into the streets & lanes, the cellars & garrets, the work shops & offices & sick rooms of our cities,—what a divine visitation, what a memorable time of healing & health would it not be!"

A noteworthy by-product of the romantic infatuation with nature was the increasingly popular "camping trip." "Camping" had formerly been something done only out of necessity by the soldier in the field or the emigrant traveling west. Now necessity became play, and upperclass Americans began to "camp" as a form of recreation, a very odd notion to an individual who had suffered over hundreds of miles of forest and prairie. Camping helped accentuate the difference between the destructive character of the city and the healing and restorative quality of nature. It encouraged, as we have seen in Dana, thoughts of the exalted and the "sublime." It was morally improving, a kind of Christian exercise, closely related to or accompanied by prayer. One could reflect upon the nature of the Infinite Power, meditate and relax from the merciless pace of daily life.

In such an age Niagara Falls was a never-to-be-forgotten spectacle. Thomas Hamilton, the Scottish traveler who found little else to admire in the United States, wrote of his first sight of the Falls, "The spectator at first feels as if stricken by catalepsy. His blood ceases to flow, or rather is sent back in overpowering pressure on the heart. He gasps, 'like a drowning man,' to catch a mouthful of air. . . . The past and the future are obliterated, and he stands mute and powerless, in the presence of that scene of awful splendour on which his gaze is riveted. . . . The results of that single moment will extend through a lifetime, enlarge the sphere of thought, and influence the whole tissue of his moral being."

Lincoln, who visited Niagara Falls in 1849 on his way home from Washington, after his brief term as a Congressman, wrote a vivid description of their awesomeness and then added, "But still there is more. It calls up the indefinite past. When Columbus first sought this continent—when Christ suffered on the cross—when Moses led Israel through the Red Sea—nay, even, when Adam first came from the hand of his Maker—then as now, Niagara was roaring here. The eyes of that species of extinct giants, whose bones fill the mounds of America, have gazed on Niagara, as ours do now. Contemporary with the whole race of men, and older than the first man, Niagara is strong, and fresh to-day as ten thousand years ago. . . . Never dried, never froze, never slept, never rested."

In all the nineteenth century's adulation of "Nature" there was buried a profound anomaly. Sexuality was the most powerful fact of nature. "Man's animal nature," was a code phrase for sexuality. "Natural man" was a man of uninhibited appetites. Yet the lovers of Nature with a capital "N" could not deal with the issue of sexuality at all. So there was another "split," another division of the ego. The yearning to merge with Nature continually ran into the uncomfortable fact that nature was full of dark passions, lusts of the blood, competition for survival. One sympathizes, to a degree, with Lowell's rather ill-humored complaint: "I look upon a great deal of the modern sentimentalism about Nature as a mark of disease. It is one more symptom of the general liver complaint. To a man of wholesome constitution the wilderness is well enough for a mood or a vacation, but not for a habit of life." It seemed to Lowell that a devotion to nature was too often accompanied by sentimentalism and "a misanthropic contempt for mankind in general."

46

American Character

The disintegrative character of American life disposed the individual American to join anything or everything to escape from an often devastating feeling of isolation. As Captain Marryat put it, "the Americans are society mad," and Moritz Busch, noting the fondness of German immigrants for fraternal organizations, observed that his countrymen could join the Whigs or the Democrats and then, since such political affiliations usually left something to be desired in fraternal good cheer, could "crawl into the Masonic tapeworm articulated in thirty-three degrees" or "help make the world happy as a member of the 'Ancient and Honorable Order of Odd Fellows,'" an imitation of the Masonic order which professed to have originated among the soldiers of the first-century Roman army and which by the 1850s counted twenty-five hundred lodges and over two hundred thousand members. "All these secret doll boxes of a pompous caste-feeling," Busch wrote, "are crammed to suffocation." Busch was the rather cynical spectator at an Odd Fellows' parade through the streets of Dayton, Ohio; "four bands, its adornment of bright-colored bandoleers and gold braid and tassels and its pompous speeches and toasts" may have failed to impress Busch, but the local paper declared that they made "an unforgettable impression upon every soul receptive to beauty and the sublime."

In New York, the Odd Fellows were forming a benevolent organization "for assisting distressed brethren, educating their orphan children and doing all sorts of good things among themselves," and they invited George Templeton Strong to join. He wrote in his diary that "the Church—if its principles be but carried out as they should be—is quite union enough . . . I'll have nothing to do with self-created substitutes, whether they are called Temperance Societies or Odd Fellow lodges. What the present age seems to want is to get by voluntary societies and unauthorized and unchristian (if not anti-christian) means and devices at the temporal and visible benefits for which, among other things, the church was instituted—which she ought to be effecting now, and which in former days she did effect, and to do so without what their devisers call bigotry, priestcraft, and superstition. . . . In short, I'm strongly inclined to think that the I. O. of O.F., with all its humbug and frippery, is intended to be—seriously expected by many of its brethren to become—a sort of cheap substitute for Christianity, and I won't touch it."

By the same token Americans loved meetings and conventions and came for hundreds of miles to attend them at great cost and with great difficulty. The chambers of commerce met, the Masons, the Odd Fellows, the temperance reformers, the ministerial associations, the tailors and the teamsters. They flocked to New York, to Boston, to Cincinnati, to Baltimore and Philadelphia. They exchanged fraternal "greetings," listened patiently to interminable speeches and wearisome reports, paraded, if that was their disposition, and returned home, exhausted and sanctified.

Related to, if distinct from, the desire for social association was the capacity for political coalescence. Isabella Bird noted that "When a number of persons hit upon a grievance, real or supposed, they unite themselves into a society, and invite delegates from other districts. With a celerity which can hardly be imagined, declarations are issued and papers established advocating party views; public meetings are held, and a complete organization is secured, with ramifications extending all over the country. A formidable and compact body thus arises."

Closely related to the endless "associations," to the forming of groups and communities, was the classic American fear of being alone—of loneliness. To Marryat, Americans seemed to dread being alone themselves and unwilling to leave others alone. "There is no part of the world, perhaps," he wrote, "where you have more difficulty in obtaining permission to be alone, and indulge in a reverie, than in America. The Americans are as gregarious as schoolboys, and think it an incivility to leave you by yourself. Everything is done in crowds, and among a crowd." Emerson and Thoreau agreed that amid all the noise and bustle and glitter of American life there was a profound loneliness—in Emerson's words, an "eternal loneliness . . . how insular and pathetically solitary are all the people we know!"

Americans were conspicuously people of the word. Gustaf Unonius expressed his admiration for "the extraordinary ease with which the American expresses himself. As a rule he is undeniably a born speaker, and on all questions that concern conditions in his country, its constitution and its institutions, he generally displays great knowledge and keenness no matter how ignorant and uncultivated he may be otherwise." In Unonius's opinion this was due to the free schools "in which citizens are educated from their early youth to take part in the government of their country and vote on all questions." George Ticknor, a sophisticated young man fresh from the delights of German scholarship, wrote of hearing Webster's oration at Plymouth Rock in 1820: "I was never so excited by public speaking before in my life. Three of four times I thought my temples would burst with the gush of blood." Emerson, one of the most famous lecturers of the age, wrote of Edward Everett: "There was an influence on the young people from the genius of Everett which was almost comparable to that of Pericles in Athens. . . . If any of my readers were at that period in Boston or Cambridge, they will easily remember his radiant beauty of person, of a classic style, his heavy large eye, marble lids, which gave the impression of mass which the slightness of his form needed; sculptured lips; a voice of such rich tones, such precise and perfect utterance, that, although slightly nasal, it was the most mellow and beautiful and correct of all the instruments of the time."

Infatuated with lectures, Americans turned out by the thousands to hear discourses on any subject under the sun or moon. Gustaf Unonius tells of a Swedish baron whose efforts in the goldfields had come to nothing who saw a large snake one day when he was resting from his labors. Staring at it, he found he could hypnotize it and dominate it completely. Fascinated by this chance discovery, he began collecting poisonous snakes as well. "Finally," Gustaf Unonius, his fellow immigrant wrote, "it occurred to him that it would be more profitable to devote himself to snake charming than to gold digging in California." He studied all he could find out about snakes, and "since everything in America has to be done with lectures, he gave at his performances regular talks on the anatomy of snakes and related matters. . . . These performances proved most profitable."

Carl Schurz, who went on the lecture circuit to help make ends meet, as did so many men of letters and political figures, wrote that he valued the experience because he "saw what I might call the middle-class culture in process of formation." He met many men and women of limited education and opportunity "in the somewhat lonesome far Western towns" where life was often "dreary enough" but who desired "to keep pace with the progress of civilization in all its aspects, by informing themselves about the products of literature, the achievements of science, and the aims and appliances of humanitarian movements. I was often astonished," he added, "at the eager activity of the minds and the largeness of the ideas disclosed by school teachers and small country tradesmen, and village doctors and little lawyers." Much was crude and some things absurdly pretentious, but Schurz saw "in those debating clubs and philosophical societies, and literary circles . . . the growing processes of people great in intellectual and moral energy."

Americans were almost as infatuated with the written word as with the spoken one—at least the word as it appeared in the ubiquitous newspapers that flourished in every village and hamlet across the United States. There was general agreement that the press was, taken as a whole, impossibly licentious, crude, and barbarous. Philip Hone's special object of contempt was James Gordon Bennett's *New York Tribune.* Hone hoped in vain that his paper would be boycotted by all decent people. "Write him down, make respectable people withdraw their support from the vile sheet," he declared, "so that it shall be considered disgraceful to read it, and the serpent will be rendered harmless." But the mixture of gossip, scandal, and political and social crusading that Bennett had made his trademark proved irresistible to New Yorkers of all classes, and although ladies and gentlemen cut him cold and his wife was forced to take refuge in England much of the time, people continued to read his scandalous sheet avidly. Bennett had been, Marryat noted, "horse-whipped, kicked, trodden under foot, spat upon, and degraded in every possible way; but all this he courts because it brings him in money."

Hone, who had been chairman of the great Boz Ball in Dickens's honor, was indignant at the author's abuse of his American admirers but he applauded his attack on the "horrible licentiousness of the daily press . . . the stupendous evil. . . . It is for sentiments like these," Hone wrote, "that this lively writer, whose works have been hitherto so popular in this country, is now vilified and misrepresented. And so will any man who has the moral courage to make battle against this frightful monster who stalks unrebuked through the land, blasting with its pestiferous breath everything bright and lovely. . . ."

At the same time, Marryat, who was no friend to the press, pointed out that Great Britain, with a population of twenty-six million, had only three hundred and seventy newspapers while the United States, with, roughly, ten million fewer people, had more than a thousand, and Isabella Bird wrote: "The contents of an American paper are very miscellaneous. Besides the news of the day, it contains congressional and legal reports, exciting fiction, and reports of sermons, religious discussions, and religious anniversaries. It prys into every department of society, and informs its readers as to the doings and condition of all."

"Without reporters," Aleksandr Lakier wrote, "not a single official or ceremonial breakfast or dinner could take place, nor a single ball of a minister, consul, or other official." If there were speeches the reporter "pulls out his little book and takes notes. . . . The next day the whole country will learn what happened, and if it is interesting, it will be reprinted. . . . One cannot take a step or two out of the ordinary that someone does not notice it and publish it." The principal newspapers, Lakier noted, had their foreign correspondents, and news from abroad was awaited with the greatest eagerness. A boat was sent out to intercept steamships from abroad and the foreign news was thrown overboard in a small tarred barrel to be picked up and rushed to the telegraph office and broadcast all over the country.

By 1854 there were some four hundred daily papers in the United States and 2,217 weekly papers. "The New York publications," George Combe wrote, "are composed of the plunder of European novels and magazines; of reports of sermons by popular preachers; of stories, horrors, and mysteries; of police reports, in which crime and misery are concocted into melo-dramas now exciting sympathy, now laughter; with a large sprinkling of news and politics . . . they may be regarded as representing to some extent the *general* mind; and certainly they are not calculated to convey a very high opinion of it."

James Watson Webb, the editor of the *New York Courier and Enquirer,* denounced the temperance champion and Kentucky Congressman Thomas Marshall, who demanded satisfaction and seriously wounded Webb in the leg. But Webb was incorrigible. When he was denounced in Congress by a Jacksonian from Maine named Cilley, he challenged Cilley to a duel. The latter refused the challenge on the grounds that Webb was not a gentleman and that Cilley could not be held accountable for remarks made in debate in Congress. At this point a Kentucky Congressman named Graves took up Webb's cause and challenged Cilley. Cilley chose rifles at eighty yards, and on the third round of fire Cilley was fatally wounded. The duel roused such a furor in the country that Congress finally bestirred itself and passed a law which "provided death to all survivors when anyone was killed, and five years' imprisonment for giving or accepting a challenge. . . ."

In 1846 the most sensational duel was between the editors of rival Whig and Democratic papers in Richmond, Virginia. John Hampdon Pleasants, a man of fifty-four with a wife and children, was editor of the *Star* and Thomas Ritchie, Jr., twenty-five, was an editor of the *Enquirer*. From insults in their papers they passed to "duelling," and Philip Hone noted, "Disgraceful and shocking as it may appear, the combatants were permitted to go into the combat with all kinds of weapons—pistols, rifles, broadswords and broadaxes, tomahawks and bowie-knives." First they fired at each other and then rushed at each other, "hacking and slashing in slaughter-house fashion." Pleasants, badly mutilated, died soon after the encounter and Ritchie was freed.

Some Southern papers, the story went, had a man on their staff "to attend exclusively to the fighting part of the business. If the writing editor branded you before the public as a liar," David Macrae wrote, "and you went in Southern fashion to demand satisfaction, he handed you over politely to the fighting editor—the gentleman who managed the pistolling department." Macrae was startled, in visiting the offices of the *Mobile Tribune* in Alabama, to see a sign on the door which read: "Positively no admittance until after two o'clock. Except to whip the editors."

The American press was clearly not a "press" in the conventional sense of the word but a phenomenon. The greatest medium for the dissemination of slander and invective ever invented, it was also a channel for the transmission of an essential modicum of factual information and, like almost everything in American life, a form of entertainment. Editors were invariably political partisans and often anxious to advance their own political ambitions. They were also, as James Preston Webb's career reminds us, poor actuarial risks. Shot at and horsewhipped, they often shot back. Violent words provoked violent acts and the destruction of presses printing unpopular material was by no means an infrequent occurrence, as we have seen with Lovejoy, Birney, and the Mormons. Perhaps Isabella Bird said it best: "Declamatory speaking and writing are the safety-valves of a free community."

In addition to newspapers, American popular reading fare included magazines and books—novels and how-to-do-it works. Magazines and journals were started up continually, some like the *Southern Literary Messenger* edited by Poe, publishing the best contemporary writing, others purveying hackwork of the most inferior kind. In 1839 two journalists, Rufus Griswold and Park Benjamin, started a weekly magazine called *Brother Jonathan,* which concentrated on reprinting, without payment, popular British novels. This soon spawned a rival, *The New World.* The two magazines entered into competition to publish the cheapest "supplements"—unbound or paperback editions of popular novels. The new technology of printing enabled them to sell such works for from 6 1/4 cents to 37 1/2 cents, with many in the twenty-five-cent range. Frederika Bremer's novels in translation were issued in such a format, along with works by Balzac and Eugène Sue's enormously popular book *The Wandering Jew.* Walter Whitman's temperance novel, *Frederick Evans,* was also published in paperback. Soon a number of magazines and newspapers followed the path blazed by *Brother Jonathan* and *The New World.* Scott's works were published at twenty-five cents a volume, as was Louis Adolphe Thiers's *History of the French Revolution.* Harper & Brother, who had been pirating English books for years, felt themselves threatened, and began to turn out their own cheap editions of popular works. Nothing, of course, equaled the popularity of Dickens's novels, which appeared in a wide variety of editions. Frank Luther Mott estimated that at least four hundred thousand sets of Dickens were sold in the United States.

Victor Hugo's *Hunchback of Notre Dame* was another imported novel, as was Bulwer-Lytton's *The Last Days of Pompeii.* The latter sold at ten dollars in a de luxe edition and in paperback for ten cents. There were literally hundreds of British novels pirated by American publishers. The appetite of their readers for them seemed insatiable; more copies of British books were often sold in the United States than in Great Britain.

The most serious rival to Samuel Goodrich, "Peter Parley," as a producer of books for girls and boys was the Reverend Jacob Abbott. A Congregational minister and the headmaster of the Mt. Vernon

School for Girls in Boston, Abbott wrote the enormously popular *The Young Christian,* followed by more than two hundred works, including the Rollo Books, designed to teach moral principles along with science, geography, and history. The Rollo series sold a million and a quarter volumes in twenty-five years. *Swiss Family Robinson,* published in 1832 in Harper's "Boys and Girls Library of Useful and Entertaining Knowledge" was another best-seller.

In addition there was a host of by now long-forgotten novels, most of them by women, all highly moral and cloyingly sentimental. Susan Warner's *The Wide, Wide World* was characteristic of the genre. Her father was an unsuccessful lawyer and the family, yearning for the respectability that in America came only with some degree of affluence, lived a desperately marginal life. Susan Warner wrote a novel of the Christian fortitude displayed by her family in the face of adversity. The *North American Review* declared, "We know not where, in any language, we shall find [the] graphic truth excelled." Church journals praised Warner for having succeeded "better than any other writer in our language in making religious sentiment appear natural and attractive, in a story that possesses the interest of romance." Published in 1850, after having been turned down by a number of publishers, it sold over half a million copies in the United States and perhaps as many abroad. Maria Susanna Cummins and Mary J. Holmes were almost equally successful, the latter lady turning out thirty sentimental novels during her career.

At this point, the reader will hardly have to be persuaded that Americans were violent people. There was mob violence, personal violence, and violent crime. Hone mentioned the case of a wild altercation in the Arkansas legislature where the speaker of the Assembly, after exchanging heated remarks with a member of the house, had left his chair, drawn a bowie knife, and stabbed his adversary to death. A jury found the speaker "Guilty of excusable homicide," and the judge discharged him.

Vigilance committees were often formed, especially in frontier communities, to try to control violence. Charles Pancoast reported the general lawlessness of Warsaw, Missouri, but no one would suggest that it was necessary to go to the frontier to find violence. Duelling, as we have just noted, was one of the most striking manifestations of violence in American life. Even the halls of Congress were not immune to threats of violence. Carl Schurz, accompanying a Wisconsin Congressman named Potter to the House of Representatives, "saw him buckle on a belt with a pistol and a bowie-knife." There was, every day, he told Schurz, the danger of an attack by Southerners on the floor or "from a gang of . . . desperadoes gathered in the galleries." Later, when a Southern firebrand challenged him to a duel, Potter chose bowie knives, at which his challenger backed down on the grounds that the bowie knife was "not a civilized weapon."

In January, 1840, Philip Hone noted in his diary: "Riot, disorder, and violence increase in our city: every night is marked by some outrage committed by gangs of young ruffians who prowl the streets insulting females, breaking into the houses of unoffending publicans, making night hideous by yells of disgusting inebriety, and— unchecked by the city authorities—commiting every sort of enormity with apparent impunity." One such gang broke into a house where a company of German immigrants was celebrating the New Year and smashed furniture and insulted the women present. Driven out by the Germans, they returned with reinforcements, vowing "Death to the Dutchmen." The defenders of the house fired on the gang, killing the leader and wounding three or four others.

Isabella Bird tells us that in New York in 1852 "one person in seven of the whole population came under the notice of the authorities, either in the ranks of criminal or paupers. . . . The existence of a 'dangerous class' in New York was manifest."

In June, 1860, the *New Orleans Daily Crescent* recapitulated the yearly crime statistics of the parish. The population of New Orleans at the time was 150,000 whites, 11,000 free blacks, and 14,500 slaves. Over the previous year the following arrests had been made, the paper reported:

For murder	62
Stabbing with intent to murder	146
Assault with deadly weapon	734
Arson and attempted arson	42
Burglary	44
Highway robbery	53
Larceny	2148
Swindling	238
Suspicious character	2110
Assaults and battery, threats and miscellaneous transgressions	47,403

Audubon, writing of the Kentucky frontier, noted: "Sometimes, in cases of reiterated theft or murder, death is considered necessary; and, in some instances, delinquents of the worst species have been shot, after which their heads have been stuck on poles, to deter others from following their example." A desperado named Mason who, operating with a band of thieves and murderers from a settlement on Wolf Island in the Mississippi, preyed on flatboats headed down the river to New Orleans, met such a fate.

What we would call today white-collar crime flourished. It ranged from employing workers under hazardous conditions in order to make money, to the bribery of state legislators and Congressmen. On the state level it was evident that while some legislators were bribed quite openly, others were more often simply persuaded to vote for certain measures by agents of interested corporations who, "under the pretense of explaining the subject to the members, flatter them, give them suppers, and open their understandings by means of plentiful libations of wine," George Combe wrote. Many of the legislators were men from country districts, "of little education and humble fortune, but of unquestionable integrity, who would reject with indignation a money bribe, but who unconsciously fall before personal flatteries and champagne." "The technical name for these practices," Combe added, "is 'lobbying.'" "The railroad cars bring up the boxes of champagne, brandy, cigars, and delicacies of all kinds" and "the members of the legislature are at liberty to partake gratuitously of the eating, the drinking, and the roaring frolics carried on in these places of resort, which are open all day and all night. . . ." In New York lobbying had been reduced to such a system that agents or lobbyists themselves often answered the roll calls on various votes on the grounds that the issues were too complex for the legislators to understand.

Tocqueville emphasized the American obsession with the idea of equality and the irony of the fact that the pressures for conformity were enormous in the "land of the free." George Combe was almost as alarmed as Tocqueville over the tyranny of the majority which, in his view, produced a kind of "moral cowardice" among politicians and public figures generally, who risked their popularity by espousing causes that flew in the face of the opinions of the majority. At the same time Combe emphasized that certain courageous individuals defied public opinion with "impunity." Fanny Kemble wrote in much the same spirit of the pressures of conformity in America—"this 'what-'ll-Mrs. Grundy say' devotion to conformity in small things and great . . . this dread of singularity which has eaten up all individuality amongst them, and makes their population like so many moral and mental lithographs, and their houses like so many thousand hideous brick twins."

Some members of the upper class could get away with unorthodox behavior if they were wealthy enough to be independent. Gustavus Dickinson, an heir of the important and wealthy Dickinson family, "married a woman socially much beneath him," Sidney George Fisher noted, "and having strong passions & no self-control, insensible to the restraint of public opinion indeed, & with plenty of money," did as he pleased to the distress of his family, more especially his mother, who took to her bed in anger and mortification. Dickinson compounded his crime of making an unsuitable marriage by abandoning his family and living openly with his mistress. "Yet there is nothing radically bad about the fellow," Fisher wrote. "He is a mere good-natured animal, wholly uneducated, with a large estate. His parents . . . encouraged him to grow up a working farmer and sportsman."

Gustaf Unonius observed that immigrants of the lower classes who came to the United States were "inclined at first to show too much servility and cringe before those who seem to be above them in social standing. But just give them time enough to get a notion of republican freedom and equality, and . . . being too humble . . . they soon grow discourteous, impertinent, and insolent toward those who are their superiors in culture and wealth, in order to prove that they know their rights and that in America one man is as good as another. . . . The attendant who brushes my shoes and the maid who makes my bed are known as 'that gentleman,' 'that lady,' and at the suppertable in the log inn the 'gentleman coachman' who drives the stagecoach is seated side by side with his lady and gentleman passengers."

Captain Marryat told the story of a young couple who set off on their honeymoon in a carriage. After several days of travel the driver of the carriage told them he would take them no further. "On inquiring the cause of the refusal, he said that he had not been treated as a gentleman; that they had had private meals every day and had not asked him to the table; that they had used him very ill and that he would drive them no more." White servants were determined to be called "help" rather than "servants." Their job was to assist their employer, not to serve their master.

One is inevitably reminded of Tocqueville's comment, "The nations of our time cannot prevent the conditions of men from becoming equal, but it depends upon themselves whether the principle of equality is to lead them to servitude or freedom, to knowledge or barbarism, to prosperity or wretchedness."

Aleksandr Lakier wrote, "When you tell an American about class divisions in other lands, he becomes ecstatic about the equal state of each and all, without distinctions of wealth, origin, or connections, in his own country. In America he considers this equality absolutely natural, and he separates out only the colored (with whom whites want to have nothing in common, not even the air they breathe) and ladies (who are considered higher beings . . .)."

David Macrae observed that in the western states where the passion for equality was even more apparent the servants not infrequently sat down to dinner with the family. "In one village hotel," he wrote, "I remember the waiters who were off duty sitting down to supper with us in their shirt-sleeves. They were as free and polite in their manners and talked as well as any in the company; and but for their shirt-sleeves would not have been distinguishable from the rest."

The American devotion to equality was well-represented in the political arena by the makeup of the New York legislature in 1840. It contained: "59 farmers, 23 lawyers, 18 merchants, 7 physicians, 2 cabinet-makers, 2 lumbermen, 1 furrier, 1 gardner, 1 mariner, 1 joiner [carpenter], 1 blacksmith, 1 post-master, 1 mechanic, 1 grocer, 1 yeoman, 1 agriculturist, 1 teacher . . ."

For a nation devoted to equality, Americans had a surprising predilection for titles. Militia colonels and captains were scrupulously addressed as "colonel" or "captain." "Professor" was an especially coveted title and was, David Macrae observed, often "absurdly employed." Thus there were tailors who termed themselves professors of tailoring; a barber in Chicago who advertised himself as a professor of haircutting, and "another man with a patent [who] called himself a professor of soap."

Another distinguishing feature of American politics was the relative youth of those participating. George Combe estimated that at a Whig caucus in Boston, 5 percent of those present were boys under fourteen, 60 percent between fourteen and twenty-eight, and only 5 percent over fifty.

Then there was the matter of boasting. "The word *world* is in great use with us Americans, when we would assert our superiority, and discourage competition," Philip Hone wrote in 1850. "The best in the world, the handsomest in the world, the fastest in the world, unmatchable; there is no use in the world for the world to try to equal us."

Tocqueville had noted earlier that "For the last fifty years no pains have been spared to convince the inhabitants of the United States that they are the only religious, enlightened, and free people . . . they conceive a high opinion of their superiority and are not very remote from believing themselves to be a distinct species of mankind."

The Frenchman attributed American boastfulness to what we would call today a collective inferiority complex. "It would seem as if, doubting their own merit, they wished to have it constantly exhibited before their eyes. Their vanity is not only greedy but restless and jealous. . . . It is impossible to conceive a more troublesome or more garrulous patriotism; it wearies even those who are disposed to respect it." Tocqueville conjectured that some of it was rooted in the relationship between Great Britain and the United States. The pathos lay in the fact that the British never doubted for a moment that they were the greatest nation on earth. Americans, while constantly proclaiming their greatness, clearly doubted it and needed a litany of reassurance. The other explanation that Tocqueville offered was that each American was so completely identified with his country (often, as we have noted, he had no other identity) that everything said about the United States was taken personally. Whatever its roots, it has been so persistent and depressing an aspect of the American character that we must constantly take note of it. It was, of course, an acute embarrassment to liberal, intellectual Americans like George Templeton Strong and Sidney George Fisher, and even Emerson burst out in uncharacteristic exasperation: "Great men, great nations, have not been boasters and buffoons, but perceivers of the terror of life and have manned themselves to face it."

It is an arresting sentence, particularly coming from the perpetually optimistic Emerson. It was in fact "the terror of life," the "terror of American history" that Americans (and often Emerson himself) seemed often unable to face. George Templeton Strong had an interesting analysis of the roots of American "brag." "We are so young a people," he wrote in his diary, "that we feel the want of nationality, and delight in whatever asserts our national 'America' existence. We have not, like England and France, centuries of achievement and calamities to look back on; we have no *record* of Americanism and we feel its want. Hence that development, in every state of the Union, of 'Historical Societies' that seize on and seal up every worthless reminiscence of our colonial and revolutionary time. We crave a history, instinctively, and being without the eras that belong to older nationalities . . . we . . . venerate every trivial fact about our first settlers and colonial governors. . . ."

When all is said and done, it was perhaps the busyness of Americans that most impressed visitors. "All men in America are busy," Captain Marryat wrote; "their whole time is engrossed by their accumulation of money; they breakfast early and repair to their stores or counting-houses; the majority of them do not go home to dinner, but eat at the nearest tavern or oyster-cellar, for they generally live at a considerable distance from the business part of the town, and time is too precious to be thrown away." The day was spent in business and even a social drink after work was devoted to "doing a little more business." The result was that "the major portion of them come home late, tired, and go to bed; early the next morning they are off to their business again." The wife, in consequence, saw little of her husband but he, since he had been hard at work making a living since his late teens, was an indifferent companion, in any event. He was capable of sharing few of those cultural and intellectual pleasures that his wife, with more leisure, had often immersed herself in.

"The money-making instinct is next to universal," David Macrae wrote. "Young ladies speculate in stocks; children are commercial before they get out of their petticoats. 'I'll trade with you for that,' is an expression you often hear amongst the school-boys: amongst the girls too sometimes. You will see a little girl of six show a toy to her companion, and say, gravely, 'Will you trade?' . . . If one business does not consume a man's energies, he will engage in two or three or four, no matter how incongruous, if they fetch more greenbacks. I found ministers and professors speculating in mines; lawyers keeping shop; and newspaper editors selling toys. In one town I remember a man of prodigious activity acting as cutler, insurance agent, medical practitioner, grain merchant and postmaster all at once."

"'Always in haste!' is the motto of these active, restless people," Moritz Busch wrote. "Yankee Doodle and his *as nimble as a rat, sir* constantly echo in the ears of the observer of their doings. They live fast—for most of them are already independent at twelve and married at twenty. . . . They love to make money fast—for that is the intention with which anyone here who has the stuff devotes himself to business. They do everything fast, so why shouldn't they work at the same rate? To be sure, the result is not always solid, but it's always clean, pretty, and modish." In the same spirit, Captain Marryat wrote: "Nothing is made in America but to last a certain time; they will go to the exact expense necessary, and no further; they know that in twenty years they will be better able to spend twenty dollars than one now. The great object is to obtain quick returns for the outlay, and, except in a few instances, durability or permanence is not thought of."

It was Busch who described "the character of the North American people" as "cold, sober, cleverly calculating, intelligently ambitious, perhaps a bit too hasty." Tocqueville had earlier made a similar observation. On the one hand he found Americans disarmingly "frank and open." On the other they were "grave" and reserved, with a "staid and frigid air," apparently incapable of spontaneous outbursts of joy and exuberance or carefree celebration. He attributed this to a constant state of tension and anxiety produced by the precariousness of most men's worldly estates, never knowing from one day to another whether fortune would sweep them up or tumble them down. "The whole life of an American," Tocqueville wrote, "is passed like a game of chance, a revolutionary crisis, or a battle."

To Emerson there was something pinched or meager in the American character. "America," he wrote, "seems to have immense resources, land, men, milk, butter, cheese, timber, and iron, but it is a village littleness;—village squabble and rapacity characterize its policy. It is a great strength on a basis of weakness."

It is, of course, critically important to keep in mind the sectional differences that were so conspicuous a part of American life. The Re-formed man was primarily and most essentially a New Englander. New England was, indeed, like the proverbial saltbox at the bottom of the sea. Captain Marryat called the region "a *school,* a sort of manufactory of various professions, fitted for all purposes—a talent bazaar where you have everything at choice. . . ." Generation after generation it kept producing men and women with, as we say today, "internalized values," individuals who could make their way in the world secure in the knowledge that their values were the correct and Godly ones. They were remarkably "free-floating," these atomized creatures, flung outward by the centrifugal forces of American society, constantly trying to re-form and coalesce into new human groups or associations. They spread out over the country, carrying with them, like a peddler's pack, their moral and psychological nurture, their "values," that God-possessed passion for redeeming the world and/or making money. They were most clearly distinguishable from the Catholic Irish and Germans and the French of St. Louis or New

Orleans, from the leisurely gentlemen or the red-necked crackers of the South. But even in the South there were substantial elements of the Puritan consciousness, the Protestant Passion, or whatever we wish to call it.

As we have seen, the West produced its own variations on both the Southern and the Yankee themes. In Washington, Richard Henry Dana was impressed by the difference in manners between individuals from the South and West and those from New England. The Southerners and Westerners had "an independence, a self-reliance, a self-sufficiency (in opposition, I mean, to the circumspection, fear of others, & the imitativeness, too characteristic of the Northern character) in the air & manner of these men. . . . They think for themselves, they speak for themselves, they dress to suit themselves, & not because such & such is the way of such & such people & in this & that circle. . . . They are not aiming after a precocious & half attainable gentility. This is not at all on their minds."

To upper-class Northerners, Southerners often seemed, like Westerners, too relaxed and casual in their manners to appear well bred. Sidney George Fisher described a Southern woman he met in Philadelphia as typically "careless in dress & person, affected, familiar, badly educated & without the appearance and manner of a high-bred lady. . . ."

Much to the annoyance of Northerners, British travelers, however much they might deplore slavery, usually found Southerners much more congenial company than the harried merchants of New England and New York. Thomas Hamilton described "the opulent and educated" Southerner as "distinguished by a high-mindedness, generosity, and hospitality" seldom to be found in the North. "He values money only for the enjoyments it can procure, is fond of gaiety, given to social pleasures, somewhat touchy and choleric, and as eager to avenge an insult as to show a kindness. . . . In point of manner, the Southern gentlemen, are decidedly superior to all others of the Union."

Another striking difference between North and South was in their respective attitudes toward education. The South was not merely indifferent to education, many Southerners were strongly opposed to it. "Even the profession of the teacher has been held so low," David Macrae wrote, "that few Southerners of any ability would give themselves to the work. . . ." Slavery, in Macrae's view, made the South conservative in everything. "The old philosophy is taught in her universities; the old creeds and professions bind the churches. . . .

The same Conservatism is visible in the social relations. Servants are under control, children are treated more as they are with us, and woman stands just where she used to." In 1856 the Virginia *Democrat* summed matters up complacently, declaring "We have got to hating everything with the prefix 'free.' But worst of all these abominations is the modern system of Free Schools. The New England system of Free Schools has been the prolific source of infidelity and treasons that have turned her cities into Sodoms and Gomorrahs, and her land into the common nestling place of howling bedlamites. We abominate the system because the schools are free." The South hated all Yankee "isms," Macrae noted, and stubbornly resisted "Northern ideas in religion, politics, and sociology, any one of which, if admitted, would have been inevitably followed by the others, to the subversion, sooner or later, of the whole system of Southern society."

Fanny Kemble, living on her husband's plantation in Georgia, thought wistfully of "the white houses, the green blinds, and the flower plots of the villages in New England" and compared them with those of a Southern town, "these dwellings of lazy filth and inert degradation." "It does seem amazing to think," she wrote, "that physical and moral conditions so widely opposite should be found among people occupying a similar place in the social scale in the same country. The Northern farmer, however, thinks it no shame to work, the Southern planter does; and there begins and ends the difference. Industry, man's crown of honor elsewhere, is here his badge of utter degradation; and so comes all by which I am surrounded—pride, profligacy, idleness, cruelty, cowardice, ignorance, squalor, dirt, and ineffable abasement.

"The Southern people are growing poorer every day," she wrote, "in the midst of their slaves and their vast landed estates; whilst every day sees the arrival amongst them of some penniless Yankee, who presently turns the very ground he stands upon into wealth, and departs a lord of riches at the end of a few years, leaving the sleepy population among whom he has amassed them floated still farther down the tide of dwindling prosperity. . . ." Yet Fanny Kemble deplored the Northern preoccupation with moneymaking.

Sidney George Fisher wrote in his diary in April, 1844, "The union of the country is factitious, and becoming less real every day. Every day the difference between the North & the South is becoming more prominent and apparent. The difference exists in everything which forms the life of a people—in institutions, laws, opinions, manners, feelings, education, pursuits, climate & soil. Edinburgh & Paris are not more dissimilar than Boston & N. Orleans. A union not founded on congeniality—moral & intellectual—a union between two people who, in fact, in all important characteristics are broadly contrasted, must be a weak one, liable to be broken when at all strained. In such a country there can be no strong national feeling, no sentiment of identity, none of the thousand ties formed by a community of origin, recollections, hopes, objects, interests & manners, which make the idea of a country sacred & dear. Such a Union is one of interest merely, a paper bond, to be torn asunder by a burst of passion or to be deliberately undone whenever interest demands it—local sectional interest, the interest of the hour, or as things go here, the interest of a party."

Fisher's pessimistic assessment was not far wide of the mark. The North and the South were the poles. The West was a fascinating amalgam of the two. It was as though there were three nations in one, a kind of political trinity. Above all, it was the West that, decade after decade, kept that "factitious" union from disintegrating.

I have argued that the so-called Protestant Ethic—thrift, piety, and hard work—explains little or nothing about the development of American society (or capitalism), Max Weber to the contrary notwithstanding, and proposed the phrase Protestant Passion as a far more accurate and expressive term to describe the essential spirit of the United States from the moment of its birth—the passion to redeem the world. The most important element in the Protestant Passion was the conviction that everything—art, literature, education, economics, food and drink, and on *ad infinitum*—had a moral referent. Moral considerations pervaded every issue. It was not enough, for example, for the South to argue that slavery was necessary, or inevitable, or merely expedient, the South was compelled to insist that slavery was a positive moral good—the best and most Christian condition for benighted blacks.

This preoccupation with the "moral" led to a good deal of double-entry bookkeeping and a heavy load of guilt, but it gave, one suspects, an essential coherence to a chaotic and disintegrative society. It was the single unifying principle overriding all other considerations, marking out a common path that all could travel. It was the resounding "Thou shalt," which constantly threatened to harden into the "Thou shalt not," the negative injunction of a diminished passion. The fact that we are today largely unsympathetic to moral imperatives and, indeed, often strongly reactive to them, should not blind us to the potency of the moral and its efficacy as a "binding principle" for our predecessors.

Of vital if somewhat mysterious importance was the New Pantheon of Democratic Heroes and Heroines. The New Age demanded, it turned out, new heroes. There were conventional soldier-heroes—Washington, Jackson, Harrison, Taylor, and Scott; but in addition there were politician-heroes—Webster, Clay, Calhoun, and, in his final career, John Quincy Adams; preacher-heroes—Charles Grandison Finney and Henry Ward Beecher prominent among them; Indian-heroes, true and fictitious—Tecumseh, Black Hawk, Osceola, Hiawatha, the Last of the Mohicans; Indian-fighter–heroes—Daniel Boone and Davy Crockett; reformer-heroes—abolitionists like Garrison and John Brown; businessman-heroes—John Jacob Astor and Cornelius Vanderbilt; orator-heroes—Edward Everett and William Ellery Channing (and Webster and Clay, of course); inventor-heroes—Morse, Fulton, and McCormick; lawyer-heroes—William Wirt, David Ogden, John Marshall himself; and an increasing number of heroines—Lucretia Mott, Elizabeth Cady Stanton, Harriet Tubman, Sojourner Truth, Fanny Kemble, Jenny Lind, Margaret Fuller, Dorothea Dix. The democratic appetite for heroes was apparently insatiable. The reason seems to have been in part because Americans, without inherited vocations and traditionally prescribed roles, had difficulty "imagining themselves," conceiving of the part that they would assume in the strange, unsettling drama of American life. They thus needed what we call today, in a disagreeably antiseptic phrase, "role models," and that, of course, is what heroes and heroines are above all: they are persons we admire and strive to emulate. If a new type or new role was created such as, for example, the inventor or engineer, it had to be defined by the appropriate "hero" in order that others might emulate him and have their own role in life defined and dramatized. America did not invent heroes, but we built a large new pantheon or a wing on the ancient pantheon and filled it with a gallery of new democratic heroes and heroines.

The picture of American "character" that emerges from all this is that of a people obsessed with making money and getting ahead; charmed by the "go-ahead" nature of the age, by the country he/she lived in; restless, energetic, self-confident, highly resourceful, aggressive, pious, nervous, anxious, perpetually optimistic and thus disposed to deep fits of gloom and despondency, endlessly boastful, highly mobile, constantly "excited," devoted to the new and novel, intolerant of the old; convinced that the United States was all-wise, all-powerful, just, and immortal; disposed to suppress all those tragic dilemmas that conflicted with the dream of happiness and success; indefatigable pursuers of pleasure and happiness. A people who adored nature and despoiled it; generous, kind, helpful to those in trouble, curious to the point of rudeness, fixated on "equality," suspicious of any claim or pretense or appearance of superiority (Moritz Busch wrote, "The arrogance of the mob rests like an alp upon anyone of intellectual distinction"), with a genuine love of liberty (with certain notable exceptions) and (in the lower and middling classes) inclined to be somewhat rough and unmannerly. A people addicted to a wide variety of stimulants and narcotics from liquor and tobacco to opium and cocaine, virtually incapable of repose, astonishingly resilient in the face of repeated setbacks, and, of course, infatuated with the spoken word, living in hastily erected, overheated houses—the women elegantly and constrictedly attired, the men increasingly drab, the family increasingly dominant.

To all of which there are, of course, numerous exceptions and almost endless variations. But the composite portrait is clearly that of a New Man and perhaps, especially, a New Woman, in a New Age.

47

American Art

The problems for the artist are always *what* to paint, *how* to paint, and *who* will pay him for his work?

In the highest periods of art the question of what to paint has been, in the main, determined for the artist. Christian iconography, for example, kept generations of artists occupied from the Middle Ages through the Renaissance. The generation of American painters whose artistic self-consciousness and creative energies were stimulated by the crisis of the American Revolution initially worked in the realm of the individual image, of portraiture, and then, in the case of Benjamin West and such pupils of his as John Singleton Copley and John Trumbull, in the grand historical style—Trumbull, of course, taking it as his mission to recreate the climactic moments of the Revolution itself.

The question of patronage remained acute. West had the ultimate patron, George III, king of England. Copley had to go to England to make his living as an artist, and even Gilbert Stuart, America's most gifted stay-at-home painter, spent a period abroad in the British Isles painting portraits on commission. Trumbull tried to pad out a modest inheritance by charging admission for the public to see his great historical pieces, by importuning Congress for funds to enable him to complete his projected Revolutionary canvases, and by running a gallery. Charles Willson Peale ran his museum as a commercial undertaking and was constantly in straitened financial circumstances.

It is not surprising then that the great generation of West, Copley, and Stuart had no immediate successors. Stuart and Trumbull lived long enough to constitute another generation, Stuart dying in 1828 at the age of seventy-three while Trumbull died in 1843 in his eighty-eighth year. For years Trumbull, as president of the American Academy of Fine Arts, dominated the artistic scene and although his own powers as a painter declined sharply, his forceful personality and his fame as a hero of the Revolution enabled him to preside over the American art world so far as one can have been said to exist. It was, in large part, as a reaction against that dominance that Samuel F. B. Morse started the National Academy of Design.

Whatever Trumbull's deficiencies as an artist may have been, he was generous in his encouragement of young painters. Among these was Washington Allston, son of a rich South Carolina planter. With the support of his indulgent father, Allston was educated at Harvard and then traveled to England, like so many artistically inclined young Americans before him, to study with Benjamin West. West had, by this time, moved from his historical set-pieces into a style that would be defined as "romantic"—natural settings with dramatic highlights, the sun streaming through clouds, the moon shining through clouds, nymphs and classical figures set amidst ruins. West had just completed a classic example of the genre, "Death on a Pale Horse." Allston was entranced. Leaving London, he joined a young artist, John Vanderlyn, a native of New York state who had grown up in the Hudson Valley region that was to give its name to an American school of romantic landscapes. Vanderlyn's father and grandfather had both been painters and his father had apprenticed him to the proprietor of a paintshop. A New York merchant had encouraged the intense and talented young man and paid his tuition at an art school. There he had acquired as a patron Aaron Burr, who sent him to Gilbert Stuart as a pupil and then underwrote a trip to France. In Paris, both Vanderlyn and Allston were thoroughly corrupted by the fashionable neoclassical school which dominated French painting. After years of study in Paris and Rome, Vanderlyn returned to the United States to waste a substantial talent painting second-rate versions of a third-rate school of painting. Allston's case was somewhat different. Completing his grand tour in Rome, where he met the famous expatriate Washington Irving and Samuel Coleridge, he returned to the United States whose atmosphere he found thoroughly uncongenial to an aspiring painter. He married a cousin of Richard Henry Dana's and took with him when he returned to England young Samuel F. B. Morse, twelve years his junior, who already considered himself a student of the older man. Wealthy, aristocratic, intellectual, a poet and a writer himself and the friend of important literary figures in England, Allston stayed in England for seven years. A man of great personal charm and moral force, he had access to the highest levels of English society, but he was obsessed with his mission to become "at least the greatest painter in America." It turned out to be difficult to do that from England. When financial problems forced him to return to the United States in 1818, Allston had already been at work for several years on the painting that was supposed to establish him (and American painting) in the forefront of the international world of art. Entitled "Belshazzar's Feast," it was an unhappy melding of classical, Renaissance, and biblical styles and themes. The subject was, of course, the biblical story of Daniel and the children condemned to the fiery furnace and the mysterious writing on the wall, "mene, mene, tekel." A consortium of Boston businessmen put up money to enable Allston to complete the painting "which was intended as a national specimen of American art."

As the years passed without the picture's being completed—some of its sponsors died without a glimpse of it—the painting took on an almost mythical quality. It was rumored to be a work of such grandeur as to herald the advent of an artistic renaissance in America. Allston doubtless came to feel the pressure of such expectations. He worked and reworked the large canvas until it became a metaphor of his own life as an artist and the uncertain state of the visual arts in the republic.

Richard Henry Dana was one of the first persons notified of Allston's death in 1843, and he recorded in his diary the details of the expression and surroundings of the dead artist. With the coming of dawn, he wrote, "we could contemplate his sublime countenance. There was the highest grandeur of intellect, with the purity & peacefulness of one in the world but not of the world. . . . Truth & beauty, for the glory of God & the elevation of man were the great objects for wh. his powers had been given him, & these he pursued, without comparison or conflict." When Dana told Allston's father that his son had died it was as though "his sanity of mind had left him. . . . At length he said, in a broken, incoherent manner, 'how is this? What does this mean?' " Dana, to comfort the father, "talked of the blessings & desirable things attending his death. He had escaped that terrible vision, the night-mare, the incubus, the tormentor of his life, his unfinished picture."

After Allston's funeral, his friends and family "assembled to enter the painting room & 'break the seal' of the great picture. An awe had come upon my mind," Dana wrote, "as though I were about to enter a sacred & mysterious place. I could hardly bring my mind to try the key." He opened the door and entered the room and there was the huge canvas "almost obscured by dust & marks & lines of chalk." Where the king should have stood, the figure was blotted out and there were indications of a constant process of repainting. "To the latest moment," Dana wrote, "he had labored upon this great work."

The fate of the picture, especially the question of whether to try to remove the pigment blotting out the central figure of the king, was much debated in and out of the family. Samuel F. B. Morse was consulted and Morse admitted that he had been giving too much time to his "electro-magnetic experiments" in the hope of making enough money to allow him to paint "with a feeling of independence, & that his chief motive was to do something wh. shd. please Allston. This had been a powerful motive, almost a ruling motive. As soon as he heard of the death," Dana noted, "he felt that he had lost a great motive for pursuing his beloved art."

Meanwhile, a new generation of artists whose modest origins and dates of birth freed them from a preoccupation with the grandiose neoclassical style appeared on the scene. A disconcerting number were immigrants—young men who, touched by the fresh stirrings of romanticism, yearned for the distant landscape of America. Morse was a kind of transitional figure. Although he dabbled in the school of elegant portraiture and proved himself an accomplished painter, he achieved his best effects with such large-scale "historical" paintings as his scene of the House of Representatives.

The herald of the new era in American painting was a young Englishman, Thomas Cole, who, revolted by the horrors of the industrial midlands of his own country, came to the United States in 1819 at the age of eighteen and worked, successively, as an engraver and as an assistant to his father in the manufacture of wallpaper in Steubenville, Ohio. Nature was his first and most ardent love. In the words of his nineteenth-century biographer, Louis LeGrand Noble, he "obeyed the call [of nature] with the quick and silent readiness of a lover, and saw, as he had never yet seen, how full her face was of divine loveliness, and confessed in sentiment that a passion for nature was his ruling passion." "Nature" was in the air. Young Cole had not read essays on nature or been consciously caught up in the literary and artistic dimensions of the romantic movement. He had "caught" it as he might have caught smallpox or a cold. Painting seemed to him the best way he could express his infatuation with the natural world. Encouraged by an itinerant German portrait painter named Stein who lent him a manual on painting, Cole made his own brushes and secured paints from a cabinetmaker. His first crude landscapes were unsalable. He tried portraits with more success and then, perhaps as a consequence of his exposure to the painting manual, tried two biblical scenes, Ruth gleaning in the fields and Belshazzar's Feast, the nemesis of Washington Allston.

When his father moved to New York City, Cole painted in the garret of the house. He displayed one of his paintings in a store window, where it was sold for ten dollars to a patron who underwrote a trip to the Hudson River Valley, the region John Vanderlyn had abandoned twenty-five years earlier. Cole came back with three paintings which he offered for sale at twenty-five dollars apiece. John Trumbull bought one of them, "The Falls of the Caterskill," and spread the word of a brilliant young painter to Asher Durand, a well-known engraver of portraits and a bank-note designer, and William Dunlap, theatrical manager, playwright, painter, and biographer, a classic American jack of all artistic trades. "This youth," Trumbull told Dunlap and Durand, "has done what I have all my life attempted in vain"—rendered a vigorous and convincing landscape. The three men went off to view Cole's paintings and Dunlap at once bought one that he sold a few weeks later to Philip Hone for fifty dollars. He salved his conscience for not passing on his profit to Cole by praising his work "in the journals of the day," and thus helped draw attention to him.

William Cullen Bryant, who might be called one of the American "inventors" of nature, was also much impressed by Cole's work. "I well remember," he wrote years later, "what an enthusiasm was awakened by those early works of his . . . the delight which was expressed at the opportunity of contemplating pictures which carried the eye over scenes of wild grandeur peculiar to our country, over our aerial mountain-tops with their mighty growth of forest never touched by the axe, along the banks of streams never deformed by culture. . . ." America was at the beginning of a long and ardent and sometimes stormy romance with nature, and the young Englishman touched a profoundly responsive chord. Encouraged by various patrons, Cole established a studio in the Catskills and there turned out a series of romantic landscapes, not painted "from nature" but "recollected in tranquillity," enhanced, made even more "sublime and beautiful" than in real life, for nature was, after all, an increasingly potent revelation of the Divine. It must therefore elevate the feelings of the viewer to the grand and noble, the exalted and eternal.

There was a little madness in Cole, as in most of America's best writers and poets and painters. He was tormented by the riddle of the relationship between the Almighty, democratic America, and Nature. In that new trinity the artist must find the key to the enigma. What was perhaps most compelling about Cole to a democrat like Bryant was that he was most emphatically a "democratic" artist, self-taught, a "natural" genius shaped by the landscape that so infatuated him. Robert Gilmor, a Baltimore patron of Cole's, gave him a loan of three hundred dollars to enable him to go to England and study the works of the outstanding painters, Sir Thomas Lawrence, John Constable, and J. M. W. Turner. He brought with him a letter to that famous literary expatriate James Fenimore Cooper, whose romantic Indians and frontiersmen, delivering their stilted dialogue in front of lovingly detailed backdrops of forests and lakes and mountains, had anticipated Cole's landscapes.

After two years in England, much of it spent sketching in galleries, Cole went on to Paris and then Italy, lingering for nine months in Florence. The effects on his work when he returned to the United States were not, on the whole, happy ones; too many ruins, too many grandiose classical statues, too much history. Soon Cole acquired his most important sponsor, the self-made merchant Luman Reed. Reed had a floor in his home reserved as a gallery and admitted the public one day a week. It was Reed who commissioned Cole to paint a series of large allegorical canvases designed to depict *The Course of Empire*, tracing the rise of a nation to power and wealth, its phase of decadence, and its eventual destruction when culture is once more absorbed by nature. It was conceived by many critics as an allegory on the superior power of nature over all human achievements, but it was interpreted by others as depicting the downfall of decadent Europe and the rise of the United States. The series, when completed, was a great success, bringing in over one thousand dollars for Cole in admissions to its public showing. James Fenimore Cooper, returned at long last to

America, described it as "Not only . . . the work of the highest genius this country ever produced, but . . . one of the noblest works of art that has ever been wrought."

Having sipped the wine of allegory, Cole became an addict. His next major venture was a series entitled *The Voyage of Life,* four landscapes depicting "Childhood," "Youth," "Manhood," and "Old Age" in the form of a figure, attended by a guardian angel, adrift in a boat. The least successful of Cole's efforts, it enjoyed the greatest popularity and was widely reproduced in engravings. The element of eccentricity to the point of madness is best represented by "Titan's Goblet," a painting that Cole completed in 1833. An enormous goblet, perhaps five miles high and several miles in circumference, rests on a rocky promontory above the ocean. Thousands of tiny human figures seem to flee from it. The symbolism remains obscure. We are told that the goblet is a symbol of the Tree of Life from a Norse legend and the branches support an ocean dotted with Greek ruins and modern buildings, but it is, for all that, a very odd conception, most eccentrically rendered.

One has the feeling that Cole was conscious of his paintings becoming visual analogues to Bryant's poems or to the essays of Emerson. But many of the landscapes of the painter who professed his infatuation with nature were only landscapes in the broadest sense of that word. They were like no landscapes ever viewed by man, certainly no landscapes in the Catskills. Cole often adopted a strange perspective as though suspended in a balloon or airplane thousands of feet in the air. The human figures in his "landscapes" grew smaller and smaller until they were hardly discernible. Even in the relatively early scene from *The Last of the Mohicans* the combatants can hardly be discerned. It is hard for the modern viewer of Cole's grandiose canvases to escape the feeling of a somewhat disordered imagination at work. Certainly in Cole's paintings and in his scattered journal entries there are abundant indications of that "melancholy" that was so much a style as well as quality of mind in the romantic imagination. His biographer's description of Cole's "Dream of Arcadia" suggests the romantic "pastoral" elements that in his view made the work great: "The temple, fair in its proportions, grand in its elevation, smoking censers and solemnities, the bridge and the horsemen, all suggest the state and the metropolis, the faith, art, science, power and luxury of Greece in palmy times." It was Cole's intention, his biographer tells us, always to incorporate in his paintings "a strong moral lesson."

Although Cole's work received what seems to us today extravagant praise and such critics as Cooper, Dunlap, and Bryant acclaimed him as one of the great masters of all times, Cole himself felt that his talent was throttled by the necessity to sell his pictures, to accept commissions, and to make accommodations to the public taste. "I am not the painter I should have been," he wrote in his journal, "had there been a higher taste. Instead of working according to the dictates of feeling and imagination, I have painted to please others in order to exist. Had fortune favored me a little more than she has, even in spite of the taste of the age, and the country in which I live, my imagination would not have been cramped, as it has been; and I would have followed out principles of beauty and sublimity in my works, which have been cast aside, because the result would not be marketable."

The reflection is rather an odd one. Considering how eccentric many of Cole's own visions were, one wonders where his private daemon would have carried him had he not been constrained to make a living. After all, to have progressed from a designer of wallpaper to become the idol of critics and connoisseurs is hardly to have been overlooked by fortune. Was it more pictures in the spirit of "Titan's Goblet" that Cole yearned to paint? Of course, his denunciation of the philistinism of his age was, in itself, part of the romantic syndrome. The conflict between the pure vision of the creative personality and the harsh realities of the mundane world has been a familiar theme in all romantic periods.

Convinced that a fuller recognition of his genius could be found abroad and suffering from a deep depression that made painting a chore, Cole took some of his best-known paintings on a tour that began in England and ended in Rome. The judgments of foreign critics were far from sympathetic and Cole returned home, became a convert to the Episcopal Church through the priest who became his biographer, Louis LeGrand Noble, and began a series of religious paintings that were to be called *The Cross and the World,* a variation on the theme of the sacred and profane. The series was never completed or even well begun, and it was succeeded by other projected series equally ambitious and similarly doomed, among them *Life, Death and Immortality.* In 1844 he wrote to a friend, "I have been dwelling on many subjects, and looking forward to the time when I can embody them on canvas. They are subjects of a moral and religious nature. On such I think it the duty of the artist to employ his abilities; for his mission, if I may so term it, is a great and serious one. His works ought not to be a dead imitation of things, without the power to express a sentiment, or enforce a truth."

Cole's last years were bitterly frustrating ones. His health and his commissions declined and he was subject to periods of deep despondency. Like Washington Allston, he struggled unsuccessfully to complete canvases that he had begun with the highest hopes. He became increasingly reclusive; his death at the age of forty-seven was apparently from pneumonia but one must conjecture that it was more the consequence of a mental and physical diminution of his powers, which were closely related to the impasse he had reached in his painting. It is perhaps dangerous to place too heavy a load of meaning on Cole's life and work, but it is clear enough that he suffered severely from the unresolved ambiguity of his own view of nature-America. Beginning modestly enough as a gifted painter of landscapes with a sensitive feeling for nature, Cole was carried on to constantly larger and more extravagant conceptions. If there was a kind of madness in the American landscape, or at the very least a terrible ambiguity, Cole surely imbibed it. It infected his work like a disease. What was Nature, after all? Cole tried, in the spirit of his times, to turn it into a symbol of redemption, and when the symbolism grew so inflated that it collapsed of its own vastly overextended weight, he turned desperately to conventional symbolism. But that proved stubbornly resistant to his limited techniques. Religious paintings no longer "worked" for Cole or, for that matter, anyone else.

Although defeated by his own excessive ambitions, Cole helped to establish a "school" by dramatizing, indeed overdramatizing, the landscape of the Hudson River Valley and the Catskill Mountains. Asher Durand forsook engraving bills to become a full-time landscape painter, superior in technique to Cole, and acknowledged his debt to his master by painting one of the most famous of American landscapes, a picture of Cole and William Cullen Bryant, the two great "discoverers" of nature, standing on a rocky ledge above a waterfall conversing on its beauties.

Durand's salvation doubtless lay in his mastery of the extremely exacting technique of engraving and his consequent inclination to paint directly from nature and render its details faithfully. Durand, like Cole, had been influenced by Bryant's nature poems and for a time he flirted with the grandiose—painting a "Scene from Thanatopsis"—but he quickly subsided into a less pretentious mode.

Durand attracted a number of other young artists, of varying degrees of talent, who shared his enthusiasm for depicting nature sensitively and accurately. The little company would descend each summer on boardinghouses in the Catskills and set out on sketching and painting expeditions. Their goal, as described by Durand, was to establish "an original school of art worthy to share the tribute of universal respect paid to our political institutions." One ambitious young painter, Worthington Whittredge, who had grown up in Ohio and studied for ten years in the salons of Düsseldorf and Rome, on returning to America and seeing Durand's landscapes shed bitter tears at having wasted his time in alien lands and, in his words, "hid myself for months in the recesses of the Catskills," determined to master the "American" style. Where Cole had become increasingly obsessed with religious themes, the Hudson River school remained more orthodox lovers of nature but with a strong religious-transcendental bent. Nature, in Durand's words, was "fraught with high and holy meaning, only surpassed by the light of Revelation."

John Frederick Kenesett, twenty years Durand's junior, had been, like him, an engraver. In his freshness of vision and spareness of style, Kenesett excelled his master's more studied and self-conscious landscapes and in his naive vision might be said to have balanced himself on that narrow boundary between "primitive" and "high" art. Such works as "Marine off Big Rock," painted in the latter part of Kenesett's career, have a directness and economy that transcend any school in their appeal. Much the same might be said of the paintings of Martin John Heade, which are more to the modern taste than the lush scenes of Cole and Durand.

Frederick E. Church was the son of a prosperous and socially prominent Hartford, Connecticut, family. He showed precocious talent as a child and his father paid for him to study for three years with Cole, who declared that the young man had "the finest eye for drawing in the world." Certainly Church was a superior draftsman and, having absorbed what Cole could teach him, he departed on a trip to South America in 1835, where he made sketches and studies that he utilized for the next twenty years. He sought the grand and spectacular much as Cole had done, but without the touch of the bizarre that distinguished most of the older man's work. Abandoning the overtly allegorical and symbolic, Church strove to make his landscapes tell their own story in the drama and grandeur of their effects, especially in his use of light and of cloud forms. Ranging far beyond the modest preoccupations of Kenesett and Heade, Church anticipated the monumental canvases of Albert Bierstadt. George Templeton Strong was especially taken with Church's Ecuadorian landscapes: "most lovely and beautiful: warm, rich, hazy air, copious masses of brilliant, many-colored equatorial foliage. . . . I think him our most promising artist," he wrote.

Bierstadt had been born in Germany and raised in Massachusetts. Initially he drew his artistic nourishment from the Hudson River painters, most particularly Church. Of them all Bierstadt was the most technically accomplished. Although he is best known for his later enormous "Rocky Mountain" canvases, his skill is most apparent in his smaller canvases and studies. There, with his ability to create brilliant effects impressionistically with a few brush strokes, he appeals most to the modern consciousness.

While Thomas Cole and, after him, Frederick Church were struggling with the "meaning" of nature and the "landscape as metaphor," other American painters had turned their attention to the details of everyday life. If Cole endeavored to romanticize the physical landscape, the so-called genre painters, deriving their inspiration in more or less equal parts from the dominant Düsseldorf school and the rough and colorful life around them, romanticized the commonplace, turned the often sordid scenes of backwoods politics into democratic epics and discovered the poetry of such ordinary activities as eel fishing or shucking corn.

William Sidney Mount was born and grew up on Long Island. He devoted his artistic career to painting the life around him—quiet, surely painted, idyllic rural scenes, many with a "story" to tell. Mount's charming, unpretentious paintings come as a welcome counterpoint to the ambitious canvases of Cole and Church. They are much closer in spirit to the scenes of Kenesett and Heade. Blacks figure prominently in many of his paintings and Mount was especially attracted by their skill at making music. In contradistinction to most of his fellow artists, he showed no interest in studying abroad or working under the guidance of a "master." His desire was "to be entirely original . . . I launched forth on my sea of adventure," he wrote, "with the firm determination to avoid the style of any artist and to create a school of my own." In this resolution Mount was placing himself close to the tradition of the naive, self-taught artist who scorned the artistic establishment. The fact was that his pictures were extremely popular. He sold whatever he painted, attained an international reputation, and apparently never experienced those agonies over the "role of the artist in America" that tormented such painters as Allston and Cole. (One of his most beguiling paintings—"Eel-fishing at Setauket"—was painted for George Templeton Strong's father.) Mount's charming scenes evoke the sense of a secure and happy man, at peace with himself and his world, who mastered a limited range, thoroughly within his competence, and this was enough to distinguish him from most of his contemporaries.

Mount had a number of followers if few peers. Prominent among the latter was Richard Caton Woodville, a man as driven and unhappy as Mount was serene. Woodville could afford to go abroad for training and, underwritten by a well-to-do papa, he spent five years in Düsseldorf, alternating between drunken sprees and feverish periods of painting. The handful of paintings that he did in his tragically short lifetime—he died at the age of thirty-one of drink and dissipation—give a tantalizing hint of the depth of his powers as a "pure painter." Woodville's "Waiting for the Stage," painted in 1851, five years before his death, is unsurpassed among genre paintings in the marvelous use of color, in the composition and the skill with which the figures are rendered.

One of the strangest American artists of the first half of the nineteenth century, a genre painter only in the loosest sense of the word, was David Gilmor Blythe, who was born and grew up in a cabin in Ohio. Apprenticed to a woodcarver, he branched out into crude portraiture and then into a series of paintings of "scenes" such as "Trial" and the "Hide-Out," where ominously distorted figures with pasty, bloated faces and dwarfish bodies play cards, cook bacon and eggs, sew, shave, drink, or engage in fierce political harangues. It is sobering to place Blythe's scenes of frontier lawyers, robbers, and greasy politicians, pictures with their haunting sense of evil, beside the idealized types of George Caleb Bingham. Somehow all the ambiguity of nineteenth-century America seems to fall into place between those extraordinary parentheses. From the little we know of Blythe's own life, he seems to have been a perpetual searcher for "some place . . . where man can live with man in unity." Instead, settling in Pittsburgh when that town was the jumping-off point for the West, Blythe made himself the artist of the poor and degraded. Morbid, depressive, a heavy drinker, he roamed that darker underworld that mocked America's cherished doctrines of equality and happiness.

In the realm of portraiture, Gilbert Stuart had a worthy successor in Thomas Sully, who had Stuart's gift for creating the quality of living flesh. Sully was a South Carolinian who, after a period of study in England, established himself in Philadelphia where he became the premier portraitist of his day, attracting clients from both sides of the Atlantic and painting in a long life (eighty-nine years) over 2,600 works, the great majority of them portraits.

A word should be said about Charles Willson Peale's artistic brood—Rembrandt, Titian I (who died at eighteen), Titian Ramsay (Titian II), Rubens, Raphaelle, Charles Linnaeus, and Benjamin Franklin. Rembrandt, the most gifted painter, painted a grandiose allegorical canvas called "The Court of Death," which, sent around the country on exhibition, brought in some nine thousand dollars in admission fees. Titian I assisted his father, wrote a work on the art of miniature painting, and died of yellow fever. Raphaelle, also a gifted painter, unable to earn a living by painting, turned to the physiognomy-trace, a device that cut out silhouettes and brought in substantial sums of money; nevertheless, Raphaelle was always poor, as improvident as his father. In spite of severe arthritis in his hands and bouts of alcoholism, he turned out a number of striking still lifes.

Titian Ramsay Peale, the reader may recall, accompanied Stephen Long on his expedition of 1819–20 and painted the flora and fauna collected by the expedition. Linnaeus became a soldier of fortune, to his pacifist father's indignation, meddling in South American revolutions. Benjamin Franklin Peale, having failed in cotton manufacturing, became an engineer and chief coiner of the U. S. Mint.

The two foremost sculptors of our period were Horatio Greenough and Hiram Powers. Greenough was one of three artistic brothers born in Boston and educated at Harvard. With the encouragement of Washington Allston, Greenough went to Rome to work in that city's ateliers. He found a patron in James Fenimore Cooper, who commissioned a marble group called "Chanting Cherubs." When it was exhibited, a hue and cry was raised over the fact that the cherubs were nude. In 1833, Greenough was commissioned by Congress, through the influence of Cooper, to do a heroic statue of Washington for the Capitol. Greenough worked for eight years on the piece, producing a huge Washington draped in a Roman toga that again stirred up a controversy. Philip Hone's mocking description was a rather typical reaction. To Hone it looked "like a great Herculean, warrior-like *Venus of the bath,* a grand martial Magog, undressed, with a huge napkin lying in his lap and covering his lower extremities, and he, preparing to perform his ablutions, is in the act of consigning his sword to the care of the attendant. . . ."

Greenough's aesthetic ideas were more interesting than his highly derivative sculptures. Again he was burdened with the task of "proving" that American art could rival that of the great masters of antiquity or the Renaissance. The fact was that Greenough was a brilliant and perceptive critic and was well aware of the difficulties that confronted him as the designated vindicator of "American art." "I *gazed* at the Apollo and Venus," he wrote, "and *learned* little by it. . . . It was not until I had run through all the galleries of Rome, and had under my eye the genial forms of Italy that I began to feel Nature's value. I had before adored her, but as a Persian does the sun, with my face to the ground." In sculpture as in architecture it seemed to him essential to "begin from the heart as a nucleus, and work outwards." Greenough was convinced that American art must flow organically from the character of American life.

Returning to the United States in 1851, Greenough proposed a colossal monument recording "The treason of Arnold—the capture and sudden death of André and the fate of Capt'n N. Hale. I believe," he added, "this idea may take a form exceedingly significant of our system highly expressive of our democratic ethics—& a caution to egotistical intrigue." He planned to "go straight to the people for the means to do it and lecture and stump it until I get the wherewithal." Less than a year after his return to New England, Greenough had a stroke; he died a few weeks later, at the age of forty-seven.

Perhaps what is most appealing about Greenough was his determination to engage life fully in an age and a country not notable for such robustness of spirit. "I would not pass away," he wrote in one of his last letters, "and not leave a sign that I, for one, born by the grace of God in this land, found life a cheerful thing, and not that sad and dreadful task with whose prospect they scared my youth." The sentence was a kind of epitaph for New England Puritanism which, in certain of its dimensions, had shrunk from a passion to an ethic. Or, as we have been disposed to argue, poured its passion into the task of social redemption.

Hiram Powers, born in the same year as Greenough in Woodstock, Vermont, began his career as a sculptor in Cincinnati, making wax figures for a Chamber of Horrors. In Washington he attracted attention by doing a series of skillful busts of Jackson, Calhoun, and

Webster, and eccentric Nicholas Longworth, Cincinnati's leading philanthropist, who, the reader may recall, gave money only to bums, down-and-outers, and those whom no one else would help. Longworth put up the money for Powers to take his family to Rome for study. There Powers remained for the rest of his life, turning out a series of technically deft but insipid "classical" pieces. The most famous of these was his "Greek Slave," a nude female figure that was a tremendous success. The allusion to American slavery and Greek independence plus its shocking nudity gave it a great popular appeal. When it was displayed in New York crowds flocked to see it and more than two hundred dollars a day was collected in admissions. Philip Hone considered it the equal of the Medici Venus. It then moved on to Boston where it was also extravagantly admired by Richard Henry Dana, among others.

In time Powers made six copies of the piece and it made his fortune. He lived to a vigorous old age in a mansion in Florence where he entertained Hawthorne and other visiting Americans and was taken as living refutation of the charge that democracy could not produce art equal to that of the great masters. Today a number of his sculptures are tucked away in a corner of the National Gallery of Art, hardly noticed.

One of the most interesting developments on the American art scene was the founding of the Art Union. Art, like newspapers and entertainment, must be democratized in a democracy, or a republic, if one preferred. The American Art Union was thus established in 1840 to encourage American art. A gallery was opened in New York where painters, engravers, sculptors, and medal makers displayed their works. At the peak of its success, the Union counted sixteen thousand members. For a five-dollar-a-month fee subscribers received a large steel engraving and four small ones, as well as a monthly bulletin, describing works for sale. Paintings and sculptures were purchased by the Union and, as new works were acquired, old ones were disposed of to the members by lot. When the American Art Union went out of business in 1853, it had distributed 2,400 works of art to its members.

48

American Originals

John James Audubon was born Jean Jacques Rabin (Rabin was his mother's name) at Les Cayes, Santo Domingo, in 1784, the natural son of Jean Audubon, a lieutenant in the French Navy, and a French Creole woman. His father took him back to France with him and formally adopted him at Nantes in 1794. Audubon himself was highly secretive about his origins, telling his children that he had been born on a Louisiana plantation. From early childhood he showed a precocious talent for drawing birds and animals, and his father sent him to study with the foremost academician of the day, David. Audubon came to the United States in 1803 to live on a farm his father owned near Philadelphia. "At length," Audubon wrote, "I reached the country in which my eyes first opened to the light; I gazed with rapture upon its noble forests, and no sooner had I landed, than I set myself to mark every object that presented itself, and became imbued with an anxious desire to discover the purpose and import of that nature which lay spread around me in luxuriant profusion. . . ."

After a year in America, Audubon went back to France and there persuaded a friend, Ferdinand Rozier, to return to the United States with him and open a general store in Louisville, Kentucky. Before heading west, Audubon married Lucy Bakewell, the carefully raised daughter of an Englishman. Kentucky turned out to be Audubon's "natural habitat." He became an expert with the Kentucky rifle and an addict of the roving life of a frontier hunter. Birds were his obsession. He sketched and painted them in their natural surroundings, observed their habits, and collected their eggs and skins. The life along the Ohio and Mississippi rivers entranced him. The store, on the other hand, proved a disaster. Audubon and poor Rozier, whose talent for business was apparently little better than Audubon's, weathered one crisis after another, often bailed out by Audubon's father or father-in-law. Finally, in 1812, Audubon and his partner declared bankruptcy. It was undoubtedly a welcome release for Audubon. During his years in Louisville as a storekeeper, Audubon met Alexander Wilson, the ornithologist, whose great work on American birds was nearing completion under the aegis of De Witt Clinton. Wilson was disconcerted to encounter the romantic-looking young Frenchman with long, flowing hair, dramatic attire, and a knowledge of the birds of the region that exceeded his own.

After his partnership with Rozier broke up, Audubon moved his wife and son to Hendersonville, where he once more tried storekeeping, this time in partnership with his brother-in-law. Again, Audubon was largely an absent partner, often gone for days or weeks with his gun and dog on the trail of some elusive avian species. "The scarcer the fruit, the more prized it is," Audubon wrote; "and seldom have I experienced greater pleasures than when on the Florida Keys, under a burning sun, after pushing my bark for miles over a soapy flat, I have striven all day long, tormented by myriads of insects, to procure a heron new to me, and have at length succeeded in my efforts."

The store languished and the depression of 1819 drove the partners into bankruptcy. At this point Audubon was the prototype of the charming n'er-do-well, a poor provider for his self-sacrificing wife and two small sons, a frontier eccentric with a French accent. But the birds he was painting were like no birds on the earth. They were marvelous, heroic birds, larger and more vivid than life, birds transformed by his brush into irresistible works of art. Fierce, terrible hawks and eagles, turkeys more splendid than eagles, herons as stately as goddesses. Small wonder that sober Alexander Wilson, a fine, if orthodox ornithologist, was put off by Audubon's paintings. They had entered quite a different dimension of reality.

While his wife worked as a governess in New Orleans, Audubon did portraits in pastel in Louisville and Cincinnati and when she opened a girls' school at Bayou Sara, he taught music and dancing to the dazzled young ladies. Finally, in 1824, he made his way to Philadelphia, startling the artists of that city by his exotic appearance and winning their support by the power of his remarkable paintings. He was urged by Prince Canino, the son of Lucien Bonaparte whom he met in Philadelphia, to undertake to have his paintings and notes published. This meant having the plates engraved from the paintings by an expert engraver and then having them hand-colored, a tedious and expensive process. There were neither the subscribers nor the engravers in the United States so Audubon, armed with letters from, among others, Andrew Jackson and Henry Clay, to some of the leading artists and patrons in England, sailed from New Orleans in 1826 with 435 paintings of 489 American birds. Audubon was then forty years old, an "American woodsman," as he liked to call himself.

Within a week of his arrival at Liverpool, Audubon found a sponsor who recognized his genius and arranged for him to have a showing of his work at the Royal Institution. Audubon appeared to those Englishmen already enamored of the American frontier as the embodiment of that romantic world. The painter's charming manners, his handsome face and flowing hair made an image of the perfect Byronic hero. The vigor and beauty—the monumental quality—of his paintings confirmed the popular notion that the closest association with nature must produce the most powerful art. Audubon, an actor to his toes and well aware of the value of the romantic aura he projected, carefully concealed the fact that he had grown up in France and once been a pupil of David. Better his admirers should believe him to be a homemade product of the Kentucky frontier. Soon he was the darling of the British aristocracy, a number of whom were amateur scientists. Appropriately, the "Turkey Cock" was the first engraving made and offered for sale. The edition was promptly sold out and Audubon began to make preparations for the publication of his birds in four elephant folio volumes, engaging the services of the great London engraver Robert Havell, Jr. It was estimated that the engravings alone would take sixteen years to complete and the cost would be one hundred thousand dollars, an enormous sum for that time. The only way to raise sufficient funds was by subscription, so Audubon, like Catlin and later Bingham, had to peddle his project among the wealthy at a thousand dollars for the set. Included were five volumes of what Audubon called *Ornithological Biography*.

Elected a member of the Linnaean Society in 1828 and a fellow of the Royal Society two years later, Audubon brought his wife and sons to England, and his oldest son, Victor, took charge of guiding his father's work through the various stages of publication. Throughout the *Biography*, Audubon scattered little vignettes of his experiences from Louisiana and Florida to Canada and Nova Scotia. Called by Audubon "Delineations of American Life and Character," they give a revealing index to the artist's own spirit. For the next thirteen years Audubon remained based in England, making three long trips to the United States that covered a total period of five years. The engraving went faster than anticipated and the first of elephant folios appeared in 1830 to enormous critical acclaim, followed a year later by the first volume of the *Ornithological Biography*. "We have all laboured at it," Audubon wrote in the preface to his volumes, "and every other occupation has been laid aside, that we might present, to the generous individuals who have placed their names on my subscription list," a work worthy of their patronage. He was especially "proud and thankful . . . to say that my own dear country gave me a support equal to that supplied by Europe." The task had at first seemed overwhelming, "But," Audubon wrote, "my heart was nerved, and my reliance on that Power on whom all must depend, brought bright anticipations of success."

The last of the bird folios was published in 1840 and Audubon returned to the United States that year, internationally famous, to make his home on the Hudson River, just north of New York City. Three years later at the age of fifty-eight he set out for the Yellowstone region and the Rocky Mountains. He also began work on a volume of American *Quadripeds*, which, as his health waned, was done largely by his sons. He died in 1851 in his sixty-sixth year, after four years of diminishing physical and intellectual capacities.

George Catlin was born in Wilkes-Barre, Pennsylvania, in 1796. His father, Putnam Catlin, had enlisted as a fifer in the Second Connecticut Regiment at the age of thirteen and had fought through the Revolution. His mother had been captured by the Indians as a child of seven in the Wyoming Valley Massacre. Putnam Catlin was an unsuccessful lawyer who abandoned law for farming and who lived more in the world of books than of torts and replevins. His son inherited his father's impractical and visionary temperament. When George was twenty-one his father sent him off to Tapping Reeve's law school at Litchfield, Connecticut. Graduated from Reeve's institution, he tried practicing law in western Pennsylvania but, as he put it later, "another and stronger passion was getting the advantage of me, that of painting, to which all my pleading soon gave way; and after having covered nearly every inch of the lawyer's table (and even encroached upon the judge's bench) with penknife, pen and ink, and pencil sketches of judges, jurors, and culprits, I very deliberately resolved to convert my law library into paint pots and brushes, and to pursue painting as my future, and apparently more agreeable profession." His father gave him his blessing along with an impressive catalogue of Renaissance artists with whose work he was enjoined to become familiar, and Catlin, after painting portraits of local worthies, set out for Philadelphia. Strikingly handsome and engaging in his enthusiasm, Catlin enlisted the interest of Charles Willson Peale and his son Rembrandt, and of Thomas Sully. He was soon elected to the Pennsylvania Academy of Fine Arts and began to get commissions for portraits, but as he put it, he "was continually reaching for some branch or enterprise of the arts, on which to devote a whole life-time of enthusiasm. . . ." The search ended when "a delegation of ten or fifteen noble and dignified-looking Indians from the wilds of the 'Far West' suddenly arrived in the city, arrayed in all their classic beauty. . . . In silent and stoic dignity, these lords of the forest strutted about the city for a few days. . . ."

After they left Catlin brooded about the dramatic visitation until he came "to the following deductions and conclusions. Man, in the simplicity and loftiness of his nature, unrestrained and unfettered by the disguises of art, is surely the most beautiful model for the painter. . . . And the history and customs of such a people, preserved by pictorial illustrations, are themes worthy of the life-time of one man, and nothing short of the loss of my life shall prevent me from visiting their country and becoming their historian. . . . I set out on my arduous and perilous undertaking with the determination of reaching, ultimately, every tribe of Indians on the Continent of North America, and of bringing home faithful portraits of their principal personages, and full notes of their character and history. I desired, also, to procure their costumes, and a complete collection of their manufactures and weapons, and to perpetuate them in a *gallery unique,* for the use and instruction of future ages."

The question was how. Such a splendid obsession must be costly. Catlin continued to paint miniatures, hoping to be able to save enough money to launch his venture. In New York he painted three miniatures of Governor De Witt Clinton, the great patron of the arts and sciences and the promoter of the Erie Canal. Clinton gave Catlin a commission to paint a series of pictures of the building of the canal. Through Clinton, Catlin also met William Leete Stone, the editor of the *New York Commercial Advertiser,* who shared Catlin's infatuation with Indians. Successful and sought-after as a portraitist, Catlin, in 1828, married a handsome and socially prominent New Jersey girl named Clara Bartlett Gregory. A year later, tormented by the conflict between his career as a miniaturist and the desire to begin what he conceived to be his lifework, Catlin had a kind of breakdown. When he recovered he set out for St. Louis where he found a patron in William Clark. Clark invited Catlin to paint some Indians who had come to engage in treaty negotiations and, apparently pleased with his work and his manner of dealing with the Indians, undertook to help him carry out his ambitious plan. Starting with the nearby Iowa, Missouri, Omaha, Sauk, and Foxes, Catlin added paintings of the principal chiefs of the Delaware, Potawatomi, Kickapoo, and Shawnee. After a winter spent with his wife in Albany, Catlin was back in St. Louis in the spring ready to start up the Platte to paint the Pawnee, Oto, and Sioux. He was increasingly impatient to penetrate those regions inhabited by tribes that had suffered least from contact with the whites. These were the tribes scattered along the Missouri to the Yellowstone country, the Minitari, Mandan, Arikara, Snake, Crows, Blackfeet, and Yankton Sioux. In 1832 Catlin boarded the brand new steamboat, the *Yellow Stone,* built expressly to carry supplies to Fort Union. At every stopping point along the river, he made sketches. When the *Yellow Stone* ran aground, Catlin set out with the fur traders. "I packed on the backs and in the hands of several men such articles for painting as I might want . . . with my sketchbook slung on my own back, and my rifle in my hands. . . ."

The Mandan village on the Missouri was the first village of aborigines whose contact with whites had been limited to the occasional trader or trapper who made his way up the river. In this tribe, so little contaminated by civilization, Catlin was in his element. Always intensely curious, the men, women, and children of the village swarmed around the lodge where Catlin was painting his first portraits of chiefs. Even before they were finished the excitement had reached such a pitch that two of the paintings were brought out and held up over the doorway so that the crowd had an opportunity to see and recognize their chiefs. "The effect upon so mixed a multitude . . . was novel and really laughable," Catlin wrote. "The likenesses were instantly recognized, and many of the gaping multitude commenced yelping; others were stamping off in the jarring dance—others were singing, and others again were crying—hundreds covered their mouths with their hands and were mute; others, indignant, drove their spears frightfully into the ground, and some threw a reddened arrow at the sun, and went home to their wigwams." When Catlin emerged from the lodge the excitement was almost as great. "Women were gaping and gazing—and warriors and braves offering me their hands,— . . . and whilst I was engaged, from the waist upwards, in fending off the throng and shaking hands, my legs were assailed (not unlike the nibbling of little fish, when I have been standing in deep water) by children, who were creeping between the legs of the bystanders for the curiosity or honour of touching me with the ends of their fingers." The astonished Indians pronounced Catlin "the greatest *medicine-man* in the world; for they said I had made *living beings*—they said they could see their chiefs alive, in two places—those that I had made were a *little* alive—they could see their eyes move—could see them smile and laugh, and if they could laugh they could certainly speak, if they should try, and they must therefore have *some life* in them." After a time the squaws of the village set up a loud lamentation, denouncing Catlin as a "dangerous man; one who could make living persons by looking at them; and at the same time, could, as a matter of course, destroy life in the same way. . . . That bad luck would happen to those whom I painted—that I was to take a part of the existence of those whom I painted, and carry it home with me amongst the white people, and that when they died they would never sleep quiet in their graves."

A kind of panic seized the village and it took all of Catlin's considerable powers of persuasion, filtered through an interpreter, to convince the Mandan that there was no danger in his magic. Soon the chiefs were competing to have their portraits painted, spending half a day donning their most splendid regalia. "The vanity of these men, after they had agreed to be painted," Catlin wrote, "was beyond description." "An Indian often lies down from morning till night in front of his portrait, admiring his beautiful face, and faithfully guarding it from day to day to protect it from accident or harm . . . owing to their superstitious notion that there may be life to a certain extent in the picture, and that if harm or violence be done to it, it may in some mysterious way affect their health or do them other injury."

Catlin spent the summer adding to his pictorial and verbal inventory of the wild tribes, soon, he realized, to be swept aside by the irresistible tide of white migration. When a party of Indian hunters returned from a buffalo hunt with "about *fourteen hundred fresh buffalo tongues*" to be exchanged for a few gallons of whiskey, Catlin noted that "Not a skin or a pound of the meat, except the tongues, was brought in. . . ." In such waste Catlin read the extinction of the seemingly limitless herds of buffalo. "The Indian and the buffalo are joint and original tenants of the soil," he wrote, "and fugitives from the approach of civilized man. . . . It is not enough in this polished and extravagant age, that we get from the Indian his land, and the very clothes from his back, but the food for his mouth must be stopped, to add a new article to the fashionable world's luxuries . . . that white men may figure a few years longer, enveloped in buffalo robes—spread them over the backs of their sleighs and trail them ostensibly amid the busy throng, as a thing of elegance that had been made for them! . . . It may be that *power* is *right,* and *voracity* a virtue; and that these people, and these noble animals, are righteously doomed to an issue that *will* not be averted." But it was clear that Catlin could not well reconcile himself to such a thought.

He longed both to establish a museum and a gallery for the display of their varied and remarkable artifacts and his portraits of their chiefs and principal braves, and also to persuade Congress to set aside a vast domain where they might be forever free and uncontaminated. "What a splendid contemplation it would be," he wrote, "by some great protecting policy of our government, to preserve their pristine beauty and wildness, in a *magnificent park,* where the world could see them for ages to come. What a beautiful specimen for America to preserve and hold up to the view of her refined citizens and the world, in future ages! A *National Park,* containing man and beast, in all the wild freshness of their native beauty! I would ask no other monument to my memory, than to be the founder of such an institution." But Catlin must have known in his heart that it was a vain and foolish vision. You could not treat human beings—beautiful, powerful, wild creatures—like animals in a cage, however vast and splendid that cage might be. Heartrending as the thought was, it must all go and the painstakingly collected artifacts, the brilliant pictures, would, in the end, be hardly more suggestive of the unimaginable reality than paper flowers are of real flowers.

Finally, Catlin had completed his remarkable visual record of more than forty tribes. He had succumbed. Like so many who ventured into that fearful and enchanted world, noble and terrible, he was never to escape its thrall. "I love a people," he wrote, "who have always made me welcome to the best they had . . . who are honest without laws, who have no jails and no poor houses . . . who never take the name of God in vain . . . who worship God without a Bible, and I believe that God loves them also . . . who are free from religious animosities . . . who have never raised a hand against me, or stolen my property, where there was no law to punish either . . . and oh! how I love a people who don't live for the love of money." It was not, of course, really the aborigines that Catlin was speaking of. He knew at first hand of the terrible hardships and cruelties that were integral to their lives, of the constancy of violent death and torture; of raids and merciless warfare. In the passage quoted, George Catlin was writing far more as the unrequited lover of a faithless white America that had betrayed his ideals than as what he so often was—a scrupulously accurate portrayer of aboriginal Americans. The ideal and the reality could not be encompassed in the same frame. They constantly threatened to tear Catlin himself apart. He had seen the Indian in "the innocent simplicity of nature" abandon his ancestral ground "and turn his face in sadness to the setting sun . . . and I have seen as often the approach of the bustling, busy, talking, elated, exultant white man, with the first dip of the plough share, making sacrilegious trespass on the bones of the dead. . . . I have seen the grand and irresistible march of civilization . . . this splendid juggernaut rolling on and beheld its sweeping desolation. And I have held converse with the happy thousands, living as yet beyond its influence, who have not been crushed, nor have yet dreamed of its approach. I have stood amidst these unsophisticated people, and contemplated with feelings of deepest regret the certain approach of this over-whelming system which will inevitably march on and prosper; reluctant tears shall have watered every rod of this fair land. . . . All this is certain."

When he had completed his plan, so far as it was practical to do so, he opened his "Indian Gallery" in New York City, showing a considerable degree of shrewdness in soliciting the support of the powerful and fashionable. He gave Daniel Webster, Philip Hone, and other New York notables an advance showing. Hone wrote that the Indian Gallery contained Catlin's "great collection of paintings, consisting of portraits of Indian chiefs, landscapes, ceremonies, etc., of the Indian tribes, and implements of husbandry, and the chase, weapons of war, costumes, etc., which he collected during his travels of five or six years in the great West. . . . I have seldom witnessed so interesting an exhibition. We had a collation of buffaloes' tongues," Hone added, "and venison and the waters of the great spring, and smoked a calumet of peace under an Indian tent formed of buffalo skins."

From New York Catlin took his gallery to Boston, Washington, and Philadelphia. It was a great initial success everywhere, but once the novelty had worn off there was a disheartening decline in admissions. Busy at a narrative of his adventures among the aborigines, finding it difficult to raise money for its publication in the United States and disappointed in the unwillingness of Congress to appropriate money for a permanent museum, Catlin decided to take his exhibition to England—"eight tons of freight, consisting of 600 portraits and other paintings . . . and several thousands of Indian costumes, weapons, etc."

In England, Catlin rented three large rooms in Egyptian Hall and his exhibition was an enormous success. Queen Victoria came to a private showing and Catlin found sponsors among the lords of the realm. He made plans to publish his account of his adventures in two large, profusely illustrated volumes, *Letters and Notes of the Manners, Customs, and Condition of the North American Indians . . . In Two Volumes with Four Hundred Illustrations.* The work was highly praised by English reviewers, one of whom called Catlin "one of the most remarkable men of the age."

Catlin, who had in him a good deal of the showman and promoter, hired English actors to perform in costume the songs and war dances of the Indians. Just at the point when dwindling admissions had forced him to consider taking his exhibition on a tour of British and Continental cities, a party of nine Ojibwa Indians arrived in London in the charge of an enterprising promoter named Rankin. Catlin at once incorporated them in his exhibition, and the genuine article gave the gallery new life; but when one of the Indians had a highly publicized affair with an English woman, Rankin and Catlin fell out and Catlin and the Ojibwa set up their own show. Moreover, the unhappy Ojibwa, dejected and homesick, were a far cry from the noble savages depicted in Catlin's paintings and, indeed, considerably less impressive than the actors who had preceded them. Charles Dickens reported that they were "mere animals and wretched creatures . . . squatting and spitting" and "their dances no better than the chorus of an Italian opera in England."

With the Ojibwa out of the way, several of them dead of white men's diseases and British climate, Catlin was about to pack up and head for home to try once more to prevail on Congress to provide an appropriate home for his artifacts when fourteen Iowa Indians arrived in a party organized by an old acquaintance of Catlin's named Meolody. Once more Catlin refurbished his exhibit. This time he hired horses for the Iowa to ride, whooping and yelling. Londoners, it turned out, were growing weary of imported Indians. Desperately, Catlin took them on tour. Expenses outran admissions, several of the Iowa died, and Catlin decided to break new ground by taking his gallery, with its human additions, to Paris. There he and his savage companions were received, with considerable fanfare, by the king and queen. "Tell these good fellows I am glad to see them," the king told the Indian interpreter; "that I have been in many of the wigwams of the Indians in America, when I was a young man, and they everywhere treated me kindly. . . ." In Paris, Catlin repeated his London triumph, but the Iowa languished in the alien surroundings; a number of them contracted pneumonia, several died, and the rest fled back to America. A few weeks after their departure, Catlin's wife, Clara, died of pneumonia, leaving him a widower with four young children to care for.

Another party of Ojibwa, who had been performing in London, hearing that the Iowa had departed, came to Paris to join Catlin. Then it was Belgium, where three of the Ojibwa died of smallpox and the others had to be placed in hospitals. Meanwhile, the collection and paintings found a temporary home in the Louvre. Catlin tried to sell it all to Louis Philippe and then to the British Museum "or some English Nobleman or Gentleman" for thirty-five thousand dollars, but he had no takers and he eked out a bare living through commissions to copy paintings from his gallery of Indian portraits. His son, George, died of pneumonia and his wife's parents reclaimed the three young girls. A committee of Congress proposed the establishment of the Smithsonian Institution as a national gallery of art and recommended that Catlin's collection be purchased for it, but the onset of the Mexican War left the plan in limbo. In the revolutionary upheavals of 1848, a Paris mob broke into Catlin's studio and destroyed several of his paintings and he barely escaped to London with his collection. From there, hounded by creditors, he returned to Paris in 1853 after the restoration of the monarchy.

In the 1852–53 session of Congress the proposal to purchase

Catlin's collection was revived. Webster, in his last days in the Senate, praised Catlin's work as did Jefferson Davis, senator from Kentucky, who had taken Black Hawk to Washington after the end of the Black Hawk War. But Davis ended his speech by saying that the feeling against Indians was so strong in his home state that he was obliged to vote against the bill which, as it turned out, was defeated by a single vote.

Impoverished and deaf, Catlin set out at the age of fifty-six for the jungles of Brazil to paint the natives of South America. Accompanied by a giant black man, an escaped slave named Caesar Bolla, who carried the artist's paints and canvases, Catlin made three trips into the interior of Brazil, over the Andes to Peru, and then across the pampas of Argentina. It was one of the most extraordinary expeditions of the century, the aging artist back once more in that world most congenial to him—the world of primitive peoples, enduring hardships and dangers that would make a saint blanch, protected among warlike and suspicious tribes, many of which had never seen a white person, by his "magic" as a man of "great medicine." He came back to Brussels to a studio on "an obscure street near the Antwerp railroad station." The American consul who sought him out found the deaf old man living on a few francs a day. "He talked to me often about his collections of paintings and sketches," the consul wrote, "and expressed a hope that all his works might be brought together and placed in the hands of the Government of the United States. . . . He evidently felt more anxiety for the future of his lifelong work than to execute orders. . . . and always took pride in calling himself the 'friend of the Indian.' . . . His life in Brussels was almost that of a recluse. . . ."

In his years in Brussels Catlin wrote two more books, *Life Among the Indians* and *Last Rambles Among the Indians.* In 1870 at the age of seventy-four, after thirty-one years abroad, Catlin came home to New York City. He opened an exhibition of his works in a gallery at Fifth Avenue and 14th Street. Joseph Henry, a friend from days long ago and now director of the Smithsonian, invited him to give an exhibition of his work there. A room in the Smithsonian was given to him as a makeshift studio and efforts were renewed to prevail on Congress to buy his collection of paintings and drawings, now numbering over twelve hundred. Too weak and ill to continue painting, Catlin moved to Jersey City to be near his daughters. He died on December 23, 1872, in his seventy-seventh year, and his last words were reported to be "What will happen to my gallery?"

George Catlin's life, tragic and disordered, paralleled, in some respects, the lives of those aborigines whom he celebrated. Its crowning irony was that he had to convert his Indians into a marketable product. He had to "sell" them, live off them. In London and in Paris he exploited the unfortunate Ojibwa and Iowa. His imagination always exceeded his means and he was as prodigal of money as he was of his talent. He spent more than half of his mature life outside of the United States, joining that company of literary and artistic figures who, it seemed, could not endure their native land or wholly escape it. He did an enormous amount of hack work merely to survive, innumerable copies of original paintings and hasty and poorly executed scenes, far inferior to his best work. He was a romantic, a visionary, an obsessive, a showman, something even of a confidence man, a hustler for the Indians. But out of the torment and disorder emerged those splendid portraits, those fine, proud, doomed heads, those splendidly caparisoned immortal figures, images that will always speak to us of what was most compelling in the life, customs, and manners of the Indians of North America. It was not primarily as an artist that George Catlin thought of himself but as the recorder of a vanishing breed and way of life. Yet in his direct and intense observation of the human and artifactual reality before him, he was assuredly an artist with a fine sense of color, a powerful and convincing mastery of the body and its proportions; a deft draftsman, able, with an economy of strokes, to capture the essence of his subject. While the artists of the Hudson River school ventured out each summer into the domesticated landscape of the Catskills, George Catlin ranged over the vast expanses of two great continents.

George Caleb Bingham was born on a sizable plantation in western Virginia. His father, Henry, owned a number of slaves and a good many acres of rich tobacco land but the hard times of 1819 left him bankrupt and he set out with his family, including his father-in-law, for Franklin, Missouri, in Boone's Lick country. George Caleb Bingham was eight years old when his father moved from the comfortable and, indeed, in many ways, luxurious life of a Virginia planter of the second or third rank to the rough Missouri frontier, which we are already familiar with through the adventures of Charles Pancoast. Henry Bingham bought a farm of a hundred and sixty acres, built a tobacco drying shed, and bought a tavern in Franklin; four years later he died, leaving his wife with six young children to care for.

Mrs. Bingham opened a school for girls to make her livelihood and George was apprenticed to a cabinetmaker in Boonville. There he also became a devout Methodist and a boy preacher. The author of a nineteenth-century sketch of Bingham's life states that "he frequently preached at the camp meetings common in those days. I have heard him tell the story that on one occasion after he had finished the sermon, one of his auditors came forward and tendered him a silver dollar, saying his sermon was well worth the money." He began to study of law also, but by the time he was twenty he had found that he could turn his precocious artistic talent to use by painting portraits for twenty dollars, frame included. A severe attack of measles resulted in the loss of his hair and Bingham thereafter wore a wig. The portrait painting flourished and Bingham developed a technique that enabled him to do a portrait in a day's sitting. When he established himself in Columbia, Missouri, one of the state's larger towns, in 1834, he had already achieved a striking mastery of line and an ability to render excellent likenesses. An article in the *Missouri Intelligencer*, March 14, 1835, told of the editor's delight in visiting Bingham's studio. The portraits that lined the room seemed to the editor the work of "an undoubted high creative genius" and the artist's presence in Columbia was evidence of "an important era, in the history of Trans-Mississippian progress, towards a state of intellectual and social refinement. . . . Of Mr. Bingham himself, we would say a word. As a painter, whatever he is, he is by means of his own unassisted application, and untutored study. His boyhood was spent on the banks of the Missouri; and never, since he reached the stature of manhood, has he been East of the Mississippi. Except those of his own execution, he never saw a portrait painted in his life. . . . We are unacquainted, save to a degree, with the works of Eastern artists, but it is tho't that the portraits of Mr. Bingham might be placed along side the finest specimens of Harding, Catlin, and Duett. . . . If we might venture a criticism upon Mr. Bingham . . . we should say, that of the three Italian schools, his style combines more of the excellencies of the Leontine and Venetian, than of the Lombard." The editor urged his readers to visit Bingham's studio, adding a fervent regional plea. "If the West will but extend a cherishing patronage, she can rear up, from the number of her youth, sons of genius, that, like the trees of her own deep forests, will attain the largest and the stateliest growth."

Bingham found patronage and commissions in St. Louis, married a childhood sweetheart from Franklin, and with her, traveled to

Natchez, Mississippi, hoping to make his living there as a portrait painter. The money he made painting portraits at forty dollars and sixty dollars apiece was all lost in the Panic of 1837 and the failure of the Agricultural Bank of Natchez. More disheartening, the long depression that followed the panic seriously depleted the ranks of citizens sufficiently prosperous to afford to have their portraits painted. Returning to Columbia, Bingham received enough commissions from friends and relatives to enable him to go to Philadelphia to study for three months in the Academy of Fine Arts. At the Academy Bingham saw paintings of the genre school stemming from the Düsseldorf ateliers. They were like a revelation to the young artist. Back home in Missouri, he began to pay close attention to the scenes around him and became deeply involved in the Tippecanoe and Tyler Too campaign of the Whigs against Van Buren and the Democrats in 1840. Bingham, with his youthful experience as a camp meeting preacher, was an effective stump speaker and he found himself much in demand as a worker for the Whig cause.

From the conclusion of the presidential campaign until 1850 the details of Bingham's life become curiously vague. In Washington he met and painted a portrait of John Quincy Adams, who wandered into Bingham's studio and engaged him in conversation about the Bible. Before he left the city in 1844 he painted "The Jolly Flatboatmen"— the first of those classic scenes of river life which are as much a part of the lore of the Mississippi as Mark Twain's *Life on the Mississippi* and *Huckleberry Finn.*

When Bingham took "The Jolly Flatboatmen" to the gallery of the American Art Union it was an instant hit. The Union purchased it, a great compliment for an unknown young artist, and had it made into an engraving for distribution to its members in the Union's yearly bulletin. The painting's reception made Bingham's reputation. He was the "Missouri Artist," a living example of the fact that American genius could sprout even in the culturally arid soil of the Western frontier.

A painting superior to "The Jolly Flatboatmen" was "Fur Traders Descending the Missouri," apparently completed in 1844. The "Fur Traders," painted at the beginning of Bingham's career as a genre painter, is certainly one of the great American paintings. The two traders, drifting through the early morning mist on the river, their faces turned toward the viewer, are caught in a timeless floating moment: the older man steering in the stern, self-contained, impassive as an Indian, his body and arms feeling the river's current; his young companion, handsome and carefree, a slight smile on his lips.

In the fall of 1844, Bingham was back in Boonville actively engaged in politics, and two years later he was the Whig candidate for the state legislature from Sabine County. Winner by three votes, he lost on a recount. That he continued to paint is indicated by the fact that he sold two paintings in 1847, "Lighter Relieving a Steamboat Aground" and "Raftsmen Playing Cards."

A by-product of Bingham's politicking was the "Stump Orator," which appeared in the records of the American Art Union in 1848, the same year that Bingham was again a candidate for the state legislature, this time successfully. It was said that "his great speech against secession was the first defiant utterance against rebellion in the Capitol in Missouri." But the painting never ceased; "Watching the Cargo" was exhibited in 1849. The bulletin of the American Art Union of that year, reviewing his most popular canvases, noted, "All these works are thoroughly American in their subjects and could never have been painted by one who was not perfectly familiar with the scenes they represented."

We know from an account in the *Missouri Statesman* in October, 1851, that Bingham in that year was working on the two large canvases that were eventually known as "County Election" and "Canvassing for a Vote." After a brief description of "County Election," the reporter wrote, "Several hours would not suffice fully to examine it, so numerous and life-like are the characters. Indeed it is full of reality, a seeming incarnation, prominent in figure, grouped and colored with admirable skill and effect. Persons of highly cultivated taste in the fine arts, and critics in general, will accord to it a remarkable degree of genius and merit. There was also in his studio a smaller painting, another political scene of great originality of conception and beauty of finish, to wit: 'Candidate Electioneering.'" The final painting in the political series, "The Verdict of the People," was painted in 1854 and intended, in Bingham's words, to *"cap the climax."*

The public reaction to Bingham's paintings wherever they were exhibited was enthusiastic. He made arrangements to have many of them engraved for general sale and he painted copies of others. The problem was how to feed his growing family. Between work on his large genre paintings and his political activities, he painted portraits again to make ends meet and began studies for a painting of

Washington crossing the Delaware, which soon became Bingham's "Belshazzar's Feast"—a work that he labored over for sixteen years. When one thinks of Bingham's astonishing productivity in a period of ten years, his protracted labors over the Washington scene are the more remarkable. On a visit to Boston in 1856, Bingham made copies of the Stuart portraits of Washington and Jefferson "and executed some private commissions."

A devoted follower of Henry Clay and an enemy of loco-focoism, Bingham painted two great banners for the Missouri Whigs to carry in the electioneering of 1844. One side of one of the banners depicted Clay "advocating 'the American System.'" Above a fortress waved the American flag and beyond it was the ocean "crowded with shipping, and farther in the front is a farmer with his plough, a railroad, a number of dingy manufacturing establishments . . . while Mr. Clay, with his hands extended towards them, exclaims . . . 'All these great interests are confided to the protection and care of government.' . . . On the reverse side of the banner is represented a prairie, in its uncultivated state . . . with a herd of buffalo roving across it. . . ."

The Boonville Club and the Boonville Juvenile Clay Club displayed an even more elaborate banner, also painted by Bingham, with a "noble farmer" on one side and "an Eagle perched high on a firm immovable rock," on the other. "A mere description of the devices on these banners, however, conveys no idea of their real beauty," an enthusiastic newspaper reporter wrote.

Bingham was devoted to the Union and hostile toward slavery. The fact that he lived in a slave state distressed him and his political involvement may well have been prompted by the depth of his concern. The Kansas-Nebraska Act, which turned the neighboring territory into a bloody battleground, added to Bingham's distress, and his departure for Europe in 1856 to work at Düsseldorf may well have been motivated in large part by his growing despair over the future of the Union. From Düsseldorf he wrote a friend, "The striking peculiarity of the school which flourishes here by its own inherent vitality, is a total disregard of the 'old masters' and a direct resort to nature for the truths which it employs. As might be expected, works springing from a principle of execution so simple and so rational are characterized by a freshness vigor and truth which captivates those of common understanding and is none the less agreeable to minds of the highest cultivation."

It was clearly Bingham's ambition to "captivate those of common understanding" as well as to appeal to "minds of the highest cultivation." The fact that he turned to historical paintings of Jefferson and Washington and portraits of Clay and Jackson suggests that the "Missouri Artist" could no longer cope with the ambiguity of his feelings about the contemporary scene. It is significant that his only major canvas after his return from Düsseldorf was a picture entitled "Order No. 11," referring to an order by the commanding general of the Department of the Border, Thomas Ewing, for the forced evacuation of the Kansas-Missouri border to stop the Jayhawker raids. The picture was painted as an indictment of Ewing and is a far cry from such earlier works as "The Jolly Flatboatmen."

If Bingham became infatuated by genre painting during his three-month visit to Philadelphia in 1837, it is nonetheless remarkable that his first or second completed canvas in that style was "Fur Traders on the Missouri." For a work of such brilliance to emerge from the Western frontier, from the crude and violent land of Missouri, seemed to some critics to verify the contention that American genius flourished most conspicuously when free of the contamination of alien ideas and styles. Bingham had read James Fenimore Cooper. His tall, handsome frontiersmen, clear-eyed and muscular, are the lineal descendants of the novelist's Natty Bumpo-Deerslayer-Hawkeye and the rest of that tribe of nature's noblemen. Even Bingham's drunks and loafers have nothing sordid about them; they are merely picturesque. For Bingham, the romance of the frontier and the forests and mountains was subordinate to the romance of democratic politics. His is a perfect romantic vision of the frontier centering on the Mississippi and the Missouri rivers, filled with the lounging figures of trappers, fiddlers, dancers, and boatmen and intense and sonorous politicians. The eyes of his subjects are dark and directly commanding, the bodies powerful and at ease under their loose garments. The strong practical hands are as arresting as the eyes, and the feet in their rough boots are rendered with as sure a tactile sense and feeling for form and surface as that of any painter in our history. The fact that this vision was clothed in its most seductive forms in a single decade suggests that Bingham worked in a kind of frenzy. Indeed, it is almost as though he were afraid that the bitter realities of American life, particularly the growing divisions between North and South which were perhaps experienced most excruciatingly in Missouri, where the involvement with slavery was balanced by a deep devotion to the Union, would overwhelm him before he could transfer his vision to canvas.

Certainly Bingham's great paintings fix a set of American images in our minds more powerfully than any other works save perhaps Trumbull's canvases of the American Revolution, but one senses behind them the profound ambivalence of the artist. Or at least the haste. In a way, Bingham is almost too good to be true. His attitude toward his own work seems eminently practical and democratic. He turned out his "pot boiler" portraits without complaint and was businesslike in arranging for the engraving of his major canvases and for their sale. It did not seem to him any more undignified or inappropriate to hawk his paintings than it would have been to sell hogsheads of tobacco or sides of beef. In his intention to appeal to the "common understanding" Bingham was brilliantly successful. The rapid decline of his powers or, perhaps more accurately, his silence, may be attributed to the fact that he no longer had subjects that commanded his remarkable energy and, perhaps equally, to the fact that he found it easier to repeat his early successes than to attempt to form new visions.

The Civil War and the five years leading up to it constituted a terrible trauma for the creative consciousness. The fact that three of the major painters of the mid-nineteenth century—Washington Allston, Thomas Cole, and George Caleb Bingham—were unable to continue to work productively in the last decades of their lives suggests very strongly that the artist-in-America labored under peculiar aesthetic and psychological difficulties. In addition to the problems that beset every painter, he was conscious every minute that he carried special responsibilities as a representative of a social and political order. One of the most serious charges leveled by the enemies of democracy was that it lowered the whole cultural and intellectual tone of a people and encouraged the dominance of the mediocre over the excellent. Each American painting had thus to bear the burden of being some kind of statement about the value of democracy. The problem was further complicated by the fact that the Eastern upper class was constantly conceding the cultural game to the Old World. As we have noted, such supporters of the arts as George Templeton Strong and Sidney George Fisher were thoroughly persuaded of the superiority of things European, more particularly those English. When Bingham's "The Jolly Flatboatmen" was exhibited at the Art Union in 1846, the *Literary World* criticized the painting, "the very name of which gives a death blow to all one's preconceived notions of HIGH ART." The painting, this critic wrote, expressed no moral, patriotic sentiment and therefore lay outside the established "standard of taste." Much preferred was a painting called "Sybil," a moody lady staring into the future. So the American artist labored under two disadvantages: he had to affirm the cultural potency of democracy and he had to submit his work to the judgment of a class of potential patrons who doubted in their hearts that democracy was consistent with true culture and refinement.

The correspondences between the lives of the three most "American" of the painters we have discussed here is instructive. Certainly they did the most powerful and original work of any painters in the first half of the nineteenth century; indeed they can lay legitimate claim to preeminence over a far longer stretch of time. Catlin and Audubon transcended the category of artists; they were, respectively, an anthropologist and an ornithologist who made records of vanishing aspects of America in paint. The primary intention was to *record*. By the same token I suppose we might say that Bingham was, in an essential way, a sociologist of the frontier. He, also, was a recorder. But the extravagance of the visions of the three men exalted their subjects to the level of the heroic. Heroic birds, heroic Indians, heroic trappers and politicians. "Fur Traders on the Missouri" is as dazzlingly mysterious as the original act of creation. Audubon's splendid totemistic birds are conceived on a scale appropriate to the vastness of the continent. Catlin's Indians fix in our imaginations the inexhaustible image of the noble savage past all degradations.

All three men associated themselves with the frontiers and the forests of North America. All three had early connections with a world of cultivation and upper-middle-class aspiration. They all married women above their own station who supported them devotedly and they all spent varying periods of time abroad—Audubon thirteen years, Catlin thirty-seven, Bingham only two. Contemplating their careers one is inclined to embrace the notion of the "natural," "democratic" artist.

Audubon, Catlin, and Bingham were "popular" artists in the exact sense of that word, their pictures viewed by tens of thousands of people and almost universally acclaimed. All three were, perforce, artist-businessmen who had to spend a substantial amount of time and energy promoting their work simply in order to make a living. For all three the painting of portraits was at various times an essential means of supporting their families. They were artistic jacks-of-all-trades, trying their hands at anything that promised to bring in a few sorely needed dollars. The intensely creative periods in their lives were, in each instance, slightly more than a decade. Audubon painted the great majority of his bird subjects in the period between 1812 and 1824; Catlin his "gallery" of over six hundred Indians between 1829 and 1837; Bingham his great genre paintings between 1844 and 1855. When one contemplates the time-energy equation represented by the almost incredible outpouring of creativity in those limited spans, the mind turns to such physical analogies as the building of the Erie Canal, one of the great engineering enterprises in history, accomplished in slightly more than ten years. It is almost as though creative energies in America were expended with such prodigality that they could be sustained only for a decade, as though the acceleration from sail to steam, from horse-drawn coach to railway car was paralleled by a similarly accelerating expenditure of human energy. In a nation whose collective life was measured in decades rather than, as in most traditional cultures, centuries, even artists and writers must respond to the ethic of accelerating production.

Another fact worth noting about the three artists whose work has so many common denominators is that they solved the problem that haunted such painters as Washington Allston and Thomas Cole—what themes to choose as "American" painters—by focusing their attention on specific objects of the "natural" world: Indians and avian species in the cases of Catlin and Audubon, pictorial essays on frontier life in the case of Bingham. They thus avoided the agonizing problem of appropriate subjects. It was only when Bingham, sick at heart over the disruption of the democracy he loved, turned to historical subjects that his great powers failed him.

So we might say that the greatest art of the era here under consideration was practical, democratic, descriptive, romantic, idyllic, and splendidly visionary, American life ennobled and enhanced: bird, Indian, and frontier politician or river boatman—all epic figures in the romance of Western democracy.

Surely there was a moral to be drawn in the contrast between Washington Allston, wealthy, highly cultivated, unquestionably gifted, with the finest training in his art that England and the Continent could provide, locked away with his private agony, "Belshazzar's Feast," or Cole, equally impotent in his Catskill retreat, and George Caleb Bingham's joyously populated canvases flowing forth one after the other, untroubled by subtle aesthetic considerations, until the onrushing North-South crisis stopped his hand.

We have already spoken of the fact that the work of certain of the so-called Hudson River school of painters, men like Kenesett and Heade, had in it substantial elements of the "naive vision," the "primitive" or untutored, natural view of the world that so often disarms us by its directness and simplicity, having the unself-conscious expressiveness of the child's view of the world grown older and somewhat more complex. Since Americans of all classes had been released by the Declaration of Independence and the intricate events that flowed from it from many of the inhibitions that traditionally prescribed and defined appropriate tasks and set the canons for crafts and arts, one might conjecture that the same spirit that disposed Americans to try their hands at any task that fancy or necessity presented them with might induce them to produce a large body of "naive," or what we somewhat misleadingly term "folk" art. And the conjecture would, of course, be true. Preeminently "people of the hand"—whittlers, fashioners, graspers, tinkerers, toolmakers, implement users—ordinary Americans ornamented the day-to-day world in which they lived with gilded weathervanes in the shapes of cocks or trotting horses; carved and painted clocks or boots or hats to advertise shops; made toys for children where no toys could be bought or there was no money to buy them; carved headstones for grave markers, eagles beyond counting, and innumerable Indians. Many, of course, were done by professionals, by carvers and gilders, but many more were done by men and women who simply felt the impulse to adorn or shape, by men whose whittling turned into carving and who carved Henry Ward Beecher or Henry Clay or Andrew Jackson or Father Time or Liberty or incised a powder horn or a whale's tooth, or made a decoy for ducks; who created animals, wild and domestic, gates in the form of flags, wooden chains whittled out of a single long stick, fanciful whirligigs set in motion by the wind to box or saw wood endlessly, or an Indian paddling a canoe, his arms revolving in the breeze.

Whittling and chewing and spitting were the common accompaniments of masculine conversation, as knitting and sewing were of the feminine sphere. The women, more bound to the domestic realm, made samplers and quilts and flowers of hair and paper and painted delicate watercolors of weeping willows to commemorate the death of a child in the family. Those homely icons, most now in museums or adorning fashionable urban apartments, speak in a peculiarly engaging way of some of the less readily perceived aspects of the American character: the constant flow of humor, of wit and ingenuity, of playfulness and exuberance, of "invention." For every Audubon or Bingham or Catlin there were tens of thousands of fabricators, Americans whose perpetually restless fingers, not for a moment deterred by any notion of "art," gave arresting shapes to wood and metal (and paint as well) in response to their owner's particular vision of his world.

By the same token, artists like Cole and Durand, whose work ascended to that level defined as "fine," began their careers as craftsmen. So clearly there was in America an invigorating reciprocity between craftsmanship and Art with a capital A. There *was* a democratic art, struggling to free itself from overblown classical analogies and European definitions of appropriate form and subject.

49

American Literature: The Precursors

Washington Irving was born in New York City in 1783, in the year of the Treaty of Paris that concluded the American Revolution. His father was a successful businessman. Irving's two brothers attended Columbia and one became a doctor and the other a lawyer and newspaper editor. Irving himself was apprenticed to one of the leading judges of New York. His interests were primarily literary, but his father and brothers were so persistent in urging him to make his way in the legal profession that he was thirty-six before he finally tried to make his living as a writer. Meanwhile, Irving and his young literary friends had entertained themselves by writing sketches and satires. Assuming the nom de plume of Diedrich Knickerbocker, Irving wrote a comic history of New Amsterdam, employing a mock heroic style that he had picked up on a European tour. Many of his sketches and essays were printed in his brother Peter's *Morning Chronicle.*

When Irving became engaged to be married, he resigned himself to having to practice law, about which he felt much as Dana, Fisher, and Strong did, that it was a career only slightly to be preferred to business, a "sordid, dusty, soul killing way of life." After the death of his fiancée in 1809, Irving went through a period of almost six years of aimless indecision. He had strong inclinations toward the life of a wealthy upper-class New Yorker but little prospect, it appeared to him, of achieving riches as a writer. The very length of his vacillation is revealing. He was teetering on the verge of a career—that of writer—which did not in fact exist. Not only were there no models of older men who made their living with their pen, but there was a negative connotation attached to writing. It was not "serious work" for a young man anxious to get ahead in the world. Business, law, medicine, and politics (the latter only accessible, in large part, through the law) were virtually the only careers open to ambitious young men. As we have seen, for those who valued their independence and their morality (or, as we would be more inclined to say today, their integrity) none of these alternatives was wholly satisfying—most were perceived to be "soul killing." Going to England to act as an agent of his father's company, Irving found his brother Peter, who had preceded him abroad, ill and undertook, almost gratefully, to nurse him back to health. The collapse of the company freed him to try to make his living as a writer.

The first fruit of this decision was his *Sketch Book* "by Geoffrey Crayon, Gent.," an account of his European travels. Published in the United States and England, it was hailed in the latter country as the first work of an American writer worthy of serious notice. Thoroughly romantic in its style, it found a ready audience in both countries. Irving had come to Europe, he confessed, because the natural scenery of America contained little of the picturesque. It was "full of youthful promise" but Europe "was rich in the accumulated treasures of age. Her very ruins told the history of times gone by, and every mouldering stone was a chronicle. I longed to wander over the ruins of renowned achievement—to tread, as it were, in the footsteps of antiquity—to loiter about the ruined castle . . . to escape, in short, from the commonplace realities of the present, and lose myself among the shadowy grandeurs of the past. . . . I will visit this land of wonders, thought I, and see the gigantic race from which I am degenerated."

Irving had become enamored of the rich treasury of European folktales and he set out to create instant folktales for America. The final piece in the *Sketch Book* was the "Legend of Sleepy Hollow, Found Among the Papers of the Late Diedrich Knickerbocker." Based on a German folk story, the tale of Rip Van Winkle, set in the Catskills, was a delightfully told tale. Now followed a series of increasingly popular travel pieces. Irving was invited to Spain by a friend, Alexander Everett, head of the American legation in Madrid, to translate a collection of documents relating to Columbus's voyages. He spent four years there, wrote an excellent biography of Columbus, *A Chronicle of the Conquest of Granada,* which appeared in 1828, and then *The Alhambra,* which appeared four years later.

In 1832 Irving returned to America and settled down on the Hudson near Tarrytown; he was almost fifty years of age and very much a literary lion. He had been in Europe for fifteen years and it was clear that his feelings for his native land were as ambivalent as its for him. He tried to make amends for his long absence by writing *A Tour of the Prairies.* With Charles Latrobe and the Count de Pourtalès, plus the Indian commissioner and a party of United States Army rangers, Irving ventured into the region of the Pawnee. The Osage and Pawnee Indians were as handsome as Greek statues and as picturesque as ruined castles. Irving has a characteristic reflection on a young Osage warrior: "such is the glorious independence of man in a savage state. This youth, with his rifle, his blanket, and his horse, was ready at a moment's warning to rove the world; he carried all his worldly effects with him, and in the absence of artificial wants, possessed the great secret of personal freedom. We of society are slaves, not so much to others as to ourselves; our superfluities are the chains that bind us, impeding every movement of our bodies, and thwarting every impulse of our souls." Americans (and Englishmen and Frenchmen and Germans and Italians) loved that kind of talk, or writing. The Count de Pourtalès was so charmed by "the wild chivalry of the prairies" that he wanted to put on "Indian dress and adopt the Indian habits." It seemed to Irving, a little belatedly, that a tour of the prairies "would be more likely to produce that manliness, simplicity, and self-dependence most in unison with our political institutions," rather than the more fashionable European tour in the course of which a young American might well grow "luxurious and effeminate."

Back in New York, Irving assumed his rightful place as a gentleman. When Philip Hone and a party of friends visited the coal mines of the Delaware & Hudson Canal Company, Irving was one of the group. "The gentle Geoffrey Crayon," Hone wrote, "has enjoyed himself to the very top of his bent. He has been in perfect raptures all the way; I have never known him so entertaining; he jokes and laughs and tells stories and actually does not sleep in the day time. In fact, the whole voyage has been one of mirth and good humor."

Irving wrote a made-to-order account of John Jacob Astor's trading post at Astoria. He used Captain Bonneville's notes for a book on the captain's adventures, and wrote a five-volume biography of Washington. When he died in 1859 at the age of seventy-six, Irving was the unchallenged dean of American letters, famous around the world. His fifteen-year absence from his homeland had been long forgiven and he was pointed to as a living refutation of the canard that a democratic society could not produce great literature. It is interesting to note that both political parties courted Irving and a more-or-less Whig President, John Tyler, prevailed on him to serve as American minister to Spain.

Irving was a thoroughgoing Whig, a gentleman, and America's first "professional" writer. If he had difficulties coping with the crudeness and disorder of American life, he kept them largely to himself, writing about the picturesque days of long ago—the Alhambra, the conquest of Granada, or the "romance of the prairies." He solved the problem of how to cope by staying away until he was rich and famous. Undoubtedly he suffered more than he lets us know over the dilemma of becoming an American "writer" as opposed to a lawyer or a businessman. But Irving and his contemporary, James Fenimore Cooper, made writing a respectable vocation in the United States as well as a highly remunerative one.

James Fenimore Cooper was six years younger than Irving. The son of a judge who gave his name to the town—Cooperstown—at the head of Lake Otsego—"Glimmerglass"—where young Cooper grew up and which he made the scene of several of his most famous novels, he was a member of the landed aristocracy who wrestled most of his life with the extremely taxing question of the artist vis-à-vis America. In striking contrast to what we might not unfairly call Irving's escapism, Cooper tried his best to come to terms with the democratic ethos. He was tossed out of Yale for a prank, went to sea on a merchant ship, and then joined the U. S. Navy as a midshipman. In 1810, after his father had been knocked over the head in a political brawl and killed, Cooper resigned his commission and married a De Lancey, heiress of one of the great families of New York. He is said to have started writing out of the need to make money when the estate left him by his father was much diminished by the depression of 1819. His first serious novel, *The Spy*, was, by the standards of the day, a sensational success, selling eight thousand copies in the space of a few months. The setting was the American Revolution and the hero was Harvey Burch, a spy for Washington. *The Pioneer*, which appeared two years later, sold thirty-five hundred copies on the day of publication. In the book, Cooper introduced the first classic American fictional hero, Natty Bumpo, the hawkeyed frontiersman who was to be featured in four more adventure novels as the Deerslayer, as Leatherstocking, and as the Pathfinder. Cooper had hit instinctively on a sure-fire best-seller theme—the encounter between frontiersman and Indian, with the "good" Indians usually on the side of the frontiersman, the frontiersman himself a curious blend of Indian and white man. What Margaret Fuller wrote of Irving's account of the plains Indians could as well be applied to Cooper: "His scenery is fit to be glanced at from a dioramic distance; his Indians are academic figures only . . . his success is wonderful but inadequate." Cooper was soon a figure of world renown. His novels were translated into virtually every European language and snapped up the moment they appeared on the bookstalls. (All Gustaf Unonius knew of Indians when he arrived on the Wisconsin frontier was what he had read in Cooper's novels.) More than any other single phenomenon they fixed in the imagination of the world the image of the frontiersman and the Indian. Exciting plots acted out against lush and lovingly detailed landscapes marked all of Cooper's pioneering novels. With the formula down, the novels tumbled out, one after another: *The Pilot, Lionel Lincoln, The Last of the Mohicans,* the most romantic of them all, in 1826; and *The Prairie,* the story of Natty Bumpo retired beyond the Mississippi, a year later.

Cooper had his own strategy for dealing with America—to get out as soon as he could and stay away as long as he dared. When he left in 1826 he was already a literary lion, the most spectacular success story in American letters. He had written six novels in six years, four of them best-sellers. He and his wife remained in Europe for seven years, based in Paris and traveling around the continent, while Cooper wrote seven books, many of them stressing the themes of American simplicity and virtue as contrasted with the corruptions of a Europe he clearly preferred. It was an odd sight: the celebrator of the American frontier moving through the salons of Europe, extravagantly admired, his work compared favorably with that of Sir Walter Scott. But Cooper plainly had the same problem as Strong, Hone, Fisher, and Dana. He was made profoundly uneasy by the crass, assertive, vulgar ways of his fellow Americans, who had no respect for family or tradition, for good manners or proper behavior. When he returned to the United States in 1833, he wrote several travel accounts and then began taking his countrymen to task for their vices in a series of books—*The American Democrat, Homeward Bound,* and *Home as Found*—all of which appeared in 1838 and proved too stiff a dose for his compatriots to swallow without vociferous complaints.

Cooper's tone was that of an affectionate parent correcting an unruly child. There were "notions" abroad, he wrote in *The American Democrat,* that were "impracticable" and which "if persevered in, cannot fail to produce disorganization, if not revolution. . . ." He felt it necessary, out of affection for his countrymen, to correct these errors and misconceptions about democracy. "The writer," Cooper declared, "believes himself to be as good a democrat as there is in America. But his democracy is not of the impracticable school. He prefers a democracy to any other system, on account of its comparative advantages, and not on account of its perfection. He knows it has evils; great and increasing evils . . . but he believes that monarchy and aristocracy have more." Beyond that he was "not a believer in the scheme of raising men very far above their natural propensities." What most concerned him was the disposition of Americans to be taken in by, indeed to feed upon, "fulsome, false and meretricious eulogiums." He had even thought of calling his work "Anti-Cant" since his purpose in writing it was to deflate all the noisy self-serving rhetoric about the glories of democracy so that it might be seen for what it was, a system full of flaws but justly claiming to be better and more humane than any other alternative yet devised.

Cooper spoke for the Classical-Christian Consciousness which was so well aware of the general human inclination to self-aggrandizement and self-importance. The accents were those of Madison or William Manning, of a John Adams or a Gouverneur Morris. The notion of equality, for example, was widely misunderstood according to Cooper. As it appeared in the Declaration of Independence, it meant simply that all men had been "created equal" in the sense of having equal protection under the law, equal political rights, equal opportunities to advance in the world. Obviously there were the widest inequalities of talent, wealth, natural gifts, etc. So far were people from being "naturally" good, "the very necessity of a government at all, arises from the impossibility of controlling the passions by any other means than that of force." A good government was not one that tried to make all men equal but one that refrained "from fortifying and accumulating social inequality as a means of increasing political inequalities." Cooper's point is worth lingering over because it is so persistent an element in a major stream of American political thought. Inequality of talents and material condition being natural and inevitable in every society, that government is fairest and most just which resists all efforts of the advantaged to use it to extend and solidify the privileges that they enjoy. In Cooper's view, and in the view of a substantial number of primarily upper-class Americans in every generation who have shared his views, that is pretty much the limit of the responsibilities of government. The opposing point of view was that money and class plus the basic human drive for power are always working to exploit those less powerful (Manning's argument); it is therefore the responsibility of a democratic government to intervene wherever necessary as the active advocate of those we might call the "unpowered," the perennial victims of society, democratic, aristocratic, or monarchical. The reason the franchise should be universal is that otherwise the powerless have not even the uncertain counter of their vote to trade for fair play. The trouble with this approach to ensuring social justice and a fair distribution of the wealth of a society is that it tends to make the disadvantaged (however we understand that rather slippery word) the wards of the government and wards tend, in the long run, to fare badly, however good the intentions of their custodians may be—the most notorious case, of course, being that of the American Indians. Manning, well aware of this, wanted workingmen to empower themselves by creating their own organizations and their own means of disseminating information. These variant views of the nature and responsibility of a democratic government are by no means new, and they will be with us throughout the remainder of this work.

Much of what Cooper said, and said on the whole lucidly and amiably, is hard to gainsay, but he tipped his hand, so to speak, with such sentences as, "There can be no question that the educated and affluent classes of a country, are more capable of coming to wise and intelligent decisions in affairs of state, than the mass of the population. Their wealth and leisure afford them opportunities for observation and comparison, while their general information and greater knowledge of character, enable them to judge more accurately of men and measures." There is a real question of whether the "educated and affluent classes of a country" are better qualified to run things than their less fortunate fellow citizens, the point being that power in the form of education and affluence is as prone to seek its own advantage (or "self-aggrandizement") as any other form of power and must be as strenuously resisted. In any event, such a statement was waving a red flag in front of the great majority of Americans, who were neither educated nor affluent.

Cooper went on to state the popular proposition that "the tendency of democracies is, in all things, to mediocrity, since the tastes, knowledge and principles of the majority form the tribunal of appeal." Another dubious proposition. Cooper reserved his greatest scorn for the democratic shibboleth that "one man is as good as another." He also delivered a stern little lecture on the duties that the servant owed to his master (among other things, "a respectful and decorous obedience").

As though Cooper were determined to leave no group of Americans or section of the country unoffended, he wrote, "The time must come when American slavery shall cease, and when that day shall arrive . . . the struggle that will follow, will necessarily be a war of extermination." This gloomy prophecy which, to be sure, Jefferson and many others had made, was coupled with the statement that "it is quite possible to be an excellent christian and a slaveholder," and the general argument that slaves were happy and well off in their servitude. In case there were any men and women who had escaped his strictures, Cooper condemned the American party system which, to most of his countrymen, was the ultimate achievement of democratic politics. Cooper then came to the heart of his grievance against American democracy. It placed itself in the greatest danger by "denying to men of education their proper place in society [leading it] . . . no political system can long continue in which this violence is done to the natural rights of a class so powerful. . . . All, who are in the least cultivated, know how irksome and oppressive is the ignorance and vulgarity, and the attempt to push into the ordinary associations, the principles of equality. . . ." In other words, Cooper was offended by the pushiness and familiarity of the lower classes. Rashest of all, he took on the American press, suggesting that hardly half of what they printed in their papers was true even in a rudimentary sense. It was but stating the obvious "to say that the country cannot much longer exist in safety, under the malign influence" of the press. His strictures against universal suffrage were obviously directed primarily at the Irish and Germans "who have few convictions of liberty, beyond those which arise from a love of licentiousness . . . and who, in their hearts and language, are hostile to the very people whose hospitality they enjoy."

Finally, he lectured Americans on their manners which, needless to say, were deplorable. Manners were "indispensable to civilization." They were in the keeping of men of good breeding and it was up to them to instruct the multitude. For those who failed to share in the prosperity of the country, he recommended the consolations of religion.

Following up *The American Democrat* with two satiric novels on America, Cooper might be said to have delivered to the American public a series of knockout punches. It was hard to say which caused the most pain and outrage, the lecture (*The American Democrat*) or the dramatizations. In *Homeward Bound* and *Home as Found,* the heroes are the Effinghams, an aristocratic New York family, quite obviously the Coopers. The villains are pushy fortune hunters and the nouveaux riches. Steadfast Dodge is a constant dabbler in one or another "philosophical, political, or religious expedient to fortify human wisdom, make men better and resist error and despotism." His principles are, it turns out, only skin deep. Speculation and chicanery were his strong suits. Aristabulus Bragg, "a plastic character" in Cooper's words, was what his name suggests, a braggart and a pretender, common and bad-mannered, though a cut above Dodge. "The whole country," one of the Effinghams remarks, "is in such a constant state of mutation, that I can only liken it to the game of children, in which, as one quits his corner another runs into it. . . ." Visiting New York, the Effinghams are dismayed to find that money rules. "All principles are swallowed up in the absorbing desire for gain—national honor, permanent security, the ordinary rules of society, law, the constitution . . . are forgotten or are perverted."

Conniving and unscrupulous as Bragg may be—"a compound of shrewdness, impudence, common-sense, pretension, humility, cleverness, vulgarity, kind-heartedness . . . selfishness, law-honesty, moral fraud, and mother-wit," the refined Eve Effingham calls him—he is far more appealing than the aristocratic Effinghams who go moping about, deploring the decline of the United States. At the end of *Home as Found* the Effinghams have a nostalgic moment at the long-deserted hut of Natty Bumpo, "a man who had the simplicity of a woodsman, the heroism of a savage, the faith of a Christian, and the feelings of a poet. A better man than he, after his fashion, seldom lived."

Americans were, predictably, enraged by Cooper's analysis of our character and institutions. Philip Hone dismissed him as "an arrogant, acrimonious writer . . . full of malicious spleen against his countrymen . . ." and contrasted Cooper's "dogmatical opinions" with the "unpretentious deportment of his distinguished rival, Washington Irving."

The newspapers were quick to denounce Cooper as an apostate. He, in turn, sued them for libel and the country was treated to the spectacle of the world-famous expositor of American virtue and simplicity in the person of Natty Bumpo and his noble Indian friends engaged in an unseemly brawl with the press he so disliked. It was certainly a sad way for Cooper to conclude his remarkable career. One can only guess at the depths of bitterness that sustained so prolonged a literary and legal assault on those editors and politicians he thought were destroying the republic by displaying and encouraging bad manners. Cooper's preoccupation with manners is, unhappily, a conspicuous American theme. We have found it amply displayed in our diarists. We will find it in latter Adamses as we have in the earlier, though the first John, it must be said, seems to have largely escaped it. It is hard to avoid the feeling that Cooper's nerves were weak and his judgment somewhat warped by his years abroad as a literary lion.

No prominent American writer has ever been so cruelly and definitively cut up by another writer as Cooper was by Mark Twain in his famous essay entitled "Fenimore Cooper's Literary Offenses." Calling *Deerslayer,* probably Cooper's most famous novel, "simply a literary *delirium tremens,*" Twain concludes, "A work of art? It has no invention; it has no order, system, sequence or result; it has no likeliness, no thrill, no stir, no seeming of reality; its characters are confusedly drawn, and by their acts and words they prove that they are not the sort of people the author claims that they were; its humor is pathetic; its pathos is funny; its conversations are—oh! indescribable; its love-scenes are odious; its English is a crime against the language. Counting these out, what is left is Art. I think we must all admit that."

It is hard to improve on Twain. What is left *is* Art and that, of course, is why it is so hard to say what Art is. Cooper, tedious as he was on the subject, *was* a gentleman. He was kind. He encouraged and patronized young writers and artists; generous and high-minded men like Horatio Greenough revered him and mourned his death. So we can forgive him, or indeed pity him for his snobbisms, knowing there must have been much suffering beneath them, and credit him with that relatively rare achievement of having delineated an enduring human type—indestructible, noble, nutty Natty, the prototype of all Western heroes.

Lowell said it best in his *Fable for Critics:* "He has drawn you one character, . . . that is new,/ One wildflower he's plucked that is wet with the dew/ Of this fresh Western world, and, the thing not to mince,/ He has done naught but copy it ill ever since. . . . And the women he draws from one model don't vary,/ All sappy as maples and flat as a prairie."

When Cooper died in 1851, a large memorial meeting was held in New York to honor him. Daniel Webster presided and Washington Irving and William Cullen Bryant were the main speakers. All was forgiven, and if his innumerable novels are not highly regarded today, the best of them still make enthralling reading for the young.

We must here take note of a remarkable literary anomaly. As we have already observed, when Richard Henry Dana was a Harvard undergraduate he had an emotional and physical breakdown, the most apparent manifestation of which was an inflammation of his eyes. He decided that a life of vigorous physical activity might restore him and he decided to sign on a Boston ship sailing to California to trade in hides. When he returned to Boston two years later, after enough adventures to satisfy any youth, he wrote *Two Years Before the Mast,* an immediate best-seller, a classic and profoundly American work that made him almost as famous in England, where it was promptly reprinted, as in America. It is, in fact, a marvelous and mysterious book, a kind of modern testament to a critically important aspect of the Protestant Passion, a witness of the capacity of New England Puritanism to come to grips with the practical world. It is the American odyssey, the record of a young man's travel in search of the meaning of his particular existence. There is in Dana's book no symbol, no metaphor of man's willful conquest of nature as in *Moby Dick.* It records rather the direct and specific details of life on a sailing vessel; the particular, tactile, olfactory, three-dimensional world of the ship. Detail so clearly observed becomes poetry and then epic. Dana's descriptions of the shaking out and setting of the sails is as sensual as a love lyric—all in all an astonishing performance for a sheltered young Boston Brahmin, a gentleman not yet twenty-five years old.

Two Years Before the Mast functions on two levels. It has an almost unbearable poignance because we know it as the transcendent moment of an enthralling if, finally, disappointed life. For two years Richard Henry Dana slipped away from the rigidly prescribed life of an upper-class Bostonian and in doing so he became the surrogate for every member of his class who yearned to escape and lacked the courage or resourcefulness (or desperation) to do so. He crossed over into a strange, disquieting other world of violent emotions often violently displayed, of colorful disorder and alarming openness, a riddle for those who "never walked but one line from their cradles to their graves." "We must come down from our heights," Dana declared, "and leave our straight paths for the by-ways and low places of life, if we are to learn truths by strong contrasts; and in hovels, in forecastles, and among our own outcasts in foreign lands see what has been wrought among our fellow-creatures by accident, hardship and vice."

Two Years Before the Mast is also a profoundly, inescapably original *American* act and was generally understood to be so by such discerning English readers as Charles Dickens. Dana anticipated both Whitman and Melville in his command of the "eloquence of facts." He knew how much more effective it was to describe each separate event in the management of the multitudinous sails of a ship than to go mooning on about the beauty of a ship under sail. Dana was brother to the engineer and inventor. We are apt to think of the sailing ships as pretechnological and the steamship as technological, but the sailing ship had a technology far more intricate and commanding than the steamship. Dana made the American infatuation with *how things worked* into poetry. In his introduction, he wrote, "There may be in some parts a good deal that is unintelligible to the general reader; but I have found from my own experience . . . that plain matters of fact in relation to customs and habits of life new to us, and descriptions of life under new aspects, act upon the inexperienced through the imagination, so that we are hardly aware of our want of technical knowledge." Dana saw and recorded everything, the Spanish hidalgos, the Indians, the Kanakas, the sailors from the Sandwich Islands, the American beachcombers living like "loafers" mixed in with the Californians, the butchering of cattle and the rough preparation of the hides.

Back in Boston, Dana was often a lawyer for sailors. His book, with its vivid depictions of the brutal life of sailors, led to important reforms in maritime law, and Dana himself worked to ameliorate the conditions on board maritime vessels.

Twenty-four years later he came back to California, now a state in the Union, and found himself a celebrity. San Francisco, a sleepy village when the *Alert* had dropped anchor in the bay those many years ago, was now "the great centre of a world-wide commerce," a city of over a hundred thousand inhabitants. The dock was "densely crowded with express-wagons and hand-carts to take luggage, coaches and cabs to take passengers . . . agents of the press, and a greater multitude eager for newspapers and verbal intelligence from the great Atlantic and European world." Through this crowd, Dana made his way to the

Oriental Hotel. In the morning, when he looked out of his hotel window at the great bustling scene that spread away to Contra Costa "and reflected on what I once was and saw here, and what now surrounded me, I could scarcely keep my hold on reality at all, or the genuineness of anything, and seemed to myself like one who had moved in 'worlds not realized.'" Soon he met two Harvard classmates and then another "Harvard man, a fine scholar and a wit, and full of cleverness and good humour. . . ." He retraced his footsteps as though in a trance. At the Presidio he met a young Army engineer, Custis Lee, a recent graduate of West Point at the head of his class, "a son of Colonel Robert E. Lee, who distinguished himself in the Mexican War." Down the California coast to Monterey and Santa Barbara, the sentimental journey continued. "How softening is the effect of time!" Dana wrote. "It touches us through the affections. I almost feel as if I were lamenting the passing away of something loved and dear—the boats, the Kanakas, the hides, my old shipmates!" "Death, change, and distance" altered everything in America and gave memory a special poignance. At San Diego, "the present, all about me, was unreal, unnatural, repellent." A vast sadness possessed him, "I alone was left of all, and how strangely was I here! What changes to me! Where were they all? What should I care for them—poor Kanakas and sailors, the refuse of civilization, the outlaws and beachcombers of the Pacific? Time and death seemed to transfigure them." And so, "borne down by depression," the middle-aged Brahmin, disappointed lawyer and politician, antislavery hero in his own right, stood poised on the Western brink of the continent, wondering what it all meant, much as the nation itself stood poised on quite another brink—the terrible devastation of war. It is a moment as moving and mysterious as the country's life. Boston and California held in the mind, stretching the mind to breaking. Dana went on dutifully to Santa Clara, to "the rich Almaden quicksilver mines," to Stockton, to the Tuolumne, the Stanislaus, the Merced, the "Big Trees," and "then to the wonderful Yosemite Valley . . . a stupendous miracle of nature." So, finally, he completed his "acts of pious remembrance" and continued on around the world, trying to restore his health or to escape Boston and America for that transcendent aqueous world of freedom and adventure. In America reality was uncommonly hard to hold to. To men like Dana it seemed it could be held only in memory.

50

People's Poetry

It is not surprising that "a people of the Word," addicted to orations, should find poetry an especially congenial form of expression. Dickens was reputed to have written an anonymous article in the *Foreign Quarterly* on American poets, "over which," in George Templeton Strong's words, "all the papers are going into severe paroxysms of patriotic wrath. Don't see why they can't keep cool," Strong added. "That we have no national school of poetry is very true, but it's our misfortune and not a fault, for we've no materials to make one out of. We've neither a legendary past nor a poetic present. Large mountains, extensive prairies, tall cataracts, long rivers, millions of dirty acres of every cosmological character don't 'constitute a state' for purposes of poetry; but 'men, high-minded men' and their memories. . . ." Strong thought it likely that in time "we shall have our poets, and that we have as fair a chance of producing the Dante or Milton or Shakespeare as any other nation, in the course of the coming five centuries, which is about a reasonable period to assign for the advent of the next of that stamp."

Strong conceded too much; "a national school of poetry" was clearly in the making. Americans were indefatigable readers *and* writers of poetry. It was only required that poems, like the Psalms, be morally improving or (a broader and looser category), like the Psalms and the Songs of Solomon, praise the Lord and/or his creation.

The dean of American poets was William Cullen Bryant, one of the most engaging men of the century. Inspired by Wordsworth, he wrote a series of nature poems that had a strong appeal to American readers and a strong influence on other poets. Bryant told his friend Richard Henry Dana (who, the reader will recall, was sometimes upset by Bryant's middle-class manners) that when he read Wordsworth "a thousand springs seemed to gush up at once in his heart, and the face of nature of a sudden to change into a strange freshness and life." It is as good a moment as we are likely to find to fix as the birth of American nature poetry and it is significant that Bryant says "the face of nature" *changed* "into a strange freshness and life."

Like most of his countrymen, Bryant, it may be assumed, saw nature, prior to the Wordsworthian revelation, as rather dark and menacing, something to be subdued and overcome, rather than something to be praised and celebrated. Starting life as a lawyer, Bryant in 1814, at the age of twenty, wrote a poem called "The Yellow Violet," which, by combining praise of nature in the violet with a moral principle, prefigured the next half-century of American poetry. Overshadowed by more striking flowers, the humble violet—"slight thy form, and low thy seat" with "gentle eye"—reminded the passerby that

> . . . they, who climb to wealth, forget
> The friends in darker fortunes tried.
> I copied them but I regret
> That I should ape the ways of pride.

The "Yellow Violet" was followed a year later by what became, along with "Thanatopsis," one of his most admired poems, "To a Waterfowl":

> Whither, midst falling dew,
> While glow the heavens with the last steps of day,
> Far, through their rosy depths, dost thou pursue
> Thy solitary way?

After reflecting on the "Power" that guides the bird, Bryant ends:

He who, from zone to zone,
Guides through the boundless sky thy certain flight,
In the long way that I must tread alone
Will lead my steps aright.

It was the perfect poem for the age. The pious Christian could read it secure in the conviction that the conveniently capitalized "He" was the Almighty of the Scriptures; the lover of nature, the incipient transcendentalist (Emerson had not yet called the new faith into being) could read it, reassured by "the Power" which might be Nature or any mildly anthropomorphic divinity.

Young men are much given to brooding about death in the period from, say, fifteen to twenty, and somewhere in this period Bryant began the most famous poem of the century about death— "Thanatopsis." The first words established the mood of the entire poem: "To him who speaks/ A various language . . ." "When thoughts of the last bitter hour come like a blight/ Over thy spirit," he abjured his reader, he or she need only "go forth under the open sky and list to Nature's teachings" (rather than to the Bible). The story that Nature told was that of losing "each human trace, surrendering up/ Thine individual being . . . To mix forever with the elements,/ To be a brother to the insensible rock. . . ." Nature is now capitalized as an upper-case divinity.

In death one joined the great legion of departed souls, kings and emperors and "the speechless babe, and the gray-headed man," all merged with Nature. The important thing was to:

So live that when thy summons comes to join
The innumerable caravan which moves
To that mysterious realm where each shall take
His chamber in the silent halls of death,
Thou go not, like the quarry-slave at night,
Scourged to his dungeon, but, sustained and soothed
By an unfaltering trust, approach thy grave
Like one who wraps the drapery of his couch
About him and lies down to pleasant dreams.

It is a fascinating exercise to reflect upon the poem as a measure of the movement from the Classical-Christian Consciousness to the Secular-Democratic. Certainly the mood is Greek, as is the word for Death. It is also patently agnostic, as indignant ministers were quick to point out. One does not learn the vital lessons of life from the Word of

God as recorded in Scripture but from Nature herself, from the stars and the trees. There is no promise of an immortal soul, of life beyond the grave, but only of peaceful dissolution and absorption back into the Nature from which one comes. "An unfaltering trust" is required, but it is not clear in "what" or "whom," so that the mood is one of stoical resignation. "Thanatopsis" is a very modern poem and gives point to the notion that poets perceive the spirit of a new age long before the theologians and philosophers. Yet it is a very American poem in the poet's injunction to "So live . . ." The implication is that one can hope to face death with equanimity only if he/she has lived a moral life. Bryant's poem engaged the issue of death which, after all, stands at the heart of Christianity (and other religions as well, of course) and threw down a bold challenge: our reality is to be found in Nature, of which we are a part and from whose limitations we cannot hope to escape.

In a sense all the poems and lectures of Emerson, all the sermons of George Ripley and Theodore Parker, were a kind of extended footnote to "Thanatopsis." Bryant was five years younger than Cooper. Like Cooper, he was a supporter and patron of the painter Thomas Cole (Cole, the reader will recall, derived much of the inspiration for his landscapes from Cooper's novels). Asher Durand's most famous painting is of the two famous nature lovers talking on a rock above a waterfall, both dressed, incidentally, as though they were strolling down Broadway. Infatuation with nature did not carry its enthusiasts so far as to permit them to dress "naturally."

A Democratic newspaper editor, a dedicated reformer (he horse-whipped an anti-Jackson editor on Broadway for what he considered libelous remarks), an ally of Weld and the Grimké sisters, a leader in the fight against capital punishment, Bryant still found time to turn out a substantial number of poems, most of them dealing with the themes of Nature, death, and mutability. Often ailing, he was to live until 1878, dying in his eighty-fourth year, an exemplary poet-politician, still laboring in good causes and writing good if not great verses. Edgar Allan Poe, the best critic of the age, wrote in 1846 that Bryant's position was "*comparatively* well settled" though "for some time past there has been a growing tendency to underestimate him. . . . It will never do to claim for Bryant a genius of the highest order . . ." but it was by no means enough to dismiss him as merely talented. Poe continued, "Mr. Bryant has genius, and that of a marked character, but it has been overlooked by modern schools" because it was not in the latest fashion. However that may be, Bryant is as important to us for what he represented as for what he achieved.

Thirteen years younger than Bryant, John Greenleaf Whittier was born in New Hampshire, taught school briefly and then, catching the attention of William Lloyd Garrison, was encouraged by him to take up a career as a newspaper editor. Of all the literary figures of the time, Whittier was the one most fully identified with the cause of antislavery. A book of his antislavery poems entitled *Voices of Freedom* was published in 1846, and he was a frequent speaker and writer in the cause. A wit and raconteur, he was notably pious. He praised nature in the lower case; his poems were full of uplifting sentiments; Burns was his idol. He wrote some memorable lines: "The age is dull and mean. Men creep,/ Not walk; with blood too pale and tame/ To pay the debt they owe to shame;/ Buy cheap, sell dear; eat, drink and sleep/ Down-pillowed, deaf to moaning want;/ Pay tithes for soul-insurance; keep Six days to Mammon, one to Cant"; a fine ballad ("Skipper Ireson's Ride": "Poor Floyd Ireson, for his hard heart,/ Tarred and feathered and carried in a cart/ By the women of Marblehead"); and a great poem, "Snowbound," which captured definitively the onset of a New England storm—"The sun that brief December day/ Rose cheerless over hills of gray,/ And, darkly circled, gave at noon/ A sadder light than waning moon./ Slow tracing down the thickening sky/ Its mute and ominous prophecy,/ A portent seeming less than threat,/ It sank from sight before it set."

One of the most interesting aspects of Whittier was his celebration of work as the ordinary man's path to redemption (accompanied, of course, by large portions of Christian piety). His *Songs of Labor* were designed to reveal "the unsung beauty of life's common things." The old curse on work was gone now that free men worked for themselves:

> The doom which to the guilty pair
>   Without the walls of Eden came,
> Transforming sinless ease to care
>   And rugged toil, no more shall bear
> The burden of old crime, or mark of primal shame.
>
> A blessing now, a curse no more:
>   Since He, whose name we breathe with awe,
> The coarse mechanic vesture wore,
>   A poor man, toiling with the poor,
> In labor, as in prayer, fulfilling the same law.

Carl Schurz described Whittier as "tall and slim, with his fine, placid face, all goodness and unpretending simplicity . . . I left him feeling as if the mere meeting with him had been a blessing—a breath of air from a world of purity and beneficence."

Henry Wadsworth Longfellow was the greatest popular poet of the century. Born the same year as Whittier, grandson of Peleg Wadsworth, a Revolutionary general, young Longfellow's social class and family connections opened all doors to him. He was notably precocious, writing passable verse at the age of thirteen. On graduating from Bowdoin College in Maine, he was offered a professorship if he would extend his Bowdoin education with travel abroad. After three years of pleasant travel in Germany, Spain, Italy, and France, he settled down to an agreeable career as a small-town college professor, writing poems and essays and teaching literature. The Bowdoin stint was followed by an appointment to Harvard, and in the congenial atmosphere of Cambridge he was soon the center of a literary circle. Like Dana and Fisher and George Templeton Strong, Longfellow suffered from "nervous sensibility," periods of immobilizing depression, but he was a born storyteller and versifier and he soon outstripped his contemporaries as *the* poet of America. He was a kind of poetic counterpart to Irving—romantic, charmed with tales of far-away and long-ago, sentimental, genteel, generous.

Longfellow passed readily and gracefully from a handsome, rather dandified young man to "the good gray poet." When Carl Schurz met him, Longfellow was in his mid-forties, but he had already adopted much the manner of a wise old man. Schurz visited him "in the cosy intimacy of his old colonial house in Cambridge," the Craigie House, which had been one of Washington's numerous headquarters, and Longfellow brought out a bottle of Rhine wine in honor of his German friend and "a couple of long German student pipes, which," Schurz wrote, "I fear he did not enjoy smoking very much, although he pretended to enjoy it, no doubt, he thought I did." They talked of German poets and poetry and Schurz considered him "one of the most beautiful men I have ever known" who "grew more beautiful every year of his advancing old age—with his flowing white hair and beard and his grand face" like "a fatherly Zeus holding a benignant hand over the world and mankind. . . . His very being seemed to be enveloped in an atmosphere of peace and noble sympathy." He was the perfect democratic poet in his unpretentious fatherly manner and in his poetry. His poems were all perfectly understandable. Many of

them were simply stories in verse. And all were morally improving—
"A Psalm of Life" was a perfect expression of his positive thinking. It
ended:

> Let us then be up and doing,
>   With a heart for any fate;
> Still achieving, still pursuing,
>   Learn to labor and to wait.

The poem had about it an air of ripe wisdom and the patience that
comes with age, but Longfellow was only thirty-one when he wrote it.
His verses invariably had a fine beat to them and were readily
committed to memory by generations of school children. How many
juveniles declaimed "The Wreck of the Hesperus"?

> Such was the wreck of the Hesperus,
>   In the midnight and the snow!
> Christ save us all from a death like this,
>   On the reef of Norman's Woe!

The poems poured out year after year: "The Village Blacksmith"
(children delighted to alter "The muscles of his mighty arms/ as strong
as iron bands" to "strong as rubber bands"), "The Skeleton in Armor"
("SPEAK! SPEAK! thou fearful guest!/ Who with thy hollow breast/
Still in rude armor drest,/ Comest to daunt me!"), "Endymion,"
"Excelsior" ("The shades of night were falling fast,/ As through an
Alpine village passed/ A youth who bore 'mid snow and ice/ A banner
with the strange device,/ Excelsior!"), "The Day Is Done" ("And the
night shall be filled with music,/ And the cares that infest the day,/
Shall fold their tents like the Arabs,/ And as silently steal away"). And,
finally, *The Song of Hiawatha,* unquestionably one of the most popular
literary accomplishments of the century—"By the shores of Gitche
Gumee,/ By the shining Big-Sea-Water,/ Stood the wigwam of Nokomis,/ Daughter of the Moon, Nokomis"—the sentimental story of
Nokomis and her daughter, Wenonah, who, seduced by "the West-
Wind, false and faithless," bore "a son of love and sorrow," Hiawatha.
Hiawatha was more like a New England reformer who "prayed
and . . . fasted . . . toiled, and suffered,/ That the tribes of men might
prosper,/ That he might advance his people!" The poem was directed
to those "who love a nation's legends/ Love the ballads of a people . . .

Ye whose hearts are fresh and simple,/ Who have faith in God and Nature,/ Who believe, that in all ages/ Every human heart is human,/ That in even savage bosoms/ There are longings, yearnings, strivings/ For the good they comprehend not. . . ."

In *Hiawatha*, God and Nature shared top billing and "improvement"—"yearnings, strivings"—was, apparently, as much a part of the Indian psyche as of the white. The death of Hiawatha, paddling "Westward! westward!" in his canoe, leaving behind him his devoted disciples and the promise to return from "the Land of the Hereafter" when many moons have passed away—"Ere I come again to see you"—plays on the Christian theme of a Savior and redeemer, "one who comes again." Longfellow's anthropology is sappy and his verse often insipid (Whitman described *Hiawatha* as a "pleasing, ripply poem") but in its elegiac mood, with its incantatory repetitions and tone of persuasive sadness, the poet *does* capture something of the tragic destiny of the American aborigine. I suspect that there are more than a few aging Americans to whom the haunting lines of *Hiawatha* will bring nostalgic tears. *The Courtship of Miles Standish* was almost as popular as *Hiawatha*. Many American schoolchildren's image of Indians was formed from reading *Hiawatha* and their vision of New England from *The Courtship of Miles Standish*.

When Rufus Griswold put out an anthology entitled *The Poets and Poetry of America* in 1842, it sold over three hundred thousand copies at the substantial price of three dollars per volume, and *Hiawatha*, published in 1855, sold fifty thousand copies in five months at a dollar a copy.

Henry Wadsworth Longfellow no longer gets high marks from the critics if, indeed, he ever did. Edgar Allan Poe accused him of plagiarism, which stirred up a storm in critical circles, and a defender of Longfellow pointed out a startling similarity between certain lines of Coleridge's "Ancient Mariner" and Poe's "The Raven." But it is interesting to note that Poe's principal charge against Longfellow is that he was too bent on making a moral point. "His didactics are all *out of place*. He has written brilliant poems by accident; that is to say, when permitting his genius to get the better of his conventional habit of thinking. . . . We do not mean to say that a didactic moral may not be well made the *under-current* of a poetical thesis, but that it can never be put so obtrusively forth as in the majority of his compositions."

By Poe's standard some of Longfellow's best poems are his late sonnets to Chaucer, Shakespeare, Milton, and Keats. In any event we are not done with him; he lived almost three-quarters of the century and he fixed the popular notion of poetry for millions of Americans. Fortunately, we do not have to adjudicate the delicate question of his stature as a pure poet. He was, with Emerson, the great literary phenomenon of the age, the superstar of poetry, and the popularity of his work reminds us of how important poetry was in feeding the American imagination. For better or worse and, on the whole I suspect for the better, for generations of Americans the word "poet" suggested the response "Longfellow."

But he was, after all, only the first among his peers in what we might call the "golden age of popular poetry." Preceded by Bryant and Whittier, he was followed or accompanied by James Russell Lowell and Oliver Wendell Holmes, whose poetry was often disconcertingly similar—one is almost tempted to say interchangeable. Bryant, Jacksonian newspaper editor as poet; Whittier, abolitionist as poet; Longfellow, professor as poet; Lowell, gentleman as poet; Holmes, doctor as poet. So the poets were all poets *plus* something.

Lowell was twelve years Longfellow's junior. A scion of the wealthy and socially prominent Lowell family, he graduated from Harvard College and from the Law School in 1840. With the confidence and generosity of his class at its best, Lowell was a witty and trenchant commentator on the political and cultural scene. He created a shrewd semiliterate New Englander countryman named Hosea Biglow whose carefully rendered dialect makes unrewarding reading in this age, but he also composed a good-natured critique of his fellow writers and poets, certain couplets of which have attached themselves like burrs to their subjects, i.e.: "There comes Poe, with his raven, like Barnaby Rudge,/ Three fifths of him genius and two fifths sheer fudge"; or Emerson—"A Greek head on right Yankee shoulders."

Bryant he considered talented, but much too "cool"—"As a smooth silent iceberg, that never is ignified . . . (There's no doubt that he stands in supreme iceolation)."

It was clear that Lowell was more drawn to Hawthorne than to Emerson. Hawthorne's genius was "so shrinking and rare/ That you hardly at first see the strength that is there:/ A frame so robust, with a nature so sweet,/ So earnest, so graceful, so lithe and so fleet,/ Is worth a descent from Olympus to meet. . . ." In Hawthorne, Nature, lacking the common clay "For making so full-sized a man as she wanted,/ . . .

to fill out her model, a little she spared/ From some finer-grained stuff for a woman prepared,/ And she could not have hit a more excellent plan/ For making him fully and perfectly man."

Some splendid lines from his later poetry made one wish Lowell had expended less of his poetic energy on the tiresome Biglow (obviously he did not tire his contemporaries) and more on lyrics and odes to his friends, such as the poem to Louis Agassiz which starts so boldly—"The electric nerve, whose instantaneous thrill/ Makes next-door gossips of the antipodes"—and his splendid commemorative "Ode" at the first Harvard commencement after the Civil War.

By 1868, when the Reverend David Macrae visited Lowell in Boston, the poet and essayist was teaching at Harvard. Macrae accompanied him to one of his classes "where 100 to 150 students were assembled, most of them keen, dark-eyed youths." Lowell, devoid of the customary academic gown, and dressed instead in "plain shooting-coat and light speckled necktie; long curling brown hair, parted in the middle; corner of a white handkerchief sticking out of his breast-pocket," leaned casually with his elbows on the lectern, "one leg bent back and swaying itself easily." He read his lecture in a "pleasant, quiet, gentlemanly way" and enlivened it "with continual sallies of wit." The troubadours and the old metrical romances were the subject of his lecture and he described the life of a wandering knight as "delightful. No bills to pay. Hero never brought to a stand-still for want of cash."

A delightful conversationalist and a master of friendship, Lowell became in time the leader, or one might say conductor, of the brilliant literary circle that included Emerson, Charles Eliot Norton, Agassiz, Longfellow, Charles Sumner, and Holmes. Holmes was surely one of the most talented and engaging of the group. Son of the historian-minister, Abiel Holmes, young Oliver Wendell, two years Longfellow's junior, graduated from Harvard and studied medicine in Paris and at Harvard, at which latter institution he became Parkman Professor, lecturing on anatomy and writing an important paper on puerperal fever. Like Lowell, who prepared for the law, Holmes had a poetical bent. When the frigate *Constitution* was discovered to be rotting away at a wharf, Holmes, then only twenty-one, wrote one of the memorable poems of the century, "Old Ironsides"—needless to say, an immediate hit that helped to save the historic ship from destruction. He had an impish sense of humor to go with his patriotic zeal and the year of "Old Ironsides" he wrote his famous poem recounting how he had written such a funny verse that his servant had suffered fits from laughing excessively:

> Ten days and nights, with sleepless eye,
> I watched that wretched man,
> And since, I never dared to write
> As funny as I can.

It was certainly quite an achievement for a lad of twenty-one to write two poems, so diverse, that would immediately enter the canon of American verse, but Holmes proved up to it. He was jolly, indefatigable and unpretentious, pouring out occasional verses for every occasion, talking like a marvel, teasing his fellow doctors with "The Stethoscope Song," about a stethoscope filled with flies that led a young doctor to false diagnoses. But "The doctors being very sore,/ A stethoscope they did devise/ That had a rammer to clear the bore,/ With a knob at the end to kill the flies."

Like a number of his fellow poets, Holmes took Webster to task for his acceptance of the Fugitive Slave Law in the Compromise of 1850:

> Illustrious Dupe! Have those majestic eyes
> Lost their proud fire for such a vulgar prize?
> Art thou the last of all mankind to know
> That party-fights are won by aiming low?
> Thou, stamped by Nature with her royal sign
> That party hirelings hate a look like thine?
> Shake from thy sense the wild delusive dream!
> Without the purple art thou not supreme?

In his gentle mocking of New England and of his countrymen, Holmes displayed the most "modern" consciousness of his circle. His poem "The Deacon's Masterpiece, or The Wonderful 'One-Hoss Shay' " was an engaging parable of the collapse of Calvinist orthodoxy. Calvinism was the one-hoss shay, "Drawn by a rat-tailed, ewe-necked bay, which simply disintegrated on the 1st of November, 'Fifty-five!' " "You see, of course, if you're not a dunce,/ How it went to pieces all at once,—/ All at once, and nothing first,—/ Just as bubbles do when they burst,/ End of the wonderful one-hoss shay,/ Logic is logic. That's all I say."

Perhaps his most famous poem was "The Chambered Nautilus," which made an analogy between the expanding chambers of the shell and constant spiritual growth of the individual:

Year after year beheld the silent toil
That spread his lustrous coil;
Still, as the spiral grew,
He left the past year's dwelling for the new . . .
Build thee more stately mansions, O my soul,
As the swift seasons roll!
Leave thy low-vaulted past!
Let each new temple, nobler than the last,
Shut thee from heaven with a dome more vast,
Till thou at length art free,
Leaving thine outgrown shell by life's unresting sea!

Only "Thanatopsis" rivaled "The Chambered Nautilus" as the quintessential expression of the mid-nineteenth-century middle-class consciousness: the exultation of Nature (with a large or a small N), the theme of moral growth—"more stately mansions," the gentle air of resignation at the end of life.

If Lowell was the ruler of the Saturday Club and Longfellow its revered sage, Holmes was its merry wit. Carl Schurz wrote of him, "His talk was so animated, bubbling and sparkling, and at the same time there was so kindly and genial a flow of wit and wisdom, that I sat there in a state of amazed delight," and asked a companion, "Who is that wonderful man?"

So there they are, not all quite cut out of the same cloth—Bryant and Whittier were, for instance, outside the magic Cambridge circle— but all "popular poets," teaching, preaching, moralizing, entertaining, rhapsodizing about Nature, cautioning about death, growing, with each passing year, somehow further removed from the frantic disorder of American life, creating their own small order, a bland and blameless miniature republic of letters. One could read all their poetry through and, aside from the issue of slavery, get very little notion of the storm and stress of American society.

It is easy to be patronizing toward that secure, intact little world of unabashed sentimentality that revolved around Harvard and friendship, a company whose members seemed mellow by their thirties, but they were, I suspect, at least as important as McGuffey's ubiquitous *Readers* in both shaping and reflecting the mind and temper of their countrymen. Moreover, they constituted a unique phenomenon; they created what has never been before or since, a "people's poetry." Their lives were by no means as sunny as their perpetually optimistic poems suggest. They experienced their own dark terrors, their failures of nerve and health, deaths of beloved wives and children, anguish over the state of the republic. One leaves them reluctantly. The feeling of nostalgia that their poetry conveys is partly in the tone of the poems themselves, partly in the America they evoke which, if it never existed, we at least once believed in and can believe in no longer. There were, as we have seen, numerous strategies for counteracting the disintegrative effects of American life—utopian communities, Masons' and Odd Fellows' lodges, new religious sects. Of them all, the Saturday Club was one of the most humane, and certainly the most genteel.

51

Breaking Out

We have already paid considerable attention to Ralph Waldo Emerson as the founder of the "Church" of Transcendentalism; now we must consider him again as America's foremost man of letters, a figure who dominated the literary scene even more conclusively than his fellow New Englander Daniel Webster dominated the political. In a sense everything in the literary line starts with Emerson. He was the great liberator. As his commencement address heralded the virtual eclipse of Unitarianism as a potent intellectual and religious movement, it laid the foundations for the new alliance between literature and morality. It elevated the poet and, perhaps above all, the lecturer, to a new priesthood. It called for a fresh and vigorous religion of literature. Prayers were metamorphosed into poems and sermons into lectures. Young men and women as diverse as Sidney George Fisher, Walter Whitman, and Margaret Fuller were thrilled by his essays and began to see the world in a startling new way. For many who read him, it was almost as though they had taken a mind-expanding drug, eaten magic mushrooms or smoked the cannabis indica. Colors seemed more vivid, the landscape revealed new beauties, birds sang more sweetly. Margaret Fuller wrote that Emerson's influence "has been more beneficial to me than that of any American, and from him I first learned what is meant by the inward life. Many springs have since fed the stream of living water, but he first opened the fountain." Lowell said truly his "prose is grand verse," for Emerson's sentences were as finely cadenced as a line of verse. It might be said that he discovered, or rediscovered, in a time of tangled thickets of verbiage, the power of the simple declarative sentence, a sentence in which the weight and quality of each word were as carefully considered as a gem on a jeweler's scale.

We can get an inkling of what Emerson meant for a generation of young men, and for young women as well, from Sidney George Fisher. In March, 1844, he noted in his diary that he had bought Emerson's essays a few days earlier and read nearly all of them. "Full of thought & originality & profound views of life & human relations," he wrote. "Emerson is the head of what are called the transcendentalists, in New England. The object of his philosophy is to investigate spiritual laws & phenomena. He is often obscure & to me unintelligible. . . . All profound thinkers are unintelligible to the multitude, the range of their thought is beyond the common intellect. . . . If there is some want of perspicuity, there is also much clearness both in Carlyle & Emerson, and their philosophy if profound is also eminently practical, as indeed truth always is and must be. They are great teachers, & I owe them thanks . . . for much light shed on my path & for many lessons of wisdom."

A few years later he wrote that he had read all that Emerson had written "a hundred times . . . and always with new pleasure. One never tires of truth and beauty, of fine thoughts, elevated sentiments and a simple, pure, sinewy and graceful style. These are the charms of the great masters in art, of Plato, Shakespeare and the Bible. It seems to me that everything I ever thought is in Emerson's writings and a thousand things besides that I never thought, but which he has planted in my mind as germs of thought. He seems to have melted all knowledge in the crucible of his intellect and given to us the essence. Physical science, history, mathematics, philosophy are in his hands instruments and illustrations, which he uses with the ease and grace of a master. He is a philosopher and poet of a high order and is the most original & profound thinker now living."

Emerson was the sage of Concord, and Nathaniel Hawthorne, who lived at the other end of town for a time, noted that Concord was filled with "a variety of queer, strangely-dressed, oddly-behaved mortals, most of whom took upon themselves to be important agents of the world's destiny. . . ." They were attracted by Emerson, "a great original thinker. . . . People that had lighted on a new thought or a thought they fancied was new, came to Emerson, as the finder of a glittering gem hastens to a lapidary, to ascertain its quality and value." For his part, Hawthorne became, in his son's words, "a sort of Mecca of Pilgrims with Christian's burden on their backs. Secret criminals of all kinds came to him for counsel and relief."

The two men were on friendly terms despite the radical differences in their respective views of life and art. Emerson wrote: "Nathaniel Hawthorne's reputation as a writer is a very pleasing fact, because his writing is not good for anything, and this is a tribute to the man."

Emerson made the keeping of a journal an art form. Year after year he recorded his feelings and commented on his times and his contemporaries in often unforgettable aphorisms. Of the sailor-preacher, Edward Taylor: "what splendor! what sweetness! what richness! what depth! what cheer! How he conciliates, how he humanizes. . . . Beautiful philanthropist! Godly poet! The Shakespeare of the sailor and the poor." On John Quincy Adams: "He is no literary gentleman, but a bruiser. . . ." On Alcott: "He is the best natured man I ever met. The rats and mice make their nests in him." On critics: "The borer on our peach trees bores that she may deposit an egg; but the borer into theories and institutions and books bores that he may bore." On railroad trains: "The Americans take to the contrivance as if it were the cradle in which they were born." On Boston religion: "Christianity is a compound of force, or the best Diagonal line that can be drawn between Jesus Christ and Abbott Lawrence." After the death of his little son, Waldo, he wrote, "Sorrow makes us all children again,—destroys all differences of intellect, the wisest know nothing." He knew himself as well as we can know him. "I have so little vital force," he wrote in his thirty-ninth year, "that I could not stand the dissipation of a flowing and friendly life; I should die of consumption in three months."

It may have been, in the last analysis, as a lecturer that Emerson's influence was most widely felt. Bronson Alcott said, "There was no lecture till Emerson made it . . . and a public to listen to the master. . . . That were a victory worth a life, since the lecture is an American invention, serving the country with impulse and thought of an ideal cast." In that new church, the lecture hall, Emerson wrote "everything is admissible, philosophy, ethics, divinity, criticism, poetry, humor, fun, mimicry, anecdotes, jokes, ventriloquism, all the breadth and versatility of the most liberal conversation; highest, lowest, personal, local topics, all are permitted, and all may be combined in one speech. . . . Here is a pulpit that makes all other pulpits tame and ineffectual—with their cold, mechanical preparation . . . —fine things, pretty things, wise things, but no arrows, no axes, no nectar, no growling, no transpiercing, no loving, no enchantment. . . . Here he may hope for ecstacy and eloquence. . . . I look upon the Lecture-room as the true church of to-day, and as the home of richer eloquence than Faneuil Hall or the Capitol ever knew." Emerson's sentence is worth lingering over. As Alcott said, the lecture is an American invention. Perhaps it is the ultimate American invention, more important than the telegraph or the airplane. There is no reason, after all, not to believe that inventors of other countries would not, in good time, have invented both. But the lecture, the secularized sermon, became the channel of redemption for vast numbers of Americans. The fact that Emerson should give credit to the lecture hall as possessing "richer eloquence" than the chambers of Congress, which had echoed with the eloquence of Fisher Ames, Alexander Hamilton, Daniel Webster, and John Quincy Adams, not to mention Faneuil Hall, with its sacred memories of James Otis, Samuel Adams, Wendell Phillips, Frederick Douglass, and dozens of others, gives us, I think, a clue to his attitude toward politics, at least as they *seemed* to reflect the real world. It could be argued that the greatest eloquence is, after all, that which speaks to some dramatic moment when the affairs of men come to a desperate crisis. It speaks to and out of historical urgencies that give words a unique potency. The lecture hall is the antithesis of such moments of crisis. Everyone settles down comfortably to be entertained and instructed or, particularly in the United States, to hear the revealed truth. Dickens's was not a random shot when he professed to despair over a people whose perpetual form of celebration was a lecture. In the lecture hall we play with reality. That indeed is the privilege of the lecturer—to allow us to investigate various truths. The lecturer does not, typically, expect us to rush out and man the barricades. The lecturer speaks to quite a different side of our nature. That Emerson gave preeminence to the lecture hall over the political forum (he compared Edward Everett with Pericles) is evidence that he had a precarious grasp on the real world.

David Macrae left us a vivid picture of Emerson the lecturer. "Emerson has the queerest New England face," Macrae wrote, "with thin features, prominent hatchet nose, and a smile of childlike sweetness and simplicity. . . . Eyes, too, full of sparkling geniality, and yet in a moment turning cold, clear, and searching like the eyes of a god." Mounting the platform, he stood at the lectern waiting for the conversation in the audience to die out, "head inclined, and his calm, deep, thoughtful eyes passing dreamily over the sea of faces, till there was perfect silence." Then he began reading from an odd collection of miscellaneous bits of paper of various shapes and sizes. "The first lesson of Nature is perpetual ascension." Physicists had declared that "a pot of earth might remain a hundred years the same, but put a seed in and all was changed. . . . 'Now, *put a man into the world*,' he cried out with sudden energy, '*and see how soon the great pot will be changed!* Man,' he continued in a more conversational tone, 'brings in the element of Reason. There goes reason to the boiling of an egg, to the fighting of battles, to the making of an alphabet.'"

"Emerson," Macrae wrote, "went on thus for an hour and a half—standing at the desk, his thin piquant face full of kindly light, and that 'slow wise smile' continually stealing over it. . . . Once or twice, when he seemed anxious to impress his thought upon the audience, the large hand that hung at his side clenched itself and began to work convulsively, jerking downwards as if stabbing some one at his knee; then suddenly, just as his thought exploded, the long arm was flung out with the finger clenched, and the great thumb sticking up like the blade of a broken sword."

If Emerson invented the lecture, the avidity with which his countrymen fastened on that form of human communication certainly gives us an essential clue to the American psyche. Perhaps it is no more than a curious American faith in words, especially words drained of any profound emotional content. Lectures then appear as sermons that offer intimations of salvation without requiring the assumption of burdensome responsibilities.

By retrieving from a diminished faith the essentially moral structure of the universe, Emerson both performed an important service for his age and hastened the secularization of America. We must also credit (or charge) Emerson with the apotheosis of the "creative personality" or "genius" whose highest expression was the poet-lecturer. The lecture was thus the essence—the lecture, which of all expressive forms, is the blandest, the most academic, the least dramatic, the most reasonable. The Greeks had tragic drama, the Italians a variety of expressive plastic and verbal forms; the Americans had the lecture, which was long on information and short on "soul."

To Emerson the poet was the hero-priest, but he was always curiously shy about his own poetry. It took some persistent urging from James Freeman Clarke to prevail on Emerson to let Clarke print some of his poems in the *Western Literary Messenger*. In an age of poetry he wrote some of the best. "Each and All" contained the famous lines: "All are needed by each one!/ Nothing is good or fair alone." "The Snow-Storm," perhaps the best known of all of Emerson's poems, contains his artistic creed:

> Come see the north wind's masonry
> Out of an unseen quarry everymore
> Furnished with tile, the fierce artificer
> Curves his white bastions . . .
> Speeding, the myriad-handed, his wild work
> So fanciful, so savage, nought cares he
> For number or proportion . . .
> And when his hours are numbered, and the world
> Is all his own, retiring, as he were not,
> Leaves, when the snow appears, astonished Art
> To mimic in slow structures, stone by stone,
> Built in an age, the mad wind's night-work,
> The frolic architecture of the snow.

"The Snow-Storm" is one of that relatively small number of poems that have altered our perception of the natural world. "The architecture of the snow" is an image that the reader can never escape.

Journal keeper, artificer, lecturer, aphorist, the liberator of others who could not truly liberate himself, Emerson calls to mind Alfred North Whitehead's definition, "style is the ultimate morality of mind." It is a phrase not particularly flattering in its application to Emerson. Something was deficient. Our greatest user of words (Thoreau was his only rival), he could lay out sentences so deceptively lucid as to be irresistible, sentences that sometimes dissolved in cloudy nonsense if seriously reflected upon. But still we cannot escape them. Or him. The deficiency was in the felt absence of suffering, of the profoundest engagement of life, a curious evasiveness. One would not dare to say that Emerson was incapable of suffering. Suffer surely he did but he *reserved* his suffering in a curiously New England way; he would not let it *enter his work*. It emerged only rarely, the merest slip of tongue or pen. Emerson's journals were the final fruit of that running spiritual audit, that daily assessment of one's state of grace or gracelessness that was almost a New England character trait, the private record of the New England soul turned into art.

Emerson became the high priest of the Secular-Democratic Consciousness, the ex-Unitarian shaman of mid-nineteenth-century refugees from the various forms of Calvinism that suddenly seemed too harsh to endure and thus, like the famous one-horse shay, collapsed one day.

It is hard not to see transcendentalism and the cult of Nature as avenues of escape from the often devastating realities of American life. But escape certainly has its function; none of us could bear to face reality uninterruptedly, and Emerson is a marvelous escape artist, a master illusionist. Moreover on one point he was surely right—the basis of all art is profoundly moral; literature is, in Carlyle's words, "but a branch of Religion and always participates in its character." In addition, Emerson was the great liberator of the imagination for his age; his words came with thrilling power to thousands of young men and women who felt cramped and thwarted by ancient dogmas and turned to him as to a stream of living water. Thus, since history is a dialectical process, it is pointless to reproach Emerson for his cloudy etherealness and reluctance to pay attention to the darker side of life. His task was clearly to establish the thesis to which a Hawthorne or Melville would propose the antithesis.

David Henry Thoreau was born in Concord in 1817, the son of a successful pencil manufacturer. Thoreau attended Harvard, where he wrote an impassioned essay on the "blind and unmanly love of wealth" that was the "ruling spirit" in America. Six days a week, he wrote, should be spent in cultivation of the moral and spiritual faculties and one day at work. He graduated without distinction (he wore a green coat because undergraduates were required to wear black). He then set out, in his father's business, to make a pencil superior to any then on the market. Having accomplished that and been assured that it would make his fortune, he abandoned the pencil business, returned to Concord, taught school with his brother, John, and in 1839 took a thirteen-day boat trip with him down the Concord and up the Merrimack rivers. When the school closed, in part because of John's bad health which culminated in his early death, and in part because Henry had little capacity for sustained effort, he lapsed into dependence on his assertive and rather domineering mother. The story was told that after his graduation from Harvard, when he asked his mother what he should do for a career and she suggested that he go traveling, he began to weep, whereupon his sister Helen comforted him, declaring, "No, Henry, you shall not go; you shall stay at home and live with us."

So his beginnings were a muddle of uncertainty and self-doubt. In an early poem he wrote:

> I am a parcel of vain strivings tied
> By a chance bond together,
> Dangling this way and that . . .

Like so many other young Americans Thoreau was tormented by the classic American question: "What may a man do and not be ashamed of it?" He planned to go west, he yearned for the freedom and adventure of an Indian's life, or what he imagined it to be. He tried a stint as a tutor for the children of Emerson's brother, William, in New York but soon came home. The great presiding influence in Thoreau's life, his spiritual "father," was Emerson. Almost unconsciously Thoreau adapted Emerson's powerfully epigrammatic sentence to his own uses (though he often sounded indistinguishable from his master).

Living with his family, tormented by a sense of guilt that he rather than his beloved older brother had received the family imprimatur in the form of a Harvard education, Thoreau nevertheless dreamed of a great future. His fate, he wrote, was linked to the stars: "It surely is some encouragement to know that the stars are my fellow-creatures, for I do not suspect but they are reserved for a high destiny." When his brother died of lockjaw, the psychological effect on Henry was enormous. He developed the same symptoms and was immobilized for months. He seems to have been attentive to only one woman, a brief and abortive romance with a girl he and his brother had both courted.

Finally, in 1845, noting that "It is time that I begin to live," Thoreau built a little cabin at Walden Pond, on a piece of property that Emerson had recently bought. It was a perfect retreat, within walking distance of home, an idyllic spot where his mother and sisters brought him home cooking. There is certainly something of the ridiculous about a twenty-seven-year-old man starting out like a Boy Scout to live in the woods a few miles from home with his mother and devoted sisters looking out for him, but Thoreau's genius converted that otherwise rather silly episode into a great epic of self-discovery. The "solitary hired man on a farm on the outskirts of Concord, who has had his second birth and peculiar religious experience," was Thoreau himself, and the God he worshiped was Nature. He went to Walden Pond on July 4, 1845, and stayed until September 6, 1847, twenty-six months in all. He went to clear his life of all triviality and superfluity, to discover its essential nature as it might be free from all outmoded conventions and crippling social inhibitions. Of course that was impossible to do, but Thoreau made the effort into art. He was, he wrote, "anxious to improve the nick of time, and notch it on my stick too; to stand on the meeting of two eternities, the past and future, which is precisely the present moment; to toe that line."

He had, as we have noted, Emerson's marvelous aphoristic turn: "As if you could kill time without injuring eternity," he wrote in *Walden.* He was a writer of sentences more than of paragraphs, pages, or books. *Walden,* and indeed all of Thoreau's books, are books written by a young man who stubbornly refused to grow up, who prolonged his adolescence and dependence almost beyond the state of endurance for other young men. "What old people say you cannot do, you try and find that you can do. . . . I have lived some thirty years on this planet, and I have yet to hear the first syllable of valuable or even earnest advice from my seniors." What, one wonders, about Emerson and Edward Channing, whom Thoreau was proud to call his masters?

"To be a philosopher," Thoreau wrote, "is not merely to have subtle thoughts, nor even to found a school, but to love wisdom as to live according to its dictates, a life of simplicity, independence, magnanimity, and trust. It is to solve some of the problems of life, not only theoretically, but practically." Clothes, food, shelter, the community, solitude—each of the common and necessary elements of life—Thoreau took up and considered from the perspective of his sylvan retreat: "The bad neighborhood to be avoided is our own scurvy selves. . . . I would rather sit on a pumpkin and have it all to myself than to be crowded on a velvet cushion. . . . Before we can adorn our houses with beautiful objects the walls must be stripped, and our lives must be stripped, and beautiful housekeeping and beautiful living be laid for a foundation. . . ." On education: "I mean that they [students] should not *play* life, or *study* it merely, while the community supports them at this expensive game, but earnestly *live* it from beginning to end."

On the land: "Enjoy the land, but own it not. Through want of enterprise and faith men are what they are, buying and selling, and spending their lives like serfs." If Thoreau from time to time turned toward society the face of a radical anarchist, he was one with Emerson and the rest of his contemporaries in affirming the moral foundations of existence—"Our whole life is startling moral. There never is an instant's truce between vice and virtue. Goodness is the only investment that never fails." Work which Thoreau was so adept at avoiding was the path of virtue. "If you would avoid uncleanliness, and all the sins, work earnestly, though it be at cleaning a stable. Nature is hard to overcome, but she must be overcome. What avails it that you are a Christian, if you are not purer than the heathen."

Two things might be said here. Thoreau, devoted as he was to Nature, much as he revelled in her, celebrated her, found divinity in her, felt, as Emerson felt and, indeed, all the transcendentalists felt, that Nature "must be overcome." What was natural in man was bestial, sensual, animal, sexual. That must be overcome. And yet, a few sentences further on, Thoreau anticipates Whitman in his charge that "we are so degraded that we cannot speak simply of the necessary functions of human nature. . . . Every man is the builder of a temple, called his body, to the god he worships."

For all the private terrors and public deformities Thoreau freed himself from, he could not escape from what Whitman called "the infidelism of sex." "We are conscious of an animal in us," he wrote, "which awakens in proportion as our higher nature slumbers. It is reptile and sensual, and perhaps cannot be wholly expelled; like the worms which, even in life and health, occupy our bodies." So it was "reptiles" and "worms"! The dangerous animal body that must be overcome. That was the schizophrenic split that all the paeans to Nature could not obscure. Nature was, after all, ambiguous; it lay, like the serpent, ready to attack man at any moment that his "higher nature" slumbered. It was the determined, anxious chastity of Emerson and Thoreau that was the final measure of their failure amid such otherwise brilliant success. Like the Fourierists and Brook Farmers, they could not cope with what Noyes called "the terrible urgency" of sex.

When at last he was ready to leave the woods, it seemed to Thoreau that he had learned "by experiment" that "if one advances confidently in the direction of his dreams, and endeavors to live the life which he has imagined, he will meet with a success unexpected in common hours. He will put some things behind, will pass an invisible boundary; new, universal, and more liberal laws will begin to establish themselves around and within him . . . and he will live with the license of a higher order of beings. . . . If you have built castles in the air, your work need not be lost; that is where they should be. Now put the foundations under them. . . . If a man does not keep pace with his companions, perhaps it is because he hears a different drummer. Let him keep pace with the music which he hears, however measured or far away. . . . However mean your life is, meet it and live it. . . . Love your life, poor as it is. . . . Cultivate poverty like a garden herb, like sage." The task was to "walk even with the Builder of the universe . . . not to live in this restless, nervous, bustling, trivial Nineteenth Century."

Thoreau did not write *Walden* at Walden. There he wrote the first draft of an account of his trip of six years earlier with his brother John on the Concord and the Merrimack and so helped to exorcise the memory of his dead brother. *A Week on the Concord and Merrimack Rivers* was published by Thoreau ten years later at his own expense in an edition of a thousand copies, of which only 215 were sold, the rest being returned to Thoreau to constitute, as he dryly said, the larger part of his library. From Walden Pond, Thoreau went not home but to Emerson's house, where he lived for almost two years.

It was during this time at Walden that the Mexican War began, a war that Thoreau bitterly opposed. As the reader will recall, the consequence of that opposition was a famous night in jail and the equally famous essay "On Civil Disobedience."

After his prolonged stay in the Emerson household, Thoreau went back to live with his father and help that amiable but rather ineffectual man with his pencil factory. He traveled, was an active member of the Transcendental Club, enjoyed a minor literary reputation, worked away at *Walden,* and finally completed and published it in 1854. By making his "I" universal, by the loving observation of the small universe of Walden with his own cue from his master, Emerson, he carried the American romance with nature to its illogical conclusion.

Despite failing health, Thoreau continued to write but he published no more books (eight were published posthumously over the next thirty years) and died in 1862 at the age of forty-five. Emerson read a eulogy at his funeral, which was later published in the *Atlantic Monthly.* Thoreau had been like a son or younger brother to Emerson. In his essay Emerson called his friend "a born protestant," who "declined to give up his large ambition of knowledge and action for any narrow craft or profession, aiming at a much more comprehensive calling, the art of living well. . . . There was something military in his nature, not to be subdued, always manly and able, but rarely tender, as if he did not feel himself except in opposition. He wanted a fallacy to expose, a blunder to pillory. . . . 'I love Henry,' said one of his friends, 'but I cannot like him; and as for taking his arm, I should as soon think of taking the arm of an elm tree.' . . . The length of his walk uniformly made the length of his writing. If shut up in the house he did not write at all." Emerson spoke of his friend's determination to observe the "ethical laws by his holy living." It is a telling phrase which reminds us that Thoreau was the austere monk of the religion of Nature. "He thought," Emerson added, "that without religion or devotion of some kind nothing great was ever accomplished. . . . The country knows not yet, or in the least part, how great a son it has lost. . . . But he, at least, is content. His soul was made for the noblest society; he had in a short life exhausted the capabilities of this world; wherever there is knowledge, wherever there is virtue, wherever there is beauty, he will find a home."

There was much truth to George Templeton Strong's criticism of American poetry. "Half the poetry of the last hundred years is, in truth, worthless," he wrote, "because it deals with Roman or Athenian or medieval institutions, not with the images, objects, subjects, thoughts, manners, and events amid which its author was living and which it was his office to illustrate and beautify. . . . There is poetry enough latent in the South Street merchant and Wall Street financier; in Stewart's snobby clerk chaffering over ribbons and laces; in the omnibus driver that conveys them all from the day's work to the night's relaxation and repose; in the brutified denizen of the Points and the Hook; in the sumptuous star courtesan of Mercer Street thinking sadly of her village home; in the Fifth Avenue ballroom. . . ." Even as Strong wrote those words a young man named Walter Whitman, a year his senior, was preparing to turn the commonplace scenes of the New York streets into poetry. Whitman's parents were of Dutch and English ancestry, his father a farmer and carpenter. Whitman had little schooling but he helped his father, read Sir Walter Scott, and started work at the age of eleven as a clerk, later learning the printer's craft and working for a number of papers on Long Island, Brooklyn, and New York. People who knew him in that period described him as a moody and untidy young man, restless and preoccupied. He identified himself strongly with Jacksonian democracy, with the temperance movement, and with the cause of the oppressed in general. By 1848, at the age of twenty-seven, he was editor of the *Brooklyn Eagle*. When he denounced the Democrats for refusing to face the slavery issue, he was dismissed, spent a few months in New Orleans, read omnivorously in the works of Goethe and Carlyle, and became a phrenologist, ascribing especially to its doctrines of the need for proper care of the body and a healthy diet. He returned from New Orleans to live with his parents.

That the gene pool of Whitman's parents was tainted is beyond doubt. One brother died in an insane asylum; another was a drunkard. A third brother was a congenital idiot. A sister had severe periods of melancholia, and Whitman described his father as "manly, mean, anger'd, unjust." He was surrounded by madness and must have often doubted his own sanity.

Upon his return to New York Whitman adopted quite self-consciously the manner of life of a workingman, dressing in rough, simple clothes, working as a carpenter-builder, constructing inexpensive homes for laborers. At the same time he turned seriously to writing. As a carpenter-builder, his time was largely his own. He wrote when he wished to, worked when he must. His brother George wrote, "He would lie abed late, and after getting up would write a few hours if he took the notion." In the midst of this apparently aimless and ambitionless life, Whitman read a volume of Emerson's essays. In one of his essays the latter had written: "I embrace the common, I explore and sit at the feet of the familiar and low. . . . What would we really know the meaning of? The meal in the firkin; the milk in the pan; the ballad in the street; the news of the boat; the glance of the eye, the form and gait of the body." And in another essay, he had written, "the language of the street is always strong. What can describe the folly and emptiness of scolding like the word *'jawing'*? I feel too the force of the double negative. . . . And I confess to some pleasure from the stinging rhetoric of a rattling oath in the mouth of trackmen and teamsters. . . . Cut these words and they would bleed; they are vascular and alive; they walk and run. Moreover, they who speak them have this elegancy, that they do not trip in their speech. It is a shower of bullets, whilst Cambridge men and Yale men correct themselves and begin again at every half sentence." In later years Whitman told the writer of boys' books, John Taylor Trowbridge, that Emerson's essays were like a revelation to him—"all that had lain smoldering so long within him, waiting to be fired, rushed into flame at the touch of those electric words." When Whitman read Emerson, he was "simmering, simmering, simmering; Emerson brought me to a boil." It was almost as though Emerson was his John the Baptist, preparing the way. That Emerson, Harvard man and ex-Unitarian, could write so powerfully about speech was a kind of marvel in itself. It was hardly surprising that he could not speak so. It took a new generation to practice what Emerson had preached (Emerson was, to be sure, only fifteen years older than Whitman, but that was enough to constitute a new literary generation).

In 1855 Whitman completed and set in type *Leaves of Grass.* Most booksellers thought it indecent and would not touch it. One told the poet he could not carry it because he was a "religious man." The volume itself was quarto size, bound in green covers with the title in gold on the front and back. Whitman's name was not given on the title page but there was a photograph of him which was destined to become one of the most famous of all American photographs: a young man in a soft broad-brimmed hat and flannel shirt open at the neck, one hand on his hip and the other in his trousers pocket.

The first poem in *Leaves of Grass,* untitled, was later called by Whitman "Song of Myself." I suspect there are no more famous words announcing the arrival of a major poet:

> I celebrate myself, and sing myself,
> And what I assume you shall assume
> For every atom belonging to me as good belongs to you.
>
> I loafe and invite my soul,
> I lean and loafe at my ease observing a spear of summer grass. . . .
>
> Creeds and schools in abeyance,
> Retiring back a while sufficed at what they are, but never fogotten,
> I harbor for good or bad, I permit to speak at every hazard,
> Nature without check with original energy.

Whitman sent a copy of *Leaves of Grass* to Emerson, and Emerson, to his eternal credit, recognized the genius of the author and wrote to Whitman: "Dear Sir—I am not blind to the worth of the wonderful gift of *Leaves of Grass.* I find it the most extraordinary piece of wit and wisdom that America has yet contributed. I am very happy in reading it, as great power makes us happy . . . I give you joy of your free and brave thought. I have great joy in it . . . I greet you at the beginning of a great career, which yet must have a long foreground somewhere, for such a start. I rubbed my eyes a little, to see if this sunbeam were no illusion. . . ."

In comments to friends, Emerson was somewhat more cautious, referring to Whitman as evidently "hurt by hard life & too animal experience" and in another letter he called *Leaves of Grass* a "wonderful book . . . with all its formlessness & faults."

Whitman had sent the book to other literary figures and a number of papers and had written three reviews himself which he arranged to have published in various papers. Otherwise the response was almost uniformly hostile. The *Boston Intelligencer* called it "a heterogeneous mass of bombast, egotism, vulgarity and nonsense. . . . The beastliness of the author is set forth in his description of himself, and we can conceive of no better reward than the lash for such a violation of decency. The author should be kicked from all decent society as below the level of the brute. He must be some escaped lunatic raving in pitiable delirium."

Charles Eliot Norton read *Leaves of Grass* at Emerson's prompting and wrote to Lowell describing Whitman as "one of the roughs, a Kosmos"; Emerson, Norton added, was enthusiastic about him "for Walt Whitman has read *The Dial Nature,* and combines the characteristics of a Concord philosopher with those of a New York fireman." Norton acknowledged the poem's power—"some superbly graphic description"—but much of it was "simply disgustingly coarse." It was the kind of book one could not leave lying about for fear that a woman might look "past the title page." To Norton it was "merely . . . a literary curiosity." Lowell concurred; the great ones "let the stream of their activity flow quietly." It seemed to him that even "Michel Angelo cocked his hat a little wee too much. . . ."

Whitman was, of course, delighted with Emerson's letter. It was balm for all the wounds inflicted by other critics. It did not occur to him not to use it to promote his book. He took a copy to his friend, Charles Dana, a cousin of Richard Henry, who was the editor of the *New York Tribune* and Dana printed it. Gentlemen did not publish the private letters of other gentlemen. When Emerson was told that the letter had appeared in the *Tribune,* he said: "Dear! dear! that was very wrong, very wrong indeed. That was merely a private letter of congratulation. Had I intended it for publication I should have enlarged the *but* very much—enlarged the *but,* enlarged the *but.*"

Months later, writing to Carlyle, Emerson had recovered his

nerve. "One book, last summer, came out in New York," he wrote, "a nondescript monster which yet had terrible eyes and buffalo strength, and was indisputably American,—which I thought to send you; but the book throve so badly with the few to whom I showed it, and wanted good morals so much that I never did. Yet I believe now again, I shall. It is called *Leaves of Grass.* . . ."

A year after the first edition Whitman brought out another, which perpetuated his earlier faux pas by printing Emerson's letter to him and a reply to Emerson. There had been twelve poems in the original edition. Now there were thirty-two. The second edition contained the poem beginning:

> Walt Whitman, a kosmos, of Manhattan the son,
> Turbulent, fleshy, sensual, eating, drinking and breeding,
> No sentimentalist, no stander above men and women or part
> from them,
> No more modest than immodest.
>
> Unscrew the locks from the doors!
> Unscrew the doors themselves from the jambs!
>
> Whoever degrades another degrades me,
> And whatever is done or said returns at last to me. . . .
>
> I speak the pass-word primeval, I give the sign of democracy,
> By God! I will accept nothing which all cannot have their
> counterpart of on the same terms.

Whitman hailed Emerson as "dear Friend and Master." He was, he wrote in his "letter," determined to confront his countrymen "with an American rude tongue. . . . Master I am a man who has perfect faith. Master, we have not come through centuries, caste, heroisms, fables, to halt in this land today. . . . As nature, inexorable, onward, resistless, impassive amid the threats and screams of disputants, so America. Let us defer. Let us all attend respectfully the leisure of These States, their politics, poems, literature, modes of training their own offspring. . . . Their shadows are projected in employments, in books, in the cities, in trade; their feet are on the flights of the steps of the Capitol; they dilate, a larger, brawnier, more candid, more democratic, lawless, positive nature to The States, sweet-bodied, completer, dauntless, flowing, masterful, beard-faced, new race of men. . . .

"Swiftly, on limitless foundation, the United States too are founding a literature." All the literature of the past would pour its riches in "for that other plainly signified literature, to be our own, to be electric, fresh, lusty, to express the full-sized body, male and female, to give the modern meanings of things, to grow up beautiful, lasting, commensurate with America, with all the passions of home, with the inimitable sympathies of having been boys and girls together. . . ." America had long lain under the "huge English flow, so sweet, so undeniable," but so overwhelming. Now America, "grandest of lands in the theory of its politics, in popular reading, in hospitality, breadth, animal beauty, cities, ships, machines, money, credit," must discover its own non-English, post-English soul. "Open the doors of The West. Call for new great masters to comprehend new arts, new perfections, new wants. . . . Here are to be obtained results never elsewhere thought possible; the modes are very grand too. The instincts of the American people are all perfect, and tend to make heroes. It is a rare thing in a man here to understand The States."

Indeed, America, in Whitman's view—literary America, at least —was choked on "formulas, glosses, blanks, minutiae. There is not a single History of the World. There is not one of America, or of the organic compacts of These States, or of Washington, or of Jefferson, nor of Language, nor any Dictionary of the English Language. There is no great author; every one has demeaned himself to some etiquette or some impotence. The churches are one vast lie; the people do not believe them, and they do not believe themselves. . . ." Americans did "the most ridiculous things for fear of being called ridiculous, smirking and skipping along, . . . no one behaving, dressing, writing, talking, loving, out of any natural and manly tastes of his own, but each one looking cautiously to see how the rest behave, dress, write, talk, love. . . ." Whitman announced to his pleased but uneasy "Master" his intention to celebrate "with joy the sturdy living forms of the men and women of These States, the divinity of sex, the perfect eligibility of the female with the male, all The States, liberty and equality, real articles, the different trades, mechanics, the young fellows of Manhattan Island, customs, instincts, slang, Wisconsin, Georgia, the noble Southern heart, the hot blood, the spirit that will be nothing less than master, the filibuster spirit, the Western man, native-born perfections, the eye for forms, the perfect models of made things, the wild smack of freedom, California, money, electric-telegraphs, free-trade, iron and the iron mines—recognize without demur those splendid resistless black poems, the steam-ships of the seaboard states, and those other resistless splendid poems, the locomotives. . . ."

Whitman reserved his greatest scorn for his age's greatest "infidelism," "the filthy law, and the books enslaved to it, that what makes the manhood of a man, that sex, womanhood, maternity, desires, lusty animations, organs, acts, are unmentionable and to be ashamed of, to be driven to skulk out of literature. . . . This filthy law has to be repealed—it stands in the way of great reforms. Of women just as much as men, it is the interest that there should not be infidelism about sex, but perfect faith." American poets must decide "whether they shall celebrate in poems the eternal decency of the amativeness of Nature, the motherhood of all, or whether they shall be the bards of the fashionable delusion of the inherent nastiness of sex, and of the feeble and querulous modesty of deprivation."

"These States" in their variety, their "needs, dangers, prejudices, and the like" were the inheritors of all the achievements of "past ages and lands," and it was their responsibility to "initiate the outlines of repayment a thousand fold." To produce new masters and new visions, to accept "old worlds and new," "evil as well as good, ignorance as well as erudition, black as soon as white, foreign-born materials as well as home-born, reject none. . . ." Show how precedents create new opportunities. "Always America will be agitated and turbulent. This day it is taking shape, not to be less so, but to be more so, stormily, capriciously, on native principles, with such vast proportions of parts! As for me, I love screaming, wrestling, boiling-hot days."

All this would be achieved on Emersonian terms "upon that vast basis of the supremacy of Individuality—that new moral American continent. . . ." And then to Emerson directly: "These shores you found. I say you have led The States there—have led Me there. I say that none has ever done, or ever can do, a greater deed for These States, than your deed. . . . Receive, dear Master, these statements and assurances through me, for all the young men. . . ."

The remarkable letter was almost as long as the remarkable poems that preceded it and, in truth, as much a poem, for if Emerson's prose was poetry so was Whitman's, as well as his poetry prose. It belongs with a half dozen of the most notable letters in our history. Emerson had pointed the way and Whitman had traveled it. The poem(s) and the letter constituted together one of the most powerful extensions of the literary consciousness in America. They broke through into a new realm of the imagination and added a new dimension to the American language, created a new set of terms, of images into which to try to tease or drive the essence of the meaning of "These States." So art or the sacred muse of song drew these two wildly disparate individuals together. Whitman was the suitor and Emerson the fascinated but apprehensive object of his suit. Together they delineated one-half of the American body, or psyche. With words like ultrasonic probes they searched the deepest organs of the body politic, the remotest reaches of the psyche. Emerson had made the terrible isolation of American life into its greatest virtue by founding the "religion of individualism." Now Whitman acclaimed the chaos and disorder of American life, finding in it a vast expansion of human possibilities. In a sense they had covered over wounds without healing them. But it was incontestable that they had made an opening. They seemed to have in common a sometimes almost tiresomely affirmative view of life in America; but Whitman, who had been hurt and enraged time after time by the brutality and crudity of the American scene, kept life at arm's length for the most part, picking for himself a romantic public role and fiercely protecting the apparently rather dry kernel of his private existence. Emerson simply suppressed his terrors. But he could not suppress Whitman. When Whitman brought out a third edition of *Leaves of Grass*, published in Boston, which was uncomfortably close to home for Emerson, Emerson tried to persuade him to omit the "Children of Adam" poems. His arguments against "the sex handicap" seemed to Whitman unassailable. But, Whitman wrote years later, Emerson did not see "that if I had cut sex out I might just as well have cut everything out—the full scheme would no longer exist—it would have been violated in its most sensitive spot."

Thoreau, after reading the second edition of *Leaves of Grass* and making a pilgrimage to meet this strange new literary Minotaur who had not even been born in New England, wrote to a friend: "There are two or three pieces in the book which are disagreeable, to say the least; simply sensual. He does not celebrate love at all. It is as if the beasts spoke. . . . But even on this side he has spoken more truth than any American or modern that I know. I have found his poem exhilarating, encouraging." As for sensuality, it was not that Thoreau did not wish it written of so much as he wished that men and women were pure enough to "read them without harm, that is, without understanding them." Some readers had expressed anxiety that the book might be read by women, "as if," Thoreau wrote, "a man could read what a woman could not." And then he reminded his correspondent that if one could be shocked by Whitman, "whose experience is it that we are reminded of?"

With such "deductions" *Leaves of Grass* sounded to Thoreau, "very brave and American. . . ." He saw its moral and didactic basis clearly enough: "I do not believe that all the sermons, so called, that have been preached in this land put together are equal to it for preaching. . . . Though rude, and sometimes ineffectual, it is a great primitive poem,—an alarum or trumpet-note ringing through the American camp." Thoreau mentioned to Whitman that he "did not think much of America or politics" which seemed to put "somewhat of a damper to him," but he had been reassured to find the author of *Leaves of Grass* not a braggart or egotist, as his book suggested he might be. "He is a great fellow," he concluded.

Whitman was never simply a rough, untutored workman, journeyman typesetter, or knock-about newspaper reporter. He knew the streets of New York intimately, the swarming, colorful, dangerous streets that we are familiar with through George Templeton Strong's diary. But he loved the opera and was a devotee of the arts, with a special interest in Egyptology. Certainly he had led a life that often seemed undirected. What can be said with some confidence is that one consistent thread through it was his compassion for the failed, for the flawed and defeated. He knew them in his own family and in a thousand other embodiments. And to the failure and to the suffering, the drifting, the "loafing," the isolation and the sense of futility, he had responded passionately. He was the poet as hero. Emerson had called for him and he had answered. It was all through his poetry, swelling up from the depths of American life, spreading everywhere, protean, inexhaustible, comprehending all, illuminating all, healing and redeeming, making the incomprehensible soul of America art, making art life—"Crossing Brooklyn Ferry," "So Long," "Out of the Cradle Endlessly Rocking." There was a kind of breathtaking presumption in Whitman's determination to encompass it all—the runaway slave whom he nursed and fed and then "pass'd north." The rich young women, hidden and watching, yearningly, "Twenty-eight young men bathe by the shore . . . float on their backs, . . . their white bellies bulge to the sun," as "An unseen hand also pass'd over their bodies. . . ." "I am of the old and young, of the foolish as much as the wise, / Regardless of others, ever regardful of others, / Maternal as well as paternal, a child as well as a man . . . / One of the Nation of many nations . . . A southerner soon as a Yankee . . . / These are really the thoughts of all men in all ages and lands, they are not original with me, / If they are not yours as much as mine they are nothing, or next to nothing, / If they are not the riddle, and the untying of the riddle they are nothing. . . ."

Emerson had given him the key, the enormous self, the self so vast that it comprehended everything, took in everything, absorbed and made art out of the totality of the universe, or, at least, out of America, made one vast enumerative poem out of confusion and disorder. Whitman celebrated "the supremacy of the Individual" who expanded until he became God. We call *Leaves of Grass* a poem and Whitman a poet, but that is only because we have no suitable category for it or him. He was a prophet, a mystic, a seer, a priest, a preacher, the voice of the people, the voice of God. Whether *Leaves of Grass* is a "good" poem, or a bad one, or no poem at all is beside the point, certainly for us. It is an American phenomenon. There is nothing to compare it to and, it is safe to say, there will never be anything like it. It is, as professors like to say of discrete phenomena, *sui generis,* of its own, a separate category. A catalogue and a distillation. It is of central importance to this work, of greater importance perhaps than Melville's *Moby Dick,* because this work has set out, far more modestly to be sure, on the same track—that is to say, we have it as our goal to place "These States" in a similar perspective, to penetrate, to encompass on the deepest level the humanity and tragedy and heroism, the *awesomeness* of our history.

Of the various debts we owe to Emerson, the fact that he prepared the way, "found these shores," for Whitman is undoubtedly the greatest. What more potent parable could we have of the strange "genius" of our humanity than the fact that our prim, Puritan-Unitarian-Harvard man could have reached into the depths of Whitman's flawed and tragic world—how far from Cambridge!—and drawn forth the most powerfully American utterance in our history and, having done so, have had the wisdom to recognize and the courage to acclaim this alarmingly "wild" offspring with his "Titanic abdomen."

Kenneth Rexroth, the American poet, commenting on the aridity of academic departments of literature, has noted that there is not one course taught on the various campuses of the University of California on America's greatest poet. But the universities are unwittingly right. Whitman has nothing to do with professors of literature. His poems carry an almost unendurable burden of emotion; they have as little to do with formal literary criticism as a fluorescent light with a sunset. It was such verse as the world had never seen before, where the passion created the form; poetry only nominally, poetry because it must have a category. As Thoreau perceived, it was a sermon more powerful than all the sermons heretofore delivered on Man in America. *Leaves of Grass* was Walter Whitman's escape from the madness that brought down two of his brothers and that threatened his sister. He took the multiple schizophrenias that constantly threatened to tear the country apart into himself. He was the "suffering servant" who bore the afflictions of "These States"—the murderous racial conflicts, the crippling sexual anxieties, the war between men and women ("I say it as great to be a woman as to be a man"), the clash of North and South, "undisguised and naked" he offered himself as the healer: "Stop this day and night with me and you shall possess the origin of all poems. . . . / You shall no longer take things at second or third hand,/ Nor look through the eyes of the dead, nor feed on the spectres in books . . . / There was never any more inception than there is now,/ Nor any more youth or age than there is now,/ And will never be any more perfection than there is now,/ Nor any more heaven or hell than there is now,/ Urge and urge and urge,/ Always the procreant urge of the world."

In healing himself, Whitman prescribed for America. A health, a wholeness, a wholesomeness breathes from the poem; a profound morality pervades it.

In the five years between the first slim volume called *Leaves of Grass* with its twelve untitled poems and the third edition, published in 1860, containing some hundred and twenty-three, Whitman worked in a kind of ecstatic fever. *Leaves of Grass* grew almost as though it had an organic life of its own, as an oak grows from an acorn. By 1860 it was, for all intents and purposes, finished, though Whitman continued to supplement and rearrange it for decades, becoming its editor and custodian as though it had its own independent life. *Leaves of Grass* exists, not to be talked about or lectured upon, but to be read as a mountain might exist to be climbed, a mountain from whose summit the whole breathtaking landscape of America would unfold. Whitman is simply there, as inexplicable an upwelling of power and compassion as Lincoln himself and as profoundly American.

Emerson, Thoreau, and Whitman were all contained in John Calvin's *Institutes*, in the strange new "individual" he placed in a direct and responsible relationship to God, in the company of saints and the priesthood of believers. They secularized the "individual"; like explorers journeying in a strange land, they traveled to its furthest reaches, mapping and describing the terrain. To put it another way, they toppled God from his throne and enthroned "The Individual," omnipotent, all-encompassing. Emerson was the theologian-priest of the new religion, Thoreau its political philosopher, Whitman its poet-hero.

52

THE DARKER SIDE

Nathaniel Hawthorne was a year younger than Emerson and in almost every way the antithesis. Born in 1804 in Salem, Massachusetts, the descendant of generations of Puritans, Hawthorne explored that half of the Puritan psyche, that half of the world—the dark side—that Emerson and the transcendentalists, for the most part, ignored: vanity, human presumption, decadence, corrupted innocence, the monstrous distortions of the ego—original sin. Hawthorne was wary of the "self," the free, autonomous "individual" constantly proclaimed by the transcendentalists. The self could too easily become self-ish, egotistical, ruthlessly feeding its own appetites, supremely confident of its own rectitude.

His own home was a silent and solitary refuge of the sort that appeared frequently in his short stories and novels. His father had died when Hawthorne was only four years old and he was thrown much on his own resources. By the time he left for Bowdoin College in Maine, bypassing Harvard, he had read most of the best-known English and French authors. He was apparently determined from the first to be a writer; everything he did, everything he observed was with that goal in mind. He mined the history of New England for scenes and characters to exemplify the major themes that preoccupied him.

He wrote and published anonymously at the age of twenty-four a novel entitled *Fanshawe* which received the obscurity it deserved, but through it he formed an association that was to be critically important to him. His sponsor and patron was Samuel Goodrich. Under the pen name of Peter Perley, Goodrich published more than a hundred rather saccharine tales of the American past primarily for children—*The Tales of Peter Perley about America.* (Henry James, in an essay on Hawthorne, referred caustically to Goodrich's attempt "to vulgarize human knowledge and adapt it to the infant mind.") Goodrich also published a literary magazine called *The New England Token* and soon Hawthorne's short stories began to appear in its pages. Hawthorne did a tour of duty as editor of Goodrich's *American Magazine of Entertaining and Useful Knowledge* and wrote *Peter Perley's Universal History,* which sold over a million copies.

In addition to his own serious short stories, Hawthorne made a speciality of children's stories, writing four in two years. After a spell at Brook Farm, he married Sophia Peabody, a remarkable person in her own right, member of a classic New England family of intellectuals and reformers, a woman far more outgoing than the shy and reserved Hawthorne. He was thirty-eight when he married. Like Thoreau he had been a kind of literary celibate. The marriage, belated though it was, was an unusually happy one. Hawthorne derived a new poise from it.

Twice-Told Tales, a collection of short stories, was a major literary success. Edgar Allan Poe praised it as a work of genius. George Templeton Strong thought the book had "great power, much imagination, fertility and felicity of thought and diction, and occasional passages of real beauty. BUT," he added, "such a dismal series of ghostly, ghastly charnel-house conceptions I never met with. . . ." Hawthorne then began work on *The Scarlet Letter* and extended his world from Salem to Lenox, where he met Herman Melville, fifteen years his junior. Melville, thirty-three years old, was married to Elizabeth Shaw, daughter of the famous chief justice of Massachusetts, Lemuel Shaw; he had been widely acclaimed for his first novel, *Typee,* which had appeared in 1846 and been a notable success. When Melville and Hawthorne met, Melville was feverishly at work on *Moby Dick.* The young man sought out the older with characteristic enthusiasm. Their relationship was strikingly similar to that between Whitman and Emerson. Melville plainly felt that Hawthorne was the spiritual kin he was seeking. In the guise of a Virginian spending the summer in

Vermont, Melville wrote a kind of impassioned love letter to Hawthorne in the form of a literary essay: "A man of a deep and noble nature has seized me in this seclusion. His wild witch voice rings through me [that was enough to startle and disconcert the reserved Hawthorne]; or, in softer cadences, I seem to hear it in the songs of the hillside birds that sing in the larch trees at my window . . . there is no man in whom humor and love are developed in that high form called genius; no such man can exist without also possessing, as the indispensable complement of these, a great, deep intellect, which drops down into the universe like a plummet." Hawthorne was such a man. His air of pervading melancholy, his patient exploration of "the dark half of the physical sphere," his "touch of Puritanic gloom" drew Melville to him. "Certain it is," Melville wrote, "that this great power of blackness in him derives its force from its appeals to that Calvinistic sense of Innate Depravity and Original Sin, from whose visitations, in some shape or other, no deeply thinking mind is always and wholly free . . . perhaps no writer has ever wielded this terrific thought with greater terror than this same harmless Hawthorne." Melville went on to compare Hawthorne with Shakespeare, insisting that "the difference between the two men is by no means immeasurable," and calling on his countrymen to recognize Hawthorne's true stature. To so acknowledge Hawthorne would "brace the whole brotherhood," "for genius, all over the world, stands hand in hand, and one shock of recognition runs the whole circle round."

The Scarlet Letter, published in 1850, was a success and *The House of Seven Gables* which followed it was also acclaimed and sold well. *The Scarlet Letter*—the letter *A* for adultery, worn by Hester Prynne while protecting her guilty lover—is far more about the nineteenth century's hypocrisy and dissimulation in regard to the matter of sexuality and sin than it is about Puritan attitudes, which, as we have seen, were generally characterized by a practical approach to sexual failings never again achieved by Americans. Henry James called it "the finest piece of imaginative writing yet put forth in the country."

The Blithedale Romance, a somewhat satirical account of his Brook Farm experience, followed a year later but was not a financial success. Having written a campaign biography for his Bowdoin classmate, Franklin Pierce, Hawthorne accepted an appointment as United States consul in Liverpool and spent four years in England; he traveled in Europe and especially in Italy, where he acquainted himself with the culture of Rome, which provided the setting for his last novel, *The Marble Faun*.

In England, Hawthorne was haunted by a recurrent dream that he had had for many years. "It is that I am still at college, or, sometimes, even, at school—and there is a sense that I have been there unconscionably long, and have quite failed to make such progress as my contemporaries have done; and I seem to meet some of them with a feeling of shame and depression that broods over me as I think of it, even when awake." Hawthorne felt the dream was the consequence of his having spent twelve years after graduating from college in "heavy seclusion—when everybody moved onward and left me behind. How strange," he added, "that it should come now, when I may call myself famous and prosperous!—when I am happy too."

The Marble Faun deals with the theme of Old World decadence and American innocence. The "marble faun" is a Pan-like Italian, Praxiteles' faun come to life. Miriam, the American girl, is overwhelmed by evil. She falls under the spell of an "ill-omened" character who has such power over her "as beasts and reptiles of subtle and evil nature sometimes exercise upon their victims," so they are bound by a bond "forged in some such unhallowed furnace as is kindled by evil passions and fed by evil deeds." Hawthorne had been away from his native soil four years when he wrote *The Marble Faun*. It is the least successful of his novels. His capacity to create and sustain a mood is attenuated by the complicated plots and subplots. One has the uneasy feeling that its primary purpose was to titillate and instruct the American tourist in Rome. Yet scattered through its often turgid pages there are passages of classic Hawthorne.

The effect of the Civil War on Hawthorne was devastating. In the words of Henry James, "The whole affair was a bitter disappointment to him, and a fatal blow to that happy faith in the uninterruptedness of American prosperity which [was] . . . the religion of the old-fashioned American in general, and the old-fashioned Democrat in particular. It was not a propitious time for cultivating the Muse." Indeed, it was as though his tragic vision of Original Sin were projected onto the stage of national history. Hawthorne's final years were clouded ones. Pinched for funds, he tried to start another novel, but he found it impossible to complete. He died in his sleep at Plymouth, New Hampshire, in 1864, at the age of sixty.

One of Hawthorne's most common themes was that of hidden or

secret sin. In "The Minister's Black Veil," when the minister is questioned by his puzzled fiancée, he replies cryptically: "If I hide my face for sorrow, there is cause enough, . . . and if I cover it for secret sin, what mortal might not do the same?" "The Prophetic Pictures" and "The Birthmark" also deal with masks and illusions. Hawthorne made himself master of that strange territory between the illusion and the reality, between the Ego and the dark demands of the Id, a land of shadows and social pretense that slips easily into the realm of tragedy and terror. We have seen him mocking the claims of science and progress in "The Celestial Railroad," where the passengers, looking for an easy shortcut to heaven by rail, find themselves headed instead for hell.

It is tempting to read Hawthorne's career in terms of the history of the period, and such a reading would clearly not be entirely beside the point. Certainly in the framework of our psychological/ philosophical fault line between the Classical-Christian Consciousness and the Secular-Democratic, Hawthorne and his work fall on the Classical-Christian side.

Henry James, writing the first critical study of Hawthorne in 1879, called him "the most beautiful and eminent representative of a literature . . . the most valuable example of the American genius." To James the moral of Hawthorne's life and work was that "the flower of art blooms only where the soil is deep, [and] that it takes a great deal of history to produce a little literature, that it needs a complex social machinery to set a writer in motion. . . . He combined in a singular degree the spontaneity of the imagination with a haunting care for moral problems. Man's conscience was his theme."

Of all the important literary figures of the nineteenth century, Edgar Allan Poe was undoubtedly the most eccentric. His own life was more bizarre than any of his tales. Born of actor parents, Poe was orphaned at the age of two (his father was an alcoholic; his mother died of tuberculosis) and ended up in the home of foster parents, the John Allans of Richmond, Virginia. Allan was a merchant who undertook to establish a branch of his business in England. Until he was eleven, young Poe attended English schools. His business having failed, Allan returned to Richmond and there Poe pursued studies designed to prepare him for college. He seems to have had a very close attachment to his foster mother and the discovery that Allan was unfaithful to her was the cause of considerable resentment on Poe's part.

Entering the University of Virginia in 1829, Poe proved an erratic student, drinking to excess and gambling. Allan refused to pay his tuition and tried to steer him in the direction of the law, but Poe was determined to write, and after a bitter quarrel with his foster father he went to Boston to try to make his living as a journalist and editor. Unable to make a go of it, he enlisted in the army under an assumed name. Although he did well as a soldier, rising to the rank of sergeant major, he was soon bored and managed to obtain a discharge on the grounds that he claimed to seek an appointment to West Point. Allan, hoping to see Poe launched on a military career, provided him with enough money to sustain him while he was waiting to be admitted to the Academy and Poe, seeking his origins, went to Baltimore where he met relatives of his dead parents, among them an aunt, Mrs. Maria Clemm, who befriended the handsome and charming young man. While he was in Baltimore his second volume of poetry was published. In 1830, when he was twenty-one, he was admitted to West Point. A new quarrel with Allan and a growing determination to pursue a career as a writer led Poe to neglect his academic work. He was dismissed from the Academy and the same year his third volume of poetry appeared, entitled simply *Poems by Edgar A. Poe.* The slim volume contained three of his most famous poems, clearly influenced by Keats and Byron—"To Helen" ("Helen, thy beauty is to me/ Like those Nicean barks of yore,/ That gently, o'er a perfumed sea,/ The weary, way-worn wanderer bore/ To his own native shore . . ."), "Israfel," and "Lenore."

For four years Poe made his home with Mrs. Clemm in Baltimore. During this period he joined the staff of the *Southern Literary Messenger,* establishing himself as a brilliant editor and increasing the circulation of the magazine fivefold. But he drank heavily and fought with the owner of the *Messenger.* In 1836, at the age of twenty-seven, he married his thirteen-year-old cousin, Virginia Clemm. His life now became a series of increasingly desperate expedients, interspersed with poems and, more frequently, short stories of the fantastic or "detective" genre. From Richmond to New York and then to Philadelphia Poe, his child bride, and his patient aunt and mother-in-law, Maria Clemm, made their way, dogged by poverty and ill health. Poe added opium to his addiction to liquor. Meantime he continued to turn out his carefully crafted poems ("The Raven" appeared in 1845), critical essays, and short stories. The poems and stories were enormously popular. In striking contrast to the tragedy and disorder of Poe's life, they were the products of a highly self-conscious theory of "art for art's sake," the artful use of literary devices, given great intensity by his own dark vision of life.

Poe wrote but never published a poem entitled "Alone," which offers a revealing clue to his temperament:

> From childhood's hour I have not been
> As others were—I have not seen
> As others saw—I could not bring
> My passions from a common spring—
> From the same source I have not taken
> My sorrow—I could not awaken
> My heart to love at the same tone—
> And all I lov'd—*I* lov'd alone. . . .

Again, there is the lonely, isolate "*I*," the romantic image of the wayfarer, burdened with an excessively sensitive and morbid nature. In reply to a query from Lowell about his conception of his role as a poet, Poe wrote: "I live continually in a reverie of the future. . . . My life has been *whim*—impulse—passion—a longing for solitude—a scorn of all things present, in an earnest longing for the future." America seemed to him a fate from which he could not escape and democracy "a very admirable form of government—for dogs." "The Conqueror Worm" ends with the apocalyptic lines:

> Out—out are the lights-out all!
>   And, over each quivering form,
> The curtain, a funeral pall,
>   Comes down with the rush of a storm,
> While the angels, all pallid and wan,
>   Uprising, unveiling, affirm
> That the play is the tragedy, "man,"
>   And its hero the Conqueror Worm.

Virginia wasted away from tuberculosis and died in 1847 at the age of twenty-three, after ten troubled years of marriage. With the death of his wife, Poe's last defenses were overthrown. He had "In the mad pride of intellectuality" believed in "the power of word" to depict every human emotion, but at Virginia's death he found all "his spells broken./ The pen falls powerless from my shivering hand . . . / I cannot write/ I cannot speak or think,/ Alas, I cannot feel. . . ."

Poe now went rapidly down hill, both physically and mentally, seeking out in a desperate spirit the company of a succession of women with whom his relations, in the words of a biographer, "were fantastic, and nothing more" (a rather opaque observation); but at the same time Poe wrote some of his most famous poems, including "The Bells" and "Annabel Lee." The future seemed to brighten when Poe joined a temperance society and became engaged to a sweetheart of his youth, with the marriage day set; but during a trip to Baltimore, Poe disappeared from sight, was found semiconscious several days later by a friend, and died four days afterward at the age of forty, delirious and tormented by visions.

Poe died famous, his poems and short stories widely acclaimed. His morbid fancies were thoroughly congenial to the spirit of the time. The tragic events of his life heightened the romantic aura that surrounded him. The psychological burdens he bore were certainly not unrelated to the general character of American life. This was specially true in his chronic financial insecurity and his inability, famous as he became, to make a living from his writing.

In his much less well-known role as a critic, the real power of Poe's intellect is most evident. He was one of the first critics to praise Hawthorne. Hawthorne's *Twice-Told Tales,* Poe wrote in 1847, belonged "to the highest region of Art—an Art subservient to genius of a very lofty order. . . . Mr. Hawthorne's distinctive trait is invention, creation, imagination, originality—a trait which . . . is positively worth all the rest. . . . He has the purest style, the finest taste, the most available scholarship, the most delicate humor, the most touching pathos, the most radiant imagination, the most consummate ingenuity; and with these varied good qualities he has done *well* as a mystic."

Behind Poe's preoccupation with the creation of particular effects—of loneliness, of terror, of degradation—there lies a Hawthorne or Melville–like concern with the nature of evil and with the strange, twilight world of human passions and anxieties, the world of sleep and of dreams, of death. "For my own part," Poe wrote, "I have never had a thought which I could not set down in words, with even more distinctness than that with which I conceived it. . . ." But there was "a class of fancies, of exquisite delicacy, which are *not* thoughts, and to which, *as yet,* I have found no language." To Poe "*pure Imagination* chooses, from either *Beauty or Deformity,* only the most combinable things hitherto uncombined. . . . One might start with Beauty or Deformity and pass into its opposite." The writer thus searched for "the absolute 'chemical combination'" that would produce art.

Criticism is not, generally speaking, one of the more enduring of the arts, but Poe's critical essays can still be read with pleasure. They are characterized by an unusually sure grasp of the essence of an author's work and, except in the case of Longfellow, by a generosity of spirit and largeness of mind which reveal Poe at his best. There are indeed two Poes: the tormented poet, the explorer of evil and degeneration, the lonely, obsessed alcoholic; and Poe the critic, cool, perceptive, writing with the grace and strength of a man in sure possession of himself and his notions of literature.

Poe is an almost irresistible subject for a psychoanalytically oriented literary critic, but theories that attempt to account for his art by reference to the multiple tragedies and disappointments of his own life are ultimately less interesting than the fact that under such circumstances he functioned so brilliantly as an artist.

In one very important sense, he was a victim of the social attitudes of the time. He was known to be the child of actors, and actors stood in very low esteem. It was also evident that John Allan, who had "social position" in Richmond, was a grudging guardian and that he had no intention of treating Poe as an adopted son and heir. Thus raised as a gentleman, sent to good schools and accustomed to associating with young men and women of assured social standing, Poe felt himself a lonely and marginal figure who did not truly belong to the class with which he found himself most closely associated. Like Sidney George Fisher and George Templeton Strong he suffered terrible anxieties about money, but unlike them he did not have the backing and support of wealthy family and friends. On the literary level we find in Poe a strange conjunction of prevailing currents in American thought or, perhaps more accurately, in the American psyche: the dramatization and romanticizing of the lonely, isolated individual; the celebration of the "poet-hero" as the superior individual; the anxiety about death; the exultation of intuition over reason (common with many of the transcendentalists as well); the disposition to play various roles and invent fictitious histories; and, finally, the inability to cope with sexuality, of which his marriage to his thirteen-year-old cousin was surely a symptom.

The life of Herman Melville was such a life as a romantic novelist might compose. Melville was born in 1819; he was the same age as Whitman, two years younger than Thoreau. His paternal ancestors had been leaders in the Massachusetts Bay colony and state for generations, and his grandfather, Thomas Melville of Boston, was the model for Oliver Wendell Holmes's "The Last Leaf":

> They say that in his prime,
> Ere the pruning-knife of Time
> Cut him down,
> Not a better man was found
> By the Crier on his round . . .

Melville's maternal grandfather was Peter Gansevoort, famous for his defense of Fort Stanwix during the Revolution (greatly outnumbered, Gansevoort had replied to the British demand for the surrender of the fort, "I have only to say that it is my determined resolution with the forces under my command, to defend this fort, at every hazard, to the last extremity, in behalf of the United States who have placed me here to defend it against all their enemies"). His father had established himself in New York but became a bankrupt and died when Melville was twelve. He and his mother suffered, in consequence, that most dreaded fate of the upper class; they fell out of it through impecuniousness. There was no thought of college. Melville went to work as a clerk at the age of fifteen, taking jobs, successively, as a farmhand and rural schoolteacher.

At eighteen Melville shipped out on a merchant vessel on the New York to Liverpool run and after another stint of teaching he signed on the whaler *Acushnet,* undoubtedly the decisive act of his life. He and a companion jumped ship in the Marquesas Islands and found their way to the remote and beautiful valley of Typee, occupied by amiable cannibals. From his wildly romantic Typee adventure Melville went on to spend months on Tahiti, finally signing on the U. S. frigate *United States* and returning home after almost three years of adventuring, equipped with enough literary raw material to last him a lifetime. The books came tumbling out. First was *Typee,* a mildly fictionalized account of his life with the island natives, featuring a romance between the narrator and Fayaway, a beautiful native girl. Melville was particularly attracted to the theme of corrupted innocence, seeing the Marquesas island girls involved with the sailors in "every species of riot and debauchery. The grossest licentiousness and the most shameful inebriety. . . . Alas for the poor savages when exposed to the influence of these polluting examples!"

Like white travelers among the American aboriginal tribes, Melville was fascinated by the "light-hearted joyousness that everywhere prevailed," the spirit of fun and play that characterized the daily life of the Typees. They spent days playing delightedly with toy popguns that Melville made for them—"Pop, Pop, Pop, Pop, now resounded all over the valley"—as the Typees had mock wars and brilliant ambushes.

In essence the book was a simple and directly written travel-romance of a thoroughly conventional kind. When it appeared in 1846, Melville was only twenty-seven years old. It was an immediate hit and Melville had the intoxicating experience of being praised and acclaimed, of having his book read and his pocket filled with cash—not much, to be sure, but enough to convince him that his vocation was writing stories of adventure on the high seas. *Omoo,* a year later, utilized in much the same manner the Tahiti experience. It too was a success. *Mardi,* which followed, is surely one of the strangest works of fiction by an American author. The simple narrative style is gone, replaced by a wildly ornate and intricate prose and a use of symbolism so extreme as to deter all but the most determined reader. Clearly Melville had, between *Omoo* and *Mardi,* undergone some profound personal transformation. He had, for one thing, married Elizabeth Shaw, the daughter of the chief justice of Massachusetts, Richard Henry Dana's nemesis in a number of Fugitive Slave cases; it was a most advantageous marriage for a young man of "ruined fortunes." Melville nonetheless suffered more than most husbands from the "angelic wife" syndrome. Despite the unfailing devotion of Elizabeth Melville to her husband, the marriage became a cold thing to Melville, who withdrew both physically—into his dark and forbidding study—and psychologically. Marriage shattered the dream of love—"breaks love's airy zone," in Melville's words. From the ecstacies of courtship, "like the bouquet of the costliest of German wines" the daily intimacy of domestic life saw love "too often evaporate . . . in the disenchanting glasses of matrimonial days and nights." It was small wonder Melville was disenchanted. When he and his wife set up housekeeping at 103 Fourth Avenue in New York the household included two brothers, his three sisters, and his mother, not to mention numerous Boston in-laws who came to visit.

Like Thoreau, indeed like all of his contemporaries with the exception of Whitman, Melville could not cope with the sexual muddle of the nineteenth century. In his old age he wrote a remarkable poem that can be taken to be about the basic schizophrenia of his age—the sexual break. Entitled "After the Pleasure Party," it read in part:

> Could I remake me! or set free
> This sexless bound in sex, then plunge
> Deeper than Sappho, in a lunge
> Piercing Pan's paramount mystery!
> For, Nature, in no shallow surge
> Against thee either sex may urge.
> Why hast thou made us but in halves—
> Co-relative? This makes us slaves.
> If these co-relatives never meet
> Selfhood itself seems incomplete.
> And such the dicing of blind fate
> Few matching halves here meet and mate.
> What Cosmic jest or Anarch blunder
> The human integral clove asunder
> And shied the fractions through life's gate?
>
> Now first I feel, what all may ween,
> That soon or late, if faded e'en,
> One's sex asserts itself . . .
> Hence the winged blaze that sweeps my soul
> Like prairie fires that spurn control,
> Where withering weeds incense the flame
> And kept I long heaven's watch for this,
> Condemning love, for this, even this?

In *Mardi* the hero, Yoomy, and a companion escape from their whaling ship—America? civilization?—and encounter and commandeer an abandoned, drifting vessel on which they set off in search of Yillah, a maiden from Orollis, the Island of Delight. From Alma and Sereniz (the Kingdom of God) they visit Borabolla, a native sage. They discuss the most arcane and erudite subjects with a succession of fantastic characters they meet on their way. The "novel" is interspersed with philosophical digressions. The narrator, or Yoomy, declares: "all generations are blended, and heaven and earth of one kin; the hierarchies of seraphs in the uttermost skies; the thrones and principalities of the zodiac; the shades that roam throughout space; the nations and families, flocks and folds of the earth; one and all, brothers in essence. . . . All things form but one whole;

the universe a Judea, and God Jehovah its head. . . . Let us compose ourselves to death as fagged horsemen sleep in the saddle. . . . No custom is strange; no creed is absurd; no foe, but who will in the end prove a friend," and much more.

To say that such interjections impede the narrative is to misstate the case; they are obviously where Melville's heart is. America appears as Vivanza—"though now in childhood, she anticipates her youth, and lusts for empire like any czar. . . . Many books and many long, long chapters are wanting to Vivanza's history; and what history is but full of blood." The reference is clearly to the United States imperial venture in Mexico. The United States is possessed and obsessed by gold and valuable ores—"the only poverty. . . . But man will still mine for it; and mining, dig his doom. . . . Shrieks and groans! cries and curses! It seems a golden Hell! . . . Oh, bitter end to all our hopes, we die in golden graves." And again, " 'Oh, curse of commerce!' cried Babbalanja, 'that it barters souls for gold.' " The book rushes to an almost incomprehensible climax. The searchers for Yillah, frustrated, turn back for Serenia, "our haven." But Yoomy and his companion leap overboard and strike out for land, pursued by the others, "And thus, pursuers and pursued flew on, over an endless sea."

Chloroform and marijuana were, as we have noted in the case of George Templeton Strong, popular drugs with young upper-class New Yorkers in this era, and it is hard to escape the suspicion that Melville, taking a clue from Coleridge (after all "over an endless sea" has a definite Coleridgean ring to it), had given rein to his fantasies under their influence.

In any event, strange as it is, *Mardi* is the essential precursor to *Moby Dick*. It is as though, having tried the style of the straight adventure narrative and found it impossibly confining, Melville broke out into a mad "space" of his own and then pulled back, startled and disconcerted by what he had wrought but nonetheless tantalized by the strangeness. The next two novels, *Redburn* in the same year, 1849, and *White-Jacket* the next year, were "realistic" in their depiction of life at sea and in the swarming, malodorous seaports that were in such sharp contrast to the purity and "cleanness" of the ocean. Obviously owing a good deal to Richard Henry Dana's *Two Years Before the Mast*, *White-Jacket* is the sociology of an American naval vessel and a bitter indictment of the practice of flogging so common on navy ships in Melville's day. Still, the symbols are here as well. The narrator's white canvas jacket, fashioned by his own hands, is both his burden and his salvation. The seed of *Moby Dick* is there in the marvelous manner in which Melville, like Dana before him, turns enumeration into art; and the seed of *Billy Budd* when White-Jacket, threatened with an unjust flogging, determines to kill the captain and then himself rather than submit.

Taking refuge at Lenox with his wife, Melville plunged on into *Moby Dick,* confident that he had at last found a middle ground between the wild fantasies and extravagant symbolism of *Mardi* and the magic of the specific and practical that he had explored in *White-Jacket.* It was there he sought out Hawthorne, who was writing *The Scarlet Letter,* entranced by the older man's explorations of the "dark sphere" and by Hawthorne's awareness of the devouring appetites of the ego, the "supreme" individual.

While he was working on *Moby Dick* in the spring of 1851, Melville took time to write to Hawthorne, who had returned home. The letters demonstrate very vividly the alternating moods of euphoria and despair Melville was experiencing. "Though I wrote the Gospels in this century," he declared, "I should die in the gutter.—I talk all about myself, and this is selfishness and egotism. . . . The reason the mass of men fear God, and *at bottom dislike* Him, is because they rather distrust His heart, and fancy Him all brain like a watch." In a piercing sentence from another letter, he wrote, "My development has been all within a few years past. I am like one of those seeds taken out of the Egyptian Pyramids, which, after being three thousand years a seed and nothing but a seed, being planted . . . grew to greenness and then fell to mould. So I."

The year of the writing of *Moby Dick* was the most arduous of Melville's life. Back in New York, his strength and energy failed him as he finished the book, sitting at his desk, in the words of his wife, "all day not eating anything until four or five o'clock." He walked or cut wood for exercise. His eyes began to fail him. He wrote a friend, "I keep one eye shut and wink at the paper with the other." And again, "My evening I spend in a sort of mesmeric state in my room—being unable to read." Several times he fainted in the street from excitement and fatigue.

After *Moby Dick* was published and Hawthorne had read and praised it, Melville wrote: "I feel that the Godhead is broken up like the bread at the Supper, and that we are the pieces. Hence this infinite fraternity of feeling. . . . My dear Hawthorne, the atmospheric skepticisms steal into me now, and make me doubtful of my sanity in writing you thus. . . . Lord, when shall we be done changing? Ah, it's a long stage, and no inn in sight, and the night coming, and the body cold. But with you for a passenger, I am content and can be happy. . . . Knowing you persuades me more than the Bible of our immortality." Melville's friendship with Hawthorne, one-sided as it was, enabled him to survive.

Mardi, however eccentric, had been a private and necessary exploration for Melville. Yillah may be interpreted as the American dream of democratic innocence, of progress and perfectability, of earthly redemption. The Mexican War was, for Melville, as for so many of his generation, the rude shattering of that dream. Yillah, on her Island of Delight, was not to be found. *Moby Dick* was the sequel. Ahab was the pursuing ego, grown monstrous and obsessive and, finally, destructively mad chasing the white whale: white, the symbol of purity, the dream of perfection, the dream pursued that turned into a crippling reality, the reality of America, the fate of all extravagant dreams not anchored in the excruciating contradictions of the human condition. The vision is so passionate and powerful that it soars above any pat "symbol system" and seems at last to include a universe which widens out to take in Yankee and Southerner, black man and Indian. The rhetoric, so dense and daunting in *Mardi,* comes back to earth and provides a welcome counterpoint to the details of a whaling vessel's own splendidly intricate economy. Like the end of *Mardi,* the end of *Moby Dick* finds only Ishmael left of the ill-fated ship and crew, Ishmael and the white whale. Whatever Moby Dick represents—the vision of American innocence, evil, the ego—the vast animal seems large enough to bear them all on his scarred white back.

What was left of Melville's reputation with the reading public was destroyed by *Moby Dick.* Few critics praised it and few people bought it. The common response was of indifference or hostility. "Dollars damn me," Melville wrote to Hawthorne, "and the malicious Devil is forever grinning in upon me, holding the door ajar. . . . What I feel most moved to write, that is banned—it will not pay. Yet, altogether, write the *other* way I cannot." Later he wrote, "Try to get a living by the Truth—and go to the Soup Societies."

It is worth noting that what were perhaps the three most powerful literary works of the century—*Two Years Before the Mast, Moby Dick,* and *Leaves of Grass*—were characterized by a common obsession with the facts—what Charles Francis Adams called "the eloquence of facts." It was always an American appetite—how things worked, their names and functions, their shapes and philosophical dimensions or intimations. The best of democracy grasped life in all its astonishing specificity. The vastest generalizations began with an ax or a plow, a steam-engine valve or the filling of a sail.

Despite the general exhaustion occasioned by the writing of *Moby Dick*, Melville followed it a year later by one of the most remarkable novels of the nineteenth century, *Pierre, or the Ambiguities. Pierre* is both an intensely autobiographical novel and an exploration of the "ambiguities" or paradoxes of American life. It is a novel of falsity and illusion. Nothing is what it appears to be. Pierre Glendenning's mother, still comparatively young and still beautiful, who is clearly in large part Melville's mother, plays at being his sister rather than his mother. Although Pierre is engaged to a lovely girl, he meets and falls in love with a young woman who appeals to him for help and turns out to be his half-sister, the illegitimate child of his sainted father who was thought to have been above all evil doing. All Pierre's efforts at noble and high-minded—"moral"—behavior simply serve to sink him deeper into a terrible quagmire of deceit and despair. He decides to marry his "sister" Isobel in order to protect her. His fiancée, Lucy, not surprisingly, goes into a decline and his mother throws him out. The most powerful moment in the novel comes with Mary Glendenning's rejection of her son. His suffering counts for nothing in the face of her "immense pride;—her pride of birth, her pride of affluence, her pride of purity, and all the pride of high-born, refined, and wealthy Life. . . ." Pierre comes to understand the "strange transition from the generous impulsiveness of youth to the provident circumspection of age . . . very slow to feel, deliberate even in love, and statistical even in piety."

Pierre ends up in New York City with both women on his hands. He has a brief spectacular success as the author of an epic poem, which encourages him to fancy himself a writer. But his next effort is demolished by the critics. Lucy's brother and her suitor, Glen, Pierre's cousin, track him down. Glen, who had profited from Pierre's misfortunes, accuses him of ruining the lives of Lucy and Isobel and attacks him. Pierre draws a pistol and shoots his cousin, crying, "For thy one blow, take here two deaths! 'Tis speechless sweet to murder thee!" Arrested and jailed, Pierre is visited by Lucy and Isobel. Lucy dies, presumably of grief, and Pierre and Isobel drink poison. The ending is so macabre as to be almost absurd. It is saved only by the intensity of Melville's own feeling.

Owing a good deal to Carlyle (whose influence on Melville's style was, *Moby Dick* aside, rather a disaster) and to Hawthorne, *Pierre* was characterized by the same flights of philosophizing that are so large a part of *Mardi*. We are hardly into *Pierre* before we encounter the following passage: "The monarchial world very generally imagines, that in demagoguical America the sacred Past has no fixed statues erected to it, but all things irreverently seethe and boil in the vulgar caldron of an everlasting uncrystalizing Present." Such a notion is, to a degree, an illusion but it is true, "that with no chartered aristocracy" it is difficult in the extreme for "any family in America [to] imposingly perpetuate itself." In consequence, "political institutions, which in other lands seem above all things intensely artificial, with America seem to possess the divine virtue of a natural law, for the most mighty of nature's laws is this, that out of Death she brings Life." Clearly a major theme of the novel is the precariousness by which the American upper class holds on to its privileges.

Good is infused with evil. "Why," the narrator asks, "in the noblest marble pillar that stands beneath the all-comprising vault, ever should we descry the sinister vein? We lie in nature very close to God; and though, further on, the stream may be corrupted by the banks it flows through; yet at the fountain's rim, where mankind stand, there the stream infallibly bespeaks the fountain." Life, far from being the simple, happy journey of the fulfilled and expanding self that the transcendentalists depicted, was filled with tragedy. "Gloom and grief" were "the selectest chamberlains to knowledge? Wherefore is it, that not to know Gloom and Grief is not to know aught that an heroic man should learn."

Melville's war with the transcendentalists' sunny view of the world was not covert. Not only did they contemplate the picturesque of the landscape, they were charmed by "the *povertiresque* in the social landscape and entertained themselves by *povertiresquely* diversifying those snug little cabinet-pictures of the world, which exquisitely varnished and framed, are hung up in the drawing-room minds of humane men of taste, and amiable philosophers of the 'Compensation' or 'Optimist' school. They deny that any misery is in the world except for the purpose of throwing the fine *povertiresque* element into its general picture. Go to! God hath deposited cash in the Bank subject to our gentlemanly order. . . ." It is a bitter and revealing passage. In the end it becomes evident to Pierre that men's most ingenious devices cannot hold off the terrors of life, "For there is no faith, and no stoicism, and no philosophy, that a mortal man can possibly evoke, which will stand the final test of a real impassioned onset of Life and Passion upon him."

Americans have never responded warmly to "prophets of doom" as we have been disposed to call them—individuals who were bold enough to suggest that the world was considerably more complex than our official creed held it to be. Nor has the American tolerance for ambiguity ever been high. Thus *Pierre, or the Ambiguities* disappeared from sight even more quickly and completely than *Moby Dick,* which always had a small company of admirers made up largely of people fascinated by whales.

In the defeat of *Moby Dick* and *Pierre,* Melville went traveling once more, seeking Hawthorne, who was comfortably ensconced in his post as United States consul at Liverpool. When Melville arrived with "a little bit of a bundle" containing a nightshirt and a toothbrush, Hawthorne found him "looking much as he used to do (a little paler, and perhaps a little sadder) [Melville did not age in the manner of other men] . . . with his characteristic gravity and reserve of manner." Hawthorne was not surprised that Melville stood in need of refreshment "after so many years of toilsome penlabor and domestic life, following so wild and adventurous a youth as his was." They walked together and sat in a hollow in the sand dunes "(sheltering ourselves from the high, cold wind) and smoked a cigar" and Melville, "as he always does, began to reason of Providence and futurity, and of everything that lies beyond human ken, and informed me that he had 'pretty much made up his mind to be annihilated'; but still he does not seem to rest in that anticipation; and, I think, will never rest until he gets hold of a definite belief. It is strange how he persists . . . in wandering to-and-fro over these deserts, as dismal and monotonous as the sand hills among which we are sitting. He can neither believe or be comfortable in his unbelief and he is too honest and courageous not to try to do one or the other . . . he has a very high and noble nature, and better worth immortality than most of us."

Hawthorne's son, Julian, wrote in the same vein: "There was a vivid genius in this man, and he was the strangest being that ever came into our circle. Through all his wild and reckless adventures, of which a small part only got into his fascinating books, he had been unable to rid himself of a Puritan conscience. . . . He was restless and disposed to dark hours, and there is reason to suspect that there was in him a vein of insanity."

Back from his hegira, Melville took up the onerous task of earning a living for his family. In debt and unemployed, he was reduced to living on a kind of dole provided by his wealthy uncles and father-in-law. He wrote a better than pot-boiling novel in 1855 about a real American hero of the Revolutionary War named Israel Potter. He lectured a bit and after almost a decade of hand-to-mouth existence for himself and his family, he got a job through political wire pulling as a customs inspector, a job which he held for almost twenty years. He wrote, for the most part, rather wooden poetry and, over the next thirty-five years, a series of short stories including the brilliant "Benito Cereno," "Bartleby, the Scrivener" and "The Encantadas." In 1888 Elizabeth Melville inherited a modest fortune from her family and Melville, then sixty-nine, retired and spen the remaining three years of his life writing, the most notable consequence being the novella *Billy Budd,* not published until 1925. America quite forgot him.

An English admirer of Melville, visiting New York in 1885, wrote: "I sought everywhere for this Triton, who is still living somewhere in New York. No one seemed to know anything of the one great writer fit to stand shoulder to shoulder with Whitman on that continent."

The comparison was an apt one. *Moby Dick* and *Leaves of Grass* are the two preeminently American literary works that stand among the masterpieces of world literature (along, of course, with *Huck Finn*). Whitman wrote the central and essential *Leaves* between 1855 and 1860. Melville wrote eight novels in the years from 1846 to 1855, the culmination being *Moby Dick* (the sixth). The five books that had preceded *Moby Dick* brought Melville $8,069.34, perhaps ten times that sum in present-day currency but little enough for the fierce labor that had gone into their creation. Such intensity clearly could not be sustained.

The democratic artist-writer was a new phenomenon in the world. He made new rules, responded to new imperatives, suffered new agonies. But why that incredible effusion, that wild outpouring of literary expression in the period 1850 to 1855: *A Week on the Concord and Merrimack Rivers* was published in 1849, *Walden* was published in 1854, *The Scarlet Letter* in 1850, *The House of Seven Gables* in 1851, *Moby Dick* in 1851, *Uncle Tom's Cabin* (which I insist belongs in that illustrious company) in 1852, *Leaves of Grass* in 1855? One feels that was hardly chance. What, then, was it—a conjunction of the planets? The intervention of the Almighty? Or the sense of crisis in the air as the nation rushed to the terrible day of judgment in the Civil War? Or none or all of these?

There is also the so-called second-generation phenomenon; the theory that it takes two generations after an event of profound significance such as the American Revolution for it to be translatable into art. By this notion the experience has to sink down to a certain substratum of the subconscious and then rise up as a kind of "natural" emanation. (James said that "it takes a great deal of history to produce a little literature.") The artists came first; they made the necessary integrations earlier. Their task was, one suspects, less formidable. The writers had to be released from the inhibiting constraints of European canons and standards. Emerson played a critical role in this release in two ways. First, in his Phi Beta Kappa address, he threw down a challenge to all American artists of the brush or pen to free themselves from English and European forms and models. "The Puritanism that cannot die, the Puritanism that made New England what it is, and is destined to make America what it should be, found its voice in Emerson," Lowell wrote. The author of *A Fable for Critics* called the Phi Beta Kappa address "an event without any formal parallel in our literary annals. . . . It was our Yankee version of a lecture by Abelard. . . . The Transcendental Movement was the protestant spirit of Puritanism seeking a new outlet and an escape from forms and creeds which compressed rather than expressed it."

Above all there was the fact that Emerson created or drew attention to the all-inclusive "I," to the "supremacy of the Individual," as Whitman put it. In doing so he created a new American category. The Protestant "I" had found its meaning and its focus in the congregation of the faithful, the literary expression of which was the Puritan diary or "soul ledger" where the moral accounts were kept. Emerson legitimated the "I," the "self" as the subject-object of art. The "Song of Myself" was the most spectacular consequence. Hawthorne aside, the rest were all liberated "I's." Thoreau was an unvarnished, unmistakable "I" as well as an "eye," and Melville was a thinly disguised "I."

Such effusions in the form of art may be assumed to follow the articulation of a new human type. All the pent-up anguish of trying to cope with what it meant to be an American was released, one suspects, by making the "I" not simply respectable, but the measure of everything. Hawthorne's literary contemporaries doubtless had such deep respect for him because he was the least of the "I's," the most genuine artist; the most complete creator of literature. He had his own "self" under astonishing control, especially compared with the agonized "self" of a Whitman or a Melville or, indeed, a Thoreau. The others were prophets, saviors, pronouncers of American salvation or doom, writers of the new Scriptures, wrestlers with the untamed psyche of America.

Perhaps the major point to make about the writers we have been considering, more specifically Emerson, Whitman, Thoreau, and Melville, is that they explored a new territory of the American psyche. The self broke free of its conventional religious constraints *but not of its moral constraints* and hung for a long moment above the continent, coruscating brilliantly, illuminating every detail of the immense landscape; then, if it did not exactly sputter out, it lost the splendid luminosity that came from the tension inherent in the profoundly ambiguous notion of "the self." The "I" turned out to be astonishingly ephemeral. It could not be sustained. There was even the shadow of suspicion that there was no "I," simply social and historical man in various and multiform manifestations.

53

The Historians

Americans have always had a special relationship to history. Other peoples have commonly been defined by culture, but America, from the beginning, was made up of such diverse nationalities that our only common denominator was our shared past, or history. To an unprecedented degree our history has been not only our identity but a form of explanation. The nature or character of other nations has generally been the consequence of centuries and sometimes millennia of cultural accumulation. America appeared instantly, as it were, in world history. (In a TV skit some years back, Dean Martin, playing George Washington, urged Betsy Ross to make haste in finishing the American flag because "the country starts tomorrow.")

Innumerable historical societies sprang up after the Revolution to preserve the records of that momentous episode and the events that preceded it. A half-dozen histories of the Revolution were written within a decade or so after the end of the war, the best of them David Ramsay's *History of the American Revolution*, later incorporated into his *Universal History*. John Marshall wrote his multivolumed *Life of Washington*, in effect a history of the Revolution; and there was a spate of state histories, some of them, like Jeremy Belknap's *History of New Hampshire*, first-rate works.

After the first flurry, there was a historical hiatus. From 1800 to the early 1830s the writing of history in America languished. The same romantic mood that disposed Washington Irving to write about the conquest of Granada or the life of Columbus militated against histories of the United States. The common view was that, except for the West, the mundane, commercial life of the states was poor material for history. Just as poets like Longfellow and Bryant chose classical or medieval subjects for their narrative poems, American historians chose remote, romantic, and picturesque subjects.

The dean of American writers of history was William Hickling Prescott, a member of the charmed circle of Boston's aristocracy. He was the grandson of William Prescott, the hero of Bunker Hill. Prescott, who was born in 1796, graduated from Harvard at the age of eighteen with badly impaired sight, the result of being hit in the eyes with a piece of bread thrown by a fellow student during a scuffle in the college dining commons. Prescott decided on a career as a scholar. Having settled on history as his field, he began a remarkable regimen of study. Since his eyesight was so bad, he had often to be read to but his program of listening included most of the important classical and modern English authors, prominent among them Tacitus, Livy and Cicero, Sir Philip Sidney, Francis Bacon, and Milton. Prescott then went on to master French, Spanish, Italian, and German, determining finally that his subject would be the Spanish conquest of America. He ordered from Spain more than a hundred books that he considered essential to such a work and employed an amanuensis named English to read aloud to him. As general background material, Prescott listened to Montesquieu's *Spirit of the Laws*, Adam Smith's *Wealth of Nations*, the concluding four volumes of Gibbon's *Decline and Fall of the Roman Empire*, the *Meditations of Marcus Aurelius*, and a dozen other works, not directly related to his projected history. His first venture was a history of the reign of Ferdinand and Isabella. In the midst of his labors, he wrote in his journal: "Preserve a calm, philosophical, elevated way of thinking on all subjects connected with the action of life. Think more seriously of the consequences of conduct. Cherish devotional feelings of reliance on the Deity. Discard a habit of sneering or scepticism. Do not attempt impossibilities, or, in other words, to arrive at certainty on questions of historic evidence . . . and [remember] that the great laws for our moral government are laid down with undeniable, unimpeachable truth."

In 1838 the *History of Ferdinand and Isabella* was published in three volumes and was an immediate success. In Tichnor's words, "A success so brilliant had never before been reached in so short a time by any work of equal size and gravity on this side of the Atlantic." It was perceived by American (and indeed by English) reviewers as having great symbolic importance. It marked American scholarship's coming of age, a work of history on a grand scale, worthy of a place beside the greatest disciples of Cleo, the Muse of History. Philip Hone was among those who considered the book a definitive answer to the sneer of the English critic Sidney Smith: "Who ever reads an American book?"

Fighting rheumatism and partial paralysis as well as continual discomfort from his eyes, Prescott began work on the *Conquest of Mexico,* which appeared in 1843, followed four years later by the *Conquest of Peru.*

Prescott viewed the writing of history as primarily a literary undertaking: "a man's style, to be worth anything," he wrote, "should be the natural expression of his mental character." Style, then, was essential in a historical work. It should be improving and teach a lesson. The lesson for Prescott was that history was the unfolding of God's purpose. Man was the agent of the Almighty. The Almighty was benign and he intended the progress of the race. Thus the Spanish Arabs must give way to the rise of Christian Spain, a higher stage in the progressive development of human society. Similarly, the Aztecs, brilliant as their civilization was, must give way to the superior culture of Christian Spain. Spain must, in turn, be eclipsed by the more humane and enlightened doctrines of the Reformation. "Folded under the dark wing of the Inquisition, Spain was shut out from the light which in the sixteenth century broke out over the rest of Europe, stimulating the nations to greater enterprise in every department of knowledge. . . . How could there be freedom of thought, where there was no freedom of utterance? . . . Every way the mind of the Spaniard was in fetters."

Among the Aztecs the power of the priesthood spelled the downfall of the civilization. "The influence of the priesthood must be greatest," Prescott wrote, "in an imperfect state of civilization, where it engrosses all the scanty science of the time in its own body."

Prescott was soon a literary lion. When he visited New York, he was entertained with a splendid dinner at the home of the philanthropist and patron of the arts Moses Grinnell. Philip Hone described him as a "rather handsome man of about six and forty, of intellectual appearance, good manners, agreeable conversation, and much vivaci-

ty." Clergy were prominent at the Grinnell dinner attended by Hone:
"—Episcopalian, Presbyterian, and Unitarian, high church and low
church, Puseyite and liberal," Hone wrote. "It was a pleasant reunion;
all the literary men of the city were there, all the distinguished men;
the learned and wise, by their own estimate or that of their compeers,
were assembled to honor the man who had raised so proud a
monument of the literary glory of his native country."

George Bancroft was another Bostonian born with a silver spoon
in his mouth. He graduated from Harvard in 1817 and followed his
friend George Tichnor, nine years his senior, to the University of
Göttingen, where, as we have noted earlier, he was deeply influenced
by the new German science of history with its intensive and systematic
examination of every shred of historical evidence. Bancroft wished to
wed it to the American concern for the moral bases of all action. A
born reformer and radical Democrat, Bancroft found it hard going in
Whig Boston when he returned from Europe. He taught at Harvard
for a year, but his zeal for educational and social reform irritated his
superiors and he was not reappointed. His next venture was to start a
progressive boys' school—the Round Hill School at Northampton—
where his most notable pupil was another proper Bostonian, John
Lothrop Motley. It was at Round Hill that the notion possessed him of
writing a large-scale history of the United States, the first volume of
which appeared in 1834. In his introduction, Bancroft explained his
purpose. "The United States of America," he wrote, "constitute an
essential portion of a great political system, embracing all the civilized
nations of the earth." At a time in history when "the force of moral
opinion" was "rapidly increasing," the United States had in its
particular charge "the practice and defence of the equal rights of
man." Bancroft was active in Democratic politics, a staunch Jackson
man. No one knew better than he the tensions and divisions that
characterized American society, but he chose to sound a note of
undiminished optimism. The prosperity of the United States was the
consequence of "even justice; invention is quickened by the freedom of
competition; and labor rewarded with sure and unexampled returns."
The relationship of the United States to other nations was characterized by "equality and honest friendship. . . . Every man may enjoy the
fruits of his industry; every mind is free to publish its convictions. . . .
There is no national debt; the community is opulent; the government economical. . . . Intelligence is diffused with unparalleled
universality. . . ." On went the litany of glories. It was Bancroft's task,

as he saw it, to "explain how the change in the condition of our land has been accomplished . . . to follow the steps by which a favoring Providence, calling our institutions into being, has conducted the country to its present happiness and glory."

Bancroft proceeded to do just that in nine substantial volumes, stopping, perhaps conveniently, just short of the Treaty of Paris. In fairness to Bancroft, it must be said that by the time he had finished his tenth and final volume, almost thirty years later, he sounded a more somber note. In the introduction to his last volume, he wrote, "It is good to look away from the strifes of the present hour, to the great days when our country had for its statesmen Washington and John Adams, Jefferson and Hamilton, Franklin and Jay. . . . the study of those times will always teach lessons of moderation and unselfish patriotism." There are certainly dangers in undertaking a history the execution of which will extend over more than three decades. Bancroft's *History* did two things: It projected the image of a virtually unblemished nation, thus reminding us that a kind of patriotic euphoria survived into the early 1830s; and it established the notion, at the end, that the great days of the Revolution and the Founding Fathers existed as a golden age for later Americans to try to emulate despite the drastic decline in the moral temper of the republic.

Cut on the streets of Boston by old friends because of his political views, Bancroft became an influential party manager, the promoter of Polk's presidential ambitions, and secretary of the navy, in which role he established the Naval Academy at Annapolis. After eighteen months in office, Bancroft resigned as secretary to accept the office of ambassador to the Court of St. James's. His history was enormously popular. Like Prescott's works (although it must be said Bancroft lacked Prescott's brilliance of style), Bancroft's volumes described a progressive movement in history and saw the United States as the agent of the divine purpose. Far more than any other work, it determined his countrymen's view of their past. That it was not universally applauded is indicated by an entry in the diary of Sidney George Fisher. Fisher, doubtlessly offended by Bancroft's democratic politics, found it "poor stuff, filled with unnecessary details, without just thought, factitious in sentiment, weak, tawdry & diffuse in style. A miserable performance truly. . . . He spins it out because he sells it by the volume." On the other hand when Bancroft gave an address before the New York Historical Society on "The Necessity, the Reality, and the Promise of the Progress of the Human Race," George Templeton

Strong, no admirer of the historian, was ready to admit it raised him "into a far higher sphere than I thought he could attain. . . ."

As the historian of the Secular-Democratic Consciousness, Bancroft was convinced that "the spirit of God breathes through the combined intelligence of the people." Nothing came to America of the demoralizing aspects of decadent European culture. Only "free people . . . separating itself from all other elements of previous civilization; the people, self-confiding and industrious; the people, wise by all traditions that favored popular happiness—the people alone broke away from European influence, and in the New World laid the foundations of our republic. . . . The people alone were present in power."

Richard Hildreth, born in Deerfield, Massachusetts, in 1807, was still another Harvard-educated historian very much in the Bancroft style. An abolitionist and temperance crusader and a monetary reformer, he wrote the antislavery tract *Despotism in America,* of which we have already taken note. He began his own history of America and published it between 1848 and 1852 in six volumes, later writing three more which carried the history through the administration of Monroe. In the introduction, Hildreth declared that it was his intention to present the founders of the nation "unbedaubed with patriotic rouge, wrapped up in no fine-spun cloaks of excuses and apology, without stilts, buskins, tinsel, or bedizenment, in their own proper person, often rude, hard, narrow, superstitious, and mistaken, but always earnest, downright, manly, and sincere . . . their best apology is to tell their story exactly as it was." Hildreth, like Bancroft, made much of the fact that he had depended primarily on "the original authorities, particularly laws, state papers, public documents, and official records, printed and manuscript," as well as "numerous valuable collections of letters and memoirs." Hildreth intended "to sketch the story even to the present times" but the task proved too extensive for him. A self-imposed austerity of style cost Hildreth readers and his work suffered by comparison with Bancroft's livelier narrative.

John Lathrop Motley was, like Prescott and Bancroft before him, a Boston Brahmin. Born in 1814, he graduated from Harvard in 1831 and, like so many of his fellows, traveled abroad to study in Germany and England. With an assured income from his family's fortune, he indulged himself in writing two minor novels, and then, after a period of service as secretary of the American legation in St. Petersburg, decided, influenced by Prescott, to devote himself to the career of historian. He chose as his general topic the story of the rise of the Dutch Republic against the tyranny of Philip V of Spain. When the history was published in 1856 in New York and London, it was a striking popular and critical success, strengthening the view that the writing of history was a particularly congenial field for American authors. The popularity of the work was increased by the fact that it was a dramatic story of the triumph of republican and Protestant principles, in the persons of the Dutch, over tyrannical and Catholic principles in the person of Philip. Like Prescott's histories, those of Motley were characterized by a brilliant narrative style. They were both absorbing reading and instructive lessons in the superiority of a free over an autocratic society.

Francis Parkman was yet another proper Bostonian. Born into a well-to-do family in 1823, he absorbed the new ethic of nature, camping, hiking, and exploring the rivers and lakes of New England. He graduated from Harvard and acquired a law degree. During the more or less obligatory European tour, he climbed Vesuvius with Theodore Parker, who, looking into the active volcano, exclaimed, "What stock in trade for an orthodox minister!" Back in the United States, Parkman suffered from bad health and bad "nerves." He therefore set out for Oregon, seeking both a cure and firsthand information about the Indians, whose chronicler he had decided to become. There is evidence that Parkman suffered from a crippling neurosis. He was certainly a hypochondriac, constantly dosing himself with dubious medicines and faithfully recording his various pains, real and imaginary. He was accompanied on his western journey by his cousin, Quincy Adams Shaw, and the two young men took dangerous risks by going among many of the more warlike and unpredictable Indian tribes virtually alone rather than putting up with the company of crude and uncultivated emigrants. The Indians were natural aristocrats, Parkman believed, the American whites lower-class barbarians. Through the good offices of a son-in-law of a chief of the Oglala Sioux, Parkman was able to spend three weeks in a Sioux village. An acute observer and a lively writer, he gained insights into Indian life and character that gave a special vividness and authenticity to his great work on *France in the New World*. The Indian, he wrote, "lives in constant fear. The world, to him, is full of spirits—or of the Great Spirit manifested in a thousand forms. He is surrounded with evil and with good—every voice of nature has its hidden meaning to his ear."

After his return from Oregon, Parkman published *The California and The Oregon Trail* (1849), which gave an intimation of his historical powers. Like Prescott, he had severe trouble with his eyes and often had to have books read to him when his eyes were too inflamed for him to read. Working under conditions of the greatest difficulty (he had to devise a stylus with wires to guide his hand in writing), Parkman published *The History of the Conspiracy of Pontiac* in 1851. Seven volumes followed before his death, all dealing with the French in America and together establishing his claim as America's premier historian.

In sharp contrast to Bancroft and Hildreth, Parkman was a thoroughgoing conservative who shared the hostility of such members of his class as Sidney George Fisher and George Templeton Strong for democracy and materialism. He expressed strong doubts "that the rule of the masses is consistent with the highest growth of the individual; that democracy can give the world a civilization as mature and pregnant, ideas as energetic and vitalizing, and types of manhood as lofty and strong, as any of the systems which it boasts to supplant."

But if Parkman was a conservative he was also a moralist. England won out over France in the New World because England represented "Liberty" and France "Absolutism . . . the one an unflinching champion of the Roman Catholic reaction; the other the vanguard of the Reform. Each followed its natural laws of growth, and each came to its natural result. . . . England imposed by the sword on reluctant Canada the boon of rational and ordered liberty. Through centuries of striving she had advanced from stage to stage of progress, deliberate and calm . . . enlarging popular liberties while bating nothing of that height and force of individual development which is the brain and heart of civilization. . . ."

All of our historians were well-to-do, upper-class New Englanders and Harvard graduates. Two overcame, heroically, tremendous physical handicaps. They were determined moralists, all resolutely Protestant and aggressively anti-Catholic. They were also thoroughgoing romantics sharing an infatuation with dramatic scenes, with heroes and heroines and feudal pomp and circumstance (Hildreth was, to be sure, an exception on the latter point).

It might be said that the historians of the first half of the nineteenth century defined America elliptically, by indirection. Unwilling or unable to deal with the United States *per se* they concentrated their attention on Spain, France, and British colonial America. Here things were far less ambiguous, far more malleable under the historian's shaping hand. It was American history by extrapolation. If it could be made clear that the United States was the culmination of a progressive process, the dilemmas that the history of the republic since 1789 posed could be avoided. In this respect the changes in Bancroft's tone from his opening to his closing volume are especially significant. America had only history to define it, only common memories to hold it together against the persistently disintegrative forces of American life. But those memories could not be too recent, it seemed. Where Francis Parkman, a conservative Whig, and George Bancroft, a radical Democrat, met was on the common ground of a colonial past, on the meaning of which both could agree. The victory of England over France and Spain was a victory of liberty over absolutism. What happened subsequently turned out to be far more complicated. That dangerous ground was better left to journalists and politicians.

While modern standards of research in original sources had developed, the historians still thought of themselves primarily as literary figures. Above all, they wrote for "a public." Without readers they had no claim on the ancient and honorable title of historian.

54

The United States and
the World

One of the central propositions of this work is the interrelatedness of the United States and the rest of the world, the notion that the United States is, in a sense, "the world." During the Revolution Americans constantly used the word "universal" as a kind of prefix to the notion of the revolution—any change that they anticipated. America, to use the phrase of a modern British critic, was the proponent of "revolutionary universalism." Samuel Thacher in his Fourth of July oration in 1797 had declared: "All hail, coming revolutions," and reminded his audience that they met to celebrate "the consequent emancipation of a world." Jedediah Morse, in much the same spirit, wrote a *Universal Geography,* and David Ramsay a *Universal History.* But the revolution, or revolutions, were supposed to be *Christian* revolutions. The aggressive atheism of the French Revolution—not to mention the bloody and disastrous course of the French upheaval—gave revolutions in general a bad name for pious Americans. The rise of the Holy Alliance and the consolidation of European thrones encouraged a spirit of withdrawal in the United States, a disposition to see Europe as hopelessly sunk in depravity and reactionary politics. That mood of disassociation had been dissipated by the dramatic Greek struggle for independence which had drawn

Lord Byron and Samuel Gridley Howe as well as thousands of other "freedom fighters" from Europe and America.

In the year 1848, a wild, revolutionary fever swept over Europe. In Great Britain, the Young Ireland Party, founded eight years earlier by Daniel O'Connell, turned from political agitation to political assassination and arson as techniques for securing Irish independence. The right of habeas corpus was suspended in Ireland by the British government and an insurrection took place in Tipperary in July of 1848.

France, experiencing somewhat belatedly its own industrial revolution, spawned a vigorous progeny of socialist theorists—Fourier, Etienne Cabet, Louis Blanc—whose ideas, as we have seen, were carried over into the United States. A severe European depression in 1846–47 provided the radical theorists with hundreds of thousands of converts among hungry peasants and unemployed workers. A banquet scheduled to be held in Paris by opponents of Louis Philippe was forbidden by the government, and angry workers and students gathered in the streets. Barricades were erected and fighting began between soldiers and the workers. Paris was soon in the hands of the workers. Louis Philippe abdicated in favor of his grandson, the Count of Paris, who was brushed aside as a republic was proclaimed—the Second French Republic, which affirmed the right to work, promising that the government would provide, through national workshops, jobs for those without employment. For months Paris was in a political ferment as the right and left wings of the revolution struggled for dominance. The national workshops, which soon had a hundred thousand or more workers enrolled in them and served as hotbeds of radical agitation, were dissolved by the provisional assembly, and once again the workers took to the streets in bloody riots. By December an uneasy order had been restored, and in a popular election, Louis Napoleon, nephew of Bonaparte, was elected president of the Republic by an enormous majority. It was the same Louis Napoleon who, exiled in America, had frequented shabby bars.

The immediate reaction in the United States to the news of the uprising of the Paris Commune was determined to a substantial degree by party lines—Democrats for, Whigs against or skeptical. When word of the collapse of the Bourbon throne reached Winfield Scott's army in Mexico City, "there was a mass meeting," Jacob Oswandel noted, "among the officers in favor of the revolution in France. Gen. Joseph Lane was called to the chair, and he made a telling speech in regard of the revolution and the free France. The utmost enthusiasm prevailed during the whole meeting."

Elsewhere faith in America's mission to encourage worldwide revolution in the name of equality and republican government instantly revived. One of the leaders of a reform movement in the Lutheran Church, John Nevin, wrote: "All signs unite to show that the new order of world history is at hand, and the way is to be prepared for it centrally in America." The old hopes of the Revolutionary era for a universal revolution, which had died out under a succession of reactionary regimes in Europe, revived.

Early in 1848 an uprising broke out in Sicily against Austrian domination and soon spread to northern Italy. In Milan rebels forced the evacuation of the city by its Austrian garrison and Venice followed, proclaiming its own republic. Soon the whole of Italy was in a turmoil. Mazzini and Giuseppe Garibaldi, who led an insurrection in Rome, were forced to accept terms from the French, and by the summer of 1849 the revolutionary upheavals had been suppressed in Italy. The insurrection in Rome involved Margaret Fuller's husband, Angelo Ossoli.

In Hungary, part of the Hapsburg Empire, a movement for independence and parliamentary government (in place of a diet dominated by the nobility and gentry) was led by Louis Kossuth, who, encouraged by word of the uprising in Paris, made a fiery speech demanding political reform and autonomy for Hungary. The Czechs were up in arms as well and the unrest spread to Vienna itself, forcing Emperor Ferdinand of Austria to flee from the city. Moravia, Transylvania, and Dalmatia experienced their own revolutionary movements. Hungary, under Kossuth's leadership, announced the establishment of the Hungarian Republic with a liberal constitution. "Democracy is epidemic now," George Templeton Strong wrote, "and even Austria has gone mad; the mob of Vienna are erecting barricades, driving out their Emperor, and murdering obnoxious ministers in a style quite worthy of Paris itself. . . . Indecision, imbecility, and groveling fear of their subjects are the prominent features of King and Kaiser all over the continent; they shrink before the cowardly and clamorous mobs that have suddenly risen up to dispute their rule as if a supernatural enemy had appeared against them. . . ."

Unsympathetic as he was with the ideals of the revolutionaries, Strong saw that "all the energy and youth and spirit and enterprise of . . . Europe have deserted the conservative side and are clamoring for innovation and ready to fight for it, especially when backed by the ignorant, brutal, degraded masses who are ready not only to fight but to rob and murder in the glorious cause. . . ."

Hungary's freedom proved short-lived. An Austrian army invaded the country from the west while Russia attacked from the east. The Hungarian army was crushed, Kossuth fled, and thirteen Hungarian generals were executed for treason. In Berlin there was fighting in the streets between angry citizens and the soldiers of King Frederick William. A National Assembly met at Frankfurt to debate the unification of Germany and the formation of a constitution and Prussia did likewise, but a year later the movement to unite Germany under a parliamentary system had collapsed.

The consequence of the political turmoil that swept Europe in 1848–49 was an outfall of defeated revolutionaries (most of them quite moderate by present-day standards). In addition to the revolutionaries, many of the lower classes of society, people who desired only to be left alone, packed up those worldly possessions they could carry and headed for the New World.

George Templeton Strong expressed no surprise when Louis Napoleon "pricked the bladder" of the Second Republic and it "collapsed." "The sublime structure of civil liberty and social order, so often and so touchingly appealed to as evidence that at least one of the lands of the Old World was capable of self-government, have crumbled quietly down and vanished into nonentity at the first kick given it by the first ambitious man of moderate abilities who had a popular name and an army to back him. . . . It's the extinguishment of the last glimmer of constitutionalism on the Continent, the retrogression of France to absolutism and the sovereignty of a standing army." It seemed to Strong especially ironic that the overthrow of the Republic should have been carried out by a man who, "ten or twelve years ago, was a disreputable, dirty, drinking, penniless foreign prince prowling about these streets and ordered out of the bar room of the old Washington Hall . . . because he was too great a loafer to be allowed to hang about even those disreputable premises. . . ."

By early 1849 the "revolutions" from which so much had been hoped had been crushed, their leaders executed or forced to flee for their lives. Walt Whitman wrote:

> God, 'twas delicious!
> That brief, tight, glorious grip
> Upon the throats of kings.

But "bitter destruction" had followed
And frightened rulers come back:
Each comes in state, with his train,
Hangman, priest, and tax-gatherer,
Soldier, lawyer, and sycophant;
An appalling procession of locusts,
And the kings strut grandly again.

Kossuth fled to Turkey after the Republic of Hungary had been crushed by Russian troops. On the petition of Congress, President Fillmore negotiated Kossuth's release from Turkey and sent a United States naval vessel, the *Mississippi*, to bring the Hungarian hero to America. Kossuth, his family, and some fifty Hungarian and Italian fighters for freedom came aboard. When Kossuth reached the United States in the fall of 1850, he was given a welcome reminiscent of that accorded to Charles Dickens. He was greeted by delegations of German, Italian, and Spanish Americans at Staten Island and the next day convoyed to New York through a harbor filled with gaily decorated boats. When he appeared at Castle Garden the building was filled and surrounded by an enthusiastic crowd estimated to number more than a hundred thousand. It was fifteen minutes before the cheers subsided sufficiently to allow Kossuth to be heard. He had come, he acknowledged, to solicit the support, moral and monetary, of the American people to carry on the fight to liberate Hungary from Austrian rule. George Templeton Strong, who attended the meeting, wrote of him, "He is a master of the art of stump oratory, and is gifted with much tact, presence of mind, and appreciation of national character. But I recollect no instances in history where a great work has been done by platform and dinner-table oratory, or much farthered thereby. . . . But this 19th century is a peculiar period, and if great men live in it they must do their work under the conditions they find around them."

After his speech Kossuth was swept up in an endless round of parades, dinners, public appearances, and newspaper interviews. Committees from cities all over the country arrived to invite him to visit them. The abolitionists sought his ear to try to persuade him to make a public statement condemning slavery. The European Democrats, a political group made up of French, Italian, German, and Austrian immigrants, sought his support, as did a party of Cuban refugees and a society of black citizens of New York. Kossuth wished to prevail on Congress to intervene on behalf of Hungary and to warn

Russia not to interfere in her internal affairs. Above all, Kossuth wanted money. Admissions were charged to hear him speak and many patriotic and political associations gave him generous contributions.

In Washington members of Congress threw a banquet in Kossuth's honor at which Daniel Webster, secretary of state, proposed a toast to "Hungarian Independence, Hungarian Control of Her Own Destinies, and Hungary as a Distinct Nationality among the Nations of Europe." The toast, when reported in European newspapers, understandably upset the Austrians. Encouraged by the large and often wildly enthusiastic crowds that turned out in every city and hamlet he visited (the cheers, not surprisingly, were more abundant than the money), Kossuth returned to Washington and appealed secretly to German societies and associations to make aid from the United States to European revolutionaries fighting for national independence a requirement for securing their vote for all candidates for national office. Then he slipped away under an assumed name, with some ninety thousand dollars contributed by sympathetic Americans.

The furor created by Kossuth's visit may be said to have exceeded any rational expectation. Undoubtedly many Americans, Northern and Southern, profoundly disturbed at the country's internal divisions and the blot of slavery on the national escutcheon, welcomed an opportunity to reaffirm their faith in the principles of the American Revolution. Like the visit of Lafayette a quarter of a century earlier, Kossuth's visit provided the occasion for a national exercise in nostalgia. In simpler days the United States had stood as an example for the world of the possibility for national independence and republican government. All subsequent struggles for freedom were the children of that initial act. The Hungarian revolution was evidence that those ideals, tarnished as they might be in the United States, still had power in the world. That one fact was enough to make Kossuth the symbol of the vision that had inspired the Founders—a Hungarian Washington, the father of his people.

Another event in Europe that drew the attention of Americans was the Crimean War, brought on in 1854 by the determination of France and Great Britain to block Russian efforts to absorb the disintegrating Ottoman Empire. The war came before long to focus on the allied siege of Sebastopol, which exacted terrible tolls from disease as well as battle. George Templeton Strong was convinced that "the civilization of Western Europe, continental Europe, at least, is effete and worn out, like that of the Roman Empire. . . ." The Crimean War thus might shatter the old system, "introduce a new element . . . into the social life of the Old World" and even lead to "a quiet, bloodless revolution in England." In Strong's view, all that was archaic, foolish, and arrogant in English life was being demonstrated in the inefficiency and criminal waste of life occasioned by the siege. Indeed, to most Americans, the Crimean War was irrefutable evidence of the wisdom of Washington's Farewell injunction to avoid all entanglements with European politics. It increased, if that was possible, the conviction of the great mass of citizens that the United States was the model of an enlightened republic and Europe hopelessly decadent and corrupt.

Counterbalancing the idealistic fervor of the Americans who favored the cause of liberty around the world was, as we have seen in the Mexican War, a deep-seated inclination to help ourselves to every acre of land within reach. The most alluring prize, once we had stolen a substantial part of Mexico, was Cuba, with which the United States carried on an extensive trade. The large, rich, badly governed Spanish island lying just off the coast of Florida exercised an irresistible charm for many Americans. In the revolutionary year of 1848, Cuba had its own freedom fighter, Narciso López, a former Spanish general and ex-governor of Madrid. López was a magnetic if somewhat eccentric figure who found a ready ear for his plans to liberate Cuba especially among Southerners, who wished to add the island, where slavery was apparently safely ensconced, to the ranks of the slaveholding states. Polk, hearing rumors of projected expeditionary forces, put out feelers to find out if Spain might be disposed to sell the island for a hundred million dollars or so. The prompt reply to the inquiry had been that Spain, "sooner than see the island transferred to *any power* . . . would prefer seeing it sunk in the ocean."

López, thwarted in his efforts to foment a revolution, fled to the United States and began rounding up men and supplies for an invasion, or, as it was called, a filibustering expedition, but Taylor had succeeded the expansion-minded Polk and soon showed that he was determined to block the efforts of Americans to "free" Cuba. The attitude of the South was suggested by the fact that Governor John Quitman of Mississippi apparently seriously considered resigning his office to lead the expedition. Jefferson Davis was approached by López and suggested Robert E. Lee, who was inclined to accept at the cost of his army commission. After Taylor's death in 1850, Fillmore continued his policy of actively discouraging any plans for invasion. Various bands of volunteers, including six hundred from Georgia and Florida, assembling at Eastern and Gulf ports, were intercepted by federal officials and forced to turn back. But the lust for Cuba could not be that easily assuaged. Two hundred Cubans paraded in New York carrying the Cuba liberation flag and thousands of sympathetic onlookers cheered them. Early in August a force composed largely of American volunteers and led by López slipped out of New Orleans headed for Cuba. Their ship ran aground fifteen miles from Havana. Leaving his second-in-command, a Colonel Crittenden, to bring on the baggage and supplies, López started by land for the city. Crittenden was intercepted by Spanish forces and driven back, and when he and fifty-one of his men attempted to escape in longboats they were picked up by a Spanish war vessel, taken to Havana, given a summary trial, and shot in the public square. López found the Cuban people too intimidated to rise to his standard. He and his men took to the hills, but 162 of his followers, most of them American, were captured and shipped to Spain. López was turned over to the Spanish authorities and garroted.

When word of the execution of Crittenden and his men reached New Orleans a riot followed in which the Spanish consular offices were smashed and stores owned by Spaniards looted. For a time there was talk of war, but Webster, as secretary of state, was tactful and conciliatory and Spain was promised indemnity for damage done the consular offices by the mob.

French and British warships meanwhile appeared in the Gulf of Mexico to protect Cuba against further raids. To a disgusted George Templeton Strong, the liberation movement was simply "a lust after other people's productive coffee-estates, a thirst for personal property, specie, jewelry, and the like, owned by somebody else, the desire of being on the winning side in a grand period of confiscation, and larceny on a large scale."

But the acquisition of Cuba by fair means or foul remained a major preoccupation of many Southerners. Franklin Pierce declared in his inaugural address that the fears of some of the founders of the republic that the expansion of the country would imperil the republic had proved groundless. "The stars upon your banner have become nearly threefold their original number," and yet the republic was stronger than ever. "With an experience thus suggestive and cheering," Pierce continued, "the policy of my administration will not be controlled by any timid forebodings of evil from expansion." Indeed "the acquisition of certain possessions" was "essential for the preservation of the rights of commerce and the peace of the world." It is hardly surprising that with such encouragement private filibustering expeditions were soon under way against Mexico and Cuba. The President's policy on Cuba as developed in consultation with his secretary of state, William Marcy, who, the reader will recall, had, as secretary of war, been so useful to Polk in acquiring a substantial portion of Mexico, was to make clear to Spain that the United States stood ready to buy Cuba but would, in no event, permit that island to pass into the possession of any other power. In addition Spain must not interfere with American commerce in any way.

A few months later the *Black Hawk*, an American vessel which regularly carried cargo and passengers between Havana, Mobile, Alabama, and New York City, was detained in Havana by customs officials and four hundred bales of cotton seized on the grounds of improper cargo manifests. When word reached Washington, Pierce and Marcy responded by imposing a set of humiliating demands on Spain. Indemnity must be made, the officials responsible fired, and a reply made within forty-eight hours. The intention was clearly to try to force Spain into a reaction that would provide the United States with a pretext for seizing Cuba. But when Spain replied in a firm but conciliatory tone, Pierce backed off. He ordered the American ministers to England, France, and Spain—Buchanan, John Mason, and Pierre Soulé—to meet and propose a policy for the United States to follow on the question of Cuba. The product of that meeting was the Ostend Manifesto of 1854, which called for the United States to buy Cuba. The Manifesto spoke piously of the poor Cubans "now suffering under the worst of all possible governments, that of an absolute despotism"; the consequence was that it was impossible to suppress the African slave trade because corrupt Cuban officials turned their heads. But if Spain, "dead to the voice of her own interest, and actuated by stubborn pride and a false sense of honor," refused to sell Cuba, the United States in the interests of peace and justice as well as of "self-preservation" would be justified, "by every law, human and divine," in "wresting it from Spain . . . upon the very same principle that would justify an individual in tearing down the burning house of his neighbor if there were no other means of preventing the flames from destroying his own home." The Ostend Manifesto became justly famous as one of the most specious and self-serving documents in American history. The fact that one of its authors was to be the next president of the United States was a most unfavorable augury. The majority of those who read this extraordinary document were well aware that far from being concerned with the freedom of the Cubans, the South feared that Spain, under pressure from England and France, would free the slaves in Cuba, making the island a potential refuge for fugitive slaves from the Gulf states. They knew also that there was considerable agitation in the South to revive the African slave trade and that Southern planters looked with envious eyes on the fertile soil of their neighbor.

The publication of the Ostend Manifesto stirred up a tempest of opposition among Northern Congressmen and for the balance of Pierce's term the question of Cuba remained in abeyance. It is not surprising that Buchanan revived it. Indeed, his inaugural, like that of his predecessor, exuded the spirit of expansion. The country was unprecedently prosperous. There was so much money in the treasury that it seemed merely common sense to use some of it to build a "military road" to the Pacific Coast lest that region come to feel neglected. Buchanan also revived the notion of a canal across the Isthmus of Panama. While we should preserve a spirit of "Christian benevolence" toward our neighbors of Central and South America, it was also true that the perpetual political unrest in Mexico was a sore trial to the patience of the United States. We should never interfere in the "domestic concerns" of any member of the "great family of nations," except in the name of "self-preservation" (what has come to be called in the present day "national security"). Self-preservation, as had already been demonstrated by the Mexican War, was a cloak commodious enough to cover any villainy. Now Buchanan indicated a desire to fling it once more over our unhappy neighbor, Mexico.

It had been the glory of the United States, Buchanan declared, that while other less enlightened nations had "extended their dominions by the sword we have never acquired any territory except by fair purchase or, as in the case of Texas, by the voluntary determination of a brave, kindred, and independent people. . . . Acting on this principle, no nation will have a right to complain if in the progress of events we shall still further extend our possessions." If our history did not abound in such hypocritical pieties, we might suspect Buchanan of shameless deception, of slipping readily into the role of confidence-man-as-president. But we must, I think, concede that he believed sincerely in the truth of what he said. Americans certainly do not have a corner on self-deception; it is an attribute of the species. But considering the gap that frequently yawned between what Americans did and what they *said* they were doing, one is tempted to consider whether we may not have carried that perhaps necessary human failing to new heights or depths. Captain Marryat asked what could be done with a people to whom its leaders did not dare to tell the truth, and it is a major premise of this work that we have been singularly indisposed to see ourselves as we really are—neither substantially better nor worse than the common run of mankind. Indeed how could it be otherwise since we are, more than any other people of the world, "the common run of mankind."

William Walker's first filibustering expedition had come in 1853 on the heels of Pierce's inaugural address, wherein he had advocated a bold policy of expansion for the United States. Walker, doubtless having in mind the example of Frémont and the Bear Republic, organized an expedition that entered Baja California and announced the establishment of the independent Republic of Sonora. When Mexico troops approached, Walker's small band took to their heels.

We find Walker next in Nicaragua, where he rose to the command of a revolutionary army. His principal rival was Cornelius Vanderbilt, who, starting life as a Staten Island ferryman, had, by a series of speculations and dubious deals revolving around steamboat monopolies, become a rich man. Vanderbilt was determined to build a transit line across Nicaragua to carry travelers to California. This was to be done through the agency of the Accessory Transit Company. Vanderbilt's agents, deciding to double-cross him and gain control of the venture, persuaded Walker to cancel Vanderbilt's charter and give one to them. In the meantime, Walker had made use of Vanderbilt's credit to pay for the passage of more than a thousand recruits to swell his forces. But Walker had met his match in Vanderbilt. When Costa Rica declared war on Walker and his American volunteers, Vanderbilt worked on Buchanan to declare Walker out of bounds. Walker deposed the president of Nicaragua and tried to assume full control of the state, but Guatemala and San Salvador joined forces with Costa Rica and Vanderbilt dispatched his own expeditionary force to aid in Walker's overthrow in 1857. With Walker out of the way, Vanderbilt regained control of his company and received a new charter from Nicaragua.

In the formal diplomatic realm, Webster, as Tyler's secretary of state, had concluded an important treaty with his opposite number, Lord Ashburton of Canada, settling the troublesome issue of the Maine boundary in 1842. The treaty was signed with much ceremony on August 9, 1842. In December of 1846 a little-noticed treaty was concluded by the American minister to New Granada (Colombia), Benjamin Bidlack. In addition to the commercial provisions of the treaty, it contained an article, Polk noted in his diary, "giving the guaranty of the U. S. for the neutrality of the Isthmus of Panama and the sovereignty of New Granada over that territory." That was further than Polk and his Cabinet were willing to go at the moment and the treaty was not ratified until June of 1848. Soon thereafter the discovery of gold in California drew attention to the notion of a canal across the Isthmus. John Clayton, secretary of state under Fillmore, undertook to try to clarify the British and American spheres of influence in Central America by a treaty that opened the possibility of an American-built canal across Nicaragua. The so-called Clayton-Bulwer Treaty, signed on April 19, 1850, stipulated that neither Great Britain or the United States "will ever obtain or maintain for itself any exclusive control over said Ship Canal . . . or colonize, or assume, or exercise any dominion over Nicaragua, Costa Rica, the Mosquito Coast, or any part of Central America. . . ." The two countries would do their best to encourage the construction of such a canal and the establishment of free ports at each end, and guarantee the canal's neutrality and accessibility.

As we have noted earlier, New England merchants had, since the first decades of the century, maintained a flourishing trade with China centering on ginseng, furs, tea, fine silks, and porcelain. The relations between New England merchants and their opposite numbers in China had been warm and friendly. Harriet Martineau wrote of talking with a Boston merchant who recalled with much pleasure his meetings with his Chinese counterpart on several voyages to China. "He said that his thoughts often wandered back with vivid pleasure to the long conversations he had enjoyed with some of his Chinese friends on the deepest themes of philosophy and the highest truths of religion, when he found them familiar with the convictions, the emotions, the hopes which, in New England, are supposed to be derived only from the Christianity of this region."

All foreign vessels were restricted to the port of Canton. After the Opium War of 1839–42 the British and French forced the Chinese to open other ports. Tyler thereupon sent Caleb Cushing, a Massachusetts lawyer and Democrat, to negotiate a treaty that would protect American interests. Cushing carried with him a letter of "Peace and Friendship" signed by the President which began: "I hope your health is good. China is a Great Empire, extending over a great part of the World. The Chinese are numerous. . . . The Twenty-six United States are as large as China, though our people are not so numerous. The rising Sun looks upon the great mountains and rivers of China. . . . The Chinese love to trade with our People, and to sell them Tea and Silk for which our People pay Silver. . . . But if the Chinese and Americans will trade, there should be rules. . . ."

What the Chinese thought of this strange missive is unknown, but a treaty was signed in Wanghia on July 3, 1844, affirming the desire to establish "firm, lasting, and sincere friendship between the two Nations. . . ." In addition to Canton, the ports of Kwangchow, Amoy, Fuchow, Ningpo, and Shanghai were opened.

The emperor replied to Tyler's letter, "I, the Emperor, having looked up and received the manifest Will of Heaven, hold the reins of *Government* over, and sooth and tranquilize the *Central Flowery King-dom,* regarding all within and beyond the border seas as one and the same Family. . . . Now bounded by perpetual *Amity* and *Concord* advantage will accrue to the *Citizens* of both *Nations,* which I trust must certainly cause the PRESIDENT also to be extremely well satisfied and delighted."

The British and French renewed their war with the Manchus in 1856 and in 1858 a new Sino-American treaty was negotiated in Tientsin which was similar to those extracted by the French and British. This treaty opened the country to Christian missionaries, who soon poured in to convert the vast company of heathens.

In 1854 what was to be in the long run America's most significant relationship in the Orient was established by Commodore Matthew Perry (son of Oliver Hazard Perry of War of 1812 fame), who commanded a squadron of American warships that sailed first to Hong Kong and Okinawa and then anchored off Japan, forbidden territory to foreign devils. Perry wrote piously in his journal, "We pray God that our present attempt to bring a singular and isolated people into the family of civilized nations may succeed without resort to bloodshed." There was a remarkable lack of self-consciousness in the man who could describe one of the world's most ancient and extraordinary civilizations in such patronizing terms. But certainly Japan was an anomaly. American ships and American sailors and commercial goods had penetrated to every corner of the globe, to every remote and exotic people. Only Japan had remained aloof and impenetrable. Now the United States had determined that its isolation must end. The requirements of trade and, perhaps more, of American self-esteem, dictated that Japan must enter into "the friendly commerce of nations." On July 8, 1853, the residents of Shimoda on the Izu Peninsula saw two steamships, with two sailing vessels in tow, off the shore. An old man later described the scene. Hearing excited cries in the town, he inquired their cause and was told "that offshore there were burning ships." Climbing a hill, he saw "that they were not Japanese but foreign. What we had mistaken for fire was smoke belching forth from these warships and they caused a great commotion. . . . When we came down the hill the whole town was astir. Some men rushed to Edo [the capital]."

Excitement and anxiety were widespread. No one dared tell the ailing Shogun of the arrival of the foreign ships. Three days later, attending a Noh play at Edo Castle, the Shogun overheard someone speaking of the astonishing event and promptly retired to his bed. Preparations began for war.

Perry meanwhile sent an emissary ashore with a letter for the Shogun proclaiming his peaceful mission. At anchor, his boats were surrounded by Japanese guard boats whose crews attempted to board Perry's flagship, the *Susquehanna*. These efforts Perry ordered repelled and the boats were driven off. Perry, who proved himself an instinctive master of oriental diplomacy, would allow only a high official on board. He was determined *"by stately and dignifed reserve, joined to perfect equity in all he asked or did"* (his third-person description of his strategy) to win over his involuntary hosts.

Finally the Shogun decided to let his lesser lords receive the letter that had been sent to him from the president of the United States via Commodore Perry. The Japanese built a pavilion in which the ceremony of the presentation of the letter was to take place. Five thousand soldiers in medieval armor with ancient guns and spears were lined up behind canvas screens and nine samurai were hidden under the pavilion with orders to kill Perry and his aides if any American duplicity was indicated. The Commodore and his staff, with escorts of sailors and marines and the music of a band, landed and presented the letter to the gorgeously attired governor of the province. He would, Perry informed the Japanese through an interpreter, return in the spring for his answer.

The ceremony completed, Perry wrote his wife, "This achievement of mine I consider an important event in my life. The Pageant was magnificent and I am the only Christian that has ever before landed peacefully on this part of Japan or in any part without submitting to the most humiliating degradation."

After Perry's departure, a Japanese official said to the court physician, "These Americans are certainly different from the British and others. They seem to be sincere and honest. I hear that their military order is strict and they know the rules of politeness. From now on the Japanese had better stand on friendly relations with them."

In Perry's absence, the highest officials of Japan and over a hundred daimyo, or feudal lords, were consulted and the general opinion was that the United States must be rebuffed and the nation prepared to repel any invasion. A few of the more powerful and "modern" Japanese lords urged that trade be established with the United States.

When Perry returned in January protracted negotiations followed as to where the actual treaty conference would be held. Perry wanted to go to the capital at Edo but this was firmly refused. During the negotiations over the site, presents were constantly exchanged and Perry received "a box of obscene paintings of naked men and women, another proof of the lewdness of this exclusive people." Perry again proved a master of psychology, being alternately imperious and conciliatory but always making it clear that he considered himself in every way the equal of his hosts.

Finally Yokohama was agreed upon as the treaty site and work was begun on a "treaty hall." When it was completed the ceremony began, an event painstakingly recorded by Japanese artists, who, incidentally, were as ubiquitous as modern press photographers in recording virtually every detail of the American fleet, the sailors and officers and numerous portraits of Perry himself. The American flag bearer was a giant black man who was as much a curiosity to the Japanese as the Commodore himself. Black mess men put on a minstrel show which delighted and astonished the Japanese, and American marines examined an enormous sumo wrestling champion—all recorded by the artists. The irrepressible Japanese sense of humor was tickled by their visitors' large, ungainly frames, their big-featured faces with downward-slanting eyes and light hair and sallow complexions. They found American noses especially intriguing and American table manners, or the lack of them, hilarious. The strange, stiff, black uniforms of the Americans contrasted with the rich and intricate costumes of the Japanese officials, and the swords of the American naval officers looked like toothpicks beside the fearsome samurai blades.

All that the Japanese were willing to concede for the time being was refuge for shipwrecked sailors, who had commonly been executed in the past, and the right of resupply or provisioning for American ships in designated ports. Perry finally won Japanese acceptance of an American representative to reside in Japan, the first modest step toward formal diplomatic relations. This agreement was known as the Treaty of Kanagawa.

When the treaty was concluded, more elaborate presents were exchanged. The Americans strung and demonstrated a telegraph wire, and presented three dozen clocks, a small-scale locomotive with a passenger car barely big enough to carry a child and three hundred feet of track, a telescope, a barrel of whiskey, and the seeds of some native American plants. For almost four months, the American vessels visited those Japanese ports open by treaty for visits but not for trade. The length of the stay was the most important aspect of the negotiations because it impressed the image of America and Americans very deeply on the Japanese consciousness. News of the visit and the pictures, which constituted a remarkable archive in themselves, and the American artifacts traded by sailors and officers circulated throughout the country. Perry, in turn, brought back evidence of the almost incomprehensibly exotic character of Japan and some advice to his countrymen. Despite their unfortunate encounters with Western Christianity in earlier times, Perry was "inclined to believe that, by just and honorable relations with the educated classes, they will in time listen with patience and respectful attention to the teachings of our missionaries. They are in most respects a refined and rational people, and would on this account be more open to conviction than their neighbors, the Chinese, over whom, in almost every essential, they hold a vast superiority. *Indeed, I have never met in any part of the world, even in Europe, with a people of more unaffected grace and dignity. . . ."* Perry was also impressed with the natural resourcefulness of the Japanese. "In the practical and mechanical arts," he wrote, "the Japanese show great dexterity, and when the rudeness of their tools and their imperfect knowledge of machinery are considered, the perfection of their manual skills appears marvelous. Their handicraftsmen are as expert as any in the world, and, with a freer development of the inventive powers of the people, and their readiness in adapting them to their own uses, the Japanese would not remain long behind the most successful manufacturing nations. Their curiosity to learn the results of the material progress of other people, and their readiness in adapting them to their own uses, would soon, under a less exclusive policy of government, which isolates them from national communion, raise them to a level with the most favored countries. Once possessed of the acquisitions of the past and present of the civilized world, the Japanese would enter as powerful competitors in the race for mechanical success in the future."

The thaw was slow. It was a year before the Japanese consented to accept an American consul, Townsend Harris, and he was coldly received. With tact, skill, and persistence, Harris finally secured an audience with the Shogun at Edo and, after a year of tortuous negotiation during which Harris narrowly escaped assassination, a commercial treaty was concluded. Harris played as crucial a part in opening up commercial relations with Japan as Perry had, and although antiforeign daimyo deposed the last Shogun, the young Emperor Meiji, brought to power by them, turned the tables on them, opened his country to foreign trade, and began the modernization of Japan, a process in which the United States was to play the most crucial role.

Townsend Harris's Treaty of 1858 with Japan provided for the visit of a Japanese delegation to the United States. It took place in the summer of 1860 and the indefatigable pen of George Templeton Strong recorded the event in New York. "From early morning . . . the town was agog about the Japanese ambassadors. Streets were already swarming as I went downtown. . . . Every other person, at least, was manifestly a rustic or a stranger. Flags everywhere. Small detachments of our valiant militia marching, grim and sweaty, to their respective positions. Dragoons, hussars, and lancers, by twos and threes, trotting about with looks of intense uneasiness." The Japanese finally appeared, sitting in their carriages "like bronze statues, aristocratically calm and indifferent. . . . Broadway was densely filled, . . . for many blocks. . . ."

Beyond trade, treaties, negotiations, diplomatic maneuverings, beyond even the ubiquitous missionaries, there was the moral and psychological dimension of the relations between the United States and "the World."

Frederick Grimké was especially concerned in his book *The Nature and Tendency of Free Institutions,* published in 1856, with "The Influence of America Upon Europe," as he headed one of his chapters. While it was doubtless true, he wrote, that "a train of accidental causes no doubt assisted in the establishment of free institutions in America," the rest of the world was profoundly interested in "what these institutions gave promise of. . . . America is the first instance in which the institutions of one country have been permitted to spread their influence abroad without the intervention of any force—without even the desire to employ any. It is consequently the first instance in which a deep and general impression has been made upon the manners and habits of thinking of other communities." The principal means of effecting this diffusion of American ideas and institutions had been by "commercial intercourse," which had had two effects. It had helped to promote "the growth of the middle class in more than one country in Europe," and this middle class had been invariably receptive to the influence of American institutions; and it had also served as a channel or channels of communication. The form of government adopted by the United States—"the most striking event of the age"—was one particularly congenial to the middle class, while "the common people" were much interested because the American system "promises to lift them higher in the scale."

America had shown that it was possible to confer "the electoral franchise upon the great body of the people," without producing chaos and disorder, and, similarly, "making all the political departments elective." These were real "discoveries."

After discussing the various areas in which American notions of government had been influential, Grimké went on to enumerate the more informal channels through which American ideas and customs had affected the world. One of the simplest was through letters written by American immigrants to their relatives and friends in the countries from which they had emigrated. America was also made known through books of travels, the most famous of which was that of Tocqueville, who taught Europeans to view American institutions "in a totally different spirit from what they had been accustomed to."

We have already noted the great flood of travel books about the United States, written in virtually every language by visitors who came to view the future and praise or deplore it. They exist as a yardstick to help measure the influence of the United States upon the consciousness of the people of the world, who, after all, created the United States by coming to it. To a degree difficult to comprehend, America was an experiment by the species far more than it was a conventional nation. Viewed in this light, our official "foreign relations" were always subordinate to that deeper flow of common interests and sympathies that connected us to the rest of the human race.

Although, as we have seen, upper-class Americans identified most closely with England, read English books—all Americans, of course, read Scott and Dickens—followed English fashions (the men at least; the women were slaves to Paris), and filled their houses with English furniture and English paintings, doggedly Democratic Americans still clung to the shreds of the once fanatical devotion to the French. But if the American elite and middle-class intellectuals like Emerson gloried in the British connection, they were increasingly influenced by German thought and German scholarship. George Tichnor and George Bancroft were only the vanguard of young American intellectuals who made their way to Göttingen and Heidelberg to immerse themselves in the exciting world of the new scholarship: in history every shred of historical evidence was painstakingly examined for clues to the whole form of the past, and the newer sciences of chemistry and physics were profiting from the same thoroughness of method and "grinding competition" that so impressed George Tichnor. German idealism, or neo-Platonism, was especially congenial to those young intellectuals breaking free from the dried husks of Calvinism or an increasingly bland and formal Unitarianism. The German philosopher Georg Wilhelm Friedrich Hegel was, Swedenborg excepted, the European philosopher who had the greatest influence on American thought. His notion that history was the progressive realization of the idea of freedom was a "natural" in America. When Emerson visited St. Louis he found that the St. Louis Philosophical Society was dedicated heart and soul to the German philosopher and the *Journal of Speculative Philosophy* was heavily Hegelian in tone.

Through Emerson and the transcendentalists, Hindu literature and philosophy were introduced to American readers. But the common sense school of philosophy, originating with the eighteenth-century Scottish philosophers Thomas Reid and Dugald Stewart, continued to dominate college courses in philosophy. Common sense philosophy had no truck with idealism. The objects that presented themselves to the senses were what they appeared to be—elements of the real world, not reflections of ideas. Individuals had an intuitive moral sense and it was the business of philosophy to strengthen and extend it.

American sculptors like Hiram Powers and Horatio Greenough still went to Rome or Florence to study and, when they could, remained there because only in Italy could a sculptor find craftsmen to give a marble form to his conceptions. Painters, however, found their way, as we have seen, to Düsseldorf, the most influential center of art training in Europe. The English and the French connections had been there from the beginning of the Union; the establishment of the German connection was the most significant intellectual event of the first half of the nineteenth century.

George Tichnor organized the first department of Spanish literature in the United States, and doubtless in the world, and wrote an impressive study of Spanish poets and writers. Washington Irving, with his *Alhambra, Conquest of Granada,* and *Life of Columbus* as well as his tour of duty as American ambassador to Spain during Tyler's administration, had helped to focus attention on the romantic history of that country, an interest that was substantially reinforced by William Prescott's great histories of the conquest of Mexico and Peru. But Spanish influence did not extend beyond architectural details and mock Moorish villas. Contemporary Spain, with her ancient and disintegrating feudalism was useful primarily in pointing a moral—the superiority of a free society over an authoritarian one and of Protestantism over Catholicism.

55

The New Politics

It seemed to George Templeton Strong after the election of 1844 that the Whig Party was "defunct, past all aid from warm blankets, galvanic batteries, and the Humane Society; it's quite dead and the sooner it's buried the better. What form of life will be generated from its decomposition remains to be seen." Clay had lost to Polk, in Strong's opinion, because in a long and distinguished public life he had provided his enemies with numerous statements and acts to use against him, "fairly or falsely, while his opponent was impregnable from the fact that he had never done or said anything of importance to anybody and the attempts made by the Whigs to injure his personal character only recoiled on their heads. Henceforth I think political wire-pullers will be careful how they nominate prominent and well-known men for the Presidency; they'll find it safer to pick up the first man they may find in the street. . . ."

With Clay defeated as the Whig standard-bearer, the mantel of party leadership had fallen to Webster. He was clearly the candidate of the most influential Whigs and it must have seemed to him that the longed-for prize was at last within his grasp. But Clay's fortunes revived and a new rival emerged. Soon it was clear that the hero of the war that the Whigs had so bitterly opposed was to be the party's choice for president in 1848. Zachary Taylor and Winfield Scott had kept the country and the army agitated by their angry rivalry. While both were experienced and able officers, fortune had smiled on Taylor by allowing him to be in command of the most dramatic victory of the war. The Whigs, only too well aware that their last triumph had been achieved with a general (poor, decrepit Harrison), were determined to repeat the experiment. "At present," Philip Hone wrote in April, 1847, "all parts and parties, professions, sexes, and conditions, call him [Taylor] away from the field of battle to take upon himself the chief magistracy. Webster and Clay, Scott and McLean, Calhoun and Polk, are shoved aside to make way for the hero of Resaca de la Palma, Palo Alto, Monterey, and Buena Vista. The lovers of peace, even the Quakers, call out for the warrior." Ladies and gentlemen and "the gentry with red flannel shirts" agreed only on "Rough and Ready" as their next leader. Polk, who was not without a sense of the ironic, must have been wryly if somewhat painfully amused at the possibility of being superseded by an individual to whom had accrued the credits of a war that Polk had engineered.

The only serious problem was that no one knew whether Taylor was a Whig or a Democrat. While it was true that he had been widely assumed during the Mexican War to be a Whig, he had never voted in any election and although he had been engaged in numerous quarrels within and without the army, he was the prototype of the nonpolitical general. This made him an ideal candidate for president. In a nation increasingly polarized over the issue of slavery, the fact that Old Rough and Ready's political views were generally obscure was, along with his victories in the Mexican War (which he had opposed), his principal asset. Although he was a wealthy Kentucky plantation owner, one of only roughly eighteen hundred Southerners who owned more than a hundred slaves, he gave hints that he was opposed to the extension of slavery. When the notion of putting him forward as a presidential candidate was first broached to him in 1846, he declared the idea "too visionary to require a serious answer." The thought had "never entered my head," he wrote, "nor is it likely to enter the head of any sane person." That response was almost enough in itself to make him worthy of the office.

An indifferent speller and grammarian, Taylor spoke with a slight stutter and was conspicuously lacking in what were then thought to be the requisite oratorical skills. Of medium height, stout, untidy, bowlegged, he walked more like a sailor than a soldier and was addicted to battered straw hats. These personal eccentricities endeared him to his soldiers and made him seem the model of democratic informality. But with all this he had a good deal of plain common sense, personal integrity, and shrewd strategic instincts. His principal military rival, Winfield Scott, Old Fuss and Feathers, was a far less appealing character. Lewis Cass, the Michigan perennial who won the Democratic nomination, was a fat, jowly figure with an ill-fitting red wig. Cass, in opposing the Wilmot Proviso, had come up with the doctrine that the settlers of any new territory should be left to decide the issue of slavery or nonslavery, a seemingly logical but potentially mischievous idea that undermined the Missouri Compromise. Cass's proposal, under the name "squatter sovereignty," became a plank in the Democratic platform. Cass had been a schoolmate of Daniel Webster's and, migrating west, had served as territorial governor of Michigan and then as senator when Michigan became a state. Philip Hone spoke for most of his class when he wrote that Cass "is the embodiment of political humbug and demagogism, administering to the worst part of the community." Hone could not forgive him for his support for the annexation of Texas and the Mexican War. The Democratic nomination of the Michigan politician was "a declaration of war against the universe," Hone wrote. The nomination of Cass led to a walkout by the Van Burenites, who acquired the nickname of Barnburners—extremists who would burn down the barn to kill the Polk-rats. Those who remained loyal to the party were termed the Hunkers, hankering after offices and political preferment rather than standing on principle. The Barnburners were ready to come forward as the Free Soil Party, with Van Buren once more a presidential nominee. The James Birney Liberty Party men rallied to Van Buren's banner, as did many disaffected antislavery men from both the Whig and Democratic parties, though Van Buren was far from being a radical on the antislavery issue.

Richard Henry Dana, whose increasing commitment to the antislavery cause had made him one of the organizers of the Free Soil Party, wrote of the convention: "Ohio met & was unanimous for Mr. Adams for Vice-President. There was an enthusiasm for him, partly on account of his father, whose memory they wished to honor & vindicate, & partly on his own account, to vindicate him, as the early champion of the Conscience Whigs, ag. the attacks & sneers of the Cotton Whigs of Mass. The feeling for J.Q. Adams was far greater than I had imagined. People crowded about the son, shook his hands, spoke of their admiration for the 'old man,' & seemed by a natural process of the mind to desire to show him the respect they could not show to the father. The other Western states was also unanimous, & the 60-odd Delegates fr. Penn. met & resolved on Adams."

It now rested with the Massachusetts delegation. Richard Henry Dana was a delegate and sported an Adams badge. "An old fellow from Wisconsin, with a sun-burnt face, hook nose, deep voice & noble, ardent countenance, seeing my badge," Dana wrote, "clapped his great hand on my shoulder & said—'Yes, Sir, we want him. He's the man for this day & time. There he is *with the crape on his hat now.*' Mr. Adams wore crape on his white hat, for his father. It went to the hearts of these men, as though he had carried his image before him. A gentleman rose & stated the opinion & feeling of the West, & moved that Ch. Fr. Adams of Mass. be unanimously nominated. Never, since my ears first admitted sound, have I heard such an acclamation. Men sprang upon the tops of the seats, threw their hats in the air, & even to the ceiling." It was an especially sweet moment for the introspective and often bitter Charles Francis.

The Van Buren-Adams Free Soil ticket advertised the irony of American politics—the son of John Quincy Adams, Van Buren's longtime political enemy, now sharing the ticket with the agent of his father's political downfall. The slavery issue was to make even stranger bedfellows. The Free Soil platform declared its intention to "maintain the rights of Free Labor against the aggressions of the Slave Power, and to secure Free Soil for a Free People." They stood on the Ordinance of 1787, which forbade slavery in the territories and determined to "limit, localize, and discourage Slavery." There must be no slavery in the territories acquired by the Mexican War or in Oregon. The Free Soilers called for strict economy in government and free grants of land to actual settlers in the West.

When the Whig convention met in Baltimore in June, 1848, Taylor's principal rivals for the nomination were Webster and Clay. With the recollection of their success with Harrison in 1840, the Whig leaders could not resist the lure of Taylor's status as a popular hero, and the two titans of their party were brushed aside for the untried general. Millard Fillmore was nominated for vice-president. "I am disappointed, but I am satisfied," Philip Hone wrote. "The Clay Whigs generally are not so easily satisfied; they are exasperated, and swear all sorts of opposition to the nomination. They will go for the Barn-burners; they will get up an opposition candidate; they will support

Cass. . . ." The Whigs could hardly have made a more cynical choice. Taylor appeared to be in no way qualified for the office of president. He had disclaimed the principal planks in the Whig platform and chose to depict himself as a man above party. Clay, on the other hand, had every legitimate right to the support of the Whigs.

The presidential race was characterized by two letters that defined the candidates' positions on two of the most important issues facing the country. Cass included his popular sovereignty doctrine in the so-called Nicholson Letter, while Taylor, in a letter to his brother-in-law, Captain John Allison, assured him and the party that he was "a Whig but not an ultra Whig." The fact that he had been widely mentioned as a potential Democratic candidate also helped him to appear as a nonpartisan figure. The acceptance by Van Buren of the nomination of the Free Soil party, by splitting the Democrats, increased Taylor's chances for election. A substantial number of Clay Whigs, indignant at the party's desertion of their hero in the twilight of his political career, joined the Democratic Barnburners.

All the by-now-familiar pageantry of presidential elections unrolled: bitter and often libelous newspaper attacks on the opposition candidates, torchlight processions, banners, buttons, campaign biographies, songs and satirical verse such as:

> *Extra Cass—*
> Pray, tell me, Rough and Ready,
> How did it come to pass
> That you were made a President,
> And I was made an ass?
> *Rough and Ready—*
> Sir, you would play the demagogue,
> And practice mystifying,
> Until enveloped in a fog,
> All human eyes defying;
> In such a guise, no friend could C you;
> And so, poor *ass,* they tho't they'd flee you.

James Fenimore Cooper wrote for the Democrats, and Whittier for the Free Soilers. Abraham Lincoln, representative from Illinois, campaigned actively for Taylor, arguing that to vote for Van Buren and the so-called Free Soilers would only give the election to Cass. A popular Free Soil song ran:

Come, ye hardy sons of toil,
And cast your ballots for Free Soil;
He wh'd vote for Zacky Taylor,
Needs a keeper or a jailor.
And he who for Cass can be
He is a Cass without the C;
The man on whom we love to look
Is Martin Van of Kinderhook.

Moritz Busch saw in Cincinnati a bus painted with a likeness of Zachary Taylor. Out of it hopped "a half dozen young female boarders in bloomer costume" to proselytize for their hero. One of the most interesting features of the campaign, which grew increasingly heated as the time for the elections drew near, was the publication of books on the candidates in German. In New Orleans a fight between Whigs and Democrats ended in the burning of the Whig headquarters. A drunken prostitute in Philadelphia, arrested by the police, gave her name as Rough and Ready and was so booked.

Taylor was attacked for trying to be all things to all men and praised for being above narrow party politics; Cass was criticized for having speculated in real estate while territorial governor.

When the votes were counted Taylor had won by a surprisingly slim margin, 163 electoral votes to 127. In popular votes Taylor had a margin of 140,000 out of some 2,580,000 cast, and Van Buren and the Free Soilers had gotten 291,263. In New York state Van Buren had drawn 120,510 votes, most of them presumably from Cass, who lost the state by 104,000. Cass took all of the Western states but lost Florida, Georgia, Kentucky, Louisiana, and Tennessee, while Taylor took all of the Northeastern states except Maine and New Hampshire.

Again the results suggested a political equilibrium between Whigs and Democrats so delicately balanced that the scale could be tipped by chance events such as Van Buren's hostility toward Cass. The Free Soilers seemed to have made substantial gains over Birney's vote four years earlier but most of it simply represented the strength of Van Buren's Barnburners in New York. Underneath the relatively calm surface, the rickety alliances that held the two major parties together were beginning to come apart.

In his inaugural address Taylor promised to take the Constitution as his guide and to do his best to emulate his illustrious predecessors, especially "the Father of his Country." While it was natural for

Americans to "sympathize in all efforts to extend the blessings of civil and political liberty," he declared in reference to the revolutions that were sweeping Europe, it was essential to follow the admonitions "of our own beloved Washington to abstain from entangling alliances with foreign nations." Beyond that he was for a modest but efficient army and navy, honesty in government, "and the utmost economy in all public expenditures." Taylor also expressed his gratitude for the "high state of prosperity to which the goodness of Divine Providence has conducted our common country." As behooved a nonpolitical general, a simple man of action, the inaugural was one of the shortest on record. To an audience accustomed to hour-long orations it seemed over before it was well begun. Whigs and Democrats agreed it was manly and forthright.

In office the new President was a model of democratic simplicity. George Francis Train, visiting Taylor at the White House not long after his inauguration, found him at his desk with his feet up on a chair. "He wore a shirt that was formerly white," Train wrote, "but which looked like the map of Mexico after the battle of Buena Vista. It was spotted and spattered with tobacco juice. Directly behind me, as I was soon made aware, was a cuspidor, toward which the President turned the flow of tobacco juice. I was in mortal terror, but I soon saw there was no danger . . . he never missed the cuspidor once, or put my person in jeopardy."

The Mexican War had brought in its wake an intensification of sectional antagonisms. The Wilmot Proviso became the most critical issue in the republic, the North supporting it, the Southern states unanimous in their opposition. When the Missouri legislature issued a blast at the Proviso and affirmed her solidarity with the South, Thomas Benton publicly expressed his dissent, going about the state to debate the issue with anyone bold enough to gainsay him. The resolutions of the legislature, he declared, were "false in their facts, incendiary in their temper, disunion in their object, nullification in their essence, high treason in their remedy, usurpation in their character." He was sixty-seven with a long, stormy political career behind him. Often laughed at and ridiculed for his rough ways and combative temperament, he showed great courage and independence by flying so boldly in the face of the majority opinion in his home state.

In the South the debate on the Wilmot Proviso led to renewed calls for secession. Some states proposed cutting off all commercial relations with the North and declaring a moratorium on debts owed by

Southerners to Northern banks or merchants. There were demands for a convention of delegates from Southern states to decide on measures to protect the interests of the slaveholding states. When the Thirty-first Congress convened in December of 1849, there were 112 Democrats, 105 Whigs, and 12 Free Soilers. Sectional feeling ran so high that it took more than sixty ballots and two weeks to elect a speaker of the House. In the debate over the right of Southerners to carry their slaves into free states or territories acquired by the Mexican War, Robert Toombs of Georgia declared to the Northerners, "We have the right to call on you to give your blood to maintain the slaves of the South in bondage. Deceive not yourselves; you cannot deceive others. This is a proslavery government. Slavery is stamped on its heart!"

To which Thaddeus Stevens, one of the founders of the Anti-Masonic Party and now a new antislavery Congressman from Pennsylvania, replied, "During the present session we have been told amid raving excitement that if we dared to legislate a certain way, the South would teach the North a lesson. . . . Are the representatives of free men to be thus treated? You have too often intimidated Congress. You have more than once frightened the tame North from its propriety and found 'doughfaces' enough to be your tools. But I hope that the race of 'doughfaces' is extinct!"

If Taylor's inaugural was uncommonly short, the same could not be said of his first annual message to Congress, a long and able address. He was firm in his resistance to any Cuban adventure and he carefully refrained from any interference in the Hungarian struggle against Austria, although his sympathies and those of the American people were entirely on the side of the Magyars. In Latin America, Venezuela had been involved in "a sanguinary civil war" which was now concluded. Efforts were being made to conclude an agreement with New Granada to send mail across the Isthmus of Panama and also, hopefully, to secure the right to build a railroad across the isthmus. It was Taylor's conviction that the United States should do everything in its power to "foster and strengthen its relations with the Central and Latin American states." Taylor also affirmed his determination to suppress the "barbarous traffic" of the African slave trade.

Taylor spoke at some length of the special relationship between the United States and the Sandwich Islands, declaring, "We desire that the islands may maintain their independence and that other nations should concur with us in this sentiment." He also urged Congress to pass protective tariffs for the "encouragement of manufactures" and to give "a new and increased stimulus to agriculture." The President suggested that a department of agriculture be established "to give this leading branch of American industry the encouragement which it merits." California had recently formed a government of its own, he reminded Congress, and given clear indications that she wished to be admitted into the Union as a state. It could be anticipated that New Mexico would soon follow suit, and Taylor urged that both be promptly admitted. California had just plunged into the gold rush, and Taylor recommended the establishment of a branch of the United States Mint in San Francisco. He had, on his own authority, appointed Indian agents to protect the rights of the aborigines in California and in the Great Basin region. The discovery of gold in California and the rapid growth of population both in that "area" and in the Oregon Territory meant that a railroad must be built to connect the East and West, Taylor declared, recommending the appointment of a commission to determine whether it should be "undertaken as a national improvement or left to individual enterprise" and which of several proposed routes should be followed.

Taylor closed his address by reminding his listeners of his injunction to "abstain from the introduction of those exciting topics of a sectional character which have hitherto produced painful apprehensions in the public mind. . . ." To agitate such issues was to imperil the Union. "In my judgment its dissolution would be the greatest of calamities. . . . Upon its preservation must depend our own happiness and that of countless generations to come."

While advocates of secession might growl and grumble, most Americans were surprised and pleased by Taylor's address. It ranks near the top of presidential papers, comprehensive and humane, an impressive achievement for a man whose interest had been confined largely to the military sphere.

Taylor's admonition to "abstain from those exciting topics of a sectional character" fell on deaf ears. The antislavery representatives were determined to press for the abolition of the slave trade in the District of Columbia and the admission of California and New Mexico as free states, while the Southerners were as unyielding in their opposition to any statement excluding or limiting slavery in any state or territory and determined to try to strengthen the Fugitive Slave Law which, through the passage of personal liberty laws in the Northern states, had been rendered nugatory. In addition, the Mormon empire of Deseret had applied to be recognized as constituting a territorial government.

In the midst of increasing party bitterness and rancor over the fate of the lands wrested from Mexico, Clay, seventy-four years old and once more in the Senate after seven years' absence, his ambition to be president defeated, undertook to fashion a final compromise. Clay's compromise provided for the admission of California to the Union as a free state; the organization as a territory of the region acquired from Mexico without mention of slavery; the adjustment of the Texas-New Mexico boundary; assumption by the United States of the debts of Texas; noninterference with slavery in the District of Columbia; abolition of the slave trade in the District; and the strengthening of the Fugitive Slave Law. He introduced his bill in January, 1850.

"The great Kentucky Senator has been making a great speech," Philip Hone wrote, "intended to pour oil upon the waves which are now agitating in fierce contentions the minds of men in the whole length and breadth of the land. . . . His speech was worthy of the statesman and patriot who has always succeeded in cases of national emergency in calming the rate of contending factions; but will it do now? I fear not. . . . His peroration was sublime; the Senate was entranced, but alas! the demon of party listens not to the voice of the charmer, charm he ever so wisely." For almost seven months the attention of the country was fixed on this "final" compromise.

It was the last act of an extraordinary drama. The writer of fiction would not presume to invent such a scene. Calhoun, Clay, and Webster had dominated the political life of the United States for more than a generation. Each had become the spokesman for a great section of the Union. Each had remarkable powers of intellect and great personal magnetism. Each had aspired to be president of the United States. Andrew Jackson aside, they were the three best-known and most popular figures of the age, attended everywhere by admiring crowds, inordinately praised and acclaimed. Calhoun's growing physical infirmity and bizarre political doctrines had caused a decline in his influence in the decade of the forties but he was still the preeminent spokesman of the South. Too weak to read his reply to Clay, he was assisted to his seat and his speech read by James Mason of Virginia. It began on the now familiar note of intractability: "I have, senators, believed from the first that the agitation of the subject of slavery would, if not prevented by some timely and effective measure, end in disunion." He had done his best to persuade Congress to pass legislation to stifle all criticism of slavery but "the agitation has been permitted to proceed, with almost no attempt to resist it, until it has reached a period when it can no longer be disguised or denied that the Union is in danger. You have thus forced upon you the greatest and gravest question that can ever come under your consideration: How can the Union be preserved?" Only by allowing Southerners to carry their "property," their slaves, wherever they wished. The last hour in which to stop all agitation against slavery had come. "Is it, then, not certain that if something decisive is not now done to arrest it, the South will be forced to choose between abolition and secession? Indeed, as events are now moving, it will not require the South to secede to dissolve the Union." It would be rent by the political and social tensions created by those opposed to slavery. One by one the bonds of Union would break; many, in fact, had already snapped, the most important of these being the unity of the Christian churches. In Calhoun's view only one measure could prevent the final cord that still held the Union together—the political cord—from breaking. That was an amendment to the Constitution which would provide for the election of *two* presidents (the old Roman tribune notion), one from the North and one from the South, who would have a mutual veto over all acts considered antithetical to their sections. The speech was Calhoun's last political statement in the Senate.

"The leader of the disunionists," Philip Hone wrote, "the slave-holders' oracle, the daring repudiator, has made his speech. The gaping gossipers have 'supped deep' on oratorical horrors. . . . If this manifesto is to be taken as the textbook of the South, all attempts at conciliation will be fruitless. It is a calm, dispassionate avowal that nothing short of absolute submission to the slave-holding States will be accepted. . . ."

Three days later Webster replied. The Senate chamber was crowded to its furthest corners and the gallery likewise packed when Webster rose to speak in support of Clay's Omnibus Bill. "I wish to speak today," he began, "not as a Massachusetts man, nor as a Northern man, but as an American, and a member of the Senate of the United States . . . it is not to be denied that we live in the midst of strong agitations, and surrounded by very considerable dangers to our institutions and our government. The imprisoned winds are let loose. . . . I do not affect to regard myself, Mr. President, as holding, or as fit to hold, the helm in this combat with the political elements; but I have this duty to perform. . . . I have a part to act, not for my own security or safety, for I am looking out for no fragment upon which to float away from the wreck, if wreck there must be, but for the good of the whole, and the preservation of all. . . . I speak today for the preservation of the Union. 'Hear me for my cause.' " Webster then proceeded to trace the historic roots of the institution of slavery from ancient days to the present, and then analyzed the nature of the moral convictions for and against slavery and the dangers of taking rigid and uncompromising stands on issues where opinions differed. One of the most dramatic moments in Webster's speech came when, describing the manner in which Southern opinion had changed on the issue of slavery from condemning it and anticipating its eventual abolition to defending it as a necessary and desirable institution, Webster turned to James Mason, the Virginia senator and grandson of George Mason and reminded him of his grandfather's eloquent attack on slavery in the debates of the Federal Convention, only recently published. The North complained "that instead of slavery being regarded as an evil, as it was then, an evil which all hoped would be extinguished gradually, it is now regarded as an institution to be cherished, and preserved, and extended. . . ." A Louisiana senator had taken pains "to run a contrast between the slaves of the South, and the laboring people of the North, giving the preference, in all points of condition, and comfort, and happiness, to the slaves of the South." Who, Webster asked, "are the laboring people of the North? They are the people who till their own farms with their own hands; freeholders, educated, independent men. . . . Let me say, Sir, that five-sixths of the whole property of the North is in the hands of laborers of the North; they cultivate their farms, they educate their children, they provide the means of independence. If they are not freeholders, they earn wages; these wages accumulate, are turned into capital, into new freeholds, and small capitalists are created. And what can these people think when . . . the member from Louisiana undertakes to prove that the absolute ignorance and the abject slavery of the South are more in conformity with the high purposes and destiny of immortal, rational human beings, than the educated, the independent free labor of the North?"

The word "secession" particularly distressed Webster. "Peaceful secession!" he exclaimed. "What would be the result? Where is the line to be drawn? What states are to secede? What is to remain an American? What am I to be? An American no longer. Am I to become a sectional man, a local man, a separatist, with no country in common with the gentlemen who sit around me here? . . . Heaven forbid! Where is the flag of the republic to remain? . . . Shall the man of the Yellowstone and the Platte be connected, in the new republic, with the man who lives on the Southern extremity of the Cape of Florida? Sir, I am ashamed to pursue this line of remark. . . . I would rather hear of natural blasts and mildews, war, pestilence, and famine, than to hear gentlemen talk of secession. To break up this great government! to dismember this glorious country! . . . No, Sir! There will be no secession!"

The Union was destined to last forever. "Its daily respiration is liberty and patriotism. . . . Large before, the country has now, by recent events, become vastly larger. This republic now extends, with a vast breadth, across the whole continent. The two great seas of the world wash the one and the other shore. We realize, on a mighty scale, the beautiful description of the ornamental border of the buckler of Achilles:—

> Now, the broad shield complete, the artist crowned
> With his last hand, and poured the ocean round;
> In living silver seemed the waves to roll,
> And beat the buckler's verge, and bound the whole.

Webster's speech was his last major address to his colleagues and his countrymen. It was a worthy companion piece to his great debate with Hayne, the final evocation of the sacredness of the Union. It did not conclude the debate over Clay's bill. That dragged on week after week. But it was the climax of Webster's remarkable public career, the apotheosis of the dream of Union, now continental, bound by the oceans, which he, more than any other individual of his time, had fixed in the public consciousness. There could be no war to preserve the Union if the notion of its inviolability had not taken such possession of the minds of Americans living North of the Mason-Dixon line and west of the Alleghenies that they were, quite literally, willing to sacrifice their lives for that *idea*. And that idea had been given reality by Webster on innumerable occasions. Yet many of Webster's fellow New Englanders denounced the speech in the bitterest terms. Webster, by placing the Union above the freeing of the slaves, incurred the wrath of the abolitionists. Worse than that, he had given sanction to the fugitive slave provisions of the compromise. Horace Mann called him "a fallen star"; Charles Sumner declared, "Webster has placed himself in the dark list of apostates." Henry Wilson wrote: "Daniel Webster will be a fortunate man if God, in his sparing mercy, shall preserve his life long enough for him to repent of this act and efface the stain on his name." But Philip Hone was thrilled by the speech and convinced that it would be applauded by "a large proportion . . . of the discreet, reflecting men of all parts of the Union. . . ."

Before the month was out Calhoun was dead. "One of the great lights of the Western World is extinguished"; Philip Hone wrote, "the compeer of Webster and Clay is removed from the brilliant trio; the South has lost her champion; slavery, its defender; and nullification and (we are compelled to say) disunion, their apologist. . . . Will the withdrawal of the leader have the effect of disbanding the forces of Southern opposition? Or will they rally under some leader equally ardent and uncompromising, but of motives less pure and action more unscrupulous? God save the Republic! should be the prayer of all good Americans in this crisis. . . ."

On July 4, 1850, President Taylor went to the celebration at the Washington Monument. The orator of the day, Senator Foote of South Carolina, was characteristically long-winded and the President, baked by the summer sun, drank large quantities of ice water. Back at the White House he suffered an attack which developed several days later into typhus fever, and on the morning of July 9 he died, the second general-president to die in office in less than a decade. Taylor's death had unfortunate political consequences. Lacking as he had been in experience, he had made a surprisingly good president. Certainly there was no indication that he, or perhaps any other man, could have brought about a resolution of the issues that divided the country, but he had a judiciousness and a personal integrity that gave a much needed weight to the actions of the government. The man who succeeded him was yet another reminder of the weakness of the American method of choosing vice-presidents.

Millard Fillmore's most conspicuous qualification for high public office was perhaps the fact that, starting life in the most modest circumstances, he had, by unremitting effort and some good fortune, achieved a degree of prominence in the Whig Party. Beginning his political career as an Anti-Mason, he had attached himself to Henry Clay and been four times a Congressman from western New York, a candidate for vice-president in the previous election, and the defeated Whig nominee for governor of his home state. Besides party loyalty, ambition, and tenacity, he had little to recommend him for the office that devolved on him with the death of Taylor. Taylor's Cabinet resigned and Fillmore appointed Webster as his secretary of state, his only other Cabinet appointment of note being John Crittenden of Kentucky as attorney general. The new administration gave whole-hearted support to Clay's compromise. Failing to pass as a package, the bill was broken down into its component parts. The troublesome question of the Texas border was combined with the admission of New Mexico as a state. The next day a bill admitting California to the Union and establishing the territory of Utah was passed, and that night there was a general celebration in Washington with bands, cannon fire, and rockets.

When the much strengthened fugitive slave bill came up for a vote, many of the Whigs in Congress, unwilling to be recorded as voting for it, absented themselves. The bill provided for commission-ers "who were to hear and determine the case of a claimant in a summary manner." The owner need not be present or even have signed an affidavit claiming the captured man to be his slave. His agent or attorney was authorized to act in his place. The runaway could not testify in his own behalf or call witnesses. Any bystander could be summoned to aid in the capture of a fugitive slave and if he refused he was subject to heavy penalties. Concealing a fugitive, hindering his arrest in any way, or attempting to free someone already in custody was punishable by heavy fines or imprisonment. Finally, it was an ex post facto law, and thus unconstitutional its opponents claimed, since it applied to a slave however long ago he may have escaped from his master.

In Congress the debate proceeded with growing animosity among members. Foote of South Carolina denounced Benton and when Benton threatened to attack him, Foote drew a pistol and was prevented from firing it only by the intervention of senators near him. "Faction, violence, intemperance, and ungentlemanly deportment prevail in both houses of Congress," Hone wrote.

The passing of Clay's compromise, the Compromise of 1850 as it came to be called, in the form of five different bills was hailed by Hone as a triumph over "disunion, fanaticism, violence, insurrection. . . . The lovers of peace, the friends of the Union, good men, conserva-tives, have sacrificed sectional prejudices, given up personal predilec-tions, given up everything, for the Union and peace. . . . But, although all good men rejoice that the affair is settled, none are satisfied. . . ."

A great Union meeting was held at Castle Garden attended, in Hone's words, by "stalwart men, commercial magnates, comfortable millionaires, Whigs and Loco-focos, assembled to stand by the Union and to support the Constitution. . . . Parties are so broken up, mixed up, and scattered that nobody knows what the result may be. The dregs have risen to the top of the pot."

George Templeton Strong noted that Congress had at last acted on "the great Southern problem . . . checked the Southern chivalry in the generation of gas, and blighted Billy Seward and his gang of incendiaries who wanted to set the country on fire with civil war. . . . Extreme people on both sides much disgusted with the result, but the great majority satisfied and relieved."

George Templeton Strong had been initially unsympathetic with the hue and cry raised by the abolitionists over the Fugitive Slave Law. "My creed on the question is: That slave-holding is no sin," he wrote, adding, "the slaves of the Southern States are happier and better off than the niggers of the North, and are more kindly dealt with by their owners than servants are by Northern masters." The abolitionists "deserve to be scourged and pilloried for sedition or hanged for treason," Strong declared, "but as the execution of justice upon them would do more harm than good and draw attention to their impotent efforts for evil, it is better to let them alone."

But, increasingly, through the pages of his diary appear expressions of irritation and anger toward the South. Having begun by defending the enforcement of the Fugitive Slave Law in the Compromise of 1850, Strong, a few weeks later, was experiencing somewhat different emotions. "South still clamorous, querulous and absurd . . . preventing people from seeing their just grounds of complaint by the preposterous vaporing, bombast, and brag wherewith they make themselves and their concerns ridiculous. They want their 50,000 runaway niggers back, after their six months or six years respectively of independence and citizenship at the North!! That is, they want 50,000 centres of resistance and insurrection scattered over their plantations to preach the rights of man and make their black brudders restless, discontented, ambitious, and dangerous. They want . . . 50,000 sparks disseminated among their powder barrels. . . . I'm beginning to think that Southern Ultraism may be let alone to cut its own throat and punish its own lunatics, without let or interference." Yet "treason" was the word Strong most commonly used in referring to the efforts to prevent the recovery of escaped slaves. "I've no sympathy for this gang of maudlin philanthropists and Quaker bravos . . . ," he wrote. They were "making the awful name of treason very cheap, especially as two-thirds of the traitors are run-away niggers themselves—keepers of oyster shops, black barbers, 'hands' on the farm."

In New York on a visit, Richard Henry Dana was invited by William Evarts to dine with him at Delmonico's. Boston-born Evarts, as assistant United States attorney in New York state, would have the responsibility of enforcing the Fugitive Slave Law. "He defends the act and the compromise on wh. it is founded, & Webster's cause, & thinks Webster is to be the next President, in each particular of wh. I disagreed with him," Dana wrote.

The Fugitive Slave Law was undoubtedly the most misconceived piece of legislation ever promoted by Southern members of Congress. It stirred up more hostility against slavery than any prior event in the history of sectional conflict because it brought with it the enactment of dozens of excruciating dramas of fugitives pursued, recaptured, and returned to slavery. Or, increasingly, of slave captors being thwarted by lovers of freedom. White men and women who were in some ways more prejudiced against blacks than Southern slaveholders often became strong partisans when they read about or witnessed the capture of a runaway and perhaps participated in the efforts to secure his freedom. Each capture or attempted capture, rescue or failure to rescue had an enormous symbolic potency. The themes of escaping from servitude to freedom, of being recaptured and returned to servitude, touched the deepest levels of response in a people determined to think of themselves as champions of freedom. From the point of view of the future of their "special institution," the South could far better have afforded to sustain its yearly losses in runaways (numerous as they were, they represented a small proportion of the slave population) than to press for the enactment of so odious a statute. In the decade between the passage of the Fugitive Slave Law and the outbreak of the Civil War, out of tens of thousands of escaped slaves only 332 were captured, the great majority in the border states of Pennsylvania and Ohio; of that number, 33 were either rescued from federal officials or released. The costs of tracking down slaves in the states farther north were exorbitant; slave catchers and attorneys had to be hired and court costs paid, plus the transportation of the slave and those accompanying him back to the plantation from which he or she had escaped.

Harriet Tubman is said to have led over three hundred slaves to freedom. It might thus be said that the efforts of Southern slaveholders over a decade to recover their black "property" with a vast expenditure of time and money did not equal the efforts of one fugitive slave woman to free them. And of course thousands more slaves escaped in that same decade. The determination of the South to have its Fugitive Slave Law clearly went beyond any possible practical consequences from the act. It was a reflection of both the region's paranoia and its desire to scourge the North by imposing on it a measure peculiarly offensive to it—in short, an act of aggression rather than a remedy for the slow drain of runaway slaves.

The passage of the Fugitive Slave Law spread panic among the thousands of ex-slaves living in Northern communities. Hundreds of them left their jobs and homes and headed for the sanctuary of Canada. In New York, eight days after the passage of the bill, James Hamlet, who had been a free man for three years, was captured and carried to Baltimore. When three blacks in Lowell, Massachusetts, prepared to leave for Canada, citizens of that town held a meeting at which a speaker declared: "I would say to the colored men of Massachusetts be calm, courteous, firm and determined. The man hunters are in the land. Your house, however humble, is your castle. You have a moral and legal right to defend its sanctity against prowling man-stealers. Do it at any cost, at any sacrifice." A number of towns where escaped slaves lived organized secret vigilance committees of armed men to resist any intrusion by slave catchers.

In Boston a meeting was held at Faneuil Hall to denounce the law. Charles Francis Adams presided and Frederick Douglass, Theodore Parker, and Wendell Phillips were among the speakers. Many legislators joined in drafting resolutions calling for the repeal of the law as unconstitutional. The Northern reaction increased the secessionist sentiment in the South. When a black man named Shadrach, who was a waiter, was arrested, taken before a commissioner, and then lodged in jail, Boston blacks set him free and started him on his way to Canada.

A Maryland plantation owner named Edward Gorsuch was a leader in the Methodist Episcopal Church. In contrast to most slave owners, Gorsuch took care to instruct his slaves in Christian doctrine and had freed some of his older slaves and hired them at wages. When four of his slaves fled and established themselves near the town of Christiana, Pennsylvania, in a small colony of blacks, Gorsuch undertook to try to recapture them. Rounding up a party of six, including a son, a nephew, and a cousin, Gorsuch set out for Christiana. While the party was still in Philadelphia word reached the fugitives at Christiana.

The most prominent black man at Christiana was William Parker. A fugitive himself, Parker "thought of my fellow servants left behind, bound in the chains of slavery . . . and I formed a resolution that I would assist in liberating everyone within my reach, at the risk of my own life, and that I would devise a plan for their entire liberation." Parker fell under the influence of Frederick Douglass and discovered that he had known him in his slave days as Frederick Bailey. Hearing Douglass speak was a revelation. "I have never listened," Parker declared, "to words from the lips of mortal man which were more acceptable to me." He and some of his fellow blacks "formed an organization for mutual protection against slaveholders and kidnappers and resolved to prevent any of our brethren being taken back into slavery. . . ." A white abolitionist described Parker as "bold as a lion, the kindest of men, and the most steadfast of friends."

When the Gorsuch party reached Christiana they found that the escaped slaves, armed with pistols and muskets, had barricaded themselves, with other blacks, in Parker's house. The slave hunters, accompanied by a United States marshal, surrounded the house and called on the fugitives to surrender. When Parker's wife blew a horn to summon neighboring blacks to their assistance, the posse began firing at the house. One of Gorsuch's slaves taunted him, "Does such a shriveled up old slaveholder as you own such a nice, genteel young man as I am?" The beleaguered blacks then sang a spiritual, "I will die on the field of battle/Die on the field of battle,/With glory in my soul." After an exchange of fire, the blacks descended on the Gorsuch party, beat Edward Gorsuch insensible, severely wounded his son, and drove the rest of the posse from the area.

The Christiana episode received wide publicity and a number of Southern newspapers took the line that if the Christiana blacks were not quickly and severely punished, the South should at once secede from the Union. Some Northern papers blamed the "riot" on the abolitionists who had encouraged "their innocent dupes, the colored mob," to offer resistance. A local newspaper ran the headline, "Civil War—The First Blow Struck." The *Boston Christian Register* declared, "All the natural rights and claims and apologies are on the fugitive's side. He only did what any white man would be applauded for doing." And Horace Greeley's influential *Tribune* took much the same line, deploring the bloodshed but insisting, "No act of Congress can make it *right* for one man to convert another into his personal property. . . ."

When Georgia slave agents arrived in Boston after the passage of the Fugitive Slave Law to recapture William and Ellen Crafts, special heroes in the continuing drama of escape, the city was once again in a ferment. No commissioner could be found to serve the warrants that the slave hunters brought with them. Instead Ellis Gray Loring drew warrants for the arrest of the agents, alleging slander and asking for ten thousand dollars in damages.

When the Boston Vigilance Committee met to plan a course of action, Wendell Phillips, Richard Henry Dana, Charles Sumner, Ralph Waldo Emerson, Garrison, and Theodore Parker were there. Ellen Crafts was taken to the Loring house in Brookline. Her husband, a cabinetmaker, continued at his trade with a loaded pistol at his side. With the agents close on his trail, Crafts was persuaded to take refuge at the home of Lewis Hayden. Hayden was another slave whose flight had become a *cause célèbre* six years earlier when Calvin Fairbank, the young Oberlin abolitionist, had recruited his schoolteacher friend, Miss Webster, to help Hayden and his family to escape. Fairbank had subsequently been sentenced to five years in the state penitentiary for his role. Now Hayden and his sons barricaded their house, armed themselves with rifles and pistols, and placed two kegs of gunpowder in the basement to blow the house and themselves up if the United States marshal and the Georgia slave hunters penetrated their defenses.

The strategy of the antislavery forces was to form a Committee of Sixty to harass the slave hunters until they left the city. The agents were arrested on a variety of charges, from slander to attempted kidnapping, pursued by a crowd of blacks, arrested for smoking on the streets and for "profane cursing and swearing," for carrying concealed weapons, and for reckless driving. The corridors of their hotel were patrolled by members of the vigilance committee, and they were pursued by shouts of "slave hunters—there go the slave hunters." Finally, frustrated and angry, they withdrew. The Crafts were sent to England, where English abolitionists befriended them.

A month later, Thomas Sims, a fugitive slave who had been working as a waiter in Boston, was arrested by a United States marshal and his posse and locked up in the court house. This time elaborate precautions were taken against any effort to rescue him. He was guarded, in Dana's words, "by a huge force of policemen, & a chain stretched entirely round" the court house itself. "More despicable wretches in appearance than the Southern agents I never beheld," Dana added, "—cruel, low-bred, dissolute, degraded beings!"

The strategy of the antislavery group was to try to have the state of Massachusetts secure custody of Sims on the ground that he had stabbed one of the officers who arrested him. What followed were a fascinating series of legal maneuvers on both sides. Barrages of writs and warrants were fired back and forth. Day after day, Sims's case was argued before one justice or another in an effort to block his return to Georgia. Meanwhile Sims was confined in a small room of the heavily guarded court house, where Dana could see him looking through the grates. "Our Temple of justice," he wrote, "is a slave pen! Our officers are slave hunters, & the voice of the old law of the State is hushed & awed into silence before this fearful Slave power wh. has gotten such entire control of the Union."

All the antislavery efforts failed and shortly before dawn Sims, surrounded by more than a hundred heavily armed city police, was spirited away to a waiting vessel. Yet the pot continued to boil and the antislavery forces renewed their efforts to pass state legislation that would negate the Fugitive Slave Law.

When Charles Sumner made it evident that he was determined to speak out in the Senate on the subject of the Fugitive Slave Law, the Southerners declared it would be the signal for dissolving the Union. But despite the efforts of his fellow senators of both parties to prevent him, Sumner used the debate on the appropriations bill to get the floor on the ground that the Fugitive Slave Law referred to the "extraordinary expenses" required for its enforcement. Richard Henry Dana wrote that many of the men and women in the gallery wept during Sumner's speech. "Old Gen. Underwood from Kentucky shed tears, & Mrs. John Bell in the gallery was in tears. The attention was unbroken, the expressions of admiration, after the close were unbounded." But only Salmon Chase, John Hale of Maine, and Benjamin Wade of Ohio voted with Sumner.

The year 1851 has a special significance for this work. It was the last year of life for one of our valued guides, Philip Hone. Ailing, financially pressed, despondent over the death of his wife, Hone's last months were further shadowed by the growing rift between the North and the South. "The dreadful question of slavery, which has cast an inextinguishable brand of discord between the North and the South of this hitherto happy land," he wrote, "has taken a tangible and definite shape on the question of the admission of the new State of California into the Union with the Constitution of her own framing and adoption. The flame is no longer smothered; the fanatics of the North and the disunionists of the South have made a gulf so deep that no friendly foot can pass it; enmity so fierce that reason cannot allay it; unconquerable, sectional jealousy, the most bitter personal hostility. . . . Passion rules the deliberations of the people's representatives to a degree which, from present appearances, will prevent the dispatch of public business of any kind. . . . The South stands ready to retire from the Union, and bloody wars will be the fatal consequence. White men will cut each other's throats, and servile insurrections will render the fertile fields of the South a deserted monument of the madness of man. On the other hand the Abolitionists of the North will listen to no terms of compromise. Equally regardless of the blessings of union, they profess to hold it of no value unless the power is conceded to them of restraining the extension of the great moral evil which overshadows the land."

In April, a few days before his death, he wrote faithfully and laboriously that only four pages remained to be completed in the twenty-eighth volume of his diary. For a month he had been burdened by "continued unmitigated illness and incapacity to perform any act of mental or physical ability . . . Volume 29 lies ready on my desk. Shall it go on? . . . Has the time come?" The last words of the diary were a "prayer," partly taken from Oliver Goldsmith, the last stanzas by Hone himself:

> This world and worldly things beloved
> My anxious thoughts employed,
> And time unhallowed, unimproved,
> Presents a fearful void.
>
> But, Heavenly Father, wild despair
> Chase from my laboring breast,
> Thy grace it is that prompts the prayer,
> That grace can do the rest.
>
> This life's brief remnant all is Thine;
> And when Thy firm decree
> Bids me this fleeting breath resign,
> Lord, speed myself to Thee!

And so it ended. Philip Hone had indeed loved "This world and worldly things" but loved them, for the most part, wisely and well. And the prejudices and partialities of his class and time aside, he had been a humane and generous man and a wonderfully expressive observer of the age.

56

The Republicans

In 1852 the Northern wing of the Democratic Party was still firmly under the control of the party's conservatives, William Marcy of New York, Lewis Cass of Michigan, and James Buchanan of Pennsylvania. The Southern wing, with its growing obduracy on the slavery issue, insisted that the protection of the government must be extended to the property of slaveholders in the territories and in free states. But there was a general disposition in both parties to accept the Compromise of 1850, placate the South by strict enforcement of the Fugitive Slave Law, and leave the issue of slavery in the territories to be solved on the basis of popular sovereignty. In both parties the official line was to treat the slavery issue as solved by the Compromise of 1850 and focus on the importance of preserving the Union at all costs.

Fillmore, as president, felt that he deserved his party's nomination. Clay, discarded by the party leaders for Taylor four years earlier, saw his hopes revived by the disposition of much of the country to accept the Compromise of 1850 and credit him with achieving it. Webster, in bad health and soured by his repeated failures to win the nomination, was nonetheless determined to make what must clearly be his final try. But the Whigs, having had one of their rare tastes of victory in 1848 with a victorious general, were determined not to let sentiment, common sense, or respect for the electorate distract them from putting forward the only general left, Old Fuss and Feathers, Winfield Scott. George Templeton Strong, after an evening with General Scott, had written, "Any man who could listen for half an hour to the General's bad French and flat jokes, his tedious egotisms, his agonizing pedantries of connoisseurship in wine and cookery, his insipid, inflated gallantries, and his painful exhibitions of suspicious sensitive conceit would pronounce him the smallest and feeblest of created men. . . ." Seeing him thus, it was hard to keep in mind "that he had proved himself a brave, prudent, skillful, brilliant, and humane commander, and a warmhearted and excellent man." Thurlow Weed and William Seward, the latter strongly identified with the Barn-burners, led the antislavery wing of the party and cast their lot with Clay or Webster.

On the Democratic side Marcy, Cass, and Buchanan vied for the nomination. For a time Marcy seemed to have the edge and his supporters floated the slogan, "May the Lord have Marcy upon us," as especially appealing to Irish voters. Cass labored under the burden of his defeat by Taylor. Buchanan—handsome, wealthy, plausible, a good speaker and a man with a long record of public service, including a term as Polk's secretary of state—had dominated Pennsylvania politics for almost two decades. The principal drawback for each candidate was the two-thirds rule of the Democratic nominating convention, which had been invoked in 1844 to block the nomination of Van Buren. Now it threatened to bar any seasoned candidate whose political activities or opinions had aroused opposition in his own party. Recognizing the probability that none of the three front-runners could muster the necessary two-thirds of the delegates, party managers began, well before the convention, to search for a compromise candidate in the event of a convention deadlock. They fastened on Levi Woodbury, a Democratic war-horse from New Hampshire. But Woodbury, despite his obvious desire to make the transition from a war-horse to a dark horse, died some months before the nominating convention and the managers—prominent among them Gideon Pillow, one of the few Democratic generals in the Mexican War and a bitter enemy of Scott's—began to look elsewhere. They did not, in fact, look very far. Only a few counties away from Woodbury's home they turned up Franklin Pierce, who spoke well, looked well, belonged to an old New Hampshire family, and could even be called "General" since he had fought with (in both senses of the word) Scott in the campaign from

Veracruz to Mexico City. He had served in the House and Senate without particular distinction but he was a practical, affable man, with few enemies. So the party managers put him on ice and began quietly to circulate his name "as worthy . . . of high place among the names of eminent citizens who will be conspicuously before the national convention."

The Democratic convention met in Baltimore on June 1, six hundred strong, with innumerable political hawks and buzzards hanging over the proceedings, jamming the hotels and crowding the streets. Fumes of booze and cigar smoke and the smell of sweating bodies were pungent in hotel lobbies and saloons. Painted ladies were much in evidence. Deals were made, votes bargained for and exchanged, favored candidates touted. The atmosphere was somewhere between that of a horse race, a boxing match, and a carnival. There were 288 votes to be cast, with 197 for the two-thirds majority. After eight ballots Cass led with 119 votes, Buchanan was second with 95, and Stephen Douglas, the flamboyant high roller from Illinois, the personification of wide-open frontier politics, was in third place at 24. Carl Schurz, the young German revolutionary who had immigrated to the United States, described Douglas as short, "broad-shouldered and big-chested" with "a stout, strong neck . . . a square jaw and broad chin; a rather large, firm-set mouth . . . quick piercing eyes with a deep, dark, scowling, menacing horizontal wrinkle between them; a broad forehead and an abundance of dark hair which . . . he wore rather long and which, when in excitement, he shook and tossed about defiantly like a lion's mane . . . the very incarnation of forceful combativeness." Schurz had seen Douglas, after a "boisterous speech" in the Senate, sit on "the lap of a brother senator and loll there, talking and laughing, for ten or fifteen minutes, with his arm around the neck of his friend. . . ."

The Lord had failed to have Marcy, who lagged at 23 votes. In nine more ballots Cass weakened and Douglas gained strength. What went on on the floor as one roll call after another droned on was simply the window dressing that concealed the negotiations in the rear of the hall, in nearby hotel rooms and odd corners. The Buchanan men tried to prevail on the Marcyites to join in a desperate effort to put the Pennsylvanian over. The supporters of Cass worked on the adherents of Douglas. Day after day the hurried conferences and anxious consultations went on, the threats, the promises, the cajolings. Finally, after three days, it became clear that the anticipated had happened—the convention was hopelessly deadlocked. Pierce's name was presented as planned by the Virginia delegates, with 29 votes to support it, but he gained no additional support for ten ballots, while Marcy made his bid, advancing to 98, still 99 shy of the number needed to nominate.

Then on the forty-sixth and forty-seventh ballots, first Kentucky and then Maryland and four delegates from Massachusetts joined Pierce's steady 29. On the forty-ninth ballot, North Carolina broke for Pierce and soon thereafter the stampede began and it was all over in an instant. Pierce for president! William Rufus King of Alabama was chosen for vice-president. "Nobody knows much of Franklin Pierce, except that he is a decent sort of man in private life," George Templeton Strong wrote. "Very possibly he may run all the better, as Polk did, for his insignificance. Democracies are not over-partial to heroes and great men. A statesman who is too much glorified becomes a bore to them. . . . Democracy is secretly jealous of individual eminence of every sort, not merely that which grows out of wealth or station. . . . So that it is not impossible that the Locos will *pierce* their enemies in 1852 as they *poked* them in 1844. . . . Scott's foibles are so many that he's vulnerable and can be made ridiculous, and this galvanized cypher, of whom nothing can be said but that he is a cypher, may very well beat him. . . ." A makeshift platform of familiar Democratic bromides was patched together and the exhausted delegates headed for home, full of Maryland seafood, fine bourbon, and a consciousness of having done their duty as loyal Democrats and patriotic Americans. An odd way to choose a candidate for the president of the self-proclaimed greatest nation on earth, some foreign observers of the scene reflected, but if such thoughts occurred to any of the delegates they kept them to themselves or confined them to their private journals.

The Whig convention, which met a few weeks later in the same city, was in striking contrast to the rowdiness and general confusion of the Democratic gathering. There were only three declared candidates —Scott, Fillmore, and Webster. Clay, so long denied, was dying at Ashland. He sent word that his choice was Fillmore, but it did nothing to deflect the supporters of Scott. With one of the great Whig champions hors de combat, only Webster was left to contest the field with the superannuated general. "The glorious Daniel" was himself an ailing man, seventy-two years old, worn out by almost a half-century of political warfare, disheartened by the repeated rebuffs of his party, by the death of a beloved son in the Mexican War which he had so strongly opposed, by high living and self-indulgence, his last the companionship of a young mistress. But the fire of ambition still burned in those compelling eyes. His friends deplored his final, undignified reaching for a prize he was too ill to claim had it been given him. But he was determined to invite this final humiliation. On the first ballot (with only a majority needed in the Whig convention) Fillmore received 133 votes as incumbent president and Scott 131. Webster had 29! Fillmore was strongly opposed to Scott, and word came to the Webster forces that if they could find 41 votes for their man, the Fillmore people would try to swing to him 106 of the votes pledged to the President, giving the New Englander the 147 needed for nomination. Thus it seemed for a time that only 12 votes out of 293 stood between Webster and his party's nomination. But those 12 votes could not be found. In the end Seward and Weed, who had parted from Webster over the Compromise of 1850, held their delegates. Nonetheless, voting went on through more than fifty ballots before enough Southern Whigs, suspicious of Scott's commitment to the Compromise, were persuaded to cast their ballots for the general. At one point Fillmore had enough votes to secure the nomination if Webster came over to *him*. But Webster and his backers dallied and the chance slipped away. Scott thus received the nomination on the fifty-third ballot. When word reached Webster, he said to Rufus Choate, his most loyal lieutenant, "How will this look in history?"

He might well have asked. Scott, never a strong candidate, suffered from a schism of "free-soil Whigs," but he suffered most of all from his own ineptitude. When the Democrats charged him with anti-Irish and anti-Catholic sentiments, he found a pretext to tour the country (allegedly to inspect sites for military hospitals, since actual campaigning by a presidential candidate was considered undignified), giving long-winded "nonpolitical" talks in which he referred to his fondness for a "rich Irish brogue" and "a sweet German accent."

"The General," George Templeton Strong wrote, "tries to look as wise as the Sphinx, but accomplishes only a puzzled, dubious gaze into vacancy, which says, 'I'm in a scrape and a bad one. . . . I'm afloat in a sea, don't understand this sort of campaigning near as well as the other, and don't see that I can do anything, unless I write letters, and my friends make such a row if I hint at such a thing that I daren't do it.' And all this time the poor General is being discussed *and* analyzed and pulled to pieces in newspapers and speeches and pamphlets through all the land. . . . What must be his sensations when he's called Fuss and Feathers in half the village newspapers of the United States?"

Henry Clay died June 29, a few days after Scott's nomination. He had been a kind of quintessential American politician—it was in his long, narrow, rather homely face, his sharp, direct gaze, high forehead, and wide, generous, sensual mouth; the consummate politician, the brilliant orator, the darling of the West. Only Webster rivaled him in popular adulation. If Webster's forte was power and dignity, Clay's was charm; the irresistible smile, turned indiscriminately on foe or friend, the warm handshake, the disarming look of complete candor. American politics were based, or said to be based, on compromise and he was the master of compromise. No more skillful party manager has ever drawn a wavering colleague aside and spoken more ingratiatingly into his ear. Clay had the quality of touching people's hearts; his oratory, less burdened with learning than Webster's or Calhoun's, struck closer to the feelings of ordinary Americans. His unhappy waffle over the admission of Texas aside, he was typically forthright and courageous. He had boldly opposed the Mexican War, not counting the political cost, and had asked for a generous peace with Mexico that would leave its territory intact. Only Webster had done more to root the idea of Union in the hearts of Americans. Clay died in the faith that, with the Compromise of 1850, he had prolonged indefinitely the life of the Union he so loved.

The "Free Soil Whigs" held a convention at Faneuil Hall to nominate their own presidential tickct. Richard Henry Dana noted in his diary on February 27: "This day the Free Soil Convention was held . . . to sustain the Wilmot Proviso." Dana had written the report and resolutions to be addressed to Congress. The Free Soilers split with the Whigs primarily over the failure of the party's platform to reject the Fugitive Slave Law and nominated Senator John Parker Hale of New Hampshire for president, thereby virtually assuring the election of Pierce.

"No election ever drew ncar so quietly, no two candidates ever developed so little enthusiasm," George Templeton Strong wrote. "Scott's stumping tour may have done good among the masses, but I'm sure it has lost him respect with sensible people everywhere. His speeches are awkward, strained, vapid, and egotistical. Pierce has a talent for silence. . . ."

Aside from Winfield Scott's "tour," which, by letting people see and hear him, worked substantially to his disadvantage, the campaign was notably lacking in excitement. Nathaniel Hawthorne wrote a campaign biography for his Bowdoin College classmate, Pierce, which was supplemented by two others, presumably written in more popular form. Again great pains were taken with the "foreign" vote, with the Whigs wooing the German and Irish Catholic vote, and the Democrats depicting Scott as the relentless enemy of all immigrants. Campaign tracts were written in Swedish and German. Pierce was dubbed "The Young Hickory of the Granite Hills"; certainly at forty-eight he was considerably junior to the sixty-six-year-old Scott, who, it might be noted, was to live another fourteen years.

It is perhaps sufficient to say that the most notable event of the fall of 1852 was not the presidential election but the death of one of the defeated nominees of the Whig Party. Daniel Webster died on October 24, 1852, four months after his final rejection as his party's presidential candidate in favor of inept old Scott. Everyone understood that it was the end of a great era; first Calhoun, then Clay, and now the titan of them all. George Templeton Strong wrote in his diary: "From the old heroic race to which Webster and Clay and Calhoun belonged down to the rising race of Sewards and Douglases and Fishes is a dismal descent."

Oratory is no longer an effective mode of public discourse so it is difficult to appreciate fully Webster's talents and his accomplishments. He dominated the political life of his native New England in a way that no other regional politician, with the possible exception of his rival, Calhoun, has ever done. To his constituents he was "God-like," "the divine Webster," a man capable of recreating the meaning of the republic with words, through speech. And what his speech had done, in stunning reiteration over decades, was make the idea of "Union" paramount in the minds of a majority of Americans north of the Mason-Dixon line. Where all the natural tendencies were toward provincialism, regionalism, and sectionalism, Webster had tied the states together in what were to prove indissoluble bonds by the power of his rhetoric. Vain, ambitious, self-indulgent, untidy, increasingly willing to serve as the tool of business interests, indefatigable in his pursuit of the ultimate goal, the presidency, which was always to elude him, he was crucified, like so many politicians of his time, on the inescapable cross of the slavery question, a question that could not forever be compromised or smoothed over in the name of Union. While there is no question that Webster compromised his own integrity out of a love of material comfort and a desire to be president, there is certainly no reason to doubt the depth and sincerity of his commitment to the Union. In that sense he belonged to an earlier age, to the age of Washington, Adams, and Madison, and, toward the end of his life, Jefferson, men to whom the preservation of the Union was the overriding consideration in all political matters. So it must be said that, with all his very human weaknesses, the country owed and owes Webster an incalculable debt. His life was, moreover, a classic American tragedy. From having been almost universally admired and indeed loved in his home region and throughout much of the nation, his name became, by the time of his death, a word of opprobrium. The most renowned moralist-philosopher of the time, Ralph Waldo Emerson, had written his political obituary when Webster supported the Fugitive Slave Law as part of the Compromise of 1850 and the *New York Evening Post* had printed only a week before his death a long poem that began:

> 'Twas the last hope of his craving ambition,
>   'Twas the last stake in that desperate game;
> All now is lost—save a last contrition,
>   Or, what is worse, self-glorying shame.

and ended:

> Call on thy pride, if thy virtue's departed,
>   Though we no longer can feed thee on faith,
> Live not like a slave by thy passions perverted
>   And creep not at last so abjectly to death.

But if all such thoughts were not forgotten on the news of his death, they were at least suppressed. The death brought back too much, raised too many questions both about the country's past and its future, about the nature of American politics and its human costs. "From all these causes, & in their various & conflicting qualities & degrees," Richard Henry Dana noted, "all men agree to mourn his death. No death since that of Washington has excited so general a grief." Three or four days later after the obsequies, after innumerable speeches and sermons, Webster's funeral was held at his estate. "A mile & a half before we reached Mr. Webster's," Dana wrote, "we found waggons, chaises & coaches, put up at sheds & barns, & standing in open fields, the horses tied to fences & trees. . . . On looking over the country from the hill top, they covered the land like grasshoppers. When I reached the house it was full, & the doors locked, while an immense crowd filled the piazzas & the yard, & was scattered over the grounds. Under a tree in front of the house stood the coffin, uncovered, & in it lay stretched, at length, 'all that is mortal of Daniel Webster.'" He wore a blue coat with gold buttons and a white neck cloth, "while the huge, massy forehead, the dome of thought, lay open, under the N. England sky, gazed upon by the thousands of his own race & nation, in silent awe."

To Dana, Webster was "a true product of N. England, & true child of her earth, & to her earth, on her most sacred spot, the home of the Pilgrims, was he to return. . . . And to this remote & not easily accessible spot, thousands, from all parts of the country, from all cities & states within reach, have made their toilsome journey, moved by a common impulse, & overshadowed by an awe wh. they feel but cannot all express. No man represented so completely, in our day, at least, the mighty, innate, inaccessible superiority of dialectic intellect. The Almighty gave him, at birth a larger & heavier brain than any of his race & a physical frame suited to its utmost needs."

Dana could not get the image of Webster out of his mind, "the great solemn countenance, lying stretched in death, in the open air, under the canopy of heaven. . . . With all his greatness & smallness, with all the praise and blame, gratitude, admiration, censure & distrust, with which we look upon his life, there is something so majestical, so large of mind & heart about him, that an emotion of pride & tears swells at the very thought of him."

Aside from the deaths of Webster and Clay the most sensational event of 1852 was the publication of *Uncle Tom's Cabin*. Harriet Beecher Stowe believed that God had called on her to write a book depicting slavery in a manner that, while sympathetic to the dilemma of white Southerners, would arouse general sympathy for slaves by revealing their common humanity with the whites. The resulting work, not very highly regarded by professors of literature, is a marvelous novel full of unforgettable characters and dramatic situations. Uncle Tom, far from being a toady to the whites, sacrifices his life to prevent the whipping of a black woman by the infamous Simon Legree. However it may be rated as "literature," it is a work of extraordinary imaginative power, a gripping story of terror and suspense interspersed with acute reflections on the relations between the races.

At the end of *Uncle Tom's Cabin* Harriet Beecher Stowe warned her readers that God's vengeance must surely be visited upon the United

States if the evil of slavery was not eradicated. That day would "burn as an oven; and he shall appear as a swift witness against those that oppress the hireling in his wages, the widow and fatherless, . . . and he shall break in pieces the oppressor," she quoted from the prophet Malachi. "Are these not dread words for a nation bearing in her bosom so mighty an injustice?" Stowe asked. "Both North and South have been guilty before God; and the *Christian church* has a heavy account to answer. . . ." The only hope lay in "repentance, justice and mercy; for, not surer is the eternal law by which the millstone sinks in the ocean, than that stronger law, by which injustice and cruelty shall bring on nations the wrath of Almighty God."

Sidney George Fisher called it "The great book of the year. . . . No book ever had such sudden & universal success. It is read by everybody with interest & delight, it is bought as fast as it can be printed, it is advertised in every paper in America & England & the Continent, it is sold in hotels & railroads, & read by all classes, in cottages & palaces, by the wayside & the fireside, & has been translated into every language of Europe, including the Russian. . . . Altogether, the work displays genius, creative, imaginative, fruitful & original." Other books of course had such qualities without such success. The real reason for the book's extraordinary popularity, Fisher wrote, "is that it reveals the true nature & contains a faithful picture of American slavery. . . . It is a correct picture of the enormities of slavery, as I know from what I have myself witnessed & heard from others thoroughly experienced & acquainted with the subject & whose prejudices were all in favor of the system." Its emotional impact on its readers was enormous; its political consequence incalculable. Only Tom Paine's *Common Sense* has ever had such a strong influence on that mysterious thing called public opinion.

In the absence of clear-cut issues, the campaign of 1852 focused on personalities and was, in consequence, somewhat more foul and malicious than the average run of presidential campaigns—though that, assuredly, is a difficult palm to award. Pierce, who had had a drinking problem and had, indeed, left the Senate because of it, was attacked as a drunkard, and, for not proclaiming slavery an unqualified blessing to humanity, an abolitionist. Poor Scott, struggling as best he could to stay afloat in waters far too deep for him, was mocked and derided for his appearance, his mannerisms, his speech. The old hero, for hero he was, was left little of reputation or self-respect by the end of the campaign. The young officer who had performed so brilliantly at Lundy's Lane, been decorated and brevetted major general at the age of twenty-eight, was only a dim memory; the regular army officer who had gone on to win laurels as a soldier-diplomat in settling the border dispute with Canada in 1838, who had reformed the army and outlawed the cruel punishments meted out as discipline to soldiers and, more recently, added to his laurels with notable and conclusive victories in the Mexican War, was mercilessly abused by the partisan press. Foolish and vain he may have been but he certainly deserved better than winding up as the tool of ambitious politicians. The death of Clay, the rejection of Webster, the humiliation of Scott, proved democracy a cruel mistress; most cruel, it sometimes seemed, to those who had served her best.

As the election returns began to come in it was clear that Scott and the Whigs had suffered a catastrophic defeat. "If Webster's ghost don't sing a comic song at Mrs. Fish's spiritual soiree tonight, or rap out an Hallelujah chorus under the table," George Templeton Strong wrote, "I'm mistaken. Pity he couldn't have lived to see this day. . . . General opinion seems to be that the Whig party is dead and will soon be decomposed into its original elements. Shouldn't wonder. Where is its leader or leaders. . . . Even the Democracy is likely to be disintegrated by the election. The Whigs have long been nothing but a hoop to keep northern and southern democracy more or less bound together by fear of a common enemy. . . . If one party dies the other must perish of inaction, for there's no principle to give either an independent life."

The electoral vote was 254 for Pierce to 42 for Scott, who won only four states—Kentucky, Massachusetts, Tennessee, and Vermont. In the popular vote he made a much more respectable showing—1,386,580 to Pierce's 1,601,474. Hale, the Free Soiler, had 156,667, substantially below Van Buren's tally in 1848, but much of this loss was accounted for by the drop in the New York Free Soil vote from roughly 120,000 in 1848 to 25,000. New York aside, the Free Soilers with little money or organization and an unknown candidate had pretty much held their own.

In Franklin Pierce's inaugural address he paid the ritual attention to the Founding Fathers and their vision of America. In the nation's birth, even though "inconsiderable in population and apparent resources, it was upheld by a broad and intelligent comprehension of rights and an all pervading purpose to maintain them, stronger than armaments. It came from the furnace of the Revolution, tempered to the necessities of the times. The thoughts of the men of that day were as practical as their sentiments were patriotic. They wasted no portion of their energies upon idle and delusive speculations, but with a firm and fearless step advanced beyond the government landmarks which had hitherto circumscribed the limits of human freedom. . . . The object sought was not a thing dreamed of; it was a thing realized. . . . The oppressed throughout the world from that day to the present have turned their eyes hitherward." The fires of liberty burned undimmed in the United States. "In this our country has . . . thus far fulfilled its highest duty to suffering humanity." The strength of the United States was based "upon eternal principles of right and justice."

Two new elements entered the political equation during the administration of Franklin Pierce—the Republican Party and the Kansas-Nebraska bill. When Stephen Douglas, like a mischievous and unprincipled child, opened that Pandora's box, the Kansas-Nebraska Act, he gave a dazzling display of his skills at political management and made evident his determination to succeed Henry Clay as the political leader of the West and a prime candidate for the presidency.

Douglas's bill divided the Nebraska territory into two prospective states, leaving to "popular sovereignty"—that is to say, to the settlers themselves—the issue of whether they would come into the Union as slave or free states. Since Kansas lay directly west of the Missouri Compromise line, the bill in effect repealed the thirty-five-year-old Missouri Compromise in anticipating that Kansas would be a slave state and Nebraska a free state. For three months the bill was debated with increasing bitterness. Finally Douglas mustered the votes to ram it through Congress, assuming that its passage would assure him of his party's presidential nomination in 1856.

The Kansas-Nebraska Act raised a storm in New England, especially among the antislavery Whigs. It also shook a number of Northerners out of the Democratic Party, most notably those with latent antislavery views. Since Stephen Douglas's middle name was Arnold, it was inevitable that effigies of him would be found hanging from lamp posts with such labels as "Stephen A. Douglas, the author of the infamous Nebraska bill; the Benedict Arnold of 1854." He was sent thirty pieces of silver by one group of indignant citizens.

The assumption of Douglas and the Southerners that Kansas would be admitted to the Union as a slave state was something that Free Soilers were determined to defeat; both Kansas and Nebraska must become free states. To this end various emigrant aid societies were organized, primarily for the purpose of sending free-soil settlers into Kansas in sufficient numbers to ensure that the territory would be organized as a free state. Hundreds of thousands of dollars were raised to finance the Kansas crusade, and thousands of emigrants, some of whom burned with antislavery missionary zeal and some of whom were only moderately antislavery in their sentiments, found the prospect of financial assistance in getting settled in the new territory irresistible and headed west. The same reaction was evident in the antislavery states of the Mississippi Valley. The *Cleveland Herald* called for a state convention to form plans to check the spread of slavery, and a Milwaukee newspaper made a similar proposal. In Maine and Vermont, Michigan and Massachusetts, such conventions of anti-Nebraska men laid the groundwork for the formation of the Republican Party.

In Boston feelings were further exacerbated by another fugitive slave episode. On the morning of May 25, 1854, an acquaintance had informed Richard Henry Dana that a fugitive slave named George Burns was in custody. "I went up immediately," Dana wrote, "& saw a negro, sitting in the usual place for prisoners, guarded by a large corps of officers. He is a piteous object, rather weak in mind & body, with a large scar on his cheek, wh. looks much like a brand, a broken hand, from wh. a large piece of bone projects, & another scar on his other hand. He seemed completely cowed & dispirited." Dana at once offered to act as his lawyer but the prisoner was afraid that any resistance, legal or otherwise, would only result in his being more severely punished by his master. Dana therefore procured a delay to give the man a chance to make a more reflective decision. When Wendell Phillips and a black clergyman visited him, Burns turned out to be a literate and intelligent man. He accepted Dana as legal counsel and told him that he had never worked for his master since he was seven years old but had been hired out. He had fled because he was convinced that his master intended to sell him to the New Orleans slave market.

That night there was a large meeting in Faneuil Hall to discuss the proper strategy for trying to prevent Burns's return to his master. The composition of the audience was revealing. Former Whigs and defenders of the Fugitive Slave Law were much in evidence. "The most remarkable exhibition," Dana wrote, "is from the Whigs, the Hunker Whigs, the Compromise men of 1850. Men who would not speak to me in 1850 & 51, & who were enrolling themselves as special policemen in the Sims affair, stop me in the street & talk treason. This all owing to the Nebraska bill. I cannot respect their feeling at all, except as a return to sanity. The Webster delusion is passing off." Amos Lawrence, the cotton tycoon, who had long opposed any measures that might alienate the South, told Dana that he and his business friends would pay any legal costs incurred in defending Burns since they were determined "it sh. be known that it was not the Free Soilers only who were in favor of the liberation of the Slaves, but the conservative, compromise men."

Two days later an attempt was made to rescue Burns. The door of the court house was broken down and a few men forced their way in. A teamster named Batchelder, who had volunteered to help guard the prisoner, was killed, but the rescuers were wounded and forced back. Thomas Wentworth Higginson, a Unitarian minister and Harvard graduate, one of Boston's "own," had been one of the ringleaders. "I knew his ardor & courage," Dana noted, "but I hardly expected a married man, a clergyman, & a man of education to lead the mob."

Theodore Parker and Samuel Gridley Howe had also offered to lead raids on the court house but the only result of Higginson's effort was that a company of United States marines, a company of artillery, and two or three companies of militia were ordered into Boston to defend the court house. The hearing on Burns's recapture was crowded and the building surrounded by "the hireling soldiers of the Standing Army of the U.S.," in Dana's words. "The lazy hounds were lounging all day out of the windows, & hanging over the stairs, but ready to shoot down good men, at a word of command."

Meanwhile a movement started to raise money to buy Burns's freedom in the event that no legal obstacles could be placed in the way of his return and the court proceedings went forward with no one admitted who had not been carefully screened by soldiers. Colonel Suttle, Burns's master, who had appeared to claim his property, was guarded by a body of young Southern law students "who sat around Col. Suttle & went in & out with him." Dana's address to the court on behalf of his client took four hours—"My friends say it is the best speech I ever made," he noted in his journal.

The excitement in the city was intense. The court's verdict was expected on Friday, June 2. Word of the trial had spread "throughout N. England, & indeed a great part of the Union. The hearts of millions of people were beating high with hope, or indignation, or doubt." The mayor of Boston, "a poor shoat, a physician of a timid, conceited scatter-brained character," in Dana's opinion, had panicked and called up fifteen hundred militia. "These troops & the three companies of regulars," he wrote, "fill the streets & squares from the C't. Hs. to the end of the wharf" where the revenue cutter that would take Burns back to slavery was tied.

The decision was brief. Everything was legal and in order. Burns was properly identified and must, by the law of the land, be returned to his master. "The decision," Dana wrote, "was a grievous disappointment to us all, & chiefly to the poor prisoner. He looked the image of despair." It remained only to have him carried to the cutter. The square in front of the court house was cleared of people by the police but "every window was filled & beyond the lines drawn by police, was an immense crowd. Whenever a body of troops passed to or fro, they were hissed & hooted by the people. . . . Near all the shops in C't. & State streets were closed & hung in black, & a huge coffin was suspended across State st. . . ." Orders were given to the troops to fire on the people if they were "turbulent & disorderly." The city was, in effect, under martial law, a powder keg with the match in the hands of the military. "Notwithstanding their numbers & the enormous military protection, the Marshal's company [with the prisoner] were very much disturbed & excited." So accompanied by jeers and hisses, the soldiers and police conveyed their charge to the United States vessel. With Burns on board and the ship headed out to sea, Dana turned back to his office. Walking down Court Street toward Bowdoin Square, he was struck a brutal blow over his right eye by a heavy club. Stupefied and bleeding, he was taken to a doctor's office and the wound treated. The attack had the incidental effect of cementing Dana's new status as a hero in the city where he had so often been treated as an outcast. "The charge wrought by the Nebraska bill is astonishing," he wrote. The "Webster Whigs" felt that "they have been deceived by the South, & that they have misled others. I do not [know] how many who hardly spoke to me from 1850 to 1853, & whom I heard of in all quarters as speaking ag. me bitterly, come up to me with the freedom & warmth of old friends, & talk as though there had never been any difference between us. This is not always easy to bear." At the time of the Sims case he noted, "we were all traitors & malignants, now we are heroes & patriots. The truth is Danl. Webster was strong eno' to subjugate, for a time, the moral sentiment of N. England. He was defeated, killed, & is now detached. He deceived half the North, but they are undeceived."

In Richmond, Burns was put in the town's slave pens, chained hand and foot as punishment for his escape, and kept there for four months when his master put him up for auction. For an hour no one bid for him but he was abused and threatened for having escaped. Indeed, Suttle had to form a bodyguard around him to protect him from a menacing crowd. Finally he was sold to a North Carolina slave dealer for $910. The Carolinian's purpose was to sell him to some Northern antislavery organization for a handsome profit. Finally, Burns's new owner arranged to sell him for $1300, but when the rumor got out on a steamer headed for Baltimore that Burns was on board and was to be sent North and turned free, his owner had to stand guard over the cabin for three hours with a loaded pistol.

Back in Boston, Burns, now a celebrity, visited the jail cell where he had been kept and Dana wrote in his diary, "What a change, what a life for an obscure negro! . . . now he visits the scene of his agony of trial, a hero, a martyr, with crowds of the learned & intelligent of a civilized community listening to his words! Who can tell what other things & which are the men that are to move the world."

On the heels of the Kansas-Nebraska Act a coalition of antislavery Democrats in Congress—Joshua Giddings and Salmon Chase of Ohio, Charles Sumner of Massachusetts, and Gerrit Smith of New York— drew up an "Appeal of the Independent Democrats in Congress to the People of the United States," which signaled the breakup of the Democratic Party. They declared the act "part and parcel of an atrocious plot" to turn the West into a "dreary region of despotism inhabited by masters and slaves," denounced the notion of popular sovereignty as a recent and unconstitutional innovation, and pledged their adherence to the Missouri Compromise. The Kansas-Nebraska Act was a "gross violation of a sacred pledge," and must be resisted by every means, "for the cause of freedom is the cause of God."

Even as staunch an enemy of abolition and "Niggerocracy" as George Templeton Strong was deeply offended by the Kansas-Nebraska Act. "I'm resisting awful temptations to avow myself a Free-Soiler," he wrote. "I've never denied or doubted the wrong of slavery. . . . I have denied that wrong because I could not affirm that all men were born free and equal, and I am no nearer the capacity to affirm that proposition. *Don't believe* all men so born. . . . Every indication of Northern sentiment points to a vigorous reaction against the Nebraska bill and the formation of a strong antislavery party at the North."

The "strong antislavery party" was not long in appearing. At Jackson, Michigan, on July 6, 1854, a convention assembled and drew up a platform that opposed the extension of slavery and referred favorably to many of the reform movements of the hour. Soon Ohio, Wisconsin, and Vermont had followed suit. In Massachusetts Charles Francis Adams and Richard Henry Dana were in the forefront of those organizing a convention that met on July 19. Two years earlier Charles Francis Adams had noted in his diary that the defection of a substantial number of Whigs from Scott to Pierce presaged the "end of the Whig party." "The minorities," he added, "afterwards would be under the necessity of uniting." As the months passed Adams noted from time to time the indications of political "transition." "Silence" and watchfulness had seemed to him the best course but now, suddenly, disparate forces rushed to an unexpected conjunction. The Massachusetts convention stated boldly: "That no man can own another man . . . That slavery must be prohibited in the territories . . . That all new States must be Free States . . . That the rights of our colored citizens going to other States must be protected." And, in reference to the Compromise of 1850, "That in the course of God's providence nothing can be called final which is wrong. . . ." So began the Republican Party. "The Republican party," an antislavery editor wrote, "is a necessity of the time. It represents a reality. . . . You cannot kill it, unless you kill, at the same time, the soul of man." The people of Massachusetts "yearn for a great principle, and for an honest man."

Despite the emergence of the Republicans, for a time the principal political beneficiary of the passage of the Kansas-Nebraska Act was the Native American Party, which emerged from political obscurity with startling force, reincarnated as the Know-Nothings. In the midterm elections of 1854 it elected dozens of state legislators and a number of Congressmen. While the *Herald* and the *Tribune* both spoke of the movement "as a mere temporary perturbation of our party system," George Templeton Strong wrote, "probably this secret organization will be short-lived, but taking its late triumphs in connection with those of the Natives ten years ago, it seems to me that its principle is likely to be an important element in political calculations for some time to come. . . . But for the Nebraska and temperance questions, they would have controlled this election entirely, and reduced the Whig and Democratic parties to insignificance." A few weeks after the midterm election Strong "met a prodigious Know-Nothing procession moving uptown . . . , a most emphatic and truculent demonstration. Solid column, eight or ten abreast, and numbering some two or three thousand, mostly young men of the butcher-boy and *prentice* type . . .

marching in quick time, and occasionally indulging in a very earnest kind of hurray. We may well have a memorable row here before the fall elections are over," he added, "and perhaps a religious war within the next decade, if this awful vague, mysterious, new element of Know-Nothingism is as potent as its friends and political wooers seem to think it. . . . If the Know-Nothings were only political, not politico-religious, I'd join them."

Dana described the movement as "made up of religious & national hostility to the R. Catholics & Irish, & a distrust of & disclination to the old parties." It seemed to Dana a great setback that the Know-Nothings should "have arisen to divide the Counsels of the North & weaken our influence on the Slave Question, at a time when a united front from the North is so necessary." Adams and Dana were anxious to absorb the antislavery elements of the Know-Nothings into a new political alliance that would be distinguished more by its resistance to the extension of slavery than by its nativist sentiments. The troubling aspect of Know-Nothingism was that it demonstrated in dramatic fashion the depth of the general disillusionment with existing party alignments.

On August 22, 1854, committees of the Know-Nothings and "Know-Somethings" and "the remnant of the Free Soilers" met and attempted to form a new party. The most that could be agreed to, since Know-Nothings dominated the gathering, was a "call" for a convention to meet in Worcester. The "call to the meeting" was framed with the intention of excluding the Know-Nothings and it was so far successful that when the convention convened it identified itself with the new Republican Party. In the face of these developments many Americans felt that the country was lapsing rapidly into barbarism. To men of a reflective turn of mind the wave of revivals set off by the depression of 1854 with their intense emotionalism, the popularity of spiritualism in various forms, and, perhaps above all, the success of Brigham Young and his Mormons, all pointed toward some new dark age. To someone as devout as George Templeton Strong, the new "religion" of human-ism seemed almost as great a threat as the Church of the Latter-Day Saints. Underlying all these disturbing phenomena was the increasing madness of the South, where neither the law nor Christian morality seemed capable of preventing the most egregious abuse of basic human rights for whites and blacks alike. And beyond the South's collective insanity there was ample evidence of a growing hostility among the urban poor toward the wealthy and well-to-do, a furious and bitter spirit manifested in constant acts of individual and mob violence. "Simple barbarism" had, in George Templeton Strong's opinion, been increasing for twenty years. "Life and property grow less and less secure. Law, legislation, and judiciary are less respected; skepticism spreads as to the existence anywhere of anybody who will not steal if he has an official opportunity. Our civilization is decaying. We are in our decadence. An explosion and crash must be at hand."

57

Bleeding Kansas

Even before Pierce had signed the Kansas-Nebraska Act into law, hundreds of emigrants had started for the new territories, many of them subsidized by the Massachusetts Emigrant Aid Company. The response of Missourians was the formation of the Society of Missourians for Mutual Protection, pledged to keep abolitionists out of Kansas. A vigilance committee was appointed to protect the rights, i.e., the slave property, of Southern emigrants to Kansas. The town of Leavenworth, in an area still reserved as Indian land, was established by Missouri settlers as the intended capital of the territory.

The free-state emigrants established their headquarters at Lawrence, where tents, log cabins, and lean-tos were the principal habitations. The Northern emigrants, many of them inured to the hardships attendant on the establishment of new communities, soon far outnumbered the Southerners, less mobile and for the most part ill equipped to pull up stakes and transport their slave property into a region whose future was at the best uncertain. The Southern strategy was, therefore, to encourage the organization of groups of irregulars, heavily armed men who attempted to intercept and turn back free-state emigrants, and to hound those already on the ground into withdrawing. The emigrant aid societies responded by issuing the new

Sharps repeating rifles to those families who went to Kansas under their sponsorship. The consequence was that a state of terror and guerrilla warfare existed in Kansas almost from the moment that the first emigrants crossed its boundaries.

Pierce appointed Andrew Reeder of Pennsylvania as the first governor of the Kansas Territory. The chief justice of the territorial court was Samuel Dexter Lecompte. One of Lecompte's first duties was to set the conditions for the election of a territorial representative to Congress. When the polls opened, thousands of Missourians crossed the state line into Kansas Territory to vote for proslavery candidates. In Douglas, a town of some thirty residents, 226 illegal ballots were cast by visitors from Missouri who came on horse- and mule-back, in wagons and buggies. Needless to say, the proslavery candidate won. The next step was to elect a territorial legislature. A census of voters showed that 8,501 persons were residents of the territory, of whom fewer than 3,000 were qualified voters. Again the Missourians came in droves—they even brought a cannon with them—and overwhelmed the bona fide settlers at the polls. Free-state newspapers and abolition-ist journals were proscribed, presses were smashed and type scattered, and antislavery preachers were barred from their pulpits. All these acts of violence were reported in detail in the Northern press, leading to redoubled efforts in the North to swell the number of Free Soil emigrants. Reeder's attempt to preserve some semblance of justice resulted in pressure on him from Pierce to resign, which Reeder resisted. He became embroiled with the legislature over the location of the territorial capitol and dissolved it. Pierce removed him and replaced him with a proslavery governor, Wilson Shannon, while the Free Soilers elected the deposed Reeder to Congress as the territory's delegate and drafted a free constitution at Topeka to be approved by popular vote as the basis of the territory's admission to the Union as a free state. When the existence of a quasi-military force in Missouri, organized for the purpose of routing the Free Soil residents of Kansas, became widely known, the Free Soilers appealed to Pierce for federal troops to protect them. Pierce, ignoring the petitioners, blamed the emigrant aid societies for the troubles in Kansas, denounced the Topeka convention, and gave the government's support to the Leavenworth "assembly."

The effect of the President's proclamation was to cast the Free Soilers in the role of lawbreakers and give encouragement to their enemies. The response in the North was a new flow of money and emigrants. Judge Lecompte termed the Topeka government "an unlawful and hitherto unheard-of organization" composed of men "who are dubbed governors, men who are dubbed lieutenant governors . . . and men who are dubbed all the other dubs with which the territory is filling." They were, thus, "guilty of high treason." Their leaders were indicted and when the people of Lawrence protested that "armed men were stopping wagons, arresting, threatening, and robbing unoffending travelers upon the highway," the only response by the governor was to order that all arms be surrendered. Thus encouraged, raiders assembled from Missouri—the Lecompton Guards, the Doniphan Tigers, the Atchison Guards, and the Kickapoo Rangers. Elsewhere throughout the South men were recruited and armed to rescue Kansas from the abolitionists. Preston Brooks, who would soon make a name for himself in Congress, contributed two hundred fifty dollars to the cause. Major Jefferson Buford, an Alabamian, undertook to raise three hundred irregulars, "sober, discreet, reliable men capable of bearing arms. . . ." Buford sold forty slaves to help equip his small force and marched it to Kansas, where they were designated by Shannon as Kansas militia and, joining five hundred other armed men, headed for Lawrence. There the force, armed with cannons, demanded that all arms in the town be surrendered. When a brass howitzer and four small cannons were given up, the invaders occupied the town, destroyed two printing presses and the town library, and bombarded and finally set fire to the Free State Hotel.

The raid aroused a wave of indignation in the North and Northwest. Money was quickly subscribed to replace the presses and more emigrant trains prepared to leave for Kansas. John Brown, his four sons, and some sixty abolitionists at Osawatomie determined to seek revenge. The party descended on a proslavery community at Dutch Henry's Crossing on Pottawatomie Creek, took twenty-five men from their homes, and killed them in a mass execution. Thus fresh fuel was added to the bonfire of hatred and reprisal. The editor of the proslavery *Border Times* headlined an issue "War! War!" and a band of men called Shannon's Sharp Shooters went to Osawatomie under the command of Henry Clay Pate, a correspondent of the St. Louis *Missouri Republican,* arrested one of Brown's sons, and pillaged some abandoned cabins. Brown, raising a counterforce, attacked and captured the raiders. "I went to take Old Brown," Pate wrote his home paper, "and Old Brown took me."

The Free Soil companies that were formed took such names as the Bloomington Rifles and the Prairie City Boys. Shannon finally called in the United States dragoons to drive the Missouri raiders out of the territory and prevent further violence. Although an effort was made to block emigration into the territory, and Free Soil parties entering Kansas were searched for weapons and disarmed, the tide continued. Most Northern groups came with plans to start communities and many of these had a decidedly utopian air about them. Miriam Colt and her husband belonged to a society of vegetarians who decided to emigrate in a body and establish an "Octagon" colony, the name referring to the central building of the community as well as to the manner in which the lands would be laid out, radiating from a central core containing "a Hydropathic Establishment, an Agricultural College, a Scientific Institute, A Museum of Curiosities and Mechanic Arts and Common Schools." In addition there were ambitious plans for factories that would manufacture farming implements and "portable houses for new settlers." The settlers would gather "frequently" in the Octagon House "for discussion of practical and philosophical issues—politics, theology and morals," thus "the greatest amount of intelligence will be kept active, and the dullness and monotony, often incident to country life, avoided."

The Colts, assured that Kansas would soon become a free state, sold their farm, invested the money in the Octagon Company, and prepared to travel to their new home with their two children and fifty-five fellow vegetarians, most of them from the "burnt-over" region of western New York. They went by train to Buffalo and thence on a lake steamer to Cleveland, Ohio; then to Indianapolis and on to St. Louis, where they boarded a steamer up the Missouri for Kansas City. At Kansas City they transferred to covered wagons for the last leg of their journey. After ten days of jolting travel, the Colts and the rest of the company arrived at the site of Octagon City. Instead of the mills, boardinghouses, and barns that they had been assured would be there to greet them they saw nothing but prairie—"Not a house to be seen"—and nothing to eat but hominy and water. High winds and heavy rains added to the general discomfort. Four thousand Osage Indians living just across the Neosho did nothing to contribute to the settlers' peace of mind. The Indians entered the half-built cabins, sat down, and let "their blankets slide from their shoulders, revealing their large, dark, brown, and nearly nude forms, to the shudder of the unaccustomed beholder," Miriam Colt wrote. She was soon wearing "the Bloomer dress," finding it the only practical garment, and when her husband described in glowing terms the "elegant building spot" and "neat little log cabin" that they would soon be lodged in, a small inner voice whispered to the weary Miriam, "this will never be."

The Border Ruffians, a "drunken, ruthless" mob, in Miriam Colt's words, were a far greater threat than the Indians, twenty-four thousand of whom, it was said, still lived in the territory, and the apprehensive settlers kept their trunks packed and their valuables buried in daily anticipation of a raid like that against Lawrence. Even the famous Kansas moons, "lovely far beyond describing," did little to lessen the pangs of homesickness and a feeling of impending disaster. First came clouds of mosquitoes and then the chills and fever, although no one associated malaria with the stinging pests. Miriam Colt was stricken, and while they were making plans to abandon the settlement and return home, the children were laid low and then her husband. Friends, some of them recently recovered from the fever, helped them to pack up, ill as they were. They began their return home just as the young corn that they had so painstakingly planted a few months before bore its first ears, but Miriam, venturing into the field to pick some for the trip, saw a "large yellow wolf" guarding the field and dared not enter it. So, still alternately wracked by chills and fever, they struggled along. "I have washed and taken care of five sick ones [including her mother and father], they all calling for water! water! at the same time," Miriam Colt wrote on July 9, 1855. Before Miriam got home, her young son, Willie, had died of dysentery. She sold some of his clothes to buy a small headstone that read "Willie, the Little Stranger," and after her husband had tried in vain to sell his gold watch to buy food, they pushed on. A week later her husband was dead also and Miriam Colt wrote in her journal, "My God! my God! why hast thou forsaken me?" His "precious garments," worn as they were, went to an auctioneer's stand to be sold so that a simple stone might mark his grave, and Miriam Colt wrote the words of Scripture in her diary, "My heart is sore pained within me; and the terrors of death are fallen upon me,—fearfulness and trembling are come upon me, and horror hath overwhelmed me."

Not every settler in Kansas endured such hardships and disaster as Miriam Colt, but many certainly did and many died, far more from malaria than from the bullets or knives of the guerrilla armies that ranged the territory.

An English journalist named Thomas Gladstone, a cousin of the famous British prime minister, visited Kansas as a reporter for the London *Times*. Gladstone, having spent weeks observing the conflict between the pro- and anti-slavery factions, wrote that the fair administration of justice "seems never to have entered the minds of those holding the legal appointments in the territory." The proslavery "judges, marshals, sheriffs, or constables," having gotten into office by fraud, used its power "for the extermination of the other party. The power of arrest, the power of imprisonment, the power of hanging, was theirs only that they might arrest, imprison, or hang Free-state men. Hence, murderers, if they have only murdered in behalf of slavery, have gone unpunished; whilst hundreds have been made to suffer for no other crime than the suspicion of entertaining Free-state sentiments."

Murder, lawlessness, and guerrilla warfare were endemic throughout the territory. By June of 1856, proslavery patrols turned all Northern emigrants back at the border, often robbing them as well; the only safe route into the state was through Iowa and Nebraska and then south. According to Gladstone, a Leavenworth tough bet a pair of boots that he would take the scalp of an abolitionist, rode out, met a resident of Lawrence named Hops driving a buggy, shot and scalped him, and took the bloody scalp back to Leavenworth. A German who denounced the murder was shot and a party that came to recover Hops's body was "arrested," placed in jail, and robbed of all they had. Whether such stories were true or false (and some were certainly true) they served to keep the territory in a constant state of agitation. The free-state settlers were divided into those who believed in nonresistance to violence and those who fought back, giving an excellent account of themselves in raids against proslavery centers. Two rival "armies" took shape, one commanded by "General" David Atchinson, a longtime Missouri senator, an enemy of Benton, and a strong supporter of Douglas's Kansas-Nebraska Act. Now he was on hand to give practical and forceful effect to the legislation that he had helped to pass. "General" James Henry Lane, recently a Congressman from Indiana, was the military and political leader of the more militant free-state men. Shannon designated Atchinson's forces as "The Army of Law and Order in Kansas Territory" and what was, in effect, the preview of a larger and bloodier struggle took place in "bleeding Kansas." Pierce gave his complete support to Shannon and the proslavery forces and urged the admission of Kansas as a slave state under the Lecompton constitution. Reporters for Northern papers sent back a stream of horror stories—a family of five children, whose father was in prison at Lecompton, on the verge of starvation; a community of more than a hundred families destitute of food or decent clothing; there seemed no end to tales of murder and suffering. Bleeding Kansas was a phenomenon almost too horrifying to contemplate. Three-quarters of a century of progress, democracy, science, reason, and widespread efforts at uplift and reform had culminated in a conflict more savage than the warfare between the "uncivilized" tribes of Africa or the age-old enmity of Huron and Iroquois. Americans had, to be sure, killed and scalped Indians, burned slaves suspected of plotting insurrection, and stolen vast expanses of land from Mexico. But now they turned on each other like mad dogs, murdering, maiming and pillaging in such a sanguinary temper that conventional warfare appeared civilized by comparison.

But in its own darkly mischievous way, Kansas served a larger purpose. If the ultimate desideratum was the freeing of the Southern slaves and the preservation of the Union in that order, the civil war which began there deepened the Northern hatred of the South, intensified Southern paranoia, and, most important of all, made abolitionism and abolitionists almost respectable by dramatizing the antislavery cause as dramatically as the Fugitive Slave Law. Kansas drew attention to the practical historical consequences of the slave system. Union sentiment was thus buttressed by antislavery sentiment, always far weaker, and the North was thereby prepared psychologically to wage a war to preserve the Union, and, for most Northerners, only incidentally, to free the slaves, perhaps more as a punishment for the South's crime of dismembering the Union than out of any particular sympathy for the slaves themselves.

58

Lincoln Reenters Politics

Undoubtedly the most important consequence of the passage of the Kansas-Nebraska Act was that it brought back into the political arena an obscure Illinois politician whose opposition to the Mexican War, popular in Illinois, had forced him out of state politics. Abraham Lincoln, son of Thomas and Nancy Lincoln, was born in Hardin County, Kentucky, in 1809. When he was eleven, his family moved to Indiana and spent the first winter there in a crude lean-to. Two years later his mother died of the "fever" so common in the Mississippi Valley. Thomas Lincoln married a widow with three children of her own, Sarah Bush Johnston. An energetic and affectionate woman, Sarah Johnston brought some order and direction into Abe Lincoln's life. If young Lincoln had ambition, Sarah fanned it; if he did not, she planted it. Abe worked at all the tasks that were part of a frontier boy's growing up, and in addition, although he had hardly more than a year of formal schooling, he read omnivorously.

In 1830 Thomas Lincoln, a typical restless frontier type, barely literate, trying one thing and then another, moved to Sangamon County in the new state of Illinois. Now twenty-one and closely attached to his stepmother, Lincoln helped with the move, the building of the new home, and the clearing of the land about it. Then he struck out for himself, helping a friend build a flatboat and taking it down the Mississippi to New Orleans, where he got his first glimpse of slavery since his youth in Kentucky. Back in Illinois, he settled at New Salem. Tall, homely, ingratiating, he made himself useful, as one of the few literate citizens in the little town of four or five hundred, by drawing up simple legal papers for his neighbors. Telling stories and listening to stories was one of the principal forms of entertainment in a frontier town, and Lincoln made himself a master of the genre. Six months after he had settled in New Salem he ran, at the age of twenty-three, for representative from Sangamon County to the state legislature and, in accord with the "principles of true republicanism," wrote a "communication" to the people of the county to make clear his "sentiments with regard to local affairs." He was for internal improvements—"the opening of good roads, and . . . the clearing of navigable streams." He supported a railroad from the Illinois River to the nearby town of Springfield, but thought the opening of the Sangamon River a more practical project. He was for constraints on usury and in favor of education. "For my part," he wrote, "I desire to see a time when education, and by its means, morality, sobriety, enterprise and industry, shall become much more general than at present."

After a reference to his youth, he added, "Every man is said to have his peculiar ambition. Whether it be true or not, I can say for one that I have no other so great as that of being truly esteemed of my fellow men, by rendering myself worthy of their esteem. How far I shall succeed in gratifying this ambition, is yet to be developed. I am young and unknown to many of you. I was born and have ever remained in the most humble walks of life. I have no wealthy or popular relations to recommend me. My case is thrown exclusively upon the independent voters of this county. . . ."

Lincoln ran eighth in a field of fifteen candidates, but in terms of his political future the most significant statistic was that he polled 277 out of 300 votes in New Salem. A month later he helped to enlist a company of thirty-day volunteers to fight in the Black Hawk War and was elected captain.

Back after a brief service, Lincoln ran a sawmill on the Sangamon, read any law book he could get his hands on, and plunged once more into local politics. He surveyed, acted as clerk and judge at elections, wrestled, and talked in his high-pitched voice to anyone who would listen—and most were glad to, for this awkward, ambitious youth was always entertaining and informative.

Illinois was a Democratic state. Lincoln was a Whig. He had, thus, to swim constantly against the current. In 1834 he was elected to the state legislature and served his political apprenticeship there for four terms—1834–41. During those years he won his license to practice law, became engaged to Ann Rutledge, whose death in 1835 undoubtedly contributed to a strong vein of morbidity in Lincoln, and moved to Springfield, where his law practice increased notably and where he met, courted, and married Mary Todd, a popular and lively young woman who had valuable social connections, the lack of which in his own background Lincoln had noted in his appeal to the voters of Sangamon County. He lectured on temperance, read Shakespeare and the Bible, and worked hard to achieve a writing and speaking style of power and directness, interspersed, of course, with homely jokes and aphorisms.

Watching the spectacular career of another ambitious Illinois lawyer, named Stephen Douglas—four years his junior, with origins almost as humble as his own—he suffered the pangs of jealousy. Indeed, being more than commonly sensitive, he suffered substantially over a number of things and out of that suffering developed a deep compassion for the deprived, the crippled, the insane, the unfortunate, the black slave and the free black. The morbid streak in Lincoln is perhaps best indicated by a poem he wrote in 1826, when he was seventeen, entitled, "My Childhood-Home I See Again." In it, after a rather conventional evocation of his childhood and the "scenes of play/And school-mates loved so well," Lincoln writes of a friend gone mad—Matthew—whose "mournful song/Upon the still night rose":

> I've heard it oft, as if I dreamed,
>   Far-distant, sweet, and lone;
> The funeral dirge it ever seemed
>   Of reason dead and gone.
> To drink its strains, I've stole away,
>   All silently and still,
> Ere yet the rising god of day
>   Had streaked the Eastern hill.

"A drop of honey catches more flies than a gallon of gall," Lincoln advised the Washingtonian Temperance Society. Don't attack and abuse the makers and sellers of liquor. They are simply doing what every enterprising American seeks to do—provide a product that the public wishes. Redeem the drunkard by sympathy and understanding, by the testimony of those who have experienced the evil and overcome it. The temperance address is an important document in the Lincoln canon, for it reveals four themes that were to run through all his political utterances and actions: the compassion of which we have already spoken; the evocation of the Scripture (in reclaiming the drunkard, Lincoln declared, "we cry, 'come sound the moral resurrection trump, that these may rise and stand up, an exceeding great army'—'Come from the four winds, O breath! and breathe upon these slain that they may live' "); reference to the American Revolution as the ground of all our ideals and hopes ("in it the world has found a solution of that long mooted problem, as to the capability of man to govern himself. In it was the germ which was vegetated, and still is to grow and expand into the universal liberty of mankind"); and, finally, the anticipation of the day of "universal gladness . . . when there shall be neither a slave nor a drunkard on the earth."

Because he would not join a church and eschewed revival meetings, Lincoln's political rivals tried to depict him as a godless man, a heathen and an unbeliever. Yet it was clear that one source of his compassion was deeply rooted in his Christian faith. In his address to the Washingtonians in 1842 he spoke of the strength to be found in the fact that "Omnipotence condescended to take on himself the form of sinful man, and, as such, to die an ignominious death for their sakes. . . ."

Lincoln's future did not lie in being a temperance lecturer, but it is certainly noteworthy that speaking on a subject on which so much repetitious eloquence had been employed he could relate it to the great themes that had already come to dominate his life. At thirty-six Lincoln was able to look back at himself twelve years earlier, a strange, friendless, uneducated, penniless boy, working on a flatboat at ten dollars per month. But Stephen Douglas, only thirty-two, controlled the Democratic Party in Illinois; had been nominated for Congress at the age of twenty-four, losing by only thirty-five votes; had served as judge on the state supreme court and that year been elected to Congress. There he made an instant impression. Diminutive, with a barrel chest and booming voice, with all the flair and extravagance associated with frontier politics, a born stump speaker and master of invective, he had also a lawyer's ability to reason on the subtlest points of constitutional law. Moreover, he was a luminary of the dominant party. Everywhere that the ambitious young Lincoln turned, he found the way blocked by the ambitious young Douglas, acclaimed by many as the most brilliant figure to rise in the Western political skies since Henry Clay had appeared as senator from frontier Kentucky almost forty years earlier.

Lincoln knew himself the better man and it sorely tried him to see his adversary pile triumph on top of triumph while he barely held his own in the uncertain waters of Illinois politics. In 1847 he won election to Congress as a Whig, but with Polk determined to force Mexico into a war to which Lincoln and the Whigs were strongly opposed, it was a bad time for a freshman congressman of the opposition party to try to impress himself on the national consciousness. He made an able speech against the war which, since his constituents heartily favored it, served only to mark him for defeat. Anticipating it, he withdrew from the coming congressional elections. The same year that Lincoln was elected to Congress the Democrat-dominated Illinois legislature sent Douglas to the Senate. On that more conspicuous stage the new senator further enhanced his reputation by his speeches in support of Polk's policies and by his ability as a party manager. Soon there were few pieces of legislation that were not referred to Douglas for his opinion.

Lincoln, referring to himself as "the lone Whig star of Illinois," lingered in the East to campaign for Taylor. The *Boston Daily Advertiser,* covering a talk by him at Worcester, Massachusetts, described him as "a very tall and thin figure, with an intellectual face, showing a searching mind, and a cool judgment. He spoke in a clear, cool, and very eloquent manner," the reporter continued, "for an hour and half, carrying the audience with him in his able arguments and brilliant illustrations—only interrupted by warm and frequent applause." It was a promising beginning. At the Whig Club in Boston, the virtually unknown Westerner gave a speech to "a full and enthusiastic meeting," a speech "which for sound reasoning, cogent argument and keen satire, we have seldom heard equaled," the *Boston Atlas* reported, noting, "the audience gave three cheers for Taylor and Fillmore, and three more for Mr. Lincoln, the Lone Star of Illinois. It was a glorious meeting." Western Whigs were relatively rare and as word of Lincoln's ability to entertain and instruct and of his eccentric, homespun appearance and manner spread, the size of his audiences grew. Even an unfriendly Free Soil paper at Taunton, Massachusetts, reported that the Lone Star had given "unlimited satisfaction to the disheart-ened Taylorites. . . . It was reviving to hear a man speak as if he believed what he was saying and had a grain or two of feeling mixed up with it. . . . His awkward gesticulations, the ludicrous management of his voice and the comical expression of his countenance, all conspired to make his listeners laugh at the mere anticipation of the joke before it appeared."

The half-dozen speeches Lincoln made in Taylor's behalf were a modest beginning for someone as ambitious as he. For every person who knew who Abraham Lincoln was, there were a thousand who knew the name of Stephen A. Douglas.

Withdrawing from the congressional election, Lincoln returned to Washington to finish out his term. He spoke in favor of the abolition of slavery in the District of Columbia and found time to file a patent for "an improved method of lifting vessels over shoals" by means of buoyant air chambers. Back in Illinois, he spent days writing letters to the new president in behalf of office-hungry Illinois Whigs and even included a petition for himself as land commissioner, a job which went to a political rival who had failed to support Taylor in the presidential campaign. In debt and out of office, Lincoln virtually abandoned politics and devoted his attention to building up his law practice. His wife's relatives were a valuable asset, but his own talents as a lawyer and his reputation for unshakable integrity were the cornerstones of his success in the legal profession. Soon he had more business than he could handle, but politics were never far from his mind, although he had to watch from the sidelines as Stephen Douglas added to his political laurels by maneuvering Clay's compromises of 1850 through Congress. Although Lincoln disliked the Fugitive Slave Law, it seemed to him part of a bargain which must be faithfully observed by the North.

In the election of 1852 Lincoln took to the hustings to make the best case he could for Scott. Then he was back at his burgeoning law practice, taking time occasionally to jot down thoughts on government or on slavery. "*Most governments,*" he noted, in one such reflection, "have been based practically, on the denial of equal rights of men . . . ours began by *affirming* those rights. *They* said, some men are too *ignorant* and *vicious,* to share in government. Possibly so, said we; and by your system, you would always keep them ignorant, and vicious. We propose to give *all* a chance; and we expect the weak to grow stronger, the ignorant, wiser; and all better, and happier together."

With the passage of the Kansas-Nebraska Act, Lincoln bestirred himself. The measure seemed to him pregnant with disaster and he began at once to write and speak in opposition to it. The senatorial seat held by Douglas's fellow Democrat was up and in the wake of the reaction against the Kansas-Nebraska Act it seemed possible that a Whig might win it. Lincoln set his sights on that prize. At Winchester, Illinois, on August 26, the *Illinois Journal* reported that "the Hon. A. Lincoln" had attacked the "Nebraska-Kansas bill," in an "ingenious, logical, and at the same time fair and candid manner. . . . His masterly effort—said to be equal to any upon the same subject in Congress,— was replete with unanswerable arguments, which must and will effectually *tell* at the coming election." At Carrollton, at Springfield, at Bloomington, Lincoln continued his assault. In the latter town he began by declaring "that Southern slaveholders were neither better, nor worse than we of the North, and that we of the North were no better than they. If we were situated as they are, they should act and feel as we do; and we never ought to lose sight of this fact in discussing the subject." It was a theme he was to return to again and again. Southerners were not evil, wicked men. They were caught in a wicked system and were as much its victims as the slaves. Soon Douglas was back after the adjournment of Congress and he and Lincoln engaged in a series of debates over the measure that was associated so closely with Douglas's name. At Bloomington again Lincoln began his response to Douglas by twitting him on his evasiveness about the Know-Nothings who had appeared with such startling suddenness on the political scene and the newspaper account of his remarks is interspersed with "[Laughter and applause]," "[Laughter]," "[Renewed laughter]."

Defending the Missouri Compromise, Lincoln scored a telling point by reading Douglas's statement, made several years prior: "All the evidences of public opinion at that day seemed to indicate that this Compromise [the Missouri] had become canonized in the hearts of the American people as a sacred thing, which no ruthless hand should attempt to disturb." Douglas replied rather lamely that "*natural* right" required that Kansas and Nebraska be opened to settlement, and, at least under the terms of the bill, prospectively, to slavery. What natural right was this, Lincoln asked: "Is not slavery universally granted to be, in the abstract, a gross outrage on the law of nature? Have not all civilized nations, our own among them, made the Slave trade capital, and classed it with piracy and murder? Is it not held to be the great wrong of the world?"

At Peoria, Douglas and Lincoln were again matched. Lincoln took his stand, he declared, on the Declaration of Independence and Jefferson's Northwest Ordinance. "Thus, away back of the constitution, in the pure fresh, free breath of the revolution, the State of Virginia, and the National congress put that policy [no slavery in the territories] in practice. Thus through sixty odd of the best years of the republic did that policy steadily work to its great and beneficent end."

Slavery, founded on human selfishness, and justice were in eternal antagonism. "Repeal the Missouri compromise,—repeal all compromises—repeal the Declaration of Independence—repeal past history, you still cannot repeal human nature. It will still be the abundance of man's heart, that slavery is wrong; and out of the abundance of his heart, his mouth will continue to speak."

Already the rival parties were contending for the domination of Kansas with "bowie-knives and six-shooters" if need be. "And if this fight should begin, is it very likely to take a very peaceful, Union-saving turn? Will not the first drop of blood so shed be the real knell of the Union? . . . Let no one be deceived. The spirit of seventy-six and the spirit of Nebraska, are utter antagonisms; and the former is rapidly being displaced by the latter."

The real issue between himself and "Judge Douglas" (did Lincoln use the title with conscious irony?), Lincoln insisted, was the question of whether "the negro is a human." The judge quite evidently did not believe so, "and consequently has no idea that there can be any moral question in legislating about him. In his view, the question of whether a new country shall be slave or free, is a matter of as utter indifference, as it is whether his neighbor shall plant his farm with tobacco, or stock it with horned cattle. Now, whether this view is right or wrong, it is very certain that the great mass of mankind take a totally different view. They consider slavery a great moral wrong; and their feeling against it, is not evanescent, but eternal. It lies at the very foundation of their sense of justice; and it cannot be trifled with. It is a great and durable element of popular action, and, I think, no statesman can safely disregard it."

And that, of course, was the critical question. Senator-Judge Stephen A. Douglas was deficient in the moral faculty, as the phrenologists would have put it; that bump was egregiously underdeveloped and that bump, Lincoln determined, would eventually bring his high-flying foe down into the dust. It was Chicago next and then Quincy. Even though Douglas was not on the platform, he was there in spirit as Lincoln summoned him up and catechized him. "The large company . . . listened with unwearied attention and an approbation emphasized by repeated outbursts of enthusiastic applause," the *Quincy Whig* reported. It was Lincoln's last shot before the midterm elections. He still lived in the hope that the senatorship would be his. The Whigs were out everywhere in large numbers and the scent of victory was in the air. But Lincoln's fate was not, of course, to be determined by the direct votes of the citizens of the state. The next senator would be appointed by the state legislature and there the opportunities of maneuver and intrigue were infinite. On the eve of the voting Lincoln had forty-four of a needed forty-seven votes committed to him, while his most serious rival had forty-one; but he was not sure that was an advantage. He knew many members of the legislature were ambitious for the post themselves and would gladly delay the outcome in hopes that sentiment might swing their way. Lyman Trumbull, a Belleville jurist, had five votes. Trumbull had been a Democrat but he was known to have strong antislavery, indeed abolitionist, leanings and to be "anti-Nebraska." An able man, he was a poor speaker and lacking in popular appeal, but the "Nebraska men" were determined, at all costs, to block Lincoln. They indicated to the governor, Joel Matteson, soon to be indicted for grand theft in a canal-building scandal, that they could muster enough votes to elect him. Matteson, with this encouragement, worked to stymie Lincoln, and Lincoln, rather than see Matteson rewarded for his perfidy, threw his votes to Trumbull, who was, in consequence, elected. Bitterly disappointed, Lincoln wrote to a friend: "The agony is over at last. . . ."

Thwarted in his bid for the senatorship that would have given him a national platform from which to engage Douglas, Lincoln turned his attention to helping to build up the newly created Republican Party for the coming presidential election. Some of his allies, among them Owen Lovejoy, brother of the martyred Elijah, proposed an alliance with the Know-Nothings, whose spectacular success in the midterm elections had introduced a disturbing new element into the political equation. Lincoln discouraged all such ideas. "I do not perceive," he wrote Lovejoy, "how anyone professing to be sensitive to the wrongs of the negroes, can join in a league to degrade a class of white men." And writing to his old friend Joshua Speed, Lincoln again disassociated himself from the Know-Nothings. "As a nation, we began by declaring that '*all men are created equal.*' We now practically read it 'all men are created equal, *except negros.*' When the Know-Nothings get control, it will read 'all men are created equal, except negroes, and *foreigners*, and *catholics.*' When it comes to this I should prefer emigrating to some country where they make no pretense of loving liberty—to Russia, for instance, where despotism can be taken pure, and without the base alloy of hypocrisy."

A few days after his letter to Lovejoy, Lincoln wrote an old friend, George Robertson, a Kentucky jurist, thanking him for the gift of a book and adding, "Our political problem now is 'Can we, as a nation, continue together *permanently—forever*—half slave, and half free?' The problem is too mighty for me."

But the more Lincoln thought about it, the more it seemed to him that this was the thistle that must be grasped, the politically unsayable that must be said, whatever the risk. As long as the people of the nation were encouraged by their political leaders to believe that the country could remain forever "half slave and half free," nothing substantial could be done toward the eventual eradication of slavery. It was such thinking or nonthinking that had enabled Douglas to propose and carry his Kansas-Nebraska Act. To say it publicly, openly, specifically, and politically must be to risk the ruin of his career. But Lincoln knew or sensed that the essence of politics is to speak the essential but unspeakable word at the proper moment. Then the whole world must listen. Too soon is ruin; too late and someone else snatches the guidon of leadership. Having tried it on Robertson, Lincoln could not get the phrase out of his mind.

59

A Decision Deferred

The Kansas legislature, in the hands of proslavery forces, passed a series of oppressive laws which caused a strong reaction in the North. On September 26, 1855, New York Whigs met with members of the fledgling Republican Party to form a political alliance and draw up a free-soil platform for the state elections, a little more than a month off. The Democrats, revealing the depths of their own division, divided into Softs and Hards. (The Softs were the conservatives, successors to the Hunkers, led by William Marcy and loyal to Pierce. The Hards were antiadministration Democrats.) In the election the Know-Nothings won out by a narrow margin over the Republicans, with the Democrats a poor third. There were similar results in other states, with the Republicans everywhere in the ascendancy. The results were a further blow to the Pierce administration, which had tried unsuccessfully to carry water on both shoulders. When Congress convened in December, the Republicans had 105 seats to 74 for the Democrats and 40 for the Know-Nothings who, having abandoned their secrecy, were now known as the American Party.

For a time there had been an intense struggle between the Know-Nothings and the new Republican Party for the allegiance of the antislavery Whigs, or Woolly-Heads. But Seward herded them into the

Republican fold and when the first Republican organization meeting of the year was held at Pittsburgh in February, it was dominated by moderates who were determined to avoid the abolitionist taint and make as wide an appeal as possible to ex-Whigs, to temperance advocates, to the German and Irish Catholics, farmers, laborers, and businessmen. Aware that they must attract a substantial number of disillusioned Democrats as well as former Whigs while holding on to the Free Soilers, the Republicans handled the slavery issue in a gingerly fashion and contented themselves with affirming their solidarity and setting the date of June 17 for the party nominating convention in Philadelphia.

The American Party, holding a nominating convention on February 22 in Philadelphia with 227 delegates in attendance, found itself so sharply divided on the slavery issue that it split into Northern and Southern wings. The main convention nominated Millard Fillmore, while the "Northern Bolters" decided to wait and see who the Republican nominees were before taking action on their own.

On the Democratic side Douglas hoped to be rewarded for the Kansas-Nebraska Act by his party's nomination but it was clear that Pierce aspired to reelection. As the time approached for the Democratic convention, scheduled to meet on June 2 in Cincinnati, James Buchanan appeared to have a substantial lead in delegate support. The strategy of Pierce and Douglas was, therefore, to combine their forces to block Buchanan and deadlock the convention. Pierce would then have his go at the nomination, and if he failed would throw his support to Douglas.

In May an event took place that greatly increased partisan bitterness. Charles Sumner, the beau ideal of the New England abolitionists, had been infuriated by the policy of the Pierce administration in Kansas. "Really, the wickedness of this case," he wrote William Jay, "is too great for belief," and a month later he wrote Gerrit Smith, "Douglas has appeared at last on the scene, and with him that vulgar swagger which adhered in the Nebraska debate. Truly, truly, this is a godless place. . . . My heart is sick." Sumner, Carl Schurz wrote, had a smile of "peculiar charm." Pierce Butler of South Carolina, his adversary, was described by Schurz as having a "rubicund face, framed in long silver-white hair," with a "merry twinkle" in his eye, fond of quoting Horace and a "jovial companion," but on the issue of slavery, he flared up "fiercely."

Sumner and Douglas were soon involved in bitter personal attacks on each other's integrity. Douglas spoke of the Massachusetts senator's "baseness" and lack of patriotism, and accused him of "a gross libel." Meanwhile the news from Kansas was all bad. Sumner wrote to William Jay once more: "The tyranny of the slave oligarchy becomes more violent day by day. To-day I am smitten by the news from Kansas." He was determined, he wrote, to "expose this whole crime at great length, and without sparing language." When Sumner began his speech to the Senate on May 19, the floor and gallery were crowded with Whigs and antislavery men from the House. Sumner described in lurid detail the "Crime Against Kansas, the rape of a virgin territory, compelling it to the hateful embrace of slavery . . . traceable to a depraved desire for a new slave state, hideous offspring of such a crime, in the hope of adding to the power of slavery in the national government. . . . Even now, while I speak, portents lower in the horizon, threatening to darken the land, which already palpitates with the mutterings of civil war." The Kansas-Nebraska Act had been passed by "the mingled meanness and wickedness of the cheat." David Atchinson, senator from Missouri, had "like Catiline, stalked into this chamber reeking with conspiracy," and found a ready accomplice in Butler of South Carolina. Sumner compared Butler and Douglas to Don Quixote and Sancho Panza. Butler's mistress was the "harlot Slavery." It was, Sumner declared, the duty of decent and honest men "to dislodge from the high places that tyrannical sectionalism of which the senator from South Carolina is one of the maddest zealots." Sumner continued in this vein, with his bitterest invective directed at Butler, for the better part of two days; he ended his tirade with these words, "In the name of the Constitution outraged, of the laws trampled down, of justice banished, of humanity degraded, of peace destroyed, of freedom crushed to earth, and in the name of the Heavenly Father, whose service is perfect freedom,—I make this last appeal."

Cass rose at once to denounce Sumner's oration as "the most un-American and unpatriotic" speech "that ever grated on the ears of the members of this high body" and Douglas followed, calling it a "Yankee bedquilt . . . of classic allusions each one distinguished for its lasciviousness and obscenity . . . unfit for decent young men to read. . . . Is it his object to provoke some of us to kick him as we would a dog in the street, that he may get sympathy upon the just chastisement?"

Exactly what Sumner hoped to accomplish by his speech is not clear. The Southerners in the Senate were notorious for the bitterness and violence of their language on the subject of abolition or antislavery in general, but Sumner's long, carefully contrived speech was no simple outburst of rage but a deliberate provocation. That the speech, which was quickly printed up for distribution, should have its admirers was not surprising. A correspondent of the *Missouri Democrat* reported that Sumner "showed that in oratorical talent he was no unworthy successor to Adams, Webster and Everett. . . ." And the *New York Post* called it "the most single combination of oratorical splendors which in the opinion of a veteran senator has ever been witnessed in that hall." Longfellow, when he read it, wrote to Sumner congratulating him on the "brave and noble speech you made, never to die out in the memories of men . . . it is the greatest voice, on the greatest subject, that has been uttered since we became a nation."

Young Preston Brooks, a Congressman from South Carolina— "amiable and friendly," tall and handsome with "black hair and sparkling eyes," a protégé and admirer of Butler—decided to "punish" Sumner for his attack on the South and on slavery and to do so apparently as a warning to other antislavery senators or representatives that Southern honor could not be so impugned. A few days later, Brooks came up to Sumner's desk, denounced the speech as a "libel on South Carolina and Mr. Butler," and then began to strike him on the head with his cane until it broke and Sumner fell unconscious, seriously injured, bleeding from wounds on his head.

The Senate refused to censure Brooks, leaving that task to the House, nor did any Southern senator rise to deplore the attack. In the South Brooks was praised and acclaimed and given any number of symbolic walking sticks by grateful constituents. In the North the episode, vividly described and long dwelt upon, served to further inflame public feeling against the South. There were meetings throughout the North to condemn Brooks's attack on Sumner, and George Templeton Strong, attending such a gathering in New York, found it crowded with "men not given to fits of enthusiasm or generous sympathy. . . . I guess the North is roused at last. . . . I hold the antislavery agitators wrong in principle and mischievous in policy. But the reckless, insolent brutality of our Southern aristocrats may drive me to abolitionism yet." "Never was the country in such a crazy state as just now," he wrote a few days later, . . . civil war is impending over Kansas; the Administration blundering us into the misery and ruin of war with England, in a quarrel about which no mortal feels interest enough to induce him to spend five dollars; North and South farther alienated than ever before. . . . We at the North are a busy money-making democracy, comparatively law-abiding and peace-loving, with the faults (among others) appropriate to traders and workers. A rich Southern aristocrat who happens to be of fine nature, with the self-reliance and high tone that life among an aristocracy favors, and culture and polish from books and travel, strikes us . . . as something different from ourselves, more ornamental and in some respects better. He has the polish of a high civilized society, with the qualities that belong to a ruler of serfs. Thus a notion has gotten footing here that 'Southern gentlemen' are a high-bred chivalric aristocracy . . . very gallant and generous, regulating themselves by 'codes of honor' (that are *wrong*, of course, but very grand). . . . Whereas I believe they are, in fact, a race of lazy, ignorant, coarse, sensual, swaggering, sordid, beggarly barbarians, bullying white men and breeding little niggers for sale."

The day after Sumner delivered his speech, proslavery forces pillaged and looted Lawrence, Kansas. Two days later John Brown and his band fell on the proslavery settlers at Osawatomie and murdered and mutilated five men in the name of "God and the Army of the North." It was in this atmosphere that the delegates to the Democratic convention met in Cincinnati on June 2. For the first fourteen ballots the votes of the delegates were more or less evenly divided between Pierce, Buchanan, and Douglas, with all three far short of the necessary two-thirds. The events in Kansas and the Sumner-Brooks episode had undoubtedly hurt Douglas. It soon became clear that a substantial number of delegates would not support him under any circumstances, and Douglas and his managers decided that, rather than sustain a defeat, they would set their sights on 1860 and withdraw from the contest, leaving most of his delegates to go to Buchanan. John C. Breckinridge of Kentucky was chosen as the party's vice-presidential candidate.

On June 17 the Republicans gathered at Philadelphia, more than a thousand strong. Many of the delegates were young men and there was a kind of vibrancy and excitement in the air that was missing from most political conventions, a feeling that great things were impending. Idealists of every stripe and degree were there, nuts, visionaries, fanatics, and a good sprinkling of seasoned Whig leaders like Weed, Thaddeus Stevens, and Charles Francis Adams. Horace Greeley, patron of a hundred nostrums, white knight of the liberal press, was conspicuous, along with such tested champions of the antislavery cause as Joshua Giddings and Henry Wilson. The mood of a religious revival, an evangelical Protestant fervor, a freshening of the spirit, swept the delegates along. David Wilmot, hero of the Proviso, brought in a platform calling for no extension of slavery into free territory and the prompt admission of Kansas into the Union as a free state. It contained accusations of murder, arson, and robbery against the Democratic proslavery faction in Kansas and pledged the party to prosecute the offenders, language omitted from the final version of the platform, which was less a conventional platform than a call to do battle for the Lord against the wickedness of slavery.

George Templeton Strong observed that "Republicanism has made strong adherents in the laboring-class, rugged, dirty-faced blackguards. . . . To be sure, it could hardly be otherwise. This is the working-man's party, emphatically the democratic party, resisting the spurious sham Democracy that subordinates labor socially and politically to capital. . . ."

The Republicans did not have a general available as a candidate so they turned to the next best thing, a soldier-explorer-hero in the person of John C. Frémont, whose exciting accounts of his exploits, written in large part by his wife, had thrilled thousands of Americans and who had been, to a modest degree, martyred by the Democratic administration of Polk for his role in the conquest of California. Frémont was young, dashing, handsome, with an attractive and ambitious wife, and with no evident political liabilities (and no political experience to speak of, unless being the son-in-law of Senator Thomas Benton qualified as political experience). The Republican leaders had settled on him months before, passing over Chase and Seward as too controversial. Indeed everything was so well managed that on the first ballot various delegates rose to withdraw the names of Frémont rivals, making him the party's candidate by acclamation. W. L. Dayton of New Jersey was chosen for vice-president.

Pandemonium followed. All the old, stale politics-as-usual had been banished. The Whig Party, to which the musty odor of reaction and defeat had clung for so long, was dead and a vigorous new party, steady on the issue of the extension of slavery, had risen in its place. It was all wildly intoxicating. "Free Speech, Free Soil and Frémont," chanted by the delegates, sounded like an unbeatable slogan. It mattered little that Frémont was a slender reed to bear such a weight of hope. George Templeton Strong, observing a Frémont rally, wrote in his diary, "Frémont won't be President, my dear, deceived, short-sighted brothers. You are bellowing to no purpose, disquieting your-self in vain. . . . Ten years hence there will be some Frémont who can make it worth one's while to hurrah for him, but *you,* my unknown vociferous friends and fellow-citizens, are premature. You don't perceive that 'the Republican party' is a mere squirm and wriggle of the insulted North, a brief spasm of pain under pressure and nothing more."

The Northern division of the Know-Nothings or Native Ameri-cans, strongly tinged with antislavery leanings, had met in New York in the middle of June and nominated Nathaniel Banks, the speaker of the House, as their candidate, with the understanding that if the Republi-cans went for Frémont, the Americans would switch to him.

The Southern Know-Nothings nominated Fillmore, who was willing to clutch at any straw. Fillmore was a moderate Whig, a strong Unionist, a temporizer, a doughface (Northern men with Southern principles), a member of the old order, although at fifty-six he was ten years younger than Buchanan. Like Buchanan, Fillmore had very little notion of the seriousness of the storm that was blowing up. Tweedle-dum and Tweedle-dee again.

The platform of the American Party declared *"Americans must rule America;* and to this end, *native*-born citizens should be selected for all state, federal, or municipal offices of government, in preference to naturalized citizens." The platform went on to call for a period of twenty-one years "continued residence" as a requirement for citizen-ship. Why the hostility to immigrants, more particularly the Irish and Germans, which had been smoldering for thirty years or more and given repeated manifestations of its pertinacity in that period, should have suddenly burst forth with such force in the mid-1850s is hard to account for. It may have been the rising tide of immigration that set it off, or the growing frustration of the Whigs at the Democratic alliance of Southern slaveholders and Northern workingmen that had repeat-edly denied them political power. The fact that the nativists were, at various times, allied with antislavery factions within the Whig Party strongly suggests that the antislavery Whigs saw the immigrant vote as a major obstacle to the containment and eventual limitation of slavery. The more central the slavery issue became, the more deeply the Irish-slaveholder coalition was resented by those to whom slavery was a critical issue.

In the campaign that followed, Kansas was the central issue. Robert Toombs, a Whig senator from Georgia, proposed a bill to ensure a fair vote on the issue of slavery versus nonslavery by the settlers in Kansas, but the House rejected it and passed its own bill calling for the admission of Kansas immediately under the free-state Topeka constitution. There the matter rested, with each house refusing to consider the other's bill.

Buchanan laid out his party's basic strategy: "The Union is in danger, and the people everywhere know it. The Black Republicans must be, as they can be with justice, boldly assailed as disunionists, and this charge must be reiterated again and again." The Southern press culled the speeches and writings of such Republican leaders as Joshua Giddings of Ohio, who had declared, "I look forward to the day when there shall be a servile insurrection in the South; when the black man . . . shall assert his freedom and wage a war of extermination against his master." James Watson Webb had written that he believed the Republicans would be forced to "drive back the slavocracy with fire and sword." An abolitionist orator addressing an audience in Faneuil Hall declared, "Remembering that he was a slaveholder, I spit on George Washington." When he was hissed, he replied, "You hissers are slaveholders in spirit!" Certainly many Northerners, especially the abolitionists, spoke of separating from the South rather than continuing to endure the stigma of slavery.

Frémont was ridiculed by the Democrats as "a man whose only merit . . . is the fact that he was born in South Carolina, crossed the Rocky Mountains, subsisted on frogs, lizards, snakes, and grasshoppers, and captured a woolly horse." He was also attacked as a secret Catholic and the uncertain circumstances of his birth were dwelt on at length.

Most Northern papers backed Frémont, and a roster of intellectuals declared for the explorer, prominent among them Lowell, Emerson, Whittier, Bryant, Longfellow, and Irving. College students too young to vote joined in the political tumult and affirmed their allegiance to the Republicans and Frémont. Despite his initial skepticism about Frémont's chances, George Templeton Strong threw himself for the first time into political affairs, helping to organize The Young Men's Eighteenth Ward Frémont Vigilance Committee. "About a dozen present," he wrote, "wire-pullers seemingly; men familiar with canvassing, who knew the best places to get posters printed, and were on intimate terms with stump-speakers and 'central organizations.' Mostly 'middle-class people' but fair and intelligent, able to talk clearly and pertinently." As a ward worker, Strong heard his first "stump-

Speech," "made up of slang, funny stories, and an occasional modulation into a high flight of Bowery theatre declamation, indignation and 'pathos and bathos delighted to see.' But it was immensely effective, kept his audience in an uproar of cheers and genuine laughter . . . I was sore with laughing when he finished."

Henry Fisher, visiting New York, reported back to his brother, Sidney, that "the capitalists there are alarmed at the progress Frémont is making, as they think his election would dissolve the Union. This is the old threat always made by the South when it is opposed. The Union is essential to the South & it knows it. Unless thro some sudden excitement & madness, they will never dissolve the Union."

On June 2 Strong noted in his diary, "Kansas battle beginning in the House. Indications that Douglas and others are scared by the storm his selfish folly has raised. . . . Can civil war between North and South be postponed twenty years longer? I fear we, or our children, have got to pass through a ruinous revolutionary period of conflict between two social systems before the policy of the U.S. is finally settled. The struggle will be fearful when it comes. . . ."

More Southern states began to threaten secession if Frémont were elected. A group of Southern governors meeting in Raleigh, North Carolina, issued a statement declaring that their states would secede if Frémont became president. Such talk infuriated Northerners. It was reported that the governor of Virginia, Henry Wise, had told someone that " if Frémont were elected, he would never be permitted to reach Washington. " Strong noted that "the 'Black Republican' party commends itself much to educated and intelligent people of the North, particularly of the sort that commonly declines any concern in 'mere' political matters. I don't think its principle has made its way down to the masses yet, or is taken hold of by them (unless in the New England states), though the working-class is deeply and directly interested in the controversy." The old-line Whigs, who put the preservation of the Union above all other considerations, met in September to throw their weight to Fillmore and declare, "It is enough to know that civil war is raging and the Union is in peril; and proclaim a conviction that the restoration of the Fillmore Presidency will furnish the best if not the only means of restoring peace." That plea undoubtedly carried weight and it seems safe to assume that for those Americans who voted for Fillmore, the Union was the highest good.

On the eve of the election Strong wrote in his diary, "The 'masses' of the North are very far from Abolitionism, whatever it may suit

Southern politicians to say. They distrust any party that is hostile to the niggerocracy and can be misrepresented as Abolitionists."

Pennsylvania, with its 27 electoral votes, was the key state for the Democrats. Hammering away on the native-son theme—Buchanan was a Pennsylvanian—and spending large sums of money in Philadelphia the Democrats carried the day in Pennsylvania by a majority of 3,000 votes out of 423,000 cast. Frémont had 114 electoral votes, Fillmore 8, and Buchanan 174, but the combined popular vote for Buchanan's two rivals far exceeded his own. He thus became a minority president in a most dangerous moment. If the 27 electoral votes of Pennsylvania had gone to Frémont, the election would have been thrown into the House, where Frémont would probably have won. He had not even had his name placed on the ballot in any state south of the Mason-Dixon line except Maryland, where he polled 281 votes and which incidentally was won by Fillmore. California, which four years earlier had cast some 75,000 votes, 40,000 of them for Pierce and 35,000 for Scott, now tallied 110,000, 53,365 to Buchanan, 36,165 to Fillmore and only 20,691 to its "liberator," Frémont.

In the aftermath of the election, the Republicans took what comfort they could from the fact that Buchanan was a "minority" president. Buchanan, in his inaugural address, referred to the passions aroused by the presidential election and added, "when the people proclaimed their will the tempest at once subsided and all was calm. The voice of the majority," he added, "speaking in the manner prescribed by the Constitution, was heard, and instant submission followed. Our country alone could have exhibited so grand and striking a spectacle of the capacity of man for self-government." The idea of popular sovereignty, which Buchanan had borrowed from Cass, he praised as "a happy conception . . . that the will of the majority shall govern" in the "question of domestic slavery in the Territories." So would Kansas determine its future. As to when that time might be, that was "of little practical importance." In any event it was a judicial matter which fell within the jurisdiction of the Supreme Court, which would soon be rendering a decision to which he, as President, "in common with all good citizens," would cheerfully submit. Few in Buchanan's audience were privy to the knowledge that the Court intended to uphold the judgment that Dred Scott had not been made a free man by virtue of having been for some months on the free soil of Illinois.

Dred Scott had been sold by his owner, Charles Blow, to Dr. John

Emerson, a St. Louis physician, for five hundred dollars in 1841. Emerson, who had obtained a commission as an army doctor, was sent to a post in Illinois and took Dred with him. From there Emerson, in time, was dispatched to Fort Snelling, on the west bank of the Mississippi River, north of the Missouri Compromise line in free territory. Emerson, in poor health, was shifted from one post to another, leaving Scott, and the woman he had married, at Fort Snelling, to hire out as servants. On Emerson's death in 1843, the Scotts, with the rest of his property, passed to Emerson's wife. Dred Scott tried to buy his freedom and that of his family but Mrs. Emerson refused. Scott then requested permission to sue for his freedom on the grounds that he had lived for a time in free territory. The judge, who had been mayor of Alton, Illinois, at the time of Elijah Lovejoy's murder, granted Scott's petition in 1846. While a strange series of trials dragged on through the lower courts, Mrs. Emerson hired out Scott and his wife as servants for five dollars a month and went to live with her sister in Springfield, Massachusetts. In a jury trial, a Missouri court returned a verdict in favor of the Scotts and Mrs. Emerson's lawyers appealed to the Missouri supreme court. That body had determined to use any relevant case that came before it to overthrow the then well-established doctrine that a slave was free by virtue of being brought into a free state or territory. They intended to declare that under the Constitution Congress had no power to legislate on the subject of slavery in the territories. As proslavery Southerners, they believed that it was the intention of the North to destroy slavery, starting with its prohibition in the territories. They therefore welcomed the Dred Scott case on review, and in 1852, six years after Scott had first instituted his suit, they issued a decision in favor of Mrs. Emerson. Scott's lawyers immediately appealed the verdict to the Supreme Court.

Andrew Jackson had appointed Roger Taney as chief justice to succeed John Marshall in 1834, and Taney had served with distinction for more than twenty years. As a young lawyer in Maryland many years before, he had defended a Methodist minister who had preached an antislavery sermon and in doing so he had quoted from the Declaration of Independence. The minister had been charged with inciting insurrection and Taney, in defending him, declared, "Slavery is a blot upon our national character and every lover of freedom confidentially hopes that it will be effectually wiped away. And until that time shall come when we can point without a blush to the language held in the Declaration of Independence, every friend of humanity will seek to lighten the galling chains of slavery." That the words were not merely the expedient rhetoric of a young attorney Taney had proved by freeing his own slaves.

The Chief Justice was described by a contemporary as "a tall, square-shouldered man, flat-breasted, in a degree to be remarked upon, with a stoop that made his shoulders even more prominent, a face without one good feature, a mouth unusually large, in which were discolored and irregular teeth, the gums of which were visible when he smiled, dressed always in black, his clothes sitting ill upon him, his hands spare with protruding veins, in a word a gaunt, ungainly man. His voice, too, was hollow, as the voice of one who was consumptive. And yet, when he began to speak, you never thought of his personal appearance, so clear, so simple, so admirably arranged were his low-voiced words. He used no gestures. He used even emphasis but sparely. There was an air of so much sincerity in all he said, that it was next to impossible to believe he could be wrong. Not a redundant syllable, not a phrase repeated, and, to repeat, so exquisitely simple. . . ." Taney was a thoroughgoing Jacksonian Democrat who distrusted "the money power" which, he had written to Jackson years before, sought "to destroy the spirit of freedom and manly indepen- dence in the working classes of society." The decisions of the Court under Taney had been in the direction of greater democracy while maintaining the authority of the Court. Now Taney, nearing his eightieth year, was to write the decision that would identify his name forever with that of Dred Scott and fatally compromise his judicial fame. In the decision of the Court, split five to four, Taney declared that the question was simply: "Can a negro, whose ancestors were imported into this country, and sold as slaves, become a member of the political community formed and brought into existence by the Constitution of the United States, and as such become entitled to all the rights, privileges and immunities guaranteed by that instrument to the citizens?" The weight of prior judicial decisions and legislative enactments "and the language used in the Declaration of Indepen- dence" had been to the effect "that neither the class of persons who had been imported as slaves, nor their descendants, whether they had become free or not, were then acknowledged as part of the people, nor intended to be included in the general words used in that memorable document. . . . They had been for more than a century before regarded as beings of an inferior order, and altogether unfit to associate with the white race, either in social or political relations; and so far inferior that they had no rights which the white man was bound to respect; and that the negro might justly and lawfully be reduced to slavery for his benefit." It followed from this that Dred Scott was not a citizen of Missouri and thus had no right to sue in its courts.

All this was bad enough, but Taney and the Court majority refused to stop there, though their colleagues had urged them to. The majority, like the majority of the Missouri supreme court, believed it was their responsibility to go further and settle for all time the question of the authority of Congress to limit the spread of slavery into the territories and, indeed, to pass judgment, almost forty years after the fact, on the constitutionality of the Missouri Compromise. Under what misapprehension, the Court in effect asked, had the plaintiff and his lawyers initiated the suit? Taney argued for the Court that the article of the Constitution which gave Congress the power to "make all needful rules and regulations respecting the territory or other property of the United States" had applied only to what then composed the states, roughly, the region east of the Mississippi. The Louisiana Territory, not yet acquired, was not, therefore, comprehended under the article. Slaves were property and Congress could never have "a mere discretionary" power "over the person or property of a citizen." The Missouri Compromise thus stood in defiance of the "due process of law" clause. In stripping all rights of a citizen, indeed all rights of a human being, from free blacks as well as slaves, the Court laid out in stark relief the condition to which blacks had been reduced in the United States. Northerners of every shade of political opinion resented the gratuitous declaring of the Missouri Compromise, which had acquired almost a sacred character in the North, to be unconstitutional. What the decision said, in effect, was that any effort whatever by Congress to limit slavery in any state or territory was unconstitutional. Under the terms of the Court's opinion, any slaveholder could take his slaves, i.e., his property, wherever he wished, immune from federal or state laws. Or that, at least, was the way in which the decision was understood. The motives of the Court were undoubtedly to try, by its ill-omened decision, to quiet the political turmoil in the country by "settling" the issue of slavery. The fact that five of the justices were Southerners and four slaveholders did not encourage the view in the North that they had judged impartially, and a storm of angry protest burst around their heads.

The *New York Tribune* declared that "Chief Justice Taney's opinion was long, elaborate, able and Jesuitical. His arguments were based on gross historical falsehoods and bold assumptions that went the whole length of the Southern doctrine," and the *New York Independent*'s headlines announced: "The Decision of the Supreme Court Is the Moral Assassination of a Race and Cannot Be Obeyed."

A Democratic paper in Pennsylvania took the line, common to most Democratic journals, that the decision settled "certain points . . . beyond the reach of the fanatics of the Nation. . . . Whoever now seeks to revive sectionalism arrays himself against the Constitution, and consequently against the Union." The *New Hampshire Patriot and Gazette* stated that the decision made "Black Republicanism" unconstitutional. "It utterly demolishes the whole black republican platform and stamps it as directly antagonistical to the constitution. . . . This is the end of the matter. . . . That decision must be carried into effect."

And so the storm raged on. Dred Scott and his wife and child, it is agreeable to note, were given their freedom by Mrs. Emerson, who had married Calvin Chaffee, a prominent abolitionist. But Dred enjoyed only a year of freedom, dying of consumption in 1858, assured of attention by posterity. The decision became a critical ingredient in the political stew that came to a boil in the presidential election of 1860.

60

The Lincoln-Douglas Debates

Encouraged by the Republican showing in 1854, Lincoln campaigned actively for Frémont and the Republican ticket in Illinois in
1856. Douglas's senate seat would come up in 1858, and if the tide
continued to run strongly for the antislavery cause, Douglas might be
vulnerable. The *Alton Weekly Courier* noted in its June 5, 1856, issue that
"Abraham Lincoln, of Sangamon, came upon the platform amid
deafening applause." A week later he was at Springfield and then at
Princeton, dwelling each time on the Declaration and the Northwest
Ordinance, on the intentions of Jefferson and the Founding Fathers on
the matter of slavery in the territories. In July he addressed a large
audience in Dearborn Park. A newspaper reported it had never seen
"an audience held for so long a time in the open air to listen to an
argumentative speech."

At Galena, a few days later, an enthusiastic reporter wrote "Hon.
Abraham Lincoln hits the nail on the head every time, and in this
instance it will be seen, he has driven it entirely out of sight. . . ." The
Democrats had charged the Republicans with being "disunionists," so
intent on stopping the spread of slavery that they were willing to drive
the South out of the Union or declare themselves out of it and thus
free of the contamination of slavery—the extreme abolitionist posi-

tion. Lincoln met that charge head on. "We, the majority, would not strive to dissolve the Union; and if any attempt is made it must be by you, who so loudly stigmatize us as disunionists. But the Union, in any event, won't be dissolved. We don't want to dissolve it, and if you attempt it, *we won't let you*. With the purse and the sword, the army and the navy and the treasury in our hands and at our command, *you couldn't do it*. . . . All this talk about the dissolution of the Union is humbug—nothing but folly. *We* WON'T dissolve the Union, and *you* SHAN'T."

Everywhere Lincoln insisted that Frémont, "our young, gallant and world-renowned commander was the man for the day," and everywhere he called upon the spirits of "the old prophets and fathers of this republic." They must be repudiated or the doctrines of the slavocracy must be repudiated; there was no other choice. But a Republican victory was not to be. Lincoln once more experienced the bitter but familiar taste of defeat. In the pain of that defeat, he gave a kind of cry of disappointment and pain. "Twenty-two years ago," he wrote, "Judge Douglas and I first became acquainted. We were both young then, he a trifle younger than I. Even then, we were both ambitious; I, perhaps, quite as much as he. With *me*, the race of ambition has been a failure—a flat failure; with *him* it has been one of splendid success. His name fills the nation; and is not unknown even in foreign lands. I affect no contempt for the high eminence he has reached. So reached, that the oppressed of my species, might have shared with me in the elevation, I would rather stand on that eminence, than wear the richest crown that ever pressed a monarch's brow." The editors of Lincoln's papers included this reflection under "Fragment on Stephen A. Douglas." Assuredly it is one of the most revealing and ironic "fragments" in all history.

But this defeat was different. The Republican Party had brought a great new political force into American life, and Lincoln, who had helped in a modest way to create it, was swept up by it. The oration he gave as the featured speaker at a Republican banquet in Chicago a month after the election had about it the exuberance of victory. The reporter of the *Democratic Press* noted, significantly, that the "Hon. Abram Lincoln" rose to speak "amid most deafening cheers." He hailed the newly elected Republican governor—"[Cheers.]" He told a joke—"[Laughter and cheers]." Another joke—"[Cheers]." He made fun of Pierce's final annual message to Congress: "Like a rejected lover, making merry at the wedding of his rival, the President felicitates hugely over the late Presidential election." He had hoped for a second term but it had been denied him. "He is in the cat's paw. By much dragging of chestnuts from the fire for others to eat, his claws are burnt off to the gristle, and he is thrown aside as unfit for future use."

And then on to more serious matters. The recent presidential election had been a struggle by the Republicans to maintain the doctrine of "the practical equality of all men" against the Democratic doctrine that "slavery is right, in the abstract workings of which, as a central idea, may be the perpetuity of human slavery, and its extension to all countries and colors." Lincoln called on "every one who really believes, and is resolved, that free society is not, *and shall not be a failure,*" to join, hands and hearts, despite whatever differences may have in the past divided them, to "reinaugurate the good old 'central ideas' of the Republic. We *can* do it. The human heart *is* with us. God is with us. We shall again be able not to declare, that 'all States as States, are equal,' nor yet that 'all citizens as citizens are equal,' but to renew the broader, better declaration, including both of these and much more, that 'all *men* are created equal.' "

As he saw the election of 1856 in better perspective, Lincoln wrote that the Republicans, newly formed, "stood up, an army over thirteen hundred thousand strong. That army is, to-day, the best hope of the nation, and of the world. Their work is before them; and from which they may not guiltless turn away."

The principal issues of Buchanan's presidency involved slavery. In the South, increasingly aggressive on the subject, there was further talk of obtaining Cuba and reviving the slave trade. John Slidell of Louisiana, Buchanan's campaign manager and his lieutenant in the Senate, introduced a bill to purchase Cuba from Spain and make two or more slave states out of the island. When an American naval cruiser, the *Dolphin,* intercepted a slave ship, the *Echo,* with three hundred Congolese natives aboard in the fall of 1858 and brought the vessel into Charleston harbor, a heated debate took place over whether it was not more humane to rescue the poor creatures from the horrors of barbarism by making them slaves on some Christian plantation than to return them to their own land. In the course of the discussion a number of Southern newspapers called for the legalizing of the slave trade. The fact was that most of the ships engaged in the illicit trade had been built in the United States and were owned by American investors.

Prompted by Slidell, Buchanan outraged the North and probably destroyed his chances for a second term by recommending in his annual message to Congress that Kansas be promptly admitted to the Union under the Lecompton Constitution and that in light of the Dred Scott decision, "Kansas is at this moment as much a slave State as Georgia or South Carolina," adding, "slavery can never . . . be prohibited in Kansas except by means of a constitutional provision. . . ."

When the midterm congressional elections of 1858 rolled around, Lincoln took to the hustings again to challenge Douglas for his Senate seat. Douglas returned to his home state defending the Kansas-Nebraska Act, despite the continued chaos in that territory, as well as the Dred Scott decision, which was in fact a serious blow to his doctrine of popular sovereignty. Lincoln followed close on his heels, searching out the fallacies in his arguments, gently deriding him, looking for the vulnerability that would bring him down. The arguments were intricate and complex and the speeches were lengthy, often more than two hours, yet everywhere large audiences listened enthralled, aware that the most momentous issue in the republic's history was being defined and debated. It is from this period that Carl Schurz's description of Lincoln dates. Schurz, encountering him campaigning on a railroad train, wrote of the "swarthy face with its strong features, its deep furrows, and its benignant, melancholy eyes . . . haggard and careworn. . . . On his head he wore a somewhat battered 'stove-pipe' hat. His neck emerged, long and sinewy, from a white collar turned down over a thin black necktie. His lank, ungainly body was clad in a rusty black dress coat with sleeves that should have been longer. . . . His black trousers, too, permitted a very full view of his large feet. On his left arm he carried a grey woolen shawl, which evidently served him for an overcoat in chilly weather. His left hand held a cotton umbrella of the bulging kind, and also a black satchel that bore the marks of long and hard usage. His right hand he kept free for handshaking, of which there was no end until everyone in the car seemed to be satisfied. I had seen, in Washington and in the West, several public men of rough appearance; but none whose looks seemed quite so uncouth, not to say grotesque, as Lincoln's."

Douglas traveled in "great style" with a retinue of secretaries, servants, and "numerous loud companions," in a "special train with cars specially decorated for the occasion." Douglas's strategy was to depict Lincoln as a "nigger-worshiper." Douglas, Lincoln declared, had stated that those who argued that the Declaration of Independence applied to Negroes as well as whites, "do so only because they want to vote, and eat, and sleep, and marry with negroes. . . . Now I protest against that counterfeit logic which concludes that, because I do not want a black woman for a *slave*, I must necessarily want her for a *wife*. I need not have her for either. I can just leave her alone." Douglas had expressed horror "at the thought of the mixing blood by the white and black races," but Lincoln pointed out that it was precisely under slavery that this "amalgamation" of the races went on most conspicuously. The number of mulattoes in the South, the children most typically of unions between white master and slave women, was mute testimony to that fact.

By the spring of 1858, Lincoln had developed and refined his arguments, tried out lines of reasoning and the effectiveness of certain phrases and sentences with the audiences he addressed. The notion of the incongruity, the ultimate impossibility, of a nation enduring "half slave and half free," which he had first expressed almost three years earlier in a letter to his friend George Robertson, pushed its way forward again. In a "fragment" of a speech, one section was headed "A house divided against itself cannot stand," and below that he wrote, "I believe the government cannot endure permanently half slave and half free. I expressed this belief a year ago; and subsequent develop-ments have but confirmed me. I do not expect the Union to be dissolved. I do not expect the house to fall; but I do expect it will cease to be divided. It will become all one thing or all the other." To defeat slavery "it was not necessary to use '*bloody bullets*' but *peaceful ballots* . . . thanks to our good constitution. . . ."

The Republican state convention met in Springfield in the middle of June, 1858, and nominated Lincoln as candidate for the Senate against Douglas in the coming midterm elections. In accepting the nomination, Lincoln, for the first time before a major audience, expressed his conviction that "a house divided against itself cannot stand." Billy Herndon, Lincoln's law partner for a time, tells us that Lincoln submitted his speech to "a company of his personal and political friends," of whom Herndon was one, and that they were unanimous in declaring it "too radical and too far in advance of the public sentiment." Lincoln is said to have replied, "That makes no difference; that expression is a truth of all human experience. . . . The proposition is indisputably true, and has been for more than six thousand years; and I will deliver it as written. I want to use some universally known figure, expressed in simple language as universally known, that it may strike the minds of men, in order to arouse them to the peril of the times. I would rather be defeated with this expression in the speech, held up and discussed before the people, than to be victorious without it."

The evocation of the biblical sentence from the third chapter of Mark was, if there is any meaning to that word, inspired. The verse is from Mark's account of the incidents leading up to the betrayal and crucifixion of Christ. The disciples thought that Jesus was "beside himself" or temporarily insane. And the scribes declared that Christ cast out devils through the power of Satan. But Jesus replied, "How can Satan cast out Satan?" And then came the lines that were to be unforgettably engraved on the minds of generations of Americans: "if a house be divided against itself, that house cannot stand." The verse that followed read, "And if Satan rise up against himself and be divided, he cannot stand, but hath an end." These biblical reverberations were not lost on the majority of Lincoln's audience or on the vastly larger number who later read his speech. To be divided against oneself is death; in the language of the psychiatrist it is schizophrenia. The United States was, in its deepest being, divided against itself unto the agony of death, death to its ideals and principles, death to the Union, death to its soul. Whatever the cost, it must look into the face of that terror. The sentence also has implications concerning Lincoln's own inner life that we can hardly ignore. Lincoln was at the beginning of his own Gethsemane, a triumph and a crucifixion. He believed it was his destiny to knit up that schism; to heal, through surgery, however bloody, that suppurating wound in the body politic; to restore the republic; to take upon himself the burden of the sins of America that the nation might once more have a good conscience before the world. The Word met the Time.

Some of Lincoln's own bitterness came out in his characterization of his rival: "They remind us that *he* [Douglas] is a very great *man*, and that the largest of *us* are very small ones. Let this be granted. But 'a *living dog* is better than a *dead lion*.' Judge Douglas, if not a *dead* lion *for this work* is at least a *caged* and *toothless* one."

To chasten himself, Lincoln reminded himself privately of his persistent ambition to win "the honors of official station," but "in the republican cause there is a higher aim than that of mere office." That was to the cause of justice and the extension of human freedom. And fame attached to that as well. It had taken a hundred years to stop the British slave trade and during that time the movement for its abolition had had its "open fire-eating opponents; its stealthy 'don't care' opponents; its dollar and cents opponents; its inferior race opponents. . . . But all of them had sunk into oblivion, flickered in the socket, died out, stank in the dark for a brief season, and were remembered no more, even the smell." But every schoolboy knew the names of William Wilberforce and Granville Sharp, the enemies of the slave trade. By the same token, he himself might not live to see the outcome of the contest that lay ahead but he was glad to be able to contribute his "humble mite to that glorious consummation." Implicit also was the thought that in such an eventuality, fame might well come posthumously to him as it had to Wilberforce.

But there were more immediate practical considerations. With the selection for senator coming on and Douglas obviously on the defensive, denouncing the "unholy and unnatural alliance" that had been formed against him, Lincoln was determined to press his attack. Douglas had declared his intention of fighting "that allied army wherever I meet them," whether within the Democratic ranks or outside, as the Russians had blasted the allies at Sebastopol. Lincoln played with Douglas's image. "Just to think of it!" he told a delighted audience, "right at the very outset of this canvass, I, a poor, kind, amiable, intelligent [laughter], gentleman [laughter and renewed cheers] I am to be slain in this way. Why, my friend, the Judge, is not only, as it turns out, not a dead lion, nor even a living one—he is the rugged Russian Bear! [Roars of laughter and loud applause.]"

On Lincoln went, patient, humorous, tireless, always recurring to "this old Declaration of Independence" and the "framers of the Constitution" and to Jefferson. In speaking of Douglas, he was gently mocking and Douglas, reading the newspaper accounts of Lincoln's speeches, was increasingly nettled and increasingly denunciatory in his responses. But this oblique debating did not entirely suit Lincoln. He desired personal confrontation. He felt confident enough of his own powers to welcome such encounters, and he was undoubtedly conscious of the effect on audiences of his own moral earnestness contrasted with his opponent's sophistries and evasions. He wrote Douglas on July 24, inviting him to agree on a debating format "during the present canvass." He would thus add Douglas's audiences to his own, thereby substantially increasing the numbers and heightening the drama. Such meetings would also guarantee national press coverage and carry Lincoln's name far beyond the limits of Illinois. By the thirty-first, Lincoln and Douglas had agreed on the procedure to be followed. There would be seven meetings, the speakers alternating in opening and closing the debates. Before they met Lincoln gave a half-dozen more speeches and at the little town of Havana he again twitted Douglas on his belligerence and his offer, several days before, to "fight," Lincoln taking the line that Douglas wished to box or wrestle him. This challenge Lincoln refused. "It might establish," he said, "that Judge Douglas is a more muscular man than myself, or it might demonstrate that I am a more muscular man than Judge Douglas. But this question is not referred to in the Cincinnati platform, nor in either of the Springfield platforms. [Great laughter.]"

The first formal debate took place at Ottawa on August 21. Some twenty thousand people were present. A fourteen-car train carried people from Chicago and eleven passenger cars came from Peru and LaSalle, besides the innumerable carriages and wagons from the surrounding countryside. Douglas was met at Peru and escorted to Ottawa by a guard of honor bearing flags and banners; Lincoln, tradition has it, came unattended and unheralded. Douglas opened the debate by challenging Lincoln to tell where he stood on the Republican platform adopted at Springfield four years earlier and charging him with a plot to "abolitionize the Old Whig party all over the State, pretending that he was then as good a Whig as ever." A lifetime of stump speaking had made Douglas a skillful and flamboyant orator. He was as armed with anecdotes and humorous stories as Lincoln, as much a master of irony and of satiric thrusts, more immediately commanding with his booming voice and dramatic gestures. Lincoln was, he declared, a friend of over twenty-five years. He praised him for his success as a grocer in Salem. They had both been poor boys who were faced from the start with "an uphill struggle . . . in life." "He was then just as good at telling an anecdote as now. He could beat any of the boys wrestling or running a foot race, in pitching quoits or tossing a copper, could ruin more liquor than all the boys of the town together [uproarious laughter], and the dignity and impartiality with which he presided at a horse race or fist fight, excited the admiration and won the praise of everybody that was present and participated. [Renewed laughter.]" Douglas, in appearing to praise his rival, had accused him of heavy drinking and being an aficionado of horse racing and prize fighting, all anathemas to many of the pious folk in the audience.

Lincoln's brief appearance in politics, Douglas reminded his audience, had been marked by his "taking the side of the common enemy (Mexico) against his own country [cries from the audience of 'that's true']." Forced out of politics for his disloyal stand on the Mexican War, "he came back up again in 1854, just in time to make this Abolition or Black Republican platform, in company with Giddings, Lovejoy, Chase, and Fred Douglass . . . [Laughter, "Hit him again," etc.]."

Douglas turned his heaviest fire on Lincoln's "house divided" speech the month before at the Republican nominating convention. This was as much as a proclamation of war against the slaveholding South. This was the essence of disunion. As for the talk about the equality of man, Douglas wished it understood that "I am opposed to negro citizenship in any and every form. [Cheers.] I believe this government was made on the white basis ["Good"]. I believe it was made by white men, for the benefit of white men and their posterity for ever, and I am in favor of confining citizenship to white men . . . instead of conferring it upon negroes, Indians and other inferior races. ["Good for you." "Douglas forever."] . . . I do not question Mr. Lincoln's conscientious belief that the negro was made his equal, and hence his brother [laughter], but for my own part, I do not regard the negro as my equal, and positively deny he is my brother. . . . He belongs to an inferior race, and must always occupy an inferior position. ["Good," "that's so," etc.]" The key to the question of the status of the Negro, free or slave, rested solely with the citizens of the individual states; that was the true democratic spirit.

When Douglas had taken his seat, Lincoln came forward to a prolonged ovation. Referring to Douglas's two-edged compliments, Lincoln confessed that he was "not very much accustomed to flattery, and it came the sweeter to me. I was rather like the Hoosier, with the gingerbread, when he said he reckoned he loved it better than any other man, and got less of it. [Roars of laughter.]"

Lincoln responded to Douglas's charge that he was simply an abolitionist in disguise by starting to read the speech he had delivered at Peoria four years earlier, and when he stumbled over the opening sentence a voice called out, "Put on your specs." Lincoln did, observing, "Yes, sir, I am obliged to do so. I am no longer a young man. [Laughter.]"

On the matter of the Negro, Lincoln conceded that he might in certain respects be inferior to the white, "But in the right to eat the bread, without leave of anybody else, which his own hand earns, *he is my equal and the equal of Judge Douglas, and the equal of every living man.*

[Great applause.]" As for the Judge's attack on the statement that "a house divided against itself cannot stand," Lincoln inquired, "Does the Judge say it *can* stand? . . . If he does, then there is a question of veracity, not between him and me, but between the Judge and an authority of a somewhat higher character. [Laughter and applause.]"

As for popular sovereignty, that was a colossal humbug. It does allow people of a territory to have slavery if they want it, "but it does not allow them *not* to have it if they *do not* want it." That, at least, would be the effect of the Dred Scott decision. The Dred Scott decision was Douglas's Achilles heel and Lincoln hammered away at it mercilessly. He had pointed out its fallacies to Douglas. "But I cannot shake Judge Douglas's teeth loose from the Dred Scott decision. Like some obstinate animal (I mean no disrespect) that will hang on when he has once got his teeth fixed, you may cut off a leg, or you may tear away an arm, still he will not relax his hold. . . . He hangs to the last, to the Dred Scott decision. [Loud cheers . . . Vociferous applause.]"

The Ottawa debate set the tone for the remaining encounters. The second one, a week later at Freeport, was distinguished by Douglas's enunciation of what came to be called the Freeport Doctrine. Lincoln had pressed him about how he could apply his doctrine of popular sovereignty—allowing the people of a state to make their own decision about entering the Union slave or free—in the face of the Dred Scott decision. Douglas's ingenious answer was that since slavery could nowhere exist without the support of the local police power, if a state or territory were opposed to slavery it would exclude it simply by not protecting it. "Hence, no matter what the decision of the Supreme Court may be on the abstract question, still the right of the people to make a slave Territory or a free Territory is perfect and complete under the Nebraska bill." Those were strange words from a man who had so recently argued that the decision of the Supreme Court in the case of Dred Scott must be obeyed if the rule of law was to be preserved. Lincoln finally had his opponent where he wished to place him. One feels a twinge of sympathy for the beleaguered Douglas. Every word he spoke had to be weighed and considered with the utmost care as to its effect on Southern opinion. And that, it turned out, was an opinion that would accept no compromises or equivocations. If Douglas were to succeed Buchanan as the candidate of the Democratic Party, and hopefully as the next president of the United States, he must have the votes of the South, but the Freeport Doctrine, while it may have won the senatorial race for Douglas, did him in south of Mason and Dixon's line. Southern newspapers were soon full of vituperation directed against both Lincoln *and* Douglas.

Lincoln had also asked Douglas if he would support the acquisition of more territory without regard to its effect on the slavery question. To this Douglas replied unequivocally. He was for expansion per se, "in North, in the South, or on the islands of the ocean, I am for it; and when we acquire it will have the people, according to the Nebraska bill, free to do as they please on the subject of slavery and every other question."

By the third debate at Jonestown, the respective positions of the candidates had been laid out in detail, examined, attacked, and defended. Much that was said was repetitious but Lincoln, having extracted the Freeport Doctrine from Douglas, made as much as he could of its contradictions and its tendency to stir up conflict as well as weaken the Union by breaking it down into conflicting and hostile jurisdictions. But again and again Lincoln had to reply to the Douglas-reiterated charge that he favored the "amalgamation" of the races. Each time he did it with decency and restraint.

Repetitious or not, the debates had by now attracted the attention of the nation. Douglas himself must have felt that the prize was no longer the senatorial seat from Illinois but something far larger—the leadership of the nation. The moral requirements of the role eluded him. For him politics was a series of discrete acts, each one calculated for its effects on his own ambitions. That there should be, at least now in this hour of crisis, some larger dimension, did not occur to him. He continued to deride his rival's evocation of the Declaration of Independence and his appeals to his countrymen's better natures. So the excitement mounted. An estimated eighteen thousand people came to the fifth debate at Galesburg, two thousand by train from Peoria.

The seventh and final debate was at Alton, where Elijah Lovejoy had been killed twenty-two years earlier. The carnival atmosphere of some of the earlier debates was missing. The committee on arrangements, sensible perhaps of the momentous issues in question, had ruled out flags and banners so that there was an air of seriousness, almost somberness about the gathering. Douglas opened on the defensive, almost plaintive, directing much of his fire against Buchanan, whose willingness to accept the fraudulent Lecompton Constitution had placed Douglas on the horns of yet another dilemma that was bound to cost him Southern support. When Lincoln replied, he dwelt on

Douglas's war with the administration. It was, he told a responsive audience, most encouraging to Republicans. "I say to them again—'Go it, husband!—Go it, bear!' [Great laughter.]"

The spirit in which Douglas so readily accommodated himself to the perpetuation of slavery was "the same as that which says, 'You work and toil and earn bread, and I'll eat.' Whether spoken by kings who wished to live off the labor of their subject," or "from one race of men as apology for enslaving another race, it is the same tyrannical principle." And as for Douglas's argument for accepting the Dred Scott decision but nullifying its practical effect "by legislating it out of all force while the law itself still stands, I repeat there has never been so monstrous a doctrine uttered from the mouth of a respectable man. [Loud cheers.]"

In addition to the famous debates Douglas and Lincoln spoke to dozens of other audiences. Douglas estimated that by the end of the campaign he had traveled more than five thousand miles and made over a hundred speeches. In the election the Republicans carried the day, but Douglas's hold on the legislature was still too strong for Lincoln to break. Douglas was chosen for the Senate by a vote of 54 to 46. Defeated, Lincoln was left free to make evident his own availability as his party's candidate in the presidential election of 1860, only two short years away. In the Senate he might well have lost some of the political virginity that was his greatest asset, have been forced to take positions on controversial issues that must lose him support. In the wake of the most exciting state campaign in memory, he was much in demand as a Republican speaker.

Although Lincoln lost to Douglas, the Buchanan administration suffered a series of setbacks. In Pennsylvania, Ohio, Indiana, and Iowa the Democrats lost heavily. A coalition of Free Soilers, Republicans, and Know-Nothings in Pennsylvania won twenty-five out of twenty-eight congressional seats. A month later in New York and New England, the Democrats were again routed. There was general agreement that the Democratic debacle was due to Buchanan's efforts to bring Kansas into the Union under the proslavery Lecompton Constitution.

With the election of 1858 behind him, Lincoln turned his attention to 1860. He was uneasy about a disposition on the part of some Illinois Republicans to court Douglas, "a proven winner," on the ground that he had opposed the Buchanan administration by voting against the Lecompton Constitution. Lincoln was convinced that it was this vote alone which had enabled Douglas to retain his Senate seat. Speaking at a Republican conclave in Chicago, he warned his audience that Douglas would absorb the Illinois Republicans and subvert them to his own ambitions. As late as September, 1859, he wrote, "What will Douglas do now? He does not quite know himself. Like a skillful gambler he will play for all the chances." His best chance was to go to the Charleston convention, hoping that the Southern delegates would not present him with some new test of loyalty to Southern principles, some test he could not accept without destroying all his support in the North. This, Lincoln was confident, the South would do. Douglas would refuse and then present himself as a man of principle and try to woo the Northern Republicans and what remained of the Democrats.

The same month Lincoln spoke at Columbus, Ohio. Here he tried to protect his flank against the persistent charge that he believed in the social equality of the black with the white. These were painful exercises for him. Of the depth of his compassion for the oppressed slave, of his determination to speak out for his equal rights before the law, there could be no doubt and it was maddening that he should have, constantly, to restate his position and to hedge it so carefully with disavowals of any disposition to support racial mingling. Finally he declared, "I am not, nor ever have been in favor of making voters or jurors of negroes or qualifying them to hold office, or intermarry with white people. . . . I have never seen a man, woman or child, who was in favor of producing a perfect equality, social and political, between negroes and white men." Yet the issue continued to follow at his heels, or, rather, to proceed him. He ended his Columbus speech with the familiar reference to the Declaration of Independence and an accusation that the Democrats were at work "blowing out the moral lights around us; teaching that the negro is no longer a man but a brute; that the Declaration has nothing to do with him; that he ranks with the crocodile and the reptile; that man, with body and soul, is a matter of dollars and cents." Thus did he suffer his own schizophrenia, disavowing and avowing, saying what he knew he must say and then saying what he believed from the same platform to the same audience and letting them sort it out as best they might.

Everything he said was reported and scanned for some flaw or inconsistency. He could never be off guard. In his own mind at least he was running for the presidency against Douglas, for Douglas was on every page and in every paragraph. When Douglas came out publicly against the Southern agitation to legalize the slave trade, Lincoln felt a spasm of anxiety. That Lincoln never let Douglas rest was a deliberate strategy. The debates with Douglas had made Lincoln a national figure, a worthy opponent of the most popular politician of the day, now that Clay and Webster had passed from the scene. So it was important to keep borrowing on Douglas's reputation. Moreover, since it was clear that Douglas would be the Democratic candidate—or, as it turned out, *a* Democratic candidate—who could be a more appropriate challenger than the man had bested him—at least in the Republican view—on one platform after another.

By the end of September Lincoln was in Indianapolis. He now for the first time in his life "appeared before a large audience in Indiana," Lincoln declared. It was here "on our own good soil of Indiana" that he "grew up to his present enormous height. [Laughter] . . . and with the trees and logs and grubs he fought until he reached his twentieth year." And so on through the Dred Scott decision, the Kansas-Nebraska Act, and Douglas's popular sovereignty.

Then it was the Wisconsin Agricultural Society at Milwaukee and the next day at Beloit and Janesville, then Elwood, and Leavenworth, taking pains to see that the now famous Lincoln-Douglas debates were printed and distributed as widely as possible. He also composed an autobiography, stressing his humble origins as a poor farm boy with little schooling and his service in the Black Hawk War, describing himself as weighing "on the average a hundred and eighty pounds; dark complexion with coarse black hair, and grey eyes—no other marks or brands recollected."

At last there was the crucial moment: his first major address as an undeclared candidate for the Republican nomination in the coming election in the critically important state of New York. More rested on the success of this single appearance than on all his other formal and informal speeches combined. Here was his most demanding audience —sophisticated Easterners, powerful men, wealthy men, temperance men and women, old Whigs, new Republicans, Free Soilers, abolitionists, Know-Nothings—looking for a political home or a political bargain. There was prejudice aplenty against the West in that sea of pale, inquiring, curious faces. Horace Greeley and William Cullen Bryant (who chaired the meeting and introduced Lincoln) were present among the fifteen hundred people who crowded into the two-year-old Cooper Union, built by Peter Cooper, the great entrepreneur of railroads and the Atlantic cable. Each person in the audience had a different expectation, a different hope or fear or vision. So that no one might miss the point, his first sentence, after an initial comment, referred to Senator Douglas. Then the argument proceeded at once to the Constitution and the Ordinance of 1787 and what those documents had to say about the extension of slavery. The "fathers" were called up, one by one, for their testimony. The argument was spare, direct, unencumbered by rhetorical flourishes. To the North his message was: "As those fathers marked it, so let it again be marked, as an evil not to be extended, but to be tolerated and protected only because of and so far as its actual presence among us makes that toleration and protection a necessity."

To the people of the South who considered themselves "a reasonable and a just people" Lincoln had conciliatory words, but he ended firmly. They had declared that they would "not abide the election of a Republican President! In that supposed event, you say, you will destroy the Union; and then, you say, the great crime of having destroyed it will be upon us! That is cool. A highwayman holds a pistol to my ear, and mutters through his teeth, 'Stand and deliver, or I shall kill you and then you will be a murderer!' " The South had been imploring the North, in effect, "to unsay what Washington said, and undo what Washington did." And then the famous ending, "Neither let us be slandered from our duty by false accusations against us, nor frightened from it by menaces of destruction to the Government nor of dungeons to ourselves. LET US HAVE FAITH THAT RIGHT MAKES MIGHT, AND IN THAT FAITH, LET US TO THE END, DARE TO DO OUR DUTY AS WE UNDERSTAND IT."

When Lincoln finished speaking there was prolonged and enthusiastic applause. A reporter for Greeley's *Tribune* was convinced that Lincoln was the greatest figure in history since St. Paul and while that was a rather extreme opinion, his statement that "no man ever before made such an impression on his first appeal to a New York audience" was closer to the truth. Bryant expressed his admiration. The *Tribune* carried the entire text and it was also printed in pamphlet form. "It has produced a greater effect here than any other single speech," a member of the audience wrote him. "It is the real platform in the eastern states and must carry the conservative element in New York, New Jersey and Pennsylvania."

61

Way Out West

In 1857 another "gold rush" drew attention to what I have called earlier the Fur West—the vast, largely arid lands of the Rocky Mountain region and the Great Basin. The gold rush of '49 was followed almost a decade later by the rush on the Fraser River in British Columbia. A San Francisco paper reported in June, 1858, "On every side, at every turn, you hear of Fraser River. Every acquaintance you meet asks whether you are going to Fraser River, or tells how he is going, or would go if he could, and enumerates your acquaintances who are going. . . . Here and there you will see fixed up in front of a store, some sign such as this: 'Selling out at cost; going to Fraser river, sure's you're born.' The Coroner of this city complains that the new diggings have put an end to suicide." In a period of five months twenty-three thousand men left San Francisco for the Fraser River diggings.

Northern California and San Francisco especially suffered from the exodus. City lots dropped in value from two thousand dollars a front foot to two hundred, and one shopkeeper displayed a skull in his window labeled A RETURNED FRASER RIVER MINER. Two other skulls beside it bore the sign HEADS OF FAMILIES RETURNED FROM BELLING-HAM BAY. The Fraser River strike proved relatively meager, averaging out to one hundred seventy dollars per miner, far from enough to pay for the food they consumed, not to mention the cost of their equipment and transportation. But the Fraser River rush had barely spent itself before word came of the discovery of gold in the Rockies. A band of Cherokee Indians on the way to California in 1849 had found flakes of gold in a tributary of the North Platte, but had abandoned it for the richer prospects in California. It was almost ten years before a miner named William Russell arrived at Cherry Creek in present-day Colorado and after months of fruitless prospecting found a few hundred dollars' worth of gold on the South Platte. The find was reported in the *Kansas City Journal of Commerce* under the headlines: "THE NEW ELDORADO!!! Gold in Kansas Territory!!!" The border towns that lived by outfitting Western emigrants did all they could to encourage the notion that gold was lying around in Rocky Mountain streams waiting to be picked up. Two camps were established in the region of Cherry Creek, and by spring tens of thousands of the hopeful were heading west, attracted by such statements as "there is no end to the precious metal. Nature seems to have turned into a most successful alchemist by converting the very sands of the streams into gold." The Midwest, in the grip of the devastating depression of 1857, supplied the majority of gold seekers, of whom it was estimated there were more than a hundred thousand in 1859. "The number of people in this section of Iowa who are going to Pikes Peak is astonishing," one seeker wrote. "A company of over sixty will leave Fairfield next week, and nearly every man you meet is bound for the Peak in a 'few weeks.'"

Again, thousands fell ill and hundreds died on the various trails. The ox-drawn wagons were supplemented by such odd vehicles as a wagon under sail, which "plowed right through the mud, but cast anchor in a deep ravine where the wind failed to fill the sail. . . ." One enthusiastic gold seeker wrote: "Today we . . . came in sight of the Arkansas River, and Jerusalem, what a sight! Wagons-wagons-Pikes Peak wagons. Well! there were a few of them—I presume three hundred ox-wagons in sight . . . I went up and spoke to the men; they told me the sad news; said there is no gold at the Peak. Some that are going on say they had met three hundred wagons coming back." Someone else noted, "The roads are lined with mining tools that have been thrown away as they would not pay for bringing back," and that "Some of the men that helped get up the excitement have been hung and others shot."

Among those heading west were Mollie and Byron Sanford,

leaving Nebraska City with a party of friends, two yoke of cows and two of oxen, supplies for six months, and "a half-dozen fine hens and a rooster." Their destination was Denver and their route along the Platte. The cows proved reluctant draft animals and when Mollie heard "By" curse them she cried for the first time in years. The stagecoach from St. Joe to Denver came speeding by, stirring up clouds of choking dust, but there were mail stations, ranches, and military posts every fifteen or twenty miles. When Mollie, riding in her little buggy, got separated from the main party, she found herself surrounded by grinning Indians who grasped her long braids, "took their hunting knives and made every demonstration of cutting them off, *or* scalping, I did not know which," she wrote. She distracted her unwelcome visitors with gifts of sugar from a can under the wagon seat, and the appearance of the rest of the train drove off "the pesky redskins," who galloped away, giving their war yelps.

By the end of June they were in Denver, "the Promised Land," where no houses were to be had and Mollie and By found "hundreds of families . . . living in wagons, tents, and shelters made of carpets and bedding. Everybody," Mollie noted, "seems glad to welcome the coming pilgrims, as we are called, anybody from 'back in the States.'" Some five thousand people were in and around what passed for "Denver City"; many were friends from Nebraska. There was a boom-town atmosphere with bands playing all day long and gamblers and saloonkeepers occupying most of the town's permanent structures. The oxen were traded for a lot, and By and his brother-in-law built a "board shanty" ten feet by twenty.

From Denver, Byron took Mollie to Gold Hill near Boulder, where her "home" was a lean-to, the earth covered with pine boughs which made the only bed she had. Byron was to do blacksmithing and Mollie was to cook for eighteen or twenty miners at an outdoor fire. "All I have furnished to cook," she wrote, "is bread, meat and coffee. The cups and plates are of tin. A long table is made in a shed made of pine boughs outside the cabin . . . I fear I shall sink under this burden. It is not what my fancy painted it." Even Byron seemed a stranger in these crude surroundings and did "all sorts of awkward things. If this does not take the romance out of me," she wrote, "then I am proof against *anything*." It was "cook, cook, bake, bake" and when the young men in the group sang "Home Sweet Home," Mollie cried herself to sleep. The cumbersome and expensive crusher, designed to break the ore out of gold-bearing rocks, turned up precious few particles of gold and Mollie, recovering from a wasting illness that lasted through weeks of summer, wrote, "I *do* take a little time now and then, amid all my work, to moralize. I will not put myself down to ceaseless drudgery. I must think and read and do something, so that I shall at least not retrograde." But homesickness for Hazel Dell was a constant ache. "I know how wrong and useless it is to feel blue," she wrote. "Well for me it is, my good angel lifts me out of these momentary fits of despondency. I guess I get too tired, or too something." The poems she wrote, tender reflections on home, and love poems to Byron that she forbore to show him for fear he would "make sport" of them, were a solace.

When Mollie returned to Denver to visit her sister, Dora, in 1860, she found it "much improved" and having a "jubilee" over the election of Lincoln. Back at Golden Hill Christmas came and still no gold, and Mollie wrote, "The men folks are all discouraged. They came here expecting to find the gold almost on the surface of the ground." Her Christmas present was a bottle of whiskey presented to her by a good-natured Irishman named Patrick, who accompanied the gift with a little speech, "It's thinkin' we did that ye might nade it in case of sickness or snakebite, ye know." But Mollie put camphor in the bottle so no one would be tempted by it and when By came in, chilled and weary and took an unsuspecting swig, he lectured to Mollie for being "*too* much temperance."

Mollie became pregnant and went back to Denver for the birth of her child, which was still-born in August. The Sanfords were caught up by the opening phases of the war. Byron was offered a lieutenant's commission in the 1st Colorado Regiment, and Denver was full of the sound of fife and drum as young men from the mines, clerks, storekeepers, and farmers flocked there, "all ready to fight for their country." Mollie slipped easily into the life of an officer's wife in a frontier military post, the mining days mercifully over.

The search for gold that brought Mollie and Byron Sanford to Denver and then to Golden Hill scattered miners and prospectors throughout the Colorado Rockies. At Clear Creek, later Idaho Springs, gold was discovered. John Gregory found gold in an area near North Clear Creek which he named Gregory's Gulch. He proved his claim and sold it in Denver for twenty-two thousand dollars, the beginning of one of the great lodes of the Rockies. Word of Gregory's strike brought general celebrations. Henry Villard, a journalist visiting there, wrote, "Individuals could be heard everywhere on the streets shouting to each other, 'We are all right now,' 'the stuff is here after all,' 'the country is safe,' etc. On the following day an exodus took place in the direction of North Clear Creek. . . . Traders locked up their stores; bar-keepers disappeared with their bottles of whiskey, and the few mechanics that were busy building houses, abandoned their work, the county judge and sheriff, lawyers and doctors, and even the editor of the *Rocky Mountain News*, joined in the general rush." Soon there were new names on the maps—Black Hawk, Central City, Nevadaville, Negro Gulch, Buckskin Joe, Oro City. Ten thousand miners and assorted camp followers crowded into California Gulch (now Leadville) following a strike there.

The rush brought with it many of the attendant evidences of civilization—saloons, prostitutes, robbers, rudimentary agencies of the law, and vigilance committees to hunt down the thieves and murderers who followed the miners. The Territories of Nevada and Dakota, carved out of Utah Territory, were hastily organized and an effort made by settlers to establish the state of Jefferson. Old trails became highways, rutted and ankle-deep in dust or mud but traversed by thousands of wagons, mules, and men. It was calculated that twelve thousand men, sixty-nine hundred wagons, and sixty-eight thousand oxen were engaged in carrying freight from such jumping-off points as St. Joe, Independence, Atchison, Leavenworth, and Nebraska City to Utah, Denver, and New Mexico. A stagecoach left St. Joe for Salt Lake City every day, a trip that took the better part of two weeks. A similar stagecoach line was established with numerous changes of horses and stops at "hotels" along the route running between St. Louis and San Francisco, a trip of 2,795 miles that took twenty-four days to complete. The arrival of the first coach on October 10, 1858, was hailed by President Buchanan as "a glorious triumph for civilization and the Union. Settlement will soon follow the course of the road, and the East and West will be bound together by a chain of living Americans which can never be broken."

No self-respecting history of the United States would dare omit mention of one of the most ephemeral phenomena of our past—the pony express. Dan Drumheller, who had come to California in 1854 as a boy of fourteen, sold a string of ponies for two hundred dollars to a man named Finny, who signed him up as a rider, on the newly formed pony express at $150 a month. "Our equipment," he wrote, "was very simple. In the front of every station when the driver was due, the horse stood out at the rack, bridled and saddled and ready to go. The saddle was a very light tree with a single cinch." The mail was carried in two leather pouches that fitted over the pommel and cantle of the saddle trees and were cinched around the horse's belly. Thirty pounds of mail, the letters written on the thinnest of paper, were carried from St. Joe in Missouri to Sacramento at the cost of two dollars fifty cents an ounce. The stations were eighteen or twenty miles apart and each rider aimed to make "one hundred miles in a day's trip of ten hours with five relays of horses." After a rest of thirty-six hours the riders headed back along the same track. Drumheller's portion of the trip was through Paiute country, "including old Winnemucca's bunch of lazy pirates." One night, arriving at a station to change horses, Dan found the station tender dead and mutilated by the Paiute. Dan had to push on with his tired horse to the next station. The fastest run ever made from St. Joe to Sacramento was six days (carrying the news of Lincoln's election), but dramatic and colorful as it was, the pony express never made a profit or justified the risk. Drumheller quit after three months of riding, and a year later, with the completion of the transcontinental telegraph line, the pony express passed into legend.

If the Far West existed on the periphery of the East's vision, it suffered no lack of self-confidence as a consequence. It followed events in the East with the closest attention. California, which had been admitted to statehood in 1850, had voted in the elections of 1852 and '56, going Democratic each time. Oregon was admitted to statehood in 1859, just in time to register its vote for Lincoln. The Democrats were strong in Oregon but it was, above all, Union sentiment that most distinguished those states. While neither would be called proslavery, both were antiblack in that they were quite indifferent to the fate of the slaves if only the Union could be preserved. The *Oregon Spectator* described its position and, by inference, that of its readers as that of "a democrat of the Jeffersonian school." Another settler, complaining about the territorial government, wrote: "Western people do not hear the declaration of Independence read every fourth of July for nothing. They remember very well that if government . . . becomes 'destructive of the ends for which it was instituted,' the people have a right to alter or abolish the same." Pure Jeffersonian doctrine was expressed by another recent settler: "We have an agricultural community, and the domestic virtues incident to an agricultural people; there is where you look for the true and solid wealth and happiness of a people." The Oregon settlers identified themselves with the theme that the natural resources of the Western country had been "given by

Heaven for . . . the expansion of republicanism—to work out the redemption of the human race—to re-image man in his godlike lineaments."

Joseph Lane, one of the most prominent politicians of the territory and then the state, declared, "We are now upon the far west; we can go no further. Many would regret that the coast did not extend two thousand miles further, that our institutions might be extended over them. They will be extended to the islands, and ultimately, I trust, they will be extended over the whole world. Democracy is progressive, our republican institutions are progressive, and they must prevail, for they are adapted to the happiness of man."

One of the early settlers and political leaders of Oregon wrote in 1857, that "the people of Oregon are eminently National in their sentiments and attachments . . . she will be a conservative National State, and in every emergency will stand by the Union and the constitution."

The slave issue had produced anxiety and irritation in Oregon because it held up the admission of that state to the Union, but the antiblack bias of the region was evident in a statute passed by the territorial legislature in 1854 to prohibit free blacks and mulattoes from establishing themselves in Oregon Territory under threat of floggings. Slave owners were given three years to get rid of all slaves. Interestingly enough the law was passed in response to charges that free blacks had been stirring up Indians to attack white settlements. In a debate over the constitutionality of the law one member of the territorial legislature declared, that "niggers . . . should never be allowed to mingle with the whites. They would amalgamate and raise a most miserable race of human beings. . . . If niggers are allowed to come among us and mingle with whites, it will cause a perfect state of pollution. Niggers always retrograde, until they get back to the state of barbarity from whence they originated. . . ."

The Kansas-Nebraska Act prompted a prolonged discussion in Oregon of the doctrine of popular sovereignty, a notion readily accepted by frontier communities which were, at the same time, adamant against slavery itself. The Oregon Whigs, in decided minority, concentrated their fire on the repeal of the Missouri Compromise. Only slightly less reprehensible than the free black was the abolitionist; indeed one of the principal arguments for excluding all blacks, slave and free, from the territory was that the abolitionists, with their "insane agitation," would appear in their wake.

In the view of many the issue was a practical one. The climate was unsuited for blacks. The editor of the *Oregon Statesman* wrote, "the African . . . is destined to be the servant and subordinate of the superior white race. . . . And we believe, also, that the wisdom of man has not yet devised a system under which the negro is as well off as he is under that of American slavery." There were even those who felt that in the event of war, Oregon should be "Identified with the Southern Liberalists, and not with Northern Fanatics."

Within the Democratic Party the delegates from Oregon and from California, attending the Democratic conventions, threw their weight on the anti-Douglas side, aligning themselves with the Southern faction in the party. Lincoln would carry California by fewer than a thousand votes—39,173 as against 38,516 for Douglas and 34,334 for Breckinridge, while Breckinridge polled only 264 fewer in Oregon than Lincoln. "If the aggressions of the North continue," one California delegate declared, "and the Union should be dissolved, the Pacific States have, thank God, the domain upon which to build up a splendid empire of their own." Such sentiments were much in evidence but not, it turned out, dominant. The deepest feeling was one of reverence for the Union. When word reached the coast of the breakup of the Democratic Convention at Charleston, the *Weekly Oregonian* of Portland reported that politicians had been thunderstruck. Many "stood around speechless, to hear the comments, and . . . had not a word to say. We saw an editor standing with his face toward the Willamette, staring at vacancy. It was a sad scene."

The pro-Union feeling in Oregon grew stronger as the danger of dissolution became more apparent. The editor of the *Oregonian* wrote, "The Union is bound together and cemented by materials which no Southern braggart, northern dough-face, or addle-brained, thick-skulled political *demagogue* can sunder," and the governor of Oregon, John Whiteaker, declared, "When I consider the few benefits that have resulted to Oregon from becoming a State; the almost entire neglect of her interests and rights by the general government, and then reflect that her population is made up of citizens representing every State of the Union . . . and find them all loyal, all unalterably attached to the Union, I feel like dismissing the idea of a separation as not being worthy a place in the mind of any American citizen." That may have been overstating the case somewhat, but it was clear there was little support in Oregon, and only slightly more in California, for a Pacific republic.

While most citizens of the Far West clung to the belief that a civil war could and must be avoided, Isaac Stevens, governor of the Washington Territory, showed a keener awareness of the nature of the crisis. "It must be constantly borne in mind," he wrote, "that we have to deal with revolution, where event succeeds event with the rapidity of a dream, where the restorer or palliative of the day becomes obsolete in the morrow, and where the most patient and wise forecasts can discern but dimly the shadow of coming events. . . . If Union seems to be accompanied with occasional discord, separation will threaten perpetual war. If in Union, there is not always harmony, in separation there will never be peace." In Washington County, Joe Meek, one of the last of the famous mountain men, wrote, "I am a Douglas man and . . . I keep the stars and stripes flying 80 feet over my house all the time . . . and go Decidedly for the union. If the union is lost every thing is lost."

Yet notably absent was any sentiment for emancipation. Even the possibility was deplored by many. One Willamette Valley Democrat wrote, typically, "I am for the union but against free negroes on this continent. But save the union if we have to cut the damned Negroes head off and give his Boddy to the dogs for I have no love for them."

New Englanders like Richard Henry Dana and Charles Francis Adams deplored the constant expansion of the country. It was the single most divisive issue: Texas, Oregon, California—every new state and territory added fuel to the bitter controversy over slavery. Fisher called them "new elements of discord." There were enough states already, enough land to contain millions more Americans. But, strangely, incomprehensibly, the new lands, the acquisition and organization of which constantly threatened to tear the nation apart, actually worked to hold the Union together. It was there in the West, in the valley of the Mississippi, along the coast of California, and in the Oregon Territory that the Union was most strongly held to, most carefully nurtured, most prized. It was like some kind of physical law—the further from the center, the stronger the attraction toward that center, the greater the determination that it must hold.

The undecided question of who might come to dominate those states and territories was what, in fact, held the North and the South together. The prospect that one section or the other might gather those prizes into its fold was an unacknowledged but powerful cement even while it exacerbated feelings between them. The North and South, divided, like Cain and Abel, by hatred, suspicion, and jealousy, remained in the Union until they might determine to whom the western inheritance would fall. The consequences of parting company without settling the inheritance were too unpredictable. They had to hang together to protect their interests. The irony of it was that the North, in large part, deplored the whole "Western question," had no ambitions independent of the limitation of slavery, and wished the whole issue of Western expansion would simply go away. It was the South that might be said to have "invented" the West. Almost single-handedly Jefferson had implanted the dream and the reality of "the West" in the American consciousness and made the "Jeffersonian Republicans" the custodians of it. To the South it seemed that the North was the proverbial dog-in-the-manger. The North did not wish to claim the West; it did not even wish it to exist. But it was determined that it should not fall to the South. That was the linchpin, the keystone of the Union. It continued to hold the "federal edifice" together long after many of the shrewdest prognosticators had predicted it must come apart. Meanwhile the West went its own particular way, wholeheartedly dedicated to the idea of Union and quite unconscious of its role in prolonging the life of the Union.

62

John Brown

In the strange, by now irresistible, current that swept the country along toward the tragic denouement, the acts of John Brown entered with their own unique potency. Brown was already a legendary figure in Kansas, where he had led free-state men in half a dozen successful raids against the proslavery forces. In May, 1859, at Chatham, Ontario, Brown held a "convention" of twelve whites and twenty-four blacks including Harriet Tubman, to ratify a "free" American constitution. It was the first step in his quixotic plan to free the slaves by force and establish a new social and political order of complete racial equality.

From Canada, Brown returned to Kansas, rather thinly disguised by a gray beard that gave him more than ever the appearance of an avenging Old Testament prophet and using the assumed name of Shubel Morgan (Shubel in Hebrew meant captive of God). Brown collected a party whose nucleus was his sons and, responding to the plea of a slave from Missouri who was to be sold at auction, crossed into that state, went to the house of the slave's owner, and gathered up five slaves and a wagon and some horses. They took five slaves from an adjacent farm, killed a white man who tried to intervene, and carried the slaves to a cabin on the Pottawatomie. The Missouri legislature offered a three-thousand-dollar reward for his capture, and President

Buchanan personally put up two hundred dollars in reward money. With money on his head, Brown and his band headed for Canada where he set the slaves free.

Heading south again, Brown conferred with Gerrit Smith, Joshua Giddings, Samuel Gridley Howe, and other abolitionist leaders. The events in Kansas had radicalized men like Gerrit Smith, who had come to believe that the slaves could be freed only by force. But Lewis Tappan, Garrison, and the pacificist wing of the movement continued to deplore all violence and urge passive resistance. By now Brown had completed his plans for a raid into Virginia which, he believed, would trigger a general slave uprising. When he went to solicit Frederick Douglass's support, Douglass refused to become involved. The two men had known each other for more than ten years and it was, indeed, Brown who had persuaded Douglass that the slaves would never be emancipated by appeals to conscience. Douglass described Brown as "lean, strong, and sinewy, of the best New England mold, built for times of trouble . . . a figure straight and symmetrical as a mountain pine" with "a strong, square mouth, supported by a broad and prominent chin. His eyes," Douglass added, "were bluish-gray, and in conversation they were full of light and fire. When on the street, he moved with a long, springing, race-horse step, absorbed by his own reflections. . . ."

This was the man who laid before Douglass his plan to accomplish by force what could not be done by moral suasion. Brown had recruited fourteen white men, his sons among them, and five free blacks. His intention was to seize the United States arsenal at Harpers Ferry, distribute the arms and ammunition stored there to Maryland and Virginia slaves, and lead them in a fight to free all slaves throughout the South.

Stephen Vincent Benét described Browns' men thus:

> There were twenty-two in all,
> Nineteen were under thirty, three not yet twenty-one,
> Kagi, the self-taught scholar, quiet and cool,
> Stevens, the cashiered soldier, Puritan-fathered,
> A singing giant, gunpowder-tempered and rash.
> Dauphin Thompson, the pippin-cheeked country boy,
> More like a girl than a warrior; Oliver Brown,
> Married last year when he was barely nineteen;
> Dangerfield Newby, colored and born a slave,
> Freeman now, but married to one not free

Who, with their seven children, waited him South,
The youngest baby just beginning to crawl;
Watson Brown, the steady lieutenant, who wrote
Back to his wife,
    "Oh, Bell, I want to see you
And the little fellow very much but must wait.
There was a slave near here whose wife was sold South.
They found him hanging in Kennedy's orchard next morning.
I cannot come home as long as such things are done here.
I sometimes think that we shall not meet again."
These were some of the men. For better or worse
They were all strong men.

On the night of October 19, 1859, Brown and his followers surprised the watchman and took possession of the arsenal, which contained a gun factory and an armory. A detachment was sent to a nearby plantation to capture Colonel Lewis Washington, a great grand-nephew of the general, whose proudest possession was the sword given his ancestor by Frederick the Great. Brown's men seized the sword, freed the colonel's slaves, and put them to guarding the colonel, but that was too drastic a reversal of roles and they let him walk away unmolested. The leading white citizens of the nearby town were rounded up and some fifty slaves prevailed on to accept arms. Brown proclaimed a general emancipation, but the anticipated slave uprising failed to materialize and soon the captors found themselves besieged by local militia, the Jefferson Guards. Dangerfield Newby was shot and one of the townspeople cut off his ears for souvenirs. Shepherd Heyward, a prosperous black man from Harpers Ferry who had joined Brown, was also killed early in the fighting. When Brown sent his son, Watson, and another man out with a white truce flag, they were both shot down. Oliver Brown, badly wounded and in agony, begged his father to kill him.

The next morning when Colonel Robert E. Lee, grandson of Henry ("Light-Horse Harry") Lee, the great chronicler of the Southern campaigns of the American Revolution, arrived with a detachment of United States soldiers to take over the military operation, most of the defenders had been killed or wounded. An assault was made, the doors of the arsenal battered down, and Brown, seriously wounded, was captured with three other survivors and hurried off to Richmond to be tried for treason and quickly convicted.

In his address to the court, given after the sentence of death was pronounced, Brown defended his action. "This court acknowledges, as

I suppose, the validity of the law of God. I see a book kissed here which I suppose to be the Bible, or at least the New Testament. That teaches me that all things whatsoever I would have that men should do to me, I should do even so to them. It teaches me, further, to 'remember them that are in bonds, as bound with them.' I endeavored to act up to that instruction. I say, I am yet too young to understand that God is any respecter of persons. I believe that to have interfered as I have done—as I have always freely admitted I have done—in behalf of His despised poor, was not wrong but right. Now, if it is deemed necessary that I should forfeit my life for the furtherance of the ends of justice, and mingle my blood further with the blood of my children and with the blood of millions in this slave country whose rights are disregarded by wicked, cruel, and unjust enactments,—I submit; so let it be done!"

When he heard of the raid on Harpers Ferry, George Templeton Strong wrote in his diary: "The leader, old Osawatomie John Brown of Kansas, seems cracked; a free-soil Balfour of Burley. Insanity won't save him from the gallows. He will undoubtedly be hanged. . . . This insane transaction may possibly lead to grave results." Strong was pleased to see a prompt and aggressive prosecution, reflecting that "we are accustomed to see defendants in a capital case treated with a hyper-delicacy of double-refined tenderness and consideration, favored with every unreasonable delay and encouraged to insist on every frivolous or fraudulent quibble." Strong believed that the Virginia court would be well advised not to make Brown a martyr by hanging him but to declare him insane and have him "locked up in an asylum." A month later, Strong wrote, "I fear this savage old wrong-headed Fifty-Monarchy-man has done us a mischief that will be memorable. The South is frightened into a frenzy, utterly without reason . . . Fanatics and sedition-mongers at the North are doing all they can to exasperate and irritate . . ."

When Brown's letters and his last words to the court were printed, Strong, like millions of his countrymen, was deeply moved. "Old John Brown," he wrote, "was hanged this morning; justly, say I, but his name may be a word of power for the next half-century. . . . Old Brown's demeanor has undoubtedly made a great impression. Many heroes of the Newgate Calendar have died game, as he did; but his simplicity and consistency, the absence of fuss, parade and bravado, the strength and clearness of his letters, all indicate a depth of conviction that one does not expect in an Abolitionist . . . and that tends to dignify and ennoble in popular repute the very questionable church of which he is protomartyr. . . . So did the first Christian martyrs wake up senators and landed gentlemen and patrician ladies. . . . One's faith in anything is terribly shaken by anybody who is ready to go to the gallows condemning and denouncing it." "The whole South seems bewildered with fright and fury," Strong added. The *Richmond Enquirer* had endorsed the suggestion that the South secede from the Union and place itself under the protection of Louis Napoleon. "This," Strong added, "transcends any atrocity I've heard attributed to Garrison or Wendell Phillips." The story was that Charleston had been "thrown into consternation by the mistake of a sentinel in taking a cow for an invading Abolitionist. . . . Cow didn't stand when challenged, was fired upon, and the community got under arms."

The *Liberator,* with its pacificist bent, called Brown's raid "a misguided, wild, and apparently insane effort."

Thoreau had met John Brown at Emerson's house in 1857 and fallen under the spell of that charismatic man. When Brown was captured after the raid on Harpers Ferry, Thoreau called a meeting of the citizens of Concord and delivered an address, "A Plea for Captain Brown." It was a touching and quixotic act. The man who rather disdained reformers and believed in a kind of moral laissez-faire, by means of which everything bad could be put right if each citizen attended honestly to his own affairs, made an impassioned defense of Brown. "He was," Thoreau declared, "a superior man. He did not value his bodily life in comparison with ideal things. He did not recognize unjust human laws but resisted them as he was bid. For once we are lifted out of the trivialness and dust of politics into the region of truth and manhood. No man in America has ever stood up so persistently and effectively for the dignity of human nature . . . in that sense he is the most American of us all." To Thoreau he was "an angel of light," a Christ-like figure of suffering and redemption. "I foresee the time," Thoreau concluded, "when the painter will paint the scene . . . the poet will sing it; the historian record it; and, with the Landing of the Pilgrims and the Declaration of Independence, it will be the ornament of some future national gallery, when at last the present form of slavery shall be no more. We shall then be at liberty to weep for Captain Brown. Then, and not till then, we will take our revenge."

It was precisely an act like Brown's, of course, that had no place in Thoreau's philosophy. This passionate intervention in history was the antithesis of the Concord philosopher's withdrawal from the taint of the Mexican War by his refusal to pay his taxes. So we may see Thoreau's plea for Brown as a kind of act of penance, a tacit acknowledgment of the limitations of Thoreau's own ethical individualism.

Herman Melville, deeply moved by Brown's dignity and courage, wrote "The Portent":

> Hanging from the beam,
>   Slowly swaying (such the law),
> Gaunt the shadow on your green,
>   Shenandoah!
> The cut is on the crown
>   (Lo, John Brown),
> And the stabs shall heal no more.
>
> Hidden in the cap
>   Is the anguish none can draw;
> So your future veils its face,
>   Shenandoah!
> But the streaming beard is shown
>   (Weird John Brown),
> The meteor of war.

Robert Purvis, the black abolitionist, declared that in white America only John Brown "that noble martyr and saint, the innocent hero of Harper's Ferry . . . believed what he professed and practiced what he believed: He nobly acted what he nobly thought, and sealed by death the lessons which he taught. He believed that the black man was a man, and he laid down his life to secure for him the rights of a man. . . . Sir, the antislavery cause is onward. . . . Slavery will be abolished in this land, and with it, that twin relic of barbarism, prejudice against color."

The mad scheme of this fierce old man—he was fifty-nine at the time of his death—thus turned out to have had in it a curious power. Misconceived, doomed from the beginning, it revealed itself as an act of enormous symbolic potency. In the dignity and simplicity of his bearing and in his moving evocation of Christian love, John Brown seemed to many Americans the culmination and apotheosis of years of struggle and sacrifice by thousands of people, white and black, in the cause of antislavery. In Strong's words: "There was something truly chivalric in old John Brown's march with his handful of followers into the enemy's country to redeem and save those he held to be unjustly enslaved at the peril of his own life." So he triumphed in death and joined the company of sainted heroes; became a legend, a song, a hymn, an epic poem.

63

The Election of 1860

As the election year of 1860 approached, the mood of the nation became increasingly tense and irascible. Nerves grew taut and tempers flared. The feeling spread that the nation was rushing toward some terrible denouement. Most people suppressed such intimations as best they could. Times had been difficult and dangerous before. The United States had a special destiny. God, under whose special protection most Americans thought the country, would somehow preserve the nation from calamity. But Kansas, Preston's crippling of Sumner, and John Brown's raid all pointed toward a final crisis.

William Seward was Lincoln's most serious rival for the Republican nomination. Shortly before Lincoln arrived in New York for his Cooper Union address, Seward had given his own "great address," staking *his* claim for the party's nomination. Certainly it was an excellent one, both the speech and the claim. Seward had been an Anti-Mason, a liberal Whig governor of New York, enlightened in his attitude toward his Irish Catholic constituents, the champion of many reforms, and an early and consistent enemy of the extension of slavery. Even Horace Greeley, his longtime political foe, declared "his natural instincts were progressive and humane." Elected to the Senate in 1848, Seward had become a hero to the abolitionists for his opposition to the

Fugitive Slave Law and his evocation of "a higher law than the Constitution," God's law, in the name of which every man of conscience was obliged to resist slavery. While he had grown cautious in his public pronouncements as the possibility of his securing the nomination of the new Republican Party for president in the election of 1860 became more apparent, he remained an outspoken critic of the Fugitive Slave Law and the Kansas-Nebraska Act. In 1858, in a speech at Rochester, New York, Seward had used a phrase which was to become as famous as Lincoln's "house divided. . . ." Describing the nature of free and slave labor he declared, "It is an irrepressible conflict between opposing and enduring forces, and it means that the United States must and will, sooner or later, become either entirely a slave-holding nation or entirely a free labor nation. Either the cotton and rice fields of South Carolina and the sugar plantations of Louisiana will be ultimately tilled by free labor and Charleston and New Orleans become marts for legitimate merchandise alone, or else the rye fields and wheat fields of Massachusetts and New York must again be surrendered by their farmers to slave culture and to the production of slaves, and Boston and New York become once more markets for trade in the bodies and souls of men."

The phrase "irrepressible conflict" gained immediate popular currency, and Seward was charged by Southerners and Democrats with advocating the forcible emancipation of slaves. Lincoln had said much the same thing, but Lincoln chose his words more carefully and wisely forbore the inflammatory contrast of a free South or an enslaved North. Indeed, it might be said that by just such a careful measure as the difference between the respective images did Lincoln finally come to outdistance Seward in his bid for his party's nomination. There were other factors involved, of course—the determination of Greeley and Bryant to find a candidate other than Seward and, beyond that, practical indications that Seward could not carry the all-important states of the Northwest, which Lincoln could. Yet Seward, with his idealism, his outspokenness, his generosity, and his devotion to principle is a singularly attractive figure. Greeley, it is interesting to note, was opposed to Seward primarily on the grounds that "his natural tendencies were toward a government not merely paternal, but prodigal." That is to say, he was too disposed to use public moneys for the relief of the poor, the needy, and the unemployed.

Two days after Lincoln's Cooper Union speech, Seward, having introduced a bill to admit Kansas to the Union as a free state, rose in the Senate to support it. The chambers were crowded with listeners, many of them standing, as Seward, a rather graceless public speaker, began. In a long and eloquent discourse, he chided the South for its talk of disunion and lay the onus of such an act squarely at its door. Senator James Hammond of South Carolina, who had replied to Seward's famous "irrepressible conflict" speech two years earlier by describing Northern workers as "the mudsills of society," declaring, "You dare not make war on cotton. . . . Cotton is king," noted "as everyone has a revolver and the South does not intend again to be surprised into hearing another Lovejoy speech [a reference to the bitter antislavery speech by Owen Lovejoy, a loyal supporter of Lincoln's election and brother of the martyred Elijah], a general fight in one or the other House with great slaughter is always on the *tapis* and may occur any day. . . . There are no relations not absolutely indispensable for the conduct of joint business between the North and the South in either House, no two nations on earth are or ever were more distinctly separate and hostile than we are."

When the Republicans met at Chicago, deep in Lincoln territory, to nominate a presidential candidate, Seward was clearly the front-runner with Lincoln a strong contender. Greeley's own choice was Edward Bates, the Missouri Congressman who had made such an eloquent speech at the convention on internal improvements in 1847. Attending the convention as a delegate from the newly formed state of Oregon, Greeley found a number of delegates strongly opposed to Seward on the grounds that his nomination would provoke the South to immediate secession. "I want to succeed this time," Horace Greeley wrote a friend, "yet I *know* the country is not Anti-Slavery. It will only swallow a little Anti-Slavery in a great deal of sweetening. An Anti-Slavery man *per se* can not be elected; but a Tariff, River-and-Harbor, Pacific-Railroad, Free Homestead man, *may* succeed *although* he is Anti-Slavery; so I will try to get a candidate who will fairly and readily unite votes to win."

Carl Schurz and the young idealists who were his co-workers at the convention were initially committed without reservation to Seward, but the sight of Thurlow Weed, with "his cold, impassive face . . . giving directions to a lot of henchmen, the looks and talk and demeanor of many of whom made me feel exceedingly uncomfortable," Schurz wrote, rather disillusioned them. Still, Seward "charmed our minds with panoramic views of our political and social conditions and problems to be solved; his telescopic eye seemed to pierce even the veil which covers future developments" and he was at the same time "adorned with the peculiar graces of superior mental culture." Among the delegates, Weed "moved as the great captain, with ceaseless activity and noiseless step, . . . now and then taking (some delegate) into a corner of the room for a secret talk, or disappearing with another through a side door for transactions still more secret . . . the most skillful political manager—others called it 'wire-puller'—of his time." Schurz thought uneasily of the relationship between Seward and Weed as similar to that between Faust and Mephistopheles and repeated to himself the words of Marguerite:

> In my inmost soul it saddens me
> When I see them in that company

By the time the balloting began a core of resistance to Seward had formed that was large enough to block his nomination. The first ballot showed 173-1/2 for Seward, 102 for Abraham Lincoln, 50-1/2 for Simon Cameron (Buchanan's principal rival in Pennsylvania), 49 for Salmon Chase of Ohio, and 48 for Bates. Opposition quickly formed to check any move for Chase or Cameron and the next ballot saw Seward with 184-1/2 and Lincoln with 181, Pennsylvania having been persuaded to switch to him and all the other candidates losing a few votes here and there. On the third ballot the swing to Lincoln became the proverbial stampede. His running mate was Hannibal Hamlin of Maine. "It can hardly be doubted," Schurz wrote later, "that Thurlow Weed's cohorts hurt Seward more than they helped him." But Schurz and the idealists stood with Seward to the end, determined to honor him for his long years of leadership in the cause of liberal politics. When Seward was defeated, however, they did not experience any scruples in devoting their energies to Lincoln's election. In the words of Schurz, "We were all lifted up by the inspiring consciousness of being, for once, wholly right. There was nothing to apologize for, nothing to defend, nothing to explain, nothing to conceal, for, as we believed with unlimited, supreme faith, our cause was clearly, undeniably the cause of liberty, right, and justice, and our party a party of high moral aims and exalted patriotism."

"He is unknown here," George Templeton Strong wrote of Lincoln. "The *Tribune* and other papers commend him to popular favor as having had but six months' schooling in his whole life; and because he cut a great many rails, and worked on a flatboat in his early

youth; all of which is somehow presumptive evidence of his statesmanship. The watchword of the campaign is already indicated. It is to be
'Honest Abe.' . . . But that monosyllable does not seem to me likely to
prove a word of power."

Sidney George Fisher also received the news of Lincoln's nomination with less than enthusiasm. "I had never heard of him before," he
wrote in his diary. As an unknown he might be able to reconcile
different factions. "The great point," he wrote, "is that Seward is *not*
nominated. He represented the extreme opinions opposed to slavery
and the South, and the selection of his name would have exasperated
the Southern people and alarmed conservatives throughout the
North." But Fisher's friend William Meredith, one of the political
leaders of the city, was dismayed by Lincoln's nomination. In Meredith's view, Lincoln was "a Western 'screamer,' represents Western
coarseness & violence. The papers say he was fond of horse racing,
foot racing, etc. . . . Such is democracy. These very qualities, connecting him in sympathy with the masses, favor his success. Education,
refinement, the birth & breeding of a gentleman would be against
him."

Charleston had been selected for the Democratic convention
before Douglas, pushed into a corner by Lincoln, had devised his
Freeport Doctrine that at once alienated the South. Douglas men tried
to move the convention to the more neutral ground of Baltimore, but
the Southerners would have none of it and the convention thus
assembled on April 23 at the Institute Hall. Jefferson Davis insisted on
a platform calling for the protection of slavery in the territories and
rejecting the doctrine of popular sovereignty. A majority of the
delegates supported Douglas in his determination to stand fast on
popular sovereignty and brought in a platform full of evasions and
contradictions, stating that neither Congress nor any territorial
legislature had the power to exclude slavery from the territories or in
any way impair the right of property in slaves. Other planks called for
the purchase of Cuba from Spain and for the building of a railroad
from the Mississippi to the Pacific. After six days of deadlock, most of
the members of the Southern delegations withdrew. The rump session
began balloting and after fifty-seven ballots were taken without
nominating a candidate, the convention adjourned to meet in Baltimore on June 18.

The following day the seceders, calling themselves the Constitutional Democrats, met and issued a call for a convention to meet at

Richmond in June. A week later an assembly under the name of the Constitutional Union party, with delegates from twenty-one states, met in Baltimore to propose a ticket of its own. Whigs left over from the absorption of most of their number by the Republicans and Know-Nothings or Americans made up the majority of the delegates. The preservation of the Union at all costs was their platform. As George Templeton Strong put it, "the conservative fogies and fossils" chose John Bell of Tennessee and Edward Everett of Massachusetts as their nominees.

Unable to agree in Charleston, the Democrats gathered again in Baltimore. After several days of wrangling over disputed delegates, the convention broke apart once more. Those remaining nominated Douglas unanimously, with Herschel Johnson as their candidate for vice-president. The seceders then met and nominated John C. Breckinridge of Kentucky and Joseph Lane of Oregon as their presidential and vice-presidential candidates respectively.

George Templeton Strong's comments on the Baltimore convention were characteristically acidulous: "Southern swashbucklers demand an ultra-nigger platform that would cost the party every Northern state; unless it be adopted, they will depart to put on their war paint and whet their scalping knives. The worst temper prevails; delegates punch each other and produce revolvers. . . . Its session has abounded thus far in scandalous, shameful brutalities and indecencies that disgrace the whole country and illustrate the pace at which we are traveling down hill toward sheer barbarism and savagery. . . . Millions yet unborn will bless the day when the Baltimore Convention of 1860 exploded and the Democratic Party ceased to exist."

There were now four presidential candidates: Lincoln for the Republicans, Douglas for what was left of the regular Democrats, Bell for the Constitutional Unionists, and Breckinridge for the Southern Democrats. Bell, originally a Jackson supporter, had defected to the Whigs and been a leader of the Southern Whigs for more than two decades. He had supported John Quincy Adams on the right of petition and voted against the admission of Kansas under the Lecompton Constitution. He was a man of integrity and intelligence, devoted above everything else to the Union and opposed to secession, "both as a Constitutional right and as a remedy for existing evils."

Breckinridge, at thirty-nine one of the youngest men ever to run for the presidency, was the scion of a family distinguished in the annals of Kentucky. He was the grandson of John Breckinridge, Jefferson's co-adjutor in framing the Virginia and Kentucky Resolutions. He had been a supporter of Henry Clay and had been elected to Congress as a Whig, although he served in Buchanan's administration. He was the candidate of the proslavery extremists—William Yancey, Robert Toombs, and the other advocates of secession. Strong wrote that Breckinridge represented "the most cruel, blind, unreasoning, cowardly, absolute despotism that now disgraces the earth. . . ."

The campaign itself was divided into Northern and Southern sections, so to speak. The Republicans, conceding the South, did not even enter tickets in most of the Southern states. Douglas, Breckinridge, and Bell were thus left to contest for that vote.

At the Republican state convention in Decatur, Illinois, a few weeks before the Republican nominating convention at Chicago, a cousin of Lincoln's, John Hanks, had brought two weathered fence rails into the convention hall with a placard attached to them proclaiming, "ABRAHAM LINCOLN, the Rail Candidate for President in 1860. Two rails from a lot of 3,000 made in 1830 by Thos. Hanks, and Abe Lincoln—whose father was the first pioneer of Macon County." The hall burst into applause and a call was raised for Lincoln to speak. He could not say for a certainty, he replied, that these were rails that he had split, "but whether they were or not, he had mauled better ones since he had grown to manhood." Loud cheers and the birth of the "rail-splitter" slogan. George Templeton Strong was not impressed. "I am tired of this shameless clap-trap," he wrote. "The log-cabin hard-cider craze of 1840 seemed spontaneous. This hurrah about rails and railsplitters seems a deliberate attempt to manufacture the same kind of furor by appealing to the shallowest prejudices of the lowest class."

The Republicans added color to their rallies by the presence of young men who called themselves the Wide Awakes, wore glazed caps and capes, and marched in parades carrying torches. Started at Hartford, the organization soon had chapters all over New England and around the country. To Strong, the New York Wide Awakes out on parade were "imposing and splendid." The men "marched in good order, each man with his torch or lamp of kerosene oil on a pole, with a flag below the light. . . . Every file had its rockets and its Roman candles, and the procession moved along under a galaxy of fire balls—white, red, and green. I have never seen so beautiful a spectacle on any political turnout." The most popular Republican slogans were

"Honest Abe for President," "Lincoln and Free Homestead," "Free Soil for Free Men," "No more Slave Territories."

The Democrats countered with "The Little Giant," "Cuba Must Be Ours," "Billy Seward and His Three Aunties, Aunty Mason, Aunty Rent, Aunty Slavery," and "We Want a Statesman and Not a Rail Splitter as President." Pins and buttons were the fashion, with miniature axes for the "Rail Splitter." Seward, always generous and loyal, did his best to convey his large constituency to Lincoln, speaking at dozens of rallies to thousands of his admirers. Lowell, Bryant, and Whittier were also active in Lincoln's behalf, and Boston and New Haven professors and intellectuals gave their support to the Illinois rail splitter.

Carl Schurz made one of the famous speeches among all the great tide of eloquence expended in the Republican cause and made it, appropriately enough, at Cooper Union. He spoke for three hours to an enthralled audience, noting with pleasure an old gentleman who, in his enthusiasm, pounded his umbrella so hard and so frequently on the floor that he smashed it to pieces before Schurz finished. The speech made Schurz, not yet a decade in America, one of the most talked-of political figures in the country.

As the Republicans appeared to gain strength, talk of secession was heard increasingly in the South. In a widely reprinted editorial, the *Charleston Mercury* made the case in October, a month before the election, that the South should, in the event of Lincoln's becoming president, immediately secede from the Union. If Lincoln was elected abolitionism would rule and the South would be plundered by the North through a new protective tariff. The value of every slave would drop at least a hundred dollars, the "*under*ground railroad will become an *over*ground railroad," and the border slave states, drained by a massive flight of slaves, would soon become free states. Most dangerous of all, a party of Southerners would form to work from within for the abolition of slavery. "Secret conspiracy, and its attendant horrors, with rumors of horrors, will hover over every portion of the South. . . . Slave property is the foundation of all property in the South. When security in this is shaken, all other property partakes of its instability. Banks, stocks, bonds, must be influenced. Timid men will sell out and leave the South. Confusion, distrust and pressure must reign. Before Messrs. LINCOLN and HAMLIN can be installed in Washington . . . the Southern States can dissolve peaceably (we know what we say) their Union with the North. Mr. LINCOLN and his Abolition cohorts, will have no South to reign over. Their game would be blocked. The foundation of their organization would be taken away; and, left to the tender mercies of a baffled, furious and troubled North, they would be cursed and crushed, as the flagitious causes of the disasters around them."

Although Lincoln was bitterly denounced by Southerners as a radical abolitionist, many abolitionists viewed him with suspicion. One black leader, a runaway slave named Ford Douglass, was indignant at Lincoln's acquiescence on the issue of black inferiority. On the Fourth of July, 1860, at an antislavery meeting at Framingham, Massachusetts, Douglass was the principal speaker. Four parties had emerged to compete for the presidency he reminded his listeners; "All of these parties ask for your support, because they profess to represent some principle. So far as the principles of freedom and the hopes of the black man are concerned, all these parties are barren and unfruitful; neither of them seeks to lift the Negro out of his fetters and rescue this day from odium and disgrace. Take Abraham Lincoln. I want to know if any man can tell me the difference between the antislavery of Abraham Lincoln and the antislavery of Henry Clay? Why there is no difference between them. Abraham Lincoln is simply a Henry Clay Whig. . . . I am a colored man; I am an American citizen, and I think I am entitled to exercise the elective franchise. I am about twenty-eight years old, and I would like to vote very much. . . . No party, it seems to me, is entitled to the sympathy of antislavery men, unless that party is willing to extend to the black man all the rights of a citizen."

"Now, friends," Douglass declared, "I am proud of the Negro race, and I thank God today that there does not course in my veins a single drop of Saxon blood . . . I am proud of the Negro race. I think that *Negro* looks just as well on paper and sounds just as sweetly to the ear as *Saxon*. . . ."

Among the fragmented Democrats there was considerable confusion. Jefferson Davis prevailed on Bell and Breckinridge to support him as a compromise candidate, but Douglas balked. His hope and the hope of the South was that no candidate would get a majority of the electoral college vote and the selection of a president would thus be thrown into the House, where various alliances were possible. Although Winfield Scott, as the Whig candidate in 1856, had done some sub rosa campaigning under the pretense of inspecting hospital sites, it was still considered improper for a presidential candidate to be involved in traveling around the country soliciting votes. Douglas defied this tradition, however, and disheartened and physically depleted as he was, he traveled about—he described himself as "a way worn backwoods traveler"—speaking wherever he found an audience. After the Charleston convention had broken up, Douglas showed an unselfish spirit in writing to various powers in the party that he would gladly give way if a candidate could be found who would assure "the unity and ascendancy of the Democratic Party . . . and the country preserved from the perils of Northern abolitionism and Southern disunion. . . . I conjure you to act with an eye to the safety and welfare of the Country, and without the slightest regard to my individual interests or aggrandizement," he wrote. "*My* interests will be but promoted, and ambition gratified . . . by that course . . . which will be most effectual in saving the country from being ruled by a sectional party."

It is agreeable to say that Douglas appeared at his best in this arduous campaign for the presidency. While he buoyed himself and his supporters up by that optimism essential to a candidate for office, he resolutely refused any compromise with the Southern secessionists or "Bolters" as he called them. He insisted early in July that there were favorable signs everywhere. The Democrats would take most of New England, New York was certain, and Pennsylvania was leaning his way. All dreams. And as the summer faded into fall, even Douglas became aware that the cause was lost. By early October, Lincoln, encouraged by a report from Seward that New York seemed safely in the Republican column, wrote to the latter, "It now really looks as if the Government is about to fall into our hands." While he waited in Springfield for the news of state elections to trickle in, he received a letter from an eleven-year-old girl named Grace Bedell in Chautauqua County, New York, who wrote, "I want you should be President of the United States very much so I hope you wont think me very bold to write to such a great man as you are. Have you any little girls about as large as I am if so give them my love. I have got 4 brothers and part of them will vote for you any way and if you will let your whiskers grow I will try to get the rest of them to vote for you (extra space here) you would look a great deal better for your face is so thin. All the ladies like whiskers and they would tease their husbands to vote for you and then you would be President." To which irresistible and properly famous epistle, Lincoln replied, "I regret the necessity of saying I have not daughters. . . . As to the whiskers, having never worn any, do you not think people would call it a piece of silly affectation if I were to begin now?" But begin he did, nonetheless.

Sidney George Fisher was convinced that the North had "become united" on the slavery issue and that in the course of the campaign it evidenced a "moral enthusiasm" on the subject which was especially offensive to the South. He himself wrote an essay which was "a philosophical argument, temperate in language, perfectly free from party feeling or sectional bias . . . which, taking the Northern ground of opposing the increase of slavery, at the same time justifies and advocates slavery." Many of Fisher's Philadelphia friends and considerable numbers of businessmen, bankers, and cotton manufacturers were greatly taken with Fisher's essay and had thousands printed up and distributed, despite his brother Henry's efforts to dissuade him from allowing it to be circulated.

Henry Middleton, Fisher's Charleston friend, objected to Fisher's essay on the grounds "that the South had equal rights with the North to the territories & to exclude Southern men from them was an insult as well as an injury. That for all these evils and dangers, a great Southern confederacy, which could, at its pleasure, extend its sway over adjacent tropical regions, over the West Indies, Mexico, & Central America, with slavery as its foundation & cotton, sugar, rice, & tobacco as its sources of wealth & prosperity, was the true remedy."

In early fall Fisher indulged himself in some cautious optimism. "The people," he wrote, "seem in good humor and no violent or dangerous feeling appears to be roused. . . . Standing aloof as a spectator, I enjoy the scene. On the whole it is satisfactory. The people are intelligent, prosperous and happy, as no other people are, they are consulting about their affairs, discussing them warmly indeed, but not in an angry, quarrelsome spirit, and notwithstanding many abuses to regret, republican institutions work well, particularly in the country." The general assumption was that Lincoln would be elected and Fisher thought such an outcome desirable, "because he is a safe man and the principles of his party are, if not entirely correct, by far the best of any other party. . . ." But by election day, Fisher's natural pessimism asserted itself. The election appeared to him "a crisis . . . of immense importance, for it *may* involve the fate of the Union, *may* be the signal for discord, destruction & bloodshed. The excitement is violent at the South." Fisher hoped for a Lincoln victory but by a narrow margin. The Republican Party, he feared, was "leavened largely with . . . a blind reckless & enthusiastic hatred of slavery, without regard to the character of the Negro race, or to the consequence of abolition."

When the popular vote was tallied it may be presumed to have been a fair replication of the profound ambivalence of America's political and psychological mood. Lincoln, with 1,866,452 popular votes, all in the populous states of the North and West, had 180 electoral votes. Douglas was next in popular vote with 1,376,957 but only 12 electoral votes. He had carried only Missouri and New Hampshire, while tallying five hundred thousand more popular votes than Breckinridge. Breckinridge had carried every state of the deep South and accumulated 72 electoral votes. Bell, with less than half of Douglas's popular vote, had more than three times as many electoral votes—39—having taken Tennessee and Virginia in addition to Kentucky.

If we assume that a disproportionate number of Douglas's votes in the North were the votes of those who preferred Union to stopping the spread of slavery and that virtually all of Bell's votes, North and South, were enemies of disunion, it seems reasonable to assume that very close to a majority of Americans, certainly in the Northern and Western states, put the preservation of the Union before all other considerations. For example, the combined vote for Bell and Douglas in Alabama was 41,526, as compared with Breckinridge's total of 48,831. In Virginia, the combined Douglas-Bell vote was 16,000 more than the vote for Breckinridge, and Bell carried the state by a narrow margin. In Kentucky, also carried by Bell, the combined Bell-Douglas vote was almost 40,000 more than the vote for Breckinridge. Strangest of all, in Pennsylvania Breckinridge polled 178,871 to Lincoln's 268,030, while in New York Douglas ran up 312,510 to Lincoln's 362,646. In Illinois Lincoln received only 12,000 more votes than Douglas out of 349,978 cast in that state. In fact in most Western states Douglas ran very well, although in none would the switch of Bell's vote to Douglas have given him a popular majority. Bell's strength in the South certainly indicated far more pro-Union sentiment in that section than the proclamations of the politicians and the fulminations of the Southern press suggested.

In Sidney George Fisher's view, the defeat of the Democrats was to be ascribed entirely to "the insane and monstrous conduct of Southern politicians. . . . As they do not seem to learn from experience, it is impossible to say how far they may yet exasperate, to their own ruin & the ruin of the country, the feelings of the Northern people."

The message conveyed to Lincoln by the popular vote was that pro-Union sentiment in the country was strong while antislavery sentiment was relatively weak. It followed from this, ineluctably, that if force was to be used to prevent the South from leaving the Union, it must be in the name of preserving the Union rather than of freeing the slaves. Emancipation must be the residual, if crucial, by-product of the effort to preserve the Union. The preservation of the Union was the primary task; everything else was of subordinate importance.

64

War

A month after the election of Lincoln, Sidney George Fisher sounded more antislavery than ever. "The opinion of the civilized world is against the institution," he wrote, "and tho cotton is king, it is only king on the Exchange. Morality is progressive, and its progress is reflected & stimulated by literature and the moral & enlightened sentiment of mankind is too strong for material interest. Civilized nations are governed not by force but by opinion. Northern opinion is averse to slavery, is becoming more hostile to it every day, & this hostility is constantly increased by the outrages of the South. . . . Strength & power are with the North, weakness and slavery are with the South."

Pierce Butler turned up in Philadelphia "eager for secession." He came to the city, he declared, only to buy arms. "He will take his daughter Fanny with him," Fisher wrote, "and has bought a rifle for *her,* too, for he says even the women in the South are going to fight. What madness, yet one cannot help admiring the knightly spirit these Southern men are displaying. They rush recklessly on fearful odds & fearful dangers and talk like men insane."

There was general skepticism in the North about the Southern threats to secede. "Republicans laugh at the vaporings of our Southern friends," Strong wrote. "It is easy to show that secession would be an act of madness and folly, but we know there are fools and madmen south of the Potomac, and they may do sore and irremediable mischief to us. . . ." But there were wild fluctuations of feeling in the North as well. The Union must be preserved at all costs. The South should be allowed to depart in peace. Many Republicans insisted that "secession . . . would do us no lasting mischief," Strong wrote. He was convinced that "Bisection is disaster and degradation, but if the only alternative is everlasting submission to the South, it must come soon, and why should it not come now? What is gained by postponing it four years longer?"

So it went, back and forth. A determination to preserve the Union, a disposition to be rid of the South. Strong, vacillating himself almost from day to day, was dismayed "to find so many Northerners holding the Union so cheap. . . . People generally treat the political peril with what seems to me unaccountable indifference. . . . We are generally reconciling ourselves to the prospect of secession by South Carolina, Georgia, Alabama, little Florida, and perhaps Mississippi, too. We shall be well rid of them. Perhaps the prevalence of this feeling—the cordial consent of the North—will keep them from seceding. . . . I think, from all indications, that the Republican leaders are frightened and ready to concede everything, to restore the Missouri Compromise line and satisfy the fugitive slave remedies of the South. A movement that way has certainly begun." In Corvallis, Oregon, the editor of the *Weekly Union* captured the mood of the country as well as anyone when he wrote, "Everything is drifting towards some almost unknown and unseen danger, and everybody seems to be stupefied into inaction, without making an effort to evade it, calmly waiting for the final crash."

Meanwhile a remarkable exchange of letters took place between Lincoln and his defeated Democratic opponent, Stephen Douglas. A month after the election Lincoln wrote to Douglas urging him to do all he could to quiet Southern fears that the Republicans wished, "*directly, or indirectly,*" to "interfere with the slaves, or with them, about their slaves." In reply Douglas insisted that the Union could never be preserved by force, adding, "An error on this point may lead to the most disastrous consequences." Then Douglas made a curious and revealing argument. What the Southern people, in his opinion, did fear, and rightly, was not the active intervention by the new administration in the institution of slavery as it existed, but the characterization of slavery as a moral wrong. To Douglas it was as though the South had one religion and the North another, and the North took the official position that the Southern religion was wrong and that of the North right and refused to allow the South to practice its own religion in the territories and new states of the Union. "We at the South do think African Slavery, as it exists with us, both morally and politically right," Douglas wrote. "This opinion is founded upon the inferiority of the Black race. . . . Under our system, as I view it, there is no rightful power in the general government to coerce a State, in case any one of them should throw herself upon her reserved rights, and resume the full exercise of her Sovereign Powers." If force was used to preserve the Union, the result would be "nothing short of a Consolidated Despotism." That was, after all, the heart of the matter. Slavery had become, in effect, the "religion" of the South. At the deepest level of their consciousness many Southerners "wanted out" of the Union regardless of the cost. They could no longer endure the psychological burden of being told that in perpetuating and defending slavery they were doing something immoral and unjust, because in their hearts they knew it to be so. If getting out of the Union was the price for having a "good conscience" it was a price they were quite willing to pay.

Since the justifiers of slavery and the secessionists won out, it is easy to forget that there were tens of thousands of Southerners who had little sympathy with slavery and who gave their wholehearted allegiance to the Union. Carl Degler has divided the Southern opponents of slavery into those whose opposition was based primarily on the view that slavery was inhuman and un-Christian and those, like Hinton Helper, who deplored its effects on white society. Eli Caruthers, a North Carolinian and a Presbyterian minister, wrote a four-hundred-page attack on slavery, one portion of which was headed, "Negroes Not a Degraded Race Suited Only for Slavery." Not only were Negroes not inherently inferior to whites, "For long generations," they "appear to have been the superior race and to be the admiration of the literary and scientific community, the mutilated and long buried monuments of their greatness have been brought to light on the Nile, the Tigris and the Euphrates. . . . Should we not honor them as a race for what they have done and for what God has done for them and by them." Even if blacks were as inferior as some whites claimed, "they certainly have as good a right," Caruthers argued, "to the free use of whatever power the creator has given them as the weak minded among the whites or as those who have been more liberally endowed."

The Manumission Society of North Carolina declared, "Negroes are *human beings* and are capable of loving, of being endeared to each other." Liberty was the right of all and "God has made no difference in this respect between *white* and *black.*" "The debt we owe to the Negroes," the pamphlet continued, could only be paid off by education in order that "they may be prepared both to enjoy and appreciate liberty."

Besides the theorists, who in some instances kept slaves themselves, there are those, like Mary Merkeley Minor Blackford of Fredericksburg, Virginia, who turned their slaves free. Seeing a son separated from his mother, Mary Blackford wrote: "How the practice of injustice hardens the feelings is perfectly wonderful; what is done under our own eyes would shock us to the last degree were it not for this hardening process. I am convinced that the time will come when we shall look back and wonder how Christians could sanction slavery." Thomas Marshall, son of the chief justice, believed that the lot of the slave was better than that of "the laborer in any part of Europe" but he was opposed to slavery "because it is ruinous to the whites. . . . The evil admits of no remedy. It is increasing, and will continue to increase, until the whole country will be inundated by one black wave. . . ."

As we have noted earlier, the greatest opposition to slavery came from Southern women. A Northerner, talking with Charleston women about the institution, reported that "their eyes fill with tears when you talk with them about slavery."

At no other time in our history had the interregnum between the election of a president in November and his assumption of office four months later been more hazardous or subjected the country to greater dangers. Even before the results of the election of 1860 had become known some Southern states had taken the initial steps toward secession. Now others began to follow suit. William Gist, the governor of South Carolina, anticipating Lincoln's election, had requested the state legislature to remain in session until definite word came. If Lincoln was the successful candidate, a state convention should be called at once to take the necessary steps to separate the state from the Union. The governor's request was greeted by band music and an informal parade. In other states boycotts of Northern goods were called for and resolutions passed that required the North to be treated as a foreign power with duties on Northern manufactures. But such feeling, as the votes for Bell and Douglas had suggested, was far from unanimous. Most states were for delaying any decisive action until Lincoln had taken office and it was clear what his policies would be.

In South Carolina, the home of secession sentiment, there was little vacillating. The federal district judge closed his court declaring, "For the last time I have, as a judge of the United States, administered the laws of the United States within the limits of South Carolina. So far as I am concerned, the Temple of Justice raised under the Constitution . . . is now closed." Senator James Chesnut of South Carolina resigned his seat, and pressure was brought upon James Hammond, the other senator of the state, to do likewise; he complied although he wrote that he considered it "an epidemic and very foolish." A friend wrote him from Charleston, "You can form no idea of the unanimity and enthusiasm here. It is wonderful and seems to be the work of inspiration."

Georgia was soon on the bandwagon. Companies of Minute Men were formed to defend the state from Northern invaders. Alexander Stephens represented the cooler and more moderate men. He wished for delay until some act by the federal government, such as the repeal of the Fugitive Slave Law, should give a valid pretext for resistance. In Alabama volunteer military associations with such names as "The Rattlesnakes" and the "Sons of the South" were formed, along with a Home Guard of all men between forty-five and sixty. In New Orleans a movement was started to forbid the sale of cotton to the North. It was confidently believed that such a measure would soon reduce the North to poverty and bring abject pleas for reconciliation on Southern terms. The story was spread about the South that the new vice-president, Hamlin, was "an octoroon mulatto" to whose election no Southern gentleman could submit. Secession talk caused a business panic in the North, which served to confirm the Southern opinion that the North could not exist without its cotton—that cotton was truly "King." The mood of the South was not sweetened by newspaper stories that slaves, hearing of Lincoln's election, had proclaimed that they would all now be free. The border states were far more cautious. They were both more vulnerable and counted more Union sentiment.

On December 20, six weeks after Lincoln's election, a South Carolina convention issued "An Ordinance dissolving the Union between the State of South Carolina and other States united with her under the compact entitled 'The Constitution of the United States.' " The bells of the churches were rung, cannons were fired, and the citizens poured into the streets to celebrate the freedom and independence of South Carolina.

In the North there was, as we have seen, a considerable sentiment for letting the South depart in peace. That, certainly, was the feeling of many abolitionists—a good riddance. Dr. Oliver Wendell Holmes, the genial Autocrat of the Breakfast Table, spoke for these when he wrote "Brother Jonathan's Lament for Sister Carolina":

> She has gone—she has left us in passion and pride—
> Our stormy-browed sister, so long at our side!
> She has torn her own star from our firmament's glow,
> And turned on his brother the face of a foe!
>
> Go then, our rash sister! afar and aloof,
> Run wild in the sunshine away from our roof;
> But when your heart aches and your feet have grown sore,
> Remember the pathway that leads to our door!

Soon his own son would be marching off to war against "Sister Carolina," and Holmes would be writing poems to "Union and Liberty" and the "Voyage of the Good Ship Union."

Poor Buchanan, meanwhile, fiddled and dithered. What was to be done? In his view, nothing. He was content to let his successor contend with that problem. If no steps were to be taken to prevent the secessionists' departure, how should the government respond when federal installations in the various Southern states were seized or attacked? Should they be reinforced or defended? Or simply surrendered as unobtrusively as possible? The problem came to focus first on the federal forts in Charleston Harbor—Fort Moultrie, Fort Sumter, and Castle Pinckney . . . all summoning up the memories of Revolutionary heroes of that state. Major Robert Anderson, in command of the U.S. garrisons, had appealed for troops and supplies, but these appeals had been ignored. Anderson was to avoid any action that might appear aggressive but to defend the forts if attacked. South Carolina warned the President not to try to reinforce the forts, and while Buchanan wavered, his Cabinet members began to resign, one because he would not promise not to. Anderson, meanwhile, feeling that the soldiers under his command were too few to defend all three forts, concentrated the men in Fort Sumter. There, it must be said for Buchanan, he did dispatch a vessel, the *Star of the West,* with supplies and reinforcements, but when shore batteries opened fire on her, her captain turned about and sailed away, leaving Anderson to his fate.

While complicated negotiations were going on, fourteen other United States forts and arsenals in seceding states were seized or besieged.

The response of the North was, on the one hand, to pledge support for the President in maintaining the power and dignity of the United States, and, on the other, to put forward a wide range of compromise proposals designed to placate the South. The best known of these, the so-called Crittenden Compromise, sought to restore the Missouri Compromise line. North of it slavery would be prohibited, south it would be left to the protection of the territorial governments, and states admitted would themselves determine whether they were to be free or slave. Slavery was not to be interfered with by Congress in any state where it existed. The owners of runaway slaves were to be compensated for their loss by the federal government. The principal effect of the compromise was to demonstrate that Northern and Southern representatives were hopelessly split. Seward next attempted a compromise and when this failed, Mississippi, Florida, and Alabama seceded on successive days in January. A week later the members of Congress from the seceding states left Washington, and the Senate passed a bill admitting Kansas to the Union as a free state.

On February 4 delegates from the six Southern states that had declared themselves out of the Union—South Carolina, Georgia, Alabama, Mississippi, Louisiana, and Texas—met at Montgomery, drafted a "constitution for the provisional government of the Confederate States of America," and elected Jefferson Davis provisional president.

Lincoln watched helplessly as the Union came to pieces and state after state seceded because a "Black Republican" had been elected president of the United States. He occupied his time as best he could lining up his Cabinet and considering other crucial appointments. He asked Seward to be secretary of state and Edward Bates, Greeley's protégé, to be attorney general; Simon Cameron, a corrupt man and a poor administrator, was nominated for secretary of war; Salmon Chase became secretary of the treasury; and Gideon Welles, a Connecticut Democrat, an old Jacksonian, and a stout antislavery man who had helped to organize the Republican Party, was secretary of the navy. Welles, intelligent, patient, and incorruptible, was one of Lincoln's best Cabinet appointments.

On February 11, Lincoln left Springfield for the long, slow journey to Washington. On the rear platform of the train carrying him from Springfield, he delivered a brief farewell to a somber crowd of friends and neighbors collected to see him off. As the train pulled away from the station his young secretary, John Nicolay, asked him to write down his words. Lincoln started to and then passed the job on to Nicolay, who completed it from memory: "My friends—No one, not in my situation, can appreciate my feeling of sadness at this parting. To this place, and the kindness of these people, I owe every thing. . . . Here my children have been born, and one is buried. I now leave, not knowing when, whether ever, I may return, with a task before me greater than that which rested upon Washington. Without the assistance of that Divine Being, who ever attended him, I cannot succeed. With that assistance I cannot fail. Trusting in Him, who can go with me, and remain with you and be every where for the good, let us confidently hope that all will yet be well."

In Tolono, in Danville; in Lafayette, Indiana, and in Lebanon, in Indianapolis; in Cincinnati, Ohio, and in London, Columbus, Newark, Cadiz Junction, Steubenville, Cleveland, Ashtabula, Conneaut, at Westfield, New York, and Dunkirk, Buffalo, Batavia, Syracuse, Rochester, Albany, Troy, Fishkill, Peekskill, New York City; at Jersey City, New Jersey, at Newark and Trenton; Independence Hall in Philadelphia, Lancaster, Harrisburg—the slow procession moved on. Sometimes there were four or five or six brief addresses a day to quiet, anxious crowds, gazing intently at the odd, gaunt man into whose hands they had delivered the fate of the republic. Would he stand firm? Could he be trusted, so untested, so untried, to steer the ship of state through such perilous waters? Four years later there would be another such procession, shadowed by grief too deep to speak. This one was a knitting together, a gathering of the remaining strands of Union. Lincoln, seeing all those faces turned up in anxiety and concern, or simply in a wondering kind of emptiness, longing for the strengthening word of hope and encouragement, must have felt troubled in his deepest being, all his resolutions tried. Yet he drew strength from their need, knowing he and only he could restore the shattered Union. Fate, in its inscrutable way, had marked him for the task and he would complete it. Republican leaders, men like Seward, Chase, and Charles Francis Adams, watched Lincoln's progress and read his speeches with more than a little apprehension. His quiet, easy, informal manner and his failure to announce a clear course for the country puzzled and alarmed them. Adams impressed on Seward how important it was that he should guide the footsteps of the inexperienced president-elect and Seward urged Adams to take a Cabinet position in the new government so that he could help too.

As Lincoln's train neared Washington there were reports of plots on his life and the president-to-be of the United States had to be smuggled from Baltimore, a hotbed of secession sympathies, to the capital in a railroad car with the curtains drawn. In Washington at Willard's Hotel, the Marine Band serenaded him and a large crowd gathered and called for him. He came out on the balcony to the dismay of the agents assigned to guard him and made some brief remarks, stressing his hopes for reconciliation. Then he turned to the preparation of his inaugural address.

An air of gloom and crisis hung over the inauguration. It could not have been otherwise. The Thirty-sixth Congress had adjourned, many of its Southern members vowing never to return. The matter of supplying Fort Sumter was becoming increasingly urgent. Finally, no one was sure what Lincoln's policy toward the seceding states would be. The ceremonies were delayed for a time because of the late adjournment of the House. Finally, with the diplomatic corps, the justices of the Supreme Court, and the House and Senate gathered at the east portico of the Capitol, Lincoln was introduced by Senator Baker of Oregon and the oath of office administered by Chief Justice Taney. As he moved to the lectern, he could find no place to put his hat and Douglas, standing near him and seeing his dilemma, stepped forward and took it from him.

The President began with words of reassurance for the South. "Apprehension seems to exist among the people of the Southern States, that by the accession of the Republican Administration, their property and their peace, and personal security are to be endangered. There has never been any reasonable cause for such apprehension. Indeed, the most ample evidence to the contrary has all the while existed, and been open to their inspection." He then quoted from his speeches and from his party's platform in support of his statement.

As the sixteenth president of the United States he began his term of office "under great and peculiar difficulty. A disruption of the Federal Union heretofore only menaced, is now formidably attempted." It was his view that "in contemplation of universal law, and of the Constitution, the Union of these States is perpetual. Perpetuity is implied, if not expressed, in the fundamental law of all national governments." It followed that "no State, upon its own mere motion, can lawfully get out of the Union—that *resolves* and ordinances to that effect are legally void; and that acts of violence, within any State or States, against the authority of the United States, are insurrectionary and revolutionary, according to circumstances."

"I therefore consider that, in view of the Constitution and the law, the Union is unbroken; and, to the extent of my ability, I will take care, as the Constitution itself expressly enjoins upon me, that the laws of the Union be faithfully executed in all the States." This would be done in a careful and conciliatory spirit. Lincoln made it clear that he would use the powers of his office "to hold, occupy, and possess the property, and places belonging to the government, and to collect those duties and imposts; but beyond what may be necessary for these objects, there will be no invasion—no using of force against, or among the people anywhere."

The central idea of secession was the rejection of majority rule, an act that was "the essence of anarchy." More than that, the two sections could not separate. "We cannot remove our respective sections from each other, nor build an impassable wall between them. A husband and wife may be divorced, and go out of the presence and beyond the reach of each other; but the different parts of our country cannot do this." His duty, as chief magistrate, was to administer the present government, as it came to his hands, and to transmit it, unimpaired by him, to his successor.

"In *your* hands, my dissatisfied fellow countrymen," he said, addressing the South, "and not in *mine,* is the momentous issue of civil war. The government will not assail *you.* You can have no conflict, without being yourselves the aggressors. *You* have no oath registered in Heaven to destroy the government, while *I* shall have the most solemn one to 'preserve, protect and defend' it.

"I am loth to close. We are not enemies, but friends. We must not be enemies. Though passion may have strained, it must not break our bonds of affection. The mystic chords of memory, stretching from every battle-field, and patriot grave, to every living heart and hearthstone, all over this broad land, will yet swell the chorus of the Union, when again touched, as surely they will be, by the better angels of our nature."

In a curious way the four-month-long hiatus between Lincoln's election and inauguration proved an advantage. It gave the most militant Southern states an opportunity to display their intransigence *before* Lincoln had ever taken office. Had he been able to assume office shortly after his election, the Southern states would undoubtedly have found cause in something that he did or did not do to justify secession. Lincoln would certainly have been immediately involved in the difficult business of reenforcing and defending government forts and posts within the seceding states, thereby appearing, to some Americans, to be acting aggressively toward the seceders. By not waiting to determine what Lincoln's policies would be on the various issues involving slavery, the seceding Southern states seemed to many people to have placed themselves clearly in the wrong. The impression was of "bad sports" who, not winning, quit the game before it was fairly begun.

It was Douglas, of course, who was responsible for Lincoln's becoming president of the United States. Lincoln, seeing the handwriting on the wall for his opposition to the Mexican War, had abandoned the political arena. For six years he wandered in the political wilderness, his hopes for high office dashed, "a failure," in his own view, at the age of thirty-nine. For a man as ambitious as Lincoln it was a kind of death. But those six years, before Douglas revived his political prospects by the Kansas-Nebraska Act, we know were years vital to Lincoln's own growth, years of deepening wisdom and compassion during which he must reconcile himself to the life of an obscure country lawyer, knowing the gifts that lay unused in him. His successful rival then gave him a second life, and Lincoln proved his political genius by fastening himself on Douglas with an unbreakable tenacity and singleness of purpose. The man who had unmade him now made him. Douglas's dreams must have come to be haunted by the spectral figure of Lincoln endlessly pursuing him—Carl Schurz called Lincoln Douglas's "avenging angel." From 1854 to 1860, for a time span almost exactly equivalent to the period of his exile, Lincoln hunted down Douglas, the man whose fame was to bear him to national prominence. He rode on Douglas's shoulders to the Republican nomination. And Douglas proved essential to the end. By helping to divide the anti-Republican vote and thus assuring Lincoln of the presidency, he made his most important contribution. The final irony was that Douglas's somewhat tainted immortality was to be as Lincoln's rival in the debates that Douglas "won," won at least in the sense that he retained his Senate seat which, by that time, was of no use to Lincoln in any event. A month after Lincoln's inauguration, Stephen Douglas, worn out from campaigning but doing his best to rally support for Lincoln's policies, caught typhoid fever and died at the age of forty-eight, after one of the most spectacular and ill-starred careers in American history.

Charles Francis Adams had been a strong supporter of Seward in the contest for the Republican Party's presidential nomination. The New Yorker, seasoned and tested in the antislavery cause, experienced in administration, democratic in his sympathies, eloquent and learned, seemed to Adams ideal presidential material, the first candidate since the days of the last Adams president to be properly qualified for the job. Adams, not a delegate to the convention, was correspondingly astonished and dismayed at the choice of Lincoln. Conceding that he was "honest and tolerably capable," Adams deplored Lincoln's lack of experience and uncouth frontier manners. Yet when Seward, anxious to establish a claim in Adams's behalf on Lincoln's attention, asked Adams to accompany him on a campaign tour through the Northwestern states, Adams accepted and spent a month touring the region with special attention to Wisconsin.

When Lincoln was elected, Adams too was returned to Congress, with more than 60 percent of the vote. Neither of his distinguished ancestors had received "so brilliant and so feeling a testimony to his character and services." Seward at once began to try to prevail on Lincoln to offer Adams the post of secretary of the navy, but Lincoln bestowed that office on Gideon Welles. He finally agreed to appoint Adams minister to England, a position the latter was quick to accept. When Adams went to visit Lincoln before his departure he was disconcerted by the President's casual, offhand manner. He tried to thank him for the appointment, but Lincoln replied, "Very kind of you to say so, Mr. Adams, but you are not my choice. You are Seward's man." It was a classic meeting of an Eastern man and a Western man. Charles Francis Adams, son of one president and grandson of another, bone and marrow of New England, cool and aloof in manner, family-proud, always conscious of his status as "an Adams"; and the frontier lawyer, his antithesis in so many ways, a man of no "family," no "background," with no "manners" and yet with a quiet self-confidence. Democratic politics played strange tricks.

The question of supplying Fort Sumter was the most crucial issue facing Lincoln. He notified Governor Pickens of South Carolina that provisions but no armaments or reinforcements were on their way to Sumter. The response of South Carolina was to demand Anderson's surrender at once. When Anderson refused, General Pierre G. T. Beauregard opened a heavy fire on the fort. Thirty-four hours later, on April 13, Anderson surrendered. Walt Whitman, returning down Broadway from the opera, "heard in the distance the loud cries of the newsboys, who came presently tearing and yelling up the street, rushing from side to side even more furiously than usual." He bought an extra and took it to the Metropolitan Hotel "where the great lamps were still brightly blazing, and, with a crowd of others . . . read the news. . . . For the benefit of some who had no papers, one of us read the telegram aloud, while all listen'd silently and attentively. No remark was made by the crowd . . . but all stood a minute or two, I remember, before they dispers'd."

Two days later Lincoln declared an "insurrection" existed and called for seventy-five thousand volunteers. The nightmare had become a reality, the Civil War had begun.

Tragedy stalks us all and brings us at last to the grave. But the human spirit is indestructible. "Man does not die like a dog in a ditch," Boris Pasternak wrote, "he lives in history." And so he does and that history, tragic though it may be, is permeated with the *moral*. What we used to call right and wrong, or good and evil. We are their battleground. But there are, through the grace of God, redemptive forces always working in history, in us. Slavery was an unmitigated evil. George Mason, a Southerner and a slaveholder, had said in the Federal Convention, "As nations can not be rewarded or punished in the next world, they must be in this. By an inevitable chain of causes & effects, Providence punishes national sins, by national calamities." The prophetic words were now to be fulfilled, and it belonged to the everlasting glory of the abolitionists that they, and they alone, through storm and fire, in the face of hatred and abuse, had insisted that slavery was, above all, a moral issue, that it was wicked and un-Christian and could never be accepted by a free people; that it was not for a moment a matter of expediency or compromise, that it was an everlasting blot on the good name of the United States, a sin in the eyes of God, and a scandal to the world.

At the same time it must be confessed that their perpetual rage against the institution of slavery threatened sometimes to consume them, that they were often unpleasantly self-righteous and lacking in charity for the South and for those of their own region who were less bold and resolute. Many of them had a rule-or-ruin philosophy that would endure no compromise or delay, and, finally, many, like the Garrisonites, would have had the North secede and abandon the slaves to their fate rather than tolerate a contaminated Union. They thus provided one half of the essential equation. The other half was provided by those men of whom Webster was the model and exemplar, who labored year after year for the cause of Union. Just as the abolitionists dramatized the horror of slavery in a thousand speeches and pamphlets, the lovers of the Union wove a magic web of words so strong that it could never be more than briefly breached. Their great achievement was to create a bedrock of Union feeling against which secession must finally smash to pieces. The strands of antislavery sentiment and of love of Union met in Lincoln and, meeting, preserved the Union and, in time, freed the slave. Americans do not believe in the tragic character of history; they believe in solutions, and so American historians have expended an astonishing amount of ingenuity trying to explain to us how the Civil War might have been avoided. One such historian recently expressed his yearning for a Douglas victory in the election of 1860. We are, in truth, a nation of wishful thinkers. The fact, unpleasant as it may be, is that the people of the United States, guilty and innocent alike, had to pay the price for the moral horror of slavery. There are historical imperatives from which none of us can escape. We must pay for greed, indifference, enslaving or exploiting others, pursuing our selfish interests at the cost of the less powerful and less fortunate. That is not sentimentalism, Christian moralizing, liberal tenderness, radical propaganda, though it may be all of these; it is, if you like, "scientific" truth.

Genius knows genius. Lincoln knew very well his own powers. To those like Carl Schurz who saw him for the first time the most striking thing about him was his physical oddity, almost uncouthness—the high-pitched but compelling voice, the scrawny neck, the too large feet and rough hands shaped by ax and maul and shovel handle and plow handle, big wrist bones below the shirt cuffs. When politicians were almost invariably stout Lincoln was alarmingly thin. He had, indeed, created and exhausted a type. He was what Harriet Martineau twenty-five years earlier had called "an American original," a quite new kind of human being, grown in the soil of the West. Washington was remarkable but recognizable—the perfection of an English country gentleman (which is, of course, why the British so admired him); Jefferson had his counterpart in a Shaftesbury or the hero he so admired, Algernon Sidney. Jackson, the first American "original" to be president, was, as someone was to say later of another American president, "pure act," rude, untutored, direct, violent, frontier gunfighter as president shooting it out with the Bank of the United States.

Lincoln, the most compelling and mysterious of our "great men," was so thoroughly and deeply what he was, so "centered," so solid, so essential that he conveyed an impression, one might almost say, of translucence. All forms and formalities became irrelevant in his presence. Convention prescribed the manner and behavior of "great men" as rigidly as it did the dress and deportment of ladies or gentlemen. Men and women who met Lincoln for the first time, expecting to encounter a typical "great man," were invariably startled and disconcerted, and the more discerning of them deeply impressed by the complete absence of any of the supposed attributes of "greatness." In an era obsessed with "nature" but bound by rigid convention, Lincoln appeared a disarmingly "natural" man. Jackson, Benton, and Douglas epitomized the West. But this Westerner fitted no category. The simple dignity, the suggestion of profound melancholy, the homely, ultimate American face, the inexhaustible face that made all others dim by comparison, that made "Lincolnesque" a physical description, that made homeliness more compelling than beauty, that made homeliness beauty, that was ageless, that was always old and always young; deepening into sadness, erupting unexpectedly into laughter. And always and always the stories, the wry, amusing, ironic stories, a constant thread running through every discourse, lightening, enlivening, illuminating, delighting.

That this crude, raw, half-civilized country could produce a Lincoln out of the most American heart of it was perhaps enough to justify the disorder, the perpetual anxiety, the chronic schizophrenia. Each nation may be said to produce a man—or a handful of men—who represent the quintessence of everything that is most notable about it, in which it appears at its best—the English, Shakespeare; the French, Descartes or Voltaire; the Germans, Goethe; the Italians, Dante. It was appropriate that in the United States, where democratic politics dominated everything, our representative man, the embodiment of our highest aspirations, should be a politician. Indeed it might be said it took a Lincoln to suggest the possibilities inherent in the often grim farce of American politics.

Acknowledgments

As with all the volumes of this work I am much indebted to the suggestions, advice, and labor of a number of people. Fawn Brodie saved me from embarrassing errors. Norman O. Brown had valuable suggestions. Patty Nelson, David Stanford and Ann Fabian continued their interest and assistance. Martha Ways was very helpful. Francis Rydell, Charlotte Cassidy and Carol English brought order out of the disorder of my manuscript. Ken Leish continues to be my ideal of an editor, while Gladys Carr's faith in the possibility of this presumptious task has helped immeasurably to make it a reality.

INDEX

About the Author

Page Smith was educated at Dartmouth College and Harvard University. He has served as research associate at the Institute of Early American History and Culture and has taught at the University of California at Los Angeles and at Santa Cruz, where he was Provost of Cowell College. He is now Professor Emeritus of that university, as well as co-director of the William James Association. Dr. Smith is the author of *The Historian and History; Daughters of the Promised Land: Woman in American History; As a City upon a Hill: The Town in American History;* the highly acclaimed two-volume biography *John Adams,* which was a selection of the Book-of-the-Month Club, a National Book Award Nominee, and a Bancroft winner; *A New Age Now Begins* and *The Shaping of America,* both Main Selections of the Book-of-the-Month Club. *The Nation Comes of Age* continues Dr. Smith's extensive *People's History* of the United States, of which *A New Age Now Begins* and *The Shaping of America* are the first volumes. Page Smith lives in Santa Cruz, California.

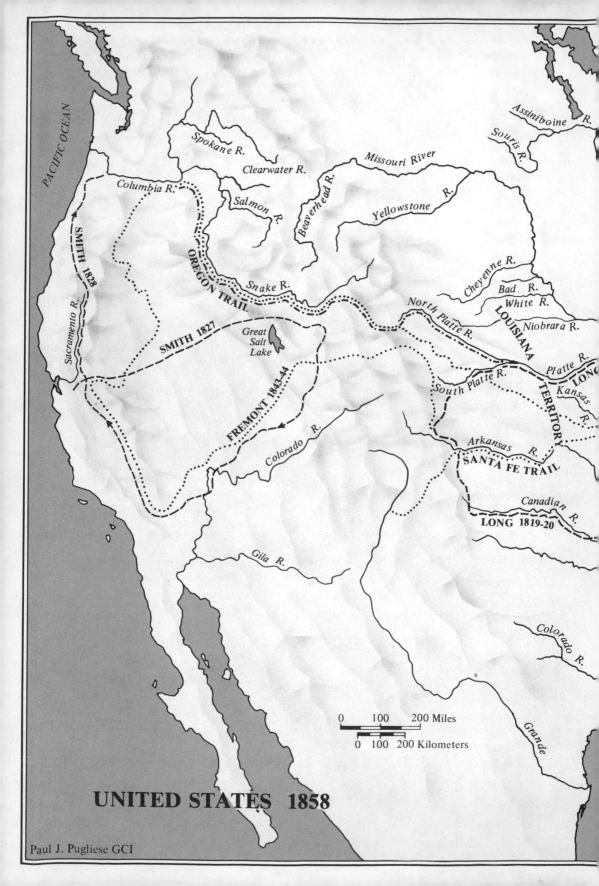

UNITED STATES 1858

Paul J. Pugliese GCI